BRISTOL CITY
The Modern Era
– A Complete Record –

Bristol City: The Modern Era – A Complete Record	1-874287-28-7
Colchester Utd: Graham to Whitton – A Complete Record	1-874287-27-9
Halifax Town: From Ball to Lillis – A Complete Record	1-874287-26-0
Portsmouth: From Tindall to Ball – A Complete Record	1-874287-25-2
Portsmouth: Champions of England – 1948-49 & 1949-50	1-874287-38-4
Coventry City: The Elite Era – A Complete Record	1-874287-03-1
Coventry City: An Illustrated History	1-874287-36-8
Luton Town: The Modern Era – A Complete Record	1-874287-05-8
Luton Town: An Illustrated History	1-874287-37-6
Hereford United: The League Era – A Complete Record	1-874287-18-X
Cambridge United: The League Era – A Complete Record	1-874287-32-5
Peterborough United: The Modern Era – A Complete Record	1-874287-33-3
West Ham: From Greenwood to Redknapp – Match by Match	1-874287-19-8
West Ham: The Elite Era – A Complete Record	1-874287-31-7
Wimbledon: From Southern League to Premiership	1-874287-09-0
Wimbledon: From Wembley to Selhurst	1-874287-20-1
Aberdeen: The European Era – A Complete Record	1-874287-11-2
The Story of the Rangers 1873-1923	1-874287-16-3
The Story of the Celtic 1888-1938	1-874287-15-5
History of the Everton Football Club 1878-1928	1-874287-14-7
The Romance of the Wednesday 1867-1926	1-874287-17-1
Red Dragons in Europe – A Complete Record	1-874287-01-5
The Book of Football: A History to 1905-06	1-874287-13-9
England: The Quest for the World Cup – A Complete Record	1-897850-40-9
Scotland: The Quest for the World Cup – A Complete Record	1-897850-50-6
Ireland: The Quest for the World Cup – A Complete Record	1-897850-80-8

BRISTOL CITY
THE MODERN ERA
— A Complete Record —

Series Editor: Clive Leatherdale
Series Consultant: Leigh Edwards

David Woods

DESERT ISLAND BOOKS LIMITED

First Published in 2000

DESERT ISLAND BOOKS LIMITED
89 Park Street, Westcliff-on-Sea, Essex SS0 7PD
United Kingdom
www.desertislandbooks.com

British Library Cataloguing-in-Publication Data
A catalogue record for this book is available from the British Library

ISBN   1-874287-28-7

Printed in Great Britain
by
Biddles Ltd, Guildford

Photographs in this book are reproduced by kind permission of
The *Bristol United Press* and John Kelland

CONTENTS

PREFACE

This book on the recent history of Bristol City Football Club starts as my Ashton Gate career was drawing to a close. However, being born and bred, as well as still living in the vicinity of the ground, I class myself as a supporter, and like the other fans I have my own favourites among the many players who have represented the club over the years.

The great John Atyeo was my hero, whilst many others I had the pleasure of playing with – Mike Gibson, Jack Connor, John Quigley, Brian Clark, Bobby Williams, Hugh McIlmoyle, Chris Crowe, and that goalscoring machine John Galley – come immediately to mind. The most complete footballer, though, was the incomparable Atyeo, and his club record of goals and appearances is a fitting testimony to his remarkable prowess. In more recent years the skills of Keith Fear, Alan Walsh, Bob Taylor, Nicky Morgan, Andy Cole and Greg Goodridge have kept the fans enthralled.

Whilst no championships have been won since 1954-55, the 32 seasons covered by this book have been anything but dull for City's immensely loyal fans. Four promotions, five relegations, two visits to Wembley, two Anglo-Scottish Cup Finals, as well as contesting a Third Division play-off final and reaching League Cup semi-finals on two occasions, have ensured a real roller-coaster ride for players and fans alike.

Jantzen Derrick

AUTHOR'S NOTE

Little appreciating the size of the task ahead when I accepted Clive Leatherdale's commission to write this book, I have had cause to be thankful that page limitations restricted my ambitions to cover the whole post-war period. As it is the narrative commences in 1967-68, which saw the start of Alan Dicks' long Ashton Gate reign.

This work would not have been possible without the invaluable assistance of long-time City supporters Tom Hopegood and Tony Ticktum. They both amazed me with their recall of games long ago, a capacity that I have progressively lost the more I have delved into Bristol football history.

As I did not start keeping a scrapbook until the 1973-74 season, I am indebted to the help of Bristol Rovers fan Malcolm Norman, who let me have his extensive collection of City cuttings covering the 1970 to 1979 period. On the photographic front, the assistance of John Kelland and John Brewer has been invaluable.

I am also indebted to the many journalists who have unknowingly provided most of the raw material for the match summaries, and amongst this fraternity I would like to record my particular appreciation for the help I have had over the years from Peter Godsiff, David Foot and the late George Baker, as well as the gentleman who fostered my interest in football history – the late Bill Pinnell, known to generations of Bristolians as 'The Traveller'.

Amongst football researchers much camaraderie exists. As well as thanking Brian Tabner for supplying official home and away Football League attendances, I would like to thank those of other allegiances – Jim Brown (Coventry), Mike Davage (Norwich), Leigh Edwards (Bournemouth), Mike Jay (Bristol Rovers), Alan Lacock (Bristol Rovers), Johnny Meynell (Halifax), Ron Parrott (Hereford), Rev Nigel Sands (Crystal Palace), Ray Shoesmith (West Ham), Colin Timbrell (Gloucestershire FA Historian and Arsenal fan), Jeff Whitehead (Colchester), as well as City supporters Mervyn Baker, Kevin Brake, Andrew Crabtree, Phil Jones, Terry Norris, Gerry Pearce, Geoff Rose, Matthew Stevens, and Mike Swain.

I would also like to express my gratitude to Lorna Parnell of the Football League, who has been of great help in supplying information and answering my queries, and also the staff at both the Bristol Central Library and the British Newspaper Library at Colindale.

Finally a big thank-you to my children, who have had to put up with a much distracted father during the progress of this book.

DAVID WOODS, January 2000

INTRODUCTION

Bristol City would appear to be one of those clubs who are unable to stabilise. Throughout their history they have rarely managed more than five seasons at any one level. Many think of the present First Division as being their natural home, but 1998-99's dire performances, and taking into account that ten of their 42 seasons at this level (albeit the old Division Two) took place before the Football League was extended, is suggestive that they are now back where they belong.

This, of course, is not how it should be in so large a city as Bristol, which in the eighteenth century was second only to London. It certainly wasn't the intention of the founders of the club in 1894, when as Bristol South End they strove to be the cream of the top locals sides – Warmley, St George, Clifton Association, Eastville Rovers, and Bedminster.

South End turned professional on joining the First Division of the Southern League in 1897, whereupon they adopted their present name after appealing to the Football Association. Finishing runners-up three times, election to the Football League was secured for 1901-02, though not before 'survival of the fittest' had reduced Bristol's professional sides to the two we have today.

Warmley, St George, and Eastville Rovers also adopted professionalism in 1897, and Bedminster (founded as Southville in 1887) followed suit twelve months later. It just wasn't possible for Bristol to support the activities of five professional clubs and gradually they, along with the renowned Clifton Association Club, who gave up the battle in December 1897, started falling by the wayside.

In the east of the City bitter rivals Warmley and St George, both formed in 1882, died in 1899 after an earlier proposed amalgamation had been rejected, but south of the river wisdom prevailed. The Bedminster board were the instigators of their amalgamation with Bristol City in the summer of 1900. Eastville Rovers, who became Bristol Rovers in 1899, doggedly soldiered on by themselves, very much in the same admirable way they still conduct their affairs.

City's early years in the Football League were their most successful. Finishing sixth in their first season, three successive fourth placings followed before promotion to the top flight was secured. In 1905-06 City only lost two League games on their way to amassing a record 66 points, as well as becoming the first club ever to win thirty League games in a season. Five years in the First Division then ensued, with the Championship being narrowly missed in 1906-07 and the FA Cup final reached in 1909. Relegation at the end of the 1910-11 campaign brought financial problems, and no sign of regaining lost status until finishing third in 1920-21. Since when, until the 1967-68 season which is the starting point of this book, it has been City's dismal lot to have operated at Third Division level for all but fourteen campaigns.

Not a record to boast about, given the club's undoubted potential, not to mention the high level of support that has been enjoyed over the years! Let us therefore read further to see what travails have taken place during the intervening period.

CONSOLIDATION
1967-1973

LEAGUE DIVISION 2   **1967-68**
Division 2   19th
League Cup   2nd Round
FA Cup   5th Round

The capture of England international Chris Crowe from Nottingham Forest had transformed City's 1966-67 campaign. Not only did their struggling side start winning, but they did so with a style and panache that thrilled the fans. The record signing of Hugh McIlmoyle from Wolverhampton Wanderers in early March appeared to be the icing on the cake: it was expected that a serious assault on reclaiming top-flight status after a 56-year gap would be made in 1967-68.

After a 1-0 home victory over Swindon in the first pre-season friendly on 3 August, a crowd of 7,719 were attracted to Ashton Gate four days later when the Supporters Club opened City's first shop. Unfortunately First Division visitors West Bromwich Albion proved much too strong as they strolled to a 4-1 success, but a 3-3 draw at Swindon the next evening kept hopes buoyant for the League campaign.

The atmosphere was electric at Ashton Gate for the opening fixture against Huddersfield Town, and all bode well after just two minutes when Crowe slid in the day's quickest goal. Unfortunately, this proved to be the calm before the storm: it was downhill all the way thereafter, with City losing 2-3 after Tony Ford had hit the post with a late penalty.

With only one win in the first eight League games, not to mention losing 0-5 at home to Everton in the League Cup, the axe fell on manager Fred Ford at an emergency board meeting. That was on the evening of 19 September, just three days after City's 2-4 home defeat by Blackpool. Unusually for a club in trouble, this sacking brought forth much protest, with letters streaming into the columns of the local *Green 'Un* and Gordon Parr leading a deputation of players to chairman Harry Dolman's house in Chew Magna to plead for Ford's reinstatement.

The decision stood, however, and whilst the search for a manager went on, club physiotherapist Les Bardsley took over for the third time as caretaker boss, with the assistance of chairman Dolman, and directors Norman Jones and Graham Whittock. Johnny Quigley was appointed captain in place of the dropped Gordon Low.

Torquay boss Frank O'Farrell was Dolman's first choice, but he turned his back, objecting to the unfair manner in which he considered his good friend Ford had been dismissed. Dolman then turned to Coventry City's assistant manager, Alan Dicks, who was interviewed by the board on 5 October and offered a three-year contract at £4,000 per annum, as well as a bonus of £1,000 should he succeed in preserving City's Second Division status.

A mediocre half-back with Millwall, Chelsea and Southend United, Dicks gained much valuable experience under Jimmy Hill at progressive-minded Coventry. At 33 years of age and having gained his full FA coaching badge in his early twenties, Dicks appeared to be the ideal man to lead City forward.

Commitments at Coventry, though, meant he was unable to take up full-time duties until 16 October, though he selected the side for the 1-1 home draw with Cardiff City two days earlier. His first signing was wing-half Ken Wimshurst from Southampton for a £12,000 fee, but his priority was a centre-forward, following Dolman's decision to transfer McIlmoyle to Carlisle United in exchange for £22,000 in late September.

Liverpool reserve Alf Arrowsmith was the initial target, but, on being rebuffed, Dicks turned to 23-year-old John Galley. Surprisingly, Rotherham boss Tommy Docherty agreed to let him go for £25,000, but on joining City in late November Galley's left ankle was in plaster.

Passed fit to make his debut on 16 December, Galley demonstrated that he was worth the wait, scoring all the goals in a 3-0 away win against Huddersfield. His haul of sixteen League goals that season proved to be a major factor in City's escape from the jaws of relegation. It was a close thing though, as many at Ashton Gate on the night of 29 March, when Rotherham took both points, were inclined to the opinion that relegation was inevitable.

Four wins from their last eight games hauled City back from the brink and, after beating Preston on 27 April to banish lingering fears of the drop, they put on a show the following week with a 4-2 win at Villa Park. It was there that keeper Barry Watling and former England and Bristol Boys skipper Geoff Merrick made their debuts.

Did You Know?

Stan Mortensen (ex-Blackpool & England) refereed when City beat Rovers at head-tennis to win the Fred Pontin Trophy at the Colston Hall in Dec 1968.

The FA Cup offered City respite from their relegation battle. Having negotiated replays to overcome Bristol Rovers and Middlesbrough, the fifth round was reached for the second successive year. Record receipts for both Ashton Gate and Eastville – £9,954 and £6,600 respectively – had been generated by the local derby clashes, whilst the fifth round game at Leeds yielded receipts of £15,250. This rough encounter, which City lost 0-2, boiled over in the second half when Gary Sprake, the Leeds keeper, was sent off for belting Chris Garland.

Among the back-room staff, former Rochdale boss Tony Collins was appointed chief scout in November, but the most significant newcomer was John Sillett, who took over coaching duties towards the end of the season. On the playing front, the departure of Quigley to Mansfield for £3,000 was viewed with alarm by most supporters, despite Dicks hoisting the club's record fee to £36,300 by bringing in Bobby Kellard from Portsmouth. Others who moved included Low to Stockport for £3,000, Lou Peters to Bournemouth for £5,000, whilst Ray Savino departed for King's Lynn in March.

Losses of £25,599 were announced for the season, despite the number of season ticket holders (at a cost of £10) rising from 1,442 to 2,017. This wasn't surprising, however, as the dross the fans were expected to watch drove average home gates down from 16,183 to 15,935. The deficit of £5,500 incurred by the hastily-arranged transfer of McIllmoyle added to the costs incurred in obtaining the services of Galley and Wimshurst. In the League Cup, receipts of £5,737 were realised from the Everton encounter, whilst in the League the largest return at Ashton Gate was for Birmingham City's visit on 30 December, when a crowd of 23,493 generated £4,818.

Match of the Season 1967-68

Charlton Athletic 1 Bristol City 2

Division 2, 20 April 1968

The emotions aroused by this game provoked a personal crisis for Alan Dicks, who had taken over from Fred Ford the previous October. With the season approaching its climax, City, with just four games left, were involved in a desperate fight to avoid relegation.

With Charlton just one place higher in the table, this clash was viewed as a game neither side could afford to lose.

It had been a struggle for Dicks to improve the club's fortunes, despite the shrewd signing of John Galley, who had started his City career with a hat-trick at Huddersfield. Wins proved hard to come by and many feared City were heading for a quick return to the lower reaches after just three seasons in Division Two.

'Do or die' at the Valley was, however, a worrying prospect for City. Charlton, unbeaten over the Easter period, were one of City's bogey sides and many fans had vivid memories of their overturning a 0-2 half-time FA Cup deficit at Ashton Gate in 1959-60 to win 3-2. Whilst Charlton were unchanged, City had Terry Bush taking over from flu victim Gordon Parr in the defensive wing-half position.

With Chris Crowe operating on the right wing, despite wearing the No 2 shirt, City made the better start in front of a near 12,000 crowd, and on a bumpy, hard pitch carried the game to their opponents. Keeper Charlie Wright did well to keep out Galley's 25-yarder, before City were rewarded with a well-taken goal after just eight minutes. Derrick hooked the ball into the middle from the left, and Galley's back-header set up Crowe, moving in from the right, to unleash a rocket into the far top corner.

Playing effectively in attack against a Charlton defence vulnerable to Galley and Garland's quick thrusts through the middle, City kept up the pressure to add another goal before half-time when a mis-hit ten-yard effort from the prolific Galley struck Paul Went and rolled into the net.

After the break, City were unfortunate not to increase their advantage when John Quigley's shot was cleared off the line by Peter Reeves. Charlton raised the tempo following the 65th-minute replacement of Matt Tees by substitute Stenson, and forced their way back into the game when Keith Peacock's corner from the left was headed low into the net by Harry Gregory. As City doggedly hung on, the tension was such that Dicks found he had temporarily lost the use of his legs.

On an afternoon of high drama City secured what was thought to be one of the most critical wins in their history, but as events turned out defeat did not mean relegation for the loser. Charlton rediscovered their form to attain fifteenth place at the season's end, while City finished in nineteenth spot to preserve their status and earn Dicks his £1,000 bonus.

LEAGUE DIVISION 2   **1968-69**
Division 2   16th
League Cup   3rd Round
FA Cup   3rd Round

After the struggles of the previous campaign, optimism among the fans wasn't high. Portents were grim, with many of the club's records being lost in July floods that saw Ashton Gate under water. However, the presence of record signing Kellard in City's line-up had 7,862 spectators turning up for the opening friendly against Southampton. The game was won 5-3, but as this was followed by a 1-3 defeat at Bournemouth and a 1-1 draw at Hereford, the jury was still out when City travelled to sun-drenched Craven Cottage for the League opener. A good performance against relegated Fulham, despite a 0-1 defeat, augured well, but with just one win from the opening twelve League games – coupled with the team earning a reputation for rough and negative play – pressure on the manager intensified. Shouts of 'Dicks must go' reverberated at home games as relegation became a serious threat. Matters came to a head in Alan Skirton's first match.

A £15,000 signing from Blackpool, Skirton had been a member of City's Youth team that had reached the semi-finals of the FA Youth Cup twelve years previously. He could do little, however, as Norwich's 1-0 win on 23 November provoked a mass demonstration demanding Dicks' head. Dolman responded by calling a crisis board meeting. The manager survived, despite having supervised just two wins from the first nineteen games and a lamentable total of thirteen goals. Dolman was concerned about the coverage of City's affairs in the local press. Having fallen out with Herbie Gillam, sports editor of the *Western Daily Press*, he accepted an invitation by Gordon Farnsworth, editor of the *Bristol Evening Post*, for a frank interview to be published in the *Green 'Un*. Unfortunately, the outcome demonstrated Dolman's paranoia over supporters having an outlet for their frustration. He complained that much of the criticism was destructive and also blamed the local press for raising false hopes of success among the fans.

Dicks decided on a bolder policy against Carlisle, but after City's attack-minded display at Brunton Park failed to reap its due reward, he reverted to type at Middlesbrough, where negative tactics brought a 1-4 defeat. The tide began to turn when both points were secured in a fortuitous 2-1 home success over Bury. With Galley regaining his form following an operation on an in-growing toenail, the following ten games – culminating in a 6-0 thrashing of Fulham – earned five wins and two draws.

Relegation fears were rekindled by a 1-2 defeat at Sheffield United, but only two defeats in the remaining nine games hoisted City up to sixteenth, eight points clear of the drop zone. The season ended at the Baseball Ground, where any optimism for the following season was shattered. City were annihilated 0-5 by champions Derby County.

A notable landmark had been achieved in the League Cup. City's 2-0 win over Newport, which ended a barren seven-year spell, was only their second success in the competition. Heady times followed with a 1-0 victory over Middlesbrough that earned another clash with First Division Leeds. The crowd of 16,359 did not have their enjoyment marred by a repeat of the previous season's ugly incidents but City proved to be no match for the defending League Cup holders.

The FA Cup took the Ashton Gate fans to Upton Park, where City faced a Hammers side which included all three of their England World Cup heroes. On a day that saw the opening of the East Stand, City gave Bobby Moore, Geoff Hurst and Martin Peters a far from easy time before losing 2-3.

Despite the number of season ticket holders increasing to 2,054, attendances continued to decline. City's operating loss of £20,252 was not so bad as the previous year, the opening of the Sunday Market in the officials' car park helping to stem the flow. Receipts of £4,426 were generated by City's largest home crowd of the season. The 20,632 who turned up for the Cardiff fixture on 28 September witnessed the first real flowering of the hooligan problem at Ashton Gate, with rival 'supporters' fighting in the Covered End.

Work on building Dolman's dream to replace the old Number Two stand – known affectionately as the Cowshed – that had been demolished in the summer of 1966, eventually started in January 1969, this at a projected cost of £180,000, which eventually rose to £235,000. At the time it was thought to be a gamble, but with the provision of a bowls area within the structure, which yielded an income of £12,000 per year, Dolman's wisdom in progressing with the project was soon vindicated. All sixteen club houses were sold, many at favourable prices, to the players and staff who occupied them. Mann the brewers lent £64,000 at an interest rate of 2.5 percent per annum over seven years, whilst the Football Association, the Supporters Club, 51 Club, and the directors themselves, who each pledged £3,000, all chipped in with loans. The Dolman Stand, as it was duly named, found itself ready for use for the start of the 1970-71 season, but as costs mounted Dicks was left with little money for new players. He was obliged to transfer Kellard to

Leicester for £49,000 in the summer of 1970 and Garland to Chelsea for £110,000 in September 1971.

Whilst the Supporters Club did not commence their Player of the Year awards until 1970-71, Kellard was City's undoubted star of 1968-69, his all-action play even winning over those fans who still bemoaned the loss of Quigley. It was fortunate then, that Dolman stymied Kellard's efforts to go back to Pompey by offering to buy his apparently unsaleable house on Hayling Island. Departures included Chris Crowe, whose idiosyncratic bouts of genius were never enough for Dicks; he negotiated his own transfer to Australian club Auburn of Sydney for a £3,000 fee.

In the Football Combination, City's reserves, after winning the Second Division Championship the previous season, finished in ninth place, whilst at youth-team level Sillett's work was beginning to bear fruit. The Colts occupied fourteenth spot (having been seventeenth in 1967-68) in the Western League, whilst the Youth team improved on last season's second round exit by reaching the third round of the FA Youth Cup. They beat Swindon 4-2, Plymouth 2-0, before losing 1-3 against Cardiff. Unfortunately, the Youths would be denied the splendid competition which since 1960-61 had been offered by the Wessex Youth League: it was allowed to die after City finished runners-up in 1967-68. During the competition's eight-season run, City's poorest campaign had been in 1963-64 when they finished fourth. Four times they won the Championship, doing the Cup and League double in 1965-66, and thrice finished as runners-up.

For the first team it was a poor season overall, best remembered for the fact that all City's forwards (Galley, Garland, Kellard, Sharpe and Skirton) scored in a 5-0 Gloucestershire Senior Professional Cup final triumph over Bristol Rovers in front of 14,735 fans at Eastville Stadium on 28 April.

The incorporation of the Football League Review into City's programme brought a threepence price increase to one shilling as the club carried on improving their publication, having radically changed its design in 1966-67. However, when Ashton Gate was used as a neutral venue in December (Exeter beat Nuneaton Borough 1-0 in a second replay of an FA Cup first round tie) a single-folded sheet of paper was produced for the 5,071 spectators who paid match receipts of £1,297.

This was the ninth occasion, and the last to date, in which Ashton Gate was used as a neutral venue in the FA Cup, though the ground – which was originally the home of Bedminster Cricket & Football Club – has also been used by other sports – Rugby Union, Rugby League, American Football, cricket, baseball, lacrosse.

Did You Know?

The Wurzels' song 'One for the Bristol City' was adopted as the official club song in September 1977.

Match of the Season 1968-69

Bristol City 6 Fulham 0

Division 2, 1 March 1969

Fulham's visit on a cold and windy St David's Day, brought to mind the fixture ten years previously when they had attracted 32,378 to Ashton Gate for a 1-1 top-of-the-table draw. At that time, Fulham – Johnny Haynes, Jimmy Hill, Roy Bentley, Jimmy Langley, Graham Leggatt *et al* – were headed for a second spell in the top flight. This time they were down at the foot of the Second Division, despite the recent £20,000 signing of Brian Dear from West Ham.

After Chris Garland had latched onto Bobby Kellard's pass to stroke the ball past Brian Williamson, City – who had only scored sixteen goals in fifteen previous League games – tore Fulham apart. George Cohen, a member of England's 1966 World Cup winning side, endured a torrid afternoon, in what was to be his final game. City scored four goals in the first half and two in the second.

Alan Skirton was much involved in the first-half action. He headed wide of an open net before his challenge for Galley's cross caused John Ryan to slice the ball between his own posts. Eleven minutes later he notched City's first successful penalty for almost two years after the Fulham keeper had grabbed Garland round the legs. It was then Skirton's cross from the left that Galley headed back for Gerry Sharpe to nod in at the far post.

After the break, Fulham offered little threat apart from a Haynes effort which Trevor Jacobs cleared off the line. Despite creating many chances it wasn't until five minutes from time that City added to the score, Garland following up to put Sharpe's blocked shot into the back of the net. Galley finished off the romp two minutes later, turning in Garland's centre as City notched up their biggest League victory since beating Notts County by the same score in December 1961.

The two vital points helped City's valiant war against the drop, but there was to be no escape for Fulham, who finished bottom, conceding over eighty goals, whilst only managing seven wins.

It would be 1970-71 before the two clubs met again, when Fulham, pressing for promotion from the Third Division, gave City two tough games in the quarter-finals of the Football League Cup.

LEAGUE DIVISION 2   **1969-70**
Division 2   14th
League Cup   2nd Round
FA Cup   3rd Round

In the summer of 1969 Dicks pulled off two brilliant buys from the North East, obtaining centre-half Dickie Rooks from Middlesbrough for £13,000 and full-back Brian Drysdale from Hartlepool for £10,000. Unbeaten in their four pre-season friendlies, City's League campaign started well when Galley headed in at the Open End for a 1-0 success over newly-promoted Watford. However, with Merrick having dislocated his elbow at Sheffield United in a 1-2 defeat, it was not long before the manager was under the cosh yet again. Ignoring the claims of the impressive Malcolm Clarke – signed from Cardiff – after he had played just two games, Dicks' outfit slumped, until perking up against bogey team Norwich City.

Despite his team winning 4-0, the Ashton Gate crowd's patience was sorely tested by Dicks' substitution of Jantzen Derrick by Danny Bartley. It took a 6-0 win over another bogey side – Charlton Athletic – three days later to change the mood. City embarked on a six-match unbeaten run which conversely ended against a Bolton side who viewed City as bit of a jinx.

With on-loan keeper Bob Wilson from Cardiff replacing the injured Mike Gibson, City went down in a 1-3 defeat at Bolton, but this proved to be but a brief interruption to a sparkling run of success. Four wins and three draws were secured from the following seven games before the Christmas break was spoilt by a 1-2 home defeat by Huddersfield. Two more losses ensued, including a 1-4 hammering at Norwich when Merrick made his long-awaited return. It was that sort of season. One defeat in eight games was the prelude to one win in the next eight. City plummeted down the table to finish fourteenth, having been at one stage as high as ninth.

Injuries took their toll, Merrick only playing one game after dislocating his elbow, whilst Galley was out of action with ankle trouble for long spells. Terry Bush, though, proved an admirable deputy with his wholehearted play and thunderbolt shooting. Gerry Sharpe was top scorer with eleven goals, but Garland caught the eye with his six, despite being embroiled in a wrangle over wages. Garland was called up for the England U-23 international squad against Wales at Ashton Gate in October. The crowd of 22,286 who saw England win 2-0 were disappointed that Garland was not picked (later that season he came on as substitute against Bulgaria).

In the League Cup – having disposed of Exeter – City were involved in a marathon second round tie with Leicester. They paid for missing their chances in the first two games and losing the toss for choice of venue for the second replay. Despite scoring first, they were undone by Andy Lochhead's hat-trick. In the FA Cup City were humiliated at Fourth Division Chester, where Billy Dearden's late goal punished them for trying to hold out for a replay.

Receipts of £5,874 were earned from the 24,905 spectators against Swindon, City's biggest home League crowd of the campaign. Season ticket sales dropped to 2,013, but with average home gates shooting up to 16,274 the club was able to declare its first profit since 1965-66 – a princely £3,856 being announced at the AGM held in the Indoor Bowls Club in the Dolman Stand.

The Youth side – containing Len Bond, Ray Cashley (an amateur full-back who impressed when taking over in goal from the injured Bond), Keith Fear, Billy Menmuir, Steve and Tom Ritchie – attracted much attention after disposing of Swindon, Cardiff, Plymouth and Bournemouth to reach the fifth round of the FA Youth Cup. A crowd of 10,178 (City's best FA Youth attendance since 18,181 turned up for the semi-final against Chelsea in April 1960) saw Leeds' youngsters beaten 2-1. Sadly, City lost 0-3 on aggregate in the semi-final against Tottenham.

The Colts finished fourteenth in the Western League, the same position as the previous year, while the Reserves, as well as reaching the final of the Somerset Professional Cup (losing 0-1 on aggregate against Bath City), made a strong bid for the Football Combination Championship before sliding back to fifth.

Though City retained their hold on the Gloucestershire Senior Professional Cup with a 2-1 home victory over Bristol Rovers, the curtain didn't come down on the season until almost two weeks later. Top Italian club Juventus came to Ashton Gate on 5 May, when goals from Gordon Parr and Skirton earned City a 2-1 win.

On the playing front, Tony Ford joined Bristol Rovers for £4,000 in December, and at the end of the season his long-time full-back partner Alec Briggs retired after thirteen years with the club. Popular Jack Connor, who had played over 400 games at the heart of City's defence, became player-coach. Manager Alan Dicks was rewarded for City's improved showing with a five-year contract at £5,000 per annum, after persuading the board to give Collins and Sillett new three-year agreements.

All in all, it was a much improved campaign after a poor start, with up-and-coming youngsters Gerry Gow, Ian Broomfield, Peter Spiring, Trevor Tainton having already played in the first team. Others, such as Ritchie, Rodgers, and the talented Fear, were hovering on the fringes, and the future prospects at Ashton Gate suddenly appeared much brighter.

```
┌─────────────────────────────────────────────────────────────┐
│                     Did You Know?                             │
│                                                               │
│  Walsall did not allow City to film the League Cup-tie at     │
│  Fellows Park in 1981 because they were due to face City      │
│  again in the League a few weeks later.                       │
└─────────────────────────────────────────────────────────────┘
```

Match of the Season 1969-70

Bristol City 6　Charlton Athletic 0

Division 2, 23 September 1969

After two years at Ashton Gate, with no sign of improvement in City's fortunes, Alan Dicks was coming under heavy fire from the fans. Scoring only two goals, whilst losing five of their first seven League games of the season, City had slumped to 21st spot in the Second Division table.

Feelings were running high, so much so that the manager had endured severe abuse in the previous game against Norwich City, despite a 4-0 success bringing the poor run to an end. The Charlton game was seen as a huge test for both the manager and the team, and over 15,000 fans were in attendance as City responded with a performance which proved to be a turning point of their campaign.

Following Alan Skirton's early header from a corner, John Galley brought the crowd to their feet with a tremendous ten-yard volley – likely the most powerful ever seen at Ashton Gate – the ball nestling in the back stanchion of the Covered End goal. These two first-half strikes were only a prelude to what was to come.

Charlton's defence disintegrated after the break as Skirton led them a merry dance, not only adding to his goal haul, but also hitting the bar with a 20-yarder and forcing keeper Tony Burns into making three expert saves. Playing great football, City stacked up the goals. Two came from free-kicks, and two others were the product of defence-shattering bursts down the right, firstly by Bobby Kellard, then by Galley.

Whilst many fans remained critical of City's slow progress, fortunes improved as the season unfolded. Indeed, the Charlton game was part of a six-match unbeaten run. Dicks was slowly fashioning a side that was becoming more difficult to beat, ending the campaign in fourteenth place with 39 points, and actually scoring more goals than they conceded.

There is little doubt that the back-to-back home wins over Norwich and Charlton enabled the directors to keep faith with Dicks, and, whilst it would be a long time in coming, such faith was to be ultimately rewarded with promotion to the top flight.

LEAGUE DIVISION 2   **1970-71**
Division 2   19th
League Cup   Semi-Final
FA Cup   3rd Round

A season of contrasts, as City came close to reaching Wembley in the League Cup, whilst only just avoiding relegation. With the transfer of Kellard to Leicester to help pay for the Dolman Stand, and with Dicks having little money to spend on players, Gow kept his place for most of the season. He looked raw to start with, but by the end of the campaign his great determination had made him worthy of a regular place. Dicks did, however, part with £5,000 to Ipswich to bring Steve Stacey back to Ashton Gate after City had previously sold him to Wrexham for £2,000.

For the first time since 1963, when the FA lifted restrictions on the playing of pre-season friendlies, City went abroad for their early preparations. Two wins and a draw against Dutch sides Holstein Kiel (2-0), Go Ahead Deventer (1-1) and Veendam (2-1), followed by home wins over West Ham (1-0) and Go Ahead Deventer (2-0) had everyone fired up for the big kick-off against relegated Sunderland.

With the Dolman Stand, though still unfinished, in use for the opening match, Ashton Gate was treated to a thrilling encounter which City won by the odd goal in seven. A 1-1 draw at Charlton followed before City chalked up a long-awaited home success over Cardiff – Sharpe's late strike brought a 1-0 win to take City up to fourth place. Unfortunately, this proved to be as good as it was going to get. A 0-4 drubbing at Filbert Street precipitated a slump that saw City in relegation peril after losing 0-1 at Bolton. With just two wins from the following thirteen games, relegation appeared inevitable, until City's youngest forward line carved out a 3-2 home win over Millwall in late-February. Ten points from the following nine games saw City claim the dizzy heights of eighteenth, after beating Portsmouth 2-0 at home on 10 April.

It was the loan signings of half-backs Brian Hill from Coventry and Les Wilson from Wolves that saved City from the drop. The duo inspired a 3-0 win at Watford on their debuts and were part of the side that recovered from a 0-2 half-time deficit to defeat promotion-chasers Luton at Ashton Gate. Even so, City only mustered a meagre 31 points and Dicks was fortunate that relegated Blackburn (27 points) and Bolton (24) were so poor.

The FA Cup offered but a brief distraction as Southampton gained belated revenge for their 1909 defeat – when City marched on to reach the final – by overcoming Cashley's goalkeeping defiance to win 3-0 at the Dell in a twice-postponed third round tie. The real loss, though, came five days later when the brilliant Gerry Sharpe, only 24, broke his leg in a tackle with Middlesbrough's Eric McMordie in City's 0-2 defeat at Ashton Gate. After weeks in hospital, when infection raised fears of amputation, Sharpe embarked on a long period of recuperation. Sadly he was forced to retire following a gallant comeback bid in the Reserves the next season. He was rewarded with a Testimonial in December 1973 and deserved better than the 3,607 crowd who turned up to see a 0-1 defeat by Derby County.

With Dicks under fire again from his many critics, it was a wonder to many that he survived the season, but no doubt City's run in the League Cup helped. Certainly it improved his position enough to fiercely resist efforts at an Emergency Board Meeting in January to dismiss Collins as an economy measure. Dicks had his way and directors Lionel Smart and Graham Whittock resigned.

The League Cup run commenced with a goalless draw at Third Division Rotherham. City were fortunate not to be numbered among the victims on a night of shocks – Carlisle 2 Manchester City 1; Bristol Rovers 2 Newcastle 1; Lincoln 2 Sunderland 1; Sheffield United 1 Leeds 0. A 4-0 win in the replay flattered City, but a 1-0 success at First Division Blackpool gave no measure of their superiority. Revenge was then gained over Leicester for the previous season's defeat – Wimshurst's extra-time winner prevented the tie extending into another marathon – taking City into the quarter-finals, where they avoided First Division Tottenham, Coventry, Crystal Palace and Manchester United.

On being paired with Third Division pacemakers Fulham, many thought City would have an easy passage into the semi-finals, and whilst this is how it often looked in a 0-0 draw at rain-swept Craven Cottage, the replay was a different matter. City were outplayed, but Sharpe's penalty proved enough to clinch the tie in front of a 23,230 crowd.

With Spurs beating Coventry 4-1, Manchester United disposing of Crystal Palace 4-2 and Bristol Rovers losing a replay 0-1 against Aston Villa, all of City's possible opponents in the hat for the semi-final draw were clubs of distinguished cup pedigree. It did not therefore much matter that they were drawn to play the favourites, Tottenham Hotspur, though the task was made more difficult by being at home in the first leg. The game was postponed for a week because of a power workers dispute, but on the evening of 16 December, 30,201 fans paying record receipts of £13,931 saw Skirton put City ahead just after half-time. Unfortunately, Alan Gilzean headed in a brilliant equaliser for Spurs to leave everything to play for in the second leg.

Did You Know?

England played a World XI at cricket at Ashton Gate in September 1980. A year later rain restricted the crowd at a floodlight cricket match to 1,539.

A stern defensive battle at White Hart Lane kept Spurs at bay for ninety minutes, but City's defence cracked in extra-time. Martin Chivers and Jimmy Pearce broke down the barrier to end City's hopes of their first major cup final for almost 62 years. The defeat also brought to an end their best cup run since reaching the semi-finals of the FA Cup in 1920, when their injury-hit side lost 1-2 to Huddersfield Town at Stamford Bridge.

The Reserves were well in the running for the Football Combination Championship, heading the table for much of the season until a late slump brought a final placing of fourth, whilst in the Western League, the Colts dropped down to fifteenth. Following their heady efforts in reaching the semi-final in 1969-70, the Youths went out of the FA Youth Cup at the first time of asking – losing 0-3 at Bournemouth.

Having played 168 games and scored 46 goals, a diseased knee ended Bush's career at 28. He later became Assistant Secretary at Ashton Gate, before taking up a position with the Transport and General Workers Union. Derrick joined French First Division side Paris Saint-Germain on a free-transfer, whilst Dicks quickly signed John Emanuel from Welsh club Ferndale, after watching his superb performance as a trialist in City's drawn Gloucestershire Cup match at Eastville Stadium.

The £2,000 proceeds of Connor's Benefit against Wolves in March, which City lost 1-2 in front of 7,800 fans, were added to the monies raised from other events held throughout the year. Among these was an Old Players' Match between City and Rovers at Eastville, which attracted a 2,000 attendance. Goals from Ian Hamilton and Alfie Biggs gave Rovers a 2-0 win, avenging defeat in a similar fixture almost seven years earlier, when a crowd totalling 3,289 saw City win 6-3 at Eastville in 1964.

A total of 12,256 spectators were present at Eastville when Fear scored for City in the last unresolved Gloucestershire Cup final, before the introduction of the penalty shoot-out. A short trip to Spain then followed, where City, having lost 1-3 to Espanol, beat Calella 2-1. Garland was selected for the Football Association's five-week tour of Australia, whilst promising youngster Peter Spiring was loaned to American side Washington Darts for the summer.

Despite a new record number of 4,176 season ticket holders, finance remained a problem. With the burden of the Dolman Stand repayments creating losses of £500 per week, accountant Tony Sully, later to replace Bert Bush as Secretary, took on the duties of Financial Secretary. Any gains made by the League Cup run were offset by a drop of over two thousand in the home League average attendance, but Kellard's £49,000 transfer to Leicester City saved the day and a profit of £15,172 was announced at the AGM held on 10 December 1971.

Match of the Season 1970-71

Bristol City 1 Tottenham Hotspur 1

League Cup, semi-final, 1st leg, 16 December 1970

A season of giant-killing in the Football League Cup saw struggling Second Division Bristol City and promotion-chasing Aston Villa of the Third Division both reach the semi-finals. For City, Welsh Cup winners in 1933-34, it was their first major semi-final since 1919-20 when they lost 1-2 against Huddersfield Town at Stamford Bridge in the FA Cup.

After many years of failure in the League Cup, now in its eleventh year, City fans were surprised at their team's success, especially as they had to overcome bogey side Leicester along the way. Apart from the Filberts, City enjoyed the luck of the draw, only once facing a top-flight side, albeit struggling Blackpool, and playing Third Division Fulham in the quarter-finals. City's struggle in the League came as a blow to the fans, who had expected the club to build on the previous season's improvement. Naturally, the consequence of this was more criticism being heaped on Alan Dicks, so City's lucrative cup run did much to keep him in a job.

After a week's delay in playing the tie, due to a power workers dispute, cup fever was rampant at Ashton Gate. City faced a Spurs side packed with star names, and the crowd of 30,201 was slightly larger than the number who attended the second leg a week later. After a dour opening, City fans dreamed of a first trip to Wembley when Alan Skirton scored with a close-range shot just after the interval. However, Alan Gilzean's far-post header from a Martin Peters cross left everything to play for in the second leg.

Given little chance at White Hart Lane, City put up a sterling defensive performance to take the game into extra-time before succumbing to goals by Martin Chivers and Jimmy Pearce. Spurs went on to cup glory, beating Villa 3-1 in the final. For City, though, nothing changed; they struggled throughout the season in the League and eventually finished just above the relegation spot.

LEAGUE DIVISION 2   **1971-72**
Division 2   8th
League Cup   1st Round
FA Cup   3rd Round

After the disappointments of the previous campaign, Chairman Dolman demanded improvement in 1971-72. New signings included Gerry Sweeney from Morton for £22,000 and Dave Merrington, a free from Burnley. Things didn't look promising when Bristol Rovers beat City 3-1 at Ashton Gate on the newly-laid pitch in a joint benefit game for Bush and Ford. However, with homebred players such as Cashley, Merrick, Spiring, and Tainton establishing themselves, matters improved once the League campaign got underway. A 5-1 win at Hillsborough surprised all, but despite the transfer of Garland to Chelsea after just four games, City sustained the momentum – twice topping the table early on. Emanuel's dynamic runs from midfield were a revelation, and a massive following travelled to Swindon on 2 October.

They were rewarded by Spiring's second-half volley that kept City in a promotion spot. The following week a 2-1 home success over Watford gave City sixteen points from eleven games and lifted them to second. Unfortunately a 1-3 defeat in the next game in front of the Match of the Day cameras at Millwall, against opponents who often proved a good yardstick of City's progress, brought Ashton Alf (as City's supporters are known) back to reality. Despite paying Wolves £15,000 to sign 23-year-old Les Wilson permanently, heavy grounds and only one further win (5-3 over Orient) prior to the New Year not only squashed promotion hopes, but left City worrying about relegation yet again.

Galley's textbook header got 1972 off to a good start with a home victory over Birmingham, but it wasn't until 19 February when Charlton were beaten 2-1 at Ashton Gate that another two-point haul came City's way. During this period City had slumped from tenth to sixteenth, but a return of the firmer pitches and the recall of winger Danny Bartley heralded much improved form. Eight wins and three draws from the last thirteen games produced a final position of eighth, City's best showing since 1965-66.

In the League Cup, though, it was a case of 'after the Lord Mayor's show'. The previous year's epic deeds meant naught at Home Park, where Plymouth made City pay for failing to take advantage of their first-half chances. In the FA Cup it was a similar story, as early chances were squandered before City succumbed to Preston's late onslaught, when Dicks' gamble on Rooks' fitness backfired.

Did You Know?

When Sunday football began in Bristol in 1966, City supporters formed a team called Bristol Casuals, while Rovers fans called their team the Pirates.

City's on-field progress was reflected in the home attendances, which rose to an average of 15,225. The biggest was 23,525 who turned up for the visit of Cardiff City, whilst the lowest was against Charlton Athletic – just 10,207. Despite season ticket sales dropping to 3,912, the selling of Garland allowed a record profit of £64,537 to be declared at the AGM.

The Gloucestershire Cup final at Ashton Gate was drawn 1-1, but Bristol Rovers took the trophy by winning the penalty shoot-out 4-2. The next day City travelled to Ferndale to play the local side as part of the deal that had brought Emanuel to the club. Sweeney got on the scoresheet in a 5-1 win. At the end of the month City embarked on an ambitious four-match overseas tour, which brought victories over a Teheran Select XI (2-0), Persepolis (1-0), Appollo Limasol (1-0) and Famagusta (3-1) in the space of seven days.

This extended City's participation in 'friendlies' for the season to thirteen. In the pre-season, besides the Rovers match, other games resulted as follows – Newport Co (a) 2-1, Wolves (h) 0-1, Torquay (a) 0-1, Port Vale (a) 1-1. During the campaign a goalless draw was played out against West Brom at Ashton Gate on 30 November, with 4,884 in attendance to support a benefit match for Terry Bush. The remaining friendlies brought a 1-0 win at Southend, whilst a home clash with Morton in May drew just 1,700 spectators, who saw Gow's second-half penalty salvage a 1-1 draw.

With Cashley established in goal, Mike Gibson – arguably the best keeper City have ever had – was allowed to join Gillingham on a free transfer, having played 383 games in nine years. Gordon Parr, who had been with the club twice as long, sampled League of Ireland football with Waterford. Recurring knee trouble brought an end to the Ashton Gate career of Rooks, a centre-half who, despite supplanting the popular Connor in City's side, had won over the hearts of the fans with his sterling displays. Merrington, who had not played a senior game due to Achilles tendon trouble, retired along with Wimshurst.

They both joined City's backroom staff, which was reshuffled in the summer of 1972 following Collins' departure to become Chief Scout at Leeds United. Sillett became Chief Coach, Wimshurst was given charge of the reserves, while Merrington took over the youth team. In the previous season they had reached the fifth round of the FA Youth Cup by beating Bournemouth (h) 1-0, Plymouth

Argyle (a) 3-2, and Stoke City (h) 2-0 (after a 1-1 away draw), before losing 1-2 at Norwich. Tony Rance became Commercial Manager and later replaced Sully as Secretary.

The Colts did not operate in 1971-72, and their return for the following season, when they finished fifteenth in the Western League, proved to be their swan-song. The Reserves, who had won the Somerset Professional Cup in 1970-71 (beating Yeovil 4-3 on aggregate), retained the trophy by beating Taunton 6-1 at Wordsworth Drive and 3-1 at Ashton Gate three days later. In the Football Combination, a run of form from December until late January, with only one point dropped in seven matches, carried City into Championship contention, but with only four wins from their last fourteen games they had to settle for a final placing of eighth.

Match of the Season 1971-72

Sheffield Wednesday 1 Bristol City 5

Division 2, 21 August 1971

By 1971 the club's vigorous scouting network was beginning to bear fruit and the introduction of up-and-coming youngsters into the side, coupled with the signing of Gerry Sweeney from Morton, prompted this outstanding performance against Sheffield Wednesday early in the season.

The campaign had started brightly with Sweeney scoring on his debut in a 3-3 home draw with Millwall, but few fans could have anticipated what was to follow at Hillsborough a week later. The lack of goals since Dicks' arrival was forgotten as City, seizing the initiative from the start, ran riot to notch up their biggest away win for five years. They were three up by half-time, Galley sparking the action by finishing a four-man move with a shot into the top corner of Peter Grummitt's net. Two more strikes after the break put City five up before Mike Prendergast headed a late goal for the Owls.

This success gave City much confidence and they maintained a top-four placing throughout the autumn, before the goals dried up. City scored only two in eight League games during December and January, which brought a slump into the bottom half of the table. A late-season recovery secured a creditable finishing position of eighth to suggest that, after so many years of struggle, City had at last come to terms with Second Division football.

For the Owls, their course was set in the opposite direction. A second consecutive season of under-achievement for this famous club saw them finish in fourteenth place, an early warning of their demise that was to bring relegation in 1974-75.

LEAGUE DIVISION 2   **1972-73**
Division 2   5th
League Cup   2nd Round
FA Cup   4th Round

Despite the lack of any signings in the summer of 1972, Ashton Alf entertained promotion thoughts for the first time in a long while as City embarked on their round of pre-season friendlies. Two hefty wins over Port Vale and Leicester kept expectations high, and a large following travelled to a wet and windy Goldstone Ground for the League opener against newly promoted Brighton.

With Rodgers back at centre-half, after almost a year's absence with a serious knee-ligament injury, Bartley hooked home a volley for a deserved point; but City failed to win any of their first five matches. They even found themselves at the bottom after losing 1-2 at home to Sheffield Wednesday, at which point Sillett told City fans that their heroes were the best footballing side in the Second Division.

A 2-0 success at fellow strugglers Orient ended the drought, to set up a nine-match unbeaten run extending over six weeks. This culminated in a 2-0 win at Oxford, by which time City were in eighth place. Three successive defeats, including the heaviest loss of the season, a 1-5 drubbing at Fulham (when young full-back Steve Ritchie made his only League appearance), brought Ashton Alf back to earth. Failure to win at home until 25 November, when Sunderland were defeated 1-0, proved costly. Despite the record £70,000 signing from West Brom of Bobby Gould – who made a less than auspicious debut in a 0-1 home defeat by Burnley – patchy form up to the turn of the year saw City slipping down the table. Considering the time of year, it was appropriate that it should be at Millwall's Cold Blow Lane on 30 December that City slumped to thirteenth after losing 0-3.

It took the intervention of the FA Cup to raise spirits. Gould's last-gasp third round equaliser at Portsmouth prompted a brilliant display in the replay which was won 4-1. City fans then enjoyed the treat of a trip to First Division Wolves, where injury-hit City were perhaps unfortunate to lose an enthralling cup-tie.

Despite an amazing on-field bust up between Gould and Gow, which prompted the latter to be sensibly pulled off by Dicks, a 3-1 home win over Brighton put the season back on track. City's young side – reinforced by the signing of Donnie Gillies from Morton just before the transfer deadline (in exchange for Steve Ritchie and £30,000) – won eight and drew three of their last fourteen games. They climbed to fifth at the campaign's end, when their total of 63 goals was enough to gain entry to the following season's Watney Cup.

In round two of the League Cup, City put up a brave show at Upton Park before losing 1-2 against First Division West Ham. In the Gloucestershire Cup, City turned the tables on the Rovers with a 5-3 penalty shoot-out victory, following a 2-2 draw at Eastville.

Season ticket sales reached a new record with 4,282 sold at prices ranging between £10.50 and £13.50 to raise £42,139, but the home average attendance dropped dramatically to 12,892 – a reflection, perhaps, of the fact that it took City over three months to notch up their first home success. A loss of £20,912 was declared at the AGM. The fearless play of the rumbustious Gould earned him ten goals, whilst Galley – described by Dicks as the best signing he ever made – managed seven from his twenty games prior to joining Nottingham Forest for £30,000 in December.

The quicksilver Spiring, whose exciting bursts from midfield promised more than they achieved, also moved on. He signed for Liverpool in March, when Bill Shankly, who was always on the lookout for young players of potential, paid £55,000 for his services. At the end of the campaign long-serving full-back Trevor Jacobs joined Bristol Rovers on a free transfer, but Swansea City had to pay £12,000 to capture centre-half David Bruton.

Emanuel's sterling performances were recognised when he was called up for the Welsh squad for the end-of-season Home Internationals. By coming on as substitute during a 0-3 defeat by England at Wembley on 15 May and again during a 0-1 loss against Northern Ireland at Goodison Park four days later, he was able to upgrade his earlier amateur appearances for his country. Emanuel thereby became City's first full international since Dermot Curtis, who was in the Republic of Ireland side that lost 1-3 against Austria in Vienna in May 1958.

The youth policy, partly financed by insurance receipts (Sharpe £15,000, Rooks £5,000, and Merrington £3,500) was by now coming along nicely. The youth team, captained by 18-year-old Gary Collier, who made his League debut in a 3-1 win at Luton in March, reached the FA Youth Cup final for the only time.

Opening with a 0-0 draw at Southampton, City won the replay 2-0. An identical score, this time against Birmingham side Northfield Juniors, allowed City the opportunity to spot the talent of Clive Whitehead among the ranks of the opposition. A 1-0 win at Everton persuaded 6,781 to attend the home quarter-final with Arsenal, when goals from Collier and Price earned a place in the semi-finals for the third time and a controversial meeting with Sheffield United.

Did You Know?

The Young Robins Club was formed in 1967 for 11-18 year olds. Subscription was 2s 6d (12½ pence). Membership quickly topped 400, including 50 girls.

After Kevin Prue's two strikes earned a 2-2 draw at Bramhall Lane, the 7,906 fans at Ashton Gate for the second leg nine days later were bemused when United refused to play extra-time following a goalless ninety minutes. Thankfully, justice was done when Martyn Rogers' goal was enough to win the decider on Birmingham's neutral St Andrew's Ground. Unfortunately, City proved to be no match for Ipswich in the final. Having lost the first leg 0-3 at Portman Road, City never looked like pulling back the deficit in the second leg a week later.

Disappointment for the 6,032 crowd, maybe, but at least they enjoyed the consolation of Rogers' 90th-minute goal as City lost 1-4 on aggregate. A reward of sorts came later for the youngsters as they travelled to Holland in the close season and won the prestigious Blauw Wit tournament in Amsterdam. They also won the Bordeaux Etudiantes Youth Tournament and added to their successes in 1971 and 1972 by collecting the honours at the Tilberg Youth Tournament for the third time. By contrast, the Reserves had a poor season, relinquishing their hold on the Somerset Professional Cup after a 1-3 defeat at Bridgwater Town in the third round. They also finished seventeenth in the Football Combination.

Match of the Season 1972-73
Sunderland 2 Bristol City 2

Division 2, 31 March 1973

During a season which saw City continue their progress of the previous campaign, no greater test came than that at windy Roker Park. In-form Sunderland were seeking their fourth successive League victory, having recovered from a mid-season slump.

Fielding the same line-up that had achieved wins at Luton and at home to Aston Villa, City were confident of success at a venue that had often proved a happy hunting ground in the past – actually winning at Roker the week following Sunderland's record 9-1 thrashing of Newcastle at St James' Park in 1908-09.

City gave as good as they got early on, but when Geoff Merrick turned Dick Malone's cross into his own net on 35 minutes the spectre of City's record 1-6 FA Cup defeat at Roker Park in 1963-64 haunted the thoughts of the small band of Robins fans in the 33,255 crowd. Fortunately the interval was reached without the team conceding further goals, but Merrick left City a mountain to climb early in the second half when he attempted to head the ball back to his keeper. The alert Dave Watson nipped in to stretch out his foot and touch the ball over the head of the advancing Ray Cashley.

Now was the time for City's great team spirit to assert itself, and this is precisely what happened under the inspiring leadership of captain Merrick. Refusing to be cowed by his earlier errors, Merrick rallied his side with a headed goal in the 59th minute and continually drove his players forward in the search for the equaliser. With time running out it looked as though all the effort was to be in vain, but then midfield dynamo John Emanuel ensured City did not leave Roker without any reward. He seized on a half-clearance to send a great first-time left-footed shot rocketing high into the net from 25 yards.

City's young side showed they had come of age in this match and this great fighting spirit was to be the basis of their promotion-winning side three years later. Four of City's final five games of the season were won, to take them up to fifth place in the table, whilst Sunderland, with an identical record but inferior goal-average, were one place lower.

City and Sunderland would be promoted together, and their clash in this game highlighted the fact that both clubs were building squads with elevation to the top flight very much in mind.

ON THE RISE
1973-1979

LEAGUE DIVISION 2   **1973-74**
Division 2   16th
League Cup   3rd Round
FA Cup   6th Round

Whilst 1973-74, with a slide to sixteenth place, didn't appear to offer evidence of an upswing in City's fortunes, the signing of 21-year-old centre-forward Paul Cheesley from Norwich City for £30,000 – following Gould's £80,000 December move to West Ham and the free-transfer summer captures of Mike Brolly from Chelsea and Jimmy Mann from Leeds – meant all the pieces of the promotion jigsaw would come together.

A memorable FA Cup run that saw Leeds beaten 1-0 in a replay at Elland Road was the undoubted catalyst for the great events of the following two years, despite City losing to Liverpool by a solitary goal in the quarter-finals at Ashton Gate. Paradoxically, the start of City's long-term decline were sown this season – namely the seeds of the boardroom battles which eventually led to the formation of Bristol City (1982) plc.

We must not get ahead of events, however, as the feeling during the summer was one of anticipation of this being City's year. A 2-1 first round win at Peterborough in the Watney Cup on 11 August fuelled these hopes, which were not dampened by a 1-4 defeat against First Division Stoke in the semi-final at the Victoria Ground four days later.

After winning both their opening matches, slick Luton's 3-1 win at Ashton Gate brought Ashton Alf back to earth, but a 3-1 win over Hull saw City perched on top of the table. This game at windswept Ashton Gate is remembered for keeper Cashley's astonishing goal. With the wind behind them, the Tigers had the better of the first half and fully deserved the lead gained by Stuart Pearson's tap-in. After the break Tom Ritchie headed City level before Cashley made his mark with a clearance that sped through the air and bounced just outside the Hull penalty area before ballooning high into the net over keeper Jeff Wealands, who was caught ten yards off his line. The distance of the kick was originally hailed as being 98 yards, but measurement of the Ashton Gate pitch a few days later revised this downwards to 95 yards 2 feet – still a record for a League goal, beating Peter Shilton's effort against Southampton six years previously by two yards.

A 1-2 defeat at Hull saw City's players use up their unexpended energy with a late-night party in their hotel. Following complaints from the other residents Dicks slapped a £20 fine on every player, but Gould, who had not been involved, refused to pay and appealed to the Football Association. Within a few months Gould, a tremendous ambassador for the club who always took the trouble to talk to the fans, was transferred, with Dicks explaining that his star player had been unable to get on with his team-mates.

A week after the Hull affair, City recorded their first ever win over Scunthorpe, this in a replay of their second-round League Cup-tie. There followed two classic encounters with First Division Coventry, but Whitehead's goal was not enough at Highfield Road as the Sky Blues won 2-1.

The League campaign nosedived after this. Despite the arrivals of Cheesley and Ernie Hunt (the latter on a two-month loan from Coventry before City paid £7,000 for the 31-year-old's services) a 0-2 defeat on their New Year's Day debut against Orient heaped the pressure back on Dicks as City slumped to fourteenth. Dolman registered his concerns by leaving written instructions as he took off for his annual mid-winter holiday in the Barbados. The gist was that more money needed to be injected into the club, that Dicks ought not to be offered more than a one-year contract, and that if Dolman's views did not prevail he would consider that he had grounds for resigning.

It was in this uncertain atmosphere that Dicks prepared for the FA Cup, but in the home third-round tie with Hull at Ashton Gate keeper Bond was unable to emulate Cashley's goalscoring exploits as City could only scrape a 1-1 draw. A rare Tainton goal brought a hard-fought win in the replay at Boothferry Park. Before the next round, City played on a Sunday for the first time because of the national power crisis and the ban on the use of floodlights.

On a sunny afternoon at Burnden Park, Hunt's volley was insufficient to prevent Bolton winning 2-1, but in the wind and rain at soggy Hereford the following Saturday, Merrick's left-footed effort carried City through to the fifth round.

Few gave City much chance against Leeds, even with home advantage, but the First Division pacesetters were fortunate to escape with a 1-1 draw in front of a crowd of 37,141 paying record receipts of £28,111. Billy Bremner rifled a 25-yard shot into the top corner to give Leeds a first-half lead, but the visitors were rocking when Fear lobbed a 65th-minute equaliser. The incredible replay victory is covered in Match of the Season.

With Liverpool the quarter-final visitors, the fans flocked to the League match against Oxford, but the real attraction was the issue of vouchers for the cup-tie and, once these had been obtained, many of the 25,904 crowd did not hang around to watch City's 0-0 draw. Sadly, the FA Cup dream ended in front of 37,671 spectators, creating a new receipts record for Ashton Gate of £28,826. Shortly after half-time Rodgers, in for the injured Merrick, failed to deal with a Kevin Keegan cross and the ball, after hitting Drysdale, bounced obligingly into John Toshack's path.

Dolman had arrived back from the West Indies in time to see the famous win at Leeds, but was shocked to learn that the other directors accepted his resignation, as they were not prepared to accede to his demands. The rift was hushed up until after the Cup run. In due course it was announced that self-made millionaire Robert Hobbs was the new Chairman, while Dolman became the club's first president since Albert Denby in 1896 had followed Col Plant and John Durant in the role.

Cup glory brought honours for Gillies and Gow, both of whom were selected for Scotland's Under-23 squad against England at Newcastle. Gillies played the whole game, whilst Gow came on for the last half-hour in a 0-2 defeat.

In the League, it needed a hat-trick of wins in early April to keep relegation at bay. A close season tour to Greece did little to improve City's form, the best results being 1-1 draws against Olympiakos and Agrinion, following a 1-2 defeat by AEK Athens. Average home League attendance increased to 14,058, and with the income from the Cup revenue, a profit of £60,527 was announced at the AGM.

The Youths only reached the third round of the FA Youth Cup, but the growing reputation of City's youth policy earned a fixture with England Youth. A crowd of only 450 were present at Ashton Gate to see England (with Whitehead in their ranks) win 2-0.

Match of the Season 1973-74

Leeds United 0   Bristol City 1

FA Cup, 5th Round replay, 19 February 1974

A season that started brightly was only redeemed by City's best run in the FA Cup since they reached the semi-finals 54 years previously.

Did You Know?

City's 8 consecutive League wins in 1997-98 was well short of their record 14 League wins in 1906-07 – a record shared with Manchester U and Preston.

Prior to the Leeds epic, a fourteen-game sequence had brought City just two wins and nine goals between October and January, not to mention a 0-5 trouncing at Oxford on Boxing Day, which left Dicks fretting about his job.

Following the 1-1 draw at Ashton Gate, Leeds were overwhelming favourites for the replay. This game, which kicked-off at 2pm on account of the miners' strike affecting national power supplies, drew a huge crowd to Elland Road. Jim Evans, City's Promotions Manager, had booked the League Liner – a special Pullman carriage chartered by the Football League – for the Tuesday afternoon replay and sold enough tickets to fill it within an hour. Widespread absenteeism was reported in the Avon area as a mass exodus took place. Some of City's 8,000 travelling fans were locked out of Elland Road when the gates were closed half an hour before the kick-off, with 47,182 customers already inside the ground.

Leeds, brimming with ten internationals, played the free-flowing soccer for which they were renowned, but City kept them at bay with a mixture of luck and tenacity before, against the odds, taking a 73rd-minute lead. The Bristol hordes could hardly believe it as Gillies, having received a super pass from Fear, clipped the ball underneath Saturday's hero, keeper David Harvey. The remaining minutes were pure torture as Leeds strove to save the game, but City somehow kept their goal intact to achieve their greatest Cup success since beating Portsmouth 39 years previously. The result earned a mention on the front page of *The Times* and kept Alan Dicks in his job.

Leeds duly clinched the championship, but suffered their first League defeat of the season in their very next game. For City, their cup luck ran out at home to Liverpool in the quarter-finals, when John Toshack's shot was all that divided the sides at the end of a close game.

LEAGUE DIVISION 2   **1974-75**
Division 2   5th
League Cup   3rd Round
FA Cup   3rd Round

Dicks' brainchild 'All-In-the-Game' competition was staged at Ashton Gate on 28 July and filmed for transmission on ITV's World of Sport a month later. City came second with 250 points in this first pilot of a competition that was to run again in 1976 and 1977. Wolves were the winners with 315 points, whilst Derby (230) were third and Chelsea fourth (195).

The football started with a 5-0 home win over Dutch side Veendam, by which time Sillett – whose one-touch football coaching was such a feature of City's young side – had rowed with Dicks and left to take over as manager of Hereford. Wimshurst stepped up as Chief Coach, whilst Merrington – who had returned to Burnley – was succeeded by Don Mackay, a former Dundee United and Southend goalkeeper.

A goalless draw at Nottingham Forest was indicative of City's season to come: despite their neat, composed football, goals were at a premium. Dicks relied on Gow, Emanuel and Sweeney to provide the cutting thrust, but it wasn't until Mann's regular inclusion in the side from late October that the team started to click.

A slow start saw City as low as fifteenth after losing 0-2 at Oxford, but four straight wins hoisted them up to fourth after Emanuel's shot secured a 1-0 home win over Manchester United, who were suffering the indignity of a season in Division Two. Although City hovered among the promotion places throughout the campaign, and completed the double over the champions-to-be with a 1-0 victory at Old Trafford, the paucity of goals proved too big a handicap. With money in short supply, Dicks' interest in Wolves striker Hugh Curran was not followed up. City soldiered on, and on Good Friday a first-ever League win at Southampton put them in a promotion spot.

With a home game against fellow promotion chasers Norwich the following day, City fans travelling home from the Dell were intoxicated by thoughts of a long-cherished First Division place. Norwich, though, without a game the day before, looked the fresher side. Inspired by the play of Martin Peters, they deservedly won thanks to Colin Suggett's goal.

A 1-1 home draw against Bristol Rovers on Easter Tuesday, followed by wins over Notts County and Sheffield Wednesday, sustained City's interest, but a controversial defeat at Orient when the floodlights failed destroyed the dream. City were left to reflect on the Norwich defeat that effectively cost them promotion. Dicks made sure that in future years his side would never again have to play three games over the Easter period.

A final position of fifth was a great improvement and for the first time in many years City were an admired Second Division club. Surprisingly, the average home attendance barely increased, whilst the number of season tickets holders dropped from 4,269 to 3,863, no doubt put off by price increases for the best seats from £15.50 to £17. A loss of £68,456 was declared at the AGM.

In the League Cup, a 2-1 home victory over Cardiff was followed by an outstanding 4-1 win at Crystal Palace, which set up a home meeting with Liverpool in the third round. Given the fact of last season's FA Cup win for Liverpool over City, this opportunity for revenge over the First Division giants failed to generate much excitement. Only 25,753 out of 37,000 tickets were sold. Following a disappointing goalless draw City were put to the sword at Anfield where Liverpool achieved a 4-0 victory.

In the light of the previous year's exploits, the FA Cup was a big disappointment as City went out at the first time of asking – a 0-2 defeat at Sheffield United a poor reward for playing some good football. Failure was also City's fate in the County tourney. Bristol Rovers followed up the previous season's 2-0 win by retaining the trophy with a 2-1 extra-time success at Eastville in front of an 11,408 crowd. City collected a cup in early May when, having beaten Blackburn 2-0 and Stoke 1-0, the Pontins Five-a-Side Tournament at Southport was won by beating Sunderland 1-0 in the final.

A second benefit match for City's great servant Cliff Morgan – who captained the side in the 1930s – brought down the curtain at Ashton Gate when only 1,796 turned up to see Leicester win 4-2. For the players, though, there remained a trip to Norway. The highlight of a four-match tour was a 10-0 thrashing of Mo, following victories over Molde (2-0), Bodo-Glimt (1-0) and Mjolner (5-2).

In the Football Combination the Reserves emulated the seniors in making a strong bid for League honours, but at the end had to be satisfied with third place after losing their last three fixtures. Although it was a disappointing finish, it was still their highest position since finishing runners-up in 1954-55. Fortunately, they made no mistake in the Somerset Professional Cup, the last season before it was renamed the Somerset Premier Cup. In the final, Taunton Town were beaten 3-0 in the second leg at Wordsworth Drive, after City had beaten them 4-0 at Ashton Gate three days earlier. The Youths, though, could not follow suit in the FA Youth Cup, losing 0-1 at Ipswich in the third round after winning 3-2 at Plymouth.

> **Did You Know?**
>
> Mark Aizlewood is City's second most capped player. His 21 Welsh caps can't match the 26 England caps won by Billy Wedlock between 1907 and 1914.

Match of the Season 1974-75

Bristol City 0 Norwich City 1

Division 2, 29 March 1975

History shows that this was the season when Dicks convinced City fans that the team he was building could take the club into the highest echelons of the English game. Indeed, it was only defeat in this vital game on Easter Saturday that ultimately denied City promotion in 1974-75.

A first-ever League win at Southampton the previous day had put City in control of their own destiny and convinced the travelling horde of fans that the promotion prize was theirs. Unfortunately promotion rivals Norwich had the advantage of resting in a Bristol hotel while City were otherwise engaged on the South Coast, and whilst this did not have any apparent effect on the result, it was a situation that Dicks was at pains to ensure wasn't to happen at Easter time again.

City's team was built on the ethos of everyone working for each other, which in the absence of a prolific attack lent them defensive resilience. Despite the lack of goals, nine wins from a twelve-game run which culminated at Southampton suggested that City were coming through with a late dash to snatch the third promotion prize.

A bumper crowd of more than 22,000 were enticed to Ashton Gate on a fine sunny afternoon, but with Keith Fear returning after suspension in place of Tom Ritchie, the promotion dream faltered against impressive opponents who demonstrated class and composure under City's ceaseless, but often punchless, pressure. Guilty of over-elaboration, many City moves broke down through players being caught in possession. Colin Suggett, earlier denied when Geoff Merrick headed off the line, won the priceless points for Norwich as early as the seventeenth minute with a low right-footed volley after Ted MacDougall had hooked back Phil Boyer's cross.

Although City won three of their remaining six fixtures, this proved to be a vital win for Norwich that gave them the boost to secure promotion, a situation that would have been reversed if the result had gone the other way.

LEAGUE DIVISION 2   **1975-76**
Division 2   2nd (Promoted)
League Cup   2nd Round
FA Cup   3rd Round

Despite only being ninth favourites, at odds of 20-1 for promotion, belief was strong, both within the club and amongst the fans, that the prize could be won. It was, however, felt that a goalscorer was needed: Cheesley had only flattered to deceive in his infrequent appearances since joining from Norwich. As it turned out, it was the harnessing of Cheesley alongside the hard-working Ritchie that proved to be the final piece of the promotion jigsaw. Indeed, it was not long before Cheesley was being noted as a candidate for England honours. Merrick was in such outstanding form that Bristol City great John Atyeo was moved to comment that he was the best defender he had ever seen. The cultured Gary Collier at centre-half, together with the energetic Sweeney and the reliable Drysdale at full-back, as well as keeper Cashley enjoying his best ever season, all combined to ensure that City's defence could mop up the pressure and supply the platform for a return to the top flight.

After failing to qualify for the knock-out stages of the Anglo-Scottish Cup – when a defeat at Chelsea, a draw at Fulham and a home win over Norwich left City second in their group – a disputed, twice-taken penalty by Sweeney at Ashton Gate brought a winning, if shaky start to the League campaign. Sunderland were then sent packing as two goals from Mann and another from Brolly brought a 3-0 win, but successive 1-3 defeats at Hull and Southampton brought City down to earth. The smallest League derby attendance for years saw Cheesley get off the mark in a 1-1 draw at Ashton Gate, before the promotion march really got under way with wins over Blackburn and Oxford. It was in those matches that the Cheesley-Ritchie partnership began to spark, as they each scored twice to take City to the top of the table.

October brought a brilliant performance at Oldham, inspired by Whitehead's thirty-minute substitute appearance. He set up a headed goal for Cheesley and scored the fourth himself to earn City the plaudits from many rival managers as being the best side outside the First Division. Following a runaway 4-1 success at York, with Cheesley notching the only hat-trick of his career, City's nine-match unbeaten run came to an end when West Brom's player-boss Johnny Giles inspired his side's 2-0 win at Ashton Gate.

Three more scoreless games followed, before the BBC Match of the Day cameras recorded City's return to form in the reverse fixture against York, when Ritchie hit a hat-trick in another 4-1 win.

> **Did You Know?**
>
> **Geoff Merrick conceded nine own-goals in seven seasons for Bristol City, out of a total of just 17 City own-goals in that period.**

He scored twice the following week in a 2-1 success at Fulham and only a 0-1 defeat at Bolton disturbed City's progress up to the turn of the year.

In the FA Cup, few were particularly concerned over City's 1-2 exit as all efforts were now concentrated on the promotion prize. Against struggling Oxford at the Manor Ground the following week it might be thought that in a 1-1 draw City lost a point, but in effect this was a point gained because, following Cheesley's early headed goal, it was only Cashley's defiance between the sticks that averted a heavy defeat.

Dicks, recalling the previous season's Easter setback, persuaded Plymouth to bring forward their home fixture against City from Easter Saturday to 24 January, the date of the fourth round of the FA Cup. The game was poor and goalless, but the point earned was vital. By this time, though Collins had returned from Leeds as Assistant Manager, Hobbs dropped a bombshell by threatening to sell Merrick and Ritchie to Arsenal, who had bid £250,000 for the pair. Dicks, his sights fixed on promotion, insisted they stayed, but with the club facing an ultimatum from the bank the directors were sorely tempted. The argument raged for two weeks, but eventually the board announced that the pair would be staying. They appealed for supporters to purchase season tickets (£33 before 30 June, £40 thereafter) for the following year. The fans responded by purchasing over £66,000 worth in a few weeks and the financial showdown with the bank was averted.

Ritchie proved his worth by netting in a 1-1 home draw with Southampton and grabbing the winner at Orient to take City back to the top of the table. Having done so, it came as no surprise to City fans that their favourites lost the next fixture, though there was no fluke about Forest's 2-0 win at Ashton Gate. Two wins and a draw followed before a crucial encounter at West Brom. This fixture should have taken place on 28 February, but the Football League sanctioned a late postponement as nine City players, plus Dicks, had gone down with flu. Many City fans had already set off for the game and knew nothing of the postponement until they reached the ground.

The game was re-scheduled for 17 March. After Sweeney's drive earned a 1-0 win, few doubted that City were headed for the First Division. A 1-1 draw with promotion rivals Sunderland at Roker

Park cast aside many of the remaining doubts, with thoughts focusing instead on the Championship. Missed chances brought a 1-2 defeat at Blackpool and a further point was dropped in a 2-2 draw with Chelsea, which allowed Sunderland to take over pole position. After another point was lost at Eastville in a dire derby clash, City were left needing two points to clinch promotion, with two games remaining.

20 April 1976 will long be remembered by those City fans present at Ashton Gate. A rare Whitehead goal early in the game clinched a nervous victory over a Portsmouth side who belied their already relegated status by putting up a mighty struggle. Noisy were the celebrations that night as City clinched their long-awaited return to the top echelon of the English game.

With the Championship still up for grabs, City were deflated in their final game as Notts County won 2-1 at Ashton Gate. In the event, Sunderland's 2-0 home success over Portsmouth meant the Rokermen could not be overhauled, finishing three points clear. Fortunately, City found their form to beat Bristol Rovers 3-2 after extra-time in the Gloucestershire Cup final at Ashton Gate.

An open-topped bus tour of the city was followed by a civic reception at the Council House, whereupon the players went off to Spain to play a 1-1 draw with Orhuela Deportiva. For their achievement in winning promotion the players were awarded a bonus of £1,000, whilst the manager was rewarded with £5,000. The most-expensive season tickets had increased in cost to £23 and City's home League average attendances jumped to 16,204. This, coupled with no outgoings on transfer fees, meant that a relatively small deficit of £5,900 was announced at the AGM.

Match of the Season 1975-76
West Brom 0   Bristol City 1

Division 2, 17 March 1976

Although it would be fair to say that promotion is not won in a single game, there comes a defining moment in every campaign. Over the course of the season, City's twice-taken penalty in the opening fixture against Bolton comes to mind, but the match that the Robins' travelling fans were convinced clinched promotion was this rearranged epic battle at the Hawthorns on St Patrick's Day.

The first half of this thrilling encounter was played at a furious pace, with table-topping City more than holding their own against fellow promotion challengers. Just before half-time, Gerry Sweeney sent the massive contingent of City fans amongst the 26,000 crowd into raptures, finishing off a clever move by netting with a cross-shot from the right into the Birmingham End goal.

After the break it was a different story, as the Baggies seized control. Ray Cashley's goal was under almost constant siege as Albion did everything but score. Heroic defending and the intervention of the woodwork prevented an equaliser, though City missed the chance of putting the result beyond doubt when Paul Cheesley miskicked in front of an open net. It was just like the Leeds cup-tie again as the final minutes dragged agonisingly by, and the fans' relief was palpable when the final whistle blew.

Despite only winning two of their final eight games, City duly fulfilled the confidence of their fans by gaining promotion in their penultimate game, but they lost out on the Championship. West Brom bounced back from this defeat to put together a great winning run to clinch the third promotion spot. Only their inferior goal-average kept them below City.

LEAGUE DIVISION 1   **1976-77**
League Division 1   18th
League Cup   2nd Round
FA Cup   3rd Round

Dicks knew he had to strengthen his squad. He released Emanuel to Newport County and Brolly to Grimsby, and had funds available from the record number of 6,639 season tickets sold. Unfortunately, Burnley midfielder Doug Collins chose to join Plymouth on a free transfer, whilst a £55,000 bid for Mansfield striker Ray Clarke was rejected, as were overtures for Newcastle's John Tudor. It was therefore the promotion-winning side that quite properly participated in the pre-season Anglo-Scottish Cup. Despite home wins over West Brom and Notts County, a 2-4 defeat at Nottingham Forest was sufficient to deny them a place in the knock-out stages.

The fans were unconcerned though, their thoughts focused on City's League opener at sun-baked Highbury. City's shock win did scant justice to their superiority over an Arsenal side that included their record new-signing Malcolm Macdonald. Lauded by Brian Moore on ITV's The Big Match, City showed their win was no fluke as they went second in the table with a 4-1 home win over Sunderland, following a 1-1 draw with Stoke in their first home match. The Stoke game was marred by an injury that finished Cheesley's career. He fell awkwardly after contesting a high ball with keeper Peter Shilton and his right knee crumpled beneath him. He attempted a comeback in a 0-1 home defeat by Birmingham two months later, but eventually, following three operations and a lengthy stay at Farnham Park Rehabilitation Centre, near Slough, was obliged to hang up his boots.

Unbeaten in the first four League games, Dicks searched in vain for a striker as the goals dried up. A 1-2 defeat at Maine Road put a halt to City's promising start. Then, after a home draw against West Ham, City mustered just two goals in the next six games, losing them all. Len Bond, back at Ashton Gate after being loaned out and playing in America, ended Cashley's run of consecutive games when taking over in goal against Leicester. Bond pulled a groin muscle taking a goal-kick at Villa Park and never played for City again, joining Brentford in the summer. John Shaw was the next keeper to be drafted in, having waited two and a half years for his senior chance. His debut coincided with Cheesley's last game. Shaw seized his opportunity so firmly that he became a fixture in the side. By 1978-79 he was being tipped for Scottish international honours.

City tumbled dramatically down the table and had sunk to twentieth (out of 22) when Dicks made his first foray into the transfer market. It wasn't a forward he wanted, however, but one of England's greatest post-war defenders – 32-year-old Norman (bite your legs) Hunter. He signed a three-year contract after City paid Leeds £40,000 for his services. Known only by his reputation as a hard man, City supporters soon began to appreciate the other side of his character that had so endeared him to the Leeds fans over the course of thirteen years and 540 League appearances.

Instead of a ruthless clogger, City supporters learned that Hunter was an accomplished footballer. Possessed of a cultured left-foot, his passing and positional play were impeccable. Every time he surged forward it was like a one-man cavalry charge. Hunter, however, did not enjoy an auspicious City debut. It was at Derby, where he had been sent off after fighting with Francis Lee some years previously. He was given a rough ride by the home fans and received a first-half booking as City slipped to a 0-2 defeat.

Hunter's first home appearance coincided with Fear's return to the side. A sound display by Merrick – who had moved to left-back in place of Drysdale to accommodate the newcomer – helped City halt their losing run with a goalless draw. The following week saw Dicks splash out £50,000 to secure 29-year-old Liverpool midfielder Peter Cormack, who had been capped nine times by Scotland. Cormack's debut was at Tottenham and he was instrumental in the goal that brought City's later winner. His long diagonal pass set Merrick scurrying down the left to cross for Fear to net.

Things looked even brighter following a 3-1 home win over Norwich. And though City lost 1-2 at Anfield they extended Liverpool to the limit. Dicks then agreed a £100,000 fee to bring Chris Garland back from Leicester. A training ground bust-up that left Jeff Blockley with a broken jaw meant that Leicester boss Jimmy Bloomfield was anxious to offload the fair-haired striker who had made a name for himself as a First Division marksman since leaving City four years previously.

Garland's first match was at home to Leeds, when 31,400 spectators, City's biggest home crowd of the season, saw very little. After ten minutes fog enveloped the ground and though rumour suggested Garland had hit the bar with a header it was no surprise that the game was called off at half-time.

With Gow needing a cartilage operation and Ritchie unable to recapture his previous form, City had to wait until 22 January for their next win. After bowing out of the FA Cup 1-4 at Ipswich and then losing 1-2 at Old Trafford, City secured the double over Arsenal, helped by Cormack's two goals. Garland's first goal after his return earned a home point against Newcastle, but the crunch came at Sunderland, who had gone thirteen games without winning and

1,017 minutes of play without scoring a goal. Both sequences ended against City, the crucial goal dumping them back in trouble.

Dicks took the players to Torremolinos for a short break. Garland's goal accounted for Manchester City on their return, but only one win in the next nine games saw City entrenched at the bottom of the table. Cormack's penalty winner against Spurs heralded better things, and seven points from seven games, whilst not lifting City clear of the drop-line, kept them in with a chance of pulling clear with two matches left.

Garland's two goals beat champions Liverpool at Ashton Gate, whereupon City's fate was suddenly thrust into their own hands. With one match left, three days later, it didn't matter what the other clubs did; all City had to do was draw at Coventry. The record books show that was what happened, but behind the 2-2 scoreline was a story that no writer of fiction could ever dream up.

Match of the Season 1976-77
Coventry City 2 Bristol City 2

Division 1, 19 May 1977

Postponed on New Year's Day because of a frozen pitch, this game provided a climax to the season that no one present will ever forget. Having waited 65 years to regain First Division status, City looked to be making a quick return back to where they had come from.

Stoke and Tottenham were already down, but the third relegation spot rested between City, Sunderland and Coventry, each with 34 points. On this last fateful evening Sunderland were away at Everton. If Sunderland won, Coventry's inferior goal-difference (introduced to replace goal-average this season) meant they too would have to win to survive. Both games were due to kick off at the same time for this Thursday evening fixture, but this failed to take account of the sheer numbers of Bristolians converging on the ground. Many of the estimated 15,000 red-and-white bedecked West Country fans travelled up the M5 more in hope than expectation, almost resigned to relegation, but they reckoned without their team's fighting qualities – not to mention the consequences of the five-minute delay to the kick-off, brought about by the massive 36,000 crowd still trying to squeeze inside Highfield Road.

Coventry went in front after fifteen minutes through Tommy Hutchison, their Scottish International winger. When he doubled his tally shortly after the break it looked all up for the Robins. Fortunately, the players did not give up the ghost, and Gerry Gow revived hopes a few minutes later by scoring from twelve yards.

Did You Know?

When City beat St Albans 9-2 in the FA Cup in 1996, it was the first time City had been involved in an 11-goal match since beating Chichester 11-0 in 1960.

It was now all City, and with just eleven minutes left Donnie Gillies shot into the far corner of the Coventry net to level matters. A battle royal then ensued, but the Robins looked the more likely winners until the heart-pounding action came to an abrupt halt four minutes from time. The electronic scoreboard was flashing up the message that Sunderland had lost 0-2, the result of which was that both teams needed only to maintain the status-quo. The remaining minutes degenerated into farce, with the Robins retaining possession in their own half, the only danger being the prospect of a back-pass going astray. So passed the final minutes, until the bemused referee, Ron Challis, blew for time with both sets of fans deliriously happy.

Survival celebrations in Bristol were interrupted the following day when Hobbs, unbeknown to his colleagues, announced that potential directors could buy themselves vacancies on the board for £25,000 each. This bombshell stirred the other four directors into action and Hobbs was deposed as chairman on 23 May. Stephen Kew succeeded him with the backing of Norman Jones, Graham Griffiths and Bill Garland.

While Bristol City's tenure in the top flight would last only three more seasons, Coventry have lived a charmed life in its glorified ranks ever since.

LEAGUE DIVISION 1   **1977-78**
League Division 1   17th
League Cup   3rd Round
FA Cup   3rd Round

City's return to the First Division precipitated a change to the club badge. The design – a robin perched on a ball surmounted by the Clifton Suspension Bridge – was adopted in July 1976. Prior to 1972, the club badge had always been the Coat of Arms of the City and County of Bristol, though a robin had been worn on the players' shirts in 1949-50. However, with the increasing marketing of club products it was decided to hold a competition to design an official badge. Organised by the *Bristol Evening Post*, it attracted 300 entries and the winner was 57-year-old rugby fan Harry Winn. He received a prize of £50 for his simple design depicting a robin on a five-bar gate. This new crest appeared in the match programme but not on the players' shirts, which continued to bear the Bristol Coat of Arms right up until the end of the promotion campaign. It would not be until the 1994-95 season that the Suspension Bridge badge was supplanted and the Bristol Coat of Arms returned to grace City's shirts once more.

In the close season the big news focused on the boardroom battle. Hobbs had gathered around him a team of businessmen to fight for his reinstatement. Daily statements from one side and then the other enlivened the local newspapers for months. At the AGM, held in the packed Patrons Bar of the Dolman Stand, when a loss for the 1976-77 season of £113,039 was announced, the attempt by Hobbs and his followers to gain control was thwarted. Two new directors, Peter West and David Callow, were elected, and the following day solicitor Richard Castle joined them.

The power-struggle continued, however. In November the board called an extraordinary meeting, where it pledged to increase the share capital from £30,000 to £110,000. The resolution was carried at this stormy meeting by 306 votes, but there was a dispute over 500 shares. Had they gone against the motion, the outcome would effectively have unseated the board and restored majority-shareholder Hobbs to power. The matter was settled in an expensive High Court action the following summer. The result stood and Hobbs conceded defeat.

Following on from the tournaments staged in 1974 and 1976, the third and last 'All in the Game' soccer skills contest was held at Ashton Gate between 14-16 July. After beating St Mirren by 210 points to 145, City were knocked out in the semi-finals 130-110 by Manchester City. The final was won by Leicester 162-132.

In the pre-season qualifying for the Anglo-Scottish Cup, a 0-1 defeat at Birmingham did not deny City reaching the quarter-finals for the first time. Wins over Bristol Rovers and Plymouth carried them through. A 0-2 defeat in the first leg at Partick Thistle did not auger well for City's chances of making progress, but two goals from Mann and one from Whitehead in the return two weeks later set up a semi-final meeting with Hibernian. The first leg at Easter Road was a tempestuous affair, ending 1-1 despite Hunter (73rd-minute tackle on Ally McLeod) and Cormack (77th-minute head-butt on Des Bremner) being sent off. Shaw was City's hero, when saving McLeod's 84th-minute spot-kick, and Ritchie the villain, when his late miss prevented City pulling off a sensational win.

Hibs chairman Tom Hart described City as the 'Butchers of Bristol', and made clear that under no circumstances would his side play the second leg. He attempted to claim the tie, and then threatened to withdraw by paying a £2,000 fine, but City's demands for £12,000 compensation, coupled with the intervention of the Scottish and English League Secretaries, brought a change of heart. City won a thriller, 5-3, in front of 6,072 soaking fans at Ashton Gate.

It looked easy in the final when City won the first leg 2-1 in heavy rain at Love Street, Paisley (City: Mabbutt 20, Cormack 74; St Mirren: Abercrombie 87) in front of 7,800 spectators on 23 November, but St Mirren were a different proposition at Ashton Gate on 5 December. A 16,110 crowd were confident of City winning their first major trophy since lifting the Welsh Cup in 1934, but Bobby Reid gave the visitors a 68th-minute lead with an overhead kick from a narrow angle. City equalised two minutes later in their first concerted attack of the half when Kevin Mabbutt headed in Whitehead's inswinging corner. St Mirren kept pressing and Frank McGarvey headed what most considered to be a valid goal before colliding with keeper Shaw. Fortunately for City, referee Derek Nippard thought otherwise, and Saints' manager Alex Ferguson found himself in hot water after the game for his ill-tempered remarks to the official. The teams for the final were:

1st leg:
ST MIRREN: Hunter, Young, Beckett, Fitzpatrick, Reid, Dunlop (Hyslop 45), Copeland, Stark, McGarvey, Abercrombie, Munro.
BRISTOL CITY: Shaw, Sweeney, Gillies, Gow, Collier, Merrick, Tainton, Ritchie, Mabbutt, Cormack, Mann.
2nd leg:
BRISTOL CITY: Shaw, Gillies, Sweeney, Gow, Collier, Merrick, Tainton, Ritchie, Mabbutt, Mann, Whitehead.
ST MIRREN: Hunter, Beckett (Richardson 74), Young, Fitzpatrick, Reid, Copeland, McGarvey, Stark, Hyslop, Abercrombie, Munro.

Did You Know?

Against Oxford U in 1968, City sub Derrick did not wear No 12. He wore No 8, the same as the player he replaced, Garland. The referee did not notice.

In the League, City struggled early on with three defeats and two draws before recording their first win, 3-2 at home to West Ham. The next nine games brought only two more victories – Hunter's left boot flying off when he netted the decisive goal in a 3-2 home win over Leeds, and a 3-1 success against Derby. By then Dicks was desperately searching for a striker. Scarcity of goals was a headache, especially away from home where Gillies' effort in a 1-1 draw at Newcastle was City's first away strike of the season. Unable to sign Alan Gowling from Newcastle, Dicks turned his attention to 28-year-old Joe Royle from Manchester City. The England international centre-forward, who had been at Maine Road for three years since his transfer from Everton, was persuaded to come to Ashton Gate on loan. He made an immediate impact on his debut, scoring all City's goals in a 4-1 hammering of Middlesbrough.

After this there was no way the City fans were going to let Royle go, and an avalanche of letters to the press eventually persuaded the reluctant Royle to sign permanently. Of course, the goals were not to flow so easily again, the trend being set in Royle's first game after City had paid a £90,000 fee for his services.

His brilliant chip was disallowed at Derby, but the big centre-forward proved to be a great provider for others as City eventually came to terms with top flight soccer. Try as he might, Royle could not find the target. He went eleven matches without scoring, hitting the woodwork, having goals disallowed in consecutive games, and squandering a spot-kick against West Brom with a shot high into the crowd. A simple tap-in versus Norwich in February ended the drought as City embarked on a six-match unbeaten run.

The loss of Collier for the rest of the season after suffering knee damage in a 1-1 draw at Old Trafford allowed David Rodgers to make a triumphant return to the side; it was his goal that brought City their first ever win at West Ham. A harsh defeat by Everton wiped the smile off City's faces, and whilst just two wins from the final eleven games did not raise the spectre of relegation, it brought a disappointing finishing position of seventeenth.

A poor disciplinary record didn't help City's cause. Tainton, Sweeney and Gow had all been sent off during the spring. Having had almost 200 misconduct points, City were fined £800 by the FA.

Failure to cope with Third Division Wrexham in both the major cup competitions raised doubts as to City's overall ability. Whilst one defeat against such opposition could be explained away, to succumb twice suggested City were far from being a genuine top-flight side. The fans' small consolation was a thrilling 4-4 home draw with Wrexham in the third round of the FA Cup.

The close-season saw an end to physiotherapist Les Bardsley's 21-year association with the club. The popular ex-Bury player left to concentrate on his thriving private practice, whilst Bill Heather was appointed in his place. Bardsley was granted a testimonial in February 1978 against a Bobby Charlton XI.

Match of the Season 1977-78
Bristol City 4 Middlesbrough 1

Division 1, 26 November 1977

Every player hopes to make a good impression on his debut, and in this game Joe Royle's hopes were more than fulfilled. On loan from Manchester City, his four-goal haul made him an instant hit with the Ashton Gate fans, and many were the letters in the local press urging the reluctant player to make a permanent move.

City's poor return of just five goals from their previous six games had prompted manager Dicks to strengthen the attack, and Royle's first game attracted almost 21,000 fans for the visit of Middlesbrough. His four goals from just four chances demonstrated what City had been lacking since Paul Cheesley's career had been ended by injury during the preceding campaign.

Whilst Royle's goals – a header, followed by a right-footed shot and two with his left – were taken with the aplomb one would expect from a top-class international striker, it was his all-round ability that impressed the most as he added a new dimension to City's game.

After mulling over a permanent move for some weeks, Royle eventually decided to come to the West Country. Unfortunately, it was a case of 'after the Lord Mayor's Show' for quite a while as it was not until early February that Royle found the net again. Two games at the turn of the year illustrated his bad luck. On Boxing Day against West Brom he hit the crossbar and had a goal disallowed, and his fifth-minute effort against Nottingham Forest was struck off because Kevin Mabbutt had strayed offside.

Whilst Royle never recaptured the goalscoring exploits that had made him an instant idol, there is little doubt that – together with Norman Hunter – he supplied the class that enabled City not only to survive awhile in the top flight, but to be good enough to challenge for a European place in 1978-79.

LEAGUE DIVISION 1   **1978-79**
Division 1   13th
League Cup   2nd Round
FA Cup   4th Round

Whilst doubts over City's true abilities never entirely disappeared, on account of their failure yet again to overcome so-called inferior opposition in cup competitions – losing to Second Division Crystal Palace in both the League and FA Cup – they found themselves near the top of the table in the wage stakes. Other than Liverpool and Everton, City's were reputedly the highest paid players in the League, on a basic £300 per week, on a par with Aston Villa, Derby, Leeds, Manchester City and Nottingham Forest.

City returned to Scandinavia, where they had won six out of six games twelve months previously, for their pre-season action. This time they again managed a clean sweep, beating Vasteras SK, Edsbro IF, Enkopnings and IFK Eskilstuna, before returning to begin their defence of the Anglo-Scottish Cup. It could not have started better as Bristol Rovers were hammered 6-1 at Ashton Gate. Wins over Cardiff and Fulham enabled City to top their qualifying group. Unfortunately, in the quarter-finals St Mirren gained revenge for last season's defeat – winning 2-1 at Ashton Gate and drawing 2-2 at Love Street.

Opening their League campaign with a 2-1 win at newly promoted Bolton, City followed up with three points from their next two games. This raised hopes, until City lost 0-2 at bottom of the table Wolves. The points continued to accumulate on a fairly regular basis, however, and helped by Shaw keeping a clean-sheet at home to Coventry on Boxing Day, goals from Royle (three), Ritchie and Cormack produced City's best-ever win in the top division. What a change this made: instead of bracing themselves for another struggle against relegation, City fans saw their team firmly ensconced in the top half of the table and were talking about qualifying for Europe.

Climbing as high as fifth at one stage, City were still in with a shout of qualifying for the Fairs Cup as late as 10 April, when a 3-1 win over Chelsea left them a challenging seventh. City were disadvantaged in having fulfilled more fixtures than many of their rivals and added just three points from their final five games. This banished thoughts of Europe and brought an end of season position of thirteenth. Though disappointing at the finish, it was City's highest final placing since 1908-09 and their fourth best overall.

Cheesley had his benefit match on 27 November, when his previous club Norwich City provided the opposition and won 6-3.

City played sixteen friendlies during this campaign. These included a 2-0 success against Bristol Rovers at Eastville in a benefit for Frankie Prince, a 0-0 home draw with Moscow Dynamo, and an end of season tour of North America. A 1-1 draw against Vancouver Whitecaps was followed with an 8-3 success over Vancouver Island and a 1-2 defeat versus Portland Timbers.

In the Gloucestershire Senior Professional Cup, City maintained their good record in the competition. They clinched their fourth successive win against Bristol Rovers in the final, having beaten their arch rivals 3-2 in 1975-76, 1-0 in 1976-77, and 3-0 in 1977-78. This time goals from Gow and Mann clinched a 2-0 away win in front of 6,661 fans on 15 May for City to claim the Cup for the 46th time.

By this time, the youth policy so ably nurtured by Sillett had been allowed to wither as Dicks had given few first-team chances to the talented youngsters in the reserves. The 'stiffs' finished eighth in the Football Combination this season, following on from placings of fifth, tenth and eighteenth respectively in the three previous years. The lack of opportunity for home produced talent following Sillett's departure in 1974 had its effect in the FA Youth Cup. Apart from reaching the fifth round in 1975-76, where they lost 1-6 in a replay at Newcastle, the Youths made little headway in the competition. They reached only the third round in 1976-77 and 1977-78. It was even worse in 1978-79 as they were blown away 1-5 at the first time of asking by Bristol Rovers.

Match of the Season 1978-79
Bristol City 5 Coventry City 0

Division 1, 26 December 1978

Both City and Coventry were in the top half of the table at the time of this Boxing Day clash, but the Sky Blues, who had been hoping to put an end to a run of poor form away from home, were no match for the rampant Robins. City provided their fans with the perfect Christmas present as they notched up their record top-flight score, which extended Coventry's miserable winless away run to eight matches, including a 1-7 mauling at West Brom.

As City turned on the style after half-time, their previous best score in this division should have been easily surpassed, but the heroics of the Sky Blues custodian Les Sealey thwarted their endeavours. Fortunately, a poor Coventry side were unable to find the net themselves, so enabling City's home 5-1 home victory over Nottingham Forest in 1910-11 to be surplanted in the club's records.

Did You Know?

At half-time in the Wolves home game in Nov 1998 the two mascots came to blows on the pitch. This was better than the game, which City lost 1-6.

The season proved to be the zenith of City's brief four-year flirtation with the elite, and this match was probably the team's best all-round performance. The first half of the campaign had seen City become an established First Division force with wins on their travels at Burnden Park, Old Trafford, and Portman Road, as well beating the likes of Liverpool and Aston Villa at Ashton Gate. The progress made was such that the team were challenging for a place in European competition right up to early April, giving little indication of the troubles that lay ahead.

City's side in 1978-79 still contained many of their promotion-winning side of 1975-76, but to this had been added the skill and experience of Hunter, Cormack and Royle. All three played a full part in City's thrilling display against Coventry, but Royle was the star with his hat-trick increasing his total goals haul for the season to seven.

Surprisingly, despite appearing in all City's remaining fixtures, Royle did not find the back of the net again this campaign. Lack of goals and a poor disciplinary record eventually wrecked the club's European ambitions. For their part, despite this heavy defeat, Coventry went on to achieve their third highest top-flight placing, finishing in tenth spot, whilst City ended a disappointing thirteenth after the promise of so much more.

DECLINE & FALL
1979-1984

LEAGUE DIVISION 1	**1979-80**
Division 1	20th (Relegated)
League Cup	4th Round
FA Cup	4th Round

Whilst many fans were worried about the loss of Norman Hunter, who in June had turned down City's offer of a two-year contract in favour of joining Barnsley as player-coach, most thought of City as an established top-flight club at this stage. Further Leeds links were severed with the departure of Terry Cooper on a free-transfer to join Bristol Rovers, but with the signing of midfielder Tony Fitz-patrick from St Mirren for a club record £250,000 in July optimism was high that City would build on their previous campaign's success and perhaps claim a European place.

Despite gaining only one point from their opening game, at home to Leeds, this optimism did not appear misplaced as the 23,331 fans present were treated to a vibrant game and an outstanding strike by City's Finnish international Pertti Jantunen. Adding to the general air of a club going places was the issue of a vastly improved programme, and at the end of the season this publication was a deserved winner of the 'Programme of the Year' award, winning all five categories – (i) most improved (ii) best value for money (iii) most attractive cover (iv) best in Division One (v) best in the League. Quite a difference from 1999–2000 when we find City's poor quality effort to be strangely at odds with the brilliant publication put together by Bristol Rovers, despite both programmes being printed by Bristol City's media department.

A 1-3 midweek defeat at Coventry tempered hopes somewhat, but a 2-0 win at Villa Park – clinched by Ritchie's late penalty – followed by a 2-0 home success over Wolves, shifted City up to sixth. Despite suffering only four defeats in their first fourteen League games, City were not playing well and though Dicks took the plaudits when he became the longest serving current manager –

rather crassly being photographed on the pitch behind his desk – the failure to adopt a vigorous 'buy and sale' policy, or bring on the youngsters, was coming home to roost. The loss of Collier, who became the first player to exercise his right under freedom of contract when joining Coventry in the summer of 1979, affected City's judgement to such an extent that ridiculously lengthy contracts were given out to mediocre players of insufficient ability to raise the club's stature. Not surprisingly, perhaps, complacency set in and City rapidly tumbled into the relegation zone once the limited abilities of their side were cruelly exposed in a 0-3 League Cup defeat at Nottingham Forest in November.

Most fans fatalistically accepted City's ultimate fate when Micky Channon's 15-yard drive for Southampton brought defeat at Ashton Gate four days before Christmas. On Boxing Day City dropped into the relegation zone for the first time when they found themselves at the wrong end of a 3-0 scoreline at West Brom. Destined not to climb out of the bottom three throughout the rest of the season, they nevertheless raised hopes with their best ever win against top-flight opposition. It came in the FA Cup, when Derby County were thrashed 6-2 at Ashton Gate.

January was otherwise a sad month. It saw the death at the age of 56 of old-time City favourite Cyril Williams, who was killed in a car smash in Somerset. A 0-3 home defeat by Ipswich provoked much anti-Dicks feeling, which resulted in the police having to break up a demonstration in the officials' car park after the match.

Only one win in eighteen matches from early November made relegation almost inevitable, but City's fate was not settled until the penultimate game on 29 April – a 2-5 defeat at Southampton. Paradoxically, a 0-0 draw in the final game at Spurs raised City up to twentieth, a position which would have brought safety but for the introduction of three-up, three-down, seven years previously.

So ended City's second spell in the top division and whilst many of the fans who journeyed to White Hart Lane for the final game were resigned to not getting back quickly, it is doubtful that even in their worst ever dreams they envisaged the nightmare that was to unfold. To the surprise of many, Alan Dicks and his assistant Tony Collins were awarded new five-year contracts, with the manager mouthing reassurances about his team doing well in 1980-81.

The season's only success came in the Anglo-Scottish Cup, but Dicks blew City's chances of reclaiming the cup by fielding under-strength sides in the two-legged final against old rivals St Mirren. In the preliminary stages a 4-0 win at Birmingham had augured well and a 0-0 draw at Plymouth followed by a 1-0 home success over Fulham left City group winners. In the quarter-finals Partick Thistle were beaten 3-1 over two legs, and though Morton escaped with a 2-2 draw at Ashton Gate, City turned the tables in the semi-final second leg, winning 1-0 at Cappielow.

A Howard Pritchard goal in the dying seconds enabled City to take the Gloucestershire Cup for the fifth successive year, before the curtain was brought down on a miserable season with a 1-3 defeat against Derek Dougan's XI in Merrick's benefit match.

In the Youth Cup a 7-1 away success over Torquay was followed by a 6-0 away demolition of Port Vale, before City came unstuck at Ashton Gate in January when Middlesbrough won 2-1.

The club's worsening financial problems were manifest in a new record loss of £161,223 being declared. Season ticket sales continued to fall, only 5,373 being sold compared to 6,807 in 1978-79, but price increases brought only a slight drop in receipts from £236,058 to £230,896. Whereas in 1978-79 season tickets for all seats had been £45, in 1979-80 centre seats in both stands cost £55, whilst wing seats in the Grandstand cost £50 compared to £45 in the Dolman.

Match of the Season 1979-80

Bristol City 2 Leeds United 2

Division 1, 18 August 1979

In a season that was to end in relegation, highlights were few and far between. Nevertheless, the optimism of the fans that the previous season's results could be equalled or bettered was reflected by the club itself, whose marketing strategy prospered under the direction of Tony Rance. In addition to the much improved, award-winning match programme, the introduction of pre-match entertainment in the form of the Bristol City cheerleaders in 1977-78 and novelties such as staging women's lacrossse at the home game with Nottingham Forest – when the English beat a Combined Scottish & Welsh side 15-3 – did much to raise the club's profile.

A crowd of just over 23,000 for the visit of Leeds were treated to a ding-dong struggle, the highlight of which was Jantunen's 20-yard drive into the Open End goal to put City 2-1 in front. Unfortunately, Alan Curtis, Leeds' new signing from Swansea, enjoyed a dream debut and he notched his second goal of the game to deprive City of a win eight minutes from time.

But this bright draw ushered in a false dawn. Eighth at the end of September, a run of fourteen games for City yielded just nine points and pushed them down into the drop-zone. Goalscoring was a persistent problem. Joe Royle, for example, despite his heading ability in laying on the chances, struggled to score goals.

LEAGUE DIVISION 2   **1980-81**
Division 2   21st (Relegated)
League Cup   2nd Round
FA Cup   5th Round

A low-key pre-season underlined City's diminished status: sand-wiched between draws at Poole and Swindon, the Robins could muster only a 1-0 win over tiny Barnstaple. This hardly offered much encouragement for a successful season. Nor did City's first competitive results of the new campaign. They found themselves eliminated in the group stage of the Anglo-Scottish Cup, following a 1-1 home draw with Notts County and a 0-1 defeat at Orient.

And as for misplaced hopes of a rapid return to the top flight, these were soon dispelled when City failed to win any of their first nine games. The departure of Joe Royle to Norwich shortly before the opening fixture left a gap in attack that was never filled. Come May, with City finishing the season with less goals than points, it was not surprising that relegation was the outcome, or that City's measly 29 goals scored marked the 1980-81 side, in the days of two points for a win, as the club's worst ever in the scoring stakes.

Given such a record, it is surprising City did not finish bottom. An even poorer Rovers team – ironically in a season when they shared Ashton Gate for five games early on, following the destruc-tion by fire of Eastville's South Stand – prevented such ignominy and gave Bristol soccer the dubious distinction of being the first provincial city ever to provide two teams being relegated from the same division together. Strangely enough, just nine years later the two clubs were to provide the reciprocal, becoming the first outside London to be promoted from the same division at the same time.

Manager Alan Dicks had seemed bullish at the start of the season, insisting he had a good enough squad to make an impact in the promotion race, but a 0-1 home defeat by Swansea on 6 September brought Dicks' long reign to an end: he was sacked two days later. Tony Collins (chief scout 1967-72 and assistant manager 1976-80) and first-team coach Ken Wimshurst acted as caretakers before Bob Houghton took over on a three-year contract worth £25,000 per annum on 29 September.

Initially, it seemed that City had pulled off a remarkable coup in obtaining the services of a man who had guided Swedish club Malmo to the European Cup final in 1979, when they lost 0-1 to Nottingham Forest, as well winning the Swedish League and Cup four times since 1974. Houghton brought in Roy Hodgson as his assistant and early home wins over Luton and Newcastle suggested City had stumbled upon a dream ticket, but this took no account of the club's rapidly worsening financial position, which was to scupper long-term progress. In the short-term, however, £100,000 was found to bring in giant Swedish international keeper Jan Moller from Houghton's former club.

Following a vibrant attacking performance against Luton in Houghton's first home match in charge, the fans grew increasingly frustrated by the new manager's defensive inclinations. Just two goals in a barren run of nine League games between 20 December and late February that yielded just one solitary win left City fighting a rearguard action to maintain their status. That battle was lost, with but two more wins chalked up before the end of the season.

Gates slumped, and with many players enjoying lengthy contracts negotiated in First Division days the club was not just fighting against a second relegation, but was soon to be embroiled in a struggle for their very survival. The coffers saw little benefit from City's short-lived participation in the League Cup – Birmingham winning 2-1 on aggregate – but progress in the FA Cup kept the wolf from the door for a while. A 2-0 win over Derby was followed by a 5-0 goal-bonanza over Carlisle before the Robins were knocked out at the fifth round stage by Nottingham Forest.

Desperate times call for desperate remedies. Welcome revenue was generated by the staging of cricket at the ground for the first time since Bedminster's departure in 1912. In September a crowd of 7,925 were in attendance to see a Rest of the World cricket XI beat an England side, but this did little to stem losses, which this season amounted to £491,969. The average home attendance almost halved from 18,932 to 9,765, whilst the number of season ticket holders was slashed from 5,373 to 2,943. Not surprisingly, by the time of the AGM in November 1981, the club was on its knees financially. An organisation known as 'Friends of Bristol City' had been formed a month previously, following a statement that the club owed debts in excess of £700,000.

The fight to reinstate Robert Hobbs flared up again, but at a shareholders meeting in December the rebel group, led by Lionel Amos and supported by Leslie Kew, Frederick Matthews, D Squires and J Drinkwater, withdrew their challenge when they accepted that they could not prevail. However, nine days later, Stephen Kew, who had been chairman for the three-and-a-half years since the overthrow of Hobbs, stood down, though he remained on the board. Long-time City supporter Archie Gooch, who had been on the board for less than a year, then took over the helm for what was to prove to be the most desperate time in the club's history.

Public interest in the annual contest for the Gloucestershire Cup continued to dwindle. The attendance for this season's final –

having attained a high of 20,097 in 1954-55 – dropped to a new low of 2,558 at Eastville on 5 May. The dramatic drop in local interest was unexpected, as it was not until 1978-79 that crowds dropped below five figures for the first time since 1965-66. Mabbutt's extra-time goal took City to within sight of their record of seven successive trophy wins notched up between 1905-06 and 1911-12.

The Reserves had a poor season, dropping to seventeenth in the Football Combination, though reaching the semi-finals of the Somerset Premier Cup.

Match of the Season 1980-81

Nottingham Forest 2 Bristol City 1

FA Cup, 5th Round, 14 February 1981

City's unexpected FA Cup run started at the Baseball Ground, when many thought Derby would avenge their 2-6 hammering in the previous year's competition. But keeper John Shaw was in superb form as City hung on for a goalless draw, and then won the replay 2-0, thanks to Tom Ritchie's inspired performance. In the next round City were unable to supply the killer finish despite being on top at Carlisle, but they had no such trouble in the replay when five goals without reply clinched a meeting with defending European Cup holders Nottingham Forest, who had beaten Bolton and Manchester United to reach this stage.

Almost 27,000 spectators assembled at the City Ground, where they saw City almost pull off a shock victory against a Forest side possibly suffering the effects of a midweek trip to Japan where they lost 0-1 to Nacional in the World Club Championship final. Kevin Mabbutt coolly stroked a goal just prior to half-time, and despite all Forest's pressure it was not until seven minutes from time that John Robertson's debatable penalty turned the tide. Ian Wallace then deprived City of a replay that would have proved a welcome boost to their depleted coffers, turning the ball in during a goalmouth scramble for a late winner.

Sadly, City's stirring FA Cup form was not translated into their League performances. Forest also had their disappointments as they exited the competition in the next round when losing a replay at Ipswich 0-1. Having already lost their grip on the European Cup, seventh place in the First Division meant Forest did not qualify for Europe in 1981-82.

LEAGUE DIVISION 3   **1981-82**
Division 3   23rd (Relegated)
League Cup   3rd Round
FA Cup   4th Round

At long last City found their man when a fee of £150,000 secured the services of centre-forward Mick Harford from Newcastle. No doubt the introduction of three points for a win was partly responsible for the club pursuing the services of a proven goalscorer, but Harford, despite his valiant endeavours, could not compensate for deficiencies elsewhere in City's team. Behind the scenes, changes amongst the backroom staff had seen the appointment of Alex Lockhart as physiotherapist and club doctor S Dasgupta took up his new duties for the home win over Plymouth.

The fans expected Third Division stability at the very least, but as the financial crisis came to a head relegation paled into insignificance in the face of threats to the club's very survival. The outcome was a season that ended with City having the dubious distinction of being the first club ever to tumble from the First to the Fourth Division in successive seasons. Although suffering just one defeat in the opening five games, the following nineteen fixtures yielded only three further wins. Rob Newman's 20-yard free-kick clinched a 1-0 success at Walsall in February, but by then much had happened to change the composition of City's line-up.

The club's chronic bank-balance necessitated the transfer of Kevin Mabbutt to Crystal Palace in September, with Welsh international centre-half Terry Boyle coming in part-exchange. Clive Whitehead, who was on an eleven-year contract said to be worth £550 per week, went to West Brom in November. There was even talk of Bob Houghton moving on early in the season. It had been rumoured that he had been offered the position of manager of the Swedish national side, but he chose to tough it out at Ashton Gate until a 1-3 home defeat by Wimbledon on 2 January caused him to throw in the towel. His assistant, Roy Hodgson, took over on a caretaker basis, but he had little opportunity of demonstrating his considerable managerial ability, which was gained when in charge of Swedish club Halmstad.

Following the announcement of the club's £700,000 plus debt, various rescue packages, including the formation of 'Friends of Bristol City', were established. But despite Park Furnishers becoming the club's first sponsors – when their name was emblazoned across the front of City's shirts in the home game against Southend – in November, by the turn of the year the situation was so bad that closure appeared imminent. A run in the FA Cup produced much needed revenue, but the decision to bring forward the kick-off time for the second round clash with Northampton to 7pm because of City's staff party had unforeseen consequences. The tie saw one of the club's lowest ever home attendances in the competition – just 2,901. The gate for the meeting with First Division Aston Villa in the next round was much better, but even so City's share of the £45,000 receipts, from 20,279 spectators, was but a drop in the ocean in the sea of debt in which they were immersed.

With the Receivers at the door and the club estimated to be insolvent with liabilities of £850,000, it was widely thought that the following week's game at Newport would be the club's last, despite the attempts by local businessmen Deryn Coller (Park Furnishers) and Ken Sage (Alusage) to save the rather long-in-the-tooth Bristol Babe. Their plan was to re-launch the club with a £1 million share-issue under a new organisation known as Bristol City (1982) plc. This scheme was initially dependent on the acceptance of a redundancy package by eight players (the so-called Ashton Gate Eight) who were on high wages and long contracts. These players – Chris Garland (who returned to play on a match-by-match basis in 1982-83), Peter Aitken, Jimmy Mann, Julian Marshall, Geoff Merrick, David Rodgers, Gerry Sweeney and Trevor Tainton – were understandably aggrieved about being offered only one-third of their entitlement, but following the intervention of Gordon Taylor (Secretary of the Professional Footballers Association) they eventually agreed to accept an improved redundancy offer (raised from £58,000 to £80,000, plus the guarantee of a testimonial match).

The new organisation took over in a temporary capacity the following day, though the now-defunct City retained the players' registration and ownership of the ground. Hodgson was left with an unenviable task, but the fans responded with admirable support as the embryonic organisation began their existence with a home draw with promotion-chasing Fulham on 6 February.

Apart from Moller, Boyle, Harford and Shaw, the remaining players were mainly raw youngsters, hence the reason for City's old nickname of the Babes being heard again. Financial restraints and shortage of players precipitated the disbandment of City's Reserve side, which resigned from the Football Combination in February.

Hodgson, aided by his new assistant Colin Toal and chief scout Richard Dinnis, bolstered the squad by the loan signings of defender Aiden McCaffery from Bristol Rovers, and midfielders Ray Gooding (Coventry) and Les Carter (Crystal Palace). In the event, the Football League, preoccupied by City's transfer debts, would not sanction the renewal of McCaffery and Gooding's monthly contracts, and they soon returned from whence they came. It was of little surprise that City were unable to escape from the jaws of relegation, especially given the March transfers of Moller to Toronto Blizzards for £85,000 and Harford to Birmingham for £125,000.

The fate of the new administration hung in the balance however, as everything hinged on a share issue in April, which was only successful at the last due to injection of money from local businessmen, plus further investment from the interim board members. Bristol City plc was finally up and running on 30 April, when it dispensed with the services of caretaker boss Hodgson and put Youth team manager Gerry Sharpe in control for what little of the season remained. The stadium was purchased for the new plc for £565,000 on 7 May.

The team fared well under Sharpe's direction, only losing once in six outings, but the directors were unimpressed. They settled on ex-City player and former Bristol Rovers manager Terry Cooper as their choice to kick-start City's revival, after conducting interviews with both him and Sharpe, as well as Stuart Morgan (Weymouth), Frank Burrows (ex-Portsmouth) and ex-City forward Joe Royle.

On the eve of the Argentine invasion of the Falkland Islands, Cooper, having persuaded Doncaster boss Billy Bremner to release him from his playing contract, inherited a club bereft of many players. Free-transfers were granted to Les Carter, Billy Down, Peter Devine, Jon Economou, Allan Hay, David Mogg, John Shaw, Gary Smith, Mark Smith and Steve Wheery.

What then of The Ashton Gate Eight, who were the recipients of a special benefit match played on 24 March, when 6,020 fans turned up to see Southampton beat Ipswich Town 2-1? Each of these sacrificial lambs found other clubs with whom to play out the season. Sweeney, after a brief spell at Trowbridge Town joined up with Aitken at York, Garland and Merrick went to Hong Kong to play for Carolina Hills, Mann turned out for Barnsley, Rodgers initially went to Torquay, along with Tainton, before moving to Lincoln, whilst Marshall went to Blackburn. After the winding up of the old club it was reported that these players shared £82,750, such sum including the receipts of the special match referred to above.

The change of regime terminated the Park Furnishers agreement, their name last being emblazoned across City's chests in the Newport game. It was not until the 0-1 home defeat by Brentford in March that the traditionalists had to put up with their favourites' shirts again being tarnished in such a way. Hirerite's sponsorship would last for more than eight years, until 1990-91. They were superseded by Thorn for three seasons, who were in turn followed by Dry Blackthorn 1993-94, Auto Windscreen's 1994-1996, Sanderson's Computer Equipment 1996-1999, and DAS 1999-2000.

Match of the Season 1981-82
Bristol City 0 Fulham 0

Division 3, 6 February 1982

This fixture will always be remembered by City fans as the game
they thought they would never see. Just seven days earlier a large
exodus of supporters flocked over the Severn Bridge to Newport
fearing that they could be witnessing City's last match, as the
burden of ever increasing debt left the club facing closure. The tide
of debt had to be stemmed and the salvage plan was subject to
eight players accepting a redundancy package before midday on
Tuesday, 2 February. As the drama unfolded in the full glare of the
television and press cameras at the Dragonara Hotel, the players
accepted an improved package. This left Roy Hodgson the task of
fielding a side to turn out against promotion-chasing Fulham.

Relief at City's survival almost doubled the attendance from the
previous home game, and the fans gave tremendous support to a
basically young and inexperienced side that did duty at Ashton
Gate on this day. Debuts were given to Wayne Bray – a 17-year-old
midfielder who had won seven England schoolboy caps and was
the youngest member of the Bristol Boys team that won the English
Schools Trophy two years previously; Jon Economou, a 20-year-old
Londoner who had waited three years for his chance; and 18-year-
old Wiltshire lad Rob Newman. With the glare of publicity still on
the club, television cameras recorded scenes and interviews with
supporters in the crowd. As for the new directors, they wore red
bowler hats, which they tossed to the fans in acknowledgement of
having succeeded with part one of the rescue plan.

On the day, the Bristol Babes more than held their own against
their experienced opponents. Unfortunately, the upsurge in enthusiasm was unable to sustain City for the rest of the season, and they
were doomed to relegation well before the end of the campaign.
Fulham, though, had cause to rue the points lost in this game as
they ultimately cost them promotion.

Demolition of the Cow Shed stand at Ashton Gate during the close season 1966

The architects' model of the proposed new stand at Ashton Gate 1968

Coach John Sillett welcomes Les Wilson and Brian Hill to Ashton Gate (March 1971)

Gow and Galley in action during City's 2-0 home win over Portsmouth (April 1971)

City's promising youngsters sign pro forms with Dicks and John Sillett (Sept 1971)

Gerry Gow scores from the spot during City's 3-2 win at Cardiff (April 1972)

City players are shown the South Bristol Technical College prospectus (1972-73)

Team talk before City's FA Cup-tie at Portsmouth (January 1973)

Bobby Gould chats to supporters queuing for Wolves FA Cup tickets (January 1973)

City lose 0-1 at Nott'm Forest. The Notts Co floodlights can also be seen (March 1973)

City players practice their golf at Ashton Gate – Fear, Rodgers, Gillies, Gow, Cashley

City, in white, on the attack during a 0-2 defeat at Middlesbrough (September 1973)

Bobby Gould heads City's first goal against Sheffield Wednesday (September 1973)

A waterlogged Hereford pitch, but City won this FA Cup-tie 1-0 (January 1974)

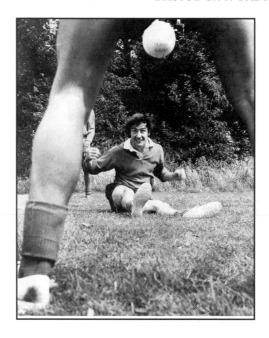

Gerry Sweeney heading the ball in training (1974)

The Bristol City squad 1974-75. Manager Alan Dicks is in the centre, front row

Portsmouth keeper David Best thwarts Keith Fear, but City win 3-1 (February 1975)

Donnie Gillies milks the applause after his goal against Portsmouth (February 1975)

Jimmy Mann's shot is blocked during this 0-1 home defeat by Norwich (March 1975)

Tom Ritchie tries a shot during the 3-0 home win over Hull (December 1975)

Tom Ritchie is foiled by the keeper during this 0-0 draw at Plymouth (January 1976)

City's players relax prior to their vital promotion match at Sunderland (March 1976)

Geoff Merrick calls as Rovers captain Frankie Prince tosses up at Eastville (April 1976)

The Bristol City squad that famously won promotion to the old Division 1 (1975-76)

LEAGUE DIVISION 4   1982-83

Division 4	14th
League Cup	2nd Round
FA Cup	1st Round

The first AGM of the new administration was held at the Colston Hall on 21 June 1982. The new board was named as follows: Des Williams (chairman), Les Kew (vice-chairman), Bob Boyd, Deryn Coller, Bob Marshall, Oliver Newland and Ivor Williams.

The money raised from the share issue had barely been enough to purchase the assets from the old company, so frugality was the word at Ashton Gate where the directors paid personally for both their drinks and those of their visitors. In such a difficult time new boss Cooper was to prove the ideal man to take the club forward. He worked tirelessly in the summer to put a team together with the limited finances at his disposal. He persuaded the directors to sanction the appointment as his assistant of Clive Middlemass, who had been a colleague at Leeds and managed Workington for two years before linking up with Cooper at Bristol Rovers. Cost cutting measures during the season ended the lengthy associations of Gerry Sharpe and Commercial Manager Jim Evans, after periods of 21 and nineteen years respectively. The board charged the Supporters Club £10,000 rent for their premises in the Grandstand, and the executive 51 Club was renamed the Directors' Club.

Cooper did well to secure the free-transfer services of 23-year-old striker Glyn Riley from Barnsley and 30-year-old winger Alan Crawford from Chesterfield, not to mention persuading Tom Ritchie to return from Sunderland to his old stomping ground. With a small playing staff of fifteen, Cooper scoured the local non-league scene, from where he picked up 22-year-old Simon Panes (top-scorer for Western League Melksham the previous season) on a short part-time contract. Of the ten players given free-transfers at the end of the previous campaign, John Shaw and Jon Economou were re-signed on fresh terms. Kevin Slabber's broken leg in a reserve game left Cooper keeping his fingers crossed that goal-keeper Shaw stayed clear from injury as the club could not afford to sign another keeper. Twins Nyere and Omele Kelly joined as youth players, while their elder brother Errington arrived from Bristol Rovers during the season. Nyere became City's then youngest ever player at the age of sixteen years, 244 days (until ousted by Marvin Brown in 1999) when coming on as an 82nd-minute substitute in a 1-3 defeat at Hartlepool on 16 October.

Cooper's confidence in his side making an immediate return to the Third Division was to prove misplaced. Ironically, the board fretted over the prospect of having to pay out more than £10,000 in promotion bonuses and took out insurance to guard against such an eventuality. Friendly wins at Bridport and Cheltenham Town preceded City's participation in the newly established Football League Trophy. Despite a home win over Torquay, losses at Exeter and Newport meant City bowed out at the group stage.

Although finding themselves in the Fourth Division for the first time in their history, City's form was initially encouraging. In the first match, at home to Hull, Russell Musker notched his first goal for the Robins with a 20-yard spectacular after Riley had marked his debut with the club's first ever goal in the Fourth Division. City lost Musker's services when he broke a leg in a 1-2 League Cup defeat at Swindon on 31 August. That was also the day former chairman Robert Hobbs died, aged 75, at his Salcombe home. A 2-2 League draw at Tranmere four days later kept hopes high, before a 1-4 mauling at Crewe set the alarm bells ringing.

Another mauling was not long in coming. This time City went down 1-7 at Northampton, a result which had Cooper eating his words about instant promotion. He revised his long-term objectives, saying 'it could take three years to get promotion'. Nor was this as bad as it was going to get. Crewe's win at Halifax on 29 October dumped City to 92nd place in the Football League. They could go no lower. On this occasion the ignominy did not last long. The point earned from a goalless draw at Aldershot the following day took City off the floor, but a 0-1 defeat at Rochdale on 4 December – when Andy Llewellyn made his debut at the age of sixteen years, 281 days – saw City hit rock bottom again. Another single-goal defeat at Chester kept City there, but a 2-2 draw at Bury took them up a place, and gradual improvement over the rest of the campaign brought an eventual finishing position of fourteenth. For this they were indebted to a nine-match unbeaten run of five wins and four draws in the spring.

It was the signing of centre-half Forbes Phillipson-Masters from Plymouth in November – following Boyle's transfer to Newport, to save on his £400 per week wages – which provided the cornerstone to City's recovery. The newcomer brought much needed stability to the defence with his no-nonsense approach. Peter Johnson from Newcastle also impressed at full-back during his run of 21 consecutive matches in a four-month loan stay, his wages being met by supporters' contributions.

In the League Cup, City overcame their first leg deficit against fellow Fourth Division Swindon by winning the home tie 2-0. This was rewarded by a two-leg clash with First Division Sheffield Wednesday. City had it all to do after conceding two early goals in the first leg at Ashton Gate, which they lost 1-2. But at Hillsborough in the return they put up a gritty display to level the tie on aggregate before going out in extra-time. City showed less resolve in the FA Cup, going out in the first round at Third Division Orient when, despite full-back Johnson opening the scoring with a fierce shot from the edge of the area, they were overwhelmed 1-4.

In the Gloucestershire Cup, City were unable to return to their winning ways. Hoping to avenge the 0-1 home defeat that ended their run of six straight victories the previous season, City were disappointed to lose 1-2 at Eastville on 21 September.

Following City's resignation from the Football Combination the previous February, the Reserves now found themselves competing in the Western League for the first time since 1964-65. This time they had to start in the lower section, but City were unable to make any impact and ended the season in thirteenth place.

The FA Youth Cup saw a slight improvement on the displays of the two previous seasons when the team had been eliminated at the first time of asking. After beating Plymouth 2-1 in a replay to avenge their defeat of the year before, City lost by the same score against Bristol Rovers, this following a 1-1 home draw seven days previously.

At the AGM in December the accounts were declared for the partial financial year of 1981-82, as well as those for 1982-83. The figures for 1982-83 showed a profit of £2,391, which was no doubt helped by the staging of a Rolling Stones Concert at Ashton Gate in June 1982. The 35,123 rock fans who turned out for the occasion produced the anomaly of Ashton Gate's largest crowd in the history of the club under the new organisation. The loss of £60,672 revealed for 1981-82 included the £43,649 cost of the share issue.

Match of the Season 1982-83
Bristol City 4 Wimbledon 2

Division 4, 23 October 1982

When the season began, City fans hoped that their club's fortunes would take a turn for the better. But it was nearly all gloom and doom throughout the first half of the campaign.

With only one win from the opening eleven League games, this surprise success over previously unbeaten Wimbledon lifted the gloom somewhat for City's hard-pressed supporters. Top of the table Dons, seeking a club record seventh straight League win, were surprisingly defensive at the outset. 'Boring Wimbledon' is the chant, before Alan Nicholls sparked City's superlative display when

---

Did You Know?

City keeper Ray Cashley scored past his opposite number, Hull's Wealands, from over 95 yards in September 1973. The goal put City 2-1 up.

---

heading in Crawford's cross. Dave Bassett's boys attempted to adopt a more expansive approach, but City took control. With player-boss Cooper and midfielder Jon Economou pulling the strings, two strikes by Riley had the game virtually won by half-time.

After the break the game was more even and Wimbledon climbed back into contention with a goal by John Leslie, before Riley – perhaps inspired by the prankster who put a dead mouse in his boot before the game – completed his first League hat-trick. Despite Dean Thomas's late penalty, City gained a deserved success over one of their relegation companions of the previous season. The only blot on the afternoon was the 70th-minute sending off of City's ex-Wimbledon man Steve Galliers.

City's shock victory did not prevent Wimbledon from easily winning the Fourth Division Championship. In doing so they established a new record of 98 points, after finishing the season with a 22-game unbeaten run, and three years later found themselves among the elite. For City, their surprise win did not spark an upturn in fortunes, though improved form in the New Year acted as a platform for promotion in 1983-84.

LEAGUE DIVISION 4   **1983-84**
Division 4   4th (Promoted)
League Cup   1st Round
FA Cup   3rd Round

Surprise was expressed when Cooper's first signing for the new season was revealed as Howard Pritchard, who had previously played for the club before moving to Swindon. He came on a free-transfer and was a revelation. A vastly improved player from the one who left Ashton Gate three years previously, Pritchard was to provide the wing thrust that was to play a major part in City's promotion. Other signings saw Cooper bring in free-transfer players in 23-year-old striker John Kerr from Tranmere and the excellent central defender Bruce Halliday from Bury, whilst another raid on the Western League produced Shepton Mallet's Gary Marshall.

During the season Musker moved to Gillingham for a £7,500 fee after having a spell on loan with Exeter, and Kerr was to decamp to Stockport, whilst in the boardroom Cooper became a co-opted member and Bob Boyd was replaced by Mike Fricker. Amongst the back room staff a reshuffle saw Mike Gibson, one of the greatest goalkeepers in City's history, promoted to reserve team manager, whilst club Secretary John Lillington, who severed a 16-year association with the club when resigning in November, was replaced by ex police sergeant and erstwhile Birmingham supporter Bob Twyford, aged 45, who commenced his duties on 19 January 1984.

Despite the absence of Rob Newman, who missed the first two matches due to suspension, and the loss of Alan Nicholls with a broken leg in a pre-season match, City opened with a 4-0 win over Mansfield at Ashton Gate, but early form was patchy. Bundled out of the League Cup by Oxford, City found themselves unable to gain any consolation in the Gloucestershire Cup when losing to Bristol Rovers for the third season in a row on 20 September. Suddenly fortunes changed, and four successive wins that started with a 5-0 home League win over Torquay United four days later, not only shot City into second place, but earnt them a £250 prize for being the Division's top scorers in September.

On top of the table for the first time thanks to a Paul Stevens goal against York on 18 October, City failed to maintain their form, despite the signing of 29-year-old Kenny Stroud from Newport County, who was sent off in his second game in a 0-1 defeat Blackpool on 1 November. Four successive defeats saw City slip to seventh, before Kerr's goal brought a 1-0 win at Darlington to halt the sequence.

The intervention of the FA Cup brought a meeting with the famous Corinthian Casuals, played on the equally famous Champion Hill ground of Dulwich Hamlet. A goalless draw in south-east London brought the amateurs to Ashton Gate on 23 November when Pritchard's hat-trick helped bring about a 4-0 win and set up a mouth-watering prospect of an away match with Bristol Rovers in the second round. Third Division Rovers took the lead in front of a 14,396 crowd paying receipts of £31,809, but after Ritchie had levelled matters, Martin Hirst, a 21-year-old Bristol University geography student, found the net with a late winner for a famous City victory over the old enemy.

The following round brought a magnificent display against Notts County in a 2-2 draw at Meadow Lane on 8 January, but in the replay in front of the largest attendance (16,107) since City's reformation, the First Division club came out on top 2-0. At this time in the League, City were in the midst of a nine-match unbeaten run that ended with a 0-1 defeat at Plainmoor on 11 February when they were third place, during which time Cooper received the award as Bell's Fourth Division Manager of the Month at City's 2-1 home win over Wrexham on 21 January. A 1-3 defeat at Exeter on 22 February in the first round of the Associate Members Cup was City's fourth game without a win, but a 2-1 home victory over Aldershot three days later was the start of a run-in that only produced two defeats in 16 games as City clinched the promotion prize.

The transfer deadline signings of winger Keith Curle from Torquay for £10,000, and striker Trevor Morgan for a similar amount from Bournemouth were crucial, especially that of the experienced Morgan, who played in all City's remaining games. They both made their debuts in the 1-1 draw with York on 3 March as City embarked on the thrilling last third of the season, which was unfortunately marred by the behaviour of their hooligan brigade in a 0-2 defeat at Reading on 7 April. Cooper, who had bravely acted as peacemaker, was so disgusted by the actions of City's mad minority that he threatened to resign.

Morgan's two goals in a 2-1 win at Sealand Road on 7 May clinched promotion when it was estimated that City fans accounted for more than 3,000 of Chester's 4,013 crowd. This success completed City's programme with them in third place, but by the time other clubs had caught up with their fixtures they had to settle for a final placing of fourth. The Reserves made a memorable season a cause for a double celebration as they won the First Division of the Western League to gain promotion to the Premier. This success was reflected in the club's balance sheet, a profit of £31,089 being revealed at the AGM held in the Supporters Club on 13 December 1984.

Match of the Season 1983-84

Bristol Rovers 1 Bristol City 2

FA Cup, 2nd Round, 10 December 1983

In a promotion season there are many highlights, and this was certainly the case in 1983-84. Despite manager Cooper's attempts to dampen the expectations of City fans at the start of the campaign, it was expected that promotion would be won. An exciting team, capable of scoring goals and defending strongly, was just the combination required for City to begin the climb back.

The promotion challenge brought a steady rise in attendances, culminating in a crowd of more than 12,000 who saw the 1-0 win over Swindon that put City on the brink of promotion in their last home game. Although promotion brought great joy to the City fans, the result that gave them their greatest satisfaction was achieved in the second round of the FA Cup when local rivals Bristol Rovers were beaten on their home ground at Eastville.

When the draw was made many thought the Rovers were favourites by virtue of their superior Third Division status, the first time in four previous pairings in the competition that the Rovers had been the higher status club. However, what many overlooked was the fact that the Rovers had never won on their own ground in these meetings. Rovers were in the Southern League when they beat Football League newcomers City 3-2 in a replay at St John's Lane in 1901-02. When they pulled off a famous 4-3 victory at Ashton Gate in 1957-58, they were the more successful Second Division club, but by the time of Second Division City's 2-1 replay win at Eastville in 1967-68 Rovers had dropped back to the Third Division. The 1945-46 competition was unique in the annals of the FA Cup, as it was the only time it has operated as a two-legged tournament. Fortunately City took advantage to gain their only home success over the Rovers in the tournament, winning 4-2 at Ashton Gate, before clinching a double with a 2-0 success at Eastville a week later.

This latest clash with the Rovers attracted a 14,396 crowd to Eastville, who paid receipts of £31,809. After a goalless first half, they saw Archie Stephens give the Rovers a 50th-minute lead with one of his typically brave headers in front of the massed ranks of City fans on the open Muller Road terrace. Terry Cooper then came on as substitute in place of Alan Crawford and City began to dictate

---

Did You Know?

Gerry Gow missed four penalty-kicks for City in season 1972-73. Of those
matches, City won 1, drew 1, and lost the other two by a single goal.

---

the play. Anguished when Glyn Riley fired against a post, the City
fans were joyful on 78 minutes as Tom Ritchie cracked in a fine
equaliser. As the minutes passed a replay looked ever more likely,
but City kept up the offensive and whilst Martyn Hirst's mis-hit
89th-minute winner was rather fortunate, there was no denying that
the success it brought was fully deserved.

In the next round City put on a fine display against First Division Notts County at Meadow Lane to achieve a 2-2 draw, before
going out of the competition 0-2 in a replay at Ashton Gate. The
Rovers went on to only narrowly miss promotion by finishing in
fifth place, whilst revenge over City in the FA Cup wasn't long in
coming. The very next season the extraordinary sequence of away
successes in the competition continued with Rovers coming back
from conceding an early goal to deservedly gain a 3-1 victory in the
second round at Ashton Gate on 8 December 1985.

Despite the players sharing more than £30,000, the club's
finances considerably improved as a result of promotion, and were
also helped by the £17,700 receipts from Billy Graham's Crusade at
Ashton Gate, when 250,000 attended over an eight-day period in
May 1984. The fans as always paid the price with season tickets in
the Grandstand increasing from £65 to £75, whilst match day rates
went up by 50p to £4 and ground admission for both the Open and
the Covered Ends also increased by the same amount to £2.

RECOVERY
1984-1989

LEAGUE DIVISION 3	**1984-85**
Division 3	5th
League Cup	2nd Round
FA Cup	2nd Round

Promotion meant Terry Cooper's contract was extended for two years. Following the release of full-back Gary Williams on a free-transfer, he set about strengthening his side. His main target was Darlington's talented goalscoring winger Alan Walsh. The Quakers wanted £85,000 for their star player, who had scored almost 100 goals in 250 games for his hometown club. Cooper offered just £10,000, and an independent tribunal allowed Cooper to get away with daylight robbery by setting a paltry £18,000 fee on 27-year-old Walsh, who was destined to be one of the best ever players to wear a City shirt. Another top capture was 30-year-old Bobby Hutchinson on a free from Tranmere. A bruised instep suffered in a 3-3 draw at Hereford in a pre-season friendly meant Hutchinson did not appear in the first team again until November, coming on as substitute at Doncaster, when Newman sustained the broken shin which kept him out of action for over three months.

With Curle having been sent off in City's 6-2 friendly win at Cheltenham, it was a depleted side that opened the League season with a 2-0 home win over Wigan, but at least the contract disputes with Riley, Ritchie and Paul Stevens had been resolved. Cooper had little choice but to give 17-year-old Lee Rogers his debut in defence, and include himself as substitute. Though inconsistent, early form was encouraging and an exhilarating 3-0 home win over the Rovers pushed City up into third place. Cooper then swooped to sign 27-year-old Steve Neville from Exeter for £12,000, with Morgan moving in the opposite direction. For three months it did not look like money well spent, as Neville struggled to find his goal touch. He broke his drought in his thirteenth game by netting both goals in City's win at Brentford.

The departure of Ritchie to team up with former colleague Gerry Gow at Yeovil was a shock. Another crowd favourite nearing the end of an illustrious City career was keeper Shaw. Concern over his form led Cooper to blood 20-year-old local lad Mike Hooper, who made his League debut in a 2-1 home win over Lincoln. The former England Boys keeper, a part-timer studying English at Swansea University, impressed enough to keep his place for the following week's FA Cup-tie against Bristol Rovers. This time his inexperience proved costly. City lost 1-3, whereupon Shaw was briefly restored until Keith Waugh arrived on loan from Sheffield United. As Cooper was unwilling to pay the £25,000 fee required to make the transfer permanent, Ian Leigh was borrowed from Bournemouth. He lasted just one game before Shaw was restored for the rest of the season. Shaw was given a free transfer at the end of the campaign, moving to Exeter. He was replaced, ironically, by Keith Waugh, whom Cooper now managed to sign on a free transfer.

A 0-1 defeat at Reading in December pushed City down to tenth, but a pulsating 4-3 home win over Plymouth on Boxing Day, followed by a 1-0 success over Burnley, carried City into the New Year on a wave of optimism. Defeat at Hull sullied the mood, and further setbacks at the hands of Walsall and Rotherham saw City fast losing touch with the pacesetters. It required Neville's first goals to restore morale, and a run of five straight wins hauled City up to fourth. By this time Cooper had strengthened his squad with the free transfer signing of 23-year-old centre-half Mark Hughes from Swansea, and on transfer deadline day spent £30,000 to purchase 27-year-old Wigan forward Steve ('Rambo') Johnson.

Hooliganism reared its ugly head when Millwall were the visitors in early March. In scenes worse than those witnessed at Reading the previous season, seats were ripped up in the Dolman Stand, causing £2,500 worth of damage, whilst outside the ground a young City fan needed 67 stitches after being slashed. Secretary Bob Twyford was so sickened by the violence that he handed in his resignation – he was eventually replaced by Jean Harrison – stating that as a former police sergeant he could not be associated with a game which attracted so many ugly characters. Following a meeting with senior police chiefs, steps were immediately taken to sort out the main trouble-spots in the ground, and the decision was taken to install close-circuit television in the summer. When leaders Bradford City arrived the week after the Millwall mayhem, an extension to the players tunnel was in place, and the police presence doubled. Unaccompanied teenagers were denied entry to the Dolman Stand.

Losing 0-1 at Plymouth on 5 April was a promotion blow, but the real damage was done eight days later at Eastville. In a match ruined by the gale-force wind blowing towards the Muller Road End, City's decision to kick against the storm in the first half betrayed a negative attitude that the Rovers exploited to win 1-0. Despite suffering only one further defeat in the remaining eight games, the damage had been done and City had to be satisfied to finish in fifth place, six points behind third-placed Hull.

In the League Cup, City disposed of Newport 5-1 on aggregate and were rewarded with a meeting with First Division West Ham in the second round. A thriller at Ashton Gate ended 2-2, with City feeling aggrieved that they did not take a lead into the second leg. At Upton Park, after holding the Hammers until half-time, a second-half collapse brought about City's biggest ever defeat in the competition – 1-6.

The FA Cup first round produced a hard-fought tie at Fisher Athletic, but Riley's early strike was enough to take City through. A winning run in the Freight Rover Trophy saw Hereford beaten 2-1 on aggregate in the first round and Port Vale dispatched 2-1 at Ashton Gate. Walsh's penalty was not enough in the Southern Area quarter-final at Ashton Gate, when just 3,167 crowd saw Newport win 2-1. City's last chance to claim some silverware this reason disappeared with the Gloucestershire Cup, which was again moved back to the end of the season. At Eastville on 21 May Walsh's penalty took the contest into extra-time, but City lost 1-3.

The Reserves also came close to winning something. Their first season in the Premier Division of the Western League, following promotion, saw them finish third. They also reached the semi-finals of the Somerset Premier Cup. In the FA Youth Cup, City were unable to improve on the previous season's first round 1-3 knock-out at home to Plymouth, losing at the first stage 0-4 at Reading.

City's promotion almost doubled the number of season tickets sold, from 1,287 to 2,073, and with average home League gates increasing from 7,287 to 8,507, it was not surprising that finances remained buoyant. A profit of £46,156 was declared at the AGM.

Match of the Season 1984-85

Bristol City 2 Bradford City 0

Division 3, 9 March 1985

City went into this game on a high, following a 4-1 away success at Bolton. Even so, the table-topping Yorkshire side were expected to provide a stern test, despite the loss of the suspended midfielder Greg Abbott. Cancer victim 18-year-old Roger Crook, who was ferried by ambulance to the game, was among the 9,222 crowd who

---

Did You Know?

**At Queen's Park Rangers in April 1977 the rain was so torrential that
City's Geoff Merrick had to rescue a dog from a large puddle.**

---

appreciated Bradford's attacking inclinations in an open game.
Howard Pritchard found himself unmarked to head the Robins'
opener midway through the first half. On two other occasions the
right-winger went close – being denied by the crossbar either side of
the interval – whilst Bradford were unfortunate when Don
Goodman's header thudded against a post. Alan Walsh made sure
of the points thirteen minutes from time, his typically fierce right-
foot shot from the edge of the penalty area clinching a vital win.
Hughes was named Man of the Match, his performance in stifling
Bradford's Northern Ireland striker Bobby Campbell earning the
plaudits of Terry Cooper, who went so far as to tip him for future
Welsh honours.

Despite this victory – which lifted the Robins to fifth – being part
of a five-match winning sequence, City were unable to make an
impression in the promotion race. The fact that they were unable to
improve on their position only served to demonstrate the calibre of
the promotion candidates. Bradford were an outstanding side, and
they soon shook off the effects of this defeat. They went on to win
a total of 28 games and clinch the Championship with 94 points,
four better than runners-up Millwall. For Roger Crook, though,
there was no happy ending: he died a few days after the match.

LEAGUE DIVISION 3   **1985-86**
Division 3   9th
League Cup   1st Round
FA Cup   2nd Round

City started the new season as second favourites for the Third
Division Championship, but before the campaign kick-off Ashton
Gate welcomed illustrious visitors in two friendlies. Manchester
United beat City 1-0 in front of a 6,707 crowd, and a week later
8,182 spectators witnessed a 3-3 draw with Liverpool.

Newcomers for City included Brian Williams, signed on a free-
transfer from Bristol Rovers, and another ex-Rovers man, Gary
Emmanuel from Swindon Town. The fans, though, were indignant
about this increasing Rovers connection. Williams was sent off in
the League curtain-raiser against Walsall at Ashton Gate, whilst
Emmanuel was barracked. A 1-5 League Cup defeat at Hereford and
a 0-5 hammering at Bournemouth put paid to Emmanuel's short
Ashton Gate career. He was soon on his way to Swansea, but
Williams would go on and establish himself in the City side for two
seasons before moving to Shrewsbury.

Conceding goals at an alarming rate early on in the season, City
suffered four straight League defeats and, not surprisingly, found
themselves bottom of the table. Heads rolled, among them centre-
half Hughes, who had been outstanding the previous season.
Cooper slated him for being overweight, and Hughes soon departed
for a bargain £3,000 to Tranmere, for whom he went on to give
noble service for many years. It was not until 7 September that City
obtained their initial League victory. Pritchard's second-half header
against Wigan launched City on a seven-match unbeaten run that
lifted them up to eighteenth.

A break from League action saw Ashton Gate stage an Under-21
International in October. Only 3,826 turned up to see England beat
Turkey 3-0. A week later a 3-6 shocker at Bury saw City at sixes and
sevens. Ex-Cardiff midfielder David Tong made his debut in a 3-0
win over a poor Wolves side at the end of the month, a result
which sparked a sequence of fifteen games with just three defeats.
Strangely, those three losses came one after the other in early
December, the first of which being a 1-2 home defeat by Exeter in
the FA Cup. City returned to winning ways with a spirited 2-0
success over Plymouth on Boxing Day.

Victories over Doncaster and Rotherham ensured a bright start to
1986, and, apart from successive defeats at Derby and Wolves, City
maintained their form throughout the coming months. Keeper John
Vaughan came in on loan from West Ham when a back injury ruled

out Waugh for two games in early March. Bristol Rovers were beaten 2-0 at Ashton Gate at the end of the month, but in the last Eastville derby before Rovers' relocation Neville's goal was sufficient only to ensure a 1-1 draw. Topsy-turvy end of season form saw City eventually finish ninth. They notched their best victory of the season at Bolton, winning 4-0, before immediately succumbing by the same score at Plymouth.

Ample consolation for a mediocre League season was found in the Freight Rover Trophy, in which City reached Wembley for the first time. In the preliminary competition things didn't look promising. City started with a goalless home draw against Plymouth in January, but a 2-1 win at Walsall two weeks later put City top of their three-club group. They enjoyed the luck of the draw in the knock-out stages, reaching the semi-finals with home wins over Northampton (3-2) and Gillingham (3-0). At this stage supporters were still largely apathetic, as seen by crowds of just 3,038 for the visit of Northampton and 5,707 for Gillingham. But all this changed for the two-legged regional final. In the first game at Hereford, in front of 7,608 spectators, it looked as though City were re-living nightmares of that 1-5 League Cup thrashing early in the season. This time they kept the margin of defeat down to 0-2, but that still left themselves a mountain to climb in the return three days later.

The second leg at Ashton Gate kept the 11,558 fans enthralled, as Hereford battled for their lives. Following a goalless first half, City's hopes seemed to be ebbing away. It took Riley's header, which slipped through the Hereford keeper's fingers after 62 minutes to get City on the move, and within minutes Pritchard saw his effort deflected into the Hereford net by the unfortunate Mike Pejic. Undismayed, Hereford were unlucky when Ian Wells hit the bar with a fierce shot, and shortly before the end of normal time Chris Price shot narrowly wide.

The visitors often looked the more likely winners in extra-time and Paul Maddy should have won it for them three minutes from time, when unmarked in the penalty area and with the goal at his mercy. Waugh dived to his left to parry Maddy's powerful shot. It was not until the dying seconds that Neville clinched the game for City. He calmly controlled Hutchinson's knock-down from Walsh's cross from the left before steering in his 25th goal of the season. The 3-2 aggregate win set up an appointment with Northern Section winners Bolton Wanderers in the national final.

An estimated 30,000 City fans travelled to Wembley on 24 May. Despite the electric atmosphere, both sets of fans made sure that it was dubbed the 'friendly final'. City had one last-minute injury scare when David Harle complained of a strained hamstring, but he

---

Did You Know?

Joe Royle's four goals on his City debut in November 1977 meant that the 4-1 victory over Middlesbrough was City's biggest win of the season.

---

recovered to be named in City's line-up. Bolton had slight doubts over Tony Caldwell and Mark Came, but they too came through to take their place at Wembley.

Match of the Season 1985-86

Bristol City 3   Bolton Wanderers 0

Freight Rover Trophy final, 24 May 1986

To reach a Wembley final for the first time in City's history has to be the highlight of this or any other season, even though it was in a relatively minor competition restricted to Third and Fourth Division teams. Unfairly dubbed the 'Mickey Mouse Cup', it provided many City fans with the highlight of their time in watching a club that had rarely lived up to its potential.

A competition for the Associate member clubs of the Football League had first come into being in 1933-34, and continued up until World War II. It was not until 1981-82 that it was revamped as the Group Cup, being known as the Football League Trophy the following year, then the Associate Members Cup. It was the coming of sponsorship that saw it renamed the Freight Rover Trophy in 1984-85, when the final was played at Wembley for the first time.

Having finished nine places above Bolton, and having done the double over the Trotters in the League, City were the form favourites to win their first Wembley final. Pre-match pessimists, though, were quick to remind everyone that experience and tradition counted for much at Wembley. The famous Wanderers had only lost once in five previous appearances at the Twin Towers, while their player-manager Phil Neal had played more games at Wembley than he had at Bolton's Burnden Park!

Early arrivals were treated to pre-match entertainment which included a 15-minute each-way game between old-timers which not surprisingly ended goalless:

MIKE MORRIS'S TV AM ROBINS XI: Ray Cashley; Gary Imlach, Jim Ferguson, Gerry Gow, Terry Mancini, Bobby Moore, George Best, Tony Currie, Bobby Gould, Richard Keys, Chris Garland.
GORDON TAYLOR'S P.F.A. TROTTERS XI: Peter Bonetti; Brendon Batson, Fred Eyre, Graham Kelly, Dave Webb, Bill McMurdo, Alan

Hudson, Frank Worthington, Malcolm Macdonald, Stan Bowles, Gordon Taylor.

The final itself was a credit to the Third Division. Bolton had the best of the opening half-hour, with George Oghani bringing a fine save from Keith Waugh and Tony Caldwell hitting the crossbar. The City fans, who formed the majority of the 54,502 crowd, erupted just before the interval when Bobby Hutchinson challenged Bolton keeper Simon Farnworth for Keith Curle's free-kick and the ball fell kindly for Riley to score from eleven yards. Despite the skill of former Scottish international Asa Hartford in midfield, Bolton had no answer to City's resolute display after the break. Howard Pritchard scored number two when Steve Neville's 73rd-minute shot was parried, and Neville capped his Man of the Match display by crossing the ball from the left for Riley to head in City's third.

City's share of the £286,281 Wembley receipts helped produce the profit of £72,937 announced at the AGM in December 1986. The club was further rewarded when taking possession of the winner's prize of a £15,000 minibus. Thousands of Bristolians took to the streets to acclaim their heroes, who made a three-hour open-topped bus tour on the Monday following the game.

Twelve months later City got through to Wembley again, but this time lost in a penalty shoot-out after a 1-1 draw with Mansfield. Bolton's Wembley experience appears not to have served them well. A year later they were relegated to Division Four.

BRISTOL CITY: Waugh, Newman, Williams, Curle, Moyes, Riley, Pritchard, Hutchinson, Harle, Walsh, Neville.
BOLTON: Farnworth; Scott, Phillips, Sutton, Came (Bell), Thompson, Neal, Oghani, Caldwell, Hartford, Gavin.
REFEREE: G Tyson.

LEAGUE DIVISION 3   **1986-87**
Division 3   6th
League Cup   2nd Round
FA Cup   3rd Round

Prospects for 1986-87 were hampered in the summer when star winger Pritchard rejected a new two-year deal and was sold to Gillingham for £22,500. Johnson was also on the move, going to Scunthorpe for £12,500. Newcomers included 6ft 4in Paul Fitzpatrick on a free from Bolton and Gary Hamson from Leeds, though the big captures were 27-year-old Barnsley winger Gordon Owen and 30-year-old centre-half John MacPhail from York. Owen cost £30,000, but MacPhail was obtained for a bargain £14,500 – Cooper once more exploiting the League Tribunal system, after being unable to agree a fee with York boss Denis Smith.

Despite MacPhail being unfit to play until the end of October, the season started well. City were unbeaten in their opening six games, which included two grand tussles with Bournemouth in the League Cup. Walsh's volley produced a 1-0 win at Dean Court, but in the second leg City needed Riley's extra-time volley to take them through after Steve Aylott's opener for the Cherries. A 3-0 League win at Chesterfield had City up in second place, but after losing 0-1 at Doncaster in their next game, the loss of Neville's goalscoring touch began to take its toll. Despite 3-0 wins at Chester and Fulham, defeats at Bournemouth and Blackpool shunted City down to eighth by the time they opened their FA Cup campaign. Southern League VS Rugby proved stubborn opponents, as City gained a flattering 3-1 home success to set up a home derby with Conference club Bath City in round two.

With work to replace the Covered End roof continuing, a boring tie was only enlivened by Paul Bodin's late strike to earn Bath a replay. Despite the fact that Bath now shared their Twerton Park home with Bristol Rovers, police concerns meant the replay was again staged at Ashton Gate. This time a richly entertaining game saw Marshall run the Bath rearguard ragged to engineer a 3-0 win. The visit of Second Division Plymouth in the third round elicited much interest, and a crowd larger than the official figure of 16,943 was thought to be present to witness a rousing 1-1 draw. It took extra-time to separate the sides in the replay before City went down 1-3, thereby missing out on mouth-watering tie at First Division leaders Arsenal.

Following successive defeats against Rotherham and Notts County in November, four wins and a draw kept City handily placed in the League, until Gary Smart's late winner for Bristol

Rovers set the New Year off to a losing start. Further defeats at Rotherham and Wigan sent Terry Cooper delving into the transfer market. Harle and Hamson had already been sold to Scunthorpe and Port Vale respectively, whilst Trevor Morgan had returned to Ashton Gate. Having watched one of British soccer's outstanding strikers play in Southampton's Reserves, Cooper persuaded his former Leeds colleague Joe Jordan to join City on a month's loan.

Making his debut in a 5-0 drubbing of Doncaster, the 35-year-old Jordan bagged his first City goals in his second match, in the Freight Rover Trophy. City had commenced their defence of the trophy by topping a group that included Exeter and Bristol Rovers and then beating Southend 1-0 at home in the first round. Jordan's goals came in a 3-0 home win over Brentford. City's luck held in the next round as Gillingham were beaten 2-0 at Ashton Gate to send them into a two-legged tie with Fourth Division Aldershot, who had gone ten games unbeaten. In the first leg, goals by Jordan and Newman secured a 2-1 win at a packed Recreation Ground. Six days later a 16,371 crowd were at Ashton Gate to see City win 2-0.

In the League, though, despite the capture of Steve Galliers on loan from Wimbledon, and Jim Harvey, for whom Cooper paid Hereford £20,000, City were erratic. A shock home defeat by a well-organised Brentford looked to have dashed all hopes of a play-off place, but slip-ups by the other contenders enabled City to reach the final day of the campaign in fifth place. It was now that their luck changed. City's old problems from the penalty spot returned with a vengeance, depriving them not only of a place in the play-offs, but also the Freight Rover Trophy.

First, that critical last League match. After taking an early lead against Swindon through Morgan's header, City were unable to turn their pressure into further goals. They paid the price midway through the second half when Peter Coyne's mis-hit volley brought Swindon level. Shortly before the final whistle Jordan was tripped in the area but Owen drove his spot-kick wide of the Covered End goal. This, coupled with Gillingham's home win over Bolton, sent City down to sixth. That would have been good enough today to earn a play-off place, but in 1986-87 the quartet comprised teams finishing third, fourth and fifth, plus the club finishing one above the relegation places in Division Two.

Looking for solace in the Freight Rover Trophy final at Wembley City were cruelly disappointing against Mansfield. Though Neville had not recovered from a broken leg sustained four months earlier at Wigan, City were at full strength with the recall of Walsh and Riley. They were favourites against opponents who had finished four places and sixteen points adrift of them. The previous season

> **Did You Know?**
>
> The best goal ever scored by an opponent at Ashton Gate? Probably that by
> Liverpool's Steve Heighway in 1978. He beat three players in a 70-yard run.

Cooper had let assistant-boss Clive Middlemass lead the team out,
but this time it was the turn of long-serving scout Jock Rae. City's
team was: Waugh, Newman, Williams, Moyes, MacPhail, Llewellyn
(Fitzpatrick), Owen, Walsh (Curle), Riley, Marshall, Jordan.

City, wearing white even though there wasn't a colour clash,
could not match the standards of the previous year. Mansfield took
control and Man of the Match Keith Cassells centred for Kevin Kent
to hammer the Stags ahead in front of a 58,586 crowd. Three
minutes from time Riley slammed in an equaliser. Extra-time
brought no further goals, so for the first time ever a Wembley final
was decided by a penalty shoot-out.

City had the advantage of going first, and Williams, Newman,
MacPhail and Curle put their kicks away. Cassells missed Mansfield's second, but strikes by Mark Kearney, Ian Stringfellow and
Gary Pollard kept them in the hunt. With City 4-3 up they needed
only to net their fifth kick to retain the trophy. Wretchedly, Owen's
blaster flew off keeper Kevin Hitchcock's boot and over the bar.
Kent dispatched his kick for the Stags to take the contest into
sudden death. This didn't take long, as Moyes saw his effort saved,
whilst Tony Kenworthy made no mistake for Mansfield.

Wembley receipts of £324,592 enabled City to declare a £156,925
profit at their AGM in December 1987, the figure boosted by season
ticket revenue increasing from £78,885 to £83,806.

The Reserves also had a successful season, improving on their
ninth place in the Western League in 1985-86 to finish third. In their
second season of the South West Counties League they did even
better, taking the Championship after finishing eighth the previous
season. In the Somerset Premier Cup they equalled last year's
accomplishment in reaching the semi-finals.

Match of the Season 1986-87
Bristol City 1 Swindon Town 1

Division 3, 9 May 1987

This was a disappointing season for City fans who had anticipated a
return to Division Two. City had flattered to deceive throughout the
campaign, just doing enough to keep hopes alive of a promotion
play-off place, thanks to a good home record that saw only three

defeats. Away from home it was a different tale: City's reasonable total of seventeen points up to the New Year was followed by a meagre return of twelve points from their subsequent twelve games.

As the season entered its decisive phase, City had looked odds-on gaining a play-off place, but a spell of only three wins in nine games left them needing victory against Swindon in their final match to be sure of taking part. The fact that the Moonrakers were only playing for their pride, having already qualified for the play-offs, convinced the 19,201 crowd – the biggest at Ashton Gate since the advent of the new company – that their supposedly more moti-vated team would easily secure the required victory.

They were to be proved wrong. Despite controlling the early play and going in front in the twelfth minute thanks to Morgan's glancing header from Owen's chip, City lost control of the game to Swindon's neat possession football. Even though Marshall's lob hit the Swindon crossbar and Newman was denied by Fraser Digby's fine save, it came as no surprise when, after 66 minutes, Swindon equalised. Llewellyn conceded a needless free-kick, from which Joe Jordan's misdirected headed clearance fell to the unmarked Peter Coyne, whose mis-hit volley went in off a post. Ultimately, however, the fate of City's season was decided by Cooper's deci-sion to take off regular penalty taker Brian Williams. Minutes later, Jordan was supposedly tripped in the area.

Scuffles ensued as Swindon bitterly contested the penalty deci-sion. Confusion reigned amongst the City players as to who should take the kick. Owen bravely volunteered, even though he had failed from the spot at Middlesbrough in the League and at home to Brentford in the Freight Rover Trophy. His concentration was not helped by the kick being delayed as the referee sought to calm the jostling that broke out amongst the players. To the dismay of City's fans, Owen placed his shot wide.

In the thirteen minutes that remained City threw everything at Swindon. Marshall had a shot cleared off the line by Mark Jones, and keeper Digby pulled off a fine save to keep out Newman's volley. In the end, though, Swindon might even have won. In the dying seconds Moyes' handball inside the area was punished by a free-kick outside.

Swindon went on to deservedly gain promotion, beating Gilling-ham 2-0 in the play-off final, after disposing of Wigan 3-2 on aggre-gate in the semi-finals. City were left to rue on the loss of too many points against inferior opposition over the season, and the fact that their relentless siege on the Walsall goal in their penultimate game failed to secure the win that would have assured a play-off berth.

LEAGUE DIVISION 3   **1987-88**
Division 3   5th
League Cup   1st Round
FA Cup   2nd Round

So near, yet so far. A hectic season saw Terry Cooper's reign end
and Joe Jordan's begin. The new manager inspired City to the final
of the play-offs. Despite Cooper's earlier comment that apart from
seeking to permanently sign on-loan midfielder Steve Galliers (he
signed for £37,500) he would not need to add to his playing staff,
this wasn't how things turned out. It was musical chairs at Ashton
Gate. The comings and goings started before a ball was kicked. A
tribunal fixed fee of £27,500 bought Tony Caldwell from Bolton.
£18,000 was recouped from Sunderland when MacPhail joined up
with his old York boss Denis Smith. A small fee brought Port Vale's
Russell Bromage to replace Brian Williams, who moved to Second
Division Shrewsbury. Trevor Morgan joined Bolton for £16,000.
    The fans, like the manager, were confident of promotion, but
were jolted by City's failure to avenge their Freight Rover defeat in
the opening game, losing 0-2 at Mansfield. A run of nine League
games unbeaten put the world to rights. City were top of the pile
after beating Chesterfield 2-1. It was not such a happy story in the
League Cup, as City lost 3-5 on aggregate to Swindon in the first
round.
    With Riley on loan at Torquay, and Harvey joining Tranmere for
£20,000, City's run ended with a 0-3 reverse at Northampton, when
Galliers and Fitzpatrick were sent off. A 3-2 home win over
Southend, followed by a 4-1 success at Grimsby, did not put a halt
to the transfer merry-go-round. Curle was sold to Reading for a club
record fee of £150,000, and captain Moyes joined Shrewsbury for
£25,000. Cooper paid £22,000 to Doncaster for defender Glenn
Humphries – who marked his debut with a 38-second own-goal in
City's 1-4 defeat at Rotherham – £55,000 for striker Carl Shutt from
Sheffield Wednesday, and £50,000 to Charlton for centre-half John
Pender. Livewire Shutt was an instant hit, scoring twice on his
debut and netting eleven goals in his first twelve games. Pender,
though, was sent off as his new side crashed 2-4 at Blackpool. Form
slumped and City endured six League games without a win until
York were beaten 3-2 in mid-December.
    Success of sorts was achieved in the FA Cup, when Caldwell,
who had not settled, bagged the goal that brought a flattering home
win over Beazer Homes League Aylesbury, when 18-year-old
reserve keeper Mark Coombe made his only first-team appearance
for City. With Waugh fit to reclaim his position from loan keeper

Mark Prudhoe (Walsall), City's luck ran out in the second round. A 0-1 home defeat by Torquay provoked shouts for Cooper's head. With assistant manager Clive Middlemass having left to take charge at Carlisle, Jordan took over as Cooper's right-hand man, whilst ex City favourite Alan Crawford, who had been at Western League Bristol Manor Farm, was appointed youth coach.

Cooper bounced back, earning the Third Division Manager of the Month award on the back of four wins and a draw up to the turn of the year, which hoisted City from twelfth to fourth. The movement of players continued, though, with Owen going on loan to Hull, before joining Mansfield for £35,000, while keeper John Vaughan was loaned from West Ham for his second spell at Ashton Gate. Winger Ralph Milne was another loan signing, but City found £50,000 to pay for him – Milne marking his debut with a clean strike in a 3-2 home win over Bury. Caldwell was loaned to Chester, and Micky Tanner transferred to Bath, whilst another £50,000 paid for the services of Steve McClaren from Derby. This proved to be the manager's last throw of the dice, as City were by then off the pace in eighth spot and out of the newly-named Sherpa Van Trophy. Having qualified second in their group, they lost 0-1 at Aldershot.

After a 0-2 defeat at Southend on 11 March, the directors met to consider Cooper's future, and his last match in charge was the following Wednesday night's Gloucestershire Cup clash with Bristol Rovers at Ashton Gate. City won 3-1 in front of 2,278 fans, as they completed a strange double in the competition, after having clinched the delayed 1986-87 final with a 2-1 success in front of just 1,376 fans in the first Twerton Park derby during December.

When Jordan took temporary charge, there were no recriminations from Cooper, only sadness that he was leaving a club where he had enjoyed every minute. With only eleven games in which to prove himself, the caretaker boss was handicapped by having Newman and Humphries suspended, whilst illness and injury ruled out Bromage, Shutt and himself. A goalless draw at Fulham got Jordan's show on the road. His first venture into the transfer market saw Reading striker Colin Gordon arrive on a month's loan. A penalty by the big fair-haired marksman, and a strike by Neville that ended his 23-week barren spell, forged a 2-0 home win over Rotherham. Aldershot were beaten by the same score, but though a 0-1 defeat at Chester seemed to have dashed City's promotion hopes, Jordan's never-say-die spirit lifted his team to five wins and a draw in their last seven games. Gordon's late goal in the final match clinched a play-off place.

Jordan was rewarded with a two-year contract before the play-offs started. City's fifth position brought them a two-legged semi-final with Sheffield United, who had finished third from bottom in the Second Division. At Ashton Gate, 25,335 fans saw Walsh notch the only goal just before half-time. In the second leg three days later, Shutt, replacing the injured Neville, shattered his hometown club by giving City the lead. United levelled on the night when Colin Morris looped a header over Waugh, but City's defence stayed firm thereafter to condemn the Blades to relegation.

City's opponents in the two-legged final were Walsall, who had beaten Notts County 4-2 on aggregate in the other semi-final. The first match was at Ashton Gate, when many of the 25,128 crowd were confident of a City win. Though Neville was fit to return, City were weakened by Gordon's return to Reading. Jordan had been unwilling to pay the £70,000 demanded for his transfer.

Walsh duly put City ahead from a free-kick, but a cruel equaliser – Andy Llewellyn's clearance struck Waugh and rebounded into the net for an own-goal in the 63rd minute – changed the complexion of the game. Two strikes by Republic of Ireland international David Kelly appeared to give Walsall what looked like an unassailable advantage. The story of City's extraordinary 2-0 win in the second leg, which meant the contest went to a third game, is taken up in Match of the Season.

In those days play-offs took no account of the away-goals rule. With the two teams finishing 3-3 on aggregate, this was just as well, as otherwise City would have gone out. A third fixture was therefore required. This also took place at Fellows Park, on 30 May, a Bank Holiday, which encouraged 4,000 City fans to make the trip. The venue had been decided not by the toss of a coin but by a penalty shoot-out, which City lost. Neither the players nor the fans were perturbed by this return to the Midlands, as they thought they had the measure of Walsall. But they reckoned without their old nemesis, Kelly. City trailed by three goals after just nineteen minutes, and Kelly completed his hat-trick to tie up a 4-0 success for the Saddlers. This amounted to City's heaviest defeat in almost three years. To add salt to the wound, Shutt was sent off shortly before the final whistle for fouling keeper Fred Barber.

Unfortunately, both the home and away games with Walsall were marred by thugs, who again tarnished City's name. The 1-3 defeat at Ashton Gate was too much to stomach for some City fans, who went on the rampage, fighting a pitched battle with police in Ashton Park and smashing the windscreens of dozens of cars. At Fellows Park there were forty arrests. Whilst some fans appeared to have justifiable complaints at the heavy handed methods, there was no excuse for the mindless thugs who overturned police vans as they fought with the local constabulary.

Did You Know?

After losing four games on the trot early in 1979, Alan Dicks took his players for a short holiday in Torremolinos. They came home and lost their fifth!

Match of the Season 1987-88
Walsall 0 Bristol City 2

Division 3, Play-Off final, 2nd leg, 28 May 1988

Having lost the play-off home leg 1-3, few City fans were persuaded by Jordan's insistence that the remaining promotion place was still up for grabs. The small band of optimists pointed to Jordan's motivational qualities, which had steered City into a play-off spot when the side looked out of contention. Jordan even picked himself to play his first full game for five months.

Jordan's battlers did not let a matter of a two-goal deficit deter them at Fellows Park, and by the end it was Walsall who were grateful to earn another chance. City's inspired players were a yard quicker to the ball and could well have brought the aggregate scores level in the opening fourteen minutes. Milne forced a fine save from Fred Barber and Walsh crashed a close-range volley against a post. Later, Shutt shot inches wide and Walsh curled a free-kick just too high as the home side were penned back by a stream of attacks. Just when it seemed that City's dominance would go unrewarded, Newman rose on the half-hour to glance Walsh's corner over the line, despite Craig Shakespeare's desperate clearance.

A half-time pep talk revived Walsall slightly, and Waugh did well to deflect David Kelly's drive for a corner. Galliers then made a goal-line clearance to deny Phil Hawker, before Shutt levelled the aggregate scores with a low drive in the 66th minute. Both sides created and wasted chances in the time remaining.

With no provision for extra-time or away goals, the promotion decider would go to a third game, the venue to be determined by a penalty shoot-out. Willie Naughton put the Saddlers ahead, but Barber blocked Walsh's reply. Trevor Christie fired Walsall two up before Newman put City on the scoresheet. Shakespeare then made it 3-1, at which point Milne's effort was saved. It was left to David Kelly to secure that ill-fated second meeting at Fellows Park.

Promotion backfired on Walsall boss Tommy Coakley and his assistant, former City favourite Gerry Sweeney. The Saddlers were not strong enough to cope with higher-grade football and were headed for instant relegation. Coakley and Sweeney lost their jobs before the season was out.

LEAGUE DIVISION 3   **1988-89**
Division 3   11th
League Cup   Semi-Final
FA Cup   3rd Round

The general consensus was that there would be no stopping City now. But that was not how things turned out. Poor form in the League even saw Jordan's job on the line, but, like Dicks before him, Jordan was rescued by City's Cup performances.

In the FA Cup, City recorded the greatest number of replays in their history, requiring *four* attempts to dispose of Aldershot in the second round, after beating Southend in round one. Although their sixth match in the competition, at Hartlepool, saw the team go out 0-1, Ashton Alf wasn't unduly concerned as City were still going strong in the League Cup.

That Wembley trail started modestly, as in both legs of the first round against Exeter the Robins scored once without reply. A 4-2 win at the Manor Ground shattered Second Division Oxford's eight-season, 27-match unbeaten home record in the League Cup. A 2-0 second-leg success booked City a home tie with Second Division Crystal Palace. An early three-goal salvo destroyed Palace, and further progress looked assured when the luck of the draw paired City with Fourth Division Tranmere. A formality it might have been on paper, but in real life Tranmere made things extremely difficult. Shutt's strike on the half-hour mark was all that separated the sides at the finish.

Faced with Second Division Bradford City in the quarter-finals, many fans expected the Robins to bow out. Bradford had accounted for Everton in the previous round, so the virtually-retired Jordan recalled himself to City's colours. He won the Man of the Match award for an inspirational display at Valley Parade, Walsh's early strike taking City through to the semi-finals for the second time in their history.

Few gave City a prayer against the might of Brian Clough's Nottingham Forest, but in the first leg on the banks of the Trent it took an unfortunate own-goal by John Pender four minutes from time to deny City an epic giant-killing cup win. City's goalscoring hero was 19-year-old Paul Mardon, whose name didn't even appear in the match programme. He had put City in front midway through the second half with a 15-yard drive for his first senior goal.

City's brave performance earned the media spotlight, and the second leg at Ashton Gate on Sunday, 26 February was shown live on ITV. The wind and rain spoilt the game as a spectacle, but the occasion is taken up in Match of the Season.

Did You Know?

John Palmer is City's briefest ever substitute. At Torquay in March 1983 he shook hands with the departing Paul Williams when the ref blew for time.

In the Sherpa Van Trophy, City's interest disappeared at the first round stage. After qualifying in second place from their Group games – which included a 0-1 reverse at Bristol Rovers – they were slaughtered at Molineux, where Wolves won 3-0. A similar scoreline had also been City's fate at Twerton Park at the start of the season, when Bristol Rovers secured the Gloucestershire Cup in front of just 1,664 fans on 17 August.

With numerous changes in personnel during the close season, both on and off the pitch, perhaps it was not surprising that League form was indifferent. Departures included Neville, who returned to Exeter as player-coach, and Marshall to Carlisle, both for £10,000 tribunal fees. Jimmy Lumsden, previously assistant to Eddie Gray at Leeds, joined City in a similar capacity, whilst physiotherapist Alex Lockhart departed for private practice. Former Everton and Chelsea midfielder Gary Stanley took up the offer of a contract after impressing whilst on trial, and striker Scott McGarvey arrived from Grimsby in exchange for Caldwell. Neither Stanley or McGarvey would prove to be a success, but John Bailey was an instant hit with his sense of fun and skilful play. The 31-year-old had been released by Newcastle three months previously, and, impressing during a trial, signed permanent forms.

Keeper Waugh's early season injury saw City borrow ex-Bristol Rover Tim Parkin from Sunderland, before Andy Leaning (27) was signed for £10,000 from Sheffield United after a period on loan. Jordan was no less active in the transfer market than Cooper had been, and it was not long before £35,000 was changing hands to secure the services of 24-year-old Mark Gavin from Bolton. Money was recouped by Fitzpatrick moving to Carlisle for £40,000. Then came the astonishing swoop by Manchester United. Few could believe that the famous Reds considered Ralph Milne to be worth £170,000. But this failed to take account of Alex Ferguson's Aberdeen years, when Dundee United's Milne was one of the brightest lights in Scottish football. Milne did enough damage to Aberdeen over the years to ensure that Ferguson marked his card. It must also be admitted that the right-winger looked a far better player at Old Trafford than he ever did at Ashton Gate.

A 1-5 home defeat by Fulham in early October was one low spot. Another was Bristol Rovers' victory on 2 January that plunged City into a trough of four successive League defeats. Tony Shepherd, on loan from Celtic, made his debut in that game against Rovers, which City lost 0-1 in front of the biggest Ashton Gate crowd for almost nine years. Notwithstanding the stirring League Cup run, the manager's position was still under review when City lost 1-2 at home to Blackpool on 15 April, but a Bob Taylor hat-trick three days later helped City to a 6-1 thrashing of Huddersfield and eased the weight on Jordan's shoulders.

Taylor became an Ashton Gate hero, a real snip at £175,000 from Leeds, while Shutt, valued at £50,000, was a makeweight in the deal. Taylor made his debut in a 1-1 draw at Bristol Rovers, forming an instant understanding with the marauding Robbie Turner, for whom City paid Wimbledon £45,000 in late January. The Taylor-Turner spearhead would drive City to promotion in 1989-90.

Many felt that City's final position of eleventh was unsatisfactory. The fact that Bristol Rovers reached the play-offs did not make things easier for Jordan. There were many occasions when Jordan's managerial capabilities were questioned, but four wins from City's last six games gave promise of better times ahead.

Match of the Season 1988-89

Bristol City 0 Nottingham Forest 1
> League Cup, semi-final, 2nd leg, 26 February 1989

This was City's second semi-final appearance in the League Cup, which started life in 1960-61. The advent of sponsorship saw it being named the Milk Cup in 1982-83, then the Littlewoods Cup 1986-87, Rumbelows Cup 1990-91, Coca-Cola Cup 1992-93 and its current incarnation as the Worthington Cup in 1998-99.

The tie stood at 1-1 after the first leg. With Forest boss Brian Clough banished from the touchline following an incident in the previous round, Gary Parker shattered City's dreams at Ashton Gate with a goal six minutes from the end of extra-time to keep Forest on course for a unique Wembley hat-trick. For City it was a heartbreaking conclusion to a game of high drama for the partisan West Country crowd of almost 30,000.

For most the game it appeared that Keith Waugh had returned to haunt Clough, as he thwarted the Forest attack with many fine saves. Waugh was an impressionable 5-year-old on the Roker Park terraces when Clough suffered the collision with Bury's goalkeeper which put paid to his playing career. Now the unemotional Clough sat poker-faced alongside his chairman Maurice Roworth as Waugh defied Forest to merit his Man of the Match award. Waugh more than anyone else almost earned gallant City a replay at Villa Park.

However, Parker's late goal should take nothing away from Jordan's braves, who came within a coat of paint of reaching Wembley. With less than a minute of normal time remaining, Alan Walsh blasted a shot against Steve Sutton's right-hand post at the Covered End. For a split second the City players thought they were Wembley bound, but the ball flew off the post to Steve Hodge, who was happy to hack it away for a corner.

The match was played in driving rain and on a glue-pot pitch. After a nervy opening, City laid siege to the Forest citadel in the first 45 minutes and were perhaps unfortunate not to be in front at the interval. It was a different story in the second half. It was virtually one-way traffic, as Forest unleashed their onslaught. City survived thanks to Waugh, and once extra-time was under way the introduction of Carl Shutt for Mark Gavin allowed City to re-impose themselves as the dominate force.

Failure to take their chances proved costly. Forest, who had sealed a place at Wembley the previous Wednesday in the Simod Cup, secured their return trip when Webb crossed from the right for Parker to fire his 12-yard shot into the roof of the Open End net. A minute later Parker almost made it two, rifling another effort against the crossbar.

At the end Clough allowed himself a smile as he advised Jordan to be careful and kissed him on the cheek. Doubtless Clough smiled even more when his team beat Luton 3-1 in the final, not to mention annexing the Simod Cup (a competition for the top two divisions of the Football League) with a 4-3 success against Everton. Forest were unable to make it a unique Wembley treble: their FA Cup bid ended in the semi-final. Liverpool beat them after both clubs had endured the traumas of Hillsborough.

Despite the extra revenue generated by their cup exploits, City's financial situation took a turn for the worse, with a loss of £185,354 as against a profit of £106,877 the previous year. Season ticket sales increased from £90,725 to £102,219, but average home League attendances fell 1,697 to 8,121.

The Reserves were unable to retain their hold on the South West Counties League Cup, which they had won the previous campaign. In the League though, they improved on their 1986-87 showing by three places to finish fourth. The Youths continued their general poor form in the FA Youth Cup that characterised the 1980s, during which they never progressed past the second round. This time they lost 2-3 at home to Plymouth, having beaten Bristol Rovers 3-1 at Ashton Gate in front of 270 spectators.

LOST OPPORTUNITIES
1989-1994

LEAGUE DIVISION 3	**1989-90**
Division 3	2nd (Promoted)
League Cup	1st Round
FA Cup	5th Round

With the loss of crowd favourite Alan Walsh to Turkish club Besik-tas for £45,000, Jordan set about rebuilding the side for a promotion challenge. The board allowed him substantial funds to spend, and spend he did, though additional revenue was generated by the sale of Galliers to Maidstone for £20,000. McClaren moved to Oxford in a straight swap for Gary Shelton. Gillingham's lightning-fast winger David Smith was snapped up for £75,000, midfielder Paul Wimble-ton (Cardiff) cost £60,000, and £175,000 was found to sign the cultured David Rennie from Leeds.

City also needed a new goalkeeper. Waugh was unhappy with his new terms and moved to Coventry for a tribunal-fixed fee of £40,000. Ronnie Sinclair came from Leeds on a free transfer, but it was Leaning who played in goal when City opened the League season with a 1-1 draw at Bury, after losing the Gloucestershire Cup final at home to Bristol Rovers. A modest start was not helped by the loss of Bailey with a fractured toe in the second match against Birmingham. A 4-5 aggregate defeat by Reading in the League Cup increased the pressure on Jordan, but September was a good month, with victories over Blackpool, Cardiff and Shrewsbury and a goalless home draw with Bristol Rovers. A 0-6 hammering in a top of the table clash at Tranmere took the icing off the cake somewhat, but City still lay fourth.

In October young striker Nigel Hawkins moved to Blackpool for £17,500, while Bailey's 25-yarder at Crewe brought City their fourth win in six games played that month. Welsh International striker Andy Jones arrived on a month's loan, but despite his useful performances the board blocked a proposed £125,000 transfer. Goals from Turner and the prolific Taylor earned the 2-0 win at Walsall that took City to the top for the first time, but failure to win another League game until mid-December saw them tumble down to sixth.

In the FA Cup, City experienced no such problem. After beating Conference club Barnet in the first round, victories over Fulham and Swindon earned a mouth-watering clash with Chelsea. Receipts of £97,780 were generated by the 24,535 crowd that crammed into Ashton Gate to witness the shock of the fourth round. Gavin's late strike clinched a sensational 3-1 win, capitalising on Turner's two-goal haul and an inspirational display by Sinclair between the posts. City's fame spread far and wide, even bringing new supporters from Scandinavia who formed their own Supporters Club. Sadly, despite being presented with a plum home tie with Fourth Division Cambridge United in the next round, City were unable to progress to the last eight. Taken aback by the quality of Cambridge's football in a goalless draw at Ashton Gate, City lost out after another marathon contest. Taylor's rasping drive in the replay earned an extra-time 1-1 draw, but after losing the toss for choice of venue, City were humiliated 1-5 back at the Abbey Stadium.

Though City lost out in the Leyand Daf Cup, 0-1 at home to Notts County in January, League form had picked up. A 4-0 success at Birmingham allowed City to reclaim top spot, and despite home defeats by Reading and Tranmere the course seemed set not just for promotion, but a long-awaited championship. Paul Miller had come on loan from Wimbledon, and Wimbleton was sold to Shrewsbury for £60,000. Seeking further reinforcements, in early March Jordan paid Millwall £50,000 for 28-year-old striker Dean Horrix.

Horrix played just three games. Tragedy struck following a 1-0 win at Shrewsbury. After a night out with friends, Horrix was a passenger in a car driven by his wife that hit a tree. Mrs Horrix escaped with a damaged hand. Her husband died instantly.

The tragedy stunned the club, but made the players even more determined to win promotion. The team could do little wrong, as a run of fourteen undefeated games kept them looking down on the rest. Despite the shrewd signing of Nicky Morgan from Stoke, plus the capture of Junior Bent from Huddersfield and Iain Ferguson on loan from Hearts, the side was stuttering without Taylor. The striker had pulled a hamstring after claiming a hat-trick in a 4-1 home demolition of Crewe. He attempted a comeback at Bolton, but his season was finished. It was this game at Burnden Park that ultimately cost City the championship. Their 0-1 defeat on what was normally considered one of their lucky grounds opened the door to the relentlessly pursuing Bristol Rovers.

As luck would have it, the penultimate game of the season was against Rovers at Twerton Park four days later. Despite the championship being at stake, City put on a gutless show, as Rovers swept to a 3-0 victory and took over at the top with a two-point lead. Whilst a 4-0 home win over Walsall in the final game ensured promotion, it could not compensate for the Twerton defeat. Rovers won 3-0 at Blackpool to secure the championship.

The promotion drive boosted City's League average attendance to 11,544. This, coupled with the revenue generated by their FA Cup exploits, yielded an annual profit of £68,550. Receipts of £66,633 were produced by City's biggest home League gate – 19,483 for the Walsall promotion-clincher.

The Reserves did their bit to convince the fans that City were on the up. They won the South West Counties League Cup, but finished third in the League and were knocked out at the semi-final stage of the Somerset Professional Cup.

Match of the Season 1989-90
Bristol Rovers 3 Bristol City 0

Division 3, 2 May 1990

It often appeared that there was a jinx on this fixture. Throughout Rovers' ten-season sojourn at Twerton Park from 1986-87, adverse weather necessitated a change to the scheduled date on no fewer than three occasions, whilst a Grandstand fire – alleged to have been started by City hooligans – forced postponement in 1990-91. Who knows, the result of this vital championship fixture might have been different if it had been played on its original date of 3 February, when a waterlogged pitch brought cancellation.

Historically, City held the advantage in League derbies with 26 wins against eighteen for the Rovers, ten of these wins coming at Eastville. At what became known as Fortress Twerton, however, City rarely gave a good account of themselves. It would not be until the most recent derby played on this ground seven years later that City broke their duck in the League. None of this bothered City fans unduly; they expected victory, knowing that a win was vital to ensure Rovers did not snatch the title at City's expense.

Apart from a 1-3 defeat at Notts County in April, Rovers had not tasted defeat in the League since going down 1-2 at Brentford in January. Twenty games had produced 45 points to put them hot on the heels of City, whose 0-1 defeat at Bolton in the previous game now offered Rovers the chance to assume top spot. Conversely for City, it meant that their fate was still in their hands. A City win would not only clinch promotion, but also ensure they finished as champions.

Did You Know?

At Plymouth in April 1985, the local constabulary prevented 700 City fans from attending the game. Their train was detained in a railway siding.

Twerton was packed with 9,813 excited fans, paying receipts of £29,950, on a warm sunny evening. Rovers' physical team quickly seized the initiative. City were back-peddling from the start and appeared to have no idea how to cope with the muscular presence of Devon White. Apart from Mark Gavin's mis-hit cross-shot in the first half and Robbie Turner's header past the post in the second, City lacked conviction. It was no surprise they fell behind midway through the first half, when Man of the Match White capitalised on Andy Llewellyn's slip to convert David Mehew's cross. Carl Saunders set up White to fire in the second from ten yards after 55 minutes. Seven minutes later referee Roger Dilkes ruled out Mehew's header, when Phil Purnell's fierce drive was handled on the line by Llewellyn, but Ian Holloway netted the resultant penalty to tie up Rovers' deserved success.

Regrettably, with the Rovers fans in good voice with the strains of 'Goodnight Irene' reverberating around the ground, some of City's so-called fans appeared unable to countenance defeat. Disturbances broke out as a few hot-heads sought to get the match abandoned. The referee was encouraged to continue by the sportsmanlike attitude of both teams, with City captain Rob Newman telling him – 'You keep the game going, and we'll keep going for you'. City boss Joe Jordan is also to be commended, preventing the situation from getting out of hand by walking round the ground and confronting the unruly City fans.

Defeat denied City the championship, but not promotion, which was secured against Walsall three days later.

LEAGUE DIVISION 2   **1990-91**
Division 2   9th
League Cup   2nd Round
FA Cup   3rd Round

With Bristol having erased the shame of being the first provincial City to have both its sides relegated from the same division in the same season by reversing the process, local interest was intense as the new campaign approached. City embarked on a tour of Scotland and the North for their pre-season preparations. Ayr, Clydebank and Carlisle were duly beaten. Revenge of sorts was achieved against an under-strength Bristol Rovers side, when City's 4-1 win secured the Gloucestershire Cup at Twerton Park. Pre-season preparations were concluded with a 1-1 home draw with Crystal Palace and a 2-0 success over Aston Villa in Newman's benefit.

The League campaign commenced at Ashton Gate, when City fought back from a half-time deficit to beat Blackburn 4-2. City's side included new signings Louie Donowa from Ipswich (£45,000), Andy May from Huddersfield (£90,000), as well as their major capture – Welsh International centre-half Mark Aizlewood, who cost £125,000 from Bradford City. Missing was Wayne Allison – who had joined City from Watford, plus a £100,000 cheque, as make-weight in a deal that saw Gavin move in the opposite direction – and Murray Jones, who arrived on a free from Crystal Palace. Also on the move was Turner, who joined Plymouth for £150,000, and Pender who in mid-October joined Burnley for £70,000.

Allison made his debut at West Brom, as substitute in City's 2-2 draw in the first round of the League Cup, but Jones was destined never to break into the first team. A 1-0 extra-time win in the second leg carried City through to a two-legged meeting with First Division Sunderland. A stirring performance at Roker earned a 1-0 win thanks to Morgan's header, but in the return leg City equalled their record 1-6 defeat in the competition.

The debacle against Sunderland coincided with City's assistant boss Lumsden's appointment as manager. Though Joe Jordan had signed a three-year contract in the summer, he resigned on 19 September to take over at Hearts in place of Alex McDonald. Three successive games were won during the period of Lumsden's temporary control, and it was perhaps unfortunate that – no sooner had he put pen to paper – City should feature in a game in which they were punished for every mistake. City's involvement in the Full Members (Zenith Data Systems) Cup did not last long, though they were perhaps unfortunate to go out 2-3 in a penalty shoot-out, at the end of a 1-1 extra-time draw at Oxford.

In the League, matters had taken a turn for the worse after City's 1-0 home win over Newcastle United in late September. The next four games yielded only one point, from a 1-1 home draw with West Ham, which kicked off at 11.30am. Despite a 2-1 success at Millwall, performances were still erratic. With Lumsden in hospital, his assistant Tony Taylor was in charge when City beat Hull 4-1 at home to record their best win of the season. Losses to Port Vale, Oxford and Charlton prompted Lumsden to make his first major signing. He paid £200,000 to Rotherham for full-back Martin Scott, who made his debut in a 1-1 home draw with Sheffield Wednesday. Other moves at the turn of the year saw Murray, after a spell on loan with Doncaster, joining Exeter for £30,000, Chris Honor going on loan to Swansea, whilst Humphries was sold to Scunthorpe for £55,000.

There was no New Year's joy for City. A 0-2 defeat at Barnsley heralded five straight losses in January, including a 1-2 exit from the FA Cup at Norwich. The 2-3 defeat at Twerton Park dumped City down to thirteenth, their lowest position of the season. Morgan ended his goal drought in the next game to inspire a 2-0 home win over West Brom. This sparked a run of three successive victories that fostered hopes of a play-off place. The Gulf War was raging when City beat Oxford 3-1, but the game was marred by the death of club chairman Des Williams with a heart attack.

Donowa's late goal that secured a 1-0 home win against Bristol Rovers set off a four-match unbeaten run and hoisted City into a play-off position. But 0-1 and 1-4 defeats at West Ham and Portsmouth in late March ultimately proved fatal to City's promotion hopes and dropped them down to eighth. All hope was finally extinguished when Teddy Sheringham's hat-trick at Ashton Gate brought Millwall a 4-1 win. When the curtain came down on the season City lay ninth, a satisfactory placing on their return to the Second Division.

For older City fans, there was a treat to be savoured on the ground of Bristol Manor Farm at the Creek, where Newman's highly successful benefit season ended with a special match. His City XI drew 2-2 with a Bristol City 1976 XI in front of 500 spectators, who saw goals from Donowa and Newman matched by strikes from Fear and Cheesley.

With the average home League attendance rising to 13,495, and season ticket sales doubling from £122,165 to £250,235, City's profits increased to a new record of £424,172.

The Reserves also did well, finishing as Champions of the South West Counties, as well as winning the League Cup and the Somerset Premier Cup.

Did You Know?

In 1988 City fans did not believe Alex Ferguson would pay £170,000 for Ralph Milne. But when with Dundee U, Milne caused havoc to Ferguson's Aberdeen.

Match of the Season 1990-91
Bristol City 1   Bristol Rovers 0

Division 2, 5 March 1991

It might even be unique statistically, but this was the season when *both* derby fixtures had to be re-arranged. The Stand fire at Twerton forced postponement of City's away game on 19 September, whilst snow and ice prevented the match at Ashton Gate going ahead on 12 February.

The Rovers won the re-arranged game at Twerton, which kicked-off at midday on 26 January, and were hoping to achieve a League double over City, even though such a feat was rare in the 36 seasons of Bristol derbies. Only twice had the Rovers managed it, whilst City's record was not much better, notching only four such 'doubles' since the two sides first met in the Football League in 1922-23.

Lying one point ahead of Rovers in the table, and with a game in hand, City were both the favourites and the form side. They had won three of their previous four games and the majority of the 22,269 fans – paying receipts of £102,821.50 – for this Tuesday evening match expected a home win. History, though, was against City. Their last home League victory over the Rovers had been back in March 1986, when the result was 2-0.

City's hero in 1991 was Louie Donowa, a late replacement for the injured David Smith. It was his goal that denied Rovers an eleventh successive unbeaten game in League derbies. Just two minutes from time he latched onto a through-ball, and though keeper Brian Parkin blocked his first effort, the ball popped up for Donowa to stoop to head it into the empty net. The late goal was a real sickener for Rovers, especially for Ian Holloway. When Andy Reece had been sent tumbling by Andy Leaning, Holloway's spot-kick was saved.

Donowa had justified his selection with a strong running display which gave Rovers' left-back Vaughan Jones a torrid time. Geoff Twentyman's marshalling qualities were a key factor in the early stages as Rovers weathered City's opening 20-minute blitz. Nicky Morgan was thrice thwarted by the woodwork, but committed Rovers were resilient and came back well in a thrilling match, which was capably refereed by Ron Groves. City managed seven shots on target and five off, against five and nine for the Rovers, whilst the corner count was to the advantage of the homesters 8-4.

At the final whistle the City fans were in raptures, their displays of celebration more reminiscent of promotion than just winning a match, even though it was against the old enemy. The only disquieting note of a memorable night were the jeers of a small number of Rovers fans during the minute's silence held in memory of City chairman Des Williams, whose heart attack had claimed his life ten days previously.

City's win broke the mould, for in subsequent seasons the Ashton Gate club re-established their former supremacy, notching up six more League derby successes, including three away, whilst Rovers have won but twice.

LEAGUE DIVISION 2 **1991-92**
Division 2   17th
League Cup   2nd Round
FA Cup   5th Round

The season started well enough with City second in the table after going unbeaten for the first five games. These included a 1-0 home win over promotion favourites Blackburn, but a run of six matches that yielded just two points saw City plummet to eighteenth after losing 1-4 at Derby on 5 October.

This was not what Ashton Alf was expecting. Confidence had been high in the close season that City would put together a promotion challenge, though the loss of the versatile Newman to Norwich for £600,000 after he had netted a cool £100,000 from his benefit year caused some disquiet. Other concerns revolved around the development of Ashton Gate in the summer, a consequence of the Taylor Report's requirement for all-seater stadiums. The cost of extending the Grandstand roof, both length and widthways, to enable it to join up with the Covered End, plus the installation of 9,000 seats, came to £670,000. The work was partly funded by the Football Trust, City's outlay being a modest £260,000. Many fans were unhappy at losing the standing terraces at the Covered End. Nor did it help when it was realised that the seats provided in this part of the ground had no backs. Fortunately the Open End was still available to those who wished to stand, a facility that remained available until the building of the Atyeo Stand in 1994 converted Ashton Gate into an all-seater stadium.

As well as the departure of Newman, others to seek pastures new included Honor, Donowa and Mardon. It was the supposed delights of the Scottish League that attracted Honor, as he joined Airdrie for £20,000, whilst Donowa and Mardon shot up the M5 to Birmingham, who paid £50,000 and £60,000 respectively. Among the new intake of players were Rochdale keeper Keith Welch, who cost £200,000, as well as free-transfer signings Gerry Harrison and Gus Caesar from Watford and Cambridge United respectively. All except Caesar were in the side that beat Bristol Rovers 3-2 in the Gloucestershire Cup final at Ashton Gate on 7 August.

The next local derby also went in City's favour: City won 3-1 in a Football League Cup, second round tie at Twerton. Sadly, the Robins did not have long to savour their victory. The return leg at Ashton Gate ended in a 2-4 extra-time defeat, which sent Rovers through on away goals. Erratic League form and Taylor's scoring drought forced Lumsden to buy and sell. He signed striker Terry Connor from Swansea for £192,000 and defender Russell Osman for

> **Did You Know?**
>
> At Aldershot in 1989, terracing behind the goal had to be evacuated because of faulty power cables. A case of more 'live wires' off the pitch than on it.

£60,000 from Southampton, and sold unsettled winger David Smith to Plymouth for £185,000. The void out on the wing was later filled by the return of Gavin from Watford for a cut-price £65,000.

Leaving aside a 1-2 home defeat by First Division Southampton in the second round of the Full Members (Zenith Data Systems) Cup, City put together a seven-match unbeaten run. It began with a 1-0 home win over Watford and ended with a 1-3 defeat at Middlesbrough, where Osman was sent off. But thereafter it was free-fall all the way, with only a 3-0 home League win over Port Vale to take the mind off relegation. The gloom was not lightened by the selling of crowd favourite Taylor to West Brom for £300,000, following the departures of Caesar to Aidrie for £30,000 and goalkeeper Sinclair to Stoke for £25,000.

Fortunately, the fans had the diversion of the FA Cup to take their minds off City's League predicament. This included its share of giant-killing, as well as an outstanding performance at Leicester. Against First Division Wimbledon in the third round at Ashton Gate, Warren Barton's late own-goal gave City a fortunate replay, which was won by May's swerving long-range drive. In the next round at Filbert Street, City's new boy, Polish International Jacki Dziekanowski, signed from Celtic for £250,000, turned in a performance that had Match of the Day commentator John Motson drooling. The draw for the fifth round took City to Nottingham Forest, where they lost 1-4.

A 1-2 defeat at Charlton meant City had not won in the League for seven games. At this point Lumsden was dismissed and Mark Aizlewood, Russell Osman and Gary Shelton took over as joint caretaker managers until ex-York and Sunderland boss Denis Smith was appointed on 9 March. It was not until Smith's third match in charge that City's long winless run, which by then had extended to eleven games, came to an end. Dziekanowski's two strikes was sufficient for a City side, strengthened by signing of Andy Cole on loan from Arsenal, to beat Wolves 2-0 at Ashton Gate.

With the further capture of Leroy Rosenior on a free from West Ham, City's new-look side embarked on an eight-match unbeaten run that lifted them to safety. A 2-1 home win over Ipswich ensured survival, whereupon the season petered out with three losses. In the last game, at Watford, City's record £250,000 buy Ray Atteveld from Everton, together with Aizlewood and Allison, were sent off.

The excitement of the final couple of months sustained average home League attendances at a relatively healthy 11,479. But despite the transfer of Rennie to Birmingham for £120,000 late in the season, a deficit of £659,284 was declared.

The Reserves won the South West Counties League for the second successive season but were unable to retain their hold on the League Cup or the Somerset Premier Cup, exiting at the quarter-final stage of both tournaments The Youths reached the third round of the FA Youth Cup for the first time since 1979-80, beating Swindon and Epsom & Ewell before losing 0-3 at Southend.

Match of the Season 1991-92
Bristol City 2 Ipswich Town 1

Division 2, 18 April 1992

A season that started with so much promise degenerated into a relegation battle. The coming of new boss Denis Smith sparked hopes of salvation with his astute signings of Andy Cole and Leroy Rosenior, and his ability to cultivate the talents of Jacki Dzienka-nowski. City's unbeaten run of eight games, of which five were won, between 17 March and 18 April, enabled them to claw themselves clear of the trap-door.

This game against Ipswich was the last in this unbeaten run. City needed the points to be sure of saving their status. The enthusiasm of City's fans was such that older supporters' minds turned to the second half of the 1966-67 season, when the coming of Chris Crowe and Hugh McIlmoyle sparked a revival.

It was thought that the clash with League leaders Ipswich would give an indication as to just how far City had progressed under their new manager, and the fans were not disappointed. Yet again the brilliant skills of Dziekanowski were displayed at their very best, and in harness with the electrifying pace of Cole, City more than matched their visitors.

Goalkeeper Keith Welch was rarely troubled as City's deadly duo Rosenior and Cole turned up trumps once more. Rosenior volleyed in the opener late in the first half; then Cole doubled City's lead in the 53rd minute after waltzing past three defenders. It was not until the closing stages that Ipswich made a fist of it, via the penalty spot, after Matt Bryant had brought down Chris Kiwomya.

For City, this result meant that they staved off relegation. In a sense it was a pity, for they now returned to their losing ways. For Ipswich, this reverse was but a blip in their march to the title, which they won by four points from Middlesbrough.

LEAGUE DIVISION 1   **1992-93**
Division 1 (New Style)   15th
League Cup   2nd Round
FA Cup   3rd Round

City's record fee of £250,000 for Atteveld did not linger in the record books for long. In July Cole was signed from Arsenal for double that amount as Denis Smith set about rebuilding for the new season. At the time the manager was hugely popular and many City fans were of the opinion that they at last had a man in charge with the charisma and the talent to take City forward. The love-affair with the new boss did not last, of course. His implementation of a defensive formation that suited neither the players nor the fans quickly brought disillusionment. So did the acquisition of centre-half David Thompson from Millwall, in exchange for Andy May, and full-back Brian Mitchell on a free from Bradford City. Once the new season began to unfold it was clear that City were back to their familiar role of strugglers.

An upheaval to the structure of the English game saw the formation of the FA Premier League, which meant that all lower divisions were upgraded. City were now a First Division club once more, though in reality the goalposts had been moved. The top clubs had long been agitating for more control, becoming ever more greedy. A breakaway was stifled in the mid-1980s, but this time, in collusion with the FA, it was successful. With the Football League's loss of their top twenty-two clubs, the rest of the competition was restructured with the remaining three divisions having their status enhanced and all their clubs becoming full members.

City's goals flowed in the League opener against Portsmouth, though keeper Leaning looked out of sorts with the requirements of the new back-pass rule. They flowed again in the first round of the League Cup, when City notched up a 5-1 win over Third Division Cardiff. Sadly, such games were the exception. Perhaps the fans should have been forewarned by a 1-2 defeat at the hands of Bristol Rovers in the Gloucestershire Cup final at Twerton Park on 5 August, but a 2-1 home friendly win against Chelsea three days later suggested all was well.

With the demise of the Full Members Cup, the Anglo-Italian Cup, which had been contested in the late 1960s and early 70s, was revamped in its place. City beat Watford 1-0 at home and then drew 1-1 at Luton to qualify for European competition for the first time.

This venture was less than successful, as City could not manage to beat any of their four Italian opponents. Both home games were lost, 0-2 to Cosenza and 1-2 to Reggiana. Away, City did slightly better, losing 3-4 at Pisa before bowing out with a 2-2 draw at Cremonese.

In domestic competition, heavy defeats by West Ham, Newcastle and Brentford, not to mention being knocked out the League Cup 3-5 on aggregate by Sheffield United, set alarm bells ringing at Ashton Gate. City's defence looked unable to adapt to the sweeper system. Danish international Bjorn Kristensen was borrowed from Newcastle but was unable to prevent a humiliating 0-4 defeat in the televised local derby at Twerton in mid-December. Some cheer came when Leroy Rosenior turned out for Sierra Leone in a goal-less draw against Toga in the African Nations Cup, but the chill of an English winter gripped City in a vice: the team was sinking like a stone.

Smith changed tactics: he abandoned the sweeper system and restored to wingers, but by the time the FA Cup came round City had gone seven League games without a win and were wallowing down in eighteenth spot. The Cup offered no relief – a 0-2 defeat at Luton was made worse by the expulsion of Scott. This was the final straw for City's board. The next day Smith was dismissed, and player-coach Russell Osman given temporary control.

Osman did not offer instant solutions, and most City fans were resigned to relegation, but slowly but surely he turned things round. The captures of Glenn Pennyfather from Ipswich and Stuart Munro (Blackburn) were crucial, and their debuts were marked by a shock 3-2 success at Portsmouth. This, though, was a false dawn and the fans had to suffer a five-match winless run before the next victory. City's forgotten man Nicky Morgan took over from Andy Cole, who had been transferred to Newcastle for a record £1.75 million the day before. It was Morgan who clinched a 1-0 win at Birmingham with a looping header. Brian Tinnion was then signed from Bradford City for a tribunal fee of £180,000, making his debut in a 1-2 defeat at Swindon. Mark Shail, a 25-year-old central defender who cost £40,000 from Yeovil, saw his first action when coming on as substitute in the 0-0 home draw with Derby.

Former favourites Gerry Sweeney and Clive Whitehead joined Osman's coaching staff and with a new crew at the helm City slowly climbed to safety. The team notched important wins over Watford, Grimsby, Bristol Rovers and Wolves to move up to four-teenth with five matches left. In contrast to the previous season, this time City remained unbeaten in their final matches, but the fact that four of those games were drawn meant an end of season posi-tion of fifteenth. Osman was rewarded with a three-year managerial contract, which he signed on 1 May. Many supporters, though, were critical of City's defensively orientated tactics under their new boss, and after the final game, against Brentford, ex-City great John Atyeo remarked: 'We may have stayed up, but at what cost for the future?' And City won the match 4-1!

None of this deterred the fans turning up six days later to support a special benefit for ex-City favourite Chris Garland, who was suffering from Parkinson's disease. The visit of Manchester United attracted a crowd of 21,716; the game ended 3-3.

The sale of Andy Cole had a predictable effect on the balance sheet as City announced a profit of £517,481 for the season. That figure included an increase in season ticket revenue from £311,452 to £325,799.

Back in the Football Combination for the first time in nine years, the Reserves had a less than successful season. They finished seventeenth and in the Somerset Premier Cup they were knocked out in round one. The Youths did better, reaching the fifth round of the FA Youth Cup after enjoying home advantage in every round. They overcame Bristol Rovers, Epsom & Ewell, Swansea, and Swindon before losing 3-4 to Norwich.

Match of the Season 1992-93
Bristol City 4 Brentford 1

Division 1, 8 May 1993

A season which again saw City flirting with relegation, culminated with this, their best win of the campaign after a run of just two defeats in thirteen games. With Brentford needing all three points to be sure of retaining their status, a better than average crowd of 12,695, including an estimated 3,000 Bees fans from West London, converged on Ashton Gate on a blustery Saturday afternoon.

Fears that Osman's side might take things easy were dispelled by City's blistering start. Attacking the Covered End, Mark Gavin and Gary Shelton exposed the Brentford defence after six minutes with a quick exchange of passes before City's No 8 set up Leroy Rosenior to score at the near post. Mark Aizlewood had a header cleared off the line by Kenny Sansom, and Rosenior hit a shot just over before Wayne Allison doubled City's advantage on 29 minutes. Gary Shelton's aggression forged the opening for Allison, on the right-hand side of the box, to fire home an angled drive.

Goals scored had replaced goal-difference to separate sides level on points, and after the break the Bees adopted a cavalier approach to try to snatch something from the game. City's keeper Keith Welch had to be alert to tip over Keith Millen's 47th-minute header, but Gary Blissett's 29th goal of the season was their sole reward. He

---

Did You Know?

The Bristol local press introduced colour photos in December 1989. The first
home game to feature colour photos was versus Rotherham. But it ended 0-0!

---

headed in from almost on the goal-line on 57 minutes, after Marcus
Gayle's header came back off the bar. By then, though, Rosenior
had further increased City's tally, as two minutes earlier he had
punished slack defending. Latching onto Mark Shail's through-ball
he curled a delightful right-footed shot inside Gerry Peyton's left-
hand post.

City's counter-attacks met with virtually no resistance, and it
was no surprise when Rosenior notched the fourth hat-trick of his
career with a typical poacher's strike, when Tinnion's shot was only
half-saved. The only surprise was that this ended the scoring. In
the remaining 23 minutes Allison and Junior Bent spurned inviting
opportunities to rattle up a massive win.

Apart from isolated spells, Brentford failed to show the spirit
necessary to prevent a return from whence they had come just
twelve months previously. They looked strangely uncoordinated,
and Bees manager Phil Holder was moved to comment after the
game that his players could not handle the pressure.

The cycle, though, was to turn full circle four years later, when
the Second Division play-offs saw Brentford beat City in both legs
of the semi-final. Alas, Brentford lost to Crewe in the play-off final.

LEAGUE DIVISION 1   **1993-94**
Division 1   13th
League Cup   1st Round
FA Cup   5th Round

The close-season signings of 29-year-old Ian Baird (£295,000) from Hearts and 27-year-old Liam Robinson (£130,000) from Bury did little to suggest that the goalscoring void created by Andy Cole's departure would be easily filled. A 1-1 home draw with Bristol Rovers in the Gloucestershire Cup, which the old enemy won 5-3 in a penalty shoot-out, followed by a 1-2 defeat by Cape Town Spurs six days later, was not encouraging. Few fans were surprised when City lost their League opener 1-3 at Wolves.

Goals from Baird and Allison brought a merited home success over Crystal Palace (the eventual champions) a week later, but only one more win in the next six games left City floundering in twentieth spot after a 0-0 draw at Portsmouth. By then City were already out of both cup competitions organised by the Football League.

In the League Cup, all looked set fair with a 1-0 win at Swansea, but in the return leg the Swans surprised everyone but themselves by winning 2-0. In the Anglo-Italian Cup, City failed to qualify from their group after losing 1-3 at Portsmouth. Fortunately, matters improved in the FA Cup, but more of that later.

Back in the League, a fourteen-game run with only two defeats took City up to eighth place by early December, but the football was anything but entertaining. Boardroom matters, in fact, took centre stage. The resignation of director Ivor Williams, who sold his five percent holding of foundation shares to the Supporters Club for £35,000, brought to public attention boardroom disagreements that had been smouldering for some eighteen months. With the announcement on 18 May 1993 of an FA Inquiry into monies claimed by City from the Football Trust for ground improvements, it became clear that rebels were waiting to strike.

These rebels, calling themselves the Reform Group, officially launched their bid for power on 30 September, and issued their blueprint for the future – 'The Way To Win' – five days later. This group consisted of board member Mike Fricker, Deryn Coller (a recent board member), Peter Burchill, John Clapp and David Russe. The literature explained that Coller had resigned from the board the previous March because he could no longer countenance what he claimed were financial irregularities which, due to block voting, he was powerless to prevent. Fricker did not resign, as he felt he had a duty to protect those who had brought to his attention the matters that led to the Inquiry.

> **Did You Know?**
>
> When City gained promotion in 1989-90, Bob Taylor became the first player since John Atyeo to score 30 goals a season – 27 in the League, 7 in cups.

Matters came to a head with an EGM at the Whitchurch Sports Centre on 12 November. About 1,000 small shareholders were present to decide the fate of the opposing parties, but in truth many appeared to be unimpressed by both factions. Particular concerns were voiced that, despite the Reform Group's declared objectives of City attaining Premiership status within five years, and winning a major trophy to gain entry to European competition within ten, no concrete proposals were put forward for the injection of cash. Hard decisions had to made, and for many the clinching factor was the fact that the FA had announced on that very day the result of their Inquiry.

The Inquiry had culminated in a seven-hour hearing at the Park Hotel, London, on 9 November. A three-man commission, headed by Southampton Vice-Chairman Keith Wiseman, supported by Alan Turvey (a divisional member from Hayes) and Barry Bright (Kent FA) interviewed Chairman Les Kew and took evidence from a range of City officials, as well as the floodlight contractor. The outcome went against City, who were fined £40,000 (£30,000 suspended for two years).

In this context it was not surprising that the Reform Group won the power struggle. The Chairman and three directors were voted off the board, Mike Fricker was re-elected, and four new members elected. David Russe was named as the new Chairman, with Fricker as his deputy. Supporters Club Chairman Garry Williams was co-opted as a member and a statement was issued: 'We must now start the task of rebuilding bridges ... of uniting this great club, its staff and its supporters, so that we can surge forward to one common goal.'

Ironically, though City had been eighth when the new regime assumed power, the team had slipped to thirteenth by the season's end, playing football that was anything but exciting and entertaining – which had been promised. Manager Osman, who had found himself in an unenviable position during the boardroom upheavals, called upon a record 38 players in all competitions during the campaign. He was willing to give chances to players released by other clubs, such as Marvin Harriott (Barnsley) and Scott Partridge (Bradford City), as well as blooding youngsters and bargain signings like Zimbabwean international Henry McKop (£15,000 from Bonner Sport in Germany).

It was in the FA Cup that City gave their fans something to shout about. Their win at Liverpool was almost on par with the victory over Leeds twenty years earlier. This time the team's head-line-making win would not have the same effect on the club's fortunes, even though it was followed by a 4-0 success at Stockport in the fourth round before City went out to Charlton 0-2 in a replay at the Valley in round five.

At the end of the season, City set off on a three-match eleven day tour of Zimbabwe, further afield than their first foreign trip in 1946 when they sailed across the North Sea to Denmark. City were unbeaten in Africa, winning one and drawing two matches.

League attendances were a cause of mounting concern. Not even City's epic win at Anfield sparked a resurgence, for just 8,171 turned up for the visit of Tranmere eleven days later. The Cup run did, however, alleviate City's financial plight. At the AGM in December 1994 a profit of £59,680 was announced.

City's reserve strength was not encouraging. The second team finished twentieth in the Football Combination, though they did reach the third round of the Somerset Premier Cup. The Youths in the FA Youth Cup went out in the second round to Aston Villa, after winning 1-0 at Reading in round one.

Match of the Season 1993-94

Liverpool 0 Bristol City 1

FA Cup, 3rd Round replay, 25 January 1994

For a club with a less than impressive Cup pedigree, triumphs of this magnitude did not occur very often. City achieved just fifteen acts of giant-killing over top-flight opposition during 88 previous seasons of FA Cup action – Middlesbrough (1903), Bolton (1903 & 1979), Arsenal (1905 & 1920), Bury (1909), Liverpool (1910), Bradford City (1920), Portsmouth (1935), Southampton (1967), Leeds (1974), Derby (1980), Chelsea (1990), Wimbledon (1992), plus a fourth round, first leg win over Brentford in 1946.

The sequence of cup-ties against Liverpool in January 1994 was special for Bristol City for the simple reason that the players out-performed the Premier League superstars in all three games.

The original tie at Ashton Gate had come to a premature halt through floodlight failure after 65 minutes. A 20,612 crowd had seen Wayne Allison's 39th-minute glancing header cancel out Ian Rush's side-footed early opener. The re-arranged fixture eleven days later brought 21,718 back to Ashton Gate, encouraged by admission prices being reduced. Both sides made changes – Liverpool bringing in Steve McManaman for Stig Bjornebye, and City replacing Ian Brown with Junior Bent, and filling the void left by the suspended Matt Bryant with Andy Llewellyn. The score and scorers were the same as in the first game: Rush prodded in from close-range midway through the second half and Allison levelled when sweeping in a right-footed effort at the far post.

Playing in their purple and green change strip, and roared on by more than 7,000 travelling fans, City were unchanged for the Anfield replay. Liverpool brought in Steve Harkness for Julian Dicks and Mark Walters for Robbie Fowler.

To hold Liverpool's all-stars at Ashton Gate twice was one thing, but to beat them in their own back yard was tantamount to mission impossible. In fairness, this was not the Liverpool team of old. Manager Graeme Souness was under much pressure on account of his side's indifferent League form, and if ever there was a time to humble the Reds, this was it.

Liverpool had their chances. City did well to survive an amazing goalmouth scramble midway through the first half, but by the end of ninety minutes the home team were well beaten. City turned in a superlative performance and deserved more than Brian Tinnion's 67th-minute curler past Bruce Grobbelaar. Rob Edwards, Liam Robinson and Tinnion all squandered first-half chances as Liverpool's defence was pulled apart by the pace of Allison and Bent. As for the much-vaunted Liverpool attack – for whom Rush needed one goal to equal Denis Law's FA Cup record of 41 – they were closely marshalled by City's defence.

McManaman switched wings to try his luck against Llewellyn, and John Barnes dropped into midfield, but to no avail as City sustained the pressure after the break. Grobbelaar was lucky to stay on the pitch when he handled outside the box to prevent Bent connecting with Dave Martin's through-ball. Four minutes later Bent blazed over with another inviting opportunity. Even after Tinnion's goal, chances continued to come City's way, but they were not taken, denying City a score-line that would have more realistically demonstrated their superiority on the day.

Upon the final whistle the Kop rose to salute City's heroes as they undertook a lap of honour. It was a sensational night for all connected with Bristol City Football Club, but not for Souness, for whom this defeat was the last straw. Two days later he resigned, to be succeeded in the Anfield hot-seat by his assistant Roy Evans.

Despite the hope that this great victory would propel City onward and upward, it was not to be. In the Cup, victory over Stockport was followed by defeat to Charlton in the fifth round. In the League, City would be relegated one season later.

6

RE-VAMP
1994-2000

LEAGUE DIVISION 1	**1994-95**
Division 1	23rd (Relegated)
League Cup	2nd Round
FA Cup	4th Round

As a consequence of the Atyeo Stand at the Open End of the ground, Osman had to look for free-transfer signings. He acquired during the close season 31-year-old keeper Phil Kite (Cardiff) and midfielders Rod McAree (a 20-year-old from Liverpool) and 21-year-old Colin Loss from Gresley Rovers. This did not augur well for the coming campaign.

The new stand, on which work had commenced in March 1994, was used for the first time in August, when Port Vale were the visitors, but it was not fully functional until six weeks later when FA Chairman Sir Bert Millichip performed the opening ceremony. This Stand was named in honour of Bristol City great John Atyeo, who had scored 350 goals in 645 appearances for the club, as well as grabbing five in his six England games. Sadly, John was no longer alive to appreciate the honour – he had died in June 1993. As with both the main stands, Dolman in 1970 and Williams in 1992, it was fitting that another City great, Billy Wedlock – who won 26 England caps between 1907 and 1914 – should be similarly honoured. The Covered End was named after him in 1996.

After pre-season away games against Wimborne (1-1), Clandown (8-0), Petersfield (7-1) and Bath (3-2) – as well as a 1-3 home defeat by Tottenham – the serious business got underway with the Gloucestershire Cup final on 3 August. The first ninety minutes were thrill-less and goalless. No extra-time was played, so the contest was settled by a penalty shoot-out. Rovers won it by the extraordinary score of 11-10, after City's keeper Keith Welch failed to score past his opposite number.

In the League Cup, City could not muster a goal in either of their first round ties with Notts County, going out 0-4 on aggregate.

City enjoyed more success in the FA Cup. After a goalless home draw with Stoke, the floodgates opened in the replay at the Victoria ground as City notched up a 3-1 extra-time victory, which earned them a home clash with Premiership side Everton. This, though, was as good as it got. The Toffees won 1-0 at Ashton Gate on 29 January, in front of a 19,816 crowd which paid club record receipts of £174,231.

By then, one manager had gone and other arrived. City's disastrous start, with only four wins in eighteen League and Cup games had ex-City player Chris Garland warning in the *Western Daily Press* that 'The Club has the sniff of doom'. He complained that the directors were forcing Osman to work with his hands tied behind his back by not generating funds for him to spend on players.

Osman's sacking on 14 November, following a 0-3 defeat at Sheffield United nine days earlier, split the fans. Many felt that he had had a raw deal. Former chairman Les Kew suggested it was Osman's support for the former board that was responsible for his dismissal. Others, mindful of Osman's dour tactics and the limited opportunities he had given to crowd favourite Dziekanowski, felt the sacking warranted. Joe Jordan assumed his duties the following day, but this too divided supporters. Many could not forgive Jordan for having walked out on the club four years earlier when he joined Hearts.

Jordan began his second term in charge with a thrilling 3-2 home win over Swindon, but a sequence of six defeats left City deep in the relegation mire by Christmas. A 3-1 home success over Stoke on 27 December stopped the rot, but with only one League win during January, City were unable to improve on their 23rd placing. Despite the signings of Gary Owers from Sunderland (a £750,000 part-exchange deal for Martin Scott), Martin Kuhl from Derby for £300,000, and Richard Dryden for £200,000 from Birmingham, form remained wretched. With only four more League wins in the final eighteen games it was little wonder that City were relegated. The only surprise was that City did not finish bottom – an even worse Notts County side propped up the table some five points below. For those fans taking the wider perspective, relegation was almost predictable. This had, after all, been the fifth season since promotion, demonstrating once again that a five-year cycle often shaped City's history.

Off the pitch, finances were worsening. A loss of £766,945 (compared to a £59,680 profit in 1993-94) was declared at a much delayed AGM, held in May 1996, though the number of season tickets holders had surprisingly increased from 2,185 (£298,983) to 2,365 (£367,248).

Did You Know?

During the home defeat by Notts Co in Dec 1995, each time a City substitution was made comedians in the crowd held up every number between 1 and 11.

Perhaps it was a consequence of the building of the Atyeo Stand, but after it was completed the state of City's pitch began to give cause for concern. So much so that the Reserves had to play on Clevedon Town's ground at the Hand Stadium. Eleven Football Combination games took place at this venue. The Reserves improved on their previous season's showing to finish fifteenth, as well as reaching the semi-finals of the Somerset Premier Cup before losing 0-2 to Bath City. In the FA Youth Cup, City's youngsters did well to progress through to the fifth round, where they put up a brave display before succumbing 1-2 to Tottenham Hotspur in front of a 1,089 Ashton Gate crowd.

The stars of this otherwise miserable season were undoubtedly Bristol City Women's Football team, who played in the South West Region Women's Football League Division One. They won the Championship, the League Cup and the Pat Sowden Cup, but missed out on promotion to the National League by losing a play-off 2-3 at Leyton Orient. City's Ladies were also the giant-killers of the Women's FA Cup. Unfortunately, Liverpool proved too strong in the semi-final, winning 5-0 on Mangotsfield's Cossham Street ground.

Match of the Season 1994-95
Bristol City 3 Swindon Town 2

Division 1, 20 November 1994

Highlights were few and far between in a season which brought a return to the nether reaches. Everything had seemed so different when Joe Jordan made a hero's return to Ashton Gate, inspiring City to this win over West Country rivals Swindon Town.

The upturn in mood at the club was palpable. Upon the final whistle of this dazzling televised spectacular it was as though the National Lottery had been won, leaving City's success-starved fans feeling like millionaires. Having notched up only five goals in their preceding ten games, City's second-half play in this contest was a revelation. Following a goalless opening half, Junior Bent got the show going in the 54th minute, reacting quickest when Swindon keeper Frazer Digby parried Wayne Allison's curling 25-yarder. Two minutes later Allison was on the scoresheet himself, drilling Scott

Partridge's pass into the bottom corner of the net. Keith Scott lifted
Swindon with an almost immediate response, scooping the ball past
Phil Kite after Paul Bodin had played him into the area. The see-
saw swung City's way again just after the hour, as Bent's industry
and commitment produced a cross which gave Allison a simple tap-
in. It was not until the final minute that Swindon's Scott, looking
yards offside, gave the margin of victory an unfair slant by forcing
the ball over the line at his second attempt.

The euphoria of Jordan's return did not endure. City never
recovered from the effects of losing the next six games. For Swindon, this defeat ended manager John Gorman's reign. He joined
City as Jordan's assistant, but his replacement in the Swindon hot-
seat – Steve McMahon – was unable to prevent the Wiltshire team
taking the drop with City.

LEAGUE DIVISION 2   **1995-96**
Division 2   13th
League Cup   2nd Round
FA Cup   1st Round

When a club is relegated they often react by being in the following season's promotion chase. City, though, buck the trend. Apart from the early 1920s this has not been their experience, and it certainly was not in 1995-96, when at one stage they looked distinctly likely to suffer a second successive demotion. It was only in the second half of the season that the fans accepted that the team had the ability to keep out of the relegation zone. A run of seven matches with only one defeat, culminating in a 2-0 win at Brighton, even had City up in eleventh spot.

An unforeseen consequence of the building of the Atyeo Stand was the rapid deterioration of the Ashton Gate pitch. It was re-laid during the summer, but with the new surface needing time to bed down, this meant the cancellation of the 99th Gloucestershire Senior Professional Cup final. All pre-season friendlies had to be played away from home, too, except that with Chelsea. A crowd of 10,422 were attracted to Ashton Gate for this meeting with the Premiership side. They were rewarded by Phil Barber's 72nd-minute goal that allowed City to recover from a 0-1 first-half deficit.

With City's losing streak continuing on their return to the re-designated Second Division, pressure on the board intensified. Chairman David Russe resigned in September and his successor, Mike Fricker, faced the harsh truths of the club losing money and support. Despite the welcome sharp-shooting of David Seal, City won only one of their opening ten League games. City were next to bottom, before a welcome 4-0 home win over Hull was achieved on 14 October.

The £175,000 signing of Darren Barnard from Chelsea, and improved performances from Paul Agostino, turned things around. City began to put some form together, though it would not be until the New Year that the side began to gel. Stirring performances by Brian Tinnion and Matt Hewlett in a 1-1 draw at Wycombe in mid-December sparked an upturn in fortunes, as City only lost eight of their remaining 26 games. Paul Agostino's superb header at Twerton Park in March helped City to their first ever League win on that ground, in what to date has proved to be last local derby played there. Further victories against Wrexham, Hull and Rother-ham carried City to the safety of mid-table.

City's finances were boosted by the team's pairing with Premier Division Newcastle in the second round of the League Cup, after

> **Did You Know?**
>
> City's most painful defeat of the 1990s? Probably in 1991 when they led
> Rovers 4-1 over two legs in the Rumbelows Cup. Yet City somehow lost!

they had required penalties to dispose of Colchester at the first
hurdle. A 15,952 Ashton Gate crowd saw City slaughtered 0-5 by
Kevin Keegan's Premiership leaders, but an improved showing in
the second leg at St James' Park enabled City to hold their heads
high, despite a 1-3 defeat. There was little joy or revenue to be had
from the FA Cup. City went down to a first round replay defeat at
Bournemouth, even though they had largely dominated the action.
In the cup competition for the League minnows (Auto Windscreens
Shield) City lost their opening group game 0-3 at Oxford, but a 2-0
home win over Barnet was enough to clinch a meeting with
Shrewsbury in the first round. No goals in 120 minutes at Gay
Meadow meant a penalty shoot-out, which City lost 6-7.

Proposals to revive City's flagging fortunes were put forward in
December by recently appointed director Scott Davidson. Along
with fellow directors John Clapp and Bob Neale, Davidson was
joined by successful local businessman John Laycock to head a new
group willing to take control. The deal was concluded in March
1996. This was followed by a share issue in the summer. Fans
responded by paying £457,080 for 4,854 supporters' shares, as well
as purchasing season tickets, joining the new membership scheme,
and participating in other fund-raising ventures. This did not
prevent a loss of £686,071 being declared for the season at the AGM.

In the Football Combination, City Reserves finished thirteenth,
whilst in the Somerset Premier Cup they lost 0-1 at home to
Mangotsfield United at the semi-final stage. The Youths meanwhile
suffered their record defeat in the FA Youth Cup when they were
annihilated 0-7 by Crystal Palace on Wimbledon's old Plough Lane
ground in front of a meagre gathering of 104 hardy fans.

Match of the Season 1995-96
Bristol Rovers 2 Bristol City 4

Division 2, 16 March 1996

Victory in a local derby is always cause for celebration, and City's
success in this game at the adopted home of the Rovers at Twerton
Park in the City of Bath was no exception. Since Rovers moved
there in 1986 it had not been a happy hunting ground for City, who
had failed to bag a win in seven League visits. In such circumstances

---

Did You Know?

After the game with WBA in April 1995 a Portaloo caught fire. The flames spread to the Covered End. The drama was more exiting than the match.

---

victory was therefore extremely sweet, but it was made even sweeter by the fact that it was the last derby, to date, played at this venue.

The Rovers, managed by John Ward, who would later steer City to promotion, started as favourites. But they went behind early on when Kevin Nugent squeezed the ball through keeper Andy Collett's legs. A crowd of almost 9,000 were treated to a thrilling contest that could have gone either way after Rovers' Andy Gurney fired a 16-yarder into the far corner of the net. Matt Hewlett's right-footed shot from eighteen yards, deflected in off Paul Miller, gave City the advantage on the stroke of half-time.

Shortly after the interval Rovers' Marcus Stewart saw his low shot ruled out through Peter Beadle being offside, and City took advantage seven minutes later. Martin Kuhl swept a pass out to Junior Bent on the right, and the winger's floated cross to the far-post was met Paul Agostino, who headed into the Rovers net. The other half of City's Aussie duo then made victory certain. Substitute David Seal met Hewlett's through-ball with a delightful chip that well and truly laid to rest the Twerton hoodoo. Billy Clarke's almost immediate response could not sway the final outcome.

Thus City won the 80th League derby. The overall record now read as follows: P80 W30 D27 L23 F115 A96. This was not to be a productive season for either club, the Rovers finishing tenth, three places and ten points above City. It was only the 25th occasion since the two clubs first met in the League in 1923 that the red and whites had finished lower than their rivals.

LEAGUE DIVISION 2   **1996-97**
Division 2   5th (play-off semi-finals)
League Cup   2nd Round
FA Cup   3rd Round

Ongoing problems with the Ashton Gate pitch saw it being re-laid yet again, this time properly, at a cost of £180,000. It looked in mint condition for City's Open Day on 21 July and was ready to stage the 99th Gloucestershire Senior Professional Cup final two weeks later. A late goal by Shaun Goater, City's new £150,000 signing from Rotherham, was enough to give City a 1-0 win over Bristol Rovers in what was probably the last such contest. Neither club was keen to carry on this local tradition, which had commenced back in 1887-88, though they agreed that their Reserves should compete for the Gloucestershire Senior Challenge Cup, which had been contested by the clubs in the north of the county since 1936-37.

Come May it was unfortunate that City concluded their official Centenary season without any other trophy. Reaching the promotion play-offs, things looked bright when they were paired with a Brentford side that appeared to have gone off the boil. The Bees, though, came good at the right time, beating City 2-1 in both legs.

An inauspicious opening to the season had brought only one win from the first five games, including a 3-3 draw at Torquay in the League Cup. The debut of former QPR winger Greg Goodridge, who cost just £50,000, brought Ashton Gate to its feet as City grabbed a 5-0 win over Luton. The signing of the inspirational Shaun Taylor from Swindon for £100,000 in early September lit the spark under City's season.

After beating Torquay by the barest margin in the second leg of the League Cup, City had the daunting task of facing First Division leaders Bolton in round two. Following a goalless draw at Ashton Gate, few gave City a chance at Burnden Park, but a goal from Owers kept City in the hunt, and it needed extra-time before Bolton eventually won 3-1.

In the League, City only lost four out of twenty games by the time the third round of the FA Cup came around. Wins against Swansea and St Albans took them to Chesterfield. A feeble display was answered by a 0-2 defeat to a side destined to become only the fifth lower division club to reach the semi-finals – a fact that, to City fans, served only to demonstrate what might have been. Also in January City's venture into the Auto Windscreens Shield got under way. While Owers' goal was enough to win their first round tie at Swansea, Goater's strike at Watford was not enough to avert a 1-2 defeat.

Did You Know?

When Sunderland won 6-1 in the Rumbelows Cup in 1990, it was City's worst home defeat since 1949. But Sunderland had 7 shots on target: City had 10!

Dismissal from the cups affected League form, and seven of the next thirteen games were lost. Among the successes during this otherwise barren spell was a 2-1 victory over Bristol Rovers on their Memorial ground home which they shared with Bristol Rugby Club. The small group of selected City fans had to travel by arranged transport from Ashton Gate, but the inconvenience was forgotten as goals by Agostino and Goater earned the win. Jordan was unable to bathe in the glow of victory for long: losing the next two games brought the curtain down on his second managerial spell at the club.

Jordan's sacking was no surprise as he had been under pressure all season. It was widely predicted that had the team lost at Millmoor in mid-September he would have been dismissed there and then. Rotherham duly went two goals up, but Owers saved the manager's bacon with a 25-yarder followed by an easy header.

Former Rovers boss John Ward was selected as Jordan's replacement. Ward was at the time assistant to Adrian Heath at Burnley, but no obstacles were put on his leaving and he took over at Ashton Gate four days after Jordan's dignified departure. Ward had easily topped the local *Evening Post* poll for the fans' choice as boss, ahead of such names as Gary Mabbutt, David Webb, Mel Machin, Sammy McIlroy and John Rudge.

In the interim, coach Gerry Sweeney took charge for City's visit to Crewe, where he oversaw a 2-1 win. Ward's first match in charge brought a 0-1 home defeat by Gillingham, but he roused his troops for an assault on the play-offs, the semi-finals of which were secured thanks to five successive wins.

The first leg with Brentford was played at a monsoonal Ashton Gate, when City were caught cold by Brentford's adventurous start. Marcus Bent went close for the visitors when his shot shaved a post, and his eighth-minute overhead kick needed a smart save from Welch. It was no surprise when Paul Smith gave Brentford the lead six minutes later by ramming in a shot to Welch's right. City clawed their way back into contention with a glancing header from Owers that went in off a post, but on the half-hour Rob Taylor restored Brentford's advantage by flicking in a header from Gus Hurdle's cross. This ended the scoring, though City felt they had cause to rue referee Uriah Rennie's readiness to let the game flow – despite several bone-crunching challenges – as they had three penalty appeals turned down.

The second leg was at Griffin Park three days later. To City's credit they were up for it, no doubt encouraged by Brentford's poor home form of late. On top throughout the first period, City levelled on aggregate shortly after the break when Barnard's fierce cross-shot found the corner of the net. Not long afterwards Goater might have put City ahead overall, but he failed to make proper contact with a free header. City paid dearly for the miss when Rob Taylor beat Welch with a curler on 67 minutes, and Marcus Bent ensured Brentford's participation in the final by stealing in front of Rob Edwards to fire the decisive goal.

There would be no happy ending for the Bees, who lost the Wembley final to a first-half goal to Crewe.

The Reserves' eighteenth position was above the relegation trap-door of the Football Combination, but that did not prevent them being removed from the competition, along with Bristol Rovers, Bournemouth, Cardiff and Swansea. Other clubs apparently did not relish all the travelling involved to the West Country.

In the Football Combination League Cup, City Reserves failed to qualify from their group, but they reached the final of the Somerset Premier Cup, losing 1-2 at Yeovil. The youngsters in the FA Youth Cup could do no better than win 2-1 at Leyton Orient, before losing their home match against Bournemouth 2-3.

The AGM reported a loss of £387,672, though the number of season tickets sold increased from 1,884 to 3,092.

Match of the Season 1996-97

Bristol City 2 Chesterfield 0

Division 2, 30 April 1997

A run of bad results in March brought four defeats in five games and marked the end of the road for manager Joe Jordan. His replacement, John Ward, performed wonders to take City to the play-offs.

Ward appeared undeterred by the 0-1 home loss by Gillingham that saw City down in ninth place. He engendered a new spirit in the club, both with the fans as well as the players, and a five-match undefeated spell left City poised to clinch a play-off berth. All they needed to do in this, their penultimate League fixture, was beat Chesterfield. A crowd in excess of 16,000 were lured to Ashton Gate for this vital game against the FA Cup giant-killers, who a few weeks earlier had been robbed of a place in the final by woeful refereeing, and who were themselves looking for a win to keep alive their own play-off hopes.

City tore into their opponents from the first whistle and Shaun Goater twice went close before he opened the scoring in the seventh minute, courtesy of his reliable right boot. Darren Barnard's centre had looked too deep, but Gary Owers' first-time knock-back left City's top scorer free to smash home from six yards. City were in no mood to sit back on their lead, and they had their fans in good voice as they continued to press home their attacks.

Chesterfield's Kevin Davies, subject to a £350,000 bid by City earlier in the year, rarely threatened. Instead it was giant striker Andy Morris who caused most problems. Keith Welch did well to tip his 30-yarder over for a corner before City doubled their lead. In the 38th minute Goater's attempted cross from the corner of the six-yard box was adjudged to have been handled by defender Sean Dyche, and Darren Barnard sent former City keeper Andy Leaning the wrong way from the spot.

Gary Owers almost made it three: his cheeky lob had the back-peddling keeper at full-stretch to tip the ball over. Goater then saw his back-heeled effort cleared off the line by Jonathan Howard as City ended the first half in as much control as anyone could remember at the halfway stage of a major game. It was low tempo thereafter, as City were content to protect their lead, but great were the scenes at the final whistle as the fans celebrated as though promotion had already been achieved.

The euphoria was not to last. City's winning impetus was lost with a 0-2 defeat in the final League fixture at Wycombe three days later. Brentford took full advantage in the play-offs.

LEAGUE DIVISION 2   **1997-98**
Division 2   2nd (Promoted)
League Cup   2nd Round
FA Cup   2nd Round

Following the late run to make the play-offs the previous season, the fans' confidence of success this term was shared by the bookies, who installed City among the promotion favourites. The signings of wing-back Mickey Bell from Wycombe for £150,000, defender Sean Dyche (£275,000 Chesterfield), as well as strikers Colin Cramb (£250,000 Doncaster) and Steve Torpey (£400,000 Swansea) upped expectations. Despite early hiccups that sparked demonstrations against the team's style of play, a tactical rethink by boss Ward set City on their way to a return to the First Division. Promotion was achieved with aplomb, with some five games remaining. The only disappointment in the minds of supporters was the sale of ace striker Shaun Goater to Manchester City on the eve of the transfer deadline. His departure was reckoned to be the major factor that denied the club the championship.

League action commenced at sun-drenched Grimsby, where Torpey's crisp shot on the turn put City ahead. A sickening clash of heads shortly afterwards ended his involvement, and Grimsby came back strongly. Keith Welch pulled off vital saves, but was powerless to stop Tommy Widdrington's equaliser. With Ward keeping faith with his preferred 5-3-2 formation for the first home game, the fans were not best pleased, despite a 2-0 success over Blackpool.

For the time being Ward persisted with his unpopular system, but it brought only one win from the subsequent five games. The fans erupted in protest after witnessing a dire 1-1 draw with Bournemouth which dumped City in nineteenth place. At first, Ward was content to tinker with the problem – introducing mercurial winger Greg Goodridge for the next game, a 3-0 home win over Luton – but he was not ready to jettison the 5-3-2 philosophy. It was not until three matches later, at half-time in the home match with York, that he finally switched to 4-4-2.

With the team suffering just one defeat in seven matches since mid-September, the fans were in good heart with a goalless draw at Walsall, but a 2-0 win at Millwall heralded even better fortunes, as City embarked on their longest winning run since their promotion campaign of 1905-06.

A run of nine successive victories (eight in the League) was ended only by a 0-1 reverse at Bournemouth in the FA Cup. A 1-1 draw in the top of the table clash at Watford a week later enabled City to maintain their long unbeaten League tag. Victories over

Chesterfield and Millwall then extended this run to eleven games before City were shot down at Craven Cottage by big spending Fulham at the end of the year.

Undeterred, City responded with a 4-1 home thrashing of rivals Grimsby, a result that took City to the top for the first time. City's reign was short: a goalless home draw with Northampton knocked them off their perch, but it was not until a three-match winless spell in February that alarm bells started ringing, especially as they had scored only three goals in six games.

It took Mickey Bell's second-half penalty to get the show back on the road in an otherwise mediocre performance at York. A 2-0 home win over Bristol Rovers that took City back to the top in mid-March convinced the sceptics that promotion was within the team's grasp. However, it was not until Grimsby's failure to win at Wycombe on 10 April that the dream was realised.

In the meantime, the decision to accept Manchester City's £500,000 offer for Shaun Goater was clearly taken over Ward's head. He brought in Oldham's Sean McCarthy and Jason Roberts from Wolves on loan. With McCarthy taking over from Goater, City's away fixture with Wycombe looked like being pivotal to the team's promotion chances. City responded well, with Cramb's two strikes earning a nail-biting 2-1 victory.

City's next fixture was at Oldham, in front of the Sky cameras. Roberts played from the start, but despite scoring and playing his part in City's win, he was back on the bench for the fixture with Carlisle. Disillusioned, he headed off without permission to play for Grenada in an international tournament, as a consequence of which Ward made the mistake of discounting him from his future plans. A 1-0 home win over Carlisle disguised the loss of this fine prospect. But as City toiled with the less mobile McCarthy up front, a mere four points from their last five games cost them dear. In mitigation, City could point to Lady Luck deserting them when a fierce equalising 'goal' by Adam Locke (a free-transfer signing from Colchester) was disallowed at Burnley. In the circumstances, it was just as well that Grimsby lent a helping hand at Wycombe.

Whilst the Championship was beyond recall, nothing could hide the fact that this had been a great season. A League double over Bristol Rovers, not to mention a 2-1 aggregate success over them in the League Cup, followed by a 2-1 home win over Premiership Leeds, meant City had some prized scalps under their belts. In the Auto Windscreens Shield, City beat Millwall before losing at Bournemouth. The Cherries were the only blot on City's season. Thrice City lost at Dean Court, whilst at Ashton Gate in the League Steve Robinson's late goal earned Bournemouth a deserved point.

| **Did You Know?** |
| At Millwall in 1997 Shaun Goater started with a brace on his teeth and a face swollen on one side. Millwall ensured he got a whack on the other side too. |

To celebrate a remarkable season, thousands of fans took to the streets on 3 May to applaud their heroes on an open-top bus tour of the city. It concluded with a civic reception at the Council House, where the players were presented with the Runners-Up Shield and medals. The occasion took a bizarre twist when they were given the wrong medals, receiving those earmarked for the First Division runners-up. Nor were the team the only ones at Bristol City with something to celebrate. Groundsman Steve Drew scooped the coveted Groundsman of the Year award for the Second Division.

With the demise of the Gloucestershire Senior Professional Cup, City Reserves contested what had been the northern competition (Gloucestershire Senior Challenge Cup). Overcoming Cheltenham via a penalty shoot-out, they demolished Bristol Rovers 6-0 (Cramb scoring all six), before beating Forest Green Rovers 2-1 in the Ashton Gate final in front of 590 spectators. The Reserves also annexed the South West Trophy League Championship, beating Bristol Rovers 3-0 in the two-legged final. The Youths disposed of Torquay and Swansea in the FA Youth Cup, but found Arsenal too strong in the third round, losing 1-3.

Match of the Season 1997-98

Bristol City 1 Watford 1

Division 2, 13 April 1998

City blew it in this Easter Monday game. They badly needed to win to pull the rug from under Watford's relentless surge for the Championship. You would not have sensed the urgency, though, as City performed as though a second draw with the Hornets this season would be good enough. Lack of ambition is always corrosive, and the City players would have to pay heavily for theirs.

Sure, City had some excuses. They lost inspirational captain Shaun Taylor in the 37th minute with knee ligament damage that was to sideline him for almost twelve months. They had also lost star striker Shaun Goater, in his case by being sold a month previously. But attitute is everything, and City demonstrated that they lacked that priceless commodity on a pudding of a pitch that two days earlier had been cut up badly by the England Monarchs American Football team.

No quarter was given during the early exchanges in front of the division's largest crowd of the season. City forced two early corners and twice went close to scoring, but having weathered the storm Watford stepped up a gear and began to impose themselves. Tommy Mooney had Watford's best chance of the first half, but his effort was cleared off the line by Louis Carey.

After the break, Colin Cramb went close for City when his back-header hit the bar, but Watford hit back and Peter Kennedy's left-footed effort was blocked by Keith Welch. City were not so fortunate on 64 minutes when Alan Hazan's cross was met by a fierce close-range strike by Kennedy. Welch saved, but Jason Lee thumped in the rebound. Four minutes later City levelled thanks to Welsh international Rob Edwards, who steered the ball home from inside the six-yard box. Though City enjoyed territorial control for the rest of the game they never looked capable of bagging a winner. For Watford, the point clinched promotion and set them on course for the Championship.

In the next game at Chesterfield, Brian Tinnion had to take over between the sticks in place of the injured Welch. City's 0-1 defeat left Watford a point behind with a game in hand. With both clubs winning their penultimate fixtures, the destination of the title went to the wire. The Hornets won a potentially difficult game at Fulham, while City failed against mid-table Preston at Deepdale. Yet again a Championship had been tossed away.

The following season Watford demonstrated their worth, gaining promotion to the Premier League via the play-offs. City meanwhile returned from whence they came. Their players proved unequal to the demands of the higher level, though the club did not exactly help matters when ridding themselves of their popular and successful manager and bringing in Benny Lennartsson in his place.

Bristol City's plate to celebrate promotion to the old Division 1 in 1976

Gerry Sweeney and Arsenal's George Armstrong at Highbury (August 1976)

The PG Tips chimpanzees during the home match with West Ham (September 1976)

Arsenal's Malcolm MacDonald meets the Wild West Show. City lost 0-2 (Oct 1977)

This style of programme was used in season 1979-80, v Southampton (Dec 1979)

The Rockin' Robins, who appeared as a colour spread in the programme (Dec 1979)

Tom Ritchie celebrates Garland's goal in the 6-2 thrashing of Derby (January 1980)

Tony Fitzpatrick celebrates the only City goal he ever scored, v Oldham (Nov 1980)

The Bristol City squad for the 1981-82 season

City's Rob Newman wins this aerial challenge at home to Fulham (February 1982)

The style of Bristol City match programme for season 1981-82 (March 1982)

Glyn Riley scores the first goal in the 3-1 home win over Mansfield (March 1983)

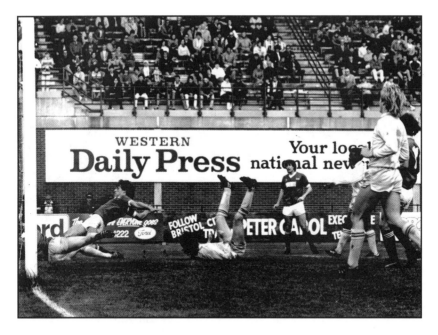

City's Glyn Riley challenges the Reading keeper for the ball at Ashton Gate (May 1986)

A ticket for Wembley for the Freight Rover Trophy Final (May 1986)

Keith Curle challenges Mansfield's keeper in the Freight Rover Final (May 1987)

Carl Shutt celebrates the first of his four goals against Fulham (December 1987)

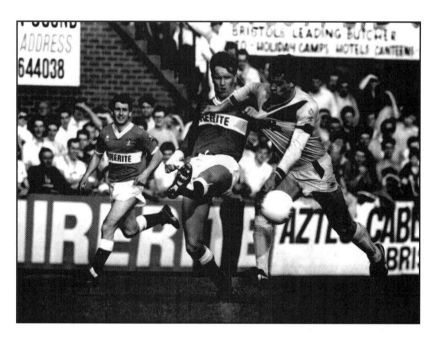

City's Colin Gordon tugs a Sheffield United shirt in this play-off semi-final (May 1988)

Alan Walsh in typical pose against Forest in the League Cup semi-final (February 1989)

Rob Newman challenges for the ball in the 4-2 win over Blackburn (August 1990)

Bob Taylor scores against Rovers in the Gloucestershire Cup Final (August 1991)

Andy Cole flicks the ball over his head against Portsmouth (August 1992)

Action from City's home defeat by Cosenza in the Anglo-Italian Cup (November 1992)

Junior Bent surges through during City's 2-0 win over Sunderland (October 1993)

Mark Shail shadows former City favourite Bob Taylor of WBA (April 1995)

LEAGUE DIVISION 1   **1998-99**
Division 1   24th (Relegated)
League Cup   2nd Round
FA Cup   3rd Round

Many City fans spent the summer dreaming of further promotion as the club splashed out on new players, helped by the financial input of former City Chairman Archie Gooch, who returned to the board after a sixteen-year absence. The new intake included Ade Akinbiyi (a club record fee of £1.2 million from Gillingham), Tony Thorpe (£800,000 Fulham), Carl Hutchings (£130,000 Brentford), Julian Watts (a free from Leicester), Danish international Soren Andersen (£410,000 Aalborg), and Moldovan international Ivan Tistimetanu (£500,000 FC Zimbru). The only player to move on was Gary Owers, who signed for Notts County.

Despite all this new blood, City's early form was disappointing. With hindsight, perhaps the 0-5 pre-season maulings at the hands of Aalborg and Borussia Monchengladbach should have alerted the club that it was not going to be easy to build on the previous season's promotion.

A 2-2 draw in the opening Division One game, at home to Oxford, was fair reward, but the rot started in the next game, when a last-minute equaliser at Queens Park Rangers robbed City of two points. Despite beating Shrewsbury 7-4 on aggregate to progress to the second round of the Worthington Cup, it was not until 26 September, when Crewe were annihilated 5-2 at Ashton Gate, that City gained their first three-point haul – in the process avenging Crewe's Worthington Cup victory a few days previously.

In the meantime, manager John Ward was showing increasing signs of desperation. Following the 1-3 defeat at Ipswich he went on record as saying that he was running out of alternatives. Thinking he needed help, the club appointed 55-year-old Swedish coach Benny Lennartsson as Director of Coaching, who took up his duties on 28 October. His appointment came as a surprise to the shareholders who had attended City's AGM just six days previously, when a loss of £312,799 was declared for season 1997-98 – despite an increase in the number of season ticket holders to 5,500.

Ward, who had been asked by the board back in September to come up with some suitable candidates for the new coaching position, had recommended the ex-Queens Park Rangers manager Ray Harford. The board, in its infinite wisdom, decided that they preferred a continental coach. With the impending announcement of Lennartsson's appointment, Ward felt that he had no option other than to resign.

Did You Know?

When City lost 0-4 at Bury in 1996, disgusted fans were barred from leaving 30 minutes early. One of them phoned local radio about being imprisoned!

Ward's final match in charge was a thrilling 2-1 Ashton Gate win over Bolton, when City's vibrant play gave every indication of a return to form. But all this had been scattered to the winds by the time of Lennartsson's first game at Bradford City eight days later. City's motorway journey north on the Friday before the game lasted nine hours, but there could be no excuse for the team's lack of application on the pitch, which resulted in a 0-5 whitewash. Sadly, such displays became the norm, even though Lennartsson tried his best to convince the fans that City were getting better.

The 1-6 home thrashing by Wolves in the next game undermined confidence even further, and despite a fortunate 2-0 win over a Sheffield United side missing eight regulars – which brought Lennartsson his first success – City rarely threatened to escape from the jaws of relegation. The diversion of the FA Cup brought another meeting with Everton, who by coincidence had won at Ashton Gate during City's last relegation season four years previously. This time Everton doubled their victory margin to 2-0, with City paying a heavy price for missing their chances.

Another last-minute goal prevented City taking all three points that their play at West Brom would have deserved, but the real damage was done by an injury to their Moldovan international Ivan Tistimetanu, which was to keep him out for the rest of the season. With Welch out of form and – following City's 2-4 defeat at Birmingham in late November – out of favour, the services of Bo Andersen, touted as one of the best continental keepers, was secured from Lyngby. In the event, the useful form of reserve Steve Phillips kept the Dane out in the cold until the end of March. By then, City had virtually thrown in the towel, though the loan signing of David Howells from Southampton had helped concoct a mini-revival. His super strike against Port Vale helped the team to a 2-0 win and sparked two further victories off the cuff. Nine points from three games, but City needed more of the same. A 0-1 loss at Bolton left the club without a prayer. Following three successive defeats, a debut goal by Lorenzo Pinamonte against Norwich at least allowed City to bow out of the First Division on a winning note.

Paradoxically, a season that ended in relegation also saw City field a club record number of six full internationals. These were Rob Edwards (Wales), Greg Goodridge (Barbados), Soren Andersen

(Denmark), Ivan Tistimetanu (Moldova), Jim Brennan (Canada) and Vilmos Sebok (Hungary). City reserve Jehad Muntasser had even represented Libya. Vilmos, who had been signed for £200,000 from Ujpest Dozsa, notched a hat-trick in Hungary's 5-0 home win over Liechtenstein in March, and also played in the away draw in Slovakia and in the 1-1 draw with England in Budapest.

In the midst of City's gloom, fans were for a while distracted by news of the club's plans to relocate to a new stadium on the site of the old Whitchurch Airport at Hengrove Park. With the proposed cost of redeveloping Ashton Gate estimated to be in the region of £25 million, the City board calculated that it would be more cost effective to build a new stadium elsewhere. With that in mind, an approach was made to the Bristol City Council about the feasibility of finding an alternative home. The Council put forward Hengrove Park as a suitable venue, upon which the club formally confirmed their interest.

However, whilst the proposed new ground has been earmarked as a possible World Cup venue, should England secure the 2006 nomination, there is still – as of January 2000 – no indication as to whether planning permission for this stadium will be granted. If that remains the case by the end of the 1999-2000 season, Bristol City will remain at Ashton Gate and commence the first phase of redevelopment with a proposed £15 million West Stand to replace the Williams Grandstand.

Season 1998-99 also marked the first season of City's Youth Academy, as part of the new FA School of Excellence scheme. Their Under-19 side finished sixth, whilst the Under-17s were runners-up in their League, but lost 1-2 at Sunderland in the third round of the FA Youth Cup. The Reserves, who played a series of friendlies throughout the season, were knocked out at the semi-final stage of the Gloucestershire Senior Challenge Cup. At the end of the season a City Under-20 side took part in the Groningen Championships, but after failing to qualify for the semi-finals from their group they were cheered by having won the Fair Play Award.

Match of the Season 1998-99
Sunderland 1 Bristol City 1

Division 1, 8 September 1998

Having won promotion and invested heavily in new players during the summer, City fans were upbeat. In the event, this miserable campaign mirrored that of 1923-24, when relegation followed promotion in the shortest possible time.

As early as September it was evident that City faced arduous times, but against championship favourites Sunderland at the Stadium of Light, they at least upset a few pundits. City's surprise draw suggested that the happy hunting they often enjoyed at Sunderland's old Roker Park home (four wins and seven draws in nineteen previous visits) might well have been transferred to the Wearsider club's new home.

The facilities at the Stadium of Light, compared to those at Ashton Gate, were enough in themselves to give City an inferiority complex. And this is how it came across in this live game on Sky TV. Without a win in their opening six games, City were overrun as John Ward's defensive ploy – leaving Ade Akinbiyi alone up front – seemed sure to bring disaster. Keith Welch's inspired display of goalkeeping kept Sunderland at bay. Welch even saved Kevin Phillips' 24th-minute spot-kick, but by then City trailed 0-1. Welch had been helpless to prevent Phillips's opener – a first-time shot into the roof of the net for his sixth goal of the season.

City's slight improvement after the break at least created some half-chances, but Welch was still by far the busier keeper. With time running out, most of City's travelling support seemed satisfied that the margin of defeat was at least respectable. But substitute Soren Andersen had other ideas. Collecting a pass from Mickey Bell on the left, Andersen swivelled and hammered in an unstoppable shot past Sunderland keeper Thomas Sorensen. It brought City their luckiest and most unexpected point of the season.

Whilst this slight setback did not deflate Sunderland, who dropped only six points at home all season on their way to the Championship, the result did nothing to encourage the Robins. Ward watched from afar as City finished bottom of the League.

LEAGUE DIVISION 2   **1999-2000**
League Cup   2nd Round
FA Cup   3rd Round

Despite giving the impression that irrespective of relegation the club would stick by Lennartsson, the board knew changes would have to be made, if only to accelerate the sale of season tickets, which the previous season had hit a new high of 7,500. It therefore came as no surprise that by early July a new manager was in situ. The only surprise was the identity of the man in question, for when it was disclosed it provoked howls of protest in some quarters. This was partly due to his connections with Bristol Rovers, for whom he had enjoyed a distinguished playing career, but also in part because of concerns over his preferred style of football. Ex-Gillingham and Bournemouth boss Tony Pulis – who had been sacked by the Gills just five days before he was appointed at Ashton Gate – was the man in question. As with the appointment of Lennartsson, City fans were asked to believe that this was the man to take the club onward and upward.

Warnings of the style of football City fans might be forced to endure appeared in the shape of graffiti on walls near the Ashton Gate ground. Pulis, to his credit, quickly demonstrated a welcoming trait of speaking about things as they were. In no time at all, fans were talking of a quick return to Division One. Even the bookies had the Robins marked as second favourites for promotion. Shape up or ship out was the maxim, but shipping players out was a problem as Pulis quickly discovered when identifying those whose attitude did not match his.

A defensively orientated approach during the League opener at Reading in the Madejski Stadium did little to endear Pulis to City's long suffering fans. As the team struggled to accumulate points in the early part of the season, criticism of the new manager mounted. However, his bullish attitude at the AGM won over most of the 500 shareholders present. It was at this meeting that a record loss of £2,352,643 was announced for the year ending 31 May 1999.

The sale of Akinbiyi – despite apparent assurances during the summer that he would not be sold – to Wolves for a new record Football League fee of £3.5 million was a blow, as was the transfer of Canadian international Jim Brennan to Nottingham Forest for £1.5 million. The loss of wing-back Brennan was covered by the presence of Mickey Bell, but the signings of Steve Jones from Charlton for £500,000 and ex-Rover Peter Beadle for £200,000 from Notts County did little to fill the hole left by Akinbiyi's departure. Hopes for the future appeared to rest largely in Tistimetanu's return from

---

Did You Know?

In September 1999, v Nottingham Forest in the Worthington Cup, Marvin Brown became City's youngest ever player at 16 years, 71 days.

---

his long lay-off, a consequence of the injury suffered at West Brom the previous season, and the loan signing of 20-year-old Tommy Black from Arsenal, who marked his debut in a goalless home draw with Wycombe by picking up the Man of the Match award.

Despite City going half a season undefeated on their own ground, the fans were forced to endure some apathetic displays at Ashton Gate, where a glut of low-scoring draws tells its own story. Highlights were few and far between, the laying of the Bournemouth hoodoo in the FA Cup being the most notable, though City's best form was reserved for the goalless derby against the Rovers in mid-October.

The jury is therefore still out on Pulis and his assistant Lindsay Parsons, and whilst many fans are not enamoured by City's style of play, there are signs that improvement is taking place. We can, as always, only trust that the club we all love remains in good hands.

GUIDE TO SEASONAL SUMMARIES

Col 1:   Match number (for league fixtures); Round (for cup-ties).
           e.g. 2:1 means 'Second round; first leg.'
           e.g. 4R means 'Fourth round replay.'

Col 2:   Date of the fixture and whether Home (H), Away (A), or Neutral (N).

Col 3:   Opposition.

Col 4:   Attendances. Home gates appear in roman; Away gates in *italics*.
        Figures in **bold** indicate the largest and smallest gates, at home and away.
        Average home and away attendances appear after the final league match.

Col 5:   Respective league positions of Bristol City and their opponents after the match.
        Bristol City's position appears on the top line in roman.
        Their opponents' position appears on the second line in *italics*.
        For cup-ties, the division and position of opponents is provided.
           e.g. 2:12 means the opposition are twelfth in Division 2.

Col 6:   The top line shows the result: W(in), D(raw), or L(ose).
        The second line shows Bristol City's cumulative points total.

Col 7:   The match score, Bristol City's given first.
        Scores in **bold** indicate Bristol City's biggest league win and heaviest defeat.

Col 8:   The half-time score, Bristol City's given first.

Col 9:   The top lines shows Bristol City's scorers and times of goals in roman.
        The second line shows opponents' scorers and times of goals in *italics*.
        A 'p' after the time of a goal denotes a penalty; 'og' an own-goal.
        The third line gives the name of the match referee.

Team line-ups: Bristol City line-ups appear on the top line, irrespective of whether
        they are home or away. Opposition teams appear on the second line in *italics*.
        Players of either side who are sent off are marked !
        Bristol City players making their league debuts are displayed in **bold**.

Substitutes: Names of substitutes appear only if they actually took the field.
        A player substituted is marked *
        A second player substituted is marked ˆ
        A third player substituted is marked "
        These marks indicate the sequence of substitutions.

N.B.   For clarity, all information appearing in *italics* relates to opposing teams.

LEAGUE DIVISION 2

Manager: Fred Ford ⇒ Alan Dicks — SEASON 1967-68

No	Date	Venue & Opponents	Att	Pos	Pt	Res	F-A	H-T	Scorers, Times, and Referees
1	19/8	H HUDDERSFIELD	18,148		0	L	2-3	1-1	Crowe 3, McIlmoyle 58 / Ellam 18, Nicholson 47, Harper 51 — Ref: R Paine
2	22/8	H QP RANGERS	20,228		0	L	0-2	0-1	Leach 11, 77 — Ref: E Jennings
3	26/8	A IPSWICH	13,702	21	0	L	0-5	0-2	Brogan 8, 14, 68, Hegan 57, Viljoen 75 — Ref: R Tinker
4	29/8	A QP RANGERS	15,448	21	0	L	1-3	1-0	McIlmoyle 8 / Morgan I 48, Allen 49, Morgan R 89 — Ref: R Spittle
5	2/9	H CARLISLE	13,842	20	2	W	1-0	1-0	Jacobs 35 — Ref: K Burns
6	5/9	H MIDDLESBROUGH	13,216	19	3	D	0-0	0-0	Ref: V Batty
7	9/9	A BLACKBURN	14,621	21	3	L	0-2	0-0	Connelly 61, Ferguson 64p — Ref: J Taylor
8	16/9	H BLACKPOOL	13,191	22	3	L	2-4	1-2	Quigley 28, Derrick 88 / Ingram 26, 86, Skirton 42, 87 — Ref: C Nicholls
9	23/9	A MILLWALL	12,121	21	4	D	1-1	1-1	Crowe 23 / Dunphy 30 — Ref: W Handley
10	30/9	H HULL	11,630	19	5	D	3-3	3-3	Garland 4, Bush 24, Sharpe 32 / Houghton 2, 44p, Chilton 27 — Ref: J Clarke

Line-ups (City roman, opponents italic)

1. Huddersfield — City: 1 Gibson, 2 Oldfield, 3 Briggs, 4 Parr, 5 Connor, 6 Low, 7 Derrick, 8 Crowe, 9 McIlmoyle, 10 Quigley, 11 Peters, 12 Bush. *Huddersfield: Oldfield, Parkin, Catlin, Nicholson, Ellam, Meagan, McHale, Shaw, Harper, Dobson, Hill.*

> After the day's quickest score, when Crowe finishes off a superb four-man move, City are stunned by Town's fight-back in an all-action game. A typical McIlmoyle header hauls City back into game, but are unable to equalise, even squandering a 70th-min pen as Ford's effort hits post.

2. QP Rangers — City: 1 Gibson, 2 Ford, 3 Briggs, 4 Parr, 5 Connor, 6 Low, 7 Derrick*, 8 Crowe, 9 McIlmoyle, 10 Quigley, 11 Peters, 12 Bush. *QPR: Springett, Clement, Harris, Keen, Keetch, Hazell, Lazarus, Morgan I, Allen, Leach, Morgan R.*

> City are outclassed by weakened opponents who include four reserves. Rangers, twice thwarted by the post in the five mins leading up to half-time, are indebted to Leach. He drives in left-wing centre before clinching victory over pathetic City by deftly heading in cross from the right.

3. Ipswich — City: 1 Gibson, 2 Carroll, 3 Briggs, 4 Parr, 5 Connor, 6 Low, 7 Savino, 8 Crowe, 9 McIlmoyle, 10 Quigley, 11 Peters. *Ipswich: Hancock, Carroll, Houghton, Jefferson, Baxter, Boulton, Spearritt, Hegan, Baker*, Viljoen, Brogan, McNeil.*

> City's rearguard, often exposed by smaller opponents, are given a harassing time. Unbeaten Ipswich canter to an easy win after Brogan's fine angled shot from the left puts them ahead. Crowe is denied towards the finish, his header from a Savino free-kick being cleared off the line.

4. QP Rangers — City: 1 Gibson, 2 Ford, 3 Briggs, 4 Parr, 5 Connor, 6 Low, 7 Savino, 8 Bush, 9 McIlmoyle, 10 Quigley, 11 Peters. *QPR: Kelly, Clement*, Harris, Keen, Hunt, Hazell, Lazarus, Morgan I, Allen, Leach, Morgan R, Watson.*

> McIlmoyle's left-foot shot, in off the far post, from the edge of the penalty area is scant reward for City's first-half performance. Quigley is the star with display of perpetual motion, but blatant defensive errors by Gibson & Ford within 55 secs in second half give Rangers the advantage.

5. Carlisle — City: 1 Gibson, 2 Jacobs, 3 Briggs, 4 Quigley, 5 Connor*, 6 Low, 7 Peters, 8 Crowe, 9 McIlmoyle, 10 Tainton*, 11 Bartley, 12 Down. *Carlisle: Ross, Neil, Caldwell, McConnell, Passmoor, McCarron, Saville*, Garbutt, Carlin, Balderstone, Sharp, Murray.*

> City are well on top against defensive opponents, but numerous wasted opportunities – notably by Crowe and McIlmoyle – restrict their first victory of the season to a solitary strike. Jacobs latched onto a poor clearance to net from ten yards with a left-foot shot for his first-ever goal.

6. Middlesbrough — City: 1 Gibson, 2 McPartland, 3 Butler, 4 Quigley, 5 Connor*, 6 Low, 7 Savino, 8 Crowe, 9 McIlmoyle, 10 Tainton, 11 Peters, 12 Bush. *Middlesbrough: Jones, Gates, Rooks, Horner, Masson, Crossan, O'Rouke, Hickton, Chadwick.*

> Quigley is again the star performer, holding City's depleted injury-hit side together after Connor, Low and Jacobs suffer early knocks. Boro supply most of the skill and are somewhat unfortunate not to win. Gibson, back to somewhere near his best form, does much to deny them.

7. Blackburn — City: 1 Gibson, 2 Jacobs, 3 Briggs, 4 Parr, 5 Low, 6 Tainton, 7 Derrick, 8 Quigley, 9 McIlmoyle, 10 Crowe, 11 Peters. *Blackburn: Blacklaw, Newton, Wilson, Clayton, Coddington, Rogers, Ferguson, Helliwell, Anderson, Darling, Connelly.*

> City are forced on the defensive throughout by opponents who miss many chances. Helliwell seizes on a poor clearance and slips ball through to Connelly to shoot opener. Low elbows Anderson off ball to concede the penalty. Rogers is booked for retaliation after being held by Quigley.

8. Blackpool — City: 1 Gibson, 2 Jacobs, 3 Briggs, 4 Parr, 5 Connor, 6 Low, 7 Crowe, 8 Derrick, 9 McIlmoyle, 10 Quigley, 11 Peters. *Blackpool: Taylor, Armfield, Mowbray, Milne, James, McPhee, Skirton, Craven, Ingram, Green, Oates.*

> City's defence falters badly in front of the Match of the Day cameras. Skirton's final goal for the Seasiders is right out of the top drawer. He completes a fine left-side run by cutting in and firing home at the Open End. Derrick slams in game's final goal with ill-concealed annoyance.

9. Millwall — City: 1 Gibson, 2 Jacobs, 3 Briggs, 4 Parr, 5 Connor, 6 Bush, 7 Crowe, 8 Derrick, 9 McIlmoyle, 10 Down, 11 Peters*, 12 Ford. *Millwall: Leslie, Gilchrist, Burnett, Jones, Kitchener, Wilson, Possee*, Dunphy, Hunt, Weller, Armstrong, Welsh.*

> Crisis club City, under the control of caretaker boss Les Bardsley following the sacking of Fred Ford, take an early lead. Crowe crashes in a fierce drive from the right into the far corner, before Dunphy fashions Millwall's skilful equaliser from 15 yards through a crowded goalmouth.

10. Hull — City: 1 Gibson, 2 Ford, 3 Briggs, 4 Quigley, 5 Connor, 6 Parr, 7 Crowe, 8 Garland, 9 McIlmoyle, 10 Sharpe, 11 Derrick, 12 Bush. *Hull: Swan, Butler D, Lees*, Jarvis, Pettit, Simpkin, Young, Wagstaff, Chilton, Houghton, Butler I, Wilkinson.*

> This defensive, error-ridden thriller ignites from the off. The Tigers take an early lead as Houghton punishes Parr's poor headed clearance to net from the edge of the penalty area, but Garland crashes home an early equaliser from Crowe's right-wing centre for his first League goal.

No	V	Opponent	Date	Att	Pos	Res	Opp Pos	Pts	HT	FT	Scorers	Referee
11	A	(PALACE)	7/10	19,938	—	—	1	5	—	—	Kember 63, Woodruff 77	Ref: R Kirkpatrick
12	H	CARDIFF	14/10	15,609	20	D	17	6	0-1	1-1	Crowe 57, Brown 42	Ref: G Hill
13	A	PORTSMOUTH	21/10	21,278	21	L	3	6	0-1	0-2	Jennings 21, Ford 89 (og)	Ref: G Roper
14	A	ROTHERHAM	4/11	5,938	21	L	20	6	0-0	0-1	Chappell 80	Ref: R Egan
15	H	DERBY	10/11	15,919	21	W	7	8	0-0	1-0	Garland 68	Ref: T Locket
16	A	PLYMOUTH	18/11	11,179	20	W	22	10	1-0	1-0	Connor 44	Ref: K Walker
17	H	CHARLTON	25/11	12,567	21	L	17	10	0-0	0-2	Went 46p, Gregory 51	Ref: H Davey
18	A	PRESTON	2/12	10,127	20	W	18	12	1-0	1-0	Garland 10	Ref: V Batty
19	H	NORWICH	5/12	13,444	20	L	6	12	0-1	0-2	Bryceland 35, Curran 90	Ref: A Dimond
20	A	HUDDERSFIELD	16/12	12,071	20	W	14	14	1-0	3-0	Galley 30, 71, 77	Ref: G Robinson
21	H	IPSWICH	22/12	17,628	20	D	5	15	1-0	1-1	Galley 17, Baxter 71	Ref: R Prichard

Lineups (as listed, left to right):

- **11 (Palace):** Jackson J, Sewell … Gibson, Ford, Briggs, Presland, Payne, McCormick, Bannister, Light, Crowe, Kember, White, Bush, Woodruff, Sharpe, Jackson C* Long
- **12 (Cardiff):** Gibson, Wilson, Coldrick, Ferguson, Clarke, Murray, Harris, Jones, Brown, King, Bird, Bush, Tashack, Derrick, Bartley, Low
- **13 (Portsmouth):** Gibson, Milkins, Pack, Ley, Smith, Tindall, Harris, McCann, Pointer, Hiron, Kellard, Jennings, Peters, Garland*, Bartley, Jennings
- **14 (Rotherham):** Gibson, Hill, Wilcackson, Burgin, Rabjohn*, Hazelden, Tiler, Pring, Galley, Sheffield, Hodgson, Crickmore, Chappell, Sharpe, Quigley, Bartley
- **15 (Derby):** Gibson, Matthews, Wright, Hopkinson, Webster*, McFarland, Saxton, Hughes, Durban, O'Hare, Hector, Waller, Barker, Garland, Quigley, Bartley
- **16 (Plymouth):** Gibson, Dunne, Everitt, Baird, Piper, Nelson, Hore, Davey, Bickle, Peacock, Neale, Harrison, Crowe, Garland, Quigley, Bartley
- **17 (Charlton):** Gibson, Wright, Curtis, Kinsey, Moore, Went, Reeves, Campbell, Tees, Gregory, Booth, Peacock, Crowe, Garland, Quigley, Bartley
- **18 (Preston):** Gibson, Kelly, Ross, Ritchie, Smith, Singleton, McLab, Lee, Spavin*, Forrest, Lyall, Temple, Gemmill, Crowe, Sharpe, Garland, Quigley, Bartley, Bush
- **19 (Norwich):** Gibson, Keelan, Stringer, Mullett, Lucas, Brown, Sharpe, Fogg, Bryceland, Manning, Curran, Kenning, Crowe, Sharpe*, Garland, Quigley, Bartley, Low
- **20 (Huddersfield):** Gibson, Oldfield, Parkin, Catlin*, Nicholson, Mielzarets, Meagan, Shaw, Dobson, Worthington, Hill, Harper, Legg, Crowe, Galley, Garland, Quigley, Bartley
- **21 (Ipswich):** Gibson, Hancock, Carroll, Houghton, Jeferson, Baxter, Viljoen, Spearritt, Hegan, Wigg*, Hunt, Brogan, Woods, Crowe, Galley, Garland, Quigley, Bartley

Match reports:

11 (Palace): City, watched by their new manager Alan Dicks, hold their own against Palace until caught out by Cliff Jackson's inswinging corner from the right. McCormick nods the ball back across the box for Kember to head in. City's comeback hopes are ended by Woodruff's chip over Gibson.

12 (Cardiff): The swirling wind proves troublesome for City, who find themselves deservedly behind when Brown beats Parr to the ball and finds the corner of the net from eight yards. Bartley's inswinging corner from the right brings the equaliser, Crowe heading home from almost on the goal-line.

13 (Portsmouth): With Alan Dicks having completed his duties with Coventry, his City career starts with this defensive-orientated display that reaps what it deserves. Jennings volleys home his ninth strike of the season early on and, at the death, Ford's own-goal completes the misery of City fans.

14 (Rotherham): City, with £12,000 signing Ken Wimshurst from Southampton, pay dearly for missing many opportunities against the Millers. A centre from Charlie Crickmore, Rotherham's £20,000 signing from Gillingham, causes confusion in the City goalmouth and sub Chappell forces the ball in.

15 (Derby): A case of the pot calling the kettle black as Dicks complains of Derby's ultra-defensive tactics. City's team of furies give the home crowd their first glimmer of hope for many weeks. Garland flings himself boldly forward to head superbly into the top corner to bring a deserved success.

16 (Plymouth): The 200 or so City fans in the crowd are overjoyed as their favourites achieve their fourth successive victory at Home Park. City's centre-half is the hero as he goes up for Crowe's inswinging corner; the ball ending up in the net as Connor's header hits Mike Everitt on the shoulder.

17 (Charlton): Peacock hits a post for Charlton early on as City struggle to settle down in an entertaining game. Went puts visitors in front with a disputed pen after Parr plays the ball cleanly away from Gregory, who later scores with an angled shot from the left. Quigley is booked in the last minute.

18 (Preston): Garland atones for an earlier miss to put City ahead at Deepdale as Parr's misplaced shot finds him free to clip the ball into the top corner. City spurn chances to increase advantage in the first half and are forced to defend after the break. Davis is booked in 70th minute for fouling Lee.

19 (Norwich): City are doubly unfortunate on 30 minutes after the ref disallows Bartley strike and awards penalty for Stringer's handball. Sharpe's kick hits the bar. Dominant City are left to rue missed opportunities. Norwich capitalise on Wimshurst's slip and then a breakaway move to win the game.

20 (Huddersfield): A magnificent hat-trick debut by John Galley, a £25,000 signing from Rotherham some two weeks previously when his leg was in plaster. He hammers in an unstoppable left-foot shot for the opener, then a perfectly placed left-foot effort, before picking up a rebound to seal a great win.

21 (Ipswich): City's chapter of penalty woes continues with their third consecutive miss as Crowe blasts wide in the 63rd min after Galley had been brought down by Baxter. Galley is unfortunate to have his soaring header struck off shortly after putting City ahead when he nudged ball over line.

LEAGUE DIVISION 2

Manager: Fred Ford ⇨ Alan Dicks

SEASON 1967-68

1 | 2 | 3 | 4 | 5 | 6 | 7 | 8 | 9 | 10 | 11 | 12 sub used

---

22 — A BIRMINGHAM, 26/12 — Att 40,429 — Pos 20 — Pt L 15 — F-A 1-4 — H-T 0-1

Scorers, Times, and Referees: Wimshurst 60, Vowden 90, Briggs 45 (og), Leggatt 53, Bridges 83, Ref: W Gow

1	2	3	4	5	6	7	8	9	10	11	12
Gibson	Parr	Briggs	Wimshurst	Connor	Bush	Crowe*	Garland	Galley	Quigley	Peters	Derrick
Heriot	Murray	Green	Wylie	Sleeuwenk'Beard		Bridges	Vincent	Pickering	Vowden	Leggatt	

City have but one chance in the first half, when Crowe's shot hits the foot of a post. It takes Wimshurst's headed goal to herald relief from siege conditions; but City's revival is ended by a late goal-burst from the League's most prolific attack. Briggs and Quigley are both booked.

---

23 — H BIRMINGHAM, 30/12 — Att 23,493 — Pos 20 — Pt W 17 — F-A 3-1 — H-T 1-0

Scorers: Crowe 43, Galley 47, 84, Vincent 62, Ref: J Osborne

1	2	3	4	5	6	7	8	9	10	11
Gibson	Parr	Briggs	Wimshurst	Connor	Bush	Derrick	Crowe	Galley	Quigley	Peters
Heriot	Murray	Martin	Wylie	Sleeuwenk'Beard		Bridges	Vincent	Pickering	Vowden	Leggatt

After outplaying Birmingham in the first half, City fully deserve the lead that Crowe gives them as he slides the ball home. Galley's rocket from the edge of the area doubles the advantage, but the Robins are restricted to breakaways after the Blues register in a goalmouth scramble.

---

24 — A CARLISLE, 6/1 — Att 8,261 — Pos 19 — Pt D 18 — F-A 0-0 — H-T 0-0

Ref: P Baldwin

1	2	3	4	5	6	7	8	9	10	11
Gibson	Parr	Briggs	Wimshurst	Connor	Bush	Derrick	Crowe	Galley	Quigley	Peters
McPartland Neil	Caldwell	McConnell	Garbutt		Marshland	Rudge	Murray	McIlmoyle*	Balderstone	McVitie	Passmoor

Carlisle, without a win for seven matches, exert early pressure on an icy pitch. McIlmoyle's header is cleared off the line by Briggs before City respond midway through the first half when Galley's header hits the crossbar. McPartland makes a superb save from Galley to deny City a win.

---

25 — H BLACKBURN, 13/1 — Att 19,900 — Pos 19 — Pt D 19 — F-A 0-0 — H-T 0-0

Ref: W Castle

1	2	3	4	5	6	7	8	9	10	11	12
Gibson	Jacobs	Parr	Wimshurst	Connor	Bush	Derrick	Crowe	Galley	Quigley	Peters	
Blacklaw	Newton	Wilson	Shaples	Coddington	Hole	Ferguson	Rogers	Gilliver*	Darling	Connelly	Mulvaney

Derrick misses two first-half chances as both teams find it tough going in the Ashton Gate mud. Ref makes several controversial decisions after the break and Quigley receives the first booking of the season in the 72nd min. Galley is thwarted right at the end by Ferguson's great tackle.

---

26 — A BLACKPOOL, 20/1 — Att 13,032 — Pos 19 — Pt D 20 — F-A 1-1 — H-T 0-1

Scorers: Galley 59, Skirton 38p, Ref: K Burns

1	2	3	4	5	6	7	8	9	10	11	12
Gibson	Jacobs*	Parr	Wimshurst	Connor	Bush	Derrick	Crowe	Galley	Quigley	Peters	Garland
Taylor	Armfield	Thompson	Milne	Rowe	McPhee	Skirton*	Green	Ingram	Oates	Suddick	Craven

Skirton, a former Ashton Gate amateur, puts Blackpool ahead from the penalty spot with a power shot to Gibson's right, after Jacobs brought down Green. In a high-standard game of many incidents, Galley runs in unchallenged at the far post to head past Taylor for City's equaliser.

---

27 — H MILLWALL, 3/2 — Att 14,673 — Pos 20 — Pt L 20 — F-A 0-2 — H-T 0-2

Scorers: Conlon 28, Possee 43, Ref: J Lewis

1	2	3	4	5	6	7	8	9	10	11
Gibson	Parr	Briggs	Wimshurst	Connor	Bush	Garland	Crowe	Galley	Quigley	Peters
Leslie	Gilchrist	Cripps	Jones	Kitchener	Burnett	Possee	Weller	Conlon	Neil	Jacks

Defensively-minded Millwall achieve a smash and grab win. Conlon bursts through to shoot home from eight yards shortly after Quigley was booked for obstructing the taking of a Lions free-kick. Possee completes the scoring, touching Conlon's speculative 30-yarder over the line.

---

28 — A HULL, 10/2 — Att 12,596 — Pos 20 — Pt L 20 — F-A 2-4 — H-T 1-0

Scorers: Galley 33, 69, Wagstaff 49, 51, 58, Butler 50, Ref: T Pallister

1	2	3	4	5	6	7	8	9	10	11	12
Gibson	Parr	Briggs	Wimshurst	Connor	Bush	Derick	Garland	Galley	Quigley	Crowe	
McKechnie	Banks	Butler D	Greenwood	Wilson	Simpkin	Houghton*	Wagstaff	Chilton	Davidson	Butler I	Henderson

After a minute's silence for the Hull trawler disaster, a poor first half is enlivened by Galley's typical header and efforts to capture a dog. Three quick strikes alters things after the break. Immediately after Galley spurns an easy chance, a fierce Wagstaff drive secures Hull's fourth goal.

---

29 — H CRYS PALACE, 24/2 — Att 13,083 — Pos 19 — Pt W 22 — F-A 2-1 — H-T 2-0

Scorers: Galley 10, Wimshurst 43, Woodruff 83, Ref: J Carr

1	2	3	4	5	6	7	8	9	10	11
Gibson	Jacobs	Briggs	Wimshurst	Connor	Bush	Derrick	Garland	Galley	Quigley	Crowe
Jackson J	Sewell	Bannister	Payne	Stephenson	McCormick	Lazarus	Kember	White	Woodruff	Tomkins

City, in dire need of points, make a great start. A superb goal from Galley, who hooks in on the turn from eight yards, is followed by Wimshurst running Crowe's through-ball past Jackson. Palace come more alive after the break, but only reward is when Woodruff converts White's pass.

---

30 — H ASTON VILLA, 27/2 — Att 17,138 — Pos 19 — Pt D 23 — F-A 0-0 — H-T 0-0

Ref: A Jones

1	2	3	4	5	6	7	8	9	10	11
Gibson	Jacobs	Briggs	Wimshurst	Connor	Bush	Derrick	Garland	Galley	Quigley	Crowe
Dunn	Bradley	Wright	Park	Chatterley	Deakin	Roberts	Mitchinson	Woodward	Godfrey	Anderson

Galley, thrice thwarted by Villa's reserve keeper, is the only City forward to have any genuine goal attempts in a disappointing match. Villa, basing everything on defence, are but a pale shadow of their great sides of the past. Anderson wastes their only chance when he bursts through.

---

31 — A CARDIFF, 2/3 — Att 15,334 — Pos 19 — Pt W 25 — F-A 1-0 — H-T 0-0

Scorers: Galley 66, Ref: D Lyden

1	2	3	4	5	6	7	8	9	10	11
Gibson	Jacobs	Briggs	Wimshurst	Connor	Parr	Crowe	Garland	Galley	Quigley	Peters
Davies	Derrett	Ferguson	Clarke	Murray	Harris	Jones	Clark	King	Toshack	Lea

Cardiff appear preoccupied with next Wednesday's European Cup match v Moscow Torpedo. Thus assisted, City are able to achieve their first victory over their Welsh opponents in ten seasons. A poor game is settled by Galley, who heads Peters' floated free-kick into the roof of the net.

32 H PORTSMOUTH 16/3 · Att 16,085 · 18 W 3–0 · 4 27
Scorers: Harris 26 (og), Garland 75, Galley 84 — Ref: J Finney
City: Gibson, Jacobs, Briggs, Wimhurst, Connor, Parr, Crowe, Garland, Galley, Quigley, Peters
Portsmouth: Milkins, Pack, Ley, Smith, Tindall, Harris, McCann, Treblicock, Hiron, Kellard, Jennings
City are gifted the lead in a game spoilt by the windy conditions. Crowe's curling centre provokes Harris to head into his own net. Pompey's comeback attempt is ended by a fine solo goal by Garland, running through from inside his own half, before Galley's header wraps things up.

33 A NORWICH 23/3 · Att 13,634 · 19 L 2–3 · 7 27
Scorers: Quigley 44, Garland 53 | Manning 14, 89, Crickmore 76 — Ref: G McCabe
City: Gibson, Jacobs, Briggs, Wimhurst, Connor, Parr, Crowe, Garland, Galley, Quigley, Peters
Norwich: Vasper, Stringer, Black, Lucas, Brown, Allcock, Foggo, Anderson, Manning, Curran, Crickmore
Vasper is caught off his line as Garland finds the net with a hopeful hook from the by-line as Allcock attempts to let the ball run out. Gibson requires treatment after a controversial equaliser, before the Canaries clinch all the points with Manning's brilliant header from Foggo's corner.

34 H ROTHERHAM 29/3 · Att 19,783 · 19 L 0–1 · 20 27
Scorers: — | Downes 5 — Ref: D Nippard
City: Gibson, Jacobs, Briggs, Wimhurst, Connor, Parr, Crowe, Garland, Galley, Quigley, Peters
Rotherham: Hill, Swift, Hague, Quinn, Watson D, Tiler, Chappell, Haselden, Downes*, Storrie, Bentley (sub Shepherd)
A hard, physical, vital relegation encounter against Tommy Docherty's defensively-organised side. Tiler and Hague receive bookings, but the game's 44 fouls are evenly distributed. City fail to match the Millers at the start and Downes rises above Connor for the game's only goal.

35 H BOLTON 2/4 · Att 11,047 · 19 D 1–1 · 12 28
Scorers: Hatton 31 (og) | Greaves 53 — Ref: B Homewood
City: Gibson, Jacobs, Briggs, Wimhurst, Connor, Parr, Crowe, Garland, Galley, Quigley, Peters* (sub Bush)
Bolton: Hopkinson, Cooper, Farrimond, Williams, Hulme, Hatton D, Rimmer, Byrom, Greaves, Lennard, Taylor
Derrick, replacing the injured Quigley, is City's star man early on before fading in the second-half snowstorms. His right-wing cross forces Hatton to head into his own net. City are on the attack throughout, but Bolton level in a breakaway when Greaves hooks in from Taylor's pass.

36 A DERBY 6/4 · Att 16,028 · 19 L 1–3 · 12 28
Scorers: Briggs 82 | Hector 42p, Barker 73, 81 — Ref: T Hill
City: Gibson, Jacobs, Briggs, Wimhurst, Connor, Parr, Derrick, Garland, Galley, Bush*, Peters* (subs Quigley, Bartley)
Derby: Boulton, Webster, Richardson, Stewart, McFarland, Hopkinson, Durban, Barker, O'Hare, Hector, Hinton
Briggs turns in Bartley's left-wing corner for his first-ever League goal, but by then County had the game won. Two goals for Barker, his second a screamer that goes in off the bar. O'Hare goes in goal for seven first-half minutes, whilst after the break Hector blasts a penalty wide.

37 H PLYMOUTH 13/4 · Att 17,076 · 19 W 2–0 · 22 30
Scorers: Galley 51, 87 — Ref: M Sinclair
City: Gibson, Jacobs, Briggs, Wimhurst, Connor, Parr, Derrick, Garland, Galley, Bush*, Quigley (sub Crowe)
Plymouth: Dunne, Sillett, Sullivan, Hore, Saxton, Etheridge, Bickle, Burnside, Tedesco, Piper, Reynolds
City squander many first-half opportunities, but Galley benefits from better service after the break when City abandon their 4-3-3 plan. The centre-forward heads in Jacobs' cross as City take lead and makes the game safe with a 15-yard shot from in off the post from Derrick's pass.

38 A BOLTON 17/4 · Att 7,289 · 20 L 0–1 · 14 30
Scorers: — | Greaves 17 — Ref: T Pallister
City: Gibson, Jacobs, Briggs, Wimhurst, Connor, Parr, Derrick, Garland, Galley, Bush*, Crowe (sub Quigley)
Bolton: Hopkinson, Ritson, Farrimond, Williams, Hulme, Hatton D, Wharton, Hill, Greaves, Bromley, Taylor
Expensive blunders by City's two most reliable players prove costly. Galley, goalscorer extraordinaire, proves his fallibility by missing two simple chances, whilst Gibson makes one of his rare errors. He gifts Greaves an easy header when letting a centre slip through his fingers.

39 A CHARLTON 20/4 · Att 11,756 · 20 W 2–0 · 19 32
Scorers: Crowe 8, Galley 29 | Gregory 69 — Ref: E Jennings
City: Gibson, Jacobs, Briggs, Wimhurst, Connor, Bush, Derrick, Garland, Galley, Crowe, Quigley
Charlton: Wright, Keirs, Kinsey, Campbell, Went, Reeves, Hince, Tees*, Treacy, Gregory, Peacock (sub Stenson)
In-form Charlton, with three points from relegation rivals over Easter, prove vulnerable to quick thrusts through the middle. Crowe's fierce shot gives City an early lead and then Galley's mis-hit shot strikes Went and rolls in to put City in command over one of their bogey sides.

40 H PRESTON 27/4 · Att 16,935 · 19 W 4–1 · 20 34
Scorers: Galley 15, Garland 17, Crowe 51, [Wimhurst 58] | Irvine 40 — Ref: B Daniel
City: Gibson, Jacobs, Briggs, Wimhurst, Connor, Bush, Derrick, Garland, Galley, Crowe, Quigley
Preston: Kelly, Patrick, Ross, Smith, Hawkins, Knighton, Temple, Irvine, Charnley, McNab, Gemmill
Requiring one point to be safe from relegation, City are surprised as Irvine heads Preston back into the match from a Gemmill corner. They then storm to their best win of the season with strikes from Crowe, who draws out Kelly before slotting home, and a great shot by Wimhurst.

41 A ASTON VILLA 4/5 · Att 15,301 · 19 W 4–2 · 15 36
Scorers: Derrick 10, Crowe 19, Garland 20, [Bush 54] | Godfrey 4, Chatterley 12 — Ref: H Richards
City: Watling, Jacobs, Briggs, Wimhurst, Connor, Merrick, Derrick, Garland*, Galley, Crowe, Bartley (sub Bush)
Aston Villa: Withers, Edwards, Aitken, Chatterley, Turnbull, Deakin, Rudge, Mitchinson, Greenhalgh, Godfrey, Anderson
With relegation pressure lifted, City storm to their first-ever victory over Villa at their 19th attempt, despite being without the injured Gibson and Galley. Both sides are committed to an attacking policy. Bush sets the seal on a great win with a thundering 15-yarder into the top corner.

42 A MIDDLESBROUGH 11/5 · Att 12,684 · 19 L 1–2 · 6 36
Scorers: Garland 87 | Webb 4, 81 — Ref: K Styles
City: Mahoney, Jacobs, Briggs, Wimhurst, Connor, Merrick, Derrick, Garland, Galley, Crowe, Bartley
Middlesbrough: Whigham, Smith, Jones, Crossan, Rooks, Spraggon, Chadwick, McMordie, Webb, Hickton, Lugg
City bring in another keeper for his debut, but he is overshadowed by Stan Webb. This match, a pale shadow of the FA Cup clashes between the sides, is settled by Webb, who marks his debut by forcing the ball over the line from six yards. He then clinches the points with a header.

Home — Away 14,417 — Average 15,935

LEAGUE DIVISION 2 (CUP-TIES)　　Manager: Fred Ford ⇨ Alan Dicks　　SEASON 1967-68

League Cup

		Scorers, Times, and Referees	F-A		H-T	1	2	3	4	5	6	7	8	9	10	11	12 sub used
2	H EVERTON	Kendall 5, 63, Royle 44, Hurst 58,	0-5	21 L	0-2	Gibson	Jacobs	Briggs	Parr	Low	Bush	Derrick	Crowe	McIlmoyle	Sharpe	Peters	(Brown 68)
13/9	22,054 1:8	Ref: J Yates				*West*	*Wright*	*Brown*	*Kendall*	*Labone*	*Harvey*	*Young*	*Ball*	*Royle*	*Hurst*	*Temple*	

City are given a soccer lesson by a superb Everton team, whose keeper does not have a shot to save until the 82nd minute. Kendall's first goal is scored from 16 yards, but his second finishes off the best move of the night. He picks his spot after a passage of play involving eight passes.

FA Cup

		Scorers, Times, and Referees	F-A		H-T	1	2	3	4	5	6	7	8	9	10	11	12 sub used
3	H BRISTOL ROV		0-0	19 D	0-0	Gibson	Parr	Briggs	Wimhurst	Connor	Bush	Derrick	Crowe	Galley	Quigley	Peters	
27/1	37,237 3:19	Ref: H New				*Taylor L*	*Hillard*	*Munro*	*Williams J*	*Taylor S*	*Stone*	*Jarman*	*Jones W*	*Biggs*	*Mabbutt*	*Jones R*	

A big letdown after all the hype. Incidents to excite a strangely quiet, near-capacity crowd are few and far between as City fail to exploit the gulf in status between the sides. Crowe's clever play produces a chance but Laurie Taylor dives to his left to keep out Galley's right-foot drive.

		Scorers, Times, and Referees	F-A		H-T	1	2	3	4	5	6	7	8	9	10	11	12 sub used
3R	A BRISTOL ROV	Crowe 37, Galley 38	2-1	19 W	2-1	Gibson	Parr	Briggs	Wimhurst	Connor	Bush	Derrick*	Crowe	Galley	Quigley	Peters	Garland
30/1	30,157 3:19	Taylor S 28 Ref: H New				*Taylor L*	*Hillard*	*Munro*	*Williams J*	*Taylor S*	*Stone*	*Jarman**	*Jones W*	*Plumb*	*Mabbut*	*Jones R*	*Ronaldson*

What a difference three days make. A rip-roaring contest with City riding their luck as Rovers' twice hit a post and Parr clears off the line from Ronaldson. After going behind to Stuart Taylor's header, Crowe equalises with a great cross-shot, and then Galley heads in to clinch victory.

		Scorers, Times, and Referees	F-A		H-T	1	2	3	4	5	6	7	8	9	10	11	12 sub used
4	A MIDDLESBROUGH	Garland 38	1-1	20 D	1-1	Gibson	Jacobs	Briggs	Wimhurst	Connor	Parr	Derrick	Garland	Galley	Quigley	Crowe	
17/2	29,086 11	Parr 8 (og) Ref: D Lyden				*Whigham*	*Horner*	*Jones*	*Masson**	*Gates*	*Spraggon*	*Kear*	*Horsfield*	*Hickton*	*Crossan*	*Downing*	*McNeil*

A hard-fought contest that brings bookings for Galley, Jacobs and Crossan. City fight back well after Parr deflects Horsfield's weak shot past Gibson. Derrick is unfortunate with his deft effort disallowed for offside. Garland earns a replay with a fierce shot from Wimhurst's free-kick.

		Scorers, Times, and Referees	F-A		H-T	1	2	3	4	5	6	7	8	9	10	11	12 sub used
4R	H MIDDLESBROUGH	Connor 4, Galley 27	2-0	20 W	2-0	Gibson	Jacobs	Briggs	Wimhurst	Connor	Parr	Derrick	Garland	Galley	Quigley	Crowe*	Peters
20/2	21,771 11	Hickton 78 Ref: D Lyden				*Whigham*	*Jones*	*Worthington* Masson	*Masson*	*Gates*	*Spraggon*	*Kear*	*Horsfield*	*Hickton*	*Crossan**	*McNeill*	*Chadwick*

City take early control as a headed goal by Connor from Crowe's inswinging corner is followed by a strike to grace any occasion. A wonderful move between Wimhurst and Derrick produces a chip forward to Galley who rises to head home. Hickton's fine shot leads to nailbiting finish.

		Scorers, Times, and Referees	F-A		H-T	1	2	3	4	5	6	7	8	9	10	11	12 sub used
5	A LEEDS		0-2	19 L	0-2	Gibson	Jacobs	Briggs	Wimhurst	Connor	Parr	Sharpe	Garland	Galley	Quigley	Crowe	
9/3	45,227 1:2	Jones 34, Lorimer 45 Ref: A Dimond				*Sprake !*	*Reaney*	*Cooper*	*Bremner*	*Charlton*	*Hunter*	*Greenhoff*	*Lorimer*	*Jones*	*Giles**	*Hibbitt*	*Madeley*

A hard-fought, tough encounter boils over after the break. Bookings for Garland, Hibbitt and Wimhurst, whilst Sprake is sent off for punching Garland. City's great spirit isn't reflected in a scoreline which is given an unfair spin by Lorimer's 20-yard screamer into the top of the net.

League Table

Pos	Team	P	Home W	D	L	F	A	Away W	D	L	F	A	Pts
1	Ipswich	42	12	7	2	45	20	10	8	3	34	24	59
2	QP Rangers	42	18	2	1	45	9	7	6	8	22	27	58
3	Blackpool	42	12	6	3	33	16	4	5	12	38	27	58
4	Birmingham	42	12	6	3	54	21	7	8	6	29	30	52
5	Portsmouth	42	13	6	2	43	18	5	7	9	25	37	49
6	Middlesbro	42	10	7	4	39	19	5	5	11	21	35	46
7	Millwall	42	9	10	2	35	16	5	6	9	27	34	45
8	Blackburn	42	13	5	3	34	16	3	6	12	22	33	45
9	Norwich	42	12	4	5	40	30	4	7	10	20	35	43
10	Carlisle	42	9	9	3	38	22	5	4	12	20	30	41
11	Crys Palace	42	11	4	6	34	19	3	7	11	22	37	39
12	Bolton	42	8	6	7	37	28	5	7	9	23	35	39
13	Cardiff	42	9	6	6	35	29	4	6	11	25	37	38
14	Huddersfield	42	10	6	5	29	23	3	6	12	17	38	38
15	Charlton	42	10	6	5	43	25	2	7	12	20	43	37
16	Aston Villa	42	10	3	8	35	30	5	6	10	19	34	37
17	Hull	42	6	8	7	25	23	6	5	10	33	50	37
18	Derby	42	8	5	8	40	35	5	5	11	31	43	36
19	BRISTOL CITY	42	8	7	7	26	25	6	3	12	22	37	36
20	Preston	42	8	7	6	29	24	4	4	13	14	41	35
21	Rotherham	42	7	4	10	22	32	3	7	11	20	44	31
22	Plymouth	42	5	4	12	26	36	4	5	12	12	36	27
		924	219	128	115	787	516	115	128	219	516	787	924

Odds & ends

Double wins: (2) Plymouth, Preston.
Double loses: (3) QP Rangers, Rotherham, Norwich.
Won from behind: (1) Aston Villa (a).
Lost from in front: (4) Huddersfield (h), QP Rangers (a), Hull (a), Norwich (a).
High spots: Beating Bristol Rov on way to 5th Round of the FA Cup. John Galley's hat-trick at Leeds Road on his City debut.
Vital win at the Valley on 20 April.
City's first-ever victory over Aston Villa at their 19th attempt.
Low spots: Dismissal of Fred Ford.
Outplayed by Everton in the League Cup.
Losing 0-5 at Ipswich on 26 August.
Blackpool's 4-2 success at Ashton Gate.
Losing a bruising encounter against Rotherham at Ashton Gate.

Player of the year: John Quigley.
Ever-presents: (0).
Hat-tricks: (1) John Galley.
Leading scorer: John Galley (18).

Appearances and Goals

Player	App Lge	Sub	LC	Sub	FAC	Sub	Goals Lge	LC	FAC	Tot
Bartley, Danny	12	1					1			1
Briggs, Alec	39	6	1		5					
Bush, Terry	20				2		1		1	2
Connor, Jack	41		1		5		2			2
Crowe, Chris	38	1	1		5		7		1	8
Davis, Richard	6									
Derrick, Jantzen	27	1	1		4		2			2
Down, Dickie	1	1								
Ford, Tony	8	1								
Galley, John	21		1		5		16		2	18
Garland, Chris	29	1	1		3		8		1	9
Gibson, Mike	40		1		5					
Jacobs, Trevor	21		1		3		1			1
Low, Gordon	8	2								
McIlmoyle, Hugh	8	1					2			2
Mahoney, Mike	1									
Merrick, Geoff	1									
Parr, Gordon	36		1		5					
Peters, Lou	22		1		2					
Quigley, John	41		1		5		2			2
Savino, Ray	3	1								
Sharpe, Gerry	5	1			1		1			1
Tainton, Trevor	4									
Watling, Barry	1									
Wimshurst, Ken	29				5		3			3
(own-goals)							2			2
25 players used	462	16	11		55		48		5	53

LEAGUE DIVISION 2 — Manager: Alan Dicks — SEASON 1968-69

1. A FULHAM — 10/8
Att 16,572 · Pos — · Pt L, 0 · F-A 0-1 · H-T 0-1
Scorers: Gilroy 8 · Ref: T Dawes

City: 1 Gibson · 2 Jacobs · 3 Briggs · 4 Wimshurst · 5 Connor · 6 Parr · 7 Crowe · 8 Garland · 9 Galley · 10 **Kellard** · 11 Bartley · 12 sub Pentecost
Fulham: Seymour · Ryan · Dempsey · Matthewson · Callaghan · Brown · Haynes* · Conway · Large · Gilroy · Barrett

Fulham, seeking a quick return to Division One, take an early lead when Joe Gilroy slides in a Johnny Haynes pass. City have as much of the play as Fulham in the sunny conditions and should have levelled on the hour when Jacobs fired wide. Bookings for Kellard and Gilroy.

2. H SHEFFIELD UTD — 17/8
Att 19,280 · Pos — · Pt D, 1 · F-A 1-1 · H-T 0-0
Scorers: Galley 68, Addison 60p · Ref: K Wynn

City: Gibson · Briggs · Merrick · Wimshurst · Connor · Parr · Crowe · Garland · Galley · Kellard · Derrick
Sheffield Utd: Hodgkinson · Badger · Shaw · Munks · Mallender · Wagstaff B · Woodward · Carlin · Addison · Currie · Reece

Interest seldom flags in this game, in which City's enthusiasm counters United's greater skill. After Briggs handles to concede a penalty, City level when Galley finishes off Wimshurst's through-ball with a thunderous twelve-yard left-foot drive. Mallender booked for kicking Galley.

3. H BOLTON — 20/8
Att 17,353 · Pos 13 (6) · Pt D, 2 · F-A 2-2 · H-T 1-1
Scorers: Garland 29, Galley 72; Wharton 39, 86 · Ref: M Sinclair

City: Gibson · Jacobs · Merrick* · Wimshurst · Connor · Parr · Crowe · Garland · Galley · Kellard · Derrick · 12 sub Briggs
Bolton: Hopkinson · Ritson · Farrimond · Williams · Hulme · Hatton · Wharton · Hill · Greaves · Bromley · Taylor

An exciting game, which features much good football. Terry Wharton brushes off Derrick's challenge to whip in Bolton's late equaliser and rob City of the win their play deserved. Garland heads in a brilliant opening goal after Bolton are caught out by Wimshurst's quick free-kick.

4. A BLACKPOOL — 24/8
Att 15,767 · Pos 14 (7) · Pt D, 3 · F-A 2-2 · H-T 2-1
Scorers: Garland 34, Kellard 37; Milne 17, Green 66 · Ref: K Burns

City: Gibson · Jacobs · Briggs · Wimshurst · Connor · Parr · Crowe · Garland · Galley · Kellard · Derrick
Blackpool: Taylor · Armfield · Mowbray · Milne · James · McPhee · Skirton · Green · White · Suddick · Hutchison

After missing two easy chances, it is third-time lucky for Garland at Bloomfield Road as his swerving left-foot shot equalises Milne's headed opener. Kellard's 20-yarder gives City the advantage at the interval, but Green races through from the halfway line to fire in a great leveller.

5. A ASTON VILLA — 26/8
Att 17,685 · Pos 16 (15) · Pt L, 3 · F-A 0-1 · H-T 0-0
Scorers: Woodward 73 · Ref: J Osborne

City: Gibson · Jacobs · Briggs · Wimshurst · Connor · Parr · Crowe* · Garland · Galley · Kellard · Sharpe · 12 sub Bush
Aston Villa: Dunn · Wright · Aitken · Edwards · Turnbull · Park · Ferguson · Mitchinson · Woodward · Godfrey* · Rudge* · Greenhaigh

City, on top in the first half, are exasperated by Villa's time-wasting and audacious possession football after the break. Villa are unfortunate when Ferguson's fine shot hits the post, but gain reward when Woodward runs through to score with ease after Godfrey dispossesses Parr.

6. H BLACKBURN — 31/8
Att 19,787 · Pos 16 (6) · Pt W, 5 · F-A 1-0 · H-T 1-0
Scorers: Galley 37 · Ref: J Yates

City: Gibson · Jacobs · Briggs · Wimshurst · Connor · Parr · Crowe · Garland · Galley · Kellard · Sharpe
Blackburn: Blacklaw · Newton · Wilson · Mulvaney · Coddington · Hole · Metcalfe · Rogers · Martin · Darling · Connelly

City's great team effort secures their first win of the season. In an absorbing match Blackburn display most of the poise and skill, but Sharpe is the master of England's Keith Newton. A brilliant Garland header enables Galley to shoot home and take Blackburn's unbeaten record.

7. A HULL — 7/9
Att 12,309 · Pos 15 (14) · Pt D, 6 · F-A 1-1 · H-T 0-0
Scorers: Galley 73; Chilton 56 · Ref: F Cowen

City: Gibson · Jacobs · Briggs · Wimshurst · Connor · Parr · Tainton* · Garland · Galley · Kellard · Sharpe · 12 sub Bush
Hull: McKechnie · Banks · Beardsley · Pettit · Wilson · Greenwood · Jarvis* · Wagstaff · Chilton · Simpkin · Butler I · Houghton

Chilton shoots Hull ahead to punish City for squandering their better chances. Garland, after being brought down, extends City's series of spot-kick failures to five as his tame 53rd-minute effort is easily saved, and shortly afterwards Wimshurst rolls his acute-angled shot against a post.

8. H DERBY — 14/9
Att 15,850 · Pos 17 (13) · Pt D, 7 · F-A 0-0 · H-T 0-0
Ref: R Tinkler

City: Gibson · Jaobs · Briggs · Wimshurst · Connor · Parr · Crowe · Garland · Galley · Kellard · Sharpe
Derby: Green · Webster · Robson · Durban · McFarland · Mackay · Walker · Carlin · O'Hare · Hector · Hinton

An action-packed contest that has everything except goals. Garland leads Dave Mackay a merry dance and might well have scored twice, but for the brilliance of keeper Les Green. Referee Ray Tinkler (Boston) is a replacement for the indisposed Peter Hayward of Bournemouth.

9. A MILLWALL — 16/9
Att 13,079 · Pos 16 (3) · Pt D, 8 · F-A 2-2 · H-T 1-1
Scorers: Wimshurst 44, Garland 72; Cripps 43, Jones 71 · Ref: W Castle

City: Gibson · Jacobs · Briggs · Wimshurst · Connor · Parr · Sharpe · Garland · Galley · Kellard · Bush
Millwall: King · Brown · Cripps · Jones · Kitchener · Barrett · Weller · Jacks · Conlon · Dunphy · Possee

City survive to achieve their sixth draw in an action-packed thriller at Cold Blow Lane. Twice the Lions lead, thanks to a Cripps header and a Jones shot, but on each occasion City level almost from the kick-off. Wimshurst lashes in from 15 yards, and Garland heads in a Briggs cross.

10. A OXFORD — 21/9
Att 13,123 · Pos 16 (14) · Pt D, 9 · F-A 0-0 · H-T 0-0
Ref: R Paine

City: Gibson · Jacobs · Briggs · Wimshurst · Connor · Parr · Sharpe · Garland* · Galley · Bush · Kellard · 12 sub Derrick
Oxford: Barron · Lucas · Beavon · Atkinson R · Kyle · Clarke · Sloan · Atkinson G · Gaston · Evanson* · Harrington · Bullock

City make hard work in claiming a point against opponents reduced to ten men on 69 minutes. Harrington follows earlier casualty Evanson, in being carried off with a suspected fractured leg. Referee fails to spot City substitute Derrick wearing the No 8 shirt throughout the second half.

Football season results table — matches 11–21

#	V	Opponent	Date	Att.	Lge Pos / Opp Pos / Pts	Res	FT	HT
11	H	CARDIFF	28/9	20,632	17 / 6 / 9	L	0-3	0-3
12	A	CHARLTON	5/10	15,394	18 / 7 / 10	D	0-0	0-0
13	H	ASTON VILLA	8/10	15,199	17 / 21 / 12	W	1-0	0-0
14	H	BIRMINGHAM	12/10	19,578	17 / 15 / 13	D	0-0	0-0
15	A	CRYS PALACE	19/10	15,033	17 / 6 / 13	L	1-2	1-0
16	H	PORTSMOUTH	26/10	16,071	16 / 17 / 14	D	2-2	0-1
17	H	HUDDERSFIELD	9/11	13,738	18 / 4 / 14	L	0-1	0-1
18	A	PRESTON	16/11	12,325	19 / 8 / 14	L	0-1	0-0
19	H	NORWICH	23/11	13,824	18 / 16 / 14	L	0-1	0-1
20	A	CARLISLE	30/11	9,263	20 / 13 / 14	L	0-3	0-1
21	A	MIDDLESBROUGH	3/12	18,038	21 / 2 / 14	L	1-4	0-2

11 — CARDIFF (28/9)
City: Gibson, Jacobs, Briggs, Wimshurst, Connor, Parr, Sharpe, Garland, Galley, Bush, Kellard, Derrick
Cardiff: Davies, Derrett, Bell, Sutton, Murray, Harris*, Jones, Clark, King, Toshack, Lea, L-Phillips
Scorers: King 65, Toshack 73, Jones 78
Ref: T Hall
City, unfortunate when a Briggs shot hits the bar just before the break, are surprised by King's brilliant 25-yard strike that puts the visitors ahead. Toshack's header then doubles their advantage, before Jones fires in a 25-yard rocket to set the seal on Cardiff's impressive success.

12 — CHARLTON (5/10)
City: Gibson, Jacobs, Briggs, Wimshurst, Connor, Parr, Sharpe, Garland, Galley, Bush, Kellard, Derrick
Charlton: Wright, Curtis, Kinsey, Campbell, Keirs, Reeves, Hince, Treacy, Gregory, Moore, Peacock*, Went
Ref: M Fussey
City's defence is kept fully extended by top of the table Charlton at the Valley after boss Dicks ignores the claims of Crowe to replace the injured Galley. Kellard and Briggs both make goal-line clearances to deny the Haddicks, who also twice hit the woodwork in the first half.

13 — ASTON VILLA (8/10)
City: Gibson, Jacobs, Briggs, Wimshurst, Connor, Parr, Sharpe, Crowe, Galley, Bush, Kellard, Derrick
Aston Villa: Dunn, Wright, Aitken, Edwards, Turnbull, Hole, Ferguson*, Godfrey, Greenhalgh, Broadbent, Anderson, Martin
Scorers: Kellard 70
Ref: M Kirkhof
City show few ideas to counter negative tactics, as they lack the players to supply pace down the flanks. Connor does well to clear Ferguson's 55th-minute shot off the line, before Kellard's terrific right-foot drive from the edge of the area secures City's first-ever home win over Villa.

14 — BIRMINGHAM (12/10)
City: Gibson, Jacobs*, Briggs, Wimshurst, Connor, Parr, Sharpe, Crowe, Galley, Kellard, Bush, Derrick
Birmingham: Herriot, Martin, Green, Wylie, Robinson, Beard, Hockey, Greenhoff, Vowden, Page, Vincent
Ref: A Oliver
Despite the absence of goals the football is of a constant high standard. Birmingham play an open game, but their high scoring attack is mainly restricted to long shots. In contrast City create many opportunities, but are denied by their own poor finishing and Jim Herriot's good form.

15 — CRYS PALACE (19/10)
City: Gibson, Ford, Briggs, Wimshurst, Connor, Parr, Tainton, Sharpe, Galley, Kellard, Bush, Derrick
Crystal Palace: Jackson J, Hoy, Loughlan, Bannister, McCormick, Blyth*, Lazarus, Kember, Woodruff, Jackson C, Taylor, Sewell
Scorers: Sharpe 17 / Woodruff 70, Lazarus 78
Ref: E Jennings
Against the shock League Cup conquerors of Leeds, City take a deserved lead. Sharpe jabs the ball in from six yards after Jackson fails to hold a low-angle drive. Gibson has no chance with Woodruff's shot from the edge of the area, but City claim foul as Lazarus notches winner.

16 — PORTSMOUTH (26/10)
City: Gibson, Ford, Briggs, Wimshurst, Connor, Parr, Tainton, Sharpe, Galley, Kellard, Bush, Derrick
Portsmouth: Milkins, Youlden, Ley, Smith, Tindall, Harris, Pointer, McCann, Haydock*, Trebilcock, Travers, Jennings
Scorers: Sharpe 56, Galley 72 / Pointer 44, McCann 47
Ref: R Challis
Former England forward Ray Pointer stabs in McCann's cross to give defensive-minded Pompey the lead. After McCann forces the ball over the line, attack-minded City do well to fight back. Sharpe nods ball over the advancing Milkins and later Galley shoots in from eight yards.

17 — HUDDERSFIELD (9/11)
City: Gibson, Ford, Briggs, Wimshurst, Connor, Parr, Sharpe, Garland, Galley, Kellard, Bush, Derrick
Huddersfield: Poole, Smith A, Legg, Nicholson, Ellam, Cherry, Smith S, Lawson, Aimson, McGill, Dobson
Scorers: Smith S 36
Ref: B Daniels
City are unchanged following the midweek friendly at Morton. Despite Garland shooting against a post on 34 minutes, City are unimpressive and give young keeper Poole little to do. After McGill's good play, Stephen Smith fires in a great 20-yard shot for Huddersfield's winner.

18 — PRESTON (16/11)
City: Gibson, Ross, Briggs*, Wimshurst, Connor, Parr, Sharpe, Garland, Galley, Bush, Kellard, Derrick
Preston: Kelly, Ritchie, Ross, McNab, Hawkins, Knighton, Temple, Spavin*, Irvine, Ingram, Gemmill, Hughes
Scorers: Gemmill 69
Ref: R Harper
City are fortunate that the referee ignores Preston's three penalty appeals as their defensive policy comes unstuck. Gemmill crashes the ball in from close range midway through the second half to bring Preston their deserved success. Kelly saves well from Garland near the call of time.

19 — NORWICH (23/11)
City: Gibson, Ford, Briggs, Wimshurst, Connor, Parr, Skirton, Sharpe, Garland, Bush*, Kellard, Derrick
Norwich: Keelan, Stringer, Butler, Howhall, Mallender, Anderson, Fogg, O'Donnell, Manning, Curran, Crickmore, Tainton
Scorers: O'Donnell 4
Ref: W Handley
City play with little conviction and the crowd react with ironic cheers on the infrequent times the ball reaches the wing. With £15,000 Alan Skirton from Blackpool making his debut, City fail to recover after Manning's short pass allows O'Donnell to shoot in from 16 yards.

20 — CARLISLE (30/11)
City: Gibson, Jacobs, Davis, Wimshurst, Connor, Parr, Skirton, Sharpe, Garland, Bush, Kellard, Derrick
Carlisle: Ross, McConnell, Caldwell, Ternent, Passmoor, Garbutt, Barton, Murray, McIlmoyle, Balderstone, McVitie
Scorers: Murray 8, McVitie 50, McIlmoyle 75
Ref: T Hill
City's much-improved performance flounders due to the alert keeping of Alan Ross and some poor finishing. A deceptive scoreline is completed by headers from McVitie and McIlmoyle, after Murray had veered past Connor to drive in a low 18-yarder for Carlisle's opener.

21 — MIDDLESBROUGH (3/12)
City: Gibson, Jacobs, Briggs, Wimshurst*, Connor, Parr, Skirton, Sharpe, Garland, Bush, Kellard, Derrick
Middlesbrough: Whigham, Smith, Jones, Spraggon, Rooks, Kinnell, Chadwick, Hickton, Horsfield, McMordie, Downing, Tainton
Scorers: Sharpe 88 [McMordie 60] / Hickton 19, 41p, Downing 56, McMordie 60
Ref: H Davey
After their praiseworthy attacking policy at Carlisle, City's return to a defensive strategy is suicidal. Hickton, who was unmarked when he lobbed in the opener, nets from the spot after being tripped by Kellard. Boro' are denied top spot by Sharpe, who fires in from 20 yards.

LEAGUE DIVISION 2

Manager: Alan Dicks

Match details

No	Date	Att	Pos	Pt	Res	F-A	H-T	Scorers, Times, and Referees
22 H BURY	7/12	9,664	18	16	20 W	2-1	1-0	Skirton 17, Galley 50 / Collins 72 / Ref: C Nicholls
23 A BIRMINGHAM	14/12	18,958	17	16	20 L	0-2	0-2	Pickering 1, 15 / Ref: A Morrisey
24 H CHARLTON	26/12	17,427	6	18	19 W	2-0	0-0	Sharpe 70, Skirton 73 / Ref: I Jones
25 A PORTSMOUTH	28/12	19,529	13	19	20 D	1-1	0-1	Galley 89 / Brown 4 / Ref: J Finney
26 H MIDDLESBROUGH	11/1	13,696	6	21	19 W	3-0	2-0	Sharpe 28, Galley 37, 70 / Ref: B Homewood
27 A HUDDERSFIELD	18/1	9,059	8	21	20 L	1-4	0-4	Galley 85 / Nic'son 10, Aimson 19, Dobs'n 33p, 42 Poole / Ref: D Laing
28 A CARDIFF	25/1	26,210	3	21	20 L	0-3	0-2	Clark 18, 44, King 61 / Ref: H New
29 H PRESTON	1/2	13,419	17	23	19 W	2-1	0-0	Sharpe 47, Galley 69 / Lee 55 / Ref: T Reynolds
30 H CARLISLE	15/2	13,785	11	25	19 W	3-0	0-0	Garland 47, 55, Sharpe 51 / Ref: K Wynn
31 H CRYS PALACE	25/2	14,695	6	26	19 D	1-1	1-0	Connor 9 / Woodruff 49 / Ref: L Callaghan

Line-ups (City players in normal type, opponents in *italics*)

No	1	2	3	4	5	6	7	8	9	10	11	12 sub used
22	Gibson / *Ramsbottom*	Jacobs / *Parnell*	Briggs / *Saile*	Wimshurst / *Kerr*	Connor / *Turner*	Parr / *Lindsay*	Skirton / *Farrell*	Sharpe / *Jones*	Galley / *Towers*	Kellard / *Collins*	Bartley / *Grundy*	
23	Gibson / *Herriot*	Jacobs / *Martin*	Briggs / *Green*	Wimshurst / *Wylie*	Connor / *Robinson*	Parr / *Page*	Skirton / *Greenhoff*	Sharpe / *Hockey*	Galley / *Pickering*	Kellard / *Vincent**	Derrick* / *Summerill**	Bartley / *Murray*
24	Gibson / *Wright*	Jacobs / *Curtis*	Briggs / *Kinsey*	Wimshurst* / *Campbell*	Connor / *Went*	Parr / *Reeves*	Skirton / *Gregory*	Sharpe / *Booth*	Galley / *Tees*	Kellard / *Moore*	Bartley / *Peacock*	/ *Bush*
25	Gibson / *Milkins*	Jacobs / *Pack*	Briggs / *Ley*	Wimshurst / *Smith*	Connor / *Hand*	Parr / *Youlden*	Skirton / *McCann*	Sharpe* / *Pointer*	Galley / *Brown*	Kellard / *Bromley*	Bartley / *Jennings*	Derrick
26	Gibson / *Whigham*	Jacobs / *Gates*	Briggs / *Smith*	Wimshurst / *Spaggon**	Connor / *Rooks*	Parr / *Kinnell*	Skirton / *Chadwick*	Garland / *Hickton*	Galley / *Horsfield*	Kellard / *McMordie*	Sharpe / *Downing*	Laidlaw
27	Gibson / *Poole*	Smith A / *Legge*	Briggs / *Nicholson*	Wimshurst / *Ellam*	Connor / *Cherry*	Parr / *Dobson*	Skirton / *Lawson*	Garland / *Aimson*	Galley / *McGill*	Kellard / *Hill*	Sharpe	
28	Gibson / *Davies*	Jacobs / *Carver*	Briggs / *Bell*	Wimshurst* / *Sutton*	Connor / *Murray*	Parr / *Derrett*	Skirton / *Jones*	Garland / *Clark*	Galley / *Lea*	Kellard / *Toshack*	Sharpe / *King*	Bush
29	Gibson / *Kelly*	Jacobs / *Ross*	Briggs / *McNab**	Wimshurst / *Spark*	Connor / *Cranston*	Parr / *Heppolette*	Skirton / *Temple*	Garland / *Spavin*	Galley / *Ingram*	Kellard / *Knighton*	Sharpe / *Lee*	Hawkins
30	Gibson / *Ross*	Jacobs / *Marsland*	Briggs / *Caldwell*	Wimshurst / *Ternant*	Connor / *Passmoor*	Parr / *Garbutt*	Skirton / *Barton*	Garland / *Murray*	Galley / *McIlmoyle*	Kellard / *Balderstone*	Sharpe / *McVitie*	
31	Gibson / *Jackson*	Jacobs / *Sewell*	Briggs / *Loughan*	Wimshurst / *Hoy*	Connor / *McCormick*	Parr / *Blyth*	Skirton / *Lazarus*	Garland / *Kember*	Galley / *Woodruff*	Kellard / *Dawkins**	Sharpe / *Taylor T*	/ *Taylor C*

Match notes

22 — Bury: On a dry, cold afternoon, Bury cause City all manner of problems after Collins hits magnificent 25-yard screamer into the top corner of the net. Connor clears a Towers flick off the line as City somewhat fortuitously hold onto the advantage gained by headers from Skirton and Galley.

23 — Birmingham: Pickering beats Gibson with a dipping 20-yarder to put the Blues in front after only 39 seconds, and later doubles their advantage when sliding in a deflection off Connor. In the second half Briggs clears Summerill's effort off the line as City continue to fight a rear-guard action.

24 — Charlton: On a chilly, windy Boxing Day the wing play of Skirton and Bartley inspire City to a convincing win over promotion-chasing Charlton. Bartley centres on the run for Sharpe to head in, and then Skirton outpaces Kinsey to net with a cross-shot into the far corner of the Open End goal.

25 — Portsmouth: For City, who turn out in all white, Gibson – in his white jockey cap, green jersey and maroon tracksuit trousers – is the height of sartorial elegance. Brown puts Pompey ahead when Gibson can only push out Pointer's shot, but City get a deserved late leveller thanks to Galley.

26 — Middlesbrough: City are unable to break their penalty hoodoo after Garland is pushed by Gates. Another change of kicker, but the result the same, as Whigham dives to his right to save Skirton's 71st-minute shot. Galley takes advantage of Kinnell's missed kick to waltz ball in for City's second goal.

27 — Huddersfield: City, after being outplayed at Leeds Road, improve after the break and gain consolation with a late Galley header. Nicholson and Aimson shoot early goals for the Town, before a harsh pen seals City's fate, when Connor is adjudged to have held down Aimson in going for a centre.

28 — Cardiff: City are outplayed by promotion-chasing Cardiff at Ninian Park, where former favourite Brian Clark scores twice. Lea is given offside when he nods in, but no such problem when Clark slides the ball home shortly after. City are well beaten by the time King heads in Toshack's chip.

29 — Preston: Sharpe turns in Garland's centre to give the City a deserved lead at an unusual-looking Ashton Gate, where the spectators are restricted to three sides because of the demolition work for the new stand. Galley runs in City's winner after Lee's low shot produces North End's equaliser.

30 — Carlisle: Carlisle are unable to improve their impressive away record, despite their superior play prior to half-time. City stun the Cumbrians with quick goals after the break. Skirton's good play gives Garland time and space to stroke the ball home, and then sets up Sharpe's near-post header.

31 — Crystal Palace: John Jackson denies City in the first half, except when Connor hurls himself forward to head in from Garland. The tactical substitution of a defender for an attacker at the break changes the complexion of the game. Clive Taylor sets up Woodruff's right-footed strike from 16 yards.

32 — H FULHAM — 1/3
Att 15,715 · 18 · W · **6-0** · 22 · 28
Scorers: Garl'd 6, 85, Ryan 27 (og), Skirton 38p, [Sharpe, 44, Galley 88]
Ref: C Thomas
City: Gibson, Jacobs, Briggs, Wimshurst, Connor, Parr, Skirton, Garland, Galley, Kellard, Sharpe
Fulham: Williamson, Cohen, Ryan, Tranter, Matthews'n* Horne, Jones, Lloyd, Dear, Haynes, Brown, Earle
A St David's Day spectacular on a cold, windy afternoon at Ashton Gate as relegation-threatened Fulham are overwhelmed. At last City break their pen hoodoo, after Williamson grabs Garland around the legs. Skirton ends City's two-year barren spell with a kick to the keeper's right.

33 — A SHEFFIELD UTD — 8/3
Att 14,887 · 19 · L · 1-2 · 9 · 28
Sharpe 55
Salmons 15, Tudor 64
Ref: J Taylor
City: Gibson, Jacobs, Briggs, Wimshurst, Connor, Parr, Skirton, Garland, Broomfield, Kellard, Sharpe
Sheffield Utd: Hodgkinson, Badger, Heaton, Hemsley, Colquhoun, Powell, Woodward, Currie, Tudor, Salmons, Reece
Alan Hodgkinson, who marks his 500th League appearance by being captain for the day, is not much troubled by City's attack in a poor game. After Sharpe shoots in from a corner to level a drive by Salmons, the contest is settled by Tudor, who reacts quickest to stab home a loose ball.

34 — H BLACKPOOL — 15/3
Att 16,060 · 18 · D · 1-1 · 11 · 29
Galley 34
Suddick 67
Ref: R Challis
City: Gibson, Jacobs, Briggs, Wimshurst, Connor, Parr, Skirton, Garland, Galley, Kellard, Sharpe
Blackpool: Taylor, Armfield, Bentley, Craven, James, McPhee, Brown, White, Green, Milne, Suddick
A gift Blackpool equaliser, as Suddick has the simple task of shooting into an empty net after Gibson fails to hold Parr's back-pass. City deservedly take the lead when an alert Galley runs in at the far post to slide home a Garland cross-shot that appeared to be going wide.

35 — A BLACKBURN — 22/3
Att 7,566 · 17 · W · 3-1 · 14 · 31
Galley 33, 73, Derrick 62
Martin 13
Ref: D Corbett
City: Gibson, Jacobs, Briggs, Wimshurst, Connor, Parr, Skirton*, Garland, Galley, Kellard, Sharpe, Derrick
Blackburn: Blacklaw, Kopel, Wilson*, Newton, Coddington, Mulvaney, Metcalfe, Martin, Fryatt, Rogers, Connelly, Darling
Against a Blackburn side including new signing Frank Kopel, City pull off their first away win of the season. After Martin's early header, City equalise when the ball rebounds off a post and ends up in the net via Galley's shins. Derrick's superb left-foot 20-yarder is a goal all the way.

36 — A NORWICH — 26/3
Att 8,682 · 17 · D · 1-1 · 16 · 32
Kellard 69p
Foggo 52
Ref: K Markham
City: Gibson, Jacobs, Briggs, Wimshurst, Connor, Parr, Derrick, Garland, Galley, Kellard, Sharpe
Norwich: Vasper, Stringer, Butler, Howshall, Mallender, Forbes, Foggo, Bennett, Conlon, Lucas, Crickmore* Anderson
Disgust at a pathetic display by players and officials alike elicits angry protests from the fans. Cushions are hurled from the stands at the end of this bore of a game. Derrick is unlucky to have his 15th-min header struck off, but a late tackle on Sharpe brings City their penalty equaliser.

37 — H HULL — 29/3
Att 13,105 · 15 · D · 1-1 · 12 · 33
Connor 41
Jarvis 73
Ref: K Walker
City: Gibson, Jacobs, Briggs, Wimshurst, Connor, Parr, Derrick, Garland, Galley, Kellard, Sharpe
Hull: McKechnie, Banks, Beardsley, Jarvis, Pettit, Simpkin, Greenwood* Lord, Wilkinson, Wagstaff, Butler I, Butler D
A game littered with mistakes on a hard surface, with City's square defence frequently catching the Tigers offside. Connor, at the near post, heads Kellard's corner just inside the far post, but Hull equalise when a defender deflects a Jarvis shot, from the edge of the area, over the line.

38 — A BOLTON — 7/4
Att 8,172 · 17 · L · 0-1 · 19 · 33
Byrom 38
Ref: J Hunting
City: Gibson, Jacobs, Briggs, Wimshurst, Connor, Parr, Crowe, Garland, Galley, Kellard*, Derrick
Bolton: Hopkinson, Cooper, Farrimond, Williams, Hulme, Marsh, Wharton, Greaves, Byrom, Rimmer, Phillips, Tainton
City are made to pay for their one defensive lapse against a Bolton side with only one win from their previous 15 games. Byrom does the damage by supplying the second header to Cooper's free-kick after Wharton is fouled. Hopkinson does well to tip over Galley's overhead kick.

39 — H MILLWALL — 8/4
Att 14,382 · 18 · D · 0-0 · 6 · 34
Ref: D Lloyd
City: Gibson, Jacobs, Briggs, Wimshurst, Connor, Parr, Skirton, Garland, Galley, Kellard, Sharpe
Millwall: Standen, Brown B, Burnett, Jacks, Kitchener, Dorney, Possee, Jones, Peterson, Bolland, Dunphy
An undistinguished end to the Easter holiday as City fail to take their chances in a moderate encounter. The chapter of wasted opportunities begins as early as the third minute when Sharpe shoots wide of an open goal and ends in the dying seconds as Galley's snap-shot hits the post.

40 — H OXFORD — 12/4
Att 11,457 · 17 · W · 2-0 · 20 · 36
Galley 74, 85
Ref: J Lewis
City: Gibson, Ford, Briggs, Wimshurst, Connor, Parr, Skirton, Garland, Galley, Kellard, Sharpe
Oxford: Barron, Beavan, Gladwin, Atkinson R, Clarke, Higgins*, Sloan, Shuker, Skeen, Atkinson G, Harrington, Hatch
City do most of the attacking in the first half, but the nearest they come to a goal is when Clarke almost puts into his own net with a back pass to Barron. United, with the advantage of the wind, look more dangerous after the break, but Galley's two late shots clinch City's victory.

41 — A BURY — 15/4
Att 6,020 · 15 · W · 2-1 · 21 · 38
Galley 36, Sharpe 68
Arrowsmith 16
Ref: M Fussey
City: Gibson, Jacobs, Briggs, Kellard, Connor, Parr, Skirton, Garland, Galley, Sharpe, Wimshurst
Bury: Forrest, Parnell, Tilley, Anderson, Turner, Parry, Farrell, Collins*, Arrowsmith, Kerr, Bartley* Jones
After Bury go ahead with a superb volley, Galley's header and a cracking shot by Sharpe condemn the Shakers to relegation. Arrowsmith is left to rue missing an open goal in the second min and having a 15th-minute pen saved by Gibson, after Connor had handled on the goal-line.

42 — A DERBY — 19/4
Att 31,644 · 16 · L · **0-5** · 1 · 38
Durban 17, 32, 44, Hinton 54, [Hector 88]
Ref: F Cowan
City: Watling, Jacobs, Briggs, Wimshurst, Connor, Parr, Skirton, Garland, Bartley, Kellard, Sharpe
Derby: Green, Webster, Robson, Durban, McFarland, Mackay, McGovern, Carlin, O'Hare, Hector, Hinton
Footballer of the Year Dave Mackay carries the Championship trophy as Derby take the field. The rampaging Rams go in front when Durban heads in after Kellard had cleared off the line. Wating punches Hinton's fierce 79th-minute pen over the bar after O'Hare is tackled by Briggs.

Home 15,463 · Away 14,729 · Average 14,729

LEAGUE DIVISION 2 (CUP-TIES)   Manager: Alan Dicks   SEASON 1968-69

League Cup

		F-A	H-T	1	2	3	4	5	6	7	8	9	10	11	12 sub used
1	H NEWPORT 14/8	W 2-0	1-0	Gibson	Jacobs	Briggs	Wimshurst	Connor	Parr	Derrick	Garland*	Galley	Kellard	Bartley	Bush
				Weare	*Williams D*	*Wilson*	*Cooper*	*Wood*	*Rowland*	*McClelland*	*Hill*	*Buck*	*Jones*	*Thomas*	

Scorers, Times, and Referees: Galley 36, Garland 48. 9,763. Ref: T. Lockett

Newport looked quite capable of emulating Swansea's shock victory at Eastville the previous evening, until a wonder goal quells their spirit. Garland turns as he is falling on the by-line and hits the ball into goal off the far post. Kellard's chip to Galley produces City's headed opener.

		F-A	H-T	1	2	3	4	5	6	7	8	9	10	11	12 sub used
2	H MIDDLESBROUGH 16 4/9	W 1-0	0-0	Gibson	Jacobs	Briggs	Wimshurst	Connor	Parr	Crowe	Garland	Galley	Kellard	Sharpe	Chadwick
				Whigham	*Smith*	*Jones*	*Gates*	*Rooks*	*Myton*	*Kear*	*McMordie*	*Hickton*	*Horsfield**	*Downing*	

Scorers, Times, and Referees: Galley 84. 13,918 / 5. Ref: R. Paine

An unexpected win for City as triumph turns into tragedy for Willie Whigham. Lauded for saving Wimshurt's seventh-min pen, after Sharpe is tripped by Smith, he later gifts Galley an easy tap-in, when failing to complete an easy catch. Boro's defensive tactics reap a just reward.

		F-A	H-T	1	2	3	4	5	6	7	8	9	10	11	12 sub used
3	A LEEDS 16 25/9	L 1-2	0-1	Gibson	Jacobs	Briggs*	Wimshurst	Connor	Parr	Bush	Garland	Galley	Crowe	Kellard	Derrick
				Sprake	*Reaney*	*Cooper*	*Bremner*	*Madeley*	*Gray*	*O'Grady*	*Lorimer*	*Jones*	*Giles*	*Johanneson*	

Scorers, Times, and Referees: Garland 70 / Johanneson 40, Jones 63. 16,359 / 1:1. Ref: S. Kayley

City are often mesmerised by a brilliant Leeds side. Bremner's pass inside of Briggs allows Johanneson to crash the ball in from ten yards, but the Peacocks relax after Jones volleys in their second. City make belated efforts to save the game after Garland rams in from Crowe's pass.

FA Cup

		F-A	H-T	1	2	3	4	5	6	7	8	9	10	11	12 sub used
3	A WEST HAM 20 4/1	L 2-3	1-1	Gibson	Jacobs	Briggs	Wimshurst	Connor	Parr	Skirton	Garland	Galley	Kellard	Sharpe	
				Ferguson	*Bonds*	*Charles*	*Cushley*	*Stephenson*	*Moore*	*Redknapp*	*Boyce*	*Hurst*	*Lindsay*	*Peters*	

Scorers, Times, and Referees: Galley 11, Skirton 88 / Peters 15, 64, Hurst 52. 32,526 / 1:6. Ref: E. Jennings

All-action City shock the Hammers with their high standard of play. Peters heads in West Ham's equaliser from Redknapp's corner after Galley, looking suspiciously offside, turns Skirton's centre over the line. Hurst hooks the ball over Gibson to put the Hammers in front.

Football League Division Two

		P	Home					Away					Pts
			W	D	L	F	A	W	D	L	F	A	
1	Derby	42	16	4	1	43	16	10	7	4	22	16	63
2	Crys Palace	42	14	4	3	45	24	8	8	5	25	23	56
3	Charlton	42	11	8	2	39	21	7	6	8	22	31	50
4	Middlesbro	42	13	7	1	36	13	6	4	11	22	36	49
5	Cardiff	42	13	3	5	38	19	7	4	10	29	35	47
6	Huddersfield	42	13	6	2	37	14	4	6	11	16	32	46
7	Birmingham	42	13	3	5	52	24	5	5	11	21	35	44
8	Blackpool	42	9	8	4	33	20	5	7	9	18	21	43
9	Sheffield Utd	42	14	4	3	41	15	2	7	12	20	35	43
10	Millwall	42	10	5	6	33	23	7	4	10	24	26	43
11	Hull	42	10	7	4	38	20	3	9	9	21	32	42
12	Carlisle	42	10	5	6	25	17	6	5	10	21	32	42
13	Norwich	42	7	6	8	24	25	8	4	9	29	41	40
14	Preston	42	8	8	5	23	19	4	7	10	15	25	39
15	Portsmouth	42	11	5	5	39	22	1	9	11	19	36	38
16	BRISTOL CITY	42	8	8	5	30	15	3	7	12	16	38	38
17	Bolton	42	8	7	6	29	26	4	7	10	26	41	38
18	Aston Villa	42	10	8	3	22	11	2	6	13	15	37	38
19	Blackburn	42	9	6	6	30	24	4	5	12	22	39	37
20	Oxford	42	8	5	8	21	23	4	4	13	13	32	33
21	Bury	42	8	4	9	35	33	3	4	14	16	47	30
22	Fulham	42	6	7	8	20	28	1	4	16	20	53	25
		924	230	129	103	733	452	103	129	230	452	733	924

Appearances and Goals

	Appearances						Goals			Tot
	Lge	Sub	LC	Sub	FAC	Sub	Lge	LC	FAC	
Bartley, Danny	6	2	1							
Briggs, Alec	39		3		1					
Broomfield, Ian	1									
Bush, Terry	7	5	1	1		1				
Connor, Jack	42		3		1		2			2
Crowe, Chris	10		2							
Davis, Richard	1									
Derrick, Jantzen	16	4	1	1		1	1			1
Ford, Tony	5									
Galley, John	39		3		1		19	2	1	22
Garland, Chris	31		3		1		6	2		8
Gibson, Mike	41		3		1					
Jacobs, Trevor	37		3		1					
Kellard, Bobby	42		3		1		3			3
Merrick, Geoff	2									
Parr, Gordon	42		3		1					
Sharpe, Gerry	36		1		1		10			10
Skirton, Alan	21				1		3		1	4
Tainton, Trevor	3	3								
Wating, Barry	1									
Wimshurst, Ken	40	1	3		1		1			1
(own-goals)							1			1
21 players used	462	15	33	2	11		46	4	2	52

Odds & ends

Double Wins: (2) Blackburn, Bury.

Double Losses: (2) Cardiff, Huddersfield.

Won from behind: (2) Blackburn (a), Bury (a).

Lost from in front: Crystal Palace (a).

High spots: Exciting 3-3 home clash with Hull.
3-0 home win v Middlesbrough on 11 January.
Demolition of Fulham 6-0 at Ashton Gate.
The all-action play of Bobby Kellard.
Beating Bristol Rov 5-0 (a) in the Gloucestershire Cup Final on 28 Apr.

Low spots: Only scoring five goals in twelve League games from 21 September to 3 December.
Negative tactics at Middlesbrough that reap their just reward.
Pathetic performance, devoid of skill or effort, at Norwich.
Annihilation by the Champions at Derby.

Player of the year: Bobby Kellard.

Ever-presents: (3) Jack Connor, Bobby Kellard, Gordon Parr.

Hat-tricks: (0).

Leading scorer: John Galley (22).

LEAGUE DIVISION 2

Manager: Alan Dicks

SEASON 1969-70

No	Date	Venue / Opponent	F-A	H-T	Att	Pos	Pt	Scorers, Times, and Referees	1	2	3	4	5	6	7	8	9	10	11	12 sub used
1	9/8	H WATFORD	W 1-0	1-0	19,362		2	Galley 32 — Ref: A Jones	Gibson	Jacobs	Drysdale	Clarke	Rooks	Parr	Skirton	Garland	Galley	Kellard	Sharpe	
		Watford							*Walker*	*Welbourne*	*Williams*	*Eddy*	*Garvey*	*Lees*	*Scullion*	*Hale*	*Garbett*	*Green*	*Lewis**	*Sinclair*
2	16/8	A HULL	L 0-2	0-0	10,170		2	Chilton 79, Blampey 84 — Ref: S Kayley	Gibson	Jacobs	Drysdale	Clarke	Rooks	Parr	Skirton	Garland*	Galley	Derrick	Bush	
		Hull							*Walker*	*McKechnie*	*Banks**	*Butler D*	*Jarvis*	*Simpkin*	*Blampey*	*Wagstaff*	*Chilton*	*Houghton*	*Butler I*	*Wilkinson*
3	23/8	H CARDIFF	L 0-2	0-0	23,237	18	2	Clark 74, Bird 82p — Ref: M Sinclair	Gibson	Jacobs	Drysdale	Merrick	Rooks	Parr	Skirton	Garland	Galley	Kellard*	Sharpe	
		Cardiff							*Davies*	*Carver*	*Bell*	*King*	*Murray*	*Harris*	*Jones*	*Clark*	*Lea*	*Toshack*	*Bird*	*Connor*
4	26/8	A SHEFFIELD UTD	L 1-2	1-2	15,539	19	2	Tainton 20 / Connor 4 (og), Tudor 15 — Ref: W Castle	Gibson	Jacobs	Drysdale	Merrick*	Connor	Parr	Tainton	Garland	Galley	Derrick	Sharpe	
		Sheffield Utd							*Hodgkinson*	*Badger*	*Heaton*	*Barlow*	*Colquhoun*	*Powell*	*Woodward*	*Addison*	*Tudor*	*Currie*	*Reece*	*Clarke*
5	30/8	A HUDDERSFIELD	L 0-3	0-2	10,206	20	2	Hoy 19, Briggs 37 (og), Dobson 70 — Ref: R Johnson	Gibson	Briggs	Drysdale	Menmuir*	Rooks	Bush	Skirton	Garland	Galley	Derrick	Sharpe	
		Huddersfield							*Poole*	*Clarke*	*Hutt*	*Nicholson*	*Ellam*	*Cherry*	*Hoy*	*Lawson*	*Worthington*	*McGill*	*Dobson*	*Tainton*
6	6/9	H PRESTON	D 0-0	0-0	13,740	20	3	Ref: A Oliver	Gibson	Briggs	Drysdale	Tainton	Rooks	Parr	Skirton	Garland	Galley	Derrick	Sharpe	
		Preston							*Kelly*	*Ross*	*Ritchie*	*Heppolette*	*Hawkins*	*McNab*	*Wilson*	*Irvine*	*Ingram*	*Gemmill*	*Lee*	
7	13/9	A MIDDLESBROUGH	L 0-2	0-2	14,513	21	3	Downing 3, Smith A 45 — Ref: R Matthewson	Gibson	Briggs	Drysdale	Tainton	Rooks	Parr	Skirton	Garland	Galley	Derrick	Kellard	
		Middlesbrough							*Short*	*Smith A*	*Jones*	*Smith G*	*Gates*	*Spraggon*	*Lugg*	*McMordie*	*Webb*	*Hickton*	*Downing*	
8	20/9	H NORWICH	W 4-0	1-0	11,879	21	5	Galley 2, 64, Skirton 62, Bartley 80 — Ref: R Darlington	Gibson	Ford	Drysdale	Tainton	Rooks	Parr	Skirton	Garland	Galley	Kellard	Bartley	
		Norwich							*Keelan*	*Stringer*	*Butler*	*Mallender*	*Forbes*	*Anderson*	*Foggo*	*Bryceland*	*Silvester*	*Bennett*	*Howshall**	*Crickmore*
9	23/9	H CHARLTON	W 6-0	2-0	15,098	18	7	Skirton 2, 58, Galley 24, 65, 87, Bartley 88 [Bartley 88] — Ref: C Thomas	Gibson	Ford*	Drysdale	Tainton	Rooks	Parr	Skirton	Garland	Galley	Kellard	Bartley	
		Charlton							*Burns*	*Curtis*	*Kinsey*	*Campbell*	*Keirs*	*Reeves*	*Kenning*	*Gilchrist*	*Crawford*	*Moore*	*Peacock*	*Briggs*
10	27/9	A MILLWALL	D 1-1	1-1	11,406	18	8	Standen 22 (og) / Possee 7 — Ref: K Wynn	Gibson	Briggs	Drysdale	Wimshurst	Rooks	Bush	Skirton	Garland	Galley	Tainton	Kellard	
		Millwall							*Standen*	*Nicholls*	*Cripps*	*Dorney*	*Kitchener*	*Burnett*	*Possee*	*Dunphy*	*Weller*	*Bolland**	*Alder*	*Neil*

Match commentaries

1. For their first-ever Second Division game, Watford have Endean and Walley suspended. Green's shot hits the post for the Hornets on 27 mins, while shortly after Eddy clears Galley's effort off the line. A fine move ends with Galley's superb header that is worthy of winning any game.

2. City are rather fortunate in the 14th minute when Chilton is ruled to have pushed his way past Rooks and Parr before firing in a superb goal. Coming more into the contest after the break, City are undone when Wagstaff's brilliant run down the right leaves Chilton a simple tap-in.

3. The nearest to a goal, in the opening 45 incident-packed mins of this game, are when a shot by Lea and a header by Galley hit the woodwork. Clark breaks the deadlock by heading in Bird's corner at the near post and then Parr's blatant unnecessary handball gifts Cardiff their penalty.

4. Injury again disrupts the career of the luckless Merrick as he dislocates his left elbow in the 32nd minute. United are rampant after Connor flicks the ball into his own net and Tudor's header, but Tainton shoots in off the far post to inspire a fight-back that has the Blades hanging on.

5. After Worthington's low centre is flicked in by Hoy, City concede their third own-goal of the campaign as Lawson's effort strikes Briggs on the head before trickling over the line. Dobson looks yards offside when receiving ball from McGill, before driving the third goal past Gibson.

6. Garland is unfortunate in the 43rd minute when his left-foot shot from Sharpe's pull-back is disallowed for offside against the winger. City create and waste many chances in the first half, but find Preston more resolute after the break as the game drifts along in a rather aimless way.

7. Alec Smith foils City's spirited first-half comeback by firing in from ten yards when Drysdale fails to clear. After Downing's magnificent six-yard header from Lugg's free-kick, City are frustrated by their own poor finishing as they sink into a relegation position for the first time.

8. Galley's simple headed goal, as Keelan and Forbes miss Ford's long centre, inspires City. The substitution of Derrick (City's best player) is greeted with much booing and slow hand-clapping, before Skirton shoots into the corner of the net from twelve yards two minutes later.

9. This surely can't last as City take their goal tally to ten in two matches. After Skirton nods the ball back, Galley hits a tremendously powerful ten-yard volley for City's opener. Charlton's harassed defenders are relieved to hear the final whistle as City receive the acclaim of their fans.

10. Jim Standen, playing his first game after finishing cricket with Worcestershire, gives City a helping hand. In his attempt to deal with Kellard's corner, he only succeeds in putting the ball in his own net. Possee's delicate header from Burnett's free-kick gives the Lions an early lead.

No		Team	Date	Att			Res	Score		HT	Scorers / Opponent scorers	Referee
11	H	BIRMINGHAM	4/10	18,694	15	13	W	2-0	10	0-0	Garland 86, Galley 90	Ref: V Batty
12	H	HULL	7/10	18,132	12	13	W	3-1	12	1-0	Garland 23, Skirton 52, Galley 86 — Chilton 54	Ref: R Kirkpatrick
13	A	PORTSMOUTH	11/10	14,900	12	18	D	0-0	13	0-0		Ref: B Daniels
14	A	LEICESTER	18/10	25,954	15	5	L	0-2	13	0-1	Fern 32, Glover 87	Ref: K Styles
15	H	CARLISLE	25/10	15,161	15	7	D	0-0	14	0-0		Ref: G Hartley
16	A	BOLTON	1/11	6,757	15	16	L	1-3	14	0-1	Sharpe 80 — Rooks 36 (og), Byrom 65, Wharton 78	Ref: R Capey
17	H	ASTON VILLA	8/11	16,165	13	22	W	1-0	16	1-0	Skirton 44	Ref: H New
18	H	OXFORD	11/11	10,698	13	14	W	2-0	18	1-0	Garland 18, Bartley 83	Ref: E Wallace
19	H	QP RANGERS	15/11	18,893	10	3	W	2-0	20	1-0	Bush 29, Garland 78	Ref: K Wynn
20	A	BLACKBURN	22/11	13,307	11	2	D	3-3	21	1-1	Sharpe 12, 75, Bush 49 — Darling 2, Rogers 69, Martin 82p	Ref: R Paine
21	H	BLACKPOOL	29/11	14,818	9	8	W	2-1	23	1-0	Rooks 35, Sharpe 74 — Hutchison 85	Ref: B Homewood

11. H BIRMINGHAM
City: Gibson, Ford, Drysdale, Rooks, Parr, Spiring*, Garland, Galley, Kellard, Bartley, Wimshurst
Opponents: Herriot, Martin, Thompson, Robinson, Pendrey, Murray, Hockey, Hateley, Vincent, Summerill
In a game largely confined to midfield, both sides find it difficult to make progress. Garland, thwarted on 17 minutes as his powerful header is saved, makes a breakthrough near the end. He fires in his first goal of the season, before Galley's header secures a third-successive home win.

12. H HULL
City: Gibson, Ford, Drysdale, Rooks, Parr, Skirton, Garland, Galley, Kellard, Bartley, Wimshurst
Opponents: McKechnie/Banks, Butler D, Barker, Simpkin, Wilkinson, Lord, Chilton*, Houghton, Butler I, Greenwood
After Chilton heads enterprising Hull back into the game, City have reason to be relieved when the popular referee Roger Kirkpatrick penalises Pettit for handling Kellard's cross. Unfortunately Skirton drives his spot-kick well wide and it needs Galley's late header to clinch the points.

13. A PORTSMOUTH
City: Gibson, Ford, Drysdale, Rooks, Parr, Skirton, Garland, Broomfield, Kellard, Bartley
Opponents: Mikins/Travers, Ley/Pointer, Hand, Harris, Trebilcock, Hiron, McCann, Bromley, Jennings
Against a Pompey side seeking to improve on their dismal return of just three points at home this season, City's decision to extend their attacking football to away games is understandable. Unfortunately glaring misses by Broomfield and Skirton means a goalless afternoon.

14. A LEICESTER
City: Gibson, Ford, Drysdale, Rooks, Parr, Skirton, Garland, Galley, Kellard, Tainton
Opponents: Shilton, Rodrigues, Nish, Roberts, Cross, Farrington, Fern, Brown, Gibson, Glover
City revert to a defensive line-up with Wimshurst as sweeper. Just after Galley's header is ruled offside, Brown twice suffers as his 73rd-min shot is disallowed and later the officials fail to note his header is over the line. Fern climbs above three defenders to head in Farrington's cross.

15. H CARLISLE
City: Gibson, Ford, Drysdale, Rooks, Parr, Skirton, Garland, Galley, Kellard, Bartley, Wimshurst
Opponents: Ross, Hemstead, Caldwell, Passmoor, Winstanley, Balderstone, Barton, Brown, Hatton, Ternent, Murray
Garland is unlucky early on when his 18-yard left-foot shot on the turn crashes against the bar. Carlisle illustrate, with their neat football, why they are so highly placed in the table, but they are fortunate to survive a second-half barrage. At the death Tainton slices a good chance wide.

16. A BOLTON
City: Wilson, Drysdale, Wimshurst, Rooks, Parr, Skirton, Garland, Sharpe, Kellard*, Tainton, Merrick
Opponents: Hopkinson, Ritson, Hallows, Williams, Hurley, Marsh, Wharton, Byrom, Greaves, Rimmer, Taylor
City never really recover after Rooks pokes the ball past loan keeper Wilson, just two minutes after Parr had cleared Byrom's shot off the line. Sharpe's low 15-yard drive elicits a belated City response, after Byrom's narrow-angled shot and Wharton's stab in from Drysdale's back-pass.

17. H ASTON VILLA
City: Gibson, Ford, Drysdale, Rooks, Parr, Skirton, Garland, Bush, Kellard, Bartley
Opponents: Phillips, Wright, Aitken, Hole, Rioch N, Edwards, McMahon, Godfrey, Martin*, Rioch B, Anderson, Simmonds
Mike Gibson has to have a pain-killing injection in his left shoulder before making a welcome return to the City team. On a blustery afternoon the standard of play is poor, but Skirton's powerful header gives City the lead. In the dying moments Bush's thundering drive hits the crossbar.

18. H OXFORD
City: Gibson, Jacobs, Drysdale, Rooks, Parr, Skirton*, Garland, Bush, Kellard, Bartley, Sharpe
Opponents: Barron, Lucas, Gladwin, Smithson, Clarke, Shuker*, Evanson, Atkinson G, Skeen, Harrington, Atkinson R, Thompson
Gibson is City's saviour as his superb performance prevents the always likely prospect of a shock result. Garland, named as deputy keeper just before the start, has an inspired 15-minute period during which time he has two shots saved as well as registering with a gem of a header.

19. H QP RANGERS
City: Gibson, Jacobs, Drysdale, Rooks, Parr, Skirton, Garland, Bush, Kellard, Bartley, Sharpe
Opponents: Kelly/Watson, Harris, Hunt, Mobley*, Hazell, Bridges, Leach, Clarke F, Marsh, Clarke C, Clement
City demonstrate that they are really on the up with this win over high-flying Rangers, who do not really threaten until the last quarter. Bush times his jump to perfection when sending a dropping header over Kelly, and Garland effortlessly slots the ball home after taking a return pass.

20. A BLACKBURN
City: Gibson, Jacobs, Drysdale, Rooks, Parr, Skirton, Garland, Sharpe, Kellard, Bartley
Opponents: Blacklaw, Kopel, Wilson, Hunter, Mulvaney, Knighton, Metcalfe, Connelly, Martin, Rogers, Darling
After Darling's powerful ten-yard opener and Sharpe's equalising shot, City have to thank Gibson for maintaining parity until half-time. Bush heads City in front just after the break, but Parr's handball enables Rovers to obtain the very least they deserve, as Martin nets from the spot.

21. H BLACKPOOL
City: Gibson, Jacobs, Drysdale, Rooks, Parr, Skirton, Garland, Sharpe, Kellard, Bartley
Opponents: Thomson, Armfield, Mowbray, McPhee, Hatton, James, Rowe, Brown*, Pickering, Suddick, Hutchison, Bentley
City, who are in command throughout, have the ball in the Blackpool net in the 27th minute, but Sharpe is ruled offside. Rooks times his jump perfectly to head in Bartley's corner, and Sharpe coolly drives the ball in from eight yards before Hutchison hooks in Suddick's cross in reply.

LEAGUE DIVISION 2   Manager: Alan Dicks   SEASON 1969-70

No	Date		1	2	3	4	5	6	7	8	9	10	11	12 sub used
22	A SWINDON 6/12		Gibson	Jacobs	Drysdale	Tainton	Rooks	Parr	Skirton	Garland	Galley	Kellard	Bartley	
			Downsboro'	*Thomas*	*Trollope*	*Butler*	*Burrows*	*Harland*	*Heath*	*Smart*	*Horsfield*	*Noble*	*Rogers*	
23	H MIDDLESBROUGH 13/12		Gibson	Jacobs	Drysdale	Tainton	Rooks	Parr	Skirton	Garland	Galley	Sharpe	Bartley	
			Whigham	*Smith A*	*Jones*	*Smith G*	*Gates*	*Spraggon*	*Downing*	*Laidlaw*	*McImoyle*	*Hickton*	*Allen*	
24	H HUDDERSFIELD 27/12		Gibson	Jacobs	Drysdale	Tainton	Rooks	Parr	Skirton	Garland	Galley*	Sharpe	Bush	
			Poole	*Clarke*	*Hutt*	*Nicholson*	*Ellam*	*Cherry*	*Smith*	*Lawson*	*Worthington*	*McGill*	*Chapman*	
25	A CARDIFF 29/12		Gibson	Jacobs	Drysdale	Tainton	Rooks	Parr	Skirton	Garland	Bush	Sharpe	Bartley	
			Davies	*Carver*	*Bell*	*Sutton*	*Murray*	*Woodruff*	*King*	*Clark*	*Harris*	*Tostack*	*Bird*	
26	A NORWICH 10/1		Gibson	Jacobs	Drysdale	Tainton	Rooks	Merrick	Skirton	Garland	Bush	Sharpe	Bartley*	Wimshurst
			Vasper	*Butler*	*Black*	*Stringer*	*Forbes*	*Lucas*	*Briggs*	*Conlon*	*Silvester*	*Paddon*	*Fogo*	
27	H MILLWALL 17/1		Gibson	Jacobs	Drysdale	Wimshurst	Rooks	Parr	Sharpe	Garland	Bush	Kellard	Bartley*	Tainton
			King	*Brown*	*Cripps*	*Dorney*	*Kitchener*	*Burnett*	*Possee*	*Dunphy*	*Weller*	*Bolland*	*Neil*	
28	A PRESTON 24/1		Gibson	Jacobs	Drysdale	Wimshurst	Rooks	Parr	Skirton*	Garland	Bush	Kellard	Sharpe	Tainton
			Kelly	*Ross*	*Ritchie*	*Heppolette*	*McNab*	*Spark*	*Lee*	*Spavin*	*Hawkins*	*Gemmill*	*Clark*	
29	A BIRMINGHAM 31/1		Gibson	Jacobs	Drysdale	Wimshurst	Rooks	Parr	Skirton	Garland	Bush	Kellard	Sharpe	
			Herriot	*Martin*	*Thomson*	*Page*	*Robinson*	*Beard*	*Murray*	*Vincent*	*Hateley*	*Hockey*	*Summerill*	
30	H PORTSMOUTH 7/2		Gibson	Jacobs	Drysdale	Wimshurst	Rooks	Parr	Skirton	Garland	Bush	Kellard	Sharpe	
			Milkins	*Hand*	*Travers*	*Pointer*	*Harris**	*McCann*	*Munks*	*Storrie*	*Hiron*	*Bromley*	*Ley*	
31	A WATFORD 14/2		Gibson	Jacobs	Drysdale	Wimshurst	Rooks	Parr	Skirton	Garland	Bush	Kellard	Sharpe	
			Walker	*Welbourne*	*Williams*	*Lugg*	*Lees*	*Whalley*	*Scullion*	*Garbett*	*Endean*	*Packer*	*Owen*	

Scorers, Times, and Referees / Match details

No	Scorers, Times, and Referees	Att	Pos	Pt	F-A	H-T
22	Burrows 25 (og); *Horsfield 72*; Ref: T Reynolds	23,522	9 *6*	D 24	1-1	1-0
23	Ref: D Corbett	15,290	9 *10*	D 25	0-0	0-0
24	Skirton 43; *Rooks 7 (og), Worthington 84*; Ref: J Lewis	20,541	10 *3*	L 25	1-2	1-1
25	*Toshack 90*; Ref: D Pugh	18,479	11 *4*	L 25	0-1	0-0
26	Garland 52; *Silvester 26, 90, Conlon 50, 56*; Ref: F Nicholson	6,523	11 *13*	L 25	1-4	0-1
27	Bush 12; *Dunphy 43*; Ref: N Burtenshaw	13,133	11 *19*	D 26	1-1	1-1
28	Sharpe 44; Ref: H Williams	11,045	11 *20*	W 28	1-0	1-0
29	Bush 22, Skirton 82; *Summerill 32, Vincent 66*; Ref: M Sinclair	20,421	11 *13*	D 29	2-2	1-1
30	Bush 34, 87, Sharpe 89; Ref: D Lyden	13,831	9 *12*	W 31	3-0	1-0
31	*Garbett 26, Lugg 74p*; Ref: A Green	12,744	11 *19*	L 31	0-2	0-1

Match reports

22. City are given a gift lead as Downsborough takes too many steps after fielding Skirton's centre. From the free-kick Kellard chips to the far post where Burrows running in sends the ball powerfully into his own goal. Horsfield drives in a low left-foot shot for Swindon's equaliser.

23. No sparkle at Ashton Gate where City, who take half-an-hour before getting in a shot, make little impression on Middlesbrough's defence. Bartley misses their best opportunity, stabbing the ball wide following a good move involving Skirton, Tainton and Jacobs near the end.

24. Another Rooks own-goal as the ball ends up in the top corner of the net after he juts out his foot to deal with Smith's shot. Worthington's 25-yard screamer clinches the Terriers win following City's leveller when Skirton rams the ball over the line after Poole pushes out Galley's shot.

25. Toshack's first goal in ten games, an injury-time header from Woodruff's long centre, ends brave City's defensive battle. On a snow-covered surface City do not create much, though Bush should have scored instead of shooting wide from eight yards with only five minutes remaining.

26. In front of the lowest Carrow Road attendance for twelve years, Silvester drives the ball in from eight yards, after Gibson parries Conlon's header. Jacobs is lying injured when Conlon heads the Canaries further in front, but Garland registers with a cross-shot shortly afterwards.

27. Bartley follows up to make sure Bush's early shot crosses the line, but City are made to pay for not taking their chances as Dunphy disposes Parr to shoot Millwall's equaliser. After King makes an excellent save to deny Bush just after the break, Millwall take control for long periods.

28. Making his Preston debut Clive Clark, signed for £25,000 from QPR, is denied by an offside decision after netting early in the second half. City achieve their first away win of the season as Sharpe heads into an open net after interplay between Bush and Garland splits Preston apart.

29. Birmingham make the most of an escape when a 27th-minute shot by Rooks is disallowed. Summerill takes the ball round Gibson and Parr's tackle to run in an equaliser to Bush's gentle header. Skirton forces home City's late equaliser after Vincent had scored direct from a corner.

30. Portsmouth's packed midfield stifle City's attack as well as providing a platform for their neat approach play. Bush nets from ten yards with a left-foot shot on the turn, but City are hard pressed to keep Pompey at bay until the centre-forward turns in Garland's pass for his second goal.

31. City, after making a bright start at snow-covered Vicarage Road, are rocked by Garbett's header from Owen's cross. Williams clears Skirton's header off the goal-line straight after the break, but all City's efforts are in vain as Gibson brings down Garbett to concede a 74-minute pen.

No		Opponent	Pos	Res	Score			Att
32	A	ASTON VILLA	10	W	2-0	22	33	26,870

Scorers: Connor 69, Sharpe 70
Ref: M Sinclair

City: Gibson, Jacobs, Wimshurst, Connor, Parr, Skirton, Garland, Bush, Kellard, Sharpe
Villa: Dunn, Wright, Hole, Curtis, Tiler, Godfrey*, Chatterley, Lochhead, Rioch B, Anderson, Martin

City are much the better side as Villa offer little in the way of attacking threat. Chatterley saves Skirton's chip off the line, but the respite is short as a min later Connor's first-time shot from 15 yards finds the net. Sharpe completes the scoring by slipping the ball in.

No		Opponent	Pos	Res	Score			Att
33	H	LEICESTER	12	D	0-0	9	34	17,044

Ref: V Batty

City: Gibson, Jacobs, Wimshurst, Rooks, Parr, Skirton, Garland, Bush, Kellard, Sharpe
Leicester: Shilton, Nish, Woollett, Sjoberg, Cross, Farrington, Fern, Brown*, Matthews, Glover, Rodrigues

A typical all-action display by Bobby Kellard, booked for the fifth time last week, gives reason for Leicester boss Frank O'Farrell to raise his £30,000 bid. A few seconds before half-time Skirton's headed goal is disallowed as Sharpe, the supplier of the pass, is adjudged offside.

No		Opponent	Pos	Res	Score			Att
34	H	BLACKBURN	9	W	4-0	10	36	12,683

Scorers: Bush 14, 57, Sharpe 38, Kellard 84
Ref: J Osborne

City: Gibson, Jacobs, Wimshurst, Rooks*, Parr, Skirton, Garland, Bush, Kellard, Sharpe
Blackburn: Blacklaw, Eccles, Wilson, Hunter, Mulvaney*, Knighton, Metcalfe, Goodwin, Martin, Connelly, Hill

Rovers seeking to add to their solitary success at Ashton Gate in 1909 are easily defeated. Improved wing play brings first-half headed goals for Bush and Sharpe, whilst after the break Bush takes deliberate aim for City's third, and Kellard drives in from the region of the penalty spot.

No		Opponent	Pos	Res	Score			Att
35	A	BLACKPOOL	10	L	0-1	3	36	13,657

Scorers: Bentley 86
Ref: A Bone

City: Gibson, Jacobs, Wimshurst, Rooks, Parr, Skirton, Garland, Bush, Kellard, Sharpe
Blackpool: Thomson, Armfield, Mowbray, Bentley, James, Burns*, Craven, Pickering, Suddick, Hutchison, Brown

After Sharpe's seventh-min miskick in front an open goal, City find themselves restricted to breakaways as Blackpool assert themselves. In the second half City's policy of playing high balls down the middle is unproductive and Bentley's tremendous 25-yarder gives Pool the points.

No		Opponent	Pos	Res	Score			Att
36	A	OXFORD	11	L	0-2	13	36	9,086

Scorers: Lewis 30, 72
Ref: C Nicholls

City: Gibson, Jacobs, Wimshurst, Connor, Parr, Skirton, Garland, Bush, Kellard, Sharpe
Oxford: Barron, Lucas, Gladwin, Smithson, Clarke, Thompson*, Sloan, Atkinson R, Skeen, Lewis, Atkinson G, Clayton

Pathetic City succumb to goals from free-kicks as Lewis twice slams the ball in. Skirton nets what appeared to be a valid equaliser, but Sharpe is marginally offside. Kellard's uncharacteristic quiet performance is likely due disciplinary concerns should he pick up another booking.

No		Opponent	Pos	Res	Score			Att
37	H	SWINDON	11	D	3-3	6	37	24,905

Scorers: Galley 46, Sharpe 67, Kellard 76p; Horsfield 8, 57, Wimshurst 84 (og)
Ref: J Hunting

City: Gibson, Jacobs, Wimshurst, Rooks, Parr, Skirton*, Garland, Galley, Kellard, Sharpe, Bush
Swindon: Downsboro', Thomas, Trollope, Butler, Burrows, Harland, Smart, Smith, Horsfield, Noble, Rogers

Swindon's third goal is unlucky for Wimshurst as the ball strikes him and goes into the net after Horsfield misses a cross. City take the lead for the only time in an enthralling match after Thomas attempts to punch the ball over the bar. Kellard beats the keeper with a kick to his right.

No		Opponent	Pos	Res	Score			Att
38	H	BOLTON	11	D	2-2	16	38	17,298

Scorers: Kellard 41p, Sharpe 86; Hulme 73, Byrom 85
Ref: E Jennings

City: Mahoney, Jacobs, Wimshurst, Connor, Parr, Skirton, Garland, Galley, Kellard, Sharpe
Bolton: Boswell, Ritson, Marsh*, Williams, Hulme, Rimmer, Wharton, Byrom, Hunt, Greaves, Taylor, Farrimond

Just 30 seconds after Byrom shoots low into the net, Sharpe rams in City's late equaliser. Offside cuts short Bolton's celebrations when Hunt fires in on six minutes, and City take the lead with a penalty, after Boswell holds Sharpe. Bolton level as Hulme smashes in a poor clearance.

No		Opponent	Pos	Res	Score			Att
39	A	QP RANGERS	10	D	2-2	8	39	11,017

Scorers: Jacobs 3, Bush 86; Bridges 50, Francis 55
Ref: H Davey

City: Mahoney, Jacobs, Wimshurst, Rooks, Parr, Skirton*, Garland, Galley*, Kellard, Sharpe, Bush
QP Rangers: Spratley, Harris, McGovern, Mobley, Hazell, Bridges, Francis, Leach, Marsh, Ferguson, Bush

Jacobs' centre is misjudged by Spratley and the ball goes into the far corner of the net for City's early lead. Bush heads in Tainton's high cross for a late equaliser after Rangers take charge. Francis takes careful aim for his goal, while Bridges fires in a shot that goes under Mahoney.

No		Opponent	Pos	Res	Score			Att
40	A	CARLISLE	11	L	1-2	12	39	6,219

Scorers: Brown 13, McVitie 16; Jacobs 26
Ref: A Morrissey

City: Mahoney, Jacobs, Wimshurst*, Tainton, Parr, Skirton, Spiring, Bush, Kellard, Sharpe
Carlisle: Ross, Hemstead, Davis, Terment, Garbutt, McVitie, Barton, Hatton, Brown, Balderstone, Ferguson

City's defence is badly at fault as Brown's weak header trickles in the net for Carlisle's opener, and then McVitie runs through to shoot home. Jacobs fires in from 25 yards to gain some reward for a spirited reply, that had caused Garbutt to head a cross onto his own post shortly before.

No		Opponent	Pos	Res	Score			Att
41	H	SHEFFIELD UTD	13	L	0-1	4	39	11,159

Scorers: Colquhoun 37
Ref: K Styles

City: Gibson, Jacobs, Drysdale, Rooks, Parr, Skirton, Spiring*, Bush, Kellard, Sharpe
Sheffield Utd: Hodgkinson, Badger, Flynn, Addison, Powell, Woodward*, Currie, Colquhoun, Salmons, Reece, Derrick

City are rescued from their lethargy when Colquhoun heads in from Woodward's corner. They dominate the play, but are left to rue many missed chances and appeals for a penalty when Sharpe is brought down by Powell in the box. Tudor blasts United's best chance over the bar.

No		Opponent	Pos	Res	Score			Att
42	A	CHARLTON	14	L	1-2	20	39	15,972

Scorers: Campbell 13, Treacy 50; Garland 88
Ref: N Burtenshaw

City: Wright, Jacobs, Drysdale, Gow, Parr, Tainton, Garland, Bush, Kellard, Sharpe
Charlton: Wright, Kinsey, Moore, Keirs, Reeves, Kenning, Treacy, Riddick, Campbell, Peacock*, Gregory

With Kellard seeking a transfer, Rooks takes over as City captain. Campbell's eight-yard shot and Treacy's superb header enable Charlton to maintain their status. Garland heads in from Kellard's free-kick at the death, but earlier Bush can only find the post from a similar situation.

Home 16,274
Away 14,205
Average 14,205

LEAGUE DIVISION 2 (CUP-TIES)

Manager: Alan Dicks

SEASON 1969-70

League Cup

				F-A	H-T	Scorers, Times, and Referees	1	2	3	4	5	6	7	8	9	10	11	12 sub used
1	A	EXETER	13/8 8,003	D 1-1	0-0	Kellard 72 / Banks 74 / Ref: T Reynolds	Gibson	Jacobs	Drysdale	Clarke	Rooks	Parr	Skirton	Garland	Bush	Kellard	Sharpe	
							Shearing	*Crawford*	*Blain*	*Balson*	*Sharples*	*Newman*	*Corr*	*Giles*	*Banks*	*Mitten*	*Walker*	

Giles hits the bar as the Grecians bustling play forces City into an abundance of errors. Kellard's soft shot from the edge of the penalty area puts City ahead, but Exeter obtain a deserved equaliser when Banks runs through onto Newman's perfect pass to slip the ball past Gibson.

				F-A	H-T	Scorers, Times, and Referees	1	2	3	4	5	6	7	8	9	10	11	12
1R	H	EXETER	19/8 10,924 4:23	W 3-2	2-0	Rooks 6, Kellard 30, Sharpe 69 / Corr 57, Parr 83 (og) / Ref: W Gow	Gibson	Jacobs	Drysdale	Merrick	Rooks	Parr	Skirton	Garland	Galley	Kellard	Sharpe	
							Shearing	*Crawford*	*Blain*	*Giles*	*Newman*	*Parker*	*Corr*	*Banks*	*Wingate*	*Mitten*	*Walker*	

Exeter show that their cup reputation is no myth after a Rooks header and Kellard's diagonal shot give City early control. Banks creates panic in the City defence and Corr finds the net after three shots had been cleared. Parr slams ball into own net to set up a nail-biting finale.

				F-A	H-T	Scorers, Times, and Referees	1	2	3	4	5	6	7	8	9	10	11	12
2	H	LEICESTER	2/9 15,883 4	D 0-0	0-0	Ref: I Jones	Gibson	Briggs	Drysdale	Tainton	Rooks	Parr	Skirton	Garland	Galley	Derrick	Sharpe	
							Shilton	*Rodrigues*	*Houghton*	*Nish*	*Sjoberg*	*Cross*	*Brown*	*Fern*	*Lochhead*	*Roberts*	*Glover*	

Garland and Tainton are denied by the woodwork in the first half as City generally dominate last season's FA Cup finalists in this fluent game. Briggs is fortunate ten minutes before time as a linesman spots his handball in the penalty area, but decides to put his flag down again.

				F-A	H-T	Scorers, Times, and Referees	1	2	3	4	5	6	7	8	9	10	11	12
2R	A	LEICESTER	10/9 20,797 2	D 0-0 aet	0-0	Ref: A Jones	Gibson	Briggs	Drysdale	Tainton	Rooks	Parr	Skirton	Garland	Galley	Derrick	Sharpe*	Spiring
							Shilton	*Rodrigues*	*Houghton*	*Nish*	*Harrison*	*Manley*	*Gibson*	*Fern*	*Lochhead*	*Mackay**	*Glover*	*Tewley*

City are unable to turn their superiority over a Leicester side, missing five regulars, into goals. Sharpe, after an earlier header is cleared off the line, should have ended the drought just before half-time, but from a perfect position lifts his shot over the bar. Garland is booked for dissent.

				F-A	H-T	Scorers, Times, and Referees	1	2	3	4	5	6	7	8	9	10	11	12
2 RR	A	LEICESTER	15/9 12,600 2	L 1-3	1-1	Galley 5 / Lochhead 13, 52, 59 / Ref: E Jennings	Gibson	Briggs	Drysdale	Tainton	Rooks	Parr	Skirton	Garland	Galley	Kellard	Bartley	
							Shilton	*Rodrigues*	*Houghton*	*Nish*	*Sjoberg*	*Cross*	*Matthews*	*Fern*	*Lochhead*	*Brown*	*Glover*	

Leicester rediscover their form in this 2nd replay at Filbert Street after City go ahead when Galley taps in Skirton's cross. Lochhead whips in Rodrigues' fierce cross for the equaliser and goes on to complete a hat-trick by shooting in from Fern's low cross and Brown's headed pass.

FA Cup

				F-A	H-T	Scorers, Times, and Referees	1	2	3	4	5	6	7	8	9	10	11	12
3	A	CHESTER	3/1 10,030 4:9	L 1-2	0-1	Skirton 70 / Webber 3, Dearden 89 / Ref: H Williams	Gibson	Jacobs	Drysdale	Tainton	Connor	Parr	Skirton	Garland	Bush	Sharpe	Bartley	
							Carling	*Cheetham*	*Birks**	*Sutton*	*Turner*	*Bradbury*	*Dearden*	*Spence*	*Webber*	*Draper*	*Provan*	*Edwards*

City pay the cost of seemingly settling for a replay against unmarked Skirton's headed response to Webber's opening eight-yard header. City, who find Chester's bustling tactics difficult to handle, play one short for five minutes in the first half after Bush collides with Carling.

Home and Away Record

	Team	P	W	D	L	F	A	W	D	L	F	A	Pts
				Home					Away				
1	Huddersfield	42	14	6	1	36	10	10	6	5	32	27	60
2	Blackpool	42	10	9	2	25	16	10	4	7	31	29	53
3	Leicester	42	12	6	3	37	22	7	7	7	27	28	51
4	Middlesboro	42	15	4	2	36	14	5	6	10	19	31	50
5	Swindon	42	13	7	1	35	17	4	9	8	22	30	50
6	Sheffield Utd	42	16	2	3	50	10	6	3	12	23	28	49
7	Cardiff	42	12	7	2	38	14	6	6	9	23	27	49
8	Blackburn	42	15	2	4	42	19	5	5	11	12	31	47
9	QP Rangers	42	13	5	3	47	24	4	6	11	19	33	45
10	Millwall	42	14	4	3	38	18	1	10	10	18	38	44
11	Norwich	42	13	5	3	37	14	3	6	12	12	32	43
12	Carlisle	42	10	6	5	39	28	4	7	10	19	28	41
13	Hull	42	11	6	4	43	28	2	6	13	29	42	41
14	BRISTOL CITY	42	11	7	3	37	13	2	6	13	17	37	39
15	Oxford	42	9	9	3	23	13	3	6	12	12	29	39
16	Bolton	42	9	6	6	31	23	3	6	12	23	38	36
17	Portsmouth	42	8	4	9	39	35	5	5	11	27	45	35
18	Birmingham	42	9	7	5	33	22	2	4	15	18	56	33
19	Watford	42	6	8	7	26	21	3	5	13	18	36	31
20	Charlton	42	7	8	6	23	28	0	9	12	12	48	31
21	Aston Villa	42	7	8	6	23	21	1	5	15	13	41	29
22	Preston	42	7	6	8	31	28	1	6	14	12	35	28
		924	241	132	89	769	438	89	132	241	438	769	924

Odds & ends

Double wins: (1) Aston Villa

Double losses: (3) Cardiff, Sheffield Utd, Huddersfield.

Won from behind: (0).

Lost from in front: (0).

High spots: Beating Norwich 4-0 at Ashton Gate.
Beating Charlton 6-0 at Ashton Gate.
Doing the double over Aston Villa.
Exciting 3-3 draws with Blackburn (a) and Swindon (h).
Beating Blackburn 4-0 at Ashton Gate.
Beating Bristol Rovers 2-1 (h) in the Gloucestershire Cup Final.

Low spots: Losing 0-1 at Chester in the FA Cup.
Losing 0-2 at Oxford.

Player of the year: Dickie Rooks.
Ever-presents: (1) Brian Drysdale.
Hat-tricks: (1) John Galley.
Leading scorer: Gerry Sharpe (11).

Appearances and Goals

	Appearances						Goals			
	Lge	Sub	LC	Sub	FAC	Sub	Lge	LC	FAC	Tot
Bartley, Danny	16	1	1		1		3			3
Briggs, Alec	4	1	3		1					
Broomfield, Ian	1									
Bush, Terry	22	4	1		1		9			9
Clarke, Malcolm	2	1	1							
Connor, Jack	5	1			1		1			1
Derrick, Jantzen	6	1	2							
Drysdale, Brian	42		5							
Ford, Tony	7									
Galley, John	20		4				9	1		10
Garland, Chris	39		5		1		6			6
Gibson, Mike	38		5		1					
Gow, Gerry	1									
Jacobs, Trevor	31		2		1		2			2
Kellard, Bobby	35		3				3	2		5
Mahoney, Mike	3									
Menmuir, Billy	3	1								
Merrick, Geoff	3		5		1					
Parr, Gordon	38		5							
Rooks, Dickie	38		5				1	1		2
Sharpe, Gerry	28	2	4		1		10	1		11
Skirton, Alan	34	1	5		1		7		1	8
Spiring, Peter	4			1						
Tainton, Trevor	25	4	3		1		1			1
Wilson, Bob	1									
Wimshurst, Ken	18	2								
(own-goals)							2			2
26 players used	462	19	55	1	11		54	5	1	60

LEAGUE DIVISION 2 — Manager: Alan Dicks — SEASON 1970-71

Key: City players in regular type (positions 1–11, plus 12 = sub used); opponents in italic below. * = player substituted.

---

1. SUNDERLAND (H) — 15/8 · Att 17,584 · W · Pt 2 · F-A 4:3 · H-T 2:1
Scorers: Sharpe 14, 86, Skirton 44, Wimsh'st 63 / Kerr 16, Baker 72, 74 — Ref: K Walker

1	2	3	4	5	6	7	8	9	10	11	12
Gibson	Jacobs	Drysdale	Wimshurst	Rooks	Parr	Skirton*	Garland	Galley	Gow	Sharpe	Tainton
Montgomery	Irvin	Harvey	Todd	Heslop	McGiven	Park	Kerr	Baker	Porterfield	Hughes	

A thrill a second clash in which skill far outweighs brawn, despite two bookings for each side. Jacobs is given a torrid afternoon by Hughes, but Sharpe secures the points for City after weathering much pressure in closing stages, following Baker's fine volley from the edge of the box.

---

2. CHARLTON (A) — 22/8 · Att 10,460 · D · Pt 3 · F-A 1:1 · H-T 0:1
Scorers: Galley 82 / Peacock 18 — Ref: C Robinson

1	2	3	4	5	6	7	8	9	10	11	12
Gibson	Jacobs*	Drysdale	Wimshurst	Rooks	Parr	Skirton	Garland	Galley	Gow	Sharpe	Tainton
Wright	Curtis	Kinsey	Moore	Keirs	Reeves	Davies*	Treacy	Gregory	Campbell	Peacock	Riddick

Galley stabs in Skirton's cross from the right to reward City's much improved second-half performance. Charlton highlight City's defensive shortcomings as Curtis clips a long ball through the middle for Peacock to steal in on the left and hook the ball first time over Gibson's head.

---

3. CARDIFF (H) — 29/8 · Att 24,969 · Pos 4 · W · Pt 5 · F-A 1:0 · H-T 0:0
Scorers: Sharpe 89 — Ref: G Kew

1	2	3	4	5	6	7	8	9	10	11	12
Gibson	Jacobs	Drysdale	Wimshurst	Rooks	Parr	Skirton	Garland*	Galley	Gow	Sharpe	Tainton
Parsons P	Carver	Bell	Sutton	Murray	Clark	Gibson	Harris	Woodruff	Toshack	King	

City achieve their first home success over the Bluebirds in eight games. Sharpe hammers in Tainton's cross from the right to end jinx. As usual Woodruff's long throws cause problems, but Rooks and Parr are in fine form. Bookings for Gow in first half and Ian Gibson after the break.

---

4. LEICESTER (A) — 2/9 · Att 20,435 · Pos 11 · L · Pt 5 · F-A 0:4 · H-T 0:4
Scorers: Farrington 20, Kellard 21, Brown 34, [Nish 44p] — Ref: R Johnston

1	2	3	4	5	6	7	8	9	10	11	12
Gibson	Jacobs	Drysdale	Wimshurst	Rooks	Parr	Skirton	Tainton	Galley	Gow	Sharpe	
Shilton	Whitworth	Nish	Kellard	Sjoberg	Cross	Farrington	Matthews	Stringfellow*	Glover	Fern	Brown

Seeking their first home success, Leicester start nervously against City. Skirton has a searing left-foot volley disallowed for barging his way past Cross before Leicester gain confidence with two quick goals. Nish completes City's rout with a penalty after Rooks fouled Stringfellow.

---

5. SHEFFIELD UTD (A) — 5/9 · Att 15,097 · Pos 8 · D · Pt 6 · F-A 3:3 · H-T 1:0
Scorers: Galley 27, 50, Gow 63 / Woodward 66, Dearden 72, Tudor 89 — Ref: B. Homewood

1	2	3	4	5	6	7	8	9	10	11	12
Gibson	Stacey	Drysdale	Wimshurst	Connor	Parr	Skirton	Garland	Galley	Gow	Sharpe	
Hodgkinson	Badger	Hemsley	Powell	Colquhoun	Salmons	Woodward	Barnwell*	Dearden	Currie	Reece	Tudor

Woodward's scorching 20-yarder sparks United's fightback in a thrill a minute game in which City squander a three-goal lead. City twice clear shots off the line before taking the lead in their third attack, when Alan Hodgkinson is punished for dropping a cross under Galley's challenge.

---

6. HULL (H) — 12/9 · Att 12,978 · Pos 8 · D · Pt 7 · F-A 3:3 · H-T 2:1
Scorers: Garland 14, Skirton 22, 57 / Chilton 44, 49, Butler 74 — Ref: B Daniels

1	2	3	4	5	6	7	8	9	10	11	12
Gibson	Stacey	Drysdale	Wimshurst	Connor	Parr	Skirton	Garland	Galley	Gow	Sharpe	
McKechnie	Beardsley	De Vries*	Wilkinson	Neill	Simpkin	Lord	Greenwood	Chilton	Wagstaff	Butler	Pearson

City sparkle until Gibson's short free-kick out of defence lets the visitors back into the game. Despite going ahead again, City become a nervy shambles and Hull gain a deserved share of the spoils when Wagstaff's chip from the right is delightfully flicked in at the near post by Butler.

---

7. QP RANGERS (A) — 19/9 · Att 13,367 · Pos 12 · L · Pt 7 · F-A 1:2 · H-T 0:0
Scorers: Garland 49 / Marsh 68, Bridges 70 — Ref: T Dawes

1	2	3	4	5	6	7	8	9	10	11	12
Gibson	Stacey	Drysdale	Wimshurst	Connor	Parr	Skirton	Garland*	Galley	Gow	Sharpe	Tainton
Parkes	Hazell	Clement	Venables	Hunt	Sibley	Bridges	Francis*	Saul	Marsh	Ferguson	

Garland takes a pass in his stride and smashes a left-footer high into net as City confirm their superiority at Loftus Road. Defensive errors then bring defeat. Marsh is left free at the far post to head in a right-wing centre; then Bridges beats the offside trap to flick a through ball into goal.

---

8. BLACKBURN (H) — 26/9 · Att 14,019 · Pos 12 · D · Pt 8 · F-A 1:1 · H-T 0:0
Scorers: Skirton 59 / Conlon 67 — Ref: J Hunting

1	2	3	4	5	6	7	8	9	10	11	12
Gibson	Stacey	Drysdale	Wimshurst	Rooks	Parr	Skirton	Garland	Galley	Gow	Sharpe	Tainton
Jones	Kopel	Wilson	Hunter	Mulvaney	Knighton	Conlon	Russell	Goodwin	Rogers	Kerr	

City get the slow handclap from disgruntled fans as they hit rock bottom form against defensive opponents. Skirton takes advantage of City's only real chance with a crisp drive past the advancing Jones, but Blackburn respond. Conlon gets past Drysdale and levels with a fierce shot.

---

9. BIRMINGHAM (H) — 29/9 · Att 15,979 · Pos 7 · W · Pt 10 · F-A 2:1 · H-T 0:0
Scorers: Galley 74, Sharpe 75 / Summerill 77 — Ref: L Callaghan

1	2	3	4	5	6	7	8	9	10	11	12
Gibson	Stacey	Drysdale	Wimshurst	Rooks	Parr	Skirton	Garland	Galley	Gow	Sharpe	Tainton
Kelly	Martin	Pendrey	Hockey	Hynd	Robinson	Francis*	Vowden	Latchford R	Vincent	Summerill	Thomson

City respond to Brum's physical approach with an aggressive second-half display. Surprisingly, only Gow is booked, and that was for abusive language. City's opener is credited to Galley, whose shot hits a post and rolls along the line before Martin nets the ball whilst trying to clear.

---

10. LUTON (A) — 3/10 · Att 15,992 · Pos 11 · L · Pt 10 · F-A 0:3 · H-T 0:2
Scorers: MacDonald 17, 33, Slough 55 — Ref: A Jones

1	2	3	4	5	6	7	8	9	10	11	12
Gibson	Stacey	Drysdale	Wimshurst*	Rooks	Parr	Skirton	Garland	Galley	Gow	Sharpe	Tainton
Read	Ryan John	Slough	Hoy	Nicholl	Moore	Ryan Jim	Court	MacDonald	Keen	Givens*	Busby

City suffer a comprehensive defeat as MacDonald scores twice, his second a classic header to finish off Jim Ryan's cross, to take his tally to seven. On the attack from the outset, Luton take the lead when Gibson diverts the ball into MacDonald's path when saving Keen's strong shot.

No	Venue	Opponent	Date	Att	Pos	Res	Score	W	D

11 — H OXFORD, 10/10 — 16,027 — 14 — L — 0-4 — 3 — 10

City: Gibson; Kearns; Stacey / Lucas; Drysdale / Shuker; Tainton / Smithson; Rooks / Clarke; Parr / Thompson; Skirton / Sloan; Garland / Atkinson G; Broomfield / Skeen; Gow / Clayton; Sharpe / Evanson

Scorers: (Smithson 70p) / Atkinson 2, Evanson 55, 65,
Ref: R Matthewson

City are unable to hold an eager Oxford side who take an early lead, when Atkinson punishes a static defence by deftly flicking Lucas' long diagonal ball into the corner of the net. Smithson completes City's rout by converting a penalty, awarded when Gibson grabs Sloan's legs.

12 — A SUNDERLAND, 17/10 — 17,335 — 17 — L — 0-1 — 9 — 10

City: Gibson / Montgomery Malone*; Stacey / Irvin; Drysdale / Todd; Wimshurst / Smith; Rooks / Pit; Parr / McGiven; Skirton / Porterfield; Garland / Kerr; Galley / Baker; Gow* / Harris; Sharpe / Hughes; Tainton / Park

Scorers: McGiven 30
Ref: R Lee

City, in all white, demonstrate much energy in attack and tightness in defence by playing in a 4-3-3 formation. Sharpe blasts wide from ten yards before Sunderland score. Kerr's centre from the left is played back by Hughes, for McGiven to send in an unstoppable 18-yarder.

13 — A MIDDLESBROUGH, 20/10 — 16,651 — 20 — L — 0-1 — 8 — 10

City: Gibson / Whigham; Stacey* / Madden; Drysdale / Jones G; Wimshurst / Smith; Rooks / Gates; Parr / Spraggon; Fear / Mills; Garland / McMordie*; Galley / McIlmoyle; Tainton / Hickton; Sharpe / Laidlaw; Merrick / Webb

Scorers: Hickton 84
Ref: W Johnson

A tough unrelenting struggle in the wind and rain at Ayresome Park as City adopt a 4-4-2 formation. Hickton denies City any reward for much wholehearted effort when he heads in the corner of the net from a disputed free-kick. Luckless Stacey, booked earlier for handball, is carried off with ankle damage.

14 — A BOLTON, 24/10 — 7,749 — 21 — L — 0-1 — 13 — 10

City: Gibson / Boswell; Drysdale / Ritson; Merrick / Farrimond; Wimshurst / Williams G; Rooks / Hurley; Parr / Hulme; Skirton / Taylor; Garland / Byrom; Tainton / Fletcher; Gow / Rimmer; Sharpe / Phillips

Scorers: Williams 86
Ref: D Lyden

A scrappy game as City again utilise a 4-4-2 formation. Bolton are jeered by their fans just prior to their late goal. Taylor's ball into the middle is back-headed by Fletcher for Williams to stride forward unchallenged to net from eight yards. Parr is booked for fouling Fletcher from behind.

15 — H SHEFFIELD WED, 31/10 — 13,093 — 21 — L — 1-2 — 14 — 10

City: Gibson / Grummitt; Drysdale / Rodrigues*; Merrick / Wilcockson; Wimshurst / Thompson; Connor / Ellis; Parr / Pugh; Skirton / Sinclair; Broomfield / Prendergast; Galley* / Warboys; Tainton / Todd; Sharpe / Sissons; Gow / Craig

Scorers: Broomfield 82 / Prendergast 54, Sissons 71
Ref: R Capey

City hold early initiative in an incident-packed game, but a chapter of misses leads to a loss of momentum after half-time. Parr's poor defensive header sets up Craig's high centre, which Prendergast heads through Gibson's arms. A goalmouth scramble allows Broomfield to score at last.

16 — A SWINDON, 7/11 — 16,678 — 20 — L — 1-2 — 12 — 10

City: Gibson / Jones; Drysdale / Thomas; Merrick / Trollope; Wimshurst / Butler; Rooks / Blick; Rodgers / Harland; Garland / Smith; Galley / Horsfield; Tainton / Noble; Sharpe / Rogers

Scorers: Galley 66 / Horsfield 72, Noble 90
Ref: R Kirkpatrick

Rodgers marks his City debut with a booking, while an alert linesman averts strife as Swindon are awarded a 63rd-minute 'goal'. The aptly named Mr Handy prevails to ensure the decision is changed to a corner. Noble blasts in Horsfield's centre for Swindon's injury-time winner.

17 — H WATFORD, 14/11 — 11,100 — 20 — W — 3-0 — 17 — 12

City: Gibson / Walker; Drysdale / Welbourne; Merrick / Williams; Wimshurst / Eddy; Rooks / Lees; Rodgers / Walley; Garland / Scullion; Broomfield / Wigg; Galley / Endean; Tainton / Packer; Sharpe / Woods*; Gow / Garbett

Scorers: Broomfield 2, Wimshurst 39, Sharpe 84
Ref: M Fussey

Despite missing many chances, City end a run of seven-successive League defeats. Broomfield latches onto a ball played over Watford's defence to net from eight yards, Wimshurst smashes in a crisp left-foot drive, and Sharpe forces ball over line after his initial shot is blocked.

18 — A MILLWALL, 21/11 — 9,173 — 20 — L — 0-2 — 11 — 12

City: Gibson / King; Drysdale / Brown B; Merrick / Cripps; Gow / Dorney; Rooks / Kitchener; Rodgers* / Burnett; Garland / Bridges; Broomfield / Dunphy; Galley / Bolland; Tainton / Possee; Sharpe / Allder; Parr

Scorers: Cripps 23, Allder 42
Ref: K Burns

City lose composure after going behind when Cripps finishes off Brown's cross from the right with a diving header. Hesitancy between Gibson and Rooks then doubles the deficit as Allder runs between them to deposit the ball in an empty net. Bookings for Drysdale and Garland.

19 — H CARLISLE, 28/11 — 13,561 — 19 — W — 2-1 — 7 — 14

City: Gibson / Ross; Drysdale / Hemstead*; Tainton / Davis; Rooks / Winstanley; Rodgers* / Sutton; Sharpe / Martin; Broomfield / Barton; Galley / Hatton; Gow / Owen; Merrick / Bartley; Balderstone Kinsella

Scorers: Galley 83, Gow 86 / Hatton 55
Ref: A Morrisey

With vouchers being issued for the Spurs cup-tie, the crowd is smaller than expected. Gow secures the points with a 20-yard screamer, but Carlisle take a deserved lead through Hatton, who manages to evade Gibson's attempts at a rugby tackle. Tennent is booked for pushing the ref.

20 — A ORIENT, 5/12 — 6,250 — 19 — D — 1-1 — 20 — 15

City: Gibson / Goddard; Drysdale / Jones; Wimshurst / Bennett; Rooks / Mancini; Parr / Allen; Skirton / Lazarus; Garland* / Riddick; Galley / Fairbrother; Gow / Dyson; Sharpe / Brabrook*; Tainton / Bullock

Scorers: Sharpe 80 / Riddick 11
Ref: M Kerhof

City obtain a deserved point on a heavy pitch, that makes passing difficult, when Skirton's back-header is hooked low into the corner of the net by Sharpe. Orient's goal is a simple affair. Riddick heads in from Brabrook's cross. A four-man move ends with Skirton heading onto the bar.

21 — H NORWICH, 12/12 — 10,637 — 20 — L — 0-1 — 7 — 15

City: Gibson / Keelan; Drysdale / Payne; Wimshurst / Black; Rooks / Stringer; Parr / Forbes; Skirton / Briggs; Garland / Livermore; Galley / Silvester; Gow / Howard; Sharpe / Padden; Tainton / Foggo

Scorers: Silvester 37
Ref: R Barker

Dominant City fall to a Canaries smash and grab win that is inspired by Keelan's great display. Norwich are unlucky on 63 mins to be given an indirect free-kick instead of a Ken Foggo score, but in a rare breakaway Silvester heads Foggo's cross high into the net to Gibson's right.

LEAGUE DIVISION 2 — SEASON 1970-71

Manager: Alan Dicks

Note: in each numbered player column (1–12) the upper (roman) name is the Bristol City player and the lower (italic) name is the opponent. The two figures in the "Pos" column are the two position numbers printed in the source. An asterisk (*) marks a substituted player.

No		Opponents	Date	Att	Pos	Pt	Res	F-A	H-T	1	2	3	4	5	6	7	8	9	10	11	12 sub used
22	H	CHARLTON	19/12	10,187	20 / 22	16	D	2-2	0-2	Gibson / Wright	Jacobs / Curtis	Drysdale / Bruck	Wimshurst / Kenning	Rooks / Went	Parr* / Shipperley*	Skirton / Davies	Garland / Treacy	Galley / Plumb	Gow / Bond	Sharpe / Peacock	Tainton / Reeves
23	A	BIRMINGHAM	9/1	15,292	20 / 14	16	L	0-2	0-2	Gibson / Latchford D	Jacobs* / Martin	Drysdale / Hockey	Wimshurst / Page	Rooks / Hynd	Parr / Robinson	Skirton / Campbell*	Spring / Bowker	Garland / Latchford R	Gow / Summerill	Sharpe / Taylor	Tainton / Thwaites
24	H	MIDDLESBROUGH	16/1	10,535	20 / 6	16	L	0-2	0-1	Gibson / Whigham	Drysdale / A Smith	Merrick / Jones	Gow / Moody	Rodgers / Gates	Parr / Spraggon	Skirton / Downing	Garland / McMordie	Galley / McIlmoyle	Derrick* / Hickton	Sharpe / Laidlaw	Broomfield
25	A	CARLISLE	30/1	7,764	20 / 6	16	L	1-2	1-1	Cashley / Ross	Jacobs / Davis	Drysdale / Gorman	Wimshurst / Tennant	Rooks / Winstanley	Fear / Sutton	Fear / Murray	Gow / Owen	Galley / Hatton	Merrick / Hatton	Garland* / Balderstone	Tainton
26	H	ORIENT	6/2	11,423	21 / 18	17	D	0-0	0-0	Cashley / Goddard	Tainton / Jones	Drysdale / Rofe	Wimshurst / Bennett	Rooks / Mancini	Parr / Allen	Spring / Lazarus*	Garland / Brisley	Galley / Bullock	Gow / Dyson	Fear / Fairbrother	Riddick
27	A	NORWICH	13/2	10,513	21 / 8	17	L	2-3	2-0	Cashley / Keelan	Tainton / Payne	Drysdale / Black	Wimshurst / Stringer	Rooks / Forbes	Parr / Anderson	Spring / Livermore	Garland* / Silvester	Galley / Bennett	Merrick / Paddon	Fear / Foggo	Broomfield
28	H	MILLWALL	20/2	10,578	19 / 11	19	W	3-2	2-0	Cashley / King	Tainton / Brown B	Drysdale / Cripps	Wimshurst / Dorney	Rooks / Kitchener	Parr / Garner	Spring / Brown S*	Broomfield / Bolland	Garland / Bridges	Merrick / Dunphy	Fear / Allder	Neill
29	A	SHEFFIELD WED	27/2	12,347	20 / 12	19	L	0-2	0-2	Cashley / Grummitt	Tainton / Todd	Drysdale / Burton	Wimshurst* / Thompson	Rooks / Prophett	Parr / Pugh	Spring / Sinclair	Broomfield / Craig	Garland / Sunley	Gow / Prendergast	Fear / Sissons	Merrick
30	H	BOLTON	6/3	10,550	19 / 20	20	D	1-1	1-1	Gibson / Clarke	Tainton / Ritson	Drysdale / McAllister	Wimshurst / Waldron	Rooks / Rimmer!	Parr / Greaves	Skirton / Hallows	Garland / Byrom	Galley / Hulme	Gow / Seddon	Fear / Manning	Merrick
31	A	PORTSMOUTH	10/3	8,676	19 / 17	21	D	1-1	1-0	Gibson / Milkins	Jacobs / Smith	Drysdale / Youlden*	Wimshurst / Hand	Rodgers / Blant	Parr / Munks	Tainton / Piper	Garland / Pointer	Galley / Hiron	Gow / Bromley	Bartley / Jennings	Trebilcock

Scorers, Times, and Referees

22 — CHARLTON: Rooks 56, Sharpe 58p; Plumb 2, 23. Ref: I Smith.
Ex Bristol Rover Dickie Plumb is denied a hat-trick on 67 minutes when his left-footer hits a post. City suffer early shocks in this bottom of the table clash, but Rooks' header brings them back into the game. The penalty trickles in after hitting underside of bar and twice bouncing on line.

23 — BIRMINGHAM: Taylor 16, Latchford R 45. Ref: G Jones.
Following a minute's silence in memory of the Ibrox disaster victims, and replacement of a broken corner flag, City are denied on five minutes when Spring's strike is disallowed because of free-kick taken prior to the ref's signal. Bob Latchford is also unlucky, hitting bar near the end.

24 — MIDDLESBROUGH: Hickton 25, Parr 80 (og). Ref: C Nicholls.
Chants of 'Dicks must go' greet Derrick's substitution shortly after Parr's unlucky own-goal. Gibson prevents a heavy defeat as City have Sharpe stretchered off on 87 mins following McMordie's tackle. Strikes by Gow and Laidlaw are disallowed on 15 and 67 mins respectively.

25 — CARLISLE: Galley 14, Hatton 19, Owen 74. Ref: S Kayley.
Cashley makes a confident start to his League career behind an uncertain defence. He has no chance with Owen's header from Gorman's cross from the left, but is caught off his line by Hatton's magnificent 25-yarder. Galley heads his hundredth League goal, after a great run by Fear.

26 — ORIENT: Ref: V Batty.
Fairbrother proves a real handful to City, who find control difficult on a well-sanded pitch in this relegation clash. City improve after the break and have a Wimshurst chip, as well as a Rooks header, cleared off line by Mancini, whilst Drysdale deals likewise with Dyson's inswinger.

27 — NORWICH: Galley 15, Fear 26; Silvester 56, Anderson 65, Bennett 68. Ref: N Paget.
Galley takes advantage of the strong wind to net with a superb 35-yard lob as City are well on top before the break. It's a different tale after the interval. Norwich storm back with the wind to their advantage and Anderson, involved in all three of their goals, scores with a low cross-shot.

28 — MILLWALL: Wimshurst 14, Gow 45, Fear 76; Cripps 47, Bridges 54. Ref: I Jones.
City field their youngest forward line as Wimshurst's 20-yarder slips through King's fingers for a gift lead and Gow forces home a low shot. Fear scores City's winner after the break. Bookings in from a free-kick and Bridges heading in at the near post.

29 — SHEFFIELD WED: Prendergast 11, 39. Ref: C Robinson.
City, after missing four good chances, allow Wednesday to go ahead. Cashley is at fault, allowing Prendergast's header to slip beneath him, but is blameless later when his wonder save presents Prendergast with his second goal. Garland is booked in the 43rd minute for abusive language.

30 — BOLTON: Garland 40, Waldron 18. Ref: A Oliver.
The Trotters score first as Rooks lays injured in the area, Alan Waldron shooting low into goal from ten yards. Garland looks offside as he lobs the ball in on the turn to equalise. Bookings for Roy Greaves and Garland, whilst Warwick Rimmer is sent off on 75 mins for fouling Garland.

31 — PORTSMOUTH: Garland 18, Hand 76. Ref: C Thomas.
City have their defensive tactics breached by Hand, whose shot is deflected away from Gibson. An illegally taken free-kick rules out Garland's superb soaring header, but three minutes later the striker gets his reward, collecting Tainton's through pass to slip the ball past Milkins.

Matches 32–42

No.	Venue	Opponent	Date	Att.	City Pos.	Result	Score	HT	Opp. Pos.	Pts
32	A	WATFORD	13/3	12,288	19	W	3-0		18	23
33	H	SWINDON	20/3	17,310	19	W	2-1		10	25
34	H	SHEFFIELD UTD	27/3	14,999	19	L	0-1		2	25
35	A	CARDIFF	3/4	24,638	19	L	0-1		2	25
36	H	LUTON	9/4	18,846	19	W	3-2		4	27
37	H	PORTSMOUTH	10/4	14,663	18	W	2-0		17	29
38	A	HULL	12/4	22,178	18	L	0-1		4	29
39	A	OXFORD	17/4	8,902	19	L	0-1		12	29
40	H	QP RANGERS	24/4	12,522	19	D	0-0		12	30
41	H	LEICESTER	27/4	16,103	19	L	0-1		1	30
42	A	BLACKBURN	1/5	3,971	19	D	2-2		21	31

Home 14,174 — Away 13,131

---

32 — WATFORD (A)
Scorers: Gow 53, Garland 66, Galley 83 — Ref: R Matthewson

With loan signings Hill and Wilson in their ranks, City settle down after a negative start. Gow is at the near post to finish off a cross. Then Garland scores with a left-foot shot before Galley's superb solo run from the centre-circle, during which he beats three men, seals City's win.

Bristol City: Gibson, Jacobs, Drysdale, Wilson, Parr, Hill, Tainton, Garland, Wimshurst, Gow, Galley
Watford: *Edmonds, Butler, Williams, Garbett, Lees, Walley, Scullion, Welbourne, Eddy, Farley*, Woods, Wigg*

33 — SWINDON (H)
Scorers: Gow 47, Galley 53 — Horsfield 64. Ref: F Nicholson

Swindon are outplayed on a quagmire of a pitch. Wilson supplies the midfield drive often lacking this season, while Tainton gives Trollope cause to regret passing a last-minute fitness test. Gow's header and Galley's shot earn goals before Parr's error allows Swindon a ray of hope.

Bristol City: Gibson, Jacobs, Drysdale, Wilson, Parr, Hill, Tainton, Garland, Wimshurst, Gow, Galley
Swindon: *Downsbrough/Thomas, Trollope, Butler, Burrows, Harland, Peplow, Gough, Horsfield, Noble, Rogers*

34 — SHEFFIELD UTD (H)
Scorers: Currie 14. Ref: G Hill

A linesman denies City a 27th-minute equaliser, ruling that Gow unfairly won the ball before Dearden to run into the area and score with great aplomb.

Bristol City: Gibson, Jacobs, Drysdale, Wilson, Parr, Hill, Tainton, Garland, Wimshurst, Gow, Galley
Sheffield Utd: *Hope, Badger, Hemsley, Colquhoun, Hockey, Woodward, Dearden, Currie, Reece, Salmons, Ford**

35 — CARDIFF (A)
Scorers: Wimshurst 4 (og). Ref: J Hunting

City make a mockery of their lowly position and dominate proceedings, but are unable to convert any of their many chances. Cardiff offer little threat, except in breakaways, but are gifted victory by Wimshurst, who deflects the ball off his head when challenging for a cross from the left.

Bristol City: Gibson, Jacobs, Drysdale, Wilson, Parr, Hill, Tainton, Garland, Wimshurst, Gow, Galley
Cardiff: *Eadie, Carver, Bell, Murray, Phillips, King, Woodruff, Gibson*, Warboys, Harris, Bird*

36 — LUTON (H)
Scorers: Rooks 59, Garland 64, MacDonald 43 — Busby 23, MacDonald 43. Ref: D Nippard

Great entertainment, superb attacking football by both sides. City's two-goal 90-second burst climaxes a contest that has everything. Luton's opening goal is perfection, as Busby finishes off MacDonald's right-wing cross. Garland hammers home the ball from the left to clinch the win.

Bristol City: Cashley, Jacobs, Drysdale, Wilson, Rooks, Merrick, Tainton, Garland, Wimshurst, Gow
Luton: *Read, Ryan John, Slough, Nichol, Moore, Ryan Jim, Busby, MacDonald, Keen, Anderson, Goodeve*

37 — PORTSMOUTH (H)
Scorers: Garland 30, Tainton 85. Ref: A Hart

A quiet afternoon for Cashley against defensively-minded opponents in this vital relegation clash. Garland slides the ball home from a Rooks header to put City ahead. After the break, Gow has a low drive disallowed for offside, but great play by Fear lays on a goal for Tainton.

Bristol City: Cashley, Jacobs, Drysdale, Wilson, Rooks, Merrick, Tainton, Garland, Wimshurst, Gow, Fear
Portsmouth: *Standen, Youden, Travers, Hand, Munks, Piper, Storrie, Hiron, Bromley, Jennings*

38 — HULL (A)
Scorers: Banks 58. Ref: W Castle

Cashley, playing over Easter due to Gibson dislocating a finger at Cardiff, saves a penalty given for Gow tripping Chilton. Despite Hull's fifth-successive failure from the spot, Cashley blocking Knighton's kick, they win this mediocre contest thanks to Banks' tame shot finding the net.

Bristol City: Cashley, Jacobs, Drysdale, Wilson, Rooks, Merrick, Tainton, Garland, Wimshurst, Gow, Fear
Hull: *McKechnie, Banks, Beardsley, Wilkinson, Neill, Houghton, Knighton, Lord, Chilton, Wagstaff, Butler, Parr*

39 — OXFORD (A)
Scorers: Clarke D 67. Ref: D Pugh

Oxford have the ball in City's net just after the start. Tainton volleys home on 39 minutes, but both efforts are disallowed for offside. Derek Clarke rises high above the advancing Cashley to head the only goal; but City's relegation fears are eased with news of Blackburn's defeat.

Bristol City: Cashley, Jacobs, Drysdale, Wilson, Rooks, Parr, Tainton, Garland, Wimshurst, Gow, Fear
Oxford: *Kearns, Lucas, Shuker, Roberts, Clarke C, Evanson, Atkinson G, Skeen, Clarke D, Cassidy, Clayton, Bartley*

40 — QP RANGERS (H)
Scorers: (none). Ref: C Fallon

Clement leads Rangers' attack in place of the injured McCulloch. City are reinforced by the return of Hill and Garland, though ankle problems forces the withdrawal of Jacobs. An uneventful contest apart from flashes of Marsh's skill, with neither side demonstrating much penetration.

Bristol City: Cashley, Jacobs, Drysdale, Wilson, Rooks, Hill, Tainton, Garland, Merrick, Gow, Skirton
QP Rangers: *Parkes, Watson, Gillard, Hunt, Hazell, Francis, Venables, Clement, Marsh, Saul, Skirton*

41 — LEICESTER (H)
Scorers: Brown 89. Ref: W Gow

Ebullient Bobby Kellard, much missed this season since his transfer, celebrates fulfilment of his ambition of reaching the top flight as Leicester clinch the title. Brown lashes in Kellard's right-wing corner for the injury-time winner. Wilson was booked 57 mins for throwing the ball away.

Bristol City: Cashley, Jacobs, Drysdale, Wilson, Rooks, Hill, Tainton, Spiring*, Garland, Gow, Skirton
Leicester: *Shilton, Whitworth, Nish, Kellard, Sjoberg*, Cross, Farrington, Brown, Fern, Carlin, Manley, Stringfellow*

42 — BLACKBURN (A)
Scorers: Galley 8, 27 — Hunter 56, Rogers 70. Ref: V James

Blackburn, doomed to Associate Member status for the first time, look dead and buried at the interval. Injury-hit City introduce 17-year-old Len Bond, who distinguishes himself on several occasions. Rovers deserve the draw, achieved by Hunter's header and Rogers' fine low shot.

Bristol City: Bond, Jacobs, Drysdale, Gow, Rooks, Hill, Tainton, Garland, Merrick, Fear, Galley
Blackburn: *Jones, Goodwin, Kopel, Hunter, Fazackerley*, Metcalfe, Conlon, Broomfield, Pickering, Rogers, Eccles, Menmuir*

LEAGUE DIVISION 2 (CUP-TIES) Manager: Alan Dicks SEASON 1970-71

League Cup

Match	F-A	H-T	1	2	3	4	5	6	7	8	9	10	11	12 sub used
2 A ROTHERHAM 7 — 8/9 — 7,384 3:8 — D 0-0 0-0			Gibson / *Tunks*	Jacobs / *Houghton*	Drysdale / *Leigh*	Wimshurst / *Bettany*	Connor / *Watson*	Parr / *Swift*	Skirton / *Brogden*	Garland / *Hague*	Galley / *Phillips**	Gow / *Bentley*	Sharpe* / *Mullen*	Tainton / *Lill*

Scorers, Times, and Referees — Ref: K Howley

Dogged defending by Connor and Parr on a night of cup shocks keep City in the competition against keen young Rotherham forwards. Garland is guilty of the 'miss of the season' after rounding the keeper in the second minute. Leigh appears from nowhere to clear the ball off the line.

Match	F-A	H-T	1	2	3	4	5	6	7	8	9	10	11	12 sub used
2R H ROTHERHAM 7 — 15/9 — 9,403 3:11 — W 4-0 1-0			Gibson / *Tunks*	Jacobs* / *Houghton*	Drysdale / *Leigh*	Wimshurst / *Bettany*	Connor / *Swift*	Parr / *Hague*	Skirton / *Brogden*	Garland / *Fantham*	Galley / *Womble*	Gow / *Bentley*	Sharpe / *Mullen**	Tainton / *Warnock*

Skirton 26, Gow 54, Garland 55, 83 — Ref: R Burns

Bettany hits a post for the visitors shortly before Skirton heads City in front. After the break, Gow's harmless shot deceives Tunks and then the move of the match sees Chris Garland running 40 yards to head in. A cool chip from Garland seals a rather flattering scoreline for City.

Match	F-A	H-T	1	2	3	4	5	6	7	8	9	10	11	12 sub used
3 A BLACKPOOL 11 — 7/10 — 10,877 1:21 — W 1-0 1-0			Gibson / *Thomson*	Stacey / *Armfield*	Drysdale / *Mowbray*	Tainton / *Hatton*	Rooks / *James*	Parr / *Alcock*	Skirton / *Burns*	Garland / *Suddick*	Galley* / *Craven**	Gow / *Hutchison*	Sharpe / *Coleman*	Broomfield / *McNicholas*

Sharpe 24 — Ref: H Williams

City's first away cup win over top-flight opposition for 61 years. Teamwork, with every player working for each other, forms the basis of City's shock success. Blackpool are decisively beaten as Sharpe spurns numerous opportunities to add to his header from Skirton's perfect cross.

Match	F-A	H-T	1	2	3	4	5	6	7	8	9	10	11	12 sub used
4 A LEICESTER 21 — 28/10 — 21,577 3 — D 2-2 1-1			Gibson / *Shilton*	Drysdale / *Whitworth*	Merrick / *Nish*	Wimshurst / *Manley*	Rooks / *Sjoberg*	Parr / *Cross*	Skirton / *Farrington*	Garland* / *Brown A*	Broomfield / *Stringfellow**	Tainton / *Kellard*	Sharpe / *Glover*	Gow /

Garland 17, Sharpe 72, Farrington 27, Nish 76p — Ref: D Pugh

Shilton secures Leicester an undeserved replay. Inspired City twice ahead, but the Filberts respond with a 25-yard shot and a disputed pen after Parr cuts across Manley. City's second is the goal of the game, Sharpe finishing a 40-yard dribble with a shot into far corner. Rooks is booked.

Match	F-A	H-T	1	2	3	4	5	6	7	8	9	10	11	12 sub used
4R H LEICESTER 21 — 3/11 — 16,575 1 — W 2-1 1-0 aet			Gibson / *Shilton*	Drysdale / *Whitworth*	Merrick / *Nish*	Wimshurst / *Manley*	Rodgers / *Sjoberg*	Parr / *Cross*	Skirton* / *Farrington*	Broomfield / *Fern*	Galley / *Stringfellow**	Tainton / *Kellard*	Sharpe / *Glover*	Gow / *Brown A*

Rodgers 15, Wimshurst 104, Nish 82p — Ref: W Gow

City demonstrate much courage and determination as Leicester take the tie into extra-time with a late equaliser. Rodgers hits a tremendous shot which cannons off Sjoberg and into the net. Leicester take the initiative in the second half, but City win in extra-time with a well-taken goal.

Match	F-A	H-T	1	2	3	4	5	6	7	8	9	10	11	12 sub used
QF A FULHAM 20 — 17/11 — 16,281 3:1 — D 0-0 0-0			Gibson / *Seymour*	Drysdale / *Pentecost*	Merrick / *Callaghan*	Wimshurst / *Brown Stan*	Rooks / *Matthewson*	Rodgers / *Dunne*	Garland / *Moreline**	Broomfield / *Halom*	Galley / *Earle*	Tainton / *Lloyd*	Sharpe / *Barrett*	Morton /

Ref: J Taylor

City are on top at rain-soaked Craven Cottage but squander many opportunities. Sharpe hits a post at the Cottage end on eight minutes. There is nearly a spectacular 30-yard up and under own-goal by Matthewson, who chased Gibson's goal-kick whilst under pressure from Broomfield.

Match	F-A	H-T	1	2	3	4	5	6	7	8	9	10	11	12 sub used
QFR H FULHAM 20 — 24/11 — 23,230 3:1 — W 1-0 1-0			Gibson / *Seymour*	Drysdale / *Pentecost*	Merrick / *Callaghan*	Gow / *Brown Stan*	Rooks / *Matthewson*	Parr / *Dunne*	Skirton / *Horne*	Garland* / *Halom*	Galley / *Earle*	Tainton / *Lloyd*	Sharpe / *Barrett*	Broomfield /

Sharpe 31p — Ref: J Taylor

Fulham chairman, comedian Tommy Trinder, sums up City's performance with his well-known catchphrase 'you lucky people'. Few would disagree as City are outplayed. Brown's trip on Skirton yields a penalty, but Fulham are denied justice of a similar award just before the end.

Match	F-A	H-T	1	2	3	4	5	6	7	8	9	10	11	12 sub used
SF H TOTTENHAM 20 — 1 16/12 — 30,201 1:3 — D 1-1 0-0			Gibson / *Jennings*	Jacobs / *Kinnear*	Drysdale / *Knowles*	Wimshurst / *Mullery*	Rooks / *England*	Parr / *Beal*	Skirton / *Gilzean*	Garland / *Perryman*	Galley / *Chivers*	Gow / *Peters*	Sharpe / *Pearce*	Tainton /

Skirton 56, Gilzean 72 — Ref: N Burtenshaw

City are thwarted by Gilzean's immaculate far-post header, rounding off Peters' pinpoint pass. Wimshurst controls the midfield as the game opens up in the second half. City score with Jennings out of position when Beal's clearance hits Peters and rolls obligingly into Skirton's path.

Match	F-A	H-T	1	2	3	4	5	6	7	8	9	10	11	12 sub used
SF A TOTTENHAM 20 — 2 23/12 — 29,982 1:4 — L 0-2 0-0 aet			Gibson / *Jennings*	Jacobs / *Kinnear*	Drysdale / *Knowles*	Wimshurst* / *Mullery*	Rooks / *England**	Parr / *Beal*	Skirton* / *Gilzean*	Garland / *Perryman*	Sharpe / *Chivers*	Gow / *Peters*	Spiring / *Neighbour*	Tainton / *Pearce*

Chivers 98, Pearce 111 — Ref: K Burns — (City lost 1-3 on aggregate)

A brave show by City as a costly error of judgement by Gibson grants Spurs a breakthrough goal. Advancing too soon to Knowles' free-kick, he is exposed as Chivers heads in. City's best chance falls to Sharpe, a fraction late as Tainton's cross presents an open goal on 61 minutes.

FA Cup

Match	F-A	H-T	1	2	3	4	5	6	7	8	9	10	11	12 sub used
3 A SOUTHAMPTON 20 — 11/1 — 24,131 1:8 — L 0-3 0-0			Cashley / *Martin*	Parr / *Kirkup*	Drysdale / *Hollywood*	Wimshurst* / *Fisher*	Rooks / *McGrath*	Rodgers / *Gabriel*	Tainton / *Paine*	Garland / *Channon*	Broomfield / *Davies*	Gow / *O'Neil*	Sharpe / *Jenkins**	Merrick / *Byrne*

O'Neil 72, Davies 79, 85 — Ref: C Nicholls

Tenacious City give the Saints many anxious moments as Cashley has a debut to remember, making many fine saves, incuding a 69th-minute penalty after Rooks' handball. He dives right to hold Mick Channon's kick, but Southampton undismayed, respond with three late strikes.

League Table

	Team	P	Home					Away					Pts
			W	D	L	F	A	W	D	L	F	A	
1	Leicester	42	12	7	2	30	14	11	6	4	27	16	59
2	Sheffield Utd	42	14	6	1	49	18	7	8	6	24	21	56
3	Cardiff	42	12	7	2	39	16	8	6	7	25	25	53
4	Carlisle	42	16	3	2	39	13	4	10	7	26	30	53
5	Hull	42	11	5	5	31	16	8	6	7	23	25	51
6	Luton	42	12	7	2	40	18	6	8	9	22	25	49
7	Middlesbro	42	13	6	2	37	16	4	8	9	23	27	48
8	Millwall	42	13	5	3	36	12	6	4	11	23	30	47
9	Birmingham	42	12	7	2	30	12	5	5	11	28	36	46
10	Norwich	42	11	8	2	34	20	4	6	11	20	32	44
11	QP Rangers	42	11	5	5	39	22	5	6	10	19	31	43
12	Swindon	42	12	7	2	38	14	3	5	13	23	37	42
13	Sunderland	42	11	6	4	34	21	4	6	11	18	33	42
14	Oxford	42	8	8	5	23	23	6	6	9	18	25	42
15	Sheffield Wed	42	10	7	4	32	27	2	5	14	19	42	36
16	Portsmouth	42	9	4	8	32	28	1	10	10	14	33	34
17	Orient	42	9	11	5	16	15	4	5	12	13	36	34
18	Watford	42	6	7	8	18	22	4	6	11	20	38	33
19	BRISTOL CITY	42	9	6	6	30	28	5	5	15	16	36	31
20	Charlton	42	7	6	8	28	30	1	8	12	13	35	30
21	Blackburn	42	5	8	8	20	28	1	7	13	17	41	27
22	Bolton	42	6	5	10	22	31	1	5	15	13	43	24
		924	225	141	96	697	444	96	141	225	444	697	924

Odds & ends

Double wins: (1) Watford.

Double losses: (5) Leicester, Oxford, Middlesbrough, Sheffield Wed, Norwich.

Won from behind: (2) Carlisle (h), Luton (h).

Lost from in front: (4) QP Rangers (a), Swindon (a), Carlisle (a), Norwich (a).

High spots: Goals galore in thrilling game against Sunderland at Ashton Gate.

Gate on the opening day of the season.

Great fight-back to beat Luton 3-2 at Ashton Gate.

Debut of Hill and Wilson in 3-0 success at Vicarage Road.

Reaching the semi-final of the League Cup.

Beating Blackpool 1-0 at Bloomfield Road in the League Cup.

Low spots: Gerry Sharpe's career-ending injury against Middlesbrough.

Losing in the semi-final of the League Cup.

Losing 0-4 against Oxford at Ashton Gate.

Finishing League programme by playing five games without a win.

Lack of goals, City failing to score in 18 League games.

Player of the year: Brian Drysdale.

Ever-presents: (1) Brian Drysdale.

Hat-tricks: (0).

Leading scorer: John Galley (12).

Appearances and Goals

Player	Appearances						Goals			
	Lge	Sub	LC	Sub	FAC	Sub	Lge	LC	FAC	Tot
Bond, Len	1									
Bartley, Danny	3	1								
Broomfield, Ian	9	2	3	2			2			2
Connor, Jack	4		2							
Cashley, Ray	11									
Derrick, Jantzen	1									
Drysdale, Brian	42		9							
Fear, Keith	10	2								
Galley, John	36		7				12			12
Garland, Chris	38		8	1			8		3	11
Gibson, Mike	30		9							
Gow, Gerry	37	1	6	2			5		1	6
Hill, Brian	7									
Jacobs, Trevor	21		4							
Menmuir, Billy		1								
Merrick, Geoff	13	4	4			1				
Parr, Gordon	31	2	8							
Rodgers, David	6		2		1				1	1
Rooks, Dickie	33		6		1		2			2
Sharpe, Gerry	24		9		1		7		3	10
Spiring, Peter	6		1				2			2
Skirton, Alan	20	2	8				4		2	6
Stacey, Steve	9		1							
Tainton, Trevor	26	11	5	2	1		1			1
Wilson, Les	10									
Wimshurst, Ken	34		7		1		3		1	4
26 players used	462	26	99	6	11	1	46		11	57

LEAGUE DIVISION 2 — Manager: Alan Dicks — SEASON 1971-72

No	Date	Venue / Opponent	Att	Pos	Res	F-A	Pt	H-T	Scorers, Times, and Referees
1	14/8	H MILLWALL	12,612		D	3-3	1	2-2	Gow 3, Sweeney 13, Garland 73 / Dunphy 17, Possee 23, Bolland 74 / Ref: J Taylor
2	21/8	A SHEFFIELD WED	12,724		W	5-1	3	3-0	Galley 12, 26, 65, Emanuel 37, Prendergast 89 / [Garland 63] / Ref: G Hill
3	28/8	H MIDDLESBROUGH	16,474	2	W	2-1	5	2-0	Wimhurst 2, Garland 29p / Maddren 71 / Ref: H Hackney
4	31/8	H CARDIFF	**23,525**	1	W	2-0	7	1-0	Galley 20, Gow 46 / Ref: J Hunting
5	4/9	A BURNLEY	13,634	2	D	1-1	8	0-0	Galley 49 / Bellamy 47 / Ref: T Dawes
6	11/9	H HULL	16,659	1	W	4-0	10	2-0	Galley 8, 79, Fear 38p, Gow 81 / Ref: S Kaley
7	18/9	A BIRMINGHAM	28,745	2	L	0-1	10	0-1	Latchford 40 / Ref: A Oliver
8	25/9	H NORWICH	18,768	4	L	0-1	10	0-0	Stringer 48 / Ref: R Armstrong
9	28/9	H BLACKPOOL	20,352	2	W	4-0	12	1-0	Galley 24, Tainton 62, Wimhurst 67 / [Gow 87pl] / Ref: C Nicholls
10	2/10	A SWINDON	21,595	2	W	1-0	14	0-0	Spiring 79 / Ref: N Burtenshaw

Line-ups (City in normal type, opponents in italic)

No	1	2	3	4	5	6	7	8	9	10	11	12 sub used
1	Cashley	Wimhurst	Drysdale*	Emanuel	Rooks	Merrick	Tainton	Garland*	Galley	Sweeney	Gow	Fear
	King	*Brown*	*Cripps**	*Dorney*	*Kitchener*	*Burnett*	*Possee*	*Bolland*	*Bridges*	*Dunphy*	*Allder*	*Coxhill*
2	Cashley	Wimhurst	Drysdale	Emanuel	Rooks	Merrick	Tainton	Garland*	Galley	Sweeney	Gow	Fear
	Grummitt	*Rodrigues*	*Burton*	*Prophett*	*Holsgrove**	*Pugh*	*Sinclair*	*Craig*	*Downes*	*Prendergast*	*Sissons*	*Thompson*
3	Cashley	Wimhurst	Drysdale	Emanuel	Rooks	Merrick	Tainton	Garland	Galley	Sweeney	Gow	Fear
	Whigham	*Maddren*	*Jones*	*Stiles*	*Boam*	*Spraggon*	*Downing*	*Hickton*	*McMordie*	*Vincent*	*Laidlaw**	*Mills*
4	Cashley	Wimhurst	Drysdale	Emanuel	Rooks	Merrick	Tainton	Garland	Galley	Sweeney	Gow	Fear
	Eadie	*Carver*	*Bell*	*Sutton*	*Murray*	*Phillips*	*Gibson*	*Clark*	*Hoy*	*Warboys*	*Foggon*	
5	Cashley	Wimhurst	Drysdale	Emanuel	Rooks	Merrick	Tainton	Fear*	Galley	Sweeney	Gow	Spiring
	Mellor	*Docherty*	*Cliff*	*Bellamy**	*Waldron*	*Dobson*	*Thomas*	*West*	*Fletcher*	*Casper*	*Kindon*	*Collins*
6	Cashley	Wimhurst	Drysdale	Emanuel	Rooks	Merrick	Tainton	Fear*	Galley	Sweeney	Gow	Spiring
	McKechnie	*Banks*	*De Vries*	*Wilkinson*	*Greenwood*	*Knighton*	*Lord*	*Houghton*	*Pearson*	*Wagstaff*	*O'Riley**	*Simpkin*
7	Cashley	Wimhurst	Drysdale	Emanuel*	Rooks	Merrick	Tainton	Garland	Galley	Sweeney	Gow	Spiring
	Kelly D	*Martin*	*Pendrey*	*Page**	*Hynd*	*Robinson*	*Campbell*	*Francis*	*Latchford R*	*Phillips*	*Taylor*	*Smith*
8	Cashley	Wimhurst	Drysdale	Emanuel*	Rooks	Merrick	Tainton	Fear	Galley	Sweeney	Gow	Spiring
	Keelan	*Payne*	*Butler*	*Stringer*	*Forbes*	*Anderson*	*Howard*	*Silvester*	*Livermore*	*Paddon*	*Foggo**	*Briggs*
9	Cashley	Wimhurst	Drysdale	Emanuel	Rooks	Merrick	Tainton	Spiring	Galley	Sweeney	Gow	Fear
	Ramsbottom	*Hatton*	*Fuschillo*	*Booth*	*Alcock*	*Suddaby*	*Ainscow*	*Green*	*James*	*Suddick*	*Wann*	
10	Cashley	Wimhurst	Drysdale	Emanuel	Rooks	Merrick	Tainton	Spiring	Galley	Sweeney	Gow	Fear
	Downsboro' / Thomas	*Trollope*	*Butler*	*Burrows*	*Mackay**	*Peplow*	*Harland*	*Jones C*	*Noble*	*Rogers*	*Bunkell*	

Match reports

1. An exciting game as Cashley blunders to let Millwall back into contention. He lets Eamonn Dunphy's gentle free-kick through his fingers and fails to come off line as Derek Possee fires the equaliser. Gow scored the first with a right-foot shot after beating three defenders in a solo run.

2. Galley sparks off City's biggest away win for five years when finishing off a four-man move with a shot into the top corner. A brilliant display against mediocre opponents, whose only consolation is a strike at the death, when Mike Prendergast heads in from Ken Burton's centre.

3. Bill Maddren's magnificent strike sets up a nail-biting finish after City take an early two-goal lead. Wimhurst nets with a poor free-kick and Garland puts away pen after John Vincent's handball. Bookings for Gow, Emanuel and Nobby Stiles as ref adheres to clampdown directive.

4. Table-topping City put on a superb show after Cardiff dominate the early stages. Against the run of play, City take the lead as Galley hooks the ball into the roof of the net after side-stepping a defender. Gow then sets the seal on a fine success by driving home Tainton's cross.

5. A lively game in the brilliant sunshine, but not a rough one despite the booking of five players. Galley is unfortunate on 14 minutes when his header is disallowed for offside, but he equalises Arthur Bellamy's shot from the edge of the box, by heading in Wimhurst's high lob.

6. City celebrate Alan Dicks' award as Bells Manager of the Month as Galley heads in Tainton's cross and then Fear punishes Francis Banks handball with a confident penalty. After the break, Galley is on target with a tap-in before Gow's header completes a handsome victory.

7. City lose their unbeaten record against superior opponents in a fast, attractive game. Tenacious defending restrict Birmingham to Bob Latchford's headed goal, so leaving City to rue the referee's decision not to award penalty when Tainton was clearly fouled just after half-time.

8. City find the Norwich defence in fine form in this top-of-the-table clash. David Stringer poaches the points for the Canaries, latching onto Merrick's poor clearance to blast in from six yards. City are denied by Kevin Keelan's superb display and Gerry Butler clearing off the line.

9. Blackpool are unlucky as a slip by debutant Paul Fuschillo allows Galley to score from a narrow angle, whilst Dennis Wann hits the bar early in each half. Terry Alcock's foul concedes a penalty after Tainton's 25-yarder and Wimhurst's free-kick had increased City's advantage.

10. Spiring's fierce right-foot volley from Tainton's cross secures City's win in a defensive-orientated contest. Neither side exhibit much control in the sweltering heat, though early on Don Rogers posed his usual threat. Merrick heads out Joe Butler's thunderous shot just prior to the break.

Match 11 — WATFORD (H), 9/10

Att	Pos	Res	Score	HT	OppPos	Pts
18,100	2	W	2-1	1-0	19	16

Scorers: Spring 38, Galley 53 — *Lindsay 82* — Ref: N Paget

City: Cashley, Wimhurst, Drysdale, Emanuel, Rooks, Merrick, Tainton, Spring, Galley, Sweeney, Gow
Walker, Butler, Williams, Welbourne, Baxter, Lees, McGettigan, Eddy, Wigg, Lindsay, Franks

City are shocked midway through the first half as Ron Wigg hits the bar, but gain reward for their almost constant attacking when Spring nudges in Drysdale's cross. Watford's adoption of a more offensive approach after the break pays off when Lindsay's shot creeps into the net.

Match 12 — MILLWALL (A), 16/10

Att	Pos	Res	Score	HT	OppPos	Pts
14,041	3	L	1-3	1-3	2	16

Scorers: Spring 38 — *Merrick 2 (og), Bridges 79, Bolland 85* — King — Ref: R Capey

City: Cashley, Wimhurst, Drysdale, Emanuel, Rooks, Merrick, Tainton*, Spring, Galley, Sweeney, Gow
Brown, Cripps, Dorney, Kitchener, Burnett, Dunphy, Bridges, Smethurst, Bolland, Possee, Fear

A disastrous start as Merrick heads into his own goal whilst attempting to clear Eamonn Dunphy's free-kick, but Spring levels with a superb shot. City are unfortunate on 77 mins when Sweeney hits the post, but succumb to a Barry Bridges' header and Gordon Bolland's 30-yarder.

Match 13 — PORTSMOUTH (A), 20/10

Att	Pos	Res	Score	HT	OppPos	Pts
12,575	3	D	1-1	0-0	11	17

Scorers: Spring 82 — *Ley 57* — Ref: B Daniels

City: Cashley, Wimhurst, Drysdale, Emanuel, Rooks, Merrick, Tainton, Spring, Galley, Sweeney, Gow
Milkins, Smith, Ley, Hand, Youlden, Munks, Piper, Reynolds, Hiron, McCann, Trebilcock

City's pattern-weaving display has Portsmouth all a dither, especially in the first half. George Ley puts Pompey in front from a free-kick after Rooks is penalised for pushing Ray Hiron, but City deservedly equalise with Spring's powerful drive after Gow dribbles past three defenders.

Match 14 — ORIENT (H), 23/10

Att	Pos	Res	Score	HT	OppPos	Pts
17,772	3	W	5-3	1-3	18	19

Scorers: Rooks 35, Spring 52, Galley 55, 90, [T'nton 71] — *B'wyer 19, 42, Brisley 26* — Ref: E Jolly

City: Cashley, Wimhurst, Drysdale, Emanuel, Rooks, Merrick, Tainton, Spring, Galley, Sweeney, Gow
Goddard, Allen, Rofe, Dyson, Hoadley, Harris, Lazarus, Brisley, Bullock, Bennett, Bowyer

City stage a remarkable recovery in this pulsating affair. Rooks' header brings City back into the match after Orient's great start with Ian Bowyer heading in and a 20-yarder from Terry Brisley. A sensational Galley volley levels matters and Tainton lashes ball in to put City ahead.

Match 15 — CHARLTON (A), 30/10

Att	Pos	Res	Score	HT	OppPos	Pts
10,101	4	L	0-2	0-1	18	19

Scorers: *Hunt 14, Treacy 60* — Ref: R Perkin

City: Cashley, Wimhurst, Drysdale, Emanuel*, Rooks, Merrick, Tainton, Spring, Galley, Sweeney, Gow
Dunn, Reeves, Warman, Bond, Went, Shipperley, Davies, Treacy, Hunt, Rogers, Peacock, Fear

Wimhurst finds his lack of pace exploited as an out-of-sorts City succumb to lowly Charlton. Peter Hunt, playing his first game of the season, gives City an early jolt with his low shot, and after the break Ray Treacy's glancing near-post finishes off Dennis Bond's corner.

Match 16 — FULHAM (H), 6/11

Att	Pos	Res	Score	HT	OppPos	Pts
17,295	5	L	1-2	0-2	17	19

Scorers: Galley 82 — *Barrett 26, Cross 40* — Ref: R Lee

City: Gibson, Wimhurst, Drysdale, Emanuel*, Rooks, Merrick, Tainton, Spring, Galley, Sweeney, Gow
Webster, Fraser, Callaghan, Brown, Matthewson, Richardson, Conway, Cross, Earle, Lloyd, Barrett, Jacobs

Roger Cross heads in Jimmy Conway's centre just prior to the interval, but offside deprives Fulham of reward for the move of the match. Gibson saves City from a heavy defeat as they are often exposed through the middle. Galley rises majestically to head in Tainton's cross.

Match 17 — QP RANGERS (A), 13/11

Att	Pos	Res	Score	HT	OppPos	Pts
14,898	7	L	0-3	0-1	3	19

Scorers: *O'Rouke 28, Merrick 73 (og), Marsh 90* — Ref: R Crabb

City: Gibson, Wimhurst, Drysdale, Emanuel, Rooks, Merrick, Tainton, Spring, Galley, Sweeney, Gow
Parkes, Clement, Hazell, Saul, Mancini, Hunt, Morgan, Francis, Leach, Marsh, O'Rouke

Rodney Marsh, with one of his infamous dives, wins penalty in the last moments. Gibson goes left to save Marsh's kick, but from the resulting corner the Rangers star man hooks the ball home. Rangers counter the Wimhurst-Tainton alliance as City's play is spoilt by poor passing.

Match 18 — CARLISLE (H), 19/11

Att	Pos	Res	Score	HT	OppPos	Pts
13,017	7	L	1-4	1-3	12	19

Scorers: Gow 3 — *Barton 20, Bowles 42, Owen 44, 88* — Ref: H Davey

City: Gibson, Jacobs, Drysdale, Emanuel, Rooks, Merrick, Tainton, Wimhurst, Fear*, Sweeney, Parr
Ross, Heinstead, Gorman, Ternent, Winstanley, Sutton, Barton, Martin, Owen, Bowles, Balderstone Davis*

Carlisle, superior in midfield and lethal in attack, win this game much as they please after Gow nets at the third attempt. Frank Barton cuts through for the equaliser and then fine approach play between Chris Balderstone and Bobby Owen allows Stan Bowles to shoot them ahead.

Match 19 — SUNDERLAND (A), 27/11

Att	Pos	Res	Score	HT	OppPos	Pts
15,655	9	D	1-1	0-1	5	20

Scorers: Wilson 75 — *Pitt 39* — Ref: G Jones

City: Gibson, Wimhurst, Drysdale, Emanuel*, Rooks, Merrick, Tainton, Gow, Broomfield, Wilson, Sweeney
Montgomery, Malone, Coleman, Harvey, Pitt, Chambers, McGiven, Kerr, Watson, Hughes, Tueart, Parr

Former England star Jackie Milburn accepts the consensus view of this being a bore. Wilson, playing his first game since signing permanently from Wolves, is City's saviour. He puts the finishing touch to a move with Broomfield after Ritchie Pitt's strong shot gives Newcastle the lead.

Match 20 — LUTON (H), 4/12

Att	Pos	Res	Score	HT	OppPos	Pts
12,921	10	D	0-0	0-0	14	21

Ref: C Robinson

City: Gibson, Wimhurst, Drysdale, Wilson, Rooks, Merrick, Tainton, Spring, Broomfield, Sweeney, Gow*
Read, Ryan John, Slough, Keen, Nicholl, Moore, Anderson, Court, Halom, Givens, Hindson, Bruton

City's punchless attack is easily controlled by the dominant form of John Moore and Chris Nicholl, whilst at the other end Gibson brings off many fine saves. Don Givens and John Ryan are unfortunate to be booked for tackles much milder than many others unpunished in the game.

Match 21 — OXFORD (A), 11/12

Att	Pos	Res	Score	HT	OppPos	Pts
8,264	9	D	0-0	0-0	17	22

Ref: K Styles/Bent

City: Gibson, Wimhurst, Drysdale, Bruton, Rooks, Merrick, Tainton, Wilson, Broomfield, Sweeney, Griffin
Burton, Lucas, Shuker, Roberts, Clarke C, Evanson, Skeen, Fleming, Clarke D, Cassidy, Aylott, Clayton*

The loss of Ray Burton – injured bringing down Broomfield – transforms the game into a thriller. Masterly display by Gibson thwarts Oxford as they lay siege to City's goal. Linesman Bent takes over from the injured referee for the last five mins. Bookings for Burton and Dick Lucas.

LEAGUE DIVISION 2 — Manager: Alan Dicks — SEASON 1971-72

No	Date		Att	Pos		Pt	F-A	H-T	Scorers, Times, and Referees
22	H BURNLEY 18/12		12,909	11 (6)	L	22	0-2	0-0	Fletcher 58, 90 — Ref: W. Castle
23	A PRESTON 27/12		19,738	11 (7)	L	22	0-1	0-1	Lyall 1 — Ref: H Hackney
24	H BIRMINGHAM 1/1		17,457	10 (7)	W	24	1-0	1-0	Galley 15 — Ref: R Crabb
25	A MIDDLESBROUGH 8/1		13,117	11 (7)	L	24	0-1	0-0	Downing 59 — Ref: R Matthewson
26	A BLACKPOOL 22/1		9,923	15 (12)	L	24	0-1	0-1	Suddick 7 — Ref: C Howell
27	H PORTSMOUTH 29/1		10,949	14 (15)	D	25	1-1	1-1	Galley 21; Bruton 35 (og) — Ref: B Homewood
28	A ORIENT 12/2		13,272	18 (16)	L	25	0-2	0-1	Bullock 34, 51 — Ref: N Paget
29	H CHARLTON 19/2		10,207	16 (18)	W	27	2-0	2-0	Galley 32, Tainton 39 — Ref: J Williams
30	A FULHAM 26/2		9,276	17 (20)	L	27	0-2	0-0	Callaghan 86, Earle 89 — Ref: R Toseland
31	H QP RANGERS 4/3		11,105	15 (6)	W	29	2-0	0-0	Rodgers 64, Galley 69 — Ref: R Toseland

Line-ups (1–11, 12 sub used)

No	Team	1	2	3	4	5	6	7	8	9	10	11	12 sub used
22	City	Gibson	Wimshurst	Drysdale	Gow	Bruton	Merrick	Tainton	Wilson	Rooks	Sweeney	Burnside*	Griffin
22	Opp	Mellor	Docherty	Thomson	Bellamy	Waldron	Dobson	Thomas	West	Fletcher	Kindon	James	
23	City	Gibson	Wimshurst	Drysdale	Wilson	Rooks	Merrick	Tainton	Spiring	Galley	Sweeney	Gow	Tarbuck
23	Opp	Kelly	McMahon	McNab	Bird	Hawkins	Spavin*	Spark	Clark	McIlmoyle	Lyall	Ingram	
24	City	Gibson	Wimshurst	Drysdale	Wilson	Bruton	Merrick	Tainton	Spiring	Galley	Sweeney	Gow	
24	Opp	Latchford D	Carroll	Pendrey	Page	Hynd	Harland	Campbell	Francis	Latchford R	Hatton	Summerill	
25	City	Gibson	Wimshurst	Drysdale	Wilson	Bruton	Merrick	Tainton	Spiring	Galley	Sweeney	Gow	
25	Opp	Platt	Craggs	Stone	Madden	Boam	Gates	Downing	McMordie	Mills	Hickton	Laidlaw	
26	City	Gibson	Jacobs	Drysdale	Wilson	Bruton	Merrick	Gow	Spiring*	Galley	Sweeney	Bartley	Tainton
26	Opp	Burridge	Hatton*	Bentley	Suddaby	James	Simpkin	Burns	Suddick	Dyson	Lennard	Hutchison	Ainscow
27	City	Bond	Jacobs	Drysdale	Gow	Bruton	Merrick	Tainton	Wilson	Galley	Sweeney	Bartley	
27	Opp	Milkins	Smith	Collins	Wilson	Hand	Blant	Piper	Reynolds	Trebilcock	Ley	Jennings	
28	City	Bond	Jacobs	Drysdale	Emanuel	Rodgers	Merrick	Tainton	Wilson	Galley	Sweeney	Gow*	Parr
28	Opp	Bowtell	Hoadley	Rofe	Bennett	Harris	Allen	Fairbrother	Dyson	Bullock	Walley	Bowyer	
29	City	Cashley	Jacobs	Drysdale	Emanuel	Rooks	Merrick	Tainton	Spiring	Galley	Sweeney	Bartley	
29	Opp	Dunn	Jones	Warman	Bond	Went	Shipperley	Davies	Treacy*	Hunt	Rogers	Flanagan	Barnard
30	City	Cashley	Jacobs	Drysdale	Wilson	Rooks	Merrick	Tainton	Spiring	Galley	Sweeney	Bartley	
30	Opp	Mellor	Moreline	Callaghan	Brown	Matthewson	Richardson	Conway	Cross	Earle	Lloyd	Barrett	
31	City	Cashley	Jacobs	Drysdale	Emanuel	Rodgers	Merrick	Tainton	Spiring	Galley	Gow	Bartley	
31	Opp	Parkes	Clement	Gillard	Hazell	Mancini	Hunt	O'Rourke	Francis	McCulloch	Marsh*	Busby	Leach

Match notes

22 H BURNLEY: Unmerciful barracking for skipper Wimshurst as City's makeshift side are subjected to much pressure by high-scoring Burnley. The playing of Rooks at centre-forward and the introduction of Burnside is not a success. Steve Kindon's electrifying run sets up Paul Fletcher's second goal.

23 A PRESTON: Peter Doherty, now assistant at Deepdale, admits his old club are unlucky to lose. City blitz the Preston goal for the entire second half, but are unable to recover from George Lyall's 45-second shoulder-high shot that Gibson knocks against the bar for Hugh McIlmoyle to nudge in.

24 H BIRMINGHAM: City are back to their best in this all-action contest with a display of non-stop running in the first half. Galley's 15-yard textbook header is one of his finest goals, whilst Gibson is outstanding after the break when Birmingham wrest control. Page, Pendrey and Tainton are booked.

25 A MIDDLESBROUGH: A poor match, devoid of thrills, on a cold, grey day at Ayresome Park, as City offer little in the way of attacking enterprise. Derrick Downing's 25-yarder benefits from a deflection off Bruton's foot to sail over Gibson's head and into the net. Gow heads off the line to save City early on.

26 A BLACKPOOL: Merrick leads City for the first time and after winning the toss finds himself much involved as Blackpool exert heavy pressure. Gibson is unsighted as Alan Suddick's ten-yard volley beats him at the near post. Jacobs is booked for his 87th-minute foul on Tommy Hutchison.

27 H PORTSMOUTH: City employ two orthodox wingers for the first time this season. Galley's shot finds the net after hitting John Collins and John Milkins, whilst Nicky Jennings' hard-hit centre canons in off Bruton. City are much relieved at the death as Norman Piper's strike is disallowed for handball.

28 A ORIENT: A phantom whistler helps Orient's unconvincing success in bog-like conditions. City stop as Ian Bowyer nods the ball back across goal for Mike Bullock to head home. Peter Allen's flighted chip sets up Bullock for another scoring header, while near the end Bowyer's strike is disallowed for offside.

29 H CHARLTON: Galley's near-post header and a five-yard effort by Tainton give City a well-deserved success. Against poor opposition, City's all-round supremacy is difficult to fault. The calm efficiency of Merrick and the commanding form of Rooks means a trouble-free afternoon for Cashley.

30 A FULHAM: Cashley's outstanding performance is unable to prevent Fulham, with Peter Mellor making his debut, obtaining a deserved success. John Conway's corner is headed on into the middle, where Fred Callaghan has time to stumble over the ball, before lashing it in from seven yards.

31 H QP RANGERS: Rangers are reduced to being a very ordinary side when Rodney Marsh limps out of the action with a pulled muscle. Cashley's great save from John O'Rourke after five minutes and Emanuel's stirring midfield display keep City in the game, before Rodgers heads in Bartley's cross.

Football season results and line-ups (rotated table). Column headings for the line-up are partly cut off at the top of the page; the City XI is listed in roman type and the opponents' XI in italic type.

No	Venue	Opponent	Date	Att	Res	Pos	Pts	FT	HT	Scorers	Referee
32	A	WATFORD	11/3	5,384	W	22	31	2-0	1-0	Bartley 5, Galley 80	Ref: D Laing
33	H	SHEFFIELD WED	18/3	12,568	W	16	33	1-0	1-0	Spring 39	Ref: B Daniels
34	A	HULL	25/3	11,700	D	18	34	1-1	0-1	Tainton 55 / Wagstaff 28	Ref: E Jolly
35	H	SWINDON	31/3	21,496	W	14	36	1-0	0-0	Galley 88	Ref: C Thomas
36	H	PRESTON	1/4	12,562	W	14	38	4-1	1-1	Spring 8, Tainton 82, Emanuel 87 [Galley 90] / Tarbuck 1	Ref: I Jones
37	A	NORWICH	4/4	34,914	D	7	39	2-2	0-1	Sweeney 84, Gow 88p / Cross 24, Bone 70	Ref: R Kirkpatrick
38	A	CARLISLE	8/4	6,596	L	6	39	0-2	0-1	Owen 14, Gorman 50	Ref: W Hall
39	H	SUNDERLAND	15/4	12,178	W	5	41	3-1	0-1	Gow 69p, Drysdale 86, Galley 90 / Kerr 19	Ref: R Perkin
40	A	LUTON	22/4	8,329	D	14	42	0-0	0-0		Ref: R Challis
41	A	CARDIFF	26/4	17,227	W	19	44	3-2	2-1	Spring 10, 65, Gow 20p / Warboys 32, Woodruff 83	Ref: D Nippard
42	H	OXFORD	29/4	10,793	W	15	46	4-2	2-1	Galley 26, 41, Gow 53p, Sweeney 65 / Clarke 16p, Cassidy 81	Ref: C Robinson

Home 15,225 · Away 14,367 · Average 15,225

---

32 WATFORD
City: Cashley, Jacobs, Drysdale, Emanuel, Merrick, Rodgers, Tainton, Spring, Galley, Gow, Bartley
Watford: Walker, Butler, Williams, Lugg, Eddy, Franks, McGettigan*, Wigg, Morrisey, Lindsay, Welbourne, Kenning

Watford's smallest crowd for six years have little to excite them. City, who create little, go ahead from a free-kick as Rodgers and Spring create an opening in Watford's defensive wall. Gow steps over the ball and Bartley follows up to place his shot into the corner of the net.

33 SHEFFIELD WED
City: Cashley, Jacobs, Drysdale, Emanuel, Merrick, Rodgers, Tainton, Spring, Galley, Gow, Bartley
Sheffield Wed: Grummitt, Thompson, Clements, Prophett, Pugh, Holsgrove, Sinclair, Craig, Joicy, Sunley, Sissons

Cashley dives to his right to save Tommy Craig's spot-kick after the break. Bookings for Dave Clements, Alan Thompson and Gow, but the ref errs – perhaps suffering from the earlier effects of being pole-axed – in not awarding the Owls another pen when Jacobs blatantly trips Sunley.

34 HULL
City: Cashley, Jacobs, Drysdale, Emanuel, Merrick, Rodgers, Tainton*, Spring, Galley, Gow, Bartley
Hull: McKechnie, Banks, De Vries, Kaye, Knighton, Neill, McGill, Lord, Pearson, Wagstaff, Butler*, Greenwood

Three remarkable saves by Cashley, including Ian Butler's point-blank header, in the ten minutes leading up to half-time. City then begin to dictate a game that was slipping away from them following Ken Wagstaff's 25-yard cross-shot. Tainton lashes in an angled drive to equalise.

35 SWINDON
City: Cashley, Jacobs, Drysdale, Emanuel, Merrick, Rodgers, Tainton, Spring, Galley, Gow, Bartley
Swindon: Downsboro', Thomas, Trollope, Bunkell, Butler, Burrows, Hubbard, Smart, Horsfield, Noble, Rogers

City are so much on top in this game that even centre-half Rodgers squanders two scoring opportunities. It is not until the dying minutes that their great display gets its reward with Galley's memorable 15-yard volley. A booking for Joe Butler, who brings down Spring on 59 minutes.

36 PRESTON
City: Cashley, Jacobs, Drysdale, Emanuel, Merrick, Parr, Tainton, Spring, Galley, Gow, Bartley
Preston: Kelly, McMahon, Connor, Bird, Spavin, McNab, Heppolette, Young*, McIlmoyle, Lamb, Tarbuck, Hughes

Spring runs in at the far post to put away Galley's flick-on from a free-kick to level matters after Tarbuck's 25-yard drive past the motionless Cashley on just 35 seconds. An untidy game, but Tainton's left-foot drive and headers from Emanuel and Galley secure City's healthy win.

37 NORWICH
City: Cashley, Jacobs, Drysdale, Emanuel, Merrick, Parr*, Tainton, Spring, Galley, Gow, Bartley
Norwich: Kelan, Payne, Black, Stringer, Forbes, Briggs, Livermore, Bone, Cross, Paddon, Foggo, Sweeney

An inspired substitution brings City a share of the spoils in front of the best Carrow Road crowd of the season. Sweeney nets with a fine header from Bartley's cross. Norwich were fortunate with their opener, as Cross was played on by Parr, but no dispute over Jim Bone's classic header.

38 CARLISLE
City: Cashley, Jacobs, Drysdale, Emanuel, Merrick, Bruton, Tainton*, Spring, Galley, Gow, Bartley
Carlisle: Clarke, Davis, Gorman, Ternent, Winstanley, Delgardo, Barton, Martin, Owen, Bowles, Webb*, Hegarty

Carlisle, even without the services of Chris Balderstone and Ray Train, are much the better side. Bobby Owen puts the Cumbrians ahead as he steers in a rebound after Cashley's error. Then John Gorman's speculative lob finds the net after the keeper pushes up under the crossbar.

39 SUNDERLAND
City: Cashley, Jacobs, Drysdale, Emanuel, Merrick, Bruton, Tainton, Spring, Galley, Gow, Bartley
Sunderland: Forster, Malone, Coleman, Horswill, Pitt, Porterfield, McGiven, Kerr, Watson, Lathan, Tueart*, Hughes

Spring falls over his own feet to gain a penalty as lucky City restore parity. Impressive Sunderland fully deserved the lead gained by Bobby Kerr's neat shot, but City snatch an unlikely victory with two late strikes. Drysdale lashes in a fine shot for his first goal for the club.

40 LUTON
City: Cashley, Sweeney, Drysdale, Emanuel, Merrick, Bruton, Tainton, Spring, Galley, Gow, Bartley
Luton: Barber, Slough, Shanks, Keen, Garner, Moore, Wainwright, Halom, Givens, Ryan, John, Hindson

A typical end-of-season affair in which City have the better chances. Spiring spurns two chances to break the deadlock and is unlucky with a first-half shot which Keith Barber touches onto the crossbar. The Luton pair of Don Givens and John Ryan are the best of the visiting players.

41 CARDIFF
City: Cashley, Sweeney, Drysdale, Emanuel, Merrick, Rodgers, Tainton, Spring, Galley, Gow, Bartley
Cardiff: Irwin, Carver, Pethard, Sutton, Phillips, Murray, Gibson, Clark, Woodruff, King, Warboys

Cashley makes his fourth-successive penalty stop in the 18th min to deny Ian Gibson after Drysdale fouled Alan Warboys. He then brings off a super save from Peter King's header near the end. City make no mistake with their penalty after Tainton was blatantly tripped by Mel Sutton.

42 OXFORD
City: Cashley, Sweeney, Drysdale, Emanuel, Merrick, Smithson, Tainton, Spring, Galley, Gow, Bartley
Oxford: Burton, Lucas, Shuker, Roberts, Thompson*, Sloan, Atkinson G, Clarke D, Cassidy, Aylott, Skeen

City end the season in confident style to celebrate skipper Merrick's 21st birthday. The midfield skills of Emanuel and Gow bring a seventh-successive home success after falling behind to Derek Clarke's penalty. Rodgers is booked for third time this season after bust-up with Clarke.

LEAGUE DIVISION 2 (CUP-TIES)

Manager: Alan Dicks

League Cup

			F-A	H-T	Scorers, Times, and Referees	1	2	3	4	5	6	7	8	9	10	11	12 sub used
1	A	PLYMOUTH	0-1	L	0-0		Cashley	Wimshurst	Drysdale	Emanuel*	Rooks	Merrick	Tainton	Fear	Galley	Sweeney	Gow	Spiring
	17/8						Furnell	Davey	Harris	Hore	Darke	Provan	Brown	Allen	Hinch	Latcham	Hutchins	
		11,248			Hinch 48													
					Ref: P Walters													

City are easily the best side in the first half, but miss two clear-cut opportunities before Argyle score. The referee turns down City's protest that Cashley was fouled when colliding with Hinch in going for Ronnie Brown's corner. Steve Davey and Galley are booked in a 67th-min fracas.

FA Cup

			F-A	H-T	Scorers, Times, and Referees	1	2	3	4	5	6	7	8	9	10	11	12 sub used
3	A	PRESTON	2-4	L	2-1		Gibson	Wimshurst	Drysdale	Wilson	Rooks*	Merrick	Tainton	Spiring	Galley	Sweeney	Gow	Bruton
	15/1						Kelly	McMahon	McNab	Bird	Hawkins	Spavin	Heppolete	Clark	McIlmoyle	Lyall	Ingram	
		13,619	11 9		Spiring 25, Wilson 37													
					Lyall 34, Ingram 81, Clark 84, 87													
					Ref: V James													

The gamble on Rooks' fitness fails as City crumble to North End's late onslaught after Spiring's bad back-pass led to Gerry Ingram's 81st-min equaliser. City are in total charge early on as Spiring ghosts in to score and then Wilson's header nullifies George Lyall's unstoppable volley.

	P		Home						Away				Pts	Odds & ends
		W	D	L	F	A	W	D	L	F	A		
1 Norwich	42	13	8	0	40	16	8	7	6	20	20	57	Double wins: (4) Sheffield Wed, Cardiff, Swindon, Watford.
2 Birmingham	42	15	6	0	46	14	4	12	5	14	17	56	Double losses: (2) Fulham, Carlisle.
3 Millwall	42	14	7	0	38	17	5	10	6	26	29	55	
4 QP Rangers	42	16	4	1	39	9	4	10	7	18	19	54	Won from behind: (4) Orient (h), Preston (h), Sunderland (h), Oxford (h).
5 Sunderland	42	11	7	3	42	24	6	9	6	25	33	50	Lost from in front: (1) Carlisle (h).
6 Blackpool	42	12	6	3	43	16	8	1	12	27	34	47	
7 Burnley	42	13	4	4	43	22	7	2	12	27	33	46	High spots: Winning 5-0 at Hillsborough on 21 August.
8 BRISTOL CITY	42	14	3	4	43	22	4	7	10	18	27	46	Great fightback to beat Orient on 23 October
9 Middlesbro	42	16	4	1	31	11	3	4	14	19	37	46	Sparkling early-season form.
10 Carlisle	42	12	6	3	38	22	5	3	13	23	35	43	
11 Swindon	42	10	6	5	29	16	5	6	10	18	31	42	Low spots: Early exit in both cup competitions.
12 Hull	42	10	6	5	33	21	4	4	13	16	32	38	A heavy home defeat v Carlisle on 19 November.
13 Luton	42	7	8	6	25	24	3	10	8	18	24	38	Losing to Bristol Rov (h) 2-4 in the first penalty shoot-out to decide the
14 Sheffield Wed	42	11	7	3	33	22	2	5	14	18	36	38	Gloucestershire Cup Final.
15 Oxford	42	10	8	3	28	17	2	6	13	15	38	38	
16 Portsmouth	42	9	7	5	31	26	3	6	12	28	42	37	
17 Orient	42	12	4	5	32	19	2	5	14	18	42	37	
18 Preston	42	11	4	6	32	21	1	8	12	20	37	36	
19 Cardiff	42	9	7	5	37	25	1	7	13	19	44	34	
20 Fulham	42	10	7	4	29	20	2	3	16	16	48	34	
21 Charlton	42	9	7	5	33	25	3	2	16	22	52	33	Player of the year: Geoff Merrick.
22 Watford	42	5	5	11	15	25	0	4	17	9	50	19	Ever-presents: (2) Bryan Drysdale; Geoff Merrick.
	924	249	131	82	760	434	82	131	249	434	760	924	Hat-tricks: John Galley (1).
													Leading scorer: John Galley (22).

	Appearances						Goals			
	Lge	Sub	LC	Sub	FAC	Sub	Lge	LC	FAC	Tot
Bartley, Danny	16						1			1
Bond, Len	2									
Broomfield, Ian	3									
Bruton, David	10			1						
Burnside, David	1									
Cashley, Ray	29									
Drysdale, Brian	42				1		1			1
Emanuel, John	33				1		2			2
Fear, Keith	5	4			1		1			1
Galley, John	37				1		22			22
Garland, Chris	4						3			3
Gibson, Mike	11									
Gow, Gerry	39				1		9			9
Griffin, Kevin	1	1								
Jacobs, Trevor	15	1								
Merrick, Geoff	42				1					
Parr, Gordon	2	3								
Rodgers, David	8						1			1
Rooks, Dickie	24				1		1			1
Spiring, Peter	28	3			1	1	9		1	10
Sweeney, Gerry	33	4			1		3			3
Tainton, Trevor	41	1			1		5			5
Wilson, Les	11				1		1		1	2
Wimshurst, Ken	25				1		2			2
24 players used	462	18	11	1	11	1	61		2	63

LEAGUE DIVISION 2

Manager: Alan Dicks

SEASON 1972-73

Results

No	Date	H/A	Opponent	Att	Pos		Pt	F-A	H-T	Scorers, Times, and Referees
1	12/8	A	BRIGHTON	16,823			D 1	1-1	1-1	Bartley 42 / Irvine 28 — Ref: T Dawes
2	19/8	H	MILLWALL	15,648			D 2	2-2	1-1	Gow 20, Spring 84 / Wood 43, Smethurst 48 — Ref: R Armstrong
3	26/8	A	SWINDON	15,552	16	13	L 2	1-2	1-1	Spring 44 / Peplow 23, 84 — Ref: K Styles
4	29/8	A	HULL	8,867	18	15	L 2	0-2	0-1	Pearson 32, Holme 75 — Ref: C Howell
5	2/9	H	SHEFFIELD WED	12,373	22	3	L 2	1-2	0-1	Gow 51 / Joicey 22, 80 — Ref: C Nicholls
6	9/9	A	ORIENT	4,482	18	21	W 4	2-0	1-0	Spring 28, Galley 73 — Ref: R Capey
7	16/9	H	MIDDLESBROUGH	12,185	17	15	D 5	1-1	1-0	Spring 27 / McMordie 55 — Ref: H Davey
8	19/9	A	QP RANGERS	11,586	16	8	D 6	1-1	1-0	Spring 15 / Francis 68 — Ref: K Walker
9	23/9	A	CARDIFF	14,102	13	22	W 8	3-1	2-1	Gow 10p, Galley 12, Drysdale 70 / Bell 22p — Ref: A Oliver
10	26/9	H	FULHAM	14,210	13	14	D 9	1-1	0-1	Gow 69 / Earle 24 — Ref: F Barrett

Line-ups (City row top, opponents in italic below); column 12 = sub used

No	1	2	3	4	5	6	7	8	9	10	11	12
1	Cashley	Wilson	Drysdale	Emanuel	Rodgers	Merrick	Tainton	Spring	Galley	Gow	Bartley	
	Powney	*Templeman*	*Spearritt*	*Murray*	*Gall*	*Goodwin*	*Napier K*	*Beamish**	*Irvine*	*Bromley*	*O'Sullivan*	*Lutton*
2	Cashley*	Wilson	Drysdale	Ritchie	Rodgers	Merrick	Tainton	Spring	Galley	Gow	Bartley	Sweeney
	King	*Brown*	*Burnett*	*Dorney*	*Kitchener*	*Bolland*	*Brown S*	*Smethurst*	*Wood*	*Possee*	*Allder*	
3	Cashley	Wilson	Drysdale	Ritchie	Rodgers	Merrick	Tainton	Spring	Galley	Gow	Bartley	Howell
	Downsbaro	*Thomas*	*Trollope*	*Butler*	*Burrows*	*Potter*	*Peplow*	*Bunkell**	*Treacy*	*Hubbard*	*Rogers*	
4	Cashley	Sweeney	Drysdale !	Ritchie	Rodgers	Merrick	Tainton	Spring*	Galley	Gow	Bartley	Broomfield
	Wealands	*Banks*	*De Vries*	*Wilkinson*	*Kaye*	*Knighton*	*Lord*	*McGill**	*Pearson*	*Holme*	*Butler*	*Houghton*
5	Cashley	Sweeney	Drysdale	Emanuel	Rodgers	Merrick	Tainton	Spring*	Galley	Gow	Bartley	Ritchie
	Grummitt	*Rodrigues*	*Clements*	*Swan**	*Holsgrove*	*Craig*	*Sunley*	*Eustace*	*Joicey*	*Prendegast*	*Sissons*	*Henderson*
6	Cashley	Wilson	Sweeney	Ritchie	Bruton	Merrick	Tainton	Spring	Galley	Gow	Bartley	
	Goddard	*Arber*	*Hoadley*	*Bennett*	*Harris*	*Allen*	*Fairbrother*	*Brisley**	*Bullock*	*Downing*	*Bowyer*	*Riddick*
7	Cashley	Wilson	Sweeney	Ritchie	Rodgers	Merrick	Tainton	Spring	Galley	Gow	Bartley	
	Platt	*Craggs*	*Spraggon*	*Stiles*	*Boam*	*Maddren*	*McMordie*	*Mills*	*Smith*	*Hickton*	*Jones*	
8	Cashley	Wilson	Sweeney	Emanuel	Rodgers	Merrick	Tainton	Spring	Broomfield	Gow	Ritchie	
	Parkes	*Clement*	*Watson*	*Venables*	*Evans*	*Hazell*	*Busby*	*Francis*	*McCulloch*	*Bowles*	*Givens*	
9	Cashley	Wilson	Drysdale	Emanuel	Rodgers	Merrick	Tainton	Broomfield*	Galley	Gow	Sweeney	
	Irvin	*Carver*	*Bell*	*Kellock*	*Murray*	*Powell*	*Gibson*	*Clark*	*Woodruff*	*Phillips*	*Reece*	
10	Cashley	Wilson	Drysdale	Emanuel	Rodgers	Merrick	Tainton	Broomfield*	Galley	Gow	Sweeney	Ritchie
	Mellor	*Cutbush*	*Callaghan*	*Mullery*	*Went*	*Dunne*	*Conway**	*Earle*	*Mitchell*	*Lloyd*	*Barrett*	*Richardson*

Match reports

1. Hardly the normal opening day conditions as City take a deserved point at a wet Goldstone Ground after newly-promoted Brighton go ahead. Irvine was at the far post to head in from a Napier corner, but Bartley is City's saviour as he hooks home a glorious volley from twelve yards.

2. Galley goes in goal as Cashley sustains a gashed ankle whilst making a 38th-minute save from Wood. Millwall take control whilst facing ten men up to the interval and it takes an unstoppable left-foot shot by Spring to earn City a share of the spoils. Bookings for Brown and Burnett.

3. A tale of goalkeeping errors. Downsborough allows himself to be distracted by Tainton's challenge to set up Spring to lash the ball in for City's equaliser, whilst a tragic error gifts Swindon victory. Peplow's gentle lob from the edge of the area slips through Cashley's hands.

4. A hectic opening sees McGill lose two teeth in a challenge with Rodgers and then Drysdale is sent off for remarks to a linesman. Pearson's magnificent volley gives the Tigers the lead, but City play well and are on top in the second half until Holme profits from a Rodgers error.

5. City almost incessantly attack in the opening half, but it is Wednesday who profit as Joicey registers with a six-yard header from Sunley's cross. Gow blasts the ball into net to level shortly after squandering a penalty awarded for Clements' push on Tainton. His soft kick was saved.

6. Orient are mesmerised by City's speed and accuracy. Gow is robbed of a score as ball is over line before Goddard clears on six minutes and shortly after Tainton's shot hits post. Bowyer fails with last minute penalty, hitting his first effort saved.

7. Quick-thinking Spring puts City in the lead following Tainton's free-kick. He moves round Stiles to meet Craggs' header from Tainton's free-kick to hammer a shot into the far corner. Middlesbrough are unlucky not to gain more than a draw, secured by McMordie's lob from 12 yards.

8. Rangers boss Gordon Jago is generous with his praise for City, following this tense and exciting game. Against unbeaten opponents, City start with a brilliant 25-yard goal and finish with Cashley making a fine save to prevent Francis adding to his equaliser from Busby's cross.

9. Cardiff are soon in trouble against dominant City. Powell trips Broomfield to concede a penalty, which Gow tucks away to the keeper's right. Then Galley, looking offside, drives the ball in. Tainton's handball lets Cardiff back into the contest, but Drysdale's low drive secures the win.

10. City are much relieved to share points with impressive Fulham. City's defence is all at sea when Earle knocks in Lloyd's cross. Peter Mellor makes a magnificent save from Gow's 65th-minute penalty, but City notch their equaliser shortly after when Gow nudges in Tainton's cross.

#	Date	Venue / Opponent	Att	Pos	Pos	Res		HT	City Scorers	Opp Scorers	Ref
11	30/9	HUDDERSFIELD	12,644	11	10						A Hart
12	7/10	A PORTSMOUTH	9,475	16	12	W	3-0	1-0	Sweeney 5, 62, Emanuel 57	—	R Toseland
13	14/10	H NOTT'M FOREST	13,861	12	13	D	1-1	0-0	Gow 81	Fraser 66	J Williams
14	21/10	A OXFORD	10,182	11	15	W	2-0	2-0	Gow 10p, Galley 39	—	R Challis
15	28/10	H LUTON	13,562	4	15	L	0-1	0-1	—	Faulkner 12	R Lee
16	4/11	A FULHAM	8,982	10	15	L	1-5	1-2	Galley 27 [Strong 70]	Earle 8, Mer'k 16 (og), Mitchell 54, 85	R Raby
17	11/11	H QP RANGERS	12,570	2	15	L	1-2	1-2	Galley 24	Givens 10, 29	M Kerkhof
18	14/11	A HUDDERSFIELD	5,962	14	17	W	1-0	0-0	Fear 67	—	E Wallace
19	18/11	A BLACKPOOL	8,341	5	17	L	0-3	0-2	—	Alcock 4, Dyson 25, Suddick 65	V Batty
20	25/11	H SUNDERLAND	10,666	20	19	W	1-0	0-0	Galley 83	—	R Crabb
21	2/12	A CARLISLE	6,526	15	21	W	2-1	1-0	Spiring 35, Fear 59	Owen 88	A Jones

---

11 — HUDDERSFIELD (30/9)

Huddersfield: Wood, Clarke, Hutt, Pugh, Dolan, Nicholson, Smith D, Barry, Gowling, Lawson*, Chapman; sub Fairclough

Alan Dicks laments that City are not positive enough, so it is surprising that he waits until the 74th minute to introduce Ritchie in place of Tainton. Huddersfield's well-organised defence offers no way through, though Galley heads against the bar as City up the tempo near the end.

---

12 — A PORTSMOUTH (7/10)

Portsmouth: Milkins, Smith, Wilson, Hand, Stephenson, Munks, Piper, Hiron, Reynolds, McCann, Lewis*; sub Price

Still without a victory at home, City gain their third win away. Wilson clears off the line in the final seconds to deny Emanuel, but City's midfielder has already had the satisfaction of registering with a terrific strike that bulges the back of the net before keeper Milkins could move.

---

13 — H NOTT'M FOREST (14/10)

Nott'm Forest: Barron, Hindley, Gemmell, Serela, Cottam, Fraser, Lyall, Robertson, Chapman, Richardson, Buckley; sub Bartley

City stretch their unbeaten run to eight games. Forest play the better football in the first half, but do not take lead until after the interval, when Cashley is caught off his line by Fraser from 20 yards. Merrick's long punt produces the leveller as Gow runs through to net from ten yards.

---

14 — A OXFORD (21/10)

Oxford: Burton, Lucas, Shuker, Roberts, Clarke C, Evanson*, Sloan, Skeen, Clarke D, Curran, Aylott; sub Bray

City obtain their first-ever goal at the Manor Ground. A debatable handling offence by Roberts allows Gow, who has missed two kicks this season, to drive the ball to Burton's right. Oxford boss Gerry Summers lays the blame for an ill-tempered game on referee Ron Challis.

---

15 — H LUTON (28/10)

Bristol City: Cashley, Sweeney, Drysdale, Ritchie, Merrick, Bruton, Emanuel*, Spiring, Galley, Gow, Bartley; sub Fear
Luton: Barber, Ryan John, Thomson, Anderson, Faulkner, Ryan Jim, Slough, Halom, Hindson, Aston

City's late desperate attempts to equalise are thwarted as Keith Barber makes brilliant saves from Bartley and Galley. Luton, superbly prompted by Peter Anderson, deserve the points secured by John Faulkner from Jim Ryan's corner. Bookings for Anderson and John Ryan.

---

16 — A FULHAM (4/11)

Bristol City: Cashley, Sweeney, Drysdale, Ritchie S, Merrick*, Bruton, Emanuel*, Spiring, Galley, Gow, Bartley; sub Fear
Fulham: Mellor, Cutbush*, Callaghan, Mullery, Went, Dunne, Strong, Earle, Mitchell, Lloyd, Barrett; sub Carlton

Debutant Steve Ritchie's poor clearance sets up Earle for a soft early goal. Despite Galley's stupendous drive, City's attempt to add to their remarkable away record is wrecked by defensive errors, and Fulham are able to turn on the style after Mitchell avails himself of such largesse.

---

17 — H QP RANGERS (11/11)

QP Rangers: Parkes, Clement, Watson, Venables, Hazell, Evans, Francis, Thomas, Leach, Bowles, Givens; sub Emanuel

Silly defensive errors continue to mar City performances as Cashley is punished for his failure to deal with Don Givens' early cross. Galley skilfully prods in his first home goal of the season, but Givens gives Merrick the slip to head in a Dave Thomas corner for the winner.

---

18 — A HUDDERSFIELD (14/11)

Huddersfield: Clarke, Hutt, Pugh, Dolan, Fairclough, Smith S, Gowling, Dungworth, Chapman*, Smith D; sub Sweeney

Huddersfield, down to ten men with Gowling off injured for the final five minutes, are outplayed. Fear chips in magnificently from 25 yards for his goal, while Rodgers sees his drive hit a post. Tainton is booked for dissent, whilst Emanuel is similarly punished for his tackle on Dolan.

---

19 — A BLACKPOOL (18/11)

Blackpool: Burridge, Hatton, Bentley, Alcock, Suddaby, Lennard, Burns, Dyson, Rafferty, Suddick, Ainscow

City are punished for their mistakes as Blackpool control proceedings at Bloomfield Road. Fear is denied by Burridge's fine save midway through the second half, but by then the Pool are 3-0 ahead. Alan Suddick moves in quickly to score after Cashley and Merrick collide.

---

20 — H SUNDERLAND (25/11)

Bristol City: Bond, Wilson, Drysdale, Tainton, Merrick, Rodgers*, Emanuel, Spiring, Galley, Gow, Sweeney; sub Spiring
Sunderland: Montgomery, Malone, Coleman, Kerr, Porterfield, Watson, Horswill, Hughes, Lathan, Chambers, Tueart

The tactical 67th-min substitution of Rodgers proves to be a masterstroke. Spiring's alertness lays on a chance for Galley to divert the ball over the line for City's first home win of the season, while Bond pulls off some smart saves to deny cultured Sunderland the point they deserve.

---

21 — A CARLISLE (2/12)

Bristol City: Bond, Sweeney, Drysdale, Bruton, Merrick, Rodgers, Emanuel, Spiring, Galley, Gow, Fear
Carlisle: Ross, Derrett, Gorman, O'Neill, Winstanley, Tiler, Train, Martin, Owen, Balderstone, Laidlaw

City earn the plaudits for an outstanding display. Carlisle boss Alan Ashman salutes them as the best team in the Division. Owen forces the ball in near the end, but City hold on to the points created by Spiring's headed opener and a 15-yard low shot that zips in by star man Fear.

LEAGUE DIVISION 2 — Manager: Alan Dicks — SEASON 1972-73

No	Date		Att	Pos	Pt	F-A	H-T	1	2	3	4	5	6	7	8	9	10	11	12 sub used
22	H BURNLEY 16/12		15,334	12 L	21	0-1	0-1	Bond	Sweeney	Drysdale	Emanuel	Bruton	Merrick	Tainton	Spiring*	Gould	Gow	Fear	Wilson
								Stevenson	Docherty	Newton	Dobson	Waldron	Thomson	Nulty	Caster	Fletcher	Collins	James	

Scorers, Times, and Referees: Dobson 4. Ref: B Daniels
An unhappy debut for Bobby Gould as he is booked for fouling Colin Waldron, who seldom gives him a chance. Burnley are the best side seen at Ashton Gate so far this season and fully deserve their win, despite Drysdale's protests that he cleared Colin Dobson's header off the line.

No	Date		Att	Pos	Pt	F-A	H-T	1	2	3	4	5	6	7	8	9	10	11	12 sub used
23	A PRESTON 23/12		7,704	13 D	22	3-3	2-3	Bond	Wilson	Drysdale	Emanuel*	Rodgers	Merrick	Tainton	Fear	Gould	Gow	Sweeney	Ritchie
								Kelly	McMahon	Connor	Bird	Hawkins	Sparrow	Wilson	Spark	McIlmoyle	Tarbuck	Bruce	

Scorers, Times, and Referees: Gould 23, Tainton 34, Ritchie 83; McMahon 1, Bruce 16, Tarbuck 37. Ref: R Perkin
A thriller from the start as John McMahon scores with a 25-yarder after twelve seconds before any City player touches the ball. Gould sparks a fight-back with an unstoppable cross-shot from Fear's centre, but City are fortunate as Dave Wilson's 30-yarder hits bar just before half-time.

No	Date		Att	Pos	Pt	F-A	H-T	1	2	3	4	5	6	7	8	9	10	11	12 sub used
24	H CARDIFF 26/12		20,490	11 W	24	1-0	0-0	Cashley	Wilson	Drysdale	Ritchie	Rodgers	Merrick	Tainton	Fear	Gould	Gow	Sweeney	
								Irwin	Dwyer	Bell	Phillips	Morgan R	Morgan P	Kellock	McCullough	Woodruff	Vincent	Reece*	Showers

Scorers, Times, and Referees: Gow 65p. Ref: J Yates
Referee John Yates is Santa Claus as he awards City a penalty when Gould appears to pull back Ritchie Morgan. Cardiff boss Jimmy Scoular calls it 'the biggest act of robbery since the theft of the crown jewels', after Gow whipped in the spot-kick low beyond Bill Irwin's right hand.

No	Date		Att	Pos	Pt	F-A	H-T	1	2	3	4	5	6	7	8	9	10	11	12 sub used
25	A MILLWALL 30/12		9,707	13 L	24	0-3	0-2	Cashley	Wilson	Drysdale	Ritchie	Rodgers*	Merrick	Tainton	Fear	Gould	Gow	Sweeney	Spiring
								King	Brown B	Cripps	Dorney	Kitchener	Burnett	Possee	Dunphy	Wood	Bolland	Allder	

Scorers, Times, and Referees: Wood 12, Possee 34, 48. Ref: W Castle
City's dangerous breaks come to nought as their high crosses into the box are food and drink for Barry Kitchener, and Millwall are well set for victory by half-time. Alf Wood nudges in from a floated free-kick and then Derek Possee turns and hammers a great shot into the top corner.

No	Date		Att	Pos	Pt	F-A	H-T	1	2	3	4	5	6	7	8	9	10	11	12 sub used
26	H SWINDON 6/1		12,481	10 W	26	3-0	2-0	Bond	Sweeney	Drysdale	Emanuel	Rodgers	Merrick	Tainton	Spiring	Gould	Gow	Fear*	Hall
								Allan	Thomas	Trollope	Bunkell	Burrows	Potter	Jenkins	Howells*	Treacy	Noble	Butler	Peplow

Scorers, Times, and Referees: Gould 15, Fear 40, Emanuel 89. Ref: K Wynn
Bobby Gould gives the team talk, after which his characteristically energetic play inspires City to their most convincing home display of the season. Swindon offer little after Gould fired City ahead, and then Fear cracks in from a 20-yard free-kick, before Emanuel blasts in the third.

No	Date		Att	Pos	Pt	F-A	H-T	1	2	3	4	5	6	7	8	9	10	11	12 sub used
27	H ORIENT 27/1		11,766	11 D	27	2-2	0-1	Bond	Sweeney	Drysdale	Emanuel	Rodgers	Merrick	Tainton	Spiring	Gould	Gow	Bartley	
								Goddard	Hoadley	Wall	Allen	Harris	Bennett	Downing	Brisley	Bowyer	Queen	Heppolette	

Scorers, Times, and Referees: Merrick 47, Gow 90; Allen 12, Queen 88. Ref: R Toseland
Orient look anything but relegation candidates early on as Peter Allen finishes with a 20-yard shot high into the net. A messy game isn't helped by an inconsistent ref who, as well as issuing deserved cautions to Phil Hoadley and Drysdale, books Peter Wall, Gerry Queen and Gould.

No	Date		Att	Pos	Pt	F-A	H-T	1	2	3	4	5	6	7	8	9	10	11	12 sub used
28	A MIDDLESBROUGH 10/2		8,511	12 L	27	1-2	0-0	Cashley	Sweeney	Drysdale	Emanuel	Bruton	Merrick	Tainton	Spiring	Gould	Gow	Bartley*	Ritchie
								Platt	Craggs*	Spraggon	Gates	Boam	Madden	McMordie	Mills	Smith	Hickton	Souness	Brine

Scorers, Times, and Referees: Emanuel 64; Hickton 61, Boam 85. Ref: M Lowe
Bruton comes close to obtaining his first-ever goal when heading just over in the 8th minute. Emanuel stars, and his equalising drive into the far corner inspires City for a while, but Stuart Boam settles the issue for Boro, the ball going in off his shoulder after his header had hit the bar.

No	Date		Att	Pos	Pt	F-A	H-T	1	2	3	4	5	6	7	8	9	10	11	12 sub used
29	H BRIGHTON 17/2		11,116	11 W	29	3-1	1-1	Cashley	Sweeney	Drysdale	Emanuel	Bruton	Merrick	Tainton	Spiring	Gould*	Gow*	Bartley	Ritchie Howell
								Hughes	Templeman	Spearritt	Bromley	Piper	Goodwin	Bridges	Murray	Beamish*	O'Sullivan	Towner	

Scorers, Times, and Referees: Tainton 8, Ritchie 77, Spiring 89; O'Sullivan 4. Ref: T Bosi
City wear black armbands in memory of former favourite 'Ginger' Peacock, who died during the week. Peter O'Sullivan slots home from eight yards, but Tainton soon equalises as he finishes off Spiring's sliced shot. Gould was unlucky on 65 mins as his shot was disallowed for offside.

No	Date		Att	Pos	Pt	F-A	H-T	1	2	3	4	5	6	7	8	9	10	11	12 sub used
30	A BURNLEY 24/2		13,630	10 D	30	1-1	0-1	Bond	Sweeney	Drysdale	Emanuel	Rodgers	Merrick	Tainton	Spiring	Gould	Gow	Fear	
								Stevenson	Cliff	Newton	Dobson	Waldron	Thomson	Nulty	Casper	Fletcher	Collins	James	

Scorers, Times, and Referees: Ritchie 65; Dobson 7. Ref: G Hill
Keeper Alan Stevenson prevents a deserved away success as City outplay Burnley in midfield. Bond is at fault early on as he fails to react quickly enough to Martin Dobson's 25-yarder, but Ritchie, after hitting a post in the first half, notches the equaliser by heading in Fear's cross.

No	Date		Att	Pos	Pt	F-A	H-T	1	2	3	4	5	6	7	8	9	10	11	12 sub used
31	H PORTSMOUTH 3/3		11,002	11 W	32	3-1	2-0	Bond	Sweeney	Drysdale	Emanuel	Rodgers	Merrick	Tainton	Ritchie	Woods	Gow	Fear	
								Milkins	Wilson	Collins	Hand	Stephenson	Munks	Foggo	Piper	Hiron	Kellard	Jennings*	Lewis

Scorers, Times, and Referees: Gow 10, 60, Fear 32; Hiron 81. Ref: A Jones
Despite another penalty miss by Gow, as his 50th-min kick hits the inside of the post, City's young side storm to another victory over Pompey. Woods has an impressive debut, whilst good play between Fear and Tainton allows star man Gow to squeeze the ball in from a narrow angle.

#		Opponent	Date	Pos	Res	Att		Pts	Score	HT
32	A	NOTT'M FOREST	10/3	11	L	8,680	12	32	0-1	0-1
33	A	SHEFFIELD WED	14/3	12	L	13,635	4	32	2-3	0-0
34	H	OXFORD	17/3	12	D	11,177	8	33	0-0	0-0
35	A	LUTON	24/3	11	W	7,102	9	35	3-1	0-1
36	H	ASTON VILLA	27/3	10	W	15,654	5	37	3-0	1-0
37	A	SUNDERLAND	31/3	8	D	33,255	13	38	2-2	0-1
38	H	CARLISLE	7/4	7	W	10,588	17	40	4-1	3-1
39	A	ASTON VILLA	14/4	9	L	19,545	3	40	0-1	0-0
40	H	BLACKPOOL	21/4	8	W	11,537	5	42	3-0	2-0
41	H	PRESTON	23/4	7	W	10,799	19	44	2-1	1-0
42	H	HULL	28/4	5	W	11,066	13	46	2-1	0-0

Home 12,892 Away 11,542 Average 11,542

---

32 A NOTT'M FOREST 10/3 — 0-1

City: Bond, Sweeney, Drysdale, Emanuel, Rodgers*, Merrick, Tainton, Ritchie, Gillies, Gow, Woods; sub Fear

Forest: Barron, Hindley, Winfield, Chapman, Serella, Fraser, McIntosh, Robertson, O'Neill, Galley, Lyall; subs Potts, Sissons*

Galley 45
Ref: R Armstrong

Erstwhile hero John Galley sends City to defeat in the second minute of first-half injury-time, bursting between Sweeney and Rodgers to score with a left-foot shot from twelve yards. City take the game forward impressively, but they offer little in the way of shots to trouble Forest.

---

33 A SHEFFIELD WED 14/3 — 2-3

City: Bond, Sweeney, Drysdale, Emanuel, Rodgers, Merrick, Tainton*, Ritchie, Gillies, Gow, Gould; sub Fear

Sheffield Wed: Grummitt, Rodrigues, Mullen, Prophet, Thompson, Craig, Henderson, Coyle, Joicey, Sunley, Sissons*; sub Potts

Gould 52, Ritchie 85; Joicey 66, 87, Sunley 68
Ref: R Capey

Gould's powerful shot from Emanuel's pass allows City to be in a better position than when this fixture was originally postponed after 55 mins on 20 Jan. Unfortunately, Merrick thrice slips to set up Wednesday's goals, and despite Ritchie firing in a late equaliser City are defeated.

---

34 H OXFORD 17/3 — 0-0

City: Cashley, Sweeney, Drysdale, Emanuel, Rodgers, Merrick, Tainton*, Ritchie, Gillies, Gow, Woods; sub Fear

Oxford: Thomas, Lucas, Shuker, Roberts, Lowe, Skeen, Gough, Fleming, Cassidy, Curran, Aylott

Ref: J Goggins

Apart from an early effort by Gillies, whose left-foot lob just clears the bar, only Hugh Curran looks likely to break the deadlock. His neat flick midway through the first half is disallowed for offside. He then blasts over the bar from four yards in the 84th minute for the miss of the game.

---

35 A LUTON 24/3 — 3-1

City: Cashley, Sweeney, Drysdale, Emanuel, Rodgers, Merrick, Fear, Ritchie, Gillies, Gow, Gould

Luton: Horn, Ryan John, Thomson, Shanks, Garner, Moore, Ryan Jim*, Anderson, Busby, Hindson, Ashton; sub Fern

Gow 47, Gillies 55, Fear 68; Garner 34
Ref: J Wrennall

City turn the game on its head with a great display after the break. John Aston gave City the run around early on, but Gow's hooked equaliser from five yards inspires a comeback. Gillies opens his scoring account with a truly great goal, an unstoppable angled drive from fully 25 yards.

---

36 H ASTON VILLA 27/3 — 3-0

City: Cashley, Sweeney, Drysdale, Emanuel, Rodgers, Merrick, Fear, Ritchie, Gillies, Gow, Gould

Aston Villa: Cumbes, Rioch N, McDonald, Rioch B, Nicholl, Turnbull, McMahon, Brown, Evans!, Lochhead, Vowden

Gillies 24, Gould 65, 70
Ref: G Kew

Another superb strike by Gillies – a perfectly-judged header from Ritchie's chip – sets Emanuel-inspired City on the way to a convincing win. Unfortunately, the referee deprives City of some of the credit by sending off Alun Evans for dissent, as well as booking three other Villains.

---

37 A SUNDERLAND 31/3 — 2-2

City: Cashley, Sweeney, Drysdale, Emanuel, Rodgers, Merrick, Fear, Ritchie, Gillies, Gow, Gould

Sunderland: Montgomery, Malone, Guthrie, Horswill, Pitt, Young, Kerr, Hughes, Watson, Porterfield, Tueart

Merrick 59, Emanuel 89; Merrick 35 (og), Watson 52
Ref: L Hayes

Merrick's never-say-die attitude, after being at fault for both of Sunderland's goals, typifies City's fighting performance He heads home from Fear's corner to inspire a fightback, which is completed near the end by Emanuel's 25-yard equaliser. Bookings for Emanuel and Denis Tueart.

---

38 H CARLISLE 7/4 — 4-1

City: Cashley, Sweeney, Drysdale, Emanuel, Rodgers, Merrick, Fear, Ritchie, Gillies*, Gow, Gould

Carlisle: Ross, Carr, Gorman, O'Neill, Winstanley, Tiler, Martin, Train, Owen, Balderstone*, Laidlaw; subs Ternent, Laidlaw

O'Neill 14 (og), Rodgers 20, Gow 27p [Gould 81]; Laidlaw 5
Ref: A Lees

Carlisle, requiring four points to be safe from relegation, have the tonic of an early goal. Joe Laidlaw bursts through to net with a crisp drive, but City level as Les O'Neill lobs ball into his own goal and then go on to improve their Watney Cup prospects with three more scoring strikes.

---

39 A ASTON VILLA 14/4 — 0-1

City: Cashley, Sweeney, Drysdale, Emanuel, Rodgers*, Merrick, Fear, Ritchie, Gillies, Gow, Gould; sub Cumbes

Aston Villa: Cumbes, Ross, Robson, Brown, Nicholl, Rioch N, McMahon, Little, Lochhead, Vowden, Hamilton

Rioch 76
Ref: D Nippard

'I've had enough,' says Gerry Gow, as his injury-time spot-kick is his fourth failure of the season. Jimmy Cumbes dives to his left to make a good save to deprive City of a point they don't deserve. Villa should have won by a five or six-goal margin, but are let down by poor finishing.

---

40 H BLACKPOOL 21/4 — 3-0

City: Cashley, Sweeney, Drysdale, Emanuel, Rodgers*, Merrick, Fear, Ritchie, Gillies, Gow, Gould

Blackpool: Wood, Hatton, Bentley, Alcock, James, Suddaby, Burns, Suddick, Rafferty, Dyson, Ainscow*; sub Lennard

Gould 10, Emanuel 12, Fear 68
Ref: C Nicholls

City get back on course for Watney Cup qualification, though Blackpool make most of the running. Ritchie's dazzling footwork sets up Gould to score with a diving header and then Emanuel registers with one of his 25-yard specials, before Fear rolls ball into net to end City's anxieties.

---

41 H PRESTON 23/4 — 2-1

City: Cashley, Sweeney, Drysdale, Emanuel, Collier, Merrick, Fear, Ritchie, Gillies, Gow, Gould

Preston: Brown, McMahon, Snookes, Bird, Hawkins, Spark, Wilson*, Lamb, McIlmoyle, Bruce, Young; sub Baxter

Merrick 27, Fear 49; Bruce 77
Ref: F Bassett

The referee gets the bird from City fans as Gow's perfect shot into the far corner on the hour is disallowed because Bobby Gould was offside. Alex Bruce runs 40 yards before scoring with a great solo effort, but City's star, Fear, has Preston in a perpetual tangle with his range of skills.

---

42 H HULL 28/4 — 2-1

City: McKechnie, Sweeney, Drysdale, Emanuel, Collier*, Merrick, Ritchie, Gillies, Gow, Gould; sub Tainton

Hull: Banks, De Vries, Kay, Neill, Knighton, McGill, Lord, Pearson, Greenwood, Wagstaff; sub ...

Neill 79 (og), Gould 83; Pearson 68
Ref: C Thomas

A drab match is brought alive by Pearson's superb 25-yard volley for the Tigers. City's need for Watney Cup goals prompts Dicks to bring on Tainton with 28 mins left, and the gamble pays off with victory when Gould shoots in. Bookings for Merrick and Hull captain Ken Knighton.

LEAGUE DIVISION 2 (CUP-TIES)

Manager: Alan Dicks

League Cup

2 A WEST HAM 22 L 1-2 0-1
Galley 89
17,688 1:12
McDowell 44, Best 85
Ref: N Paget

	1	2	3	4	5	6	7	8	9	10	11	12 sub used
City	Cashley	Wilson	Drysdale	Sweeney	Rodgers*	Merrick	Tainton	Spiring	Galley	Gow	Ritchie	Broomfield
West Ham	*Grotier*	*McDowell*	*Lampard*	*Bonds*	*Taylor*	*Moore*	*Tyler*	*Best*	*Holland*	*Brooking*	*Robson*	

Galley excels as centre-half after the loss of Rodgers following a clash of heads with Billy Bonds. John McDowell fires in a tremendous shot to put the Hammers in front and then Clyde Best hammers in a 20-yard drive, before City gain a deserved reward thanks to Galley scoring header.

FA Cup

3 A PORTSMOUTH 10 D 1-1 0-0
Gould 90
15,177 17
Piper 63
Ref: R Crabb

	1	2	3	4	5	6	7	8	9	10	11	12 sub used
City	Bond	Sweeney	Drysdale	Emanuel	Rodgers*	Merrick	Tainton	Spiring	Gould	Gow	Fear*	Hall
Portsmouth	*Horn*	*Wilson*	*Collins*	*Hand*	*Stephenson*	*Munks*	*Piper*	*Reynolds*	*Hiron*	*Kellard*	*Jennings*	

A perfectly-placed linesman awards Gould's headed equaliser in the dying seconds as Pompey claim ball hasn't crossed the line. City, on top in the first half, are made to pay for missed chances when Norman Piper's banana shot floats over the defensive wall to nestle in the top corner.

3R H PORTSMOUTH 10 W 4-1 1-0
Gould 27, Tainton 74, Sweeney 84, [Gow 89pl]
16,699 17
Hiron 86
Ref: R Crabb

	1	2	3	4	5	6	7	8	9	10	11	12 sub used
City	Bond	Sweeney	Drysdale	Emanuel	Rodgers	Merrick	Tainton	Spiring	Gould	Gow	Bartley	Lewis
Portsmouth	*Horn*	*Wilson*	*Collins**	*Smith*	*Hand*	*Munks*	*Piper*	*Reynolds*	*Hiron*	*Kellard*	*Price*	

City overwhelm Pompey with a brilliant display, though Gow admits to impeding Graham Horn (booked for his protests) as Gould heads in. Tainton's header doubles City's advantage, whilst Gow's penalty after David Munks had fouled Tainton cancels out Ray Hiron's late header.

4 A WOLVES 11 L 0-1 0-1
30,849 1:8
Richards 45
Ref: A Grey

	1	2	3	4	5	6	7	8	9	10	11	12 sub used
City	Cashley	Sweeney	Drysdale	Emanuel	Rodgers*	Merrick	Tainton	Spiring	Gould	Gow	Bartley	Ritchie
Wolves	*Parkes*	*Taylor*	*McAlle*	*Shaw*	*Munro*	*Jefferson*	*McCalling*	*Sunderland*	*Richards*	*Dougan*	*Wagstaffe*	

An enthralling cup clash well controlled by Alf Grey, despite early bookings for Derek Jefferson, Gould and Ritchie. City are unfortunate to lose, as they do well to overcome losing Rodgers with a hamstring injury. John Richards scores right on the interval with a low cross-shot.

League Table

			Home					Away					
		P	W	D	L	F	A	W	D	L	F	A	Pts
1	Burnley	42	13	6	2	44	18	11	8	2	28	17	62
2	QP Rangers	42	16	4	1	54	13	8	9	4	27	24	61
3	Aston Villa	42	12	5	4	27	17	6	9	6	24	30	50
4	Middlesbro	42	12	6	3	29	15	5	7	9	17	28	47
5	BRISTOL CITY	42	10	7	4	34	18	5	9	7	29	33	46
6	Sunderland	42	12	6	3	35	17	5	6	10	24	32	46
7	Blackpool	42	12	6	3	37	17	6	4	11	19	34	46
8	Oxford	42	14	2	5	36	18	5	5	11	16	25	45
9	Fulham	42	11	6	4	32	16	5	6	10	26	33	44
10	Sheffield Wed	42	14	4	3	40	20	3	6	12	19	35	44
11	Millwall	42	12	5	4	33	18	4	5	12	22	29	42
12	Luton	42	6	9	6	24	23	9	2	10	20	30	41
13	Hull	42	9	7	5	39	22	5	5	11	25	37	40
14	Nott'm Forest	42	12	5	4	32	18	2	7	12	15	34	40
15	Orient	42	11	6	4	33	18	1	6	14	16	35	36
16	Swindon	42	8	9	4	28	23	3	5	13	18	37	36
17	Portsmouth	42	7	6	8	21	22	5	5	11	21	37	35
18	Carlisle	42	10	5	6	40	24	1	7	13	10	28	34
19	Preston	42	6	8	7	19	25	5	4	12	18	39	34
20	Cardiff	42	11	4	6	32	21	0	7	14	18	37	33
21	Huddersfield	42	7	9	5	21	20	1	8	12	15	36	33
22	Brighton	42	7	8	6	32	31	1	5	15	14	52	29
		924	232	133	97	722	434	97	133	232	434	722	924

Appearances & Goals

	Appearances						Goals			
	Lge	Sub	LC	Sub	FAC	Sub	Lge	LC	FAC	Tot
Bartley, Danny	12	2					1			1
Bond, Len	10		2		2					
Broomfield, Ian	3					1				
Bruton, David	6		1							
Cashley, Ray	32		1							
Collier, Gary	3									
Drysdale, Brian	34		1		3		1			1
Emanuel, John	33	1	1		3		5			5
Fear, Keith	20	4			1		7			7
Galley, John	20		1				6	1		7
Gillies, Donny	11						2			2
Gould, Bobby	19				3		8		2	10
Gow, Gerry	42		1		3		12		1	13
Hall, Colin						1				
Jacobs, Trevor	3									
Merrick, Geoff	41		1		3		3			3
Ritchie, Tom	24	7	1			1	4			4
Ritchie, Steve	1									
Rodgers, David	34		1		3		1			1
Spiring, Peter	20	2	1		3		7			7
Sweeney, Gerry	39	1	1		3		2		1	3
Tainton, Trevor	33	4	1		3		2		1	3
Wilson, Les	21	1	1		1					
Woods, Eddie	1	1								
(own-goals)							2			2
24 players used	462	25	11	1	33	2	63	1	5	69

Odds & ends

Double wins: (3) Cardiff, Portsmouth, Carlisle.
Double losses: (1) Sheffield Wed.
Won from behind: (4) Brighton (h), Luton (a), Carlisle (h), Hull (h).
Lost from in front: (1) Sheffield Wed (a).
High spots: Drawing 1-1 at Turf Moor on 24 February.
Beating Aston Villa 3-0 at Ashton Gate on 27 March.
Great early away form with six wins and three draws from the opening 13 games.
Beating Swindon 3-0 at Ashton Gate on 6 January.
Bobby Gould's last-minute goal in the FA Cup at Fratton Park.
Beating Bristol Rov 5-3 on penalties to win the Gloucestershire Cup on 1 May.
Low spots: Failure to win a home match until 25 November.
Losing 1-5 at Fulham on 4 November.
Unlucky 0-1 defeat v Wolves in the FA Cup.

Player of the year: John Emanuel.
Ever-presents: (1) Geoff Merrick.
Hat-tricks: (0).
Leading scorer: Gerry Gow (13).

LEAGUE DIVISION 2

Manager: Alan Dicks

SEASON 1973-74

Results

No	Date	Att	Pos (City / Opp)	Pt	Res	F-A	H-T	Scorers, Times, and Referees
1	H BOLTON 25/8	13,665		2	W	1-0	1-0	Gould 7; Ref: J Bent
2	A ORIENT 1/9	7,216		4	W	1-0	0-0	Rodgers 88; Ref: R Armstrong
3	H LUTON 8/9	12,208	9 / 6	4	L	1-3	1-2	Gould 39p; Aston 2, Ryan John 4, Finney 48; Ref: R Perkin
4	A SWINDON 11/9	14,222	2 / 7	6	W	1-0	1-0	Gould 7; Ref: R Toseland
5	A PRESTON 15/9	10,790	4 / 16	7	D	1-1	0-1	Fear 78; Young 20; Ref: J Taylor
6	H HULL 18/9	10,711	1 / 19	9	W	3-1	0-1	Ritchie 47, Cashley 55, Gould 82; Pearson 24; Ref: B Daniels
7	H SHEFFIELD WED 22/9	13,829	1 / 17	11	W	2-0	1-0	Gould 17, Fear 65; Ref: D Turner
8	A MIDDLESBROUGH 29/9	17,069	2 / 1	11	L	0-2	0-0	Murdoch 60, Armstrong 84; Ref: J Wrennal
9	A HULL 2/10	7,235	4 / 12	11	L	1-2	0-2	Rodgers 78; Greenwood 5, Wagstaff 37; Ref: H Davey
10	H WEST BROM 6/10	14,325	6 / 17	12	D	1-1	1-1	Gould 31; Brown T 25; Ref: D Nippard

Line-ups (City in roman, opponents in *italics*)

No	1	2	3	4	5	6	7	8	9	10	11	12 sub used
1	Cashley	Sweeney	Merrick	Emanuel	Rodgers	Collier	Tainton	Ritchie	Gould	Gow	Fear*	Gillies
1	*Siddall*	*McCallister*	*Dunne*	*Rimmer*	*Jones P*	*Nicholson**	*Byron*	*Jones G*	*Greaves*	*Lee*	*Phillips*	*Waldron*
2	Cashley	Sweeney	Merrick	Emanuel	Rodgers	Collier	Tainton	Ritchie	Gould	Gow	Fear	
2	*Goddard*	*Hoadley**	*Downing*	*Allen*	*Linton*	*Walley*	*Fairbrother*	*Brisley*	*Bullock*	*Queen*	*Payne*	*Fisher*
3	Cashley	Sweeney	Merrick	Emanuel	Rodgers*	Collier	Tainton	Ritchie	Gould	Gow	Fear	Drysdale
3	*Horn*	*Shanks*	*Thomson*	*Anderson*	*Faulkner*	*Garner*	*Ryan Jim*	*Ryan John*	*Butlin*	*Finney*	*Aston*	
4	Cashley	Sweeney	Merrick	Emanuel	Rodgers	Collier	Tainton	Ritchie	Gould	Gow	Fear	
4	*Allan*	*Thomas*	*Trollope*	*Stroud*	*Burrows*	*Butler*	*Moss*	*McGovern**	*Treacy*	*Legg*	*Jenkins*	*Bunkell*
5	Cashley	Sweeney	Drysdale	Emanuel	Rodgers*	Merrick	Tainton	Ritchie	Gould	Gow	Fear	Gillies
5	*Kelly*	*McMahon*	*McNab*	*Baxter*	*Hawkins*	*Stiles*	*Lamb*	*Bruce*	*Holden*	*Burns**	*Young*	*Morley*
6	Cashley	Sweeney	Drysdale	Emanuel	Rodgers	Merrick	Tainton	Ritchie	Gould	Gow	Fear	
6	*Wealands*	*Banks*	*De Vries*	*Kaye*	*Deere*	*Blampey*	*McGill*	*Lord*	*Pearson*	*Wagstaff*	*Greenwood*	
7	Cashley	Sweeney	Drysdale	Emanuel	Rodgers	Merrick	Tainton	Ritchie	Gould	Gow	Fear	
7	*Springett*	*Rodrigues*	*Shaw*	*Thompson*	*Holsgrove*	*Craig T*	*Potts*	*Sunley*	*Joicey*	*Prendergast*	*Knighton*	
8	Cashley	Sweeney	Drysdale	Emanuel	Rodgers	Merrick	Tainton	Ritchie	Gould	Gow	Fear	Gillies
8	*Platt*	*Craggs*	*Spraggon*	*Madden*	*Boam*	*Souness*	*Murdoch*	*Mills*	*Hickton*	*Foggon*	*Armstrong*	
9	Cashley	Sweeney	Drysdale	Emanuel	Rodgers	Merrick	Tainton	Ritchie	Gould*	Gow	Fear	Gillies
9	*Wealands*	*Banks*	*De Vries*	*Kaye*	*Deere*	*Blampey*	*McGill*	*Lord*	*Pearson*	*Wagstaff**	*Greenwood*	*Hawley*
10	Cashley*	Sweeney	Drysdale	Emanuel	Rodgers	Merrick	Tainton	Ritchie	Gould	Gow	Fear	Gillies
10	*Latchford*	*Nisbet*	*Merrick*	*Cantello*	*Wile*	*Robertson*	*Hartford*	*Brown T*	*Brown A*	*Shaw*	*Johnston*	

Match reports

1. H BOLTON — This dour struggle is decided early on when the ball rolls slowly into the net after Paul Jones' clearance cannons off Gould. City are not direct enough and, whilst they have two penalty appeals turned down after the break, it is newly promoted Bolton who create the better chances.

2. A ORIENT — Refusing to leave the pitch with a badly cut eyebrow, Rodgers is City's hero as he heads in from Fear's free-kick. Cashley should have been beaten early on by both Barry Fairbrother and Terry Brisley, but City, with much the best of the action thereafter, fully merit their success.

3. H LUTON — City's early season euphoria is quickly shattered by Luton's quick one-two. A push on Tainton allows Gould to atone from the spot for having sliced wide of an open goal, but Tom Finney's great twelve-yard volley ties up a deserved success for the vastly superior Hatters.

4. A SWINDON — With an imaginative and skilful display City, in their all-white strip, canter to an easy win over previously unbeaten Swindon. Jimmy Allen pulls off many fine saves to keep City at bay, but even he is powerless when the game's first corner is headed on for Gould to hook the ball in.

5. A PRESTON — Trailing to Neil Young's brilliant 15-yard header, City have Cashley to thank for keeping them in the game. Faced by only ten men after Preston's 75th-minute loss of Alan Kelly with a shoulder injury, Fear takes advantage of Stuart Baxter's keeping to head in a Gillies cross.

6. H HULL — Cashley emerges as City's unlikely goal-scoring hero, following Ritchie's headed equaliser to Stuart Pearson's tap in. The Tigers' slick play counts for nought as Cashley's 95-yard 2ft clearance finds the net and then Gould shoots in a rebound to raise City to the top of the table.

7. H SHEFFIELD WED — Fear's rounding of Peter Springett to shoot in City's second goal produces much protest. Just as well that Owls boss Derek Dooley intervenes to usher his players away from the referee as Bristol Channel's video of the game proves that Fear was onside when collecting the through ball.

8. A MIDDLESBROUGH — Boro' look much the better side in this top of the table clash against ultra-defensive City. After surviving a first-half hammering City can only admire Bobby Murdoch's thundering 20-yard drive, and then concede top place on goal average as David Armstrong breaks clear to shoot in.

9. A HULL — Lethargic City's defensive shortcomings bring skilful Hull their deserved success. After Roy Greenwood's speculative cross-shot from the right strikes Drysdale before going in off a post, the failure of Rodgers to effect a simple clearance allows Ken Wagstaff to shoot home.

10. H WEST BROM — After heading in an equaliser to Tony Brown's flicked in opener, Gould takes over in goal when Cashley sustains an arm injury just after the interval. A rough game, with Emanuel playing on with a cracked jaw, sees City twice hit the post, whilst offside rules out a Tony Brown effort.

Match records 11–21

11 · A MILLWALL · 13/10
Pos 4 · Att 7,543 · Opp 20 · Pts 14
W 2-0 (HT 0-0) — Gould 68, **Whitehead** 69
Ref: J Williams
City: Bond, Drysdale, Tainton, Sweeney, Collier, Merrick, **Whitehead**, Ritchie, Gould, Gow, Gillies
Millwall: King, Cripps, Brown, Dorney, Kitchener, Burnett, Bolland, Clark, Wood, Dunphy, Hill

After a poor first half City click into top gear with a display of non-stop attacking action. Gould is on hand to calmly slot in a rebound when Gillies shoots against a post, then Whitehead crowns a sparkling debut by running through to collect a through pass and beat the keeper.

12 · A ASTON VILLA · 20/10
Pos 3 · Att 26,918 · Opp 4 · Pts 15
D 2-2 (HT 2-1) — Fear 25, Ritchie 32 / Little 20, Graydon 49
Ref: V James
City: Bond, Drysdale, Tainton, Sweeney, Collier, Merrick, Whitehead*, Ritchie, Gould, Gow, Fear
Aston Villa: Cumbes, Gidman, Brown, Hockey, Nicholl, Ross, Graydon, Brown, Vowden*, Little, Morgan

Following Brian Little's headed opener, errors by the Villa custodian reward attack-minded City's fight-back. Jimmy Cumbes, late in getting down to Fear's shot, is at fault again when he drops the ball for Ritchie to tap in. Ray Graydon's 30-yard screamer caps a compelling contest.

13 · H SWINDON · 23/10
Pos 2 · Att 14,474 · Opp 20 · Pts 17
W 1-0 (HT 1-0) — Fear 3
Ref: B Homewood
City: Bond, Drysdale, Tainton, Sweeney, Collier, Merrick, Whitehead, Ritchie, Gould, Gow, Fear, Gillies
Swindon: Allan, Thomas, Butler, Dixon*, Burrows, Stroud, Moss, McGovern, Treacy, Legg, Jenkins, Collins

Swindon boss Les Allen is of the opinion that City are promotion bound, following the completion of an accomplished double over his side. After Fear spurts through the middle to head in Drysdale's free-kick, Swindon's dogged defending restricts City to the barest winning margin.

14 · H BLACKPOOL · 27/10
Pos 4 · Att 13,896 · Opp 11 · Pts 17
L 0-1 (HT 0-0) — Dyson 62
Ref: W Gow
City: Bond, Drysdale, Tainton, Sweeney, Rodgers, Merrick, Whitehead*, Ritchie, Gould, Gow, Fear, Gillies
Blackpool: Burridge, Bentley, Curtis, Alcock, James, Suddaby, Burns, Suddick, Dyson, Hatton, Walsh

City coach John Sillett berates his players for Blackpool's decisive goal, as a sloppy pass, a wild tackle, and failure to guard the far post, allows Keith Dyson to put away a low cross. In truth though it is the homesters' failure to turn their dominance into goals that costs them the points.

15 · A FULHAM · 3/11
Pos 5 · Att 9,613 · Opp 13 · Pts 17
L 1-2 (HT 0-0) — Tainton 83 / Conway 52, Busby 56
Ref: D Richardson
City: Bond, Drysdale, Tainton, Sweeney, Rodgers, Merrick, Emanuel*, Ritchie, Gould, Gow, Fear, Gillies
Fulham: Webster, Cutbush, Slough, Mullery, Went, Lacy, Conway J'n, Earle, Busby, Lloyd, Barrett

In front of the Big Match cameras City are forced to adopt a more positive approach after Bond drops a cross for John Conway's opening goal. Tainton hammers in City's late reply, but by then Viv Busby had steered Fulham into clear water following Steve Earle's 50-yard mazy run.

16 · H CRYS PALACE · 10/11
Pos 9 · Att 15,488 · Opp 22 · Pts 17
L 0-1 (HT 0-1) — Whittle 24
Ref: G Hill
City: Bond, Drysdale, Tainton, Sweeney, Rodgers, Merrick, Whitehead*, Ritchie, Gould, Gow, Fear, Gillies
Crystal Palace: Hammond, Mulligan, Wall, Walley, Barry, Jeffries*, Cooke, Possee, Swindlehurst, Taylor P, Rogers, Whittle

City fans should be inured against results such as this, as yet again they find themselves as the fall guys. In front of the Match of the Day cameras Alan Whittle's low shot earns Palace, thanks to Paul Hammond's acrobatic goalkeeping display, their first League win of the season.

17 · H SUNDERLAND · 17/11
Pos 8 · Att 14,965 · Opp 10 · Pts 19
W 2-0 (HT 0-0) — Sweeney 68, Gillies 88
Ref: D Civil
City: Bond, Drysdale, Tainton, Sweeney, Rodgers, Merrick, Whitehead, Ritchie, Gould, Gow, Fear*, Gillies
Sunderland: Montgomery, Malone, Bolton, Horswill, Watson, Ashurst*, Kerr, Belfitt, Halom, Porterfield, Tueart, Hughes

Champagne show as the FA Cup holders are overrun by what is, with an average age of 21.5 years, probably City's youngest-ever side. Gillies' pull back allows Sweeney to hammer City ahead, and just before time Gillies finishes off a 50-yard run with a perfect shot into the net.

18 · A CARLISLE · 24/11
Pos 9 · Att **6,020** · Opp 8 · Pts 19
L 1-2 (HT 1-1) — Ritchie 37 / Winstanley 15, O'Neill 74
Ref: H Hackney
City: Bond, Drysdale, Tainton, Sweeney, Rodgers, Merrick, Whitehead*, Ritchie, Gould, Gow, Fear*, Emanuel
Carlisle: Ross, Carr, Gorman, O'Neill, Winstanley, Ternent, Martin, Balderstone, Owen, Clarke*, Laidlaw, Train

Following a mishap on the way to Carlisle, when the team coach was forced to swerve, Sweeney is only passed fit after having his cut eye stitched. Ritchie shoots from in from Whitehead's centre, but his two spurned chances after the break are costly as Les O'Neill's low shot is decisive.

19 · H NOTTS CO · 1/12
Pos 10 · Att 10,436 · Opp 3 · Pts 20
D 2-2 (HT 1-2) — Gillies 35, Fear 68 / Masson 42p, Mann 59
Ref: G Kew
City: Bond, Drysdale, Tainton, Sweeney, Rodgers, Merrick, Whitehead*, Ritchie, Gould, Gow, Fear, Gillies
Notts County: McManus, Brindley, Worthington, Masson, Needham, McVay, Nixon*, Randall, Bradd, Probert, Mann, Vinter

After dominating the first half and being rewarded with a magnificent 25-yard strike by Gillies, City are unlucky to not be ahead at the break. Don Masson's penalty is rough justice for Rodgers who appears to be pushed in the back before involuntarily handling County's free-kick.

20 · A PORTSMOUTH · 8/12
Pos 11 · Att 13,178 · Opp 15 · Pts 20
L 0-1 (HT 0-1) — Davies 56
Ref: A Hart
City: Bond, Drysdale, Tainton, Sweeney, Rodgers, Merrick, Whitehead, Ritchie, Gould, Gow, Fear
Portsmouth: Milkins, Roberts, Collins, Piper, Went, Manley, Marinello, Kellard, Davies, Reynolds, Mellows

The hire of a generator for the duration of the power drama ensures return to a 3pm kick-off. Ron Davies' 20-yard volley wins the game for Pompey, but City are unfortunate. Denied a 51st-min pen when Fear's shot is diverted, Sweeney's late left-foot effort is disallowed for offside.

21 · A CARDIFF · 15/12
Pos 9 · Att 9,368 · Opp 18 · Pts 22
W 1-0 (HT 0-0) — Gillies 78
Ref: R Kirkpatrick
City: Bond, Sweeney, Merrick, Tainton, Rodgers, Emanuel, Whitehead, Ritchie, Gould, Gow, Gillies
Cardiff: Irwin, Dwyer, Bell, Powell, Murray, Woodruff, Farrington, McCulloch, Reece, Smith*, Anderson, Phillips

'A travesty of a match' is Cardiff boss Frank O'Farrell's opinion of this lamentable affair. Gillies atones for a first-half miskick in front of an open goal, by running in and driving the ball past Bill Irwin giving City a win that their hard, determined tackling just about deserves for them.

LEAGUE DIVISION 2

Manager: Alan Dicks

Column headings: No | Date | (Venue / Opponent) | Att | Pos | Pt | F-A | H-T | Scorers, Times, and Referees | 1 | 2 | 3 | 4 | 5 | 6 | 7 | 8 | 9 | 10 | 11 | 12 sub used

---

No. 22 — H MIDDLESBROUGH — 22/12 — Att 13,116 — Pos 9 (1) — Pt 23 — D 1-1 — H-T 0-1

Pos	1	2	3	4	5	6	7	8	9	10	11	12 sub used
City	Bond	Sweeney	Merrick	Emanuel	Rodgers*	Collier	Tainton	Ritchie	Gillies	Gow	Fear	**Durrell**
Middlesbrough	*Platt*	*Creamer*	*Spraggon*	*Souness*	*Boam*	*Maddren*	*Murdoch*	*Mills*	*Hickton*	*Foggon*	*Armstrong*	

Scorers: Gillies 58; Mills 6. Ref: C Thomas

Clive Thomas is at the centre of controversy in awarding City a free-kick instead of a pen following David Armstrong's 61st-minute handball offence, which clearly takes place inside the area. Gillies punishes David Mills for his 45-yard back-pass with a great shot into the far corner.

No. 23 — A OXFORD — 26/12 — Att 7,742 — Pos 13 (18) — Pt 23 — L 0-5 — H-T 0-2

Pos	1	2	3	4	5	6	7	8	9	10	11	12 sub used
City	Bond	Sweeney	Merrick	Emanuel	Rodgers	Collier	Tainton	Ritchie	Gillies	Gow	Fear*	Durrell
Oxford	*Burton*	*Lucas*	*Shuker*	*Roberts*	*Clarke C*	*Evanson*	*Clarke D*	*Atkinson G*	*Cassidy*	*Curran*	*Aylott*	

Scorers: [Cassidy 47, Clarke C 60] Atkinson G 13, 80, Curran 38. Ref: M Sinclair

The City defence is found wanting as four of Oxford's goals come from set pieces. Graham Atkinson puts the U's ahead with a shot that goes in off Rodgers. All City can offer, as they suffer their worst defeat since April 1969, is a late effort from Emanuel which is headed off the line.

No. 24 — A LUTON — 29/12 — Att 11,398 — Pos 13 (3) — Pt 23 — L 0-1 — H-T 0-1

Pos	1	2	3	4	5	6	7	8	9	10	11	12 sub used
City	Bond	Tainton	Drysdale	Sweeney	Collier	Merrick	Fear	Ritchie*	Gillies	Gow	Durrell	**Griffin**
Luton	*Horn*	*Shanks*	*Thomson*	*Anderson*	*Faulkner*	*Garner*	*Ryan Jim*	*Husband*	*Butlin*	*West*	*Aston*	

Scorers: Anderson 37. Ref: K Burns

Again City are caught out by a set piece, this time Peter Anderson is unmarked almost on the penalty spot to register with a looping header from skipper Bobby Thomson's free-kick. Bond makes a magnificent 57th-min save in pushing Barry Butlin's shot on the turn round the post.

No. 25 — H ORIENT — 1/1 — Att 19,126 — Pos 14 (2) — Pt 23 — L 0-2 — H-T 0-0

Pos	1	2	3	4	5	6	7	8	9	10	11	12 sub used
City	Bond	Tainton	Drysdale	Sweeney	Collier	Merrick	Gillies	**Hunt**	**Cheesley**	Gow	Durrell	**Payne**
Orient	*Goddard*	*Boyle*	*Roffey*	*Allen**	*Hoadley*	*Walley*	*Fairbrother*	*Brisley*	*Bullock*	*Heppolette*	*Downing*	

Scorers: Collier 65 (og), Merrick 83 (og). Ref: W Castle

A pointless three-match holiday programme extinguishes City's promotion hopes. Bond brings off many fine saves to frustrate a skilful Orient side, but even he cannot prevent deflections from Terry Brisley's free-kick and Derek Downing's cross bringing the visitors deserved success.

No. 26 — H PRESTON — 12/1 — Att 11,450 — Pos 13 (16) — Pt 24 — D 0-0 — H-T 0-0

Pos	1	2	3	4	5	6	7	8	9	10	11	12 sub used
City	Cashley	Collier	Drysdale	Sweeney	Rodgers	Merrick	Tainton	Ritchie	Cheesley	Gow	Gillies*	**Hunt**
Preston	*Brown*	*McMahon*	*McNab*	*Sadler*	*Baxter*	*Bird*	*Treacy*	*Hawkins*	*Holden*	*Burns*	*Bruce*	

Ref: R Challis

City's inability to break down Preston's defensive line-up results in a dull game. A tally of 39 free-kicks to City and 29 against says much, and it is disappointing that Preston boss Bobby Charlton declares himself as being satisfied that his side's work rate gets them a share of the spoils.

No. 27 — A BOLTON — 20/1 — Att 23,614 — Pos 15 (18) — Pt 24 — L 1-2 — H-T 1-2

Pos	1	2	3	4	5	6	7	8	9	10	11	12 sub used
City	Cashley	Collier	Drysdale	Sweeney	Rodgers	Merrick	Tainton	Ritchie	Cheesley*	Gillies	Hunt	**Griffin**
Bolton	*Siddall*	*Ritson*	*McAllister*	*Allardyce*	*Jones P*	*Nicholson*	*Byrom*	*Jones G**	*Greaves*	*Whatmore*	*Thompson*	*Olinyk*

Scorers: Hunt 3; Merrick 9 (og), Greaves 35. Ref: P Partridge

Hunt's left-foot volley from 20 yards gets City's first Sunday game off to a good start, but defensive errors and a shot-shy attack bring defeat. Merrick heads Sam Allardyce's cross into his own net, whilst failure to close down Roy Greaves allows him to shoot in from 25 yards.

No. 28 — H CARDIFF — 2/2 — Att 24,487 — Pos 14 (15) — Pt 26 — W 3-2 — H-T 1-2

Pos	1	2	3	4	5	6	7	8	9	10	11	12 sub used
City	Cashley	Sweeney	Drysdale	Gow	Collier	Merrick	Tainton	Ritchie	Gillies	Cheesley*	Hunt	**Rodgers**
Cardiff	*Irwin*	*Dwyer*	*Bell*	*Impey*	*Murray*	*Villars*	*Farrington*	*McCulloch*	*Phillips*	*Carlin*	*Anderson*	

Scorers: Tainton 5, Sweeney 75p, 90; Phillips 16, McCulloch 27. Ref: K Baker

In front of a large crowd obtaining vouchers for the Leeds cup-tie, City gain a late winner when Sweeney heads in Gary Bell's clearance off the line. Earlier Sweeney, with his first two step run, had netted his first League penalty following Don Murray's manhandling of Ritchie.

No. 29 — A SHEFFIELD WED — 10/2 — Att 15,784 — Pos 15 (19) — Pt 26 — L 1-3 — H-T 1-1

Pos	1	2	3	4	5	6	7	8	9	10	11	12 sub used
City	Cashley	Collier	Drysdale	Gow	Rodgers	Merrick	Tainton	Ritchie	Gillies	Sweeney	Hunt*	**Cheesley**
Sheffield Wed	*Ferguson*	*Cameron*	*Knighton*	*Thompson*	*Eustace**	*Shaw*	*Henderson*	*Sunley*	*Joicey*	*Craig*	*Potts*	*Coyle*

Scorers: Ritchie 29; Joicey 12, Henderson 58, Shaw 82. Ref: R Porterhouse

City show little to worry Leeds in this poor show. Apart from Ritchie's waist-high volley equaliser, City are unable to counter the simple, but effective, play of their opponents. The speed of Tommy Potts sets up the Owls' opener, as his low centre hits Brian Joicey's leg and bounces in.

No. 30 — A WEST BROM — 23/2 — Att 18,928 — Pos 16 (5) — Pt 27 — D 2-2 — H-T 1-1

Pos	1	2	3	4	5	6	7	8	9	10	11	12 sub used
City	Cashley	Sweeney	Drysdale	Gow	Collier	Merrick	Tainton	Ritchie	Fear	Gillies	Hunt	**Rodgers**
West Brom	*Latchford*	*Nisbet*	*Thompson*	*Cantello*	*Wile*	*Robertson*	*Johnston*	*Brown T*	*Astle*	*Hartford*	*Glover*	

Scorers: Hunt 17, Tainton 55; Wile 21, Astle 72. Ref: A Morrisey

A memorable free-kick routine puts City in front as Gillies flicks the ball up for Hunt, who lets it bounce once, before letting fly with a left-foot volley. Tainton is lucky when his mis-hit 12-yarder trickles in, but City have to settle for a point as Albion register with a couple of headers.

No. 31 — H MILLWALL — 26/2 — Att 9,605 — Pos 13 (12) — Pt 29 — W 5-2 — H-T 1-1

Pos	1	2	3	4	5	6	7	8	9	10	11	12 sub used
City	Cashley	Sweeney	Drysdale	Gow	Collier	Merrick*	Tainton	Ritchie	Fear	Gillies	Hunt	**Rodgers**
Millwall	*King*	*Brown*	*Jones*	*Dorney*	*Kitchener*	*Alder*	*Bolland*	*Clark*	*Wood*	*Smethurst*	*Hill*	

Scorers: Fear 5, 62, 64, Jones 58 (og), Smethurst 12, Hill 50 [Tainton 73]. Ref: R Crabb

A remarkable game of seven goals, with not a header among them, as City put on a super show after falling behind to Gordon Hill's brilliant overhead kick. Fear completes City's first hat-trick in two years, following an own-goal equaliser when Eddie Jones lofts the ball in.

Season Match Log (Matches 32–42)

---

32 H OXFORD 2/3 — D 0-0 (HT 0-0) — 14 · 19 · 30 — Att **25,904**
City: Cashley, Sweeney, Drysdale, Gow, Collier, Rodgers, Tainton, Ritchie, Fear, Gillies, Hunt
Oxford: Burton, Light, Shuker, Roberts, Clarke C, Briggs, Gough, Atkinson, Curran, Clarke D, Aylott
Again the lure of cup-tie vouchers swells the crowd, but most of the entertainment is before the start when Dicks receives his award as the February Manager of the Month. In a dreary bore of a game, the nearest thing to a goal is Steve Aylott's 27th-minute chip that hits the bar.
Ref: J Yates

---

33 H ASTON VILLA 16/3 — L 0-1 (HT 0-0) — 16 · 15 · 30 — Att **12,759**
Scorers: Morgan 70
City: Cashley, Sweeney, Drysdale, Gow, Collier, Merrick, Tainton, Ritchie, Fear, Gillies, Hunt
Aston Villa: Cumbes, Gidman, Aitken, McMahon, Nicholl, Turnbull, Little, Ross, Morgan, Hamilton, Leonard
City suffer a cup hangover as they fail to pose any problems for Villa. Cashley's boob costs City a share of the points, as he drops Chris Nicholl's 55-yard free-kick to set up Sammy Morgan's easy tap-in. A poor game, littered with poor passing and a general lack of desire.
Ref: A Robinson

---

34 A BLACKPOOL 19/3 — D 2-2 (HT 2-1) — 16 · 5 · 31 — Att **7,710**
Scorers: Emanuel 30, Gow 39 / James 18, Davies 48
City: Cashley, Sweeney, Drysdale, Gow, Collier, Merrick, Tainton, Ritchie, Fear, Gillies, Emanuel; sub Whitehead
Blackpool: Burridge, Hatton, Bentley, Alcock, James, Suddaby, Burns, Suddick, Davies, Evanson*, Ainscow; sub Walsh
As well as thundering in an equaliser to Glyn James' headed opener, Emanuel's inspiring midfield display boosts City in an all-action game at Bloomfield Road. City should have won after Gow shoots in from three yards, but Wynn Davies seizes on defensive indecision to tap home.
Ref: J Hough

---

35 A CRYS PALACE 23/3 — L 1-3 (HT 0-0) — 16 · 21 · 31 — Att **16,840**
Scorers: Whitehead 69 / Possee 60, 67, Rogers 63p
City: Cashley, Sweeney, Drysdale, Gow, Collier, Merrick, Tainton, Ritchie*, Fear, Gillies, Emanuel; sub Whitehead
Crystal Palace: Hammond, Mulligan, Jump, Johnson, Barry, Blyth, Jeffries, Possee, Whittle, Rogers, Taylor P
City's only response to Palace's goal rush is a Ritchie half-volley that hits a post and Whitehead's climbing far-post header to Tainton's cross. Palace clinch a double over City with two headed goals from Derek Possee and a Don Rogers pen after Emanuel brings down Alan Whittle.
Ref: R Lee

---

36 H FULHAM 30/3 — L 0-1 (HT 0-0) — 16 · 8 · 31 — Att **10,946**
Scorers: Mullery 74
City: Cashley, Sweeney, Drysdale, Gow, Collier, Rodgers, Tainton, Ritchie, Fear*, Gillies, Emanuel; sub Whitehead
Fulham: Mellor, Cutbush, Strong, Moore, Lacy, Dunne, Conway, Jim Mullery, Busby, Lloyd, Barrett
Beware the Ides of March, a warning that has gone unheeded by City, who have failed to win a single game during the past month. Fulham celebrate manager Alec Stock's 57th birthday with a double over City when Alan Mullery hooks the ball in from Bobby Moore's free-kick.
Ref: P Reeves

---

37 H CARLISLE 6/4 — W 2-0 (HT 1-0) — 16 · 5 · 33 — Att **9,570**
Scorers: Cheesley 31, Gillies 75
City: Cashley, Sweeney, Drysdale, Gow, Collier, Merrick, Tainton*, Hunt, Cheesley, Gillies, Emanuel; sub Fear
Carlisle: Ross, Carr, Winstanley, McCartney, Green, Balderstone, Martin, Train, Owen, Clarke, Laidlaw
Against a skilful Carlisle side Cheesley obtains his first City goal with a magnificent 15-yard header from Tainton's free-kick. After Cashley makes a brilliant save to keep out Bobby Owen's close-in effort, Gillies relieves City's relegation fears with a cross-shot into the far corner.
Ref: J Taylor

---

38 H NOTT'M FOREST 12/4 — W 1-0 (HT 1-0) — 16 · 9 · 35 — Att **13,125**
Scorers: Cheesley 5
City: Cashley, Sweeney, Drysdale, Gow, Collier, Merrick, Tainton, Ritchie, Cheesley*, Gillies, Emanuel; sub Fear
Nott'm Forest: Peacock, O'Kane, Serella, Bolton, Chapman, Cottam, Richardson*, McKenzie, Lyall, Galley, Bowyer; sub Dennehy
City should have had more than Cheesley's low drive to show for their early supremacy, before the loss of their scorer just before the break allows Forest to take control. Cashley brings down Duncan McKenzie to concede a penalty, but George Lyall blasts the kick high and wide.
Ref: R Toseland

---

39 A SUNDERLAND 13/4 — W 2-1 (HT 1-1) — 16 · 7 · 37 — Att **28,884**
Scorers: Ritchie 2, Emanuel 79 / Longhorn 21
City: Cashley, Sweeney, Drysdale, Gow, Collier, Merrick, Tainton, Ritchie, Fear, Gillies, Emanuel
Sunderland: Montgomery, Malone, Bolton, Longhorn, Watson, Belfitt, Kerr, Hughes, Halom, Porterfield*, Towers; sub Ashurst
Cashley makes two fantastic saves to preserve Ritchie's 80-second headed opener, but he has no chance with Dennis Longhorn's overhead kick. With the keeper prostrate, following a collision with Dave Watson, Emanuel silences the Roker Roar with his 30-yarder into an open net.
Ref: K McNally

---

40 A NOTT'M FOREST 16/4 — D 1-1 (HT 0-0) — 15 · 8 · 38 — Att **12,756**
Scorers: Ritchie 50 / McKenzie 48
City: Cashley, Sweeney, Drysdale, Gow, Collier, Merrick, Tainton, Ritchie, Fear, Gillies, Emanuel
Nott'm Forest: Peacock, O'Kane, Winfield, Chapman, Cottam, Jackson, McKenzie, Lyall, Galley, McIntosh, Bowyer
Cashley's world-class save from Ian Bowyer's twelve-yard 88th-minute thunderbolt allows City to complete an unbeaten Easter. After Duncan McKenzie brings the game to life, by smashing John Galley's through-ball into the net, Ritchie levels when Fear heads on Drysdale's free-kick.
Ref: P Willis

---

41 H PORTSMOUTH 20/4 — L 0-2 (HT 0-1) — 16 · 14 · 38 — Att **11,143**
Scorers: Davies 12, Stewart 77
City: Cashley, Sweeney, Drysdale, Gow, Collier, Merrick, Tainton, Ritchie, Fear, Gillies*, Emanuel; sub Hunt
Portsmouth: Best, Roberts, Wilson, Hand, Went, Stephenson, Marinello, Kellard, Davies, Piper, Stewart
Despite mustering only three shots, Pompey achieve their first away win of the season. Collier's failure to clear gifts Ron Davies his low drive, and whilst City have their chances, it is Peter Marinello's great run and perfect pass that sets up Andy Stewart's unstoppable 15-yard clincher.
Ref: T Bosi

---

42 A NOTTS CO 27/4 — L 1-2 (HT 0-2) — 16 · 10 · 38 — Att **6,991**
Scorers: Gillies 84 / Rodgers 11 (og), Bradd 42
City: Cashley, Sweeney, Drysdale, Gow, Rodgers, Merrick, Tainton, Ritchie, Fear, Gillies*, Emanuel; sub Whitehead
Notts Co: McManus, Brindley, O'Brien, Stubbs, Masson, Bolton, Randall, McVay, Needham, Bradd, Probert
The players' inability to master a bumpy pitch and stiff breeze results in a poor match. Rodgers amazingly jabs the ball into his own net and an abysmal offside trap allows Les Bradd to waltz the ball home, before Fear's left-flank run and cross allows Gillies to shoot in from ten yards.
Ref: A Gray

Home Average 14,058
Away Average 13,325

LEAGUE DIVISION 2 (CUP-TIES) Manager: Alan Dicks SEASON 1973-74

League Cup

2 — A SCUNTHORPE · 6 · D · 9/10 · 4,418 · 4:18 · F-A 0-0 · H-T 0-0
Scorers, Times: — Ref: J Hunting

1	2	3	4	5	6	7	8	9	10	11	12 sub used
Bond	Sweeney	Drysdale	Gow	Collier	Merrick	Tainton*	Ritchie	Gould	Gillies	Fear	Woods
Barnard	*Lynch*	*Welbourne*	*Simpkin*	*Barker*	*Davidson*	*Houghton*	*Pilling*	*Collier*	*Keeley*	*Warnock*	

Safety-first City only create two opportunities, one in each half. Fear should have given Geoff Barnard no chance early on, but his shot was smothered, then Ritchie's header elicits a brilliant save. Outplayed for most of the tie, City are indebted to their defence for replay survival.

2R — H SCUNTHORPE · 4 · W · 16/10 · 7,837 · 4:17 · F-A 2-1 · H-T 0-1
Scorers, Times: Fear 77, Sweeney 80 / Welbourne 45 — Ref: T Reynolds

1	2	3	4	5	6	7	8	9	10	11	12 sub used
Bond	Tainton	Drysdale	Sweeney	Collier	Merrick	Whitehead	Ritchie	Gould	Gillies*	Fear	
Barnard	*Lynch*	*Welbourne*	*Simpkin*	*Barker*	*Miney*	*Houghton*	*Pilling*	*Fletcher*	*Keeley*	*Warnock*	

At last City overcome their Scunthorpe hoodoo, but not without a fright. It takes Fear's 67th-minute appearance off the subs bench to provide the spark to overcome Don Welbourne's headed opener. Fear levels with a brilliant chip over the Iron's wall, and Sweeney shoots in winner.

3 — H COVENTRY · 4 · D · 30/10 · 19,196 · 1:7 · F-A 2-2 · H-T 1-1
Scorers, Times: Gould 10, 52 / Smith 22, Cartwright 69 — Ref: A Oliver

1	2	3	4	5	6	7	8	9	10	11	12 sub used
Bond	Sweeney	Drysdale	Emanuel	Rodgers	Merrick	Tainton	Ritchie	Gould	Gow	Fear*	Gillies
Glazier	*Coop*	*Holmes*	*Mortimer*	*Parker*	*Dugdale*	*Smith*	*Alderson*	*Stein*	*Cartwright*	*Hutchison*	

Gould is robbed of a likely hat-trick as the referee turns down a clear penalty when he is shoved by Alan Dugdale just four minutes from the end of this spectacular cup-tie. Gould twice puts City ahead with hard-hit drives, but two headed replies allow Coventry to survive for a replay.

3R — A COVENTRY · 5 · L · 6/11 · 13,049 · 1:10 · F-A 1-2 · H-T 1-2
Scorers, Times: Whitehead 42 / Alderson 20, Stein 32 — Ref: A Oliver

1	2	3	4	5	6	7	8	9	10	11	12 sub used
Bond	Tainton	Drysdale	Sweeney	Rodgers	Merrick	Whitehead	Ritchie	Gould	Gow	Gillies*	Fear
Glazier	*Coop*	*Holmes*	*Mortimer*	*Philpotts*	*Dugdale*	*Cartwright*	*Alderson*	*Stein*	*McGuire*	*Hutchison*	

City earn the praise, but not the spoils, as they make an honourable exit. 'What a prospect' says Coventry boss Joe Mercer of Whitehead, who gains reward for his teasing, tormenting and tantilising display when firing in from the edge of the area to haul City back into the game.

FA Cup

3 — H HULL · 14 · D · 5/1 · 8,968 · 9 · F-A 1-1 · H-T 1-1
Scorers, Times: Merrick 18 / Galvin 20 — Ref: R Crabb

1	2	3	4	5	6	7	8	9	10	11	12 sub used
Bond	Tainton	Drysdale	Fear	Collier	Merrick	Griffin	Ritchie	Gillies	Gow	Durrell*	Emanuel
Wealands	*Banks*	*McGill*	*Galvin*	*Deere*	*Burnett*	*Holme*	*Lord*	*Pearson*	*Wagstaff*	*Greenwood*	

Just 90 seconds after Merrick heads City in front, Bond drops a simple cross to allow Chris Galvin to prod in Hull's equaliser. Content to settle for a replay, the Tigers are fortunate just before the call of time when Gow shoots over the top after Jeff Wealands gifts an easy chance.

3R — A HULL · 14 · W · 8/1 · 5,340 · 9 · F-A 1-0 · H-T 0-0
Scorers, Times: Tainton 54 — Ref: V James

1	2	3	4	5	6	7	8	9	10	11	12 sub used
Cashley	Tainton	Drysdale	Sweeney	Collier	Merrick	Rodgers	Ritchie	Gillies	Gow	Woods	
Wealands	*Banks*	*McGill*	*Galvin*	*Deere*	*Burnett*	*Holme*	*Lord*	*Hemmerman*	*Wagstaff*	*Greenwood*	

City never stop harrying and chasing against opponents who appear to give up after Gow's cross sets up Tainton to blast in from eight yards. Denied two possible penalties in the first half, City are fortunate to escape, conceding one in the last minute when Tainton pulls Chris Galvin.

4 — A HEREFORD · 15 · W · 26/1 · 17,431 · 3:16 · F-A 1-0 · H-T 1-0
Scorers, Times: Merrick 17 — Ref: E Jolly

1	2	3	4	5	6	7	8	9	10	11	12 sub used
Cashley	Collier	Drysdale	Sweeney	Rodgers	Merrick	Tainton	Ritchie	Gillies*	Cheesley	Hunt	Fear
Hughes	*Radford*	*Naylor**	*McLaughlin*	*Jones*	*Tavener*	*Redrobe*	*Tyler*	*Hinch*	*Evans*	*Rudge*	*Jenkins*

Playing against the wind and driving rain, as well as the slope, in the first half, City are fortunate when Ronnie Radford is penalised despite his shirt being pulled. From Hunt's chipped in free-kick from near the left corner flag, Merrick is at the far post to shoot in with his trusty left foot.

5 — H LEEDS · 16 · D · 16/2 · 37,141 · 1:1 · F-A 1-1 · H-T 0-1
Scorers, Times: Fear 65 / Bremner 42 — Ref: J Taylor

1	2	3	4	5	6	7	8	9	10	11	12 sub used
Cashley	Sweeney	Drysdale	Gow	Collier	Merrick	Tainton	Ritchie	Fear	Gillies	Hunt	
Harvey	*Yorath*	*Cherry*	*Bremner*	*McQueen*	*Hunter*	*Lorimer*	*Jordan*	*Jones*	*Giles**	*Madeley*	*Clarke*

Leeds are fortunate to survive to face Fear again after City's talented striker had led them a merry dance. He lobs in a great equaliser to Billy Bremner's 25-yarder, as well as hitting the bar in the first half with a great shot on the turn, and laying on chances for Tainton and Gillies.

5R — A LEEDS · 16 · W · 19/2 · 47,182 · 1:1 · F-A 1-0 · H-T 0-0
Scorers, Times: Gillies 73 — Ref: J Taylor

1	2	3	4	5	6	7	8	9	10	11	12 sub used
Cashley	Sweeney	Drysdale	Gow	Collier	Merrick	Tainton	Ritchie*	Fear	Gillies*	Hunt	Rodgers
Harvey	*Cherry*	*Cooper*	*Bremner*	*Ellam*	*Hunter*	*Lorimer*	*Clarke*	*Jones*	*Giles**	*Madeley*	*Jordan*

Unlike the first meeting, this time it is Leeds who are the dominant side. City's desperate rearguard action is akin to the Siege of the Alamo, but after the post denies Peter Lorimer on 60 minutes, it is like the Relief of Mafeking for a while when Gillies shoots in his left-footed winner.

QF — H LIVERPOOL · 16 · L · 9/3 · 37,671 · 1:2 · F-A 0-1 · H-T 0-0
Scorers, Times: Toshack 48 — Ref: D Turner

1	2	3	4	5	6	7	8	9	10	11	12 sub used
Cashley	Sweeney	Drysdale	Gow	Collier	Rodgers	Tainton	Ritchie	Fear	Gillies	Hunt*	Emanuel
Clemence	*Smith*	*Lindsay*	*Thompson*	*Cormack*	*Hughes*	*Keegan*	*Hall*	*Heighway**	*Toshack*	*Callaghan*	*Boersma*

In the quarter-finals for the first time since 1920, City at 25-1 make the 5-2 favourites work hard for their success. Until John Toshack shoots in from ten yards, the ball falling into his path when Rodgers fails to deal with Kevin Keegan's cross, there is little to choose between the sides.

		Home					Away					
	P	W	D	L	F	A	W	D	L	F	A	Pts
1 Middlesbro	42	16	4	1	40	8	11	7	3	37	22	65
2 Luton	42	12	5	4	42	25	7	7	7	22	26	50
3 Carlisle	42	13	5	3	40	17	7	4	10	21	31	49
4 Orient	42	9	8	4	28	17	6	10	5	27	25	48
5 Blackpool	42	11	5	5	35	17	6	8	7	22	23	47
6 Sunderland	42	11	6	4	32	15	8	3	10	26	29	47
7 Nott'm Forest	42	12	6	3	40	19	3	9	9	17	24	45
8 West Brom	42	12	6	3	28	24	6	7	8	20	21	44
9 Hull	42	9	9	3	25	15	4	8	9	21	32	43
10 Notts Co	42	8	6	7	30	35	7	7	7	25	25	43
11 Bolton	42	12	5	4	30	17	3	7	11	14	23	42
12 Millwall	42	10	6	5	28	16	4	8	9	23	35	42
13 Fulham	42	11	4	6	26	20	5	6	10	13	23	42
14 Aston Villa	42	8	9	4	33	21	5	6	10	15	24	41
15 Portsmouth	42	9	8	4	26	16	5	4	12	19	46	40
16 BRISTOL CITY	42	9	5	7	25	20	5	5	11	22	34	38
17 Cardiff	42	8	7	6	27	20	2	9	10	22	42	38
18 Oxford	42	8	8	5	27	21	2	8	11	8	25	36
19 Sheffield Wed	42	9	6	6	33	24	3	5	13	18	39	35
20 Crys Palace	42	6	7	8	24	24	5	5	11	19	32	34
21 Preston *	42	7	8	6	24	23	2	6	13	16	39	31
22 Swindon	42	6	7	8	22	27	1	4	16	14	45	25
	924	212	143	107	665	441	107	143	212	441	665	923

* 1 pt deducted

Appearances / Goals

	Appearances						Goals			
	Lge	Sub	LC	Sub	FAC	Sub	Lge	LC	FAC	Tot
Bond, Len	15		4		1		1			1
Cashley, Ray	27		5		1		2			2
Cheesley, Paul	7	1	1		1					
Collier, Gary	31		2		6	2				
Drysdale, Brian	32	2	4		6					
Durrell, Joe	2	2			1					
Emanuel, John	24	2	1		2		2			2
Fear, Keith	32	3	2	2	4	1	8	1	1	10
Gillies, Donny	28	8	3	1	6		6		1	7
Gould, Bobby	16		4				7		2	9
Gow, Gerry	41		4		5		1			1
Griffin, Kevin		2	1							
Hunt, Ernie	9	2	2		4		2			2
Merrick, Geoff	40		4		5			2		2
Rodgers, David	26	2	2		3	1	1			1
Ritchie, Tom	39		4		6		6			6
Sweeney, Gerry	42		4		5		3	1		4
Tainton, Trevor	42		4		6		5		1	6
Whitehead, Clive	9	3	2				2	1		3
Woods, Eddie				1		1				
(own-goals)							1			1
20 players used	462	27	44	4	66	6	47	5	5	57

Odds & ends

Double wins: (4) Swindon, Millwall, Sunderland, Cardiff.
Double loses: (4) Luton, Fulham, Crystal Palace, Portsmouth.

Won from behind: (3) Hull (h), Cardiff (h), Millwall (h).
Lost from in front: (1) Bolton (a).

High spots: Cashley's goal at Ashton Gate against Hull on 18 Sep.
Ernie Hunt's goal at the Hawthorns on 23 February.
Keith Fear's hat-trick against Millwall on 26 February.
Both FA Cup games against Leeds.
FL Cup game against Coventry at Ashton Gate on 30 October.

Low spots: Losing to Crystal Palace at Ashton Gate on 10 November.
Being annihilated at Oxford on 26 December.
Failure to beat Liverpool in the FA Cup.
Losing 0-2 against Bristol Rovers in the Gloucestershire Cup on 29 Apr.

Player of the Year: Gerry Gow.
Ever-presents: (1) Trevor Tainton.
Hat-tricks: (1) Keith Fear.
Leading scorer: Keith Fear (10).

LEAGUE DIVISION 2   Manager: Alan Dicks   SEASON 1974-75

No	Date	Att	Pos	Pt	F-A	H-T	Scorers, Times, and Referees	1	2	3	4	5	6	7	8	9	10	11	12 sub used
1	A NOTT'M FOREST 17/8	11,339	21	1	D 0-0	0-0	Ref: J Rice	Cashley	Sweeney	Drysdale	Gow	Rodgers	Merrick	Tainton	**Mann**	Gillies	Cheesley	Whitehead	Whitehead
								Peacock	O'Kane	Richardson	Chapman	Cottam	Jones	Dennehy	Lyall	Martin*	Robertson	Bowyer	Woodcock

Poor entertainment as City are happy to settle for a point against Forest, for whom Miah Dennehy's cross-shot hits the inside of a post early on. Midway through the second half Cheesley's great 30-yard strike is booked for the top corner, but Dennis Peacock pulls off a superlative save.

No	Date	Att	Pos	Pt	F-A	H-T	Scorers, Times, and Referees	1	2	3	4	5	6	7	8	9	10	11	12 sub used
2	H ORIENT 24/8	10,985		2	D 0-0	0-0	Ref: D Nippard	Cashley	Sweeney	Drysdale	Gow	Collier	Merrick	Tainton	Ritchie*	Gillies	Cheesley	Whitehead	Mann
								Jackson	Fisher	Raffey	Hoadley	Harris	Walley*	Fairbrother	Heppolette	Bullock	Queen	Possee	Downing

A combination of missed chances, misfortune and inspired keeping by John Jackson prevents a rout at Ashton Gate. City produce a brilliant display of passing football, but the promise of goals never materialises as Orient, missing five regulars, hang on to snatch an unlikely point.

No	Date	Att	Pos	Pt	F-A	H-T	Scorers, Times, and Referees	1	2	3	4	5	6	7	8	9	10	11	12 sub used
3	A OLDHAM 31/8	9,860	11	2	L 0-2	0-0	Jones 46, Cashley 47 (og); Ref: R Clay	Cashley	Sweeney	Drysdale	Gow	Collier	Merrick	Tainton	Ritchie	Gillies	Cheesley	Whitehead*	Hunt
								Ogden	Wood	Whittle	Blair	Mulvaney	Bailey	Garwood	Bell	Jones	Robins	Groves	

City's tale of woe in front of goal continues, as shortly after Sweeney puts a 57th-minute penalty wide, Hunt is unlucky with a neatly headed effort that is disallowed. Cashley is at fault for the Latics' opener, as he cannot stop himself trying to save Maurice Whittle's indirect free-kick.

No	Date	Att	Pos	Pt	F-A	H-T	Scorers, Times, and Referees	1	2	3	4	5	6	7	8	9	10	11	12 sub used
4	H BOLTON 7/9	9,300	14	4	W 2-1	1-1	Gillies 33, Drysdale 79; Ritson 32; Ref: A Turvey	Cashley	Sweeney	Drysdale	Gow	Collier	Merrick	Tainton	Ritchie	Gillies	Fear	Emanuel	
								Siddall	Ritson	Dunne	Nicholson	Jones P	McAllister	Byrom	Jones G*	Greaves	Whatmore	Thompson	Taylor

A freak goal wins this game after John Ritson drives in Tony Dunne's cross to put the Trotters in front. Gillies shoots in from Fear's chip for the leveller, but Barry Siddall keeps City out until Drysdale's long shot is taken over the keeper's head and into the net by the gale-force wind.

No	Date	Att	Pos	Pt	F-A	H-T	Scorers, Times, and Referees	1	2	3	4	5	6	7	8	9	10	11	12 sub used
5	A CARDIFF 14/9	8,858	10	6	W 1-0	0-0	Fear 46; Ref: J Hunting	Cashley	Sweeney	Drysdale	Gow	Collier	Merrick	Whitehead	Ritchie	Gillies	Fear	Emanuel	
								Healey	Larmour	Pithard	Villars	Murray	Phillips	McInch	Charles	Showers	Reece*	Anderson	Attley

Cardiff are unlucky not to take an early lead as Derek Showers heads in from Willie Anderson's free-kick. The referee orders the kick to be re-taken as Jimmy McInch had returned to the pitch without permission. City through are full value for their success, obtained by Fear's header.

No	Date	Att	Pos	Pt	F-A	H-T	Scorers, Times, and Referees	1	2	3	4	5	6	7	8	9	10	11	12 sub used
6	H SOUTHAMPTON 21/9	15,708	7	8	W 2-0	1-0	Sweeney 15, Merrick 56; Ref: T Bosi	Cashley	Sweeney	Drysdale	Gow	Collier	Merrick	Whitehead	Ritchie	Gillies	Fear	Emanuel	
								Turner	Mills	Peach	Fisher	Bennett	Blyth	O'Brien*	Channon	Osgood	Gilchrist	Steele	Stokes

City's positive, attacking football should have brought more than two goals, whilst the Saints are unhappy about their three strikes that are struck off. After Sweeney shoots City ahead, Merrick ties up the points as his 40-yard free kick, which is meant as a cross, ends up in the net.

No	Date	Att	Pos	Pt	F-A	H-T	Scorers, Times, and Referees	1	2	3	4	5	6	7	8	9	10	11	12 sub used
7	H YORK 24/9	11,867	7	9	D 0-0	0-0	Ref: D Civil	Cashley	Sweeney	Drysdale	Gow	Collier	Merrick	Whitehead	Ritchie	Gillies	Fear	Emanuel	
								Crawford	Hunter	Oliver	Holmes	Swallow	Topping	Lyons	Cave	Seal	Jones*	Wann	Hinch

When Whitehead blasts the ball in off the crossbar in the 42nd minute, it doesn't seem to matter that the ref changes his mind after first giving a goal. It is surely only a matter of time, but the goals just don't come as Graeme Crawford and the woodwork frustrate all of City's efforts.

No	Date	Att	Pos	Pt	F-A	H-T	Scorers, Times, and Referees	1	2	3	4	5	6	7	8	9	10	11	12 sub used
8	A MILLWALL 28/9	5,750	13	9	L 0-1	0-0	Dorney 51; Ref: A Robinson	Cashley	Sweeney	Drysdale	Gow	Collier	Merrick	Whitehead	Ritchie	Gillies*	Fear	Emanuel	**Brolly**
								King	Brown B	Jones	Donaldson	Kitchener	Dorney	Bolland	Saul	Smethurst*	Alder	Hill	Wood

On an uneven pitch City are robbed as the referee disallows Ritchie's 80th-minute in off his thigh equaliser, claiming he had played the ball with his arm. Well on top early on, City go behind when Alan Dorney out jumps two defenders to head powerfully into the top corner.

No	Date	Att	Pos	Pt	F-A	H-T	Scorers, Times, and Referees	1	2	3	4	5	6	7	8	9	10	11	12 sub used
9	A SHEFFIELD WED 5/10	10,318	13	10	D 1-1	0-0	Merrick 57; Holsgrove 50; Ref: R Matthewson	Cashley	Sweeney	Drysdale	Gow	Collier	Merrick	Tainton	Ritchie	Gillies	Fear	Emanuel	
								Springett	Rodrigues	Shaw	Dowd	Holsgrove	Knighton	Potts	Harvey	Joicey	Craig	Sunley*	Prudham

Luckless Gillies heads against the post and then fails in front of an open goal in the three minutes leading up to the interval. City, who hardly allow Wednesday a chance, can do nothing about John Holsgrove's cracking drive, but Merrick salvages a point by heading in Fear's chip.

No	Date	Att	Pos	Pt	F-A	H-T	Scorers, Times, and Referees	1	2	3	4	5	6	7	8	9	10	11	12 sub used
10	H SUNDERLAND 12/10	13,084	12	11	D 1-1	0-1	Gow 77; Halom 32; Ref: K Baker	Cashley	Sweeney	Drysdale	Gow	Collier	Merrick	Tainton	Ritchie	Gillies*	Fear	Emanuel	Whitehead
								Montgomery	Malone	Bolton	Moncur	Watson	Porterfield	Kerr	Hughes	Halom	Robson	Towers	

Classy Sunderland are knocked out of their first-half stride by a City side whose all-action display after the interval is crowned by Gow's 20-yd free-kick equaliser. The Wearsider's boss Bob Stokoe is less than happy though, as he claims that his defence was still lining up their wall.

11 · A FULHAM · 19/10 — D 1-1 (1-0) · Att 8,960 · Pos 11 · Pts 8/12

Fear 9 · Mullery 57 — Ref: R Kirkpatrick/P White

City: Cashley, Sweeney, Drysdale, Gow, Collier, Tainton, Merrick, Ritchie, Cheesley, Fear, Emanuel
Fulham: Mellor, Cutbush, Strong, Mullery, Lacy, Conway/Jim Slough, Moore, Busby, Lloyd, Bray, Barratt

Fear gives impressive City the lead when stroking the ball in, but they are made to pay for their lack of a killer touch as Alan Mullery's 22-yard thunderbolt crashes past Cashley. After sustaining a back injury earlier in the half, the referee is replaced by the senior lineman in the 71st min.

12 · A OXFORD · 23/10 — L 0-2 (0-0) · Att 5,772 · Pos 15 · Pts 13/12

Heron 57, Sims 69 — Ref: R Crabb

City: Cashley, Sweeney, Drysdale, Whitehead, Collier, Tainton, Merrick, Ritchie, Cheesley, Fear, Emanuel
Oxford: Milkins, Light, Shuker, Roberts, Clarke C, Aylott, Briggs, Fleming, Clarke D, Sims, Heron*

What a let down! Just when City are beginning to look the part they flop. Against hard-chasing opponents, City are fortunate the score does not match last season's drubbing. Cashley lets John Sims' overhead slip through his fingers after earlier being beaten by Brian Heron's header.

13 · H NOTTS CO · 26/10 — W 3-0 (0-0) · Att 10,343 · Pos 10 · Pts 15/14

Sweeney 78p, Mann 81, Cheesley 88 — Ref: C Newsome

City: Cashley, Sweeney, Drysdale, Mann, Collier, Tainton, Merrick, Ritchie, Cheesley, Fear, Emanuel
Notts Co: Brown, Brindley, O'Brien, Masson, Needham, Carter, Stubbs, Probert !, Bradd, Mann, Scanlon

City never look back after Sweeney nets from the spot when Brian Stubbs brings down Ritchie, though the sending off of Eric Probert, for protesting too much over the penalty, obviously helps. City have the luck early on when Ian Scanlon, faced by an empty net, hits the post.

14 · A PORTSMOUTH · 2/11 — W 1-0 (0-0) · Att 9,596 · Pos 6 · Pts 20/16

Gow 65 — Ref: M Taylor

City: Cashley, Sweeney, Drysdale, Gow, Collier, Tainton, Merrick, Ritchie, Cheesley, Fear, Emanuel
Portsmouth: Best, Roberts, Wilson, Piper, Went, Stephenson, Marinello, Reynolds, Stewart, Hand*, Mellows/Foggo

Gow saves City's blushes after their early impressive display fails to produce any goals. Pushed back on defensive after the break, Gow's right-foot 25-yard drive completely beats David Best in the Pompey goal. City's numerous back-passes during the closing stages win few friends.

15 · H OXFORD · 5/11 — W 3-0 (0-0) · Att 10,036 · Pos 5 · Pts 14/18

Mann 47, Merrick 54, Ritchie 76 — Ref: B Homewood

City: Cashley, Sweeney, Drysdale*, Gow, Collier, Tainton, Merrick, Ritchie, Cheesley, Fear, Emanuel
Oxford: Milkins, Light, Shuker, Roberts, Evanson, Briggs, Aylott, Fleming, Clarke D, McCulloch, Sims

Gow ensures his 200th appearance is an occasion to remember with his whiplash tackling and accurate passing. Although failing to score he has major roles in the build-up to Mann's crisp low-shot, and Merrick's header. After a mediocre start, City are brilliant after the interval.

16 · H MANCHESTER U · 9/11 — W 1-0 (1-0) · Att 28,104 · Pos 4 · Pts 1/20

Emanuel 31 — Ref: A Hart

City: Cashley, Sweeney, Drysdale*, Gow, Collier, Tainton, Merrick, Ritchie, Cheesley, Fear, Emanuel
Manchester U: Stepney, Forsyth, Houston, Greenhoff, Sidebottom, Buchan, Macari, McIlroy, Pearson, McCalliog, Daly*/Graham

Ritchie's stirring display reduces United to a state of panic, though it is Emanuel who secures the points by firing in as Fear's shot is cleared off the line. Tommy Doherty is surely joking with his comment that 'City were the most defensive home side United had played this season'.

17 · A WEST BROM · 16/11 — L 0-1 (0-1) · Att 11,936 · Pos 4 · Pts 6/20

Mayo 22 — Ref: A Morrisey

City: Cashley, Sweeney, Tainton, Gow, Collier, Whitehead*, Merrick, Ritchie, Fear, Mann, Emanuel !
West Brom: Osborne, Nisbet, Wilson, Trewick, Wile, Rushbury, Glover, Shaw, Mayo, Hughes, Johnston ! / Cheesley

Little goes right at the Hawthorns as City's attempts to counter Mayo's shot into an open goal, after the ball rebounds off the referee, are twice thwarted by the post. Emanuel receives his marching orders in the 79th minute, when retaliating against Willie Johnston, who is also sent off.

18 · H BLACKPOOL · 23/11 — L 0-1 (0-1) · Att 11,584 · Pos 7 · Pts 9/20

Hatton 35p — Ref: G Kew

City: Cashley, Sweeney, Tainton, Gow, Collier, Merrick, Gillies, Ritchie, Fear*, Griffin, Emanuel
Blackpool: Burridge, Hatton, Harrison !, Curtis, Hart, Suddaby, Evans, Ainscow, Bentley, Parker, Evanson*/Alcock

Despite their blistering, all-action football after the break City's long-time need for a striker is even more obvious. Unfortunately it is all try and not enough skill and Blackpool are able to maintain the advantage given them by Hatton's spot-kick, following Merrick's push on Tony Evans.

19 · A HULL · 30/11 — L 0-1 (0-1) · Att 9,612 · Pos 8 · Pts 5/20

Lord 14 — Ref: D Turner

City: Cashley, Sweeney, Merrick, Gow*, Rodgers, Collier, Tainton, Ritchie, Fear*, Mann, Emanuel
Hull: Wealands, Banks, De Vries, Galvin*, Croft, Blampey, McGill, Lord, Wood, Hawley, Gillies/Greenwood

A poor game, decided by Malcolm Lord's brilliant chip as Cashley is punished for his tendency to stand well off his line. The absence of a consistent striker grows more serious by the week, though Fear's is unlucky to have his 33rd-minute hook shot disallowed for handball.

20 · H ASTON VILLA · 7/12 — W 1-0 (1-0) · Att 13,390 · Pos 8 · Pts 7/22

Mann 28 — Ref: B Daniels

City: Cashley, Sweeney, Merrick, Gow*, Rodgers, Collier, Tainton, Ritchie, Cheesley, Griffin, Mann
Aston Villa: Cumbes, Robson, Aitken, Ross, Nicholl, Brown, Graydon, Little A, Little B, Hamilton, Carrodus/Whitehead

Ex Rover Ray Graydon is the butt of the crowd's barracking by the week, though City hang onto Mann's headed goal, which is their only on-target effort. With Griffin in agony with badly bruised ribs and Ritchie hobbling with a knee injury, the superb play of Collier and Rodgers keeps Villa at bay.

21 · H NOTT'M FOREST · 14/12 — W 1-0 (1-0) · Att 10,006 · Pos 7 · Pts 13/24

Cheesley 32 — Ref: J Taylor

City: Cashley, Drysdale, Sweeney, Rodgers, Merrick, Tainton, Ritchie, Cheesley, Griffin, Griffin, Robertson
Nott'm Forest: Middleton, O'Kane, Greenwood, Chapman, Jones, Richardson, Dennehy, Martin*, Butlin, Bowyer, O'Neill/Robertson

Cheesley caps his best display of the season with a great volley as he causes all manner of problems for Forest in the first half. After the break though, it is different and it takes all the best endeavours of the defence with the best record in the League to achieve two back-to-back wins.

LEAGUE DIVISION 2   Manager: Alan Dicks   SEASON 1974-75

No	Date	Att	Pos	Pt	F-A	H-T	Scorers, Times, and Referees	1	2	3	4	5	6	7	8	9	10	11	12 sub used
22	A NORWICH 21/12	16,981	3	24	2-3	2-1	Ritchie 41, Mann 42 / *Suggett 16, Boyer 65, 67* / Ref: A Porter	Cashley	Collier	Drysdale	Sweeney	Rodgers	Merrick	Tainton	Ritchie	Cheesley	Griffin*	Mann	Durrell
								Keelan	*Machin*	*Sullivan*	*Morris*	*Forbes*	*Stringer*	*Miller*	*MacDougall*	*Boyer*	*Suggett*	*Powell**	*Steele*

Norwich are all at sea after being hit by City's two-goal 90-second blitz, but Cheesley's miss in firing wide when clean through a minute before the break lets them off the hook. Cashley is at fault as Colin Suggett gets Norwich off to a good start by scoring directly from a corner.

No	Date	Att	Pos	Pt	F-A	H-T	Scorers, Times, and Referees	1	2	3	4	5	6	7	8	9	10	11	12 sub used
23	H CARDIFF 26/12	12,484	18	25	0-0	0-0	Ref: R Toseland	Cashley	Sweeney	Drysdale	Mann	Collier	Merrick	Tainton	Ritchie	Cheesley	Fear	Durrell	
								Irwin	*Dwyer*	*Pethard*	*Buchanan*	*Morgan*	*Larmour*	*Reece*	*Smith*	*Showers*	*Whitham*	*Anderson*	

A poor game as both sides suffer a Christmas hangover, but Cardiff end their long losing sequence in Severn derbies. Durrell is robbed of a winner five minutes from time when his volley from the edge of the penalty area is disallowed due to an offside decision against Sweeney.

No	Date	Att	Pos	Pt	F-A	H-T	Scorers, Times, and Referees	1	2	3	4	5	6	7	8	9	10	11	12 sub used
24	A BRISTOL ROV 28/12	20,911	14	27	4-1	0-1	Fear 58, 90, Mann 72, Tainton 77 / *Fearnley 26* / Ref: G Hill	Cashley	Sweeney	Drysdale	Mann	Collier	Merrick	Tainton	Ritchie	Fear	Cheesley	Durrell*	Griffin
								Sheppard	*Bater*	*Parsons*	*Aitken*	*Taylor*	*Prince*	*Fearnley*	*Coombes*	*Warboys*	*Staniforth**	*Britton*	*Jones*

Rovers fail to take full advantage of the gale-force wind at their backs in the first half, and Gordon Fearnley's opener from a suspiciously offside position is never going to be enough. For City it is a different story after the break and Fear's great 25-yard volley ties up great win.

No	Date	Att	Pos	Pt	F-A	H-T	Scorers, Times, and Referees	1	2	3	4	5	6	7	8	9	10	11	12 sub used
25	A ASTON VILLA 11/1	22,422	4	27	0-2	0-1	*Little 35, Hamilton 83* / Ref: R Challis	Cashley	Sweeney	Drysdale	Mann	Collier	Merrick	Tainton	Ritchie	Cheesley*	Durrell	Whitehead	
								Cumbes	*Robson*	*Aitken*	*Ross*	*Nicholl*	*McDonald*	*Graydon*	*Little B*	*Leonard*	*Hamilton*	*Pimblett*	

Jim Cumbes, who has only one save to make, needs the services of a team-mate to clear Ritchie's last-minute volley off the line. Brian Little's curved 20-yarder puts Villa ahead, and after the floored Fear's penalty appeal is ignored, Ian Hamilton nudges home Ray Graydon's cross.

No	Date	Att	Pos	Pt	F-A	H-T	Scorers, Times, and Referees	1	2	3	4	5	6	7	8	9	10	11	12 sub used
26	H HULL 18/1	10,423	11	29	2-0	1-0	Collier 11, Gillies 75 / Ref: J Yates	Cashley	Sweeney	Drysdale	Emanuel	Collier	Merrick	Tainton	Ritchie	Fear	Gillies	Durrell	
								Wealands	*Banks*	*Daniel*	*Galvin*	*Deere*	*Burnett !*	*McGill*	*Lord*	*Wood*	*Grimes*	*Greenwood*	

Collier heads in from Brolly's free-kick for his first senior goal. Following the sending off of Dennis Burnett ten minutes later for bringing down Fear, who only had the keeper to beat, City are often frustrated by their hard-working opponents, until Gillies turns in Fear's cross.

No	Date	Att	Pos	Pt	F-A	H-T	Scorers, Times, and Referees	1	2	3	4	5	6	7	8	9	10	11	12 sub used
27	A MANCHESTER U 1/2	47,118	1	31	1-0	0-0	Gillies 90 / Ref: M Lowe	Cashley	Sweeney	Drysdale	Emanuel	Collier	Merrick	Tainton	Ritchie	Fear	Gillies	Brolly	
								Stepney	*Forsyth*	*Houston*	*Daly**	*James*	*Buchan*	*Morgan*	*McIlroy*	*Baldwin*	*Macari*	*McCalliog*	*Young*

A first-half bomb warning adds to the frenzied atmosphere of this clash. The closest United come to a goal is an early 30-yarder by Steve James that hits the crossbar, but for City Gillies hooks the ball low into the Stretford End net in the third min of injury time to clinch victory.

No	Date	Att	Pos	Pt	F-A	H-T	Scorers, Times, and Referees	1	2	3	4	5	6	7	8	9	10	11	12 sub used
28	H PORTSMOUTH 8/2	13,804	18	33	3-1	0-1	Stephenson 49 (og), Sweeney 51, Hiron 38 [Gillies 63] / Ref: J Bent	Cashley	Sweeney	Drysdale	Emanuel	Collier	Merrick	Tainton	Mann	Fear	Gillies	Brolly	
								Best	*Roberts*	*Hand*	*Piper*	*Went*	*Stephenson*	*Marinello*	*Lewis**	*Graham*	*Hiron*	*Mellows*	*Foggo*

Pompey's attack-minded approach is deserving of a better fate, but City at last find some goalscoring form. Ray Hiron's low drive puts the visitors in front, but Alan Stephenson's deflection of Fear's free-kick into his own net sets up City for scoring shots by Sweeney and Gillies.

No	Date	Att	Pos	Pt	F-A	H-T	Scorers, Times, and Referees	1	2	3	4	5	6	7	8	9	10	11	12 sub used
29	A BLACKPOOL 15/2	8,687	5	33	0-2	0-2	*Ainscow 27, Bentley 43* / Ref: K Styles	Cashley	Sweeney	Drysdale	Emanuel	Collier	Merrick	Tainton	Mann	Fear	Cheesley	Brolly	
								Burridge	*Curtis*	*Harrison*	*Hart*	*Alcock*	*Hatton*	*Walsh*	*Ainscow*	*Davies*	*Bentley*	*Evanson*	

The instructions of Blackpool manager Harry Potts for his players to attack the Second Division's best defence from the outset pays dividends. Collier's weak back-pass lets Alan Ainscow in to flick the ball past Cashley, whilst a poor clearance sees Bill Bentley fire in from 22 yards.

No	Date	Att	Pos	Pt	F-A	H-T	Scorers, Times, and Referees	1	2	3	4	5	6	7	8	9	10	11	12 sub used
30	H WEST BROM 22/2	14,180	8	35	2-1	0-1	Sweeney 64p, Fear 79 / *Shaw 12* / Ref: C Thomas	Cashley	Sweeney	Drysdale	Emanuel	Collier	Merrick	Tainton	Mann	Fear	Gillies	Brolly	
								Osborne	*Thompson*	*Wilson*	*Cantello*	*Robertson*	*Rushbury*	*Shaw*	*Brown T*	*Mayo**	*Hughes*	*Johnston*	*Trewick*

The finest game at Ashton Gate so far this season as City recover from David Shaw's stabbed-in opener from Willie Johnston's free-kick. Fear is the catalyst of City's deserved success. He is tripped by David Rushbury for Sweeney's penalty, and then scores with a stunning 18-yard chip.

No	Date	Att	Pos	Pt	F-A	H-T	Scorers, Times, and Referees	1	2	3	4	5	6	7	8	9	10	11	12 sub used
31	H OLDHAM 1/3	12,461	18	37	3-1	2-0	Wood 21 (og), Brolly 24, Fear 88 / *Robins 90* / Ref: T Bune	Cashley	Sweeney	Drysdale	Emanuel	Collier	Merrick	Tainton	Mann	Gillies	Fear	Brolly	
								Ogden	*Wood*	*Whittle*	*Edwards**	*Hicks*	*Holt*	*McVitie*	*Bell*	*Robins*	*Chapman*	*Groves*	*Branagan*

City swamp Oldham with a scintillating first-half display. Emanuel is unlucky with a 19th-min shot that finds the net, as the referee orders the free-kick to be retaken. Ian Wood heads into his own goal to open the scoring, though the full-back protests later that Fear also got a touch.

Bristol City — match record (games 32–42)

#	V	Opponent	Date	Att.	Pos		Res	Pts	FT	HT	Scorers	Referee
32	A	YORK	8/3	7,567	6	14	L	37	0-1	0-1	Pollard 43	Ref: A Hamil
33	H	MILLWALL	15/3	12,393	5	19	W	39	2-1	1-0	Fear 35, Mann 80 / Clark 89	Ref: W Gow
34	A	BOLTON	22/3	11,387	5	8	W	41	2-0	1-0	Gillies 32, Ritchie 71	Ref: C Seel
35	A	SOUTHAMPTON	28/3	21,019	3	13	W	43	1-0	1-0	Gillies 40	Ref: G Kew
36	H	NORWICH	29/3	22,118	5	4	L	43	0-1	0-1	Suggett 17	Ref: J Hunting
37	H	BRISTOL ROV	1/4	28,953	5	19	D	44	1-1	0-1	Sweeney 77 / Collier 33 (og)	Ref: D Nippard
38	A	NOTTS CO	5/4	7,227	4	13	W	46	2-1	1-1	Gillies 34, 65 / Probert 19	Ref: P Partridge
39	H	SHEFFIELD WED	12/4	12,514	5	22	W	48	1-0	0-0	Fear 78	Ref: C Newsome
40	A	ORIENT	15/4	6,486	5	11	L	48	0-1	0-1	Possee 39	Ref: L Shapter
41	A	SUNDERLAND	19/4	30,530	5	3	L	48	0-3	0-1	Bolton 43, Robson 64, Belfitt 88	Ref: E Wallace
42	H	FULHAM	26/4	11,538	5	9	W	50	3-1	0-1	Ritchie 54, Sweeney 58p, Gillies 85 / Barrett 20	Ref: J Taylor

Home 14,061 Away 13,921 Average 13,921

Line-ups and match reports

32 — York (A):
City: Cashley, Sweeney, Drysdale, Emanuel, Collier, Merrick, Tainton, Mann, Gillies*, Fear, Brolly, Ritchie
York: *Crawford, Calvert, Oliver, Holmes, Woodward, Topping, Lyons, Cave, Seal, Jones, Pollard*
City lose ground in the promotion race as their all out second-half attacks fail to bring any reward. Mann is unlucky ten minutes from time with a superb shot which cannons off the angle of bar and post. Brian Pollard fires in the only goal when Cashley pushes out Jimmy Seal's header.

33 — Millwall (H):
City: Cashley, Sweeney, Drysdale, Emanuel, Collier, Merrick, Tainton, Mann, Gillies, Fear, Brolly, Ritchie
Millwall: *King, Donaldson, Moore, Dorney, Kitchener, Saul, Hazell, Clark, Jones, Summerill, Smethurst*, Kelly C*
The loss of Eddie Jones with an ankle injury following Merrick's 62nd-minute tackle inspires ten-man Millwall's battling second-half display. Clark's tap in gives the Lions some reward, but by then City have the points as Mann's 20-yard scorcher adds to Fear's prodded in opener.

34 — Bolton (A):
City: Cashley, Sweeney, Drysdale, Emanuel, Collier, Merrick, Tainton, Mann, Gillies, Fear, Brolly, Ritchie
Bolton: *Siddall, Ritson, Dunne, Greaves, Jones P, Allardyce, Byrom, Curran*, Lee, Reid, Thompson, Whatmore*
Frustrated with the award of a free-kick instead of a penalty when clearly brought down inside the area, Gillies gets his revenge 21 minutes later by heading in Brolly's cross. City's tenacious midfield display is the basis of their victory, which is assured by Ritchie's six-inch tap in.

35 — Southampton (A):
City: Cashley, Sweeney, Drysdale, Emanuel, Collier, Merrick, Tainton, Mann, Gillies, Ritchie, Brolly
Southampton: *Turner, Andruszewski, Peach, Bennett, Holmes, Blyth, McCalliog*, Channon, Osgood, Steele, Stokes, Crabbe*
City move into a promotion spot with the aid of rather lucky goal as the ball soars high over the keeper when Tainton's free-kick hits Gillies on the shoulder. Southampton are outplayed throughout as City's committed display brings them a deserved first-ever League success at the Dell.

36 — Norwich (H):
City: Cashley, Sweeney, Drysdale, Emanuel*, Collier, Merrick, Tainton, Mann, Gillies, Fear, Brolly, Gow
Norwich: *Keelan, Butler, Powell, Morris, Forbes, Stringer, McGuire, Boyer, MacDougall, Suggett, Peters*
Tired City stumble against a classy Norwich side, who did not play yesterday. The Canaries show class and composure under City's almost ceaseless, but often punchless pressure. Colin Suggett drives in the decider after Ted MacDougall hooks back Phil Boyer's deep cross.

37 — Bristol Rov (H):
City: Cashley, Sweeney, Drysdale, Emanuel*, Collier, Merrick, Tainton, Mann, Gillies, Fear, Brolly, Gow
Bristol Rov: *Eadie, Jacobs, Bater, Aitken*, Day, Prince, Stephens, Smith, Warboys, Staniforth, Dobson, Stanton*
Another wasteful City performance as they are unable to translate their superiority into goals. After Colin Dobson's centre ends up in the net via Collier's shoulder, it takes Wilf Smith's misguided back-pass to give Sweeney the chance to slot in City's late equaliser from seven yards.

38 — Notts Co (A):
City: Cashley, Sweeney, Drysdale, Emanuel*, Collier, Merrick, Tainton, Mann, Gillies, Ritchie, Brolly, Gow
Notts Co: *Brown, Brindley, O'Brien, McVay, Needham, Benjamin, Carter, Randall, Bradd, Probert, Scanlon*
Mann's free-roving role behind the front-runners has County in knots. Eric Probert finds a gap in City's defensive wall to put the Magpies, ahead, but City twice heads in to keep promotion prospects alive, though Tainton admits his 35-yard pass for the last was really a shot.

39 — Sheffield Wed (H):
City: Cashley, Sweeney, Drysdale, Gow, Collier, Merrick, Tainton, Mann*, Gillies, Ritchie, Brolly, Fear
Sheffield Wed: *Fox, Cameron, Knighton, Mullen, Dowd, Shaw, Potts, Harvey, Ferguson, Henson, Joicey*
Near the end of this tension-filled game Fear is relieved that the referee takes an amused view of his act of supplication on being pulled up for taking a quick free-kick. Wednesday's stubborn defensive display is overcome by Fear's outrageous skill as he backheels in Tainton's cross.

40 — Orient (A):
City: Cashley, Sweeney, Drysdale, Gow, Collier, Merrick, Tainton, Mann, Gillies, Ritchie, Brolly, Fear
Orient: *Jackson, Fisher, Grealish, Bennett, Gray*, Walley, Cunningham, Possee, Bullock, Queen, Heppolette, Roeder*
A muddy pitch stifles City's talents in a match which exceeds its finishing time by some twelve minutes due to floodlight failure near the end. City do not create many chances and they lose ground in the promotion race as Derek Possee, who is well offside, rams in Glen Roeder's pass.

41 — Sunderland (A):
City: Cashley, Sweeney, Drysdale, Emanuel, Collier, Merrick, Tainton, Mann, Gillies, Ritchie, Fear*, Brolly
Sunderland: *Montgomery, Malone, Guthrie, Moncur, Watson, Bolton, Kerr, Hughes, Belfitt, Robson, Towers*
The problem of poor finishing that has dogged City all season is the only difference between the sides at Roker Park. City are frustrated when Ritchie's twenty-yard drive is kept out by a post shortly before Joe Bolton opens the scoring with a weak drive which somehow beats Cashley.

42 — Fulham (H):
City: Cashley, Sweeney, Drysdale, Gow, Collier, Merrick, Tainton, Ritchie, Gillies, Fear, Whitehead, Brolly
Fulham: *Mellor, Cutbush, Fraser, Mullery, Lacy, Moore, Scrivens, Dowie*, Busby, Lloyd, Barrett, Bullivant*
City's game against the FA Cup finalists is marred by second-half crowd disturbances and a dart throwing incident which halts play. Against attractive opponents Ritchie's powerful header sparks City's stirring revival before the misguided antics of the few spoil things for the many.

LEAGUE DIVISION 2 (CUP-TIES) Manager: Alan Dicks SEASON 1974-75

League Cup

				F-A	H-T	1	2	3	4	5	6	7	8	9	10	11	12 sub used
1	H	CARDIFF	W	2-1	1-0	Cashley	Sweeney	Drysdale	Gow	Collier	Merrick	Tainton	Mann	Gillies	Cheesley	Whitehead*	Ritchie
	19/8	8,813				*Irwin*	*Pethard*	*Charles*	*Phillips*	*Murray*	*Smith*	*Villars*	*Showers*	*Reece**	*McInch*	*Anderson*	*Impey*

Scorers, Times, and Referees: Sweeney 30, Merrick 56 / McInch 74 / Ref: K Burns

City chalk up their seventh-successive win over the Welshmen, who are flattered by the narrow scoreline. Sweeney jabs City ahead when Gillies has his shot pushed out by Bill Irwin, and Merrick's trusty left foot doubles the advantage before Jimmy McInch fires in Cardiff's reply.

				F-A	H-T	1	2	3	4	5	6	7	8	9	10	11	12 sub used
2	A	CRYS PALACE 14	W	4-1	0-1	Cashley	Sweeney	Drysdale	Gow	Collier	Merrick	Tainton*	Ritchie	Gillies	Fear	Emanuel	Whitehead
	10/9	16,263 3:9				*Hammond*	*Barry*	*Jump*	*Johnson*	*Jeffries*	*Blyth*	*Lindsay*	*Whittle*	*Swindleh'rst**	*Chatterton*	*Taylor*	*Rogers*

Scorers, Times, and Referees: Sweeney 54p, Gow 60, Whiteh'd 84, Whittle 11p [Gillies 89] / Ref: R Challis

Sweeney makes amends for giving away Palace's penalty when fisting the ball off the line, by netting City's spot-kick opener after Fear is nudged from behind by Derek Jeffries. Following Gow's 30-yard drive in off the post, City go on to their biggest away win for three years.

				F-A	H-T	1	2	3	4	5	6	7	8	9	10	11	12 sub used
3	H	LIVERPOOL 13	D	0-0	0-0	Cashley	Sweeney	Drysdale	Gow	Collier	Merrick	Tainton*	Ritchie	Gillies	Fear	Emanuel	Whitehead
	8/10	25,753 1:2				*Clements*	*Smith*	*Lindsay*	*Lawler*	*Boersma*	*Hughes*	*Keegan*	*Hall*	*Highway*	*Kennedy*	*Callaghan*	

Ref: R Perkin

Visions of a Cup upset flash through City minds just two minutes from the end of this impressive team performance. Fear cleverly slips in front of Tommy Smith to collect a superb Gillies through-pass, but Ray Clemence advances swiftly to divert the ball off target with his knee.

				F-A	H-T	1	2	3	4	5	6	7	8	9	10	11	12 sub used
3R	A	LIVERPOOL 11	L	0-4	0-1	Cashley	Sweeney	Drysdale	Gow	Collier	Merrick	Tainton	Ritchie	Cheesley	Fear*	Emanuel	Whitehead
	16/10	23,694 1:1				*Clements*	*Smith*	*Lindsay*	*Lawler*	*Boersma*	*Hughes*	*Keegan*	*Cormack*	*Highway*	*Kennedy*	*Callaghan*	

Scorers, Times, and Referees: Heighway 39, 76, Kennedy 49, 82 / Ref: R Perkin

Steve Heighway heralds City's departure from the Cup with an unstoppable 18-yarder after exchanging two passes in a breathtaking run. The final scoreline is rather unfair to City who take the offensive early on, but are gradually worn down by their opponents impressive covering.

FA Cup

				F-A	H-T	1	2	3	4	5	6	7	8	9	10	11	12 sub used
3	A	SHEFFIELD UTD 5	L	0-2	0-1	Cashley	Sweeney	Drysdale	Mann	Collier	Merrick	Tainton	Ritchie	Fear*	Cheesley	Durrell	Griffin
	4/1	20,163 1:14				*Brown*	*Badger*	*Hemsley*	*Nicholl*	*Franks*	*Eddy*	*Woodward*	*Speight**	*Dearden*	*Currie*	*Field*	*Bradford*

Scorers, Times, and Referees: Dearden 16, Currie 90 / Ref: R Matthewson

City produce plenty of good football against top-flight United, but lack the finishing ability to turn their dash into goals. Bill Dearden's brave header to Tony Currie's angled shot gives United an early lead, but it isn't until the dying seconds that Currie kills City off with his 20-yarder.

League Table

	Team	P	Home					Away					Pts
			W	D	L	F	A	W	D	L	F	A	
1	Manchester U	42	17	3	1	45	12	9	6	6	21	18	61
2	Aston Villa	42	16	4	1	47	6	9	4	8	32	26	58
3	Norwich	42	14	6	1	34	17	6	10	5	24	20	53
4	Sunderland	42	14	6	1	41	8	5	7	9	24	27	51
5	BRISTOL CITY	42	14	5	2	31	10	7	3	11	16	23	50
6	West Brom	42	13	4	4	33	15	5	5	11	21	27	45
7	Blackpool	42	12	6	3	31	17	2	11	8	7	16	45
8	Hull	42	12	8	1	25	10	3	6	12	15	43	44
9	Fulham	42	9	8	4	29	17	4	8	9	15	22	42
10	Bolton	42	9	7	5	27	16	6	5	10	18	25	42
11	Oxford	42	14	3	4	30	19	1	9	11	11	32	42
12	Orient	42	8	9	4	17	16	3	11	7	11	23	42
13	Southampton	42	10	6	5	29	20	5	5	11	24	34	41
14	Notts Co	42	7	11	3	34	26	5	5	11	15	33	40
15	York	42	9	7	5	28	18	5	3	13	23	37	38
16	Nott'm Forest	42	9	7	5	24	23	5	7	9	19	32	38
17	Portsmouth	42	9	7	5	28	20	3	6	12	16	34	37
18	Oldham	42	10	7	4	28	16	0	8	13	12	32	35
19	Bristol Rov	42	10	4	7	25	23	2	7	12	17	41	35
20	Millwall	42	8	9	4	31	19	2	3	16	13	37	32
21	Cardiff	42	7	8	6	24	21	2	6	13	12	41	32
22	Sheffield Wed	42	3	7	11	17	29	2	4	15	12	35	21
		924	232	139	91	658	378	91	139	232	378	658	924

Odds & ends

Double wins: (5) Bolton, Southampton, Notts Co, Portsmouth, Manchester U.

Double losses: (2) Blackpool, Norwich.

Won from behind: (6) Bolton (h), Bristol Rov (a), Portsmouth (h). West Brom (h), Notts Co (a), Fulham (h).

Lost from in front: (1) Norwich (a).

High spots: Doing the double over Manchester U.
Beating Bristol Rov 4-1 at Eastville on 28 December.
Beating Crystal Palace 4-1 at Selhurst Park in the FL Cup on 10 Sep.
Winning 1-0 at Southampton on 28 March.

Low spots: Losing 0-1 at home to Norwich on 29 March.
Losing 1-2 against Bristol Rov (a) in the Gloucestershire Cup on 29 Apr.

Player of the year: Gary Collier.
Ever-presents: (3) Ray Cashley, Geoff Merrick, Gerry Sweeney.
Hat-tricks: (0).
Leading scorer: Donnie Gillies (10).

Appearances and Goals

Player	Appearances						Goals		
	Lge	Sub	LC	Sub	FAC	Sub	Lge	LC FAC	Tot
Brolly, Mike	13	2					1		1
Cashley, Ray	42		4		1				
Cheesley, Paul	13	2	2	1			2		2
Collier, Gary	41		4		1		1		1
Drysdale, Brian	38		4		1		1		1
Durrell, Joe	3	1							
Emanuel, John	31		3				1		1
Fear, Keith	29	2	3		1		8		8
Gillies, Donnie	28	1	3		1		9	1	10
Gow, Gerry	22	2	4				2	1	3
Griffin, Kevin	4					1			
Hunt, Ernie			1			1			
Mann, Jimmy	29	1	1		1		6		6
Merrick, Geoff	42		4		1		3	1	4
Ritchie, Tom	32	1	3	1	1		4		4
Rodgers, Dave	5								
Sweeney, Gerry	42		4		1		6	2	8
Tainton, Trevor	38		4		1		1		1
Whitehead, Clive	10	4	1	3				1	1
(own-goals)							2		2
19 players used	462	17	44	4	11	1	47	6	53

LEAGUE DIVISION 2

SEASON 1975-76

Manager: Alan Dicks

No	Date	V	Opponents	Att	Pos	Pt	F-A	H-T	Scorers, Times, and Referees	1	2	3	4	5	6	7	8	9	10	11	12 sub used
1	16/8	H	BOLTON	10,510		2	W 1-0	0-0	Sweeney 62p — Ref: M Taylor	Cashley	Sweeney	Drysdale	Gow	Collier	Merrick	Tainton	Ritchie	Mann	Cheesley	Brolly	
										Siddall	*Ritson*	*Dunne*	*Greaves*	*Jones P*	*Walsh*	*Byrom*	*Curran*	*Jones G*	*Reid*	*Thompson*	
2	19/8	H	SUNDERLAND	12,199		4	W 3-0	2-0	Brolly 7, Mann 9, 68 — Ref: C White	Cashley	Sweeney	Emanuel	Gow	Collier	Merrick	Tainton	Ritchie	Mann	Cheesley	Brolly	
										Swinburne	*Ashurst*	*Bolton*	*Longhorn*	*Clarke*	*Moncur*	*Kerr*	*Holden*	*Halom*	*Robson*	*Porterfield**	*Gibb*
3	23/8	A	HULL	5,076	3	4	L 1-3	0-2	Ritchie 47 / Greenwood 26, 31, Fletcher 73 — Ref: C Seel	Cashley	Sweeney	Emanuel	Gow	Collier	Merrick	Tainton	Ritchie	Mann	Cheesley	Brolly	
										Wealands	*Banks*	*De Vries*	*Galvin*	*Croft**	*Roberts*	*Grimes*	*Lord*	*Wood*	*Fletcher*	*Greenwood*	*McGill*
4	26/8	A	SOUTHAMPTON	16,833	7	4	L 1-3	0-2	Gow 87 / Stokes 16, 90, Peach 28 — Ref: B Daniels	Cashley	Sweeney	Emanuel	Gow	Collier	Merrick	Tainton	Ritchie	Mann	Cheesley	Brolly*	Gillies
										Middleton	*Rodrigues*	*Steele*	*Holmes*	*Bennett*	*Blyth*	*O'Brien*	*Channon*	*Stokes*	*McCalliog*	*Peach*	
5	30/8	H	BRISTOL ROV	17,940	6	5	D 1-1	1-1	Cheesley 19 / Bannister 3 — Ref: R Matthewson	Cashley	Sweeney	Drysdale	Gow	Collier	Merrick	Tainton	Ritchie	Mann	Cheesley	Brolly	
										Eadie	*Smith*	*Williams*	*Aitken*	*Taylor*	*Prince*	*Stephens**	*Pulis*	*Warboys*	*Bannister*	*Evans*	*Fearnley*
6	6/9	A	BLACKBURN	10,381	5	7	W 2-1	0-0	Sweeney 57p, Mann 79 / Parkes 54 — Ref: J Yates	Cashley	Sweeney	Drysdale	Gow	Collier	Merrick	Tainton	Ritchie	Mann	Cheesley	Brolly	
										Jones	*Heaton*	*Burgin*	*Metcalfe**	*Hawkins*	*Fazackerley*	*Beamish*	*Oates*	*Hickman*	*Parkes*	*Martin*	*Hoy*
7	12/9	H	OXFORD	10,373	1	9	W 4-1	1-0	Cheesley 22, 85, Ritchie 68, 73 / Tait 86 — Ref: K Salmon	Cashley	Sweeney*	Drysdale	Gow	Harding	Merrick	Tainton	Ritchie	Mann	Cheesley	Brolly	Emanuel
										Milkins	*Light*	*Shuker*	*Bodell*	*Clarke C*	*Jeffrey*	*McGrogan*	*Duncan*	*Clarke D*	*Foley**	*Aylott*	*Tait*
8	20/9	A	CHELSEA	18,644	4	10	D 1-1	1-1	Cheesley 41 / Garner 25 — Ref: G Kew	Cashley	Gillies	Harris	Gow	Collier	Merrick	Tainton	Ritchie	Mann	Cheesley	Brolly	
										Sherwood	*Harris*	*Hay*	*Stanley*	*Droy*	*Dempsey*	*Britton*	*Wilkins R*	*Basan*	*Hutchinson*	*Garner !*	
9	27/9	H	BLACKPOOL	10,246	4	12	W 2-0	2-0	Cheesley 20, Gow 43p — Ref: J Bent	Cashley	Gillies	Drysdale	Gow	Collier	Merrick	Tainton	Ritchie	Mann	Cheesley	Brolly	
										Wood	*Curtis**	*Bentley*	*Hart*	*Suddaby*	*Hatton*	*Ronson*	*Suddick*	*Walsh*	*Ainscow*	*Moore*	*Harrison*
10	4/10	A	NOTTS CO	10,802	5	13	D 1-1	0-0	Mann 59 / Needham 68 — Ref: R Lewis	Cashley	Gillies	Drysdale	Gow	Collier	Merrick	Tainton	Ritchie	Mann	Cheesley	Brolly	
										McManus	*Richards P*	*O'Brien*	*Bolton*	*Needham*	*Stubbs*	*Carter**	*Probert*	*Bradd*	*McVay*	*Scanlon*	*Vinter*

Match notes

1. A poor City performance brings an unlikely win thanks to a twice-taken penalty, following the up-ending of Mann by Paul Jones. After referee rules that Sweeney's saved first kick be retaken due to Tony Dunne's encroachment, City's full-back takes full advantage of his second chance.

2. Brolly's crisp six-yard shot sparks the best display so far of Dicks' managerial reign as Sunderland are shattered by City's class, skill and pace. Ashton Gate has never been a lucky venue for the Wearsiders, but it is doubtful that they have ever suffered a more comprehensive defeat here.

3. City fail to show much form as they suffer their first League defeat of the season. Cashley is caught in no-man's land by Roy Greenwood's angled chip, but can do nothing when Peter Fletcher cheekily lobs the ball over his shoulder before turning and firing in an explosive volley.

4. Bobby Stokes hammers in a last-minute strike to end Bristol City's late fight back that almost secured a point. Mann is thwarted by a post and Emanuel shoots over from four yards, whilst in between City get some reward as Gow finishes off a superb move between Ritchie and Gillies.

5. After Bruce Bannister's deft footwork turns in Alan Warboy's off-target shot, Bristol City recover to dominate matters. It is no surprise when Cheesley slides in the equaliser from Tainton's through-ball, but thereafter Jim Eadie's inspired form prevents any alteration to the score-line.

6. Despite depriving Blackburn of their unbeaten record, Dicks is far from happy with his side's performance. After Tony Parkes' 15-yard cross-shot gives Rovers the lead, it takes Sweeney's well-hit penalty, following Andy Burgin's trip on Cheesley, to get City turning on the style.

7. City soar to the top of affairs against a bewildered Oxford side still seeking their first away win in over a year. City's non-stop running pays off as Cheesley heads in the opener, and whilst Derek Clarke's header hits the bar for United shortly after, it is mainly one-way traffic thereafter.

8. City let ten-man Chelsea off the hook by settling for point after the 76th-minute dismissal of Bill Garner for his trip on Cashley. A game of some promise early on, as Cheesley nets from 15 yards to equalise Garner's header, degenerates into a physical shambles with five bookings.

9. City dominate the first half, but shortly after Cheesley fires into the far corner of the net from just inside the box to give them the lead, Paul Hart is unlucky when his header hits a post. Gow is fortunate with his weak spot-kick that beats George Wood, after Bill Bentley fells Ritchie.

10. Mann's drive is brilliantly cleared off the goal-line by David McVay just before half-time, but he is not to be denied for long. County concede for the first time this season in a home League match. Mann shoots the ball in from 15 yards, after Cheesley deliberately leaves Gow's cross.

Fixtures log — Matches 11–21

No	Venue	Opponent	Date	Att	Pos	Opp	Pts	Score	Res	HT
11	A	OLDHAM	7/10	9,552	2	7	15	4-2	W	1-1
12	H	CHARLTON	11/10	12,659	2	13	17	**4-0**	W	2-0
13	A	YORK	18/10	5,073	1	21	19	4-1	W	3-0
14	H	WEST BROM	25/10	19,133	2	14	19	0-2	L	0-0
15	A	LUTON	1/11	11,446	2	12	20	0-0	D	0-0
16	H	ORIENT	7/11	14,553	3	11	21	0-0	D	0-0
17	A	NOTT'M FOREST	15/11	11,582	3	12	21	0-1	L	0-1
18	H	YORK	22/11	11,228	3	22	23	4-1	W	2-1
19	A	FULHAM	29/11	11,400	2	7	25	2-1	W	2-0
20	H	CARLISLE	6/12	12,446	3	19	26	0-0	D	0-0
21	H	HULL	13/12	10,361	3	14	28	3-0	W	1-0

11. OLDHAM (A)
City: Cashley, Gillies, Drysdale, Gow, Collier, Merrick, Tainton, Ritchie, Mann, Cheesley, Whitehead
Oldham: Odgen, Branagan, Whittle, Wood, Hicks, Holt, Bell, Jones*, Robins, Chapman, Brolly*; Groves, Young
Scorers: Mann 14, Gillies 70, Cheesley 79; Whittle 35p, Jones* 49 [Whiteh'd 83]
Ref: R Perkin
Mann runs round keeper Chris Ogden to slip in the opener, but Oldham take the lead with a penalty and a free-kick as Merrick twice brings down George Jones. Cheesley's headed goal is lauded as the best of the season as City's refreshing attacking policy brings a well-merited win.

12. CHARLTON (H)
City: Cashley, Gillies, Drysdale, Gow, Collier, Merrick, Tainton, Ritchie, Mann, Cheesley, Whitehead
Charlton: Tutt, Penfold, Warman, Bowman, Giles, Young, Powell, Hales, Flanagan, Hunt, Berry
Scorers: W'head 26, Gow 37p, Chees'ly 74, 78
Ref: T Reynolds
Gow's penalty, after Cheesley is brought by down Peter Hunt, is a vast improvement on his Blackpool effort. Graham Tutt is sent the wrong way as he cracks the ball to the keeper's right at the East End. The move of the match ends with Cashley's tap-in to conclude the day's scoring.

13. YORK (A)
City: Cashley, Gillies, Drysdale, Gow, Collier, Merrick, Tainton, Ritchie, Mann, Cheesley, Whitehead
York: Crawford, Oliver, Downing, Cave, Swallow, Topping, Pollard, Holmes*, Seal, Lyons, McMordie; Hunter
Scorers: Cheesley 1, 31, 55p, Ritchie 41; Cave 65
Ref: J Butcher
A memorable match for Cheesley, who notches City's first hat-trick for 20 months as his mis-hit pen finds a way through Graeme Crawford's legs. He gets off the mark by smashing in from 18 yards, then adds another with a diving header at the far post to put away Whitehead's cross.

14. WEST BROM (H)
City: Cashley, Gillies*, Drysdale, Gow, Collier, Merrick, Tainton, Ritchie, Mann, Cheesley, Whitehead; Sweeney
West Brom: Osborne, Mulligan, Wilson, Cantello, Wile, Robertson, Martin, Brown T, Brown A, Giles, Johnston
Scorers: Brown A 70, Brown T 88
Ref: G Trevett
A well-organised Baggies side inflict City's first home League defeat of the season. Alastair Brown beats three men in a run from midfield before firing the opener into the far corner, then Tony Brown's perfect low-shot from the right makes sure of ending City's short stay at the top.

15. LUTON (A)
City: Cashley, Gillies, Drysdale, Gow, Collier, Merrick, Tainton, Ritchie, Mann, Cheesley, Whitehead*; Husband
Luton: Barber, Ryan John, Thomson, Chambers, Faulkner, Futcher P, Ryan Jim*, King, Anderson, West, Aston
Ref: H Davey
City improve on last week's performance, but after spurning their chances they are fortunate to survive Luton's revival. Unlucky when Mann's 30-yard dipper hits the bar on 54 minutes, City are indebted to Cashley for getting his fingertips to Andy King's cracking drive near the end.

16. ORIENT (H)
City: Cashley, Gillies, Drysdale, Gow, Collier, Merrick, Tainton, Ritchie, Mann, Cheesley, Whitehead*; Fear
Orient: Jackson, Fisher, Grealish, Bennett, Hoadley, Walley, Cunningham, Roeder, Queen, Mooney, Heppolette
Ref: D Turner
'City are the best team we have played' says Orient boss George Petchey, but such words are of little consolation. Frustrated by Orient's battling midfield, City's third-successive scoring blank raises concerns. Only Cheesley poses a threat, twice being thwarted by great saves.

17. NOTT'M FOREST (A)
City: Cashley, Gillies*, Drysdale, Gow, Collier, Merrick, Tainton, Ritchie, Mann, Cheesley, Whitehead*; Sweeney
Nott'm Forest: Middleton, Anderson, Clark, McGovern, Chapman, Richardson, Robertson, O'Neill, O'Hare, Butlin, Bowyer
Scorers: Butlin 6
Ref: P Partridge
The goal drought continues as despite City's second-half domination they cannot counter Barry Butlin's perfectly-placed shot from a narrow angle. Forest boss Brian Clough opines that City deserved a point, but for all their pressure after the break they only create two real chances.

18. YORK (H)
City: Cashley, Gillies, Drysdale, Gow, Collier, Merrick, Tainton, Ritchie, Mann, Cheesley*, Whitehead; Hosker
York: Crawford, Creamer, Woodward, McMordie, Swallow, Topping, Lyons*, Holmes, Seal, Hinch, Downing
Scorers: Ritchie 21, 36, 72, Merrick 78; Seal 42
Ref: A Glasson
In front of the Match of the Day viewers City end their goal drought in fine style against attack-minded opponents. Ritchie grabs his first-ever hat-trick, cashing in on centre-half Barry Swallow's mistakes for two of his goals, after getting off the mark by heading in Mann's centre.

19. FULHAM (A)
City: Cashley, Gillies, Drysdale*, Gow, Collier, Merrick, Tainton, Ritchie, Mann, Cheesley, Fear; McNeill
Fulham: Mellor, Fraser, Strong, Mullery, Howe, Moore, Dowie, Conway, Busby, Slough, Barrett
Scorers: Ritchie 11, 26; Mullery 90p
Ref: J Taylor
Not a lucky venue for City in the past, the fates are with them this time as they survive a terrific pounding. Fulham's only reward is a last min pen when Alan Slough is up-ended, but by then Ritchie had run from the halfway line for City's opener and added another with a fine header.

20. CARLISLE (H)
City: Cashley, Gillies, Drysdale, Gow, Collier, Merrick, Tainton, Ritchie, Mann, Cheesley, Fear; Laidlaw
Carlisle: Ross, Carr, Gorman, Train, Green, Parker, McCartney, Martin, Clarke*, Barry, McVitie
Ref: R Crabb
Carlisle's disciplined defence seems more like Hadrian's Wall to City's frustrated forwards. Ross saves the Cumbrians near the finish with a great dive to his left to keep out Mann's thundering 35-yarder, but it is not all one way as McVitie and Martin miss easy second-half chances.

21. HULL (H)
City: Cashley, Gillies, Drysdale, Gow, Collier, Merrick, Tainton, Ritchie, Mann, Cheesley, Fear; Hawley
Hull: Wealands, Daniel, Banks, Galvin, Croft, Roberts, Grimes, Gibson*, Wood, Fletcher, Greenwood
Scorers: Ritchie 30, Mann 53, Cheesley 90
Ref: B Perkin
Playing their best football of the year in this brilliant win, City go into the second half of the season firmly entrenched in a promotion place, with a lead of four points over Notts County. Cheesley ends his seven-match goal drought by heading in Fear's corner in the last seconds.

LEAGUE DIVISION 2

Manager: Alan Dicks

SEASON 1975-76

No	Date		Att	Pos	Pt	F-A	H-T	1	2	3	4	5	6	7	8	9	10	11	12 sub used	Scorers, Times, and Referees
22	20/12	A BOLTON	19,164	3 / 2	L 28	0-1	0-0	Cashley / *Sidall*	Sweeney / *Ritson*	Drysdale / *Dunne*	Gow / *Greaves*	Collier / *Jones P*	Merrick / *Allardyce*	Tainton / *Waldron*	Ritchie / *Whatmore*	Mann* / *Jones G*	Cheesley / *Reid*	Fear / *Smith**	Brolly / *Byrom*	Whatmore 80 — Ref: R Toseland
23	26/12	H PLYMOUTH	21,471	3 / 18	D 29	2-2	1-1	Cashley / *Aleksic*	Sweeney / *Darke*	Drysdale / *Burrows*	Gow / *Sutton*	Collier / *Green*	Merrick / *Delve*	Tainton / *Randell*	Ritchie / *Johnson*	Mann / *Mariner*	Cheesley* / *Rafferty*	Fear / *McAuley*	Whitehead	Merrick 35, Collier 58 — Mariner 27, 48 — Ref: D Wallace
24	27/12	A PORTSMOUTH	14,315	3 / 22	W 31	1-0	1-0	Cashley / *Lloyd*	Sweeney / *Lawler*	Drysdale / *Mellows*	Gow / *Roberts*	Collier / *Went*	Merrick / *Cahill*	Tainton / *Eames*	Ritchie / *Piper*	Mann / *Foster*	Brolly / *Reynolds*	Fear / *McGuinness**	Hand	Ritchie 8 — Ref: B Daniels
25	10/1	A OXFORD	7,594	3 / 20	D 32	1-1	1-0	Cashley / *Burton*	Sweeney / *Taylor*	Drysdale / *Shuter*	Gow / *Lowe*	Collier / *Clarke C*	Merrick / *Jeffrey**	Tainton / *Houseman*	Ritchie / *Aylott*	Mann / *Clarke D*	Cheesley / *McCulloch*	Fear / *Briggs*	Foley	Cheesley 5 — Clarke C 73 — Ref: T Bune
26	17/1	H BLACKBURN	12,168	2 / 19	W 34	1-0	1-0	Cashley / *Jones*	Sweeney / *Wilkinson*	Drysdale / *Wood*	Gow / *Metcalfe*	Collier / *Hawkins*	Merrick / *Fazackerley*	Tainton / *Mullen**	Ritchie / *Oates*	Mann / *Svarc*	Brolly / *Parkes*	Fear / *Wagstaffe*	Hird	Mann 6 — Ref: K Ridden
27	24/1	A PLYMOUTH	17,887	2 / 11	D 35	0-0	0-0	Cashley / *Aleksic*	Sweeney / *Darke*	Drysdale / *Burrows*	Gow / *Horswill*	Collier / *Green*	Merrick / *Delve*	Tainton / *Randell**	Ritchie / *Sutton*	Mann / *Mariner*	Brolly / *Rafferty*	Fear / *McAuley*	Johnson	Ref: T Bosi
28	7/2	H SOUTHAMPTON	22,316	2 / 6	D 36	1-1	1-0	Cashley / *Turner*	Sweeney / *Rodrigues*	Drysdale / *Peach*	Gow / *Holmes*	Collier / *Blyth*	Merrick / *Steele*	Tainton / *Fisher*	Ritchie / *Channon*	Mann / *Osgood*	Brolly / *McCalliog*	Fear / *Stokes*		Ritchie 32 — Holmes 77 — Ref: D Reeves
29	14/2	A ORIENT	5,785	1 / 15	W 38	1-0	0-0	Cashley / *Jackson*	Sweeney / *Fisher**	Drysdale / *Payne*	Gow / *Grealish*	Collier / *Hoadley*	Merrick / *Walley*	Tainton / *Cunningham*	Ritchie / *Queen*	Mann / *Bullock*	Cheesley* / *Heppolette*	Fear / *Possee*	Gillies / *Allder*	Ritchie 74 — Ref: K Baker
30	21/2	H NOTT'M FOREST	15,302	3 / 12	L 38	0-2	0-1	Cashley / *Wells*	Sweeney / *O'Kane**	Drysdale / *Clark*	Gow / *McGovern*	Collier / *Chapman*	Merrick / *Bowyer*	Tainton / *Curran*	Ritchie / *O'Neill*	Mann / *O'Hare*	Cheesley / *Butlin*	Fear* / *Robertson*	Gillies / *McCann*	Curran 17, O'Hare 50 — Ref: R Lewis
31	24/2	H OLDHAM	14,631	1 / 8	W 40	1-0	1-0	Cashley / *Platt*	Sweeney / *Wood*	Drysdale / *Whittle*	Gow / *Bell*	Collier / *Edwards*	Merrick / *Holt*	Tainton / *Blair*	Ritchie / *Shaw*	Mann / *Hicks*	Cheesley / *Chapman*	Fear / *Groves*		Cheesley 5 — Ref: B James

22 — A BOLTON: 'A cracking match that would not have disgraced the First Division' is the verdict of Bolton boss Ian Greaves. A rousing tussle, with both sides committed to attack, is settled by a wretched defensive error. Neil Whatmore rolls the ball in after intercepting Collier's weak back-pass.

23 — H PLYMOUTH: A thrilling clash in which the 13th-minute loss of Cheesley with a strained back possibly explains City's inept finishing. Paul Mariner shows how to do it with a brilliant flicked header and a superb shot on the turn, though Merrick's goal is also a gem as he heads in Fear's free-kick.

24 — A PORTSMOUTH: Pompey look anything but relegation candidates as City cling onto Ritchie's early effort when he ran through the middle to shoot in. Pity then that Fear shot a 5th-min chance wide from just two yards, as otherwise City fans may then not have had to suffer such a nerve-racking finale.

25 — A OXFORD: It is so easy at the start as Cheesley heads in Gow's perfect cross, but thereafter Cashley is the hero with many great saves. Colin Clarke's header takes a deflection for United's deserved leveller, but Peter Houseman is unlucky with his last-minute effort being ruled offside.

26 — H BLACKBURN: With only Mann's miskicked shot from five yards to show for all their domination, City face the possibility of yet another anxious finale. Loan signing Dave Wagstaffe (Wolves) brings Blackburn back into the contest after the break, but City manage to successfully match their efforts.

27 — A PLYMOUTH: Cashley finds darts and a knife in his goal area before the game starts, but thankfully unruly spectators do not cause problems during play. Argyle are constantly thwarted, as City create few friends with their defensive approach and do not manage so much as a single shot on target.

28 — H SOUTHAMPTON: On Match of the Day again, City's brilliant first-half play is rewarded as Ritchie stabs in Cheesley's low cross. Peter Osgood, distinctively clad in a brighter yellow than his colleagues, inspires the Saints as Nick Holmes nets with an easy shot to extend their unbeaten run to 13 games.

29 — A ORIENT: Shortly after offside rules out Cheesley's tap-in, Ritchie's near-post header takes City back to the top of the table. Orient run out of steam near the end, having been out of action for a month due to an influenza epidemic, though Laurie Cunningham forces Cashley to save his late effort.

30 — H NOTT'M FOREST: Terry Curran's pace and the skills of John O'Hare and Martin O'Neill cause City many problems as they are repeatedly carved apart by their slick opponents. Curran shoots in from twelve yards to open the scoring, and O'Hare delicately steers the ball past Cashley to tie matters up.

31 — H OLDHAM: City's second-half jitters return, but fortunately Oldham can only manage one shot on target. Cheesley, who could have notched a hat-trick in the first eight minutes, secures the points with his early header, but after Tainton's 30-yarder hits the post five minutes later, the game declines.

Bristol City — Match Records (Nos. 32–42)

No	Date	V	Opponent	Res	Score	HT	Att	Pos	Opp Pos	Pts
32	6/3	H	LUTON	W	3-0	0-0	15,872	1	7	42
33	12/3	A	CHARLTON	D	2-2	0-0	12,711	1	12	43
34	17/3	A	WEST BROM	W	1-0	1-0	26,278	1	5	45
35	20/3	H	FULHAM	D	0-0	0-0	19,546	1	12	46
36	23/3	A	SUNDERLAND	D	1-1	0-0	38,395	1	2	47
37	27/3	A	CARLISLE	W	1-0	1-0	7,563	1	18	49
38	3/4	A	BLACKPOOL	L	1-2	1-1	8,273	1	10	49
39	10/4	H	CHELSEA	D	2-2	1-1	25,319	2	11	50
40	16/4	A	BRISTOL ROV	D	0-0	0-0	26,480	1	16	51
41	20/4	H	PORTSMOUTH	W	1-0	1-0	27,394	2	22	53
42	24/4	H	NOTTS CO	L	1-2	0-1	24,614	2	7	53

Home Average 16,204 — Away 14,059

---

32. H LUTON — 6/3 — W 3-0
Scorers: Ritchie 54, 57, Cheesley 71. Ref: J Hough
City: Cashley, Sweeney, Drysdale, Gow, Collier, Merrick, Tainton, Ritchie, Gillies, Cheesley, Whitehead
Luton: Barber, Ryan John, Buckley, Chambers, Faulkner, Futcher P, Husband, King, Futcher R, West, Aston*, Fuccilla*, McNeill
Cashley's stunning 52nd-minute save to keep out Ron Futcher's header is the turning point after Gow's first-half penalty had crashed against the bar. Ritchie's two well-taken shots give City the initiative, while Cheesley's unstoppable drive is a tonic to their influenza-weakened side.

33. A CHARLTON — 12/3 — D 2-2
Scorers: Gow 61, Sweeney 83; Berry 64, Young T 66. Ref: L Burden
City: Cashley, Sweeney, Drysdale, Gow, Collier, Merrick, Tainton, Ritchie, Gillies, Cheesley*, Whitehead
Charlton: Wood, Berry, Young D, Young T, Giles, Curtis, Powell, Hales, Hope, Peacock, Flanagan
City ride their luck at the Valley where Charlton striker Derek Hales has efforts struck off for offside in the 15th and 70th mins. City make all the running though and Gow deservedly puts them ahead with a perfectly-placed low shot, but it takes Sweeney's rasping drive to save a point.

34. A WEST BROM — 17/3 — W 1-0
Scorer: Sweeney 45. Ref: M Sinclair
City: Cashley, Sweeney, Drysdale, Gow, Collier, Merrick, Tainton, Ritchie, Gillies, Cheesley, Whitehead*
West Brom: Osborne, Mulligan, Robson, Brown T, Wile, Robertson, Martin, Cantello*, Mayo, Giles, Johnston, Brown A
The City hordes who swelled the Hawthorns crowd on St Patrick's Day are convinced that City are promotion bound after this pulsating clash. Alastair Brown and John Wile see their shots cannon off the woodwork in the final few minutes as City hang onto Sweeney's drive.

35. H FULHAM — 20/3 — D 0-0
Ref: A Morrissey
City: Cashley, Sweeney, Drysdale, Gow, Collier, Merrick, Tainton, Ritchie, Gillies, Cheesley, Whitehead
Fulham: Mellor, Cutbush, Strong, Mullery, Lacy, Howe, Mitchell, Conway, Busby, Slough, Barrett
Jaded-looking City play out a dreary draw, but increase their hold at the top of the table to four points. Fulham's packed midfield holds City at bay, though Sweeney on running through to net near the end is frustrated as his effort is disallowed due to Whitehead being given offside.

36. A SUNDERLAND — 23/3 — D 1-1
Scorers: Sweeney 47; Holden 85. Ref: R Lee
City: Cashley, Sweeney, Drysdale, Gow, Collier, Merrick, Tainton, Ritchie, Gillies, Cheesley*, Whitehead
Sunderland: Montgomery, Malone, Bolton, Train, Ashurst, Moncur, Kerr, Hughes, Holden, Robson, Greenwood, Mann
Mel Holden's late headed equaliser which preserves Sunderland's 13-month unbeaten home record, is likely to prove costly for City in their Championship quest. Sweeney's right-foot rocket shot that finishes off a brilliant seven-pass move is worthy of earning more than a point.

37. A CARLISLE — 27/3 — W 1-0
Scorer: Gow 16p. Ref: K Styles
City: Cashley, Sweeney, Drysdale, Gow, Collier, Merrick, Tainton, Ritchie, Gillies, Fear*, Whitehead
Carlisle: Ross, Carr, Gorman, O'Neill*, Green, Owen, Lathan, Bonnyman, Clarke, Laidlaw, Martin, McVitie, Mann
After missing four open-goal opportunities Ritchie is much relieved as City manage to hang onto Gow's penalty, awarded after Bill Green pulls back Whitehead. In truth Carlisle offer little threat, though Cashley does well to divert Joe Laidlaw's ten-yard drive just before the break.

38. A BLACKPOOL — 3/4 — L 1-2
Scorers: Ritchie 4; Moore 42, Walsh 77. Ref: G Courtney
City: Cashley, Sweeney, Drysdale, Gow, Collier, Merrick, Tainton, Ritchie, Gillies, Cheesley*, Whitehead
Blackpool: Wood, Bentley, Hatton, McEwan, Suddaby, Alcock, Evanson, Suddick, Walsh, Ainscow, Moore, Mann
City's zest for attack brings an early reward as Ritchie shoots them ahead with a shot on the run from 14 yards, but their defence is awry when Kevin Moore taps in Pool's equaliser. Missed chances prove costly as Micky Walsh heads in keeper George Wood's 90-yard clearance.

39. H CHELSEA — 10/4 — D 2-2
Scorers: Ritchie 6, 74; Swain 43, Stanley 75. Ref: J Hunting
City: Cashley, Sweeney, Drysdale, Gow, Collier, Merrick, Tainton, Ritchie, Gillies, Cheesley, Whitehead*
Chelsea: Bonnetti, Harris, Wilkins G, Stanley, Wicks, Hay, Britton, Wilkins R, Finnieston, Swain, Lewington, Mann
The Match of the Day cameras are at Ashton Gate for the third time this season as Kenny Swain's spectacular 20-yard chip equalises Ritchie's tapped-in opener. Another Ritchie tap-in restores City's advantage, but Gary Stanley secures Chelsea's deserved point by heading past Cashley.

40. A BRISTOL ROV — 16/4 — D 0-0
Ref: T Reynolds
City: Cashley, Sweeney, Drysdale, Gow, Collier, Merrick, Tainton, Ritchie, Gillies, Cheesley, Whitehead
Bristol Rovers: Eadie, Williams, Bater, Day, Taylor, Prince, Stephens, Smith, Warboys, Bannister, Britton
Jim Eadie denies City, with saves from Tainton and Whitehead being rated world class by his boss Don Megson. Whilst the Rovers fail to muster a shot on target, a draw is fair result for a tension-racked game even more difficult by a none-too-even ground and a tricky breeze.

41. H PORTSMOUTH — 20/4 — W 1-0
Scorer: Whitehead 3. Ref: B Homewood
City: Cashley, Sweeney, Drysdale, Gow, Collier, Merrick, Tainton, Ritchie, Gillies, Cheesley, Whitehead
Portsmouth: Figgins, Ellis, Roberts, Denyer, Cahill, Eames, McGuinness, Piper, Graham, Kamara, Mellows
Whitehead's glorious right-foot shot from ten yards clinches City's return to the elite for the first time since 1911. Already-relegated Pompey prove tougher opponents than expected as further goals to ease the tension refuse to come. At the whistle City's delirious fans invade the pitch.

42. H NOTTS CO — 24/4 — L 1-2
Scorers: Whitehead 74; O'Brien 15, Benjamin 73. Ref: A Turvey
City: Cashley, Sweeney, Drysdale, Gow, Collier, Merrick, Tainton, Ritchie, Gillies*, Cheesley, Whitehead
Notts Co: McManus, Richards, O'Brien, Smith, Needham, Stubbs, McVay, Sims, Bradd, Mann, Scanlon*, Benjamin
The promotion celebrations are soured as a competitive and skilful County bring City back to reality. O'Brien stuns Cashley with his 30-yard volley into the top corner of the net and whilst Whitehead prods in for City, it is too late as Benjamin's header had added to County's haul.

LEAGUE DIVISION 2 (CUP-TIES)

Manager: Alan Dicks

SEASON 1975-76

League Cup

					F-A	H-T	Scorers, Times, and Referees	1	2	3	4	5	6	7	8	9	10	11	12 sub used
2	A	WEST HAM	9/9	19,837 1:2	5 D 0-0	0-0	Ref: A Robinson	Cashley *Day*	Sweeney *McDowell*	Drysdale *Lampard*	Gow *Bonds*	Collier *Taylor T*	Merrick *Lock*	Tainton *Holland**	Ritchie *Paddon*	Mann ! *Jennings*	Cheesley *Brooking*	Brolly* *Robson*	Gillies *Ayris*

Reduced to ten men for the last half-hour gritty City hold the Hammers at Upton Park. Mann is the villain as he fells Billy Jennings with a crisp punch to earn his sending-off, whilst Cashley is the hero by saving Graham Paddon's 64th-min spot-kick following Merrick's handball.

					F-A	H-T	Scorers, Times, and Referees	1	2	3	4	5	6	7	8	9	10	11	12 sub used
2R	H	WEST HAM	24/9	19,849 1:3	4 L 1-3	1-0	Cheesley 19 Brooking 72, Best 75, Taylor A 78 Ref: A Robinson	Cashley *Day*	Sweeney *McDowell*	Drysdale *Lampard*	Gow *Bonds*	Collier *Taylor T*	Merrick *Lock*	Tainton *Taylor A*	Ritchie *Paddon*	Mann *Best*	Cheesley *Brooking*	Brolly* *Holland*	Gillies

City dominate the first half, but fail to take their chances. After Ritchie is brought down in the 32nd minute, Sweeney's double miss from the spot turns the game. Tommy Taylor's encroachment gives Sweeney another chance, but Mervyn Day dives to his right to pull off a fine save.

FA Cup

					F-A	H-T	Scorers, Times, and Referees	1	2	3	4	5	6	7	8	9	10	11	12 sub used
3	A	COVENTRY	3/1	15,653 1:14	3 L 1-2	0-1	Brolly 78 Cross 14, Merrick 74 (og) Ref: A Robinson	Cashley *Blyth*	Sweeney *Coop*	Drysdale *Brogan*	Gow *Craven*	Collier *Dugdale*	Merrick *Holmes*	Tainton *Cartwright*	Ritchie *Green**	Mann *Cross*	Brolly *Murphy*	Fear *Hutchison*	*Oakley*

Despite Fear shooting against the bar at the start, Coventry dominate the first half, but after the break the tables are turned. Tainton is denied an obvious 71st-min pen on being sent tumbling, but whilst Brolly registers with a screamer, Merrick's headed own-goal keeps City out of the hat.

League Table

		P	Home					Away					Pts
			W	D	L	F	A	W	D	L	F	A	
1	Sunderland	42	19	2	0	48	10	5	6	10	19	26	56
2	BRISTOL CITY	42	11	7	3	34	14	8	8	5	25	21	53
3	West Brom	42	10	9	2	29	12	10	4	7	21	21	53
4	Bolton	42	12	5	4	36	14	8	7	6	28	24	52
5	Notts Co	42	11	6	4	33	13	8	5	8	27	28	49
6	Southampton	42	18	2	1	49	16	3	5	13	17	34	49
7	Luton	42	13	6	2	38	15	6	4	11	23	36	48
8	Nott'm Forest	42	13	1	7	34	18	4	11	6	21	22	46
9	Charlton	42	11	5	5	40	34	4	7	10	21	38	42
10	Blackpool	42	9	9	3	26	22	4	7	10	14	27	42
11	Chelsea	42	7	9	5	25	20	5	7	9	28	34	40
12	Fulham	42	9	8	4	27	14	4	6	11	18	33	40
13	Orient	42	10	6	5	21	12	3	5	13	16	27	40
14	Hull	42	9	5	7	29	23	5	6	10	16	26	39
15	Blackburn	42	8	6	7	27	22	4	8	9	18	28	38
16	Plymouth	42	13	4	4	36	20	0	8	13	12	34	38
17	Oldham	42	11	8	2	37	24	4	7	10	20	44	38
18	Bristol Rov	42	7	9	5	20	15	5	4	12	18	37	38
19	Carlisle	42	9	8	4	29	22	3	5	13	16	37	37
20	Oxford	42	7	7	7	23	25	4	4	13	16	34	33
21	York	42	8	3	10	28	34	2	5	14	11	37	28
22	Portsmouth	42	4	6	11	15	23	4	1	15	17	38	25
		924	229	131	102	684	422	102	131	229	422	684	924

Odds & ends

Double wins: (4) Blackburn, Oldham, York, Portsmouth.

Double losses: (1) Nott'm Forest.

Won from behind: (2) Blackburn (a), Oldham (a).

Lost from in front: (1) Blackpool (a).

High spots: Beating York 4-1 at Ashton Gate.

Winning 1-0 v West Brom at the Hawthorns.

Brilliant display v Hull at Ashton Gate.

Clinching promotion with a 1-0 home success over Portsmouth.

Beating Bristol Rov (h) 3-2 in the Gloucestershire Cup Final on 4 May.

Low spots: Losing out on the Championship due to a poor end of season run that saw six points dropped in the last five games.

Player of the Year: The Whole Team.

Ever presents: (5) Ray Cashley, Gerry Gow, Geoff Merrick, Tom Ritchie, Trevor Tainton.

Hat-tricks Paul Cheesley (1), Tom Ritchie (1).

Leading scorer: Tom Ritchie (18).

Appearances and Goals

	Appearances						Goals			
	Lge	Sub	LC	Sub	FAC	Sub	Lge	LC	FAC	Tot
Brolly, Mike	14	1	2				1	1		2
Cashley, Ray	42		2		2					
Cheesley, Paul	38		2		1		15		1	16
Collier, Gary	40		2		2		1			1
Drysdale, Brian	39		2		2					
Emanuel, John	3	1								
Fear, Keith	13	2	2		1					
Gillies, Donnie	22	3			2		1			1
Gow, Gerry	42		2		2		5			5
Harding, Steve	2									
McNeil,		2								
Mann, Jimmy	30	6	2		1		7			7
Merrick, Geoff	42		2		1		2			2
Ritchie, Tom	42		2		1		18			18
Sweeney, Gerry	32	2	2		1		5			5
Tainton, Trevor	42	2	2		1					
Whitehead, Clive	19	3					4			4
17 players used	462	20	22	2	11		59	1	1	61

LEAGUE DIVISION 1 — Manager: Alan Dicks — SEASON 1976-77

Match details

No	Date	V	Opposition	Att	Pos	Pt	F–A	H–T	Scorers, Times, and Referees
1	21/8	A	ARSENAL	41,082	2	2	W 1-0	0-0	Cheesley 65 — Ref: G Kew
2	24/8	H	STOKE	25,316	3	3	D 1-1	0-0	Gillies 49, Smith 86 — Ref: D Lloyd
3	28/8	A	NEWCASTLE	31,775	8	4	D 0-0	0-0	Ref: D Richardson
4	4/9	H	SUNDERLAND	20,865	2	6	W 4-1	3-1	Mann 30, Tainton 34, Ritchie 42, Robson 41 [Gillies 56] — Ref: J Taylor
5	11/9	A	MANCHESTER C	35,891	7	6	L 1-2	0-2	Fear 85 / Tueart 27, Barnes 28 — Ref: R Perkin
6	18/9	H	WEST HAM	28,535	5	7	D 1-1	1-0	Fear 10 / Taylor A 69 — Ref: L Burden
7	25/9	A	EVERTON	25,761	10	7	L 0-2	0-0	Dobson 72, Latchford 88 — Ref: R Newsome
8	2/10	H	IPSWICH	21,022	16	7	L 1-2	0-1	Tainton 53 / Whymark 32, Osborne 72 — Ref: T Spencer
9	16/10	H	LEICESTER	19,746	19	7	L 0-1	0-0	Worthington 59 — Ref: L Shapter
10	23/10	A	ASTON VILLA	37,094	20	7	L 1-3	1-0	Ritchie 26 / Nicholl 52, Gidman 65, Graydon 80 — Ref: R Kirkpatrick

Line-ups (Bristol City, and opposition in *italics*)

No	Team	1	2	3	4	5	6	7	8	9	10	11	12 sub used
1	City	Cashley	Sweeney	Drysdale	Gow	Collier	Merrick	Tainton	Ritchie	Mann	Cheesley	Whitehead	Gillies
1	*Arsenal*	*Rimmer*	*Rice*	*Nelson*	*Ross*	*O'Leary*	*Simpson*	*Ball*	*Armstrong*	*MacDonald*	*Radford*	*Cropley**	*Storey*
2	City	Cashley	Sweeney	Drysdale	Gow	Collier	Merrick	Tainton	Ritchie	Mann	Cheesley*	Whitehead	Gillies
2	*Stoke*	*Shilton*	*Dodd*	*Pejic*	*Mahoney*	*Smith*	*Bloor*	*Salmons*	*Greenhoff*	*Conroy*	*Hudson*	*Crooks**	*Bowers*
3	City	Cashley	Sweeney	Drysdale	Gow	Collier	Merrick	Tainton	Ritchie	Mann	Gillies	Whitehead	
3	*Newcastle*	*Mahoney*	*Mattrass*	*Kennedy*	*Hudson*	*Bird*	*Nulty*	*Barrowclough*	*Oates*	*Cannell*	*Tudor*	*Craig T**	*Howard*
4	City	Cashley	Sweeney	Drysdale	Gow	Collier	Merrick	Tainton	Ritchie*	Mann	Gillies	Whitehead	Gillies
4	*Sunderland*	*Swinburne*	*Ashurst*	*Bolton*	*Towers*	*Clarke*	*Moncur*	*Kerr*	*Hughes*	*Greenwood*	*Robson*	*Train*	
5	City	Cashley	Sweeney	Drysdale	Gow	Collier	Merrick	Tainton	Ritchie*	Mann	Gillies	Whitehead	Fear
5	*Manchester C*	*Corrigan*	*Docherty*	*Donachie*	*Doyle*	*Watson*	*Conway*	*Barnes*	*Kidd*	*Royle*	*Hartford*	*Tueart*	
6	City	Cashley	Sweeney	Drysdale	Gow	Collier	Merrick	Tainton	Fear	Mann	Gillies	Whitehead	
6	*West Ham*	*Day*	*Coleman*	*Lampard**	*Bonds*	*Green*	*Taylor T*	*Jennings*	*Paddon*	*Taylor A*	*Brooking*	*Holland*	*McGiven*
7	City	Cashley	Sweeney	Drysdale	Gow	Collier	Merrick	Tainton	Ritchie	Mann	Gillies	Whitehead	
7	*Everton*	*Davies*	*Darracott*	*Jones*	*Lyons*	*McNaught*	*Hamilton*	*King*	*Dobson*	*Latchford*	*Goodlass*	*Telfer*	
8	City	Cashley	Sweeney	Drysdale	Gow	Collier	Merrick	Tainton	Ritchie	Mann	Gillies*	Whitehead	
8	*Ipswich*	*Cooper*	*Burley*	*Mills*	*Talbot*	*Hunter*	*Beattie*	*Osborne*	*Gates**	*Bertschin*	*Whymark*	*Woods*	*Lambert*
9	City	Bond	Sweeney	Drysdale	Bain	Collier	Merrick*	Tainton	Ritchie	Mann	Gillies	Whitehead	Fear
9	*Leicester*	*Wallington*	*Whitworth*	*Rofe*	*Kember*	*Sims*	*Woollett*	*Weller*	*Sammels*	*Worthington*	*Alderson*	*Garland*	
10	City	Bond	Sweeney	Drysdale	Gow*	Collier	Rodgers	Tainton	Ritchie	Mann	Gillies	Whitehead	
10	*Aston Villa*	*Burridge*	*Gidman*	*Smith*	*Phillips*	*Nicholl*	*Mortimer*	*Graydon*	*Little*	*Gray*	*Cropley*	*Carrodus*	*McNeill*

Match reports

1. Arsenal (A): City fans are in dreamland as their favourites make a winning return to the top flight. Full of running, poise and flair, City outclass Arsenal, but squander many excellent chances until Whitehead's cross sets up Cheesley to ram an eight-yard header into the net to clinch a famous victory.

2. Stoke (H): A phantom turnstile perhaps as an attendance of 32,537 is originally announced? A great City performance as they overcome the early loss of Cheesley after colliding with Peter Shilton. A poor back-pass allows Gillies to shoot past Shilton, but Denis Smith heads in Stoke's equaliser.

3. Newcastle (A): Unable to match their peerless approach work with any finishing power, City are denied top spot as their penalty appeals, after John Bird's chopping down of Ritchie, are ignored. The Magpies offer little and their futile efforts bring a chorus of slow handclapping from their fans.

4. Sunderland (H): City equal their highest-ever League position as Sunderland prove as mesmerised. Bryan Robson's splendid cross-drive is the visitors' only response as Mann's tremendous 23-yarder, Tainton's half-volley, Ritchie's header, and Gillies' low shot from 20 yards bring City a scintillating success.

5. Manchester C (A): A cold windy afternoon at Maine Road as Dennis Tueart chips Cashley for the opener, and then Peter Barnes leaves defenders floundering before finishing with a low cross-shot. Fear calmly slots in Whitehead's pull-back, but it is too late for City, who top the Fair Play League.

6. West Ham (H): The PG Tips performing chimps do their act before the match, but as they depart, the idiots fighting in the Covered End take over. Ten-man West Ham overcome the loss of Pat Holland with a broken shin just before half-time to gain a well-merited point when Alan Taylor shoots in.

7. Everton (A): City are badly missing their injured striker Paul Cheesley. A skilful midfield display, but City never look like pulling back Martin Dobson's header and Bob Latchford's shot, though Dai Davies was forced to make a brilliant save to keep out Garry Collier's first-half shot on the turn.

8. Ipswich (H): Playing with stitches in his face following a nightclub incident, Cashley's shaky display hands the points to cultured Ipswich. Failure to call gifts Bertschin the chance to slot the ball in, then, after Tainton's 25-yard equaliser, his weak punch allows Roger Osborne to head the winner.

9. Leicester (H): Leicester have the greater skill and deserve Frank Worthington's winner when he slides in a simple chance after Chris Garland's sits on the ball in a mêlée. Bond impresses in goal for punchless City, whilst debutant Bain takes the eye with his unruffled play and cultured passing.

10. Aston Villa (A): A gripping match at Villa Park is turned upside down by Bond's groin muscle strain shortly after Ritchie's eight-yarder puts City in front. Villa take the points with headed goals from Chris Nicholl and John Gidman, and a great twelve-yard shot on the turn from Ray Graydon.

11 · H BIRMINGHAM · 26/10 — 20 L 0-1 · 10 7 · 21,474

City: Shaw, Gillies, Drysdale, Sweeney, Collier, Merrick, Tainton, Ritchie, Mann, Cheesley, Whitehead
Birmingham: Latchford, Rathbone, Page, Emmanuel, Gallagher, Pendrey, Jones, Francis, Burns, Hibbitt, Connolly
Burns 71 · Ref: R Crabb

The crowd look to Cheesley to restore City's fortunes, but he plainly isn't fit after his serious injury sustained against Stoke nine weeks ago. Keeper Shaw looks impressive on his debut, but in being unable to hold a Trevor Francis drive, sets up Kenny Burns to run the ball in.

12 · A DERBY · 30/10 — 20 L 0-2 · 17 7 · 22,252

City: Shaw, Sweeney, Merrick, Bain, Collier, Hunter, Tainton, Ritchie, Mann, Gillies, Whitehead
Derby: Moseley, Thomas, Newton, Macken, McFarland, Todd, Powell, King, Rioch, George*, James, Hector
George 17, Hector 83 · Ref: T Bosi

England international Norman Hunter (Leeds £40,000) adds authority to City's defence, despite being booked in the 32nd minute for his late tackle on Charlie George. County deservedly take the points thanks to George's clever header, and Kevin Hector's perfect volley.

13 · H COVENTRY · 6/11 — 20 D 0-0 · 15 8 · 17,306

City: Shaw, Gillies, Merrick, Sweeney, Collier, Hunter, Tainton, Ritchie, Mann, Fear, Whitehead
Coventry: Blyth, Coop, McDonald, Yorath, Lloyd, Holmes, Beck, Murphy, Ferguson, Powell, Hutchison
Ref: C Thomas

Only Ritchie manages to cause Jim Blyth any problems early on, but after the break the rapport between Merrick, with his overlapping play, and Fear gets City moving. Unfortunately, despite a five-fold increase in the shots ratio, City have to settle for a draw as the goals don't come.

14 · A TOTTENHAM · 13/11 — 19 W 1-0 · 20 10 · 28,795

City: Shaw, Gillies, Merrick, Sweeney, Collier, Hunter, Tainton, Ritchie, Mann, Fear, Cormack
Tottenham: Jennings, Naylor, Gorman, Hoddle, Young, Osgood, Conn, Perryman, Duncan, Pratt, Taylor
Fear 84 · Ref: K Baker

In the day's only First Division game City easily contain Spurs, but despite the presence of Peter Cormack (Liverpool £50,000), offer little in attack themselves. City only manage one shot on target, but this is enough to clinch their unlikely win as Fear slides in Merrick's low cross.

15 · H NORWICH · 20/11 — 17 W 3-1 · 18 12 · 19,243

City: Shaw, Gillies, Merrick*, Sweeney, Collier, Hunter, Tainton, Ritchie, Fear, Cormack, Whitehead · Mann
Norwich: Keelan, Ryan, Sullivan, Paddon, Jones, Powell, Neighbour, Osgood, Boyer, Suggett, Peters
Ritchie 34, Cormack 40, Sweeney 47p, Boyer 79 · Ref: A Robinson

Shortly after Ritchie knocks the ball over the line following a goalmouth scramble, Cormack celebrates his home debut with an easy tap-in. Phil Boyer gives Shaw no chance with his close-in shot, but by then Jim Ryan's holding of Ritchie had brought City the reward of a penalty.

16 · A LIVERPOOL · 27/11 — 19 L 1-2 · 1 12 · 44,323

City: Shaw, Gillies, Merrick, Sweeney, Collier, Hunter, Tainton, Ritchie, Cormack, Fear*, Whitehead · Mann
Liverpool: Clemence, Neal, Jones, Thompson, Kennedy, Hughes, Keegan, McDermott, Highway, Toshack, Callaghan
Ritchie 25, Keegan 45, Jones 56 · Ref: G Nolan

Beaten, but not disgraced at Anfield, where Ritchie gives Liverpool a jolt with an early lob over Ray Clemence. Denied a pen when Joey Jones floors Ritchie, City are rocked by Kevin Keegan's headed equaliser just two mins later. Jones fires in from 25 yards for Pool's hard-earned win.

17 · H MIDDLESBROUGH · 18/12 — 19 L 1-2 · 9 12 · 15,145

City: Shaw, Gillies, Merrick, Sweeney, Collier*, Hunter, Tainton, Fear, Garland, Cormack, Whitehead · Mann
Middlesbrough: Platt, Craggs, Cooper, Souness, Boam, Maddren, McAndrew, Mills, Brine, Wood*, Armstrong, Boersma
Merrick 48, Armstrong 24p, Brine 53 · Ref: R Perkin

A pre-match Christmas Concert and a half-time circus display fails to attract the fans, who will have to watch Match of the Day. Merrick gets his revenge for a disputed penalty, when he is adjudged to have tripped David Mills, by equalising with a low left-foot shot from twelve yards.

18 · A WEST BROM · 27/12 — 19 D 1-1 · 10 13 · 30,497

City: Shaw, Gillies, Merrick, Sweeney, Collier*, Hunter, Tainton, Ritchie, Garland*, Cormack, Fear
West Brom: Osborne, Mulligan, Robson, Brown T, Wile, Robertson, Martin, Treacy, Cross, Trewick, Johnston
Ritchie 59, Cross 53 · Ref: A Jones

A hard-earned point by methodical City at the Hawthorns, where it isn't until after the break that the goals come. After David Cross heads the Baggies in front, Ritchie knocks in Whitehead's cross for City's equaliser.

19 · A MANCHESTER U · 19/1 — 20 L 1-2 · 9 13 · 43,051

City: Shaw, Gillies, Merrick, Sweeney, Collier*, Hunter, Tainton, Fear, Garland, Cormack*, Gow
Manchester U: Stepney, Nicholl, Houston, McIlroy, Greenhoff B, Buchan, Coppell, Greenhoff J, Pearson, Macari, Hill
Fear 4, Pearson 48, Greenhoff B 80 · Ref: A Hamil

An absorbing contest, in which Fear heads City in front from Whitehead's cross. Dispute over both United goals as Gillies complains of being pushed in the back when Stuart Pearson headed in, while Lou Macari is seemingly offside when Brian Greenhoff deflects in United's winner.

20 · H ARSENAL · 22/1 — 20 W 2-0 · 5 15 · 25,905

City: Shaw, Gillies, Merrick, Sweeney, Collier, Hunter, Tainton, Fear, Garland, Cormack, Whitehead
Arsenal: Rimmer, Rice, Nelson, Storey, O'Leary, Simpson, Hudson, Brady, MacDonald, Stapleton, Rostron
Cormack 22, 63 · Ref: M Baker

Breathtaking City complete the double over a skilful, but goal-shy Arsenal. Cormack is denied a hat-trick as Jimmy Rimmer pulls off a magnificent 81st-minute save to keep out his header, but the keeper had no chance with his headed opener or his shot into the net off the bar.

21 · H NEWCASTLE · 5/2 — 20 D 1-1 · 8 16 · 22,995

City: Shaw, Gillies, Merrick, Sweeney, Collier, Hunter, Tainton, Fear, Garland, Cormack, Whitehead* · Gow
Newcastle: Mahoney, Nattrass, Kennedy, Cassidy, McCaffery, Nulty, Barrowclough, Cannell*, Burns, Gowling, Blackhall, Oates
Garland 83, Burns 68 · Ref: D Civil

Justice is satisfied, given that Garland appeared to have dived, as City player Mike Mahoney saves Sweeney's weak penalty just before half-time. Mickey Burns puts Newcastle in front with a superb backheader, but Garland levels by sliding in his first goal since returning to City.

LEAGUE DIVISION 1

SEASON 1976-77

Manager: Alan Dicks

Results

No	Date	V	Opponent	Att	Pos (opp / City)	Pt	Res	F-A	H-T	Scorers, Times, and Referees
22	11/2	A	SUNDERLAND	21,407	22 / 20	16	L	0-1	0-0	Holden 59 — Ref: E Garner
23	19/2	H	MANCHESTER C	27,018	3 / 18	18	W	1-0	0-0	Garland 51 — Ref: C White
24	26/2	A	WEST HAM	29,713	18 / 20	18	L	0-2	0-1	Bonds 27p, Merrick 60 (og) — Ref: A Turvey
25	5/3	H	EVERTON	21,108	15 / 21	18	L	1-2	1-1	Cormack 2p; Latchford 45, Gillies 68 (og) — Ref: D Turner
26	12/3	A	IPSWICH	24,548	2 / 22	18	L	0-1	0-0	Wark 59p — Ref: K Baker
27	15/3	H	DERBY	18,552	18 / 22	19	D	2-2	0-2	Sweeney 63, Fear 85; Daly 28, Hales 34 — Ref: B Daniels
28	19/3	H	QP RANGERS	21,956	15 / 20	21	W	1-0	0-0	Collier 78 — Ref: A Robinson
29	26/3	A	LEICESTER	16,454	6 / 19	22	D	0-0	0-0	Ref: R Capey
30	2/4	H	ASTON VILLA	27,276	8 / 20	23	D	0-0	0-0	Ref: D Nippard
31	5/4	H	WEST BROM	23,474	5 / 20	23	L	1-2	0-1	Fear 58p; Hunter 2 (og), Cross 51 — Ref: L Shapter

Line-ups (Bristol City / *Opponent*)

No	1	2	3	4	5	6	7	8	9	10	11	12 sub used
22	Shaw / *Siddall*	Gillies / *Henderson*	Merrick / *Bolton*	Sweeney* / *Towers**	Collier / *Clarke*	Hunter / *Ashurst*	Gow / *Kerr*	Ritchie / *Elliot*	Garland / *Holden*	Cormack / *Lee*	Whitehead / *Rowell*	*Arnott*
23	Shaw / *Corrigan*	Gillies / *Clements*	Merrick* / *Donachie*	Sweeney / *Doyle*	Collier / *Watson*	Hunter / *Power*	Gow / *Owen*	Fear / *Kidd*	Garland / *Royle*	Cormack / *Hartford*	Whitehead / *Tueart*	Tainton
24	Shaw / *Day*	Gillies / *Bonds*	Merrick / *Lampard*	Sweeney / *Otulakowski*	Collier / *Green*	Hunter / *Lock*	Gow / *Taylor*	Fear / *Radford*	Garland* / *Devonshire*	Cormack / *Brooking*	Whitehead / *Jennings*	Tainton
25	Shaw / *Lawson*	Gillies / *Jones*	Merrick / *Pejic*	Sweeney / *Lyons*	Collier / *McNaught*	Hunter / *King*	Gow / *Hamilton*	Fear* / *Dobson*	Garland / *Latchford*	Cormack / *McKenzie*	Whitehead / *Goodlass*	Ritchie
26	Shaw / *Cooper*	Gillies / *Burley*	Merrick / *Mills*	Sweeney / *Talbot*	Collier / *Hunter*	Hunter / *Tibbott*	Ritchie / *Osborne*	Mann / *Wark**	Garland / *Mariner*	Cormack / *Whymark*	Whitehead / *Woods*	*Gates*
27	Shaw / *Boulton*	Gillies / *Langan*	Merrick / *Webster*	Sweeney / *Daly*	Collier / *Daniel*	Hunter / *Todd*	Mann / *Powell*	Ritchie / *Hector*	Garland* / *Hales*	Gow / *George*	Whitehead / *James*	Fear
28	Shaw / *Parkes*	Gillies / *Clement*	Merrick / *Gillard*	Sweeney / *Hollins*	Collier / *McLintock*	Hunter / *Webb*	Tainton / *Eastoe*	Mann / *Cunningham*	Fear / *Masson*	Gow / *Bowles**	Whitehead / *Givens*	*Shanks*
29	Shaw / *Wallington*	Gillies / *Whitworth*	Merrick / *Rofe**	Sweeney / *Kember*	Collier / *Woollett*	Hunter / *May*	Tainton / *Birchenall*	Mann / *Sammels*	Fear / *Worthington*	Gow / *Alderson*	Whitehead / *Earle*	*Yates*
30	Shaw / *Burridge*	Gillies / *Gidman*	Merrick / *Robson*	Sweeney / *Young*	Collier / *Nicholl*	Hunter / *Mortimer*	Tainton / *Deehan*	Mann / *Little*	Fear* / *Gray*	Gow / *Cropley*	Whitehead / *Carrodus*	Garland
31	Shaw / *Godden*	Gillies / *Mulligan*	Merrick / *Statham*	Sweeney / *Martin*	Collier / *Wile*	Hunter / *Robertson*	Tainton / *Robson*	Mann / *Cunningham*	Fear / *Cross*	Gow / *Giles*	Whitehead / *Johnston*	Garland

Match notes

22 — Sunderland (A): City are the fall guys in this vital relegation clash as not only do Sunderland achieve their first win in 13 League and Cup matches, but they notch their first goal in 1,017 mins of play. Mel Holden does well to nod in Bobby Kerr's deep centre between Shaw and the near post.

23 — Manchester City (H): Hunter for England is the cry after an almost faultless display that inspires City to climb out of the bottom three for the first time this year. His chipped free-kick allows Garland to hammer home the only goal from eight yards to end Manchester City's 17-match unbeaten run.

24 — West Ham (A): Sweeney's header and a fierce shot on the turn by Gillies are the only efforts to trouble Mervyn Day. A lacklustre game is decided by Billy Bonds' penalty, after Gow sends Alan Taylor sprawling, and Merrick's own-goal as Shaw partially saves Alan Devonshire's cross.

25 — Everton (H): Despite the tonic of Cormack's early penalty at the Open End following Andy King's run on Whitehead, City fade badly after Bob Latchford's headed equaliser. Gillies firmly steers Latchford's cross into his own net to tie up Everton's deserved success ahead of their League Cup Final.

26 — Ipswich (A): City have keeper Shaw to thank for keeping them in this contest, but he can do little about John Wark's penalty after Paul Mariner is brought down by Hunter. Ipswich boss Bobby Robson succinctly sums up City's performance viz – 'they competed all the way, but lacked penetration'.

27 — Derby (H): Gillies' switch to centre-forward after the break sparks City's recovery. Derby, so impressive early on when Gary Daly volleyed in from 25 yards, are made to pay for their complacent attitude in the second half. Sweeney's 25-yard shot on the run and Fear's drive earn City's point.

28 — QP Rangers (H): The brilliance of both keepers restricts the goals in this action-packed thriller. Phil Parkes has no chance as Collier's 12-yard shot on the turn secures City's valuable win, but the game is marred when Stan Bowles sustains a broken ankle on falling awkwardly three minutes from time.

29 — Leicester (A): Despite the extra shooting practice put in by Fear and Gillies during the week City fail to score for the tenth time this season. This game should have been won with ease, but the fact that only five of City's 16 goal attempts were on target suggests further practice is necessary.

30 — Aston Villa (H): City made most of the first-half running, but it takes Sweeney's goal-line clearance to prevent Villa snatching an undeserved 43rd-minute lead. Despite their overall dominance, City create little apart from headers from Gillies and Hunter, which are cleared off the line by John Robson.

31 — West Brom (H): After Hunter steers Derek Statham's cross into his own net, City squander many chances before David Cross shows how to finish with a low cross-drive. Fear's penalty gets City back into the game, but muffs a second spot-kick 13 mins from time when his weak effort is easily saved.

No		Opponent	Date	Att	Pos	Opp Pos	Res	HT	FT	Pts	Scorers	Referee
32	A	BIRMINGHAM	9/4	19,626	22	12	L	0-2	0-3	23	Francis 11p, 23, 89p	Ref: R Chadwick
33	H	TOTTENHAM	12/4	27,568	22	21	W	0-0	1-0	25	Cormack 66p	Ref: C Thomas
34	A	NORWICH	16/4	17,839	22	13	L	1-1	1-2	25	Cormack 40, Peters 11, Reeves 84	Ref: L Hayes
35	A	STOKE	20/4	12,277	22	16	D	1-0	2-2	26	Ritchie 40, Garland 67, Smith 56, Bloor 68	Ref: K Styles
36	A	QP RANGERS	26/4	14,576	22	16	W	0-0	1-0	28	Ritchie 64	Ref: M Taylor
37	A	LEEDS	30/4	21,461	22	10	L	0-1	0-2	28	Thomas 9, Gray E 47	Ref: G Nolan
38	H	MANCHESTER U	7/5	28,864	22	6	D	1-0	1-1	29	Garland 6, Greenhoff J 50p	Ref: R Toseland
39	H	LEEDS	10/5	23,335	21	10	W	0-0	1-0	31	Garland 69	Ref: T Bune
40	A	MIDDLESBROUGH	14/5	14,849	22	10	D	0-0	0-0	32		Ref: K Walmsley
41	H	LIVERPOOL	16/5	37,265	19	1	W	1-1	2-1	34	Garland 43, 75, Johnson 30	Ref: K Burns
42	A	COVENTRY	19/5	36,892	18	19	D	0-1	2-2	35	Gow 54, Gillies 79, Hutchison 15, 52	Ref: R Challis

Home Average 23,522 — Away 27,151

---

32 — A BIRMINGHAM, L 0-3
Bristol City: Shaw, Gillies, Merrick, Sweeney, Collier, Hunter, Tainton, Mann*, Fear, Gow, Whitehead, Garland
Birmingham: Montgomery, Calderwood, Pendry, Kendall, Gallagher, Want, Jones, Francis, Burns, Hibbitt, Connolly

Ex England boss Alf Ramsay, now a Birmingham director, pays City a back-handed compliment in that 'they play too much football'. City gain no reward for outplaying the Blues after the break and Merrick's handball gifting Trevor Francis his hat-trick recalls first-half nightmares.

33 — H TOTTENHAM, W 1-0
Bristol City: Shaw, Gillies, Merrick, Sweeney, Collier, Hunter, Tainton, Cormack, Ritchie, Gow, Whitehead, Garland*
Tottenham: Daines, Naylor, Holmes*, Pratt, Osgood, Perryman, Hoddle, Jones, Armstrong, Taylor, Keeley

Cormack hands City a lifeline as he sends the keeper the wrong way to put his spot-kick into the right-hand side of the Covered End goal after Terry Naylor floors Whitehead. A well-deserved win for City who are now just two points behind Tottenham with a game in hand.

34 — A NORWICH, L 1-2
Bristol City: Shaw, Gillies, Merrick, Sweeney, Collier, Hunter, Tainton, Cormack, Ritchie, Gow, Whitehead, Mann
Norwich: Keelan, Ryan, Sullivan, Suggett, Jones, Powell, Neighbour*, Reeves, Gibbins, Steele, Peters, Evans

City's enterprising approach work is again wasted by lack of striking power. Martin Peters drives in from 25 yards for the Norwich opener, but after Cormack shoots in City's leveller, Kevin Reeves latches onto Colin Sullivan's impeccable through-ball to knock in a late winner.

35 — A STOKE, D 2-2
Bristol City: Shaw, Gillies, Merrick, Sweeney, Collier, Hunter, Tainton, Ritchie*, Garland, Cormack, Whitehead, Fear
Stoke: Shilton, Dodd, Marsh, Mahoney, Smith, Bloor, Robertson, Salmons, Tudor, Crooks, Ruggiero

Headers by Ritchie and Garland double City's previous best away scoring return this season. Shaw is responsible for both Stoke equalisers, being stranded when Denis Smith heads in Geoff Salmons' inswinger, he is again at fault when Alan Bloor's header squeezes beneath him.

36 — A QP RANGERS, W 1-0
Bristol City: Shaw, Gillies, Merrick, Sweeney, Collier, Hunter, Tainton, Ritchie, Garland, Gow, Whitehead, Cormack*
QP Rangers: Parkes, Clement, Gillard, Hollins, McLintock, Webb, Eastoe, Francis, Masson*, Givens, Kelly, Thomas

City turn in a tenacious display against an over-elaborate Rangers side at muddy Loftus Road to claim their first away win in just over five months as Ritchie slides in Garland's pass. Merrick raises a laugh from the rain-drenched fans by rescuing a dog from a large puddle.

37 — A LEEDS, L 0-2
Bristol City: Shaw, Gillies, Merrick, Sweeney, Collier, Hunter, Tainton, Ritchie, Garland, Gow, Whitehead, Cormack*
Leeds: Stewart, Stevenson, Gray F, Cherry, McQueen, Madeley, Thomas, McGhie, Jordan*, Currie, Gray E, Harris

It looks like the end as this passionless display leaves City three points from safety. Sweeney's suicidal square ball across the edge of his own penalty area sets up Gwyn Thomas to shoot in a debut goal, and later Eddie Gray at the near post to tap in Gordon McQueen's headed pass.

38 — H MANCHESTER U, D 1-1
Bristol City: Shaw, Gillies, Merrick*, Sweeney, Collier, Hunter, Tainton, Ritchie*, Gillies, Garland, Whitehead, Mann
Manchester U: Stepney, Nicholl, Houston*, Jackson, Greenhoff B, Buchan, Coppell, Greenhoff J, McCreery, Macari, McIlroy!, Albiston

Utd boss Tommy Docherty is unhappy about City's physical approach, though Stuart Houston 23rd-min departure with a broken leg is due to an awkward fall. After Garland slides the ball in, Whitehead and Ritchie both hit the woodwork before Collier's high kick concedes a penalty.

39 — H LEEDS, W 1-0
Bristol City: Shaw, Gillies, Merrick, Sweeney, Collier, Hunter, Tainton, Ritchie, Garland, Gow, Whitehead, Mann
Leeds: Stewart, Stevenson, Hampton, Cherry, McQueen, Madeley, Thomas*, McNiven, Gray F, Currie, Gray E, Harris

No sign of the fog that caused this fixture to be abandoned at half-time on 4 December when the score was tied at 0-0. Garland turns in his best display of the season, and he is rewarded by hammering in a twelve-yard left-foot drive from Merrick's free-kick for City's deserved winner.

40 — A MIDDLESBROUGH, D 0-0
Bristol City: Shaw, Merrick*, Sweeney, Collier, Hunter, Tainton, Gillies, Ritchie, Garland, Gow, Whitehead, Cormack
Middlesbrough: Platt, Craggs, Bailey, Souness, Boam, Maddren, McAndrew, Mills, Wood*, Hedley, Armstrong, Boersma

The presentation of a silver salver to Jack Charlton to mark the end of his four-year reign as Middlesbrough boss is the highlight of a dreadful match. City obtain their first point at Ayresome Park for 68 years, thanks to the crossbar which keeps out a 55th-minute lob from David Mills.

41 — H LIVERPOOL, W 2-1
Bristol City: Shaw, Sweeney, Gillies, Collier, Hunter, Tainton, Mann, Ritchie, Garland, Gow, Whitehead, Cormack*
Liverpool: Clemence, Neal, Smith, Lindsay, Kennedy, Hughes, Callaghan, Case, Fairclough, Johnson, McDermott, Heighway

Following his diving header to finish off Whitehead's low diagonal pass, Garland gives City a First Division lifeline. He takes full advantage as Ray Clemence pushes the ball onto his head. A great win over the League Champions, who took the lead from David Johnson's header.

42 — A COVENTRY, D 2-2
Bristol City: Shaw, Gillies, Sweeney, Collier, Hunter, Tainton, Mann, Ritchie, Garland, Gow, Whitehead*, Cormack
Coventry: Sealey, Oakey, McDonald, Yorath, Holton, Coop, Smith, Beck, Wallace, Ferguson, Hutchison, Powell

City gain the necessary point to ensure First Division survival, but against opponents seeking a win to preserve their status it is a close run thing. Recovering from a 0-2 deficit City have Coventry on the ropes, but news of Sunderland's defeat leaves both sides content with a point.

LEAGUE DIVISION 1 (CUP-TIES)

Manager: Alan Dicks

SEASON 1976-77

League Cup

			F-A	H-T	Scorers, Times, and Referees	1	2	3	4	5	6	7	8	9	10	11	12 sub used
2	A	COVENTRY	0-1	0-1		Cashley	Sweeney	Drysdale	Gow	Collier	Merrick	Tainton	Ritchie	Mann	Gillies	Whitehead	
		8 L			*Ferguson 41*	*Blyth*	*Coop*	*McDonald*	*Craven*	*Holmes*	*Dugdale*	*Cartwright*	*Yorath*	*Ferguson*	*Beck*	*Murphy*	
		13,878 18			Ref: D Reeves												

Despite City's early exit from the League Cup, the fans rise at the end to acclaim their performance. Dominant City rain in 26 goal attempts (twelve on target) compared with Coventry's five (three). Mick Ferguson heads high into the net from eight yards to break City's hearts.

FA Cup

			F-A	H-T	Scorers, Times, and Referees	1	2	3	4	5	6	7	8	9	10	11	12 sub used
3	A	IPSWICH	1-4	0-3	*Fear 66*	Shaw	Gillies	Merrick	Sweeney	Collier	Hunter	Tainton	Ritchie	Fear	Cormack	Whitehead	
		19 L			*Mariner 16, 37, Whymark 42, Gates 82*	*Cooper*	*Burley*	*Mills*	*Talbot*	*Roberts*	*Beattie*	*Osborne*	*Wark*	*Mariner*	*Whymark**	*Woods*	*Gates*
		25,139 2			Ref: J Hunting												

An inglorious exit as City's defensive attitude costs them dear. Paul Mariner's 20-yard chip to put Ipswich two up is the goal of the match, but his opening header isn't bad either. Fear slides in Tainton's cross for City's sole response as Ipswich extend their unbeaten run to 15 games.

Home / Away League Table

	P	W	D	L	F	A	W	D	L	F	A	Pts
			Home						Away			
1 Liverpool	42	18	3	0	47	11	5	8	8	15	22	57
2 Manchester C	42	15	5	1	38	13	6	9	6	22	21	56
3 Ipswich	42	15	4	2	41	11	7	4	10	25	28	52
4 Aston Villa	42	17	3	1	55	17	5	4	12	21	33	51
5 Newcastle	42	14	6	1	40	15	4	7	10	24	34	49
6 Manchester U	42	12	6	3	41	22	6	5	10	30	40	47
7 West Brom	42	10	6	5	38	22	6	7	8	24	34	45
8 Arsenal	42	11	6	4	37	20	5	5	11	27	39	43
9 Everton	42	9	7	5	35	24	5	7	9	27	40	42
10 Leeds	42	8	8	5	28	26	7	4	10	20	25	42
11 Leicester	42	8	9	4	30	28	4	9	8	17	32	42
12 Middlesbro	42	11	6	4	25	14	3	7	11	15	31	41
13 Birmingham	42	10	6	5	38	25	3	6	12	25	36	38
14 QP Rangers	42	10	7	4	31	21	3	5	13	16	31	38
15 Derby	42	9	9	3	36	18	0	10	11	14	37	37
16 Norwich	42	12	4	5	30	23	2	5	14	17	41	37
17 West Ham	42	9	6	6	28	23	2	8	11	18	42	36
18 BRISTOL CITY	42	8	7	6	25	19	3	6	12	13	29	35
19 Coventry	42	7	9	5	34	26	3	6	12	14	33	35
20 Sunderland	42	9	5	7	29	16	2	7	12	17	38	34
21 Stoke	42	9	8	4	21	16	1	6	14	7	35	34
22 Tottenham	42	9	7	5	26	20	3	2	16	22	52	33
	924	240	137	85	753	430	85	137	240	430	753	924

Appearances & Goals

Player	Appearances Lge	Sub	LC	Sub	FAC	Sub	Goals Lge	LC	FAC	Tot
Bain, John	2									
Bond, Len	2									
Cashley, Ray	8		1							
Cheesley, Paul	3						1			1
Collier, Gary	42			1	1		1			1
Cormack, Peter	19	1					6			6
Drysdale, Brian	11				1					
Fear, Keith	17	9				1	6		1	7
Garland, Chris	19	2					7			7
Gillies, Donny	36	1	1		1		3			3
Gow, Gerry	27	3	1		1		1			1
Hunter, Norman	31									
McNeill, Brian		1								
Mann, Jimmy	25	5	1				1			1
Merrick, Geoff	39		1		1					
Ritchie, Tom	29	1			1		7			7
Rodgers, David	1									
Shaw, John	32				1					
Sweeney, Gerry	42		1		1		2			2
Tainton, Trevor	36	2	1		1		2			2
Whitehead, Clive	41				1					
21 players used	462	25	11		11		38		1	39

Odds & ends

Double wins: (3) Arsenal, Tottenham, QP Rangers.

Double losses: (3) Everton, Ipswich, Birmingham.

Won from behind: (1) Liverpool (h).

Lost from in front: (4) Aston Villa (al), Liverpool (al), Manchester U (al), Everton (h).

High spots: Beating Arsenal 1-0 at Highbury.

Destroying Sunderland 4-1 at Ashton Gate.

Winning 1-0 v Queens Park Rangers (a).

Coming from behind to beat Liverpool 2-1 at Ashton Gate.

Drawing 2-2 at Coventry to stay up.

Beating Bristol Rov (a) 1-0 in the Gloucestershire Cup Final on 24 May.

Low spots: Losing 0-2 at Leeds.

Succumbing to Ipswich (a) 1-4 in the FA Cup.

Paul Cheesley's injury v Stoke (h) that ended his promising career.

Player of the year: Norman Hunter.

Ever-presents: (2) Gary Collier, Gerry Sweeney.

Hat-tricks: (0).

Leading scorers: Keith Fear (7), Chris Garland (7).

LEAGUE DIVISION 1 Manager: Alan Dicks SEASON 1977-78

No	Date	Att	Pos	Pt	F-A	H-T	Scorers, Times, and Referees	1	2	3	4	5	6	7	8	9	10	11	12 sub used
1	H WOLVES 20/8	25,291	–	L / 0	2-3	1-1	Cormack 37p, 57p / Carr 20p, Sunderland 65, Patching 73 Parkes / Ref: R Crabb	Shaw	Gillies	Merrick	Gow	Collier	Hunter	Tainton	Ritchie	Garland	Cormack	Whitehead	Mann
								Palmer	*Daly*	*Daley*	*Parkin*	*McAlle*	*Patching*	*Carr*	*Richards*	*Kindon*	*Sunderland*		
2	A NOTT'M FOREST 23/8	21,743	–	L / 0	0-1	0-0	Withe 82 / Ref: A Jenkins	Shaw	Gillies	Merrick*	Gow	Collier	Hunter	Tainton	Ritchie	Mabbutt*	Cormack	Whitehead	Mann
								Middleton	*Anderson*	*Clark*	*McGovern*	*Lloyd*	*Burns*	*O'Neill*	*Bowyer*	*Withe*	*Woodcock*	*Robertson*	
3	A LEICESTER 27/8	17,011	18 / 10	D / 1	0-0	0-0	Ref: B Daniels	Shaw	Sweeney	Merrick	Gow	Collier	Hunter	Tainton	Ritchie	Mabbutt	Cormack	Whitehead	
								Wallington	*Whitworth*	*Rofe*	*Kember*	*Sims*	*Woollett*	*Alderson*	*Sammels*	*Worthington*	*Kelly*	*Weller*	
4	H ASTON VILLA 3/9	22,359	17 / 16	D / 2	1-1	0-1	Mabbutt 80 / Little 21 / Ref: D Smith	Shaw	Sweeney	Merrick	Gow	Collier	Hunter	Tainton	Ritchie	Mabbutt	Cormack	Whitehead	Mann
								Rimmer	*Gregory*	*Robson*	*Mortimer*	*McNaught*	*Phillips*	*Deehan*	*Little*	*Grey*	*Cropley*	*Carrodus*	
5	A NORWICH 10/9	12,836	19 / 9	L / 2	0-1	0-0	Gibbins 86 / Ref: P Richardson	Shaw	Sweeney	Merrick	Gillies	Collier	Hunter	Tainton	Garland*	Mabbutt	Cormack	Whitehead*	Gibbins
								Keelan	*Ryan*	*Sullivan*	*Machin*	*Jones*	*Powell*	*Neighbour*	*Reeves*	*Busby*	*Suggett*	*Davies*	
6	H WEST HAM 17/9	21,344	17 / 20	W / 4	3-2	2-1	Mabbutt 8, Ritchie 24, 66 / Robson 7, Pike 87 / Ref: L Burden	Shaw	Sweeney	Merrick	Gillies	Collier	Hunter	Tainton	Ritchie	Mabbutt	Cormack	Whitehead*	
								Day	*Lampard*	*Brush*	*Holland*	*Taylor T*	*Lock*	*Taylor A*	*Robson*	*Curbishley*	*Brooking*	*Devonshire* Pike*	
7	A MANCHESTER C 24/9	41,897	18 / 1	L / 4	0-2	0-1	Barnes 24, Owen 76 / Ref: R Perkin	Shaw	Gillies	Sweeney	Gow	Collier	Hunter	Tainton	Ritchie	Mabbutt	Cormack	Whitehead	Mann
								Corrigan	*Clements*	*Doyle*	*Owen*	*Watson*	*Booth*	*Barnes*	*Channon*	*Kidd*	*Hartford*	*Power*	
8	H QP RANGERS 1/10	20,641	18 / 13	D / 5	2-2	1-2	Tainton 31, Cormack 60p / Masson 8, Eastoe 15 / Ref: A Lees	Shaw	Gillies	Sweeney	Mann	Collier	Hunter	Tainton	Ritchie	Mabbutt	Cormack	Whitehead	Williams
								Parkes	*Clement*	*Gillard**	*Hollins*	*Needham*	*Abbott*	*Eastoe*	*Busby*	*Masson*	*Bowles*	*Givens*	
9	H LEEDS 8/10	25,514	17 / 8	W / 7	3-2	1-1	Ritchie 21, Mabbutt 65, Hunter 79 / Hankin 20, 84 / Ref: A Glasson	Shaw	Gillies	Sweeney	Mann	Collier	Hunter	Tainton	Ritchie	Mabbutt	Cormack	Whitehead	Graham
								Stewart	*Cherry*	*Gray F*	*Lorimer*	*McQueen*	*Madeley*	*Gray E*	*Hankin*	*Jordan*	*Currie*	*Graham*	
10	A EVERTON 15/10	39,230	18 / 3	L / 7	0-1	0-1	King 24 / Ref: M Lowe	Shaw	Gillies	Sweeney	Mann	Collier	Hunter	Tainton	Ritchie	Mabbutt	Cormack	Whitehead*	Gow
								Wood	*Jones*	*Pejic*	*Lyons*	*Higgins*	*Buckley**	*King*	*Dobson*	*Latchford*	*Pearson*	*Telfer Darracott*	

Match notes

1. A game of four penalties possibly creates a record of sorts, though Alan Sunderland has to finish off Willie Carr's spot-kick when it hits the bar. Newly-promoted Wolves dominate the midfield and Martin Patching shoots Steve Daley's cross low into the net to tie up their deserved win.

2. City's ultra-defensive display in deploying two sweepers gives 18-year-old Mabbutt few chances to shine on his debut. Forest, who manage five shots on target compared to City's none, are kept at bay until John Robertson's free-kick is headed in by John Withe from ten yards.

3. City's weak finishing, only one shot on target, prevents an improved performance not producing more than a draw. Lucky when Jon Sammels twice hits the post within a minute early on, City pay for their good fortune when two pen appeals, following fouls on Whitehead, are ignored.

4. Villa start the brighter and it is no surprise when Brian Little flicks the ball into the net over Shaw's head, after dashing past Sweeney to take Frank Carrodus' pass in his stride. Mabbutt's superb header from Whitehead's cross is scant reward for City's second-half domination.

5. City's well-organised defensive display comes to naught as substitute Roger Gibbins heads in Jimmy Neighbour's deep pass from the right for the Canaries' late winner. Tony Powell's 34th-minute trip on Whitehead just outside the penalty area deprives City of their best scoring chance.

6. Demonstrating a refreshing attacking tendency, City do well to beat a fluent West Ham side. After Mabbutt heads in to equalise Pop Robson's long-distance opener, Ritchie's 20-yard shot and second-half tap-in put City in charge, until Geoff Pike's late header brings an anxious finale.

7. After the goal feast in a 4-6 defeat by an England XI on Tuesday, City's attack is off target against the League leaders at Maine Road. Mabbutt admits that he should have scored at least four as wasteful City are punished by a Peter Barnes stab-in and Gary Owen's crisp low 20-yard shot.

8. A brilliant contest as City recover from Don Masson's left-footed opener and Peter Eastoe's easy tap-in. Tainton is the hero with his first goal for a year, a cracking shot from 20 yards, giving City hope, and winning the penalty when sent tumbling by Ron Abbott's clumsy challenge.

9. Yet another memorable match as City respond to Ray Hankin's first-time drive from the edge of the penalty area. Ritchie coolly eludes Dave Stewart to tuck in an immediate leveller, and Hunter sets the seal on City's success by lashing in the ball home through a crowded goalmouth.

10. City put up a brave fight at Goodison after Everton threaten to overwhelm them in the first half. Keeper Shaw performs wonders for City, but he is caught out when Bob Latchford's failure to control the ball sets up Andy King for a 20-yard snap-shot that flies in off the inside of a post.

11 H ARSENAL 22/10 — 24,864 — Pos 18 (8) — Pts 7 — L 0-2 (HT 0-1)
Scorers: Rix 45, MacDonald 90
Ref: K Baker
City: Shaw, Gillies, Sweeney, Gow, Collier, Merrick, Tainton, Ritchie, Mabbutt, Mann, Whitehead
Arsenal: Jennings, Rice, Nelson, Price, Young, Simpson, Brady, Hudson, MacDonald, Stapleton, Rix
Alan Dicks blames reaction to Wednesday's stormy encounter at Hibs in the Anglo-Scottish Cup as part of the reason for Arsenal's first away win of the season. Shaw is caught in no man's land by Graham Rix's chip, and Gow's back-pass sets up Malcolm MacDonald to roll the ball in.

12 A CHELSEA 29/10 — 22,313 — Pos 20 (17) — Pts 7 — L 0-1 (HT 0-0)
Scorers: Aylott 55
Ref: P Reeves
City: Shaw, Merrick, Wilkins G, Gow*, Collier, Hunter, Tainton, Ritchie, Gillies, Cormack, Whitehead
Chelsea: Bonetti, Harris, Wilkins G, Britton, Droy, Wicks, Aylott*, Wilkins R, Langley, Swain, Cooke, Walker
City squander their chances at Stamford Bridge where the lively Gillies is unlucky in having a shot cleared off the line as well as being denied by the crossbar. Chelsea are outplayed, but still pocket the points as Charlie Cooke's cross sets up Trevor Aylott to head in their winner.

13 A NEWCASTLE 5/11 — 23,321 — Pos 20 (21) — Pts 8 — D 1-1 (HT 0-0)
Scorers: Gillies 78, Martin 74
Ref: N Glover
City: Shaw, Merrick, Sweeney, Gow, Collier, Hunter, Tainton, Ritchie, Mabbutt*, Mann, Whitehead
Newcastle: Hardwick, Nattrass, Barker, Walker, Bird, Blackley, Barrowclough, Martin, Burns, Gowling, Craig
Shortly after Dennis Martin heads in for a makeshift Newcastle side, Gillies nets City's first away goal of the season with a twelve-yard drive through a crowded goalmouth. On top early on, City's best chance is spurned by Mann, who shoots straight at the keeper when clean through.

14 H DERBY 12/11 — 20,196 — Pos 19 (18) — Pts 10 — W 3-1 (HT 2-1)
Scorers: Ritchie 32, 45, Gillies 56 / Rioch 14
Ref: B Homewood
City: Shaw, Merrick, Sweeney, Gow, Collier, Hunter, Tainton, Ritchie, Mabbutt, Mann, Whitehead
Derby: Middleton, Langan, Nish, Rioch, McFarland, Todd, Powell, Hector, Hughes, Masson, Ryan
Great entertainment, following a minute's silence before the kick-off in respect of Harry Dolman, who died on Wednesday. Ritchie heads in two superb goals to celebrate his 200th game, and Gillies ties up City's success with great 30-yard strike to rival Bruce Rioch's opening effort.

15 A LIVERPOOL 19/11 — 41,053 — Pos 19 (6) — Pts 11 — D 1-1 (HT 1-1)
Scorers: Gow 27 / Dalglish 13
Ref: A Hamil
City: Shaw, Merrick, Sweeney, Gow, Collier, Hunter, Tainton, Ritchie, Mabbutt, Mann, Gillies
Liverpool: Clemence, Neal, Jones, Thompson, Kennedy, Hughes, Dalglish, Fairclough, Highway, Toshack, Callaghan
Gow's tremendous 30-yard volley gives City heart after Kenny Dalglish's low 16-yard shot had put Liverpool ahead with his first goal in eight games. City, for whom Hunter is inspired, turn in one of their best-ever defensive performances as Pool gain their first point in four games.

16 H MIDDLESBROUGH 26/11 — 20,536 — Pos 18 (13) — Pts 13 — W 4-1 (HT 2-1)
Scorers: Royle 11, 27, 59, 83, Mills 43
Ref: A Robson
City: Shaw, Merrick, Sweeney, Gow, Collier, Hunter, Tainton, Ritchie, Royle, Whitehead*, Cormack
Middlesbrough: Cuff, Craggs, Cooper, Souness, Boam, Ramage, Mahoney, Mills, Ashcroft, McAndrew, Armstrong*, Cummins
Joe Royle's remarkable City debut nearly doesn't happen as following a mix up over transfer forms. He is only cleared to play on the morning of the match. Four goals from four games, a header followed by a right-footed effort, then two left-footers, guarantees him instant cult status.

17 A COVENTRY 3/12 — 22,307 — Pos 17 (5) — Pts 14 — D 1-1 (HT 0-1)
Scorers: Ritchie 79 / Ferguson 32
Ref: K Salmon
City: Shaw, Merrick, Sweeney, Cormack, Collier, Hunter, Tainton, Ritchie, Royle, Wallace, Whitehead
Coventry: Blyth, Oakey, McDonald, Yorath, Holton, Coop, Nardiello, Wallace, Ferguson, Powell, Hutchison
City all but overwhelm high-riding Coventry, but glaring misses mean they have to be satisfied with a point. Mick Ferguson drives in from eight yards to put the Sky Blues ahead, but not long after Royle is thwarted by the post, Ritchie taps in as Jim Blyth spills the No 9's shot.

18 H IPSWICH 10/12 — 24,375 — Pos 14 (11) — Pts 16 — W 2-0 (HT 1-0)
Scorers: Tainton 5, Gillies 86
Ref: D Reeves
City: Shaw, Merrick, Sweeney, Gow, Collier, Hunter, Tainton, Ritchie, Royle*, Mariner, Whitehead
Ipswich: Cooper, Mills, Tibbott, Talbot, Hunter, Osman, Gates, Viljoen, Mariner, Wymark, Woods
Having won the Anglo-Scottish Cup on Monday with a 3-2 aggregate win over St Mirren, City extend their unbeaten League run to six games. Tainton's 25-yarder and a late header from Gillies, make up for Paul Cooper diving to his right to save Sweeney's ninth-minute spot-kick.

19 A DERBY 17/12 — 21,802 — Pos 16 (12) — Pts 16 — L 0-1 (HT 0-1)
Scorers: Todd 24
Ref: M Baker
City: Shaw, Merrick, Sweeney, Gow, Collier, Hunter, Tainton, Ritchie, Royle, Hughes, Whitehead
Derby: Middleton, Langan, Nish*, Daly, McFarland, Todd, Curran, Hughes, Masson, George, Ryan, Powell
Royle is robbed of a goal to celebrate his £90,000 transfer from Man City. The referee adjudges that he fouls Colin Todd before coming away with the ball and chipping a brilliant 40th-min right-foot shot over John Middleton. Derby are fortunate to win courtesy of Todd's easy tap-in.

20 H WEST BROM 26/12 — 29,292 — Pos 15 (6) — Pts 18 — W 3-1 (HT 0-1)
Scorers: Gow 60, Ritchie 65, 75 / Brown T 3
Ref: T Reynolds
City: Shaw, Merrick, Sweeney, Gow, Collier, Hunter, Tainton, Ritchie, Royle, Gillies, Whitehead*
West Brom: Godden, Mulligan, Statham, Brown T, Wile, Robertson, Martin, Brown A, Regis*, Robson, Johnston, Cunningham
Ritchie leaves no room for doubt with his 20-yard strike in the 75th minute, after earlier turning Hunter's long-range drive into the net. Tony Brown bursts through on his own for Albion, but Royle frustrates City's first-half efforts to equalise by lofting his spot-kick into the crowd.

21 A BIRMINGHAM 27/12 — 24,110 — Pos 16 (18) — Pts 18 — L 0-3 (HT 0-0)
Scorers: Gallagher 48, Towers 66, Francis 76
Ref: D Lloyd
City: Shaw, Gillies, Sweeney, Gow, Collier, Merrick, Tainton, Ritchie, Royle, Mabbutt, Cormack
Birmingham: Montgomery, Calderwood, Pendrey, Towers, Howard, Gallagher, Page*, Francis, Bertschin, Hibbitt, Dillon, Connolly
Joe Gallagher fires in Birmingham's first goal in five games, shortly after Ritchie's shot is struck-off because Royle is offside. City, unlucky with Collier's goal claim following a mêlée, are finished off by Trevor Francis, who runs from the halfway line for his 100th League goal.

LEAGUE DIVISION 1

Manager: Alan Dicks

SEASON 1977-78

Lineups (first row = Bristol City, second row = opponents)

No	Date	1	2	3	4	5	6	7	8	9	10	11	12 sub used
22	H NOTT'M FOREST 31/12	Shaw	Sweeney	Merrick	Gow	Collier	Hunter	Tainton	Ritchie	Royle	Gillies*	Mann	Mabbutt
		Shilton	Anderson	Barrett	McGovern	Needham	Burns	O'Neill	Gemmill	Withe	Woodcock	Robertson	
23	A WOLVES 2/1	Shaw	Sweeney	Gillies	Gow	Collier	Merrick	Tainton	Ritchie	Royle	Mabbutt	Mann	
		Bradshaw	Palmer	Parkin	Daley	Hazell	McAlle	Hibbitt	Carr	Richards	Bell	Black	
24	H LEICESTER 14/1	Shaw	Sweeney	Merrick	Gow	Collier	Hunter	Tainton	Ritchie	Royle	Mabbutt	Whitehead	
		Wallington	Williams	Rofe	Kelly	Sims	Webb	Goodwin	Earle	Smith	Salmons	Armstrong	
25	A ASTON VILLA 28/1	Shaw	Sweeney	Merrick	Gow	Collier	Hunter	Tainton	Ritchie	Royle	Gillies*	Whitehead	Mann
		Rimmer	Gidman	Smith	Phillips	McNaught	Mortimer	Craig	Little	Deehan	Cowans	Carrodus	
26	H NORWICH 4/2	Shaw	Sweeney	Merrick	Gow	Collier	Hunter	Mann	Ritchie	Royle	Cormack	Whitehead	
		Keelan	Bond	Sullivan	Ryan	Jones	Powell	Maguire	Suggett	Gibbins	Reeves*	Peters	Neighbour
27	A MANCHESTER U 8/2	Shaw	Sweeney	Merrick	Gow	Collier*	Hunter	Mann	Ritchie	Royle	Cormack	Whitehead	Tainton
		Roche	Nicholl	Albiston	McIlroy	Houston	Buchanan*	Coppell	Jordan	Pearson	Macari	Hill	Greenhoff J
28	A WEST HAM 11/2	Shaw	Sweeney	Merrick	Gow	Rodgers	Hunter	Mann	Ritchie	Royle	Cormack	Whitehead	Taylor A
		Day	McDowell	Lampard	Bonds	Taylor T	Green	Devonshire	Robson	Cross	Brooking	Hales*	
29	H MANCHESTER C 17/2	Shaw	Sweeney	Merrick	Gow*	Rodgers	Hunter	Mann	Ritchie	Royle	Cormack	Whitehead	Tainton
		Corrigan	Clements	Donnachie	Booth	Watson	Owen	Channon	Bell	Kidd	Harford	Barnes	
30	A QP RANGERS 25/2	Shaw	Sweeney	Merrick	Gow	Rodgers	Hunter	Tainton	Ritchie	Royle	Mann	Whitehead	
		Parkes	Clement	Gillard	Hollins	Howe	Abbott	Shanks	Busby	James	Bowles	Givens	
31	A LEEDS 4/3	Shaw	Sweeney	Merrick	Gow	Rodgers	Hunter	Tainton	Ritchie	Royle	Mann	Whitehead*	Gillies
		Harvey	Reaney*	Hampton	Flynn	Cherry	Madeley	Gray F	Thomas	Currie	Clarke	Graham	Parkinson

Scorers, Times, and Referees / Results

No	Scorers, Times, and Referees	Att		Pos	Pt	F-A	H-T
22	Mabbutt 72 / Needham 12, W'dcock 26, O'Neill 58 / Ref: L Shapter	31.506	1	17	18	L 1-3	0-2
23	Ref: J Worrall	25,283	15	18	19	D 0-0	0-0
24	Ref: C Downey	19,458	22	17	20	D 0-0	0-0
25	Deehan 80 / Ref: R Lewis	29,676	10	18	20	L 0-1	0-0
26	Ritchie 10, Royle 13, Whitehead 15 / Ref: R Crabb	16.993	10	17	22	W 3-0	3-0
27	Cormack 42 / Hill 28p / Ref: C Seel	43,457	11	15	23	D 1-1	1-1
28	Mann 45, Royle 62 / Robson 13 / Ref: C Thomas	19,934	19	14	25	W 2-1	1-1
29	Royle 1, 6 / Kidd 23, Shaw 70 (og) / Ref: A Glasson	25,416	2	12	26	D 2-2	2-1
30	Gow 53, Sweeney 60 / Bowles 17p, Busby 49 / Ref: M Sinclair	17,051	20	13	27	D 2-2	0-1
31	Ritchie 53, Gillies 82 / Ref: T Farley	24,830	6	11	29	W 2-0	0-0

Match reports

22 — Mabbutt shoots in and also hits the bar near the end as City stage a mini-revival during the final 20 minutes. It is too late however as John Needham's header, Tony Woodcock's cool shot, and Martin O'Neill's great run had put superior Forest on course for their eighth away win.

23 — Stylish City gain a deserved draw at Molineux. Royle is robbed by the linesman who rules Mabbutt is offside as his 20-yarder dips over Paul Bradshaw in the fifth minute, whilst Wolves are unlucky when Alan Black hits a post and Gillies clears off the line from Norman Bell.

24 — The Ashton Gate pitch presents a sorry spectacle to Match of the Day viewers as it is a morass of sand, mud and peat, following yesterday's decision to protect the surface in case of frost. Royle misses City's three best chances, but a draw is a fair result for a dull, unexciting game.

25 — John Deehan punishes wasteful City with an easy paced shot from 20 yards after wrong footing Hunter. A combination of Jimmy Rimmer's excellent goalkeeping and abysmal finishing, notably by Ritchie, Royle and Gillies, make City's superior performance count for naught.

26 — Royle notches his first goal since his debut, a simple tap-in after Whitehead's fierce low-hit centre cannons off David Jones. The pitch, which cuts up badly, is blamed for curtailing City's breathtaking opening following Whitehead's rasping left-foot drive into the top corner of the net.

27 — The magnificent seven (six City) is the bookings tally, among whom are Ritchie and Cormack who dispute the award of Gordon Hill's penalty following Merrick's heading duel with Joe Jordan. Cormack side-steps two players before crashing in City's deserved equaliser from six yards.

28 — City have reserve centre-half David Rodgers to thank for their first away win of the season. He outjumps everyone in the Hammers' penalty area to set up Royle to head in the decisive goal, after Mann had equalised with one of his typical power drives from all of 25 yards.

29 — Royle has the visitors in a spin, not only does he notch a 45-second header and a great strike, but also brings a great save out of Joe Corrigan as well as hitting the post. Man City's fight-back gains a deserved point when Tommy Booth's shot hits the post and rebounds off Shaw.

30 — Stan Bowles registers with his second spot-kick attempt after Shaw is adjudged to have moved when he fires high over the bar. Gow, unlucky with a 24th-minute shot cleared off the line and a 48th-minute effort that hits the post, gets City back in the game when squeezing the ball in.

31 — Merrick's vital goal-line clearance to prevent Arthur Graham from scoring, just after the interval, is the game's turning point. Royle is a real handful as City complete a double over Leeds. He sets up Ritchie's half-volley as well as laying on the pass for Gillies to fire in from ten yards.

Bristol City — match-by-match record (games 32–42)

#	H/A	Opponent	Date	Att.	Pos	†	Pts	Res	FT	HT
32	H	EVERTON	11/3	25,614	12	2	29	L	0-1	0-1
33	A	ARSENAL	18/3	28,163	13	4	29	L	1-4	1-4
34	H	CHELSEA	21/3	20,062	11	15	31	W	3-0	2-0
35	H	BIRMINGHAM	25/3	21,434	12	15	31	L	0-1	0-1
36	A	WEST BROM	27/3	23,741	13	8	31	L	1-2	1-0
37	H	NEWCASTLE	1/4	17,142	14	22	33	W	3-1	1-0
38	A	MIDDLESBROUGH	8/4	14,667	15	14	33	L	0-2	0-1
39	H	LIVERPOOL	15/4	31,244	15	4	34	D	1-1	0-1
40	A	IPSWICH	22/4	22,579	16	15	34	L	0-1	0-0
41	H	MANCHESTER U	25/4	26,035	16	10	34	L	0-1	0-0
42	H	COVENTRY	29/4	21,191	15	7	35	D	1-1	0-0

Home 23,357 — Away 25,572 — Average 23,357

---

32. H EVERTON — 11/3 — 25,614
City: Shaw, Sweeney, Merrick, Gow, Rodgers, Hunter, Tainton, Ritchie, Royle, Mann, Whitehead*, Gillies
Everton: Wood, Jones, Pejic, Lyons, Kenyon, Ross, King, Dobson, Latchford, McKenzie*, Thomas, Telfer
Ross 45
Ref: A Robinson
Despite almost constant pressure Trevor Ross's 25-yard strike in first-half injury-time brings City's six match unbeaten run to a halt. Luckless City have two penalty appeals turned down, while two of Everton's three bookings are for professional fouls that prevent clear runs on goal.

33. A ARSENAL — 18/3 — 28,163
City: Shaw, Sweeney, Merrick, Gow, Rodgers, Hunter, Tainton, Ritchie, Royle, Mann, Whitehead
Arsenal: Jennings, Rice, Nelson, Price, O'Leary, Young, Brady, Sunderland*, MacDonald, Stapleton, Hudson, Rix
Tainton 32
Stapleton 11, 38, Sunderland 15, [Price 23]
Ref: C Maskell
City are pleased to escape with only a 1-4 drubbing following Arsenal's opening three-goal salvo. Tainton's right-foot shot from the edge of the penalty area is City's sole reply to Frank Stapleton's six-yard shot, Alan Sunderland's searing drive and David Price's deft header.

34. H CHELSEA — 21/3 — 20,062
City: Shaw, Sweeney, Merrick, Gow, Rodgers, Hunter, Tainton!, Ritchie, Royle*, Cormack, Mann, Gillies
Chelsea: Bonetti, Locke, Harris, Britton, Droy!, Wicks, Finnieston*, Swain, Langley, Lewington, Hay, Garner
Cormack 27p, Gow 38, Rodgers 80
Ref: L Burden
Tainton's 83rd-min dismissal for kicking at Steve Wicks, and Micky Droy's departure two mins later for a savage tackle on Ritchie mars an otherwise thrilling game. Droy's push on Ritchie gifts Cormack his pen, before Gow's delightful chip and a Rodgers header seals City's win.

35. H BIRMINGHAM — 25/3 — 21,434
City: Shaw, Sweeney!, Merrick, Gow, Rodgers, Hunter, Mann, Ritchie, Gillies, Cormack, Whitehead*, Mabbutt
Birmingham: Montgomery, Calderwood, Pendry, Towers, Gallagher, Howard, Page, Francis, Bertschin, Hibbitt*, Connolly, Broadhurst
Francis 31
Ref: A Turvey
Despite the sending off of Sweeney for kicking Tony Towers, and the booking of six players (four City), it is not a bad-tempered affair. Trevor Francis secures the Blues victory with a left-foot drive, but Ritchie is unlucky to have his shot disallowed at the death for a dubious handball.

36. A WEST BROM — 27/3 — 23,741
City: Shaw, Gillies, Merrick, Gow, Rodgers, Hunter, Tainton, Ritchie, Royle*, Cormack, Mann, Mabbutt
West Brom: Godden, Mulligan, Statham, Brown T, Wile, Robertson, Martin, Cunningham, Regis, Trewick, Johnston
Hunter 42
Johnston 62, Brown 89
Ref: N Midgley
After taking the lead from Hunter's free-kick, City are made to pay the price for slack marking. Willie Johnston intercepts Shaw's short goal-kick to level matters, then Tony Brown cuts in front of Rodgers to lift a through ball into the net from twelve yards for Albion's late winner.

37. H NEWCASTLE — 1/4 — 17,142
City: Shaw, Sweeney, Merrick, Gow, Rodgers, Hunter, Tainton, Ritchie, Royle, Cormack, Mann, Mabbutt
Newcastle: Mahoney, Nattrass, Kennedy, Barton, Bird*, Blackhall, Barrowclough, Burns, Nulty, McGhee, Walker, Scott
Nulty 18 (og), Ritchie 49, Hunter 53
Barrowclough 84
Ref: D Civil
Shaw's failure to get his hands to Micky Burns' 36th-minute chipped free-kick is fortuitous as unbeknown to the players the award was indirect. Hunter stars for City with his hard cross ending up in the net off Geoff Nulty, and then getting on the scoresheet with a 15-yard volley.

38. A MIDDLESBROUGH — 8/4 — 14,667
City: Shaw, Stevens, Gillies, Gow, Rodgers, Merrick, Tainton, Ritchie, Royle, Cormack, Whitehead*, Mabbutt
Middlesbrough: Brown, Craggs, Bailey, Mahoney, Boam, Ramage, Mills, Cummins, Shearer, McAndrew, Armstrong
Ramage 43, Cummins 76
Ref: N Ashley
Shaw is pelted by stones and pieces of glass ten minutes from the end, by which time defensive-minded City are already well beaten. Yorkshire fast bowler Alan Ramage prods home Boro's first from ten yards, then Stan Cummins doubles the advantage when Shaw spills a free-kick.

39. H LIVERPOOL — 15/4 — 31,244
City: Shaw, Gillies, Merrick, Gow, Rodgers, Hunter, Tainton*, Ritchie, Royle, Cormack, Mann, Mabbutt
Liverpool: Clemence, Neal, Smith, Thompson, Kennedy, Hughes, Dalglish, Case, Heighway, McDermott, Souness
Cormack 74
Heighway 28
Ref: T Bune
A goal that will be remembered for years to come is the accolade as Steve Heighway beats Hunter, Merrick and Shaw in a 70-yard solo run before putting the ball in an open net. After shooting high and wide from a 41st-min penalty, Cormack fires in a left-foot half volley equaliser.

40. A IPSWICH — 22/4 — 22,579
City: Shaw, Merrick, Merrick, Gow!, Rodgers, Hunter, Tainton*, Ritchie, Royle, Cormack*, Mann, Mabbutt
Ipswich: Cooper, Burley, Mills, Talbot, Hunter, Osman, Osborne, Wark, Mariner, Geddis, Woods
Mills 64
Ref: B Daniels
After Gow's 82nd-min sending off for retaliation following a Russell Osman foul, City nearly save a point when Tainton hits the bar. A poor game, in which Ipswich's thoughts appear focussed on next week's FA Cup Final, is settled by a 20-yarder from the right foot of Mick Mills.

41. H MANCHESTER U — 25/4 — 26,035
City: Shaw, Sweeney, Merrick, Mann, Rodgers, Hunter, Tainton, Ritchie, Royle, Cormack*, Whitehead*, Mabbutt
Manchester U: Roche, Albiston, Houston, McIlroy, McQueen, Nicholl, Coppell, Jordan, Pearson, Greenhoff B, Grimes
Pearson 50
Ref: T Spencer
Substitute Mabbutt twice almost snatches a goal after coming on for the last twelve minutes, but United hold on to Stuart Pearson's deft back-header that finishes off Ashley Grimes' chipped free-kick. City miss their chances, but in truth are outplayed by much superior opponents.

42. H COVENTRY — 29/4 — 21,191
City: Shaw, Sweeney, Merrick, Gow, Rodgers, Hunter, Tainton, Ritchie, Royle, Mann, Whitehead*, Mabbutt
Coventry: Blyth, Roberts, McDonald, Yorath, Osgood, Coop, Green*, Wallace, Ferguson, Powell, Hutchison, Beck
Royle 61
Wallace 63
Ref: A Gunn
The chances go begging at Ashton Gate, where Shaw's agile display has the Coventry strikers shaking their heads in exasperation. Royle ends his goal famine to rifle City ahead with a right-footed shot from ten yards, but Ian Wallace quickly equalises with a looping header.

Home 23,357
Away 25,572
Average 23,357

LEAGUE DIVISION 1 (CUP-TIES)

Manager: Alan Dicks   **SEASON 1977-78**

League Cup

			F-A	H-T	Scorers, Times, and Referees	1	2	3	4	5	6	7	8	9	10	11	12 sub used
2	H STOKE 29/8	18 11,877 2:7	W 1-0	1-0	Mabbutt 9 Ref: M Sinclair	Shaw *Shilton*	Sweeney *Dodd*	Merick *Marsh*	Gow* *Kendall*	Collier *Smith*	Hunter *Bloor*	Tainton *Goodwin*	Ritchie *Richardson*	Mabbutt *Gregory*	Cormack *Waddington*	Whitehead *Crooks*	Gillies
3	A WREXHAM 26/10	18 10,183 3:4	L 0-1	0-0	Shinton 52 Ref: B Martin	Shaw *Davies*	Gillies *Evans*	Sweeney *Dwyer*	Gow *Davis*	Collier *Roberts*	Merrick *Thomas*	Tainton *Shinton*	Ritchie *Sutton*	Fear* *Lyons*	Mann *Whittle*	Whitehead *Cartwright*	Bain

Much prone to over elaboration and sloppy defending, City are fortunate that Stoke are unable to take advantage. Ritchie's determined run, outside of Alan Bloor, to the by-line sets up City's passage to the next round – his chip allowing Mabbutt to head in from seven yards.

City are thoroughly outplayed by Third Division opponents who twice hit the woodwork. Scarcely able to move out of their own half due to the sheer pace of Wrexham's attacks, City succumb just after the interval when Bobby Shinton neatly heads in Graham Whittle's cross.

FA Cup

			F-A	H-T	Scorers, Times, and Referees	1	2	3	4	5	6	7	8	9	10	11	12 sub used
3	H WREXHAM 7/1	18 19,644 3:1	D 4-4	2-2	Mabbutt 6, 89, Ritchie 13, Cormack 83 *Shi'n 18, 68, M'ick 23 (og), McNeil 54* Ref: R Perkin	Shaw *Davies*	Sweeney *Hill*	Gillies* *Dwyer*	Gow *Davis*	Collier *Roberts*	Merrick *Thomas*	Tainton *Shinton*	Ritchie *Sutton*	Royle *McNeil*	Mabbutt *Whittle*	Mann *Griffiths*	Cormack
3R	A WREXHAM 9/1	18 15,614 3:1	L 0-3	0-3	*McNeil 25, Whittle 31, Thomas 45* Ref: R Perkin	Shaw *Davies*	Sweeney *Hill*	Gillies *Dwyer*	Gow *Davis*	Collier *Cegielski*	Merrick *Thomas*	Tainton *Shinton*	Ritchie *Sutton*	Royle *McNeil**	Mabbutt *Whittle*	Cormack *Griffiths*	Lyons

City snatch a last-gasp replay as Mabbutt sweeps in a low shot in the final minute. The first six goals are all headers, including Merrick's own-goal to bring Wrexham level. The Welshmen control the game thereafter, until Cormack jabs the ball home to inspire City's late comeback.

City are fortunate to escape with only a three-goal beating as Bobby Shinton squanders two second-half pens. Dixie McNeil's header, Graham Whittle's scorching 18-yarder and a Mike Thomas' chip complete yet another humiliating visit to the Racecourse ground for Bristol City.

League Table

	Team	P	W	D	L	F	A	W	D	L	F	A	Pts
				Home						Away			
1	Nott'm Forest	42	15	6	0	37	8	10	8	3	32	16	64
2	Liverpool	42	15	4	2	37	11	5	7	5	28	23	57
3	Everton	42	14	4	3	47	22	8	7	6	29	23	55
4	Manchester C	42	14	3	4	46	21	6	8	7	28	30	52
5	Arsenal	42	14	5	2	38	12	7	5	9	22	25	52
6	West Brom	42	13	5	3	35	18	5	9	7	27	35	50
7	Coventry	42	13	5	3	48	23	5	7	9	27	39	48
8	Aston Villa	42	11	4	6	33	18	7	6	8	24	24	46
9	Leeds	42	12	4	5	39	21	6	6	9	24	32	46
10	Manchester U	42	9	6	6	32	23	7	4	10	35	40	42
11	Birmingham	42	8	5	8	32	30	8	4	9	23	35	41
12	Derby	42	10	7	4	37	24	4	6	11	17	35	41
13	Norwich	42	10	8	3	28	20	1	10	10	24	46	40
14	Middlesbro	42	8	8	5	25	19	4	7	10	17	35	39
15	Wolves	42	7	8	6	30	27	5	4	12	21	37	36
16	Chelsea	42	7	11	3	28	20	4	3	14	18	49	36
17	BRISTOL CITY	42	9	6	6	37	26	2	7	12	12	27	35
18	Ipswich	42	10	5	6	32	24	1	8	12	15	37	35
19	QP Rangers	42	8	8	5	27	26	1	7	13	20	38	33
20	West Ham	42	8	6	7	31	28	4	2	15	21	41	32
21	Newcastle	42	4	6	11	26	37	2	4	15	16	41	22
22	Leicester	42	4	7	10	16	32	1	5	15	10	38	22
		924	223	132	107	741	490	107	132	223	490	741	924

Appearances and Goals

Player	Lge	Sub	LC	Sub	FAC	Sub	G Lge	G LC	G FAC	Tot
Bain, John	27		2		2					
Collier, Gary	25	1	1			1				
Cormack, Peter			1		1		6		1	7
Fear, Keith	2									
Garland, Chris	24	3	1		2		4			4
Gillies, Donnie		1	1	2			4			4
Gow, Gerry	37		2		1		3			3
Hunter, Norman	38		1							
Mabbutt, Kevin	16	10	1		2		4	1	2	7
Mann, Jimmy	26	5		1	1		1			1
Merrick, Geoff	37		2		2					
Ritchie, Tom	41		2		2		11		1	12
Rodgers, David	15						1			1
Royle, Joe	26			2	2		8			8
Shaw, John	42		2		2					
Stevens, Paul	1									
Sweeney, Gerry	38		2		2		1			1
Tainton, Trevor	36	2	2		2		3			3
Whitehead, Clive	31	2	2		2		2			2
(own-goals)							1			1
19 players used	462	24	22	2	22	1	49	1	4	54

Odds & ends

Double wins: (2) West Ham, Leeds.

Double losses: (4) Nott'm Forest, Everton, Arsenal, Birmingham.

Won from behind: (5) West Ham (h), Leeds (h), Derby (h), West Brom (h), West Ham (a).

Lost from in front: (2) West Brom (a), Wolves (h).

High spots: Beating West Ham 3-2 at Ashton Gate on 17 September.

A memorable encounter with Leeds at Ashton Gate on 8 October.

Four goals for Joe Royle on his debut v Middlesbrough on 26 Nov.

Beating Hibernian (h) 5-3 in the Anglo-Scottish Cup on 1 November.

Winning the Anglo-Scottish Cup 3-2 on aggregate v St Mirren.

Beating Bristol Rov (h) 3-0 in the Gloucestershire Cup Final on 2 May.

Low spots: First-half annihilation by Arsenal at Highbury on 18 March.

Losing to Wrexham in both the FA and the FL Cup.

Player of the year: Norman Hunter.

Ever-presents: (1) John Shaw.

Hat-tricks: (1) Joe Royle.

Leading scorer: Tom Ritchie (12).

LEAGUE DIVISION 1   Manager: Alan Dicks   SEASON 1978-79

(City players in roman; opposition line-ups and the substitute used shown in italics.)

No	Date	V	Club	Att	Pos (City / Opp)	Pt	F–A	H-T	Scorers, Times, and Referees	1	2	3	4	5	6	7	8	9	10	11	12 sub used
1	19/8	A	BOLTON	21,355	—	2	W 2-1	0-1	Mann 64, Ritchie 86 / Gowling 32 / Ref: R Perkin	Shaw	Sweeney	Cooper	Mann	Rodgers	Hunter	Tainton	Ritchie	Royle	Cormack	Garland	
										McDonagh	*Nicholson*	*Walsh*	*Greaves*	*Jones P*	*Allardyce**	*Morgan*	*Whatmore*	*Gowling*	*Worthington*	*Train*	*Dunne*
2	22/8	H	NORWICH	19,968	—	3	D 1-1	0-1	Cormack 66p / Ryan 45p / Ref: M Baker	Shaw	Sweeney	Cooper	Mann	Rodgers	Hunter	Tainton	Ritchie	Royle	Cormack	Garland*	Whitehead
										Keelan	*Bond*	*Sullivan*	*Ryan John*	*Hoadley*	*Powell*	*Neighbour*	*Reeves*	*Chivers*	*Robson*	*Peters*	
3	26/8	H	ASTON VILLA	23,881	5 / 6	5	W 1-0	0-0	Rodgers 66 / Ref: T Spencer	Shaw	Sweeney	Gillies	Mann	Rodgers	Hunter	Tainton	Ritchie	Royle	Pritchard	Whitehead	
										Rimmer	*Gidman*	*Smith*	*Evans A*	*McNaught*	*Mortimer*	*Shelton**	*Little*	*Gregory*	*Cowans*	*Carrodus*	*Shaw G*
4	2/9	A	WOLVES	16,121	7 / 19	5	L 0-2	0-1	Rodgers 13 (og), Hibbitt 85 / Ref: R Chadwick	Shaw	Sweeney	Gillies	Mann	Rodgers	Hunter	Tainton	Ritchie	Royle*	Gow	Whitehead	Cormack
										Bradshaw	*Daniel*	*Palmer*	*Parkin*	*Berry*	*McAlle*	*Hibbitt*	*Carr*	*Richards*	*Bell*	*Daley*	
5	9/9	A	TOTTENHAM	34,035	12 / 15	5	L 0-1	0-1	Rodgers 19 (og) / Ref: C Maskell	Shaw	Sweeney	Gillies	Mann	Rodgers	Hunter	Tainton	Ritchie	Royle	Gow	Whitehead	
										Daines	*McAllister*	*Gorman*	*Holmes*	*Lacy*	*Perryman*	*Villa*	*Ardiles*	*Lee*	*Pratt*	*Taylor*	
6	16/9	H	SOUTHAMPTON	21,795	8 / 12	7	W 3-1	1-1	Rodgers 21, Ritchie 74, 88 / Holmes 40 / Ref: A McDonald	Shaw	Sweeney	Gillies	Mann	Rodgers	Hunter	Tainton	Ritchie	Royle*	Cormack	Mabbutt	
										Wells	*Golac*	*Peach*	*Williams*	*Nicholl*	*Waldron*	*Ball*	*Boyer*	*MacDougall**	*Holmes*	*Curran*	*Hayes*
7	23/9	A	IPSWICH	19,054	6 / 18	9	W 1-0	0-0	Ritchie 66p / Ref: B Daniels	Shaw	Sweeney	Gillies	Gow	Rodgers	Hunter	Tainton	Ritchie	Royle	Mann	Mabbutt	
										Cooper	*Burley*	*Mills*	*Talbot*	*Osman*	*Beattie*	*Wark*	*Muhren*	*Mariner*	*Whymark**	*Woods*	*Brazil*
8	30/9	H	EVERTON	22,502	5 / 2	10	D 2-2	2-1	Gow 4, Hunter 23 / Latchford 11, 67 / Ref: L Shapter	Shaw	Sweeney	Gillies	Gow	Rodgers	Hunter	Tainton	Ritchie	Royle	Walsh	Mabbutt	
										Wood	*Todd*	*Pejic*	*Lyons*	*Wright*	*Ross*	*King*	*Dobson*	*Latchford*	*Walsh*	*Thomas !*	
9	7/10	A	QP RANGERS	15,707	9 / 15	10	L 0-1	0-0	Busby 90 / Ref: M Taylor	Shaw	Sweeney	Gillies	Gow	Rodgers	Hunter	Tainton	Ritchie	Royle	Mann	Whitehead	
										Parkes	*Shanks*	*Gillard*	*Hollins*	*Howe*	*Cunningham*	*Eastoe*	*Francis*	*Harkouk**	*Bowles*	*McGee*	*Busby*
10	14/10	H	NOTT'M FOREST	26,947	11 / 3	10	L 1-3	1-2	Ritchie 11p / Birtles 4, Robertson 25p, 54p / Ref: C Thomas	Shaw	Sweeney	Gillies*	Gow	Rodgers	Hunter	Tainton	Ritchie	Royle	Mann	Whitehead	
										Shilton	*Anderson*	*Clark*	*McGovern*	*Lloyd*	*Burns*	*O'Neill*	*Gemmill*	*Birtles*	*O'Hare*	*Robertson*	*Whitehead*

Match commentaries

1. City's commitment to a more attacking policy bears early fruit as Ritchie's dribble past three defenders ends with him slotting home a late winner. Newly-promoted Bolton deserve Alan Gowling's fierce opener, but after Mann fires in from almost 25 yards City take control.

2. Hunter has a nightmare first half, getting booked for a foul on Kevin Reeves and then tripping Jimmy Neighbour to concede Norwich's pen. Whitehead peps City, but it takes the rather lucky award of a spot-kick to level matters after Mann's hopeful shot had hit Phil Hoadley's hand.

3. City's new-look side, with Whitehead operating at left-back and Sweeney in midfield, play with greater fluency than in their previous two games. Teenager Pritchard has an outstanding debut and it is from his cross that Rodgers runs in from a deep position to head in City's winner.

4. Rodgers sets Wolves on the way to their first win of the season, glancing Willie Carr's cross off of his head into the net. Despite controlling midfield City fail to create many chances, though Paul Bradshaw has to be at his best in the closing seconds to save Gow's close-range shot.

5. Woeful finishing prevents City benefiting from their classy approach play as Spurs are often outplayed. It is City who turn on the Argentinian style soccer for the Match of the Day viewers, but Rodgers gifts Tottenham the points, flicking the ball into the net for yet another own-goal.

6. Four bookings for City and one for Southampton as petulance predominates in the oppressive heat. In a game of few chances it is curious that all the shots on target produce goals. Rodgers opens the scoring with a powerful header that bounces down over the line after hitting the bar.

7. The only surprise is that it takes a spot-kick to decide this game as City carve out a host of chances with Mabbutt (twice) and Mann being thwarted by the woodwork. Ritchie places his first-ever penalty low to Paul Cooper's left following on from Kevin Beattie's tug on Mabbutt.

8. City lose their way after David Thomas is sent off for dissent when the referee refuses penalty claims following Sweeney's 51st-minute handball. Bob Latchford rescues a point for Everton by hammering the ball into the net when Mickey Walsh's header rebounds off the post.

9. City's unwillingness to settle for a point costs them dear in the dying seconds as they are caught out by a Rangers counter attack. Don Shanks' centre is missed by two defenders and Peter Eastoe heads the ball back for Martyn Busby to fire in a low drive past Shaw from 20 yards.

10. A magnificent game, but City are unable to stop Forest extending their record unbeaten run to 36 games, despite twice hitting the woodwork and dominating the corner count 19-2. Garry Birtles scores the only goal from open play when shooting in a left-footed opener from ten yards.

Season results and line-ups (match-by-match record)

11. A — MANCHESTER U — 21/10 — Att: 47,211 — W 3-1 (HT 1-0)
League pos: 9 (opp 6) · Pts: 12
Scorers: Mabbutt 11, 50, 88 — *Greenhoff J 70* · **Ref:** J Butcher
Bristol City: Shaw, Sweeney, Gillies, Gow, Rodgers, Hunter, Tainton, Ritchie, Royle, Mann, Mabbutt
Manchester U: Roche, Albiston, Houston, McIlroy*, McQueen, Buchan, Coppell, Greenhoff J, Jordan, Macari, Greenhoff B

Mabbutt breaks his away scoring duck in style by firing in a hat-trick. City give United's collection of stars a lesson in team work at Old Trafford where Shaw saves Jimmy Greenhoff's controversial penalty after Tainton is harshly adjudged to have pushed Sammy McIlroy.

12. H — ARSENAL — 28/10 — Att: 26,958 — L 1-3 (HT 1-2)
League pos: 11 (opp 7) · Pts: 12
Scorers: Rodgers 29 — *Brady 15, 60p, Stapleton 27* · **Ref:** A Hamil
Bristol City: Shaw, Sweeney, Gillies, Gow, Rodgers, Hunter, Tainton, Ritchie, Royle, Mann*, Mabbutt, Whitehead
Arsenal: Jennings, Rice, Nelson, Price, O'Leary, Young, Brady, Stapleton, Heeley, Rix, Walford

With Royle out with a groin strain his heading ability is sorely missed as City's attack fails to function. Liam Brady provides the best display of individual artistry seen for years at Ashton Gate, and it's his fall on being challenged by Hunter that produces the spot-kick that kills City off.

13. A — MIDDLESBROUGH — 4/11 — Att: 20,461 — D 0-0 (HT 0-0)
League pos: 11 (opp 14) · Pts: 13
Ref: P Richardson
Bristol City: Shaw, Sweeney, Gillies, Gow, Rodgers, Hunter, Tainton, Ritchie, Royle, Bain, Mabbutt
Middlesbrough: Stewart, Craggs, Bailey, Mahoney, Boam, McAndrew, Proctor, Mills, Hodgson, Burns, Armstrong

A poor game at Ayresome Park, where City are unlucky in the 27th minute when Royle has his full-blooded header struck off for climbing over Stuart Boam. City's defence deals easily with Boro's efforts to extend their three-match winning run, but offer little in attack themselves.

14. H — BOLTON — 11/11 — Att: 18,608 — W 4-1 (HT 1-1)
League pos: 10 (opp 19) · Pts: 15
Scorers: Ritchie 45, Royle 57, 58, Rodgers 84 — *Walsh 4* · **Ref:** A Robinson
Bristol City: Shaw, Sweeney, Gillies, Gow, Rodgers, Hunter, Tainton, Ritchie, Royle, Bain*, Mabbutt, Whitehead
Bolton: McDonagh, Nicholson, Dunne*, Greaves, Walsh, Smith, Morgan, Reid, Gowling, McNab, Whatmore

Royle opens his goal account for the season with a crisp 18-yarder that Peter Nicholson deflects into the net. Mike Walsh punishes lax marking to head Bolton into an early lead, but City's aggression and team work make victory inevitable following Ritchie's deftly nodded equaliser.

15. A — ASTON VILLA — 18/11 — Att: 27,621 — L 0-2 (HT 0-0)
League pos: 12 (opp 7) · Pts: 15
Scorers: — *Deehan 58, Cowans 70* · **Ref:** N Glover
Bristol City: Shaw, Sweeney, Gillies, Gow, Rodgers, Hunter, Tainton, Ritchie, Royle!, Bain*, Mabbutt, Whitehead
Aston Villa: Rimmer, Gidman, Williams, Evans*, McNaught, Mortimer, Shelton, Linton, Deehan, Cowans, Gregory, Gibson

City lose the midfield battle as John Deehan's great hooked shot and an 18-yard low cross-shot by Gordon Cowans enable Villa to collect their first home win since the opening day of the season. Royle's punch at Allan Evans in the 76th minute results in his first dismissal in 13 years.

16. H — WOLVES — 21/11 — Att: 18,295 — L 0-1 (HT 0-0)
League pos: 12 (opp 21) · Pts: 15
Scorers: — *Daley 89* · **Ref:** D Lloyd
Bristol City: Shaw, Sweeney, Gillies, Gow, Rodgers, Hunter, Tainton, Ritchie, Royle, Mann*, Mabbutt, Whitehead
Wolves: Bradshaw, Palmer, Parkin, Daniel, Hazell, Berry, Hibbitt, Carr, Bell, Daley, Eves, Cormack

Steve Daley gives new Wolves manager John Barnwell a flying start as he rifles in a left-footed shot past Shaw in the last minute. Ritchie and Mabbutt force Paul Bradshaw to pull off some early saves, but in a poor game City's attack again fails to function properly without Royle.

17. A — BIRMINGHAM — 25/11 — Att: 21,152 — D 1-1 (HT 1-0)
League pos: 13 (opp 21) · Pts: 16
Scorers: Mabbutt 26 — *Tarantini 69* · **Ref:** B Martin
Bristol City: Shaw, Sweeney, Gillies, Gow, Rodgers, Hunter, Tainton, Ritchie, Royle, Mann, Mabbutt
Birmingham: Freeman, Tarantini, Dennis, Towers*, Gallagher, Page, Dillon, Buckley, Givens, Calderwood, Fox, Barrowclough

£250,000 Argentinian full-back Alberto Tarantini rescues a point for bottom club Birmingham as he heads in from Steve Fox's perfect corner. City outplay the Blues, but are unable to add to Mabbutt's opener, when he backheaded Mann's cross past the helpless Neil Freeman.

18. H — DERBY — 2/12 — Att: 18,096 — W 1-0 (HT 0-0)
League pos: 11 (opp 12) · Pts: 18
Scorers: Gillies 84 · **Ref:** L Burden
Bristol City: Shaw, Sweeney, Gillies, Gow, Rodgers, Hunter, Tainton!, Ritchie, Royle, Mann, Mabbutt
Derby: Middleton, Langan, Buckley, Daly, McFarland*, Moreland*, Clarke, Powell, Duncan, Caskey, Clarke, Hill

It takes the 75th-minute sending off of Tainton, after kicking Jonathan Clarke, to spark City into action. Gillies snatches the points with a long shot that is deflected beyond the reach of John Middleton. Derby never look like adding to their single away success in the past twelve months.

19. A — LEEDS — 9/12 — Att: 22,529 — D 1-1 (HT 1-1)
League pos: 11 (opp 9) · Pts: 19
Scorers: Royle 23 — *Flynn 28* · **Ref:** N Midgley
Bristol City: Shaw, Sweeney, Gillies, Gow, Rodgers, Hunter, Mann, Ritchie, Royle, Cormack, Mabbutt
Leeds: Harvey, Cherry, Stevenson, Flynn, Hart, Madeley, Gray E, Hankin, Thomas, Currie, Harris, Hill

After Royle shoots them ahead, City are indebted to their back four as Leeds take control. Shaw has no chance as Brian Flynn fires in from the edge of the pen area, but thereafter City soak up the pressure and almost notch a winner as Ritchie and Royle both waste breakaway chances.

20. H — LIVERPOOL — 16/12 — Att: 28,347 — W 1-0 (HT 0-0)
League pos: 11 (opp 1) · Pts: 21
Scorers: Royle 77 · **Ref:** K Salmon
Bristol City: Shaw, Sweeney, Gillies, Gow, Rodgers, Hunter, Tainton, Ritchie, Royle, Cormack, Mabbutt, Whitehead
Liverpool: Clemence, Neal, Kennedy A, Thompson, Kennedy R, Hansen, Dalglish, Case, Heighway*, McDermott, Souness, Johnson

Old Evertonian Royle nudges memories of Merseyside derby days as he shakes off Liverpool's tight marking to hook City's match clincher into the net. City finish as deserved winners on a surface better suited to their quick-tackling display, than to Liverpool's one-touch football.

21. A — CHELSEA — 23/12 — Att: 19,867 — D 0-0 (HT 0-0)
League pos: 10 (opp 22) · Pts: 22
Ref: H Robinson
Bristol City: Shaw, Sweeney, Gillies, Gow, Rodgers, Hunter, Tainton, Ritchie, Royle, Cormack, Whitehead
Chelsea: Iles, Harris, Stride, Nutton, Wicks, Bumstead, Stanley, McKenzie, Osgood, Langley, Britton

Without a win in seven games, and beaten 2-7 at Middlesbrough last Saturday, Chelsea prove to be stubborn opponents as they deny City their first-ever win at Stamford Bridge. The Pensioners supply plenty of speed and bustle in the first half, but after the break City take control.

LEAGUE DIVISION 1

Manager: Alan Dicks

SEASON 1978-79

No	Date	H/A	Team	Att	Pos	Pt	Res	F-A	H-T	Scorers, Times, and Referees	1	2	3	4	5	6	7	8	9	10	11	12 sub used
22	26/12	H	COVENTRY	23,335	7	24	W	5-0	2-0	Royle 17, 21, 50, Ritchie 52 [Cormack 74] — Ref: A Glasson	Shaw	Sweeney	Gillies	Gow	Rodgers	Hunter	Tainton	Ritchie	Royle	Cormack	Whitehead	
										Keeper Les Sealey performs miracles to keep the score down, but is unable to stop Royle's hat-trick. Ritchie's perfect pass sets up Royle to shoot in with clinical ease, then follows a stylish volley, before his header puts City well on the way to achieving their best ever top-flight win.	*Sealey*	*Coop*	*McDonald*	*Blair*	*Holton*	*Osgood*	*Hunt*	*Wallace*	*Thompson*	*Powell*	*Hutchison*	
23	30/12	H	MANCHESTER C	25,693	7	25	D	1-1	1-0	Ritchie 9 [Futcher R 66] — Ref: D Reeves	Shaw	Sweeney	Gillies	Gow	Rodgers	Hunter*	Tainton	Ritchie	Royle	Cormack	Whitehead	Mann
										City's 100th top-flight win is denied by opponents who have now gone eleven games without a win. Keeper Joe Corrigan is fortunate as three shots are repelled by his woodwork, but after Ritchie's header puts City in front, Ron Futcher's looping header saves the Maine Road men.	*Corrigan*	*Ranson*	*Donachie*	*Power*	*Watson*	*Futcher P*	*Channon*	*Owen*	*Futcher R*	*Hartford*	*Barnes*	
24	1/1	A	WEST BROM	31,738	7	25	L	1-3	1-2	Cormack 22p [Brown A 10, 82, Wile 43] — Ref: K Styles	Shaw	Sweeney	Gillies	Gow	Rodgers	Collier	Tainton	Ritchie	Royle*	Cormack	Whitehead	Mann
										Albion's new multi-studded astro-boots enable them to make a nonsense of the Siberian conditions at the Hawthorns. Alistair Brown fires the Baggies ahead, but Cormack levels with a twice-taken penalty, after Ritchie's header had been punched off the line by Brendon Batson.	*Godden*	*Batson*	*Statham*	*Brown T*	*Wile*	*Robertson*	*Robson*	*Brown A*	*Regis*	*Cantello*	*Cunningham*	
25	13/1	H	TOTTENHAM	29,122	7	26	D	0-0	0-0	Ref: P Reeves	Shaw	Sweeney	Gillies	Gow	Rodgers	Hunter	Tainton	Ritchie	Royle*	Cormack	Whitehead	
										Referee Peter Reeves is criticised by both managers for allowing this parody of a match to take place. Spurs' Argentinian pair Osvaldo Ardiles and Ricardo Villa are the only players able to master the icy conditions, and the nearest to a goal is Colin Lee's header which hits the crossbar.	*Kendall*	*Holmes*	*McAllister*	*Villa*	*Lacy*	*Perryman*	*Pratt*	*Ardiles*	*Lee*	*Jones*	*Taylor*	
26	3/2	H	IPSWICH	17,599	7	28	W	3-1	2-0	Whitehead 19, Tainton 26, Gow 89 [Mariner 90] — Ref: C Newsome	Shaw	Cooper	Gillies	Gow	Rodgers	Hunter	Tainton	Mabbutt	Royle	Cormack	Whitehead	
										After this impressive win the talk is of City gaining a place in Europe next term. Rodgers receives the plaudits of Ipswich boss Bobby Robson for reducing the Ipswich attack to virtual impotence. Whitehead volleys City in front, shortly after Shaw had pulled off two remarkable saves.	*Cooper*	*Mills*	*Tibbott*	*Parkin**	*Osman*	*Butcher*	*Wark*	*Muhren*	*Mariner*	*Whymark*	*Woods*	*Geddis*
27	10/2	A	EVERTON	29,116	7	28	L	1-4	1-1	Whitehead 10 [King 33, 65, 68, Wright 70] — Ref: G Owen	Shaw	Sweeney	Cooper	Gow	Rodgers	Hunter	Tainton	Ritchie	Royle	Cormack	Whitehead	
										City, who outplay Everton for long spells, are made to pay for not making the most of their greater opportunities after Whitehead slams in Gow's mis-hit shot. Andy King heads in Everton's leveller and completes a hat-trick by shooting in two of his three further chances.	*Wood*	*Robinson*	*Higgins*	*Lyons*	*Wright*	*Ross*	*Todd*	*Dobson*	*Latchford*	*King*	*Thomas*	
28	20/2	A	SOUTHAMPTON	19,845	7	28	L	0-2	0-2	[Hayes 9, Holmes 29] — Ref: B Homewood	Shaw	Sweeney	Cooper	Gow	Rodgers	Hunter	Tainton	Ritchie*	Royle	Cormack	Whitehead	Mabbutt
										Mabbutt's two glaring misses during his half-hour substitute appearance probably cost City a point. Hunter's 100th City game is marred by conceding the free-kick which led to Nick Holmes blasting the Saints into a two-goal lead, and a 38th-min booking for a foul on Austin Hayes.	*Gennoe*	*Golac*	*Peach*	*Baker*	*Nicholl*	*Waldron*	*Ball*	*Boyer*	*Hayes*	*Holmes*	*Curran*	
29	24/2	A	NOTT'M FOREST	28,008	7	28	L	0-2	0-2	[Needham 7, Birtles 15] — Ref: D Richardson	Cashley	Sweeney	Cooper	Gow	Rodgers	Collier	Tainton	Ritchie	Royle	Cormack*	Whitehead	Mabbutt
										Alan Dicks' ban on his players arguing with the referees backfires in this game as David Needham is palpably offside as he heads in Tony Woodcock's chip. Cashley does well on his return to the side, but he is powerless as Garry Birtles heads in John Robertson's magnificent cross.	*Shilton*	*Anderson*	*Clark*	*McGovern*	*Lloyd*	*Needham*	*O'Neill**	*Gemmill*	*Birtles*	*Woodcock*	*Robertson*	*Francis*
30	3/3	H	MANCHESTER U	24,583	10	28	L	1-2	1-0	Gow 18 [Ritchie 53, McQueen 76] — Ref: A Robinson	Cashley	Sweeney	Gillies	Gow	Collier	Hunter	Tainton	Garland	Royle	Mann	Whitehead	
										Cashley's injury just after the break costs City this game as his left arm is virtually useless following Andy Ritchie's shoulder charge. It is doubtful that a fit Cashley would have prevented Utd's well-struck equaliser, but he would certainly have stopped Gordon McQueen's header.	*Bailey*	*Nicholl*	*Albiston*	*McIlroy*	*McQueen*	*Buchan*	*Coppell*	*Greenhoff J*	*Ritchie*	*Grimes*	*Thomas*	
31	10/3	A	ARSENAL	24,288	13	28	L	0-2	0-2	[Rix 31, Stapleton 43] — Ref: H Robinson	Shaw	Sweeney	Gillies	Gow*	Collier	Hunter	Tainton	Garland	Royle	Mann	Whitehead	Ritchie
										A sunshine break in Torremolinos fails to change City's fortunes as they succumb to a fifth successive League defeat. The adoption of a 4-4-2 formation for the first time this season, even though a more adventurous policy is adopted at half-time, suggests they get what they deserve.	*Jennings*	*Rice*	*Nelson*	*Talbot*	*O'Leary*	*Walford*	*Brady*	*Heeley**	*Stapleton*	*Price*	*Rix*	*McDermott*

Season fixtures 32–42 (Bristol City)

#	Venue	Opponent	Date	Pos	W/D/L	FT	HT		Att
32	H	MIDDLESBROUGH	17/3	14	D	1-1	0-0	16 29	13,559
33	A	NORWICH	24/3	14	L	0-3	0-3	9 29	13,238
34	H	BIRMINGHAM	31/3	14	W	2-1	1-0	21 31	16,453
35	H	QP RANGERS	3/4	11	W	2-0	0-0	20 33	16,671
36	A	DERBY	7/4	9	W	1-0	1-0	18 35	17,090
37	H	CHELSEA	10/4	7	W	3-1	3-1	22 37	19,784
38	A	COVENTRY	14/4	8	L	2-3	0-3	7 37	17,681
39	H	WEST BROM	17/4	9	W	1-0	1-0	2 39	30,191
40	A	LIVERPOOL	21/4	9	L	0-1	0-1	1 39	43,191
41	H	LEEDS	28/4	11	D	0-0	0-0	5 40	26,041
42	A	MANCHESTER C	5/5	12	L	0-2	0-1	15 40	29,739

Home Average 22,306 — Away 24,717

---

32. MIDDLESBROUGH (H) — Gow 56; Armstrong 83. Ref: C Downey
City: Shaw, Sweeney, Gillies, Gow, Rodgers, Hunter, Tainton, Ritchie, Royle, Mabbutt, Whitehead
Middlesbrough: *Platt, Craggs, Johnson, Mahaney, Boam, McAndrew, Hodgson, Proctor, Ashcroft, Burns*, Armstrong, Jankovic*
With the Match of the Day cameras again at Ashton Gate, City show to a painful degree their now chronic incapacity to finish off uninspired opposition. Fortunate to have only conceded Gow's low cross-shot, Boro' steal a point with David Armstrong's crisp left-footed drive.

33. NORWICH (A) — Neighbour 9, Evans 26, Reeves 31. Ref: A Cox
City: Shaw, Sweeney, Gillies, Gow, Rodgers, Hunter, Tainton, Ritchie, Royle, Mabbutt, Whitehead
Norwich: *Hansbury, Bond, Davies*, McGuire, Hoadley, Powell, Neighbour, Reeves, Robson, Paddon, Evans, Cormack, Symonds*
Playing against a strong wind at the start, City's elementary blunders allow Norwich to shoot in all three of their goals. City never look capable of taking a point off the draw specialists, and boss Dicks flies off to Holland to check on the form of Ajax's mercurial winger Geert Meijer.

34. BIRMINGHAM (H) — Meijer 5, Garland 89; Gallagher 47. Ref: M Sinclair
City: Shaw, Sweeney, Cooper, Gow, Rodgers, Hunter, Mann, Ritchie, Royle*, Mabbutt*, Meijer*, Garland
Birmingham: *Freeman, Page, Dennis, Towers, Gallagher, Tarantini, Ainscow, Broadhurst, Givens*, Dillion, Barrowclough, Calderwood*
A Dutch treat as City's new £92,000 signing gets his English career off to a great start with a left-footed shot into the far right-hand corner of the Open End goal. After Joe Gallagher heads the Blues level, Garland clinches City's first win in eight with a great 20-yard banana shot.

35. QP RANGERS (H) — Mabbutt 55, 68. Ref: D Lloyd
City: Shaw, Sweeney, Cooper, Mann, Rodgers, Hunter, Mann*, Ritchie, Royle, Mabbutt, Meijer, Whitehead
QP Rangers: *Richardson, Clement, Wallace, Roeder, Howe, Hollins, Shanks*, Busby, Walsh, McGee, Goddard, Allen*
Meijer again excels with his varied crosses and telling through balls, but Derek Richardson smothers his low drive to prevent him getting on the scoresheet. Cooper's forays down the left contribute to City's dominating display, which is rewarded by Mabbutt twice shooting in.

36. DERBY (A) — Ritchie 79. Ref: D Clarke
City: Shaw, Sweeney, Cooper, Gow, Rodgers, Hunter, Mann, Ritchie, Royle, Mabbutt, Meijer, Whitehead
Derby: *Middleton, Langan, Buckley, Daly*, Webb, Wicks, Carter, Powell, Greenwood, Moreland, Crawford, Caskey*
A stamina-sapping game on a morass of a pitch, covered with 100 tons of sand – Derby boss Tommy Docherty claiming it was done without his knowledge - to dry out the waterlogged surface. Ritchie's far-post header to Meijer's cross is fitting testament to City's great durability.

37. CHELSEA (H) — Rodgers 50, Mabbutt 66, Meijer 68; Langley 60p. Ref: A Seville
City: Shaw, Sweeney, Cooper, Gow, Rodgers, Hunter, Mann*, Ritchie, Royle, Mabbutt, Meijer, Whitehead
Chelsea: *Borota, Wilkins G, Stride, Bannon, Droy, Nutton, Harris, Wilkins R, Aylott, Langley, Fillery*
City notch up their fourth win in ten days over the basement clubs. Rodgers breaks the deadlock by blasting the ball in after every other player fails to read the referee's excellent advantage following a push on Royle, but Chelsea level from the spot after Ritchie sends Fillery sprawling.

38. COVENTRY (A) — Mabbutt 76, Gow 88; Powell 5p, Hutchison 7, Hunt 29. Ref: K Hackett
City: Shaw, Sweeney, Cooper, Gow*, Rodgers*, Hunter, Mann, Ritchie, Royle, Mabbutt, Meijer
Coventry: *Sealey, Roberts, McDonald, Yorath*, Holton, Coop, Nardiello, Blair, Hunt, Powell, Hutchison, Hagan*
City take over the mantle of superiority after the break, but run out of time in their efforts to equalise. Cooper is stunned to concede Powell's pen after going up for the ball with Brian Roberts, but no dispute over Steve Hunt's spectacular overhead that puts Coventry firmly in control.

39. WEST BROM (H) — Mabbutt 69. Ref: J Martin
City: Shaw, Sweeney, Whitehead, Gow, Rodgers*, Hunter, Mann*, Ritchie, Royle, Mabbutt, Meijer
West Brom: *Godden, Batson, Statham, Mills, Wile, Robertson, Robson, Brown A, Regis, Cantello, Cunningham*
Albion look anything but possible champions as they exhibit little of the flair that has made them such an outstanding team. City claim the points that their dominating display deserves, when Mabbutt follows up to stab in a rebound after Tony Godden palms out his free-header.

40. LIVERPOOL (A) — Dalglish 6. Ref: P Partridge
City: Shaw, Sweeney, Whitehead, Gow*, Collier, Hunter, Tainton, Ritchie, Royle, Mabbutt, Meijer
Liverpool: *Clemence, Neal, Kennedy A, Thompson, Kennedy R, Hansen, Dalglish, Case, Johnson*, McDermott, Souness, Heighway, Jantunen*
With only one win in their previous five meetings Liverpool, who were beginning to view City encounters with some apprehension, are a trifle fortunate to win this one. An untidy goal settles the issue as Kenny Dalglish pounces on David Johnson's mis-kick to slide the ball in.

41. LEEDS (H) — Ref: L Burden
City: Shaw, Sweeney, Whitehead, Gow, Collier, Hunter, Tainton, Ritchie, Royle, Mabbutt, Meijer
Leeds: *Harvey, Hird, Gray F, Hampton!, Hart, Cherry, Harris, Hankin, Madeley, Gray E, Graham*
Mabbutt reacts angrily to Leeds boss Jimmy Adamson's comment that Peter Hampton's 69th-minute over the top tackle did not warrant him being sent off. A typically poor end of the season game is only notable by the presentation of a silver salver to Norman Hunter by City fans.

42. MANCHESTER C (A) — Deyna 41, Hartford 83. Ref: T Mills
City: Shaw, Sweeney, Whitehead, Gow, Collier, Hunter, Tainton, Ritchie, Royle, Mabbutt*, Meijer
Manchester C: *Corrigan, Reid, Donachie, Henry, Watson, Bell, Channon, Deyna, Silkman, Hartford, Power, Mann*
City outplay the Blues at Maine Road, but fail miserably in front of goal after producing some of their best approach play of the season. Kazru Deyna side-steps Shaw to clip the ball into an open goal and then Asa Hartford ties up Man City's flattering win with a 15-yard low drive.

LEAGUE DIVISION 1 (CUP-TIES)

Manager: Alan Dicks

League Cup

					F-A	H-T	Scorers, Times, and Referees
2	H	CRYS PALACE	5	L	1-2	0-1	Ritchie 54
	10,924 2:6						Murphy 16, Swindlehurst 82
							Ref: A. Glasson

	1	2	3	4	5	6	7	8	9	10	11	12 sub used
	Shaw	Sweeney	Gillies	Mann	Rodgers	Hunter	Tainton	Ritchie	Royle*	Pritchard	Whitehead	Garland
	Burridge	*Hinshelwood*	*Sansom*	*Chatterton*	*Cannon*	*Gilbert*	*Murphy*	*Nicholas*	*Swindlehurst*	*Elwiss*	*Hilaire*	

Woeful City are made to pay for squandering two good early chances as Jerry Murphy fires the Glaziers in front. Ritchie's jabbed-in equaliser makes up for offside disallowing his shot two minutes earlier, but David Swindlehurst's firm header brings a deserved success for the Palace.

FA Cup

					F-A	H-T	Scorers, Times, and Referees
3	H	BOLTON	7	W	3-1	0-0	Gow 62, Rodgers 65, Ritchie 82
	17,392 17						Smith 64
							Ref: L. Shapter

	1	2	3	4	5	6	7	8	9	10	11	12 sub used
	Shaw	Sweeney	Gillies	Gow	Rodgers	Hunter	Tainton	Ritchie	Royle	Cormack	Whitehead	
	McDonagh	*Nicholson*	*Dunne*	*Greaves*	*Jones P*	*Walsh*	*Morgan*	*Smith*	*Gowling*	*Worthington*	*McNab*	

City clear the third-round hurdle for the first time in four years after Gow sparks the game into life with a right-footed shot past Jim McDonagh. Brian Smith gives Bolton hope as he nips in for a fine solo goal, but Rodgers side-foots the ball home almost immediately.

					F-A	H-T	Scorers, Times, and Referees
4	A	CRYS PALACE	7	L	0-3	0-1	Nicholas 21, Fenwick 55, Kember 87
	21,463 2:1						Ref: K. McNally

	1	2	3	4	5	6	7	8	9	10	11	12 sub used
	Shaw	Sweeney	Gillies	Gow	Rodgers	Hunter !	Tainton	Ritchie !	Royle	Cormack*	Whitehead	Mann
	Burridge	*Hinshelwood*	*Sansom*	*Kember*	*Cannon*	*Gilbert*	*Nicholas*	*Murphy*	*Swindlehurst*	*Fenwick*	*Walsh*	

Ref Kevin McNally is criticised for sending off Hunter and Ritchie in the 52nd and 88th mins respectively, as well as booking four other players as City make an inglorious exit. Kenny Sansom lays on the decisive second goal for Terry Fenwick to steer into the corner of the net.

Football League Division One — Final Table

Pos	Team	P	W (H)	D	L	F	A	W (A)	D	L	F	A	Pts
1	Liverpool	42	19	2	0	51	4	11	6	4	34	12	68
2	Nott'm Forest	42	11	10	0	34	10	10	8	3	27	16	60
3	West Brom	42	13	5	3	38	15	11	6	4	34	20	59
4	Everton	42	12	7	2	32	17	5	10	6	20	23	51
5	Leeds	42	11	4	6	41	25	7	10	4	29	27	50
6	Ipswich	42	11	4	6	34	21	9	5	7	29	28	49
7	Arsenal	42	11	8	2	37	18	6	6	9	24	30	48
8	Aston Villa	42	8	9	4	37	26	9	7	7	22	23	46
9	Manchester U	42	9	5	5	29	25	6	8	7	31	38	45
10	Coventry	42	11	7	3	41	29	3	9	9	17	39	44
11	Tottenham	42	7	8	6	19	25	6	7	8	29	36	41
12	Middlesbro	42	10	5	6	33	21	5	5	11	24	36	40
13	BRISTOL CITY	42	11	6	4	34	19	4	4	13	13	32	40
14	Southampton	42	9	10	2	35	20	3	6	12	12	33	40
15	Manchester C	42	9	5	7	34	28	4	8	9	24	28	39
16	Norwich	42	7	10	4	29	19	0	13	8	22	38	37
17	Bolton	42	10	5	6	36	28	2	6	13	18	47	35
18	Wolves	42	10	4	7	26	26	3	4	14	18	42	34
19	Derby	42	8	5	8	25	25	2	6	13	19	46	31
20	QP Rangers	42	4	9	8	24	33	2	4	15	21	40	25
21	Birmingham	42	5	9	7	24	25	1	1	19	13	39	22
22	Chelsea	42	3	5	13	23	42	2	5	14	21	50	20
		924	209	144	109	716	501	109	144	209	501	716	924

Odds & ends

Double wins: (3) Bolton, Ipswich, Derby.
Double losses: (3) Wolves, Nott'm Forest, Arsenal.

Won from behind: (2) Bolton (a), Bolton (h).
Lost from in front: (2) Everton (a), Manchester U (h).

High spots: Winning 3-1 at Old Trafford on 21 October.
Beating Coventry (h) 5-0 (City's record top-flight win).
Hammering Bristol Rov (h) 6-1 in the Anglo-Scottish Cup on 5 August.
Winning 2-0 at Eastville to secure the Gloucestershire Cup on 15 May.

Low spots: Poor form after the turn of the year that saw the chance of
European qualification slip from City's grasp.
Losing to Crystal Palace in both the FA and the League Cup.

Player of the year: Gerry Gow.
Ever-presents: (1) Gerry Sweeney.
Hat-tricks: (2) Kevin Mabbutt, Joe Royle.
Leading scorer: Tom Ritchie (11).

Appearances and Goals

Player	Lge	Sub	LC	Sub	FAC	Sub	Lge	LC	FAC	Tot
Bain, Jimmy	3	1								
Cashley, Ray	2									
Collier, Gary	9									
Cooper, Terry	11									
Cormack, Peter	14	3			2		3			3
Garland, Chris	4	1		1			1			1
Gillies, Donnie	27		1		2		1			1
Gow, Gerry	38		1		2		5	1		6
Hunter, Norman	39		1				1			1
Jantunen, Pertti		1								
Mabbutt, Kevin	26	1					9			9
Mann, Jimmy	23	5	1			1	1			1
Meijer, Geert	9						2			2
Pritchard, Howard	1		1							
Ritchie, Tom	39	1	1		2		9	1	1	11
Rodgers, David	36		1		2		5		1	6
Royle, Joe	40		1		2		7			7
Shaw, John	40		1		2					
Sweeney, Gerry	42		1		2					
Tainton, Trevor	37	1	1		2		1			1
Whitehead, Clive	22	8	1		2		2			2
21 players used	462	21	11	1	22	1	47	1	3	51

LEAGUE DIVISION 1
Manager: Alan Dicks
SEASON 1979-80

No	Date	Opponent	Att	Pos	Pt	F-A	H-T	Scorers, Times, and Referees	1	2	3	4	5	6	7	8	9	10	11	12 sub used
1	H 18/8	LEEDS	23,331		D 1	2-2	1-1	Ritchie 34p, Jantunen 65 / *Curtis 9, 82* / Ref: D Lloyd	Shaw	Sweeney	Whitehead	Gow	Rodgers	Merrick	Fitzpatrick	Ritchie	Mabbutt	Jantunen	Meijer	Cherry
									Harvey	*Hird*	*Stevenson*	*Flynn*	*Parkinson*	*Hampton*	*Curtis*	*Cherry*	*Hankin*	*Harris*	*Graham*	
2	A 21/8	COVENTRY	19,208		L 1	1-3	1-1	Ritchie 37p / *English 24, Powell 63p, Hutchison 83* / Ref: N Ashley	Shaw	Sweeney	Whitehead	Gow	Rodgers*	Merrick	Fitzpatrick	Ritchie	Mabbutt	Jantunen	Meijer	Tainton
									Blyth	*Jones*	*McDonald*	*Blair*	*Holton*	*Gillespie*	*Hutchison*	*English*	*Ferguson*	*Powell*	*Hunt**	*Hateley*
3	A 25/8	ASTON VILLA	25,526 *13*	11	W 3	2-0	1-0	Mabbutt 17, Ritchie 89p / Ref: G Nolan	Shaw	Sweeney	Whitehead	Gow	Rodgers	Merrick	Fitzpatrick	Ritchie	Mabbutt*	Jantunen	Royle	Mann
									Rimmer	*Swain*	*Gibson*	*Evans*	*McNaught*	*Williams*	*Morley*	*Little**	*Deehan*	*Cowans*	*Shelton*	*Linton*
4	H 1/9	WOLVES	19,428 *8*	6	W 5	2-0	1-0	Gow 8, Royle 72 / Ref: J Martin	Shaw	Tainton	Whitehead	Gow	Sweeney	Merrick	Fitzpatrick	Ritchie	Mabbutt	Jantunen	Royle	Mabbutt
									Bradshaw	*Palmer*	*Parkin*	*Daniel*	*Berry*	*Hughes*	*Hibbitt*	*Carr*	*Rafferty*	*Clarke*	*Patching*	
5	A 8/9	IPSWICH	16,878 *6*	10	L 5	0-1	0-0	*Woods 53* / Ref: K Salmon	Shaw	Tainton	Whitehead	Gow	Sweeney	Merrick	Fitzpatrick	Ritchie	Royle	Jantunen*	Mabbutt	Cormack
									Cooper	*Burley*	*Mills*	*Osborne*	*Osman*	*Butcher*	*Wark*	*Muhren*	*Marine**	*Brazil*	*Woods*	*Gates*
6	H 15/9	STOKE	16,917 *14*	10	D 6	0-0	0-0	Ref: C Thomas/R Gifford	Shaw	Tainton	Whitehead	Gow	Sweeney	Merrick	Fitzpatrick	Ritchie	Royle*	Mann	Meijer	Richardson
									Johns	*Evans*	*Scott*	*Irvine*	*Smith*	*Doyle*	*Dodd*	*Heath*	*O'Callaghan*	*Crooks*	*Richardson*	
7	H 22/9	NOTT'M FOREST	22,767 *2*	10	D 7	1-1	1-0	Mann 35 / *Mills 72* / Ref: M Baker	Shaw	Tainton	Whitehead	Gow	Sweeney	Merrick	Fitzpatrick	Ritchie*	Mabbutt	Mann	Cormack	Royle
									Shilton	*Anderson*	*Gray*	*McGovern*	*Lloyd*	*Burns*	*Mills*	*O'Hare*	*Birtles*	*Woodcock*	*Robertson*	
8	A 29/9	EVERTON	24,733 *12*	8	D 8	0-0	0-0	Ref: G Napthine	Shaw	Tainton	Whitehead	Gow	Sweeney	Merrick	Fitzpatrick	Ritchie	Mabbutt	Mann	Mabbutt	Hay
									Wood	*Barton**	*Bailey*	*Lyons*	*Higgins*	*Ross*	*Hartford*	*Stanley*	*King*	*Kidd*	*Eastoe*	*Wright*
9	A 6/10	LIVERPOOL	38,213 *8*	12	L 8	0-4	0-3	*Johnson 4, Dalglish 31, Kennedy R 35, [McDermott 80]* / Ref: P Partridge	Shaw	Tainton	Whitehead	Gow	Sweeney	Merrick	Fitzpatrick	Ritchie	Royle	Jantunen*	Mabbutt	Cormack
									Clemence	*Neal*	*Kennedy A*	*Thompson*	*Kennedy R*	*Hansen*	*Dalglish*	*Case*	*Johnson*	*McDermott*	*Souness*	
10	H 9/10	COVENTRY	15,300 *12*	10	W 10	1-0	0-0	Ritchie 58 / Ref: A Cox	Shaw	Sweeney	Whitehead	Gow	Rodgers	Merrick	Fitzpatrick	Ritchie	Royle	Mann	Tainton	Cormack
									Sealey	*Coop*	*McDonald*	*Gooding*	*Holton*	*Gillespie*	*Nardiello*	*Wallace*	*Hutchison*	*Powell*	*Hunt*	

Match reports

1. After an uneasy opening City settle down to play some polished football. Ex Swansea striker Alan Curtis has a dream debut for Leeds as he fires in both of his chances. Keith Parkinson pushes Ritchie in the back for his penalty, whilst Jantunen nets with an unstoppable 20-yard drive.

2. Tom English jabs Coventry ahead, but City equalise after David Jones brings down Finnish international Jantunen. The ball hits Merrick's arm to gift Coventry their penalty kick, but few can argue with the final result as the Sky Blues have a shots on target advantage of eleven to two.

3. City's slick football before the interval is replaced by resolute defending after the break. Mabbutt nips in to head in the opener, then with Villa down to ten men following the loss of the injured Gary Williams, Ritchie easily scores from the spot after being brought down by Ivor Linton.

4. Despite being over-run City's patched-up defence keeps a clean sheet for a third successive League and Cup match. Wolves are frustrated by Shaw's great display between the sticks and their own poor finishing, as City take the points with easy open goal shots for Gow and Royle.

5. Arnold Muhren gives a lesson in first-time passing as City's outplayed midfield gets bogged down. Three magnificent saves by Shaw keep City in with a chance of saving the game, but the unequal deadlock is broken when George Burley's cross sets up Clive Woods to shoot in.

6. Sweeney is the crowd's scapegoat for City's lacklustre display against a Stoke side who field an extra defender in place of ex Rovers' forward Paul Randall. The only entertainment is a pulled calf muscle that causes the referee to hand over to Roger Gifford after just two minutes.

7. City create little against a Forest side who miss a host of chances, but Mann's cannonball shooting almost brings an unlikely victory. He puts City ahead with a stupendous 35-yarder that dumbfounds Peter Shilton, then hits the bar from 25 yards, before Gary Mills shoots in for Forest.

8. A more adventurous approach might well have secured both points against a laboured Everton side seeking their first home win of the season. Royle puts in a hard-working performance against his old club, but it is skipper Gow who wastes City's best chance by shooting over the bar.

9. Liverpool take control of their 3,000th League game when David Johnson is free to head in Alan Kennedy's free-kick, but 16 minutes later Ritchie's header forces Ray Clemence to pull off a great save. Over-run in midfield before the break, City recover in a more even second half.

10. City, who have yet to put a fluent game together this season, are again unconvincing as Ritchie's low left-foot drive brings a rather lucky win. Dicks defends his 4-4-2 line-up as being necessary to tighten the defence, but City's clean sheet owes more to their opponents' poor finishing.

11 H MANCHESTER U — 13/10 — 11 D 1-1 — 11 *1* 11 — 28,305
Rodgers 38 / *Macari 21* — Ref: A Gunn

| Shaw | Sweeney | Whitehead | Gow | Rodgers* | Merrick | Fitzpatrick | Ritchie | Royle | Mann | Tainton | Mabbutt |
| *Bailey* | *Nichol* | *Albiston* | *McIlroy* | *McQueen* | *Buchan* | *Grimes* | *Wilkins* | *Coppell* | *Macari* | *Thomas* | |

City are unfortunate in not being able to add to their first-half score when Rodgers stabbed in the equaliser, as Utd run out of steam. In the final ten mins both Mann and Ritchie hit the bar, whilst Mann has two shots scrambled off the line, and Gary Bailey makes a great save from Royle.

---

12 A CRYS PALACE — 20/10 — 13 D 1-1 — 3 *12* — 27,499
Royle 67 / *Cannon 79p* — Ref: J Sewell

| Shaw | Sweeney | Whitehead | Gow* | Rodgers | Merrick | Fitzpatrick | Ritchie | Royle | Mann | Tainton | Mabbutt |
| *Burridge* | *Hinshelwood* | *Sansom* | *Nicholas* | *Cannon* | *Gilbert* | *Murphy* | *Kember* | *Walsh* | *Flanagan* | *Hilaire* | |

Vince Hilaire robs City of both points with a theatrical fall that gives Palace a controversial second penalty, 27 minutes after Shaw had saved Mike Flanagan's earlier effort. Royle's goal, which is brilliantly lobbed over the advancing John Burridge, is deserving of being a winner.

---

13 H ARSENAL — 27/10 — 16 L 0-1 — 8 *12* — 22,927
Sunderland 66 — Ref: D Civil

| Shaw | Sweeney | Whitehead | Mabbutt | Rodgers | Merrick | Fitzpatrick | Ritchie | Royle | Mann | Tainton |
| *Jennings* | *Rice* | *Nelson* | *Talbot* | *O'Leary* | *Young* | *Brady* | *Sunderland* | *Stapleton* | *Hollins* | *Rix* |

Alan Sunderland consigns City to their first home defeat in 15 matches, effortlessly stabbing in a rebound after Shaw blocks his first effort. Arsenal are the more accomplished side as City only put their game together during the final 20 minutes when Mabbutt wastes two chances.

---

14 A LEEDS — 3/11 — 11 W 3-1 — 17 *14* — 17,377
Mabbutt 20, 51, Merrick 54 / *Gray 1* — Ref: K Walmsley

| Shaw | Sweeney | Whitehead | Mabbutt | Hay* | Merrick | Fitzpatrick | Ritchie | Royle | Mann | Tainton | Meijer |
| *Lukic* | *Cherry* | *Stevenson* | *Hampton** | *Hart* | *Madeley* | *Chandler* | *Entwhistle* | *Hankin* | *Curtis* | *Gray* | *Harris* |

Despite Eddie Gray driving in the opener after just 28 seconds, City gain a comprehensive win at Elland Road and move to within six points of the top of the table. A trio of headers clinches the points in front of a restless crowd who chant for the sacking of Leeds boss Jimmy Adamson.

---

15 H DERBY — 10/11 — 15 L 0-2 — 19 *14* — 16,943
Moreland 34, Duncan 44 — Ref: L Shapter

| Shaw | Sweeney | Whitehead | Kenyon | Hay* | Merrick | Fitzpatrick | Ritchie | Royle | Mann | Tainton | Meijer |
| *McKellar* | *Langan* | *Buckley* | *Clark* | *McCaffery* | *Osgood* | *Emery* | *Powell* | *Duncan* | *Davies* | *Moreland* | |

Inept City are killed off just before half-time with Vic Moreland's header and a toe-poke from John Duncan bringing Derby their first away win in 16 games. City's switch to all-out attack, on Meijer's appearance after the break, alters little as the Derby keeper hasn't a save to make.

---

16 A MIDDLESBROUGH — 17/11 — 16 L 0-1 — 7 *14* — 14,517
Armstrong 71 — Ref: K McNally

| Shaw | Sweeney | Gillies | Tainton | Rodgers | Merrick | Fitzpatrick | Ritchie | Mabbutt* | Mann | Garland | Pritchard |
| *Platt* | *Craggs* | *Peters* | *Nattrass* | *Ashcroft* | *McAndrew* | *Cochrane* | *Bell* | *Hodgson* | *Burns* | *Armstrong* | |

Boro' captain Tony McAndrew is lucky not to be sent off in the 23rd min for a dreadful tackle on Mabbutt, who is replaced at half-time. City, who play attractive football without really threatening, are killed off when David Armstrong finishes his 40-yard dash with a low cross-shot.

---

17 H MANCHESTER C — 24/11 — 14 W 1-0 — 13 *16* — 18,549
Rodgers 29 — Ref: D Hutchinson

| Shaw | Sweeney | Whitehead | Gow | Rodgers | Merrick | Fitzpatrick | Tainton* | Royle | Mann | Garland | Ritchie |
| *Corrigan* | *Ranson* | *Donachie* | *Bennett* | *Caton* | *Stepanovic* | *Henry* | *Daley* | *Robinson* | *Power!* | *Deyna* | |

Tony Fitzpatrick, City's record £250,000 signing from St Mirren, is the star of this exciting game as his classic cross sets up Rodgers to head the only goal. Manchester skipper Paul Power is sent off for foul and abusive language in the 79th minute following an offside dispute.

---

18 A BOLTON — 1/12 — 14 D 1-1 — 22 *17* — 12,074
Rodgers 47 / *Greaves 90* — Ref: J Bray

| Shaw | Sweeney | Whitehead | Gow | Rodgers | Merrick | Fitzpatrick | Tainton | Royle | Mann | Garland |
| *McDonagh* | *Nicholson* | *Burke* | *Greaves* | *Jones* | *Walsh* | *Morgan* | *Whatmore* | *Dowling** | *Cantello* | *McNab* | *Carter* |

Poetic justice perhaps after City have a lucky escape in the 84th minute when the referee waves play-on as Peter Nicholson is felled in the area. In the third minute of injury-time Ray Greaves shoots in Bolton's leveller from eight yards, with City appealing that Nicholson is offside.

---

19 H TOTTENHAM — 8/12 — 17 L 1-3 — 6 *17* — 25,090
Ritchie 84p / *Miller 21, Hoddle 72p, 90* — Ref: D Letts

| Shaw | Sweeney | Whitehead | Gow | Rodgers | Merrick | Fitzpatrick | Tainton | Royle | Mann | Garland | Ritchie |
| *Daines* | *Hughton* | *Miller* | *Pratt* | *Smith* | *Perryman* | *Ardiles* | *Jones* | *Lee* | *Hoddle* | *Villa* | |

Talk of relegation is in the air as City are outclassed and over-run. Osvaldo Ardiles appears to take a dive for Spurs' penalty, but he lays on the goal of the match at the death, as he twists and turns past three men before setting up Hoddle to finish off his classic cross with a diving header.

---

20 A NORWICH — 15/12 — 19 L 0-2 — 5 *17* — 11,657
Taylor 25, Robson 46 — Ref: G Flint

| Shaw | Sweeney | Whitehead | Gow | Rodgers* | Merrick | Fitzpatrick | Tainton | Royle | Mann | Garland | Cormack |
| *Keelan* | *Bond* | *Downs* | *Ryan* | *Brown* | *Jones* | *Mendham** | *Taylor* | *Robson* | *Paddon* | *Peters* | *Lythgoe* |

Another poor performance as City slither to defeat on the first really heavy pitch of the season. Defensive blunders are City's undoing as a poor header by the concussed Rodgers leads to Alan Taylor shooting in the first goal, then Cormack's back-pass gifts Keith Robson the second.

---

21 H SOUTHAMPTON — 21/12 — 19 L 0-1 — 5 *17* — 14,185
Channon 53 — Ref: D Reeves

| Shaw | Sweeney | Whitehead | Gow | Kenyon | Merrick | Fitzpatrick | Tainton | Royle | Mann* | Mabbutt |
| *Wells* | *Golac* | *Peach* | *Williams* | *Watson* | *Nicholl* | *Ball* | *Boyer* | *Channon* | *Holmes* | *Hebberd* |

Mabbutt is robbed of a clear scoring opportunity in the 86th minute when he is grabbed around the waist by Chris Nicholl, who only receives a yellow card for his professional foul. On a snow-covered pitch Southampton deserve the points gained by Mike Channon's 15-yard drive.

LEAGUE DIVISION 1   Manager: Alan Dicks   SEASON 1979-80

No	Date		Att	Pos	Pt	F-A	H-T	1	2	3	4	5	6	7	8	9	10	11	12 sub used
22	A 26/12	WEST BROM	19,490	20 L 16	17	0-3	0-0	Shaw / *Godden*	Sweeney / *Batson*	Whitehead / *Pendrey*	Gow / *Trewick*	Kenyon / *Wile*	Merrick / *Robertson*	Fitzpatrick / *Robson*	Tainton / *Deehan*	Royle / *Regis*	Mabbutt / *Owen*	Mann* / *Barnes*	Meijer
23	H 29/12	ASTON VILLA	18,799	20 L 6	17	1-3	0-0	Shaw / *Rimmer*	Sweeney / *Swain*	Whitehead / *Gibson*	Gow / *Ormsby*	Rodgers / *McNaught*	Merrick / *Mortimer*	Pritchard / *Bremner*	Tainton / *Little*	Mabbutt / *Donovan*	Mann / *Cowans*	Garland / *Shaw*	
24	H 1/1	BRIGHTON	19,896	20 D 18	18	2-2	1-0	Shaw / *Moseley*	Tainton / *Gregory*	Whitehead / *Williams*	Gow / *Horton*	Rodgers / *Foster*	Merrick / *Stevens*	Pritchard / *Ryan*	Fitzpatrick / *Ward*	Mabbutt* / *Clarke*	Mann / *Lawrenson*	Garland / *O'Sullivan*	Ritchie
25	A 12/1	WOLVES	18,835	20 L 12	18	0-3	0-1	Shaw / *Bradshaw*	Tainton / *Palmer*	Whitehead / *Parkin*	Gow / *Daniel*	Rodgers / *McAlle*	Merrick / *Berry*	Pritchard / *Atkinson*	Fitzpatrick* / *Carr*	Ritchie / *Gray*	Mann / *Richards*	Garland / *Thomas*	Sweeney
26	H 19/1	IPSWICH	15,004	20 L 5	18	0-3	0-1	Shaw / *Cooper*	Tainton / *Burley*	Whitehead / *Mills*	Gow / *Thijssen*	Rodgers / *Osman*	Sweeney / *Butcher*	Pritchard / *Wark*	Fitzpatrick / *Muhren*	Royle / *Mariner*	Jantunen / *Brazil*	Garland / *Gates*	Gates
27	A 2/2	STOKE	14,510	20 L 19	18	0-1	0-0	Shaw / *Fox*	Gillies / *Evans*	Whitehead / *Johnson*	Tainton / *Irvine*	Rodgers / *Smith*	Kenyon / *Dodd*	Pritchard / *Heath*	Fitzpatrick / *Richardson*	Ritchie* / *Chapman*	Sweeney / *Crooks*	Garland / *Cook*	**Doyle**
28	A 9/2	NOTT'M FOREST	23,421	20 D 6	19	0-0	0-0	Cashley / *Shilton*	Sweeney / *Anderson*	Whitehead / *Gunn*	Tainton / *McGovern*	Rodgers / *Lloyd*	Merrick / *Burns*	Pritchard / *O'Neill*	Fitzpatrick / *Bowles*	Royle / *Birtles*	Ritchie / *George*	Doyle / *Robinson*	
29	H 19/2	EVERTON	16,317	20 W 19	21	2-1	0-1	Cashley / *Hodge*	Sweeney / *Gidman*	Whitehead / *Bailey*	Gow / *Wright*	Rodgers / *Lyons*	Merrick / *Ross*	Pritchard / *Megson*	Fitzpatrick / *Eastoe*	Royle / *Hartford*	Ritchie / *Kidd*	Tainton / *McBride*	
30	A 23/2	MANCHESTER U	43,329	20 L 2	21	**0-4**	0-3	Cashley / *Bailey*	Bailey / *Nicholl*	Whitehead / *Houston*	Gow / *McIlroy*	Rodgers / *McQueen**	Merrick / *Buchan*	Pritchard / *Coppell*	Fitzpatrick / *Wilkins*	Royle* / *Jordan*	Ritchie / *Macari*	Tainton / *Grimes*	Mabbutt / *Ritchie*
31	H 1/3	CRYS PALACE	16,549	20 L 10	21	0-2	0-0	Cashley / *Fry*	Sweeney / *Hinshelwood*	Whitehead / *Sansom*	Gow / *Nicholas*	Rodgers / *Cannon*	Merrick / *Gilbert*	Pritchard / *Murphy*	Fitzpatrick / *Francis*	Royle / *Walsh*	Ritchie* / *Flanagan*	Tainton / *Hilaire*	Mabbutt

Scorers, Times, and Referees

22 — West Brom: Owen 75, Barnes 80, 89. Ref: R Toseland
'The best three goals I've ever had scored against me' is Shaw's praise for the Albion strikers. Gary Owen's 25-yard chip is followed by Peter Barnes' two goals, a left-footed flick after a 50-yard dribble, and a ferocious low drive after another fine scamper down the touchline.

23 — Aston Villa: Gow 75p. Shaw 51, 54, 76. Ref: D Hedges
City play much good football, but they are unable to finish off the chances that Pritchard supplies from the wing. Gary Shaw's second goal for Villa is a magnificent 35-yard strike, but he is lucky with his first that goes in off his neck following a corner, as his namesake is impeded.

24 — Brighton: Gow 23p, 71p. Clarke 55, Rodgers 75 (og). Ref: M Robinson
City create the greater number of chances, but Rodgers slices Peter Ward's cross into his own net to enable Brighton to sustain their revival of 13 points from the last nine games. Whitehead causes panic with his overlaps and he is twice scythed down for Gow to slot in from the spot.

25 — Wolves: Gray 17, Richards 75, Daniel 89. Ref: R Chadwick
The message is clear – buy or be relegated as the best City can manage in this game is Garland's 25-yarder that hits the post in the 84th min. A brilliant 22-yard chip by John Richards is the goal of the game, while the impressive Peter Daniel finishes off the best move of the match.

26 — Ipswich: Gates 42, Brazil 73, Mariner 87. Ref: J Warner
Alan Brazil's outstanding strike as he turns inside two defenders before zipping a shot into the far corner of the net is the turning point, just six mins after Garland's crisp low left-footed effort hits the base of the far post. Paul Mariner's shot through Shaw's legs completes City's demise.

27 — Stoke: Rodgers 56 (og). Ref: M Lowe
Whilst Rodgers unluckily diverts Garth Crook's pull-back into his own goal, City can have few complaints over losing this vital encounter. Stoke have three goals disallowed, including Paul Richardson's successful 62nd-min spot-kick having to be retaken due to encroachment.

28 — Nott'm Forest: Ref: D Owen
A massed defence and a gluey surface combine to frustrate Forest, who are never able to demonstrate their prime attacking quality of pace. City offer little in attack, though Peter Shilton denies Royle a goal, and then when Rodgers' header beats him, Bryn Gunn heads clear.

29 — Everton: Ritchie 58, Rodgers 68. Ross 45. Ref: C Downey
City demonstrate great resolve in overcoming the setback of conceding Trevor Ross's gloriously angled shot right on half-time, after Royle and Tainton had both been denied by the post. Pritchard's cross sets up Ritchie's headed equaliser, then Rodgers hooks in to clinch the points.

30 — Manchester U: Jordan 7, 48, McIlroy 39, Mer'k 43 (og). Ref: G Tyson
On Match of the Day City look like title contenders with their neat, composed football. United though have Joe Jordan, and he arrives at the far post to head home after Ashley Grimes' corner had been deflected, and completes the scoring with an arrogant header from a Grimes cross.

31 — Crys Palace: Nicholas 57, Flanagan 87. Ref: V Callow
City waste their opportunities before Peter Nicholas sets Palace on the way to both points by shooting in a loose ball after Vince Hilaire muffs his kick. Neither side show much in the way of First Division quality as Mike Flanagan heads in to complete Palace's rather flattering success.

City Match Record (matches 32–42)

No.	H/A	Date	Opponent	Pos	Res			FT	HT	Scorers
32	A	11/3	ARSENAL	20 / 4	D		22	0-0	0-0	
33	H	15/3	LIVERPOOL	21 / 1	L		22	1-3	0-1	Mabbutt 63 / Kennedy R 5, Dalglish 55, 89
34	A	22/3	DERBY	21 / 20	D		23	3-3	2-1	Ritchie 20, 28p, Mann 58 / Biley 45, 48, 54p
35	H	5/4	WEST BROM	21 / 10	D		24	0-0	0-0	
36	A	7/4	BRIGHTON	21 / 17	W		26	1-0	0-0	Ritchie 52
37	H	12/4	BOLTON	21 / 22	W		28	2-1	1-0	Ritchie 39p, Mann 60 / Allardyce 75
38	A	19/4	MANCHESTER C	21 / 17	L		28	1-3	0-3	Rodgers 69 / Robinson 13, Denya 32, Tueart 40
39	H	22/4	MIDDLESBROUGH	20 / 10	W		30	3-1	1-1	Royle 12, Ritchie 48, 88 / Armstrong 4
40	H	26/4	NORWICH	21 / 15	L		30	2-3	0-1	Rodgers 65, Ritchie 88 / Robson 25, 74, Peters 46
41	A	29/4	SOUTHAMPTON	21 / 8	L		30	2-5	0-0	Mabbutt 68, 70 (Channon 84) / Boyer 46, 51, 66, Hayes 50
42	A	3/5	TOTTENHAM	20 / 14	D		31	0-0	0-0	

Home 18,932 Away 21,981 Average

---

32 — A ARSENAL, 11/3 — Att. 21,559 — Ref: R Challis

City: Cashley, Sweeney, Whitehead, Mann, Gillies, Merrick, Mabbutt, Fitzpatrick, Royle, Ritchie, Tainton
Arsenal: Jennings, Devine, Nelson, Talbot, O'Leary, Young, Brady, Vaersen, Stapleton, Price, Rix

Joe Royle, thrice denied by Pat Jennings in the first half, remains optimistic that City can still beat the drop. It is really a point gained at Highbury as it is Arsenal who create most of the chances. City are indebted to Cashley's agility and courage as he keeps the Gunners at bay.

33 — H LIVERPOOL, 15/3 — Att. 27,523 — Ref: R Lewis

City: Cashley, Sweeney, Whitehead, Mann, Gillies, Merrick, Mabbutt, Fitzpatrick, Royle, Ritchie, Tainton
Liverpool: Clemence, Neal, Kennedy A, Thompson, Kennedy R, Hansen, Dalglish, Case, Johnson, McDermott, Souness

Flawless Liverpool turn on the style as City are outclassed in front of the Match of the Day cameras. Pool's shot on sight policy unsettles City, and Ray Kennedy opens the scoring with a fine shot from the edge of the box. Mabbutt's hooked shot from Royle's header is City's sole reply.

34 — A DERBY, 22/3 — Att. 17,020 — Ref: T Farley

City: Cashley, Sweeney, Whitehead, Mann, Gillies, Merrick, Mabbutt, Fitzpatrick, Royle, Ritchie, Tainton
Derby: McKellar, Langan, Buckley, Powell S, McFarland, Osgood, Emery*, Powell B, Biley, Swindlehurst, Emson, McCaffery

Merrick claims loss of balance in bringing down Dave Swindlehurst for County's penalty, whilst City's spot-kick follows Keith Osgood's felling of Mabbutt. Ritchie nets the opener with a shot from 15 yards, and Mann completes the action with an untypically close-range effort.

35 — H WEST BROM, 5/4 — Att. 16,873 — Ref: L Burden

City: Cashley, Sweeney, Whitehead*, Gow, Rodgers, Merrick, Fitzpatrick, Ritchie, Royle, Mabbutt, Tainton
WBA: Godden, Batson, Cowdrill, Moses, Wile, Robertson, Robson, Deehan, Regis, Owen, Barnes

The Baggies unbeaten seven-match run comes under threat at Ashton Gate, and they are visibly shaken by City's second-half verve. Gow is in brilliant form in City's midfield, but again the finish is missing as the home fans protest with banners advocating change of management.

36 — A BRIGHTON, 7/4 — Att. 23,115 — Ref: C Maskell

City: Cashley, Sweeney, Whitehead, Gow, Rodgers, Merrick, Fitzpatrick, Ritchie, Royle, Mann, Pritchard
Brighton: Moseley, Gregory, Williams, Horton, Foster, Ryan, McNab, Wood, Clarke*, Lawrenson, O'Sullivan, Suddaby

With Derby losing at Coventry and Man City dropping another home point, Ritchie's side-footer from five yards renews hope of escaping relegation. A poor game, but with Gow and Whitehead limping, City do well to become only the second side to win at the Goldstone this year.

37 — H BOLTON, 12/4 — Att. 14,270 — Ref: C Newsome

City: Cashley, Sweeney, Whitehead, Gow, Rodgers, Merrick, Fitzpatrick, Ritchie, Royle, Mann, Pritchard* Tainton
Bolton: McDonagh, Graham, Bennett, Hoggan, Jones, Walsh, Nowak, Whatmore*, Carter, Reid, Allardyce Wilson

City's best run of the season, six points from four games, keeps survival hopes alive, but Bolton's failure to win condemns them to relegation. Gow's chip hits Paul Jones on the arm for City's spot-kick, then Mann finds his range again from long distance to double City's advantage.

38 — A MANCHESTER C, 19/4 — Att. 32,745 — Ref: P Reeves

City: Cashley, Sweeney, Whitehead, Gow, Rodgers, Merrick, Fitzpatrick, Ritchie, Royle, Mann, Pritchard* Tainton
Man City: Corrigan, Ranson, Reid, Futcher, Caton, Power, Henry, Daley, Deyna, Tueart, Robinson

City squander all but one of their chances, whilst the Blues convert theirs. Rodgers heads in from Merrick's free-kick, but by then seven good opportunities had been spurned. Man City are fortunate with their opener as Mick Robinson knocks the ball down with hand before slotting in.

39 — H MIDDLESBROUGH, 22/4 — Att. 12,013 — Ref: A Glasson

City: Cashley, Sweeney, Whitehead, Mann, Rodgers, Merrick, Pritchard, Fitzpatrick, Royle, Ritchie, Tainton
Middlesbrough: Stewart, Craggs, Bailey, Johnston, Ashcroft*, Angus, Cochrane, Proctor, Hodgson, Jankovic, Armstrong Hedley

City are fortunate not to find themselves beyond redemption before Royle opens their account with a fierce volley. Shortly after David Armstrong's headed opener, City are relieved when their nervously conceded own-goal is struck off due to an early offside infringement.

40 — H NORWICH, 26/4 — Att. 16,596 — Ref: A Seville

City: Cashley, Sweeney, Whitehead, Gow, Rodgers, Merrick*, Pritchard, Fitzpatrick, Royle, Ritchie, Tainton
Norwich: Hansbury, Bond, Symonds, Barham, McDowell, Jones, Woods, Fashanu, Robson, Paddon, Peters

Ritchie makes some recompense for his spot-kick failure after just 25 seconds, with a late tap-in, but by then it is too late as City's top-flight status hangs by a thread. Injury reduces City to ten men in the 78th minute, following Justin Fashanu's head-butt on the unfortunate Rodgers.

41 — A SOUTHAMPTON, 29/4 — Att. 16,309 — Ref: M Bidmead

City: Cashley, Sweeney, Whitehead, Gow, Gillies, Tainton, Fitzpatrick, Ritchie*, Royle, Mann, Mabbutt
Southampton: Wells, Golac, Waldron, Williams S, Watson, Nicholl, Hebberd, Boyer, Channon, Holmes, Hayes* Rogers

City are sent sliding out of the First Division by Soton's blitz at the start of the second half. Phil Boyer heads in to start the rot, and then fires home twice more to grab his third hat-trick of the season. Mabbutt responds for City with a close-range shot, and a ferocious 18-yarder.

42 — A TOTTENHAM, 3/5 — Att. 23,585 — Ref: M Scott

City: Shaw, Sweeney, Whitehead, Gow, Hay, Merrick, Fitzpatrick*, Ritchie, Royle, Mann, Gillies
Tottenham: Daines, Hughton, Miller, Hazard, McAllister, Perryman, Ardiles, Jones, Falco, Hoddle, Galvin

Already doomed City only have themselves to blame for not bowing out with a win, even though they have cause to thank the woodwork for repelling a Glenn Hoddle effort. Mabbutt misses City's best chance, as with only Barry Daines to beat his lob falls the wrong side of the post.

LEAGUE DIVISION 1 (CUP-TIES)   Manager: Alan Dicks   SEASON 1979-80

League Cup

No.	Date	Venue	Opponent	Pos	Att		Res	F-A	H-T	Scorers, Times, and Referees
2:1	28/8	H	ROTHERHAM	11	6,981	3:7	W	1-0	1-0	Ritchie 38p — Ref: A Robinson
2:2	4/9	A	ROTHERHAM	6	7,327	3:1	D	1-1	0-1	Mabbutt 87 / Fern 31 — Ref: M Scott (City won 2-1 on aggregate)
3	26/9	A	PETERBOROUGH	10	7,067	4:7	D	1-1	0-1	Gow 76 / Parkinson 44 — Ref: M Peck
3R	2/10	H	PETERBOROUGH	8	9,125	4:5	W	4-0	2-0	Jantunen 1, Royle 22, 82, Mabbutt 88 — Ref: A Selville
4	30/10	H	NOTT'M FOREST	16	25,695	2	D	1-1	0-1	Sweeney 86 / O'Hare 29 — Ref: C Downey
4R	14/11	A	NOTT'M FOREST	15	20,462	3	L	0-3	0-2	O'Neill 12, Anderson 43, W'dcock 60 — Ref: J Worrall

Line-ups (Bristol City in bold / opponents in italic)

Match	1	2	3	4	5	6	7	8	9	10	11	12 sub used
2:1 City	Shaw	Tainton	Whitehead	Gow	Sweeney	Merrick	Fitzpatrick	Ritchie	Royle	Jantunen	Meijer	
2:1 Rotherham	*Mountford*	*Forrest*	*Tiler*	*Rhodes*	*Green*	*Breckin*	*Gooding*	*McEwan*	*Gwyther*	*Fern*	*Finney*	
2:2 City	Shaw	Tainton	Whitehead	Gow	Sweeney	Merrick	Fitzpatrick	Ritchie	Royle	Jantunen	Mabbutt	
2:2 Rotherham	*Mountford*	*Forrest*	*Tiler*	*Rhodes*	*Green*	*Breckin*	*Gooding*	*McEwan*	*Gwyther*	*Fern*	*Finney*	
3 City	Shaw	Tainton	Whitehead	Gow	Sweeney	Merrick	Fitzpatrick	Ritchie	Mabbutt	Mann	Cormack*	Royle
3 Peterborough	*Waugh*	*Carmichael*	*Phillips*	*Chard*	*Smith*	*Foster*	*Gynn*	*Kellock*	*Quow*	*Robson*	*Parkinson*	
3R City	Shaw	Whitehead	Phillips	Gow*	Hay	Merrick	Fitzpatrick	Tainton	Royle	Jantunen	Mabbutt	
3R Peterborough	*Waugh*	*McVay*	*Chard*	*Smith**	*Foster*	*Gynn*	*Kellock*	*Parkinson*	*Robson*	*Carmichael*		*Guy*
4 City	Shaw	Sweeney	Whitehead	Mabbutt	Rodgers*	Merrick	Fitzpatrick	Ritchie	Royle	Mann	Gow	Hay
4 Nott'm Forest	*Shilton*	*Anderson*	*Gray*	*McGovern*	*Lloyd*	*Burns*	*O'Hare*	*Francis*	*Birtles*	*Woodcock*	*Robertson*	
4R City	Shaw	Sweeney	Kenyon	Mabbutt	Hay	Merrick	Fitzpatrick	Ritchie	Royle*	Mann	Tainton	Gillies
4R Nott'm Forest	*Shilton*	*Anderson*	*Gray*	*McGovern*	*Lloyd*	*Needham*	*O'Neill**	*Francis*	*Birtles*	*Woodcock*	*Robertson*	*Bowyer*

2:1 — After a one minute silence in memory of Lord Mountbatten, murdered by an IRA bomb, the Millers prove difficult to beat. It takes John Breckin's push on Ritchie for City to gain an advantage, the striker creating an English football record with penalties in four successive games.

2:2 — Mabbutt's late headed goal from Jantunen's wickedly curved cross takes City through to the next round, two minutes after a hairline offside decision had ruled out Gerry Forrest's shot. City are fortunate not to concede any more than Rodney Fern's tap-in, as they are often over-run.

3 — Royle's verve and mobility in a 20-minute substitute appearance saves City, as he heads down Sweeney's cross for Gow to lob the ball in from 20 yards. Although both Mabbutt and Gow hit the woodwork in the first half, Andy Parkinson's cross-shot deservedly gives Posh the lead.

3R — Jantunen's 25-yarder that puts City ahead after just 55 seconds, sparks a vintage first-half display that sees Sweeney hitting the bar and Royle heading in from Fitzpatrick's long pass. After the break though, Posh's great spirit has City hanging on until two late strikes ease the tension.

4 — Sweeney's acute-angled chip is a great finale to a pulsating cup-tie. John O'Hare stumbles the ball into the net for Forest's untidy goal after City's fine start had been disrupted by a seven-minute delay in bringing on Hay, following the early departure of Rodgers with a broken nose.

4R — City are devoid of ambition and never offer a threat as Forest take their unbeaten League Cup run to 21 games. Viv Anderson's first-time hook shot into the top corner of the net is the best of the goals as the European Champions outclass City, who can only manage two shots on target.

FA Cup

No.	Date	Venue	Opponent	Pos	Att		Res	F-A	H-T	Scorers, Times, and Referees
3	5/1	H	DERBY	20	13,384	21	W	6-2	3-0	G'land 6, 85, P'd 12, 61, W'head 39, [Mann 88] / Davies 84, Daly 87 — Ref: D Civil
4	26/1	H	IPSWICH	20	19,608	5	L	1-2	1-1	Whitehead 38 / Wark 45, Mariner 87 — Ref: T Bune

Line-ups (Bristol City in bold / opponents in italic)

Match	1	2	3	4	5	6	7	8	9	10	11	12 sub used
3 City	Shaw	Tainton	Whitehead	Gow	Rodgers	Merrick	Pritchard	Fitzpatrick	Ritchie	Mann	Garland	
3 Derby	*McKellar*	*Emery*	*Buckley*	*Daly*	*Powell S*	*Osgood*	*Clark**	*Powell B*	*Greenwood*	*Davies*	*Moreland*	*Emson*
4 City	Shaw	Tainton	Whitehead	Gow	Rodgers	Merrick*	Pritchard	Fitzpatrick	Mabbutt	Sweeney	Garland	Doyle
4 Ipswich	*Cooper*	*Burley*	*Mills*	*Thijssen*	*Osman*	*Butcher*	*Wark*	*Muhren*	*Mariner*	*Brazil*	*Gates*	

3 — Goals galore as City notch up their record Cup win over top-flight opposition. Pritchard's return to the side works wonders, notching two goals himself, a stab in and a fierce shot into the roof of the net, as well having sent over the corner for Garland to head in City's opener.

4 — City pay the penalty for missed chances as Shaw fumbles Frans Thijssen's mis-hit shot to present Paul Mariner with his late winner. Ipswich ride their luck at times, but John Wark's equaliser is pure magic as Mike Mills' left-wing run and cross ends with a perfect diving header.

Final League Table

Pos	Team	P	Home					Away					Pts
			W	D	L	F	A	W	D	L	F	A	
1	Liverpool	42	15	6	0	46	8	10	4	7	35	22	60
2	Manchester U	42	17	3	1	43	8	7	7	7	22	27	58
3	Ipswich	42	14	4	3	43	13	8	5	8	25	26	53
4	Arsenal	42	8	10	3	24	12	10	6	5	28	24	52
5	Nott'm Forest	42	16	4	1	44	11	4	4	13	19	32	48
6	Wolves	42	9	6	6	29	20	10	3	8	29	27	47
7	Aston Villa	42	11	5	5	29	22	5	9	7	22	28	46
8	Southampton	42	14	2	5	53	24	4	7	10	12	29	45
9	Middlesbro	42	11	7	3	31	14	5	5	11	19	30	44
10	West Brom	42	9	8	4	37	23	2	11	8	17	27	41
11	Leeds	42	10	7	4	30	17	3	7	11	16	33	40
12	Norwich	42	10	8	3	38	30	3	6	12	20	36	40
13	Crys Palace	42	9	9	3	26	13	3	7	11	15	37	40
14	Tottenham	42	11	5	5	30	22	4	5	12	22	40	40
15	Coventry	42	12	2	7	34	24	4	5	12	22	42	39
16	Brighton	42	8	8	5	25	20	3	7	11	22	37	37
17	Manchester C	42	8	8	5	28	25	4	5	12	15	41	37
18	Stoke	42	9	4	8	27	26	2	10	9	17	32	36
19	Everton	42	7	7	7	28	25	2	10	9	15	26	35
20	BRISTOL CITY	42	6	6	9	22	30	3	7	11	15	36	31
21	Derby	42	9	4	8	36	29	2	4	15	11	38	30
22	Bolton	42	5	11	5	19	21	0	4	17	19	52	25
		924	228	134	100	722	437	100	134	228	437	722	924

Odds & ends

Double wins: (0).
Double losses: (4) Ipswich, Liverpool, Norwich, Southampton.
Won from behind: (3) Leeds (a), Everton (h), Middlesbrough (h).
Lost from in front: (0).
High spots: Drawing 2-2 with Leeds at Ashton Gate on 18 August.
Winning 3-1 at Elland Road on 3 November.
Beating Derby 6-2 in the FA Cup on 5 January.
Beating Bristol Rov (h) 1-0 in the Gloucestershire Cup Final on 6 May.
Low spots: Relegation.
Losing 2-3 at home to Norwich on 26 April.
Lack of ambition in 0-3 FL Cup defeat at Nott'm Forest.
Losing 1-5 on aggregate v St Mirren in the Final of the Anglo-Scottish Cup.
Player of the year: Geoff Merrick.
Ever-presents: (0).
Hat-tricks: (0).
Leading scorer: Tom Ritchie (14).

Appearances and Goals

Player	Lge	Sub	LC	Sub	FAC	Sub	Lge	LC	FAC	Tot
							(Goals)			
Cashley, Ray	14									
Cormack, Peter	1	3	1							
Doyle, Ian	1	1				1				
Fitzpatrick, Tony	41		6		2					
Garland, Chris	10		2		2				2	2
Gillies, Donnie	7	1			1					
Gow, Gerry	31		4		2		4	1		5
Hay, Alan	3	1	2	1						
Jantunen, Pertti	7		3					1	1	2
Kenyon, Roger	4		1							
Mabbutt, Kevin	21	6	5	1	1		6	2		8
Mann, Jimmy	28	1	3	1			3	1		4
Meijer, Geert	3	3	6				1			1
Merrick, Geoff	39		6		2					
Pritchard, Howard	15	1			2				2	2
Ritchie, Tom	35	3	5				13	1		14
Rodgers, David	26		1		2		6			6
Royle, Joe	34	1	5	1	2		3	2		5
Shaw, John	28		6		2					
Sweeney, Gerry	40	1	6	1	2					
Tainton, Trevor	34	5	6	2	2		1			1
Whitehead, Clive	40	5	5	2	2				2	2
22 players used	462	27	66	4	22	1	37	8	7	52

LEAGUE DIVISION 2 — Manager: Dicks ⇔ Bob Houghton — SEASON 1980-81

Match summary

No	Date	Venue	Opponent	Att	Pos	Pt	Res	F-A	H-T	Scorers, Times	Ref
1	16/8	A	PRESTON	6,293		1	D	1-1	0-0	Mann 54; *Elliott 59*	M Scott
2	19/8	H	WEST HAM	14,001		2	D	1-1	1-1	Ritchie 15; *Cross 19*	D Lloyd
3	23/8	H	BRISTOL ROV	16,612	12	3	D	0-0	0-0	—	B Daniels
4	30/8	A	WATFORD	10,759	18	3	L	0-1	0-0	*Patching 78*	K Hackett
5	6/9	H	SWANSEA	9,761	21	3	L	0-1	0-1	*James L 21*	R Challis
6	13/9	A	SHEFFIELD WED	15,260	22	3	L	1-2	1-1	Ritchie 37; *Pearson 40, King 53*	B Hill
7	20/9	H	NOTTS CO	8,253	22	3	L	0-1	0-0	*Masson 82*	K Salmon
8	27/9	A	QP RANGERS	8,551	22	3	L	0-4	0-2	*Neal 15, 70, Langley 44, Shanks 72*	J Hunting
9	4/10	A	GRIMSBY	8,781	22	3	L	0-1	0-0	*Drinkell 80*	N Midgley
10	7/10	H	LUTON	7,571	21	5	W	2-1	0-1	Ritchie 58p, Mabbutt 63; *Saxby 38*	C Newsome

Line-ups (City in roman, opponents in *italic*)

No	1	2	3	4	5	6	7	8	9	10	11	12 sub used
1	Cashley	Sweeney	Hay	Tainton	Rodgers	Merrick*	Whitehead	Fitzpatrick	Mabbutt	Ritchie	Mann	Garland
1	*Tunks*	*Taylor*	*Cameron*	*Burns*	*Baxter*	*Blackley*	*Bell*	*Coleman*	*Elliott*	*Potts*	*McGhee*	
2	Cashley	Sweeney	**Baddeley**	Tainton	Rodgers*	Merrick	Fitzpatrick	Mabbutt	Ritchie	Mann	Whitehead	Garland
2	*Parkes*	*Stewart*	*Brush*	*Bonds*	*Martin*	*Devonshire*	*Holland*	*Goddard*	*Cross*	*Brooking*	*Pike*	
3	Cashley	Sweeney	Whitehead	Tainton	Gow	Merrick	Fitzpatrick	Mabbutt	Ritchie	Mann	Pritchard	Pritchard
3	*Thomas*	*Gillies*	*Bater*	*Mabbutt*	*Hughes*	*Lee*	*McCaffery*	*Bar'wclough*	*Williams*	*Bates*	*Penny* *	*Pulis*
4	Cashley	Sweeney	Whitehead	Gow	Hay	Merrick	Tainton	Ritchie	Mabbutt	Mann	Pritchard*	Garland
4	*Steele*	*Henderson*	*Jackett*	*Patching*	*Sims*	*Bolton*	*Blissett*	*Poskett*	*Jenkins*	*Train*	*Rostron*	
5	Cashley	Sweeney	Whitehead	Gow	Hay	Merrick	Tainton	Ritchie	Mabbutt	Doyle	Garland*	Pritchard
5	*Stewart*	*Attley*	*Hadziabdic*	*Mahoney*	*Stevenson*	*Phillips*	*Giles*	*James L*	*James R*	*Charles*	*Robinson* *	*Waddle*
6	Cashley	Sweeney	Whitehead	Tainton	Rodgers	Merrick	Fitzpatrick	Gow	Whitehead	Ritchie	Mabbutt	Campbell
6	*Bolder*	*Blackhall*	*Grant*	*Smith*	*Pickering*	*King*	*Taylor*	*Johnson*	*Owen* *	*Pearson*	*Mellor*	
7	Cashley	Sweeney	Whitehead	Tainton	Rodgers !	Merrick	Fitzpatrick	Gow	Whitehead	Ritchie	Mabbutt	Wood
7	*Avramovic*	*Benjamin*	*O'Brien*	*Kelly* /	*Kilcline*	*Richards*	*McCulloch*	*Masson*	*Harkouk !*	*Hunt*	*Hooks*	
8	Cashley	Sweeney	Hay	Tainton	Gow	Merrick	Mann	Fitzpatrick	Mabbutt	Ritchie	Pritchard*	**Smith**
8	*Woods*	*McCreary*	*Gillard*	*Waddock*	*Wicks*	*Roeder*	*Neal*	*Shanks*	*Langley*	*Currie*	*Burke*	
9	Cashley	Sweeney	Hay	Gow	Whitehead	Merrick	Tainton	Fitzpatrick	Ritchie	Mabbutt	Whitehead*	**Mann**
9	*Batch*	*Cruzman*	*Crosby*	*Waters*	*Wigginton*	*Moore K*	*Ford*	*Kilmore* *	*Drinkell*	*Mitchell*	*Cumming*	*Brolly*
10	Cashley	Sweeney	Hay	Tainton	Whitehead	Merrick	Tainton	Fitzpatrick	Mabbutt	Ritchie	Mann	**Smith**
10	*Findlay*	*Stephens*	*Donaghy*	*Grealish*	*Saxby*	*Price*	*Hill*	*Stein*	*Harrow*	*West*	*Moss*	

Match reports

1 — A PRESTON (16/8): After four seasons of top-flight struggle, City are given a sharp reminder that life is likely to be no easier at this level. Poor defensive play and an attack that is handled with consummate ease by Preston make City's gaining of a point, thanks to Mann's 25-yarder, somewhat of a miracle.

2 — H WEST HAM (19/8): Trevor Brooking writes off City's chances of being promotion contenders. Ritchie stabs City ahead as they play with style, but the Hammers equalise as Rodgers is injured. City are lucky when Paul Goddard's strike is disallowed for offside as West Ham take control after half-time.

3 — H BRISTOL ROV (23/8): The hot sunshine takes the steam out of this derby clash. Rovers get the point they came for with an ultra-defensive performance. Apart from occasional Gary Mabbutt inspired breaks, City are not troubled, but despite almost constant attacking are lost for ideas to beat Martin Thomas.

4 — A WATFORD (30/8): Mistakes at both ends by Alan Hay prove costly. He hesitates too long on his own line as Martin Patching rushes forward to prod in and then shoots over the bar in the final move of the game. Awful City are outclassed by a Watford side putting in 21 shots on goal to City's mere three.

5 — H SWANSEA (6/9): The City fans turn on chairman Stephen Kew and manager Alan Dicks after another anaemic display. Playing without direction or spark, they are outplayed by a more skilful Swansea. Leighton James, the game's most talented player, curls a 20-yard shot into the net for the only goal.

6 — A SHEFFIELD WED (13/9): City, under caretaker boss Ken Wimshurst, are deprived of a point in an indifferent game as Cashley concedes a bizarre goal. Jeff King's effort from 20 yards is going wide before taking deflections off Tainton and then Rodgers to trickle in. A debut goal for 17-year-old John Pearson.

7 — H NOTTS CO (20/9): Rodgers, after being twice booked, is sent off in the 71st min for Don Masson to blast in from 18 yards. Rachid Harkouk is dismissed for violent conduct with two minutes left. Paul Hooks always troubles City with his pace and he sets up County's winner for Don Masson.

8 — A QP RANGERS (27/9): The Robins still seek their first win of the season as fellow relegation strugglers Rangers tear holes in their 3-4-3 formation. City win the first-half corner count 10-1, but in a game which could easily have produced a dozen goals, they are again let down by their wayward finishing.

9 — A GRIMSBY (4/10): Mabbutt blames himself for ruining new boss Bob Houghton's first game in charge. Just two minutes from the end of this colourless encounter he glides his careful shot wide of the far post. Kevin Drinkell powers in a magnificent header from former City player Mike Brolly's corner.

10 — H LUTON (7/10): City obtain their first win of the season after a poor first-half display. Luton play neat football and Cashley does well to keep them out before Mike Saxby thumps home a rebound. A controversial penalty changes the game and City secure victory when Mabbutt scores from close in.

11 — H NEWCASTLE — 11/10 — 10,468 — Pos 21 — W — Opp 9 — 2-0 (0-0) — Pts 7
Ritchie 71, 89p — Ref: D Reeves

City: Cashley, Sweeney, Hay, Gow, Whitehead, Merrick, Tainton, Fitzpatrick, Mabbutt, Ritchie, Smith
Newcastle: Carr, Kelly, Davies, Martin, Boam, Mitchell, Shoulder*, Wharton, Shinton, Rafferty, Hibbitt, Cartwright

Houghton cites looking through old videos as the key to sparking a revival. He changes City's style so as to get the ball forward quicker as Newcastle's unbeaten seven-match run is ended. Ritchie scores with a rocket header and then nets a penalty after the best move of the game.

12 — A BOLTON — 18/10 — 8,988 — Pos 21 — D — Opp 14 — 1-1 (1-1) — Pts 8
Mabbutt 19; Gowling 17 — Ref: T Morris

City: Cashley, Sweeney, Hay, Gow, Whitehead, Merrick, Tainton, Fitzpatrick, Mabbutt, Ritchie, Smith
Bolton: Poole, Graham, Nicholson, Cantello, Jones, Walsh, Reid, Carter, Gowling, Kidd, Burke

Youngster Gary Smith misses two great chances as City have to settle for a point. The homesters look a dreadfully poor side, but go ahead as Alan Gowling tucks away Mike Carter's cross. City respond immediately as Mabbutt nets with a superb side-foot volley from Tainton's pass.

13 — A WREXHAM — 21/10 — 4,179 — Pos 21 — L — Opp 12 — 0-1 (0-0) — Pts 8
McNeil 80p — Ref: J Bray

City: Cashley, Sweeney, Hay, Gow, Whitehead, Merrick, Tainton, Fitzpatrick, Mabbutt, Ritchie, Smith*, Garland
Wrexham: Davies, Hill, Jones, Davis, Cegleiski, Carrodus, Fox, Sutton, McNeil, Vinter, Cartwright

A drab game which always looked likely to be settled with a penalty. Dreadful City only muster one shot on target and Mabbutt is fortunate to remain on the field after a bad tackle. Tainton concedes spot-kick on being adjudged to have climbed on Mike Vinter's shoulders to head clear.

14 — H DERBY — 25/10 — 12,049 — Pos 21 — D — Opp 8 — 2-2 (1-0) — Pts 9
Mabbutt 34, 70; Wilson 86, Emson 90 — Ref: A Robinson

City: Cashley, Sweeney, Hay, Mann*, Whitehead, Merrick, Tainton, Fitzpatrick, Mabbutt, Ritchie, Garland, Smith
Derby: Jones, Emery, Buckley, Sheridan, Powell S, Osgood, Skivington*, Clark, Biley, Hector, Wilson, Emson

A nightmare conclusion for City, as lapses of concentration allow Derby to poach two goals at the death. Mabbutt picks up Steve Emery's poor back-pass to put City ahead and then doubles the advantage to volley in Tainton's cross, before Merrick's pass-back sets up the shock finish.

15 — A ORIENT — 1/11 — 4,698 — Pos 21 — L — Opp 7 — 1-3 (1-1) — Pts 9
Mabbutt 13; Chiedozie 12, Parsons 69, Moores 87 — Ref: C Maskell

City: Cashley, Sweeney, Hay, Mann, Whitehead, Merrick, Tainton, Fitzpatrick, Mabbutt, Ritchie, Garland
Orient: Day, Fisher, Roffey, Taylor, Gray, Parsons, Chiedozie, Moores, Mayo, Bowles, Margerrison

City look impressive with their crisp counter-attacking, but are let down by lack of height in defence. The injured Rodgers is sorely missed as Orient fling everything high into the box. City's efforts to draw level are curtailed by Ian Moores, who skilfully flicks in with his back to goal.

16 — H BLACKBURN — 8/11 — 9,026 — Pos 20 — W — Opp 5 — 2-0 (0-0) — Pts 11
Garland 47, Tainton 85 — Ref: L Shapter

City: Cashley, Sweeney, Hay, Mann, Whitehead, Merrick, Tainton, Fitzpatrick, Mabbutt*, Ritchie, Garland, Pritchard
Blackburn: Butcher, Branagan, Rathbone, Parkes, Keeley, Fazackerley, Brotherston, McKenzie, Garner, Speight, Stonehouse

Sparkling attacking play by City against relentless opponents willing to play open football produces great entertainment for the fans. Garland impresses and fully deserves his headed goal from Whitehead's free-kick. Tainton ties up the points as he cuts inside to whip his shot into the far corner.

17 — A WEST HAM — 11/11 — 25,210 — Pos 21 — L — Opp 1 — 0-5 (0-2) — Pts 11
Goddard 11, 89, Martin 16 [Brooking 72, Cross 85] — Ref: J Martin

City: Cashley, Sweeney, Hay, Mann, Marshall, Merrick, Tainton*, Fitzpatrick, Whitehead, Ritchie, Pritchard, Smith
West Ham: Parkes, Stewart, Lampard, Bonds, Martin, Devonshire, Holland, Goddard, Cross, Brooking, Pike

City are overwhelmed in midfield by the supremely-talented Hammers, especially after the withdrawal of Tainton in the 69th minute. Smith has no chance to adjust to the pace of the game and within three minutes Trevor Brooking puts the result beyond doubt with a close-range shot.

18 — H PRESTON — 15/11 — 8,467 — Pos 21 — D — Opp 13 — 0-0 (0-0) — Pts 12
Ref: M Baker

City: Cashley, Sweeney, Hay, Mann, Whitehead, Marshall, Tainton, Fitzpatrick*, Garland, Ritchie, Merrick
Preston: Tunks, Westwell, McAteer, Burns, Blackley, Bell, Baxter, Coleman*, Elliott, Bruce, McGee, Taylor

Preston offer little as an attacking force, whilst their keeper Roy Tunks performs miracles to keep City at bay. Pritchard picks up a booking for returning to the field after treatment without the ref's permission. 'Bristol City are too good to go down,' says North End boss Nobby Stiles.

19 — A CAMBRIDGE — 22/11 — 4,922 — Pos 21 — L — Opp 8 — 1-2 (0-2) — Pts 12
Mann 90; Lyons 18, 40 — Ref: K Baker

City: Cashley, Sweeney, Hay, Mann, Whitehead, Marshall, Tainton, Fitzpatrick*, Garland, Ritchie, Merrick
Cambridge: Key, Donaldson, Murray, Smith, Fallon, Gibbins, O'Neil, Spriggs, Reilly, Lyons, Christie

City are flattered by the scoreline as Mann's goal from close range gives them an undeserved reward for a dismal performance. This rather dull game is only enlivened by two goals from John Lyons who shoots home from twelve yards before his header puts the game out of City's reach.

20 — H OLDHAM — 29/11 — 8,485 — Pos 21 — D — Opp 13 — 1-1 (0-1) — Pts 13
Fitzpatrick 53; Heaton 43 — Ref: T Spencer

City: Cashley, Sweeney, Hay, Whitehead, Rodgers, Merrick*, Tainton, Fitzpatrick, Mabbutt, Ritchie, Garland, Pritchard
Oldham: Platt, Hoolickin*, Blair, Keegan, Clements, Hurst, Heaton, Futcher, Steel, Palmer, Atkinson, Sinclair

A well-organised offside-trap frustrates City, who rue Mabbutt's early failure to score with only the keeper to beat. Oldham are dangerous on the break and Paul Heaton runs clear to beat Cashley, before Fitzpatrick snaps up his first City goal after Mabbutt's left-foot volley hits the bar.

21 — A SHREWSBURY — 6/12 — 4,435 — Pos 21 — L — Opp 14 — 0-4 (0-1) — Pts 13
Biggins 39, Tong 63, Atkins 72, [Edwards 87] — Ref: A Challinor

City: Shaw, Sweeney, Hay, Aitken, Rodgers, Marshall, Tainton, Fitzpatrick, Mabbutt, Ritchie, Whitehead
Shrewsbury: Wardle, King, Larkin, Turner*, Griffin, Keay, Tong, Atkins, Biggins, Petts, Cross, Edwards

City are made to pay dearly for wasting chances created by their skilful, penetrative football. Ian Atkins creates Shrewsbury's opening goals, before scoring himself. City's misfortune is complete as Matthews blasts home the fourth, straight after Aitken's shot was headed off the line.

LEAGUE DIVISION 2

Manager: Dicks ⇨ Bob Houghton

SEASON 1980-81

No	Date	Att	Pos	Pt	F-A	H-T	1	2	3	4	5	6	7	8	9	10	11	12 sub used
22 H BOLTON	13/12	7,850	12	15	3-1	1-1	Shaw	Sweeney	Hay	Aitken	Rodgers	Marshall	Tainton	Fitzpatrick	Mabbutt	Ritchie	Whitehead*	Garland
							Poole	*Graham*	*McElhinney*	*Wilson*	*Jones*	*Brennan*	*Nicholson**	*Whatmore*	*Hoggan*	*Kidd*	*Gowling*	*Thomas*
23 A NEWCASTLE	20/12	14,131	13	16	0-0	0-0	Shaw	Sweeney	Hay	Aitken	Rodgers	Marshall	Tainton	Fitzpatrick	Mabbutt	Ritchie	Garland*	Pritchard
							Carr	*Carney*	*Johnson*	*Martin*	*Boam*	*Mitchell*	*Shinton*	*Trewick*	*Waddle*	*Shoulder*	*Wharton*	
24 H CARDIFF	26/12	15,039	18	17	0-0	0-0	**Moller**		Hay	Aitken	Rodgers	Marshall	Tainton	Fitzpatrick	Mabbutt !	Ritchie	Garland	
							Healey	*Jones !*	*Roberts*	*Hughes*	*Pontin*	*Dwyer*	*Lewis*	*Kitchen*	*Stevens*	*Ronson*	*Buchanan*	
25 A CHELSEA	27/12	18,514	3	18	0-0	0-0	**Moller**		Hay	Aitken	Rodgers	Marshall	Tainton	Fitzpatrick	Garland*	Ritchie	Smith	
							Borota	*Locke*	*Rofe*	*Bumstead*	*Pates*	*Chivers*	*Hutchings**	*Fillery*	*Lee*	*Mayes*	*Rh's-Brown*	*Walker*
26 H CAMBRIDGE	10/1	9,869	11	18	0-1	0-1	**Moller**		Hay	Aitken	Rodgers	Marshall	Tainton	Fitzpatrick	Mabbutt	Ritchie	Pritchard	
							Key	*Donaldson*	*Murray*	*Smith*	*Fallon*	*Finney*	*Streete*	*Spriggs*	*Reilly*	*Taylor*	*Christie*	
27 H WATFORD	17/1	8,982	14	19	0-0	0-0	Shaw	Sweeney	Hay	Aitken	Rodgers	Marshall	Tainton	Fitzpatrick	Mabbutt	Ritchie*	Pritchard	**Chandler**
							Sherwood	*Rice*	*Harrison*	*Taylor*	*Sims*	*Jackett*	*Callaghan*	*Blissett*	*Armstrong*	*Train*	*Poskett*	
28 A BRISTOL ROV	31/1	10,087	22	20	0-0	0-0	Shaw	Sweeney	Hay	Aitken	Rodgers*	Marshall	Tainton	Fitzpatrick	Mabbutt	Mann	Whitehead	Pritchard
							Kite	*Gillies*	*Jones*	*Cooper*	*Hughes*	*Emmanuel*	*Bar'clough*	*Williams G*	*Lee*	*Randall*	*Mabbutt*	
29 H SHEFFIELD WED	7/2	11,494	10	22	1-0	0-0	**Moller**	Stevens	Sweeney	Aitken	Marshall	Nicholls	Tainton	Mann	Mabbutt	Pritchard	Whitehead	
							Bolder	*Blackhall*	*Grant*	*Smith*	*Shirtliff*	*Sterland*	*Mirocevic*	*Johnson**	*Leman*	*McCulloch*	*Curran*	*Pearson*
30 H QP RANGERS	21/2	11,036	8	22	0-1	0-0	**Moller**	Stevens	Hay	Aitken	Marshall	Nicholls	Tainton	Fitzpatrick	Mabbutt	Mann*	Whitehead	Pritchard
							Burridge	*Shanks*	*Gillard*	*Fenwick*	*Wicks*	*Hazell**	*Langley*	*King*	*Stainrod*	*Currie*	*Silkman*	*Waddock*
31 A NOTTS CO	28/2	7,609	2	22	1-2	1-2	**Moller**	Stevens	Hay	Aitken	Marshall	Nicholls	Tainton	Fitzpatrick	Mabbutt	Pritchard	Whitehead	
							Avramovic	*Benjamin*	*O'Brien*	*Kelly**	*Kilcline*	*Richards*	*McCulloch*	*Masson*	*Christie*	*Hunt*	*Hooks*	*Harkouk*

Scorers, Times, and Referees

22 — Mabbutt 4, 47, Aitken 72; Gowling 15p; Ref: D Hutchinson

23 — Ref: C Seel

24 — Ref: R Lewis

25 — Ref: J Warner

26 — Marshall 5 (og); Ref: H King

27 — Ref: N Ashley

28 — Ref: R Toseland

29 — Pritchard 49; Ref: D Vickers

30 — Waddock 59; Ref: M Heath

31 — Nicholls 37; O'Brien 3p, Christie 15; Ref: P Willis

Match reports

22 City maintain their dominance over opponents seeking to add to their only win at Ashton Gate as long ago as 1904. Alan Gowling equalises for Bolton from the spot after Shaw fells him, but his second-half error results in Aitken chipping in a brilliant goal to keep the City fans happy.

23 Bob Houghton reckons his side will be out of the bottom three by the end of January, but the evidence of this miserable match, against a poor Newcastle side without a goal in four games, suggests he is somewhat over optimistic. At least, City manage to end a run of five away defeats.

24 Poor holiday fare with defences in control. Swedish international keeper Jan Moller demonstrates why City spent £120,000 on him with a late stop from Gary Stevens. Two sendings off right on half-time, Linden Jones for his bad tackle on Mabbutt and the City player for retaliation.

25 City's teenage striker Garry Smith misses a great chance in the dying seconds of securing a first-ever win at Stamford Bridge. With only the keeper to beat, he delays too long and fails to get in a shot. City have the better chances in an even contest, but are let down by poor finishing.

26 Misunderstanding between Moller and Marshall floor City as the centre-half heads into the empty net as the keeper comes out. Cambridge, making their first visit to Ashton Gate, put up a great defensive performance for the remaining 85 mins to end City's six-match unbeaten run.

27 Watford manager Graham Taylor is forthright in stating that the windy conditions were too much for all 22 players. Coronation Street's Peter Adamson is among the crowd that see this poor advert for the skill of the combatants. Once again City fail to make the most of their chances.

28 If not exactly a non-event, two disciplined defences make sure there are no dynamics to excite Eastville's largest and noisiest crowd of the season. City's elation at securing a point is tempered by the fact that Rodgers suffers a broken leg in a 54-min collision with Vaughan Jones.

29 Wednesday play superbly after half-time, but are beaten when Pritchard touches home a ball from Sweeney, just a minute after Marshall had his strike disallowed. Sweeney gets back quickly to make the goal-line save over Andy McCulloch's powerful shot.

30 City fans, given leaflets before the game asking them to purchase ten-year season tickets for £500, are hardly encouraged by this display as the home strikers are easily contained. Substitute Gary Waddock procures the points for the visitors after...

31 The referee sets the City on their way to defeat with a controversial re-take decision for encroachment after Moller saved Ray O'Brien's low shot to his left. City go on to give one of their best displays of the season after Nicholls shoots in, but customary poor finishing lets them down.

No	V	Opponent	Date	Att	Pos	Pts	P	Res	FT	HT
32	H	GRIMSBY	10/3	6,898	5	23	21	D	1-1	0-1
33	A	LUTON	14/3	8,745	7	23	21	L	1-3	1-2
34	A	SWANSEA	17/3	10,832	7	24	21	D	0-0	0-0
35	H	WREXHAM	21/3	6,948	15	24	21	L	0-2	0-1
36	A	DERBY	28/3	14,798	5	24	21	L	0-1	0-0
37	H	ORIENT	4/4	6,201	12	26	21	W	3-1	0-0
38	A	BLACKBURN	11/4	9,970	3	26	21	L	0-1	0-0
39	H	CHELSEA	18/4	10,011	9	27	21	D	0-0	0-0
40	A	CARDIFF	20/4	5,575	20	29	21	W	3-2	1-1
41	H	SHREWSBURY	25/4	6,042	14	30	21	D	1-1	1-0
42	A	OLDHAM	2/5	4,785	15	30	21	L	0-2	0-0

Home Average 9,765 — Away 9,863

32. GRIMSBY — Cumming 75 (og) / Cumming 12. Ref: D Civil
Lineups (City / *opponent*): Moller/*Batch*, Stevens/*Moore D*, Hay/*Crombie*, Aitken/*Waters*, Marshall/*Wigginton*, Nicholls/*Moore K*, Tainton/*Brolly*, Mann/*Whymark*, Mabbutt/*Drinkell*, Pritchard*/*Mitchell*, Whitehead/*Cumming*, Smith/*Cumming*
City fail to get the breaks they deserve in the mud as they are denied by the brilliance of Grimsby keeper Nigel Batch. He foils City's almost incessant attacks, until colleague Bob Cumming, scorer of the opener with a crisp drive, beats him whilst being put under pressure by Tainton.

33. LUTON — Pritchard 8 / *White 24, 35, Moss 75p*. Ref: L Burden
Lineups: Moller/*Findlay*, Stevens/*Stephens*, Hay/*Donaghy*, Aitken/*Grealish*, Marshall/*Saxby*, Whitehead/*Price*, Tainton*/*Hill*, Fitzpatrick/*Stein*, Mabbutt/*White*, Pritchard/*Antic*, Smith/*Moss*, Mann
Jake Findlay is lucky to stay on the pitch as Tainton is robbed of almost certain goals by blatant professional fouls. Pritchard punishes him for the first infraction by firing home the resultant 25-yard free-kick, but City are incensed in not being given a 42nd-min penalty for his second.

34. SWANSEA — Ref: A Hamil
Lineups: Moller/*Stewart*, Stevens/*Evans*, Hay/*Hadziabdic*, Aitken/*Rajkovic*, Marshall/*Charles*, Sweeney/*Stevenson*, Tainton/*Craig*, Fitzpatrick/*James R*, Mabbutt/*Curtis**, Pritchard/*James L*, Whitehead/*Mahoney*, Mann/*Robinson*
City's inability to take chances continues to be their downfall. Swansea-born Marshall gives his best display for City, while the immaculate control of Mabbutt, the speed of Whitehead and the surging thrusts of Fitzpatrick and Aitken give promise of goals that do not materialise.

35. WREXHAM — *Carrodus 45, Fox 77*. Ref: C Thomas
Lineups: Moller/*Davies*, Stevens/*Hill*, Hay/*Dwyer*, Aitken/*Jones*, Marshall/*Cegielski*, Sweeney/*Carrodus*, Tainton/*Fox*, Fitzpatrick/*Arkwright*, Mabbutt/*Vinter*, Pritchard/*Buxton*, Whitehead/*Cartwright*, Mann
City's hopes of avoiding relegation are buried in the Ashton mud as they give their worst display for more than ten years. Injury-hit Wrexham, missing Mel Sutton and Dixie McNeil, make most of their few chances after defensive hesitation lets in Frank Carrodus to bundle the ball in.

36. DERBY — *Swindlehurst 69*. Ref: D Richardson
Lineups: Moller/*Jones*, Stevens/*Emery*, Hay/*Buckley*, Aitken/*Powell S*, Marshall/*McFarland*, Sweeney/*Powell B*, Tainton/*Wilson*, Fitzpatrick*/*Hector*, Mabbutt/*Duncan*, Smith/*Swindlehurst*, Chandler/*Emson*, Mann
City fail to score for the 22nd time this season as again their stylish approach play does not produce any reward. David Swindlehurst shoots in from Paul Emson's pull-back for Derby, whilst City boss Houghton laments the fact that scoring chances fell to the wrong players on his side.

37. ORIENT — Hay 56, Mann 63, Mabbutt 73 / *Jennings 78*. Ref: C Newsome
Lineups: Moller/*Day*, Stevens/*Fisher*, Hay/*Roffey*, Aitken/*Taylor T*, Marshall/*Gray*, Sweeney/*Moores*, Tainton/*Chidozie**, Mann/*Bowles*, Mabbutt/*Jennings*, Smith/*Hughton*, Chandler/*Taylor P*, *Mayo*
City find their goalscoring form in the second half as they achieve their first win in nine games. A comedy of errors for City's third as Bobby Fisher loses possession in the area to present an easy chance. Mabbutt heads home after Tainton stumbles and balloons the ball into the air.

38. BLACKBURN — *Burke 56*. Ref: G Courtney
Lineups: Moller/*Arnold*, Stevens/*Branagan*, Hay/*Rathbone*, Aitken/*Kendall*, Marshall/*Keeley*, Sweeney/*Fazackerley*, Tainton/*Garner*, Mann/*Crawford*, Mabbutt/*Lowey*, Smith/*Burke*, Chandler/*Speight*
City more than match promotion-chasing Blackburn in soccer skills, but again are unable to turn pressure into goals. Hay's mistake gifts Rovers a corner from which Marshall Burke nets with a close-range header to leave City some five points from safety with just four games left.

39. CHELSEA — Ref: A Glasson
Lineups: Moller/*Borota*, Stevens/*Chivers*, Hay/*Pates*, Aitken/*Bumstead*, Marshall/*Droy**, Sweeney/*Nutton*, Musker/*Driver*, Mann/*Fillery*, Mabbutt/*Lee*, Fitzpatrick/*Mayes*, Chandler/*Hutchings*, *Locke*
Peter Borota looks like a clown with his acrobatics and frying pan gloves, but he has the last laugh. He prevents City from turning one of their most creative displays of the season into victory with many outstanding saves. Locke clears a shot off the line, the only time Borota was beaten.

40. CARDIFF — Mabbutt 39, Mann 58, 90 / *Grapes 7, Kitchen 70*. Ref: M Baker
Lineups: Moller/*Healey*, Stevens/*Jones*, Hay/*Sullivan*, Aitken/*Grapes*, Marshall/*Pontin*, Sweeney/*Dwyer*, Musker*/*Lewis*, Fitzpatrick/*Kitchen*, Mabbutt/*Stevens*, Mann/*Ronson*, Chandler/*Micallef*, Tainton
Cardiff obtain a fortunate equaliser as ref ignores offside flag, but justice is done at the death. Mann's sensational 35-yard injury-time free-kick earns City their first away win for a year as well as rekindling hopes of Second Division survival. Bookings for Phil Dwyer, Hay and Mabbutt.

41. SHREWSBURY — Mann 15 / *Cross 49*. Ref: C Downey
Lineups: Moller/*Wardle*, Stevens/*King*, Whitehead*/*Leonard*, Aitken/*Turner*, Marshall/*Griffin*, Sweeney/*Keay*, Musker/*Tong*, Fitzpatrick/*Atkins*, Mabbutt/*Dungworth*, Mann/*Biggins**, Chandler/*Cross*, Smith/*Bates*
Moller is at fault as he concedes a goal on losing the ball to John Dungworth, but his blushes are saved by City, who went in front with a trademark Mann goal, a 20-yard left-foot thunderbolt into the top corner. A poor showing by City, who incorrectly assumes he has been fouled.

42. OLDHAM — *Wylde 48, Heaton 49*. Ref: R Bridges
Lineups: Moller/*McDonnell*, Stevens/*Sinclair*, Williams/*Blair*, Aitken/*Keegan*, Marshall/*Clements*, Sweeney/*Futcher*, Tainton/*Wylde*, Musker/*Heaton*, Mabbutt/*Steel*, Mann*/*Palmer*, Chandler/*Atkinson*, Smith
City make the early running, Chandler causing the Latics defence many problems, but fall apart as Oldham banish their relegation fears after the break. Roger Wylde is put clear to slip the ball in, and then Paul Heaton is there to snap a chance from a shot Moller could only half save.

LEAGUE DIVISION 2 (CUP-TIES) Manager: Dicks ⇨ Bob Houghton SEASON 1980-81

League Cup

	F-A	H-T	Scorers, Times, and Referees
2:1 A BIRMINGHAM 12 L	1-2	0-1	Ritchie 70 / Ainscow 23, Gemmill 49p / Ref: D Richardson
12,163 1:7			
2:2 H BIRMINGHAM 18 D	0-0	0-0	Ref: M Bidmead / (City lost 1-2 on aggregate)
6,955 1:13			

Team line-ups (1–11, 12 sub used):

Match	1	2	3	4	5	6	7	8	9	10	11	12 sub used
2:1 City	Cashley	Sweeney	Whitehead	Tainton	Gow	Merrick	Fitzpatrick*	Ritchie	Mabbutt	Mann	Pritchard	Hay
2:1 Birmingham	Wealands	Langan	Dennis	Curbishley	Gallagher	Todd	Ainscow	Bertschin	Worthington	Gemmill	Dillion	
2:2 City	Cashley	Sweeney	Whitehead	Gow	Hay	Merrick	Tainton	Ritchie	Mabbutt	Doyle*	Garland	Jantunen
2:2 Birmingham	Wealands	Langan	Dennis	Curbishley	Gallagher	Todd	Ainscow	Bertschin	Worthington	Gemmill	Dillion	

2:1 — A controversial penalty award against Sweeney sparks City's display of passion and quality as Birmingham are outplayed in the second half. Ritchie heads in from Gow's cross to pull back a goal, but Birmingham hang onto the advantage of Alan Ainscow's twelve-yard cross-shot.

2:2 — City, adopting a 4-2-4 formation, start with verve and enthusiasm. Early missed chances upset their attacking plan and they just fade away as Birmingham take control. The cheers of City fans when Jantunen is brought on, turn to boos when they realise that young Doyle is taken off.

FA Cup

	F-A	H-T	Scorers, Times, and Referees
3 A DERBY 21 D	0-0	0-0	Ref: D Lloyd
19,071 5			
3R H DERBY 21 W	2-0	1-0	Mabbutt 18, Ritchie 54 / Ref: D Lloyd
13,649 5			
4 A CARLISLE 21 D	1-1	0-1	Mabbutt 49 / Coady 38 / Ref: D Richardson
10,057 3:23			
4R H CARLISLE 21 W	5-0	0-0	Mabbutt 47, 59, Ritchie 66p, 70 / Ref: D Richardson
12,801 3:23			
5 A NOTT'M FOREST 21 L	1-2	1-0	Mabbutt 40 / Robertson 83p, Wallace 88 / Ref: K Walmsley
26,732 1:8			

Team line-ups (1–11, 12 sub used):

Match	1	2	3	4	5	6	7	8	9	10	11	12 sub used
3 City	Shaw	Sweeney	Hay	Aitken	Rodgers	Marshall	Tainton	Fitzpatrick*	Mabbutt	Garland	Pritchard	
3 Derby	Jones	Emery	Richards	Clark*	McFarland	Ramage	Powell S	Hector	Biley	Swindlehurst Emson	Reid	
3R City	Shaw	Sweeney	Hay	Aitken	Rodgers	Marshall	Tainton	Fitzpatrick	Mabbutt	Ritchie	Pritchard	
3R Derby	Jones	Emery	Richards	Clark	Osgood	Ramage	Powell S	Hector	Biley	Swindlehurst Reid*	Emson	
4 City	Moller	Sweeney	Hay	Aitken	Rodgers	Marshall	Tainton*	Fitzpatrick	Mabbutt	Ritchie*	Whitehead	Pritchard
4 Carlisle	Swinburne	Haigh	Coady	McDonald	Houghton	Parker	Coughlin	Campbell	Bannon*	Beardsley	Staniforth	Hamilton
4R City	Moller	Swinburne [Mann 79]	Hay	Aitken	Rodgers	Marshall	Tainton*	Fitzpatrick	Mabbutt	Ritchie	Whitehead	Mann
4R Carlisle	Swinburne	Haigh	Coady	McDonald	Houghton	Parker	Coughlin	Campbell	Bannon	Beardsley	Staniforth*	Hamilton
5 City	Moller	Stevens	Sweeney	Aitken	Marshall	Nicholls	Tainton	Mann	Mabbutt	Pritchard	Whitehead	
5 Forest	Shilton	Anderson	Gray F	Gray S	Burns	Gunn	Mills	Wallace	Francis	Walsh	Robertson	

3 — John Shaw keeps the 400-1 outsiders in the Cup, making two brilliant saves to stop Kevin Hector and Alan Biley. A typical cup-tie, full of commitment and endeavour, but lacking much in the way of goalmouth incidents. Bookings for Alan Ramage, Roy McFarland and Hay.

3R — A confident win by City, who are inspired by a star performance by Ritchie. A tenacious run down the left by Pritchard sets up a cross for Mabbutt to drive in from 20 yards. Derby only have a couple of opportunities before Ritchie ensures passage to the last 32 with a simple tap-in.

4 — City are well on top, especially in the second half when they threaten to take Carlisle apart. A replay would have been unnecessary if chances had been taken, though Moller is called upon to make a great save when Gordon Staniforth's shot is deflected by Marshall in the 81st minute.

4R — Mabbutt opens the floodgates, though he spurns a hat-trick opportunity for Sunderland-bound Ritchie to mark his farewell appearance with a penalty. Carlisle's best chance occurs in the final minute, but the long arms of Moller deny Paul Bannon when he looks almost certain to score.

5 — Forest, out of sorts following their midweek trip to Japan, are rescued by a late Houdini act. City look likely giant-killers when Mabbutt coolly strokes the ball home, but a debatable pen against Marshall turns the tide. Ian Wallace nets in a goalmouth scramble to deprive City of a replay.

Appearances and Goals

	Appearances						Goals			
	Lge	Sub	LC	Sub	FAC	Sub	Lge	LC	FAC	Tot
Aitken, Peter	22						1			1
Baddeley, Kevin					5					
Cashley, Ray	20		2							
Chandler, Ricky	7	1								
Doyle, Ian	1									
Fitzpatrick, Tony	34		1		4		1			1
Garland, Chris	10	5	1		1		1			1
Gow, Gerry	11		2							
Hay, Alan	36		1		4		1			1
Jantunen, Perti		1			1	1				
Mabbutt, Kevin	38		2		5		9		5	14
Mann, Jimmy	22	3	1		1		6		1	7
Marshall, Julian	26				5					
Merrick, Geoff	17	1	2							
Moller, Jan	17				3					
Musker, Russell	4									
Nicholls, Alan	4				1		1			1
Pritchard, Howard	15	6	1		3	1	2			2
Ritchie, Tom	27		2		3		5	1	3	9
Rodgers, David	14				4					
Shaw, John	5		2							
Smith, Gary	7	7								
Stevens, Paul	14				1					
Sweeney, Gerry	38	2			5					
Tainton, Trevor	40	1	2		5		1			1
Whitehead, Clive	31		2		3					
Williams, Gary	1									
(own-goals)							1			1
27 players used	462	25	22	2	55	2	29	1	9	39

League Table

			Home					Away					
		P	W	D	L	F	A	W	D	L	F	A	Pts
1	West Ham	42	19	1	1	53	12	9	9	3	26	17	66
2	Notts Co	42	10	8	3	26	15	9	9	4	23	23	53
3	Swansea	42	12	5	4	39	19	9	9	6	25	25	50
4	Blackburn	42	12	8	1	28	7	10	7	7	14	22	50
5	Luton	42	10	6	5	35	23	8	6	7	26	23	48
6	Derby	42	9	8	4	34	26	6	7	8	23	26	45
7	Grimsby	42	10	8	3	21	10	5	7	9	23	32	45
8	QP Rangers	42	11	7	3	36	12	4	6	11	20	34	43
9	Watford	42	13	5	3	34	18	3	6	12	16	27	43
10	Sheffield Wed	42	14	4	3	38	14	3	7	11	15	37	42
11	Newcastle	42	11	7	3	22	13	6	6	9	8	32	42
12	Chelsea	42	8	7	7	27	15	6	9	9	19	26	40
13	Cambridge	42	13	1	7	36	23	4	5	12	17	42	40
14	Shrewsbury	42	9	7	5	33	22	2	10	9	13	25	39
15	Oldham	42	7	9	5	19	16	5	6	10	20	32	39
16	Wrexham	42	5	8	8	22	24	7	6	8	21	21	38
17	Orient	42	9	8	4	34	20	4	6	13	21	36	38
18	Bolton	42	10	5	6	40	27	4	5	12	21	39	38
19	Cardiff	42	7	7	7	23	24	5	5	11	21	36	36
20	Preston	42	8	7	6	28	26	3	7	11	13	36	36
21	BRISTOL CITY	42	6	10	5	19	15	1	6	14	13	36	30
22	Bristol Rov	42	4	9	8	21	24	1	16	16	13	41	23
		924	217	144	101	668	405	101	144	217	405	668	924

Odds & ends

Double wins: (0).

Double losses: (4) Notts Co, QP Rangers, Wrexham, Cambridge.

Won from behind: (2) Luton (h), Cardiff (a).

Lost from in front: (2) Sheffield Wed (a). Luton (a).

High spots: Beating Bolton 3-1 at Ashton Gate on 13 December. Winning 3-2 at Ninian Park on 20 April. Beating Carlisle 5-0 in the FA Cup. Reaching the 5th Round of the FA Cup. Beating Bristol Rov (a) 1-0 in the Gloucestershire Cup Final on 5 May.

Low spots: Losing 0-5 at West Ham on 11 November. Low spots: Scoring fewer goals (29) than points (30). Relegation to the Third Division.

Player of the Year: Kevin Mabbutt.

Ever-presents: (0).

Hat-tricks: (0).

Leading scorer: Kevin Mabbutt (14).

LEAGUE DIVISION 3 — Manager: Houghton ⇨ Hodgson ⇨ Sharpe — SEASON 1981-82

Player position columns: 1, 2, 3, 4, 5, 6, 7, 8, 9, 10, 11, 12 sub used
(Top line = Bristol City; italic line = opponents)

No		Date	Opponent	Att	Pos	Pt	F-A	H-T	Scorers, Times, and Referees
1	A	29/8	CARLISLE	3,924		D 1	2-2	0-2	Harford 58, Mann 81 / Lee 5, Robson 43 / Ref: A Robinson
2	H	5/9	DONCASTER	6,996		D 2	2-2	2-0	Mabbutt 39, Harford 44 / Dawson 81, Mell 89 / Ref: A Seville
3	A	12/9	FULHAM	4,196	19→12	L 2	1-2	1-0	Mann 9 / Davies 65, Brown 90 / Ref: I Borrett
4	H	19/9	NEWPORT	8,021	13→2	W 5	2-1	0-1	Mann 58, 86 / Aldridge 30 / Ref: D Vickers
5	H	22/9	PLYMOUTH	7,383	6→23	W 8	3-2	1-2	Harford 2, Nicholls 61, Mann 72 / Sims 15, Hodges 32 / Ref: H Taylor
6	A	26/9	PORTSMOUTH	10,203	13→11	L 8	0-2	0-1	Tait 6, Berry 86 / Ref: M James
7	A	29/9	GILLINGHAM	3,887	15→17	D 9	1-1	0-0	Harford 77 / Price 60 / Ref: K Salmon
8	H	3/10	WALSALL	6,049	20→4	L 9	0-1	0-1	Penn 3 / Ref: L Burden
9	H	10/10	PRESTON	5,454	19→22	D 10	0-0	0-0	Ref: L Shapter
10	A	17/10	OXFORD	4,087	20→11	L 10	0-1	0-1	Cassells 45p / Ref: J Moules
11	H	20/10	READING	5,178	17→10	W 13	2-0	0-0	Devine 54, Tainton 79 / Ref: H King

Line-ups and match reports

1 — A CARLISLE
Bristol City: Moller, Stevens, Merrick, Rushbury*, Rodgers, Marshall, Tainton, Musker, Mabbutt, Harford, Devine; sub: Crabbe
Carlisle: Swinburne, Ashurst, Cody, Houghton, Parker, Coughlin, Campbell, Lee, Robson, Crabbe; sub: Bannon
City recover after a nightmare first half at Brunton Park. Rob Lee is unmarked as he heads home and then, just before the break, Pop Robson nips in between City's tall defenders to nod in Carlisle's second. Harford, City's £150,000 signing, sparks comeback with a glancing header.

2 — H DONCASTER
Bristol City: Moller, Stevens, Russell, Mann, Rodgers, Marshall, Tainton, Musker, Mabbutt, Harford, Devine
Doncaster: Boyd, Dawson, Snodin, Lally, Pugh, Harle, Warboys, Lister*, Mell; sub: Douglas
Two late blunders by Rodgers, shortly after Harford's header hits the post, cost City their first three-point haul in a game they dominate. His failure to cut out a centre gives Richard Dawson an easy chance, and a weak back-pass sets up Stewart Mell to lob the ball over Moller.

3 — A FULHAM
Bristol City: Moller, Stevens, Hay, Mann, Rodgers, Merrick, Tainton, Musker, Harford, Mabbutt, Devine
Fulham: Peyton, Hopkins, Strong, Beck, Brown, Gale, Davies, Wilson, Coney, O'Sullivan, Lewington
Fulham control the midfield and keep the City defence under almost constant pressure. Mann produces City's only shot on target when his blockbuster free-kick produces an early lead, while Roger Brown's superb injury-time header presents a deserving winner to the Cottagers.

4 — H NEWPORT
Bristol City: Moller, Stevens, Sweeney, Aitken, Rodgers, Marshall, Tainton, Mann, Mabbutt, Harford, Hay
Newport: Kendall, Elsey, Lees, Davies, Oakes, Bailey, Vaughan, Johnson, Gwyther, Aldridge*, Moore; sub: Tynan
Passions run high as the ref allows City's free-kick equaliser, despite having blown for an encroachment. Moller's save from Gwyther's spot-kick just before half-time is the turning point, and Mann's spectacular 25-yard winning drive into the top corner knocks County off top spot.

5 — H PLYMOUTH
Bristol City: Moller, Stevens, Sweeney, Aitken, Rodgers*, Nicholls, Tainton, Mann, Mabbutt, Harford, Hay; sub: Musker
Plymouth: Crudgington, Nisbet, Uzzell, Harrison, Foster, Cooper, Hodges, Kemp, Sims, Randell, Dennis*; sub: Murphy
Plymouth's failure to put up a defensive wall allows Mann to save City's blushes with a stunning 35-yard free-kick. City are fortunate as they never look like getting back into game after previously goalless Argyle snatch the lead with a John Sims header and a tap in by Kevin Hodges.

6 — A PORTSMOUTH
Bristol City: Moller, Stevens, Sweeney, Aitken, Rodgers, Nicholls, Tainton, Mann, Mabbutt, Harford, Hay
Portsmouth: Knight, McLaughlin, Viney, Kamara, Aizlewood, Ellis, Hemmerman, Doyle, Rafferty, Berry, Tait
A terrible performance by City, as they fall to Mick Tait's header and Steve Berry's mis-hit 30-yard shot from the left touchline that dips into the top corner. Harford puts himself about in the manner of an old fashioned centre-forward, but he needs a supply of good quality crosses.

7 — A GILLINGHAM
Bristol City: Moller, Stevens, Hay, Aitken, Rodgers, Nicholls, Tainton, Mann, Mabbutt, Harford, Musker
Gillingham: Hillyard, Sitton, Ford, Bruce, Weatherly, Bowman, Adams, Duncan, Tydeman*, Lee, Price; sub: Sharpe
Harford's looping header from Stevens' right-wing cross underlines just what a dangerous striker he is with the right service. Unfortunately in this dismal match such service is in short supply and City are somewhat fortunate to respond to Kenny Price's freak ricochet from a clearance.

8 — H WALSALL
Bristol City: Moller, Stevens, Hay, Aitken, Rodgers, Whitehead, Tainton, Mann, Mabbutt, Harford, Musker
Walsall: Green, Macken, Mower, Beech, Serella, Hart*, Rees, Waddington S, Penn, Buckley, Caswell; sub: Loveridge
The Saddlers, who have not conceded an away League goal this season, take an early lead. Don Penn is at the near post to put away Mark Rees' cross. City are unlucky when Mabbutt clears the bar with a 17th-minute penalty, but Walsall deserve to avenge their recent cup defeat.

9 — H PRESTON
Bristol City: Moller, Stevens, Hay, Aitken, Rodgers, Sweeney, Musker, Mann, Mabbutt, Harford, Whitehead
Preston: Litchfield, Coleman, McAteer, Clark, Booth, O'Riordan, Kelly, Buckley, Bruce, Anderson*, Dunn; sub: Farnelly
In front of the Match of the Day cameras Whitehead demonstrates much of his old guile and pace, but City are nearly made to pay for not making the most of their early domination. Preston almost snatch a late victory, but John Kelly squanders his chance of a debut goal.

10 — A OXFORD
Bristol City: Moller, Stevens, Hay, Aitken, Rodgers, Sweeney, Devine, Mann, Mabbutt, Harford, Whitehead
Oxford: Burton, Doyle, Fogg, Jeffrey, Wright, Shotton, Jones*, Foley, Cassells, Thomas, Smithers; sub: Kearns
Following Fred Ford's death yesterday, this fixture is somewhat appropriate. Oxford's match-winning pen is a travesty as Andy Thomas falls to the ground without any contact being made. City attack relentlessly after the break, having eight shots on target, but the goals don't come.

11 — H READING
Bristol City: Moller, Stevens, Hay, Aitken, Rodgers, Sweeney, Tainton, Mann, Harford, Devine, Whitehead
Reading: Fearon, Williams, Lewis, Wood, Hicks, Hetzke*, Earles, Dixon, Heale, Beavon, Sanchez; sub: Kearney
City produce their most fluent football of the season as Harford wins everything in the air. After the speedy Devine slots home his first League goal, City hit a purple patch and Tainton, Whitehead, Aitken and Harford all go close before Tainton sweeps in a deflection at the far post.

12 LINCOLN A 24/10 — 3,819 · 16 18 16 · W 2-1 (2-0)
Harford 33, 39 / Bell 60
Ref: K Walmsley
City: Moller, Stevens, Tainton, Aitken, Rodgers, Sweeney, Devine, Mann, Mabbutt, Harford, Whitehead — Gilbert
Lincoln: Naylor, Thompson, McVay, Cockerill, Peake, Carr, Commack*, Shipley, Hobson, Cunningham, Bell
As well as heading both goals for City's first away win of the season, Mick Harford picks up a statuette for helping Lincoln to promotion last term. The Imps deserved their goal, as seconds earlier the ref awarded them a free-kick instead of allowing Tony Cunningham's brilliant lob.

13 CHESTERFIELD H 31/10 — 8,110 · 15 3 17 · D 0-0 (0-0)
Ref: A Ward
City: Moller, Stevens, Williams, Aitken, Rodgers, Boyle, Tainton, Mann, Harford, Devine, Whitehead — Crawford, Walker
Chesterfield: Turner, Turk, O'Neill, Wilson, Green, Fidley, Windridge*, Henderson, Bonnyman, Kowaiski
Terry Boyle has an outstanding debut after signing from Crystal Palace in a swap deal that saw Kevin Mabbutt move the other way. Much skill and good play by both sides belies the scoreline and causes City boss Bob Houghton to bemoan the introduction of three-points-for-a-win.

14 MILLWALL A 3/11 — 5,002 · 17 4 17 · L 0-2 (0-1)
Boyle 43 (og), West 60
Ref: J Deakin
City: Moller, Stevens, Williams, Aitken, Rodgers, Boyle, Tainton, Mann, Harford, Devine, Chandler — West
Millwall: Gleasure, Martin, Warman, Chatterton, Allardyce, Slough, Hayes, Anderson, McKenna, Horrix
Boyle puts his crisp header into the wrong net from Alan West's free-kick, while another West shot hits Aitken on his knee before going in. It could have been worse for a City side too stereotyped and predictable as Millwall miss a 41st-min penalty which Nick Chatterton blasts wide.

15 BRENTFORD A 7/11 — 6,758 · 14 15 20 · W 1-0 (0-0)
Harford 82
Ref: A Gunn
City: Moller, Stevens, Williams, Aitken, Rodgers, Boyle, Tainton, Mann, Harford, Devine, Chandler — Booker
Brentford: McKellar, Salman, Tucker, McNichol, Whitehead, Hurlock, Kamara, Bowen, Johnson*, Roberts — Bowles
Brentford boss Fred Callaghan is scathing of City's negative tactics just five days after the departing Whitehead criticised Houghton as being too defensively minded. City, after hardly mustering an attack in the first half, obtain a late winner when Harford heads in Devine's corner.

16 SOUTHEND H 14/11 — 6,310 · 17 8 20 · L 0-2 (0-0)
Cusack 79p, Pennyfather 90
Ref: D Hutchinson
City: Moller, Stevens, Williams, Aitken, Rodgers, Boyle, Tainton, Mann*, Harford, Devine, Chandler — Sweeney, Greaves
Southend: Keeley, Stead, Yates, Pennyfather, Moody, Cusack, Gray*, Poutney, Spence, Mercer — Nelson
Keith Mercer insists he is no cheat on being awarded a penalty. He refutes City players' allegations that he dived following a Rodgers tackle outside the box. Southend, the better side throughout, make sure of their success when Glenn Pennyfather's half-hit shot trickles over the line.

17 BURNLEY H 28/11 — 5,255 · 19 20 20 · L 2-3 (1-1)
Mann 16p, Garland 52
Young 3, McGee 77, 90p
Ref: C Thomas
City: Moller, Stevens, Williams, Aitken, Rodgers, Boyle, Devine, Mann, Harford, Garland, Musker — Potts
Burnley: Stevenson, Laws, Wharton, Cassidy, Overson, Phelan, Dobson, Steven*, Hamilton, McGee — Young
Two decisions by referee Clive Thomas, in his last League season, decide this enthralling contest. City are denied a valid claim for an 85th-minute penalty, whilst Burnley's, five minutes later, is given to enable them to obtain due reward for their fine display of one-touch football.

18 SWINDON A 5/12 — 7,236 · 20 19 21 · D 0-0 (0-0)
Ref: J Martin
City: Moller, Stevens, Williams, Aitken, Boyle, Nicholls, Devine, Mann, Chandler, Harford, Tainton
Swindon: Allan, Baddeley, Hughes, Lewis, Graham, Emmanuel, Carter, Rowland, Rideout — Pritchard
City's young defenders emerge with credit from this game, in which the attackers of both sides are devoid of ideas. Mann breaks clear in the last minute, but his left-foot shot flashes just wide. Howard Pritchard missed Swindon's best chance on five mins when his header hit the bar.

19 BRISTOL ROV A 29/12 — 12,155 · 21 8 21 · L 0-1 (0-1)
McCaffery 4
Ref: T Bune
City: Moller, Stevens, Williams B, Aitken, Rodgers, Boyle, Tainton, Mann, Chandler, Harford, Devine — Williams D, Stephens
Bristol Rov: Thomas, Jones, Williams B, McCaffery, Parkin, Mabbut, Barrett*, Gillies, Penny, Slatter — Sweeney
Rovers end 18 years of City dominance in League encounters in an exciting clash that sees Archie Stephens hit a post as well as having his header cleared off the line. Aidan McCaffery is Rovers' hero, as he beats Moller with a low drive from Timmy Parkin's flick on from a corner.

20 WIMBLEDON H 2/1 — 4,781 · 21 23 21 · L 1-3 (1-1)
Stevens 45
Ketteridge 38, Lazarus 63, 77
Ref: K Barrett
City: Moller, Stevens, Williams, Aitken, Rodgers, Boyle, Tainton, Mann, Harford, Devine, Chandler — Joseph, Sweeney
Wimbledon: Beasant, Clement, Thomas, Smith, Morris, Downes, Ketteridge, Leslie, Lazarus, Hodges — Devine*
City disintegrate completely in the second half and suffer a humiliating defeat to end Houghton's Ashton Gate reign. Stevens gets his first League goal for City, who thrice hit the woodwork, but they are torn apart by Francis Joseph, who sets up two of Wimbledon's strikes.

21 HUDDERSFIELD H 16/1 — 5,142 · 20 8 22 · D 0-0 (0-0)
Ref: A Hamil
City: Moller, Stevens, Williams, Aitken, Boyle, Nicholls, Devine, Mann, Chandler*, Harford, Chandler — Fletcher, Garland
Huddersfield: Taylor, Brown, Burke, Stanton, Sutton, Harvey, Lillis, Kennedy, Hotte, Cowling
It takes the 75th-minute appearance of sub Garland to wake City up and he is deprived of a penalty near the end when he falls over the keeper's arm. A poor game, after which Terriers boss Mike Buxton says 'if any of my players are happy with their play I will throw them off the coach'.

22 NEWPORT A 30/1 — 5,915 · 21 17 23 · D 1-1 (1-1)
Harford 16
Vaughan 12
Ref: C White
City: Moller, Stevens, Williams, Aitken, Boyle*, Sweeney, Tainton, Mann, Chandler, Harford, Musker — Moore, Hay
Newport: Kendall, Lees, Relish, Davies, Oakes, Johnson, Vaughan, Elsey, Aldridge*, Waddle — Tynan
The City fans who travel to Newport fearing it might be the club's final game are rewarded by players who give their all in a match they should have won. Nigel Vaughan drives in a low shot to put County ahead, but City equalise as Harford glances Mann's corner past Mark Kendall.

23 FULHAM H 6/2 — 9,312 · 22 2 24 · D 0-0 (0-0)
Ref: M Heath
City: Moller, Stevens, Hay, Newman*, Williams, Nicholls, Musker, Bray, Chandler, Harford, Economou — Lewington, Smith
Fulham: Peyton, Lock, Strong, O'Driscoll, Brown, Gale, Tempest, Wilson, Coney, O'Sullivan
A triumph for the club given up for dead earlier in the week, as they never look remotely in danger of losing against high-riding Fulham. Denuded by the departure of the Ashton Gate Eight, the Bristol Babes match Fulham for skill and often outplay them with their enthusiasm.

Column key: No | Date | 1 | 2 | 3 | 4 | 5 | 6 | 7 | 8 | 9 | 10 | 11 | 12 sub used | Scorers, Times, and Referees | Att | Pos | Pt | F-A | H-T

---

24 · A PLYMOUTH · 9/2 — L · F-A 1-2 · H-T 0-1 · Att 5,260 (11) · Pos 22 · Pt 24

1	2	3	4	5	6	7	8	9	10	11	12
Moller	Stevens	Hay	Newman	Williams	Nicholls	Musker	Bray	Chandler	Harford	Economou	
Cruddington	*Nisbet*	*Uzzell*	*Harrison*	*James*	*Cooper*	*Hodges*	*Cook*	*Sims*	*Randell*	*Rogers*	*Smith*

Scorers: Chandler 71 / Cook 38, Hodges 64. Ref: G Napthine

Moller stands between Plymouth and an avalanche of goals at Home Park. He makes eight outstanding saves as Plymouth mount incessant pressure and even gets a hand to Jeff Cook's opener. City's only respite is when Chandler gets his first League goal with a great solo effort.

---

25 · A WALSALL · 13/2 — W · F-A 1-0 · H-T 1-0 · Att 4,020 (8) · Pos 22 · Pt 27

1	2	3	4	5	6	7	8	9	10	11	12
Moller	Stevens	Hay	Newman	Williams	Nicholls	Musker	Bray	Chandler	Harford	Economou*	Smith
Green	*Macken**	*Mower*	*Beech*	*Serella*	*Hart*	*Reest*	*Lowrey*	*Penn*	*Buckley*	*Cashwell*	*Round*

Scorers: Newman 34. Ref: T Mills

Walsall's aggressive tactics are condemned by City boss Roy Hodgson as the Babes bring off the Third Division shock result of the day. City's goal by Newman is reminiscent of those by Mann before his enforced departure – a 20-yard free-kick that the Walsall keeper does not see.

---

26 · H PORTSMOUTH · 20/2 — L · F-A 0-1 · H-T 0-0 · Att 9,407 (16) · Pos 22 · Pt 27

1	2	3	4	5	6	7	8	9	10	11	12
Moller	Stevens	Williams	Newman	McCaffery	Nicholls	Musker	Carter	Chandler	Harford	Hay	
Knight	*McLaughlin*	*Bryant*	*Barnard*	*Aizlewood**	*Garner*	*Hammerman*	*Rafferty*	*Gregory*	*Bason*	*Crown*	*Bartlett*

Scorers: Rafferty 80. Ref: M Baker

City play attractive, fluent football in a one-sided game, but are unable to put their chances away. Pompey make City pay as a poor back-pass by Nicholls gives Bill Rafferty the solitary goal. Newman and Chandler are both unfortunate with efforts which came back off the woodwork.

---

27 · H EXETER · 23/2 — W · F-A 3-2 · H-T 2-1 · Att 6,617 (18) · Pos 22 · Pt 30

1	2	3	4	5	6	7	8	9	10	11	12
Moller	Stevens	Hay	Newman*	McCaffery	Nicholls	Musker	Carter	Chandler	Harford	Economou	
Bond	*Mitchell**	*Sparrow*	*Rogers M*	*Foster*	*Roberts L*	*Fisher*	*Rogers P*	*Kellow*	*Delve*	*Pullar*	*Pratt*

Scorers: Harford 17, 30, Chandler 82 / Roberts 29, Rogers P 81. Ref: D Reeves

Against the most entertaining side in the country, whose 26 League games have produced 105 goals, City are imperiously driven forward by Musker. City's opener is their best goal for years, as Chandler's cross from the right is headed in with the speed of a bullet by Mick Harford.

---

28 · A PRESTON · 27/2 — W · F-A 3-1 · H-T 1-1 · Att 6,424 (22) · Pos 18 · Pt 33

1	2	3	4	5	6	7	8	9	10	11	12
Moller	Stevens	Williams	Bray	McCaffery	Nicholls	Musker*	Carter	Chandler	Harford	Hay	Newman
Hodge	*Taylor**	*McAteer*	*Bell*	*Booth*	*O'Riordan*	*Kelly*	*McGee*	*Elliott*	*Naughton*	*Bruce*	*Anderson*

Scorers: McCaffery 45, Bray 50, Harford 90 / Kelly 23. Ref: G Courtney

Three superb goals, stern defending and a large amount of luck brings a vital win. Preston monopolise the play, but City have all the breaks after John Kelly scores from twelve yards in a goalmouth scramble. Bray notches his first City goal as his 35-yarder loops over the keeper.

---

29 · H OXFORD · 6/3 — L · F-A 0-2 · H-T 0-0 · Att 8,155 (4) · Pos 21 · Pt 33

1	2	3	4	5	6	7	8	9	10	11	12
Moller	Stevens	Williams	Bray	McCaffery	Nicholls	Gooding	Carter	Cassells*	Harford	Hay	Newman
Burton	*Doyle*	*Farr*	*Jeffery*	*Briggs*	*Shotton*	*Brock*	*Foley*	*Thomas*	*Seacole*	*Kearns*	

Scorers: Shotton 50, Kearns 83. Ref: A Robinson

City fail to adjust to the muddy conditions as Oxford's greater skill and direct approach brings about a disappointing defeat. Carter is denied his first League goal by Roy Burton's great save on 15 mins. Oxford give new manager Jim Smith a great start with a slick second-half display.

---

30 · A READING · 10/3 — L · F-A 1-3 · H-T 0-0 · Att 3,552 · Pos 21 · Pt 33

1	2	3	4	5	6	7	8	9	10	11	12
Moller	Stevens	Williams	Bray	McCaffery	Nicholls	Musker	Carter	Chandler	Gooding*	Hay	Newman
Fearon	*Williams J*	*White*	*Webb*	*Hicks*	*Hetzke*	*Beavon*	*Earles*	*Dixon*	*Sanchez*	*Donnellan**	*Lewis*

Scorers: Dixon 62 (og) / Dixon 54, 86, Beavon 56. Ref: V Callow

City's lightweight side are again found out by the muddy conditions. Reading's Kerry Dixon ends a barren eight-match spell with a bizarre hat-trick. A cracking drive is followed by a headed own-goal, before finishing with a shot from the right past the badly-positioned Moller.

---

31 · H LINCOLN · 13/3 — L · F-A 0-1 · H-T 0-1 · Att 6,570 (5) · Pos 22 · Pt 33

1	2	3	4	5	6	7	8	9	10	11	12
Moller	Stevens	Hay	Newman	McCaffery	Williams	Bray	Carter	Chandler	Gooding	Economou	
Felgate	*Carr*	*Turner P*	*Cockerill*	*Peake*	*Thompson*	*Shipley*	*Turner W*	*Hobson*	*Cunningham*	*Hibbard*	

Scorers: Cunningham 35. Ref: D Civil

Lincoln extend their unbeaten run to ten games with a sweetly hit left-foot shot from 12 yards. Moller blames a long-standing shoulder injury for failing to keep a clean sheet in his final game, but it is doubtful that any keeper would have been able to save Tony Cunningham's strike.

---

32 · A CHESTERFIELD · 20/3 — L · F-A 0-1 · H-T 0-0 · Att 4,240 (1) · Pos 22 · Pt 33

1	2	3	4	5	6	7	8	9	10	11	12
Shaw	Stevens	Hay	Newman	Williams	Nicholls	Musker	Bray	Carter	Harford	Economou	
Turner	*Stirk*	*O'Neill*	*Wilson*	*Green**	*Pollard*	*Windridge*	*Henderson*	*Bonnyman*	*Ridley*	*Crawford*	*Athersych*

Scorers: Wilson 68. Ref: N Glover

City are made to pay for their misses against top of the table Chesterfield. Harford hits the post with his shot when clean through in the 55th minute, and then Economou and Bray spurn good chances before Danny Wilson settles the game for the Spireites with a spectacular 20-yarder.

---

33 · H BRENTFORD · 27/3 — L · F-A 0-1 · H-T 0-0 · Att 6,243 (7) · Pos 22 · Pt 33

1	2	3	4	5	6	7	8	9	10	11	12
Shaw	Stevens	Hay	Newman*	Williams	Nicholls	Musker	Bray	Chandler	Carter	Economou	Boyle
McKellar	*McNichall*	*Hill*	*Salman*	*Whitehead*	*Hurlock*	*Kamara J*	*Johnson*	*Bowen*	*Bowles*	*Roberts*	

Scorers: Bowen 67. Ref: D Lloyd

City's lack of experience shows against a Brentford side reduced to ten men early on. Chandler is unfortunate when hitting the woodwork twice in the second half, but Keith Bowen makes no mistake and steers the ball into a vacant net after a mix up between Shaw and Boyle.

---

34 · A SOUTHEND · 3/4 — L · F-A 0-3 · H-T 0-0 · Att 3,416 (9) · Pos 22 · Pt 33

1	2	3	4	5	6	7	8	9	10	11	12
Shaw	Stevens	Williams	Boyle	McCaffery	Nicholls!	Economou*	Bray	Carter	Carter	Hay	Newman
Cawston	*Stead*	*Yates*	*Pountney*	*Moody*	*Hadley*	*Greaves*	*Phillips*	*Nelson**	*Mercer*	*Otulakowski*	*Spence*

Scorers: Greaves 68, 75, Phillips 73p. Ref: A Ward

City look capable of taking a point from this undistinguished game until Nicholls gets involved in an off-the-ball incident with Steve Phillips to gift Southend their penalty. Danny Greaves heads Southend in front and then punishes slack marking at a free-kick to coolly slot in their third.

League match record (matches 35–46)

No	Venue	Opponent	Date	Att	Pos	—	Pts	Res	FT	HT
35	H	CARLISLE	6/4	4,329	22	3	34	D	1-1	0-1
36	A	EXETER	10/4	4,580	22	15	34	L	0-4	0-2
37	H	BRISTOL ROV	12/4	11,451	22	13	34	L	1-2	0-1
38	H	SWINDON	17/4	6,929	23	21	34	L	0-3	0-1
39	A	CHESTER	21/4	1,210	22	24	35	D	0-0	0-0
40	A	BURNLEY	24/4	7,063	23	5	35	L	0-2	0-0
41	A	GILLINGHAM	1/5	4,183	23	11	38	W	2-1	1-0
42	A	HUDDERSFIELD	4/5	3,468	23	14	38	L	0-5	0-3
43	A	WIMBLEDON	8/5	2,114	23	22	39	D	0-0	0-0
44	H	MILLWALL	12/5	3,404	23	8	42	W	4-1	2-1
45	H	CHESTER	15/5	4,475	23	24	45	W	1-0	1-0
46	A	DONCASTER	18/5	4,252	23	19	46	D	2-2	0-2

Average: Home 6,511 — Away 5,077

---

35 — CARLISLE (H) 6/4 — D 1-1 (0-1)
Scorers: Chandler 79 / Lee 8. Ref: M Robinson

City: Shaw, Stevens, Williams, Musker, Boyle, Nicholls, Bray, Chandler, Newman, Carter, Hay; sub Economou
Carlisle: Swinburn, Parker, Rushbury, Larkin, Ashurst, Craig, Ritchie, Haigh, Robson, Lee, Stainforth

A battling City performance as Hodgson's decision to field a more attacking formation presents Carlisle with a dream start. Dave Rushbury's cross-field pass sets up Bob Lee's angled drive, but Chandler makes up for his open-goal miss against Southend by lobbing in the equaliser.

36 — EXETER (A) 10/4 — L 0-4 (0-2)
Scorers: Kellow 29, 65p, Pratt 41, Rogers P 76. Ref: D Hedges

City: Shaw, Stevens, Williams, Musker, Boyle, Nicholls, Bray, Chandler, Newman, Carter*, Hay; sub Economou
Exeter: Bond, Rogers M, Sparrow, Giles, Foster, Roberts P, Pratt, Rogers P, Kellow, Delve, Hatch

Enterprising Exeter take their League goals total to 60 with a clinical demolition of City who, whilst lively in midfield, show little confidence in attack. After Kellow's diving header puts Exeter ahead, Pratt seizes on a Williams slip as he attempts to control Shaw's short throw-out.

37 — BRISTOL ROV (H) 12/4 — L 1-2 (0-1)
Scorers: Bray 66 / Williams D 3, Randall 54. Ref: R Lewis

City: Shaw, Stevens, Williams, Musker, Boyle, Nicholls, Bray, Chandler, Newman, Carter, Hay; sub Devine
Bristol Rov: Kite, Jones, Slatter, Randall, Parkin, Bailey, Barrett, Williams D, Stephens*, Mabbutt, Williams G; McCaffery

Rovers are fortunate to hang on in an incident-packed derby following Bray's carefully placed 20-yarder. City have eight shots on target to three for the Rovers, but they have no one to match the ability of David Williams, who finds the corner of the net with a sweet 25-yard drive.

38 — SWINDON (H) 17/4 — L 0-3 (0-1)
Scorers: Pritchard 25, Emmanuel 49, 62. Ref: J Bray

City: Shaw, Stevens, Hay, Allan, Boyle, Nicholls, Williams, Bray, Chandler, Carter, Newman; sub Devine
Swindon: Allan, Henry*, Baddeley, Emmanuel, Lewis, Stroud, Pritchard, Carter, Rideout, Greenwood, Graham; Quinn

City hit a new low as they illustrate to their dwindling band of fans that they are not good enough to retain their status. Fatal hesitation by Williams allows Howard Pritchard to shoot Swindon ahead, while Gary Emmanuel twice runs through City's defence to add a couple more.

39 — CHESTER (A) 21/4 — D 0-0 (0-0)
Ref: N Wilson

City: Shaw, Stevens, Hay, Musker, Boyle, Nicholls, Williams, Bray*, Chandler, Carter, Newman; sub Devine
Chester: Millington, Burns, Storton, Zelem, Blackwell, Satcliffe, Jones, Steven, Ludlam, Henderson, Allen

Shaw keeps City in the game by saving John Allen's thundering drive and a Bryn Jones header in the first half, as well as coming off his line to deny Peter Henderson after the break. City could have stolen the points as four clear chances go begging in the last five minutes.

40 — BURNLEY (A) 24/4 — L 0-2 (0-0)
Scorers: Laws 60, Dobson 80. Ref: G Owen

City: Shaw, Stevenson, Hay, Musker, Boyle, Nicholls, Williams, Devine, Chandler, Carter*, Economou; sub Newman
Burnley: Stevenson, Laws, Wharton, Cassidy, Overson, Holt, Dobson, Steven, McGee, Young, Ludlam

Manager Hodgson is proud of his side after an outstanding effort reaps no reward because of continued failings in front of goal. City miss chances before Brian Laws hammers in a low cross to put Burnley ahead. Martin Dobson seals the points by turning the ball over the line.

41 — GILLINGHAM (A) 1/5 — W 2-1 (1-0)
Scorers: Williams 41, Economou 85 / Lee 75. Ref: T Spencer

City: Shaw, Stevens, Hay, Musker, Boyle, Nicholls, Williams, Devine, Chandler, Stevens, Carter; subs Newman, Economou
Gillingham: Hillyard, White, Adams, Bruce, Weatherly, Shaw*, Powell, Tydeman, Grewcock, Cascarino, Lee; Sage

A carnival atmosphere at Ashton Gate as three days after the announcement that the future of the club has been secured, City achieve their first win in 13 games. City, under caretaker boss Gerry Sharpe, benefit with both Williams and Economou scoring their first goals for the club.

42 — HUDDERSFIELD (A) 4/5 — L 0-5 (0-3)
Scorers: Stanton 62, Wilson 88, Boyle 3 (og.), Cowling 11, Robins 29. Ref: M Scott

City: Shaw, Cox, Hay, Musker, Boyle, Nicholls, Williams, Devine, Chandler, Stevens, Economou; subs Carter*, Newman
Huddersfield: Cox, Brown, Burke, Stanton, Valentine, Harvey, Lillis, Kennedy, Robins, Wilson, Cowling; Ketteridge

City's relegation is assured as their adventurous approach is spoilt by wretched defending. Boyle deflects in Micky Kennedy's corner, while hesitation by Williams allows Dave Cowling to head into the vacant net. Then Stevens gifts Huddersfield their fifth goal with a poor back-pass.

43 — WIMBLEDON (A) 8/5 — D 0-0 (0-0)
Ref: D Axcell

City: Shaw, Beasant, Hay, Musker, Boyle, Nicholls, Williams, Bray, Devine, Stevens, Economou; sub Newman
Wimbledon: Beasant, Leslie, Armstrong, Smith, Morris, Downes, Shaw*, Thomas, Joseph, Hodges, Evans; Belfield*

Wimbledon have the better chances, with Francis Joseph hitting the post early on and John Leslie having a 67th-minute strike disallowed for offside. Chandler, with two more misses, continues his run of bad luck, while Williams mars much excellent play with his casual attitude.

44 — MILLWALL (H) 12/5 — W 4-1 (2-1)
Scorers: Newman 22, 35p, Chandler 55, 65 / Dibble 45. Ref: C Newsome

City: Shaw, Gleasure, Hay, Musker, Boyle, Nicholls, Williams, Bray*, Devine, Chandler, Newman; subs Economou, Smith
Millwall: Gleasure, Roberts, Robinson, Chatterton, Kitchener*, Alldyce, Massey, Shinton, Harrix, Dibble, West; Hayes

Shaw inspires City to their best win of the season as he leaps to his left to save Nicky Chatterton's 49th-minute spot-kick. Newman takes Peter Gleasure by surprise with a 20-yarder for the first goal, and Chandler holds off two defenders as he controls a 40-yard pass to net on 55 minutes.

45 — CHESTER (H) 15/5 — W 1-0 (1-0)
Scorers: Chandler 39. Ref: A Glasson

City: Shaw, Williams*, Hay, Musker, Boyle, Nicholls, Williams*, Stevens, Devine, Chandler, Newman; subs Economou, Smith
Chester: Millington, Dean, Raynor, Zelem, Cottam, Ludlam, Allen, Williams*, Simpson, Jones, Henderson; Blackwell

Poor finishing as well as acrobatic goalkeeping by Grenville Millington prevents a more convincing win. Boyle cracks a header against the bar and Economou's cracking drive hits the post. A great winning goal as Chandler wins the ball in the centre-circle and runs through to stroke in.

46 — DONCASTER (A) 18/5 — D 2-2 (0-2)
Scorers: Thompson 81, Chandler 84 / Snodin 5, 20. Ref: R Bridges

City: Shaw, Humphries S, Down, Musker, Boyle, Nicholls, Williams S, Bray*, Stevens, Chandler, Economou; subs Newman, Thompson, Smith
Doncaster: Humphries S, Allanson*, Russell, Lister, Humphries G, Wagginton, Pugh, Liddell, Mell, Snodin, Little; Douglas

A touch of deja-vu, but this time it is Doncaster who suffer as City hit back with two late goals to snatch a draw. Despite conceding two opportunist strikes, City fight back to dominate the second half. Thompson caps his debut with a well-struck goal from the edge of the area.

LEAGUE DIVISION 3 (CUP-TIES) Manager: Houghton ⇒ Hodgson ⇒ Sharp SEASON 1981-82

League Cup

		1	2	3	4	5	6	7	8	9	10	11	12 sub used
	Scorers, Times, and Referees												

1:1 H WALSALL — 1/9 — Att 3,944 — W 2-0 (HT 2-0)

	1	2	3	4	5	6	7	8	9	10	11	12 sub used
City	Moller	Stevens	Merrick	Mann	Rodgers	Marshall	Tainton	Musker	Mabbutt	Harford	Devine	
Walsall	*Green*	*Macken*	*Mower*	*Beech*	*Serella*	*Hart*	*Waddington S Caswell*	*Penn*		*Buckley*	*Preece*	

Scorers: Harford 28, Mann 44; Ref: D Letts

Moller's brilliant save – his arm seeming to stretch to push Alan Buckley's 63rd-min header round the post – frustrates a Walsall side who create many chances. Mann unleashes one of his long-distance thunderbolts to give City a healthy advantage to take into the second leg.

1:2 A WALSALL — 15/9 — 19 Att 2,830 22 — L 0-1 (HT 0-0)

	1	2	3	4	5	6	7	8	9	10	11	12 sub used
City	Moller	Stevens	Sweeney	Aitken	Rodgers	Merrick*	Musker	Mann	Mabbutt	Harford	Devine	
Walsall	*Green*	*Macken*	*Mower**	*Beech*	*Serella*	*Hart*	*Rees*	*Waddington S Penn*	*Buckley*	*Caswell*	*Round*	

Scorers: Penn 84; Ref: K Hackett
(City won 2-1 on aggregate)

A nerve-jangling finale after Hay shoots at the keeper to waste an early chance for City. Walsall get a late lifeline when Don Penn runs the ball in from what looks like an offside position. City are then reduced to kick-anywhere tactics and are rather fortunate to survive to make progress.

2:1 A CARLISLE — 6/10 — 19 Att 4,111 7 — D 0-0 (HT 0-0)

	1	2	3	4	5	6	7	8	9	10	11	12 sub used
City	Moller	Stevens	Hay	Aitken	Rodgers	Sweeney	Whitehead	Mann	Mabbutt	Harford	Musker	
Carlisle	*Swinburne*	*Parker*	*Rushbury*	*Haigh*	*Ashurst*	*Larkin*	*Coughlin*	*Beardsley*	*Lee*	*Crabbe**	*Staniforth*	*Hamilton*

Ref: D Owen

City's non-stop running prevents Carlisle, who had won their four previous home games, from settling. The Cumbrians set out at a frantic pace, but by the finish City look the more likely winners. Mabbutt misses City's best chance, when slicing a close range shot on 37 minutes.

2:2 H CARLISLE — 27/10 — 16 Att 5,220 7 — W 2-1 (HT 0-1)

	1	2	3	4	5	6	7	8	9	10	11	12 sub used
City	Moller	Stevens	Tainton	Aitken	Rodgers	Sweeney	Devine	Mann	Mabbutt	Harford	Whitehead	
Carlisle	*Swinburne*	*Parker*	*Rushbury*	*Campbell*	*Ashurst*	*Larkin*	*Crabbe*	*Robson*	*Lee*	*Beardsley*	*Staniforth*	

Scorers: Rodgers 49, Mann 89p; Staniforth 35p; Ref: A Robinson
(City won 2-1 on aggregate)

'Poetic justice' says David Rodgers, as the ref gives City a controversial last-minute penalty. Whitehead admits that Tony Larkin's challenge on him was perfectly fair, whilst Rodgers, who had volleyed in City's equaliser, is adamant that Dave Rushbury blatantly dived for his award.

3 A QP RANGERS — 10/11 — 14 Att 9,215 2:3 — L 0-3 (HT 0-2)

	1	2	3	4	5	6	7	8	9	10	11	12 sub used
City	Moller	Stevens	Williams	Aitken	Rodgers	Boyle	Tainton	Mann	Harford	Devine	Musker	
QPR	*Burridge*	*Gregory*	*Fenwick*	*Wilkins*	*Hazell*	*Roeder*	*Micklewhite*	*Flanagan**	*Allen*	*Stainrod*	*Gillard*	*Stewart*

Scorers: Flanagan 8, Stainrod 40, Allen 47; Ref: J Bray

On the artificial surface at Loftus Road, Stevens complains he has been pushed out of City's wall when Mike Flanagan fires in. Impressive Rangers make sure of passage to the fourth round with a cracking shot by Simon Stainrod and Clive Allen's header either side of half-time.

FA Cup

1 H TORQUAY — 20/11 — 17 Att 5,221 4:8 — D 0-0 (HT 0-0)

	1	2	3	4	5	6	7	8	9	10	11	12 sub used
City	Moller	Stevens	Williams	Aitken	Rodgers	Boyle	Tainton	Mann	Harford	Devine	Chandler	
Torquay	*O'Keefe*	*Jones*	*Pethard*	*Brown*	*Wilson*	*Larmour*	*Fell*	*Lawrence*	*Cooper*	*Rioch*	*Sermanni*	

Ref: L Burden

Struggling City find no relief in the FA Cup as Torquay offer most of the ideas in a dull first-round tie. Further disappointment for Chandler, who is still waiting to score his first City goal. He had an effort disallowed at Brentford and quite rightly two ruled out for offside in this clash.

1R A TORQUAY — 25/11 — 17 Att 4,334 4:8 — W 2-1 (HT 0-0)

	1	2	3	4	5	6	7	8	9	10	11	12 sub used
City	Moller	Stevens	Williams	Aitken	Rodgers	Boyle	Tainton	Mann	Harford	Devine	Chandler	
Torquay	*O'Keefe*	*Jones*	*Pethard*	*Brown*	*Wilson*	*Larmour*	*Bowker*	*Lawrence*	*Cooper*	*Rioch*	*Sermanni*	

Scorers: Mann 62, 81; Lawrence 69; Ref: L Burden

Mann's explosive shooting earns City passage through to the second round in a thrilling replay. Torquay, with eleven shots on target compared to City's three, threaten to run riot. Moller though, is in outstanding form, but even he can do nothing about United's brilliant headed equaliser.

2 H NORTHAMPTON — 15/12 — 20 Att 2,901 4:24 — W 3-0 (HT 1-0)

	1	2	3	4	5	6	7	8	9	10	11	12 sub used
City	Moller	Stevens	Williams	Aitken	Rodgers	Boyle	Tainton	Mann	Chandler	Harford	Devine	
Northampton	*Poole*	*Saunders*	*Saxby*	*Brady*	*Gage*	*Sandy*	*Coffill*	*Buchanan*	*Heeley*	*Phillips*	*Mahoney**	*Alexander*

Scorers: Tainton 24, Harford 64, 85; Ref: A Hamil

A poor game in which Tainton nets with a 20-yarder and Harford has a superb header disallowed. Northampton fall away after Mark Heeley's shot is judged not to have crossed the line. Harford strikes with a header and then a firm shot after seizing on Gary Saxby's poor back-pass.

3 A PETERBOROUGH — 6/1 — 21 Att 6,811 4:6 — W 1-0 (HT 0-0)

	1	2	3	4	5	6	7	8	9	10	11	12 sub used
City	Moller	Stevens	Williams	Aitken	Boyle	Nicholls	Tainton	Mann	Chandler	Harford	Musker	
Peterborough	*Freeman*	*Butler*	*Collins*	*Gynn*	*Smith*	*Rodaway*	*Syrett*	*Kellock*	*Cooke*	*Massey**	*Chard*	*Cliss*

Scorers: Chandler 64; Ref: B Stevens

Chandler's first goal in senior football makes him worth his weight in gold to hard up City. The former England Schoolboy International shoots past Neil Freeman after swivelling on Harford's headed pass. Posh are on top in the first half and Phil Chard hits City's post in the second min.

4 H ASTON VILLA — 23/1 — 22 Att 20,279 1:16 — L 0-1 (HT 0-0)

	1	2	3	4	5	6	7	8	9	10	11	12 sub used
City	Moller	Stevens	Williams	Aitken	Boyle	Sweeney	Tainton	Mann	Garland*	Harford	Musker	Chandler
Aston Villa	*Rimmer*	*Swain*	*Gibson*	*Evans*	*Williams*	*Mortimer*	*Blair*	*Shaw*	*Withe*	*Cowans*	*Morley*	

Scorers: Shaw 78; Ref: B Hill

On top in the first half and given more space than by Third Division sides, City play neat and constructive football against top flight Villa, but are not particularly threatening in attack. Gary Shaw is fortunate with the only goal as Aitken's shin deflects his mis-hit shot past Moller.

Football League Division Three — Final Table

	Team	P	Home W	D	L	F	A	Away W	D	L	F	A	Pts
1	Burnley	46	13	7	3	37	20	8	10	5	29	25	80
2	Carlisle	46	17	4	2	44	21	6	7	10	21	29	80
3	Fulham	46	12	9	2	44	22	6	6	8	33	29	78
4	Lincoln	46	13	7	3	40	16	8	7	8	26	24	77
5	Oxford	46	10	8	5	28	18	9	6	8	35	31	71
6	Gillingham	46	14	5	4	44	26	6	6	11	20	30	71
7	Southend	46	11	7	5	35	23	7	8	8	28	28	69
8	Brentford	46	8	6	9	28	22	11	5	7	28	25	68
9	Millwall	46	12	4	7	36	28	6	9	8	26	34	67
10	Plymouth	46	12	5	6	37	24	6	6	11	27	32	65
11	Chesterfield	46	12	4	7	33	27	6	6	11	24	31	64
12	Reading	46	11	6	6	43	35	6	5	12	24	40	62
13	Portsmouth	46	11	10	2	33	14	3	9	11	23	37	61
14	Preston	46	10	7	6	25	22	6	6	11	25	34	61
15	Bristol Rov *	46	12	4	7	35	28	6	5	12	23	37	61
16	Newport	46	9	10	4	28	21	5	6	12	26	33	58
17	Huddersfield	46	10	5	8	38	25	5	7	11	26	34	57
18	Exeter	46	14	4	5	46	33	2	5	16	25	51	57
19	Doncaster	46	9	9	5	31	24	4	8	11	24	44	56
20	Walsall	46	10	7	6	32	23	3	7	13	19	32	53
21	Wimbledon	46	10	6	7	33	27	4	5	14	28	48	53
22	Swindon	46	9	9	9	37	36	4	8	11	18	35	52
23	BRISTOL CITY	46	7	6	10	24	29	4	7	12	16	36	46
24	Chester	46	2	10	11	16	30	5	1	17	20	48	32
		1104	258	155	139	827	594	139	155	258	594	827	1499

* deducted 2 pts

Appearances and Goals

Player	Lge	Sub	LC	Sub	FAC	Sub	Gls Lge	Gls LC	Gls FAC	Tot
Aitken, Peter	19		5		4					
Boyle, Terry	22	1	1		5					
Bray, Wayne	19						2			2
Carter, Les	16									
Chandler, Ricky	30		3		3	1	7		1	8
Devine, Peter	19	2	3		3		1			1
Down, Billy	1									
Economou, Jon	17	2			2		1			1
Garland, Chris	1	1			1		1			1
Gooding, Ray	3									
Harford, Mick	30		5		5		11	1	2	14
Hay, Alan	33	1	2							
Mabbutt, Kevin	11		4				1			1
McCaffery, Aidan	6						1			1
Mann, Jimmy	22	6	5		5	1	6	2	2	10
Marshall, Julian	3		1		1					
Merrick, Geoff	3		2							
Moller, Jan	31		5		5					
Musker, Russell	32	1	4		3					
Newman, Rob	15	6					3			3
Nicholls, Alan	27				1			1		1
Rodgers, David	18		5		3					
Shaw, John	15									
Smith, Mark	1	4								
Stevens, Paul	46		5		5		1			1
Sweeney, Gerry	8	2	3		1		1			1
Tainton, Trevor	19		3		5		1		1	2
Thompson, Steve		1								
Whitehead, Clive	6		2				1			1
Williams, Gary	33		1		5		1			1
(own-goals)							1			1
30 players used	506	27	55		55	1	40	4	6	50

Odds & ends

Double wins: (0).

Double losses: (5) Portsmouth, Oxford, Southend, Burnley, Bristol Rov.

Won from behind: (3) Newport (h), Plymouth (h), Preston (a).

Lost from in front: (2) Fulham (a), Burnley (h).

High spots: The ability of Mick Harford.

The survival of Bristol City.

City's fine end-of-season run under caretaker manager Gerry Sharpe.

Low spots: Losing to Bristol Rov in the Gloucestershire Cup as well as succumbing twice in the League.

The financial crisis.

Further relegation.

Player of the Year: Mick Harford.

Ever-presents: (1) Paul Stevens.

Hat-tricks: (0).

Leading scorer: Mick Harford (14).

LEAGUE DIVISION 4 — Manager: Terry Cooper — SEASON 1982-83

No	Date	1	2	3	4	5	6	7	8	9	10	11	12 sub used
1	H HULL 28/8	Shaw	Stevens	Williams G	Newman	Boyle	Riley	Economou	Musker	Cooper	Ritchie	Crawford	
		Norman	*Swann*	*Thompson*	*Richards*	*Skipper*	*Booth*	*Marwood*	*Askew**	*Whitehurst*	*Mutrie*	*Roberts G*	*Flounders*
2	A TRANMERE 4/9	Shaw	Stevens	Newman	Williams G	Boyle	Riley	Economou	Bray	Cooper	Ritchie	Crawford	
		Endersby	*Burgess*	*Mooney**	*Parry*	*Hamilton*	*Williams J*	*Powell*	*Hutchinson*	*Kerr*	*Mungall*	*Griffiths*	*Ferguson*
3	A CREWE 7/9	Shaw	Stevens	Newman	Williams G	Boyle	Riley	Economou*	Bray	Cooper	Ritchie	Crawford	
		Smith	*Moore*	*Bowers*	*Salathiel*	*Scott*	*Palios*	*Haselgrave*	*Sutton*	*Goodwin*	*Evans*	*Craven*	*Thompson*
4	H BLACKPOOL 11/9	Shaw	Stevens	Newman	Williams G	Boyle	Riley	Economou*	Cooper	Bray	Ritchie	Crawford	
		Hesford	*Simmonite*	*Brackbank*	*Deary*	*Hetzke*	*Serella*	*Noble*	*Hockaday*	*Stewart*	*Pashley*	*Butler*	*Chandler*
5	A NORTHAMPTON 19/9	Shaw [Denyer 89]	Stevens	Newman	Williams G	Boyle	Riley	Economou*	Bray	Cooper	Ritchie	Thompson	
		Freeman	*Brady*	*Phillips*	*Gage*	*Burrows*	*Heeley**	*Saunders*	*Saxby*	*Massey*	*Syrett*	*Buchanan J*	*Crawford* / *Denyer*
6	H SCUNTHORPE 25/9	Shaw	Nicholls	Williams G	Newman	Boyle	Riley	Newman*	Economou	Cooper	Ritchie	Crawford	Panes
		Neenan	*Keeley*	*Pointon*	*Fowler*	*Boxall*	*Hunter*	*O'Berg*	*Angus*	*Duncan*	*Telfer**	*Leman*	*Parkinson*
7	H TORQUAY 28/9	Shaw	Stevens	Williams G	Nicholls	Boyle	Economou	Thompson	Newman	Ritchie	Riley	Crawford*	Panes
		Horne	*Doyle*	*Smith*	*Wilson*	*Wigginton*	*Brown*	*Grapes*	*Steeples**	*Cooper*	*Anderson*	*Gallagher*	*Rioch*
8	A PETERBOROUGH 2/10	Shaw	Stevens*	Johnson	Williams G	Boyle	Riley	Economou!	Thompson	Panes	Ritchie	Newman	Chandler
		Seaman	*Quow*	*Collins*	*Firm*	*Gynn*	*Rodaway*	*Slack*	*Linton*	*Cooke*	*Benjamin*	*Chard*	*Cliss*
9	H YORK 9/10	Shaw	Newman	Johnson	Nicholls	Boyle	Bray	Economou	Thompson	Chandler	Riley	Crawford	Panes
		Jones	*Evans*	*Dawson*	*Stragia*	*Crosby*	*Hood*	*Pollard*	*Ford*	*Walwyn*	*Byrne*	*Senior**	*Busby*
10	A HARTLEPOOL 16/10	Shaw	Newman	Johnson	Nicholls	Ritchie	Riley	Cooper	Williams G	Chandler	Thompson*	Crawford	Kelly N
		Watson	*Brown*	*Stimpson*	*Lowe*	*Bird*	*Linighan A*	*Bainbridge*	*Dobson*	*Linacre*	*Lawrence*	*Barker*	
11	A HALIFAX 19/10	Shaw	Newman	Johnson	Nicholls	Boyle	Riley	Cooper	Ritchie	Chandler	Williams G	Crawford	
		Smelt	*Nobbs*	*Goodman*	*Evans*	*Smith*	*Hendrie*	*Wood**	*Davison*	*Spooner*	*Nuttall*	*Ward*	*Hallybone*

No	Date	Scorers, Times, and Referees	Att	Pos	Pt	F-A	H-T
1	H HULL 28/8	Riley 38, Musker 75 / *Flounders 85* / Ref: K Cooper	4,853		W 3	2-1	1-0
2	A TRANMERE 4/9	Ritchie 49, 51 / *Hamilton 24, Kerr 39* / Ref: P Tyldsley	1,528		D 4	2-2	0-2
3	A CREWE 7/9	Ritchie 46p / *Evans 2p,63, Moore 68, Craven 77* / Ref: R Banks	1,409	18	L 4	1-4	0-1
4	H BLACKPOOL 11/9	Ref: A Crickmore	5,340	13	D 5	0-0	0-0
5	A NORTHAMPTON 19/9	Riley 80 / *Massey 17, 52, Syrett 27, 34, 46, 90.* / Ref: K Salmon	2,967	11	L 5	1-7	0-3
6	H SCUNTHORPE 25/9	*O'Berg 55, Parkinson 75* / Ref: T Holbrook	4,025	6	L 5	0-2	0-0
7	H TORQUAY 28/9	*Gallagher 2* / Ref: B Norman	3,318	3	L 5	0-1	0-1
8	A PETERBOROUGH 2/10	*Benjamin 15, Gynn 22, 84* / Ref: K Baker	2,739	17	L 5	0-3	0-2
9	H YORK 9/10	Crawford 8, Chandler 61 / *Byrne 41, Ford 82* / Ref: C Thomas	3,730	13	D 6	2-2	1-1
10	A HARTLEPOOL 16/10	Riley 34 / *Bird 15, Lawrence 35p, Dobson 69* / Ref: J Key	1,449	11	L 6	1-3	1-2
11	A HALIFAX 19/10	Ritchie 42, Newman 50 / *Davison 27, 36* / Ref: M Scott	1,465	19	D 7	2-2	1-2

Match commentaries

1. Musker chooses the right time to get his first City goal, his 20-yard spectacular coming as Hull look likely to snatch an equaliser to cancel out Riley's thunderous opener. Billy Whitehurst hits the post for the Tigers on 69 mins, but Flounders' stunning header is the least they deserve.

2. City's only chance in the first half is Crawford's cross-shot that hits the bar, shortly after Bryan Hamilton's 25-yarder puts Tranmere ahead. Coach Clive Middlemass masterminds City's stirring fight-back and Ritchie is denied a hat-trick winner when his shot is cleared off the line.

3. 'We forgot the basics' laments boss Cooper as City fall apart, despite Ritchie's dubious pen equalising Crewe's similarly contentious award. Clive Evans is unmarked as he heads in from a corner to restore Crewe's lead and further errors see them obtain their first win in 14 games.

4. Ritchie, who once set a British record of scoring with a penalty in four successive matches, accepts the blame for letting the points slip from City's grasp in this game. Ritchie's 76th-min spot-kick hits the outside of the post after Dave Serella is harshly penalised for a tackle on Riley.

5. A totally undisciplined performance produces one of City's most humiliating defeats. John Shaw is left cruelly exposed time and time again by abysmal marking. Dave Syrett, with one goal in his previous five appearances, avails himself of two free headers and two close-range shots.

6. Scunthorpe maintain their League hoodoo over City at Ashton Gate with a fierce 12-yard shot by Paul O'Berg and Noel Parkinson's brilliant volley. City, turning out in shirts without the sponsor's name, rue Riley's three missed chances and Newman's shot being hooked off the line.

7. Problems in the laundry department perhaps as City again play in plain shirts. Bruce Rioch is far and away the best player on view in a match threatened by a first-half cloudburst, as Torquay, with eight shots on target compared to City's four, are deserving winners of a dull game.

8. City suffer their fourth successive defeat after an enforced chocolate lunch when the team coach breaks down on way to the game. The Posh are presented with an easy win by City's sloppy first-half display and the 43rd-minute sending off of Economou for swearing at a linesman.

9. This thriller, encouraged by the referee's exemplary use of the advantage rule, produces a fair result as York have 17 shots (twelve on target) compared with City's 18 (eight). Many fans miss the start of the second half as the break is shortened to enable York to catch the 5.14pm train.

10. City, denied a 50th-min equaliser when Newman's free-kick hits the bar and bounces down over the line, are made to pay for missed chances. All of Pool's goals are from dead-ball situations and their high balls into the box highlight City's need for a commanding central defender.

11. An alert linesman flags vigorously to catch referee's attention that Newman's header from Crawford's corner had crossed the line before being cleared by Keith Nobbs. Bobby Davison seizes on errors by Ritchie and then Williams to net with two shots to take his season's tally to nine.

12 sub used

12 · H WIMBLEDON · 23/10 — 3-0 (W) · 22 · 4,744 · 2 · 10

City: Shaw · Newman · Johnson · Nicholls · Boyle · Riley · Economou · Ritchie · Chandler · Cooper · Crawford
Opponents: Beasant · Peters · Thomas · Gage · Tagg* · Morris · Evans · Ketteridge · Leslie · Downes · Hodges · Galliers !

City turn the form book upside down to take the League's last unbeaten record. Riley, shocked to find a mouse in his boot, scores the first hat-trick of his career. Boring Wimbledon is the chant, until they play a more expansive game after Nicholls heads in Crawford's cross.

Nicholls 31, Riley 34, 44, 68 / Leslie 66, Thomas 87p
Ref: D Civil

---

13 · A ALDERSHOT · 30/10 — 0-0 (D) · 23 · 2,826 · 8 · 11

City: Shaw · Newman · Johnson · Nicholls · Boyle · Riley · Economou · Thompson · Cooper · Chandler · Crawford
Opponents: Johnson · Andruszewski · Gillard · Scott · Wooler · Jopling · Santord · Banton · Goddard · McDonald · Brodie

A ragged, disjointed City display that is only brightened by the flank play of Johnson and the midfield skills of Newman. Boss Cooper is critical of the officials for disallowing Thompson's 44th-minute volley from Johnson's pull-back, because Chandler is in an offside position.

Ref: B Hill

---

14 · H CHESTER · 2/11 — 0-0 (D) · 21 · 4,215 · 12 · 12

City: Shaw · Newman · Johnson · Nicholls · Boyle · Riley · Economou · Thompson* · Chandler · Cooper · Crawford · Williams G
Opponents: Salmon · Bradley · Needham · Storton · Zelem · Dean · Sloan · Blackwell · Ludlam · Thomas · Cooke

A dismal encounter whose only highlight is referee Lester Shapter's pulled muscle bringing about his replacement by senior linesman Ken Deane for the second half. Cooper's misplaced pass gifts John Thomas a 71st-minute chance to break deadlock, but Shaw makes a great save.

Ref: L Shapter/K Deane

---

15 · H STOCKPORT · 6/11 — 2-2 (D) · 21 · 4,648 · 18 · 13

City: Shaw · Newman · Johnson · Nicholls · Boyle · Riley · Economou · Williams G · Thompson* · Cooper · Crawford · Kelly N
Opponents: Lloyd · Rutter · Sherlock · Emerson · Bowles · Thorpe · Williams · Phillips · Quinn · Park · Coyle

Brian Lloyd denies 16-year-old Nyerere Kelly a story-book home debut as he spreads to block the youngster's 85th-minute effort. Newman slams Tony Coyle's low cross into own net for Stockport's leveller to end twelve minutes of hectic action that has warmed the frozen fans.

Riley 58, Chandler 64 / Quinn 65, Newman 69 (og)
Ref: C Downey

---

16 · A MANSFIELD · 13/11 — 1-0 (W) · 22 · 2,035 · 10 · 14

City: Shaw · Newman · Johnson · Nicholls · Stevens · Riley · Economou · Williams G · Cooper · Chandler · Crawford · Kelly N
Opponents: Arnold · Blackhall · Kennedy · Woodhead* · Ayre · Calderwood · Matthews · Caldwell · Waddle · Hutchinson · Nicholson · Dungworth

A bad day for Newman who is made to pay for his good fortune of staying on the pitch after bringing down Dave Caldwell in the 54th minute. He touches ball over line as Shaw fails to hold Gary Nicholson's cross to deprive City of their first away win and then finds his wallet stolen.

Riley 21 / Newman 79 (og)
Ref: D Owen

---

17 · H COLCHESTER · 27/11 — 0-2 (L) · 23 · 4,371 · 6 · 14

City: Shaw · Stevens · Johnson · Nicholls · Phill-Masters · Riley · Newman · Thompson · Cooper · Chandler* · Crawford · Kelly N
Opponents: Walker · Ward · Coleman* · Longhorn · Wignall · Hunter · Allinson · Osborne · McDonough · Bremner · Leslie · Adcock

Phillipson-Masters has an unhappy debut, but Nicholls is at fault with United's opener. Glaring misses by Riley, Chandler and Kelly as well as Mike Walker's superb goalkeeping prevent City getting back into the game. Ian Allinson gives a lesson in finishing to complete City's misery.

Bremner 27, Allinson 85
Ref: T Bune

---

18 · A ROCHDALE · 4/12 — 0-1 (L) · 24 · 1,307 · 19 · 14

City: Shaw · Llewellyn · Johnson · Nicholls · Phill-Masters · Riley · Newman · Thompson · Chandler · Cooper · Crawford
Opponents: Pearce · Keenan · Snookes · Farrell · McElhinney* · Thompson D · Greaves · Hidditch · Wellings · Hamilton · Weir · Nicholson

Peter Farrell puts City at the bottom of the League as he rises unmarked to send in a looping header over Shaw, who captains the side in Ritchie's absence. The goal is a tragedy for City's improved defence, in which Phillipson-Masters, Nicholls and Cooper are outstanding.

Farrell 75
Ref: A Challinor

---

19 · A CHESTER · 11/12 — 0-1 (L) · 24 · 1,306 · 9 · 14

City: Shaw · Llewellyn · Johnson · Nicholls · Phill-Masters · Riley · Newman · Thompson · Cooper · Crawford · Garland
Opponents: Salmon · Dean · Lane · Storton · Bradley · Johnson · Williams* · Cooke · Thomas · Ludlam · Wilson · Zelem

Garland, signed on non-contract forms, makes a successful return to City's side by playing the last half-hour in place of Panes. A spectacular own-goal settles a poor match. Cooper swings his right foot at Clive Wilson's angled low drive and the ball crashes into the top corner.

Cooper 55 (og)
Ref: D Allison

---

20 · A BURY · 18/12 — 2-2 (D) · 23 · 2,196 · 1 · 15

City: Shaw · Cooper · Johnson · Nicholls · Phill-Masters · Riley · Economou · Ritchie · Chandler · Newman · Crawford · Garland
Opponents: Brown · Gardner · Bramhall · Halliday · Davies · Gore · Hilton* · Madden · Parker · Jakub · Firth · Potts

Against top of the table Bury the goal-shy City attack at long last find some form. Chandler, revelling in the ankle-deep snow, puts City back in the game with a glancing header from Cooper's well-flighted free-kick. The 50th-minute injury of Paul Hilton is the turning point of the game.

Chandler 61, Crawford 66 / Madden 46, Parker 48
Ref: J Lovatt

---

21 · H PORT VALE · 27/12 — 1-3 (L) · 23 · 6,852 · 5 · 15

City: Shaw · Newman · Johnson · Nicholls · Phill-Masters · Riley · Economou · Ritchie · Cooper · Chandler · Crawford · Garland
Opponents: Siddall* · Tartt · Bromage · Hunter · Sproson · Cegielski · Fox · Moss · Newton · Greenhoff · Armstrong · Ridley

Despite a purposeful opening, City rarely seem likely to break down the visitors' uncompromising defence. Terry Armstrong's 25-yarder puts Vale ahead with their only shot of the first half. Wayne Cegielski takes over in goal for final three minutes as Barry Siddall is stretchered off.

Phillipson-Masters 55 / Armstrong 44, Moss 56, Newton 61
Ref: A Glasson

---

22 · A HEREFORD · 28/12 — 3-1 (W) · 22 · 3,548 · 23 · 18

City: Shaw · Newman · Johnson · Nicholls · Phill-Masters · Riley · Kelly N · Ritchie · Chandler · Cooper · Crawford · White
Opponents: Powell · Price · Bray · Hicks · Pejic · Musial · Harvey · Lane · Phillips · McNeil · White

The boot is on the other foot as City benefit from Hereford's woeful finishing to gain their first away win in 23. Chandler claims the goal that puts City on course for three vital points when his touch to Ritchie's shot deceives Andy Powell. The Bulls have 22 shots to just seven by City.

Chandler 5, 11, Kelly N 40 / McNeil 12
Ref: A Seville

---

23 · H SWINDON · 1/1 — 1-1 (D) · 22 · 8,927 · 4 · 19

City: Shaw · Newman · Johnson · Nicholls · Phill-Masters · Riley · Kelly N · Garland · Chandler* · Cooper · Crawford · Riley
Opponents: Allan · Baverstock · Baillie · Emmanuel ! · Lewis · Graham · Pritchard · Batty · Rideout · Rowland · Barnard

Gary Emmanuel is sent off after protesting at City's equaliser, when Nicholls appeared to kick the ball out of the keeper's hands for Riley to tap the ball in. Ritchie has his shirt on back-to-front in the first half after a hurried twelfth-min change as City have two No 7s on the pitch.

Riley 89 / Pritchard 64
Ref: M Robinson

LEAGUE DIVISION 4   Manager: Terry Cooper   SEASON 1982-83

No	Date		Att	Pos	Pt	F-A	H-T	Scorers, Times, and Referees
24	A	DARLINGTON 3/1	1,425	22	D 20	2-2	2-2	Chandler 9, Garland 44 — Walsh 14, 35. Ref: D Scott
25	A	HULL 15/1	6,835	1	L 20	0-1	0-0	Mutrie 79. Ref: T Mills
26	H	TRANMERE 18/1	3,776	20	W 23	1-0	0-0	Riley 55. Ref: J Martin
27	H	NORTHAMPTON 22/1	4,874	15	L 23	1-3	1-2	Ritchie 41p — Phillips 21, Syrett 36, Massey 50. Ref: R Lewis
28	A	SCUNTHORPE 5/2	3,624	5	D 24	1-1	0-0	Nicholls 49 — Parkinson 82. Ref: A Hamil
29	H	PETERBOROUGH 12/2	3,922	12	W 27	1-0	1-0	Ritchie 38p. Ref: L Burden
30	H	HALIFAX 15/2	3,403	10	W 30	3-0	2-0	Ritchie 15, Cooper 37, Economou 71. Ref: B Daniels
31	A	YORK 19/2	2,879	8	L 30	0-3	0-0	Byrne 62, 86, Pollard 85p. Ref: J Hough
32	H	HARTLEPOOL 26/2	4,207	21	W 33	2-0	1-0	Ritchie 7p, Economou 47. Ref: J Bray
33	A	WIMBLEDON 5/3	2,591	3	L 33	1-2	0-2	Kelly E 47 — Newman 25 (og), Leslie 30. Ref: M Dimblebee
34	H	ALDERSHOT 12/3	4,281	16	W 36	2-0	1-0	Crawford 42, Riley 52. Ref: A Hamil

Line-ups (positions 1–11, plus 12 sub used) and match reports

24 — Darlington
City: Shaw, Williams G, Johnson, Nicholls, [—], Phill-Masters*, Garland, Ritchie, Cooper, Chandler, Crawford; sub: Newman
Darlington: Cuff, Liddle, Young, Smith, Rhodes, Kamara, Gilbert, McLean, Honour, Walsh, McFadden

Garland slides in Chandler's angled ball to level matters after Alan Walsh naps a pair with his 20-yard free-kick before coolly slotting home a through ball. Facing a gale-force wind after the break City defend well and come closest to a winner, but Pat Cuff saves Newman's header.

25 — Hull
City: Shaw, Williams G*, Johnson, Nicholls, Phill-Masters, Riley, Garland, Ritchie, Cooper, Chandler, Crawford
Hull: Davies, Swann, Askew, Roberts D, Skipper, Booth, Marwood, McClaren, Whitehurst*, Mutrie, Roberts G; sub: McNeil

Forbes Phillipson-Masters, due to sign permanently for City next week, collects his eighth booking of the season as a backs to the wall display almost frustrates the Tigers. Following a free-kick, Les Mutrie gives City no chance with his shot from Peter Skipper's headed pass.

26 — Tranmere
City: Shaw, Williams G, Johnson, Nicholls, Newman, Riley, Ritchie, Chandler, Garland, [—], Crawford
Tranmere: Endersby, Mongall, Burgess, Mooney, Hamilton*, Oliver, Powell, Aspinall, Kerr, Brown D, Griffiths; sub: Woods S

Cooper's shrewd positional switch of Chandler to midfield so as to allow Riley to revert to attack brings City their first home success for three months. Tranmere are outplayed for long periods and City deserve more than the one goal scored by Riley's unstoppable eight-yard volley.

27 — Northampton
City: Shaw, Williams G, Johnson, Nicholls, Newman, Riley, Ritchie, Garland*, Economou, Chandler, Crawford; sub: Cooper
Northampton: Freeman, Tucker, Phillips, Gage, Brady, Coffill, Saunders, Patching, Muir, Syrett, Massey

Neil Freeman, in his farewell performance before joining the police, thwarts City with a string of outstanding saves. Ritchie gives City some hope with a penalty after Peter Coffill's rash tackle on Johnson, but Steve Massey finishes off a lovely move to clinch the points for Town.

28 — Scunthorpe
City: Shaw, Newman, Williams G, Nicholls, Phill-Masters, Riley, Ritchie, Garland, Economou, Chandler, Crawford
Scunthorpe: Neenan, Oates, Pointon, Boxall, Baines, Hunter, O'Berg, Cammack, Mann, Parkinson, Leman

City's loss of Peter Johnson, who returns to Newcastle following a three-month loan spell, is compensated by Phillipson-Masters' availability after serving his suspension. Scunthorpe, including old City favourite Jimmy Mann, gain a draw with Noel Parkinson's 20-yard free-kick.

29 — Peterborough
City: Shaw, Newman, Williams G, Nicholls, Phill-Masters, Riley, Ritchie, Economou, Cooper, Musker, Crawford
Peterborough: Seaman, Winters, Collins, Gym, Firm, Slack, Clarke, Rodaway, Cooke, Benjamin, Chard

Musker makes a successful return to first-team action after over five months out with a broken leg. He provides midfield authority behind Ritchie and Riley. There is little between the sides, but a handball by John Winters allows Ritchie to put away the match-winning penalty.

30 — Halifax
City: Shaw, Newman, Williams G, Nicholls, Phill-Masters, Riley*, Cooper, Ritchie, Economou, Musker, Crawford; sub: Chandler
Halifax: Smelt, Nobbs, Wood, Evans, Smith, Hendrie, Ward, Kendall*, Allatt, Nuttall, Staniforth; sub: Goodman

Ritchie's low 18-yard shot past Lee Smelt sets up City's escape from the re-election zone. Playing delightful one-touch football on a freezing pitch they dominate opponents boasting six wins from their seven previous games. Dave Evans claims the last touch in City's other goals.

31 — York
City: Shaw, Jones, Williams G, Nicholls, Phill-Masters, Riley, Ritchie, Economou*, Chandler, Musker, Crawford
York: [?], Evans, Hay, Stragia, Smith, Hood, Ford, Crosby, Walwyn, Byrne, Pollard; sub: Bray

City's chance of saving anything from this game is destroyed when, with the ball having already been cleared, Williams trips Keith Walwyn to concede a senseless penalty. City are unable to contrive a single shot on target against a York side achieving their tenth successive home win.

32 — Hartlepool
City: Shaw, Newman, Williams G, Nicholls, Phill-Masters, Riley, Cooper, Ritchie, Economou, Musker, Crawford
Hartlepool: Blackburn, Brown, Stimpson, Robinson, Barker, Linighan A, Lowe, Smith, Dobson, Lawrence*, Linacre; sub: Langridge

City are lucky when Riley's early tumble results in a penalty, from which Ritchie gives keeper Eddie Blackburn no chance. A poor game in which Hartlepool only create one clear chance. Newman's 50-yard run ends with a perfect through-ball for Economou to score from ten yards.

33 — Wimbledon
City: Shaw, Newman, Williams G, Nicholls, Phill-Masters, Riley, Ritchie, Economou, Kelly E*, Musker, Crawford
Wimbledon: Beasant, Peters, Sparrow, Barnett, Smith, Hatter*, Evans, Belfield, Leslie, Hodges, Gage; sub: Fishenden

New signing Errington Kelly inspires a battling second performance with a superb angled drive just after the break. Kelly makes his presence felt right from the start with a spectacular overhead kick, but City are on the rack when Newman slices Gary Barnett's cross into his own net.

34 — Aldershot
City: Shaw, Newman, Williams G, Nicholls, Phill-Masters, Riley, Smith, Kelly E*, Economou, Economou, Crawford; sub: Llewellyn
Aldershot: Johnson, Andruszewski, Gillard, Briley, Whitlock, Jopling, Shrubb, Banton, Goddard, McDonald, Robinson*; sub: Lucas

City, without Ritchie who is suffering from food poisoning, struggle early on. Phillipson-Masters draws the defence for Crawford to head in from Newman's free-kick, then Nigel Smith's raking pass to the left-wing allows Crawford to send in a perfect cross for Riley to head in.

Bristol City — Season Match Log (Matches 35–46)

No	Venue	Date	Opponent	Pos	Res	Score	Att		Pts
35	A	18/3	STOCKPORT	21	D	2-2	2,036	14	37
36	A	20/3	TORQUAY	17	W	2-0	3,209	13	40
37	H	26/3	MANSFIELD	15	W	3-1	4,945	12	43
38	H	2/4	HEREFORD	15	D	1-1	6,278	24	44
39	A	4/4	PORT VALE	15	D	1-1	6,573	4	45
40	H	9/4	ROCHDALE	15	D	0-0	4,780	22	46
41	A	16/4	BLACKPOOL	14	W	4-1	2,209	16	49
42	H	23/4	BURY	15	W	2-1	5,230	4	52
43	A	29/4	COLCHESTER	15	L	1-3	2,196	5	52
44	H	2/5	DARLINGTON	15	D	2-2	4,877	17	53
45	H	7/5	CREWE	13	W	2-1	4,785	23	56
46	A	14/5	SWINDON	14	L	0-2	5,313	8	56

Average Home 4,799 — Away 2,768

---

35 — STOCKPORT (A) 18/3 — D 2-2
Scorers: Riley 17, Ritchie 70 / Power 18, Emerson 55. Ref: F Roberts

Riley's goal, a glancing header which strikes a defender, is City's only effort on target in the first half, whilst Shaw has to make six saves in the same period. Dean Emerson's well-struck drive gives County a well-deserved lead, but depleted City fight back well for a headed equaliser.

City: Shaw; Llewellyn, Williams G, Nicholls, Newman, Riley, Economou!, Ritchie, Williams P*, Cooper, Crawford; sub Palmer
Stockport: Lloyd; Rutter, Sherlock, Emerson, Sword, Thorpe, Williams, Phillips, Coyle, Power, Smith

36 — TORQUAY (A) 20/3 — W 2-0
Scorers: Crawford 8, Riley 74. Ref: C Thomas

Phillipson-Masters inspires City to their best away performance of the season. Plain sailing as Crawford heads in Riley's cross and later returns the compliment with a through-ball for Riley to coolly lob in. The shortest sub appearance on record as Palmer only has time to shake hands.

City: Shaw; Newman, Williams G, Nicholls, Phillipson-Masters, Riley, Economou, Ritchie, Williams P**, Cooper, Crawford; sub Palmer
Torquay: Horn; Smith, Young, Wilson, Little, Rioch, Jones, James, Bishop, Anderson, Gallagher

37 — MANSFIELD (H) 26/3 — W 3-1
Scorers: Riley 54, Williams P 61, Crawford 83 / Caldwell 34. Ref: T Spencer

Paul Williams from Western League, lauded as the most exciting Ashton Gate prospect in years, caps his home debut by stabbing Cooper's cross over the line. Mansfield, with three regulars missing, are swept aside in the second half after dominating the first.

City: Shaw; Newman, Williams G, Nicholls, Phillipson-Masters, Riley*, Economou, Ritchie, Williams P*, Cooper, Crawford; sub Palmer
Mansfield: Arnold; Blackhall, Kearney, Rhodes, Bird*, Calderwood, Woodhead, Bell, Dungworth, Caldwell, Reynolds; sub Kennedy

38 — HEREFORD (H) 2/4 — D 1-1
Scorers: Ritchie 41 / Phillips 33. Ref: B Stevens

Hereford look likely winners until Mel Pejic's 68th-min dismissal for foul on Crawford. Stewart Phillips' sweet left foot shot puts the visitors ahead shortly after Gary Williams hits the post. Ritchie finishes off Crawford's clever pass for City's leveller and later the post denies Riley.

City: Shaw; Llewellyn, Williams G, Nicholls, Phillipson-Masters, Riley, Economou, Ritchie, Williams P, Cooper, Crawford; sub Palmer
Hereford: Wilmot; Price, Bartley, Larkin, Pejic!, Maddy, Harvey, Lane, Phillips, Carter, White

39 — PORT VALE (A) 4/4 — D 1-1
Scorers: Riley 33 / Armstrong 21. Ref: A Robinson

Gary Williams and Wayne Bray, often criticised in the past for their casual approach, inspire City's heroic performance on a quagmire pitch. Terry Armstrong seizes on ball stuck in the mud to put Vale in front, but City respond with Riley's looping header from Bray's curling cross.

City: Shaw; Newman, Williams G, Nicholls, Phillipson-Masters, Bray, Riley, Ritchie, Williams P, Cooper, Crawford; sub Kelly N
Port Vale: Siddall; Tartt, Bromage, Hunter, Ridley, Cegielski, Fox, Steel, Newton, Lawrence M*, Armstrong; sub Earle

40 — ROCHDALE (H) 9/4 — D 0-0
Ref: D Hedges

For the first time in many months the shouts of rubbish are heard as City fail to beat mediocre Rochdale. City waste many chances, making 18 goal attempts compared to Rochdale's six. Boss Cooper confronts a disgruntled fan in a vain attempt to encourage cheers rather than jeers.

City: Shaw; Newman, Williams G, Nicholls, Phillipson-Masters, Bray*, Riley, Ritchie, Williams P, Cooper, Crawford; sub Kelly N
Rochdale: Crawford; Keenan, Carr, Farrell, Higgins, Williams, Thompson D, Greenhoff J, French, Hilditch

41 — BLACKPOOL (A) 16/4 — W 4-1
Scorers: Hetzke 9 (og), Ritchie 59p, Riley 65, [Crawford 70] / McNiven 24. Ref: D Shaw

Ritchie's successful spot-kick, after Colin Greenall brings down Riley, changes the course of the game. After Steve Hetzke's 30-yard volley into his own net, David McNiven heads in Pool's leveller and then Terry Pashley hits the crossbar as City struggle to remain on equal terms.

City: Shaw; Newman, Williams G, Nicholls, Phillipson-Masters, Riley, Economou, Ritchie, Williams P, Cooper, Crawford; sub Bray
Blackpool: Hesford; Bardsley, Pritchett, Deary, Hetzke, Greenall, Hockaday, McNiven, Stewart, Noble*, Pashley; sub Bamber

42 — BURY (H) 23/4 — W 2-1
Scorers: Breckin 56 (og), Nicholls 64 / Johnson 2. Ref: J Deakin

The fates are again kind to the City as, following Steve Johnson's spectacular overhead kick to give Bury an early lead, they equalise when David Brown, John Breckin and Paul Williams collide in going for Riley's cross. Nicholls secures the points for the City with a simple tap-in.

City: Shaw; Newman, Williams G, Nicholls, Phillipson-Masters, Riley, Economou, Ritchie, Williams P, Cooper*, Crawford; sub Kelly E
Bury: Brown; Gardner, Breckin, Hilton M, Bramhall, Halliday, Cantello*, Madden, Johnson, Jakub, Potts; sub Parker

43 — COLCHESTER (A) 29/4 — L 1-3
Scorers: Ritchie 43p / Allinson 35p, Bowen 38, McDonagh 88. Ref: T Ward

A harsh spot-kick award as keeper Shaw is adjudged to have tripped Ian Allinson heralds the end of City's nine-match unbeaten run. Despite getting back into the contest when Ritchie nets from a penalty after Riley is fouled, City's uninspired midfield make things easy for the U's.

City: Shaw; Newman, Williams G, Nicholls, Phillipson-Masters, Riley, Kelly E*, Ritchie, Williams P, Cooper, Crawford; subs Economou, McDonaugh 88
Colchester: Walker; Cook*, Packer, Leslie, Wignall, Coleman, Allinson, Osborne, Bowen, Adcock, Hull

44 — DARLINGTON (H) 2/5 — D 2-2
Scorers: Crawford 14, Phillipson-Masters 86 / Todd 18, Kamara 24. Ref: K Barratt

Darlington keeper Fred Barber takes the glory in an open, free-flowing game. Despite restricting the Quakers to two shots, the City have to rely on a mis-hit volley from Phillipson-Masters to save a point after Alan Kamara had jinked his way through for a spectacular solo goal.

City: Shaw; Newman, Williams G, Cooper, Phillipson-Masters, Riley, Kelly E*, Ritchie, Williams P, Economou, Crawford
Darlington: Barber; Kamara, Liddle, Smith, Wakefield, Barton, Honour, McLean, Todd, Walsh, Young

45 — CREWE (H) 7/5 — W 2-1
Scorers: Newman 76, 89 / Chapman 61. Ref: M James

Newman's fine volley and glancing header in the closing stages secures City's rather fortunate win. Crewe waste a second-minute pen when Nigel Walker blasts well wide after Economou's handball, but bedraggled City look out of it when Daryl Chapman heads the visitors in front.

City: Shaw; Newman, Williams G, Nicholls, Crawford, Riley, Ritchie, Smith*, Cooper, Economou, Palmer; sub Llewellyn
Crewe: Smith; Brady, Bowers, Edwards, Scott, Hart, Haslegrave, Chapman, Walker, Waller, Cliss; sub Llewellyn

46 — SWINDON (A) 14/5 — L 0-2
Scorers: — / Barnard 39, Pritchard 71. Ref: L Shapter

Palmer is frustrated by the post in the early stages and then after the interval Paul Batty clears his header off the line. Barnard shoots Swindon ahead and then the impressive Pritchard, who earlier had hit the woodwork, puts the game beyond City's grasp with a superb cross-shot.

City: Shaw; Llewellyn, Williams G, Nicholls, Palmer, Bray*, Ritchie, Economou, Cooper, Williams P, Crawford; sub Jones
Swindon: Stevens; Baillie, Baddeley, Batty, Henry, Graham, Pritchard, Barnard, Quinn, Rowland, Blacker

LEAGUE DIVISION 4 (CUP-TIES)

Manager: Terry Cooper

SEASON 1982-83

Milk Cup

	F-A	H-T	Scorers, Times, and Referees
1:1 A SWINDON 31/8 — 3,736	L 1-2	0-1	Boyle 80 / Rideout 11p, 89 / Ref: J Deakin

	1	2	3	4	5	6	7	8	9	10	11	12 sub used
City	Shaw	Stevens	Newman	Williams G	Boyle	Riley	Economou	Musker*	Cooper	Ritchie	Crawford	Bray
Opp	*Allan*	*Henry*	*Baddeley*	*Emmanuel*	*Lewis*	*Graham*	*Pritchard**	*Hughes*	*Rideout*	*Rowland*	*Barnard*	*Carter*

A gritty City display after Cooper is lucky not to be sent off for his handling offence that gifts Swindon their penalty, and the loss of Musker with a broken ankle. Boyle equalises with a looping back-header, but Rideout's magnificent 35-yard drive gives Swindon a 2nd leg advantage.

	F-A	H-T	Scorers, Times, and Referees
1:2 H SWINDON 14/9 — 3,786 (15 10)	W 2-0	2-0	Boyle 29, Ritchie 43 / Ref: A Robinson (City won 3-2 on aggregate)

	1	2	3	4	5	6	7	8	9	10	11	12 sub used
City	Shaw	Stevens	Newman	Williams G	Boyle	Cooper	Riley	Chandler	Bray	Ritchie	Thompson	
Opp	*Allan*	*Henry**	*Baddeley*	*Emmanuel*	*Lewis*	*Graham*	*Pritchard*	*Hughes*	*Rideout*	*Rowland*	*Barnard*	*Quinn*

Boyle's powerful header into the top corner sparks a rousing battle. Ritchie is full of praise for the referee who overrules the linesman to allow his goal after forcing ball through keeper's hands. "The ball was never in the keeper's possession so I had every right to go for it' says Ritchie.

	F-A	H-T	Scorers, Times, and Referees
2:1 H SHEFFIELD WED 4/10 — 4,458 (23 2:3)	L 1-2	0-2	Newman 78 / Taylor 2, 6 / Ref: D Hedges

	1	2	3	4	5	6	7	8	9	10	11	12 sub used
City	Shaw	Newman	Williams G	Nicholls	Boyle	Riley	Bray	Economou	Chandler*	Thompson	Crawford	Panes
Opp	*Bolder*	*Sterland*	*Bailey*	*Smith*	*Lyons*	*Shelton*	*Megson**	*Taylor*	*Bannister*	*Owen*	*Simmons*	*Pickering*

City again self-destruct, before Newman's twelve-yard thunderbolt gives some hope for the second leg. Williams' poor back-pass gifts Kevin Taylor the simplest of goals and debutant Tony Simmons is given too much room as he sends over a cross for Taylor to volley in his second.

	F-A	H-T	Scorers, Times, and Referees
2:2 A SHEFFIELD WED 26/10 — 7,920 (22 2:1)	D 1-1 aet	0-0	Chandler 64 / Taylor 109 / Ref: N Midgeley (City lost 2-3 on aggregate)

	1	2	3	4	5	6	7	8	9	10	11	12 sub used
City	Shaw	Newman	Thompson*	Nicholls	Boyle	Riley	Economou	Ritchie	Chandler	Cooper	Crawford	Kelly N
Opp	*Bolder*	*Sterland*	*Bailey*	*Smith*	*Lyons*	*Shirtliff P R* Megson*	*Taylor*	*Bannister*	*McCulloch*	*Owen*	*Pickering*	

Gallant City, reduced to ten men with the loss of the limping Ritchie 23 mins before the end, put up a heroic performance. Chandler volleys in a rebound to bring the aggregate scores level, but Kevin Taylor ends City's hopes in extra-time with a delightful chip to leave Shaw stranded.

FA Cup

	F-A	H-T	Scorers, Times, and Referees
1 A ORIENT 20/11 — 2,772 (22 3:21)	L 1-4	1-3	Johnson 17 / Foster 20, Godfrey 28, 38, Sussex 70 / Ref: M James

	1	2	3	4	5	6	7	8	9	10	11	12 sub used
City	Shaw	Stevens	Johnson	Nicholls	Newman	Riley	Economou	Ritchie*	Williams G	Cooper	Crawford	Thompson
Opp	*Day*	*Roffey*	*Peach*	*Foster*	*Cunningham*	*Dann*	*Osgood*	*Godfrey*	*Houchen*	*Sussex*	*Taylor*	

Johnson, with a glorious shot from the edge of the area, scores only the second goal of his career, but confusion with Ritchie off injured in the 20th min leaves City down to ten men when Orient equalise. Colin Foster latches onto Tony Cunningham's free-kick to scramble the ball in.

League table

		P	Home					Away					Pts
			W	D	L	F	A	W	D	L	F	A	
1	Wimbledon	46	17	4	2	57	23	12	7	4	39	22	98
2	Hull	46	14	8	1	48	14	11	7	5	27	20	90
3	Port Vale	46	15	4	4	37	16	11	6	6	30	18	88
4	Scunthorpe	46	13	7	3	41	17	10	7	6	30	25	83
5	Bury	46	15	4	4	43	20	8	8	7	31	26	81
6	Colchester	46	17	5	1	51	19	7	4	12	24	36	81
7	York	46	18	4	1	59	19	4	9	10	29	39	79
8	Swindon	46	14	3	6	45	27	5	8	10	16	27	68
9	Peterborough	46	13	6	4	38	23	4	7	12	20	29	64
10	Mansfield	46	11	6	6	32	26	5	7	11	29	44	61
11	Halifax	46	9	8	6	31	23	7	4	12	28	43	60
12	Torquay	46	12	3	8	38	30	5	4	14	18	35	58
13	Chester	46	8	6	9	28	24	7	5	11	27	36	56
14	BRISTOL CITY	46	10	8	5	32	25	3	9	11	27	45	56
15	Northampton	46	10	8	5	43	29	4	4	15	22	46	54
16	Stockport	46	11	8	4	41	31	3	4	16	19	48	54
17	Darlington	46	8	5	10	27	30	5	8	10	34	41	52
18	Aldershot	46	11	5	7	40	35	1	10	12	21	47	51
19	Tranmere	46	8	8	7	30	29	5	3	15	19	42	50
20	Rochdale	46	11	8	4	38	25	0	8	15	17	48	49
21	Blackpool	46	10	8	5	32	23	3	4	16	23	51	49
22	Hartlepool	46	11	5	7	30	24	2	4	17	16	52	48
23	Crewe	46	9	5	9	35	32	3	3	18	18	39	41
24	Hereford	46	8	6	9	19	23	2	2	18	23	56	41
		1104	283	142	127	915	587	127	142	283	587	915	1512

Odds & ends

Double wins: (0).
Double losses: (2) Northampton, Colchester.
Won from behind: (3) Mansfield (h), Bury (h), Crewe (h).
Lost from in front: (0).
High spots: Beating Wimbledon 4-2 at Ashton Gate on 23 October.
Drawing 2-2 at Bury on 18 December to move off the bottom.
Low spots: Heavy defeat at Northampton on 19 September.
Reaching the bottom of the League on losing at Rochdale on 4 Dec.
Losing 1-2 v Bristol Rovers (a) in the Gloucestershire Cup on 21 Sep.

Player of the year: Glyn Riley.
Ever-presents: (1) John Shaw.
Hat-tricks: (1) Glyn Riley.
Leading scorer: Glyn Riley (16).

Appearances & Goals

Player	Appearances						Goals			
	Lge	Sub	LC	Sub	FAC	Sub	Lge	LC	FAC	Tot
Boyle, Terry	14		4					2		2
Bray, Wayne	9	1	2	1						
Chandler, Ricky	20	3	3				6	1		7
Cooper, Terry	37	1	3		1		1			1
Crawford, Alan	44		3		1		7			7
Economou, Jon	34	3	3				2			2
Garland, Chris	7	2					2			2
Johnson, Peter	20				1				1	1
Jones, Mark		1								
Kelly, Errington	4	1	1				1			1
Kelly, Nyrere	2	4			1		1			1
Llewellyn, Andy	5	2								
Musker, Russell	6		1							
Newman, Rob	42		4	1	1		3	1		4
Nicholls, Alan	39		2		1		3			3
Palmer, John	2	6								
Panes, Simon	2	2				1				
Phill-Masters, Forbes	25						2			2
Riley, Glyn	43		4	1	1		16			16
Ritchie, Tom	37		3		1		12	1		13
Shaw, John	46		4		1					
Smith, Nigel	2									
Stevens, Paul	10		2		1					
Thompson, Steve	10	1	3							
Williams, Gary	35	1	3		1		1			1
Williams, Paul	11						2			2
(own-goals)										
26 players used	506	28	44	3	11	1	59	5	1	65

CANON LEAGUE DIVISION 4 — Manager: Terry Cooper — SEASON 1983-84

Results

No	Date	H/A	Opponents	Att	Pos	W/D/L	Pt	F–A	H–T	Scorers, Times	Referee
1	27/8	H	MANSFIELD	5,759	—	W	3	4–0	2–0	Crawford 13, 42, Riley 49, 87	H King
2	3/9	A	BURY	2,015	—	L	3	1–2	1–2	Kerr 8; Madden 19, 23	J Key
3	6/9	A	COLCHESTER	2,120	7	D	4	0–0	0–0	—	M James
4	10/9	H	HARTLEPOOL	5,310	6	W	7	2–0	0–0	Pritchard 46, Riley 53	D Reeves
5	16/9	A	WREXHAM	1,731	7	L	7	1–3	0–1	Crawford 75; Edwards 21, Gregory 52, Hunt 89	D Allison
6	24/9	H	TORQUAY	5,266	6	W	10	5–0	1–0	Crawford 41, 59, 66, Riley 64, Ritchie 81p	L Robinson
7	27/9	H	READING	6,322	4	W	13	3–1	0–1	Ritchie 61, Pritchard 63, 88; Senior 15	J Deakin
8	1/10	A	HEREFORD	5,943	2	W	16	2–0	1–0	Ritchie 42, Kerr 64	K Baker
9	8/10	H	HALIFAX	6,698	2	W	19	3–0	3–0	Riley 1, Crawford 15, Kerr 42	J Martin
10	14/10	A	TRANMERE	2,520	3	L	19	0–2	0–1	Williams G 21, Halliday 59 (og)	M Peck
11	18/10	H	YORK	10,888	1	W	22	1–0	1–0	Stevens 39	K Cooper

Line-ups (City in roman, opponents in italics)

No	1	2	3	4	5	6	7	8	9	10	11	12 sub used
1 City	Shaw	Stevens	Williams G	Phill-Masters	Halliday	Riley	Pritchard	Ritchie	Kerr*	Musker	Crawford	Williams P
1 Opp	*Arnold*	*Whitworth*	*Kearney*	*Foster*	*Matthews*	*Calderwood*	*Barrowclough*	*Hutchinson*	*Dungworth**	*Caldwell*	*Lowery*	*Woodhead*
2 City	Shaw	Stevens	Williams G	Phill-Masters	Halliday	Riley	Pritchard	Ritchie	Kerr*	Musker	Crawford	Williams P
2 Opp	*Brown*	*Gardner*	*Pashley*	*Coleman*	*Hilton P*	*Bramhall*	*Potts**	*Madden*	*Entwhistle*	*Jakub*	*Carrodus*	*Spence*
3 City	Shaw	Newman	Williams G	Phill-Masters	Halliday	Riley*	Pritchard	Stevens	Ritchie	Crawford	Williams P	
3 Opp	*Chamberlain*	*Cook*	*Farrell*	*Hadley*	*Wignall*	*Houston*	*Groves*	*Osborne*	*Bowen*	*Adcock*	*Hull*	
4 City	Shaw	Newman	Williams G*	Phill-Masters	Halliday	Riley	Pritchard	Ritchie	Kerr	Economou	Crawford	Stevens
4 Opp	*Blackburn*	*Brown*	*Wilson*	*Buckley*	*Linighan A*	*Weir*	*Lowe*	*Whitfield*	*Waddle**	*Johnson*	*Robinson*	*Staff*
5 City	Shaw	Newman	Williams G	Halliday	Phill-Masters	Riley	Pritchard	Stevens	Williams P*	Economou	Crawford	Musker
5 Opp	*Wardle*	*King*	*Cunnington*	*Hunt*	*Keay*	*Wright*	*Edwards*	*Evans*	*Edwards*	*Gregory*	*Heath*	
6 City	Shaw	Stevens	Williams G	Halliday	Phill-Masters	Riley	Pritchard	Ritchie	Kerr	Economou	Crawford	Fifield
6 Opp	*Turner*	*Collins*	*Holmes*	*Sheridan*	*Little*	*Carr*	*Hughes*	*Pugh*	*Bishop**	*Anderson*	*Sims*	
7 City	Shaw	Stevens	Williams G	Halliday	Phill-Masters	Riley	Pritchard	Ritchie	Kerr*	Economou	Crawford	Cooper
7 Opp	*Judge**	*Williams*	*White*	*Beavon*	*Hicks*	*Wood*	*Price*	*Harris*	*Senior*	*Sanchez*	*Crown*	*Matthews*
8 City	Shaw	Stevens	Williams G	Halliday	Phill-Masters	Riley	Pritchard	Ritchie	Kerr	Economou	Crawford	
8 Opp	*Rose*	*Price*	*Leonard*	*Hicks*	*Pejic*	*Delve*	*Harvey*	*Emery**	*Phillips*	*Kearns*	*Black*	*Beacock*
9 City	Shaw	Stevens	Williams G	Halliday	Phill-Masters	Riley	Pritchard	Ritchie	Kerr	Economou*	Crawford	Cooper
9 Opp	*Smelt*	*Nobbs*	*Wood*	*Evans**	*Smith!*	*Hendrie*	*Nuttall*	*Mell*	*Staniforth*	*Kendall*	*Ward*	*Cook*
10 City	Shaw	Stevens	Williams G	Halliday	Phill-Masters	Riley	Pritchard	Ritchie	Kerr	Economou*	Crawford	Cooper
10 Opp	*Davies*	*McMahon*	*Burgess*	*Parry*	*Mungall*	*Williams J**	*Ferguson*	*Aspinall*	*Hilditch*	*Brown*	*Hamilton*	
11 City	Shaw	Stevens	Williams G	Halliday!	Phill-Masters	Riley	Pritchard	Ritchie	Kerr	Economou	Crawford	Cooper
11 Opp	*Astbury*	*Evans*	*Hay!*	*Sbragia*	*MacPhail*	*Senior*	*Ford*	*Crosby*	*Walwyn*	*Byrne*	*Pollard*	*Busby*

Match reports

1. v Mansfield. Mansfield boss Ian Greaves says City are a different class than the Stags in this one-sided game. Riley is unfortunate when his shot hits the post in the 85th minute, but he makes no mistake shortly after to net from 16 yards after racing onto a splendid pass by substitute Paul Williams.

2. v Bury. Despite Kerr's header slipping through David Brown's hands, City are second best before the break. Bury equalise with a shot that owes something to a deflection off Halliday, but Craig Madden's winning header is all his own work. No reward for City's second-half dominance.

3. v Colchester. City end the U's 100 per cent record, but bore the spectators in the process. Colchester, with top scorer Allinson having been sold to Arsenal, lack the fire-power to trouble a blanket defence. They have two shots on goal, whilst City are scarcely any better in mustering just one more.

4. v Hartlepool. Pritchard looks for a penalty when toppled by Alan Weir, but leaps to his feet on hearing no whistle to strike the ball past a stunned Eddie Blackburn. Hartlepool's negative tactics so infuriate Economou that he takes off his shirt to hand it to former Everton player Mick Buckley.

5. v Wrexham. Ex City keeper Bob Wardle, on a month's loan from Liverpool, derives special satisfaction in beating his old club. City have 70 per cent of the possession, but give away silly goals. Halliday fails to block Dave Gregory's cross and Andy Edwards shoots home in Wrexham's first attack.

6. v Torquay. "Too many players were trying to score" is Cooper's comment. An alert linesman signals that Crawford's header is over the line as City open their account. A push on Economou condemns Torquay to their second successive 0-5 away defeat as Ritchie makes no mistake from the spot.

7. v Reading. Cooper vintage half-hour show lifts City to a hard-earned win. Ritchie replies to Trevor Senior's headed opener, when unwittingly deflecting Steve Wood's clearance. Laurie Sanchez, replacing the injured Alan Judge on 65 minutes, is beaten by Pritchard's header from Cooper's chip.

8. v Hereford. Ritchie's headed goal is City's only shot on target in the first half as Crawford is withdrawn to a deeper role to strengthen the defence. Much relieved when John Delve's 53rd-minute header is disallowed for offside, City break quickly for Pritchard to cross for Kerr to hook the ball in.

9. v Halifax. City celebrate the award of a £250 cheque for being the Fourth Division's top scorers last month as Riley shoots in on 44 seconds. City are unable to capitalise after the break against opponents handicapped by the 53rd-min sending-off of Tom Smith for a professional foul on Riley.

10. v Tranmere. City dominate the early play, but on falling behind to Gary Williams' 25-yarder they are often outplayed. Mark Hilditch fires against a post shortly before Halliday heads an own-goal. Les Parry is unfortunate to concede a 78th-min penalty for handball, but Ritchie's kick is saved.

11. v York. Former City player Alan Hay is sent off for dissent shortly after the only goal – a superb move between Stevens and Kerr ending with an angled drive. Halliday goes off injured following this early crunching tackle by Keith Walwyn, but the striker bravely plays on for an hour.

League match record (games 12–23)

#	V	Date	Opponent	Pos	Att	OppPos	Result	Pts	FT	HT	Scorers	Referee
12	A	22/10	ALDERSHOT	1	3,195	17	L	22	0-1	0-1	Lawrence 12	Ref: D Axcell
13	H	29/10	PETERBOROUGH	2	7,380	6	L	22	0-1	0-0	Buchanan 75	Ref: J Worrall
14	A	1/11	BLACKPOOL	6	4,344	5	L	22	0-1	0-1	Windridge 19	Ref: N Ashley
15	H	5/11	DONCASTER	7	6,145	3	L	22	1-2	1-1	Stroud 25 / Kowalski 7, Harle 68	Ref: A Buksh
16	A	12/11	DARLINGTON	5	1,888	21	W	25	1-0	0-0	Kerr 67	Ref: A Challinor
17	H	26/11	CHESTERFIELD	4	5,835	16	W	28	2-0	0-0	Ritchie 53p, Pritchard 59	Ref: D Vickers
18	A	3/12	NORTHAMPTON	7	2,823	10	L	28	0-1	0-1	Belfon 18	Ref: A Ward
19	A	17/12	ROCHDALE	7	1,501	20	W	31	1-0	0-0	Pritchard 86	Ref: R Nixon
20	H	26/12	STOCKPORT	4	9,246	13	W	34	3-1	2-0	Riley 20, Crawford 37, Stroud 52 / Sword 85	Ref: T Spencer
21	A	28/12	CREWE	5	3,457	15	D	35	2-2	1-2	Ritchie 10p, Pritchard 55 / Crabbe 14, King 44p	Ref: D Richardson
22	H	31/12	CHESTER	3	7,565	24	W	38	4-2	0-1	Crawford 60, Stevens 76, Ritchie 81, [Riley 86] / Camden I, Brett 87	Ref: T Bune
23	H	21/1	WREXHAM	6	6,444	18	W	41	2-1	1-0	Ritchie 9p, Crawford 79 / Gregory 89p	Ref: J Moules

Line-ups (City, then opponents in italics)

12 Aldershot — City: Shaw, Stevens, Williams G, Newman!, Riley, Phill-Masters, Pritchard, Ritchie, Kerr*, Economou, Crawford, Cooper | *Coles, Shrubb, Mazzon, Briley*, Jopling, Amporlo, Lucas, Banton, Lawrence, McDonald, Burvill, O'Sullivan*
Riley fails with two good chances, but in between these misses Les Lawrence gives Aldershot the lead with a simple tap-in. City, up against it following Newman's 41st-minute dismissal for a tackle on Dale Banton, are unfortunate when Crawford's header hits the bar near the end.

13 Peterborough — City: Shaw, Stevens, Williams G, Newman, Riley, Phill-Masters, Pritchard, Ritchie, Stroud, Economou*, Crawford, Newman | *Seaman, Chard, Imlach, Benjamin, Wile, Slack, Pike, Tydeman, Hankin, Waddle, Clarke*, Buchanan*
A woeful City performance as Terry Cooper, who has just been appointed to the board, admits that there is not much chance of signing a proven goalscorer. Substitute David Buchanan settles a poor game in Posh's favour, meeting Ian Benjamin's cross with a firm diving header.

14 Blackpool — City: Shaw, Stevens, Williams G, Newman, Riley*, Phill-Masters, Pritchard, Ritchie, Stroud!, Williams P, Crawford, Williams G | *Siddall, Bardsley, Ferns, Rodaway, Greenall, Hetzke, Windridge, Mercer, Stewart!, Deary, McNiven*
After Steve Hetzke's handball, Pritchard is left to rue his early penalty miss. Barry Siddall easily saves the half-hit shot and shortly after Dave Windridge shoots in from 20 yards. Paul Stewart on 74 minutes and Stroud shortly after are both sent off for second bookable offences.

15 Doncaster — City: Shaw, Stevens, Williams G, Newman, Riley*, Phill-Masters, Pritchard, Ritchie, Stroud, Williams P, Crawford, Economou | *Boyd, Russell, Harle, Snodin I, Lister, Humphries, Miller, Moss, Douglas, Snodin G, Kowalski*
After the shock of Andy Kowalski's opening volley, City monopolise possession. Shaw is fortunate not to be sent off after bringing down Ernie Moss on 55 minutes, but Doncaster snatch an unlikely victory when David Harle is on hand to tap in after Shaw saves from the No 8.

16 Darlington — City: Shaw, Stevens, Williams G, Newman, Riley*, Phill-Masters, Pritchard, Ritchie, Stroud, Economou, Crawford, Kerr | *Barber, Craggs, Johnson, Honour*, Smith, Barton, Cartwright, Todd, Davies, Walsh, McLean, Wakefield*
Kerr heads in Pritchard's cross at the far post to end City's sequence of four defeats. City are forced to weather much early Darlington pressure as Alan Walsh causes many problems, but are not further troubled until John Craggs long-range effort hits the crossbar near the end.

17 Chesterfield — City: Shaw, Stevens, Williams G, Newman, Riley*, Phill-Masters, Pritchard, Ritchie, Stroud, Kerr, Williams P*, Marshall | *Brown J, Kendal, O'Neill*, Scrimgeour, Stimpson, Bellamy, Birch, Spooner, Newton, Clayton, Baines, Klug*
Ritchie turns the game for a depleted City without five regulars. He scores with a perfectly-placed penalty after being floored when cleverly beating Barrie Stimpson. Chesterfield are unlucky when Steve Spooner's 18th-minute shot is ruled out for offside against John Clayton.

18 Northampton — City: Shaw, Stevens, Williams G, Newman, Riley!, Phill-Masters, Pritchard, Ritchie, Stroud, Kerr, Cooper, Williams P* | *Gleasure, Tucker, Mundee, Gage, Lewis, Burrows, Jeffrey, O'Neill, Austin, Belfon*, Muir, Hayes*
Despite much excellent play City lack the killer touch in front of goal, though Hirst is unfortunate when his shot is cleared off the line on the half-hour mark. Halliday is sent off for a second caution in a minute as City strive to counter Frankie Belfon's fierce drive.

19 Rochdale — City: Shaw, Stevens, Williams G, Newman, Halliday, Phill-Masters, Pritchard, Ritchie, Stroud, Riley, Crawford*, Cooper | *Conroy, Greenhoff B, Chapman, Farrell, Williams, Doyle, Higgins, Hamilton, Johnson, Allatt*, Thompson D, Griffiths*
Pritchard seizes on Bill Humphries' sliced clearance to shoot in from 15 yards for City's late winner. With only one previous home defeat this season Rochdale are fortunate when Stroud's ferocious drive hits a post, but it is City's poor finishing that nearly lets them off the hook.

20 Stockport — City: Shaw, Stevens, Williams G, Newman, Halliday, Phill-Masters, Pritchard*, Ritchie*, Hirst, Riley, Crawford, Cooper | *Salmon, Rutter, Sherlock, Emerson, Thorpe, Bowles, Williams, Jones, Quinn, Sword, Evans*
Riley bounces back to form following the birth of his first child earlier this month. He sets City on course for a convincing win with a close-range shot. Stockport's attempts to spring the offside trap are frequently exposed and it is no surprise when Stroud is free to crash in a drive.

21 Crewe — City: Shaw, Stevens, Williams G, Newman, Halliday, Phill-Masters, Pritchard, Ritchie, Hirst*, Riley, Crawford, Cooper | *Naylor, Brady, Bowers, King, Hart, Williams, Pullar*, Crabbe, Waller, Leonard, Cliss, Edwards*
City are run ragged in the first half after Bowers fouls Pritchard to concede Ritchie's pen. Crabbe's 20-yard chip puts Crewe level and then they take the lead after Phillipson-Masters brings down Waller. City's stirring second-half fight-back is rewarded by Crawford's fine volley.

22 Chester — City: Shaw, Stevens, Williams G, Newman, Halliday, Phill-Masters, Pritchard, Ritchie, Hirst*, Riley, Crawford, Cooper | *Harrington, Evans, Blackwell, Brett, Holden, Zelem I, Allen, Storton, Camden, Elliott, Sutcliffe!*
Brett's late goal is Chester's only shot of the second half after their X-certificate tackling gifts City victory following the dismissal of Zelem and Sutcliffe either side of half-time. Harrington is unlucky with City's leveller, knocking the ball into the net after blocking Crawford's shot.

23 Wrexham — City: Shaw, Stevens, Williams G, Newman, Halliday, Phill-Masters, Pritchard, Ritchie, Hirst*, Riley, Crawford, Cooper | *Millington, King, Cunnington, Hunt, Heath, Keay, Williams, Wright, Arkwright, Steel, Gregory, Salathiel*
Crawford celebrates heading in City's second goal, but to many fans it appears that Pritchard's head supplied the last vital touch as they both try to force home a ball that had cannoned off the crossbar. Ritchie's penalty follows on from a handball that deprives Riley of a goal.

CANON LEAGUE DIVISION 4

Manager: Terry Cooper — SEASON 1983-84

24 · A SWINDON · 24/1 — Att 6,692 · Pos 16 · Pt 42 · D · F-A 1-1 · H-T 0-0

Pos	1	2	3	4	5	6	7	8	9	10	11	12 sub used
City	Shaw	Stevens	Williams G	Halliday	Phill-Masters	Stroud	Pritchard	Ritchie	Riley	Hirst*	Crawford	Cooper
Swindon	*Andrews*	*Henry*	*Baddeley*	*Batty*	*Gibson*	*Rowland*	*Hockaday*	*Emmanuel*	*Quinn*	*Nelson*	*Barnard*	

Scorers: Riley 83 / Quinn 51 — Ref: C Downey

Riley's superbly-struck volley from the edge of the penalty area earns City a precious point from a match that appeared lost. Injury-hit Swindon raise their game in the derby atmosphere and on-loan keeper Ian Andrews has an inspired League debut. Jimmy Quinn hooks in a fine volley.

25 · A HARTLEPOOL · 28/1 — Att 1,881 · Pos 24 · Pt 43 · D · F-A 2-2 · H-T 1-2

Pos	1	2	3	4	5	6	7	8	9	10	11	12 sub used
City	Shaw	Stevens	Williams G	Halliday	Phill-Masters	Stroud	Pritchard	Ritchie	Riley	Hirst	Crawford*	Cooper
Hartlepool	*Blackburn*	*Smithies*	*Barker*	*Hogan*	*Linighan A*	*Linighan D*	*Kennedy*	*Linacre J*	*Robinson D*	*Dobson*	*Staff*	

Scorers: Riley 32, Pritchard 67 / Dobson 4, Staff 12 — Ref: D Allison

Financially-threatened Hartlepool deserve more for their early domination than Paul Dobson's bicycle kick and Paul Staff's rifle shot. Hirst shoots from the corner of the area before Pritchard secures City's fortunate draw after running through to slip the ball past Eddie Blackburn.

26 · H BURY · 31/1 — Att 7,770 · Pos 11 · Pt 46 · W · F-A 3-2 · H-T 1-0

Pos	1	2	3	4	5	6	7	8	9	10	11	12 sub used
City	Shaw	Stevens	Williams G	Newman	Phill-Masters	Stroud	Pritchard	Ritchie	Hirst	Riley	Crawford	Cooper
Bury	*Butcher*	*Gardner*	*Pashley*	*Park*	*Hilton P*	*Bramhall*	*White*	*Madden*	*Entwhistle**	*Jakub*	*Deacy*	*Carrodus*

Scorers: Ritchie 41p, Riley 59, Crawford 72 / Hilton 58, Jakub 68 — Ref: A Robinson

Bury are content to defend in numbers until Paul Hilton's ill-judged tackle on Ritchie produces a penalty opener. Hilton atones for his error by heading in Terry Pashley's cross, whilst Crawford is all on his own as he shoots City's winner. Nick Deacy limps off in the closing stages.

27 · H HEREFORD · 4/2 — Att 7,222 · Pos 21 · Pt 49 · W · F-A 1-0 · H-T 1-0

Pos	1	2	3	4	5	6	7	8	9	10	11	12 sub used
City	Shaw	Stevens	Williams G	Newman	Phill-Masters	Stroud	Pritchard	Ritchie	Hirst*	Riley	Crawford	Cooper
Hereford	*Rose*	*Emery*	*Dalziel**	*Hicks*	*Pejic*	*Larkin*	*Hendrie*	*Harvey*	*Phillips*	*Kearns*	*Butler*	*Bray*

Scorers: Crawford 42 — Ref: C Thomas

Cooper only has £20,000 to spend after City make hard work of this win. Superb saves by Kevin Rose keeps the Bulls (only one win in their previous 16 games) in with a chance. Ian Dalziel lies injured as Pritchard sets up Crawford to head in at the far post for City's first double.

28 · A TORQUAY · 11/2 — Att 4,309 · Pos 13 · Pt 49 · L · F-A 0-1 · H-T 0-0

Pos	1	2	3	4	5	6	7	8	9	10	11	12 sub used
City	Shaw	Stevens	Williams G	Newman	Phill-Masters	Stroud	Pritchard	Ritchie	Newman	Hirst	Crawford*	Cooper
Torquay	*Turner*	*Pugh*	*Anderson*	*Carr*	*Impey*	*Lennox*	*Hughes*	*Curle*	*Bishop*	*Sims*	*Barnes*	

Scorers: Sims 70 — Ref: V Callow

City exert much early pressure in a game which is a fine advertisement for basement soccer, but Shaw brings their ten-match unbeaten League run to an end. His mistimed punch from Brian Hughes' corner gifts John Sims his match-winning header to please new boss Dave Webb.

29 · H BLACKPOOL · 14/2 — Att 7,599 · Pos 7 · Pt 50 · D · F-A 1-1 · H-T 0-1

Pos	1	2	3	4	5	6	7	8	9	10	11	12 sub used
City	Shaw	Stevens	Williams G	Newman	Phill-Masters	Stroud	Pritchard	Ritchie	Hirst*	Newman	Crawford	Cooper
Blackpool	*Pierce*	*Moore*	*Ferns*	*Radaway*	*Hetzke*	*Walsh*	*Britton*	*Mercer*	*Stewart*	*Windridge*	*McNiven**	*Dyer*

Scorers: Stroud 80 / Hetzke 33 — Ref: D Hedges

City dominate the second half in their attempts to equalise Steve Hetzke's 20-yard free-kick, but the flow of the game is effected by the award of 43 free-kicks for mainly petty offences. Blackpool at last fail to clear one of City's 14 corners and Stroud rifles a superb shot in off the post.

30 · A PETERBOROUGH · 18/2 — Att 3,356 · Pos 8 · Pt 50 · L · F-A 1-4 · H-T 1-1

Pos	1	2	3	4	5	6	7	8	9	10	11	12 sub used
City	Shaw	Stevens	Williams G	Newman	Phill-Masters	Stroud	Pritchard	Ritchie	Newman	Hirst	Crawford*	Cooper
Peterborough	*Seaman*	*Chard*	*Imlach*	*Beech*	*Wile*	*Firm*	*Benjamin*	*Tydeman*	*Hankin*	*Waddle*	*Worrall*	

Scorers: Crawford 23 / Waddle 33, 81, Hankin 46, Worrall 70 — Ref: A Gunn

City skipper Tom Ritchie admits, after this defeat, that City may not have a strong enough squad to go up. Crawford shoots City ahead, but defensive errors allow the Posh to take charge. Gary Worrall, on loan from Manchester United, strikes a magnificent goal from a narrow angle.

31 · H ALDERSHOT · 25/2 — Att 7,140 · Pos 5 · Pt 53 · W · F-A 2-1 · H-T 2-1

Pos	1	2	3	4	5	6	7	8	9	10	11	12 sub used
City	Shaw	Stevens	Newman	Newman	Phill-Masters	Stroud	Pritchard	Ritchie	Riley	Newman	Hirst	Cooper
Aldershot	*Coles*	*Shrubb*	*Gillard*	*Briley*	*Souter*	*Jopling*	*Burvill*	*Banton*	*Lawrence*	*McDonald*	*Mazzon*	

Scorers: Ritchie 20p, Riley 24 / Lawrence 44 — Ref: L Shapter

Ian Gillard and Don Souter complain of being punched and kicked by City fans as they leave the pitch after this vital promotion clash. Riley produces two flashes of inspiration to win the game. He topples dramatically for Ritchie's penalty, then nets with an 18-yarder into the corner.

32 · A YORK · 3/3 — Att 5,096 · Pos 1 · Pt 54 · D · F-A 1-1 · H-T 0-0

Pos	1	2	3	4	5	6	7	8	9	10	11	12 sub used
City	Shaw	Stevens	Newman	Halliday	Phill-Masters	Stroud	Pritchard	Ritchie	Riley	**Morgan**	Cooper	
York	*Jones*	*Senior*	*Hay*	*Shragia*	*MacPhail*	*Hood*	*Ford*	*Crosby*	*Walwyn*	*Byrne*	*Pearce*	

Scorers: Morgan 79 / Phillipson-Masters 46 (og) — Ref: I Hendrick

Trevor Morgan, City's new £10,000 striker from Bournemouth, maintains his remarkable scoring-debut sequence. He stoops to head in from Pritchard's free-kick to level matters after Phillipson-Masters' misfortune to deflect John Byrne's vicious cross into his own net.

33 · A DONCASTER · 6/3 — Att 4,954 · Pos 2 · Pt 54 · L · F-A 0-1 · H-T 0-1

Pos	1	2	3	4	5	6	7	8	9	10	11	12 sub used
City	Shaw	Stevens	Newman	Halliday	Phill-Masters	Stroud	Pritchard	Ritchie	Hirst	Riley*	Curle	Hirst
Doncaster	*Peacock*	*Yates*	*Breckin*	*Snodin I*	*Harle*	*Humphries*	*Miler**	*Moss*	*Douglas*	*Kowalski*	*Snodin G*	*Woods*

Scorers: Douglas 4 — Ref: A Robinson

City never look like ending Doncaster's 15-match unbeaten run after Colin Douglas handles the ball before shooting. Stevens clears a header off the line after the break, but City are unlucky not to gain the award of a free-kick on the edge of the box instead of a penalty.

34 · H DARLINGTON · 10/3 — Att 7,046 · Pos 18 · Pt 57 · W · F-A 1-0 · H-T 0-0

Pos	1	2	3	4	5	6	7	8	9	10	11	12 sub used
City	Shaw	Stevens	Newman	Halliday	Phill-Masters	Stroud	Pritchard	Ritchie	Riley	Morgan	Curle	Hirst
Darlington	*Barber*	*Craggs*	*Johnson*	*Gilbert*	*Smith*	*Barton*	*Cartwright*	*Todd*	*Hannah*	*Wilson*	*McLean**	*Honour*

Scorers: Morgan 84 — Ref: D Letts

According to City's full-backs, John Hannah's 58th-min free-header from Kevin Todd crosses the line before Shaw claws the ball out. A goal then would have been rough justice for City who gain a late winning reward for their almost constant attacking with Morgan's right-foot volley.

Season match record (games 35–46)

#	Venue	Date	Opponent	HT	Result (FT)	Pos	Att	Opp Pos	Pts
35	H	13/3	ROCHDALE	0-1	D 1-1	4	7,101	21	58
36	A	17/3	HALIFAX	0-0	W 2-1	4	1,204	21	61
37	H	24/3	TRANMERE	0-0	D 1-1	4	6,613	9	62
38	A	27/3	MANSFIELD	0-0	W 1-0	3	1,828	23	65
39	H	31/3	COLCHESTER	1-0	W 4-1	2	6,612	9	68
40	A	7/4	READING	0-2	L 0-2	2	8,780	3	68
41	H	14/4	NORTHAMPTON	1-1	W 4-1	2	6,655	16	71
42	H	17/4	CREWE	2-0	W 2-1	2	8,184	14	74
43	A	21/4	STOCKPORT	0-0	D 0-0	2	2,645	13	75
44	A	28/4	CHESTERFIELD	0-0	D 1-1	3	2,975	14	76
45	H	5/5	SWINDON	1-0	W 1-0	3	12,810	16	79
46	A	7/5	CHESTER	1-0	W 2-1	3	4,013	24	82

Home 7,287 · Away 3,447 · Average 7,287

---

35. ROCHDALE (H) 13/3 — D 1-1
City: Shaw, Stevens, Newman, Halliday, Phill-Masters, Stroud, Pritchard, Ritchie, Riley, Morgan, Curle*, Hirst
Rochdale: Conroy, Oates, Chapman, Reid, McMahon, Williams, Thompson D, Hamilton, O'Connor, Allatt, Griffiths
Scorers: Riley 80; O'Connor 43. Ref: R Lewis
Enterprising Rochdale belie their lowly position against inept City. Malcolm O'Connor's rasping drive puts the visitors ahead, and they are unlucky on 72 mins when Vernon Allatt's header is struck off for pushing. Riley's heads in City's equaliser and later the post denies Pritchard.

36. HALIFAX (A) 17/3 — W 2-1
City: Shaw, Stevens, Newman, Halliday, Phill-Masters, Stroud, Pritchard, Ritchie, Riley, Morgan, Curle, Hirst
Halifax: Smelt, Kendall, Wood, Evans, Smith, Hendrie, Gallagher B, Little, Staniforth, Cook*, Ward, Mell
Scorers: Pritchard 48, Riley 76; Evans 89. Ref: J Lovatt
Pritchard opens the scoring with a coolly-executed volley and creates the second with a brilliant pass to Riley. A first half littered with offsides is best forgotten, but after the break City's defence is in control until a twice-taken free-kick by David Evans is deflected off Riley into the net.

37. TRANMERE (H) 24/3 — D 1-1
City: Shaw, Stevens, Newman, Halliday, Phill-Masters G, Stroud*, Pritchard, Ritchie, Riley, Morgan, Hirst, Cooper
Tranmere: Davies, Higgins, Burgess, Philpotts, Williams G, Palios, Ferguson, Aspinall, Hilditch, Hutchinson, Goodlass, Cooper
Scorers: Morgan 85; Hutchinson 49. Ref: D Burgess
Tranmere boss Bryan Hamilton tips City for promotion after his impressive side take a deserved point, but City equalise when Cooper's measured pass sets up Morgan's low drive. Mark Hilditch crosses for Bobby Hutchinson to hammer in.

38. MANSFIELD (A) 27/3 — W 1-0
City: Shaw, Stevens, Newman, Halliday, Phill-Masters, Stroud, Pritchard, Ritchie, Riley, Morgan, Hirst
Mansfield: Hitchcock, Woodhead, Whitworth, Lowery, Ayre, Foster, Barrowclough, Matthews, Juryeff, Caldwell, Nicholson*, Calderwood
Scorers: Newman 56. Ref: D Shaw
Newman clips a curling right-foot free-kick round Mansfield's wall to clinch a City victory far more emphatic than the score suggests. Re-election-threatened Mansfield look the poorest side City have faced this season, but Shaw has to be alert to parry Tony Lowery's low shot.

39. COLCHESTER (H) 31/3 — W 4-1
City: Shaw, Stevens, Newman, Halliday, Phill-Masters, Stroud, Pritchard, Ritchie, Riley, Morgan, Hirst
Colchester: Chamberlain, Cook, Phillips*, Hedman, Wignall, Houston, Groves, Osborne, Bowen, Adcock, Leslie, Hadley
Scorers: Ritchie 26p, 63, Riley 67, 81; Wignall 78. Ref: M Heath
Despite Ritchie's penalty, after another of Riley's theatrical falls, City's play is racked with tension before a bout of one-touch football allows Ritchie to score with a low shot. In a rare U's raid Steve Wignall nets with a superb header, but Riley fires in to ensure City have the final say.

40. READING (A) 7/4 — L 0-2
City: Shaw, Stevens, Newman, Halliday, Phill-Masters, Stroud, Pritchard, Ritchie, Riley, Morgan, Hirst*, Cooper
Reading: Judge, Williams, Richardson, Price, Hicks, Wood, White, Harris, Senior, Sanchez, Crown, Cooper
Scorers: Sanchez 10, Horrix 36. Ref: D Vickers
A day of shame for so called City fans as terrace violence leads to the game being held up for 15 mins in the second half. Reading are good value for their win secured by a Lawrie Sanchez shot and Dean Horrix's freak effort. His attempted cross curls over Shaw's head into the net.

41. NORTHAMPTON (H) 14/4 — W 4-1
City: Shaw, Stevens, Newman, Halliday, Phill-Masters*, Stroud, Pritchard, Ritchie, Riley, Morgan, Crawford*, Cooper
Northampton: Gleasure, Lewis, Forster, Gage, Burrows*, Hayes I, Jeffrey, O'Neill, Mundee, Austin, Muir, Belfon
Scorers: Crawford 32, 58, Riley 83, Ritchie 87p; O'Neill 44p. Ref: K Cooper
Crawford's return, after knee-ligament trouble, inspires an impressive win on a day other promotion rivals Aldershot and Blackpool falter. The referee, finding cause to book six players, aids City's cause by sending off Austin Hayes in the 23rd minute for his second bookable offence.

42. CREWE (H) 17/4 — W 2-1
City: Shaw, Stevens, Newman, Halliday, Phill-Masters, Stroud, Pritchard, Ritchie, Riley, Morgan, Hirst, Crawford
Crewe: Naylor, Edwards, Davies, Hirst, Scott, Hart, Cliss, Bishop, Waller, Leonard*, Williams, Thomas
Scorers: Hirst 29, Pritchard 31; Leonard 61. Ref: E Scales
Hirst puts himself in good heart for his geography degree finals next month with his first League goal. A sweetly-struck volley from the edge of the penalty area helps City overcome battling Crewe for whom Mark Leonard scores after latching onto Ian Bishop's hopeful through-ball.

43. STOCKPORT (A) 21/4 — D 0-0
City: Shaw, Stevens, Newman, Halliday, Phill-Masters, Stroud, Pritchard, Ritchie, Riley, Morgan, Hirst
Stockport: Salmon, Thorpe, Rutter, Emerson, Sword, Bowles, Williams, Evans, Kerr, Taylor, Coyle
Ref: D Scott
City fans are sure City are promotion bound as they chant 'going up, going up' after this exciting draw at Edgeley Park. Although there are no goals, this is one of the best games seen at Stockport this season. Action swings from end to end with goalmouth thrills coming thick and fast.

44. CHESTERFIELD (A) 28/4 — D 1-1
City: Shaw, Stevens, Newman, Halliday, Phill-Masters, Stroud, Pritchard, Ritchie, Riley, Morgan, Riley*, Hirst
Chesterfield: Brown J, Bellamy, Brown N, Kendal, Baines, Hunter, Brown P, Scrimgeour, Newton, Klug, O'Neill, Curle
Scorers: Phillipson-Masters 78; Kendal 77. Ref: K Baker
In a lacklustre encounter, without the competitive spirit expected, giant centre-half Phillipson-Masters pops up with his first goal of the season to push City closer to promotion. His header from Newman's free-kick cancels out Steve Kendal's shot from a suspiciously-offside position.

45. SWINDON (H) 5/5 — W 1-0
City: Shaw, Stevens, Newman, Halliday, Phill-Masters G, Stroud, Pritchard, Ritchie, Riley, Morgan, Crawford
Swindon: Endersby, Henry, Baillie, Batty, Baddeley, Graham, Barnard, Emmanuel, Quinn, Hockaday, Nelson
Scorers: Pritchard 46. Ref: B Stevens
City celebrate Cooper signing a new two-year contract with this derby win, that has the fans erroneously thinking that promotion had been achieved. Swindon dominate the first half, but City take control after Pritchard crashes in Crawford's pass to finish off a brilliant move.

46. CHESTER (A) 7/5 — W 2-1
City: Shaw, Stevens, Newman, Halliday, Phill-Masters, Stroud, Pritchard, Ritchie, Riley, Morgan, Crawford
Chester: Harrington, Dixon, Lane, Williams M, Zelem, Elliott, Allen, Sanderson, Coy, Wharton*, Brett, Bulmer
Scorers: Morgan 32, 87; Zelem 81. Ref: P Scott
Needing a point to secure promotion City live up to Cooper's pledge in going for a win at Sealand Road. Morgan's low drive from a free-kick punishes Chester for up-ending Pritchard, and he slots home the winner after Peter Zelem had silenced the 3,000 City fans with his header.

CANON DIVISION 4 (CUP-TIES)   Manager: Terry Cooper   SEASON 1983-84

Milk Cup

				F-A	H-T	1	2	3	4	5	6	7	8	9	10	11	12 sub used	Scorers, Times, and Referees
1:1	A	OXFORD	3,924	D 1-1	0-1	Shaw	Stevens	Williams G	Halliday	Phill-Masters	Riley	Pritchard	Ritchie	Kerr*	Musker	Crawford	Williams P	Riley 86
						Hardwick	*Hinshelwood*	*Grant*	*Thomas**	*Briggs*	*Shotton*	*Lawrence*	*Whatmore*	*Biggins*	*Hebberd*	*Brock*	*Vinter*	*Brock 16* / Ref: E Scales

Kevin Brock takes advantage of a rebound to put disappointing Oxford in front after Shaw's great block of an Andy Thomas shot. Halliday is City's star man with an almost faultless display at the back. Riley smashes home City's deserved equaliser following Musker's corner.

				F-A	H-T	1	2	3	4	5	6	7	8	9	10	11	12	Scorers, Times, and Referees
1:2	H	OXFORD	5,163 3:6	L 0-1	0-1	Shaw	Newman	Williams G	Halliday	Phill-Masters	Riley	Pritchard	Ritchie*	Kerr	Economou	Crawford	Williams P	Thomas 1
						Hardwick	*Hinshelwood*	*McDonald*	*Thomas*	*Briggs*	*Shotton*	*Lawrence*	*Vinter**	*Biggins*	*Hebberd*	*Brock*	*Barnett*	Ref: L Burden

(City lost 1-2 on aggregate)

An impressive first-half display by the City, despite being caught napping after just 16 secs when Andy Thomas races clear to shoot past Shaw. Oxford, denied a 25th-min pen when Phillipson-Masters handles the ball, take control after the break following Ritchie's exit due to injury.

FA Cup

				F-A	H-T	1	2	3	4	5	6	7	8	9	10	11	12	Scorers, Times, and Referees
1	A	CORINTHIAN CAS (at Dulwich H'let)	2,118 IL	D 0-0	0-0	Shaw	Stevens	Williams G	Halliday	Newman	Kerr	Pritchard	Ritchie	Williams P	Economou*	Hirst	Cooper	
						Chapman	*Fulton*	*Stevenson*	*Coldspring*	*Bateman*	*Pardew*	*Armitt*	*Green*	*Merron*	*Gray*	*Watson*		Ref: M James

City are made to fight for survival against the famous amateurs in this tie played on the Champion Hill ground of Dulwich Hamlet. Casuals skipper Peter Bateman puts an early chance over the bar and they put on the pressure straight after the break, before City turn the tide.

				F-A	H-T	1	2	3	4	5	6	7	8	9	10	11	12	Scorers, Times, and Referees
1R	H	CORINTHIAN CAS	5,339 IL	W 4-0	2-0	Shaw	Stevens	Williams G	Halliday	Newman	Economou*	Pritchard	Ritchie	Riley	Kerr	Stroud	Cooper	Riley 7, Pritchard 20, 46, 55,
						Chapman	*Fulton*	*Stevenson*	*Coldspring*	*Cleaver*	*Pardew*	*Armitt*	*Green*	*Merron**	*Gray*	*Watson*	*Bateman*	Ref: M James

Riley calms any City worries with an early tap-in after Ritchie's shot hits the post. Casuals bow out of the Cup in the best tradition of gracious losers as Pritchard notches the second hat-trick of his career. Bernie Merron insists on shaking hands with City players when being substituted.

				F-A	H-T	1	2	3	4	5	6	7	8	9	10	11	12	Scorers, Times, and Referees
2	A	BRISTOL ROV	14,396 3:2	W 2-1	0-0	Shaw	Stevens	Williams G	Halliday	Phill-Masters	Stroud	Pritchard	Ritchie	Hirst	Riley	Crawford*	Cooper	Ritchie 78, Hirst 89
						Kite	*Slater*	*Williams B*	*Bater*	*Parkin*	*McCaffery*	*Holloway*	*Williams G*	*Stephens*	*Randall**	*Barrett*	*White*	*Stephens 50* / Ref: K Baker

Hirst's mis-hit shot from Riley's pull-back earns City a deserved victory at Eastville Stadium. City refuse to be dismayed after Archie Stephens puts the Rovers ahead with magnificent header. Riley hits the post before Ritchie cracks in a fine equaliser after swiveling to lose his marker.

				F-A	H-T	1	2	3	4	5	6	7	8	9	10	11	12	Scorers, Times, and Referees
3	A	NOTTS CO	11,042 1:20	D 2-2	1-1	Shaw	Stevens	Williams G	Halliday	Phill-Masters	Riley	Pritchard	Ritchie	Stroud	Hirst	Crawford*	Cooper	Crawford 3, Ritchie 64
						McDonagh	*Goodwin*	*Worthington*	*Richards*	*Hunt*	*Kilcline*	*O'Neill*	*Clarke*	*Christie*	*Harkouk**	*Chiedozie*	*McCulloch*	*Christie 34p, 49* / Ref: N Glover

City's superb performance belies their lowly status. Crawford is free at the far post to head in Pritchard's cross for an early lead. County level with a penalty after Rachid Harkouk appears to dive, but City are denied a similar award in the 75th minute when Ritchie is brought down.

				F-A	H-T	1	2	3	4	5	6	7	8	9	10	11	12	Scorers, Times, and Referees
3R	H	NOTTS CO	16,107 1:20	L 0-2	0-0	Shaw	Stevens	Williams G	Halliday	Phill-Masters	Riley	Pritchard	Ritchie	Stroud	Hirst	Crawford*	Cooper	Kilcline 48, McCulloch 73
						McDonagh	*Goodwin*	*Worthington*	*Richards*	*Hunt*	*Kilcline*	*O'Neill*	*McCulloch*	*Christie*	*Harkouk*	*Chiedozie*		Ref: N Glover

The fans who are undeterred by price increases of up to 40 per cent receive poor reward as City are muscled out of the Cup. Pritchard is controversially ruled offside on hammering home Ritchie's pass shortly after Brian Kilcline bundles the ball in off a post to put Notts ahead.

League Table

	Team	P	W	D	L	F	A	W	D	L	F	A	Pts
				Home					Away				
1	York	46	18	4	1	58	16	13	4	6	38	23	101
2	Doncaster	46	15	6	2	46	22	9	7	7	36	32	85
3	Reading	46	17	6	0	51	14	5	10	8	33	42	82
4	BRISTOL CITY	46	18	3	2	51	17	6	7	10	19	27	82
5	Aldershot	46	14	6	3	49	29	8	3	12	27	40	75
6	Blackpool	46	15	4	4	47	19	6	5	12	23	33	72
7	Peterborough	46	15	5	3	52	16	3	9	11	20	32	68
8	Colchester	46	14	7	2	45	14	3	9	11	24	39	67
9	Torquay	46	13	7	3	32	18	5	6	12	27	46	67
10	Tranmere	46	11	5	7	33	26	6	10	7	20	27	66
11	Hereford	46	11	6	6	31	21	5	9	9	23	32	63
12	Stockport	46	12	5	6	34	25	5	6	12	26	39	62
13	Chesterfield	46	10	11	2	34	24	5	4	14	25	37	60
14	Darlington	46	13	4	6	31	19	4	4	15	18	31	59
15	Bury	46	9	7	7	34	32	6	3	14	27	32	59
16	Crewe	46	10	8	5	35	27	4	6	13	21	40	59
17	Swindon	46	11	7	5	34	23	4	6	13	24	33	58
18	Northampton	46	10	8	5	32	32	3	6	14	21	46	53
19	Mansfield	46	9	7	7	44	27	4	6	13	22	43	52
20	Wrexham	46	7	6	10	34	33	4	9	10	25	41	48
21	Halifax	46	11	6	6	36	25	1	6	16	19	64	48
22	Rochdale	46	8	9	6	35	31	3	4	16	17	49	46
23	Hartlepool	46	7	8	8	31	28	3	2	18	16	57	40
24	Chester	46	7	5	11	23	35	0	8	15	22	47	34
		1104	285	150	117	932	573	117	150	285	573	932	1506

Appearances and Goals

Player	Lge	Sub	LC	Sub	FAC	Sub	Lge	LC	FAC	Tot
			Appearances					Goals		
Cooper, Terry	1	20								
Curle, Keith	5	1								
Crawford, Alan	31		2		3		15		1	16
Economou, Jon	11	1	1		2					
Halliday, Bruce	41		2		5					
Hirst, Martyn	22	2			4		1		1	2
Kerr, John	13	1	2		2		4			4
Marshall, Gary		1								
Morgan, Trevor	15						5			5
Musker, Russell	2	1								
Newman, Rob	29	1	2		2		1			1
Phill-Masters, Forbes	44		2		3		1			1
Pritchard, Howard	46		2		5		10		3	13
Riley, Glynn	42		2		4		16	1	1	18
Ritchie, Tom	45		2		5		12		2	14
Shaw, John	46		2		5					
Stevens, Paul	45	1	1		5					
Stroud, Ken	34				4					
Williams, Gary	29	1	2		5		2			2
Williams, Paul	5	3			1	2	3			3
19 players used	506	33	22	2	55	5	70	1	8	79

Odds & ends

Double wins: (5) Mansfield, Hereford, Halifax, Darlington, Chester.

Double losses: (2) Peterborough, Doncaster.

Won from behind: (2) Reading (h), Chester (h).

Lost from in front: (2) Bury (a), Peterborough (a).

High spots: Achieving promotion.

Beating York 1-0 at Ashton Gate on 18 October.

Winning 2-1 at Chester to clinch promotion on 7 May.

Overcoming Bristol Rov in the FA Cup.

Low spots: Heavy defeat at Peterborough.

Losing FA replay v Notts County (h) 0-2.

Losing 2-3 v Bristol Rov (h) in the Gloucestershire Cup Final on 20 Sep.

Player of the year: Howard Pritchard.

Ever presents: (2) Howard Pritchard, John Shaw.

Hat-tricks: (2) Alan Crawford, Howard Pritchard.

Leading scorer: Glyn Riley (18).

CANON LEAGUE DIVISION 3 — Manager: Terry Cooper — SEASON 1984-85

Match summary

No		Date	Att	Pos	Pt	Res	F–A	H–T	Scorers, Times, and Referees
1	H WIGAN	25/8	8,122		3	W	2-0	0-0	Riley 60, 84 — Ref: M James
2	A NEWPORT	1/9	5,279		4	D	0-0	0-0	Ref: R Lewis
3	H SWANSEA	8/9	8,700	10 (23)	5	D	2-2	1-1	Walsh 16p, Crawford 66 / Mardenborough 21, Saunders 70 — Ref: D Vickers
4	A CAMBRIDGE	15/9	2,444	6 (21)	8	W	3-2	1-1	Walsh 8, Newman 72, Crawford 74 / Moyes 36, Greaves 69 — Ref: J Ball
5	A DERBY	19/9	11,314	8 (23)	8	L	0-1	0-1	Wilson 32 — Ref: E Scales
6	H ORIENT	22/9	6,941	7 (23)	11	W	3-2	1-1	Newman 15, Walsh 47, Crawford 78 / Silkman 24, Cornwell 88 — Ref: L Shapter
7	A WALSALL	29/9	4,754	10 (13)	11	L	1-4	0-1	Walsh 54 / Kelly 3, 65, O'Kelly 61p, Bamber 73 — Ref: J McAulay
8	H ROTHERHAM	2/10	6,586	10 (7)	11	L	0-1	0-1	Birch 38p — Ref: M Cotton
9	A YORK	6/10	4,890	9 (2)	14	W	2-0	1-0	Morgan 38, Walsh 71 — Ref: G Aplin
10	H GILLINGHAM	13/10	7,088	8 (7)	17	W	2-0	1-0	Riley 13, Morgan 59 — Ref: A Selville
11	A BRADFORD C	20/10	4,569	5 (4)	18	D	1-1	0-1	Pritchard 50 / Campbell 12 — Ref: D Richardson

Line-ups (positions 1–12; opponent shown in italic)

No	1	2	3	4	5	6	7	8	9	10	11	12 sub used
1 City	Shaw	Stevens	Newman	Rogers	Phill-Masters	Hirst	Pritchard	Riley	Morgan	Walsh	Crawford	
1 Wigan	*Tunks*	*Butler*	*Constive*	*Kelly*	*Cribley*	*Methven*	*Bailey*	*Barrow*	*Johnson*	*Lowe !*	*Langley **	*Bruce*
2 City	Shaw	Stevens	Newman	Rogers	Phill-Masters	Hirst	Pritchard	Riley	Morgan*	Walsh	Crawford	Curle
2 Newport	*Plumley*	*Jones*	*Matthewson*	*Reid*	*Saxby*	*Boyle*	*Carter*	*Pulis*	*Kent*	*Chamberlain**	*Lewis*	*Green*
3 City	Shaw	Stevens	Newman	Rogers	Halliday	Hirst	Pritchard	Riley*	Morgan	Walsh	Crawford	Curle
3 Swansea	*Rimmer*	*Evans*	*Marustik*	*Lewis*	*Stevenson*	*Richardson*	*Saunders*	*Robinson*	*Richards*	*Mardenboro***	*Pascoe*	*Rajkovic*
4 City	Shaw	Stevens	Newman	Rogers	Halliday	Hirst	Pritchard	Cartwright*	Morgan	Walsh	Crawford	Greaves
4 Cambridge	*Branagan*	*Clark*	*Beattie*	*Fallon*	*Moyes*	*Daniels*	*Massey*	*Cooke*		*Comfort*	*Pyle*	*Greaves*
5 City	Shaw	Stevens	Newman	Halliday	Phill-Masters	Hirst	Pritchard	Riley*	Morgan	Walsh	Crawford	Curle
5 Derby	*Steele*	*Palmer*	*Buckley*	*Powell*	*Hindmarch*	*Burns*	*Taylor*	*Wilson*	*Davison*	*Hooks*	*Robertson*	
6 City	Shaw	Stevens	Newman	Halliday	Phill-Masters	Hirst	Pritchard	Riley	Morgan	Walsh	Crawford	Cornwell
6 Orient	*Wilmot*	*Hales*	*Stride*	*Corbett*	*Foster*	*Banfield*	*Silkman*	*Brooks*	*Sussex*	*Cadette**	*Godfrey*	*Cornwell*
7 City	Shaw	Stevens	Newman	Halliday	Phill-Masters	Hirst	Pritchard	Riley	Morgan	Walsh	Crawford	Jones
7 Walsall	*Cherry*	*Hart*	*Mower*	*Shakespeare*	*Brazier*	*Hawke**	*Handysides*	*O'Kelly*	*Bamber*	*Kelly*	*Childs*	*Jones*
8 City	Shaw	Stevens	Newman	Curle	Phill-Masters	Hirst	Pritchard	Riley	Morgan	Walsh	Crawford	
8 Rotherham	*Mimms*	*Forrest*	*Mitchell*	*Trusson*	*Johnson*	*Pickering*	*Birch*	*Gooding*	*Dungworth*	*Simmons*	*Kilmore*	
9 City	Shaw	Stevens	Newman	Curle	Phill-Masters	Hirst	Pritchard	Ritchie	Morgan	Walsh	Riley	Cooper
9 York	*Jones*	*Evans*	*Hay*	*Stragia*	*MacPhail*	*Haslegrave*	*Ford*	*Hood**	*Walwyn*	*Byrne*	*Nicholson*	*Atkinson*
10 City	Shaw	Stevens	Newman	Curle	Phill-Masters	Riley	Pritchard	Ritchie	Morgan	Walsh	Crawford	
10 Gillingham	*Hillyard*	*Hinnigan*	*Sage*	*Oakes*	*Johnson*	*Shaw*	*Robinson*	*Shearer*	*Leslie**	*Mehmet*	*Cascarino*	*Weatherly*
11 City	Shaw	Stevens	Newman	Curle	Phill-Masters	Riley*	Pritchard	Ritchie	Morgan	Walsh	Stroud	Crawford
11 Bradford C	*McManus*	*Cherry*	*Withe*	*McCall*	*Jackson*	*Evans*	*Hendrie*	*Goodman*	*Campbell*	*Abbot*	*Ellis*	*Crawford*

Match notes

1. WIGAN — Wigan's David Lowe is sent off after swinging an elbow in frustration at the control City apprentice Lee Rogers exhibits over him on his debut. Clever running into space after the interval exposes the ponderous Wigan defence and the irrepressible Riley twice heads in.

2. NEWPORT — City weather much pressure and old adversary Tony Pulis is convinced that Newport will not let them off the hook again in next week's League Cup match. Roy Carter has his shot disallowed just before half-time, while sub Phil Green later sends a diving header against a post.

3. SWANSEA — Swansea, who have not won an away match for two seasons, almost end this run as Shaw has to make a fine save from Chris Marustik ten mins from time. Dean Saunders handles the ball to concede a penalty, but the striker makes amends by shooting in the Swans' second equaliser.

4. CAMBRIDGE — City maintain their unbeaten record in sensational style in this half-a-minute clash. Trailing 1-2 after Danny Greaves' debut goal, Newman crashes in a stunning right-foot volley from the edge of the penalty area, and then Crawford slides in the winner under Keith Branagan's body.

5. DERBY — The referee incurs City's wrath by failing to spot Rob Hindmarch's blatant handball right on half-time and disallowing Pritchard's 77th-minute shot. Kevin Wilson, the League's top scorer, shoots the only goal, firing in from the edge of the area on collecting Kevin Taylor's through-ball.

6. ORIENT — The fans jeer every square ball as City concentrate on slowing down the pace and keeping possession in the second half. Despite the boost of Newman's early scoring volley, City struggle to find any rhythm before the break. Orient level with Barry Silkman's shot from a narrow angle.

7. WALSALL — In the ascendancy after Walsh turns in Hirst's pass for an equaliser, City are sunk by a disputed pen. Richard O'Kelly makes no mistake from the spot as heated protests that Gary Childs took a blatant dive fall on deaf ears. David Kelly notches Walsall's third with a well-judged chip.

8. ROTHERHAM — It's not City's night as offside rules out efforts by Newman in the 69th minute and Morgan at the death, as well as being twice thwarted by the woodwork. After Stevens up-ends Kevin Kilmore with a clumsy tackle, Shaw is sent the wrong way by Alan Birch's penalty decider.

9. YORK — John Shaw provides the perfect answer to his critics with a brilliant display against the previously-unbeaten League leaders. He dives to his left to keep out John MacPhail's 19th-minute spot-kick after Curle is harshly penalised for handball. Walsh ties up City's victory with a fierce volley.

10. GILLINGHAM — Exhilarating City are fortunate with Riley's headed opener as Phillipson-Masters gets away with chopping down John Leslie in the build-up. Morgan heads in from a kneeling position at the Open End, before Mark Weatherly has his 20-yard drive disallowed by an offside decision.

11. BRADFORD C — A point is City's just reward for a sterling second-half fight-back. Bobby Campbell's volley is the wrong side of keeper Shaw for their early dominance and the City, with the wind behind them after the break, draw level as Pritchard bundles the ball over the line from Walsh's corner.

#		Opponent	Date	Att				Res	FT	HT
12	H	BOLTON	23/10	7,713	4	16	21	W	3-2	2-2
13	A	MILLWALL	27/10	7,039	6	1	22	D	1-1	0-0
14	H	BRENTFORD	3/11	7,674	7	8	23	D	1-1	0-0
15	A	DONCASTER	6/11	3,947	8	5	24	D	1-1	0-0
16	H	BRISTOL ROV	10/11	18,675	3	7	27	W	3-0	1-0
17	A	PRESTON	24/11	3,912	8	18	27	L	2-3	1-1
18	H	LINCOLN	1/12	7,270	6	18	30	W	2-1	2-0
19	A	BOURNEMOUTH	15/12	4,987	8	9	30	L	1-2	1-1
20	A	READING	22/12	4,101	10	13	30	L	0-1	0-0
21	H	PLYMOUTH	26/12	10,402	8	17	33	W	4-3	3-2
22	H	BURNLEY	29/12	8,282	7	20	36	W	1-0	0-0
23	A	HULL	1/1	9,753	8	2	36	L	1-2	1-1

Match 12 — BOLTON (H)
City: Shaw, Stevens, Newman, Phill-Masters, Curle, Stroud, Pritchard, Ritchie, Morgan, Walsh, Crawford
Bolton: Farnworth, Borrows, Phillips, Joyce, Berry, Valentine, Thompson, Chandler, Oghani, Foster, Bell
Scorers: Pritchard 2, Walsh 41p, 73 / Foster 19, Oghani 22. Ref: J Bray
George Oghani's close-range volley puts lively Bolton in front, after Pritchard's left-foot curler gives the homesters a dream start. A lucky win for City, courtesy of a harsh penalty decision for Peter Valentine's tackle on Pritchard and Walsh's free-kick slipping from Farnworth's grasp.

Match 13 — MILLWALL (A)
City: Shaw, Llewellyn, Newman, Curle, Phill-Masters, Riley, Pritchard, Ritchie, Morgan, Walsh, Stroud
Millwall: Sansome, Stevens, Roffey, Brisley, Smith, Lowndes, Bremner, McLeary*, Lovell, Otulakowski, Neal D
Scorers: Morgan 69 / Lovell 87. Ref: B Hill
City come close to ending Millwall's unbeaten record. After battling to stay on terms in the first half, Morgan stabs the ball home to give City the lead. Steve Lovell, denied by the woodwork on 66 minutes, chests down Dave Cusack's cross to drive in the Lions' late equaliser.

Match 14 — BRENTFORD (H)
City: Shaw, Llewellyn, Newman, Curle, Phill-Masters, Riley, Pritchard, Ritchie, Morgan, Walsh, Stroud
Brentford: Swinburne, Fisher, Murray, Roberts P, Hurlock, Salman, Kamara, Booker, Cassells, Alexander, Roberts G
Scorers: Walsh 67 / Kamara 69. Ref: R Gifford
Brentford keeper Trevor Swinburne has an inspired game, but he is unable to do anything about Walsh's vicious left-foot shot from the edge of the area. Chris Kamara makes the most of a free header to level matters, just after Curle had cleared Keith Booker's header off the line.

Match 15 — DONCASTER (A)
City: Shaw, Llewellyn, Newman*, Curle, Phill-Masters, Riley, Pritchard, Ritchie, Morgan, Walsh, Stroud | Hutchinson
Doncaster: Peacock, Russell, Yates, Snodin I, Brown T, Philliben, Buckley, Butterworth, Douglas, Harle, Snodin G
Scorers: Walsh 62 / Harle 85. Ref: N Wilson
Hutchinson's long-awaited City debut, after an instep injury, comes two months late and about an hour too soon! Lacking match practice, he replaces the injured Newman as early as the 19th minute. Another Walsh special puts City ahead, but David Harle taps in a simple equaliser.

Match 16 — BRISTOL ROV (H)
City: Shaw, Llewellyn, Newman*, Curle, Phill-Masters, Riley, Pritchard, Ritchie, Morgan, Walsh, Stroud | Hutchinson
Bristol Rov: Cashley, Slatter, Williams B, Jones M, Parkin, McCaffery, Holloway, Williams D, Stephens, Randall*, Bater, O'Connor
Scorers: Stroud 10, Riley 50, 62. Ref: A Ward
City score with their first three shots on target. Stroud's blistering right-foot volley from the edge of the area puts City in front, while Riley twice shoots in to punish Rovers for switching to a sweeper system. An Archie Stephens 87th-min header forces Shaw to make his only save.

Match 17 — PRESTON (A)
City: Shaw, Llewellyn, Jones M, Curle, Halliday, Riley, Pritchard, Ritchie, Morgan, Walsh, Stroud | Litchfield, Jones M
Preston: Brown, McAteer, Jones D, Welsh, Clark, Gray, McGee, Williams D, Stephens, Naughton, Houston, Hutchinson
Scorers: Riley 9, Phillipson-Masters 54 / Naughton 22, Houston 81, Jones 88. Ref: T Mills
North End snatch an improbable victory with two goals in the final nine minutes. Andy McAteer's centre appears to curve out before Graham Houston forces the ball over the line and then Mark Jones shoots in from an acute angle. In the dying seconds Morgan fires against the bar.

Match 18 — LINCOLN (H)
City: Hooper, Llewellyn, Halliday, Curle, Phill-Masters, Riley, Pritchard, Neville*, Morgan, Walsh, Stroud
Lincoln: Naylor, Redfearn, McCarrick, Shipley, Walker, Thompson, McGinley, Turner P, Hobson, Jack, Mair*, Strodder
Scorers: Walsh 9, Ritchie 21 / Strodder 88. Ref: N Butler
Cooper complains of poor vocal support following this lacklustre game. The similar styles of Neville and Riley produce a lack of balance in attack. Gordon Mair heads against the bar for Lincoln before Gary Strodder exploits Hooper's weakness on crosses to head in from a corner.

Match 19 — BOURNEMOUTH (A)
City: Shaw, Llewellyn, Halliday, Curle, Phill-Masters, Riley, Pritchard, Neville*, Morgan, Walsh, Stroud
Bournemouth: Smeulders, Nightingale, Savage, Williams, Brown, Howlett, O'Driscoll, Russell, Graham, Thompson, Morrell
Scorers: Riley 1 / Graham 10, Savage 81. Ref: C Downey
City outplay Bournemouth, but are unable to add to Riley's 48-second opener. He shoots from a rebound after John Smeulders blocks Neville's effort. Milton Graham guides in the Cherries' equaliser from 25 yards, six mins after a marginal offside decision had ruled out Riley's header.

Match 20 — READING (A)
City: Shaw, Llewellyn, Halliday, Curle, Phill-Masters, Riley, Pritchard, Neville, Morgan, Walsh, Stroud
Reading: Westwood, Williams, Richardson, Beavon*, Hicks, Wood, Duncan, Juryeff, Senior, White, Crown, Horrix
Scorers: — / White 76. Ref: D Brazier
Fans cite the transfer of Trevor Morgan as a reason for City's recent slump, but the truth is that many players are out of form. City improve after a dismal first half, but Reading take the points. Mark White volleys into an empty net after Shaw is beaten in the air by Trevor Senior.

Match 21 — PLYMOUTH (H)
City: Waugh, Llewellyn, Halliday, Curle, Phill-Masters, Riley, Pritchard, Hutchinson, Rogers, Walsh, Stroud | Neville
Plymouth: Crudgington, Nisbet, Cooper, Ham, Rogers, Harrison, Hodges, Summerfield, Staniforth, Tynan, Goodyear!
Scorers: Hutchinson 19, 36, Walsh 26, 87p / Tynan 24, 42, 53. Ref: M Robinson
This action-packed match is settled by a dubious penalty as Pritchard makes the most of Gordon Staniforth's innocuous challenge. Argyle, for whom Clive Goodyear is sent off on 78 mins for a second bookable offence, fail to capitalise on Tommy Tynan's stunning hat-trick shot.

Match 22 — BURNLEY (H)
City: Waugh, Stevens, Llewellyn, Curle, Phill-Masters, Riley, Pritchard, Hutchinson, Neville*, Walsh, Stroud | Biggins
Burnley: Hansbury, Palmer, Hampton, Phelan, Kennedy, Hird, Grewcock, Malley, Lawrence*, Biggins, Devine, Ritchie
Scorers: Pritchard 88. Ref: K Miller
A different Burnley than normal as their defensive tactics produce a dreary game. Many disgruntled spectators had already headed for home when Hutchinson flicks on Walsh's corner and Pritchard is at the far post to head in a late winner as Neville still seeks his first City goal.

Match 23 — HULL (A)
City: Waugh, Stevens, Llewellyn, Curle, Phill-Masters, Riley, Pritchard, Hutchinson, Neville*, Walsh, Stroud | Ring, Williams N
Hull: Norman, McNeil, Pearson, Swann, Skipper, McEwan, Flounders, McClaren, Whitehurst*, Askew, Williams N
Scorers: Riley 6 / Whitehurst 16, McEwan 59p. Ref: A Robinson
The referee's insistence of blowing his whistle for virtually every challenge explains the ridiculously high total of 59 free-kicks. The official incurs City's wrath in regard to Hull's penalty, ruling that Waugh holds down Andy Flounders. Riley shoots in on the turn to put City ahead.

CANON LEAGUE DIVISION 3

Manager: Terry Cooper

Results and Statistics

No	Date	Venue / Opponent	Scorers, Times, and Referees	Att	Pos (City / Opp)	Result	Pt	F-A	H-T
24	26/1	H CAMBRIDGE	Pritchard 31, Walsh 57, Riley 73; Ref: T Spencer	6,547	7 / 24	W	39	3-0	1-0
25	2/2	H WALSALL	Walsh 80; Kelly 5, Shakespeare 67; Ref: D Hedges	7,240	10 / 13	L	39	1-2	0-1
26	9/2	A ORIENT	Walsh 77; Ref: M James	2,754	8 / 21	W	42	1-0	0-0
27	16/2	A ROTHERHAM	Riley 31; Simmons 38, Stevens 72 (og); Ref: K Redfern	4,901	8 / 2	L	42	1-2	1-1
28	23/2	A BRENTFORD	Neville 9, 27; Booker 26; Ref: J Ashworth	4,526	7 / 17	W	45	2-1	2-1
29	26/2	H DERBY	Riley 14, Marshall 33, Crawford 82; Ref: D Reeves	8,727	6 / 13	W	48	3-0	2-0
30	2/3	H MILLWALL	Lovell 88; Ref: T Holbrook	10,875	6 / 3	L	48	0-1	0-0
31	5/3	A BOLTON	Neville 5, 43, 68, Riley 17; Joyce 48; Ref: C Seel	3,774	6 / 15	W	51	4-1	3-0
32	9/3	H BRADFORD C	Pritchard 22, Walsh 77; Ref: H King	9,222	5 / 1	W	54	2-0	1-0
33	16/3	A GILLINGHAM	Hutchinson 36, 63, Neville 84; Cascarino 68; Ref: J Martin	6,369	5 / 3	W	57	3-1	1-0
34	23/3	H YORK	Walsh 18; Ref: J Moules	8,655	4 / 11	W	60	1-0	1-0

Line-ups (positions 1–12, "12" = sub used)

No	Team	1	2	3	4	5	6	7	8	9	10	11	12
24	City	Shaw	Stevens*	Llewellyn	Curle	Phill-Masters	Riley	Pritchard	Neville	Hutchinson	Walsh	Stroud	Crawford
24	Cambridge	Branagan	Fallon	Bennett	Lockhart	Moyes	Osgood	Comfort	Sinton	McDonough	Pyle	Finney*	Daniels
25	City	Leigh	Stevens	Llewellyn	Curle	Phill-Masters*	Riley	Pritchard!	Neville	Hutchinson	Walsh	Stroud	Crawford
25	Walsall	Cherry	Caswell	Hawker	Shakespeare	Brazier	Hart	Handysides	Kelly	Elliott S	O'Kelly	Childs	
26	City	Shaw	Stevens	Llewellyn	Curle	Phill-Masters	Riley	Pritchard	Neville	Hutchinson	Walsh	Stroud	Crawford
26	Orient	Wilmot	Hales*	Castle	Cunningham	Foster	Silkman	Godfrey	Harvey	Jones	Donnellan	Corbett	Sussex
27	City	Shaw	Stevens	Llewellyn	Curle	Phill-Masters	Riley	Hirst*	Neville	Hutchinson	Walsh	Stroud	Hughes
27	Rotherham	Mimms	Forrest	Mitchell	Trusson	Johnson	Crosby	Birch	Gooding	Richardson	Simmons	Kilmore*	Dungworth
28	City	Shaw	Stevens	Newman	Curle	Hughes	Riley	Pritchard	Neville	Hutchinson	Walsh	Stroud	Lynch
28	Brentford	Phillips	Fisher	Murray	Roberts P	Wignall	Hurlock	Kamara	Torrance*	Booker	Salman	Cooke	
29	City	Shaw	Stevens	Newman	Curle	Hughes	Riley	Marshall	Neville	Hutchinson	Walsh	Stroud	Crawford
29	Derby	Steele	Stevens	Blades	Powell*	Pratley	Streete	Micklewhite	Davison	Christie	Lewis	Robertson	Hooks
30	City	Shaw	Stevens	Newman	Curle	Hughes	Riley*	Marshall	Neville	Hutchinson	Walsh	Stroud	Marshall
30	Millwall	Sansome	Stevens	Hinshelwood	Briley	Smith	Cusack	Lowndes	Fashanu	Chatterton	Lovell	Otulakowski	
31	City	Shaw	Stevens	Newman	Curle	Hughes	Riley	Pritchard	Neville	Hutchinson	Walsh	Stroud	Marshall
31	Bolton	Farnworth	Borrows	Phillips	Joyce	Came	Deakin	Oghani	Chandler	Evans	Caldwell	Bell	
32	City	Shaw	Stevens	Newman	Curle	Hughes	Riley	Pritchard	Neville	Hutchinson	Walsh	Stroud	Marshall
32	Bradford C	Harvey	Cherry*	Withe	McCall	Jackson	Evans	Hendrie	Goodman	Campbell	Singleton	Ellis	Holmes
33	City	Shaw	Stevens	Newman	Curle	Hughes	Riley	Pritchard	Neville	Hutchinson	Walsh	Stroud	Marshall
33	Gillingham	Fry	Sage	Himigan*	Oakes	Musker	Shaw	Cochrane	Shearer	Robinson	Mehmet	Cascarino	Weatherly
34	City	Shaw	Stevens	Newman	Curle	Hughes	Riley	Pritchard	Neville	Hutchinson	Walsh	Stroud	Hughes
34	York	Jones	Senior	Hay	Hood	MacPhail	Haslegrave*	Pearce	Banton	Butler	Crosby	Nicholson	Richards

Match Reports

24 — CAMBRIDGE (H): After an enforced winter break Bobby Hutchinson takes over as the City captain, following Tom Ritchie's move to Yeovil. Pritchard's volley puts City ahead in a dull first half, but after the break Walsh's vicious twelve-yarder and Riley's close-range header finish off poor opposition.

25 — WALSALL (H): City are reduced to ten men for the last two minutes when Pritchard is sent off for a retaliatory kick on Phil Hawker. Loan keeper Leigh has a nightmare start when Kelly shoots in as he fails to hold a simple back-pass. Magnificent strike by Craig Shakespeare from a disputed free-kick.

26 — ORIENT (A): Walsh strikes with a typical opportunist effort, shooting in from yards, to stifle Orient's comeback hopes. City adapt well on a snowbound pitch. Neville and Hutchinson have first-half efforts cleared off the line, but after the break Kevin Godfrey's shot strikes Llewellyn on the line.

27 — ROTHERHAM (A): Stevens is horrified as the ball loops into the net when his foot deflects Ian Richardson's cross for Rotherham's winner. The Millers impress as both teams play attractive football, and they equalise Riley's whiplash shot on the turn, when Tony Simmons picks his spot with a low volley.

28 — BRENTFORD (A): At long last Steve Neville opens his Bristol City goal account. He is unmarked when heading in Walsh's free-kick and then doubles his tally on shooting in from six yards. After spurning a hat-trick opportunity, Neville should have been awarded a penalty when held by Steve Wignall.

29 — DERBY (H): Sparkling City outplay big-spending Derby. Walsh, unfortunate when he hits his 64th-minute thunderous indirect free-kick into the roof of the net, supplies the crosses for headed goals by Marshall and Crawford. The non-stop running of Neville and Riley give Derby a busy night.

30 — MILLWALL (H): Alan Walsh and Keith Curle will have nightmares about this crushing blow to City's promotion hopes. Walsh's pen is saved by Paul Sansome after Neville is chopped down by Nicky Chatterton, while Curle is caught out of position when Steve Lovell lobs in Millwall's late winner.

31 — BOLTON (A): Neville looks offside when put clear by Riley's header to shoot in the opening goal, but no doubt about his tap-in and a later header for the third League hat-trick of his career. In an all-action first half Walsh has a goal disallowed for pushing and Stroud clears a header off the line.

32 — BRADFORD C (H): Bradford City are undone by their attack-minded approach. Pritchard is unmarked to head home Neville's cross, and is then denied by the crossbar either side of half-time. Don Goodman's header hits the post for Bradford after the break, but Walsh fires in to tie up a vital win.

33 — GILLINGHAM (A): Hutchinson's two headed goals cap an inspired performance by the City skipper. In heavy snow after the interval Gillingham prove vulnerable to City's fast breaks. Tony Cascarino volleys the Gills back into the match, but Neville breaks clear to settle the issue with his cool finish.

34 — YORK (H): York, without six first choice players, contain out-of-touch City with ease. The match is settled by a controversial goal as both Hutchinson, early in the build-up, and Walsh, at the finish look offside. Even the referee looks long and hard at the linesman before allowing Walsh's shot.

35 H DONCASTER 30/3   4 W 1-0   13 63   7,965 — Riley 25 — Ref: D Vickers

Shaw	Stevens	Newman	Curle	Hughes	Riley	Pritchard	Neville*	Hutchinson	Walsh	Stroud	Johnson
Peacock	Russell	Snodin G*	Snodin I	Brown T	Kowalski	Butterworth	Deans	Douglas	Travis	Lister	Philliben

With the pitch covered by pools of water the referee calls a temporary halt to proceedings on 22 minutes as heavy rain continues to fall. Riley gives Dennis Peacock no chance with his firm downward header. Doncaster improve in the second half and give City some anxious moments.

---

36 A PLYMOUTH 5/4   5 L 0-1   15 63   9,959 — Staniforth 79 — Ref: M Robinson

Shaw	Stevens	Newman	Curle	Hughes	Riley*	Pritchard	Neville*	Hutchinson	Walsh	Stroud	Johnson
Crudgington	Nisbet	Uzzell	Coughlin	McElhinney	Burrows	Rogers	Hodges	Tynan	Staniforth	Goodyear	

Police prevent 700 City fans seeing this contest as a late arriving train is ordered into a siding after early skirmishes on the terraces. Gordon Staniforth settles the game by netting a rebound. A fractional offside decision rules out Newman's tap-in, and Curle's volley hits the crossbar.

---

37 H HULL 8/4   4 W 2-0   2 66   11,964 — Johnson 46, Pritchard 79 — Ref: T Bune

Shaw	Stevens	Newman	Curle	Hughes	Riley	Pritchard	Johnson	Hutchinson	Walsh	Stroud	Johnson
Norman	Swann	Pearson	Williams N*	Skipper	McEwan	Flounders	McClaren	Whitehurst	Askew	Jobson	Saville

A firm downward header from Pritchard's cross allows Steve Johnson, City's £20,000 signing from Wigan, to mark his first full appearance with a goal. City's dazzling play deserves more than just another score, when Pritchard nips in front of a defender to shoot in Johnson's header.

---

38 A BRISTOL ROV 13/4   5 L 0-1   6 66   12,957 — Holloway 67 — Ref: M Dimblebee

Shaw	Stevens	Newman	Curle	Hughes	Riley*	Pritchard	Johnson	Hutchinson	Walsh	Stroud	Neville
Green	Slatter	Williams B	Bater	Parkin	Jones	Holloway	Raynor	Randall	Bannon	O'Connor	

City's ridiculous decision to play against the gale-force wind after winning the toss costs them this game. The Rovers, undeterred by the conditions after the break, punish City's offside tactics. Mark O'Connor breaks clear from a free-kick and crosses for Ian Holloway to shoot in.

---

39 H PRESTON 20/4   5 W 4-0   20 69   6,937 — Riley 13, 87, Walsh 32p, 70 — Ref: D Letts

Shaw	Stevens	Newman	Curle	Hughes	Riley	Pritchard*	Johnson	Hutchinson	Walsh	Stroud	Neville
Campbell	Farrelly	Jones M	Gibson	Atkins	Clark	Kelly	Houghton*	Twentyman	Brazil	Houston	Johnson

A controversial penalty gives City the lead after Bob Atkins is adjudged to have climbed on Pritchard's back. Man of the match Walsh fails to heed referee's signal when he blasts in an indirect free-kick, but makes amends after the interval when he breaks from halfway to shoot home.

---

40 A WIGAN 23/4   5 D 2-2   17 70   2,423 — Johnson 38, Walsh 81p / Bennett 75, Walsh 80 — Ref: J Key

Shaw	Stevens	Newman	Curle !	Hughes	Neville	Pritchard	Johnson	Hutchinson	Walsh	Stroud	Hirst
Tunks	Butler	Knowles	Kelly	Walsh	Methven	Lowe	Aspinall W?ren	Newell	Jewell*	Langley	Bennett

After Johnson's magnificent ten-yard volley, City concede two unnecessary petty fouls. Curle is sent off for butting Kevin Langley just prior to Steve Walsh forcing in a rebound for Wigan. Colin Methven handles a harmless through-ball for the pen equaliser.

---

41 A LINCOLN 27/4   4 L 0-1   19 71   1,908 — Johnson 60 / Thompson 31 — Ref: A Selville

Shaw	Stevens	Newman	Curle	Hughes	Neville	Pritchard	Neville*	Hutchinson	Walsh	Stroud	
Naylor	McCarrick	Collins	Redfearn	North M	Thompson	McGinlay	Shipley	Hobson	Thomas	Mair	

With Millwall only drawing at Burnley, City miss a great chance of making up ground in the promotion race. Steve Thompson's lobbed header puts the Imps in front and it takes Johnson's curling and dipping free-kick to save City from an embarrassing defeat against a poor opposition.

---

42 H NEWPORT 30/4   4 W 2-1   17 74   5,952 — Riley 41, Newman 75 / Chamberlain 45 — Ref: G Napthine

Shaw	Stevens	Newman	Curle	Hughes	Riley	Pritchard	Johnson*	Hutchinson	Walsh	Stroud	Hirst
Kendall	Jones	Relish*	Pulis	Boyle	Matthewson	Kent	Emmanuel	Cooper	Kellow	Chamberlain	Giles

City gain revenge for last Thursday's Freight Rover Cup defeat. Newman's thunderous 30-yarder settles this dull contest. Newport, who fail to force a single corner, score with their only shot on target. Neville Chamberlain shoots after Steve Cooper had headed the ball over the keeper.

---

43 H BOURNEMOUTH 4/5   4 W 2-0   11 77   7,083 — Marshall 45, Riley 61 — Ref: P Vanes

Shaw	Stevens	Newman	Curle	Hughes	Neville	Pritchard	Marshall	Hutchinson	Walsh	Stroud*	Hirst
Smeulders	Nightingale	Savage	Beck	Lewis	Schiavi	Shaw	Russell	Rafferty	Thompson	Morrell	

The Cherries' keeper John Smeulders has a nightmare. He is deceived by Marshall's 25-yarder which bounces up to strike him on the arm before rolling into the net, and later carries the ball outside the area to concede a free-kick, which he punches straight onto Riley's head.

---

44 A BURNLEY 6/5   4 W 1-0   23 80   4,570 — Neville 78 — Ref: P Willis

Shaw	Stevens	Newman	Curle	Hughes	Riley	Hirst	Neville	Hutchinson	Walsh	Stroud	Halliday
Hansbury	Scott	Hampton	Phelan	Overson	Hird	Grewcock*	Rhodes	Taylor	Biggins	Hutchison	Miller

Neville hammers in a scorching half-volley to keep alive City's faint promotion hopes. Burnley are restricted to long-range efforts in the first half, but manage to exert more pressure on City's defence after the break. On going ahead City bring on sub Halliday to boost their midfield.

---

45 H READING 11/5   4 L 2-3   9 80   7,038 — Neville 7, Riley 33 / Newman 26 (og), Horrix 60, Gilkes 72 — Ref: L Shapter

Shaw	Stevens	Newman	Curle	Hughes	Riley	Pritchard	Neville	Hutchinson	Walsh*	Stroud	Hirst
Westwood	Williams	Ritchardson	Beavon	Hicks	Wood	Burvill	White	Peters	Horrix	Christie*	Gilkes

City's back four are cruelly exposed by a slick Reading side. Neville obtains his first home goal when jabbing in Riley's perfect pass. Mike Gilkes rounds Shaw to slot in Reading's winner, but by then news of the Bradford City disaster at Valley Parade was diverting public attention.

---

46 A SWANSEA 17/5   5 D 0-0   20 81   11,187 — Ref: J Bray
Home Average 8,507 — Away 5,753

Shaw	Stevens	Newman	Curle	Hughes	Riley	Pritchard*	Neville	Hutchinson	Walsh	Stroud	
Rimmer	Lewis	Sullivan	Price	Stevenson	Marustik	Turner	Parlane	Waddle	McHale	Pascoe	

City retain sole possession of their unwanted record as the Swans gain the point necessary to save them from sliding from the First to the Fourth in consecutive seasons. A magnificent, exciting game, in which keepers Jimmy Rimmer and Shaw play at the top of their form.

CANON DIVISION 3 (CUP-TIES) Manager: Terry Cooper SEASON 1984-85

Milk Cup

			F-A	H-T	Scorers, Times, and Referees	1	2	3	4	5	6	7	8	9	10	11	12 sub used
1:1	H	NEWPORT	W 2-1	1-1	Crawford 34, Riley 73	Shaw	Stevens	Newman	Rogers	Phill-Masters	Hirst	Pritchard	Riley	Morgan	Walsh	Crawford	
		5,644			*Chamberlain 13*	*Jones G*	*Jones L*	*Matthewson*	*Reid*	*Boyle*	*Saxby*	*Lilygreen**	*Chamberlain*	*Carter*	*Kent*	*Lewis*	*Green*
					Ref: H Taylor												

An entertaining match to which Newport fully contribute with their slick passing. County take the lead with a controversial goal as Neville Chamberlain's shot cannons off the underside of the crossbar, but City draw level with Crawford's glancing header from Pritchard's cross.

			F-A	H-T	Scorers, Times, and Referees	1	2	3	4	5	6	7	8	9	10	11	12 sub used
1:2	A	NEWPORT	W 3-0	2-0	Morgan 17, 37, Riley 69	Shaw	Stevens	Newman	Rogers	Halliday	Hirst	Pritchard	Riley	Morgan*	Walsh	Crawford	Curle
		3,276 17				*Kendall*	*Jones L*	*Matthewson*	*Reid**	*Boyle*	*Saxby*	*Carter*	*Pulis*	*Kent*	*Green*	*Lewis*	*Lilygreen*
					Ref: J Martin												
					(City won 5-1 on aggregate)												

Scintillating City storm into the second round with a blend of aggression and skill that could upset any club in the competition. Morgan is razor sharp as he lobs in the first goal and then registers again with a thunderous 25-yarder. Riley rounds Mark Kendall to tie up a convincing win.

			F-A	H-T	Scorers, Times, and Referees	1	2	3	4	5	6	7	8	9	10	11	12 sub used
2:1	H	WEST HAM	D 2-2	2-2	Morgan 20, Walsh 33	Shaw	Stevens	Newman	Halliday	Phill-Masters	Hirst	Pritchard	Riley	Morgan	Walsh	Crawford	
		15,609 1:7			*Cottee 28, Walford 37*	*McAlister*	*Stewart*	*Walford*	*Allen*	*Martin*	*Gale*	*Bonds*	*Goddard*	*Cottee*	*Dickens*	*Pike*	
					Ref: V Callow												

City are unlucky not to be taking a lead into the return leg as the Hammers are outplayed after the break. Surprisingly all the goals come before the interval. Steve Walford notches West Ham's second equaliser with a 30-yarder after Morgan opens the scoring with a real pile-driver.

			F-A	H-T	Scorers, Times, and Referees	1	2	3	4	5	6	7	8	9	10	11	12 sub used
2:2	A	WEST HAM	L 1-6	1-1	Walsh 34p [Whitton 68, Walford 78]	Shaw	Stevens	Newman	Masters	Curle	Riley	Pritchard	Ritchie*	Morgan	Walsh	Crawford	Smith
		11,376 1:5			*Cottee 24, 75, Goddard 48, 56,*	*McAlister*	*Stewart*	*Walford*	*Allen*	*Martin*	*Gale*	*Whitton*	*Goddard*	*Cottee*	*Bonds**	*Pike*	*Barnes*
					Ref: K Baker												
					(City lost 3-8 on aggregate)												

City are hit by West Ham's remarkable resurgence after confidently taking the game forward before the break. Walsh's penalty equaliser, after Ray Stewart palms the ball over the bar, rewards City's thoughtful play, but Paul Goddard's brilliant 25-yarder changes everything.

FA Cup

			F-A	H-T	Scorers, Times, and Referees	1	2	3	4	5	6	7	8	9	10	11	12 sub used
1	A	FISHER ATH	W 1-0	1-0	Riley 9	Shaw	Llewellyn	Halliday	Curle	Phill-Masters	Riley	Pritchard	Ritchie	Morgan	Walsh	Stroud	Chambers
		2,000 SLP:8				*Bowtell*	*Davis*	*Collins**	*Sharp*	*Shiners*	*Dark*	*Lewington*	*Murrock*	*Dennehy*	*Sansom*	*Bayram*	
					Ref: M Bodenham												

It looks easy as Riley has time and space to shoot an early goal, but Fisher come back strongly. Despite Morgan heading against the bar, Fisher refuse to be overawed. Dave Sansom's 36th-minute low drive forces Shaw to make a good save and by the end City are glad to have survived.

			F-A	H-T	Scorers, Times, and Referees	1	2	3	4	5	6	7	8	9	10	11	12 sub used
2	H	BRISTOL ROV	L 1-3	1-3	Halliday 4	Hooper	Llewellyn	Halliday	Curle	Phill-Masters	Riley	Pritchard	Hirst*	Hutchinson	Walsh	Stroud	Ritchie
		19,367 7			*O'Connor 8, Randall 18, 42*	*Cashley*	*Slatter**	*Williams B*	*Bater*	*Parkin*	*McCaffery*	*Holloway*	*Williams D*	*Stephens*	*Randall*	*O'Connor*	*Williams G*
					Ref: A Robinson												

City off to a fine start as Halliday heads in from Walsh's exquisitely chipped free-kick, but Mark O'Connor gets his head to Ian Holloway's cross to loop an equaliser over the flat-footed Hooper. Rovers coast to an easy win after Paul Randall twice shows his pace to slide the ball in.

#	Team	P	Home W	D	L	F	A	Away W	D	L	F	A	Pts
1	Bradford City	46	15	6	2	44	23	13	4	6	33	22	94
2	Millwall	46	18	5	0	44	12	8	7	8	29	30	90
3	Hull	46	16	4	3	46	20	9	8	6	32	29	87
4	Gillingham	46	15	5	3	54	29	10	3	10	26	33	83
5	BRISTOL CITY	46	17	2	4	46	19	7	7	9	28	28	81
6	Bristol Rov	46	15	6	2	37	13	6	6	11	29	35	75
7	Derby	46	14	7	2	40	20	5	7	12	25	34	70
8	York	46	13	5	5	42	22	7	4	12	28	35	69
9	Reading	46	8	7	8	31	29	11	5	7	37	33	69
10	Bournemouth	46	16	3	4	42	16	3	8	12	15	30	68
11	Walsall	46	9	7	7	33	22	9	6	8	25	30	67
12	Rotherham	46	11	6	6	36	24	5	11	7	19	31	65
13	Brentford	46	13	5	5	42	27	3	9	11	20	37	62
14	Doncaster	46	11	5	7	42	33	6	3	14	30	41	59
15	Plymouth	46	11	7	5	33	23	4	7	12	29	42	59
16	Wigan	46	12	6	5	36	22	3	8	12	24	42	59
17	Bolton	46	12	5	6	38	22	4	1	18	31	53	54
18	Newport	46	9	6	8	30	30	4	7	12	25	37	52
19	Lincoln	46	8	11	4	32	20	3	7	13	18	31	51
20	Swansea	46	7	5	11	31	39	5	6	12	22	41	47
21	Burnley	46	6	8	9	30	24	5	13	13	30	49	46
22	Orient	46	7	7	9	30	36	4	6	13	21	40	46
23	Preston	46	9	5	9	33	41	4	2	17	18	59	46
24	Cambridge	46	2	3	18	17	48	2	6	15	20	47	21
		1104	274	136	142	889	614	142	136	274	614	889	1520

Odds & ends

Double wins: (6) Cambridge, Orient, York, Gillingham, Bolton, Burnley.

Double losses: (3) Walsall, Rotherham, Reading.

Won from behind: (2) Cambridge (a), Bolton (h).

Lost from in front: (5) Preston (a), Bournemouth (a), Hull (a). Rotherham (a), Reading (h).

High spots: The skilful play of Alan Walsh.
3-0 win over Bristol Rov at Ashton Gate on 10 November.
Beating Hull 2-0 at Ashton Gate on 8 April.

Low spots: Missing out on promotion.
Succumbing to an Ian Holloway strike at Eastville on 13 April.
Losing to Bristol Rov in both the FA and the Gloucestershire Cup.

Player of the year: Alan Walsh.

Ever-presents: (0).

Hat-tricks: (1) Steve Neville.

Leading scorer: Alan Walsh (22).

Appearances / Goals

Player	App Lge	Sub	LC	Sub	FAC	Sub	Goals Lge	LC	FAC	Tot
Cooper, Terry		10								
Crawford, Alan	10	6	4				4	1		5
Curle, Keith	37	3	4		2					
Halliday, Bruce	11	1	2							
Hirst, Martyn	13	3	3							
Hooper, Mike	1									
Hughes, Mark	19	1								
Hutchinson, Bobby	29	2					4			4
Johnson, Steve	6	2					3			3
Leigh, Ian	1									
Llewellyn, Andy	22			1	2					
Marshall, Gary	3	2					2			2
Morgan, Trevor	17		4		2		3	3		6
Neville, Steve	26	2			2		8			8
Newman, Rob	34		4		2		3			3
Phill-Masters, Forbes	25		3		2		1			1
Pritchard, Howard	39		4		2		6			6
Riley, Glynn	44	1	4		2		18	2	1	21
Ritchie, Tom	10			1	2		1		1	2
Rogers, Lee	6									
Shaw, John	41		4		2					
Smith Gary						1				
Stevens, Paul	30		4							
Stroud, Kenny	34	1					1			1
Walsh, Alan	45		4		2		20	2		22
Waugh, Keith	3									
26 players used	506	34	44	2	22	1	74	8	2	84

CANON LEAGUE DIVISION 3 — Manager: Terry Cooper — SEASON 1985-86

Column headings: No | Date | Att | Pos | Pt | F-A | H-T | 1 | 2 | 3 | 4 | 5 | 6 | 7 | 8 | 9 | 10 | 11 | 12 sub used | Scorers, Times, and Referees

City line-ups are shown in roman, opposition line-ups in italic (the Pos figure given on the opposition row is the opponents' league position).

No	H/A / Opponent	Date	Att	Pos	Pt	Res	F-A	H-T	1	2	3	4	5	6	7	8	9	10	11	12 sub used
1	H WALSALL	17/8	7,196		0	L	2-3	1-1	Waugh	Llewellyn	Williams B !	Curle	Hughes	Riley	Marshall*	Hutchinson	Emmanuel	Neville	Walsh	Johnson
	Walsall								_Cherry_	_Hart_	_Mower_	_Shakespeare_	_Brazier_	_Hawker_	_Handysides_	_Cross_	_O'Kelly_	_Elliott_	_Daley*_	_Childs_
2	A BOURNEMOUTH	24/8	4,969		0	L	0-5	0-4	Waugh	Llewellyn	Newman	Curle	Hughes	Hutchinson	Emmanuel	Williams B	Johnson	Walsh	Neville	
	Bournemouth								_Smeulders_	_Heffernan_	_Sulley_	_Newson_	_Brown_	_Nightingale_	_O'Driscoll_	_Russell_	_Clarke_	_Thompson_	_Morrell_	
3	H GILLINGHAM	26/8	5,883	24	0	L	1-2	1-0	Waugh	Llewellyn	Newman	Curle	Rogers	Hutchinson	Pritchard	Williams B	Johnson	Walsh	Neville*	
	Gillingham			14					_Hillyard_	_Sage_	_Elsey_	_Oakes_	_Weatherly*_	_Shaw_	_Cochrane_	_Shearer_	_Collins_	_Musker_	_Cascarino_	_Byrne_
4	A ROTHERHAM	31/8	3,255	24	0	L	0-2	0-1	Waugh	Llewellyn	Newman	Curle	Rogers	Hirst*	Pritchard	Hutchinson	Johnson	Walsh	Neville	
	Rotherham			10					_O'Hanlon_	_Forrest_	_Dungworth_	_Trusson*_	_Smith_	_Pickering_	_Birch_	_Martin_	_Tynan_	_Simmons_	_Emerson_	_Gooding_
5	H WIGAN	7/9	5,673	23	3	W	1-0	0-0	Waugh	Llewellyn	Newman	Curle	Rogers	Williams B	Pritchard	Hutchinson	Johnson	Neville*	Walsh	Riley
	Wigan			6					_Stewart_	_Butler_	_Knowles_	_Jewell*_	_Beesley_	_Methven_	_Lowe_	_Aspinall_	_Newell_	_Langley_	_Griffiths_	_Cook_
6	A CARDIFF	14/9	4,412	20	6	W	3-1	1-0	Waugh	Llewellyn	Newman	Curle	Rogers	Williams B	Pritchard	Hutchinson	Johnson	Neville	Walsh*	Riley
	Cardiff			17					_Rees_	_McLoughlin_	_Carver_	_Gibbins_	_Ford_	_Mullen_	_Gummer_	_Farrington_	_Vaughan_	_Withey_	_Giles*_	_Micallef_
7	H DERBY	17/9	7,750	20	7	D	1-1	1-0	Waugh	Llewellyn	Newman	Curle	Rogers	Williams B	Pritchard	Hutchinson	Riley	Walsh	Neville*	Marshall
	Derby			12					_Wallington_	_Street_	_Buckley_	_Williams_	_Hindmarch_	_MacLean_	_Davison_	_Micklewhite_	_Christie_	_McClaren_	_Chandler_	
8	A YORK	21/9	3,904	19	8	D	1-1	0-1	Waugh	Llewellyn	Newman	Curle	Rogers	Williams B	Pritchard	Hutchinson	Riley*	Neville*	Walsh	Marshall
	York			11					_Astbury_	_Senior*_	_Hay_	_McAughtrie_	_MacPhail_	_Haslegrave_	_Ford_	_Mills_	_Walwyn_	_Houchen_	_Canham_	_Gabbiadini_
9	H BLACKPOOL	28/9	6,570	16	11	W	2-1	1-1	Waugh	Llewellyn	Newman	Curle	Rogers	Williams B	Pritchard	Hutchinson	Riley*	Walsh	Neville*	Johnson
	Blackpool			12					_O'Rourke_	_Moore_	_Walsh*_	_Conroy_	_Law_	_Greenall_	_Davies_	_Deary_	_Stewart_	_O'Keefe_	_Dyer_	_Stonehouse_
10	A NEWPORT	1/10	3,776	18	12	D	1-1	0-0	Waugh	Llewellyn	Newman	Curle	Rogers	Williams B	Pritchard	Hutchinson	Johnson*	Walsh	Neville	Marshall
	Newport			16					_Kendall_	_Pulis_	_Jones P_	_Reck_	_Peacock_	_Boyle_	_Mardenboro'*_	_Lewis_	_James_	_Staniforth_	_Gill_	_Tyler_
11	H CHESTERFIELD	5/10	6,416	18	13	D	0-0	0-0	Waugh	Llewellyn*	Newman	Curle	Rogers	Williams B	Pritchard	Hutchinson	Johnson	Walsh	Neville	Riley
	Chesterfield			13					_Marples_	_Scrimgeour_	_O'Neill_	_Batty_	_Baines_	_Hunter_	_Reid_	_Moss_	_Walker_	_Henderson_	_Williamson_	

Scorers, Times, and Referees

1. WALSALL — Walsh 7p, Neville 87 / Cross 27, Daley 50, O'Kelly 88p. Ref: J Deakin
The loss of Williams on half-time for his second bookable offence, as well as the 87th-minute departure of the injured Johnson adds to City's woes as they are outplayed by the slick Saddlers. Emmanuel palms away Steve Elliott's header to present Walsall with their spot-kick winner.

2. BOURNEMOUTH — Clarke 1, 9, 89, Russell 7, 40. Ref: A Ward
City's much maligned defence only holds out for 45 seconds before Colin Clarke fires in from Colin Russell's pass. Three down in just nine minutes, City make a spirited recovery but a long ball down the right exposes Hughes, and Clarke runs through to complete his hat-trick.

3. GILLINGHAM — Hutchinson 40 / Cascarino 48, 87. Ref: M Robinson
A vast improvement, but Llewellyn's mis-hit back-pass puts Tony Cascarino clean through to shoot in Gillingham's late winner. City dominate matters, but only Hutchinson's fine drive manages to evade Ron Hillyard, despite having ten on-target efforts, compared to Gillingham's three.

4. ROTHERHAM — / Forrest 12, Tynan 57p. Ref: R Nixon
City's slump continues at Millmoor, with their worst display yet. After Steve Forrest bursts unchallenged into the penalty area to fire in, only Waugh's bravery and poor Rotherham finishing keeps the score down, until Hirst's trip on Alan Birch produces Tommy Tynan's penalty.

5. WIGAN — Pritchard 68. Ref: M Reed
City's tremendous attitude and commitment brings a well-deserved victory over high-flying Wigan. After gaining no reward for a superb opening, Pritchard grabs the spoils with a prodigious leap to meet Walsh's looping cross and send a well-directed header past Billy Stewart.

6. CARDIFF — Walsh 44, 77, Pritchard 85 / Withey 74. Ref: V Callow
Pritchard stakes his claim for further Welsh international honours with a sparkling display at Ninian Park. Pritchard's flick to Llewellyn sets up Walsh to shoot in at the far-post, then Waugh is the hero as he saves Jimmy Mullen's poorly-struck spot-kick after Curle's 68th-min handball.

7. DERBY — Newman 36 / Davison 57. Ref: D Hedges
City lose their way after the interval, only putting in two shots as Derby up the pace. Newman, City's hero before the break with a well-placed header, is the villain for County's equaliser as he allows Gary Micklewhite to float over a perfect far-post cross for Bobby Davison to nod in.

8. YORK — Pritchard 74 / MacPhail 45p. Ref: J Hough
Pritchard's volley over the bar is City's only first-half effort, as Waugh's push on Keith Houchen allows John MacPhail to put York ahead from the spot. City's spirited revival after the break is rewarded by Pritchard who is able to pick his spot with a header from Marshall's cross.

9. BLACKPOOL — Neville 24, Pritchard 73 / O'Keefe 16. Ref: A Robinson
Blackpool are deservedly caught out by their well-drilled offside trap as the referee decides to ignore a belated flag for Walsh to cross for Pritchard to head in City's winner. Pool's over-physical approach wins few friends, but Eamon O'Keefe's 25-yard volley is much appreciated.

10. NEWPORT — Neville 72 / Boyle 89. Ref: H Taylor
Neville gathers Walsh's 70-yard pass and outstrips two defenders before slotting the ball past the advancing Mark Kendall. A superb goal to put City ahead, but the advantage is wasted as failure of their offside trap leaves Terry Boyle all alone to head in Peter Jones' long free-kick.

11. CHESTERFIELD — Ref: M James
Unimaginative City offer precious little against unyieldingly defensive opposition. Derbyshire wicket-keeper Chris Marples saves the few efforts that come his way, while Shaun O'Neill almost snatches a shock win for the Spireites with a cross that Williams clears off the line.

No		Opponent	Date	HT	Res	Score	Pos		Pts	Att
12	A	NOTTS CO	12/10	0-2	L	0-4	19	5	13	4,332
13	H	DARLINGTON	19/10	0-0	W	1-0	17	24	16	5,873
14	A	BURY	22/10	0-1	L	3-6	18	12	16	2,460
15	H	WOLVES	26/10	2-0	W	3-0	16	23	19	7,138
16	A	DONCASTER	2/11	1-1	D	1-1	14	11	20	2,871
17	A	LINCOLN	6/11	1-1	D	1-1	15	20	21	1,379
18	H	BRENTFORD	9/11	0-0	D	0-0	16	10	22	6,598
19	A	SWANSEA	23/11	2-1	W	3-1	14	23	25	4,414
20	H	BOLTON	30/11	1-0	W	2-0	12	18	28	6,251
21	A	READING	14/12	0-0	L	0-1	13	1	28	5,785
22	H	BOURNEMOUTH	21/12	1-0	L	1-3	13	16	28	5,621
23	H	PLYMOUTH	26/12	2-0	W	2-0	12	5	31	8,296

---

12 — A NOTTS CO, 12/10 — 0-4 (L)

City: Waugh, Rogers, Newman, Curle, Moyes, Williams B !, Pritchard, Hutchinson, Johnson*, Walsh, Neville, Riley
Opp: *Leonard, Richards, Clarke, Benjamin, Sims, Yates, McParland*, Goodwin, Young, Waitt, Hunt, Daws*

Scorers: Hunt 22, 29, 60, McParland 70
Ref: C Trussell

County's 6ft 5in tall striker Mick Waitt gives City's defence, with new centre-half David Moyes, a torrid time. Three headed flicks, two from near-post corners, lay on three of County's goals as poor City, with Williams sent off in the 78th min for kicking David Hunt, slump to defeat.

---

13 — H DARLINGTON, 19/10 — 1-0 (W)

City: Waugh, Rogers, Newman, Curle, Moyes, Williams B, Pritchard, Hutchinson, Riley, Walsh, Neville
Opp: *Barber, Evans, Morgan, Tupling, Green, Pallister, Roberts, Aldred, Paskett*, MacDonald, McLean, Airey*

Scorers: Walsh 64
Ref: M Cotton

Walsh answers his critics with a moment of match-winning brilliance as his 25-yard curling free-kick hits the back of the net. In a game that produces little in the way of ill feeling, despite the abundant goalmouth action, referee Malcolm Cotton astonishingly books seven players.

---

14 — A BURY, 22/10 — 3-6 (L)

City: Waugh, Rogers, Newman*, Curle, Moyes, Williams B, Pritchard, Hutchinson, Riley, Walsh, Neville
Opp: *Butcher, Dixon, Pashley, Bramhall, Valentine, Dobson, White, Madden, Beckford, Jakub, Young, Johnson*

Scorers: Walsh 47p, Neville 58, Riley 60 / Dobson 37p, 81, Beckford 46, White 53, [Young 72, Madden 88]
Ref: F Roberts

Cooper blames his side for throwing the match away by not closing the game up after Riley had headed City level at 3-3. Bury, who lost their previous game 0-5 at Blackpool, manage 16 shots on target to City's six, but in the first half it was the Robins who created the better chances.

---

15 — H WOLVES, 26/10 — 3-0 (W)

City: Waugh, Rogers, Newman, Curle, Llewellyn, Riley, Pritchard, Hutchinson, Tong, Walsh, Neville
Opp: *Barrett, Herbert, Barnes, Streete, Clarke, Stoutt, Purdie, Ryan, Ainscow, King, Wassell*, Chapman*

Scorers: Riley 2, Hutchinson 40, Walsh 85p
Ref: A Buksh

How the mighty have fallen as Wolves produce what must rank as one of their poorest-ever displays at Ashton Gate. Walsh's penalty, after Neville had been floored by Nicky Clarke, completes the scoring, but City have only themselves to blame in not managing more than three.

---

16 — A DONCASTER, 2/11 — 1-1 (D)

City: Waugh, Llewellyn, Newman, Curle, Moyes, Riley, Pritchard, Hutchinson, Tong, Walsh, Neville
Opp: *Rhodes, Deans*, Rushbury, Humphries, Brown T, Cusack, Buckley, Douglas, Butterworth, Harle, Dobbin, Travis*

Scorers: Riley 7 / Brown 59
Ref: A Robinson

City, who demonstrate that they can play with flair and creativity away from home without sacrificing defence, are let down by their strikers. Riley heads in Neville's cross, but golden opportunities are spurned before Tony Brown nods the ball over the line for Doncaster's equaliser.

---

17 — A LINCOLN, 6/11 — 1-1 (D)

City: Waugh, Llewellyn, Newman, Curle, Moyes, Riley, Pritchard, Hutchinson, Tong, Walsh, Neville
Opp: *Judge, McNeil, McCarrick, Redfearn, Stroddar, Measham*, Taman, Turner, Latchford, McGinley, Ward, Richards G*

Scorers: Neville 37 / Redfearn 28
Ref: L Dilkes

City's offside trap again proves costly as their cavalry charge at a Lincoln free-kick leads to Curle's clearance rebounding into the net off of Neil Redfearn. Neville rescues City's point as he slams Pritchard's low cross into an empty net, after Alan Judge is drawn out of position.

---

18 — H BRENTFORD, 9/11 — 0-0 (D)

City: Waugh, Llewellyn, Newman, Curle, Moyes, Riley, Pritchard, Hutchinson, Walsh*, Neville, Johnson
Opp: *Phillips, Salman, Murray, Evans, Wignall, Hurlock, Lynch, Cooke !, Booker, Butler, Torrance*

Ref: M Scott

Curle denies uncompromising Brentford's quest for victory by blocking George Torrance's goal-bound shot in the dying moments. Lucky not to concede a 57th-minute spot-kick as Robbie Cooke goes tumbling. Curle is the victim a minute later as the No 8 is sent off for lashing out.

---

19 — A SWANSEA, 23/11 — 3-1 (W)

City: Waugh, Llewellyn, Newman, Curle, Moyes, Riley, Pritchard, Hutchinson, Tong, Walsh*, Neville, Budd*
Opp: *Rimmer, Hough, Sullivan, Gibbins, Harrison, Emmanuel, McHale, Randell, McCarthy, Waddle, Melville*

Scorers: Hutchinson 38, 40, Walsh 50 / Harrison 20
Ref: A Seville

After Chris Harrison gives crisis club Swansea the lead with a looping header, City are fortunate to be ahead at the break. Hutchinson adds to his close-in effort by turning sharply and blasting past Jimmy Rimmer and the near post from an unbelievably acute angle.

---

20 — H BOLTON, 30/11 — 2-0 (W)

City: Waugh, Llewellyn, Newman, Curle, Moyes, Riley, Pritchard, Hutchinson, Tong, Walsh, Neville
Opp: *Farnworth, Joyce, Scott, Rudge, Came, Sutton, Fitzpatrick, Oghani !, Caldwell, Hartford, Bell*, Walker*

Scorers: Riley 9, Neville 85
Ref: N Butler/D Delaney

David Delaney, who replaces the injured Noel Butler in the 23rd minute, sends off George Oghani eight minutes later for kicking Waugh. City, for whom Walsh and Pritchard are denied by the woodwork, add to Riley's early 18-yarder when Neville taps in Walsh's powerful low cross.

---

21 — A READING, 14/12 — 0-1 (L)

City: Waugh, Llewellyn, Newman, Curle, Moyes, Riley !, Moyes, Hutchinson, Tong, Walsh, Neville
Opp: *Westwood, Peters, Bailie, Beavan, Hicks, Wood, Rogers, Senior, Horrix, Bremner, Gilkes*

Scorers: Gilkes 84
Ref: I Hemley

'Is this game for men or not?' opines boss Terry Cooper as City have six players booked and Riley sent off in the 75th minute after a fracas with Dean Horrix. City cope well against Reading's pressurising style, but eventually succumb as Michael Gilkes hits home Bremner's cross.

---

22 — H BOURNEMOUTH, 21/12 — 1-3 (L)

City: Waugh, Llewellyn, Newman, Curle, Moyes, Riley, Pritchard, Hutchinson, Tong, Walsh, Neville
Opp: *Leigh, Heffernan, Sulley, Newson, Brown, Beck, O'Driscoll, Howlett, Clarke, Thompson, Morrell*

Scorers: Hutchinson 11 / Heffernan 65, Howlett 73, Newson 78
Ref: R Lewis

Everyone dressed as Father Christmas is allowed in free, but most of the goodwill on the terraces disappears in the second half as Walsh fires a penalty against the post. Gary Howlett delivers the killer-blow with a superbly struck 30-yard shot which sails on the wind into the top corner.

---

23 — H PLYMOUTH, 26/12 — 2-0 (W)

City: Waugh, Llewellyn, Newman, Curle, Moyes, Riley, Pritchard, Hutchinson, Tong, Walsh, Neville
Opp: *Crudgington, Nisbet, Cooper L, Cooper I, Goodyear, McElhinney, Summerfield, Hodges*, Coughlin, Cooper S, Clayton, Nelson, Rawbotham*

Scorers: Walsh 7p, Neville 37
Ref: D Vickers/J Carter

A Boxing Day feast of attacking football as City make a mockery of their poor League position. Kevin Summerfield's rash challenge on Pritchard allows Walsh to score from the spot, then Neville heads in to double the advantage, before the injured ref is replaced at half-time.

CANON LEAGUE DIVISION 3

Manager: Terry Cooper — SEASON 1985-86

No	Date		Opponent	Att / Pos / Pt	F-A	H-T	1	2	3	4	5	6	7	8	9	10	11	12 sub used
24	28/12	A	GILLINGHAM	4,672 / 8 / 32	1-1	0-0	Waugh	Newman	Williams B	Curle	Moyes	Rogers	Pritchard	Hutchinson	Tong	Walsh	Neville	Musker
			Hillyard				*Sage*	*Elsey*	*Oakes*	*Weatherly*	*Himigan*	*Byrne*	*Strearer*	*Robinson**	*Mehmet*	*Cascarino*		

Newman 77, Cascarino 88. Ref: D Reeves

'We're like a Christmas Club' says Cooper as City let victory slip in the dying minutes. Moyes deflects Tony Cascarino's low shot into the net to level Newman's headed opener, after Waugh's brilliant 25th-minute penalty save from Dave Mehmet had kept City level at the break.

No	Date		Opponent	Att / Pos / Pt	F-A	H-T	1	2	3	4	5	6	7	8	9	10	11	12 sub used
25	7/1	H	DONCASTER	5,395 / 7 / 35	4-1	1-0	Waugh	Newman	Williams B	Curle	Moyes	Marshall	Pritchard	Hutchinson	Tong	Walsh	Neville	Dobbin
			Rhodes				*Stead*	*Holmes**	*Humphries*	*Flynn*	*Cusack*	*Buckley*	*Douglas*	*Joyce*	*Woods*	*Brown T*		

Pritchard 6, Walsh 50p, 70, Neville 72, Douglas 65. Ref: G Ashby

After Colin Douglas volleys in following Waugh's weak punch, Walsh ends Doncaster's stubborn resistance with a breathtaking 70th-minute acute-angled shot. For a side near the top of the table Doncaster offer little, though City are somewhat flattered by the margin of their success.

No	Date		Opponent	Att / Pos / Pt	F-A	H-T	1	2	3	4	5	6	7	8	9	10	11	12 sub used
26	11/1	H	ROTHERHAM	6,672 / 13 / 38	3-1	2-0	Waugh	Newman	Williams B	Curle	Moyes	Marshall	Pritchard	Hutchinson	Tong	Walsh	Neville	Eley
			O'Hanlon				*Barnsley*	*Dungworth*	*Gooding*	*Smith**	*Pickering*	*Birch*	*Emerson*	*Tynan*	*Simmons*	*Pugh*		

Williams 34, Walsh 38, Neville 49, Tynan 52. Ref: H King/L Loosemore

Referee Howard King's replacement by Les Loosemore in the 20th minute enlivens a dull first half in which Williams' deflection of Tony Tynan's clearance and Walsh's 15-yard prod-in put City in charge. After the break Tynan's crisp half-volley gives Rotherham some reward.

No	Date		Opponent	Att / Pos / Pt	F-A	H-T	1	2	3	4	5	6	7	8	9	10	11	12 sub used
27	18/1	A	WALSALL	4,952 / 6 / 38	1-2	1-0	Waugh	Newman	Williams B	Curle	Moyes	Llewellyn	Pritchard*	Hutchinson!	Tong	Walsh	Neville	Riley Kelly
			Cherry				*Gunn*	*Hawker*	*Shakespeare*	*Brazier*	*Hart*	*Chilts*	*Cross*	*Daley**	*Elliott*	*Naughton*		

Neville 36, Cross 53p, Elliott 66. Ref: D Scott

Cheating players, loutish fans and pathetic refereeing at Fellows Park in the week that the Popplewell report is produced. The alert Neville shoots City ahead as the keeper fumbles Walsh's effort, but the game turns as Hutchinson is sent off for protesting Cross's dive for the penalty.

No	Date		Opponent	Att / Pos / Pt	F-A	H-T	1	2	3	4	5	6	7	8	9	10	11	12 sub used
28	25/1	H	CARDIFF	7,541 / 20 / 41	2-1	2-1	Waugh	Newman	Williams B	Curle	Moyes	Riley	Marshall	Hutchinson	Tong	Walsh	Neville	McLoughlin
			Smelt				*Marustik*	*Giles*	*Ford*	*Stevenson*	*Mullen*	*Christie**	*Vaughan*	*Wheeler*	*Farrington*	*Micallef*		

Neville 23, Marshall 36, Wheeler 34. Ref: T Holbrook

A patchy performance as Neville fires in from Curle's long free-kick to give City an early lead, before Paul Wheeler heads in the Bluebirds equaliser. Riley's accurate cross sets up Marshall to restore City's advantage, but Lee Smelt performs heroics to prevent any further addition.

No	Date		Opponent	Att / Pos / Pt	F-A	H-T	1	2	3	4	5	6	7	8	9	10	11	12 sub used
29	1/2	A	WIGAN	3,402 / 4 / 42	1-1	0-1	Waugh	Newman	Williams B	Curle	Moyes	Riley	Llewellyn	Barrow	Tong	Walsh	Neville	Aspinall
			Tunks				*Butler*	*Knowles*	*Kelly**	*Cribley*	*Methven*	*Lowe*	*Tanner**	*Jewell*	*Langley*	*Cook*		

Newman 68, Cook 39. Ref: K Redfern

Three brilliant saves by Roy Tunks from Walsh preserve Wigan's invincible home record. Williams clears off the line early on, before Paul Cook's thunderous drive puts Wigan in front. Marshall's introduction has an immediate impact as Newman heads in from his right-wing cross.

No	Date		Opponent	Att / Pos / Pt	F-A	H-T	1	2	3	4	5	6	7	8	9	10	11	12 sub used
30	4/2	H	BURY	5,074 / 21 / 45	4-1	1-1	Waugh	Newman	Williams B	Curle	Moyes	Llewellyn	Marshall	Hutchinson	Tong	Walsh	Neville	Bramhall
			Hughes				*Dixon*	*Pashley*	*Robinson*	*Valentine*	*Hill*	*Harris**	*Madden*	*Cross*	*Jakub*	*Young*		

Riley 29, 67, Neville 47, Walsh 48, Madden 33. Ref: C Downey

Walsh celebrates his new contract with a vicious left-foot drive from twelve yards as City take Bury apart after the break. Riley is the star with his two strikes, evading a scything tackle to shoot in the opener, and then controlling the ball on his chest before firing into the roof of the net.

No	Date		Opponent	Att / Pos / Pt	F-A	H-T	1	2	3	4	5	6	7	8	9	10	11	12 sub used
31	22/2	H	YORK	6,392 / 12 / 46	2-2	1-1	Waugh	Llewellyn	Williams B	Curle	Moyes	Riley	Marshall	Hutchinson	Tong	Walsh	Neville	Butler
			Leaning				*Senior*	*Hood*	*McLaughtrie*	*MacPhail*	*Mills*	*Ford*	*Banton**	*Walwyn*	*Haslegrave*	*Canham*		

Moyes 1, Neville 70, MacPhail 44p, Canham 89. Ref: J Deakin

York deserve their leveller before the break thanks to John MacPhail's pen after Williams handles Keith Walwyn's header on the line. Neville sprints 40 yards to head in Walsh's cross with a diving header, but Tony Canham's mis-hit 25-yard swerver destroys City's promotion hopes.

No	Date		Opponent	Att / Pos / Pt	F-A	H-T	1	2	3	4	5	6	7	8	9	10	11	12 sub used
32	1/3	A	BLACKPOOL	3,366 / 8 / 46	1-2	0-1	Waugh*	Llewellyn	Williams B	Curle	Moyes	Riley	Bryant	Hutchinson	Tong	Walsh	Neville	Marshall O'Keefe
			O'Rourke				*Moore*	*Walsh*	*Conroy*	*Law*	*Greenall*	*Britton*	*Deary*	*Stewart*	*Butler**	*Dyer*		

Bryant 66, Butler 8, Deary 63p. Ref: J Lloyd

Marshall demonstrates his versatility between the sticks as Waugh's earlier back injury forces the keeper's 42nd-min departure. He has no chance with Pool's controversial pen following Moyes' supposed handball, but Bryant celebrates his City debut with a brilliant half-volley.

No	Date		Opponent	Att / Pos / Pt	F-A	H-T	1	2	3	4	5	6	7	8	9	10	11	12 sub used
33	4/3	H	NEWPORT	4,395 / 18 / 49	3-1	1-0	Vaughan	Llewellyn	Williams B	Curle	Moyes	Riley	Marshall	Hutchinson*	Tong	Walsh	Neville	Johnson Peacock
			Kendall				*Pulis*	*Jones F*	*Berry*	*Carter*	*Boyle*	*Mardenboro' Relish**	*Gill*	*Staniforth*	*Butler**	*Lewis*		

Walsh 11, Marshall 83, Curle 89, Mardenborough 52. Ref: J Moules

Curle celebrates yesterday's birth of his first child with a blistering 70-yard dribble to take him past the challenges of Tony Pulis and Peter Jones and side-foot in City's memorable last-minute goal. On top in the first half, City register with their only second-half shots on target.

No	Date		Opponent	Att / Pos / Pt	F-A	H-T	1	2	3	4	5	6	7	8	9	10	11	12 sub used
34	8/3	A	CHESTERFIELD	2,547 / 15 / 50	0-0	0-0	Vaughan	Llewellyn	Williams B	Curle	Moyes	Riley	Marshall	Hutchinson	Newman	Walsh	Neville	Caldwell
			Marples				*Hewitt*	*O'Neill*	*Spooner**	*Baines*	*Hunter*	*Brown P*	*Moss*	*Williamson*	*Henderson*	*Scrimgeour*		

Ref: I Hemley

On the evidence of this season's meetings, games with Chesterfield should carry a warning to fans in that they could be bored to death. In following Reading's 4-2 win at Saltergate on Tuesday, John Duncan's side adopt a rigid defensive approach throughout the whole game.

35 — NOTTS CO (H) 15/3

Att: 5,701 · Pos: 7/9 · W 3-0 · Pts 53
Scorers: Walsh 45, Moyes 72, Riley 88
Ref: R Gifford

City	Opponent
Waugh	*Mimms*
Llewellyn	*Smalley*
Williams B	*Richards*
Curle	*Benjamin*
Moyes	*Sims*
Riley	*Yates*
Marshall	*Barnes*
Hutchinson	*Goodwin*
Newman	*Waitt*
Walsh	*Harkouk**
Neville	*Hunt*
	McParland

County, who come equipped to spoil with five men strung out across the back, and an efficient offside trap, do not force Waugh to make a save until three shots break the deadlock, and Riley's lunge at a low centre seals City's success.

36 — DERBY (A) 19/3

Att: 11,113 · Pos: 7/3 · L 0-2 · Pts 53
Scorers: Gregory 27, Christie 45
Ref: M Reed

City	Opponent
Waugh	*Steele*
Llewellyn	*Blades*
Williams B	*Buckley*
Curle	*Williams*
Moyes	*Pratley*
Riley	*MacLaren*
Marshall*	*Micklewhite*
Hutchinson	*Christie*
Newman	*Davison*
Walsh !	*Gregory*
Neville	*Chandler*
	Pritchard

Walsh receives his marching orders for the first time in his career for protesting over Trevor Christie's high tackle as the No 8 goes on to score off the inside of the post just before half-time. Derby's expensive side deserve their win which was set up by John Gregory's twelve yard double.

37 — WOLVES (A) 22/3

Att: 3,696 · Pos: 10/24 · L 1-2 · Pts 53
Scorers: Walsh 62; Mutch 69, Edwards 90
Ref: P Willis

City	Opponent
Waugh	*Barrett*
Llewellyn	*Palmer*
Williams B	*Barnes*
Underhill	*Streete*
Moyes	*Zelem*
Riley	*Purdie*
Marshall	*Lockhart*
Hutchinson	*Holmes*
Newman	*Mutch*
Walsh	*Edwards D*
Neville*	*Chapman*
	Pritchard

In a swirling wind City have the skill, but lack commitment against a poor Wolves side. Walsh's left-footed shot from twelve yards should have set City on the victory road, but Dean Edwards volleys Wolves' winner at the death, after Andy Mutch had levelled from an acute angle.

38 — BRISTOL ROV (H) 29/3

Att: 12,171 · Pos: 9/16 · W 2-0 · Pts 56
Scorers: Neville 26, Walsh 71
Ref: K Cooper

City	Opponent
Waugh	*Green*
Llewellyn	*Scales*
Williams B	*Bater*
Curle	*Tanner*
Moyes	*Parkin*
Riley	*Jones*
Pritchard	*Francis**
Hutchinson	*Penrice*
Harle*	*Morgan*
Walsh	*White*
Neville	*Stevenson*
Newman	*Purnell*

Despite almost total possession City find chances hard to come by as the Rovers' defence battles manfully to stem the tide. City's opener is lucky as Vaughan Jones' headed clearance rebounds off Neville, but no fluke about Walsh's turn and 15-yard angled drive that ties matters up.

39 — LINCOLN (H) 5/4

Att: 5,375 · Pos: 10/19 · D 1-1 · Pts 57
Scorers: Neville 48; White 16
Ref: R Bridges

City	Opponent
Waugh	*Swinburne*
Llewellyn	*Hodson*
Williams B	*Redfearn*
Curle	*White*
Bryant	*West**
Riley	*Strodder*
Pritchard	*McInnes*
Hutchinson	*Turner*
Harle	*Gamble*
Walsh	*Kilmore*
Neville	*Mair*
Marshall	*Toman*

Trevor Swinburne frustrates City with a string of great saves after Bryant's failure to cut out a through-ball allows Devon White to run through and fire past Waugh. Neville slams in City's equaliser from close range, but the nearest to a winner is Riley's disallowed 55th-min header.

40 — BRENTFORD (A) 13/4

Att: 3,701 · Pos: 9/11 · W 2-1 · Pts 60
Scorers: Riley 30, Pritchard 38; Millen 17
Ref: M Heath

City	Opponent
Waugh	*Phillips*
Llewellyn	*Salman*
Williams B	*Murray*
Curle	*Millen*
Moyes	*Wignall*
Riley	*Booker*
Pritchard	*Holloway*
Hutchinson	*Sinton*
Harle	*Butler*
Walsh	*Cooke*
Neville*	*Burke**
Marshall*	*Lynch*

City's fine attacking performance is rewarded courtesy of a corner flag from which a rebound allows Marshall to cross for Pritchard's sweetly-timed volley. Defensive problems persist though, and the lead as Keith Millen rises high to plant a firm header past Waugh.

41 — SWANSEA (H) 19/4

Att: 6,013 · Pos: 11/22 · L 0-1 · Pts 60
Scorers: Price 80
Ref: D Vickers

City	Opponent
Waugh	*Hughes*
Llewellyn	*Lewis*
Williams B	*Sullivan*
Curle	*Price P*
Moyes	*Gibbins*
Riley*	*Emmanuel*
Pritchard	*Hutchison*
Hutchinson	*Pascoe*
Harle	*McHale*
Walsh	*Waddle*
Neville	*Hough*
Moore	

The diminutive Moore cheers up the City fans with his touches after coming on for the last 22 minutes of a match that leaves boss Cooper speechless. Neville's 54th-minute curler that hits the bar is City's best effort as Swansea take the points with Paul Price's 15-yard low drive.

42 — BRISTOL ROV (A) 22/4

Att: 9,922 · Pos: 10/16 · D 1-1 · Pts 61
Scorers: Neville 74; Scales 80
Ref: L Shapter

City	Opponent
Waugh	*Green*
Llewellyn	*Scales*
Williams B	*England*
Curle	*Tanner**
Moyes	*Parkin*
Riley	*Jones*
Pritchard	*Francis*
Hutchinson	*Penrice*
Harle	*Morgan*
Walsh	*White*
Neville	*Purnell*
	Noble

Ron Green's heroics in keeping out Moyes' point-blank header come to naught as Neville latches onto the rebound to put City deservedly in front. Fittingly, though, John Scales' fierce cross-shot ensures that it is Rovers who have final say as the curtain descends on Eastville derbies.

43 — BOLTON (A) 26/4

Att: 4,493 · Pos: 9/16 · W 4-0 · Pts 64
Scorers: Riley 19, Neville 31, 54, Llewellyn 67
Ref: J Ashworth

City	Opponent
Waugh	*Farnworth*
Llewellyn	*Scott*
Williams B	*Phillips*
Curle	*Sutton*
Moyes	*Came*
Riley	*Bell*
Pritchard	*Darby*
Newman	*Oghani*
Harle	*Entwistle*
Walsh	*Hartford*
Neville	*Gavin*

Newman stars with his long probing passes in an action-packed second half that contains 23 of the game's 29 shots on target. Llewellyn completes the scoring with his first League goal. Taking a return pass from Riley on the edge of the box he coolly beats Simon Farnworth.

44 — PLYMOUTH (A) 29/4

Att: 24,888 · Pos: 9/2 · L 0-4 · Pts 64
Scorers: Tynan 32, 64, Nelson 54, Coughlin 61
Ref: J Deakin

City	Opponent
Waugh	*Crudgington*
Llewellyn	*Nisbet*
Williams B	*Cooper L*
Curle	*Goodyear*
Moyes	*McElhinney*
Riley	*Matthews*
Pritchard	*Hodges*
Newman	*Coughlin*
Harle	*Tynan*
Walsh	*Summerfield*
Neville	*Nelson*

Cooper's prediction of an exciting shoot-out between two attacking sides is made to look a sick joke as City can only manage one worthwhile goal attempt. Tommy Tynan wins everything in the air, but he uses his feet to set Argyle on course to clinching promotion with an easy opener.

45 — READING (H) 3/5

Att: 7,814 · Pos: 9/1 · W 3-0 · Pts 67
Scorers: Neville 7, Walsh 34p, 40p
Ref: M James

City	Opponent
Waugh	*Westwood*
Llewellyn	*Williams*
Williams B	*Richardson*
Newman	*Beavon*
Moyes	*Peters*
Riley	*Wood*
Pritchard	*Hurlock*
Hutchinson	*Harris*
Harle	*Senior*
Walsh	*White*
Neville	*Rogers*

City's sizzling soccer makes a mockery of the League table as only Gary Westwood saves the Champions from a landslide. Hutchinson heads down Llewellyn's free-kick for Neville to open the scoring, whilst Gary Peters up-ends Neville for the first penalty and handles for the second.

46 — DARLINGTON (A) 15/5

Att: 1,615 · Pos: 9/13 · D 1-1 · Pts 68
Scorers: Riley 60; Roberts 44
Ref: M Peck

City	Opponent
Waugh	*Astbury*
Llewellyn	*Aldred*
Williams B	*Tupling*
Curle	*Ward*
Moyes	*Green*
Honor	*Lloyd*
Marshall	*Roberts*
Newman	*Woodcock*
Harle	*Airey*
Walsh	*McLean*
Neville*	*Robinson*
Tanner	*Riley*

Following Curle's innocuous 85th-minute tackle, Waugh saves both Dave McLean's first spot-kick, and Dave Woodcock's effort. Walsh sets up City's goal by putting Riley clear to shoot into the net between two defenders, after Alan Roberts had slotted in Darlington's easy opener.

Home 6,600 · Away 5,214 · Average 6,600

CANON DIVISION 3 (CUP-TIES)

Manager: Terry Cooper

SEASON 1985-86

Milk Cup

Match	F-A	H-T	Scorers, Times, and Referees	1	2	3	4	5	6	7	8	9	10	11	12 sub used
1:1 A HEREFORD 21/8 2,449	L 1-5	0-3	Johnson 77 / K'ms 1, Price 15, H'vey 42p, Ph'lps 60, 78 Rose / Ref: K Barratt	Waugh	Llewellyn	Williams B	Curle	Hughes	Riley	Marshall*	Hutchinson	Emmanuel	Neville	Walsh	Johnson
				Rose	*Price*	*Dalziel*	*Halliday*	*Cegielski*	*Pejic*	*Harvey*	*Dewe*	*Phillips*	*Kearns*	*Butler*	*Marshall*
1:2 H HEREFORD 3/9 2,373 4:11	W 2-0	1-0	Johnson 6, Hutchinson 83 / Ref: R Gifford (City lost 3-5 on aggregate)	Waugh	Llewellyn	Newman	Curle	Rogers	Williams B*	Pritchard	Hutchinson	Johnson	Walsh	Neville	Marshall
				Rose	*Price*	*Dalziel*	*Halliday*	*Pejic*	*Cegielski*	*Harvey*	*Maddy*	*Phillips*	*Kearns*	*Butler*	

Clinical finishing by Hereford as they notch up their first victory over City, after taking the lead in just 41 secs following Riley's back-pass. Incredibly City have more shots and force three times as many corners as Hereford, but defensive frailties highlight the need for new blood.

City win back their respect as only keeper Kevin Rose comes between them and a sensational recovery. Hope is rekindled early on as Johnson heads in from Williams' pass, but despite incessant pressure, City's only further reward is Hutchinson's late flick in from Pritchard's cross.

FA Cup

Match	F-A	H-T	Scorers, Times, and Referees	1	2	3	4	5	6	7	8	9	10	11	12 sub used
1 A SWINDON 17/11 10,468 4:7	D 0-0	0-0	Ref: K Miller	Waugh	Llewellyn	Newman	Curle	Rogers	Riley	Pritchard	Hutchinson	Tong	Walsh	Neville	Gardiner
				Allen	*Henry*	*Ramsey*	*Barnard*	*Cole*	*Calderwood*	*Rowland*	*Hall**	*Gordon*	*Wade*	*Hockaday*	
1R H SWINDON 20/11 8,979 4:7	W 4-2	1-0	Neville 26, 57, 60, Riley 77 / Ramsey 46, Barnard 52 / Ref: K Miller	Waugh	Llewellyn	Rogers	Curle	Newman	Pritchard	Hutchinson	Tong	Hockaday	Riley	Neville	Hall
				Allen	*Henry*	*Cole*	*Calderwood*	*Ramsey*	*Roberts*	*Rowland**	*Barnard*	*Gordon*	*Gordon*	*Wade*	
2 H EXETER 7/12 8,052 4:18	L 1-2	1-1	Walsh 17p / Kellow 25, Crawford 60 / Ref: H King	Waugh	Llewellyn*	Newman	Curle	Rogers	Riley	Pritchard	Hutchinson	Tong	Walsh	Neville	Williams B
				Shaw	*Jackson*	*Viney*	*McNichol*	*McCaffery*	*Marker*	*Ling*	*Harrower**	*Kellow*	*Keough*	*Crawford*	*Pratt*

Cup football at its best with a feast of open attacking football and countless near misses at both ends. Whilst City have the edge with ten shots on target, compared to Swindon's three, they have cause to be thankful to Newman for clearing an in-swinging corner off the goal-line.

Another magnificent Cup battle, but this time the game has everything. Goals aplenty, near misses – Brian Wade hitting a post in the tenth minute – Waugh's penalty save from Andy Rowland midway through the second half, and two strong City appeals for spot-kick awards.

Alan Crawford admits that his stunning 15-yard winner that shocks his former team-mates was a hit and hope effort. Aidan McCaffery pulls back Riley to give away the penalty, but City's failure to clear Jim McNichol's free-kick allows Tony Kellow to net a close-range leveller.

				Home					Away					
		P	W	D	L	F	A	W	D	L	F	A	Pts	
1	Reading	46	16	3	4	39	22	13	4	6	28	29	94	
2	Plymouth	46	17	3	3	56	20	9	6	8	32	33	87	
3	Derby	46	13	7	3	45	20	10	8	5	35	21	84	
4	Wigan	46	17	4	2	54	17	6	10	7	28	31	83	
5	Gillingham	46	14	5	4	48	17	8	8	7	33	37	79	
6	Walsall	46	15	7	1	59	23	7	2	14	31	41	75	
7	York	46	16	4	3	49	17	4	7	12	28	41	71	
8	Notts Co	46	12	6	5	42	26	7	8	8	29	34	71	
9	BRISTOL CITY	46	14	5	4	43	19	4	9	10	26	41	68	
10	Brentford	46	8	8	7	29	29	9	10	4	29	32	66	
11	Doncaster	46	7	10	6	20	21	9	6	8	25	31	64	
12	Blackpool	46	11	6	6	38	19	6	11	6	28	36	63	
13	Darlington	46	10	7	6	39	33	5	6	12	22	45	58	
14	Rotherham	46	13	5	5	44	18	2	7	14	17	41	57	
15	Bournemouth	46	9	6	8	41	31	6	3	14	24	41	54	
16	Bristol Rov	46	9	8	6	27	21	5	4	14	24	54	54	
17	Chesterfield	46	10	6	7	41	30	3	8	12	20	34	53	
18	Bolton	46	10	4	9	35	30	5	4	14	19	38	53	
19	Newport	46	7	8	8	35	33	4	10	9	17	32	51	
20	Bury	46	11	7	5	46	26	1	6	16	17	41	49	
21	Lincoln	46	7	9	7	33	34	3	7	13	22	43	46	
22	Cardiff	46	7	5	11	22	29	5	4	14	31	54	45	
23	Wolves	46	6	6	11	29	47	5	4	14	28	51	43	
24	Swansea	46	9	6	8	27	27	2	4	17	16	60	43	
		1104	268	145	139	941	609	139	145	268	609	941	1511	

Odds & ends

Double wins: (2) Cardiff, Bolton.
Double losses: (2) Walsall, Bournemouth.

Won from behind: (3) Blackpool (h), Swansea (a), Brentford (a).
Lost from in front: (5) Walsall (h), Gillingham (h), Bournemouth (a).
Walsall (a), Wolves (a).

High spots: Winning 3-1 at Cardiff on 14 September.
Beating Plymouth 2-0 at Ashton Gate on 26 December.
Beating Bury 4-1 on 4 February.
Winning 4-0 at Bolton on 26 April.
Beating Hereford 3-0 in the Freight Rover Trophy on 9 May.
Winning the Freight Rover Trophy at Wembley Stadium by beating
Bolton 3-0 on 24 May.
Beating Bristol Rov 1-0 in the Gloucestershire Cup Final on 9 Sep.

Low spots: Losing 0-5 at Bournemouth on 24 August.
Losing 3-6 at Bury on 22 October.
Losing at Hereford 1-5 in the FL Cup.
Losing at Hereford 0-2 in the Freight Rover Trophy on 6 May.

Player of the year: Bobby Hutchinson.
Ever-presents: (1) Steve Neville.
Hat-tricks: (1) Steve Neville.
Leading scorer: Steve Neville (22).

Appearances and Goals

	Appearances						Goals			
	Lge	Sub	LC	Sub	FAC	Sub	Lge	LC	FAC	Tot
Bryant, Richard	2						1			1
Curle, Chris	44		2		3		1			1
Emmanuel, Gary	2		1		3					
Harle, David	8									
Hirst, Martyn	1									
Honor, Chris	1									
Hughes, Mark	2		1							
Hutchinson, Bobby	42		2		3		5	1		6
Johnson, Steve	8	5	1	1				2		2
Llewellyn, Andy	38		2		3		1			1
Marshall, Gary	14	5	1	1			2			2
Moore, Gordon		1								
Moyes, David	27						2			2
Newman, Rob	37		2		3		3			3
Neville, Steve	46		2		3		19		3	22
Pritchard, Howard	32	2	1		3		6			6
Riley, Glyn	33	8	1		3		10		1	11
Rogers, Lee	21	1								
Tanner, Michael	2									
Tong, David	19				3					
Underhill, Graham	1									
Vaughan, John	2									
Walsh, Alan	44		2		3		18		1	19
Waugh, Keith	44		2		3					
Williams, Brian	36	2	1			1	1			1
25 players used	506	23	22	2	33	1	69	3	5	77

TODAY LEAGUE DIVISION 3 — SEASON 1986-87

Manager: Terry Cooper

Match results

No	Venue	Opponent	Date	Result	F-A	H-T	Pt	Pos	Att	Scorers, Times, and Referees
1	H	BURY	23/8	D	2-2	2-2	1		8,239	Hutchinson 17, Moyes 33 / Taylor 18, Greenwood 43 — Ref: M Dimblebee
2	A	GILLINGHAM	30/8	D	1-1	1-1	2		4,185	Hamson 32 / Shearer 45 — Ref: M Bodenham
3	H	WIGAN	6/9	W	2-1	1-1	5	9 / 23	6,730	Walsh 34, Moyes 83 / Griffiths 43 — Ref: A Buksh
4	A	CHESTERFIELD	13/9	W	3-0	1-0	8	2 / 15	2,605	Owen 32, Newman 53, Harle 86 — Ref: J McAulay
5	A	DONCASTER	17/9	L	0-1	0-0	8	7 / 4	2,236	Dobbin 46 — Ref: M Scott
6	H	CARLISLE	20/9	W	3-0	2-0	11	5 / 18	7,040	Moyes 17, Walsh 32, 49 — Ref: K Cooper
7	A	BOURNEMOUTH	27/9	L	0-2	0-0	11	7 / 2	5,975	Savage 50p, 89p — Ref: D Hedges
8	H	DARLINGTON	30/9	D	1-1	0-0	12	9 / 14	6,667	Newman 64 / Mills 82 — Ref: K Miller
9	A	CHESTER	4/10	W	3-0	1-0	15	7 / 21	2,819	Harle 16, Hamson 57, Neville 84 — Ref: R Guy
10	H	YORK	11/10	W	3-0	0-0	18	5 / 8	7,951	Walsh 67, 87, Neville 72 — Ref: K Burge
11	H	MIDDLESBROUGH	25/10	D	2-2	2-2	19	9 / 2	8,800	Walsh 13, 19p / Slaven 25, Laws 36 — Ref: J Martin

City line-ups

No	1	2	3	4	5	6	7	8	9	10	11	12 sub used
1	Waugh	Llewellyn	Newman	Curle	Moyes	Riley	Owen	Hutchinson	Harle	Walsh	Neville	
2	Waugh	Newman	Llewellyn	Curle	Moyes	Riley	Owen	Hutchinson	Harle	Walsh	Hamson	
3	Waugh	Llewellyn	Newman	Curle	Moyes	Riley	Owen	Hutchinson*	Harle	Walsh	Hamson	Fitzpatrick
4	Waugh	Llewellyn	Newman	Curle	Moyes	Riley	Owen	Hutchinson	Harle	Walsh	Hamson	
5	Waugh	Llewellyn	Newman	Curle	Moyes	Riley	Owen	Hutchinson	Harle	Walsh	Hamson*	Neville
6	Waugh	Llewellyn	Williams B	Curle	Moyes	Riley	Owen	Hutchinson	Harle	Walsh	Neville	Newman
7	Waugh	Llewellyn	Williams B	Curle	Moyes!	Riley	Owen	Hutchinson	Harle	Walsh	Neville	
8	Waugh	Llewellyn	Williams B	Curle	Moyes	Riley	Owen	Hutchinson	Harle	Walsh	Neville	Newman
9	Waugh	Newman	Williams B	Curle	Moyes	Hamson	Owen	Hutchinson	Harle	Walsh	Neville	
10	Waugh	Llewellyn	Williams B	Curle	Newman	Hamson	Owen	Hutchinson*	Harle	Walsh	Neville	
11	Waugh	Llewellyn	Williams B	Rogers	MacPhail	Hamson	Owen*	Marshall	Harle	Walsh	Neville	

Opponent line-ups

No	1	2	3	4	5	6	7	8	9	10	11	12 sub used
1	Hughes	Ross	Pashley	Flynn	Valentine	Young	Robinson A	Butler	Taylor	Jakub	Greenwood	Eves
2	Hillyard	Haylock	Elsey	Pearce	Weatherly	Hinnigan	Pritchard*	Shearer	Robinson	Collins	Cascarino	
3	Tunks	Butler	Knowles	Hamilton	Cribley	Beesley	Lowe	Thompson	Jewell	Cook*	Griffiths	Hildicth
4	Brown J	Hewitt	Williamson	Bellamy	Scrimgeour	Reid	Kendall	Moss	Walker	Henderson	Coyle*	Kowalski
5	Rhodes	Stead	Rushbury	Redfearn	Brown	Cusack	Russell	Dobbin	Woods	Clayton	Burke	
6	Endersby	Haigh	McCartney	Wright	Saunders*	Halsall	Baker	Cooke	Paskett	Bishop	Worrall	Lynam M
7	Peyton	Williams	Morrell	Savage	Newson	Whitlock	O'Driscoll	Howlett	Richards	O'Connor	Puckett	
8	Astbury	Evans	Morgan	Hine	Green	Lloyd	Roberts A	Ward	Currie	Mills	Robinson	
9	Stewart	Greenough	Lane	Holden	Abel	Butler	Kelly	Barrow	Richardson	Houghton*	Graham	Rimmer
10	Leaning	Senior	McKenzie	Strajia	McAughtrie	Hood	Ford	Banton	Gabbiadini*	Mills	Canham	Butler
11	Pears	Laws	Cooper	Mowbray	Parkinson	Pallister	Slaven	Stephens	Hamilton	Gill	Ripley	Riley

Match reports

1. Bury — Gordon Owen, a £30,000 capture from Barnsley, wastes no time making an impression as it's his corners which bring City's goals. Yet twice, after Hutchinson's sprints for his superbly-headed opener, Bury ruthlessly exploit all too familiar defensive frailties to wipe out City's lead.

2. Gillingham — Moyes enjoys his physical battle with Tony Cascarino, as City gain a deserved point at the Priestfield Stadium. Cooper complains that the linesman had already signalled time in the first half before Howard Pritchard's corner leads to David Shearer shooting in from close range.

3. Wigan — Moyes silences the chants of City's irate fans as he rises unchallenged at the far post to meet Walsh's corner and send an unstoppable header past Roy Tunks. City are fortunate to garner full points with an indifferent performance after Walsh's quick turn and shot had put them ahead.

4. Chesterfield — City find their form at last with 90 minutes of incisive attacking football. Waugh saves Brian Scrimgeour's 62nd-minute pen after Curle fells Ernie Moss, but by then City are already two in front, Owen shooting in the opener from a free-kick and Newman nodding home a rebound.

5. Doncaster — City fail their physical at Belle Vue as rugged Doncaster deservedly take the points. Waugh pulls off a string of fine saves to keep City in contention, and it is rough justice that he should be caught too far off his line as Jim Dobbin's 30-yarder sails over his head and into the net.

6. Carlisle — Walsh and Owen have a field day as Carlisle's formation, with both full-backs tucked into the middle, leaves plenty of space on the flanks. Walsh lays on the cross for Moyes to head in at the far post, before getting in on the scoring stakes himself by twice shooting in easy chances.

7. Bournemouth — The dismissal of Moyes for arguing over the late penalty sparks crowd unrest, the referee calling a slightly premature halt to the proceedings as the fans spill onto the pitch. Williams' foul on Sean O'Driscoll gifts the first penalty, whilst Moyes' tackle on Carl Richards brings the second.

8. Darlington — Newman shows neat control to break the deadlock against defensive opponents. Accepting the ball from Hutchinson he steers in a shot from the edge of the area, before City's charity show leaves Cooper fuming as Owen's misplaced pass leads to David Mills lashing in the equaliser.

9. Chester — David Harle, sent off ten times in his career, shows he is much more than his reputation suggests. He opens the scoring with a superb first-time volley, supplies the cross for Hamson to tap in the second, and is involved in the build-up as Neville notches City's third with a diving header.

10. York — City's switch to a 4-2-4 pattern following Hutchinson's ankle injury sparks a revival after an atrocious first half. John Atyeo, making his first visit to Ashton Gate in a decade, is impressed as Walsh registers with tremendous 25-yard drive, and a great shot on the turn from close in.

11. Middlesbrough — Walsh gives City the lead with an unstoppable volley, and then registers from the spot after Neville is brought down, before Bernie Slaven seizes on a poor back-pass to get Boro' back into the game. Brian Laws levels with a 35-yard free-kick that takes a deflection off of Walsh.

York City — Match Record (matches 12–23)

No	H/A	Date	Opponent	Att	Pos	Res	Opp Pos	Pts	FT	HT	Scorers	Referee
12	A	1/11	BLACKPOOL	4,370	10	L	4	19	0-1	0-0	Butler 75	P Tyldesley
13	H	4/11	MANSFIELD	6,407	10	D	8	20	0-0	0-0	—	J Moules
14	A	8/11	FULHAM	4,459	8	W	17	23	3-0	2-0	Neville 15, 88, Walsh 28p	K Barratt
15	H	22/11	ROTHERHAM	6,756	9	L	22	23	0-1	0-1	Pugh 26	R Wiseman
16	A	29/11	NOTTS CO	3,987	11	L	4	23	0-2	0-2	Goodwin 7, McParland 13	P Don
17	A	2/12	NEWPORT	3,205	9	W	20	26	1-0	1-0	Neville 21	M Cotton
18	A	14/12	SWINDON	7,637	7	W	6	29	2-1	0-1	Neville 52, 87, White 25	M Reed
19	H	20/12	BOLTON	8,028	6	W	14	32	4-1	2-1	Neville 18, Riley 40, Newm'n 48, Walsh 70, Elliott 7	B Hill
20	A	26/12	PORT VALE	4,168	6	D	24	33	0-0	0-0	—	V Callow
21	H	27/12	WALSALL	10,193	7	W	10	36	2-1	0-1	MacPhail 63p, Fitzpatrick 66, Kelly 7	K Cooper
22	H	1/1	BRISTOL ROV	17,122	7	L	14	36	0-1	0-0	Smart 87	J Deakin
23	A	3/1	ROTHERHAM	3,170	7	L	14	36	0-2	0-0	Evans 54, Campbell 65	G Tyson

12 — A 1/11 BLACKPOOL

City: Waugh, Newman, Williams B, Rogers, MacPhail, Hamson, Llewellyn, Marshall*, Harle, Walsh, Neville!, Riley
Blackpool: Siddall, Davies, Walsh, Law, Methven, Deary, Mayes, Thompson*, Stewart, Dyer, Taylor, Butler

City cut out their defensive frailties at the expense of their attack. Unfortunately Neville's dismissal for a kick at Mike Walsh just before the break undermines much effort. Brian Butler's twenty-yarder strikes Hamson as he attempts to close down, and the ball is deflected past Waugh.

13 — H 4/11 MANSFIELD

City: Waugh, Newman, Williams B, Rogers, MacPhail, Hamson, Llewellyn, Marshall*, Harle, Walsh, Neville, **Withey**
Mansfield: Hitchcock, Graham, Logan, Lowery, Kenworthy, Kent, Keaney, Stringfellow, Cassells, McKernon

City's uninspired display illustrates how much the zest and enthusiasm of the injured Hutchinson is missed. Kevin Hitchcock saves the Stags after the interval when City at last put their game together, but he is fortunate that MacPhail's 50th-minute header is disallowed for offside.

14 — A 8/11 FULHAM

City: Waugh, Newman, Williams B, Moyes, MacPhail, Hamson, Llewellyn, Marshall, Harle, Walsh, Neville, Riley
Fulham: Vaughan, Marshall, Hopkins, Scott*, Oakes, Parker, Barnett, Hoddy, Coney, Kerrins, Davies, Achampong

It is thanks to Waugh that Fulham's blistering start is contained. Neville volleys in the opener, then a fortunate penalty after the ball rears up to hit Dean Coney's hand puts City in control. Another Walsh penalty is saved, but Neville coolly steers in City's final goal six minutes later.

15 — H 22/11 ROTHERHAM

City: Waugh, Newman, Williams B, Moyes, MacPhail, Riley, Marshall, Hutchinson, Harle*, Walsh, Withey, **Owen**
Rotherham: O'Hanlon, Dungworth, Crosby, Gooding, Warburton, Slack, Pugh, Williams, Evans, Haycock, Douglas

Millers' boss and ex City favourite Norman Hunter has a good day after receiving a rousing reception from the Ashton Gate fans. Just before a hailstorm makes conditions farcical, a reverse-pass by Gareth Evans sends Daral Pugh through City's square defence to prod the ball home.

16 — A 29/11 NOTTS CO

City: Waugh, Newman, Williams B, Moyes, MacPhail, Hamson, Owen, Hutchinson, Fitzpatrick, Walsh, Neville
Notts Co: Leonard, Smalley, Davis, Thompson, Yates, Benjamin, McParland, Goodwin, Waitt, Kevan, Clarke

City beat themselves at the outset as David Clarke's cross glances off Mark Goodwin to spin gently past Waugh, and then the infamous offside trap fails against Ian McParland to shoot home. Mick Leonard makes a fine save as Walsh fails from the spot for the fourth successive time.

17 — A 2/12 NEWPORT

City: Waugh, Newman, Williams B, Moyes, MacPhail, Hamson, Owen, Hutchinson, Fitzpatrick, Walsh, Neville, Riley
Newport: Kendall, Jones L, Jones P, O'Shea, Berry, Mullen*, Mardenboro', Gibbins, Carter, Staniforth, Lewis, Vinter

After a wretched November, City bounce back on the promotion trail with a slender but deserved success at Somerton Park. City's much-maligned defence does well to withstand Newport's late rally as they hang on to Neville's early goal, when he turned in Walsh's low cross.

18 — A 14/12 SWINDON

City: Waugh, Newman, Williams B, Moyes, MacPhail, Marshall, Owen*, Hutchinson, Fitzpatrick, Walsh, Neville, Riley
Swindon: Digby, Henry, Hockaday, Jones, Franklin, Calderwood, Bamber, Kamara, White, Gilligan*, Barnard, Wade

Even Neville is not sure how his mis-hit 87th-min shot reached the back of the net as the ball trickled through a muddy goalmouth and over the line via a post. A lucky goal perhaps, but certainly a deserved reward for Cooper's brave policy of attacking the Railwaymen with two wingers.

19 — H 20/12 BOLTON

City: Waugh, Newman, Williams B, Moyes, MacPhail, Riley, Marshall, Hutchinson*, Fitzpatrick, Walsh, Neville, **Llewellyn**
Bolton: Salmon, Neal, Phillips, Joyce, Came, Scott, Caldwell, Thompson, Elliott, Hartford, Gavin

As so often with Bolton's visits to Ashton Gate the entertainment is first class. The Trotters are let down by their finishing after Steve Elliott heads them in front. Steve Thompson has his pen saved by Waugh with the score at 3-1, then Walsh adds City's fourth with a right-foot drive.

20 — A 26/12 PORT VALE

City: Waugh, Newman, Williams B, Moyes, MacPhail, Marshall, Riley, Hutchinson, Fitzpatrick, Walsh, Neville
Port Vale: Williams A, Banks, Bromage, Walker, Hazell, Sproson, Smith, Earle, Jones, Bowden, Hamson

No chance of skilful football on a quagmire pitch at Vale Park. After a bright start when City swarmed all over the bottom club, it is Vale who create the better chances with Paul Smith squandering a clear opportunity and Waugh doing well to save Ray Walker's low 25-yard drive.

21 — H 27/12 WALSALL

City: Waugh, Newman, Williams B, Moyes, MacPhail, Riley, Marshall*, Hutchinson, Curle!, Walsh, Neville, **Hawker**
Walsall: Barber, Dornan, Mower, Shakespeare, Forbes, Hart, Train*, Cross, Kelly, Christie, Naughton

City show great spirit after going behind to David Kelly's volley and having Curle sent off in the 36th minute for his wild challenge on Fred Barber. Fitzpatrick runs clear to slot in the winner after Neville, who has a late strike disallowed for offside, appeared to dive for the penalty.

22 — H 1/1 BRISTOL ROV

City: Waugh, Newman, Williams B, Moyes, MacPhail, Riley*, Marshall, Curle, Fitzpatrick, Walsh, Neville, **Hutchinson**
Bristol Rov: Carter, Jones, Scales, Weston*, Twentyman, Carr, Dryden, Smart, Morgan, Mehew, Tanner, Micallef

Gary Smart makes City pay for wasting their chances as he settles this derby with a superb 20-yard strike. City dominate the play, but Rovers demonstrate much resolve, especially when David Mehew takes over in goal from the injured Tim Carter for the last 15 mins of the first half.

23 — A 3/1 ROTHERHAM

City: Waugh, Newman, Williams B, Moyes, MacPhail, Riley, Curle, Hutchinson, Fitzpatrick*, Walsh, Neville, **Marshall**
Rotherham: Newcombe, Douglas, Crosby, Gooding, Dungworth, Green, Pugh, Williams, Evans, Trussan, Campbell

City go down to their second defeat in the three days since Cooper was named Third Division manager of the month. After the galling derby defeat, City fall to a moderate Millers side, who score twice on the break with a Gareth Evans volley and Winston Campbell's close-range shot.

Column headers: No | Date | Att | Pos | Pt | F-A | H-T | Scorers, Times, and Referees | 1 | 2 | 3 | 4 | 5 | 6 | 7 | 8 | 9 | 10 | 11 | 12 sub used

---

24 — A WIGAN — 24/1 — Att 3,092 — Pos 8 — Pt 36 — L 1-3 (H-T 1-2)

Scorers, Times, Referees: Walsh 25. *Hilditch 38, Campbell 44, 75.* Ref: T Holbrook

	1	2	3	4	5	6	7	8	9	10	11	12
City	Waugh	Newman	Williams B	Moyes	MacPhail	Fitzpatrick	Marshall	Curle	Morgan	Walsh	Neville*	Riley
Wigan	*Tunks*	*Hamilton*	*Knowles*	*Cook*	*Cribley*	*Holden*	*Hilditch*	*Thompson*	*Campbell*	*Jewell*	*Griffiths*	

All zip goes out of the City side with Neville's 42nd-min departure with a broken leg following Andy Holden's crunching tackle. Walsh heads City in front, but Bobby Campbell nets with a fierce shot and an easy header, after Mark Hilditch had turned in a rebound to bring Wigan level.

---

25 — H CHESTERFIELD — 31/1 — Att 6,426 — Pos 8 — Pt 39 — W 1-0 (H-T 0-0)

Scorers, Times, Referees: Walsh 55. Ref: A Gunn

	1	2	3	4	5	6	7	8	9	10	11	12
City	Waugh	Curle	Williams B	Moyes	MacPhail*	Newman	Marshall	Morgan	Fitzpatrick	Walsh	Owen	Riley
Chesterfield	*Marples*	*Hewitt*	*Rogers*	*Bellamy*	*Bloomer*	*Reid*	*Coyle*	*Airey*	*Caldwell*	*Henderson*	*Greaves**	*Bernadeau*

An inept display against a side crushed 0-3 by lowly Rochdale in the Freight Rover Trophy just four days ago cannot be explained away by an icy pitch. Managing only two shots on target in one of the worst games in living memory. City secure victory with Walsh's low 15-yard drive.

---

26 — H DONCASTER — 7/2 — Att 8,982 — Pos 7 — Pt 42 — W 5-0 (H-T 2-0)

Scorers, Times, Referees: Walsh 17, 68, 88, Owen 34, Newman 47. Ref: J Ireland

	1	2	3	4	5	6	7	8	9	10	11	12
City	Waugh	Newman	Williams B	Moyes	MacPhail	Curle	Owen	Fitzpatrick*	Morgan	Walsh	Jordan	Tanner
Doncaster	*Rhodes*	*Stead*	*Brown**	*Redfearn*	*Humphries*	*Cusack*	*Russell*	*Miller*	*Clayton*	*Burke*	*Holmes*	*Gaynor*

Jordan breathes new life into City's season with a memorable debut that inspires everyone around him. Walsh nets his fourth career hat-trick, his first for City all shot in with typical aplomb, whilst a similar finish by Owen and a header from Newman completes City's nap hand.

---

27 — A CARLISLE — 14/2 — Att 2,500 — Pos 5 — Pt 45 — W 2-1 (H-T 2-0)

Scorers, Times, Referees: Morgan 9, Jordan 30. *McGarvey 66p.* Ref: P Harrison

	1	2	3	4	5	6	7	8	9	10	11	12
City	Waugh	Llewellyn	Williams B	Moyes	Moyes	Morgan	Owen	Jordan	Morgan	Walsh	Newman	Paskett
Carlisle	*Nixon*	*Lomax*	*Gorman*	*Haigh*	*Wright**	*Halsall*	*Baker*	*Cooke*	*McGarvey*	*Bishop*	*Worrall*	*Poskett*

Morgan strikes the sweetest of right-foot volleys to set City on course for their third successive League win. Jordan heads in to double the advantage, but Carlisle (nine shots on target to City's four) take control after Williams concedes the spot-kick for bringing down John Cooke.

---

28 — H BOURNEMOUTH — 21/2 — Att 14,538 — Pos 4 — Pt 48 — W 2-0 (H-T 1-0)

Scorers, Times, Referees: Newson 29 (og), Owen 77p. Ref: P Wright

	1	2	3	4	5	6	7	8	9	10	11	12
City	Waugh	Newman	Williams B	Curle	Llewellyn	Morgan	Owen	Galliers	Morgan	Walsh	Jordan	Heffernan
Bournemouth	*Peyton*	*Newson*	*Morrell*	*O'Connor*	*Williams*	*Whitlock*	*O'Driscoll*	*Pulis*	*Aylott*	*Richards**	*Cooke*	

The tension is palpable as City show they now have the steel, as well as the flair, to win promotion. A significant victory over the impressive Cherries comes courtesy of Mark Newson's errors, as he heads Llewellyn's free-kick into his own net, then fells Owen to concede the penalty.

---

29 — A DARLINGTON — 28/2 — Att 2,044 — Pos 7 — Pt 49 — D 0-0 (H-T 0-0)

Scorers, Times, Referees: Ref: K Walmsley

	1	2	3	4	5	6	7	8	9	10	11	12
City	Waugh	Newman	Williams B	Moyes	Llewellyn	Curle	Owen	Fitzpatrick	Morgan	Walsh	Jordan	Davis
Darlington	*Astbury*	*Evans*	*Morgan**	*Hine*	*Lloyd*	*Robinson*	*Tupling*	*Ward*	*Currie*	*MacDonald*	*Riley*	*Davis*

Cooper says 'the result defies belief' as City fail to exploit their complete dominance. A string of brilliant Mike Astbury saves, Phil Lloyd's goal-line clearance, and Walsh twice shooting against the woodwork, sums up City's frustration as the visitors fail to get a shot on target.

---

30 — H BLACKPOOL — 3/3 — Att 10,980 — Pos 5 — Pt 52 — W 3-1 (H-T 3-1)

Scorers, Times, Referees: Walsh 26, Newman 36, Fitzpatrick 43. *Stewart 34.* Ref: K Baker

	1	2	3	4	5	6	7	8	9	10	11	12
City	Waugh	Newman	Williams B	Moyes	Llewellyn	Curle	Owen	Fitzpatrick	Morgan	Walsh	Jordan	Riley
Blackpool	*Siddall*	*Matthews*	*McAteer*	*Law*	*Methven*	*Deary*	*Davies*	*Thomson*	*Stewart*	*Madden*	*Taylor*	

The deadlock breaking 30-yard bender that leaves Barry Siddall motionless in the Open End goal is described by Walsh as the best free-kick he has ever taken. Paul Stewart skilfully shoots in Blackpool's equaliser, but Newman restores City's advantage by forcing in Walsh's header.

---

31 — A MIDDLESBROUGH — 7/3 — Att 10,220 — Pos 5 — Pt 52 — L 0-1 (H-T 0-1)

Scorers, Times, Referees: *Mowbray 35.* Ref: D Hutchinson

	1	2	3	4	5	6	7	8	9	10	11	12
City	Waugh	Newman	Williams B	Moyes	Llewellyn	Curle	Owen	Fitzpatrick*	Morgan	Walsh	Jordan!	Riley
Middlesbrough	*Pears*	*Coyle*	*Cooper*	*Mowbray*	*Parkinson*	*Kernaghan*	*Slaven*	*Stephens*	*Hamilton*	*Gill*	*Hodgson!*	

An ill-tempered battle with Jordan's 70th-min sending off being followed 13 mins later by the dismissal of David Hogdson for kicking Curle in the stomach. Owen spurns City's best chance of equalising Tony Mowbray's header, shooting wide from the spot just before half-time.

---

32 — H NEWPORT — 14/3 — Att 9,137 — Pos 5 — Pt 55 — W 4-0 (H-T 2-0)

Scorers, Times, Referees: Morgan 23, Jordan 26, Newman 84 [Williams 87pl]. Ref: T Ward

	1	2	3	4	5	6	7	8	9	10	11	12
City	Waugh	Newman	Williams B	Moyes	Llewellyn	Curle	Owen	Tanner	Morgan	Walsh*	Jordan	Marshall
Newport	*Freestone*	*Jones L*	*Lewis*	*Berry*	*Carter**	*Compton*	*Giles*	*Gibbins*	*Stanforth*	*Mills*	*Millett*	*Mardenboro'*

Another goal to remember as Newman brightens up a dull second half with a curving right-foot volley that finds the corner of the Covered End net. Williams completes the scoring with his first City pen after his short centre had struck Newport player-manager John Lewis on the arm.

---

33 — A BRENTFORD — 17/3 — Att 4,051 — Pos 6 — Pt 56 — D 1-1 (H-T 1-0)

Scorers, Times, Referees: Owen 27. *Maddy 46.* Ref: M Bodenham

	1	2	3	4	5	6	7	8	9	10	11	12
City	Waugh	Newman	Williams B	Moyes	Llewellyn	Curle	Owen	Tanner!	Morgan	Walsh	Jordan	Riley
Brentford	*Phillips*	*Perryman*	*Murray*	*Millen*	*Droy*	*Maddy*	*Carroll*	*Sinton*	*Cooke*	*Stevens*	*Turner*	

City are lucky to survive Tanner's 85th-minute dismissal for his attempt to butt Paul Maddy. In the second half it is only desperate defending and good luck that keeps Brentford at bay, after Maddy's shot on the turn had levelled Owen's close-range opener from Jordan's astute header.

---

34 — A YORK — 21/3 — Att 2,874 — Pos 6 — Pt 57 — D 1-1 (H-T 0-1)

Scorers, Times, Referees: Tanner 48. *Canham 3.* Ref: A Robinson

	1	2	3	4	5	6	7	8	9	10	11	12
City	Waugh	Newman	Williams B	Moyes	Llewellyn	Curle*	Owen	Tanner	Morgan	Walsh	Riley	Marshall
York	*Leaning*	*McKenzie*	*Senior*	*Pickering*	*McAughtrie*	*Haslegrave*	*Ford*	*Gabbiadini**	*Sbragia*	*Walwyn*	*Canham*	*Hood*

Though Owen is robbed of a winner by a linesman failing to note that his 53rd-minute shot is well over the line before Tony Canham hooks clear, City's inept performance scarcely deserves the point earned by Tanner's speculative 30-yarder after Canham had headed York in front.

Season fixtures 35–46 (match-by-match summary grid). Reading order: match no., venue, date, opponents; City line-up (top) with opposition line-up (italic, below); scorers; referee; result and half-time score; attendance; league position; and running points.

35 — H CHESTER, 28/3 — 1-0 (0-0) — W
City: Waugh, Newman, Williams B, Moyes, Llewellyn, Fitzpatrick, Owen, Tanner, Morgan, Walsh, Riley
Chester: Stewart, Greenough, Woodthorpe, Fazackerley, Abel, Butler*, Kelly, Barrow, Rimmer, Houghton, Graham, Croft
Morgan 70. Ref: D Vickers. Att 8,230 — Pos 6 (15) — Pts 60
"Waugh preserves City's points by stopping Ricky Greenough's curler in the dying mins, as well keeping his side in the game midway through the second half with the save of the season from Graham Abel's perfectly-struck shot. Morgan out-jumps his marker to head in City's winner."

36 — A BURY, 31/3 — 2-1 (2-1) — W
City: Waugh, Newman, Williams B, Moyes, Llewellyn, Fitzpatrick, Owen*, Honor, Morgan, Walsh, Riley
Bury: Farnworth, Hill, Fairbrother, Hart, Valentine, Higgins, Harris*, Hoyland, Greenwood, McIlroy, Lee, Marshall, Robinson L
Morgan 13, Owen 37; Greenwood 19. Ref: N Ashley. Att 2,200 — Pos 5 (13) — Pts 63
"City survive a second-half onslaught to take the points earned by Morgan's headed opener, and Owen's dream volley, after Greenwood's power header had brought the Shakers level. 'A match of First Division standard' says Sammy McIlroy who inspires a skilful Bury side."

37 — H FULHAM, 4/4 — 0-0 (0-0) — D
City: Waugh, Newman, Williams B, MacPhail, Llewellyn, Fitzpatrick*, Owen, Harvey, Morgan, Walsh, Jordan
Fulham: Vaughan, Parker, Carr, Lewington, Oakes, Hicks, Barnett, Hopkins, Coney, Pike, Elkins, Honor
Ref: J Bray. Att 8,551 — Pos 5 (20) — Pts 64
"Fulham show great resolve following a 0-6 humiliation at the hands of Port Vale in their previous game. City's promotion drive comes off the rails as they adapt poorly to the conditions posed by the incessant rain. Walsh fails to connect with their one real chance just four yards out."

38 — A MANSFIELD, 11/4 — 0-2 (0-0) — L
City: Waugh, Newman, Williams B, Moyes, Llewellyn, MacPhail, Owen, Harvey, Morgan, Walsh, Jordan
Mansfield: Hitchcock, Graham, Kenworthy, Lowery, Foster, Pollard, Kent, Danskin*, Stringfellow, Cassells, Kearney, Anderson
Kearney 68p, 75. Ref: J Watson. Att 2,888 — Pos 7 (9) — Pts 64
"City hit a new low at windswept Field Mill, where the Mansfield goalie is untroubled until five minutes from time. MacPhail insists that the ball hits his chest for the penalty, but there is no doubt that his deflection of a Keith Cassells centre sets up Mark Kearney's headed second."

39 — A BRISTOL ROV, 18/4 — 0-0 (0-0) — D
City: Waugh, Newman, Williams B, Moyes, Llewellyn, MacPhail, Marshall, Galliers, Morgan, Walsh, Jordan
Bristol Rov: Bradshaw, Jones, Rushbury, Cawley, Twentyman, Tanner, Purnell, Penrice, Turner*, Meacham, Hibbitt, Scales
Ref: J Key. Att 4,695 — Pos 7 (21) — Pts 65
"Those that stay away get it right as the lowest-ever attendance for a Bristol derby in the League watches this passionless encounter. The only excitement comes just before the end when Jeff Meacham's shot is disallowed as Gary Penrice lets the ball run over the line before crossing."

40 — H PORT VALE, 20/4 — 1-0 (1-0) — W
City: Waugh, Newman, Williams B, Moyes, Llewellyn, MacPhail, Owen, Galliers, Harvey, Morgan, Walsh, Riley
Port Vale: Williams A, Webb, Bromage, Walker, Hazell, Sproson, Smith, Earle, Jones*, Beckford, Maguire, Bowden
Walsh 10. Ref: M Dimblebee. Att 8,669 — Pos 7 (13) — Pts 68
"After Walsh cleverly makes space in a crowded penalty area before curling a left-footer past Alex Williams, City often look second best against Vale. It takes skipper Williams' last ditch 79th-minute challenge on the clean through John Bowden to save the points for City."

41 — H GILLINGHAM, 22/4 — 2-0 (2-0) — W
City: Waugh, Newman, Williams B, Moyes, Llewellyn, MacPhail, Owen, Galliers, Riley, Morgan, Marshall
Gillingham: Kite, Haylock, Pearce, Berry, Weatherly, Gernon, Robinson, Shearer, Lovell*, Elsey, Cascarino, Pritchard
Williams 19p, Marshall 32. Ref: H King. Att 10,260 — Pos 6 (7) — Pts 71
"The Gills dispute Williams' penalty as Irvin Gernon is caught out by Riley's turn, but there is no argument about City's early superiority against promotion rivals. Marshall gives Paul Haylock a nightmare opening, and the lively winger's firm header doubles City's advantage."

42 — A BOLTON, 25/4 — 0-0 (0-0) — D
City: Waugh, Newman, Williams B, Moyes, Llewellyn, MacPhail, Owen*, Galliers, Riley, Morgan, Marshall, Jordan
Bolton: Felgate, Neal, Scott, Joyce, Sutton, Came, Caldwell, Brookman, Elliott, Hartford, Gavin*, Jordan, Stevens, Curle
Ref: M Robinson. Att 4,414 — Pos 6 (19) — Pts 72
"City's promotion quest is likely to end in failure because of an unexpected inability to hit the back of the net. Another Waugh clean sheet should have been enough to ensure victory against relegation-haunted Bolton, but despite constant pressure City only create two good chances."

43 — H BRENTFORD, 28/4 — 0-2 (0-2) — L
City: Waugh, Newman, Williams B, Moyes, Llewellyn, MacPhail, Marshall, Galliers, Riley, Morgan, Walsh*, Curle
Brentford: Phillips, Joseph, Millen, Droy*, Perryman, Carroll, Sinton, Cooke, Blissett, Turner, Nogan, Curle
Carroll 73, Blissett 86. Ref: G Ashby. Att 9,050 — Pos 7 (11) — Pts 72
"A nightmare for City as Steve Perryman's well-organised side notch up a deserved success. Robbie Carroll's well-struck drive puts the Bees ahead, and then, shortly after Jordan heads against the bar, Gary Blissett puts the game beyond City's grasp by taking the ball round Waugh."

44 — H NOTTS CO, 2/5 — 3-1 (1-1) — W
City: Waugh, Newman, Williams B, Moyes, Llewellyn, MacPhail, Owen, Galliers, Morgan, Marshall, Jordan
Notts Co: Leonard, Smalley, Davis, Kevan, Hunt, Benjamin*, McParland, Goodwin, Young, Campbell, Thompson, Clarke
Marshall 30, Jordan 73, Morgan 82; McParland 44. Ref: K Burge. Att 9,189 — Pos 5 (6) — Pts 75
"Aggrieved City are roused from their slumbers just after the break when their penalty appeals, after Marshall is tripped by Mike Leonard, fall on deaf ears. Jordan puts them ahead with a brilliant diving header, and then slips a well-weighted pass for Morgan to neatly slot the ball in."

45 — A WALSALL, 4/5 — 1-1 (1-1) — D
City: Waugh, Newman, Williams B, Moyes, Llewellyn, MacPhail, Owen, Galliers, Morgan, Marshall*, Jordan, Curle
Walsall: Barber, Taylor, Mower, Shakespeare, Forbes, Hart, Childs, Cross, Kelly, Christie, Hawker
Morgan 88; Kelly 74. Ref: W Flood. Att 7,683 — Pos 5 (8) — Pts 76
"With Marshall again being denied a clear penalty, as well as Fred Barber's heroics, it takes Morgan's late header to keep play-off hopes on course. Walsall go ahead in a rare breakaway when David Kelly puts in a shot that loops over Waugh, after taking a deflection off of Williams."

46 — H SWINDON, 9/5 — 1-1 (1-0) — D
City: Waugh, Newman, Williams B*, Moyes, Llewellyn, MacPhail, Owen, Galliers, Morgan, Marshall, Jordan, Curle
Swindon: Digby, Hockaday, King, Jones, Parkin, Calderwood, Bamber, Kamara, Quinn*, Coyne, Berry, Ramsey
Morgan 12; Coyne 66. Ref: D Reeves. Att 19,201 — Pos 6 (3) — Pts 77
"City's ambitions are in tatters as Owen's late penalty miss allows Gillingham (1-0 winners over Bolton) to oust them from a play-off place. Marshall hits the bar before Peter Coyne's mis-hit volley brings Swindon level. Morgan's glancing header gets City off to a good start, then..."

Average 9,441 | Home 9,441 | Away 4,151

TODAY DIVISION 3 (CUP-TIES) — SEASON 1986-87

Manager: Terry Cooper

Littlewoods Cup

	V	Opponent	Att		F-A	H-T	Scorers, Times, and Referees
1:1	A	BOURNEMOUTH	2,631	W	1-0	0-0	Walsh 46 — Ref: N Butler

1	2	3	4	5	6	7	8	9	10	11	subs used
Waugh	Llewellyn	Newman	Curle	Moyes	Riley	Owen	Hutchinson	Harle	Walsh	Hamson	
Peyton	*Pulis*	*Morrell*	*Savage*	*Heffernan*	*Whitlock*	*O'Driscoll*	*Howlett*	*Aylott*	*Richards*	*Puckett*	

Walsh's magnificent volley, struck on the turn, from the edge of the penalty area draws the acclaim, but City's defence also deserve credit for responding to the Bury game criticism with a clean sheet. Bournemouth manage five shots on target, whilst City are only able to muster two.

	V	Opponent	Att		F-A	H-T	Scorers, Times, and Referees
1:2	H	BOURNEMOUTH	4,776	D	1-1	0-0 aet	Riley 97 / Aylott 60 — Ref: H King (City won 2-1 on aggregate)

1	2	3	4	5	6	7	8	9	10	11	subs used
Waugh	Llewellyn	Newman*	Curle	Moyes	Riley	Owen	Hutchinson	Harle*	Walsh	Hamson^	Fitzpat'k/Marshall
Peyton	*Pulis*	*Morrell*	*Heffernan*	*Whitlock*	*Savage*	*O'Driscoll*	*Howlett*	*Aylott*	*Richards*	*Puckett*	*Lewis*

With yesterday's death of Ivor Guy, many fans think that something akin to his 70-yarder at Ninian Park during the war will be necessary to crack Bournemouth's resistance. In the event however Riley saves City's blushes with a close-in volley from Owen's right-wing cross.

	V	Opponent	Att		F-A	H-T	Scorers, Times, and Referees
2:1	H	SHEFFIELD UTD	8,366	D	2-2	1-2	Neville 15, Walsh 87p / Morris 33p, Foley 39 — Ref: L Shapter

1	2	3	4	5	6	7	8	9	10	11	subs used
Waugh	Llewellyn	Williams B	Curle	Moyes	Riley*	Owen	Hutchinson	Neville	Walsh	Fitzpatrick	Marshall
Burridge	*Barnsley*	*Pike*	*Arnott*	*Stancliffe*	*Smith*	*Morris*	*Frain*	*Dempsey*	*Foley*	*Beagrie*^	*Withe*

A thrilling cup-tie that lives up to all expectations as slick Sheffield outplay City in the first half, yet at the end they are hanging on for dear life. Both teams complain about harshly-awarded penalties, after Neville's 30-yard chip over a stranded John Burridge had put City ahead.

	V	Opponent	Att		F-A	H-T	Scorers, Times, and Referees
2:2	A	SHEFFIELD UTD	5,587	L	0-3	0-1	Foley 33, Morris 57, Dempsey 86 — Ref: H Taylor (City lost 2-5 on aggregate)

1	2	3	4	5	6	7	8	9	10	11	subs used
Waugh	Llewellyn	Williams B	Curle	Moyes	Hamson	Owen	Hutchinson*	Harle^	Walsh	Neville	Newman/Withy
Burridge	*Barnsley*	*Pike*	*Dempsey*	*Stancliffe*	*Eckhardt*^	*Morris*	*Frain*	*Withe*^	*Foley*	*Beagrie*	*Wigley/Smith*

United's Colin Morris, best man at Waugh's wedding, runs through onto Steve Foley's pass to slot in the killer goal as City fail to match their 1st leg form. United's other goals are two long-range efforts, Foley's 22-yard left-foot volley, and Mark Dempsey's angled drive from 25 yards.

FA Cup

	V	Opponent	Att		F-A	H-T	Scorers, Times, and Referees
1	H	VS RUGBY	7,069	W	3-1	0-0	Marshall 74, Hutchinson 82, Walsh 89 / Lane 57p — Ref: K Cooper

1	2	3	4	5	6	7	8	9	10	11	subs used
Waugh	Newman	Williams B	Moyes	MacPhail	Riley	Hamson*	Hutchinson	Harle	Walsh	Withey	Marshall
Marsden	*Potter*	*Ferns*	*Lane*	*Geddes**	*Martin*	*Ingram*	*Flannagan*	*Morris*	*Conway*	*Draper*	*Gardener*

Keith Cooper's excellent application of the advantage rule prevents impressive VS Rugby claiming the greatest result of their 30-year history. City's blushes are saved as the referee waves play on when Marshall rides a scything tackle to hammer a 25-yard swerver past Ian Marsden.

	V	Opponent	Att		F-A	H-T	Scorers, Times, and Referees
2	H	BATH CITY	10,053	D	1-1	0-0	Neville 59 / Bodin 88 — Ref: A Seville

1	2	3	4	5	6	7	8	9	10	11	subs used
Waugh	Newman	Williams B	Moyes	MacPhail	Marshall	Owen	Hutchinson	Fitzpatrick	Walsh	Neville	Stevens/Shaw
Mogg	*England*	*Bodin*	*Sherwood*	*Fulbrook*	*Barton*	*O'Donnell*	*Adams**	*Grimshaw*	*Crawford**	*Payne*	

A dull local derby in which City, performing in new kit with a white hoop across their red jersey, have the edge. Neville injects some life into the proceedings by hammering the ball past David Mogg, but Paul Bodin replies with a fine volley (Bath's only shot on target) to earn a replay.

	V	Opponent	Att		F-A	H-T	Scorers, Times, and Referees
2R	A	BATH CITY	9,058	W	3-0	1-0	Owen 34p, 86, Neville 80 — Ref: A Seville

1	2	3	4	5	6	7	8	9	10	11	subs used
Waugh	Newman	Williams B	Moyes	MacPhail	Marshall	Owen	Hutchinson	Fitzpatrick	Walsh	Neville	Shaw
Mogg	*England*	*Sherwood*	*Stevens*	*Fulbrook*	*Barton*	*O'Donnell*	*Adams**	*Grimshaw*	*Bodin*	*Payne*	

Marshall runs Bath ragged in this richly entertaining replay. After David Mogg is adjudged to have tripped Walsh for the spot-kick opener, City go on to a deserved success with Neville side-footing in Marshall's cross, and Owen's shot being deflected into the net off Paul Stevens.

	V	Opponent	Att		F-A	H-T	Scorers, Times, and Referees
3	H	PLYMOUTH	16,943	D	1-1	0-0	Riley 56 / Summerfield 49 — Ref: J Martin

1	2	3	4	5	6	7	8	9	10	11	subs used
Waugh	Newman	Williams B	Moyes	MacPhail	Riley	Riley	Llewellyn	Fitzpatrick	Walsh	Withey	Brimacombe
Crudgington	*Nisbet*	*Cooper L*	*Goodyear*	*McElhinney**	*Matthews*	*Hodges*	*Coughlin*	*Tynan*	*Summerfield*	*Nelson*	

Fitzpatrick's fluffed header at the end of a second half of rousing action, deprives City of Cup glory. In front of a crowd which appears to be much larger than the official figure of 16,943. Riley shoots in City's leveller, after Kevin Summerfield's angled drive had put Argyle in front.

	V	Opponent	Att		F-A	H-T	Scorers, Times, and Referees
3R	A	PLYMOUTH	14,142	L	1-3	0-0 aet	Marshall 108 / Summerfield 94, Nelson 109, Tynan 118 — Ref: R Gifford

1	2	3	4	5	6	7	8	9	10	11	subs used
Waugh	Newman	Williams B	Moyes	MacPhail	Tanner*	Riley	Llewellyn	Fitzpatrick	Walsh	Withey	Bur'ws/Row'm
Crudgington	*Nisbet*	*Uzzell*	*Goodyear*	*McElhinney**	*Matthews**	*Hodges*	*Coughlin*	*Tynan*	*Summerfield*	*Nelson*	

After Kevin Summerfield's lashed-in opener, Marshall's slammed-in atonement for shooting wide from a glorious opportunity in the dying minutes of normal time, is in vain as Waugh's error in allowing a tame Gary Nelson shot to slide under his body puts City out of the Cup.

		P	Home						Away					Pts
			W	D	L	F	A	W	D	L	F	A	
1	Bournemouth	46	19	3	1	44	14	10	7	6	32	26	97
2	Middlesbro	46	16	5	2	38	11	12	5	6	29	19	94
3	Swindon *	46	14	5	4	37	19	11	7	5	40	28	87
4	Wigan	46	15	3	3	47	26	10	5	8	36	34	85
5	Gillingham	46	16	5	2	42	14	7	4	12	23	34	78
6	BRISTOL CITY	46	14	6	3	42	15	7	8	8	21	21	77
7	Notts Co	46	14	6	3	52	24	7	7	9	25	32	76
8	Walsall	46	16	4	3	50	27	6	5	12	30	40	75
9	Blackpool	46	11	7	5	35	20	9	9	9	39	39	64
10	Mansfield	46	9	9	5	30	23	6	7	10	22	32	61
11	Brentford	46	9	7	7	39	32	6	8	9	25	34	60
12	Port Vale	46	8	6	9	43	36	7	6	10	33	34	57
13	Doncaster	46	11	8	4	32	19	3	7	13	24	43	57
14	Rotherham	46	10	6	7	29	28	5	6	12	19	34	57
15	Chester	46	7	9	7	32	28	6	8	9	29	31	56
16	Bury	46	9	7	7	30	26	5	6	12	24	34	55
17	Chesterfield	46	11	5	7	36	33	2	10	11	20	36	54
18	Fulham	46	8	8	7	35	41	4	9	10	24	36	53
19	Bristol Rov	46	7	8	8	26	29	6	4	13	23	46	51
20	York	46	11	8	4	34	29	1	5	17	21	50	49
21	Bolton **	46	8	5	10	29	26	2	10	11	17	32	45
22	Carlisle	46	7	5	11	26	35	3	3	17	13	43	38
23	Darlington	46	6	10	7	25	28	1	6	16	20	49	37
24	Newport	46	4	9	10	26	34	4	4	15	23	52	37
		1104	260	156	136	859	612	136	156	260	612	859	1500

* promoted
after play-offs
** relegated
after play-offs

	Appearances						Goals			
	Lge	Sub	LC	Sub	FAC	Sub	Lge	LC	FAC	Tot
Curle, Keith	24	4	1	1	4		2			2
Fitzpatrick, Paul	18	1	1		4					
Galliers, Steve	9									
Harle, David	15		3		1		2			2
Hamson, Gary	12		3		1		2			2
Harvey, Jimmy	2									
Honor, Chris	1	1								
Hutchinson, Bobby	18	1	4		3		1	1		2
Jordan, Joe	19						3			3
Llewellyn, Andy	30	1	4		2		1			1
MacPhail, John	26				5					
Marshall, Gary	18	6		2	3	2	2		2	4
Morgan, Trevor	19						7			7
Moyes, David	41		4		5		3			3
Neville, Steve	19	1	2		4		8	1	2	11
Newman, Rob	43	2	2	1	5		6			6
Owen, Gordon	34	1	4		2		5		2	7
Riley, Glyn	22	6	3		3		1	1	1	3
Rogers, Lee	3									
Tanner, Mike	4	1			1					
Walsh, Alan	41		4		5		16	2	1	19
Waugh, Keith	46		4		5					
Williams, Brian	41	2	2		5		2			2
Withey, Graham	1	1			1	1	1			1
(own-goals)							1			1
24 players used	506	26	44	5	55	2	63	4	9	76

Odds & ends

Double wins: (4) Chesterfield, Carlisle, Chester, Newport.
Double losses: (1) Rotherham.

Won from behind: (3) Swindon (a), Bolton (h), Walsall (h).
Lost from in front: (1) Wigan (a).

High spots: Superb game with Bolton at Ashton Gate on 20 December.
Jordan's debut against Doncaster on 7 February.
Newman's volley against Newport at Ashton Gate on 14 March.
Beating Bristol Rov 3-0 in the Freight Rover Trophy on 16 December.
Reaching Wembley for the second consecutive year.

Low spots: Gary Smart's superb strike that brings Bristol Rov their victory at Ashton Gate on 1 January.
Failure to beat Swindon on 9 May costing City a Play-Off place.
Losing the Freight Rover Trophy Final to Mansfield in the first ever penalty shoot-out at Wembley Stadium.

Player of the year: Rob Newman.
Ever-presents: Keith Waugh.
Hat-tricks: (1) Alan Walsh.
Leading scorer: Alan Walsh (19).

BARCLAYS LEAGUE DIVISION 3 — Manager: Cooper ⇨ Joe Jordan — SEASON 1987-88

Column key: No | Date | Att | Pos | Pt | F-A | H-T | Scorers, Times, and Referees | 1 | 2 | 3 | 4 | 5 | 6 | 7 | 8 | 9 | 10 | 11 | subs used
(Opponent line-ups shown in *italics*.)

---

1. A — 15/8 — MANSFIELD
Att 5,441 | Pt: L, 0 | F-A 0-2 | H-T 0-2
Scorers: Cassells 9, Stringfellow 20 — Ref: J McAuley

	1	2	3	4	5	6	7	8	9	10	11	subs used
City	Waugh	Llewellyn	Bromage	Moyes	Newman	Tanner	Marshall	Fitzpatrick*	Caldwell*	Walsh	Jordan	Owen/Harvey
Mansfield	*Hitchcock*	*Graham*	*Kearney*	*Lowery*	*Foster*	*Coleman*	*Kent*	*Hodges**	*Stringfellow*	*Cassells*	*Chambers*	

City lack the sparkle and pace to live up to their pre-match boast to avenge their Wembley defeat. After Keith Cassells latches onto a through ball to fire the Stags in front, his mis-hit shot catches City's defence flat-footed and Ian Stringfellow is on hand to tuck away an easy chance.

---

2. H — 22/8 — PRESTON
Att 7,655 | Pt: W, 3 | F-A 3-1 | H-T 1-0
Scorers: Owen 12, 53, Walsh 49p — *Brazil 82* — Ref: D Vickers

	1	2	3	4	5	6	7	8	9	10	11	subs used
City	Waugh	Llewellyn	Bromage	Moyes	Newman	Tanner	Marshall	Fitzpatrick	Owen	Walsh	Jordan	Worthgton*/Wrightson
Preston	*Brown*	*Branagan**	*Bennett*	*Atkins*	*Jones*	*Allardyce*	*Miller*	*Swann*	*Lowery*	*Brazil*	*Rathbone**	

Owen's skill tears North End apart after an early slice of luck when his free-kick is cruelly deflected past David Brown. Jordan's exquisite pass sets up Walsh's pen after Fitzpatrick is sent sprawling, but failure of City's notorious offside trap allows Gary Brazil to head in for Preston.

---

3. A — 29/8 — BRENTFORD
Att 4,328 | Pos 7 (*21*) | Pt: W, 6 | F-A 2-0 | H-T 0-0
Scorers: Newman 60p, Owen 85 — Ref: H King

	1	2	3	4	5	6	7	8	9	10	11	subs used
City	Waugh	Llewellyn	Bromage	Moyes	Newman	Tanner	Neville	Fitzpatrick	Owen	Walsh	Jordan	
Brentford	*Phillips*	*Joseph*	*Murray*	*Millen*	*Lee*	*Feeley*	*Smith*	*Sinton*	*Cooke*	*Blissett*	*Carroll**	*Perryman*

The result is better than the performance, but at least City improve on their dreadfully boring first-half display. Neville's clip by Colin Lee allows Newman to send Gary Phillips the wrong way from the spot, before Owen side-foot's in Llewellyn's low cross to make victory secure.

---

4. H — 31/8 — PORT VALE
Att 8,716 | Pos 3 (*13*) | Pt: W, 9 | F-A 1-0 | H-T 0-0
Scorers: Neville 89 — Ref: P Don

	1	2	3	4	5	6	7	8	9	10	11	subs used
City	Waugh	Llewellyn	Bromage	Moyes	Newman	Tanner	Marshall*	Fitzpatrick	Owen	Walsh*	Jordan	Neville/Caldwell
Port Vale	*Williams*	*Webb*	*Pearson*	*Banks**	*Hazell*	*Sproson*	*Maguire*	*Earle*	*Jones*	*Beckford*	*Hamson**	*Finney/Hooper*

Whilst Vale dominate the proceedings for last year, Andy Jones' 39th-minute header against the bar is the nearest they come to gaining any reward. Neville capitalises on Bob Hazell's one mistake to volley in City's late steal past Alex Williams from the edge of the penalty area.

---

5. A — 5/9 — BURY
Att 2,376 | Pos 4 (*9*) | Pt: D, 10 | F-A 1-1 | H-T 1-1
Scorers: Neville 32 — *Hoyland 10* — Ref: F Roberts

	1	2	3	4	5	6	7	8	9	10	11	subs used
City	Waugh	Llewellyn	Bromage	Moyes	Newman	Tanner	Neville	Fitzpatrick	Owen	Walsh	Jordan	
Bury	*Hughes*	*Hill*	*Pashley*	*Hoyland*	*Valentine*	*Hart*	*Lee*	*Greenwood**	*Taylor*	*McIlroy*	*Brotherston*	*Colville/Higgins*

City are on the rack until Jordan's class turn and pass sets-up Neville to shoot a leveller past Phil Hughes. Unfortunately Jordan heads wide in front of an open goal on 75 minutes, and Bury hang onto a point gained by Jamie Hoyland's 25-yard opener that took a deflection off Newman.

---

6. H — 12/9 — BRISTOL ROV
Att 14,746 | Pos 7 (*14*) | Pt: D, 11 | F-A 3-3 | H-T 1-1
Scorers: Walsh 38, Fitzpatrick 65, Moyes 73 — *Jones 9, Reece 58, Holloway 83* — Ref: K Barratt

	1	2	3	4	5	6	7	8	9	10	11	subs used
City	Waugh	Llewellyn	Bromage	Moyes	Newman	Galliers	Marshall	Fitzpatrick	Owen	Walsh	Jordan	
Bristol Rov	*Carter*	*Alexander*	*Tanner*	*Hibbitt*	*Twentyman*	*Jones*	*Holloway*	*Reece*	*White*	*Penrice*	*Purnell*	

Six of the best in a derby-day spectacular as City have cause to rue three other efforts that are disallowed. Vaughan Jones shoots Rovers ahead from a free-kick, but Marshall's right-wing scamper and perfect cross sets up Walsh to head in City's impressive equaliser at the far post.

---

7. A — 15/9 — WALSALL
Att 6,425 | Pos 7 (*3*) | Pt: D, 12 | F-A 1-1 | H-T 0-0
Scorers: Llewellyn 81 — *Kelly 86* — Ref: H Taylor

	1	2	3	4	5	6	7	8	9	10	11	subs used
City	Waugh	Llewellyn	Bromage	Moyes	Newman	Galliers	Owen	Fitzpatrick	Owen	Walsh	Jordan	
Walsall	*Barber*	*Dornan*	*Taylor*	*Shakespeare*	*Forbes*	*Hart*	*Goodwin*	*Cross*	*Kelly*	*Christie*	*Jones P*	

City should have been able to hold onto the lead that Llewellyn gives them with a spectacular 35-yard left-foot shot that dips perfectly into the top corner of Fred Barber's net. Unfortunately David Kelly whips inside of Bromage to notch Walsall's leveller with a superb low cross-shot.

---

8. A — 19/9 — NOTTS CO
Att 5,705 | Pos 5 (*3*) | Pt: W, 15 | F-A 1-0 | H-T 0-0
Scorers: Newman 63p — Ref: M Bailey

	1	2	3	4	5	6	7	8	9	10	11	subs used
City	Waugh	Llewellyn	Bromage	Moyes	Newman	Galliers	Neville	Fitzpatrick	Owen	Walsh	Jordan	Thompson
Notts Co	*Leonard*	*Smalley*	*Fairclough*	*Kevan*	*Yates*	*Hart*	*Mills*	*McParland*	*Birtles*	*Pike*	*Lund**	

City have to thank their defence for a determined performance at Meadow Lane to keep Notts at bay. Newman's penalty clinches the points, following Paul Hart's curtailment of Owen's scamper through County's rearguard, and thereafter City have much the better of the contest.

---

9. A — 26/9 — GILLINGHAM
Att 10,080 | Pos 6 (*5*) | Pt: D, 16 | F-A 3-3 | H-T 1-2
Scorers: Owen 27, 66, Fitzpatrick 60 — *Lovell 9, Smith 14, Elsey 61* — Ref: P Wright

	1	2	3	4	5	6	7	8	9	10	11	subs used
City	Waugh	Llewellyn	Bromage	Moyes	Newman	Galliers	Neville	Fitzpatrick	Owen*	Walsh	Jordan*	Smith D
Gillingham	*Kite*	*Haylock*	*Pearce*	*Quow*	*West*	*Greenall*	*Pritchard*	*Shearer**	*Lovell**	*Pike*	*Elsey!*	*Berry/Eves*

Karl Elsey's header is the best goal of this exciting game, but shortly after he was sent off for a minor brush with Fitzpatrick. The Gills hang on for a deserved point when Neville smashes the rebound against a post after Newman blasts a controversial 80th-min pen straight at Phil Kite.

---

10. H — 29/9 — CHESTERFIELD
Att 9,080 | Pos 1 (*16*) | Pt: W, 19 | F-A 2-1 | H-T 1-0
Scorers: Owen 39, Newman 63 — *Waller 65* — Ref: K Burge

	1	2	3	4	5	6	7	8	9	10	11	subs used
City	Waugh	Llewellyn	Bromage	Moyes	Newman	Galliers	Neville	Fitzpatrick	Owen*	Walsh	Jordan*	Caldwell
Chesterfield	*Muggleton*	*Rogers*	*Henderson*	*Bradshaw*	*Benjamin*	*Wood*	*Coyle*	*Reid*	*Waller*	*Caldwell*	*Bloomer*	

With Walsh ripping Chesterfield to shreds it looked as though the visitors might be heading for a repeat of their recent 0-10 humiliation at Gillingham. Chances are scored however and City have to be satisfied that Owen's blaster and Newman volley's take them top of the table.

---

11. A — 3/10 — NORTHAMPTON
Att 6,234 | Pos 5 (*1*) | Pt: L, 19 | F-A 0-3 | H-T 0-1
Scorers: *Chard 6, 59, Bunce 77* — Ref: K Morton

	1	2	3	4	5	6	7	8	9	10	11	subs used
City	Waugh	Llewellyn	Bromage	Moyes	Newman	Galliers!	Neville	Fitzpatrick!	Owen*	Walsh	Jordan*	Marshall/Caldwell
Northampton	*Gleasure*	*Reed*	*Logan*	*Chard*	*Wilcox*	*McPherson*	*Bunce*	*Benjamin*	*Gilbert*	*Morley*	*McGoldrick*	

Whilst Fitzpatrick is unlucky to be sent off in the 62nd min for his mistimed tackle, the same cannot be said for Galliers nine mins earlier who argues with the ref. Phil Chard seals City's fate with a header that has Waugh well beaten, after earlier registering with a 20-yard free-kick.

Season match log (matches 12–23)

Home/Away, date, attendance, club league position, opponents' league position, club points, result, full-time score, half-time score, scorers (club / opponents), referee, line-ups (club / opponents, opponents in italic) and match report.

---

12. H SOUTHEND — 10/10
Att 8,606 · Pos 3 · Opp 23 · Pts 22 · W 3-2 (HT 1-1)
Scorers: Newman 40p, 87, Fitzpatrick 66 / Robinson 36, McDonough 47
Ref: P Danson

Club: Waugh, Curle, Bromage, Moyes, Newman, Galliers, Marshall*, Fitzpatrick, Owen, Walsh, Jordan; sub Neville/Llewellyn
Opp: Steele, Martin, Johnson, Burrows, Westley, Hall, Robinson, Pennyfather, Nagan, McDonough, Ling; sub Grocock

Cooper's instructions for Newman to move forward for the last seven minutes pays off as he drills in a narrow angled 15-yarder to defeat an impressive Southend side. A good day for Newman as David Martin's trip on Moyes allowed him to shoot City's earlier spot-kick leveller.

---

13. A GRIMSBY — 17/10
Att 3,100 · Pos 3 · Opp 17 · Pts 25 · W 4-1 (HT 4-0)
Scorers: Newman 3, 27, Neville 39, Jordan 40 / McGarvey 80
Ref: E Parker

Club: Waugh, Curle, Llewellyn, Newman, Bromage, Tanner, Marshall*, Fitzpatrick, Owen, Walsh, Jordan; sub Neville
Opp: Sherwood, Toale, Agnew, Turner, Slack, Burgess, Watson, Robinson, Walsh, O'Riordan, McGarvey; sub Grocock*

Jordan's diving header caps City's most clinical display of finishing in a long time, as well as bringing to end the leanest spell of his illustrious career. After going ahead when Newman's mis-hit shot from ten yards finds the corner of the net, City's movement of the ball is a revelation.

---

14. H SUNDERLAND — 20/10
Att 15,387 · Pos 6 · Opp 1 · Pts 25 · L 0-1 (HT 0-1)
Scorers: — / Owers 1
Ref: M Reed

Club: Waugh, Llewellyn, Newman, Moyes, Curle, Galliers, Marshall*, Owen, Neville, Walsh, Jordan; sub Caldwell/Tanner
Opp: Hesford, Kay, Agboola, Corner, MacPhail, Owers, Comforth, Doyle, Gates, Atkinson^, Gabbiadini; sub Lemon/Gray*

On his return to Ashton Gate, John MacPhail gives an almost faultless performance in the heart of the Sunderland defence. He contributes to a superb defensive display that deservedly takes the Rokerites to the top of the table, thanks to Gary Owers putting away a rebound off Waugh.

---

15. A ROTHERHAM — 24/10
Att 3,397 · Pos 6 · Opp 15 · Pts 25 · L 1-4 (HT 1-3)
Scorers: Caldwell 14 / Humphries 1 (og), Airey 20, 85, Evans 30
Ref: J Rushton

Club: Waugh, Curle, Llewellyn, Moyes, Newman, Humphries, Tanner^, Fitzpatrick*, Owen, Caldwell, Jordan; subs Walsh/Honor
Opp: Douglas, Scott, Grealish, Dungworth, Green, Pugh, Williams, Evans, Airey, Campbell, Haycock*

Humphries has a nightmare City debut, stooping to head a Colin Douglas cross into his own goal after just 38 seconds. Caldwell's first-time shot from Tanner's chip brings City level, but United ruthlessly exploit aerial weakness, where Moyes is no match for the powerful Carl Airey.

---

16. A BLACKPOOL — 3/11
Att 3,140 · Pos 8 · Opp 13 · Pts 25 · L 2-4 (HT 1-1)
Scorers: Shutt 21, 51 / Morgan 1, Taylor 59, Madden 88, 90p
Ref: K Redfern

Club: Waugh, Newman, Bromage, Humphries, Pender!, Owen, Fitzpatrick, Shutt, Galliers, Marshall*, Jordan; sub Walsh
Opp: Siddall, Davies, Morgan, Bradshaw, Methven, Deary, Cunningham, Madden, Walwyn, Taylor, McAteer; sub Lancashire*

A pulsating, rough and tumble match is ultimately decided by Pender's 87th-minute sending off for hauling back Mark Taylor. After Steve Morgan gets the match off to a dramatic start by shooting in from 25 yards after just 76 seconds, Shutt marks his debut by heading City level.

---

17. A ALDERSHOT — 7/11
Att 4,324 · Pos 14 · Opp 18 · Pts 25 · L 1-2 (HT 0-1)
Scorers: — / Langley 30, Berry 90
Ref: P Foakes

Club: Prudhoe, Newman, Bromage, Humphries, Pender, Owen, Fitzpatrick, Shutt, Galliers, Marshall*, Jordan; sub Walsh
Opp: Coles, Berry, Phillips, Roberts, Anderson, Wignall, Ring, Langley, Johnson, Burvill, McDonald; sub Riley*

City might be thought unlucky to lose in injury-time for the second successive game, but they are their own worst enemies. They miss enough chances (ten on target compared to three for the Shots) to have won at a canter, whilst a poor back-pass gifts Tommy Langley his goal.

---

18. H CHESTER — 21/11
Att 8,103 · Pos 12 · Opp 10 · Pts 26 · D 2-2 (HT 1-2)
Scorers: Newman 44, Shutt 68 / Rimmer 23p, 38
Ref: J Moules

Club: Prudhoe, Newman, Bromage, Humphries, Pender, Owen*, Fitzpatrick, Shutt, Galliers, Marshall, Jordan; sub Neville
Opp: Stowell, Woodthorpe, Fazackerley, Lundon, Abel, Maddy, Bennett, Barrow, Rimmer, Croft, Painter*

Ricky Greenough's foul on Bromage sparks City's revival as Newman follows up his penalty, which Mike Stowell tips onto the post, to tap-in the rebound. Shutt's superb header brings City level, then he has a shot kicked off the line, before a late Neville header almost brings victory.

---

19. A WIGAN — 28/11
Att 2,879 · Pos 13 · Opp 9 · Pts 27 · D 1-1 (HT 1-0)
Scorers: Walsh 20 / Holden 49
Ref: J Watson

Club: Prudhoe, Newman, Bromage, Humphries, Pender, Owen, Fitzpatrick, Shutt, Galliers, Marshall, Jordan; sub Walsh
Opp: Hughes, Butler, Knowles, Hamilton, Beesley, Holden, Senior, Pilling, Campbell, Jewell, Cook; sub Ainscow*

Jordan celebrates his first game as assistant boss by helping City regain lost pride following their abject display in the 1-3 Freight Rover defeat at Wolves. Walsh's header rewards City's early dominance, but their defence has to show its mettle after Andy Holden's lashed-in leveller.

---

20. H YORK — 12/12
Att 6,235 · Pos 12 · Opp 24 · Pts 30 · W 3-2 (HT 2-1)
Scorers: Galliers 8, 47, Fitzpatrick 32 / Banton 9, 63
Ref: G Ashby

Club: Waugh, Newman, Bromage, Humphries, Pender, Owen, Fitzpatrick*, Shutt, Galliers, Marshall*, Jordan; sub Walsh
Opp: Smallwood, Hood, Johnson, Wilson, Whitehead, Tuthill*, Mills, Bradshaw, Helliwell, Banton, Canham; subs Himsworth/Clegg*

Galliers answers his critics by picking his spot to put City ahead, and then netting what proves to be the winner with a tame shot that slides under the keeper's body. City are hard pressed in the closing stages after hesitant defending had allowed Dale Banton to shoot past Waugh.

---

21. H FULHAM — 15/12
Att 6,150 · Pos 6 · Opp 5 · Pts 33 · W 4-0 (HT 3-0)
Scorers: Shutt 28, 31, 38, 81 / —
Ref: P Vanes

Club: Waugh, Honor!, Bromage, Humphries, Pender, Owen, Fitzpatrick*, Shutt, Galliers, Newman, Jordan; subs Walsh/Llewellyn
Opp: Stannard, Langley, Thomas, Eckhardt, Hicks, Skinner, Wilson, Rosenior, Davies, Walker!, Pike*

Honor has the sympathy after a 50th-minute fracas with Clive Walker results in them both being sent off, but Shutt has the glory. After his ten minute hat-trick, he side-foots a rebound past a grounded Jim Stannard to become the first City player in ten years to net four goals in a game.

---

22. A DONCASTER — 19/12
Att 1,819 · Pos 5 · Opp 23 · Pts 36 · W 2-1 (HT 1-1)
Scorers: Walsh 32, Shutt 82 / Deane 10
Ref: N Midgley

Club: Waugh, Honor, Bromage, Humphries, Pender, Owen, Fitzpatrick*, Shutt, Galliers, Tanner, Jordan; sub Walsh/Kimble
Opp: Rhodes, Stead, Miller, Raffell, Burke, Brannigan, James, Kinsella, Deane, Turnbull; subs Flynn/Chamberlain*

Under new boss Dave Mackay, Doncaster hold the early initiative as Brian Deane heads in Garry Kimble's cross and Lee Turnbull rattles the bar, before Walsh's stunning volley gets City into the game. Shutt slams in the winner after Pender's point-blank header is blocked on the line.

---

23. A GILLINGHAM — 26/12
Att 6,261 · Pos 5 · Opp 11 · Pts 37 · D 1-1 (HT 1-0)
Scorers: Newman 23p / Smith 54
Ref: D Vickers

Club: Waugh, Honor, Bromage, Humphries, Pender, Owen, Fitzpatrick, Shutt, Galliers, Tanner^, Jordan; sub Newman*
Opp: Kite, Haylock, Pearce, West, Greenall, Peacock, Pritchard, Eves, Elsey, Lovell*, Smith D; subs Weatherly/Cooper*

After Phil Kite concedes a pen for his foul on Shutt, Newman fools the keeper with a side-footed spot-kick rather than his normal blaster. Dave Smith's leveller is the highlight of a lively game, an unstoppable 25-yarder into the roof of City's net from Gavin Peacock's tapped free-kick.

BARCLAYS LEAGUE DIVISION 3 Manager: Cooper ⇨ Joe Jordan SEASON 1987-88

Each player cell shows the City player, with the opposition player in *italics* (same shirt number). The position column shows City's league position / opponents'.

No	Date	V	Team	Att	Pos	Res	Pt	F-A	H-T	1	2	3	4	5	6	7	8	9	10	11	subs used
24	28/12	H	BRIGHTON	16,058	4 / *5*	W	40	5-2	3-0	Waugh / *Keeley*	Honor* / *Brown*	Newman / *Dublin*	Humphries / *Jasper*	Pender / *Roughie*	Galliers / *Gatting*	Marshall* / *Nelson*	Fitzpatrick / *Trusson*	Shutt / *Brenner*	Walsh / *Wilkins*	Neville / *Wood*	Llewellyn/Jordan
25	1/1	H	BRENTFORD	12,877	7 / *6*	L	40	2-3	0-3	Waugh / *Phillips*	Llewellyn / *Joseph*	Newman / *Stanislaus*	Humphries / *Millen*	Pender / *Evans*	Galliers / *Jones*~*	Marshall* / *Turner*	Tanner / *Sinton*	Shutt / *Birch*	Walsh / *Blissett*	Neville / *Rix*	Jordan / *Perryman*
26	9/1	A	PRESTON	5,729	8 / *19*	L	40	0-2	0-1	Waugh / *Brown*	Llewellyn / *Rathbone*~*	Bromage / *Bennett*	Humphries / *Atkins*	Mardon / *Chapman*	Galliers / *Allardyce*	Hawkins* / *Mooney*	Newman / *Swann*	Shutt / *Ellis*	Walsh / *Brazil*	Neville* / *Joyce*	Tanner/Jordan / *Miller*
27	16/1	H	NOTTS CO	9,558	8 / *2*	W	43	2-1	0-1	Waugh / *Leonard*	Honor / *Smalley*	Bromage / *Withe*	Mardon* / *Kevan*	Pender / *Yates*	Galliers / *Birtles*	Marshall* / *Mills~*	Newman / *McParland*	Shutt / *Lund*	Walsh / *Pike*~*	Neville / *Thorpe*	Jordan/Llewellyn / *Fairclough/Barnes*
28	6/2	H	BURY	9,158	8 / *10*	W	46	3-2	0-1	Vaughan / *Farnworth*	Honor / *Hill*	Bromage / *Pashley*	Mardon / *Hoyland*	Pender / *Valentine*~*	Galliers / *Higgins*	Milne / *Lee~*	Newman / *Robinson*	Shutt / *Taylor*	Walsh / *Fairbrother*	Neville / *Bishop*	Hart/Greenwood
29	9/2	H	WALSALL	8,545	7 / *3*	D	47	0-0	0-0	Vaughan / *Barber*	Llewellyn / *Jones M*	Bromage / *Mower*	Mardon / *Shakespeare*	Pender / *Forbes*	Galliers* / *Hart*	Milne / *Jones P*	Newman / *Goodwin*	Shutt* / *Christie~*	Walsh / *Kelly*	Neville~ / *Naughton*	Honor/Caldwell / *O'Kelly*
30	13/2	A	BRIGHTON	8,782	7 / *5*	L	47	2-3	0-1	Vaughan / *Keeley*	Llewellyn / *Brown*	Bromage / *Dublin*	Mardon / *Curbishley*	Pender / *Rougvie*	Honor / *Gatting*	Milne / *Nelson*	Newman / *Trusson*	Shutt* / *Bremner*	Walsh / *Wilkins*	Neville* / *Crumplin*	Caldwell
31	20/2	H	MANSFIELD	9,528	8 / *16*	L	47	1-2	1-2	Waugh / *Hitchcock*	Honor / *Graham*	Bromage / *Ryan*	Mardon / *Lowery*~*	Pender / *Foster*	McClaren / *Coleman*	Milne / *Owen*	Newman / *Kenworthy*	Caldwell / *Kent*	Walsh / *Cassells*	Neville* / *Charles*	Marshall / *Garner*
32	27/2	H	NORTHAMPTON	8,578	9 / *6*	D	48	2-2	1-2	Waugh / *Gleasure*	Llewellyn / *Reed*	Honor / *Wilson*	Humphries / *Donald*	Pender / *Wilcox*	McClaren / *Slack*	Milne / *Singleton*	Newman / *Longhurst*~*	Caldwell / *Gilbert*	Walsh / *Adcock*	Neville* / *Chard*	Marshall / *McGoldrick*
33	1/3	A	CHESTERFIELD	1,657	8 / *19*	W	51	4-1	2-1	Waugh / *Brown J*	Llewellyn / *Rogers*	Honor / *McGeeney*	Humphries / *Wood*	Pender / *Benjamin*	McClaren / *Hunter*	Milne / *Coyle*	Newman / *Phillips*	Caldwell / *Waller~*	Walsh / *Arnott*	Neville* / *Eley~*	Galliers / *Morris/Bloomer*
34	5/3	H	GRIMSBY	8,343	8 / *21*	D	52	1-1	0-0	Waugh / *Sherwood*	Llewellyn / *Dixon*	Honor / *Agnew*	Humphries / *Cunnington*	Pender / *Burgess*	McClaren / *Jobling*	Milne / *Robinson*	Shutt* / *Saunders~*	Caldwell / *North~*	Walsh / *O'Riordan*	Galliers* / *McGarvey*	Neville/Honor / *McDermott/Stubbs*

Scorers, Times, and Referees

24 — P'der 20, N'man 31, Fitzp'k 42, Walsh 82 [Jordan 89] / *Nelson 53, Wood 76* · Ref: K Burge
Superb entertainment as City end Brighton's unbeaten 17-match run. Walsh, who starts the rout with a pinpoint free-kick to set-up Pender's headed opener, kills off Brighton's fight-back with a stunning shot from 25 yards, before producing a perfect cross for Jordan's late header.

25 — Shutt 53, Galliers 65 / *Blissett 19, 20, Sinton 39* · Ref: J Deakin
The Brentford jinx strikes as Boss Cooper is announced as Bell's Manager of the Month for December. Yet again away success over the Bees is not matched by victory at Ashton Gate, where the highlight of City's spirited second-half display is a crisp volley from the inspired Galliers.

26 — *Rathbone 8, Brazil 62* · Ref: T Simpson
On Preston's artificial pitch City soon find themselves behind when Waugh badly misjudges Mick Rathbone's free-kick. Despite the advantage of a strong wind after the break, Gary Brazil's side-foot into the corner of the net from twelve yards leaves City a well-beaten side at the finish.

27 — Walsh 57, Jordan 76 / *Lund 12* · Ref: P Durkin
Jordan's diving header ends County's twelve match unbeaten run after City had been outplayed in the first half. A linesman's flag denies Newman a 20th-min volleyed equaliser to Gary Lund's stroked-in opener, but Walsh eventually levels after the break with a rare headed goal.

28 — Galliers 51, Milne 56, Walsh 74 / *Valentine 12, Hoyland 57* · Ref: M Bodenham
Milne's arrogant side-foot volley is candidate for goal of the season as City turn on the style after their dismal first-half showing. Enterprising Bury are a yard quicker than the City before the interval and thoroughly deserving of Peter Valentine's looping header that puts them in front.

29 — (0-0) · Ref: D Reeves
The gale force wind ruins this encounter with gusts ripping sheeting off the Dolman Stand and bending the corner flags double. City have nine shots on target, whilst Walsall manage just one, but the nearest to a goal is Shutt's early drive which Craig Shakespeare clears off the line.

30 — Walsh 65, Caldwell 82 / *Nelson 7, 55, Rougvie 54* · Ref: J Carter
Battling bravely against the driving wind and rain to keep the half-time deficit to Gary Nelson's volley, City allow Albion to blast in a quick double just after the break. Walsh shoots in from Newman's pass to inspire a fight-back, but more is needed than Caldwell's side-footed effort.

31 — Foster 36 (og) / *Kent 3, Graham 29* · Ref: J Lloyd
Don't despair! Steve McLaren (£50,000 ex Derby) has the class to put City back in the promotion race according to Norman Hunter. In this game though, their defence errs to let Kevin Kent shoot into an open net and then allowing Mike Graham to tap in from Waugh's palm out.

32 — Walsh 13, Reed 85 (og) / *Adcock 38, Chard 42* · Ref: R Wiseman
McClaren comments that he has never seen four more weirder goals than those conceded by City in this game and last week against Mansfield. Tony Adcock prods in Northampton's first when Llewellyn fails to clear, then City's defence is all at sea as Phil Chard heads in the second.

33 — Milne 15, Caldwell 27, Walsh 63, [Pender 68] / *Phillips 35* · Ref: P Harrison
Galliers returns from suspension to breathe new life into City's promotion challenge. Milne's fine low shot gets City off to a good start, and then Caldwell side-foots in a low cross, before Steve Phillips turns in a rebound after Waugh had pushed Les Hunter's header against a post.

34 — Walsh 76 / *O'Riordan 65* · Ref: M James
City's fourth successive home match without a victory makes nonsense of promotion talk. It's sheer torture for the fans who bear witness to lethargic City's worst display of the season, their only consolation being Walsh's superbly struck equaliser to Don O'Riordan's headed opener.

#		Date	Opponent	Att.	Pos			Score	W/L/D		Scorers	Lineups (with subs)	Report

35 A 11/3 SOUTHEND — 3,562 — 8 22 52 — 0-2 L 0-1
Crown 24, Westley 49
Ref: D Hedges
Waugh, Steele, O'Shea; Llewellyn, Johnson, Newman, Westley; Humphries, Westley; Pender, Martin; McClaren, Butler; Milne* Brush; Galliers, Hall; Caldwell, Crown; Honor, McDonough* Neal; Neville* Ling; Marshall/Fitzpatrick
Southend, who have only kept one clean sheet in home in the League this season, hardly come under threat, as David Crown's shot on the turn, and Shane Westley's header bring them easy success. Newman's vicious half-volley ten minutes from time is City's only worthwhile attempt.

36 A 19/3 FULHAM — 4,896 — 8 11 53 — 0-0 D 0-0
Ref: V Callow
Waugh, Stannard, Eckhardt; Llewellyn, Eckhardt; Newman, Elkins; Humphries, Skinner; Pender, Oakes; McClaren, Hopkins; Milne* Barnett*; Galliers, Scott; Fitzpatrick, Marshall; Neville, Walker*; Caldwell, Hoddy/Gore
With Joe Jordan replacing Terry Cooper as manager following Tuesday night's 3-1 Gloucestershire Cup success, City manage their first clean sheet in seven League games. City demonstrate plenty of commitment, but lack the cutting edge to take advantage of a weakened Fulham side.

37 H 26/3 ROTHERHAM — 7,517 — 7 18 56 — 2-0 W 0-0
Gordon 57p, Neville 89
Ref: P Foakes
Waugh, Crichton; Llewellyn, Douglas; Honor, Crosby; Humphries, Grealish; Pender, Johnson !; Newman, Green; McClaren, Buckley; Milne, Pepper; Galliers, Wylde*; Gordon*, Haycock; Walsh, Dungworth ^ Airey/Mendonca; Neville, Dungworth; Marshall
Nigel Johnson's miserable afternoon culminates in his being sent off for felling McClaren, after earlier tripping Neville to concede Gordon's spot-kick. Neville ends his 23-week goal drought, and seals City's deserved success, by racing clear to blast a fierce shot past Paul Crichton.

38 H 2/4 ALDERSHOT — 8,712 — 7 19 59 — 2-0 W 1-0
Milne 38, Walsh 85
Ref: J Moules
Waugh, Lange; Llewellyn, Berry; Newman, Barnes D; Humphries, Joseph; Pender, Smith; McClaren, Wignall; Milne*, Bedford; Galliers, Langley; Gordon*, Riley; Walsh, Ring*; Neville, Burvill; Anderson; Bromage/Shutt
Walsh's speculative hook-shot into the top corner lends some sanity to the scoreline after City had been frustrated by their own poor finishing and Aldershot's offside tactics. Milne spurned two good chances before driving in a 20-yard opener after Lange pushed out Neville's shot.

39 A 4/4 CHESTER — 2,858 — 7 15 59 — 0-1 L 0-1
Bennett 7
Ref: J Penrose
Waugh, Stewart; Llewellyn, Butler; Newman, Lundon; Humphries, Fazakerley; Pender, Abel; McClaren, Lightfoot; Milne, Lowey; Galliers !, Barrow; Gordon, Bennett; Walsh, Croft; Neville* Graham; Shutt
City's ill discipline and their unreliable offside trap seriously damage play-off aspirations. Their defence is in disarray early on when McClaren trips Milton Graham as he cuts into the area, then eight minutes from time Galliers is sent off following his protests over a blocked free-kick.

40 H 9/4 BLACKPOOL — 6,460 — 7 12 62 — 2-1 W 1-0
McClaren 25, Gordon 66p
Taylor 50
Ref: I Hemley
Waugh, Siddall; Llewellyn, Matthews; Newman, Morgan*; Humphries, Coughlin; Pender, Methven; McClaren, Walsh; Milne, Deary; Galliers, Rooney; Gordon, Walwyn; Walsh, Cunningham Taylor*; Neville; Bradshaw/Madden
McClaren stars in City's midfield, much like old favourite Bobby Etheridge whose death at the age of 54 was announced this week. After Neville is thrice denied by Barry Siddall's point-blank saves, City's early frustration is relieved as McClaren's shot finds the back of the net.

41 A 12/4 BRISTOL ROV — 5,947 — 7 14 62 — 0-1 L 0-1
Penrice 48
Ref: R Groves
Waugh, Martyn; Llewellyn, Alexander; Newman, Twentyman; Humphries, Clark; Pender, Mehew; McClaren, Jones; Milne*, Holloway; Galliers, Reece; Gordon, White; Walsh, Penrice; Neville, Purnell
After a first half dominated by City's greater individual class, the Rovers better teamwork receives its reward after the break. Gary Penrice settles this derby with a coolly-taken shot in the heat of a goalmouth scramble, but is later unlucky to have a 20-yard side-foot effort struck-off.

42 A 18/4 PORT VALE — 2,671 — 8 11 63 — 1-1 D 0-0
Newman 80
Mills 57
Ref: T Mills
Waugh, Grew; Llewellyn, Webb; Newman, Hughes; Humphries, Walker; Pender, Hazel; McClaren, Sproson; Milne, Ford; Mardon, Earle; Gordon* Riley; Walsh, Beckford; Neville, Mills; Newman; Shutt
A ding-dong struggle, in which Llewellyn twice clears off the line, while McClaren's shot is rebuffed by a post, ends all square. Simon Mills' opening shot takes a wicked deflection, but Newman celebrates being captain for the first time by heading in City's deserved equaliser.

43 A 23/4 SUNDERLAND — 18,225 — 8 1 66 — 1-0 W 1-0
Gordon 18
Ref: D Shaw
Waugh, Carter; Llewellyn, Hardwick; Newman, Gray; Humphries, Ord; Pender, MacPhail; McClaren, Owers; Milne, Lemon; Neville, Pascoe; Gordon* Gates*; Walsh, Gabbiadini; Neville* Armstrong; Shutt/Bromage; Bertschin/Doyle
Jackie Milburn rates City's defensive display at Roker Park to be the best he has ever seen. Apart from breakaways it's all hands to the pumps – Llewellyn twice kicking off the line – as City hang onto to the advantage gained by Gordon's stoop to head in from Milne's cross.

44 H 30/4 WIGAN — 7,340 — 7 6 69 — 4-1 W 2-1
Neville 13, Galliers 43, Marshall 70, [Jordan 75]
Jewell 30
Ref: D Elleray
Waugh, Hughes; Llewellyn, Senior^; Newman, Knowles; Humphries, Hamilton; Pender, McEwan; McClaren, Beasley; Milne, Thompson D Thompson C* Piling; Galliers, Pascoe; Shutt, Thompson C* Piling; Walsh*, Jewell; Neville* Butler; Jordan/Marshall; Cook/Campbell
With victory vital to both sides City dramatically revive their play-off prospects by taking their chances in an entertaining game, whilst Wigan waste theirs. After Paul Jewell's headed equaliser, Galliers runs from the half-line before restoring City's lead with a delightful chip.

45 A 2/5 YORK — 2,620 — 6 24 72 — 1-0 W 0-0
Milne 87
Ref: C Trussell
Waugh, Endersby; Llewellyn, McMillan; Newman, Johnson; Bromage; Humphries, Tutill; Pender, Clegg; McClaren, McKenzie; Milne, Howlett; Galliers, Bradshaw; Shutt*, Helliwell; Walsh, Staniforth; Marshall, Himsworth; Neville* Jordan/Fitzpatrick
Milne's exquisite late chip rewards City's commitment in a game where they have won many times over. Marshall's 16th-minute header hits both crossbar and post, whilst offside rules out Neville's shot and Shutt fires over an open net from just four yards.

46 H 7/5 DONCASTER — 18,373 — 5 24 75 — 1-0 W 0-0
Gordon 79
Ref: P Vanes
Waugh, Samways; Llewellyn, Miller; Newman, Brevett; Humphries, Robinson L Robinson R Raffell; Pender, Robinson R Raffell; McClaren, Raffell; Milne, Kinsella*; Galliers, Turnbull; Gordon, Deane; Walsh, Chamberlain Kimble*; Neville* Jordan; Rankine/Holmes
The nerves are jangling for players and fans alike at Ashton Gate, where City eventually clinch a play-off place after Gordon has his 62nd-minute penalty saved by Mark Samways. Gordon makes amends by shooting into an empty net after his lunge robs Samways' of the ball.

Home 9,818 Away 4,886 Average 4,886

BARCLAYS DIVISION 3 (CUP-TIES)

Manager: Cooper ⇒ Joe Jordan

Littlewoods Cup

		F-A	H-T	Scorers, Times, and Referees	1	2	3	4	5	6	7	8	9	10	11	subs used
1:1 A SWINDON 18/8, 6,807		L 0-3	0-0	Quinn 65, 68, 85 / Ref: A Buksh	Waugh / *Digby*	Llewellyn / *O'Regan*	Bromage / *King*	Moyes / *Kamara*	Newman / *Parkin*	Tanner / *Calderwood*	Marshall* / *Kelly*	Fitzpatrick / *Quinn*	Owen ! / *Quinn*	Walsh / *Bamber*	Jordan / *Barnard*	Neville / *Henry*
1:2 H SWINDON 25/8, 7,013		W 3-2	3-1	Owen 9, 12, Tanner 26 / Bamber 25, Berry 54p / Ref: K Cooper / (City lost 3-5 on aggregate)	Waugh / *Digby*	Llewellyn / *O'Regan*	Bromage / *King*	Moyes / *Kamara*	Newman / *Parkin*	Tanner / *Calderwood*	Marshall* / *Coyne* *	Fitzpatrick / *Berry*	Owen / *Quinn*	Walsh / *Bamber*	Jordan* / *Barnard*	Neville/Caldwell / *Henry*

1:1 commentary: City earn the first-half applause for their quality football, but fail to capitalise as they are twice thwarted by the woodwork. After the break Owen's dismissal is soon followed by Town's opener as Jimmy Quinn makes up for blazing an earlier spot-kick over the bar with a close-range shot.

1:2 commentary: Fraser Digby's 19th-minute save from Walsh's spot-kick concludes a brilliant opening spell in which Swindon are torn apart. The bar keeps out an early Moyes effort before Owen registers with a header and a 25-yarder before he is also denied by the woodwork in the 18th minute.

FA Cup

		F-A	H-T	Scorers, Times, and Referees	1	2	3	4	5	6	7	8	9	10	11	subs used
1 H AYLESBURY UTD 14/11, 8,263 BHLP		W 1-0	0-0	Caldwell 62 / Ref: D Hutchinson	Coombe / *Garner*	Llewellyn / *Robinson*	Bromage / *James*	Humphries / *Hackett*	Pender / *Hutter*	Galliers / *Botterill*	Owen / *McBean* *	Newman / *Duggan*	Shutt / *Hercules*	Walsh* / *Phillips*	Caldwell / *Harthill*	Marshall / *Davie*
2 H TORQUAY 5/12, 9,027 4:4		L 0-1	0-0	Caldwell 85 / Ref: K Barratt	Waugh / *Allen*	Honor / *McNichol*	Bromage / *Pearce*	Humphries / *Hastegrave*	Pender / *Cole*	Galliers / *Impey*	Fitzpatrick* / *Dawkins*	Newman / *Lloyd*	Shutt / *Caldwell*	Walsh / *Loram*	Jordan* / *Dobson*	Marshall/Neville

1 commentary: Aylesbury, missing two key players through suspension, embarrass City without quite having the ability to pull off a shock victory. Peter McBean and Cliff Hercules both squander open-goal opportunities, before Caldwell heads in City's winner from Owen's perfect far-post cross.

2 commentary: Following Wednesday's success in beating the Rovers in the delayed 1986-87 Gloucestershire Cup Final, City find Torquay a much tougher proposition. The fans chant for Cooper's head as United notch up a deserved success when Dave Caldwell heads in Mark Loram's centre.

Play-offs

		F-A	H-T	Scorers, Times, and Referees	1	2	3	4	5	6	7	8	9	10	11	subs used
SF 1 H SHEFFIELD UTD 15/5, 25,335		W 1-0	1-0	Walsh 43 / Ref: J Martin	Waugh / *Benstead*	Llewellyn / *Wilder*	Newman / *Powell*	Humphries / *Webster*	Pender / *Stancliffe*	McClaren / *Barnsley*	Milne / *Heatherston^ Withe* *	Galliers / *Cadette*	Gordon* / *Cadette*	Walsh / *Downes*	Neville^ / *Beagrie*	Shutt/Jordan / *Phillskirk/Pike*
SF 2 A SHEFFIELD UTD 18/5, 19,066		D 1-1	1-0	Shutt 17 / Morris 47 / Ref: G Courtney	Waugh / *Benstead*	Llewellyn / *Powell*	Newman / *Pike*	Humphries / *Webster*	Pender / *Stancliffe*	McClaren / *Barnsley* *	Milne / *Morris*	Galliers / *Cadette*	Gordon* / *Williams*	Walsh / *Downes*	Shutt^ / *Beagrie*	Jordan/Marshall / *Agana*
F:1 H WALSALL 25/5, 25,128		L 1-3	1-0	Walsh 38 / Waugh 63 (og), Kelly 79, 90 / Ref: J Worrall	Waugh / *Barber*	Llewellyn / *Taylor*	Newman / *O'Kelly* *	Humphries / *Pender*	Pender / *Goodwin*	McClaren / *Hawker*	Milne / *Christie*	Galliers / *Hart*	Shutt / *Christie*	Walsh / *Kelly*	Neville* / *Naughton*	Jordan / *Jones M*
F:2 A WALSALL 28/5, 13,941		W 2-0	2-0	Newman 30, Shutt 66 / Ref: G Tyson	Waugh / *Barber*	Llewellyn / *Taylor*	Newman / *Dornan*	Humphries / *Shakespeare Forbes*	Pender / *Goodwin*	McClaren / *Hawker*	Milne / *Hart*	Galliers / *Christie*	Shutt* / *Kelly*	Walsh / *Naughton*	Jordan	Caldwell
F:R A WALSALL 30/5, 13,007		L 0-4	0-3	Kelly 11, 17, 63, Hawker 19 / Ref: G Courtney	Waugh / *Barber*	Llewellyn / *Taylor*	Newman / *Dornan^*	Humphries / *Shakespeare Forbes*	Pender / *Goodwin^*	McClaren / *Hawker*	Milne / *Hart*	Galliers / *Christie*	Shutt! / *Kelly*	Walsh / *Naughton*	Jordan	Jones M/Sanderson

SF 1 commentary: City's attractive approach play is too often marred by poor centres. Waugh is the busier of the two goalkeepers, but Walsh's blistering far-post volley gives City an important advantage which could have been better if he had not been denied by the woodwork just after the half-time break.

SF 2 commentary: Llewellyn saves City with goal-line clearances. On top before the break, Walsh is unlucky when his long-range free-kick hits a post, but Shutt's stooping header does the trick. After the break, though, it is a different story when Waugh is beaten by a spectacular volley from his best man.

F:1 commentary: All City have to show for their first-half dominance is Walsh's long-range free-kick. A fortunate equaliser for the Saddlers when Llewellyn's clearance strikes Waugh and rebounds over the line, but the final goal is a gem. David Kelly finishes off his great 50-yard run with fine aplomb.

F:2 commentary: Walsh is unlucky with an early volley that crashes against a post, but Newman's header brings the reward that City's attacking play deserves. After the break Shutt's low drive levels the aggregate score, but Walsall win the penalty shoot-out 4-1 to secure home advantage for the replay.

F:R commentary: Few would have predicted this defensive collapse just when it mattered most. David Kelly started the rot when shooting into an unguarded net, with Phil Hawker is also left free to head in from a corner. Shutt receives his marching orders for a punch at Walsall's keeper just before time.

Appearances / Goals

Player	Lge	Sub	LC	Sub	FAC	Sub	Lge	LC	FAC	Tot
									Goals	
Bromage, Russell	28	2	2		1		3	1		4
Caldwell, Tony	8	8	2		1	1				
Coombe, Mark				1						
Curle, Keith	3									
Fitzpatrick, Paul	22	2	2		1		5			5
Galliers, Steve	35		2		2		5			5
Gordon, Colin	8						4			4
Harvey, Jimmy		1								
Hawkins, Nigel	1									
Honor, Chris	14	3			1					
Humphries, Glenn	24				2					
Jordan, Joe	17	11	2		1		4			4
Llewellyn, Andy	36	6	2		1		1			1
McClaren, Steve	16						1			1
Mardon, Paul	8									
Marshall, Gary	13	6	2			2	1			1
Milne, Ralph	19						4			4
Moyes, David	15		2				1			1
Neville, Steve	37	3	2		2	1	5			5
Newman, Rob	44		2		2		11			11
Owen, Gordon	17	1	2		1		6	2		8
Pender, John	28		2		2		2			2
Prudoe, Mark	3									
Shutt, Carl	18	4	2		2		10			10
Tanner, Mike	10	2	2						1	1
Vaughan, John	3									
Walsh, Alan	39	3	2		2		12			12
Waugh, Keith	40		2		2					
(own-goals)							2			2
27 players used	506	52	22	3	22	3	77	3	1	81

League Table

	Team	P	W	D	L	F	A	W	D	L	F	A	Pts
			Home					**Away**					
1	Sunderland	46	14	7	2	51	22	13	5	5	41	26	93
2	Brighton	46	15	7	1	37	16	8	8	7	32	31	84
3	Walsall *	46	15	6	2	39	22	8	7	8	29	28	82
4	Notts Co	46	14	4	5	53	24	9	6	8	29	25	81
5	BRISTOL CITY	46	14	6	3	51	30	7	6	10	26	32	75
6	Northampton	46	12	8	3	36	18	6	11	6	34	33	73
7	Wigan	46	11	8	4	36	23	9	4	10	34	38	72
8	Bristol Rov	46	14	5	4	43	19	4	7	12	25	37	66
9	Fulham	46	10	5	8	36	24	9	4	10	33	36	66
10	Blackpool	46	13	4	6	45	27	4	10	9	26	35	65
11	Port Vale	46	12	8	3	36	19	6	3	14	22	37	65
12	Brentford	46	9	8	6	27	23	7	6	10	26	36	62
13	Gillingham	46	8	9	6	45	21	6	8	9	32	40	59
14	Bury	46	9	8	6	33	26	6	7	10	25	31	59
15	Chester	46	9	8	6	29	30	5	8	10	22	32	58
16	Preston	46	10	6	7	30	23	5	7	11	18	36	58
17	Southend	46	10	6	7	42	33	4	7	12	23	50	55
18	Chesterfield	46	10	5	8	25	28	5	5	13	23	42	55
19	Mansfield	46	10	6	7	25	21	4	6	13	23	38	54
20	Aldershot	46	12	3	8	45	32	3	5	15	19	42	53
21	Rotherham **	46	8	8	7	28	25	4	8	11	22	41	52
22	Grimsby	46	6	7	10	25	29	6	7	10	23	29	50
23	York	46	4	7	12	27	45	4	2	17	21	46	33
24	Doncaster	46	6	5	12	25	36	2	4	17	15	48	33
		1104	255	153	144	869	616	144	153	255	616	869	1503

* promoted after play-offs
** relegated after play-offs

Odds & ends

Double wins: (4) Notts County, Chesterfield, York, Doncaster.
Double losses: (1) Mansfield.

Won from behind: (5) Southend (h), York (h), Doncaster (a), Notts County (h), Bury (h).
Lost from in front: (1) Blackpool (a).

High spots: An exciting derby with Bristol Rov on 12 September.
Carl Shutt's four-goal haul v Fulham on 15 December.
Beating Brighton 5-2 at Ashton Gate on 28 December.
Ralph Milne's goal against Bury at Ashton Gate on 6 February.
An exciting 1-0 win against Doncaster to clinch a play-off place.
Beating Sheffield Utd 1-0 at Ashton Gate on 15 May in the 1st leg of the play-off semi-final.
Hanging on to a 1-1 draw at Bramhall Lane on 18 May in the 2nd Leg of the play-off semi-final.
Beating Walsall (a) 2-0 in the 2nd Leg of the play-off final on 28 May.
Beating Bristol Rov (a) 2-1 on 2 Dec in the delayed 1986-77 Glos Cup final, and winning this season's competition 3-1 (h) on 15 March.

Low spots: Losing 1-4 at Rotherham on 24 October.
Losing 0-1 against Bristol Rov on 12 April.
Losing 1-3 (h) v Walsall on 25 April in the 1st leg of the play-off final.
Losing 0-4 at Fellows Park on 30 May in the replay of the play-off Final.

Player of the year: Alan Walsh.
Ever-presents: (0).
Hat-tricks: (1) Carl Shutt.
Leading scorer: Alan Walsh (12) (Note: Not including play-offs).

BARCLAYS LEAGUE DIVISION 3   Manager: Joe Jordan   SEASON 1988-89

Opponent line-ups (the lower line of each match) appear in italics in the original.

No	Date	Att	Pos	Pt	Res	F-A	H-T	1	2	3	4	5	6	7	8	9	10	11	subs used
1	A NOTTS CO 27/8	6,285		1	D	0-0	0-0	Waugh	Llewellyn	Bromage	Humphries	Pender	McClaren*	Milne*	Galliers	Newman	Walsh	Caldwell	Honor
								Leonard	Morton	Withe	O'Riordan	Yates	Law	Mills	McParland*	Birtles	Pike	Thorpe	Lund
2	H CHESTERFIELD 3/9	7,547		4	W	4-0	1-0	Waugh	Llewellyn	Bromage	Mardon	Pender	McClaren*	Newman*	Galliers	Shutt	Walsh	Hawkins	Fitzpatrick
								Brown	Hewitt	McGeeney*	Henderson	Rogers	Hunter*	Eley	Arnott	Waller	Morris	Thompson	Bloomer/Wood
3	A CHESTER 10/9	2,831	11	4	L	0-2	0-0	Waugh	Llewellyn	Bromage	Mardon	Pender	McClaren	Newman	Galliers	Shutt*	Walsh	McGarvey*	Milne
			2					Stewart	Glenn	Woodthorpe	Hinnigan	Abel	Lightfoot	Jakub	Barrow	Benjamin	Johnson	Newhouse*	Dale
4	H PRESTON 17/9	7,913	12	5	D	1-1	1-1	Carter	Llewellyn*	Bromage	Humphries	Pender	McClaren	Milne*	Galliers	Newman	Walsh	McGarvey	Shutt*/Honor
			19					Brown	Rathbone	McAteer	Atkins	Jones	Allardyce	Miller	Joyce	Ellis	Brazi	Patterson	
5	A BLACKPOOL 20/9	3,412	12	6	D	2-2	2-1	Carter	Llewellyn	Bromage	Newman*	Pender	McClaren	Milne*	Galliers	Shutt	Walsh	McGarvey	Hawkins
			20					Siddall	Burgess	Morgan	Deary	Methven	Elliott	Davies	Cunningham	Garner*	Coughlin*	Taylor	Thompson/Walwyn
6	H PORT VALE 24/9	7,235	16	6	L	0-1	0-1	Carter	Llewellyn*	Bromage	Newman*	Pender	McClaren	Milne	Galliers	Shutt*	Walsh	McGarvey	Hawkins
			2					Grew	Webb	Hughes	Walker	Mills	Sproson	Ford	Earle	Futcher	Beckford	Riley	Hawkins
7	H SWANSEA 1/10	7,786	12	9	W	2-0	1-0	Leaning	Llewellyn*	Bromage	Newman*	Pender	McClaren	Milne	Galliers	Shutt*	Walsh	Hawkins	Mardon/McGarvey
			17					Wilmot	Hough	Legg	Melville*	Knill	James	Thornber	Raynor	Allon*	Bodak	Lewis	D'Auria/Love
8	A GILLINGHAM 4/10	2,966	7	12	W	1-0	1-0	Leaning	Llewellyn*	Bromage*	Newman	Pender	McClaren	Gavin	Galliers	McGarvey	Walsh	Hawkins*	Mardon/Jordan
			20					Kite	Burley	Haylock	Peacock	Clarke	Walker	Perry	Quow*	Lovell	Weatherly	Smith D	Cooper
9	H FULHAM 8/10	8,160	11	12	L	1-5	0-2	Leaning	Llewellyn*	Bromage	Newman	Pender	McClaren	Gavin	Galliers	McGarvey*	Walsh	Hawkins	Jordan/Humphries
			6					Stannard	Peters	Langley	Wilson	Eckhardt	Thomas	Marshall	Skinner	Sayer	Gordon*	Barnett	Mauge
10	A HUDDERSFIELD 15/10	5,952	11	15	W	1-0	0-0	Leaning	Llewellyn*	Bailey	Humphries	Pender	McClaren	Newman	Galliers	Shutt*	Walsh	Jordan	McGarvey/Mardon
			16					Hardwick	Trevitt	Hutchings	May	O'Doherty	Mitchell	O'Regan	Winter	Withe	Maskell	Bent*	Marsden
11	A NORTHAMPTON 22/10	3,668	7	18	W	3-1	0-1	Leaning	Newman	Bailey	Humphries	Pender	McClaren	Newman	Galliers	Shutt*	Walsh	Gavin*	McGarvey/Mardon
			17					Gleasure	McGoldrick	Thomas	Donald	Flexney	McPherson	Singleton	Reed*	Withe	Adcock	Sandeman*	Johnson/Wilson

Scorers, Times, and Referees

1. Ref: K Morton
2. Walsh 43, 71, Newman 51p, Llewellyn 63. Ref: H King
3. Lightfoot 66, Dale 85. Ref: M Peck
4. Bromage 14, Rathbone 44. Ref: I Hemley
5. McGarvey 32, 39, Davies 30, Taylor 78. Ref: G Aplin
6. Walker 6. Ref: R Lewis
7. Walsh 31, Milne 77. Ref: L Shapter
8. Gavin 1. Ref: D Axcell
9. Newman 85p, Peters 18, Sayer 35, 86, Eckhardt 56, [Marshall 80]. Ref: R Gifford
10. Walsh 85. Ref: A Dawson
11. Milne 52, McGarvey 73, 90, McGoldrick 45. Ref: J Lloyd

Match Reports

1. **Notts Co (A) 0-0** — Mindful of Jordan's efforts to sign a new keeper, Waugh was one of those rare days when everything goes right. He pulls off a string of spectacular saves to keep impressive County at bay, and has luck on his one error, as Galliers is on hand to clear off the line.

2. **Chesterfield (H) 4-0** — City's exhilarating display provides proof that Jordan's policy of playing five at the back is not necessarily a negative tactic. Walsh twice registers with headers, popping up unmarked for the opener, and then finishing off Shutt's pin-point cross to complete City's emphatic win.

3. **Chester (A) 0-2** — McGarvey's hopes of making an impressive debut are dashed by Chester's impressive trio of uncompromising central defenders. City fail to match Chester's endeavour, and they concede their first goal in the 426th min of the season when Chris Lightfoot heads in from close range.

4. **Preston (H) 1-1** — Jordan's refashioned defence looks decidedly creaky and it is thanks to on-loan keeper Tim Carter that City salvage a point. After Bromage stabs in McGarvey's pass, Mick Rathbone catches City cold, meeting Andy McAteer's cross at the far post to shoot past Carter from ten yards.

5. **Blackpool (A) 2-2** — City sparkling attack is let down by some sloppy defending at Bloomfield Road. Blackpool go ahead against the run of play when Mike Davies steals in to beat Carter from eight yards, but McGarvey twice shoots in to put City ahead, before Mark Taylor heads in Pool's late equaliser.

6. **Port Vale (H) 0-1** — Ron Futcher who opted to join ambitious Vale in preference to City looks to have made the right choice on the evidence of this game. City's defence stands off to watch as Ray Walker, after getting the luck of the bounce at the edge of the penalty area, strides forward to beat Carter.

7. **Swansea (H) 2-0** — Swansea have cause to be aggrieved when Walsh's lethal left-foot breaks the deadlock, as two minutes earlier Paul Raynor was penalised for a foul on Leaning after bundling the ball in the net. Milne heads in to make victory certain, and Walsh crashes a late volley against the crossbar.

8. **Gillingham (A) 1-0** — City are under siege for much of this poor match after Gavin takes just 85 seconds to celebrate his debut by shooting low past Phil Kite. The Gills are twice thwarted by the bar and then denied by McClaren's goal-line clearance, whilst Gavin and Walsh hit the woodwork for City.

9. **Fulham (H) 1-5** — City have 80% of the possession and loads of chances, but Fulham score from all their shots on target. McGarvey heads against the bar and misses three other chances before Leaning's handling offence outside the area allows Andy Peters to shoot in Fulham's opener from a free-kick.

10. **Huddersfield (A) 1-0** — Any doubts to Walsh's right to merit a place amongst City's greats are dispelled by his superlative strike that settles this game. He gathers a clearance beyond the halfway line and spurts clear of the Terriers' defence to sweep a perfect low 20-yard shot into the far corner of the net.

11. **Northampton (A) 3-1** — Playing in borrowed blue shirts City notch up their first win at Northampton since 1961. After Eddie McGoldrick easily shoots in from Tony Adcock's pass, City make their dominance count with Milne's ten-yard equaliser being followed by two simple tap-ins from McGarvey.

Match Records

12 — ALDERSHOT (H) 25/10
Att: 8,685 | Opp pos: 24 | Pts: 19 | City pos: 8 | D | 1-1 | HT 0-1
Scorers: McGarvey 65 / Burvill 20 — Ref: A Seville

Pos	City	Aldershot
1	Waugh	Lange
2	Newman	Berry
3	Bailey	Barnes
4	Humphries	Burvill
5	Pender	Smith
6	McClaren	Wignall
7	Milne	Phillips
8	Galliers	Riley
9	McGarvey	Claridge
10	Walsh	McDonald
11	Jordan*	Randall
Sub	Shutt	

After four successive away wins in League and Cup, City's display against bottom of the table Aldershot is disappointing. Glyn Riley cleverly creates the opening for Glen Burvill to shoot the visitors in front, but after the break McGarvey heads in Newman's cross to save a point.

13 — MANSFIELD (A) 29/10
Att: 3,808 | Opp pos: 10 | Pts: 20 | City pos: 11 | D | 2-2 | HT 2-1
Scorers: McGarvey 30, Walsh 63 / Kent 24, Charles 63 — Ref: A Flood

Pos	City	Mansfield
1	Waugh	Cox
2	Newman	McKernon
3	Bailey	Ryan
4	Humphries	Kent
5	Pender	Foster
6	McClaren	Coleman
7	Milne	Owen
8	Galliers	Kearney
9	McGarvey*	Hodges
10	Walsh	Cassells*
11	Gavin	Charles
Sub	Shutt	Stringfellow

City are absolutely brilliant in the first half as McGarvey's header and Walsh's vicious right-foot drive bring about recovery from Kevin Kent's drilled-in opener. Steve Charles, though, levels with a close-range volley after the break to reward Mansfield for their great resilience.

14 — BOLTON (H) 5/11
Att: 8,809 | Opp pos: 12 | Pts: 21 | City pos: 9 | D | 1-1 | HT 1-0
Scorers: Newman 10 / Morgan 58 — Ref: J Carter

Pos	City	Bolton
1	Waugh	Felgate
2	Llewellyn	Brown
3	Bailey	Cowdrill
4	Humphries	Savage*
5	Pender	Brookman
6	McClaren	Winstanley
7	Milne	Crombie
8	Newman	Thompson
9	Shutt*	Morgan
10	Walsh	Stevens
11	Gavin	Darby
Sub	McGarvey	Storer

Trevor Morgan returns to give his former team-mates a lesson in the art of scoring goals after dominant City fail to add to Newman's drilled-in opener. He has just one opportunity, breaking clear to hammer in a low-drive that Waugh can only deflect into the bottom corner of the net.

15 — WOLVES (H) 8/11
Att: 11,336 | Opp pos: 7 | Pts: 21 | City pos: 12 | L | 0-1 | HT 0-0
Scorers: — / Mutch 89 — Ref: G Ashby

Pos	City	Wolves
1	Waugh	Kendall
2	Newman	Bellamy
3	Bailey	Venus
4	Humphries	Streete
5	Pender	Robertson
6	McClaren*	Robinson
7	Milne	Thompson
8	Galliers	Downing
9	Shutt*	Bull
10	Walsh	Mutch
11	Gavin	Dennison
Sub	Llewellyn/McGarvey	

The utterly absorbing contest between two well-matched sides, each managing five shots on target, is settled at the death. Andy Mutch is given space to score with an overhead as City's static defence allows the ball, from Robert Dennison's right-wing corner, to bounce in front of goal.

16 — WIGAN (A) 12/11
Att: 2,675 | Opp pos: 20 | Pts: 24 | City pos: 10 | W | 1-0 | HT 0-0
Scorers: Gavin 76 — Ref: A Wilkie

Pos	City	Wigan
1	Waugh	Adkins
2	Newman	Senior
3	Bailey	Tankard
4	Humphries	Hamilton !
5	Pender	Beesley
6	Stanley*	McEwan
7	McGarvey*	Thompson
8	Galliers	Butler
9	Shutt	Entwhistle
10	Walsh	Diamond
11	Gavin	Rimmer
Sub	Llewellyn/Hawkins	

With Milne transferred to Man Utd for £170,000, City have difficulty in breaking down a side reduced to ten men. David Hamilton is sent off as early as the eighth min for his tackle on Galliers, but City have to repel unlikely Wigan pressure before Gavin volleys in his ten-yard winner.

17 — SHEFFIELD UTD (A) 26/11
Att: 11,248 | Opp pos: 2 | Pts: 24 | City pos: 12 | L | 0-3 | HT 0-1
Scorers: Deane 12, 78, Agana 63 — Ref: T Holbrook

Pos	City	Sheffield Utd
1	Waugh	Benstead
2	Stanley	Wilder
3	Bailey	Pike
4	Humphries	Booker
5	Newman	Stancliffe
6	McClaren	Smith
7	McGarvey*	Roberts
8	Galliers	Todd
9	Shutt	Agana
10	Walsh	Deane
11	Gavin	Bryson
Sub	Hawkins	

United's greater prowess in and around the penalty area brings City's run of away success to an end. After Brian Deane rises unchallenged to head in United's opener, City come close to an equaliser on a number of occasions, before Tony Agana ends all hope with a stunning volley.

18 — READING (H) 3/12
Att: 8,045 | Opp pos: 13 | Pts: 27 | City pos: 10 | W | 2-1 | HT 0-1
Scorers: Walsh 56, Hawkins 77 / Senior 39 — Ref: J Deakin

Pos	City	Reading
1	Waugh	Phillips
2	Newman	Franklin
3	Bailey	Richardson
4	Humphries	Elsey
5	Pender	Hicks
6	McClaren	Whitlock
7	McGarvey*	Knight
8	Galliers	Tait*
9	Shutt*	Senior
10	Walsh	Moran
11	Gavin	Gilkes
Sub	Hawkins	Taylor

Backed by a strong wind and driving rain Gavin inspires City's second-half fight-back after surviving Steve Richardson's crunching tackles. He takes on the Reading defence before delivering a perfect cross for Walsh to volley in an equaliser to Trevor Senior's headed opener.

19 — CARDIFF (H) 17/12
Att: 7,493 | Opp pos: 18 | Pts: 30 | City pos: 7 | W | 2-0 | HT 1-0
Scorers: Newman 4, Hawkins 82 — Ref: R Lewis

Pos	City	Cardiff
1	Waugh	Wood
2	Newman	Rodgerson*
3	Bailey	Platnauer
4	Humphries*	Wimbleton
5	Pender	Abraham
6	McClaren	Boyle
7	McGarvey*	Curtis*
8	Stanley	Bartlett
9	Shutt*	Gilligan
10	Walsh	Gummer
11	Gavin	Lynex
Sub	Llewellyn/Hawkins	Bater/Wheeler

Newman's majestic shot past George Wood from the edge of the area sets up City's victory in the Severnside derby. Cardiff, unlucky before the break on the award of a free-kick rather than a pen, are finished by a defensive mix-up allowing Hawkins to shoot in City's killer second.

20 — BURY (A) 26/12
Att: 3,368 | Opp pos: 4 | Pts: 30 | City pos: 10 | L | 1-2 | HT 1-1
Scorers: McGarvey 9 / Hoyland 22, Robinson 58p — Ref: J Key

Pos	City	Bury
1	Waugh	Farnworth
2	Honor	Hill
3	Bailey	Bishop
4	Humphries*	Hoyland
5	Pender	Valentine
6	McClaren	Lee
7	McGarvey	Robinson
8	Stanley	Elliott
9	Shutt*	McIlroy
10	Walsh	Parkinson
11	Gavin	
Sub	Hawkins	

Making light of the driving rain in the early stages City take the lead when McGarvey turns neatly on Shutt's cross to hammer the ball home. After Jamie Hoyland had levelled matters with his looping header, Newman brings down Bury's match-winning penalty.

21 — SOUTHEND (A) 31/12
Att: 4,012 | Opp pos: 16 | Pts: 33 | City pos: 9 | W | 2-1 | HT 1-0
Scorers: McGarvey 7, Walsh 80 / Bennett 83 — Ref: D Hedges

Pos	City	Southend
1	Waugh	Sansome
2	Honor	Johnson
3	Bailey	Martin
4	Humphries	Butler
5	Pender	Westley
6	McClaren	Clements
7	McGarvey	Hall
8	Stanley*	Lee
9	Shutt*	Robinson
10	Walsh	Crown
11	Gavin	Ling
Sub	Galliers	McDonough

A hard-earned, but deserved victory at Roots Hall, where Pender is dominant at the heart of City's defence. McGarvey pounces as Paul Sansome can only parry a cross, and then Walsh heads in from four yards to double City's advantage, before Southend make their late reply.

22 — BRISTOL ROV (A) 2/1
Att: 23,191 | Opp pos: 5 | Pts: 33 | City pos: 10 | L | 0-1 | HT 0-0
Scorers: — / Penrice 54 — Ref: J Carter

Pos	City	Bristol Rov
1	Waugh	Martyn
2	Honor	Alexander
3	Bailey	Twentyman
4	Humphries	Yates
5	Pender	Smith*
6	McClaren	Jones
7	McGarvey*	Holloway
8	Stanley*	Reece
9	Shutt*	White
10	Walsh	Penrice
11	Gavin^	Purnell
Sub	Shepherd/Hawkins	McClean

What used to be mission impossible is not anymore, as the Rovers come to Ashton Gate and conquer with ease. With Liverpool boss Kenny Dalglish watching from the stand, the grounded Devon White sticks out a foot to divert the ball for Gary Penrice to shoot in from 20 yards.

23 — CHESTERFIELD (A) 14/1
Att: 3,488 | Opp pos: 22 | Pts: 33 | City pos: 11 | L | 0-1 | HT 0-0
Scorers: — / Bloomer 47 — Ref: T Fitzharris

Pos	City	Chesterfield
1	Waugh	Cherry
2	Honor	Hewitt
3	Bailey	Prindiville
4	Humphries	Shaw
5	Pender	Brien
6	McClaren	Rogers
7	McGarvey*	Eley^
8	Shepherd	Arnott
9	Shutt	White
10	Walsh	Bloomer
11	Gavin	Waller
Sub	Galliers	MacDonald; Jordan/Morris

Jordan will need all his inspirational qualities to raise City for their League Cup quarter-final after this dreary display. Bob Bloomer shoots into an open goal to put the Spireites ahead, but Walsh's disallowed header is all City can muster for their total domination of the closing stages.

BARCLAYS LEAGUE DIVISION 3 — Manager: Joe Jordan — SEASON 1988-89

No	Date	Team	Att	Pos	Res	Pt	F-A	H-T	Scorers, Times, and Referees	1	2	3	4	5	6	7	8	9	10	11	subs used
24	21/1	H CHESTER	9,586 *8*	13	L	33	0-1	0-0	Johnson 66 — Ref: J Martin	Waugh	Honor	Bailey	Newman	Pender	McClaren	Shepherd	Galliers	Shutt	Walsh*	Gavin	McGarvey
										Stewart	*Butler**	*Woodthorpe*	*Hinigan*	*Abel*	*Lane*	*Jakub*	*Barrow*	*Johnson*	*Graham**	*Dale*	*Newhouse/Lightfoot*
25	28/1	A PRESTON	6,091 *7*	13	L	33	0-2	0-0	Mooney 58, 61 — Ref: T Simpson	Waugh	Honor	Bailey	Newman	Pender	McClaren	Galliers	Turner	Shutt	Walsh	Gavin	
										Tunks	*Williams N*	*Rathbone*	*Jones*	*Wrightson*	*Atkins*	*Mooney*	*Joyce*	*Ellis*	*Brazil*	*Patterson*	
26	3/2	A SWANSEA	6,523 *3*	12	D	34	1-1	1-0	Turner 15; James 86p — Ref: R Bridges	Waugh	Honor	Bailey	Newman	Pender	Mardon	Galliers	Turner	McGarvey*	Walsh	Stanley*	McClaren/Gavin
										Bracey	*Lewis*	*Coleman*	*Melville*	*Knill*	*James*	*Thornber**	*Davies*	*Phillips*	*Wade*	*Hutchison*	*Hough/Raynor*
27	11/2	H GILLINGHAM	7,319 *24*	11	W	37	1-0	0-0	Jordan 74 — Ref: M Bodenham	Waugh	Honor	Bailey	Newman	Pender	Mardon	Galliers	Dolan*	McGarvey*	Walsh	McClaren	Jordan/Gavin
										Kite	*Burley*	*Stimson*	*Reeves*	*Walker*	*Manuel*	*O'Shea*	*Docker*	*Lovell*	*Lillis**	*Smith D*	*Shipley*
28	18/2	A FULHAM	4,408 *9*	13	L	37	1-3	1-1	McGarvey 27; Walker 8, Davies 50, Marshall 65 — Ref: M Bailey	Waugh	Honor	Bailey	Newman	Pender	Mardon	Dolan	McClaren	Gavin	Walsh	Stanley	
										Stannard	*Langley*	*Elkins*	*Skinner*	*Rougvie*	*Thomas*	*Scott*	*Marshall*	*Cole**	*Davies*	*Walker*	*Donnellan*
29	21/2	A ALDERSHOT	1,960 *23*	11	W	40	1-0	1-0	Walsh 32 — Ref: P Foakes	Waugh	Stanley*	Bailey	Newman	Pender	Shutt	Honor	McClaren	Walsh	Turner	Dolan*	Jordan/Mardon
										Lange	*Brown*	*Barnes*	*Burvill*	*Smith*	*Wignall*	*Stewart*	*Puckett*	*Claridge*	*Mazzon*	*Randal**	*Riley*
30	4/3	H NORTHAMPTON	7,197 *16*	12	W	43	3-1	3-0	Shutt 27, Walsh 33, Turner 43; Walsh 85 (og) — Ref: L Dilkes	Waugh	Honor*	Bailey*	Newman	Pender	Mardon	Llewellyn	McClaren	Shutt	Walsh	Turner	Stanley
										Gleasure	*Williams*	*Wilson*	*Thomas*	*Badley**	*McPherson*	*Quow*	*Collins**	*Gilbert*	*Adcock*	*Berry*	*Culpin/Sandeman*
31	11/3	A BOLTON	4,423 *19*	14	L	43	0-2	0-0	Darby 83, 86 — Ref: T Mills	Waugh	Honor*	Bailey	Newman	Pender	Mardon	Llewellyn	McClaren	Shutt	Walsh	Gavin	
										Felgate	*Brown*	*Cowdrill*	*Brookman**	*Crombie*	*Winstanley*	*Chandler*	*Thompson*	*Thomas*	*Jeffrey*	*Darby*	*Storer*
32	18/3	H NOTTS CO	6,407 *10*	14	L	43	0-4	0-1	Barnes 33, 53, O'Riordan 60, Draper 65 — Ref: R Gifford	Waugh	Honor	Bailey	Newman	Pender	Mardon	Gavin*	McClaren	Shutt	Walsh	Turner	Galliers
										Cherry	*McStay*	*Withe*	*O'Riordan*	*Yates*	*Law*	*Turner*	*Barnes**	*Lund*	*Pike*	*Draper*	*Thorpe/Fairclough*
33	21/3	H MANSFIELD	5,065 *14*	11	W	46	2-0	1-0	Newman 27p, 84 — Ref: P Vanes	Waugh	Honor	Bailey	Humphries	Pender	Newman	Galliers	McClaren*	Hawkins*	Walsh	Turner	Mardon/Jordan
										Cox	*McKernan*	*Kearney*	*Hodges**	*Foster*	*Coleman*	*Hathaway*	*Charles*	*Kent*	*Cassells*	*Ryan*	*Owen*
34	25/3	A BRISTOL ROV	8,435 *5*	11	D	47	1-1	1-1	Penrice 26 / Walsh 24 — Ref: P Wright	Waugh	Honor	Bailey	Humphries*	Pender	Newman	Galliers*	McClaren	Taylor	Walsh	Turner	Mardon/Hawkins
										Martyn	*Alexander*	*Twentyman*	*Yates*	*Reece*	*Jones*	*Holloway*	*Bailey*	*McClean*	*Penrice*	*Purnell**	*White*

24 CHESTER — Ex City forward Steve Johnson shows the aggression so lacking amongst Jordan's featherweight attackers as he heads powerfully past Waugh. Chester, beaten in their three previous games, are fully deserving of their success as they squander several good chances to add to their lead.

25 PRESTON — City's sixth defeat in seven matches begs the question of whether sufficient members of Jordan's squad have the hunger for success to go with their undoubted ability. On Deepdale's artificial surface Brian Mooney's 20-yarder, and his simple tap-in bring Preston their deserved success.

26 SWANSEA — A hero when volleying past Lee Bracey, Turner turns villain near the end when he prevents City from ending their lean spell. Much of City's hard work goes to waste as Turner gifts Robbie James his fierce pen when jumping with his arm raised to clear Tommy Hutchison's free-kick.

27 GILLINGHAM — Jordan secures victory as he races clear onto Walsh's pass to smash an unstoppable 20-yarder into the far corner of the net. The Gills threaten whenever David Smith is in possession, and they are unlucky not to secure a penalty when the speedy winger is blatantly tripped by Mardon.

28 FULHAM — Grateful Fulham cash in to end four games without a win as City suffer a Cup hangover. McGarvey neatly heads in an equaliser after Clive Walker had blasted in from an acute angle, but City's motivation fades away after a bout of head tennis ends with John Marshall nodding in.

29 ALDERSHOT — There are more live wires off the pitch than on as the terracing behind one goal has to be evacuated in the first half because of a power cable fault. Walsh's feared left foot settles this poor game, curling a powerful shot round the Aldershot wall after Shutt is tripped 25 yards out.

30 NORTHAMPTON — After a shaky start Shutt's memorable angled drive into the roof of the net from 25 yards revives City. Robbie Turner wins over the Ashton Gate fans with his all-action display. His challenge setting up Walsh's precision strike, and then heading in Llewellyn's superb far-post cross.

31 BOLTON — City get what they deserve for offering little more than a packed defence at Burnden Park. Twice Bailey has to hook off the line, whilst Mike Jeffrey hits the post, but Julian Darby's prod-in, and his far-post header deservedly bring Bolton their first win over City in more than 14 years.

32 NOTTS CO — City give a dreadful, passionless display against mid-table County, who are not discouraged by Waugh's saving of Geoff Pike's early penalty. Mark Draper is unmarked as he lashes in the final goal, after Paul Barnes had outpaced City's spread-eagled defence to clip in the opener.

33 MANSFIELD — With the game already won Jordan is surprisingly booed as he brings himself on for the exhausted Hawkins. Newman is City's man of the match, netting with a penalty after George Foster whips his legs away, and quelling Mansfield's second-half revival with his late cross-shot.

34 BRISTOL ROV — City's joy as Walsh fires in from six yards, is soon cut short by Penrice's shot into an empty net. Geoff Twentyman's goal-line clearance, and keeper Nigel Martyn's save from Newman's 41st-min penalty, prevents City's first League win over Rovers for more than three years.

Bradford City — season match-by-match record (games 35–46)

No	Venue	Date	Opponent	Att	City Pos	Opp Pos	Res	Pts	FT	HT	Scorers	Referee
35	H	27/3	BURY	8,496	10	8	W	50	3-0	1-0	Turner 44, 63, Taylor 89	Ref: W Burge
36	A	1/4	CARDIFF	6,358	11	18	D	51	1-1	0-1	Taylor 79 / Platnauer 18	Ref: R Wiseman
37	A	4/4	BRENTFORD	4,627	13	11	L	51	0-3	0-2	Sealy 1, 51, Cockram 30p	Ref: H King
38	H	8/4	SOUTHEND	6,213	14	19	L	51	0-2	0-1	Ling 10, 60	Ref: J Moules
39	H	11/4	BRENTFORD	4,339	14	9	L	51	0-1	0-0	Evans 83	Ref: M Reed
40	H	15/4	BLACKPOOL	5,090	14	21	L	51	1-2	1-0	Taylor 36 / Walwyn 66, 72	Ref: R Pawley
41	H	18/4	HUDDERSFIELD	4,542	13	9	W	54	6-1	5-0	Taylor 2, 16, 27, Walsh 4p, Gavin 15, [McClaren 76] / Maskell 62	Ref: P Alcock
42	A	21/4	PORT VALE	6,923	13	3	W	57	1-0	0-0	Taylor 59	Ref: N Midgley
43	H	29/4	WIGAN	5,555	13	20	L	57	0-1	0-0	Tankard 88	Ref: G Pooley
44	A	1/5	WOLVES	17,351	14	1	L	57	0-2	0-1	Bull 35, 89	Ref: D Hedges
45	A	5/5	READING	3,620	11	17	W	60	2-1	1-1	Turner 43, Pender 60 / Hicks 42	Ref: K Cooper
46	H	13/5	SHEFFIELD UTD	10,769	11	2	W	63	2-0	0-0	Turner 55, Taylor 75	Ref: M James

Line-ups (City listed first, opponent in italics; * = substituted, ! = sent off):

35 BURY — Waugh, Honor, Humphries, Bailey, Pender, Newman, McClaren, Mardon, Taylor, Walsh, Turner / *Farnworth, Pashley, Hoyland, Bishop, Wassall, Clements, Lee, Robinson, Hulme*, McIlroy*, Parkinson, Greenwood/Atkin*
Bury supply the neat football, but it is City who have the killer touch after Newman's 42nd-min pen is saved by Simon Farnworth. Turner is on hand to hammer in City's opener, and then turns up to head in McClaren's cross, before Taylor gets in on the act with an unstoppable drive.

36 CARDIFF — Waugh, Honor, Humphries, Bailey, Pender, Newman, McClaren, Mardon, Taylor, Walsh, Turner / *Wood, Rodgerson, Morgan, Platnauer, Boyle, Stevenson, Kelly, Bater, Gilligan, Wheeler*, Lynex, Walsh*
Taylor (£225,000 ex Leeds) demonstrates his worth by controlling the ball on his chest, before swivelling to deliver a low-shot that takes the Cardiff keeper by surprise. Waugh keeps City in contention, but even he can do nothing about Nicky Platnauer's deflected free-kick.

37 BRENTFORD — Waugh, Honor, Humphries, Bailey, Pender, Newman, McClaren, Mardon*, Taylor, Walsh, Turner, Galliers / *Parks, Buttigieg, Stanislaus*, Bates, Evans, Cockram, Jones, Sealy, Purdie*, Blissett, Smillie, Pearce/Godfrey*
After braving the sleet, snow and swirling winds to reach Griffin Park, the fans have to endure City's disjointed and undisciplined play. Right from the kick-off City are in trouble, the unmarked Tony Sealy shooting in after just twelve seconds, and it is downhill all the way thereafter.

38 SOUTHEND — Waugh, Honor, Humphries, Bailey, Pender, Newman, McClaren*, Bromage, Hawkins, Walsh*, Turner, Mardon/McGarvey / *Sansome, Roberts, Johnson, Butler, Prior, Brush, Martin, Hall, Crown, McDonough, Ling*
City, embarrassed by a Southend side fighting to keep clear of relegation, are made to pay for poor marking and lack of concentration. Martin Ling, after being allowed the space in the first half to convert Derek Hall's cross, nips in to rob Bailey and coolly slip the ball past Waugh.

39 BRENTFORD — Waugh, Honor, Humphries, Bailey, Pender, Newman, McClaren, Bromage, Taylor, Walsh, Turner / *Parks, Feeley, Stanislaus*, Bates, Evans, Cockram, Jones, Sealy, Purdie*, Blissett, Smillie, Pearce/Godfrey*
No doubt those missing from the gaping terraces will have thought they did well in skipping this defeat. However City's ten to three shots on target advantage, suggests that Brentford are fortunate that Tony Evans' late header from Allan Cockram's free-kick brings all three points.

40 BLACKPOOL — Waugh, Honor, Humphries, Bailey, Pender, Newman, McClaren, Bromage, Taylor, Walsh, Turner*, Hawkins / *Siddall, Burgess, Matthews*, Elliott, Methven, Deary, Davies, Coughlin, Garner, Gore, Madden, Walwyn*
Taylor's first-half volley fails to halt City's slump from cup heroes to possible relegation candidates. Keith Walwyn's 61st-minute arrival brings Blackpool their first win in eleven games on a day that 95 fans are crushed to death attending the FA Cup Semi-Final at Hillsborough.

41 HUDDERSFIELD — Waugh, Honor*, Humphries, Bailey, Pender, Newman, McClaren, Galliers, Taylor, Walsh, Turner, Gavin / *Hardwick, Trevitt, May, Mitchell, O'Doherty ! Duggan, Winter, Byrne*, Cecere, Maskell, Smith, McInerney*
City's super show follows a minute's silence for the Hillsborough victims. Taylor completes his hat-trick with two low shots, after opening his account with a header and being up-ended for Walsh's penalty. Ken O'Doherty is sent off for his second bookable offence on 82 minutes.

42 PORT VALE — Waugh, Honor*, Humphries, Bailey, Pender, Newman, McClaren, Galliers, Taylor, Walsh, Turner, Humphries/Eaton / *Grew, Mills, Hughes, Walker, Webb, Glover, Jeffers, Earle, Jones*, Beckford, Riley, Futcher*
City would not have been flattered by a four-goal winning margin as Taylor and Turner turn in a brilliant performance at Vale Park. Mark Grew repeatedly comes to Vale's rescue as his defence is torn apart time and again, but he cannot keep out Taylor's firm downward header.

43 WIGAN — Waugh, Honor*, Humphries, Bailey, Newman, McClaren, Galliers, Gavin, Taylor, Walsh, Turner*, Humphries/Eaton / *Adkins, Senior, Atherton, Tankard, Beesley, Pilling, Thompson, Rimmer, Entwistle, Page, Griffiths*
Wigan snatch the points, with Allen Tankard's superb 35-yard left-footed late strike, after City had been denied by the woodwork on five occasions. Nigel Adkins' great display between the sticks ensures City's home record is the worst since their relegation season of 1981-82.

44 WOLVES — Waugh, Humphries, Bailey, Newman, McClaren, Pender, Galliers !, Gavin, Taylor, Walsh, Turner, Hawkins*/Eaton / *Hansbury, Bellamy, Thompson, Streete, Robertson, Vaughan, Gooding, Downing, Bull, Mutch, Dennison*
Galliers' over-the-ball tackle on Steve Bull leaves City a man short from the 65th minute, but they are not finished off until just before time. Bull slams in Andy Mutch's chipped pass for his 49th goal of the season, after earlier scoring with a perfectly-angled shot past Waugh.

45 READING — Waugh, Honor*, Bromage, Humphries, Pender, Newman, McClaren, Galliers, Taylor, Walsh, Turner / *Francis, Jones*, Richardson, Beavon, Hicks, Whitlock, Knight*, Elsey, Senior, Payne, Gilkes, Williams/Moran*
Waugh's 79th-minute save from Stuart Beavon's spot-kick sentences Reading to their sixth successive defeat. After McClaren does well early on to clear off the line, headers from Martin Hicks and Turner keeps things level at the break, before Pender's header secures City's victory.

46 SHEFFIELD UTD — Leaning, Honor, Bromage, Newman, McClaren, McClaren, Galliers, Galliers, Taylor, Walsh, Turner, Powell / *Tracey, Wilder, Pike, Moore, Stancliffe, Carr, Roberts, Todd*, Agana, Deane, Bryson*
A pitch invasion four minutes from the end takes the headlines away from City's win. Turner's volley, and Taylor's follow-up when Simon Tracey parries his first effort, produce a defeat United can live with, as only a massive deficit could have robbed them of automatic promotion.

Home 8,121 Away 5,410 Average 8,121

BARCLAYS DIVISION 3 (CUP-TIES)

Manager: Joe Jordan

SEASON 1988-89

Littlewoods Cup

	Scorers, Times, and Referees	F-A	H-T	1	2	3	4	5	6	7	8	9	10	11	subs used
1:1 H EXETER 30/8 — 6,005	Newman 6p — Ref: K Cooper	W	1-0	1-0	Waugh	Llewellyn	Bromage	Humphries*	Pender	McClaren	Milne	Galliers	Newman	Walsh	Caldwell*	Honor/Hawkins
					Gwinnett	*Banks*	*Viney*	*Rogers*	*Taylor*	*Cooper*	*Rowbotham*	*Hiley*	*Langley*	*Neville*	*Harrower*	
1:2 A EXETER 7/9 — 2,749	Walsh 84 — Ref: V Callow — (City won 2-0 on aggregate)	W	1-0	0-0	Waugh	Llewellyn	Bromage	Mardon	Pender	McClaren	Newman	Galliers	Shutt	Walsh	Jordan*	Milne
					Gwinnett	*Banks*	*Viney*	*Rogers*	*Taylor*	*Cooper*	*Rowbotham*	*Hiley*	*Batty*	*Neville*	*Harrower*	
2:1 A OXFORD 28/9 — 3,705 2:12	Walsh 6, Hawkins 44, Shutt 60, Milne 89 — Saunders 28, 65 — Ref: R Wiseman	W	4-2	2-1	Leaning	Llewellyn	Bromage	Newman	Pender	McClaren	Milne	Galliers	Shutt*	Walsh	Hawkins	Mardon Purdie
					Hucker	*Bardsley*	*Smart*	*Phillips L*	*Hill*	*Greenall*	*Heath*^*	*Foyle*	*Saunders*	*Mustoe*	*Rhoades-B'rn*	
2:2 H OXFORD 11/10 — 6,255 2:10	Shutt 37, McClaren 58 — Ref: B Stevens — (City won 6-2 on aggregate)	W	2-0	1-0	Leaning	Humphries	Bailey	Newman	Pender	McClaren	Gavin*	Galliers	Shutt	Walsh	Jordan*	Hawkins/Mardon Hill/Heath
					Judge	*Bardsley*	*Phillips J*	*Phillips L*	*Briggs*	*Greenall*	*Purdie*	*Foyle*	*Saunders*	*Mustoe^*	*Rh'des-B'n**	
3 H CRYS PALACE 1/11 — 12,167 2:8	Shutt 12, Milne 19, 22, Walsh 82 — Pardew 89 — Ref: J Rushton	W	4-1	3-0	Waugh	Newman	Bailey	Humphries	Pender	McClaren	Milne	Galliers	Shutt	Walsh	Barber	
					Parkin	*Pemberton*	*Hone*	*Pardew*	*Hopkins*	*O'Reilly*	*Refearn*	*Thomas*	*Bright*	*Salako*	*Barber*	
4 H TRANMERE 29/11 — 11,110 4:10	Shutt 30 — Ref: A Buksh	W	1-0	1-0	Waugh	Stanley	Bailey	Newman	Pender	McClaren	Hawkins	Galliers	Shutt*	Walsh	Gavin	Jordan Williams/Malkin
					Nixon	*Higgins*	*McCarrick*	*Martindale*	*Moore^*	*Vickers*	*Murray**	*Bishop*	*Steel*	*Muir*	*Mungall*	
QF A BRADFORD C 18/1 — 15,330 2:18	Walsh 2 — Ref: B Hill	W	1-0	1-0	Waugh	Honor	Bailey	Newman	Pender	McClaren	Palin	Shepherd	Jordan*	Walsh	Gavin	Shutt Jewell/Oliver
					Tomlinson	*Mitchell*	*Abbott**	*Banks^*	*Jackson*	*Evans D*	*Palin*	*Sinnott*	*Ormondroyd*	*Kennedy*	*Leonard*	
SF 1 A NOTT'M FOREST 15/2 — 30,016 1:4	Mardon 65 — Pender 86 (og) — Ref: T Holbrook	D	1-1	0-0	Waugh	Honor	Bailey	Newman	Pender	McClaren	Carr	Mardon	McClaren	Walsh	Jordan	Shutt
					Sutton	*Laws*	*Pearce*	*Chettle*	*Wilson*	*Hodge*		*Webb*	*Clough*	*Chapman*	*Parker*	
SF 2 H NOTT'M FOREST 26/2 — 28,084 1:7	Parker 114 — Ref: J Worrell — (City lost 1-2 on aggregate)	L	0-1 aet	0-0	Waugh	Honor	Bailey	Newman	Pender	Mardon	Galliers	McClaren	Gavin*	Walsh	Jordan	Shutt
					Sutton	*Laws*	*Pearce*	*Walker*	*Wilson*	*Hodge*	*Carr*	*Webb*	*Clough*	*Chapman*	*Parker*	

Exeter are unfortunate to lose to Newman's penalty after Lee Rogers was adjudged to have handled McClaren's cross. The visitors create the better chances in a poor game, Darren Rowbotham and Shaun Taylor going close, before Llewellyn's goal-line clearance robs Richard Cooper.

City's tactics to defend their first-leg advantage produces a game as dull as Exeter's sub-standard floodlights. Milne's mazy run creates the perfect opening for Walsh to return to his more normal scoring mode, his trusty left foot confirming City's place in the second round.

City's splendid all-round team performance ends Oxford's eight season (27 game) record of not having been beaten at home in the League Cup. Milne seals City's victory with a cracking 20-yarder past Peter Hucker at the finish of his superb run at Oxford's retreating defence.

City are fortunate to survive Oxford's impressive start, but once Jordan abandons his safety-first tactics designed to preserve the first-leg lead things improve. McClaren shoots in from 18 yards after earlier providing the through ball for Shutt's great 15-yard left-foot shot on the run.

Palace are demoralised as City repeat the purple patch they struck at Mansfield with an early three-goal salvo. Shutt's flying header is followed by Milne's double strike, as he registers with a first-time curler around Brian Parkin, before drilling in Walsh's low cross from close range.

Shutt brings the tie to life by finishing with a perfectly-struck right-foot shot after beating a couple of defenders. Tranmere abandon their sweeper system after the break, but City have the chances (six on target, compared to Tranmere's one) without being able to add to their score.

Given little chance of succeeding where Everton and Spurs had failed in cup competitions this season, Jordan inspires City's great display at Valley Parade. Walsh's reliable left foot decides the outcome after only 85 seconds, as City's defence restrict Bradford to two on-target shots.

Despite the handicap of facing one of their bogey teams, City turn in a magnificent backs-to-the-wall performance. Mardon's 15-yard drive should have inflicted Forest's first defeat in 12 games, but Pender turns Neil Webb's flick into his own net to leave the tie neatly balanced.

Shown live on ITV this game is marred by the tragic death of drummer Colin Burgess just before the start. An epic struggle in the wind and rain, nearly settled by Walsh's shot against the post at the end of normal time, is resolved by Gary Parker's fierce drive late into extra-time.

FA Cup

	Scorers, Times, and Referees	F-A	H-T	1	2	3	4	5	6	7	8	9	10	11	subs used
1 H SOUTHEND 19/11 — 7,027 21	Walsh 22, McGarvey 32, Shutt, 80 — Ling 57 — Ref: M James	W	3-1	2-0	Waugh	Honor	Bailey	Humphries	Pender	Newman	McGarvey	Galliers	Shutt	Walsh	Gavin	Smith/Ramsey
					Sansome	*Edinburgh*	*Johnson*	*Martin**	*Westley*	*Hall*	*Clark^*	*Robinson*	*Crown*	*Bennett*	*Ling*	
2 A ALDERSHOT 10/12 — 3,793 4:23	Shutt 90 — McDonald 76p — Ref: J Borrett	D	1-1	0-0	Waugh	Newman	Bailey	Humphries	Pender	Mardon	Mazzon*	Galliers*	Shutt	Walsh	Gavin	Jordan Ring
					Lange	*Brown*	*Phillips*	*Burvill*	*Smith*	*Wignall*	*Anderson*	*Claridge*	*McDonald*	*Randall*	*Stanley*	

It's easy for City until Martin Ling shoots in following Waugh's penalty save. Fortunately Shutt curtails Southend's fight-back by grabbing another of his customary classic cup goals. He arrives at speed to meet Gavin's right-wing cross and send a soaring header into the net.

Deep into injury-time Shutt saves City, as his soft header to Walsh's free-kick squirms through Tony Lange's hands and trickles into the net. Ian McDonald, denied the bar just after half-time, puts Aldershot in front with a controversial penalty after Pender blocks Steve Claridge.

Cup matches

2R H ALDERSHOT 13/12 | 10 | 0-0 | 0-0 | aet | 7,299 4.23

City: Waugh, Newman, Bailey, Humphries, Llewellyn*, McClaren, Pender, McGarvey, Galliers*, Walsh, Gavin, Stanley
Aldershot: Lange, Brown, Phillips, Burvill*, Brown, Wignall, Smith, Mazzon, Ring, McDonald, Randall, Chandler

Nothing goes right for City, even losing the toss for choice of venue for the second replay. There is plenty of effort, but no one is able to find the telling pass necessary to eliminate an Aldershot side, for whom Steve Claridge strikes twice, belying their lowly League position.
Ref: J Borrett

2 A ALDERSHOT 20/12 | 7 | 2-2 | 0-1 | aet | 3,801 4.23
Shutt 90, Newman 110p / Randall 14, Claridge 111

City: Waugh, Newman, Bailey, Llewellyn*, McGarvey, Stanley, Pender, McClaren, Galliers, Walsh, Gavin, Shutt/Honor
Aldershot: Lange, Ring, Phillips*, Brown, Mazzon, Anderson, Smith, Wignall, Claridge, McDonald, Randall, Barnes/Chandler

Shutt's mid-air volley produces a last-gasp equaliser, after Adrian Randall's speculative 35-yard drive had put the Shots in front. In extra-time Claridge drives the ball in to punish City for thinking the tie won with Newman's pen after David Barnes had clattered into the back of Gavin.
Ref: D Axcell

2R H ALDERSHOT 22/12 | 7 | 1-0 | 1-0 | W | 6,246 4.23
Shutt 10

City: Waugh, Honor, Bailey, Newman, McGarvey, McClaren, Pender, Shutt, Stanley*, Walsh, Gavin, Galliers
Aldershot: Lange, Brown, Barnes, Ring*, Mazzon, Anderson, Smith, Wignall, Claridge, McDonald, Randall, Chandler

City's longest-ever cup-tie is settled early on as Honor's deflected cross gives Shutt the time to bring the ball down before blasting it in. Newman completely subdues the dangerous Steve Claridge, and Aldershot are left to rue letting City off the hook in the previous games.
Ref: H King

3 A HARTLEPOOL 7/1 | 10 | 0-1 | 0-0 | L | 4,033 4.16
Baker 70p

City: Waugh, Honor, Bailey, Newman, McGarvey*, McClaren, Pender, Shepherd, Walsh, Gavin, Jordan
Hartlepool: Moverley, Nobbs, McKinnon, Tinkler, Stokes, Baker, Honour, Toman, Borthwick, Grayson*, Barratt, Allon

City stumble out of the FA Cup as their lightweight attack rarely threaten a worthwhile shot at the Victoria ground. Skipper Pender's needless pull on Joe Allon's shirt after the ball had been cleared gifts Pool the penalty that deservedly takes them on a rare visit to the fourth round.
Ref: P Jones

League table

	Team	P	W	D	L	F	A	W	D	L	F	A	Pts
			Home					Away					
1	Wolves	46	18	4	1	61	19	8	10	5	35	30	92
2	Sheffield Utd	46	16	3	4	57	21	9	6	8	36	33	84
3	Port Vale *	46	15	3	5	46	21	9	9	5	32	27	84
4	Fulham	46	12	7	4	42	28	10	2	11	27	39	75
5	Bristol Rov	46	9	11	3	34	21	10	8	5	33	30	74
6	Preston	46	14	7	2	56	31	8	10	6	23	29	72
7	Brentford	46	14	5	4	36	21	4	9	10	30	40	68
8	Chester	46	12	6	5	38	18	7	5	11	26	43	68
9	Notts Co	46	11	7	5	37	22	7	6	10	27	32	67
10	Bolton	46	12	8	3	42	23	4	8	11	21	31	64
11	BRISTOL CITY	46	10	8	5	32	25	6	6	11	21	30	63
12	Swansea	46	11	8	4	33	22	5	4	14	18	31	61
13	Bury	46	11	7	5	27	22	5	6	12	28	45	61
14	Huddersfield	46	10	8	5	35	25	4	6	13	28	48	60
15	Mansfield	46	10	8	5	30	22	4	6	13	16	30	59
16	Cardiff	46	10	9	4	30	16	4	6	13	14	30	57
17	Wigan	46	9	5	9	28	22	5	9	9	27	31	56
18	Reading	46	10	6	7	37	29	5	5	13	31	43	56
19	Blackpool	46	10	6	7	36	29	4	7	12	20	30	55
20	Northampton	46	11	2	10	41	34	5	4	14	25	42	54
21	Southend	46	10	9	4	33	26	3	6	14	23	49	54
22	Chesterfield	46	9	5	9	35	35	5	2	16	16	51	49
23	Gillingham	46	7	3	13	25	32	1	5	17	22	49	40
24	Aldershot	46	7	6	10	29	29	7	1	10	19	49	37
		1104	268	146	138	902	593	138	146	268	593	902	1510

* promoted after play-offs

Appearances and Goals

Player	Lge	Sub	LC	Sub	FAC	Sub	Lge	LC	FAC	Tot
Bailey, John	35		5		6					
Bromage, Russell	13		3		3					
Caldwell, Tony	1						1			1
Carter, Tim	3		1							
Dolan, Eamonn	3									
Eaton, Jason		2								
Fitzpatrick, Paul		1								
Galliers, Steve	30	3	9		4	1	3			3
Gavin, Mark	26	3	6		6		2	1		3
Hawkins, Nigel	7	10	2	2	1					
Honor, Chris	24	2	3	1	3					
Humphries, Glenn	20	2	3		3					
Jordan, Joe	2	7	5	1			1			1
Leaning, Andy	6		4							
Llewellyn, Andy	13	3	4		1		1			1
Mardon, Paul	13	7	3	2						
McClaren, Steve	44	1	9		4		1			1
McGarvey, Scott	20	6	4		6		9		1	10
Milne, Ralph	10	1	3	1			2		3	5
Newman, Rob	46		9		6		6	1	1	8
Pender, John	45		9		6		1			1
Shepherd, Tony	2	1	1		1					
Shutt, Carl	21	3	5	2	5	1	1	4	4	9
Stanley, Gary	8	2	2	1	2	2				
Taylor, Bob	12						8			8
Turner, Robbie	19						6			6
Walsh, Alan	46		9		6		11	4	1	16
Waugh, Keith	37		7		6					
28 players used	506	54	99	9	66	6	53	15	7	75

Odds & ends

Double wins: (4) Gillingham, Huddersfield, Northampton, Reading.
Double losses: (4) Chester, Fulham, Wolves, Brentford.
Won from behind: (3) Reading (h), Reading (a), Northampton (a).
Lost from in front: (2) Bury (a), Blackpool (h).
High spots: 4-0 home success over Chesterfield on 3 September.
Beating Huddersfield 6-1 at Ashton Gate on 18 April.
Carl Shutt's goal that ends marathon four-game FA Cup battle with Aldershot.
Beating Oxford 4-2 at the Manor Ground in the FL Cup.
Beating Bradford City (a) 1-0 to reach the Semi-Finals of the FL Cup.
Record-breaking seven successive wins to reach the semi-finals of the FL Cup.
Low spots: Losing 0-1 v Bristol Rov at Ashton Gate on 2 January.
Losing 0-3 against Brentford at Griffin Park on 11 April.
Succumbing to a late extra-time goal in the 2nd leg of the FL Cup Semi-Final at Ashton Gate.
Losing 0-3 v Bristol Rov in the Gloucestershire Cup Final on 17 Aug.

Player of the year: Keith Waugh.
Ever-presents: (1) Alan Walsh.
Hat-tricks: (0).
Leading scorer: Alan Walsh (16).

BARCLAYS LEAGUE DIVISION 3

Manager: Joe Jordan

SEASON 1989-90

No	Date	Att	Pos	Pt	F-A	H-T	Scorers, Times, and Referees	1	2	3	4	5	6	7	8	9	10	11	subs used
1	A BURY 19/8	3,399	1	D 1	1-1	0-0	Taylor 57 / Greenwood 88 / Ref: J Lloyd	Leaning / Farnworth	Llewellyn / Hill	Bailey / Withe	Wimbleton* / Hoyland	Pender / Valentine	Rennie / Knill	Gavin* / Lee	Newman / Feeley*	Taylor / Cunningham Robinson	Smith / Robinson	Turner* / Parkinson^	Eaton/Mardon / McIlroy/Greenwood
2	H BIRMINGHAM 26/8	8,938		W 4	1-0	0-0	Taylor 74 / Ref: M James	Leaning / Thomas	Llewellyn / Ashley	Bailey / Matthewson Atkins	Wimbleton /	Pender / Sprason	Rennie / Overson	Gavin / Peer	Newman / Bailey	Taylor / Gordon	Smith / Frain	Shelton / Sturridge* Yates	
3	A NORTHAMPTON 2/9	4,088	15 10	L	0-2	0-0	Thomas 46, Adcock 89p / Ref: J Moules	Leaning / Gleasure	Llewellyn / Sandeman	Honor / Wilson	Wimbleton* / Thomas	Pender / Wilcox	Rennie / McPherson Quow	Gavin* /	Newman / Collins	Taylor / Donald	Smith / Adcock	Shelton / Berry	Turner/Mardon
4	H BLACKPOOL 9/9	7,172	8 7	W	2-0	0-0	Wimbleton 50p, Newman 65 / Ref: R Bigger	Leaning / McIlhargey Burgess	Llewellyn /	Bromage / Morgan	Wimbleton / Gore	Pender / Briggs	Rennie / Methven	Shelton* / Wright	Newman / Thompson	Taylor / Garner	Smith / Matthews	Turner / Bradshaw* Elliott	Gavin / Mardon
5	A CARDIFF 16/9	5,970	6 24	W	3-0	1-0	Shelton 45, Taylor 54, Turner 62 / Ref: K Breen	Leaning / Wood	Llewellyn / Rodgerson Daniel	Bromage /	Wimbleton / Lynex*	Pender / Abraham	Rennie / Perry	Shelton* / Curtis	Newman / Morgan	Taylor / Gilligan	Smith / Kelly	Turner / Sendall Fry	Mardon
6	H BRISTOL ROV 23/9	17,432	5 2 11	D	0-0	0-0	Ref: J Deakin	Leaning / Martyn	Llewellyn / Alexander!	Bromage* / Twentyman Yates	Wimbleton /	Pender / Mehew	Rennie / Jones	Shelton / Holloway	Newman / Reece	Taylor / White	Smith* / Penrice	Turner / Wilmott	Mardon/Gavin
7	H SHREWSBURY 26/9	9,188	4 5 14	W	2-1	1-0	Taylor 43, 86 / Purdie 60 / Ref: A Buksh	Leaning / Perks	Llewellyn / Green	Mardon / Priest	Wimbleton / Kelly	Pender / Pratley	Rennie / Moyes	Shelton* / Brown	Newman / Bell	Taylor / Purdie	Smith / McGinlay* Naughton	Turner / Griffiths	Gavin
8	A TRANMERE 29/9	8,977	4 1 14	L	0-6	0-2	[Bishop 85, 89] / Malkin 40, 41, Rennie 55 (og), Muir 77 / Ref: P Danson	Leaning / Nixon	Llewellyn / Higgins	Bailey / McCarrick	Wimbleton / Martindale* Hughes	Pender* /	Rennie / Vickers	Shelton / Morrissey	Newman / Harvey	Taylor / Malkin	Smith / Muir	Turner! / Thomas	Humphries/Gavin / Bishop
9	A BRENTFORD 7/10	7,421	5 19 17	W	2-0	1-0	Wimbleton 35p, Turner 77 / Ref: D Hedges	Leaning / Parks	Llewellyn / Bates*	Bailey / Fleming	Wimbleton / Millen	Pender / Evans	Rennie / Ratcliffe	Gavin / Jones	Newman / May	Taylor / Holdsworth Blissett*	Smith / Godfrey	Turner / Cockram/Cadette	
10	H SWANSEA 14/10	8,794	6 18 17	L	1-3	1-1	Taylor 15 / Raynor 1, Salako 66, 79 / Ref: K Barratt	Leaning / Freestone	Llewellyn / Hough	Bailey / Coleman	Wimbleton / Melville	Pender / Boyle	Rennie / James	Gavin / Harris	Newman / Curtis	Taylor / Hutchison	Smith / Salako	Eaton / Raynor	
11	H NOTTS CO 17/10	8,331	5 12 20	W	2-0	1-0	Eaton 16, Short 80 (og) / Ref: L Shapter	Leaning / Cherry	Llewellyn / Palmer	Bailey / Platnauer	Shelton / Short	Humphries / Yates	Rennie / Robinson	Gavin / Draper*	Newman / Turner	Taylor / Lund	Smith* / Barnes	Eaton / Chapman*	Wimbleton / Stant/McStay

Match 1 (Bury): City's encouraging display is blotted by lax defending as Nigel Greenwood is unmarked when he curls in Bury's late equaliser. Pender's push deprives Taylor of the fruits of his close-range shot, but within minutes Bailey's pass allows City's No 9 to celebrate with a legitimate strike.

Match 2 (Birmingham): The Brummies look the more effective side, but lack the finishing power as they fail to put away three good first-half chances. Off-form Taylor's match-winning spectacular overhead kick to connect with Newman's headed pass is an early candidate for goal of the season.

Match 3 (Northampton): 'What a load of rubbish' is the cry from the sizeable contingent of travelling fans at the end of this dismal affair. City cannot manage a single shot on target, whilst sloppy defending loses a chance of a point as Dean Thomas' free-kick finds its way through a gaping hole in City's wall.

Match 4 (Blackpool): Fielding seven back-four players, Pool's defensive intentions come to naught when Colin Methven's push on Taylor produces City's penalty. Jordan's decision to play his first team in the reserves midweek is vindicated as Newman nudges in the second to erase memories of last week.

Match 5 (Cardiff): Shortly after Wimbleton fires his spot-kick against a post, Shelton volleys in to set up a comfortable win. Class and courage are personified by City's strike force. Taylor's brilliant turn and rasping shot demonstrating class, whilst Turner has the courage to net with a fearless header.

Match 6 (Bristol Rov): City find out yet again that no amount of money can buy the teamwork and organisation that makes the Rovers such a powerful force. Whilst by no means a one-sided contest, the Rovers look the better unit as they overcome Ian Alexander's 34th-min dismissal for his second offence.

Match 7 (Shrewsbury): Shrewsbury live up to their top of the table billing with some slick control and neat passing, but City chase and harry their opponents into submission. Taylor, who lashed in City's opener, clinches the points with a header, after Jon Purdie had earlier slid in Shrewsbury's leveller.

Match 8 (Tranmere): An absorbing contest for 40 minutes, becomes an embarrassing rout after Chris Malkin turns in Tony Thomas' cross. Reduced to ten men following Turner's 53rd-minute sending off for elbowing Steve Vickers in the face, City loose Shelton just before the end with a calf strain.

Match 9 (Brentford): City spoil Brentford's 100th birthday with a deserved victory at Griffin Park. Poor finishing means City have to be satisfied with Wimbleton's penalty following Jamie Bates' push on Smith, and Turner's powerful close-range header, which is fumbled over the line by Tony Parks.

Match 10 (Swansea): John Salako (on loan from Palace) inspires Swansea to their first away points and goals of the season. Blunders at the back are City's undoing, starting after just 45 seconds as Salako exposes Newman's poor marking with an accurate cross for the unattended Paul Raynor to head in.

Match 11 (Notts Co): City's skilful first-half display is rewarded when Eaton caps a sweeping move, involving half-a-dozen players, with a perfect left-foot shot to open his League account. Under pressure as Notts County hit back, City are much relieved when Gavin's cross cannons in off Craig Short.

No		Date	Opponent	Result		Score	Pos	Att
12	A	21/10	MANSFIELD	L	0-1	8	18 / 20	2,941
13	H	28/10	WIGAN	W	3-0	6	23 / 23	6,365
14	A	31/10	CREWE	W	1-0	4	21 / 26	3,554
15	A	4/11	WALSALL	W	2-0	1	20 / 29	5,286
16	H	11/11	BOLTON	D	1-1	3	6 / 30	11,994
17	A	25/11	READING	D	1-1	4	14 / 31	5,353
18	H	2/12	ROTHERHAM	D	0-0	6	2 / 32	9,509
19	H	16/12	ORIENT	W	2-1	3	14 / 35	7,486
20	A	26/12	FULHAM	W	1-0	3	11 / 38	6,089
21	H	30/12	HUDDERSFIELD	L	1-2	3	5 / 38	7,681
22	H	1/1	PRESTON	W	2-1	3	20 / 41	11,803
23	A	13/1	BIRMINGHAM	W	4-0	1	9 / 44	11,277

Line-up columns: Leaning | Llewellyn | Bailey | Shelton | Humphries | Rennie | Gavin | Newman | Taylor | Smith | (Eaton/Turner/Jones) | Wimbleton/Mardon

---

12 A MANSFIELD 21/10 — L 0-1
City: Leaning, Llewellyn", Bailey, Shelton, Humphries, Rennie, Gavin, Newman, Taylor, Smith, Eaton*, Wimbleton/Mardon
Opp: Cox, Hunt, Gray, Christie, Foster, O'Riordan, Kent, Stringfellow, Wilkinson, Charles, Kearney
Christie 15
Ref: T Fitzharris
Such is City's inconsistency they can now manage to look like two different sides in the same match. Impressive after the break, City were fortunate not to have been losing by more than Trevor Christie's easy header at half-time as Steve Charles saw his shot rebound off of a post.

13 H WIGAN 28/10 — W 3-0
City: Leaning, Llewellyn, Bailey, Shelton, Humphries, Rennie, Gavin, Newman, Eaton, Smith*, Turner, Mellon
Opp: Adkins, Senior, Tankard, Rimmer, Atherton, Patterson, Thompson^, Ward^, Daley, Hilditch, Griffiths, Kelly/Johnson
Shelton 5, Rennie 41, Turner 65
Ref: J Martin
City have to be thankful for Turner's strength and aerial dominance in the howling wind and incessant rain at Ashton Gate. His frustration on heading against the bar after 30 minutes is relieved as he shoots in City's third, after earlier sending over the cross for Rennie's headed goal.

14 A CREWE 31/10 — W 1-0
City: Leaning, Llewellyn, Bailey, Shelton, Humphries, Rennie, Gavin, Newman, Taylor, Smith*, Turner, Eaton
Opp: Edwards P, Murphy, Swain, Smart, Dyson, Callaghan^, Jasper, Hignett, Clayton^, Walters, Cutler/Fishenden
Bailey 18
Ref: R Pawley
City's tremendous work rate and resolve, aided and abetted by Leaning's heroics and Bailey's tremendous 25-yarder, bring a hard-earned win at Gresty Road. Andy Sussex is denied by a post, whilst Leaning makes a great one-handed stop to keep out Chris Cutler's eight-yard header.

15 A WALSALL 4/11 — W 2-0
City: Leaning, Llewellyn, Bailey, Shelton, Humphries, Rennie, Gavin, Newman, Taylor, Smith, Turner, Saville
Opp: Green, Wilder, O'Hara, Lemon, Forbes, Skipper, Kelly, Rimmer, Bertschin, Goodwin*, Thorpe
Taylor 6, Turner 65
Ref: T West
City's one blot on an exhilarating performance that takes them to the top of the table is their failure to kill off the game in a one-sided first half. Walsall offer little, though Stewart Rimmer should have equalised Taylor's opening header, before Turner heads in from Gavin's great cross.

16 H BOLTON 11/11 — D 1-1
City: Leaning, Llewellyn, Bailey, Shelton, Humphries, Rennie, Gavin, Newman, Taylor!, Smith, Turner
Opp: Felgate, Brown, Cowdrill, Comstive, Crombie, Winstanley, Henshaw, Thompson, Reeves, Phillistkirk, Darby
Newman 10, Brown 33
Ref: M Pierce
With the Berlin Wall coming down last night City find a wall of their own to conquer after Newman's early volley is countered by Phil Brown's low 25-yard drive. A disciplined response to Taylor's 43rd-minute sending off for elbowing Mark Winstanley, allows City to gain a point.

17 A READING 25/11 — D 1-1
City: Leaning, Llewellyn, Bailey, Shelton, Humphries, Rennie, Gavin, Newman, Eaton*, Smith, Turner, Wimbleton
Opp: Francis, Jones, Richardson, Beavon, Hicks, Whitlock, Knight, Tait*, Senior, Conroy^, Payne, Taylor/Moran
Rennie 10, Senior 56
Ref: H King
City are undone by their failure to put away their host of chances following Rennie's 25-yard drive into the top corner of the Reading net. The absence of the suspended Taylor proves costly as City's appeals for offside go unheeded when Trevor Senior taps in from Lee Payne's cross.

18 H ROTHERHAM 2/12 — D 0-0
City: Leaning, Llewellyn, Bailey, Shelton, Humphries, Rennie, Gavin, Newman, Jones, Smith, Turner
Opp: O'Hanlon, Barnsley, Robinson, Grealish, Johnson, Scott, Buckley, Pepper, Williamson, Evans, Hazel
Ref: A Smith
The advent of colour soccer photos in the local press might not be marked by any goals, but there is plenty to shout about in this finely-balanced contest. Only the finishing lacks quality as both City and Rotherham post their promotion credentials to hold the crowd's interest.

19 H ORIENT 16/12 — W 2-1
City: Sinclair, Llewellyn, Bailey, Shelton, Humphries, Rennie, Gavin, Newman, Taylor, Smith*, Jones*, Wimbleton/Turner
Opp: Heald, Sitton, Dickenson, Beesley, Day, Hoddle, Howard, Castle, Hull, Cooper, Pike^, Nugent
Taylor 8, 20, Castle 53
Ref: K Cooper
Bob Taylor's two goals in this hard-earned win takes his tally since joining City to 21 in 32 appearances. He is however rather fortunate with his opener as he appears to make contact with Paul Heald instead of the ball when challenging for a defensive header held up in the wind.

20 A FULHAM 26/12 — W 1-0
City: Sinclair, Llewellyn, Bailey, Shelton, Humphries, Rennie, Gavin, Newman, Taylor, Smith*, Turner*, Wimbleton/Jones
Opp: Stannard, Donnellan !, Burns, Skinner*, Nebbeling, Eckhardt, Marshall, Scott, Sayer^, Watson, Walker, Mauge/Milton
Taylor 32
Ref: G Pooley
Gavin finds himself branded a cheat at sun-drenched Craven Cottage after Leo Donnellan had been rightly sent off in the 38th min for felling City's winger. Turner's well-timed leap and flicked header sets up Taylor with a typically accurate shot from 18 yards to give City the points.

21 H HUDDERSFIELD 30/12 — L 1-2
City: Sinclair, Llewellyn, Bailey, Shelton, Humphries, Rennie, Gavin, Newman, Taylor*, Smith, Turner*, Jones / Onuora
Opp: Martin, Marsden, Hutchings, May*, Mitchell, Lewis, O'Regan, Bray, O'Connell, Maskell, Smith
Jones 74, Smith 11, Maskell 86
Ref: E Parker
Jones hooks in an equaliser to Mark Smith's 25-yard opener as City dominate after the break, before falling for a late sucker-punch. City pay the penalty for looking for all three points rather than holding out for a draw as Craig Maskell holds off Humphries to fire in Town's winner.

22 H PRESTON 1/1 — W 2-1
City: Sinclair, Llewellyn, Bailey, Shelton, Humphries, Rennie, Gavin, Newman, Taylor, Smith, Turner*, Wimbleton
Opp: Kelly, Williams, Bogie, Flynn, Hughes, Mooney, Swann, Joyce, Patterson, Harper
Swann 36 (og), Newman 71, Mooney 85
Ref: R Gifford
Jaded City get a boost as Gary Swann's headed flick to Llewellyn's cross sends the ball into the back of the Preston net. Thereafter Alan Kelly's acrobatics keep City at bay, until Newman compensates for his disallowed 69th-minute effort with a ferocious shot from close range.

23 A BIRMINGHAM 13/1 — W 4-0
City: Sinclair, Llewellyn, Bailey, Shelton, Humphries, Rennie, Gavin, Newman, Taylor, Smith, Turner
Opp: Thomas, Clarkson, Frain, Atkins, Overson, Matthewson, Bell^, Bailey, Sturridge, Gleghorn, Langley, Hopkins
Taylor 43, 86, Turner 65, Newman 71
Ref: S Bell
Birmingham, who had previously conceded just five League goals at home, are annihilated by City's breathtaking display. Taylor starts and finishes the rout, netting with a low drive just before the interval, he races between two defenders to nonchalantly stroke in City's fourth.

BARCLAYS LEAGUE DIVISION 3 — Manager: Joe Jordan — SEASON 1989-90

No	Date		Att	Pos	Pt	F-A	H-T	Scorers, Times, and Referees	1	2	3	4	5	6	7	8	9	10	11	subs used
24	H 20/1	BURY	10,992	6	W 47	1-0	1-0	Smith 35 / Ref: K Cooper	Sinclair *Kelly*	Llewellyn *Hill*	Bailey *Clements*	Shelton *Hoyland*	Humphries *Greenall*°	Rennie *Knill*	Gavin *Lee*	Newman *Robinson*	Taylor* *Hulme*	Smith *Feeley*	Turner *Withe*°	Miller / *Bishop/Greenwood*

A minute's silence in memory of the son of City's assistant boss Jimmy Lumsden, precedes this keenly-fought encounter. Newman's 44th-min penalty, which is saved by Gary Peters, prevents City adding to Smith's shot into an empty net, following a poor back-pass by Kenny Clements.

No	Date		Att	Pos	Pt	F-A	H-T	Scorers, Times, and Referees	1	2	3	4	5	6	7	8	9	10	11	subs used
25	H 30/1	CHESTER	8,769	15	W 50	1-0	0-0	Newman 57 / Ref: R Wiseman	Sinclair *Stewart*	Llewellyn *Reeves*	Bailey *Woodthorpe*	Shelton *Hinnigan*	Humphries *Lightfoot*	Rennie *Lane*	Gavin *Butler*°	Newman *Barrow*	Taylor* *Abel*	Smith *Dale*°	Turner *Croft*	Miller / *Newhouse/Hamilton*

After a first half facing a gale-force wind, Newman has the City fans singing in the rain with a goal fit to win any match. As the wind subsides, Shelton touches a short free-kick to Smith, who turns the ball back for Newman to find the top corner of the net with a classic 30-yard shot.

No	Date		Att	Pos	Pt	F-A	H-T	Scorers, Times, and Referees	1	2	3	4	5	6	7	8	9	10	11	subs used
26	H 10/2	CARDIFF	11,982	22	W 53	1-0	1-0	Shelton 4 / Ref: T Ward	Sinclair *Hansbury*	Llewellyn *Rodgerson*	Bailey *Daniel*	Shelton *Barnard*	Humphries *Abraham*	Rennie *Gibbins*	Gavin *Morgan*°	Newman *Griffin*	Taylor* *Pike*	Mellon* *Perry*°	Turner *Kelly*	Miller/Honor / *Lynex/Chandler*

The bonus of an early goal when Shelton looked suspiciously offside on shooting in from ten yards, City might well have had cause to rue their missed chances. Fortunately though, Jon Morgan does not have any of Shelton's luck, as offside rules out his 67th-minute leveller.

No	Date		Att	Pos	Pt	F-A	H-T	Scorers, Times, and Referees	1	2	3	4	5	6	7	8	9	10	11	subs used
27	H 24/2	READING	10,616	13	L 53	0-1	0-0	Leworthy 70 / Ref: K Morton	Leaning *Francis*	Llewellyn *Jones*	Bailey *Richardson*	Shelton *Wood*	Humphries *Hicks*	Rennie *Conroy*	Mellon *Gooding*	Newman *Tait*	Taylor *Senior*°	Smith *Gilkes*	Turner* *Moran*	Eaton/Honor / *Leworthy*

City's uninspired display reaps what it deserves against a Reading side who had only won once away in the League before this game. After David Leworthy's six-yard volley puts the Royals in front, Rennie squanders City's chance of a point by spooning his penalty high and wide.

No	Date		Att	Pos	Pt	F-A	H-T	Scorers, Times, and Referees	1	2	3	4	5	6	7	8	9	10	11	subs used
28	A 3/3	CHESTER	2,502	15	W 56	3-0	2-0	Taylor 4, 24, 84 / Ref: I Cruikshanks	Sinclair *Stewart*	Llewellyn *Reeves*	Bailey *Woodthorpe*	Shelton *Hinnigan*°	Humphries *Lightfoot*	Rennie *Lane*	Mellon* *Butler*	Newman *Barrow*	Taylor° *Dale*	Smith *Pugh*°	Horrix *Croft*	Honor/Eaton / *Painter/Danzey*

New signing Dean Horrix (£50,000 ex Millwall) makes a confident debut, his incisive break and measured cross allowing Taylor to head in the opener from six yards. Chester have their chances, but lack a marksman of Taylor's calibre, who completes his hat-trick with another header.

No	Date		Att	Pos	Pt	F-A	H-T	Scorers, Times, and Referees	1	2	3	4	5	6	7	8	9	10	11	subs used
29	H 6/3	TRANMERE	14,376	3	L 56	1-3	0-1	Shelton 59 / McCarrick 7, Muir 48, Bishop 50 / Ref: V Callow	Sinclair *Nixon*	Llewellyn *Higgins*	Bailey *McCarrick*°	Shelton *Bishop*	Humphries *Hughes*	Honor* *Vickers*	Mellon* *Malkin*	Newman *Harvey*	Taylor *Steel*	Smith *Muir*	Horrix *Thomas*	Jordan / *Martindale*

Slick Tranmere register their eighth successive win after Mark McCarrick's shot from the edge of the pen area clips Jimmy Harvey's heel and loops into the net. Shelton's neat turn and angled shot is City's sole response to further Rovers goals and Chris Malkin's shot against a post.

No	Date		Att	Pos	Pt	F-A	H-T	Scorers, Times, and Referees	1	2	3	4	5	6	7	8	9	10	11	subs used
30	A 10/3	SHREWSBURY	4,785	2	W 59	1-0	0-0	Smith 87 / Ref: G Aplin	Sinclair *Perks*	Llewellyn *Green*	Bailey *Lynch*	Shelton *Kelly*	Humphries *Finley*	Rennie *Moyes*	Mellon* *Weir*	Newman *Wimbleton*°	Taylor* *Hartford*°	Smith *McGinlay*	Horrix *Naughton*	Honor / *Melrose/Gorman*

'We are going up as Champions, I don't know what the panic is about' says John Bailey before this thoroughly deserved success. Smith fires in low past Steve Perks to bring City's reward for their domination of the proceedings, having five shots on target compared to Shrewsbury's one.

No	Date		Att	Pos	Pt	F-A	H-T	Scorers, Times, and Referees	1	2	3	4	5	6	7	8	9	10	11	subs used
31	A 13/3	BLACKPOOL	3,227	23	W 62	3-1	1-0	Taylor 18, 55, Shelton 90 / Brook 47 / Ref: P Jones	Sinclair *Wood*	Llewellyn *Wright*°	Bailey *Morgan*	Shelton *Groves*	Humphries *Methven*	Rennie *Elliott*	Mellon *Gore*	Newman *Brook*	Taylor *Eyres*	Smith *Garner*	Horrix *Richards*	Eaton / *Davies*

City respond to the death of Dean Horrix in a car crash last Saturday night with a Championship display at Bloomfield Road. Gary Brook's volleyed-in equaliser is but a small interlude in City's domination, and Shelton's swerving low shot into the corner ties up a well-deserved win.

No	Date		Att	Pos	Pt	F-A	H-T	Scorers, Times, and Referees	1	2	3	4	5	6	7	8	9	10	11	subs used
32	H 17/3	BRENTFORD	10,813	11	W 65	2-0	1-0	Gavin 15, Rennie 60 / Ref: A Simmons	Sinclair *Parks*	Llewellyn *Cousins*	Bailey *Peters*	Shelton *Buttigieg*	Humphries *Evans*	Rennie *Buckle*	Gavin *Gayle*°	Newman *Godfrey*°	Taylor *Holdsworth*	Smith* *Blissett*	Mellon *Smillie*	Turner / *Cadette/Driscoll*

Gavin displays his arrogant skills after racing onto Smith's through-ball to outpace Jason Cousins and shoot in the opener. It is just a case of when City would score again, and inevitably Gavin's touch tees up Rennie to fire in a 15-yarder which even Tony Parks is powerless to stop.

No	Date		Att	Pos	Pt	F-A	H-T	Scorers, Times, and Referees	1	2	3	4	5	6	7	8	9	10	11	subs used
33	A 20/3	SWANSEA	7,051	16	W 68	5-0	2-0	Taylor 26, 27, 76, Newman 49, Honor 83 / Ref: M Bodenham	Sinclair *Bracey*	Llewellyn *Trick*	Bailey *Coleman*	Shelton *Melville*	Humphries* *James*	Rennie *Thornber*	Gavin *Harris*	Newman *Davey*°	Taylor *Curtis*	Smith *Raynor*°	Turner *Hutchison*	Honor/Eaton / *D'Auria/Phillips*

City's penchant this season for beating their bogey teams is confirmed by this rare win at the Vetch. 'Champions' chant the massed ranks of the travelling fans as Taylor's hat-trick (an instinctive header sandwiched between two shots) sends City's promotion bid into overdrive.

No	Date		Att	Pos	Pt	F-A	H-T	Scorers, Times, and Referees	1	2	3	4	5	6	7	8	9	10	11	subs used
34	A 24/3	NOTTS CO	9,598	4	D 69	0-0	0-0	Ref: D Scott	Sinclair *Cherry*	Llewellyn *Norton*	Bailey *Platnauer*	Shelton *Short*	Humphries* *Yates*	Rennie *Robinson*	Gavin *O'Riordan*	Newman *Turner*	Taylor *Bartlett*	Smith *Thomas*	Turner *Johnson*	Honor

It is not often a goalless draw is greeted by scenes of unbridled celebration, but this is what happens amongst the City fans at Meadow Lane. Another giant step towards promotion, but in truth City get much more than they deserve after failing to register a single shot on target.

Bristol City — Match-by-match record (Matches 35–46)

---

35 | H | NORTHAMPTON | 27/3 | 11,965 | 23rd | 72 pts | L | 3:1 | (HT 2:1)

Turner 5, Shelton 17, Taylor 61 / Barnes 43 — Ref: K Cooper

City: Sinclair, Llewellyn, Bailey, Shelton, Humphries, Rennie, Gavin, Newman, Taylor*, Smith, Turner, Ferguson
Northampton: *Gleasure, Chard, Wilson, Terry, Wilcox, McPherson*, Berry, Collins, Leaburn, Barnes, Thorpe, Donald*

Close-range shots from Turner and Shelton make it seem so easy early on, but over-elaboration and sloppy passing allow Northampton to get back into the game. After Bobby Barnes waltzes through unchallenged to score, it needs Taylor's poaching skills to make sure of the points.

---

36 | H | MANSFIELD | 31/3 | 11,773 | 19th | 73 pts | D | 1:1 | (HT 0:0)

Taylor 87 / Kearney 70 — Ref: T Lunt

City: Sinclair, Llewellyn, Bailey, Shelton, Humphries, Rennie, Gavin, Newman, Taylor, Smith, Turner*, Ferguson
Mansfield: *Beasley, Murray, Kearney, Christie, Foster, Smalley, Kent*, Clarke*, Wilkinson, Fairclough, Charles, Hodges/Chambers*

After Mark Kearney puts Mansfield in front with a simple six-yard header, Taylor nets his 29th goal of the season to salvage City a point from a game that appeared to be lost. His powerful far-post header finishes off Gavin's cross to deny the Stags their first away win for six months.

---

37 | A | ROTHERHAM | 3/4 | 5,526 | 7th | 76 pts | W | 2:1 | (HT 0:1)

Johnson 49 (og), Taylor 70 / Buckley 26 — Ref: T Holbrook

City: Sinclair, Llewellyn, Bailey, Shelton, Humphries, Rennie, Gavin, Newman, Taylor, Smith*, Turner, Ferguson
Rotherham: *O'Hanlon, Barnsley, Robinson, Goodwin, Johnson, Heard*, Buckley, Dempsey, Williamson, Mendonca*, Cash, Hazel/Evans*

Llewellyn chooses the perfect moment to become City's first 30-goal striker since the days of John Atyeo. His brilliant header opens up a seven-point gap at the top of the Third Division after Smith's shot cannons in off Nigel Johnson to equalise Rotherham's deserved chipped-in opener.

---

38 | A | WIGAN | 7/4 | 3,331 | 14th | 79 pts | W | 3:2 | (HT 1:1)

Smith 15p, Taylor 49, Ferguson 64 / Baraclough 12, Parkinson 64 — Ref: A Bennett

City: Sinclair, Llewellyn, Bailey*, Shelton, Humphries, Rennie, Gavin, Newman, Taylor, Smith, Turner, Ferguson
Wigan: *Hughes, Senior, Tankard, Parkinson, Atherton, Johnson, Thompson, Patterson, Baraclough, Hilditch, Griffiths*, Page*

With news of the death of the great Peter Doherty (City boss 1958-60) in Blackpool, City are involved in a ding-dong struggle not far away in Wigan. The saving of Smith's second pen in the 18th minute makes things more difficult, but Ferguson fires in a 15-yard angled-shot winner.

---

39 | H | CREWE | 10/4 | 13,800 | 10th | 82 pts | W | 4:1 | (HT 3:0)

Gavin 12p, Taylor 23, 29, 62 / Murphy 74 — Ref: G Pooley

City: Sinclair, Honor, Llewellyn, Shelton*, Humphries, Rennie, Gavin, Newman, Taylor*, Smith, Turner/Mellon, Ferguson
Crewe: *Greygoose, Swain, McKearney, Smart, Callaghan, Hignett, Jasper, Murphy, Foreman*, Gardiner, Cutler*, Joseph/Jones R*

Taylor's brilliant 30-yard volley which completes his hat-trick, takes City's No 9 to the top of the Football League scoring charts. Jordan's shrewd tactical brain halts Crewe's 14-match unbeaten run, but City are concerned over the loss of Taylor with a 67th-min hamstring injury.

---

40 | A | PRESTON | 14/4 | 7,601 | 20th | 83 pts | D | 2:2 | (HT 1:1)

Morgan 44, Harper 76 / Flynn 44, Harper 76 — Ref: D Hutchinson

City: Sinclair, Honor, Llewellyn, Shelton, Humphries, Rennie, Gavin, Newman, Morgan, Smith, Ferguson
Preston: *Kelly, Williams, Swann, McIlroy, Flynn, Wrightson, Mooney, Hughes, Joyce, Atkins*, Bogie, Harper*

After Nicky Morgan's (£30,000 ex Stoke) early tap-in from Smith's low cross, Preston equalise when Mike Flynn ghosts in at the far post to head over the line. Shelton's free-kick takes a wicked deflection off Gavin to put City back in front, before Harper heads Preston level again.

---

41 | H | FULHAM | 16/4 | 16,139 | 16th | 86 pts | W | 5:1 | (HT 2:1)

Morgan 36, Smith 41, Newman 57, [Ferguson 60, Shelton 79] / Eckhardt 12 — Ref: H King

City: Sinclair, Llewellyn, Bailey, Shelton*, Humphries, Rennie, Gavin, Newman, Morgan, Smith, Ferguson
Fulham: *Stannard, Eckhardt, Pike, Skinner*, Newson, Thomas, Cole*, Scott, Milton, Barnett, Nebbeling, Walker/Davies*

Sinclair's collision with Smith sees Jeff Eckhardt swoop onto the loose ball to put Fulham in front, but with both wingers in top form City fight back for victory. Gavin's free-kick against the bar sets up Morgan's superb close-range equaliser, whilst Smith lays City's last goal on a plate.

---

42 | A | ORIENT | 21/4 | 7,273 | 14th | 87 pts | D | 1:1 | (HT 0:1)

Newman 61 / Howard 32 — Ref: G Singh

City: Sinclair, Llewellyn, Bailey, Shelton*, Humphries, Rennie, Gavin, Newman, Morgan, Smith, Ferguson*
Orient: *Heald, Hales, Sitton, Beesley, Whitbread, Newson, Baker, Howard, Nugent, Harvey, Hull*, Carter/Campbell*

Orient are kept at bay by Shelton's tireless running and bone-shaking tackles. After Newman's sweet volley counters Terry Howard's twelve-yard drive, out of sorts City are denied a club record equalling 13th away win when Turner's header is disallowed because of a Morgan foul.

---

43 | H | HUDDERSFIELD | 24/4 | 17,791 | 8th | 88 pts | D | 1:1 | (HT 0:1)

Morgan 52 / Duggan 19 — Ref: M James

City: Sinclair, Llewellyn, Bailey, Shelton, Humphries, Rennie, Gavin, Newman, Morgan, Smith, Ferguson*
Huddersfield: *Hardwick, May, Hutchings, Kelly, Mitchell, Duggan, O'Regan, Marsden, Byrne*, Maskell, Edwards, Smith*

The champagne remains on ice as City fail to get the win to secure promotion. Boosted by Andy Duggan's header the visitors prove difficult to break down, but Morgan's tap-in, after Gavin's brilliant turn and shot is parried by Steve Hardwick, takes City's unbeaten run to 14 games.

---

44 | A | BOLTON | 28/4 | 11,098 | 6th | 88 pts | L | 0:1 | (HT 0:1)

Green 32 — Ref: T Mills

City: Sinclair, Llewellyn, Bailey, Shelton, Humphries, Rennie, Gavin, Newman, Taylor*, Smith, Morgan, Turner
Bolton: *Felgate, Brown, Cowdrill, Green, Came, Winstanley, Storer*, Thompson, Reeves, Phillisfirk, Darby, Gregory*

David Felgate's faultless display between the sticks leaves City's nerves a jangling as Rovers beat Shrewsbury 1-0 to put them just a point behind. Scott Green keeps Bolton's play-off ambitions alive as he cuts inside to unleash a shot which spins viciously to wrong-foot Sinclair.

---

45 | A | BRISTOL ROV | 2/5 | 9,813 | 1st | 88 pts | L | 0:3 | (HT 0:1)

White 25, 55, Holloway 62p — Ref: L Dilkes

City: Sinclair, Llewellyn, Bailey*, Shelton, Humphries, Rennie, Gavin, Newman, Morgan, Smith, Turner*, Honor/Ferguson
Bristol Rov: *Parkin, Alexander, Twentyman, Yates, Mehew, Jones, Holloway, Reece, White, Saunders, Purnell*

Ex manager Cooper and player Andy Llewellyn confidently predict a City success, but in the event Rovers romp to an easy victory. It's all too much for City's yob element who attempt to bring proceedings to a halt, but Jordan deserves great credit for his efforts to diffuse the situation.

---

46 | H | WALSALL | 5/5 | 19,483 | 24th | 91 pts | W | 4:0 | (HT 2:0)

Shelton 3, Gavin 38p, Rennie 84, [Morgan 86] — Ref: T Fitzharris

City: Sinclair, Llewellyn, Bailey*, Shelton, Humphries, Rennie, Gavin, Newman, Morgan, Smith, Ferguson
Walsall: *Green, Dorman, Hawker, Smith*, Forbes, Skipper, Ford, Rimmer*, Taylor, O'Hara, Bremner/Goldsmith, Honor/Bent*

Erroneous news that Rovers had lost at Blackpool had City fans thinking the Championship prize was theirs. It wasn't to be however, as City's sparkling display was sealed by Rennie's brilliant chip and Morgan's bullet header. The fans celebrate in scenes reminiscent of 1976, after City's sparkling display was sealed.

Average: Home 11,544 | Away 6,254

League Cup

					F-A	H-T	1	2	3	4	5	6	7	8	9	10	11	subs used
1:1	H	READING	22/8	6,318	L 2-3	1-2	Leaning	Llewellyn	Bailey	Wimbledon	Pender	Rennie	Gavin	Newman	Taylor	Smith	Eaton	
							Francis	*Williams*	*Richardson*	*Beavon*	*Hicks*	*Wood*	*Jones*	*Taylor*	*Senior*	*Gilkes*	*Payne*	

Scorers, Times, and Referees: Wimbledon 42p, Smith 66 / *Gilkes 15, 29, 80* / Ref: K Burge

City's generous defence allows Michael Gilkes the easiest of hat-tricks after he puts Reading in front with a low shot via Trevor Senior's nod-on. Smith smashes in a fierce 25-yarder to cap City's second-half fight-back, but Gilkes has loads of space to shoot home the Royals' winner.

					F-A	H-T	1	2	3	4	5	6	7	8	9	10	11	subs used
1:2	A	READING	29/8	4,457	D 2-2	2-0	Leaning	Llewellyn	Honor	Wimbledon*	Pender	Rennie	Gavin*	Newman	Taylor	Smith	Shelton	Mardon/Eaton
							Francis	*Williams*	*Richardson*	*Beavon*	*Hicks*	*Wood*	*Jones*	*Taylor*	*Senior*	*Gilkes*	*Payne**	*Conroy*

Scorers, Times, and Referees: Taylor 16, 31 / *Senior 47, Gilkes 62* / Ref: P Alcock / (City lost 4-5 on aggregate)

Trevor Senior levels the aggregate score from a suspiciously offside position, after Taylor's opening shot and later header had put City in charge. City are denied taking the tie into extra-time by Michael Gilkes' exquisitely-taken shot, and Mardon's failure in front of an open net.

FA Cup

Rd				Att		F-A	H-T	1	2	3	4	5	6	7	8	9	10	11	subs used
1	H	BARNET	18/11	7,538	3 C:2	W 2-0	2-0	Leaning	Llewellyn	Bailey	Shelton	Humphries	Rennie	Gavin	Newman	Taylor	Smith*	Turner	Eaton
								Guthrie	*Wilson*	*Stacey*	*Poole*	*Reilly*	*Payne**	*Stein**	*Murphy*	*Bull*	*Cooper*	*Badley*	*Clarke/Gridelet*

Scorers, Times, and Referees: Taylor 21, Turner 41 / Ref: M Bodenham

City need their better finishing ability to beat Conference side Barnet, as the visitors produce the more attractive football. The alert Taylor takes full advantage as Peter Guthrie fumbles Rennie's low drive, whilst Turner volleys in from six yards to finish off Smith's accurate cross.

Rd				Att		F-A	H-T	1	2	3	4	5	6	7	8	9	10	11	subs used
2	H	FULHAM	9/12	7,662	6 12	W 2-1	0-1	Sinclair	Llewellyn	Bailey	Wimbledon	Humphries	Rennie	Gavin	Newman	Taylor	Smith	Turner	
								Stannard	*Donnellan*	*Mauge**	*Lenington**	*Nebbeling*	*Peters*	*Marshall*	*Scott*	*Sayer*	*Watson*	*Langley*	*Skinner/Barnett*

Scorers, Times, and Referees: Taylor 56, Wimbledon 80p / *Scott 43* / Ref: D Vickers

A classic cup-tie is settled when Smith's stumble following Leo Donnellan's challenge brings a penalty. City dominate the play, but are made to pay for missed chances when the referee has no doubts about Peter Scott's 25-yard opener that hits the underside bar before bouncing down.

Rd				Att		F-A	H-T	1	2	3	4	5	6	7	8	9	10	11	subs used
3	H	SWINDON	6/1	17,422	3 2:5	W 2-1	2-1	Sinclair	Llewellyn	Bailey	Shelton	Humphries	Rennie	Gavin	Newman	Taylor	Smith	Turner	Turner
								Digby	*Kerslake*	*Bodin*	*McLoughlin*	*Calderwood*	*Gittens*	*Jones T**	*Shearer*	*White*	*MacLaren*	*Foley*	*Hackaday*

Scorers, Times, and Referees: Taylor 22, Newman 35 / *Shearer 41* / Ref: K Burge

This stirring contest is a fine advert for West Country soccer, despite the treacherous underfoot conditions. Taylor waltzes the ball past Fraser Digby to put City ahead, and then tries to lay claim to the second goal when the ball pins about in the box before going in the net off Newman.

Rd				Att		F-A	H-T	1	2	3	4	5	6	7	8	9	10	11	subs used
4	H	CHELSEA	27/1	24,535	1 1:6	W 3-1	1-0	Sinclair	Llewellyn	Bailey	Shelton	Humphries	Rennie	Gavin	Newman	Taylor	Smith	Turner	Turner
								Beasant	*Clarke*	*Dorigo*	*Roberts*	*Johnson*	*Monkou**	*McAllister*	*Bumstead*	*Dixon*	*Wilson K*	*Le Saux*	*Lee*

Scorers, Times, and Referees: Turner 4, 52, Gavin 89 / *Wilson 84* / Ref: D Phillips

Goal-stopper Sinclair and goal-scorer Turner inspire City in this magnificent cup-tie. Two relatively simple goals underline Turner's goal-taking ability, but he also sets up City's third with an exquisite turn and 20-yard shot that is pushed out by Dave Beasant for Gavin to steer in.

Rd				Att		F-A	H-T	1	2	3	4	5	6	7	8	9	10	11	subs used
5	H	CAMBRIDGE	17/2	20,676	1 4:12	D 0-0	0-0	Sinclair	Llewellyn	Bailey	Shelton	Humphries	Rennie	Gavin	Newman	Taylor	Smith	Turner	Turner
								Vaughan	*Fensome*	*Kimble*	*Bailie**	*Chapple*	*Daish*	*Cheetham*	*Leadbitter*	*Dublin*	*Taylor*	*Philpott*	*O'Shea*

Ref: S Lodge

City blow their great chance of reaching the Quarter-Finals as they turn in a most disappointing display. It might have been different if Gavin had not been denied by the post early on, but Cambridge are much the better side, impressive in all departments and quicker on the ball.

Rd				Att		F-A	H-T	1	2	3	4	5	6	7	8	9	10	11	subs used
5R	A	CAMBRIDGE	21/2	9,796	1 4:12	D 1-1 aet	0-0	Sinclair	Llewellyn	Bailey	Shelton	Humphries	Rennie	Gavin	Newman	Taylor	Smith	Turner	Turner
								Vaughan	*Fensome*	*Kimble*	*Bailie*	*Chapple*	*Daish*	*Cheetham*	*Leadbitter*	*Dublin*	*Taylor*	*Philpott*	*Philpott*

Scorers, Times, and Referees: Taylor 94 / *Dublin 91* / Ref: S Lodge

Determination sees City survive a memorable night of cut-and-thrust soccer at the Abbey Stadium. John Taylor's cross that hits the woodwork is surprisingly the nearest to a goal until extra-time, when Bob Taylor's rasping drive into the top corner levels Dion Dublin's headed opener.

Rd				Att		F-A	H-T	1	2	3	4	5	6	7	8	9	10	11	subs used
5 RR	A	CAMBRIDGE	27/2	9,047	1 4:14	L 1-5	0-1	Vaughan	Llewellyn	Bailey	Shelton	Humphries	Rennie	Gavin*	Newman	Taylor	Smith	Turner	Mellon
								Leaning	*Fensome*	*Kimble*	*Bailie**	*Chapple*	*Daish*	*Cheetham**	*Leadbitter*	*Dublin*	*Taylor*	*Philpott*	*O'Shea/Robinson*

Scorers, Times, and Referees: Taylor 75 / *Leadbitter 44, Philpott 49, Dublin 51, 68* / Ref: J Moules   [Taylor 72]

After losing the toss for venue it is back to the Abbey Stadium where City are blown away after failing to take their first-half chances. Chris Leadbitter's close-range overhead kick opens the scoring, whilst John Taylor's cool 72nd-minute chip completes City's humiliation.

League table

Pos	Team	P	Home					Away					Pts
			W	D	L	F	A	W	D	L	F	A	
1	Bristol Rov	46	15	8	0	43	14	11	7	5	28	21	93
2	BRISTOL CITY	46	15	5	3	40	16	12	5	6	36	24	91
3	Notts Co *	46	17	4	2	40	18	8	7	8	33	35	87
4	Tranmere	46	15	5	3	54	22	8	6	9	32	27	80
5	Bury	46	11	7	5	35	19	10	4	9	35	30	74
6	Bolton	46	12	7	4	32	19	6	8	9	27	29	69
7	Birmingham	46	10	7	6	33	19	8	5	10	27	40	66
8	Huddersfield	46	11	5	7	30	23	6	9	8	31	39	65
9	Rotherham	46	12	6	5	48	28	5	7	11	23	34	64
10	Reading	46	10	9	4	33	21	5	10	8	24	32	64
11	Shrewsbury	46	10	9	4	38	24	6	6	11	21	30	63
12	Crewe	46	10	5	8	32	24	5	9	9	24	29	62
13	Brentford	46	11	4	8	41	31	7	3	13	25	35	61
14	Orient	46	9	6	8	28	24	7	4	12	24	32	58
15	Mansfield	46	13	2	8	34	25	3	5	15	16	40	55
16	Chester	46	11	5	7	30	23	2	8	13	13	32	54
17	Swansea	46	10	6	7	25	27	4	6	13	20	36	54
18	Wigan	46	10	6	7	29	22	3	8	12	19	42	53
19	Preston	46	10	7	6	42	30	4	3	16	23	49	52
20	Fulham	46	8	8	7	33	27	4	7	12	22	39	51
21	Cardiff	46	6	9	8	30	35	6	5	12	21	35	50
22	Northampton	46	7	7	9	27	31	4	7	12	24	37	47
23	Blackpool	46	8	6	9	29	33	2	10	11	20	40	46
24	Walsall	46	6	8	9	23	30	3	6	14	17	42	41
		1104	257	156	139	829	585	139	156	257	585	829	1500

* promoted
after play-offs

Odds & ends

Double wins: (10) Birmingham, Blackpool, Cardiff, Shrewsbury, Brentford, Wigan, Crewe, Walsall, Fulham, Chester.

Double losses: (1) Tranmere.

Won from behind: (3) Rotherham (a), Wigan (a), Fulham (h).

Lost from in front: (0).

High spots: Winning 5-0 at Swansea on 20 March. Beating Rotherham 2-1 at Millmoor on 3 April. Beating Wigan at Springfield Park 3-2 on 7 April. Beating Crewe 4-1 at Ashton Gate on 10 April. Beating Fulham 5-1 at Ashton Gate on 16 April. Beating Chelsea 3-1 in the FA Cup.

Low spots: Losing 0-6 at Prenton Park on 29 September. Losing to Swansea at Ashton Gate on 14 October. Losing to Bristol Rov 0-5 at Twerton Park on 2 May. Losing 1-5 against Cambridge in the FA Cup on 27 February. Losing 1-2 at Ashton Gate v Bristol Rov in the Glos Cup on 8 August.

Player of the Year: Bob Taylor.

Ever-presents: (2) Rob Newman, Andy Llewellyn.

Hat-tricks: (3) Bob Taylor.

Leading scorer: Bob Taylor (34).

Appearances and Goals

Player	Appearances						Goals			
	Lge	Sub	LC	Sub	FAC	Sub	Lge	LC	FAC	Tot
Bailey, John	38		1		7		1			1
Bent, Junior		1								
Bromage, Russell	3									
Eaton, Jason	6	5	1	1			1			1
Ferguson, Iain	8	3					2			2
Gavin, Mark	36	4	2		7		3		1	4
Honor, Chris	4	10	1				1			1
Horrix, Dean	3									
Humphries, Glenn	36	1			7		1			1
Jones, Andy	2	2								
Jordan, Joe	2		1							
Leaning, Andy	19		2		2					
Llewellyn, Andy	46		2		7					
Mardon, Paul	2	5				1				
Mellon, Micky	7	2			7					
Miller, Paul		3				1				
Morgan, Nicky	7						4			4
Newman, Rob	46		2		7		8		1	9
Pender, John	10		2		7	2				
Rennie, David	45		2		7		4			4
Shelton, Gary	43	1	1		6		9			9
Sinclair, Ronnie	27				5					
Smith, David	45		2		7		4	1		5
Taylor, Bob	37		2		7		27	2	5	34
Turner, Robbie	26	7			7		6		3	9
Wimbleton, Paul	10	6	2		1		2	1	1	4
(own-goals)							3			3
26 players used	506	50	22	2	77	4	76	4	11	91

BARCLAYS LEAGUE DIVISION 2   Manager: Jordan ⇒ Jimmy Lumsden   SEASON 1990-91

No	Date	V	Opponent	Att	Pos	Pt	F-A	H-T	1	2	3	4	5	6	7	8	9	10	11	subs used
1	25/8	H	BLACKBURN	13,794		3	W 4-2	0-1	Sinclair	Llewellyn	Aizlewood	May	Shelton	Rennie	Newman	Donowa	Taylor	Morgan	Smith	Allison
									Gennoe	*Atkins*	*Sulley**	*Irvine*	*Hill*	*Moran*	*Richardson*	*Millar*	*Stapleton*	*Gayle*	*Shepstone**	*Johnrose/Oliver*
2	2/9	A	SWINDON	12,686		6	W 1-0	1-0	Sinclair	Llewellyn	Aizlewood	May	Shelton	Rennie	Newman	Bent	Taylor	Morgan*	Smith	Allison
									Digby	*Kerslake*	*Bodin*	*Simpson*	*Calderwood*	*Gittens*	*Jones*'	*Shearer*	*Close**	*MacLaren*	*Foley*	*McLaughlin/Hockaday*
3	8/9	H	PLYMOUTH	14,283	5	7	D 1-1	1-0	Sinclair	Llewellyn	Aizlewood	May	Shelton	Rennie	Newman	Bent	Taylor*	Morgan	Smith	Allison
									Wilmot	*Brown*	*Morgan*	*Marker*	*Burrows*	*Hodges*	*Byrne*	*Fiore*	*Turner*	*Thomas*	*Pickard*	
4	15/9	A	WEST BROM	12,081	9	7	L 1-2	0-2	Sinclair	Llewellyn	Aizlewood	May	Shelton	Rennie	Newman	Bent	Taylor*	Morgan	Smith	Allison
									Naylor	*Hodson*	*Harbey*	*Robson**	*Bradley*	*Stradder*	*Ford*	*West*	*Bannister*	*McNally*	*Shakespeare**	*Goodman*
5	22/9	H	BRIGHTON	11,522	10	10	W 3-1	2-0	Sinclair	Llewellyn	Aizlewood	May	Shelton	Rennie	Newman	Bent	Taylor	Morgan*	Smith	Allison
									Digweed	*Crumplin*	*Chapman*	*Wilkins*	*McCarthy*	*Gatting*	*Nelson**	*Barham*	*Small*	*Codner*	*Walker*	*Byrne*
6	29/9	H	NEWCASTLE	15,858	10	13	W 1-0	1-0	Sinclair	Llewellyn	Aizlewood	May	Shelton	Rennie	Newman	Bent	Taylor	Morgan	Smith*	Allison
									Burridge	*Scott*	*Bradshaw*	*Aitken*	*Kristensen*	*Ranson*	*Gourley*	*Simpson**	*Quinn*	*McGhee*	*Gallacher**	*Clark/Robinson*
7	3/10	A	LEICESTER	9,815	20	13	L 0-3	0-1	Sinclair	Llewellyn	Aizlewood	May	Shelton	Rennie	Newman	Bent	Taylor	Morgan	Smith*	Allison, North
									Hooper	*Mauchlen**	*Paris*	*Ramsey*	*Walsh*	*James*	*Wright*	*Reid*	*Oldfield*	*Mills*	*Kelly*	
8	6/10	A	WOLVES	17,791	6	13	L 0-4	0-2	Sinclair	Llewellyn	Aizlewood	May	Shelton	Rennie	Newman	Donowa	Humphries*	Taylor	Smith*	Bailey
									Stowell	*Ashley**	*Thompson*	*Bellamy*	*Hindmarch*	*Downing*	*Steele*'	*Cook*	*Bull*	*Westley*	*Dennison*	*Bennett/McLoughlin*
9	13/10	H	WEST HAM	16,838	3	14	D 1-1	0-0	Leaning	Llewellyn	Bailey	Aizlewood	Shelton	Rennie	Donowa	Newman	Taylor	Morgan	Smith	
									Miklosko	*Potts*	*Dicks*	*Foster*	*Martin*	*Bishop*	*Parris*	*Quinn*	*Slater**	*Allen*	*Morley*	*McAvennie*
10	20/10	H	OLDHAM	14,031	1	14	L 1-2	1-2	Leaning	Llewellyn	Bailey	Aizlewood	Shelton	Rennie	May	Newman	Taylor*	Morgan	Smith	Allison/Donowa
									Hallworth	*Warhurst*	*Barlow*	*Henry*	*Barrett*	*Jobson*	*Adams*	*Currie**	*Marshall*	*Redfearn*	*Holden R*	*Moulden*
11	24/10	A	MILLWALL	10,335	5	17	W 2-1	0-1	Sinclair	Llewellyn	Bailey	Aizlewood	Shelton	Rennie	May	Newman	Allison	Morgan*	Smith	Taylor
									Horne	*Stevens*	*Cunningham*	*McCarthy*	*Wood*	*McLeary*	*Carter*	*Waddock*	*Sheringham*	*Rae**	*O'Callaghan**	*Allen*

Scorers, Times, and Referees

1. Aizlewood 51, Taylor 68, Morgan 72, Gayle 25, 55; Ref: A Buksh
   Presented with his Golden Boots award, Taylor continues amongst the goals. The lethal marksman transforms the match as City throw off the shackles of their tense and inhibited first-half display. Smith's pace and far-post cross finds Morgan to head in to complete a thrilling victory.

2. Bent 32; Ref: V Callow
   City confirm early-season optimism with a marvellous display at the County Ground as Jordan counters Swindon's diamond formation by pushing Shelton forward and having May shadow Steve Foley. Taylor's 50-yard pass releases Bent to send a side-foot shot past Fraser Digby.

3. Morgan 16, Thomas 67; Ref: P Jones
   Sinclair is City's hero with his fantastic stop from Andy Thomas' close-range header two minutes from time, adding to his exploits in saving a second-min pen. Nicky Marker's failure to control a low cross allows Morgan to prod City ahead, but Thomas fires in an unstoppable leveller.

4. Newman 85, Bannister 38, Harbey 42; Ref: R Nixon
   Jordan's pep talk revives City after their passionless first-half display leaves them trailing to Gary Bannister's volley and Graham Harbey's blistering 20-yarder. Unfortunately Aizlewood's tame 54th-min spot-kick means no reward for City until Newman shoots in from close range.

5. Smith 10, Taylor 37, 88, Small 89; Ref: J Lloyd
   Following Jordan's shock departure to Hearts, City's entertaining style and attacking flair has Brighton twice clearing off the line and grateful not to concede more. Sinclair's failure to spot Mike Small behind him when he rolls the ball in the area gifts Brighton their late consolation.

6. Smith 22; Ref: L Shapter
   Despite penning Newcastle back with a succession of exciting moves, City fail to add to Smith's powerful drive past John Burridge. The visitors dominate territorially after the break, but Aizlewood and Rennie ensure that their highly-rated strike force barely have a sniff at goal.

7. James 2, Kelly 57, 76; Ref: I Borrett
   Mike Hooper defies his old club with a masterly display of keeping, after Llewellyn's poor clearance leads to Tony James heading Leicester in front. Paul Ramsey's goal-line clearance also frustrates City, as David Kelly's header and shot makes sure of the points for the Filberts.

8. Thompson 3, Bull 16, 67, 80; Ref: P Don
   City are simple meat for the Wolves after Steve Bull's rasping drive cannons off the crossbar for Andy Thompson to head into an open net. Morgan, denied by the post on the half-hour, is denied again with a 51st-minute penalty, and Bull completes his hat-trick with a low drive.

9. Morgan 63, McAvennie 61; Ref: J Deakin
   Jimmy Lumsden's decision to re-shuffle his side, with Aizlewood in the central defensive role he prefers, brings stability after three heavy defeats. Ex Hammer Morgan heads in City's equaliser, after Frank McAvennie had been allowed to race through and shoot past Leaning.

10. Morgan 29, Adams 16, 42; Ref: T Ward
    The classy Latics win the fans' approval as much for their sportsmanship as their football. Morgan blasts in City's goal from close range, but Neil Adams wins the game for Oldham. His stooping header is followed by a far-post tap-in after Dave Currie outmanoeuvres three defenders.

11. Horne 57 (og), Aizlewood 83, Waddock 8; Ref: M Bodenham
    After hitting the woodwork in the first half, Allison justifies his selection in place of the out-of-form Taylor with a firm header that Brian Horne fumbles in. A thrilling game, played in excellent spirit, is settled by Aizlewood, who steers the ball in through a crowd of defenders.

Match Record (continued)

No.	H/A	Date	Opponent	League Pos.	Result	FT	HT	Att.	Scorers (City)	Scorers (opponents)	Referee
12	A	27/10	PORT VALE	13 / 17 / 17	L	2-3	1-2	7,451	Smith 19p, Allison 84	Walker 1, 25p, Beckford 89	Ref: A Wilkie
13	H	3/11	WATFORD	11 / 24 / 20	W	3-2	1-0	11,576	Allison 18, 48, Falconer 75 (og)	Porter 55, Holdsworth 70	Ref: T Holbrook
14	A	10/11	OXFORD	13 / 20 / 20	L	1-3	1-2	6,837	Shelton 44	Simpson 4, 87, Foyle 7	Ref: G Singh
15	H	17/11	HULL	10 / 22 / 23	W	4-1	1-0	9,346	May 38, Newman 75, Morgan 88, Allison [Shelton 89]	Finnigan 76	Ref: M Bailey
16	A	24/11	IPSWICH	11 / 12 / 24	D	1-1	0-1	9,919	Taylor 88	Dozzell 20	Ref: J Kirkby
17	H	1/12	CHARLTON	13 / 20 / 24	L	0-1	0-1	10,984		Lee 44	Ref: P Durkin
18	H	8/12	SHEFFIELD WED	12 / 3 / 25	D	1-1	1-1	11,254	Shirtliff 15 (og)	Wilson 6	Ref: P Tyldesley
19	A	15/12	BLACKBURN	9 / 16 / 28	W	1-0	0-0	7,072	Newman 47		Ref: P Vanes
20	A	22/12	NOTTS CO	11 / 5 / 28	L	2-3	1-1	6,586	Bent 34, Smith 51	Regis 12, 85, Draper 82	Ref: P Foakes
21	H	26/12	PORTSMOUTH	8 / 22 / 31	W	4-1	1-1	11,892	Morgan 24, 49, Shelton 71, Rennie 76	Clarke 44	Ref: G Williard
22	H	29/12	MIDDLESBROUGH	7 / 4 / 34	W	3-0	1-0	14,023	May 20, Morgan 75, Allison 85		Ref: G Ashby
23	A	1/1	BARNSLEY	9 / 6 / 34	L	0-2	0-2	8,961		Rammell 18, Taggart 26	Ref: T Fitzharris

Line-ups and reports

12 — Port Vale (A)
City: Sinclair, Llewellyn, Bailey*, Aizlewood, Shelton, Rennie, May, Newman, Allison, Morgan*, Smith, Donowa
Port Vale: Wood, Mills S, Hughes*, Walker, Aspin, Parkin, Glover, Porter, Jepson, Beckford, Jeffers, Cross
Whilst Lumsden complains over a liberal allocation of injury-time, conceding goals in the first and last minutes against mediocre opposition speaks for itself. Darren Beckford runs in unchallenged to nod in Vale's late winner, not long after Allison had slammed in City's equaliser.

13 — Watford (H)
City: Sinclair, Llewellyn, Bailey, Aizlewood, Shelton, Rennie, May, Newman, Allison, Morgan*, Smith, Donowa
Watford: James, Gibbs, Williams*, Porter, Holdsworth, Dublin, Thomas, Wilkinson, Falconer, Devonshire*, Gavin*, Harrison/Drysdale
Allison gets back at his old club with a headed opener and a vicious low-drive from outside the penalty area. Watford looked the more likely victors after Gary Porter's 30-yarder and David Holdsworth's header, but May's cross strikes Willie Falconer on the far post for City's winner.

14 — Oxford (A)
City: Sinclair, Llewellyn, Bailey*, Aizlewood, Shelton, Rennie, May, Newman, Allison, Morgan*, Smith, Taylor/Donowa
Oxford: Kee, Robinson, Evans C, Lewis, Foster, Melville, Magilton, Stein, Foyle, Nogan*, Simpson, Phillips
A give-away as Oxford win a game in which they are second best throughout. After Shelton's dispatch of Allison's pass, Oxford soak up constant pressure and survive countless scares before Paul Simpson makes the game safe with a perfect chip from the edge of the penalty area.

15 — Hull (H)
City: Sinclair, Llewellyn, Aizlewood, May, Shelton, Rennie, Bent, Newman, Allison, Morgan, Smith, Jenkinson
Hull: Hesford, Brown, Jacobs, Mail, Swan, Wilcox, Finnigan, Payton, Bamber*, Palin, McParland
With Tony Taylor in charge, whilst Lumsden is in hospital with disc trouble, City turn on the style after May hits the bar and Smith's 26th-min penalty is saved. Morgan's skilful close-control lays on May's exquisite right-footed opener, and gets in on the act himself with a firm header.

16 — Ipswich (A)
City: Sinclair, Llewellyn, Aizlewood, May, Shelton, Rennie, Bent, Newman, Allison*, Morgan, Smith, Taylor
Ipswich: Forrest, Yallop, Humes, Stockwell, Gayle, Linighan, Dozzell, Redford, Hill, Kiwomya, Thompson
City run Ipswich ragged, particularly in a one-sided second half, though they are fortunate when Neil Thompson blasts a 49th-min pen over the top, after Aizlewood had fisted out Chris Kiwomya's chip. The irrepressible Bent sets up Taylor to notch City's late leveller with a low drive.

17 — Charlton (H)
City: Sinclair, Llewellyn, Aizlewood, May, Shelton, Rennie, Bent*, Newman, Taylor, Morgan*, Smith, Humphries/Allison
Charlton: Bolder, Pitcher, Minto, Peake, Balmer, Caton, Lee R, Curbishley, Dyer, Watson, Mortimer
Seldom in recent seasons have City been as comprehensively outplayed as they are in this match. City had the luck on their side in the fourth min, when Paul Mortimer fires against the bar, but Robert Lee makes no mistake just before half-time with a low 18-yard drive past Sinclair.

18 — Sheffield Wed (H)
City: Sinclair, Llewellyn, Scott, May, Shelton, Rennie, Bent*, Newman, Taylor, Morgan*, Smith, Allison
Sheffield Wed: Pressman, Harkes, King, Palmer, Shirtliff, Pearson, Wilson, Sheridan, Hirst, Francis*, Worthington, Williams
Scott (£200,000 ex Rotherham) is voted man of the match by City's 51 Club after producing a goal-line clearance to earn his side a point in the snow and bitter wind. Peter Shirtliff's lunging interception of Smith's hard low-cross only succeeds in turning the ball past his own keeper.

19 — Blackburn (A)
City: Sinclair, Llewellyn, Scott, May, Shelton, Rennie, Bent, Newman, Allison*, Morgan, Smith, Shepstone/Skinner
Blackburn: Grew, Atkins, Sulley, Reid, Hill, Moran, Richardson*, Millar, Stapleton, Johnrose, Wilcox*
Newman gives his forwards a lesson in finishing with a firm low-drive from twelve yards that leaves Mark Grew rooted the spot. 'One of these days we are going to score six or seven' is Llewellyn's comment as City's ascendancy produces a quiet afternoon for keeper Sinclair.

20 — Notts Co (A)
City: Leaning, Llewellyn, Scott, May, Shelton, Rennie, Bent, Newman, Taylor, Morgan, Smith, Allison
Notts Co: Cherry, Palmer, Harding, Short/Craig/Yates, O'Riordan*, Thomas, Turner, Bartlett, Regis, Draper, Johnson
City take Christmas giving too far as Rennie's hesitation allows Dave Regis to latch onto Steve Cherry's long free-kick and score County's impressive winner. A sickening end to a match City should have won as chances were missed after Smith screwed in a low shot past Cherry.

21 — Portsmouth (H)
City: Leaning, Llewellyn, Scott, May, Shelton, Rennie, Bent*, Newman, Taylor*, Morgan, Smith, Aizlewood/Allison
Portsmouth: Knight, Neil, Beresford, Kuhl, Butters, Awford, Anderton*, Clarke, Whittingham/Aspinall, Chamberlain, Daniel/Powell
The fans who brave the atrocious weather for an 11.30am kick-off are rewarded by the quality play of both sides. Two opportunist strikes by Morgan puts the skids under Pompey, then Shelton's ten-yarder and Rennie's perfectly-struck shot from 30 yards seals City's exciting win.

22 — Middlesbrough (H)
City: Leaning, Llewellyn, Scott, May, Shelton, Rennie*, Aizlewood, Newman, Allison, Morgan, Smith, Donowa
Middlesbrough: Pears, Cooper, Phillips, Mowbray, Coleman, Proctor, Slaven, Mustoe, Baird, Ripley, Hendrie
The blend of Morgan's deft touches and Allison's raw power prove too much for Boro's defence, as the Second Division's best away side are blitzed. May gets City rolling with a 15-yard hooked shot, then a brilliant Morgan header is followed by Allison coolly side-footing the ball in.

23 — Barnsley (A)
City: Leaning, Llewellyn, Scott*, May, Shelton!, Rennie, Bent, Newman, Aizlewood, Morgan*, Smith, Taylor/Donowa
Barnsley: Baker, Banks, Taggart, Fleming, Smith, Tiler, O'Connell, Rammell*, Saville, Agnew, Archdeacon, Deehan
Whilst Shelton is harshly dismissed for dissent on being denied a 29th-min free-kick, it is defensive blunders that are responsible for City's defeat. Newman's failure to clear allows Andy Rammell to shoot past Leaning, then Gerry Taggart escapes the attentions of Rennie to head in.

BARCLAYS LEAGUE DIVISION 2   Manager: Jordan ⇨ Jimmy Lumsden   SEASON 1990-91

No	Date	Att	Pos	Pt	F-A	H-T	Scorers, Times, and Referees	1	2	3	4	5	6	7	8	9	10	11	subs used
24	H 12/1	16,169	12	34	0-4	0-1	Hazard 38, White 61, 90, Shearer 89 Ref: B Stevens	Leaning *Digby*	Llewellyn *Kerslake*	Scott* *Bodin*	May *Hazard*	Shelton *Lorenzo*	Aizlewood *Gittens*	Rennie *Jones*	Newman *Shearer*	Allison *White*	Morgan* *MacLaren*	Smith *Foley*	Donowa/Taylor
25	A 19/1	8,074	12	34	0-1	0-0	Robinson 74 Ref: R Gifford	Leaning *Walter*	Llewellyn *Brown*	Scott *Morgan*	May *Marker*	Bryant *Burrows*	Aizlewood *Salman*	Rennie* *Barlow*	Newman *Hodges*	Allison *Robinson*	Morgan *Adcock*	Smith *Morrison*	Donowa
26	A 26/1	7,054	13	34	2-3	2-2	Scott 34p, Newman 38 Mehew 11, 21, Saunders 63 Ref: K Barratt	Leaning *Kelly*	Llewellyn *Alexander**	Scott *Twentyman*	May *Yates*	Bryant *Mehew*	Aizlewood *Jones*	Donowa *Holloway*	Newman *Reece*	Taylor *White*	Morgan *Saunders*	Smith* *Pounder*	Bent *Bloomer*
27	H 2/2	11,492	9	37	2-0	1-0	Morgan 14, Taylor 60 Ref: J Martin	Leaning *Rees*	Llewellyn *Hodson*	Scott *Anderson*	May *Roberts*	Bryant *Strodder*	Aizlewood *Raven !*	Shelton *Ford*	Newman *Goodman*	Taylor *Bannister*	Morgan* *Parkin*	Smith *Shakespeare*	Allison
28	A 16/2	5,212	8	40	2-1	0-1	May 48, Newman 53 Payton 8 Ref: J Watson	Leaning *Wright*	Llewellyn *Norton*	Scott *Jacobs*	May *De Mange**	Bryant *Buckley*	Aizlewood *Shotton*	Shelton *Jenkinson ^*	Newman *Payton*	Taylor *Swan*	Morgan *Palin*	Smith* *Atkinson*	Donowa *Wilcox/Hunter*
29	H 23/2	10,938	8	43	3-1	2-1	Shelton 30, 66, Taylor 32 Nogan 16 Ref: J Deakin	Leaning *Veysey*	Llewellyn *Robinson*	Scott *Smart**	May *Foyle*	Bryant *Melville*	Aizlewood *Magilton*	Shelton *Phillips*	Newman *Lewis ^*	Taylor *Nogan*	Morgan *Simpson*	Smith	Ford/Stein
30	A 2/3	5,477	9	43	1-2	1-2	Smith 16 Dyer 42, 44 Ref: P Jones	Leaning *Bolder*	Llewellyn *Pitcher*	Scott *Reid*	May *Peake*	Bryant *Webster*	Aizlewood* *Kernaghan*	Shelton *Lee R*	Newman *Grant**	Taylor* *Dyer*	Morgan *Mortimer*	Smith *Minto*	Rennie/Allison *Leaburn*
31	A 5/3	22,269	8	46	1-0	0-0	Donowa 88 Ref: R Groves	Leaning *Parkin*	Llewellyn *Alexander**	Scott *Twentyman*	May* *Clark*	Bryant *Mehew*	Aizlewood *Jones*	Shelton *Holloway*	Newman *Reece*	Taylor *White*	Morgan *Saunders*	Donowa *Pounder*	Rennie/Allison *Willmott*
32	H 9/3	11,474	5	49	4-2	2-1	Taylor 27, 39, Shelton 49, Morgan 70 Dozzell 18, Goddard 75 Ref: H King	Leaning *Forrest*	Llewellyn *Yallop**	Scott *Thompson*	May* *Stockwell*	Bryant *Linighan*	Aizlewood *Palmer*	Shelton *Zondervan*	Newman *Goddard*	Taylor *Whitton*	Morgan *Dozzell*	Donowa *Milton*	Smith *Hill*
33	H 12/3	13,297	5	52	1-0	0-0	Taylor 88 Ref: R Bigger	Leaning *Muggleton*	Llewellyn *North*	Scott *Gibson ^*	May *Mauchlen*	Bryant *Walsh*	Aizlewood *James*	Shelton* *Wright*	Newman *Ramsey*	Taylor *Oldfield*	Morgan^ *Mills*	Donowa *Kelly**	Smith/Allison *Kitson/Reid*
34	A 16/3	13,560	5	53	0-0	0-0	Ref: D Phillips	Leaning *Burridge*	Llewellyn *Watson S*	Scott *Neilson*	May *Aitken*	Bryant *Scott*	Aizlewood *Kristensen*	Shelton *Hunt*	Newman *Peacock**	Taylor *Quinn*	Morgan^ *Howey ^*	Smith* *Brock*	Donowa/Allison *O'Brien/McGhee*

24 — Angry City fans look for scapegoats after Leaning stands for Swindon and a victory of record-breaking proportions. By the end it is difficult to work out who is playing where, and Swindon cash in with Duncan Shearer's far-post header and Steve White's opportunist shot.

25 — Having been fed a diet of fast, attacking soccer in recent seasons, the massed ranks of the City fans are given a rare glimpse of the alternative. Lumsden's decision to field a five-man defence is totally negative as impotent City deservedly go down to Paul Robinson's point-blank header.

26 — Trailing to David Mehew's double, a shot from twelve yards, followed by a sharp volley, City get back on level terms. Scott's twice-taken pen (both netted) and Newman's dispatch of Donowa's through-ball brings the match alive, which Carl Saunders settles with a nod over the line.

27 — Although City play with conviction on a difficult snow-covered pitch, Albion look anything but a relegation-threatened side. Morgan's simple tap-in and Taylor's low shot beneath the keeper at the end of a direct run brings City the points, even though Albion fashion twice the chances.

28 — Andy Payton punishes City's tentative start by firing in his 19th goal of the season. After the interval man-of-the-match Morgan sets up both City goals with unselfish headers. May's crisp volley and Newman's point-blank shot producing City's fourth away win of the campaign.

29 — Unaware of the sudden death of Chairman Des Williams, City produce some brilliant football to overcome Lee Nogan's crisp 15-yard opener. Shelton's perfectly-curved shot beyond the reach of Ken Veysey levels matters, then he shoots in the goal of the game to tie up City's success.

30 — Careless City are a soft touch at Selhurst Park after failing to add to Smith's weak low-shot which bobbled over the keeper's hands. Bryant's lapse of concentration allows Alex Dyer to run the ball in for the equaliser, and then register with a perfectly-executed chip not long after.

31 — Donowa's first City goal could hardly have come at a better time, as his late stooped header, after Brian Parkin fails to gather his innocuous shot, ends five years of derby blues. Morgan is thrice denied by the woodwork, whilst Leaning saves Ian Holloway's 75th-minute spot-kick.

32 — Taylor's goal-poaching ability turns the match after Jason Dozzell capitalises on acres of space to send a glorious 25-yard drive past Leaning. A perfectly-placed header and an acrobatic overhead confirms the striker's resurgence of confidence as City move into a play-off position.

33 — Jimmy Lumsden admits it is sheer robbery as Taylor volleys in City's late winner after the prone Tony James had played all the City attackers onside. City have Leaning to thank for keeping them in the game, as Leicester create virtually all the clear chances of a disappointing game.

34 — Leaning throws himself to palm away Mike Quinn's 87th-min point-blank header and preserve City a well-deserved point from a drab game. City miss the better chances, both Newman and Morgan firing over, while Taylor and Donowa delayed shooting with the goal at their mercy.

No		Date	Opponent	Att.	Res	Score	Pos	Pts	Scorers / Opposition scorers
35	A	20/3	WEST HAM	22,951	L	0-1	7/2	53	Gale 67 — Ref: P Alcock
36	H	23/3	WOLVES	15,499	D	1-1	7/10	54	Bryant 54; Dennison 62 — Ref: M Pierce
37	A	30/3	PORTSMOUTH	10,417	L	1-4	8/20	54	Morgan 62; Clarke 44, 60, 86p, Whittingham 49 — Ref: D Axcell
38	H	1/4	NOTTS CO	13,466	W	3-2	7/8	57	Allison 44, Donowa 76, Shelton 84; Johnson 30, O'Riordan 75 — Ref: T Lunt
39	A	6/4	MIDDLESBROUGH	13,844	L	1-2	8/5	57	Taylor 2; Ripley 20, 89 — Ref: R Nixon
40	H	13/4	BARNSLEY	12,081	W	1-0	7/9	60	Newman 26 — Ref: D Frampton
41	A	20/4	OLDHAM	14,086	L	1-2	9/2	60	Newman 86; Marshall 65, Redfearn 83p — Ref: A Dawson
42	A	23/4	BRIGHTON	7,738	W	1-0	8/6	63	Shelton 89 — Ref: R Wiseman
43	H	27/4	MILLWALL	16,741	L	1-4	8/5	63	Morgan 44; Sheringham 55, 65, 81, Thompson 60 — Ref: P Tyldesley
44	H	4/5	PORT VALE	11,555	D	1-1	9/17	64	Rennie 15; Earle 78 — Ref: P Durkin
45	A	8/5	SHEFFIELD WED	31,716	L	1-3	9/3	64	Allison 71; Hirst 34, 63, Francis 54 — Ref: P Harrison
46	A	11/5	WATFORD	13,029	W	3-2	9/20	67	Morgan 48, Newman 53, Donowa 87; Wilkinson 57, 65 — Ref: J Lloyd

Home — Away 11,421 — Average 13,495

35 — West Ham (City line-up): Leaning, Llewellyn!, May, Bryant, Aizlewood, Shelton, Newman, Taylor, Morgan, Donowa*, Allison
Opposition: Miklosko, Potts, Gale, Foster, Hughton, Bishop, McAvennie! / Slater*, Parris, Keen, Quinn^, Allen/Rosenior
City are impressive at Upton Park, where they match, and often outplay, the Hammers. Tony Gale's brilliant chip from a disputed free-kick settles the match six minutes after the dismissal of Frank McAvennie and Llewellyn, for little more than jostling for position at a throw-in.

36 — Wolves: Leaning, Llewellyn*, May, Bryant, Aizlewood, Shelton, Newman, Taylor, Morgan*, Donowa, Allison
Opposition: Stowell, Bennett, Hindmarch, Clarke, Downing, Birch, Cook!, Bull, Mutch, Dennison, Bent/Allison
City squander a host of chances, including a 29th-minute spot-kick which Scott blazes over the bar, as they fail to capitalise on Paul Cook's dismissal for dissent over the pen. Bryant's stooping header puts City in front, but Robbie Dennison's 25-yard free-kick levels matters.

37 — Portsmouth: Leaning*, Llewellyn*, May, Bryant, Aizlewood, Shelton, Newman, Taylor, Morgan*, Donowa, Allison/Rennie
Opposition: Knight, Russell, Murray, Butters, Magure, Wigley, Kuhl*, Whittingham, Clarke, Anderton*, Beresford/Black
Despite creating chances, City's overall performance is disappointing. Donowa's poor finish when clean through early on is costly as Colin Clarke (later to complete his hat-trick with a dubious penalty) sweeps in Ray Daniel's cross to put Portsmouth ahead against the run of play.

38 — Notts Co: Leaning, Llewellyn, May, Bryant, Aizlewood, Shelton, Newman, Taylor, Morgan*, Donowa, Allison
Opposition: Cherry, Short, Chris Paris, Short/Craig Yates, O'Riordan, Thomas, Turner, Bartlett, Johnson, Draper, Johnson
Shelton's blistering volley keeps City in the promotion race, but it is guts rather than skill which triumphs. County are much the better side in the first half, but City equalise Tommy Johnson's driven-in opener when Allison hammers the ball past Steve Cherry at the second attempt.

39 — Middlesbrough: Leaning, Rennie, May, Bryant, Aizlewood*, Shelton, Newman, Taylor, Morgan*, Allison, Bent/Mardon
Opposition: Dibble, Parkinson, Kernaghan, Coleman, Hendrie, Slaven*, Proctor, Baird, Mustoe, Ripley, Walsh
The referee hands the points to lucky Boro' as he fails to spot handball offences in the dying minutes when Colin Walsh keeps out Rennie's shot, and Jimmy Phillips stops Taylor's follow-up effort. Straight away the ball reaches the other end for Stuart Ripley to shoot past Leaning.

40 — Barnsley: Leaning, Llewellyn*, May, Bryant, Mardon, Shelton, Newman, Taylor, Morgan*, Allison, Bent
Opposition: Baker, Dobbin*, Fleming, Smith, Tiler, O'Connell, Rammell, Saville, Agnew, Archdeacon, Deehan/Robinson
The play-off prize still beckons for City after this win, which was more emphatic than the score suggests. Barnsley pack their goalmouth for Shelton's indirect free-kick, which is squared to Newman, whose shot from no more than eight yards finds a gap and whistles low into the net.

41 — Oldham: Leaning, Llewellyn*, May*, Bryant, Aizlewood, Shelton, Newman, Taylor*, Morgan, Allison, Bent/Morgan
Opposition: Hallworth, Halle*, Barrow, Henry, Barrett, Jobson, Adams, Warhurst, Marshall, Redfearn, Currie
City will not grieve over the synthetic pitch at Boundary Park, which is being removed at the end of the season. After Ian Marshall stoops to head the Latics in front, Mardon is incensed over the penalty award when he is adjudged to have handled whilst clearing a shot off the line.

42 — Brighton: Leaning, Llewellyn*, Mardon, Bryant, Aizlewood, Shelton, Newman, Allison, Morgan, Taylor, May
Opposition: Digweed, Crumplin, Wilkins, Pates, Chivers, Barham, Byrne, Small, Codner, Walker
Shelton's carefully-placed shot from Allison's head-down saves City's blushes at the Goldstone Ground, where poor finishing threatened to scupper play-off hopes. Brighton offer little, though John Byrne's deflected shot cannons off the bar with Leaning stranded 13 mins from time.

43 — Millwall: Leaning, Llewellyn*, Mardon*, Bryant, Aizlewood, Shelton, Newman, Allison, Morgan, Taylor, Bent
Opposition: Horne, Stevens, Dawes, Waddock, McCarthy, Stephenson, Goodman, Sheringham, Kerr, Briley
Naive defending aids Millwall's second-half fight-back which transforms this vital encounter. Three times City are undone by straightforward corners, as their defence fails to counter David Thompson's havoc-producing long runs and prodigious leaps that yield telling headers.

44 — Port Vale: Leaning, May, Rennie, Bryant, Aizlewood, Shelton, Newman, Allison, Morgan, Taylor*, Donowa
Opposition: Wood, Mills S, Walker, Parkin*, Aspin, Kent, Earle, Van der Laan, Glover, Porter, Millar
With Lumsden persisting with the sweeper system, City pay the price for their failure to put away good chances after Rennie drives a fine shot through a packed defence low into the net. Simon Mills' second attempt at a cross eludes Leaning, and Robbie Earle heads into the top corner.

45 — Sheffield Wed: Leaning, May, Rennie, Bryant, Aizlewood, Shelton*, Newman, Allison, Morgan, Taylor*, Bent
Opposition: Turner, Nilsson*, King, Madden, Anderson, Wilson, Sheridan, Hirst, Francis^, Worthington, Harkes/Williams
With others dropping points, City need to win their last two games to clinch a play-off place, but they are mere bit players at Hillsborough's promotion party. Allison's glorious 25-yard strike is little consolation for being thoroughly outclassed by a Trevor Francis inspired Owls side.

46 — Watford: Leaning, Llewellyn, May, Bryant, Aizlewood, Rennie, Newman, Allison, Morgan, Smith*, Donowa
Opposition: James, Gibbs, Ashby, Soloman, Roeder*, Dublin, Falconer, Wilkinson, Butler, Porter, Nicholas/Callaghan
Still in with a slight chance of a play-off place, City find that Donowa's tapped-in winner is of no avail as other results go against them. After enjoying the better of the first half, City's superiority is confirmed by Morgan's shot that is deflected past David James just after the break.

BARCLAYS DIVISION 2 (CUP-TIES)　　Manager: Jordan ⇨ Jimmy Lumsden　　SEASON 1990-91

Rumbelows Cup

		F-A	H-T	Scorers, Times, and Referees	1	2	3	4	5	6	7	8	9	10	11	subs used
1:1 A WEST BROM	8,721	D 2-2	1-1	Morgan 30, 47 / *Bannister 8, Hackett 84* / Ref: J Key	Sinclair	Llewellyn	Aizlewood	May	Shelton	Rennie	Bent	Newman	Taylor*	Morgan	Smith	Allison
					Naylor	*Hodson*	*Harbey*	*Robson*	*Burgess*	*Strodder*	*Ford*	*Goodman*	*Bannister*	*Bradley**	*Shakespeare*	*Hackett*

After Craig Shakespeare breaks clear to present Gary Bannister with a simple goal, City outplay Albion for long periods. Morgan lashes in a loose ball for the equaliser, and then clips a precise shot over Stuart Naylor, but City are deprived of a win by Gary Hackett's superb volley.

		F-A	H-T	Scorers, Times, and Referees	1	2	3	4	5	6	7	8	9	10	11	subs used
1:2 H WEST BROM	9,851	W 1-0 aet	0-0	Smith 113 / Ref: R Gifford / (City won 3-2 on aggregate)	Sinclair	Llewellyn	Aizlewood	May	Shelton	Rennie	Bent	Newman	Taylor	Morgan*	Smith	Allison
					Naylor	*Hodson*	*Harbey*	*Robson**	*Burgess*	*Strodder !*	*Ford*	*West*	*Bannister*	*Bradley*	*Shakespeare*	*Hackett/Foster*

Smith's rasping extra-time shot settles this cup-tie against ten-man Albion, who had lost Gary Strodder for a second bookable offence seven minutes earlier. Albion's physical approach often has City riding their luck, and Aizlewood is forced to clear Gary Bannister's shot off the line.

		F-A	H-T	Scorers, Times, and Referees	1	2	3	4	5	6	7	8	9	10	11	subs used
2:1 A SUNDERLAND 8	10,358 1:13	W 1-0	1-0	Morgan 18 / Ref: D Phillips	Sinclair	Llewellyn	Aizlewood	May	Shelton	Rennie	Bent	Newman	Taylor	Morgan	Smith	Allison
					Norman	*Kay*	*Brady**	*Bennett*	*Ball*	*Owers`*	*Bracewell*	*Armstrong*	*Davenport*	*Gabbiadini*	*Hardyman*	*Ord/Hauser*

Slick City silence the Roker roar as they outplay Sunderland. The only surprise is that they do not add to Morgan's early goal, when he headed in Taylor's flick-on from Llewellyn's cross. City should have done more with eight shots on target compared to Sunderland's total of two.

		F-A	H-T	Scorers, Times, and Referees	1	2	3	4	5	6	7	8	9	10	11	subs used
2:2 H SUNDERLAND 12	11,776 1:16	L 1-6	1-2	Morgan 5 / *Hauser 1, Ball 44, Owers 49, G'dini 65, 82 / Norman [Cullen 77]* / Ref: J Martin / (City lost 2-6 on aggregate)	Leaning	Llewellyn	Aizlewood	May	Shelton	Rennie	Donowa	Newman	Taylor*	Morgan	Smith	Allison
					Gunn	*Kay*	*Smith*	*Bennett*	*Ball*	*Owers*	*Bracewell**	*Armstrong*	*Davenport*	*Gabbiadini*	*Hauser**	*Cullen/Ord*

City fail to celebrate Lumsden's managerial appointment as they go down to their worst home defeat since Norwich's visit in January 1949. The result somewhat flatters Sunderland (seven shots on target) as City (ten shots on target) are made to pay for defensive shortcomings.

FA Cup

		F-A	H-T	Scorers, Times, and Referees	1	2	3	4	5	6	7	8	9	10	11	subs used
3 A NORWICH 9	12,630 1:10	L 1-2	1-1	Allison 41 / *Rosario 4, Fleck 70* / Ref: R Lewis	Leaning	Llewellyn*	Bailey	May	Shelton	Aizlewood	Rennie	Newman	Allison	Taylor*	Smith	Donowa/Bent
					Gunn	*Culverhouse*	*Bowen*	*Butterworth* Polston*		*Crook*	*Gordon*	*Fleck*	*Sherwood*	*Rosario*	*Phillips*	*Goss*

After recovering from an unkind goal, when a speculative 25-yard effort by David Phillips strikes Robert Rosario and ends up in the net, City's good football is deserving of a replay. Allison heads City level from Smith's cross, but Robert Fleck's 25-yarder takes the Canaries through.

Home / Away League Table

Pos	Team	P	W	D	L	F	A	W	D	L	F	A	Pts
			Home					Away					
1	Oldham	46	17	5	1	55	21	8	8	7	28	32	88
2	West Ham	46	15	6	2	41	18	9	5	7	19	16	87
3	Sheffield Wed	46	12	10	1	43	23	10	6	7	37	28	82
4	Notts Co *	46	14	4	5	45	28	9	7	7	31	27	80
5	Millwall	46	11	6	6	43	28	9	7	7	27	23	73
6	Brighton	46	12	4	7	37	31	9	3	11	26	38	70
7	Middlesbro	46	12	4	7	36	17	8	5	10	30	30	69
8	Barnsley	46	13	7	3	39	16	6	5	12	24	32	69
9	BRISTOL CITY	46	14	5	4	44	28	6	2	15	24	43	67
10	Oxford	46	10	9	4	41	29	4	10	9	28	37	61
11	Newcastle	46	8	10	5	24	22	6	7	10	25	34	59
12	Wolves	46	11	6	6	45	35	2	13	8	18	28	58
13	Bristol Rov	46	11	7	5	29	20	4	6	13	27	39	58
14	Ipswich	46	9	8	6	32	28	4	10	9	28	40	57
15	Port Vale	46	10	4	9	32	24	5	8	10	24	40	57
16	Charlton	46	8	7	8	27	25	5	10	8	30	36	56
17	Portsmouth	46	10	6	7	34	27	4	5	14	24	43	53
18	Plymouth	46	10	10	3	36	20	2	7	14	18	48	53
19	Blackburn	46	8	6	9	26	27	6	4	13	25	39	52
20	Watford	46	8	6	9	24	32	7	7	9	21	27	51
21	Swindon	46	8	8	7	31	30	4	8	11	34	43	50
22	Leicester	46	12	4	7	41	33	2	4	17	19	50	50
23	West Brom	46	7	11	5	26	21	3	7	13	26	40	48
24	Hull	46	6	10	7	35	32	4	5	14	22	53	45
		1104	253	163	136	866	615	136	163	253	615	866	1493

* promoted
after play-offs

Odds & ends

Double wins: (4) Blackburn, Brighton, Watford, Hull.

Double losses: (2) Oldham, Charlton.

Won from behind: (6) Blackburn (h), Millwall (a), Hull (a), Oxford (h), Ipswich (h), Notts Co (h).

Lost from in front: (4) Charlton (a), Middlesbrough (a), Millwall (h), Notts Co (a).

High spots: Beating Blackburn 4-1 at Ashton Gate on 25 August.
Beating Hull at Ashton Gate 4-1 on 17 November.
Beating Blackburn 1-0 at Ewood Park on 15 December.
Beating Pompey 4-1 at Ashton Gate on 26 December.
Louie Donowa's goal that beats Bristol Rov on 5 March.
Moving into a play-off position after beating Ipswich 4-2 on 9 March.
Winning 1-0 at Sunderland in the FL Cup.
Beating Bristol Rov (a) 4-1 in the Gloucestershire Cup Final on 15 Aug.

Low spots: Missing out on the play-offs.
Losing 0-2 at West Brom on 15 September.
Losing at home to Swindon 0-4 on 12 January.
Bundled out of the FL Cup by Sunderland's 1-6 blitz at Ashton Gate.

Player of the year: Andy Llewellyn.
Ever-presents: (1) Rob Newman.
Hat-tricks: (0).
Leading scorer: Nicky Morgan (17).

Appearances and Goals

Player	Appearances Lge	Sub	LC	Sub	FA	Sub	Goals Lge	LC	FA	Tot
Aizlewood, Mark	41		4		4		2			2
Allison, Wayne	18	19			3	1	6		1	7
Bailey, John	6	1								
Bent, Junior	15	5	3			1	2			2
Bryant, Matt	22						1			1
Donowa, Louie	11	13	1			1	3			3
Humphries, Glenn	1	1								
Leaning, Andy	29		1		1					
Llewellyn, Andy	42		4			1				
Mardon, Paul	6	1								
May, Andy	44	1	4			1	3			3
Morgan, Nicky	43		4				13	4		17
Newman, Rob	46		4			1	8			8
Rennie, David	29	3	4				2			2
Scott, Martin	27						1			1
Shelton, Gary	43		4			1	8			8
Sinclair, Ronnie	17		3							
Smith, David	32	2	4			1	5	1		6
Taylor, Bob	34	5	4			1	11			11
(own-goals)							3			3
19 players used	506	53	44	3	11	2	68	5	1	74

BARCLAYS LEAGUE DIVISION 2

Manager: Lumsden ⇨ Denis Smith — SEASON 1991-92

No	Date		Att	Pos	Pt	F-A	H-T	Scorers, Times, and Referees	1	2	3	4	5	6	7	8	9	10	11	subs used
1	A	SOUTHEND	6,720	D	−	1	1-1	0-1	Benjamin 32 — Ref: R Lewis	**Welch**	**Llewellyn**	**Scott**	**May**	**Bryant**	**Aizlewood**	**Shelton**	**Rennie**	**Allison**	**Taylor**	**Smith**	Tilson
	17/8								*Sansome*	*Austin*	*Powell*	*Martin*	*Edwards*	*Prior*	*Ansah*	*Sussex*	*O'Callaghan**	*Benjamin*	*Angell*	
2	H	BRIGHTON	11,299				2-1	1-0	Scott 22, Bryant 66 / Bissett 87 — Ref: D Frampton	**Welch**	**Llewellyn**	**Scott**	**May**	**Bryant**	**Aizlewood**	**Shelton**	**Rennie**	**Allison**	**Taylor**	**Smith**	Barham/Bissett
	20/8				4	W				*Digweed*	*Crumplin*	*Chapman*	*Wilkins*	*Chivers*	*O'Reilly*	*Iovan**	*Byrne*	*Wade**	*Codner*	*Walker*	
3	H	BLACKBURN	11,317	2	7	W	1-0	1-0	Allison 43 — Ref: R Bigger	**Welch**	**Llewellyn**	**Scott**	**May**	**Bryant**	**Aizlewood**	**Shelton**	**Rennie**	**Allison**	**Taylor***	**Smith**	Morgan / Gayle/Richardson
	24/8			21						*Mimms*	*Atkins*	*Sulley*	*Reid*	*Moran*	*Dobson !*	*May*	*Agnew*	*Livingstone**	*Speedie*	*Garner**	
4	A	PORT VALE	7,057	4	8	D	1-1	0-1	Morgan 67 / Mills S 43 — Ref: M Reed	**Welch**	**Llewellyn**	**Scott**	**May**	**Bryant**	**Aizlewood**	**Shelton**	**Rennie**	**Allison**	**Taylor***	**Smith**	Morgan / Mills B
	31/8			10						*Grew*	*Mills S*	*Hughes*	*Walker*	*Aspin*	*Glover*	*Porter*	*Van der Laan Houchen**		*Foyle*	*Swan*	
5	H	BRISTOL ROV	20,183	2	11	W	1-0	0-0	Allison 64 — Ref: M Bodenham	**Welch**	**Llewellyn**	**Scott**	**May**	**Bryant**	**Aizlewood**	**Shelton**	**Rennie**	**Allison**	**Morgan**	**Smith**	Bent
	4/9			22						*Parkin*	*Boothroyd*	*Twentyman*	*Yates*	*Clark*	*Archer*	*Skinner**	*Reece*	*White*	*Stewart*	*Purnell*	*Saunders*
6	A	LEICESTER	17,815	5	11	L	1-2	1-2	Morgan 36 / Gibson 17, Fitzpatrick 37 — Ref: P Don	**Welch**	**Llewellyn**	**Scott**	**Edwards**	**Bryant**	**Aizlewood**	**Bent***	**Rennie**	**Allison**	**Morgan**	**Smith**	Harrison
	7/9			2						*Poole*	*Mills*	*Platnauer*	*Fitzpatrick*	*Walsh*	*James*	*Oldfield*	*Gibson*	*Wright**	*Kelly*	*Kitson**	*Russell/Gordon*
7	H	TRANMERE	11,235	5	12	D	2-2	2-1	Allison 10, Shelton 25 / Brannan 27, Irons 48 — Ref: P Vanes	**Welch**	**May**	**Scott**	**Edwards**	**Bryant**	**Aizlewood***	**Shelton**	**Rennie**	**Allison**	**Morgan**	**Smith**	Bent
	14/9			9						*Nixon*	*Higgins*	*Brannan*	*Irons*	*Mungall*	*Vickers*	*Morrissey**	*Aldridge*	*Malkin*	*Martindale*	*Thomas*	*Cooper /McNab*
8	H	MILLWALL	10,862	6	13	D	2-2	1-2	Bryant 44, Scott 86p / McCarthy 34, Colquhoun 35 — Ref: C Wilkes	**Welch**	**May**	**Scott**	**Edwards***	**Bryant**	**Aizlewood***	**Shelton**	**Rennie**	**Allison**	**Morgan***	**Smith**	Taylor/Harrison
	17/9			22						*Davison*	*Dawes*	*Cooper*	*Bogie*	*McCarthy*	*Wood*	*Colquhoun*	*Falco**	*Rae*	*Stephenson*	*Armstrong*	
9	A	IPSWICH	9,910	10	13	L	2-4	1-1	Allison 4, Smith 56 / Thjson 37, Linighan 65, Kiwomya 87 [Goddard 89] — Ref: A Buksh	**Welch**	**Llewellyn**	**Scott**	**May**	**Bryant**	**Caesar**	**Shelton**	**Rennie**	**Allison**	**Connor**	**Smith**	Edwards/Connor
	21/9			2						*Forrest*	*Johnson**	*Thompson*	*Stockwell**	*Yallop*	*Linighan*	*Zondervan*	*Goddard*	*Whitton*	*Dozzell*	*Kiwomya*	*Milton/Lowe*
10	H	PORTSMOUTH	9,830	14	13	L	0-2	0-2	Beresford 34, 43p — Ref: D Elleray	**Welch**	**Llewellyn**	**Scott**	**May**	**Bryant**	**Caesar***	**Shelton***	**Rennie**	**Allison**	**Morgan**	**Smith**	Edwards/Connor
	28/9			7						*Knight*	*Awford*	*Beresford*	*Burns*	*Symons*	*Butters*	*Neill*	*Chamberlain Clarke**	*Whitton*	*Wigley*	*Anderton*	*Powell*
11	A	DERBY	11,880	18	13	L	1-4	0-1	Edwards 74 / Aizlewood 17 (og), Micklewhite 47, [Davison 62, 78] — Ref: W Flood	**Welch**	**Llewellyn**	**Scott**	**May***	**Bryant**	**Aizlewood**	**Edwards**	**Rennie**	**Allison**	**Connor**	**Smith**	Bent
	5/10			8						*Shilton*	*Sage*	*Forsyth*	*Williams G*	*Coleman*	*Comyn*	*Micklewhite*	*Ormondroyd*	*Davison*	*Williams P*	*McMinn*	

1. Southend: A delayed kick-off to let in the hordes of City fans, who make the atmosphere at Roots Hall like that of a home game. Ian Benjamin clips in a rebound to celebrate Southend's Second Division debut, but Taylor drives a low right-foot shot past Sansome for City's well-earned point.

2. Brighton: All seating now at the Covered End, but the fans are on their feet as Scott fires City in front against last season's play-off finalists with a direct free-kick which took a deflection. Bryant's first-time shot has City coasting, until Nicky Bissett's diving header brings Brighton's late response.

3. Blackburn: Against the promotion favourites, City fully deserve the points their skilful play merits, even though the winning strike is a fluke. Chesting down Shelton's chip and swinging a mighty boot, Allison's resulting miskick totally deceives Bobby Mimms as the ball trickles into the net.

4. Port Vale: Sub Morgan is City's hero as his deft headed deflection makes sure that Mark Grew has no chance of stopping Scott's forceful 30-yard volley. Trailing to an early candidate for 'goal of the season', a perfect 35-yard strike from full-back Simon Mills, Morgan's arrival revives City.

5. Bristol Rov: Geoff Twentyman says 'It was a case of the right place, but the wrong man' after he fails to make his shot count when clean through in the dying seconds. Just as well really, because City's dominant display fully deserved the points secured by Allison's low-shot past Brian Parkin.

6. Leicester: Leicester survive a second-half battering to deprive impressive City of their unbeaten record. Ex Robin Paul Fitzpatrick prods in Leicester's winner from close range, after Colin Gibson's 30-yard thunderbolt had been equalised by Morgan's steering in of Rennie's low cross.

7. Tranmere: City are ironed out of the full compliment of points as Kenny Irons evades Shelton's lunging tackle to cut in and beat Welch with the most innocuous of shots. Despite Smith having his second-min effort harshly disallowed, a draw is a fair result as Tranmere play some great soccer.

8. Millwall: After Taylor is elbowed across his throat, Scott drills a perfect spot-kick into the corner of the net to cap City's comeback. Millwall punish City for their offside tactics when Mick McCarthy volleys in the opener, and then an overlap results in John Colquhoun sliding in another.

9. Ipswich: When Smith's right-wing free-kick beats everyone to put City 2-1 ahead, Ipswich were being jeered by their own supporters, but by the final whistle it is a different story. After half an hour of frenzied goalmouth action, they acclaim an emphatic victory, despite a missed penalty.

10. Portsmouth: It is thanks to Welch (£200,000 ex Rochdale) that the score is kept within tolerable limits. While David Elleray's officious handling does little to aid City's cause, the fact is that even if Lumsden himself had been in charge Pompey's impressive side would still have won at a canter.

11. Derby: Woeful City are a shambles and Derby could easily have doubled their score after Aizlewood helps in Gary Micklewhite's shot. Rob Edwards (£130,000 ex Carlisle) volleys in a consolation, before slack marking allows Bobby Davison to shoot Derby's fourth past the helpless Welch.

12. WATFORD (H) 12/10 — 7,882 · 11 20 16 · W 1-0 (1-0)
Connor 43
Ref: H King
City: Leaning, Llewellyn, Scott, May, Caesar, Osman, Connor, Rennie, Allison, Morgan*, Smith, Taylor/Harrison
Watford: James, Gibbs, Drysdale, Dublin, McLaughlin, Putney, Hessenthaler*, Blissett*, Butler, Porter, Nicholas, Bazeley/Devonshire
Russell Osman, on loan from Soton, exudes class, as City find the resolution and luck to turn the tide of recent bad results. Connor's boundless energy and enthusiasm takes him between two defenders to send in a well-struck shot that slips through the grasp of the diving David James.

13. BARNSLEY (A) 19/10 — 6,566 · 8 19 19 · W 2-1
May 24, Shelton 80 · Currie 77
Ref: R Hart
City: Leaning, Llewellyn, Scott, May, Caesar, Osman, Shelton, Rennie, Allison, Morgan*, Smith, Connor
Barnsley: Butler, Robinson, Archdeacon, Fleming, Saville*, Taggart, O'Connell, Pearson*, Currie, Rammell, Graham/Williams
Completely on top in the first half, City have to work hard after the break. Osman pulls off the save of the season with a spectacular diving header to deflect David Currie's 48th-minute shot onto the crossbar, whilst skipper Shelton scores the winner with a perfect 25-yard chip.

14. NEWCASTLE (H) 26/10 — 8,613 · 9 20 20 · D 1-1
Taylor 86 · Clark 13
Ref: D Gallagher
City: Leaning, Llewellyn, Scott, May, Caesar, Osman*, Shelton, Rennie, Taylor, Morgan*, Connor, Smith/Allison
Newcastle: Wright, Neilson*, Stimson, O'Brien, Scott, Maguire, Clark*, Peacock*, Howey, Hunt, Roche, Makel/Robinson
With Ossie Ardilles now manager of Newcastle, City are again confounded by deployment of the diamond formation. Fortunately the Magpies fail to add to Lee Clarke's early strike, and City's improved play after the interval is rewarded by Taylor's powerful header to poach a point.

15. CAMBRIDGE (A) 2/11 — 4,810 · 9 3 21 · D 0-0 (0-0)
Ref: R Shepherd
City: Leaning, Llewellyn, Scott, Caesar, Bryant, Aizlewood, Shelton, Rennie, Taylor, Allison, Connor
Cambridge: Vaughan, Fensome, Kimble, Dennis, O'Shea, Daish, Taylor, Bailie, Dublin, Claridge, Philpott
Only the woodwork and some disappointing finishing by Allison prevents Lumsden pulling off a notable tactical success. Unfortunately, whilst his five man defence frustrates Cambridge's bombardment style, the outcome is a grim spectacle that is no advert for Second Division soccer.

16. PLYMOUTH (H) 5/11 — 7,735 · 9 24 24 · W 2-0
Morgan 14, Allison 27
Ref: K Barratt
City: Leaning, Llewellyn, Scott, May, Bryant, Aizlewood !, Shelton, Rennie, Allison, Morgan, Smith
Plymouth: Wilmot, Salman, Clement, Marker, Hopkins, Morgan, Edworthy, Marshall, Evans*, Fiore, Cross*/Barlow/Scott
With the new lights fully operational for the first time, Aizlewood fails to get away with aiming a head butt at Andy Clement in the 31st minute following a late tackle on Scott. Fortunately Morgan's deft right-footed flick and Allison's ferocious 18-yard drive, already had City in control.

17. SUNDERLAND (H) 9/11 — 10,570 · 9 14 27 · W 1-0
Allison 25
Ref: B Hill
City: Leaning, Llewellyn, Scott, May, Bryant, Aizlewood, Shelton, Rennie, Allison, Morgan*, Smith, Connor/Osman
Sunderland: Norman, Kay, Rogan, Bennett, Ball, Davenport, Bracewell*, Rush*, Armstrong, Byrne, Pascoe, Russell/Owers
Andy Leaning (Evening Post Player of the Month for October) frustrates classy Sunderland. Allison, who somehow contrives to turn a clear heading chance into a handball offence, manages to keep his composure to put away Morgan's flick-on after his first shot had been parried.

18. OXFORD (A) 16/11 — 5,780 · 10 24 28 · D 1-1
Allison 52 · Simpson 60
Ref: P Taylor
City: Leaning, Llewellyn, Scott, May, Bryant, Aizlewood, Shelton, Rennie, Allison, Connor*, Smith, Taylor
Oxford: Keeley, Robinson, Smart, Lewis, Foster, Melville, Magilton, McClaren, Rush*, Nogan, Simpson, Aylott
As the fog descends at the Manor Ground, rumour has it that Rennie clears Steve Foster's late header off the line to save City a point. Allison finds space to slot the ball under John Keeley, but Paul Simpson is allowed to burst through unchallenged and volley powerfully past Leaning.

19. MIDDLESBROUGH (A) 23/11 — 12,928 · 11 2 28 · L 1-3
Taylor 40 · Payton 4, Slaven 30, 59
Ref: P Jones
City: Leaning*, Llewellyn, Scott, May, Bryant, Osman !, Shelton, Rennie*, Allison, Connor*, Smith, Taylor/Caesar
Middlesbrough: Pears, Fleming, Phillips, Kernaghan, Mohan, Mustoe, Slaven, Proctor, Wilkinson, Payton*, Ripley, Pollock
City bounce back to play some great football in the first half after failure of their offside trap allows Andy Payton to race away and slot in the opener. Taylor's header gets City back into the game, but Boro' are resurgent after the break, even before Osman's 64th-minute dismissal.

20. CHARLTON (H) 30/11 — 9,123 · 11 9 28 · L 0-2
Pardew 22, Gorman 59
Ref: G Ashby
City: Leaning, Llewellyn, Scott, Connor*, Bryant, Osman, Shelton, Rennie*, Allison, Taylor, Smith, May/Edwards
Charlton: Bolder, Pitcher, Minto, Pardew !, Webster, Gatting, Lee, Bumstead, Rosenior, Gorman*, Walsh, Leaburn
'What a load of rubbish' is the cry, as, apart from Bryant's 38th-minute shot, which is disallowed for offside, City offer little. Even Alan Pardew's late dismissal for a spitting offence fails to revive City, who produce their most feeble and half-hearted home performance in a long while.

21. GRIMSBY (A) 7/12 — 4,866 · 12 16 28 · L 1-3
Rennie 34 · Woods 2, Jones 69, Smith 88
Ref: R Poulain
City: Leaning, Llewellyn, Scott, May, Bryant, Osman, Bent, Rennie, Allison, Taylor, Smith, Gavin
Grimsby: Reece, Ford, Jopling, Futcher, Agnew, Dobbin, Childs, Gilbert, Smith, Cockerill*, Woods, Jones
Captain for the first time, Martin Scott distinguishes himself with a cracking shot against the bar, then sets up Rennie's goal with his through-ball, before blundering at the death. With City besieging the Grimsby goal in search of a late equaliser, his misplaced pass sets up Mark Smith.

22. BRISTOL ROV (A) 21/12 — 6,306 · 15 18 28 · L 2-3
Rennie 11, Bent 89 · White 44, Pounder 45, Saunders 81
Ref: P Durkin
City: Leaning*, Llewellyn, Scott, Osman, Bryant, Aizlewood, May, Rennie, Allison, Taylor, Smith, Gavin
Bristol Rov: Kelly, Alexander, Twentyman, Yates, Cross, Skinner, Mehew, Reece, White, Saunders, Pounder, Bent
Leaning protests he is fouled as Devon White transforms this pulsating derby by heading the Rovers' third. Within a minute he turns provider as his header sets up Tony Pounder to smash the ball home from ten yards. City's approach play is breathtaking, but alas their finishing is not.

23. SWINDON (H) 26/12 — 14,636 · 16 9 29 · D 1-1
Taylor 48 · Shearer 9
Ref: R Gifford
City: Leaning, Llewellyn, Scott, May, Bryant, Aizlewood, Osman, Rennie, Allison, Taylor, Smith, Gavin
Swindon: Hammond, Kerslake, Jones, Ling, Calderwood, Taylor, Hazard*, Shearer, Simpson, MacLaren, White*, Mitchell/Summerbee
After Duncan Shearer turns in the opener, it is like old times as Gavin's determination takes him clear onto Rennie's pass to impudently roll the ball into Taylor's path, for the simplest of equalisers. Swindon, unlucky in being denied two obvious pens, are without a win in nine games.

BARCLAYS LEAGUE DIVISION 2 — Manager: Lumsden ⇨ Denis Smith — SEASON 1991-92

No	H/A	Club	Date	Att	Pos	Pt	Res	F-A	H-T	Scorers, Times, and Referees	1	2	3	4	5	6	7	8	9	10	11	subs used
24	H	PORT VALE	28/12	9,235	12 / 14	32	W	3-0	2-0	Allison 1, Osman 14, Bent 49 — Ref: A Smith	Leaning	Llewellyn	Scott*	May*	Bryant	Aizlewood	Osman	Rennie	Allison	Taylor	Gavin	Bent/Edwards
											Grew	*Mills S*	*Hughes D*	*Williams*	*Aspin*	*Glover*	*Jalink*	*Van der Laan Swan**	*Houchen**	*Codner*	*Jeffers*	*Mills B/Porter*
25	A	BRIGHTON	1/1	7,555	13 / 23	33	D	0-0	0-0	Ref: G Pooley	Leaning	Llewellyn	Scott	May	Bryant	Aizlewood	Osman	Rennie	Allison	Taylor	Gavin	Gavin
											Beeney	*Crumplin*	*Gallacher*	*Chapman*	*Chivers*	*Bissett*	*Robinson*	*Farrington**	*Gall*	*Walker*	*Meade*	*Meade*
26	A	BLACKBURN	11/1	12,964	14 / 1	33	L	0-4	0-3	Newell 2, 43, Scott 30 (og), Speedie 74 — Ref: A Wilkie	Leaning	May	Scott	Osman	Bryant	Aizlewood	Edwards	Rennie*	Allison	Taylor*	Gavin	Bent/Morgan
											Mimms	*Brown*	*Wright*	*Cowans*	*Hill*	*Moran**	*Wilcox*	*Atkins**	*Speedie*	*Newell*	*Sellars*	*Reid/Hendry*
27	H	SOUTHEND	18/1	9,883	14 / 2	34	D	2-2	0-1	Dziekanowski 67, Powell 77 (og), Angell 4, Ansah 72 — Ref: I Hemley	Leaning	Caesar	Scott	Osman	Bryant	Aizlewood	May	Edwards*	Morgan	Dziekanowski	Gavin	Bent
											Sansome	*Austin*	*Powell*	*Butler*	*Scully*	*Prior*	*Ansah*	*Cornwell*	*Tilson*	*Benjamin*	*Angell*	
28	H	BARNSLEY	1/2	9,508	16 / 21	34	L	0-2	0-0	Archdeacon 68, O'Connell 89 — Ref: P Alcock	Leaning	Butler	Scott	May	Bryant	Osman	Bent	Morgan*	Dziekanowski	Aizlewood	Gavin	Mellon
											Robinson	*Fleming*	*Smith*	*Taggart*	*Bishop*	*Banks*	*Graham*	*Archdeacon*	*Currie*	*O'Connell*		*Mellon*
29	A	SWINDON	4/2	9,860	16 / 5	34	L	0-2	0-0	Jones 51, Shearer 81 — Ref: K Burge	Leaning	May	Scott	May*	Bryant	Osman	Bent	Shearer	Morgan*	Dziekanowski Mellon	Allison	Allison
											Hammond	*Kerslake*	*Badin*	*Ling*	*Calderwood*	*Taylor*	*Hazard*	*Jones*		*MacLaren*	*Mitchell*	
30	A	NEWCASTLE	8/2	29,484	18 / 22	34	L	0-3	0-0	Kelly 54, 61, O'Brien 55 — Ref: J Parker	Leaning	Wright	Scott	May*	Bryant	Osman	Bent	Rennie	Allison	Dziekanowski Gavin	Shelton	Shelton
											Wright	*Ranson*	*Stimson*	*O'Brien*	*Scott*	*Neilson*	*Watson*	*Peacock*	*Kelly*	*Wilson**	*Brack*	*Roche*
31	A	CHARLTON	22/2	5,900	21 / 8	34	L	1-2	1-0	Shelton 43, Walsh 81, Webster 88 — Ref: G Singh	Welch	Osman	Scott	May	Bryant	Aizlewood	Bent*	Shelton*	Allison	Dziekanowski Edwards	Mellon/Gavin	Mellon/Gavin
											Bolder	*Pitcher*	*Barness*	*Pardew*	*Webster*	*Gatting*	*Lee*	*Bumstead**	*Leaburn*	*Nelson*	*Walsh*	*Gorman*
32	H	GRIMSBY	29/2	8,992	20 / 17	35	D	1-1	1-0	Aizlewood 43, Woods 80 — Ref: J Brandwood	Welch	Osman	Scott	May	Bryant	Aizlewood	Bent	Edwards	Allison	Morgan	Gavin	Woods/Agnew
											Reece	*McDermott*	*Jopling*	*Knight*	*Lever*	*Cunnington*	*Childs**	*Gilbert*	*Rees*	*Smith*	*Dobbin**	*Woods/Agnew*
33	A	WOLVES	7/3	12,542	22 / 12	36	D	1-1	1-1	Osman 42, Bull 45 — Ref: A Gunn	Welch	Llewellyn	Scott	May	Bryant	Osman	Gavin	Edwards	Allison	Dziekanowski* Allison	McIntyre*	Morgan/Mellon
											Stowell	*Ashley*	*Venus*	*Bennett*	*Mountfield*	*Downing**	*Birch*	*Cook*	*Bull*	*Mutch*	*Dennison**	*Rankine/Burke*
34	A	PLYMOUTH	10/3	9,734	23 / 20	36	L	0-1	0-0	Marshall 48 — Ref: M Pierce	Welch	Llewellyn	Scott	May	Bryant	Osman	Mellon	Edwards	Morgan*	Allison	Gavin	Bent
											Wilmot	*Salman*	*Spearing*	*Van Rossum*	*Marker*	*Morrison*	*Hodges*	*Garner*	*Regis*	*Marshall*	*Morgan*	

Match notes

24. Even though Taylor squanders a hat-trick of chances, as he seeks to re-discover his form of two years ago, Lumsden enthuses over his lively display. An open attractive game, to which Vale contribute much, ignites from the off with Allison shooting in from Llewellyn's low cross.

25. Short-shy City fail to deliver a KO after dominating the game against a Brighton side with only one point from their previous five games. Gavin misses from close in, but Allison is the biggest culprit as his lack of know-how when faced by an advancing keeper again costs City dear.

26. City's sweeper system fails as Blackburn enjoy oceans of space. Scott Sellars makes an 80-yard run to set up Rovers' opener for Mike Newell to shoot in. City respond with Rennie firing against the bar, but Scott concedes the softest of own-goals on stretching for Newell's cross.

27. Jacki Dziekanowski (City's record signing - £250,000 ex Celtic) makes amends for his failure to put away a first-minute chance by making no mistake when Bent rolls the ball into his path. Gavin claims City's second, but his cut-back from the by-line is deflected in off Chris Powell.

28. A hapless City performance conjures up fears of a grim battle for Second Division survival as no-nonsense Barnsley took a stranglehold on a drab encounter. Brendan O'Connell's exquisite curler finishes off City, after Owen Archdeacon had put Barnsley ahead with a low shot.

29. In many ways the two sides are closely matched, but Swindon have a play-maker and a regular scorer, two priceless commodities that City lack. Play-maker Micky Hazard sets up the first goal for Tom Jones to rifle in, whilst marksman Duncan Shearer pops up to nod in the second.

30. City are the supporting cast at St James Park for Kevin Keegan's first-match in charge of the Magpies. Sadly, inept City prove in no mood to change the predictable script after Leaning palms weakly at Steve Watson's corner for David Kelly to head in from point-blank range.

31. Lumsden's luck hits rock bottom at Upton Park, where a City win looks probable until Shelton has to hobble off with a knee injury early in the second half. Colin Walsh curls in a 25-yard free-kick for Charlton's unlikely equaliser, then Simon Webster rifles in a dream volley.

32. Lumsden's departure has City's own gang of three in charge, and one of them, Mark Aizlewood, is almost on his knees when heading in Gavin's corner. City give their all, but lack the ability to threaten Grimsby's defence. It is no surprise when Neil Woods fires in an equaliser.

33. City are the better side at Molineux, where Edwards is denied by the woodwork, but Wolves have Steve Bull who takes full advantage when Osman slips in the mud. A glorious rocket shot to equalise Osman's low volley takes his record against City to eleven goals from five games.

34. New manager Denis Smith now knows the full extent of his task to keep City up, as woeful lack of firepower consigns them to a sorry defeat. Allison's 85th-minute looping header, that comes back off the bar, is City's best attempt to redress Dwight Marshall's close-range winner.

Match-by-match record (matches 35–46)

35 — H CAMBRIDGE 14/3
9,579 — Pos 23 — L 1-2 — 3 — 36
Scott 17
Heathcote 69, Norbury 84
Ref: J Deakin

City: Welch, Llewellyn*, Scott, Aizlewood, Bryant, Osman, Mellon*, Edwards, Cole, Allison, May; subs Harrison/Bent
Cambridge: Sheffield, Clayton*, Kimble, Baillie*, Chapple, Daish, Heaney, Dennis, —, Claridge, Leadbitter; subs Norbury/Heathcote

Mellon's glaring 73rd-min miss when Cole lays on an open goal, and Welch's failure to collect a cross six mins from time gift-wrap the points for a Cambridge side lacking several key players. Mick Norbury lashes home the winner when Dion Dublin's header rebounds off the bar.

36 — H WOLVES 17/3
11,623 — Pos 21 — W 2-0 — 11 — 39
Dziekanowski 84, 87
Ref: P Scobie

City: Welch, Llewellyn, Scott, Aizlewood, Bryant, Osman, Mellon, Edwards*, Cole, Allison, May; subs Dziekanowski
Wolves: Stowell, Ashley, Venus, Bennett, Mountfield, Madden, Birch, Cook, Bull, Rankine, Thompson*; subs Mutch

Pride returns to Ashton Gate as the fans and players unite in turning the tide. Dziekanowski's appearance just after the break triggers off the action and he secures the points with a brilliant 18-yard volley, and then a waltz past keeper Mike Stowell after swapping passes with Cole.

37 — A SUNDERLAND 21/3
18,968 — Pos 20 — W 3-1 — 17 — 42
Cole 7, Allison 19, 39
Atkinson 73
Ref: S Lodge

City: Welch, Llewellyn, Scott, Aizlewood, Bryant, Osman, Mellon*, Dziek'owski*, Cole, Allison*, May; subs Rosenior/Edwards
Sunderland: Norman, Kay, Rogan, Ball, Ord*, Rush*, Bracewell, Davenport, Armstrong, Byrne, Atkinson; subs Goodman/Mooney

Taking advantage of a strong wind Cole puts the skids under Sunderland. After lashing his shot against the crossbar, he keeps his cool to head the rebound over Tony Norman. A deserved win for City, Brian Atkinson's amazing 40-yarder for Sunderland no more than a consolation.

38 — H OXFORD 28/3
12,402 — Pos 20 — D 1-1 — 21 — 43
Dziekanowski 89
Bannister 73
Ref: D Shadwell

City: Welch, Llewellyn, Scott, Aizlewood, Bryant, Osman, Mellon*, Edwards, Cole, Allison, May; subs Atteveld/Rosenior
Oxford: Veysey, Smart, Williams, Lewis, Evans, Melville, Magilton, Beauchamp, Aylott, Durnin*, Penney; subs Bannister

Welch has little to do, other than to pick the ball out of the net after Atteveld's (£250,000 ex Everton) careless back-pass had put Gary Bannister clear. City, who force 17 corners, as well as managing eight shots on target, deserve more than Dziekanowski's late point saver.

39 — A TRANMERE 31/3
5,797 — Pos 19 — D 2-2 — 15 — 44
Cole 71, Rosenior 75
Nolan 53, Steel 70
Ref: R Dilkes

City: Welch, Llewellyn, Scott, Aizlewood, Bryant, Osman, Mellon, Dziek'owski*, Cole, Allison*, May; subs Rosenior/Edwards
Tranmere: Nixon, Higgins, Nolan, Irons, Harvey, Vickers, Morrissey*, Aldridge, Steel, Nevin, Thomas; subs Malkin

Dziekanowski is City's inspiration with his skilful play and direct runs at the Tranmere defence. His slick pass into Cole's stride, enables the Arsenal youngster to slot the ball past Eric Nixon, then his fierce shot on the run is blocked to enable Rosenior to knock in the equaliser.

40 — H LEICESTER 4/4
13,020 — Pos 17 — W 2-1 — 6 — 47
Rosenior 5, Cole 55
Oldfield 18
Ref: G Poll

City: Welch, Llewellyn, Scott, Aizlewood, Bryant, Osman, Mellon, Dziek'owski*, Cole, Rosenior*, May; subs Edwards/Allison
Leicester: Poole, Mills, Whitlow, Hill, Walsh, Grayson, Thompson*, Oldfield, Wright, Ormondroyd, Gee; subs Russell

The skills of Cole, Dziekanowski and Rosenior suggest that Denis Smith's pledge to survive with style is a realistic prospect. Rosenior's power header gets City off to a good start, then Cole's stunning close-in shot ties up the win, after David Oldfield's volley had levelled for Leicester.

41 — H MIDDLESBROUGH 7/4
12,814 — Pos 17 — D 1-1 — 6 — 48
Cole 66
Hendrie 18
Ref: J Carter

City: Welch, Llewellyn*, Scott*, Aizlewood, Bryant, Osman, Mellon, Dziek'owski, Cole, Rosenior!, May; subs Atteveld/Allison
Middlesbrough: Pears, Fleming, Phillips, Kernaghan, Mohan, Peake, Pollock, Payton*, Wilkinson, Hendrie, Falconer; subs Ripley

All the passion and commitment needed to avoid relegation go into City's comeback following Rosenior's 44th-min sending-off for kicking out at Alan Kernaghan. Dziekanowski's exquisite pass inside the full-back allows Cole to cut in from the right and shoot past Steve Pears.

42 — A MILLWALL 11/4
6,989 — Pos 16 — W 3-2 — 15 — 51
Rosenior 53, 75, Cole 64
Barber 20, Atteveld 88 (og)
Ref: P Wright

City: Welch, Llewellyn, Scott, Aizlewood, Bryant, Osman*, Mellon, Dziek'owski*, Cole, Rosenior, May; subs Atteveld/Allison
Millwall: Davison, Cunningham, Dawes, Stevens, Verveer, Cooper*, Stephenson, Goodman*, Allen, Barber, Roberts; subs McClashan/McGinlay

Rosenior's aerial power and work-rate, combined with Cole's pace, direct running and clinical finishing rip the Lions apart. Cole's brilliant back-heel sends Allison galloping into the area to slide the ball sideways for Rosenior to fire in what proves to be City's match-winning goal.

43 — H IPSWICH 18/4
16,914 — Pos 17 — W 2-1 — 1 — 54
Rosenior 37, Cole 53
Whitton 83p
Ref: J Martin

City: Welch, Llewellyn, Scott, Aizlewood, Bryant, Osman, Mellon, Dziek'owski, Cole, Rosenior, May; subs Dazzel/Kiwomya
Ipswich: Forrest, Zondervan, Thompson, Stockwell*, Wark*, Whelan, Milton, Goddard, Dozzell, Kiwomya, Whitton; subs Palmer/Johnson

Ipswich make a late fight of it following their late pen after Bryant fells Chris Kiwomya, but this is the only time Welch is stretched. City's potent duo turn up trumps again, Rosenior volleying in the opener, and Cole beating three defenders before slotting the ball past Craig Forrest.

44 — A PORTSMOUTH 20/4
17,168 — Pos 17 — L 0-1 — 9 — 54
Wigley 15
Ref: G Ashby

City: Welch, Llewellyn*, Scott, Aizlewood, Bryant, Osman, Mellon*, Dziek'owski, Cole, Rosenior, May; subs Aspinall/Powell
Portsmouth: Knight, Awford*, Daniel, McLoughlin, Symons, Doling, Neill, Kuhl, Powell, Aspinall, Wigley*; subs Burns/McFarlane

City's bad habits resurface as other results erase relegation fears. Portsmouth without four regulars offer little, yet their promotion hopes are sustained by a gift-goal and City's poor finishing. Steve Wigley taps in Pompey's three-pointer after a mix-up between Osman and Welch.

45 — H DERBY 25/4
16,751 — Pos 17 — L 1-2 — 3 — 54
Atteveld 44
Gabbiadini 11, Micklewhite 81
Ref: K Breen

City: Welch, Llewellyn*, Scott*, Aizlewood!, Bryant, Osman*, Mellon, Dziek'owski*, Cole, Rosenior, May; subs Allison!/Edwards/Gavin
Derby: Sutton, Kavanagh, Forsyth, Williams P, McMinn, Comyn, Johnson, Kitson*, Gabbiadini, Ramage, Simpson; subs Gavin/Micklewhite

Whilst City can now match any Second Division side for flair, defensive queries have been raised by recent games. Amid the fizz and sparkle of this richly entertaining game, the ease with which Derby's skilful attackers penetrated early on had Denis Smith scampering to the touchline.

46 — A WATFORD 2/5
10,582 — Pos 17 — L 2-5 — 10 — 54
Cole 27, 48 [Bliss'tt 88, Gibbs 89]
Drysdale 32, Bazeley 54, Putney 58
Ref: K Morton

City: Leaning, Llewellyn!, Scott, Atteveld!, Bryant, Osman, Llewellyn, Dziek'owski*, Cole, Allison!, May; subs Mellon/Edwards
Watford: James, Gibbs, Drysdale, Dublin, Holdsworth, Ashby*, Hessenthaler, Nogan, Bazeley, Butler*, Putney; subs Blissett/Porter

Whilst the officious attitude of Bury St Edmunds ref Kelvin Morton had a major bearing on all three dismissals, the manager needs to act fast to curb City's worrying lack of discipline. Twice Cole turns City's superior play into goals, only for the advantage to be quickly tossed away.

Home Average 11,479
Away Average 10,530

BARCLAYS DIVISION 2 (CUP-TIES) — Manager: Lumsden ⇨ Denis Smith — SEASON 1991-92

Rumbelows Cup

			F-A	H-T	Scorers, Times, and Referees
2:1	A	BRISTOL ROV	10 W	3-1	2-1	Morgan 6, Smith 38, Allison 75
25/9		5,155 23			Llewellyn 37 (og)
					Ref: K Cooper
2:2	H	BRISTOL ROV	18 L	2-4	1-1 aet	Morgan 14, Smith 114
8/10		9,880 21			White 15, 72, Mehew 85, 92
					Ref: J Deakin
					(City lost on away goals)

Match	1	2	3	4	5	6	7	8	9	10	11	subs used
2:1 City	Welch	Llewellyn	Scott	May	Bryant	Caesar	Shelton*	Rennie	Allison	Morgan	Smith	Edwards
2:1 Rovers	*Parkin*	*Alexander*	*Twentyman*	*Yates*	*Clark*	*Archer*	*Boothroyd*	*Cross*	*White*	*Saunders*	*Stewart**	*Browning*
2:2 City	Welch	Llewellyn	Scott	Harrison*	Bryant*	Aizlewood	Edwards	Rennie	Allison	Morgan	Smith	Bent/Taylor
2:2 Rovers	*Parkin*	*Alexander**	*Twentyman*	*Yates*	*Cross*	*Skinner*	*Mehew**	*Reece*	*White*	*Browning*	*Pounder*	*Clark/Purnell*

2:1 — 'We've cracked the derby problem' insists Rennie after this slick City success. With ten shots on target compared to five for the Rovers, City deserve the victory clinched by Smith's volley and Allison's right-footed shot, after the Rovers had equalised Morgan's drilled-in opener.

2:2 — City fans, in dreamland when Morgan's precise shot puts their favourites 4-1 up on aggregate early on, wake up to a nightmare. Resolute Rovers go through on away goals, a fitting reward to their great spirit, after the most famous fight-back in the history of the Bristol derby.

FA Cup

				F-A	H-T	Scorers, Times, and Referees
3	H	WIMBLEDON	13 D	1-1	0-1	Barton 88 (og)
4/1		12,679 1:17				Fashanu 37
						Ref: K Cooper
3R	A	WIMBLEDON	14 W	1-0	1-0	May 10
14/1		3,747 1:17				Ref: K Cooper
4	A	LEICESTER	15 W	2-1	1-0	Bent 27, Dziekanowski 58
25/1		19,313 5				Kitson 87
						Ref: P Vanes
5	A	NOTT'M FOREST	19 L	1-4	0-1	Dziekanowski 75
15/2		24,615 1:15				[Sher'ham 73p] Llewellyn 4 (og), Clough 47, Pearce 67
						Ref: N Midgley

Match	1	2	3	4	5	6	7	8	9	10	11	subs used
3 City	Leaning	Llewellyn*	Scott	May	Bryant	Aizlewood	Osman	Rennie	Allison	Taylor	Gavin	Bent
3 Wimbledon	*Segers*	*McGee*	*Phelan*	*Barton*	*Scales*	*Fitzgerald*	*Newhouse*	*Earle*	*Fashanu*	*Sanchez*	*Anthrobus*	
3R City	Leaning	Caesar	Scott	Osman	Bryant	Aizlewood	Bent*	May	Morgan	Edwards	Gavin	Taylor
3R Wimbledon	*Segars*	*McGee*	*Phelan*	*Barton*	*Scales*	*Fitzgerald*	*Newhouse*	*Earle*	*Fashanu*	*Sanchez*	*Anthrobus**	*Clarke*
4 City	Leaning	Llewellyn	Scott	May	Bryant	Osman	Bent	Dziekanowski	Morgan*	Aizlewood	Gavin	Allison
4 Leicester	*Muggleton*	*Mills*	*Reid*	*Smith*	*Walsh*	*Fitzpatrick**	*Oldfield*	*Thompson*	*Wright*	*Willis*	*Kitson*	*Ward*
5 City	Leaning		Scott	Aizlewood	Bryant	Osman	Bent	Shelton	Allison	Dziekanowski	Gavin	Charles/Glover
5 Forest	*Crossley*	*Laws*	*Pearce*	*Walker*	*Wassall*	*Keane*	*Crosby*	*Gemmill*	*Clough**	*Sheringham · Black*	*Kitson*	

3 — The drama and passion of cup football are conspicuously absent from this game as Wimbledon dominate with their unadventurous, but effective football. Drama at the end though with Warren Barton's attempted clearance flying into his own net to give City a lucky reprieve.

3R — A display full of guts and commitment wins City a fierce battle at Selhurst Park. May's low right-foot swerving-drive from 25 yards proves decisive, as despite all of rampaging Wimbledon's pressure (eight shots on target compared to City's three) an equaliser is rarely threatened.

4 — 'He may come from a different country, but at times it looks as if he is from a different planet.' Such is John Motson's comment on Match of the Day as Polish international Dziekanowski scores one goal and makes another with a skilful display on a treacherous Filbert Street pitch.

5 — Allison is denied a goal by a close offside decision as City recover from a nightmare start, when Roy Keane's shot cannoned off a post onto Llewellyn's shin and into the net. Class tells after the break, Nigel Clough increasing Forest's advantage when Aizlewood fails to hack clear.

			Home					Away					
		P	W	D	L	F	A	W	D	L	F	A	Pts
1	Ipswich	46	16	3	4	42	22	8	9	6	28	28	84
2	Middlesbro	46	15	6	2	37	13	8	5	10	21	28	80
3	Derby	46	11	4	8	35	24	12	5	6	34	27	78
4	Leicester	46	14	4	5	41	24	9	4	10	21	31	77
5	Cambridge	46	10	9	4	34	19	9	8	6	31	28	74
6	Blackburn *	46	14	5	4	41	21	7	6	10	29	32	74
7	Charlton	46	9	7	7	25	23	11	4	8	29	25	71
8	Swindon	46	15	3	5	38	22	3	12	8	31	33	69
9	Portsmouth	46	15	6	2	41	12	4	6	13	24	39	69
10	Watford	46	9	5	9	25	23	9	6	8	26	25	65
11	Wolves	46	11	6	6	36	24	7	4	12	25	30	64
12	Southend	46	11	5	7	37	26	6	6	11	26	37	62
13	Bristol Rov	46	11	9	3	43	29	5	5	13	17	34	62
14	Tranmere	46	9	9	5	37	32	5	10	8	19	24	61
15	Millwall	46	10	4	9	32	32	7	6	10	23	39	61
16	Barnsley	46	11	4	8	27	25	5	7	11	19	32	59
17	BRISTOL CITY	46	10	8	5	30	24	3	7	13	25	47	54
18	Sunderland	46	10	8	5	36	23	3	6	14	25	42	53
19	Grimsby	46	7	5	11	25	28	7	6	10	22	34	53
20	Newcastle	46	9	8	6	38	30	4	5	14	28	54	52
21	Oxford	46	10	6	7	39	30	3	5	15	27	43	50
22	Plymouth	46	11	5	7	26	26	2	4	17	16	38	48
23	Brighton	46	7	7	9	36	37	5	4	14	20	40	47
24	Port Vale	46	7	8	8	23	25	3	7	13	19	34	45
		1104	262	144	146	824	594	146	144	262	594	824	1512

* promoted after play-offs

Odds & ends

Double wins: (1) Sunderland.

Double losses: (3) Portsmouth, Derby, Charlton.

Won from behind: (1) Millwall (a).

Lost from in front: (4) Ipswich (a), Bristol Rov (a), Charlton (a), Cambridge (h), Watford (a).

High spots: Beating Bristol Rov at home in the League and away in the League Cup.
Beating Wolves 2-0 at Ashton Gate on 17 March.
Winning at Roker Park on 21 March.
Beating Leicester in the FA Cup.
Beating Bristol Rov 3-2 at Ashton Gate in the Gloucestershire Cup on 7 August.

Low spots: Losing 0-4 at Blackburn on 11 January.
Failing to change the script at St James Park on 8 February.
Having three players sent off at Watford on 2 May.
Losing 1-4 against Nott'm Forest in the FA Cup.
Losing on away goals against Bristol Rov in the League Cup.

Player of the year: Martin Scott.
Ever-presents: (1) Martin Scott.
Hat-tricks: (0).
Leading scorer: Wayne Allison (11).

Appearances and Goals

	Appearances						Goals			
	Lge	Sub	LC	Sub	FAC	Sub	Lge	LC	FAC	Tot
Aizlewood, Mark	34		1		4		1			1
Allison, Wayne	37	6	2		2	1	10	1		11
Atteveld, Ray	4	3					1			1
Bent, Junior	7	10	1	1	3	1	2	1		3
Bryant, Matt	43		2		4		2			2
Caesar, Gus	9	1	1		1					
Cole, Andy	12						8			8
Connor, Terry	9	2					1			1
Dziekanowski, Jacki	16	1					4	2		6
Edwards, Rob	12	8	1	1	2		1			1
Gavin, Mark	12	2	2		3					
Harrison, Gerry		4	1							
Leaning, Andy	20		2		4					
Llewellyn, Andy	37		1		3					
May, Andy	44	1	1		3		1		1	2
McIntyre, Jim	1									
Mellon, Micky	12	4								
Morgan, Nicky	15	4	2		2		3	2		5
Osman, Russell	30	1	1		4		2			2
Rennie, David	27		2		1		2			2
Rosenior, Leroy	5	3					5			5
Scott, Martin	46		2		4		3			3
Shelton, Gary	18	1	1		1		3			3
Smith, Dave	17	1	2		2		1		2	3
Taylor, Bob	13	5	1		1	1	4			4
Welch, Keith	26		2		2					
(own-goals)							2		1	3
26 players used	506	57	22	3	44	3	56	5	5	66

BARCLAYS LEAGUE DIVISION 1 Manager: Smith ⇨ Russell Osman SEASON 1992-93

Column key: No | Date | Att | Pos | Pt | F-A | H-T | Scorers, Times, and Referees | 1 | 2 | 3 | 4 | 5 | 6 | 7 | 8 | 9 | 10 | 11 | subs used

---

1 — H 15/8 PORTSMOUTH Att 15,251 · Pos — · Pt 1 (D) · F-A 3-3 · H-T 2-2

Team	1	2	3	4	5	6	7	8	9	10	11	subs used
City	Leaning	Mitchell	Scott	Thompson	Bryant	Osman	Mellon	Dziekanowski	Morgan*	Cole	Shelton	Harrison
Opp	*Knight*	*Awford*	*Powell*	*McLoughlin*	*Symons*	*Russell*	*Neill*	*Chamberlain*	*Walsh**	*Whittingham*	*Burns*	*Clarke/Dolling*

Scorers: Dziekanowski 3, 50, Cole 28 · Whittingham 8, 15, 56 · Ref: R Gifford

With the advent of the Premier League, the newly-designated 1st Div gets off to a hectic start. Dziekanowski's dipping volley past Alan Knight sets the tone. Cole turns on a brilliant display, but Leaning is undone by the new pass-back ruling as he puts on a decidedly shaky performance.

---

2 — A 22/8 LUTON Att 7,926 · Pos — · Pt 4 · F-A 3-0 (W) · H-T 1-0

Team	1	2	3	4	5	6	7	8	9	10	11	subs used
City	Welch	Mitchell	Scott	Thompson	Bryant	Osman	Mellon	Dziekanowski	Rosenior	Cole	Shelton*	Harrison/Edwards
Opp	*Petterson*	*Linton*	*James**	*Kamara*	*Peake*	*Dreyer*	*Claridge*	*Hughes*	*Gray*	*Preece*	*Campbell**	*Oakes/Johnson*

Scorers: Mellon 13, Dreyer 50 (og), Cole 75 · Ref: R Bigger

Smith is pleased that City's defence, superbly marshalled by Osman, achieves a clean sheet. Cole, described by Luton boss David Pleat as 'an erratic talent, capable of great things', has a hand in all three goals. His quick break and well-timed pass sets up Mellon to shoot in the opener.

---

3 — H 29/8 SUNDERLAND Att 14,076 · Pos 10/*15* · Pt 5 · F-A 0-0 (D) · H-T 0-0

Team	1	2	3	4	5	6	7	8	9	10	11	subs used
City	Welch	Mitchell	Scott	Thompson	Bryant	Aizlewood	Mellon	Dziekanowski	Cole	Rosenior*	Shelton	Allison
Opp	*Carter*	*Kay*	*Ragan**	*Owers*	*Butcher*	*Ball*	*Cunningham*	*Goodman*	*Byrne*	*Ord*	*Davenport*	

Scorers: Ref: M Bodenham

Against a Sunderland side fielding five central defenders, City, outnumbered in midfield, struggle throughout. Even so Rosenior's first-half header thuds against a post, whilst Thompson's 80th-minute effort appeared over the line after crashing down off the underside of the bar.

---

4 — A 6/9 DERBY Att 12,738 · Pos 7/*24* · Pt 8 · F-A 4-3 (W) · H-T 1-2

Team	1	2	3	4	5	6	7	8	9	10	11	subs used
City	Welch	Mitchell	Scott	Thompson	Bryant	Osman	Mellon	Harrison*	Dziekanowski	Cole*	Shelton	Bent
Opp	*Sutton !*	*Kavanagh*	*Forsyth*	*Pembridge*	*Coleman*	*Wassall*	*Gabbiadini**	*Kitson*	*Johnson**	*Williams*	*Simpson*	*Micklewhite/Comyn*

Scorers: Scott 36p, Bent 75, Comyn 78 (og) · Simpson 10, 12 79 [Allison 88] · Ref: P Harrison

For incident, controversy and attacking football, this live TV spectacular could hardly have been bettered. Early on it looked a case of how many were Derby going to get, but Steve Sutton's dismissal for pulling at Shelton's shirt to prevent a 35th-minute goal transforms the game.

---

5 — H 12/9 SOUTHEND Att 9,515 · Pos 8/*16* · Pt 8 · F-A 0-1 (L) · H-T 0-0

Team	1	2	3	4	5	6	7	8	9	10	11	subs used
City	Welch	Mitchell	Scott	Thompson	Bryant	Osman	Mellon	Dziekanowski	Allison*	Rosenior	Shelton	Bent
Opp	*Sansome*	*Edwards*	*Powell*	*Cornwell*	*Scully*	*Prior*	*Ansah*	*Martin*	*Locke*	*Benjamin*	*O'Callaghan*	

Scorers: Benjamin 75 · Ref: V Callow

City are at their frustrating worst, devoid of ideas and prone to sloppy errors at the back. With Mitchell unable to make any impact on the right, City's wing-back system never looks effective, and they pay the cost as Ian Benjamin bursts through to slide his shot under the diving Welch.

---

6 — H 15/9 WEST HAM Att 14,094 · Pos 9/*5* · Pt 8 · F-A 1-5 (L) · H-T 0-3 [Allen C 44, 86]

Team	1	2	3	4	5	6	7	8	9	10	11	subs used
City	Welch	Llewellyn	Scott	Thompson	Bryant	Edwards	Harrison	Butler	Diek'owski*	Cole*	Shelton	Allison/Connor
Opp	*Miklosko*	*Breacker*	*Thomas*	*Potts*	*Martin*	*Allen M*	*Robson**	*Morley*	*Allen C*	*Keen*	*Small*	

Scorers: Scott 54 · Robson 6, Morley 27, 89, · Ref: J Martin

City's difficulties with the sweeper system are exposed as the slick Hammers hand out shock treatment. For home fans it is painful to watch the ease with which Mitchell Thomas' cut-back enables Mark Robson to shoot past Welch.

---

7 — A 19/9 NEWCASTLE Att 29,434 · Pos 12/*1* · Pt 8 · F-A 0-5 (L) · H-T 0-2 [Carr 64, Brock 87]

Team	1	2	3	4	5	6	7	8	9	10	11	subs used
City	Welch	Llewellyn	Scott	Thompson	Bryant	Aizlewood*	Reid	Diek'owski*	Rosenior	Allison	Shelton	Connor/Bent
Opp	*Wright*	*Venison*	*Beresford*	*O'Brien*	*Scott*	*Howey*	*Carr**	*Peacock*	*Kelly*	*Clark*	*Sheedy**	*Quinn/Brock*

Scorers: O'Brien 40, Peacock 44p, 68p · Ref: T Fitzharris

'That's Geordie Magic' screams the scoreboard as City's humiliation comes to an end. After surviving 40 mins of incessant Magpie pressure, the dam bursts when Liam O'Brien punishes Thompson's innocuous challenge with a glorious 30-yard free-kick that has the net billowing.

---

8 — H 26/9 BARNSLEY Att 8,041 · Pos 10/*24* · Pt 11 · F-A 2-1 (W) · H-T 1-1

Team	1	2	3	4	5	6	7	8	9	10	11	subs used
City	Welch	Mitchell	Scott	Thompson	Bryant	Edwards	Connor*	Diek'owski*	Allison	Mellon*	Shelton*	Bent/Harrison
Opp	*Butler*	*Robinson*	*Fleming*	*Taggart !*	*Bishop*	*Redfearn*	*Burton*	*Archdeacon*	*Pearson*	*Liddell**	*O'Connell*	*Currie/Bullimore*

Scorers: Allison 45, Scott 84p · O'Connell 35 · Ref: P Durkin

Despite losing the services of Gerry Taggart for wrestling Allison out of a clear sixth-minute scoring opportunity, only Welch stands between Barnsley and a well-deserved victory. Instead, Scott's penalty wins it for City, after Edwards goes down under Mark Robinson's challenge.

---

9 — A 3/10 TRANMERE Att 5,975 · Pos 13/*5* · Pt 11 · F-A 0-3 (L) · H-T 0-1

Team	1	2	3	4	5	6	7	8	9	10	11	subs used
City	Welch	Mitchell	Scott	Thompson	Bryant	Reid*	Connor*	Diek'owski*	Allison	Clark	Shelton*	Harrison/Rosenior
Opp	*Nixon*	*Higgins*	*Brannan*	*Martindale*	*Mungall*	*Vickers*	*Morrissey*	*Aldridge*	*Malkin*	*McNab*	*Nevin*	

Scorers: Aldridge 38, 71p, Nevin 56 · Ref: K Barratt

Smith believes Cole's return, after a month-long knee injury, will soon have City on the road to recovery. City, who show the style, but lack the finish, are caught forward in numbers when John Aldridge gets away to give Scott the slip and thump in an 18-yard opener past Welch.

---

10 — H 10/10 CHARLTON Att 9,286 · Pos 12/*2* · Pt 14 · F-A 2-1 (W) · H-T 1-1

Team	1	2	3	4	5	6	7	8	9	10	11	subs used
City	Welch	Mitchell	Scott	Thompson	Osman	Edwards	Harrison	Diek'owski	Rosenior	Cole	Shelton*	Reid/Allison
Opp	*Bolder*	*Balmer*	*Minto*	*Pardew**	*Webster*	*Pitcher*	*Leaburn*	*Bumstead*	*Aldridge*	*Dyer*	*Grant*	*Warden*

Scorers: Dziekanowski 16, Harrison 90 · Leaburn 8 · Ref: J Rushton

Harrison's right-foot rocket from 25 yards, midway through four mins of injury-time, gives City a hard-earned win over previously-unbeaten Charlton. Heads could have dropped after Carl Leaburn's four-yard tap-in, but Dziekanowski sidefoots home Cole's cross from ten yards.

---

11 — A 17/10 CAMBRIDGE Att 3,896 · Pos 11/*18* · Pt 14 · F-A 1-2 (L) · H-T 0-1

Team	1	2	3	4	5	6	7	8	9	10	11	subs used
City	Welch	Mitchell	Scott	Thompson	Bryant	Osman*	Harrison	Diek'owski	Rosenior	Cole	Shelton	Allison
Opp	*Sheffield*	*Rowett*	*Kimble*	*Fowler*	*Heathcote*	*O'Shea*	*Raynor*	*Ainsworth*	*White*	*Cheetham**	*Philpott*	*Francis*

Scorers: Cole 48 · Kimble 41p, Ainsworth 84 · Ref: K Morton

City are undone by United's up and under tactics. After Cole's cleverly-angled shot equalised Alan Kimble's pen (Bryant hauling down Mike Cheetham), Gareth Ainsworth heads in from six yards to make City pay for their failure to turn to good account their superior approach play.

Bristol City — Match-by-Match (matches 12–23)

#	V	Date	Opponent	Att	Pos	Result	Pts	Score details	Ref
12	H	24/10	LEICESTER	10,436	11 · 7	W 2-1	17	Cole 74, Grayson 87 (og) / *Davison 5*	D Frampton
13	A	31/10	BRENTFORD	8,726	15 · 19	L 1-5	17	Cole 25 / *Millen 17, 47, Chalmers 44, Blissett 55, 60*	P Scobie
14	A	4/11	MILLWALL	5,924	15 · 7	L 1-4	17	Cole 43 / *Cooper 13, Allen 18, May 24, Moralee 29*	R Pawley
15	H	7/11	BIRMINGHAM	10,019	14 · 17	W 3-0	20	Rosenior 44, Shelton 47, Cole 87	P Alcock
16	A	14/11	GRIMSBY	5,651	15 · 8	L 1-2	20	Cole 53 / *Watson 80, Mendonca 89*	J Key
17	H	21/11	SWINDON	14,081	15 · 2	D 2-2	21	Shelton 44, Rosenior 58 / *Maskell 32, Summerbee 57*	P Jones
18	H	28/11	NOTTS CO	9,086	13 · 21	W 1-0	24	Shelton 89	M Pierce
19	A	5/12	WATFORD	6,746	13 · 15	D 0-0	25		I Borrett
20	A	13/12	BRISTOL ROV	7,112	15 · 19	L 0-4	25	*Channing 23, Stewart 65, Saunders 68, Taylor 78*	J Martin
21	H	19/12	PETERBOROUGH	7,333	17 · 11	L 0-1	25	*Welsh 28*	P Vanes
22	H	26/12	OXFORD	10,737	17 · 16	D 1-1	26	Rosenior 31 / *Beauchamp 4*	R Gifford
23	A	28/12	WOLVES	16,419	18 · 7	D 0-0	27		A Ward

12 — LEICESTER
City: Welch, Mitchell, Scott, Thompson, Bryant*, Osman, Harrison, Dziekanowski, Rosenior, Cole, Shelton (subs Allison/Edwards)
Leicester: *Hoult, Grayson, Whitlow*, Smith, Walsh, Hill, Oldfield, Thompson, Davison, Ormondroyd, Joachim** (subs *Gee/Lowe*)

Dziekanowski's skill is the only source of encouragement in City's display which began disastrously and stuttered to an unlikely triumph. Simon Grayson volleys a spectacular own-goal for City's winner, after Cole's headed equaliser owed something to Russell Hoult's dive.

13 — BRENTFORD
City: Welch, Mitchell, Scott, Thompson, Edwards, Osman, Harrison, Dziek'owski, Rosenior, Cole, Allison* (subs Connor/Gavin)
Brentford: *Peyton, Statham, Hughton, Millen, Westley, Chalmers*, Luscombe, Manuel, Gayle, Blissett, Smillie* (subs *Ratcliffe/Jones*)

A Halloween horror show at Griffin Park, as City's static defence concedes four goals following corners. Reduced to ten men for the last three minutes, when Harrison is injured, City's only consolation, following a bright start, is Cole's waltz around Gerry Peyton for the early leveller.

14 — MILLWALL
City: Welch, Bryant, Scott, Thompson, Edwards, Osman, Harrison, Shelton, Rosenior*, Cole, Gavin (subs Allison/Bent)
Millwall: *Keller, Cunningham, Dawes, May, Cooper, Rae, Roberts, Moralee*, Allen, Byrne*, Barber* (subs *Dolby/Goodman*)

City contribute more to this sparkling match than the score suggests, but on-going defensive frailties and poor finishing brings another heavy away defeat. Whilst Cole fails with an open-goal chance early on, Colin Cooper has no such problem when cracking in Millwall's opener.

15 — BIRMINGHAM
City: Welch, Bryant, Scott, Thompson, Edwards, Osman, Harrison, Shelton, Rosenior, Cole, Gavin
Birmingham: *Sealey, Clarkson !, Frain, Danowa*, Hicks, Matthewson, Rodgerson, Tait, Speedie, Sturridge*, Rowbotham !* (subs *Potter/Cooper*)

City already had the game won when Darren Rowbotham's outburst of dissent over Ian Clarkson's dismissal for a high tackle on Edwards, makes it a double 56th-minute sending off. Headers from Rosenior and Cole, as well as Shelton's close-in shot, brings a well-merited victory.

16 — GRIMSBY
City: Welch, Bryant, Scott, Thompson, Edwards, Mitchell, Harrison, Shelton, Rosenior, Cole, Mellon (subs Rodger/Woods)
Grimsby: *Beasant, McDermott, Croft, Futcher*, Lever*, Dobbin, Watson, Gilbert, Groves, Mendonca, Rees*

Welch is in top form at Blundell Park, but even he can do nothing about Tommy Watson's gloriously headed equaliser, or the cruelly-deflected late winner, fired home from 25 yards by Clive Mendonca. A cruel return for a battling performance that saw City ahead with Cole's volley.

17 — SWINDON
City: Welch, Mitchell*, Scott, Thompson, Bryant, Osman, Shelton, Dziekanowski, Rosenior, Cole, Harrison
Swindon: *Hammond, Kerslake, Horlock, Hoddle*, Calderwood, Taylor, Hazard, Summerbee, Maskell, Ling, White*

On a rain-soaked pitch City twice battle back from behind and on the number of clear chances created should have won. Swindon's open-passing style, encouraged by the skills of Glenn Hoddle and Micky Hazard, allows City the freedom to fully express his abilities.

18 — NOTTS CO
City: Welch, Harrison, Scott, Kristensen, Bryant, Osman, Shelton, Dziekanowski, Rosenior*, Cole, Edwards (sub Allison)
Notts Co: *Cherry, Palmer, Djikstra, Thomas, Turner, Johnson*, Wilson, Draper*, Agana, Bartlett, Smith* (subs *O'Riordan/Slawson*)

Back from their first competitive venture into Europe, a 3-4 defeat at Pisa in the Anglo-Italian Cup, City's defence is more resilient against Notts. Shelton fires in a minute before the end of normal time, but City have to endure seven minutes of injury-time before victory is theirs.

19 — WATFORD
City: Welch, Harrison, Scott, Kristensen, Bryant, Osman, Shelton, Dziek'owski*, Rosenior*, Cole, Edwards (subs Mellon/Allison)
Watford: *Sucking, Putney, Drysdale, Dublin, Holdsworth, Ashby, Hessenthaler, Willis, Charlery, Porte*, Nogan* (subs *Bazeley/Johnson*)

Cole is always the brightest spark that threatened to turn City's hard-working team-effort into three points. Unfortunately his finishing doesn't match some brilliant runs and City have to be satisfied with a point from this thrilling encounter to end their long barren spell away from home.

20 — BRISTOL ROV
City: Welch, Harrison, Scott, Kristensen, Bryant, Osman, Shelton, Dziekanowski, Rosenior*, Cole, Edwards* (subs Allison/Gavin)
Bristol Rov: *Parkin, Alexander, Tillson, Yates, Hardyman, Browning, Channing, Stewart, Taylor, Saunders, Waddock*

Humiliation again for City as Malcolm Allison inspires Rovers to their fifth League derby win since moving to Bath. Now without a victory in seven League visits to Fortress Twerton, City never looked like winning this one after Justin Channing struck a low 30-yard drive past Welch.

21 — PETERBOROUGH
City: Welch, Harrison, Scott, Edwards*, Osman, Shelton, Bent, Rosenior*, Cole, Gavin (subs Mitchell/Allison)
Peterborough: *Bennett, Luke, Robinson, Halsall, Welsh, Sterling, Cooper, Adcock, Philliskirk, Ebdon*

The storm clouds are gathering for Denis Smith as City run out of luck. Steve Welsh claims his first League goal when putting away Tony Philliskirk's head-down from a contentious free-kick, then seconds later Rosenior has his effort disallowed for a supposed foul on the keeper.

22 — OXFORD
City: Welch, Harrison, Scott, Mitchell, Osman, Shelton, Bent*, Rosenior*, Cole, Gavin (sub Allison)
Oxford: *Reece, Smart, Ford, Lewis, Melville, Magilton, Beauchamp, Penney*, Cusack, Durnin, Allen*

The police have a lot to answer for as not for the first time the fans are inconvenienced by an early kick-off. However despite the 11.30am start the only thing wrong with the game is City's failure to convert a host of chances. Fortunately though Rosenior is able to head in City's equaliser.

23 — WOLVES
City: Welch, Mitchell, Scott !, Harrison, Osman, Bryant, Shelton, Bent*, Rosenior, Cole (subs Allison/Dziekanowski)
Wolves: *Jones, Ashley*, Edwards, Blades, Madden, Rankine, Burke, Cook, Bull, Venus, Mutch* (sub *Downing*)

After dominating the first half it takes all of City's resolve to prise a point from Wolves. Shrugging off Scott's 54th-minute dismissal, City contain the Steve Bull-Andy Mutch alliance, and almost win at the last when Dziekanowski bursts clear to force a smart save from Jones.

BARCLAYS LEAGUE DIVISION 1 — Manager: Smith ⇨ Russell Osman — SEASON 1992-93

No	Date		Att	Pos	Pt	F-A	H-T	Scorers, Times, and Referees	1	2	3	4	5	6	7	8	9	10	11	subs used
24	9/1	H NEWCASTLE	15,446	18	27	1-2	1-2	Allison 18 / Harrison 20 (og), Scott 31 / Ref: K Burge	Welch	Harrison*	Scott	Llewellyn	Bryant	Osman	Shelton	Peacock*	Allison	Cole	Gavin	Mellon/Aizlewood, Bracewell
									Smicek	Venison	Beresford	O'Brien	Scott	Howey	Lee	Kelly	Peacock	Clark	Sheedy*	
25	16/1	A BARNSLEY	5,423	18	27	1-2	0-2	Cole 74 / O'Connell 8, 22, Ref: I Cruikshanks	Welch	Llewellyn	Aizlewood	Harrison	Bryant	Osman	Bent*	Shelton	Allison	Cole	Gavin	Rosenior
									Butler	Robinson	Taggart	Fleming	Bishop	Archdeacon	Rethern	O'Connell	Currie	Biggins	Rammell	
26	27/1	A WEST HAM	12,118	18	27	0-2	0-0	Morley 67, Robson 74, Ref: B Hill	Welch	Atteveld*	Scott	Llewellyn	Bryant	Osman	Shelton	Harrison	Allison	Cole	Gavin*	Dziek'owski/Rosenior, Holmes/Parris
									Miklosko	Breacker	Brown	Potts	Gale	Allen M	Robson*	Butler	Morley	Bunbury*	Keen	
27	30/1	H LUTON	8,877	19	28	0-0	0-0	Ref: J Carter	Welch	Llewellyn	Scott	Aizlewood	Bryant	Osman*	Shelton*	Dziekanowski	Rosenior	Cole	Harrison	Mellon/Allison, Oakes/Benjamin
									Chamberlain	Dreyer	James	Johnson	Hughes	Peake	Telfer	Williams*	Rees*	Gray	Preece	
28	6/2	A PORTSMOUTH	10,675	17	31	3-2	1-1	Shelton 15, Bryant 73, Gavin 83 / Walsh 8, Whittingham 48, Ref: P Foakes	Welch	Llewellyn	Munro	Aizlewood	Bryant	Pennyfather	Shelton	Dziekanowski	Allison*	Cole	Harrison*	Gavin/Rosenior, Powell/Russell
									Knight	Awford	Daniel	McLoughlin*	Symons	Burns	Price!	Chamberlain	Walsh	Whittingham	Aspinall*	
29	10/2	A SOUTHEND	3,836	18	32	1-1	1-1	Cole 16 / Collymore 44, Ref: D Elleray	Welch	Llewellyn	Munro	Aizlewood	Bryant	Pennyfather	Shelton	Dziek'owski*	Allison	Cole	Gavin	Rosenior
									Sansome	Edwards	Hyslop	Cornwell	Scully	Prior	Ansah	Tilson	Jones	Collymore	Angell	
30	20/2	A SUNDERLAND	17,083	20	33	0-0	0-0	Ref: R Dilkes	Welch	Llewellyn	Munro	Aizlewood	Bryant	Pennyfather	Shelton	Dziekanowski	Allison	Cole	Osman	Ord/Rush
									Norman	Kay	Smith*	Atkinson	Butcher	Ball	Mooney*	Goodman	Colquhoun	Gray, Mike	Armstrong	
31	27/2	A CHARLTON	7,261	20	33	1-2	1-0	Cole 3 / Gorman 78, Gatting 90, Ref: G Poll	Welch	Llewellyn	Munro	Aizlewood	Bryant	Pennyfather*	Shelton	Dziek'owski*	Allison	Cole	Gavin	Osman/Rosenior, Gorman/Warden
									Salmon	Pitcher	Gatting	Pardew	Webster	Balmer*	Houghton	Minto	Leaburn	Nelson*	Walsh	
32	6/3	H TRANMERE	8,845	21	33	1-3	0-2	Cole 49 / Malkin 37, 78, Nevin 45, Ref: M Pierce	Welch	Llewellyn*	Munro	Aizlewood!	Bryant*	Pennyfather	Shelton	Dziekanowski	Scott	Cole	Gavin	Allison/Rosenior, Hughes
									Nixon	Higgins	Brannan*	Irons	Mungall	Vickers*	Morrissey	Martindale	Malkin	McNab	Nevin	
33	9/3	H MILLWALL	8,771	21	33	0-1	0-1	Barber 26, Ref: K Barratt	Welch	Munro	Scott	Aizlewood*	Bryant	Osman	Shelton	Dziek'owski*	Rosenior	Cole	Gavin	Rosenior/Harrison, Moralee/Dolby
									Keller	Cunningham	Dawes	Rae	Cooper	Stevens	Roberts	Allen	Bogie*	Byrne*	Barber	
34	13/3	A BIRMINGHAM	15,611	20	36	1-0	1-0	Morgan 44, Ref: A Flood	Welch	Munro	Scott	Osman	Bryant	Pennyfather	Shelton	Bent	Rosenior	Morgan	Gavin	Rodgerson/Fenwick
									Catlin	Hiley	Frain	Parris	Mardon	Matthewson*	Moulden	Gayle	Peschisolido	Tait*	Smith	

24. City, with ten shots on target compared to Newcastle's two, should have beaten the leaders. Unfortunately the Magpies quickly bounce back from Allison's header. Harrison deflects a cross into his own net, then City's slipshod offside trap fails and Kevin Scott fires in the winner.

25. City are entitled to feel aggrieved by Hartlepool referee Ian Cruikshanks as Cole is denied a blatant fifth-min penalty, and Allison is cynically brought down when clean through after the break. Barnsley take the points with Brendan O'Connell's low shot being followed by his header.

26. The difficult task caretaker boss Russell Osman faces to turn the tide in a miserable season is amply demonstrated at Upton Park where City finish up a well-beaten side. Hard work is not enough as Osman's negative tactics are thwarted by Morley's tap-in and Robson's header.

27. City's failure to beat a Luton side with very little to offer suggests that they are firmly on a relegation course. Dziekanowski is the most creative player, and it is his pass that sends Scott through to fire wide from one of only two chances created by City's first-half dominance.

28. The new signings help turn the tide against a side reduced to ten men after 82 mins when Chris Price receives the red card for his desperate foul to stop Cole. Three quality goals, shots by Shelton and Gavin, as well as Bryant's header, bring City their first away success since Sep.

29. Only the crowd of below 4,000 is in keeping with a bottom of the table clash as on this form both rampaging Southend and slick City should escape the jaws of relegation. A fair result as Stan Collymore's glorious 15-yarder counters Cole's flick in from Bryant's towering header.

30. Munro (ex Blackburn) caps another solid performance with two crucial interceptions in this dour struggle at Roker Park. A 72nd-min goal-line clearance from Brian Atkinson's header, being followed six minutes later by a point-saving tackle on Don Goodman as he prepares to shoot.

31. Whilst the result does not go City's way and despite away fans having to pay £14 for admission it is fitting that Charlton have returned to the Valley. For City, though, it is like the Valley of Death as their light brigade is halted by Gatting's headed winner two minutes into injury-time.

32. City's attractive play counts for nought as individual errors, and Nixon's saving of Scott's 65th-minute spot-kick, increases relegation fears. Welch, at fault when helping Chris Malkin's header into the net, errs again when he allows Pat Nevin's under-hit shot to sneak inside the post.

33. Cole pledges to score the goals to keep City up after squandering three guilt-edged chances, including a second-half penalty, in this exciting game. Phil Barber's angled drive past the unprotected Welch settles the contest as Kasey Keller is in unbeatable form for Milwall.

34. Nicky Morgan, City's forgotten man, is back with a typical skilful performance. He crashes an early volley against the crossbar before sinking Birmingham on the stroke of half-time. Gavin's quickly taken free-kick catches out the home defence and Morgan flights in a looping header.

Bristol City 1992–93 — match-by-match record (matches 35–46)

No	Venue	Date	Opponent	Att	Pos	Opp Pos	Pts	Res	FT	HT
35	H	20/3	WATFORD	8,265	20	14	39	W	2-1	1-1
36	A	24/3	SWINDON	13,353	22	4	39	L	1-2	0-1
37	H	28/3	GRIMSBY	6,755	19	10	42	W	1-0	0-0
38	A	3/4	NOTTS CO	6,634	20	18	43	D	0-0	0-0
39	H	6/4	BRISTOL ROV	21,854	15	24	46	W	2-1	1-0
40	A	10/4	OXFORD	6,145	17	16	46	L	0-2	0-1
41	H	12/4	WOLVES	11,756	14	9	49	W	1-0	0-0
42	A	17/4	PETERBOROUGH	5,169	15	13	50	D	1-1	0-0
43	H	20/4	DERBY	8,869	15	9	51	D	0-0	0-0
44	H	24/4	CAMBRIDGE	8,998	16	23	52	D	0-0	0-0
45	A	1/5	LEICESTER	19,294	16	5	53	D	0-0	0-0
46	H	8/5	BRENTFORD	12,695	15	22	56	W	4-1	2-0

Average 11,004 · Away 10,137

---

35 · WATFORD (H) 20/3 — W 2-1 (1-1)
Scorers: Bent 12, Pennyfather 85 · Charley 41 · Ref: J Lloyd
Bristol City: Welch, Llewellyn, Scott, Osman, Bryant, Pennyfather, Harrison, Bent, Rosenior, Morgan, Gavin; Edwards/Allison
Watford: Sucking, Soloman, Ashby, Dublin, Hessenthaler Nagan*, Haldsworth Bazeley*, Furlong, Charley, Porter; Willis/Lavin

Morgan again stars as the replacement for the departed Cole, as a welcome change of luck brings to an end City's four-month wait for a home success. Lunging in to block Barry Ashby's attempted clearance, Pennyfather watches the ball rebound into the net for City's late winner.

36 · SWINDON (A) 24/3 — L 1-2 (0-1)
Scorers: Rosenior 83 · Marwood 19, Bodin 60p · Ref: D Gallagher
Bristol City: Welch, Scott, Munro, Osman, Bryant!, Pennyfather, Harrison, Bent, Rosenior, Morgan, Tinnion; Allison
Swindon: Digby, Summerbee Bodin, Hoddle, Taylor, Calderwood, Marwood, MacLaren, Mitchell*, Ling*, White; Hunt/Close

Bryant's dismissal a minute before half-time is a handicap City cannot overcome in a niggly West Country derby. Following Brian Marwood's headed opener and Paul Bodin's pen when Steve White is tripped, the most City can manage is Rosenior's tap-in finish to Tinnion's low cross.

37 · GRIMSBY (H) 28/3 — W 1-0 (0-0)
Scorers: Morgan 70 · Ref: K Cooper
Bristol City: Welch, Scott, Munro, Osman, Bryant, Pennyfather, Harrison, Bent, Rosenior, Morgan, Tinnion
Grimsby: Willmott, Croft*, Agnew, Futcher, Rodger, Childs, Gilbert, Groves, Mendonca*, Rees; Woods/Daws

Given the pressure of the relegation battle, City's football is more attractive than could have been expected as they notch up a priceless win. The Mariners only come to life after City's star man Morgan had steamed in to finish off Tinnion's perfect cross with a powerful header.

38 · NOTTS CO (A) 3/4 — D 0-0 (0-0)
Scorers: — · Ref: R Lewis
Bristol City: Welch, Scott, Munro, Osman, Bryant, Pennyfather, Harrison, Bent, Rosenior, Morgan, Tinnion; Allison
Notts Co: Cherry, Short, Chris Johnson, Thomas, Cox, Walker, Lund*, Draper, Wilson*, Devin, Smith; Reeves/Agana

Whilst Osman blames the blustery wind and poor surface for the low quality of the football, no one can accuse this City team of lacking commitment. Tinnion's rasping 30-yard drive, which Steve Cherry does well to save, is City's best effort as they battle to hold onto a point.

39 · BRISTOL ROV (H) 6/4 — W 2-1 (1-0)
Scorers: Morgan 35, Tinnion 79p · Taylor 81 · Ref: M Reed
Bristol City: Welch, Scott, Munro, Osman, Bryant, Pennyfather, Harrison, Allison, Rosenior, Morgan, Tinnion
Bristol Rovers: Kelly, Alexander!, Tillson, Ford, Yates, Clark, Pounder, Mehew*, Reece, Taylor, Stewart*, Waddock; Evans/Channing

City are deserved winners of a match more memorable for atmosphere rather than the calibre of the football. John Taylor drills in a low shot for Rovers, but City's earlier penalty, after Ian Alexander's sending off for handling Tinnion's goal-bound shot, ultimately proves decisive.

40 · OXFORD (A) 10/4 — L 0-2 (0-1)
Scorers: — · Druce 30, Beauchamp 66 · Ref: J Carter
Bristol City: Welch, Scott, Munro, Aizlewood, Thompson, Pennyfather, Harrison, Allison, Rosenior, Morgan, Tinnion; Bent/Harrison
Oxford: Kee, Smart, Collins, Evans, Magilton, Melville, Beauchamp, Cusack, Druce*, Narbett, Penney

City dominate with their neat possession football, but a generous defence renders all their effort worthless. Welch, caught in no man's land by David Collins' back header, has no chance when his defence parts like the Red Sea to let Joey Beauchamp race through and shoot in off a post.

41 · WOLVES (H) 12/4 — W 1-0 (0-0)
Scorers: Bent 81 · Ref: P Wright
Bristol City: Welch, Osman*, Scott, Aizlewood, Bryant, Pennyfather*, Harrison, Bent, Allison, Morgan, Tinnion; Bent/Harrison
Wolves: Stowell, Simkin, Venus, Downing, Mountfield, Blades*, Thompson, Cook, Rankine*, Mutch, Dennison; Birch/Madden

With four of the six injured at Oxford coming off the treatment table, the walking wounded demonstrate the great spirit that is guiding City away from the danger zone. Defensive solidarity is rewarded near the end as Bent squirms between two defenders to shoot in from close range.

42 · PETERBOROUGH (A) 17/4 — D 1-1 (0-0)
Scorers: Tinnion 50 · Barnes 68 · Ref: J Rushton
Bristol City: Welch, Scott, Aizlewood, Bryant, Osman, Shelton, Harrison, Bent, Allison, Morgan*, Tinnion; Atteveld
Peterborough: Bennett, Bradshaw, Spearing, Cooper, Greenman, Welsh, Sterling, Ebdon, Philliskirk*, Barnes, Iorfa

After Tony Philliskirk's 25-yard volley hits a post, City are disrupted by Morgan's 26th-minute departure with a dislocated ankle. After the break though it is all City, Tinnion's superb strike puts them in front before Bobby Barnes' hooked volley brings the Posh a surprise equaliser.

43 · DERBY (H) 20/4 — D 0-0 (0-0)
Scorers: — · Ref: D Frampton
Bristol City: Welch, Osman, Munro, Aizlewood, Bryant, Shelton, Pennyfather*, Bent, Allison, Bent, Tinnion; Atteveld/Shail
Derby: Taylor, Patterson, Nicholson, Forsyth, Short, Pembridge, Sturridge, Kuhl, Kitson, Gabbiadini, Simpson

Osman's battle-scarred troops, inhibited by injury in every department, not only snuff out Derby's multi-million pound team, but create the better chances. Pennyfather's 25-yard volley crashes against a post, whilst Allison spurns a great opportunity by heading wide from six yards.

44 · CAMBRIDGE (H) 24/4 — D 0-0 (0-0)
Scorers: — · Ref: K Cooper
Bristol City: Welch, Harrison, Osman, Aizlewood, Bryant, Shail, Shelton, Atteveld, Allison, Bent*, Tinnion; Rosenior/Edwards
Cambridge: Filan, Heathcote, Kimble, Raynor, Chapple, Dennis*, Claridge, Butler, Clayton, Lyne*; Rush/Bartlett

The sweeper system didn't work when Smith tried it, and it doesn't work in this game as City do not have the players to make the formation effective. Cambridge have the better of the contest, but mind-numbing boredom such as this will have the fans staying away in their droves.

45 · LEICESTER (A) 1/5 — D 0-0 (0-0)
Scorers: — · Ref: A Wilkie
Bristol City: Welch, Osman, Munro, Aizlewood, Shail, Atteveld, Shelton, Gavin, Allison, Rosenior, Tinnion
Leicester: Poole, Mills, Whitlow, Smith, Walsh, Oldfield, Hill, Thompson*, Joachim*, Lowe, Philpott; James/Lewis

A deserved point, with both sides being denied by the woodwork, guarantees safety and earns Osman the manager's chair. Just two goals in the last twelve games is impressive, but at what cost as City's style of play is not the sort to encourage any but the most committed spectator.

46 · BRENTFORD (H) 8/5 — W 4-1 (2-0)
Scorers: Rosenior 6, 55, 67, Allison 28 · Blissett 57 · Ref: M James
Bristol City: Welch, Llewellyn, Edwards, Aizlewood, Shail, Atteveld, Shelton, Rosenior, Allison, Gavin, Tinnion; Harrison/Bent
Brentford: Peyton, Statham, Sansom, Millen, Evans, Bennett*, Manuel*, Blissett, Gayle, Smillie; Allon/Ratcliffe

A goal feast against a strangely subdued Bees side requiring a point to stay up. Allison shows where the net is as he strides through to guide the ball wide of Gerry Payton, but the star is Rosenior as he scores a hat-trick of goals with not a header among them.

BARCLAYS DIVISION 1 (CUP-TIES) Manager: Smith ⇨ Russell Osman SEASON 1992-93

Coca-Cola Cup

		F-A	H-T	Scorers, Times, and Referees	1	2	3	4	5	6	7	8	9	10	11	subs used
1:1 A CARDIFF 18/8	7,708	L 0-1	0-1	Dale 3; Ref: A Smith	Welch	Mitchell	Thompson	Scott	Bryant	Edwards	Mellon	Dziekanowski	Rosenior	Cole	Shelton	
					Grew	*James*	*Millar*	*Searle*	*Perry*	*Brazil*	*Ramsey*	*Griffith*	*Pike**	*Dale*	*Blake*	*Gibbins*
1:2 H CARDIFF 25/8	10,174	W 5-1	3-0	Cole 8, 13, 89, Rosenior 23, Allison 65; Dale 53; Ref: P Vanes (City won 5-2 on aggregate)	Welch	Mitchell	Thompson	Scott	Bryant	Aizlewood	Mellon	Dziekanowski Calloway*	Cole	Rosenior*	Shelton^	Allison/Harrison
					Grew	*James*	*Millar*	*Searle*	*Perry*	*Brazil*	*Gibbins*	*Bird*		*Dale*	*Blake*	*Baddeley*
2:1 H SHEFFIELD UTD 22/9	6,932 P:19	13 W 2-1	2-1	Connor 19, Scott 41p; Rogers 37; Ref: G Poll	Welch	Mitchell	Thompson	Scott	Bryant	Edwards	Connor*	Dziekanowski	Allison	Mellon	Shelton	Harrison
					Kelly	*Gage*	*Gannon*	*Cowan**	*Gayle*	*Beesley*	*Bradshaw*	*Rogers*	*Cork**	*Deane*	*Hodges*	*Hartfield/Bryson*
2:2 A SHEFFIELD UTD 7/10	7,588 P:16	13 L 1-4	1-2	Cole 12 (Deane 66, 74); Whitehouse 5, Bradshaw 33,; Ref: A Wilkie (City lost 3-5 on aggregate)	Welch	Mitchell	Thompson	Scott	Osman	Edwards	Harrison	Rosenior*	Allison	Cole	Shelton^ Whitehouse*	Dziekanowski/Gavin
					Kelly	*Ward*	*Cowan*	*Gannon*	*Gayle*	*Beesley*	*Bradshaw*	*Rogers*	*Littlejohn*	*Deane*	*Cork*	

Welch's confident handling and assured footwork keeps City's hopes alive, despite Nathan Blake seizing on Mitchell's misplaced pass to lay the winner on a plate for Carl Dale. After weathering an alarmingly shaky opening, Dziekanowski fails to convert City's three best chances.

City are absolutely brilliant as they put on one of their best-ever displays. Cole, whose speed off the mark, strength in holding off defenders, and coolness in front of goal, stamp him as a very special player, completes his hat-trick when racing clear and shooting past Mark Grew.

Smith abandons the sweeper system, but plays Connor and Edwards in wide midfield roles, instead of answering the call for wingers. City, without five regulars, produce a wholehearted display to claim a Premier Division scalp thanks to Tom Cowan being penalised for handball.

City always look in with a chance, until Brian Deane ends his ten-match lean spell. After Dane Whitehouse's easy tap-in when Welch fails to hold a low centre, Cole equalises for City with a bullet header, before Carl Bradshaw levels the aggregate scores again with a 20-yard volley.

FA Cup

		F-A	H-T	Scorers, Times, and Referees	1	2	3	4	5	6	7	8	9	10	11	subs used
3 A LUTON 19/1	6,094 22	18 L -2	0-1	Gray 31, Hughes 82; Ref: G Willard	Welch	Harrison	Llewellyn	Scott !	Bryant	Osman	Shelton	Mellon*	Allison	Cole	Gavin^	Rosenior/Aizlewood
					Chamberlain Dreyer	*James*	*Johnson**		*Hughes*	*Peake*	*Telfer*	*Benjamin^*	*Rees*	*Gray*	*Preece*	*Harvey/Oakes*

City's season is now at rock bottom after this humiliating surrender at Kenilworth Road. Scott's 70th-min sending-off for hitting out at Phil Gray capped a team effort bereft of skill, cohesion and passion. Ceri Hughes' shot in off the crossbar sealed Luton's passage to the next round.

Final League Table 1992–93

		P	Home W	D	L	F	A	Away W	D	L	F	A	Pts
1	Newcastle	46	16	6	1	58	15	13	3	7	34	23	96
2	West Ham	46	16	5	2	50	17	10	5	8	31	24	88
3	Portsmouth	46	19	2	2	48	9	7	8	8	32	37	88
4	Tranmere	46	15	4	4	48	24	8	6	9	24	32	79
5	Swindon *	46	15	5	3	41	23	8	6	9	33	36	76
6	Leicester	46	14	5	4	43	24	8	5	10	28	40	76
7	Millwall	46	14	6	3	46	21	4	10	9	19	32	70
8	Derby	46	11	2	10	40	33	8	7	8	28	24	66
9	Grimsby	46	12	6	5	33	25	5	7	11	25	32	64
10	Peterborough	46	7	11	5	30	26	9	3	11	25	37	62
11	Wolves	46	11	6	6	37	26	5	7	11	20	30	61
12	Charlton	46	10	8	5	28	19	6	5	12	21	27	61
13	Barnsley	46	12	4	7	29	19	5	5	13	27	41	60
14	Oxford	46	8	7	8	29	21	6	7	10	27	35	56
15	BRISTOL CITY	46	10	7	6	29	25	5	7	12	20	42	56
16	Watford	46	8	7	8	27	30	5	6	11	30	41	55
17	Notts Co	46	10	7	6	33	21	2	9	12	22	49	52
18	Southend	46	9	8	6	33	22	4	5	14	21	42	52
19	Birmingham	46	10	4	9	30	32	3	8	12	22	40	51
20	Luton	46	6	13	4	26	26	4	8	11	22	36	51
21	Sunderland	46	9	6	8	34	28	4	5	14	16	36	50
22	Brentford	46	7	6	10	28	30	6	4	13	24	41	49
23	Cambridge	46	8	6	9	29	32	3	10	10	19	37	49
24	Bristol Rov	46	6	11	6	30	42	4	5	14	25	45	41
		1104	263	147	142	859	590	142	147	263	590	859	1509

* promoted after play-offs

Odds & ends

Double wins: (1) Birmingham.
Double losses: (4) West Ham, Newcastle, Tranmere, Millwall.

Won from behind: (5) Derby (a), Barnsley (h), Charlton (h), Leicester (h), Portsmouth (a).
Lost from in front: (3) Grimsby (a), Newcastle (h), Charlton (a).

High spots: Opening day thriller v Portsmouth.
Winning 1-0 at St Andrews on 13 March.
Beating Bristol Rov 2-1 on 6 April.
A brilliant performance in destroying Cardiff 5-1 in the League Cup.

Low spots: Humiliating 0-5 defeat at Newcastle on 19 September.
Losing 0-4 at Twerton Park on 13 December.
Succumbing to Luton in the FA Cup.
Losing 1-2 away to Bristol Rov in the Final of the Gloucestershire Cup on 5 August.

Player of the year: Keith Welch.
Ever-presents: (0).
Hat-tricks: (1) Leroy Rosenior.
Leading scorer: Andy Cole (16).

Appearances and Goals

Player	Lge	Sub	LC	Sub	FAC	Sub	Goals Lge	LC	FAC	Tot
Aizlewood, Mark	19		1	1	1	1				
Allison, Wayne	22	17	2	1	1	1	4	1		5
Atteveld, Ray	5	2								
Bent, Junior	13	7			1		3			3
Bryant, Matt	41		3		1		1			1
Cole, Andy	29		3	1	1		12	4		16
Connor, Terry	2	3								
Dziekanowski, Jacki	24	2	3		1		3			3
Edwards, Rob	14	4	3							
Fowler, Jason		1								
Gavin, Mark	16	3	1		1		1			1
Harrison, Gerry	24	9	1	2	1		1			1
Kristensen, Bjorn	4									
Leaning, Andy	1									
Llewellyn, Andy	12		1		1					
Mellon, Micky	7	3		1			1			1
Mitchell, Brian	15	1	4							
Morgan, Nicky	10						3			3
Munro, Stuart	16									
Osman, Russell	33	1		1						
Pennyfather, Glenn	14						1			1
Reid, Nicky	3	1								
Rosenior, Leroy	29	9	3		1		7	1		8
Scott, Martin	35	1	4		1		3	1		4
Shail, Mark	3	1								
Shelton, Gary	42		4	1	1		4			4
Thompson, David	17		4							
Tinnion, Brian	11		4		1		2			2
Welch, Keith	45		4		1					
(own-goals)							3			3
29 players used	506	65	44	5	11	2	49	8		57

Opponent line-ups are shown in *italics* below each match's line-up. In the "subs used" column, the team's own substitutes are shown first and the opponents' in *italics*.

No	Date	Att	Pos	Pt	F-A	H-T	1	2	3	4	5	6	7	8	9	10	11	subs used
1	A 14/8 WOLVES	21,052		0	L 1·3	0·1	Welch	Munro	Scott	Aizlewood	Shail	Hewlett*	Wyatt*	Shelton	Baird	Robinson	Tinnion	Kamara/Allison
							Stowell	*Rankine*	*Venus !*	*Cook*	*Mountfield*	*Blades*	*Birch*	*Thomas*	*Bull*	*Kelly**	*Keen*	*Regis*
2	H 21/8 CRYS PALACE	12,068		3	W 2·0	0·0	Welch	Munro	Scott	Aizlewood	Shail	Hewlett	Wyatt	Shelton	Baird	Robinson*	Tinnion	Allison
							Martyn	*Humphrey*	*Coleman*	*Southgate*	*Young*	*Thorn*	*Whyte**	*Bowry !*	*Armstrong*	*Williams*	*Rodger**	*Shaw/Gordon*
3	A 28/8 DERBY	15,643	21	3	L 0·1	0·0	Welch	Munro	Scott	Aizlewood	Shail	Edwards	Bent*	Brown I	Baird	Tinnion	Shelton	Allison
							Taylor	*Charles*	*Forsyth*	*Short*	*Craig*	*Wassall*	*Kuhl*	*Williams*	*Kitson*	*Gabbiadini*	*Pembridge*	
4	H 4/9 SOUTHEND	7,392	12	6	W 2·1	1·0	Welch	Munro	Scott	Harrison	Shail	Osman	Bent	Robinson*	Baird	Tinnion	Edwards	Brown I
							Sansome	*Locke*	*Powell*	*Badley*	*Edwards*	*Sussex*	*Ansah*	*Payne*	*Lee**	*Otto**	*Angell*	*Hunt/Harding*
5	A 11/9 OXFORD	5,420	19	6	L 2·4	1·2	Welch	Munro	Scott	Aizlewood !	Shail	Osman*	Bent*	Allison	Baird	Tinnion	Edwards	Gavin/Rosenior
							Reece	*Smart*	*Ford M*	*Lewis*	*Robinson*	*Rogan*	*Magilton*	*Beauchamp**	*Cusack**	*Penney*	*Allen*	*Dyer/Collins*
6	H 14/9 LEICESTER	7,899	21	6	L 1·3	0·2	Welch	Munro	Scott	Aizlewood	Shail	Osman	Robinson*	Brown I	Baird	Tinnion	Edwards	Allison/Rosenior
							Ward	*Mills*	*Whitlow*	*Carey*	*Walsh*	*Hill*	*Oldfield*	*Thompson*	*Speedie*	*Agnew*	*Ormondroyd*	
7	H 18/9 CHARLTON	7,484	20	7	D 0·0	0·0	Welch	Borrows	Munro	Shail	Bryant	Scott*	Martin*	Allison	Baird	Tinnion*	Gavin	Robinson/Edwards
							Salmon	*Pitcher*	*Minto*	*Garland**	*McLeary*	*Chapple*	*Robinson*	*Newton*	*Gorman*	*Grant*	*Walsh*	*Balmer*
8	A 25/9 PORTSMOUTH	10,702	20	8	D 0·0	0·0	Welch	Borrows	Munro	Shail	Bryant	Edwards	Martin*	Allison	Baird	Robinson	Tinnion	Osman
							Knight	*Gittens*	*Blake**	*McLoughlin*	*Symons*	*Awford*	*Neill*	*Stimson*	*Durnin*	*Walsh*	*Kristensen*	*Powell*
9	H 2/10 BOLTON	7,704	15	11	W 2·0	1·0	Welch	Borrows	Munro	Shail	Bryant	Tinnion	Martin*	Allison	Baird	Robinson*	Scott	Edwards/Gavin
							Branagan	*Brown*	*Phillips*	*Kelly**	*Seagraves*	*Stubbs !*	*Lee*	*McAteer*	*Thompson**	*McGinley*	*Patterson*	*Darby/Green*
10	A 5/10 LUTON	5,956	8	14	W 2·0	0·0	Welch	Borrows	Munro	Shail	Bryant	Tinnion*	Martin	Gavin	Baird	Robinson	Scott	Edwards
							Sommer	*Johnson*	*James*	*Williams*	*Peake*	*Dreyer*	*Telfer*	*Oakes**	*Hartson*	*Hughes*	*Harper*	*Houghton*
11	A 9/10 NOTTS CO	6,418	10	14	L 0·2	0·0	Welch	Borrows	Munro	Shail	Bryant	Tinnion	Martin	Gavin*	Baird	Robinson	Scott	Allison
							Cherry	*Gallagher*	*Thomas*	*Turner*	*Walker*	*Palmer*	*Devlin*	*Draper*	*McSwegan*	*Lund*	*Legg*	

Scorers, Times, and Referees

1. Scott 57 / Bull 9, 87, Mountfield 71. Ref: R Poulain
2. Baird 69, Allison 84. Ref: A Smith
3. Gabbiadini 68. Ref: P Harrison
4. Tinnion 22p, Osman 57 / Sussex 71. Ref: C Wilkes
5. Baird 43, 83 / Allen 11, Magilton 30p, 63p, Dyer 72. Ref: J Brandwood
6. Scott 87 / Speedie 1, 89, Walsh 13. Ref: P Alcock
7. Ref: G Singh
8. Ref: G Willard
9. Allison 15, Scott 76. Ref: M Peck
10. Tinnion 54p, Baird 56. Ref: K Morton
11. McSwegan 70p, Draper 79. Ref: T Lunt

Match reports

1. Fears of a goal avalanche, when Bull fires the opener into the top corner of the net, subside after Wolves fail to put away further good chances before half-time. Scott shoots in City's equaliser, but Welch misses Paul Cook's free-kick and is stranded as Derek Mountfield heads in.
2. Two superb goals go some way towards masking an often dreary preceding hour as City failed to take advantage of Bobby Bowry's 19th-min sending off for elbowing Shelton. Tinnion, unlucky to have a 72nd-minute lob disallowed, supplies the crosses for both City's headed goals.
3. Ian Brown (£28,000 ex Chelmsford), who skies over from six yards in the 35th minute, and his City colleagues are left to rue how they didn't get something out of this game. Marco Gabbiadini hammers in John Harkes' square pass to make City pay for wasting a string of chances.
4. Osman's decision to dispense with the services of the popular Dziekanowski not only brings down the ire of the Ashton Gate fans on his head, but also results in his headed goal being greeted in stony silence. Tinnion's penalty gives City a huge lift after Adam Locke felled Robinson.
5. Denis Smith's Oxford side come out on top at the end of this controversial match. David Penney escapes with a booking for his horrific 45th-min foul that sends Bent to hospital, whilst Aizlewood is sent off for bringing down Chris Allen to concede Jim Magilton's second spot-kick.
6. After David Speedie's 80-sec headed opener and Steve Walsh's lob, City control the play, but are let down by poor finishing. Allison is in his usual wasteful form, but Scott registers from 15 yards before Speedie finishes off his run by drilling in Leicester's late goal past Welch.
7. 'Put the blame on me' says Allison. Confronted by an open goal in the 78th min, he delays his shot long enough for the keeper to spring across his line and effect a save. Baird's shot against the post late on sums up City's frustrations against a Charlton side happy to settle for a point.
8. Fratton Park is no place for the faint hearted, as the new harder-edged City show that they are no longer a side that struggles when the going gets tough. Five players are booked, including City's Borrows, Munro and Edwards, as a well-deserved point is prised from the seaside.
9. The team put all thought of a possible boardroom take-over out of their minds. Allison, who heads in City's opener, makes an impressive contribution apart from his usual poor finishing that keeps Bolton (Alan Stubbs sent off 34 mins) in the contest until Scott blasts in.
10. City demonstrate that the one place where they do not need to make changes is on the field as the team is now beginning to justify claims of better things. Tinnion shoots in from the spot after Gavin is brought down, then Baird produces the finishing touch to the No 8's low cross.
11. Bryant's blunder halts City's revival with a challenge that sends Gary McSwegan sprawling in the box, with the ball still out on the wing. Welch gets his hand to the consequential penalty, but can't keep it out, and he is again beaten by Mark Draper's close-in shot nine mins later.

Match-by-match record (matches 12–23)

No		Opponent	Date				Att		Result	Scorers	Referee
12	H	BARNSLEY	16/10	15	17	14	6,923	0-1	L 0-2	Bryson 35, Relearn 52	Ref: T Holbrook
13	A	TRANMERE	22/10	13	1	15	7,123	1-1	D 2-2	Shail 16, Allison 84 / Nevin 7, Brannan 63	Ref: K Leach
14	H	SUNDERLAND	30/10	12	14	18	8,162	0-0	W 2-0	Allison 82, Baird 90	Ref: P Danson
15	H	BIRMINGHAM	2/11	9	10	21	9,192	1-0	W 3-0	Allison 30, 53, 90	Ref: R Gifford
16	A	MIDDLESBROUGH	6/11	9	10	24	9,687	1-0	W 1-0	Tinnion 40p	Ref: A Dawson
17	H	MILLWALL	13/11	8	10	25	8,416	1-0	D 2-2	Allison 38, 59 / Rae 71, Beard 78	Ref: J Rushton
18	A	WATFORD	20/11	10	17	26	6,045	0-1	D 1-1	Martin 76 / Soloman 33	Ref: I Borrett
19	A	PETERBOROUGH	27/11	8	24	29	5,084	2-0	W 2-0	Robinson 8, 37	Ref: A Smith
20	H	MIDDLESBROUGH	4/12	8	13	30	8,441	0-0	D 0-0		Ref: G Poll
21	A	LEICESTER	11/12	10	5	30	13,394	0-2	L 0-3	Speedie 13, 61, Joachim 45	Ref: L Dilkes
22	H	WOLVES	18/12	9	12	33	15,151	1-0	W 2-1	Allison 30, Brown 73 / Kelly 90	Ref: G Ashby
23	A	WEST BROM	27/12	9	16	36	22,888	1-0	W 1-0	Tinnion 43	Ref: I Cruikshanks

12. H BARNSLEY — 16/10

City: Welch, Borrows, Shail, Munro, Bryant, Tinnion, Martin*, Allison, Baird, Rosenior*, Scott, Edwards/Robinson
Barnsley: Watson, Fleming, Wilson, Baden, Bishop, Anderson, O'Connell*, Redfearn, Bryson, Biggins, Eaden, Liddell

A black day as City's inept display, against visitors who had lost their four previous games, provokes much barracking of both the players and directors. Baird had a 67th-minute effort disallowed for offside as City succumb to Ian Bryson's 15-yd volley, and Neil Redfearn's 25-yd drive.

13. A TRANMERE — 22/10

City: Welch, Nixon, Shail, Munro!, Bryant, Tinnion, Martin*, Bent*, Baird, Allison, Scott, Edwards/Robinson
Tranmere: Watson, Higgins, Nolan, Brannan, Irons, Garnett, Kenworthy*, Muir, Malkin, Nevin, Thomas, Branch

City survive Munro's 53rd-minute dismissal for his second bookable offence with a great show of discipline and team spirit. There is hardly a dull moment in this encounter from the moment Pat Nevin's volley hits the back of the net until Allison heads in for City's well-earned point.

14. H SUNDERLAND — 30/10

City: Welch, Chamberlain, Shail, Munro, Bryant, Tinnion, Martin*, Bent*, Baird, Allison, Scott, Edwards/Robinson
Sunderland: Ball, Gray Mart*, Bennett, Melville, Owers, Atkinson, Goodman, Gray P, Smith M*, Armstrong, Gray, Mike/Russell

Sunderland fade after a bright start, and City should have broken the deadlock well before Allison drove in the opener. Cheers instead of jeers are heard at long last as Baird secures the points by skipping past two challenges before burying the ball in the second minute of injury-time.

15. H BIRMINGHAM — 2/11

City: Welch, Miller, Shail, Munro, Bryant, Tinnion, Martin, Bent, Allison, Robinson, Scott
Birmingham: Hiley, Parris, Potter, Dryden, Fenwick, Donowa, Shutt, Saville*, Jenkinson, Smith, Wallace

Allison finds his goal touch to claim his first hat-trick in stunning style as rampant City make it a night to remember. Of City's seven on-target efforts, six come from Allison, including the trio of shots for his hat-trick, whilst the Blues can only manage an early drive straight at Welch.

16. A MIDDLESBROUGH — 6/11

City: Welch, Pears, Shail, Scott, Bryant, Tinnion, Martin, Bent*, Allison, Robinson, Edwards, Pennyfather
Middlesbrough: Moore, Fleming, Gannon, Mohan, Whyte, Kavanagh*, Hignett, Wilkinson, Mustoe, Moore, Illman/Barron

City's first win at Ayresome Park since a 2-0 success on 9 Nov 1907 comes courtesy of Tinnion's pen after Robinson was up-ended by Curtis Fleming. Despite all of Middlesbrough's extra possession and pressure they only manage six shots on target compared to City's four.

17. H MILLWALL — 13/11

City: Welch, Scott, Shail, Munro, Bryant, Tinnion, Martin, Bent*, Allison, Robinson, Edwards, Pennyfather
Millwall: Keller, Cunningham, Dolby*, Roberts, Vn'n Hwe* Stevens, Rae, Huxford, Mitchell, Goodman, Beard, Barber/Kennedy

With last night's EGM resolving the boardroom battle in favour of the rebels, the team gets down to the serious business of playing football. After Allison's two strikes, City are stunned when Alex Rae's tap-in and a defensive mix-up that allows Mark Beard to guide the ball past Welch.

18. A WATFORD — 20/11

City: Welch, Sucking, Shail*, Scott, Bryant, Tinnion, Martin, Bent, Allison, Robinson, Edwards, Munro
Watford: Lavin, Dublin, Johnson, Holdsworth, Watson, Dyer, Soloman, Charlery, Porter, Willis

In a dour first half, City, who offer little apart from a Bent strike which is disallowed, are caught flat-footed when Jason Soloman heads in from Bruce Dyer's cross. Waking from their lethargy after the interval, City equalise when Martin crashes the ball into the roof of the net.

19. A PETERBOROUGH — 27/11

City: Welch, Bennett, Munro, Scott, Bryant, Tinnion, Martin, Bent, Robinson, Allison, Edwards, Pennyfather
Peterborough: Greenman, McDonald, Bradshaw, Howarth, Welsh, Adcock*, Hackett*, Ebdon, McGlashan, Cooper, Funnell/Barnes

With their eighth clean sheet in 13 outings and only two defeats in the same period, City are one of the Division's form sides. The irrepressible Robinson twice shows his poacher's instincts to blast in from close range and leave City nicely placed for an assault on the promotion prize.

20. H MIDDLESBROUGH — 4/12

City: Welch, Pears, Llewellyn, Munro, Bryant, Tinnion*, Martin, Bent*, Robinson, Allison, Edwards, Pennyfather/Brown I
Middlesbrough: Fleming, Mustoe, Mohan, Whyte, Stamp, Hignett, Wilkinson, Peake, Moore, Vickers

City are unable to complete a double over a Middlesbrough side without a win in ten games. A frustrating afternoon, but a draw is a fair result, even against a Boro team now without a goal in seven outings, as City lack the guile to break down the visitors' five-man midfield.

21. A LEICESTER — 11/12

City: Welch, Ward, Llewellyn, Munro, Bryant, Tinnion, Pennyfather Brown I*, Martin, Robinson, Allison, Edwards, Fowler
Leicester: Grayson, Lewis, Coatsworth*, Agnew, Hill, Joachim*, Thompson, Speedie, Roberts, Philpott, Oldfield/Eustace

Julian Joachim's stunning 25-yarder with the outside of his right foot, sandwiched between David Speedie's sharply taken close-range shots, ends City's eight-match unbeaten run. Speedie's histrionics on being tackled by Pennyfather earns an unwarranted booking for the City man.

22. H WOLVES — 18/12

City: Welch, Stowell, Llewellyn, Munro, Bryant, Tinnion!, Pennyfather Brown I*, Martin, Robinson, Allison, Edwards, Bent
Wolves: Thompson, Edwards, Venus, Bennett, Simkin, Dennison, Whyte, Birch, Bull, Kelly, Cook*, Keen/Rankine

Ian Brown, he of the electric pace, grabs his first League goal when running onto Allison's flick to slide the ball in under the diving keeper. City's superiority is not threatened by Tinnion's harsh 78th-min dismissal until David Kelly fires past Welch in the second min of injury-time.

23. A WEST BROM — 27/12

City: Welch, Lange, Llewellyn, Munro, Bryant, Tinnion, Pennyfather Brown I, Martin, Robinson, Allison, Edwards, Bent
West Brom: Burgess, Lilwall, Mardon, Raven, Ashcroft, Heggs*, O'Regan, Taylor, Mellon*, Hamilton, Donovan/Coldicott

Despite often riding their luck, City's fighting spirit and a composed defensive display brings all three points thanks to Tinnion's shot which takes a deflection off Paul Raven. Welch produces his best display of the season to spoil the day for ex City men, Mellon, Mardon and Taylor.

ENDSLEIGH LEAGUE DIVISION 1   Manager: Russell Osman   SEASON 1993-94

No	Date		Att	Pos	Pt	F-A	H-T	Scorers, Times, and Referees	1	2	3	4	5	6	7	8	9	10	11	subs used
24	28/12	H	20,725	8	36	1-4	0-0	Edwards 59 / Collymore 58, 74, Webb 69, Woan 86 / Ref: M Pierce	Welch	Llewellyn	Scott	Munro	Bryant	Tinnion	Pennyfather	Brown I*	Robinson^	Allison	Edwards	Baird/Martin
								NOTT'M FOREST	*Crossley*	*Lyttle*	*Webb*	*Cooper*	*Chettle*	*Stone*	*Phillips*	*Gemmill*	*Bohinen*	*Collymore*	*Woan*	

'Stan' is the man as he shows after being kept quiet for nearly an hour. Collymore scores Forest's first and third – a curling power drive – before turning provider to allow Ian Woan time to pick his spot. Edwards tucks away City's sole reply when Mark Crossley spills Allison's header.

No	Date		Att	Pos	Pt	F-A	H-T	Scorers, Times, and Referees	1	2	3	4	5	6	7	8	9	10	11	subs used
25	1/1	A	5,469	17	36	0-1	0-0	Groves 86 / Ref: P Jones	Welch	Crichton	McDermott	Munro*	Bryant	Pennyfather	Martin	Gavin^	Baird	Allison	Edwards	Shail/Robinson
								GRIMSBY	*Crichton*	*McDermott*	*Croft*	*Futcher*	*Handyside*	*Ford*	*Gilbert*	*Livingstone*	*Mendonca*	*Groves*		

City are punished for their one mistake when their flat-footed defence allows Paul Groves the space to fire in Grimsby's winner. Edwards comes closest for City with a volley that thunders against the crossbar, but Grimsby's shots advantage of 10-2 suggests that the best side won.

No	Date		Att	Pos	Pt	F-A	H-T	Scorers, Times, and Referees	1	2	3	4	5	6	7	8	9	10	11	subs used
26	3/1	H	11,132	8	37	0-0	0-0	Ref: P Durkin	Welch	Munro	Scott	Shail	Bryant	Tinnion	Martin	Robinson	Baird*	Allison	Edwards	Brown I
								STOKE	*Marshall*	*Clarkson*	*Sandford*	*Cranson*	*Overson*	*Origgson*	*Foley*	*Bannister*	*Regis*	*Butler**	*Gleghorn*	*Gynn*

Concerns are growing over City's modest scoring record, and against a Stoke side under the control of Joe Jordan the ball just wouldn't go in. After a dire first half, Robinson's open-goal miss on 73 mins, when Baird headed down Scott's centre, sums up City's frustrations in the rain.

No	Date		Att	Pos	Pt	F-A	H-T	Scorers, Times, and Referees	1	2	3	4	5	6	7	8	9	10	11	subs used
27	15/1	A	5,222	23	38	1-1	0-1	Scott 50 / Rammell 44 / Ref: N Barry	Welch	Munro	Scott	Shail	Osman	Tinnion	Martin	Bent	Robinson	Allison	Edwards	Brown I
								BARNSLEY	*Butler*	*Eaden*	*Fleming*	*Wilson*	*Taggart*	*Bishop*	*O'Connell*	*Redfearn*	*Rammell*	*Payton*	*Archdeacon*	

City's vehement offside protests fall on deaf ears, as Welch's parry of Owen Archdeacon's shot gives Andy Rammell an easy tap-in to put the Tykes in front. No protests over Scott's magnificent equaliser though, his 30-yard drive is still rising when it hits the back of Lee Butler's net

No	Date		Att	Pos	Pt	F-A	H-T	Scorers, Times, and Referees	1	2	3	4	5	6	7	8	9	10	11	subs used
28	22/1	H	7,458	14	38	0-2	0-1	Legg 35, Agana 80 / Ref: D Gallagher	Welch	Llewellyn	Scott	Shail	Munro	Tinnion	Martin	Bent	Robinson*	Allison	Edwards	Rosenior/Pennyfather
								NOTTS CO	*Cherry*	*Gannon*	*Sherlock*	*Palmer*	*Foster*	*Turner*	*Devlin*	*Draper*	*Lund*	*Legg*	*Agana*	

Even a magnificent cup tussle with Liverpool cannot raise the level of City's League crowds, and those who stayed away from this affair obviously knew what was coming. County, with only one win on their travels, deservedly win this one with Legg's shot and Agana's header.

No	Date		Att	Pos	Pt	F-A	H-T	Scorers, Times, and Referees	1	2	3	4	5	6	7	8	9	10	11	subs used
29	5/2	H	8,171	5	41	2-0	0-0	Tinnion 74, Allison 84 / Ref: V Callow	Welch	Llewellyn	Scott	Shail	Munro	Tinnion	Martin	Pennyfather	Robinson*	Allison	Edwards	Brown I
								TRANMERE	*Nixon !*	*Higgins*	*Mungall*	*Brannan*	*Hughes*	*O'Brien*	*Morrissey*	*Aldridge*	*Nevin**	*Malkin*	*Thomas*	*Coyne*

Keeper Eric Nixon's sending off for bringing down Brown sees substitute Danny Coyne first employed to take Tinnion's 20-yard free-kick out of the net. Allison then makes sure that City get the points their play deserves by rounding Coyne and shooting home from a narrow angle.

No	Date		Att	Pos	Pt	F-A	H-T	Scorers, Times, and Referees	1	2	3	4	5	6	7	8	9	10	11	subs used
30	12/2	A	16,696	15	42	0-0	0-0	Ref: R Poulain	Welch	Harriott	Scott	Shail	Munro	Tinnion	Martin*	Pennyfather	Robinson*	Allison	Edwards	Brown I/Bryant
								SUNDERLAND	*Chamberlain*	*Owers*	*Gray, Mike*	*Ball*	*Ferguson*	*Melville*	*Russell*	*Goodman**	*Gray P*	*Smith M*	*Atkinson*	*Lawrence*

Russell Osman believes he has unearthed a diamond in Marvin Harriott, signed on a free from Barnsley. The new arrival certainly sparkled in his first test at Roker Park, being one of the few plus points in a game which, despite the strong wind, fell well below the fans' expectations.

No	Date		Att	Pos	Pt	F-A	H-T	Scorers, Times, and Referees	1	2	3	4	5	6	7	8	9	10	11	subs used
31	22/2	A	12,417	1	42	1-4	1-1	Shail 21 / Gordon 25p, Salako 60, Armstrong 73, 84 / Ref: G Willard	Welch	Harriott	Scott	Shail	Bryant	Tinnion	Martin	Munro	Robinson	Allison	Edwards	Brown I
								CRYS PALACE	*Martyn !*	*Humphrey*	*Gordon*	*Southgate*	*Young*	*Coleman*	*Shaw*	*Matthew*	*Armstrong*	*Stewart**	*Salako*	*Whyte*

On an icy pitch both sides stick commendably to their passing game, and City give as good as they get until Welch's collision with Paul Stewart sees John Salako curl a shot into the net. Shail gets City off to a good start with his header, but then handles to concede the penalty.

No	Date		Att	Pos	Pt	F-A	H-T	Scorers, Times, and Referees	1	2	3	4	5	6	7	8	9	10	11	subs used
32	26/2	A	4,615	12	45	1-0	1-0	Allison 45 / Ref: G Poll	Welch	Harriott	Scott	Shail*	Bryant	Tinnion	Martin	Munro	Robinson	Allison	Edwards	Pennyfather
								SOUTHEND	*Sansome*	*Locke*	*Powell*	*Gridelet**	*Edwards*	*Bressington*	*Hunt*	*Sussex*	*Jones**	*Otto*	*Lee*	*Ansah/Payne*

'We're good enough for the play-offs' says Robinson, after City's gritty display at Roots Hall. After Gary Jones hits a post early on, Robinson does the work for City's match-winning goal, but after rounding the advancing Paul Sansome, it is Allison who shoots in from five yards.

No	Date		Att	Pos	Pt	F-A	H-T	Scorers, Times, and Referees	1	2	3	4	5	6	7	8	9	10	11	subs used
33	5/3	H	8,723	5	46	0-0	0-0	Ref: K Cooper	Welch	Harriott	Scott*	Munro	Bryant	Tinnion	Martin	Hoyland	Bent*	Allison	Edwards	Partridge/Rosenior
								DERBY	*Taylor*	*Charles*	*Nicholson*	*Kuhl**	*Short*	*Williams*	*Cowans*	*Pembridge*	*Kitson*	*Gabbiadini*	*Ratcliffe*	*Johnson*

Bent wastes two chances to end this stalemate, the best being an open goal from six yards, which he volleys over the top on the stroke of half-time. Paul Williams is a major stumbling block to City's efforts, but really they have only themselves to blame for not winning this one.

No	Date		Att	Pos	Pt	F-A	H-T	Scorers, Times, and Referees	1	2	3	4	5	6	7	8	9	10	11	subs used
34	15/3	H	6,635	23	46	0-1	0-1	Byrne 31 / Ref: R Gifford	Welch	Harriott	Scott	Hoyland	Bryant	Tinnion	Munro*	Hewlett*	Robinson	Allison	Edwards	Bent/Partridge
								OXFORD	*Whitehead*	*Elliott*	*Ford M*	*Ford R*	*Smart*	*Dyer*	*Lewis*	*Beauchamp*	*Moody*	*Byrne*	*Allen*	

City's bright start is blighted by their inability to put away their chances, and the longer the game goes on the more static becomes their play. Oxford by contrast take what is on offer, and John Byrne's three-yard header lifts them off the bottom of the table – but they will go down.

Match-by-match records (fixtures 35–46)

35 — H 19/3 PORTSMOUTH — Att 6,352 — Pos 17 — Pts 49 — W 1-0
Scorers: Allison 54 — Ref: T Holbrook

City: Welch, Hoyland, Munro, Shail, Bryant, Tinnion, Harriott, Hewlett, Robinson*, Scott, Baird
Opp: Knight, Dobson, Stimson, McLoughlin, Daniel, Awford, Pethwick*, Chamberlain Creaney, Wood*, Russell, Powell/Hall

Osman pleads with City fans to lay off 18-year-old Hewlett, who has become a target of the boo boys due to his languid style. In this game, won by Allison's low shot, he should have notched a hat-trick, but after his first touch lets him down with one opening, he twice shoots wide.

36 — A 26/3 BOLTON — Att 10,221 — Pos 16 — Pts 50 — D 2-2
Scorers: Allison 18, 68 / Lee 26, Coyle 44 — Ref: J Rushton

City: Welch, Hoyland, Munro, Shail, Bryant, Tinnion, Harriott, Hewlett, Robinson*, Scott, Milsom
Opp: Davison, Phillips, Stimson, Kelly, Seagraves, Stubbs, Lee*, McAteer, Coyle, Walker, Green/Winstanley

Allison's brave diving header puts City ahead at Burnden Park, but sloppy defending gives away the advantage. Shots by David Lee and Owen Coyle find the back of Welch's net, before Allison strikes again. Receiving the ball in midfield he ends his 50-yard run with an exquisite shot.

37 — A 30/3 STOKE — Att 13,192 — Pos 8 — Pts 50 — L 0-3
Scorers: Adams 8, 77, Biggins 54p — Ref: M Reed

City: Welch, Hoyland, Munro*, Shail, Bryant, Tinnion, Harriott, Hewlett*, Martin, Allison, Milsom !/Robinson
Opp: Prudhoe, Butler, Sandford, Cranson, Adams, Orlygsson*, Foley, Carruthers, Biggins*, Clark, Walters, Gleghorn/Regis

Milsom is unlucky to be sent off for his second bookable offence having only been on the field for 13 mins, but by then Stoke had the game won. City's comprehensive defeat is completed by Micky Adams' 30-yarder, after Shail's clumsy tackle earlier gifted Stoke their penalty.

38 — H 2/4 WEST BROM — Att 8,624 — Pos 20 — Pts 51 — D 0-0
Ref: P Alcock

City: Welch, Hoyland, Munro, Shail, Bryant, Tinnion, Harriott, Hewlett, Robinson, Allison, Edwards, Hoyland
Opp: Naylor, Burgess, Edwards, O'Regan, Parsley, Raven, Hunt*, Hamilton, Taylor, Donovan, Smith, Shrodder

City throw away all hopes of a place in the play-off frame, as a blank scoresheet means that whilst they have kept 21 clean sheets this season, they have also failed to hit the net on 17 occasions.

39 — A 4/4 NOTT'M FOREST — Att 24,162 — Pos 2 — Pts 52 — D 0-0
Ref: E Parker

City: Welch, Harriott, Scott, Shail, Munro, Tinnion, Martin, Wyatt, Milsom, Allison, Edwards
Opp: Crossley, Lyttle, Pearce, Cooper, Chettle, Stone, Phillips, Bohinen*, Lee, Rosario, Black, Woan

City's defence turns in a quality display to thwart a Forest side, who sorely miss the suspended Stan Collymore. Robert Rosario misses Forest's best chance from just two yards before the break, whilst in the second half Wyatt cuts inside to get a 20-yard shot on target for City.

40 — H 9/4 GRIMSBY — Att 5,480 — Pos 12 — Pts 55 — W 1-0
Scorers: Scott 90p — Ref: M Pierce

City: Welch, Harriott, Scott, Shail, Munro, Tinnion, Martin*, Wyatt, Partridge, Allison, Edwards, Hewlett
Opp: Crichton, Ford, Agnew, Handyside, Rodger, Shakespeare Childs*, Gilbert, Livingstone*, Mendonca, Groves, Croft/Woods

City leave it late to win this game, Scott's penalty at the death ending 380 minutes of goal famine. Before the dramatic finale it appeared that all City's hard work in the heavy rain would go unrewarded, but keeper Paul Crichton's up-ending of Allison ensures a deserved outcome.

41 — A 16/4 BIRMINGHAM — Att 20,316 — Pos 23 — Pts 56 — D 2-2
Scorers: Partridge 5, 20 / Claridge 60p, Donowa 75 — Ref: S Lodge

City: Welch, Harriott, McKop, Shail, Munro, Tinnion, Martin, Wyatt*, Partridge, Allison, Edwards, Robinson
Opp: Bennett, Hiley, Rogers, Donowa, Barnett, Daish, Ward, Claridge, De Souza*, Willis, Doherty, Shutt

Partridge (ex Bradford City) nicks the ball off Liam Daish to fire in his first League goal, and then finds the net again with an easy tap-in. After Allison brings down Steve Claridge for the penalty, ex City player Louie Donowa saves a point for the Blues with his shot past Welch.

42 — H 19/4 LUTON — Att 5,350 — Pos 20 — Pts 59 — W 1-0
Scorers: Edwards 20 — Ref: M Reed

City: Welch, Harriott, Scott, Munro, Hewlett, Tinnion, Martin, Wyatt, Partridge, Barclay*, Edwards, Robinson
Opp: Sommer, Linton*, James, Greene, Dreyer, Millen, Mooney, Hughes, Dixon, Aunger*, Preece, Hartson/Thorpe

Whilst Luton manage six on-target efforts compared to City's three, it is the homesters who control the play. After a shapeless start City find their stride, and Robinson twice fires wide before Edwards crashes the ball in from close range, when Juergen Sommer drops Hewlett's corner.

43 — H 23/4 WATFORD — Att 8,324 — Pos 19 — Pts 60 — D 1-1
Scorers: Partridge 10 / Furlong 51 — Ref: M Bodenham

City: Welch, Harriott, Scott, Munro, Robinson, Hewlett, Martin, Wyatt, Partridge, Barclay*, Edwards*, Tinnion/Wyatt
Opp: Digweed, Lavin, Dublin, Hessenthaler Foster, Millen, Johnson, Mooney, Hughes, Furlong, Porter, Drysdale

Robinson can still do everything but find the net, his 20-yard shot being parried by Perry Digweed for Partridge to drive in from six yards. Paul Furlong punishes City for their inability to score more against the League's worst defence, lobbing in a deserved equaliser from 18 yards.

44 — A 30/4 MILLWALL — Att 11,189 — Pos 6 — Pts 61 — D 0-0
Ref: K Cooper

City: Welch, Harriott, Scott, Munro, Hewlett, Tinnion, Martin, Wyatt, Partridge, Bent, Edwards, Robinson/Wyatt
Opp: Keller, Cunningham Huxford, Hurlock, Van den H'we Stevens, Rae*, Allen*, Moralee, Mitchell, Roberts, Kerr/Berry

Whilst Martin has a good game against his old club, and the diminutive Bent causes all sorts of problems, City do not manage to get a single shot on target at the New Den. Hewlett blasts City's best chance high and wide as their superbly-organised defence claims another clean sheet.

45 — A 3/5 CHARLTON — Att 6,713 — Pos 10 — Pts 61 — L 1-3
Scorers: Partridge 40 / Nelson 45, Chapple 47, Scott 66 (og) — Ref: I Hemley

City: Welch, Harriott, Scott, Munro, Shail, Tinnion, Martin, Wyatt*, Partridge, Bent, Edwards*, Robinson/McKop
Opp: Salmon*, Brown, Sturgess, Garland, McLeary, Chapple, Bennett, Pitcher, Leaburn, Nelson, Robinson*, Vaughan/Grant

Scott's deflection of a low cross into his own net completes City's misery at the Valley. Classy one-touch football and Partridge's neat tuck-in from Bent's centre had City in control early on, but Garry Nelson's unstoppable volley in first-half injury-time changes the course of the game.

46 — H 8/5 PETERBOROUGH — Att 7,790 — Pos 24 — Pts 64 — W 4-1
Scorers: Bent 1, 15, Robinson 46, 78 / Furnell 58 — Ref: P Durkin

City: Brown W, Harriott, Scott, Shail, Munro, Tinnion, Martin*, Wyatt, Partridge, Bent, Edwards, Robinson/McKop
Opp: Cooksey, Carter, Spearing, Williams, Howarth, Clark, McGarry, Bradshaw, Iorfa, McGlashan, Brissett*, Furnell

Wayne Brown (age 17) has a great debut between the sticks as Bent and Robinson find their shooting boots. Robinson takes his League tally to four (all against the Posh) – his lob for City's third being followed by his fierce 25-yard effort that swerves to beat the keeper at his near post.

Average: Home 8,852 — Away 11,288

ENDSLEIGH DIVISION 1 (CUP-TIES)

Manager: Russell Osman

Coca-Cola Cup

						F-A	H-T	Scorers, Times, and Referees	1	2	3	4	5	6	7	8	9	10	11	subs used
1:1	A	SWANSEA	17/8	3,746	2	W 1-0	0-0	Robinson 46 Ref: K Burge	Welch	Munro	Scott*	Aizlewood	Shail	Hewlett	Wyatt	Shelton	Baird	Robinson	Tinnion	Osman
									Freestone	*Clode*	*Cook**	*Walker*	*Harris*	*Pascoe*	*Hodge*	*Bowen*	*Torpey*	*Cornforth*	*Hayes*	*Ford*
1:2	H	SWANSEA	24/8	4,633	2:10	L 0-2	0-1	Bowen 37, 81 Ref: D Frampton (City lost 1-2 on aggregate)	Welch	Munro	Scott	Aizlewood	Shail	Hewlett*	Wyatt*	Shelton	Baird	Robinson	Tinnion	Allison/Osman
									Freestone	*Clode*	*Ford*	*Walker*	*Harris*	*Pascoe*	*Chapple*	*Bowen*	*Torpey*	*Cornforth*	*Hayes*	

1:1 — Just when the cup-tie is in danger of falling flat, up pops Robinson to add some fizz. With both teams searching in vain for any pattern to their play the game bursts into life after the break when Robinson races onto Welch's long clearance to shoot past Roger Freestone from ten yards.

1:2 — Captain Shail admits that City's display lets the players and the club down as Swansea demonstrate a much greater will to win. Jason Bowen shoots in the opener past Welch, then really celebrates his 21st birthday in style with a classic diving header to finish off Colin Pascoe's cross.

FA Cup

						F-A	H-T	Scorers, Times, and Referees	1	2	3	4	5	6	7	8	9	10	11	subs used
3	H	LIVERPOOL	19/1	21,718	P:6	D 1-1	0-0	Allison 72 Rush 62 Ref: M Bodenham	Welch	Llewellyn	Scott	Shail	Munro	Tinnion	Martin	Bent	Robinson	Allison	Edwards	
									Grobbelaar	*Jones*	*Dicks*	*Nichol*	*Redknapp*	*Ruddock*	*Clough*	*Fowler**	*Rush*	*Barnes*	*McManaman*	*Bjornebye*
3R	A	LIVERPOOL	25/1	36,720	P:5	W 1-0	0-0	Tinnion 67 Ref: M Bodenham	Welch	Llewellyn	Scott	Shail	Munro	Tinnion	Martin	Bent*	Robinson	Allison	Edwards	Pennyfather
									Grobbelaar	*Jones*	*Harkness*	*Nichol*	*Redknapp**	*Ruddock*	*Clough*	*Walters*	*Rush*	*Barnes*	*McManaman*	*Hutchison*
4	A	STOCKPORT	9/2	7,691	3:2	W 4-0	1-0	Shail 4, Allison 48, 60, 67 Ref: P Vanes	Welch	Rosenior	Scott	Shail	Munro	Tinnion	Martin	Pennyfather	Robinson	Allison	Edwards	James/Connelly
									Edwards	*Todd*	*Wallace**	*Frain*	*Flynn*	*Barras*	*Miller**	*Ward*	*Francis*	*Beaumont*	*Preece*	
5	H	CHARLTON	19/2	20,416	3	D 1-1	1-0	Tinnion 12 Robson 60 Ref: K Hackett	Welch	Munro	Scott	Shail	Bryant	Tinnion	Martin	Pennyfather*	Robinson	Allison	Edwards	Bent
									Salmon	*Brown*	*Minto*	*Pardew*	*McLeary*	*Balmer*	*Robson*	*Pitcher*	*Leaburn*	*Grant*	*Nelson*	
5R	A	CHARLTON	2/3	8,205	2	L 0-2	0-1	Pitcher 34p, Grant 90 Ref: V Callow	Welch	Munro	Scott	Shail*	Bryant	Tinnion	Martin	Bent	Robinson	Allison	Edwards	Rosenior
									Vaughan	*Brown*	*Minto*	*Pardew*	*Chapple*	*Balmer*	*Robson*	*Pitcher*	*Leaburn*	*Grant*	*Nelson*	

3 — With the first match abandoned after 65 minutes due to floodlight failure, prices were reduced, hence receipts in the region of £77K compared to £155K eleven days ago. Allison's close-in shot equalises Rush's toe-poke and at the finish Liverpool are happy to have hung on for a replay.

3R — Super City pull off a shock victory at Anfield and receive the accolade of the wonderful Liverpool fans as they complete a lap of honour at the finish. City match their opponents shot for shot, but Tinnion finds the finish with a stunning side-foot effort into the bottom corner of the net.

4 — An amazing cup-tie as Stockport's near relentless first-half pressure comes to naught. Allison's hat-trick (a header, followed by two shots) plus Shail's early head-in from Tinnion's centre constitute all City's on target efforts, while Stockport get no return from any of their seven attempts.

5 — Most City fans were in high expectation of success against high-flying Charlton, but those with longer memories were apprehensive. Tinnion's 25-yard free-kick around the visitors' wall gets City off to a great start, but they are struggling by the time Mark Robson shoots Charlton level.

5R — Despite all the confident talk beforehand, City never get going at the Valley. Darren Pitcher's spot-kick straight down the middle, after Allison brings down Steve Brown, and Kim Grant's late strike take Charlton deservedly through to a quarter-final meeting with Manchester United.

Football League Division One — Final Table

	Team	P	Home						Away					Pts
			W	D	L	F	A		W	D	L	F	A	
1	Crys Palace	46	16	4	3	39	18		11	5	7	34	28	90
2	Nott'm Forest	46	12	9	2	38	22		11	5	7	36	27	83
3	Millwall	46	14	8	1	36	17		9	5	9	22	32	74
4	Leicester *	46	11	9	3	45	30		8	7	8	27	29	73
5	Tranmere	46	15	3	5	48	23		6	6	11	21	30	72
6	Derby	46	15	3	5	44	25		5	8	10	29	43	71
7	Notts Co	46	16	3	4	43	26		4	5	14	22	43	68
8	Wolves	46	10	10	3	34	19		7	7	9	26	28	68
9	Middlesbro	46	12	6	5	40	19		6	7	10	26	35	67
10	Stoke	46	14	4	5	35	19		4	9	10	22	40	67
11	Charlton	46	14	3	6	39	22		5	5	13	22	36	65
12	Sunderland	46	14	2	7	35	22		6	6	12	19	35	65
13	BRISTOL CITY	46	11	7	5	27	18		5	9	9	20	32	64
14	Bolton	46	10	8	5	40	31		5	6	12	23	33	59
15	Southend	46	10	5	8	34	28		7	3	13	29	39	59
16	Grimsby	46	7	14	2	26	16		6	6	11	26	31	59
17	Portsmouth	46	10	6	7	29	22		7	4	12	23	36	58
18	Barnsley	46	9	3	11	25	26		7	4	12	30	41	55
19	Watford	46	10	5	8	39	35		5	4	14	27	45	54
20	Luton	46	12	4	7	38	25		2	7	14	18	35	53
21	West Brom	46	9	7	7	38	31		5	5	14	22	38	51
22	Birmingham	46	9	7	7	28	29		4	5	14	24	40	51
23	Oxford	46	10	5	8	33	33		3	5	15	21	42	49
24	Peterborough	46	6	9	8	31	30		2	4	17	17	46	37
		1104	276	144	132	864	586		132	144	276	586	864	1512

* promoted after play-offs

Appearances and Goals

	Appearances						Goals			
	Lge	Sub	LC	Sub	FAC	Sub	Lge	LC	FAC	Tot
Aizlewood, Mark	5				2					
Allison, Wayne	35	4	1		5		15		4	19
Baird, Ian	16	3	2				5			5
Barclay, Dominic	2									
Bent, Junior	17	3			3	1	2			2
Borrows, Brian	6									
Brown, Ian	5	6					1			1
Brown Wayne	1									
Bryant, Matt	27	1			2					
Edwards, Rob	31	7			5		2			2
Fowler Jason		1								
Gavin, Mark	6	2								
Harriott, Marvin	17									
Harrison, Gerry	1									
Hewlett, Matt	11	1				2				
Hoyland, Jamie	6									
Kamara, Abdul		1								
Llewellyn, Andy	15					2				
McKop, Henry	2	2								
Martin, David	33	1			5		1			1
Milsom, Paul	1	2								
Munro, Stuart	43	1	2		5					
Osman, Russell	4	1		2			1			1
Partridge, Scott	7	2			2	1	4			4
Pennyfather, Glenn	7	5			5					
Robinson, Liam	31	10	2		1	1	4	1		5
Rosenior, Leroy	1	4								
Scott, Martin	45		2		5		5			5
Shail, Mark	35	1	2		5		2		1	3
Shelton, Gary	3		2							
Tinnion, Brian	40	1	2		5		5		2	7
Welch, Keith	45		2		5					
Wyatt, Mike	8	2	2							
31 players used	506	61	22	3	55	3	47	1	7	55

Odds & ends

Double wins: (3) Southend, Luton, Peterborough.

Double losses: (3) Oxford, Leicester, Notts County.

Won from behind: (0).

Lost from in front: (2) Crystal Palace (a), Charlton (a).

High spots: Beating Peterborough 4-1 at Ashton Gate on 8 May. Beating Liverpool in FA Cup Replay at Anfield. A smash and grab FA Cup win at Stockport.

Low spots: Forest's 4-1 win at Ashton Gate on 28 December. Floodlight failure at Ashton Gate on 8 January just as City were taking control of FA Cup game v Liverpool. Losing 0-2 at Charlton in FA Cup 5th Round Replay. Losing Gloucestershire Cup Final against Bristol Rov 3-5 in penalty shoot-out following 1-1 draw at Ashton Gate on 5 August.

Player of the year: Wayne Allison.

Ever-presents: (0).

Hat-tricks: (2) Wayne Allison.

Leading scorer: Wayne Allison (20).

ENDSLEIGH LEAGUE DIVISION 1

Manager: Osman ⇨ Joe Jordan — SEASON 1994-95

No	Date		Opponent	Att	Pos	Pt	Res	F-A	H-T	Scorers, Times, and Referees
1	13/8	H	SUNDERLAND	11,127		1	D	0-0	0-0	Ref: P Alcock
2	20/8	A	BOLTON	12,127		4	W	2-0	1-0	Baird 25, Allison 68. Ref: J Watson
3	27/8	H	PORT VALE	8,940	7	5	D	0-0	0-0	Ref: G Pooley
4	30/8	A	BURNLEY	11,207	12	6	D	1-1	0-1	Allison 89, Robinson 41. Ref: K Lupton
5	3/9	A	CHARLTON	9,019	16	6	L	2-3	0-1	Allison 58, 70, Mortimer 26, Whyte 63, 69. Ref: T West
6	10/9	H	NOTTS CO	6,670	10	9	W	2-1	1-1	Bent 16, Scott 54p, Jemson 45. Ref: J Brandwood
7	13/9	H	DERBY	8,029	13	9	L	0-2	0-1	Kitson 22, Carsley 53. Ref: P Vanes
8	17/9	A	SOUTHEND	3,663	17	9	L	1-2	0-1	Baird 82, Thomson 9, Whelan 61. Ref: M Pierce
9	24/9	H	MIDDLESBROUGH	8,642	20	9	L	0-1	0-0	Hendrie 69. Ref: J.Lloyd
10	1/10	A	LUTON	6,633	17	12	W	1-0	0-0	Baird 56. Ref: P Foakes
11	8/10	H	MILLWALL	7,499	13	15	W	1-0	0-0	Baird 56. Ref: J Rushton

Line-ups (1–11 and subs used)

No	1	2	3	4	5	6	7	8	9	10	11	subs used
1	Welch	Harriott	Scott	Shail	Bryant	Fowler	McAree*	Bent*	Baird	Allison	Edwards	Partridge
	Norman	Kubicki	Gray, Mart.*	Bennett	Ferguson	Melville	Owers	Goodman	Gray P	Gray, Mike	Ball	Atkinson
2	Welch	Harriott	Scott	Shail	Bryant	Fowler	McAree*	Bent*	Baird	Allison	Edwards	Munro/Partridge
	Branagan	McDonald*	Phillips	McAtee	Kernaghan	Stubbs	Lee	Patterson	Paatelainen	McGinlay*	Sneekes	Thompson/Coyle
3	Welch	Harriott	Scott	Shail	Bryant	Fowler	Loss	Bent	Baird*	Allison*	Edwards	Partridge/Brown l
	Musselwhite	Sandeman	Tankard	Porter	Griffiths	Glover D	Kent	Van der Laan	Foyle	Glover L	Naylor*	Burke
4	Welch	Harriott	Scott	Shail	Bryant	Fowler	Loss*	Bent	Baird	Allison	Edwards	Partridge
	Beresford	Parkinson	Vinnicombe	Davis	Winstanley	Joyce	Harper	Gayle	Heath	Robinson*	McMinn	Harrison
5	Welch	Harriott	Scott	Shail	Bryant	Fowler	Loss*	Bent	Baird	Allison	Edwards	Walsh/Grant
	Ammann	Brown	Sturgess	Mortimer	Chapple	McLeary	Newton	Nelson	Garland*	Whyte	Robson*	Walsh/Grant
6	Welch	Harriott	Scott	Shail	Bryant	Fowler*	Partridge	Bent	Baird*	Allison	Edwards	Loss/McKop
	Cherry	Gallagher	Turner	Emenalo	Johnson	Yates	Jemson*	Legg	Matthews	McSwegan	Kuhl	Lund
7	Welch	Harriott	Scott	Shail	Bryant	Fowler*	Partridge	Bent	Baird*	Allison	Edwards	Loss/Simpson
	Taylor	Charles	Forsyth	Hodge	Short	Williams	Cowans	Gabbiadini	Kitson*	Pembridge	Carsley	Simpson
8	Welch	Harriott	Scott	Shail	Bryant	Tinnion	Partridge	Bent	Baird	Simpson	Edwards	Tilson/Forester
	Sansome	Hone	Powell	Gridelet*	Edwards	Willis	Dublin	Whelan	Regis	Otto	Thomson*	Tilson/Forester
9	Welch	Harriott	Scott	Shail	Bryant	Tinnion*	McAree	Bent	Baird*	Simpson	Edwards	Partridge
	Pears	Cox	Fleming	Vickers	Whyte	Hignett	Mustoe	Pollock	Wilkinson	Hendrie	Moore	
10	Welch	Harriott	Scott	Shail	Bryant	Munro	Simpson	Bent*	Baird	Tinnion	Edwards	Partridge
	Sommer	James	Johnson M	Waddock	Thomas*	Peake	Telfer	Oakes	Dixon*	Preece	Marshall	Hughes/Harston
11	Welch	Harriott	Scott	Shail	Bryant	Munro	McAree*	Seal*	Baird	Simpson	Tinnion	Partridge/Wyatt
	Carter	Cunningham	Thatcher	Van Blerk	McCarthy	Roberts	Beard*	Rae !	Kerr	Mitchell*	Kennedy	Chapman/Savage

Match reports

1. Sunderland: Thrills and spills aplenty, but no goals in this humdinger. Unfortunately Osman's refreshing decision to opt for attack highlights the same deficiencies as last season. Despite laying almost constant siege on the visitors' goal in the first half, City are still unable to supply the finish.

2. Bolton: City at last demonstrate the art of finishing as they withstand Bolton pressure and hit back on the break. John McGinlay receives the Adidas Golden Boot award for his 33 goals last season, but reputations count for nothing as Allison blasts in from 18 yards to seal City's victory.

3. Port Vale: On the day that sees the old Open End transformed by the opening of the Atyeo Stand, both teams face a new hazard in Graham Pooley who takes the new FA get-tough directive to heart. He books three players in the first 14 mins and by the end has handed out seven yellow cards.

4. Burnley: Allison saves a point for City in the second minute of injury-time with a perfect low drive to Marlon Beresford's left, but this is a game that they should have won. Cruelly robbed of a play-on advantage, City are hit as Liam Robinson's looping header finishes off a counter-attack.

5. Charlton: A thrilling finish as Allison hits the inside of a post as well as having a goal ruled out for offside, but City are left to regret not starting in a similar inspiring vein. With two goals apiece in the second half, Paul Mortimer's low 20-yard drive before the break is the crucial difference.

6. Notts Co: A game sprinkled with strange refereeing decisions, but City are not complaining about Scott's pen even though Bent was clearly outside the box when brought down. Loss hits the post as City regain the control that was briefly threatened by Nigel Jemson's free-kick equaliser.

7. Derby: City come in a poor second against a Derby side expertly marshalled in defence by Paul Williams. The Paul Kitson and Marco Gabbiadini partnership pulls the strings up front, as illustrated by Welch's parry of Gabbiadini's shot, which leaves Kitson a simple tap-in for the opener.

8. Southend: City have the chances, but can only register with Baird's late shot, whilst Southend make better use of their opportunities. A defensive mix-up allows Andy Thompson to burst through and bury the ball, whilst Ronnie Whelan's 20-yard floated free-kick finds the top corner of City's net.

9. Middlesbrough: This latest setback brought more criticism cascading down from the Ashton Gate stands. Conceding daft goals doesn't help, and that was certainly the case when Scott was left on his backside as John Hendrie collected Curtis Fleming's long ball to run in and shoot past Welch.

10. Luton: City plunder a win as their only worthwhile attempt on goal condemns the Hatters to their third successive home defeat. A cruel reward for Luton's stylish play as Baird ends City's three-match drought by side-footing in from six yards when Juergen Sommer fails to hold Bent's shot.

11. Millwall: City celebrate with a win after FA chairman Sir Bert Millichip officially opened the Atyeo stand in front of 23 old-timers of the Atyeo era, including the great Geoff Bradford of Bristol Rovers. Whilst Baird's header might not have been up to Atyeo's standard, it is welcome enough.

12 — READING (A) 15/10

9,389 · 15/2 · L · 0-1 · 0-0
Gilkes 90
Ref: K Leach

Welch	Harriott	Humphries	Shail	Bryant	Munro	Allison	Seal*	Baird	Tinnion	Edwards
Hislop	Bernal	Kerr	Wdowczyk	Williams	Holsgrave*	Gilkes	Gooding	Quinn	Hartenberger* Osborn	Murphy/Parkinson

Two minutes of stoppage time had already been played when Michael Gilkes finally got behind City's defence and crashed in a rising shot. A cruel end to a bright City performance that brings their usual quota of chances, including Allison's 81st-minute effort against a goal post.

13 — GRIMSBY (A) 22/10

4,024 · 20/11 · L · 0-1 · 0-0
Childs 61
Ref: A Dawson

Welch	Harriott	Humphries	Shail	Bryant	Munro*	Allison	Seal*	Baird	Tinnion	Edwards
Crichton	Croft	Jobling	Handyside	Lever	Groves	Watson	Dobbin	Livingstone	Woods	Shakespeare* Childs	McAree/Partridge

The ironic cheers from the away fans summed up City's performance, as they struggled to reply to Gary Childs' headed goal. Whilst Partridge has a low shot disallowed, City offer little threat to a Grimsby side weakened by injuries and the departure of manager Alan Buckley.

14 — PORTSMOUTH (H) 29/10

7,238 · 21/14 · D · 1-1 · 1-0
Scott 15p
Powell 80
Ref: A Flood

Welch	Harriott	Scott*	Shail	Bryant	Tinnion	Partridge	Baird	Allison	Edwards
Knight	Gittens	Stimson	Kristensen	Symons	McGrath	Pethick	Preki*	Powell	Creaney* Dobson	Munro/Seal, Rees/Hall

Scott's penalty, after Allison is tripped by keeper Alan Knight, should have made City hungry for goals, but nothing else on target from them for the rest of the match tells its own story. Pompey manage six, and one of them, Darryl Powell's volley, escapes Welch for a deserved point.

15 — WOLVES (H) 1/11

10,401 · 21/1 · L · 1-5 · 1-2 · [65, 87]
Baird 32
Walters 12, Thompson 36p, Kelly 63,
Ref: C Wilkes

Welch	Munro	Shail !	Bryant	Tinnion	Bent*	Seal	Baird	Paterson	Edwards
Stowall	Smith	Thompson	Ferguson	Blades	Venus	Walters	Thomas	Bull*	Kelly	Froggatt Stewart

After Baird crashes the ball into the net for City's stunning equaliser, Shail's sending-off for hauling down Steve Bull and the subsequent penalty changes the course of game. David Kelly continues his remarkable scoring record against City with a hat-trick inside 24 minutes.

16 — SHEFFIELD UTD (A) 5/11

11,568 · 22/15 · L · 0-3 · 0-2
Hartfield 6, Gage 11, Whitehouse 75
Ref: W Burns

Welch	Harriott*	Humphries	Shail	Bryant	Fowler	Wyatt	Seal*	Baird	Paterson	Edwards
Kelly	Gage	Nilsen	Hartfield	Gayle	Marshall	Rogers	Veart*	Starbuck	Blake*	Whitehouse Hodges/Scott

The writing's on the wall for City as they are unable to stop United winning their first game in nine. Charlie Hartfield starts the rot with a drive in off the post, then comes Kevin Gage's 30-yard thunderbolt, before Dane Whitehouse shoots in from ten yards to complete an easy success.

17 — SWINDON (H) 20/11

9,086 · 22/15 · W · 3-2 · 3-2
Bent 54, Allison 56, 63
Scott 58, 89
Ref: P Wright

Kite	Harriott	Scott	Hansen	Bryant	Tinnion	Fowler	Bent	Partridge	Allison	Edwards
Digby	Robinson	Bodin	Tiler	Kitcline*	MacLaren*	Horlock	Beauchamp	Fjortoft	Mutch	Scott	Murray/O'Sullivan

Following Osman's sacking, Jordan's second spell in charge commences with this dazzling live TV spectacular. Bent pops in Frazer Digby's parry of Allison's curling 25-yarder for the opening goal, whilst Keith Scott ends the proceedings by forcing the ball in at the second attempt.

18 — OLDHAM (A) 26/11

7,277 · 22/16 · L · 0-2 · 0-0
Richardson 47, McCarthy 57
Ref: K Breen

Kite	Harriott	Scott	Hansen	Bryant	Tinnion	Fowler*	Bent	Partridge	Allison	Edwards
Gerrard	Makin	Pointon	Henry	Jobson	Redmond	Richardson	Ritchie	McCarthy	Graham	Holden*	Brennan/Banger

Goal-shy City throw the game away, but where they fail Oldham succeed with two quick-fire efforts for a happy first home game for new boss Graeme Sharp. Lee Richardson sends a rising shot into the roof of City's net, then Sean McCarthy follows up to put in his rebound off the post.

19 — GRIMSBY (H) 3/12

6,030 · 23/4 · L · 1-2 · 0-0
Partridge 60
Gilbert 47, Childs 73
Ref: K Cooper

Welch	Parris	Scott	Shail	Bryant	Tinnion	Watson*	Bent	Partridge	Allison	Edwards
Crichton	Croft	Jobling	Handyside	Lever*	Groves	Childs	Dobbin	Livingstone	Woods*	Gilbert	Rodger/Lester

A dream come true for Partridge as he scores against his hometown club with a left-footed shot beyond Paul Crichton's drive. It isn't enough though as Dave Gilbert beats Welch from the edge of the box, and Gary Childs hits an unstoppable volley to secure the points for Grimsby.

20 — BARNSLEY (A) 7/12

4,305 · 23/6 · L · 1-2 · 1-1
Bent 33
Liddell 32, Archdeacon 84
Ref: E Wolstenholme

Welch	Scott	Shail	Hansen	Bryant	Tinnion	Parris	Bent	Partridge	Allison*	Edwards
Butler	Eaden	Fleming	Archdeacon	Taggart	Davis	O'Connell*	Redfearn	Jackson*	Liddell	Sheridan	Payton/Bullock

After Bent had slotted in Scott's defence-splitting pass for a quick equaliser to Andy Liddell's close-range shot, City took the game to their highly-placed rivals. Unfortunately Owen Archdeacon fired in a late goal to deprive City of the point that their spirited performance deserved.

21 — BOLTON (H) 10/12

6,144 · 23/4 · L · 0-1 · 0-1
Patterson 1
Ref: G Singh

Welch	Harriott	Scott	Shail	Bryant	Tinnion	Parris	Bent	Partridge	Allison*	Edwards
Branagan	Green	Phillips	McAteer	Coleman	Stubbs	Lee	Sneekes*	Paatelainen	McGinlay	Patterson	Partridge/Watson, Coyle

City's efforts to keep a clean sheet last just 29 seconds as David Lee's cross is allowed to drift across the area for Mark Patterson to fire in a shot that takes a deflection off Harriott. Without a single shot on target in the first half, City manage two after the break to match Bolton's total.

22 — SUNDERLAND (A) 17/12

11,661 · 23/16 · L · 0-2 · 0-0
Howey 56, 75
Ref: D Allison

Welch	Munro	Scott	Shail	Bryant	Partridge	Parris	Bent	Baird	Allison*	Edwards
Chamberlain	Owers	Kubicki	Bennett	Ball	Melville	Ferguson	Russell	Howey	Smith	Armstrong*	Gray, Mike

Sunderland, with only one previous home success this season, have the luck on their side to quell City's battling display. The referee fails to spot Lee Howey using his hand to push in Sunderland's opener; then the No 9's shot leaves Welch helpless after taking a deflection off Scott.

23 — WEST BROM (A) 26/12

21,071 · 23/18 · L · 0-1 · 0-0
Munro 81 (og)
Ref: T West

Welch	Hansen	Munro	Shail	Bryant	Tinnion	Partridge	Parris	Bent	Baird	Owers*
Naylor	O'Regan	Lilwall	Bradley	Mardon	Edwards	Donovan	Ashcroft	Heggs*	Hunt	Hamilton	Taylor

A cruel Boxing Day knockout as all City's hard work is undone by a farcical own-goal. Munro and Lee Ashcroft tussled for the ball, which ricocheted off the City man's shin towards Welch. The keeper completely missed his attempted clearance as the ball rolled on into the goal.

ENDSLEIGH LEAGUE DIVISION 1

Manager: Osman ⇨ Joe Jordan — SEASON 1994-95

Results summary

No	Date	Venue	Opponent	Pos	W/D/L	F-A	H-T	Att	Opp Pos	Pt
24	27/12	H	STOKE	23	W	3-1	0-0	8,500	11	22
25	31/12	A	TRANMERE	23	L	0-2	0-2	7,439	3	22
26	2/1	H	WATFORD	23	D	0-0	0-0	9,423	9	23
27	14/1	A	PORTSMOUTH	23	D	0-0	0-0	8,808	19	24
28	21/1	H	SHEFFIELD UTD	23	W	2-1	0-0	10,211	6	27
29	4/2	H	BARNSLEY	22	W	3-2	0-0	6,408	9	30
30	11/2	A	WOLVES	22	L	0-2	0-1	25,451	2	30
31	15/2	A	SWINDON	20	W	3-0	1-0	9,992	21	33
32	18/2	H	OLDHAM	20	D	2-2	2-1	7,851	13	34
33	25/2	H	LUTON	21	D	2-2	0-1	7,939	10	35
34	4/3	A	MIDDLESBROUGH	21	L	0-3	0-1	17,371	2	35

Match details

24 — STOKE (H), 27/12
- Scorers/Times: Bryant 66, Allison 78, 80 / Cranson 83. Ref: P Vanes
- Line-up (1–11): Welch, Hansen, Munro, Shail*, Bryant, Tinnion, Paris, Bent, Baird*, Allison, Owers. Subs used: Dryden/Partridge
- Stoke: Sinclair, Butler, Sandford, Cranson, Dreyer^, Orlygsson, Sigardsson, Clarkson, Biggins*, Williams, Gleghorn. Subs: Peschisolido/Shaw

City end a run of six straight defeats with this stylish win. Bryant's unstoppable 30-yarder relieves the tension, then Allison's near-post header finishes off Tinnion's corner, before the No 10 slides in Bent's cross. Stoke's solitary reply comes from Ian Cranson's close-range header.

25 — TRANMERE (A), 31/12
- Scorers/Times: Jones 7, Irons 41. Ref: P Richards
- Line-up (1–11): Welch, Hansen, Munro, Shail, Bryant, Tinnion, Kuhl, Bent, Baird, Allison*, Owers. Subs used: Partridge
- Tranmere: Nixon, Stevens, Irons, McGreal, Higgins, O'Brien, Morrissey, Jones G, Malkin, Nevin, Thomas

After Gary Jones shoots Tranmere ahead from eight yards, City do everything bar score. Nixon is in superb form and does well to keep out a 20-yard pile-driver from Kuhl (£300,000 ex Derby). Kenny Irons completes City's frustrations by nodding in from John Morrissey's cross.

26 — WATFORD (H), 2/1
- Ref: J Kirkby
- Line-up (1–11): Welch, Hansen, Munro, Shail, Bryant, Tinnion, Kuhl, Bent, Baird*, Allison, Edwards. Subs used: Seal
- Watford: Miller, Lavin, Bazeley, Foster, Holdsworth, Ramage, Hessenthaler, Gibbs, Shipperley, Porter, Mooney

City start the new year with the same old problem. They dominate an unspectacular game on a glue-pot pitch, but are unable their translate their possession into goals. Despite a corner count of 15-5 in their favour, City fail to cause Kevin Miller any real concern before the break.

27 — PORTSMOUTH (A), 14/1
- Ref: M Bailey
- Line-up (1–11): Welch, Hansen, Munro, Shail*, Bryant, Tinnion, Kuhl, Bent, Fleck*, Allison, Owers. Subs used: Dryden/Baird
- Portsmouth: Knight, Russell, Daniel, McGrath, Symons, Butters, Pethick, Preki, Powell, Creaney, Wood*. Sub: Hall

It's the same old recurring nightmare as again City's domination does not translate itself into goals. Tinnion is unlucky with a 15th-minute free-kick, as his curling left-foot effort from 30 yards hits the post, but throughout the whole game only Fleck manages to get a shot on target.

28 — SHEFFIELD UTD (H), 21/1
- Scorers/Times: Gayle 55 (og), Shail 75 / Gayle 67. Ref: P Alcock
- Line-up (1–11): Welch, Hansen, Dryden, Shail, Bryant, Tinnion, Edwards, Bent, Fleck, Allison*, Owers. Subs used: Partridge
- Sheffield Utd: Mercer, Gage !, Nilsen, Hartfield, Gayle, Whitehouse, Rogers, Veart, Starbuck, Hodges*, Scott^. Subs: Beesley/Flo

Following Kevin Gage's dismissal for kicking out after being fouled by Edwards, the Blades level from Phil Starbuck's resultant free-kick. Brian Gayle bundles the ball in, but Shail becomes City's unlikely scoring hero with a shot from 18 yards to end Utd's ten-match unbeaten run.

29 — BARNSLEY (H), 4/2
- Scorers/Times: Dryden 53, Bryant 66, Allison 83 / Rammell 48, Wilson 86. Ref: G Singh
- Line-up (1–11): Welch, Hansen, Munro, Dryden, Bryant, Tinnion, Kuhl, Bent, Fleck, Allison*, Owers. Subs used: Baird
- Barnsley: Watson, Eaden, Fleming, Wilson, Shotton, Moses, O'Connell*, Redfearn, Rammell, Liddell, Sheridan. Sub: Bullock

After a poor first half, Andy Rammell leaves City's defence trailing to steer in the opener. Allison makes sure of the points with a well-struck shot off the instep which curls in from 20 yards, but Barnsley's player-manager Danny Wilson has the last word with a 25-yard thunderbolt.

30 — WOLVES (A), 11/2
- Scorers/Times: Dennison 25, Kelly 62. Ref: M Riley
- Line-up (1–11): Welch, Hansen, Munro, Bryant, Dryden, Tinnion, Kuhl, Bent, Fleck, Allison*, Owers. Subs used: Baird
- Wolves: Jones, Blades, Thompson, Emblen*, De Wolf, Law, Rankine^, Kelly, Goodman, Cowans, Dennison. Subs: Bennett/Mills

City create many chances, but waste them all, while Wolves make their limited number count. Robbie Dennison's shot and David Kelly's header do the necessary for the Molineux men, but the nearest City come to a goal is Allison's second-half header that comes back off the bar.

31 — SWINDON (A), 15/2
- Scorers/Times: Bent 7, Fleck 51, Bryant 57. Ref: J Lloyd
- Line-up (1–11): Welch, Hansen, Munro, Bryant, Shail, Tinnion, Kuhl, Bent*, Fleck, Allison, Owers. Subs used: Baird
- Swindon: Hammond, Robinson, Murray, O'Sullivan, Nijholt, Thomson*, Horlock, Beauchamp, Fjortoft, Thorne, Ling. Sub: McMahon

With City's Women's team hogging the limelight after beating Huddersfield 4-3 to reach the Cup semi-finals, the men turn on their own great show to destroy Swindon at the County Ground. Bent is the star as he leads Swindon a merry dance after driving the ball in from eight yards.

32 — OLDHAM (H), 18/2
- Scorers/Times: Allison 8, 34 / Halle 28, Ritchie 82. Ref: G Pooley
- Line-up (1–11): Welch, Hansen, Munro, Shail, Bryant*, Tinnion, Kuhl, Bent, Fleck, Allison, Owers*. Subs used: Dryden/Baird
- Oldham: Gerrard, Snodin, Pointon, Henry, Moore, Redmond, Halle, Ritchie, Banger*, Richardson, Brennan*. Subs: Holden/McCarthy

Oldham are absolutely brilliant as they give City a soccer lesson in all but the art of finishing. How the Latics didn't win after so completely dominating the second-half action is a mystery, but it is unlikely that City will ever be so comprehensively outplayed at Ashton Gate again.

33 — LUTON (H), 25/2
- Scorers/Times: Owers 65, Bent 85 / Oakes 29, 54. Ref: A Flood
- Line-up (1–11): Welch, Hansen, Munro, Dryden, Bryant, Tinnion, Kuhl, Bent, Fleck, Allison, Owers. Subs used: Dryden/Baird
- Luton: Sommer, James, Johnson M, Waddock, Thomas, Peake, Telfer, Oakes, Dixon, Preece*, Marshall. Sub: Williams

The Hatters appear to be cruising after two long-range goals by Scott Oakes, and Juergen Sommer's save of Tinnion's 43rd-minute penalty. Owers then pulls one back from a seemingly offside position, before Bent salvages a point with a brilliant left-footed shot from twelve yards.

34 — MIDDLESBROUGH (A), 4/3
- Scorers/Times: Fuchs 10, 48, 65. Ref: J Parker
- Line-up (1–11): Welch, Hansen, Munro, Shail, Bryant*, Tinnion, Kuhl, Bent, Fleck*, Allison !, Owers. Subs used: Baird/Dryden
- Middlesbrough: Miller, Cox, Whyte, Vickers*, Pearson, Blackmore, Robson, Moreno, Fuchs^, Mustoe, Moore. Subs: Hignett/Wilkinson

City are shown the gap between the top and bottom – and finish a distant second. Allison's controversial dismissal for the 34th-minute challenge on Steve Vickers doesn't help, especially as by then Uwe Fuchs had waltzed around Welch and expertly buried his opener with his right foot.

Matches 35–46

Bottom summary: Home 8,805 · Away 10,220 · Average 8,005

---

35 · H · CHARLTON · 7/3
Pos 20 · W · 2-1 · Pts 38 · Att 6,118 · (14)
Kuhl 33, Tinnion 60 / *Pardew 90*
Ref: J Holbrook

City: Welch, Hansen, Munro*, Dryden, Bryant, Tinnion, Kuhl, Bent, Fleck*, Allison, Owers — Baird
Charlton: *Salmon, Brown^, Stuart*, Jones, Rufus, Balmer, Robson^, Nelson, Pardew, Whyte, Mortimer — Leaburn/Robinson*

For a change it is City who supply the killer instinct to move out of the bottom four. Kuhl's long-range effort and Tinnion's angled drive are City's only on-target efforts, whilst all Charlton have to show for their six shots is Alan Pardew's close-range strike in the dying seconds.

---

36 · A · PORT VALE · 11/3
Pos 21 · L · 1-2 · Pts 38 · Att 7,645 · (15)
Owers 10 / *Scott 7, Naylor 75*
Ref: N Barry

City: Welch, Hansen*, Munro, Dryden, Bryant, Tinnion, Kuhl, Bent, Fleck*, Allison, Owers — Seal/Shail
Port Vale: *Musselwhite, Sandeman, Tankard, Porter, Aspin, Scott, Guppy, Van der Laan, Naylor, Walker, Glover — Foyle**

Andy Porter's drive is deflected into the net off the head of Kevin Scott to give Vale an early lead, but City dominate the first half after Owers' levels with a perfect chip. It is a different story after the break though, and Ray Walker shoots in from close range to reward ascendant Vale.

---

37 · H · BURNLEY · 18/3
Pos 21 · D · 1-1 · Pts 39 · Att 6,717 · (24)
Partridge 13 / *Eyres 65*
Ref: M Pierce

City: Welch, Hansen, Munro, Dryden, Bryant, Edwards, Kuhl, Bent, Partridge*, Allison, Owers — Wyatt
Burnley: *Russell, Harrison, Winstanley, Davis, Vinnicombe !, Randall^, Hoyland, Thompson, Nogan*, Pender, Eyres — Robinson/Parkinson*

It all looks so easy early on as City, already a goal to the good due to Wayne Russell's clearance rebounding off Partridge, have a further advantage with Chris Vinnicombe's 23rd-min sending-off. A dismal second-half display is punished by David Eyres' shot from close range.

---

38 · A · NOTTS CO · 21/3
Pos 22 · D · 1-1 · Pts 40 · Att 5,692 · (24)
Baird 63 / *White 78*
Ref: P Harrison

City: Welch, Hansen, Munro*, Dryden, Bryant, Tinnion, Edwards, Bent, Baird !, Partridge, Owers
Notts Co: *Cherry, Mills, Short*, Russell*, Forsyth, Hogg, Devlin, White, Agana, Nichol, Legg — Turner/Johnson*

After Baird supplies the finishing touch to Partridge's half-hit shot, the scourge of Bristol derbies returns to haunt City. Devon White pounces on Steve Nichol's scuffed effort to nod the loose ball into the top corner to save a point for the newly-crowned Anglo-Italian Cup winners.

---

39 · H · SOUTHEND · 25/3
Pos 21 · D · 0-0 · Pts 41 · Att 6,159 · (16)
Ref: J Brandwood

City: Welch, Hansen, Munro*, Dryden, Bryant, Tinnion, Edwards, Bent, Baird, Partridge, Owers — Flatts
Southend: *Royce, Hone, Powell, Whelan, Badley, Edwards, Jones G*, Sussex, Hails, Tilson, Dublin — Battersby*

Where is the passion to stop City sliding into the Second Division without even a whimper? There was little sign of it on the pitch as two more points slip away in this instantly-forgettable match. A linesman's flag curtails Baird's 56th-min celebrations after turning in Bent's overhead.

---

40 · A · DERBY · 1/4
Pos 21 · L · 1-3 · Pts 41 · Att 14,555 · (8)
Allison 41 / *Gabbiadini 6, Williams 15, Wrack 61*
Ref: J Kirkby

City: Welch, Hansen, Munro*, Dryden, Bryant, Tinnion, Edwards, Bent, Baird, Allison, Owers
Derby: *Hoult, Yates^, Wassall, Trollope, Kavanagh, Williams, Harkes, Pembridge, Mills, Gabbiadini, Simpson^ — Wrack/Sturridge*

A 31st birthday to forget for Baird as he squanders his chances, while Derby capitalise on City's poor defending. Shail's slip allowed Marco Gabbiadini in to beat Welch, while both Paul Williams (bullet header) and Darren Wrack (angled shot) are unmarked when scoring their goals.

---

41 · H · TRANMERE · 8/4
Pos 23 · L · 0-1 · Pts 41 · Att 6,723 · (2)
Aldridge 39p
Ref: P Vanes

City: Welch, Hansen, Munro*, Dryden, Bryant, Tinnion, Kuhl, Bent, Flatts, Allison, Owers — Partridge
Tranmere: *Nixon, Stevens, Mungall, McGreal, Garnett, O'Brien, Brannan, Aldridge, Jones G, Irons, Nevin*

City are left to rue missed chances as they go down to their first home League defeat since early December. After Munro is adjudged to have wrestled Pat Nevin to the ground, John Aldridge incurs the wrath of the crowd with his celebration following his successful spot-kick.

---

42 · A · STOKE · 15/4
Pos 23 · L · 1-2 · Pts 41 · Att 10,158 · (16)
Shail 18 / *Andrade 28, Peschisolido 89*
Ref: D Allison

City: Welch, Hansen, Munro*, Dryden, Bryant, Tinnion, Martin*, Bent, Flatts, Allison, Owers — Baird/Edwards
Stoke: *Sinclair, Butler, Sigurdsson, Wallace, Clarkson, Orlygsson, Allen^, Downing^, Peschisolido, Andrade, Gleghorn — Keen/Carruthers*

Heartbreak as Paul Peschisolido breaks free of City's square defence to round Welch and shoot in Stoke's last-minute winner. A strike that almost guarantees Stoke's survival, whilst City, now seven points short of safety with just four matches remaining, look beyond all hope.

---

43 · H · WEST BROM · 17/4
Pos 23 · W · 1-0 · Pts 44 · Att 8,777 · (17)
Bent 80
Ref: D Orr

City: Welch, Hansen, Munro, Dryden, Bryant, Edwards*, Kuhl*, Bent, Flatts, Allison, Owers — Partridge/Martin
West Brom: *Naylor, Burgess, Agnew, O'Regan, Strodder, Raven^, Donovan, Coldicott, Hunt, Taylor, Hamilton — Smith^/Rees*

Most of the excitement occurs after the game as fire fighters battle to prevent flames from a portaloo spreading to the Covered End. On the pitch, sub Partridge is City's star man, and it is his low centre which ends up in the net after Bent and Paul Agnew challenge for the ball.

---

44 · A · WATFORD · 22/4
Pos 23 · L · 0-1 · Pts 44 · Att 7,190 · (10)
Phillips 62
Ref: S Mathieson

City: Welch, Hansen, Munro*, Dryden, Bryant, Flatts, Kuhl, Bent*, Partridge, Allison, Owers — Tinnion/Baird
Watford: *Miller, Lavin, Page, Holdsworth, Millen, Ramage, Hessenthaler, Payne, Porter, Beadle*, Phillips — Bazeley*

Still in with a chance of survival before this game, City's continuing lack of a killer punch condemns them to the drop. Watford, with five shots on target and ten off-target efforts, also suffer from the same malaise, but Kevin Phillips at least manages to register with a diving header.

---

45 · H · READING · 29/4
Pos 23 · L · 1-2 · Pts 44 · Att 9,474 · (2)
Tinnion 87 / *Lovell 18, Nogan 58*
Ref: P Wright

City: Welch, Hansen*, Munro, Dryden, Bryant, Tinnion, Martin, Bryant*, Partridge*, Allison, Owers — Seal/Fowler
Reading: *Hislop, Bernal, Osborn, Widowczyk*, Williams, McPherson, Gilkes, Gooding, Lovell, Nogan, Taylor — Parkinson*

Inept, passionless City are easily swept away by Reading after Stuart Lovell puts the Royals in front when deftly heading in Simon Osborn's free-kick. Lee Nogan then gets the final touch to another free-kick, before the disaffected Tinnion shoots City's reply into an empty net.

---

46 · A · MILLWALL · 7/5
Pos 23 · D · 1-1 · Pts 45 · Att 8,805 · (12)
Allison 26 / *Dixon 21*
Ref: T West

City: Welch, Hansen*, Munro, Dryden, Bryant*, Partridge*, Martin, Kuhl, Baird, Allison, Edwards — Hewlett/Paterson
Millwall: *Keller, Beard, Thatcher, Roberts, Witter, Stevens*, McRoberts^, Rae, Dixon, Oldfield, Van Blerk — Forbes/Taylor*

With the country in nostalgic vein due to the build-up to the 50th-anniversary celebrations of VE Day, City capture some of the old bulldog spirit themselves. Allison seizes on Tony Witter's misplaced headed back-pass to steer in City's leveller to Kerry Dixon's twelve-yard shot.

ENDSLEIGH DIVISION 1 (CUP-TIES)   Manager: Osman ⇨ Joe Jordan   SEASON 1994-95

Coca-Cola Cup

				F-A	H-T	Scorers, Times, and Referees
2:1	H	NOTTS CO 20/9	2,546 17 23 L	0-1	0-0	Devlin 87 / Ref: P Wright
2:2	A	NOTTS CO 27/9	2,721 20 24 L	0-3	0-1	Jemson 16, Lund 48, 74 / Ref: G Cain / (City lost 0-4 on aggregate)

Lineups – Coca-Cola Cup

	1	2	3	4	5	6	7	8	9	10	11	—	subs used
2:1	Welch	Herriott	Scott	Shail	Bryant	Tinnion	McAree	Bent	Loss*	Partridge	Edwards		Brown 1
	Cherry	*Sherlock*	*Murphy*	*Turner*	*Johnson*	*Yates*	*Devlin*	*Legg*	*McSwegan**	*Simpson*			*Jemson/Agana*
2:2	Welch	Munro	Scott	Shail	Paterson	Tinnion	McAree*	Bent*	Lund	Bryant	Edwards		Fowler/Brown 1
	Cherry	*Mills*	*Johnson*	*Turner*	*Yates*	*Murphy*	*Devlin*	*Legg*	*Lund*	*Jemson**	*Agana*		*Matthews*

With City's three blanks in four home outings it is perhaps not surprising that the public mood is reflected in the lowest Ashton Gate League Cup attendance. In this game it is the same old tale as City cannot score, giving County's Andy Legg the chance to show how from 15 yards.

City's defensive problems are now becoming almost as worrying as those up front. Nigel Jemson gets behind Paterson to control Gary Mills' 40-yard pass on his chest and shoot past Welch from eight yards to destroy any hopes City may have had in overcoming a first-leg deficit.

FA Cup

				F-A	H-T	Scorers, Times, and Referees
3	H	STOKE 7/1	9,683 23 12 D	0-0	0-0	Ref: K Cooper
3R	A	STOKE 18/1	11,579 23 14 W	3-1 aet	0-1	Bent 71, Baird 93, Tinnion 119 / Scott 17 / Ref: K Cooper
4	H	EVERTON 29/1	19,816 23 P:17 L	0-1	0-0	Jackson 79 / Ref: T Holbrook

Lineups – FA Cup

	1	2	3	4	5	6	7	8	9	10	11	—	subs used
3	Welch	Hansen	Munro	Shail	Bryant	Tinnion	Kuhl	Bent	Baird*	Allison	Owers		Partridge
	Sinclair	*Butler*	*Sandford*	*Cranson*	*Overson*	*Orlygsson*	*Clarkson*	*Downing**	*Scott*	*Peschisolido*	*Gleghorn*		*Sturridge/Sigurdsson*
3R	Welch	Hansen	Munro	Shail	Bryant	Tinnion	Kuhl*	Bent	Baird	Allison*	Owers		Edwards/Partridge
	Sinclair	*Clarkson**	*Sandford*	*Cranson*	*Overson*	*Orlygsson*	*Butler*	*Wallace*	*Scott*	*Peschisolido*	*Gleghorn*		*Carruthers*
4	Welch	Hansen	Munro	Shail	Bryant*	Tinnion	Edwards	Bent	Partridge*	Allison	Owers		Seal/Dryden
	Southall	*Jackson*	*Burrows*	*Home*	*Watson*	*Unsworth*	*Limpar*	*Parkinson*	*Barlow*	*Rideout*	*Hinchcliffe**		*Stuart*

Stoke only seem interested in hanging on for a replay as Owers (£300,000 ex Sunderland) and Kuhl control the midfield in this low-key cup-tie. Partridge nearly supplies the breakthrough as he leaves Ronnie Sinclair floundering, only for Lee Sandford to kick his shot off the line.

After a jaded first-half display in which they never look like responding to Keith Scott's back header, City suddenly find the form to leave Stoke trailing in their wake. Bent equalises with a powerful cross shot, and Baird hits the ball on the rise to put City ahead early in extra-time.

'We needed all the luck of the Cup to get through' says Everton boss Joe Royle. City should have won, both Partridge and Allison being denied by a post, but Matt Jackson's spectacular 20-yard left-foot volley into the roof of the Covered End goal wins it for the Toffee men.

		P	Home W	D	L	F	A	Away W	D	L	F	A	Pts
1	Middlesbro	46	15	4	4	41	19	8	9	6	26	21	82
2	Reading	46	12	7	4	34	21	11	3	9	24	23	79
3	Bolton *	46	16	6	1	43	13	5	8	10	24	32	77
4	Wolves	46	15	5	3	39	18	6	8	9	38	43	76
5	Tranmere	46	17	4	2	51	23	5	6	12	16	35	76
6	Barnsley	46	15	6	2	42	19	5	6	12	21	33	72
7	Watford	46	14	6	3	33	17	5	7	11	19	29	70
8	Sheffield Utd	46	12	9	2	41	21	4	11	8	33	34	68
9	Derby	46	12	6	5	44	23	6	6	11	22	28	66
10	Grimsby	46	12	7	4	36	19	5	7	11	26	37	65
11	Stoke	46	10	7	6	31	21	6	8	9	19	32	63
12	Millwall	46	11	8	4	36	22	5	6	12	24	38	62
13	Southend	46	13	2	8	33	25	5	6	12	21	48	62
14	Oldham	46	12	7	4	34	21	4	6	13	26	39	61
15	Charlton	46	11	6	6	33	25	5	5	13	25	41	59
16	Luton	46	8	6	9	35	30	8	4	11	26	34	58
17	Port Vale	46	11	5	7	30	24	4	8	11	28	40	58
18	Portsmouth	46	9	8	6	31	28	6	5	12	22	35	58
19	West Brom	46	13	3	7	33	24	3	7	13	18	33	58
20	Sunderland	46	5	12	6	22	22	7	6	10	19	23	54
21	Swindon	46	9	6	8	28	27	3	6	14	26	46	48
22	Burnley	46	8	7	8	36	33	3	6	14	13	41	46
23	BRISTOL CITY	46	8	8	7	26	28	3	4	16	16	35	45
24	Notts Co	46	7	8	8	26	28	2	5	16	19	38	40
		1104	275	153	124	838	551	124	153	275	551	838	1503

* promoted after play-offs

promoted
after play-offs

Odds & ends

Double wins: (1) Swindon.

Double losses: (6) Derby, Middlesbrough, Reading, Grimsby, Wolves, Tranmere.

Won from behind: (1) Barnsley (h).

Lost from in front: (1) Stoke (a).

High spots: Doing the double over Swindon.
Oldham's brilliant display at Ashton Gate on 18 February.
Beating Stoke 3-1 at Ashton Gate on 27 December.
Winning FA Cup replay at Stoke after extra-time.

Low spots: Wolves 5-1 win at Ashton Gate on 1 November.
Matt Jackson's 20-yard volley that deprives City of an FA Cup upset against Everton.
Losing the Gloucestershire Cup Final 11-10 on penalties v Bristol Rov at Twerton on 3 August.

Player of the year: Matt Bryant.
Ever-presents: (0).
Hat-tricks: (0).
Leading scorer: Wayne Allison (13).

Appearances / Goals

	App Lge	Sub	LC	Sub	FAC	Sub	Goals Lge	LC	FAC	Tot
Allison, Wayne	37						13			13
Baird, Ian	28	9	1		2		6		1	7
Bent, Junior	40	1	2		3		6		1	7
Brown, Ian	1					2				
Bryant, Matt	37		2		3		3			3
Dryden, Richard	15	4	2	1	1	1	1			1
Edwards, Rob	29	1	2	1	1	1				
Flatts, Mark	4	2								
Fleck, Robert	10						1			1
Fowler, Jason	10	3		1						
Hansen, Vergard	29				3					
Harriott, Marvin	19	1								
Hewlett, Matt		1								
Humphries, Mark	4									
Kite, Phil	2									
Kuhl, Martin	17				2		1			1
Loss, Colin	3	2	1							
McAree, Rodney	4	2	2							
McKop, Henry		1			1					
Martin, David	3	1			1					
Munro, Stuart	29	2	1		3					
Owers, Gary	21				3		2			2
Parris, George	6									
Partridge, Scott	14	19	1		1	2	2			2
Paterson, Scott	2	1	1		1					
Seal, David	5	4				1				
Scott, Martin	18		2		3		2			2
Shail, Mark	37	1	2		3		2			2
Simpson, Fitzroy	4									
Tinnion, Brian	33	2	2		3		2		1	3
Watson, Kevin	1									
Welch, Keith	44		2		3					
Wyatt, Mike	1	2								
(own-goals)							1			1
33 players used	506	59	22	3	33	5	42		3	45

ENDSLEIGH LEAGUE DIVISION 2 Manager: Joe Jordan SEASON 1995-96

Match results

No		Opponent	Date	Att	Pos	Pt	F-A	H-T	Scorers, Times, and Referees
1	H	BLACKPOOL	12/8	7,617	—	D 1	1-1	1-1	Seal 20 / Quinn 1 / Ref: G Pooley
2	H	STOCKPORT	26/8	7,331	—	W 4	1-0	1-0	Seal 29 / Ref: A D'Urso
3	A	SHREWSBURY	29/8	2,558	16 / 18	L 4	1-4	1-0	Agostino 21 [Rowbotham 88] / Reed 47, Spink 55, Dempsey 57, / Ref: U Rennie
4	A	PETERBOROUGH	2/9	4,621	16 / 19	D 5	1-1	0-1	Farrell 3 / Ref: M Riley
5	H	BRIGHTON	9/9	7,585	22 / 14	L 5	0-1	0-1	Berry 8 / Ref: G Singh
6	H	BRENTFORD	12/9	5,054	22 / 17	D 6	0-0	0-0	Ref: A Wiley
7	A	BRADFORD C	16/9	5,165	22 / 4	L 6	0-3	0-1	Showler 37, Shutt 62, 66 / Ref: T Heibron
8	A	NOTTS CO	23/9	5,251	22 / 4	D 7	2-2	0-0	Agostino 57, Seal 85 / Legg 49, White 55 / Ref: P Taylor
9	H	WYCOMBE	30/9	5,564	22 / 11	D 8	0-0	0-0	Ref: J Brandwood
10	A	SWINDON	7/10	12,378	23 / 1	L 8	0-2	0-1	O'Sullivan 12, Allison 88 / Ref: R Gifford
11	H	HULL	14/10	5,354	21 / 24	W 11	4-0	1-0	Bent 25, 61, Starbuck 58, Barnard 80 / Ref: P Rejer

Line-ups (City player / *opponent*)

No	1	2	3	4	5	6	7	8	9	10	11	subs used
1	Welch /*Capleton*	Hansen /*Brown R*	Munro /*Barlow*	Dryden /*Lydiate*	McLeary /*Mellon*	Kuhl /*Bradshaw*	Barber /*Quinn**	Bent /*Bonner*	Agostino /*Gouck*	Seal /*Ellis*	Partridge /*Preece*	Partridge /*Bryan*
2	Welch /*Edwards*	Hansen /*Connelly*	Shail /*Todd*	McLeary /*Bennett*	Dryden /*Flynn*	Kuhl /*Gannon*	Bent /*Beaumont*	Armstrong /*Ware*	Seal /*Helliwell**	Agostino /*Armstrong*	Barber* /*Williams**	Plummer/Partridge /*Mike/Eckhard*
3	Welch /*Clarke*	Hansen /*Scott*	Shail* /*Reed*	McLeary /*Taylor*	Dryden /*Withe*	Kuhl /*Stewart*	Bent /*Berkley*	Armstrong /*Rowbotham*	Seal /*Spink*	Agostino /*Walton*	Barber* /*Dempsey*	Bryant/Plummer
4	Welch* /*Sheffield*	Bryant /*Williams*	Munro /*Rioch*	McLeary* /*Ebdon*	Dryden /*Breen*	Kuhl /*Heald*	Bent /*Le Bihan**	Armstrong /*Manuel*	Seal /*Power**	Agostino /*Farrell*	Fowler* /*Morrison**	Shail/Kite/Partridge /*M'dale/Carter/McG'sh*
5	Kite /*Rust*	Bryant /*Myall**	Munro /*Chapman*	Shail /*Wilkins*	Dryden /*Foster*	Kuhl /*McCarthy*	Bent /*Storer*	Armstrong* /*McDougall*	Seal /*Bull**	Agostino* /*Minton*	Fowler* /*Berry**	Owers/Plum'r/P'tridge /*Smith/Byrne/Andrews*
6	Kite /*Dearden*	Hansen /*Statham*	Edwards /*Grainger*	Shail /*McGhee*	Bryant /*Bates*	Kuhl /*Ashby*	Bent* /*Mundee*	Owers /*Smith*	Seal /*Forster*	Agostino* /*Hooker*	Armstrong /*Taylor**	Partridge/Plummer /*Asaba*
7	Kite /*Ward*	Hansen /*Huxford*	Edwards /*Jacobs*	Dryden /*Mitchell*	Bryant /*Mohan*	Kuhl /*Ford*	Owers* /*Wright*	Bent /*Youlds**	Seal* /*Shutt*	Ormondroyd /*Showler*	Armstrong /*Murray*	Agostino
8	Dykstra /*Ward*	Hansen /*Gallagher*	Edwards /*Walker*	Dryden /*Nichol*	Bryant /*Strodder*	Kuhl /*Murphy*	Plummer* /*Simpson*	Owers* /*Galloway**	Agostino* /*White*	Baird* /*Atkins*	Starbuck /*Legg*	Bent/Seal /*Short/Agana*
9	Dykstra /*Hyde*	Paterson /*Rowbotham*	Hansen /*Hardyman*	Bryant /*Howard*	Dryden /*Cousins*	Edwards /*Patterson*	Owers* /*Carroll*	Bent /*Brown*	Nugent /*De Souza*	Williams* /*Williams**	Starbuck /*Farrell*	Seal /*McGavin*
10	Dykstra /*Digby*	Starbuck /*Culverhouse*	Edwards /*Bodin*	Dryden /*McMahon*	Bryant /*Seagraves*	Kuhl /*Taylor*	Bent /*Robinson*	Owers /*O'Sullivan*	Nugent /*Finney*	Paterson* /*Allison*	Barnard /*Horlock*	Agostino
11	Dykstra /*Wilson*	Starbuck* /*Watson*	Edwards /*Lawford*	Dryden /*Hobson**	Bryant /*Humphries*	Kuhl* /*Abbott*	Bent /*Peacock**	Owers /*Williams*	Nugent /*Brown*	Paterson /*Windass*	Barnard /*Mann*	Agostino/Tinnion /*Lee/Fewings/Lowth'pe*

Match reports

1. Rocked by the day's fastest goal on just twelve secs when James Quinn swivelled to send his shot past Welch, City are fortunate not to be three down before Seal's super 25-yard chip settles their nerves. Thereafter City enjoy the greater share of the possession, but can't force a winner.

2. This game won't go down as one of the best, but the match-winning strike surely must. Collecting the ball out on the left, Seal strides a couple of spaces before letting fly with a 30-yard right-footed drive which curled and dipped beyond the dive of Neil Edwards and into the top corner.

3. Gay Meadow is anything but a happy place for City as they suffer one of their most humiliating defeats in recent years. After Agostino had swept in Bent's low centre City dominated the first half, but Ian Reed's shot through a crowded penalty area sparks a second-half collapse.

4. With Welch being taken to hospital with a back injury in the 81st minute, it is fortunate that Jordan had opted for a keeper on the bench for only the second time this season. Seal conjures up a drive of immense power for City's deserved point following Sean Farrell's angled opener.

5. 'You won't see better football than that in this Division' is the opinion of Brighton boss Liam Brady after watching his side tear City apart. Only one goal, Greg Berry drilling the ball past the unprotected Kite, but it should have been more as City's midfield offered little resistance.

6. City show more commitment than on Saturday, but the nearest to a goal is early on. Bent must be kicking himself for being caught offside when Armstrong and Seal set him up for an easy tap-in, whilst for Brentford, Nicky Forster put his 35th-minute free header against a post.

7. Woeful City are left in tatters with a display bereft of confidence, imagination, as well as simple ability. Bradford, unfortunate perhaps when Tommy Wright's earlier effort is disallowed for offside, take a lucky lead when Kite allows Paul Showler's shot to spin out of his grasp.

8. Appealing for offside when Andy Legg runs through, City's defence fails again when Devon White fires in from a narrow angle. Fortunately the Aussies save the day. Seal stabbing in a loose ball to secure a point, after Agostino had earlier held off two challenges to shoot into the net.

9. Only Paul Hyde's super save from Bent's volley in the closing seconds denies City the win that their improved play after the break deserved. With Paterson operating as a sweeper, City look solid at the back, and the presence of Nugent adds much needed aggression to the attack.

10. Dykstra makes amends for conceding a 32nd pen when his trailing leg tripped Mark Robinson after winning the ball. He saves Paul Bodin's spot-kick with his legs, but is unable to do anything about either of the close-in shots that put Swindon four points clear at the top of the table.

11. The fans chant 'sign him on' as Starbuck ends his month's loan from Sheffield Utd. He nets with a perfectly-angled drive from Bent's pass to put City two up after Hull had threatened in the first half with Linton Brown failing in front of an open goal, as well as being denied by a post.

12 | A | YORK | 21/10 | 19 | 18 14 | W 1-0 | 3,367

City lineup: Dykstra, Paterson!, Edwards, Bryant, Kuhl, Owers, Nugent, Barnard, **Carey***, Shail
York: *Warrington, McMillan, Hall, Jordan*, Barras, Williams, Barnes, Peverall, Murty, Bushell/Baker*

Nugent 24
Ref: D Allison

Skipper Gary Owers inspires City's victory at Bootham Crescent as York go down to their third defeat in four games since their epic League triumph over Man Utd. Nugent chests down a long through-ball to shoot into one corner of the goal as Andy Warrington dived the other way.

---

13 | H | WALSALL | 28/10 | 21 | 16 14 | L 0-2 | 6,475

City lineup: Dykstra, Paterson*, Edwards, Bryant, Kuhl, Owers, Nugent, Barnard, Carey*, Agostino/Shail
Walsall: *Walker, Evans*, Rogers, Marsh, Palmer*, Bradley", O'Connor, Lightbourne, Wilson, Watkins/Mtam'k/B'tter*

Houghton 8, Wilson 33
Ref: B Knight

City have the chances, but both Agostino and Owers are denied by the woodwork as their mini-revival comes to an end. Caught on the break when Scott Houghton's low shot finds the back of the net, City succumb again as Kevin Wilson's cracking shot takes a deflection past Dykstra.

---

14 | H | CHESTERFIELD | 31/10 | 18 | 8 17 | W 2-1 | 4,408

City lineup: Dykstra, Paterson, Edwards, Bryant, Kuhl, Owers, Nugent, Barnard, Agostino*, Seal
Chesterfield: *Mercer, Rogers, Dyche, Williams, Law, Davies, Roberts", Morris*, Howard", Hazell/Lornor/Perkins*

Barnard 15, Morris 53 (og), Robinson 6
Ref: D Orr

Phil Robinson's unstoppable volley is followed by Barnard's great left-footed shot from a 30-yard free-kick, before Billy Mercer hands the points to City. He completely misses the ball as Andy Morris's sliced skywards clearance bounces down and rebounds into the roof of the net.

---

15 | A | OXFORD | 4/11 | 19 | 12 17 | L 0-2 | 5,665

City lineup: Dykstra, McLeary*, Shail, Bryant, Kuhl, Owers, Nugent, Barnard, Agostino*, Tinnion/Seal
Oxford: *Whitehead, Robinson", Ford M, Elliott, Gilchrist, Massey, Moody, Rush", Ford B, Beauchamp/Murphy, Angel*

Angel 83, Murphy 90
Ref: I Hemley

A calamitous error by Shail ends City's brave resistance. He has plenty of time to deal with Mark Angel's drive that comes back off a post, but pushes the ball straight back to the No 11, who fires in an unstoppable shot. Matt Murphy finishes off City from a narrow angle in injury-time.

---

16 | H | CARLISLE | 18/11 | 20 | 21 18 | D 1-1 | 5,423

City lineup: Welch, Edwards, Dryden, Shail", Kuhl, Owers, Nugent, Barnard, Partridge*, Agostino/Plummer
Carlisle: *Caig, Edmondson, Gallimore, Thorpe, Bennett, Hayward, Prokas, Currie, Reeves, Aspinall*, Murray/Thomas*

Nugent 56, Currie 48
Ref: M Pierce

After ten successive games with a sweeper, City lack the killer touch to take advantage of the greater attacking options that a switch to a flat back four produces. Nugent equalises David Currie's free-kick opener from 30 yards, with a shot that deflects in off Darren Edmondson.

---

17 | A | ROTHERHAM | 25/11 | 18 | 19 21 | W 3-2 | 2,649

City lineup: Welch, Edwards, Bryant, Shail", Kuhl, Owers, Nugent, Barnard, Seal*, Dryden/Partridge
Rotherham: *Muggleton, Smith, Garner, Monington, Blades, Berry, McGlashan, Jeffrey, Goater, Roscoe*

Barnard 26, Owers 64, Seal 65; Goater 20, 84
Ref: I Cruikshanks

An all-action match that climaxes with Owers' handball gifting Rotherham an 86th-min penalty. Shaun Goater, though, misses his hat-trick as he lifts the rebound over the top after Welch had beaten out his spot-kick. A well-deserved win for City who top the shooting stakes 15-10.

---

18 | A | CREWE | 5/12 | 19 | 2 21 | L 2-4 | 2,977

City lineup: Welch, Edwards, Bryant, Shail, Kuhl, Owers, Nugent, Barnard, Seal*, Tinnion
Crewe: *Gayle, Collins, Booty, Westwood", Macauley, Savage", Murphy, Adebola, Lennon, Unsworth/Smith*

Nugent 30, Dryden 75 [Carey 90 (og)]; Adebola 60, Booty 61, Lennon 85
Ref: P Richard

A cruel end to a hugely entertaining game after Nugent had slid in City's opener to threaten Crewe's unbeaten home record. In the dying secs Carey turns a cross into his own net shortly after Neil Lennon had fired Crewe into the lead with his drive from just inside the penalty area.

---

19 | H | NOTTS CO | 9/12 | 20 | 2 21 | L 0-2 | 5,617

City lineup: Welch, Carey, Edwards, Shail", Kuhl, Owers, Nugent, Barnard*, Seal*, Agost'o/Tin'/McLeary
Notts Co: *Ward, Mills, Baraclough, Turner, Strodder, Murphy, Gallagher", Simpson, Devlin, Arkins, Legg*, Agana/White*

Strodder 9, White 89
Ref: R Gifford

After Gary Strodder gets to Andy Legg's long throw before Welch to head in County's opener, City dominate, but fail to turn their midfield control into goals. The wags in the crowd display their displeasure by holding up every number from 1 to 11 when substitutions are made.

---

20 | A | WYCOMBE | 16/12 | 18 | 9 22 | D 1-1 | 4,020

City lineup: Welch, Carey, Hewlett, Bryant, Kuhl, Owers, Nugent, Barnard, Tinnion, Agostino
Wycombe: *Roberts, Rowbotham, Bell, Howard, Evans, Cousins, Carroll, Garner*, De Souza, Blissett, Farrell, McGavin*

Tinnion 70, Blissett 13
Ref: P Taylor

Instead of collapsing after Dave Farrell's centre is turned in by Gary Blissett, City take a grip on the match which tightens as the match progresses. Tinnion earns a point with one of his best-ever goals – a great 30-yard drive over the outstretched fingers of keeper Ben Roberts.

---

21 | A | BURNLEY | 23/12 | 17 | 5 23 | D 0-0 | 9,327

City lineup: Welch, Carey, Hewlett, McLeary, Bryant*, Kuhl, Owers, Nugent, Agostino*, Tinnion/Seal
Burnley: *Beresford, Brass, Vinnicombe*, Hoyland, Winstanley", Harrison", Weller", Joyce, Cooke", Nogan, Eyres, Adams/McMinn/Swan*

Ref: K Lynch

Gary Owers has City's best chance just before half-time, but his stumble over Marlon Beresford's outstretched leg allows time for Jamie Hoyland to run back and block his eventual shot. City's stylish display is let down by the fact that they can only muster one shot on target.

---

22 | H | SWANSEA | 26/12 | 17 | 22 26 | W 1-0 | 6,845

City lineup: Welch, Carey, Hewlett*, McLeary, Paterson, Kuhl, Owers, Nugent, Agostino*, Tinnion/Plummer
Swansea: *Freestone, Jones, Clode, Walker, Edwards, Penney", Hurst", Ampadu, Torpey, Comforth, B'well/Eboro Pascoe/Chapple, Seal*

Kuhl 90
Ref: J Rushton

After close on a dozen games of flattering to deceive, City at last turn their possession into points, even if it does take until the third minute of injury-time. Kuhl seizes on a half clearance from Tinnion's centre, to squeeze a left-foot shot past Roger Freestone from twelve yards.

---

23 | A | BOURNEMOUTH | 6/1 | 16 | 12 27 | D 1-1 | 3,667

City lineup: Welch, Carey, Edwards, Shail*, Kuhl, Owers, Nugent, Barnard*, Tinnion, Paterson/Seal
Bournemouth: *Andrews, Young, Beardsmore, Murray*, Nah, Holland, Robinson, Jones", Bailey, Mean/Santos, Bent, Brissett*

Maskell 39, Morris 52
Ref: I Hemley

City are robbed ten minutes from time as the officials fail to note that a header from Edwards was over the line before the ball was cleared. After Tinnion's low centre sets up Maskell for an easy tap-in, Mark Morris is unchallenged when rising high to firmly head past Welch.

ENDSLEIGH LEAGUE DIVISION 2 — Manager: Joe Jordan — SEASON 1995-96

Match results

No	Date	H/A	Opponent	Att	Pos		Pt	Res	F-A	H-T	Scorers, Times, and Referees
24	13/1	H	CREWE	6,790	16	2	30	W	3-2	2-1	Paterson 4, Nugent 25, 67 / Booty 18, Westwood 59 / Ref: M Fletcher
25	16/1	H	BRISTOL ROV	20,007	16	13	30	L	0-2	0-0	Beadle 73, 75 / Ref: G Singh
26	20/1	A	BLACKPOOL	4,838	16	3	30	L	0-3	0-1	Morrison 34, Ellis 56, Preece 73p / Ref: T West
27	23/1	A	WREXHAM	2,673	17	10	31	D	0-0	0-0	Ref: A Wiley
28	10/2	H	BOURNEMOUTH	6,217	17	12	34	W	3-0	2-0	Seal 13, Tinnion 21, Agostino 57 / Ref: K Leach
29	13/2	H	SHREWSBURY	5,269	15	10	37	W	2-0	0-0	Agostino 70, 89 / Ref: B Knight
30	17/2	A	BRENTFORD	5,213	15	19	38	D	2-2	0-1	Agostino 48, Barnard 56 / McGhee 35, Taylor 67 / Ref: F Stretton
31	20/2	H	PETERBOROUGH	5,014	16	17	38	L	0-1	0-0	Charlery 55 / Ref: J Brandwood
32	24/2	H	BRADFORD C	5,400	13	11	41	W	2-1	1-0	Seal 20, Kuhl 79 / Wright 64 / Ref: P Rejer
33	27/2	A	BRIGHTON	4,739	11	23	44	W	2-0	1-0	Kuhl 37, 49 / Ref: A D'Urso
34	2/3	A	SWANSEA	4,109	11	21	44	L	1-2	0-2	Walker 46 (og) / Chapple 9, Molby 28 / Ref: G Pooley

Line-ups (City player / *opponent*)

No	1	2	3	4	5	6	7	8	9	10	11	Subs used
24	Welch / *Gayle*	Carey / *Collins*	Edwards / *Booty*	McLeary / *Westwood*	Paterson / *Barr*	Kuhl / *Whalley*	Maskell / *Rivers*	Hewlett / *Murphy^*	Nugent / *Adebola*	Bent / *Lemon*	Tinnion / *Edwards**	Garvey/Unsworth
25	Welch / *Parkin*	Carey / *Channing*	Edwards / *Gurney*	McLeary / *Browning*	Paterson / *Clark*	Kuhl / *Tilson*	Maskell* / *Armstrong*	Hewlett* / *Miller*	Nugent / *Stewart*	Owers / *Matthew*	Tinnion / *Beadle*	Bent/Br'nard/Agostino
26	Welch / *Banks*	Carey / *Bryan*	Edwards / *Brown*	McLeary / *Linighan*	Paterson / *Mellon*	Kuhl / *Quinn^*	Maskell* / *Lydiate*	Hewlett* / *Bonner^*	Nugent! / *Morrison*	Owers / *Ellis*	Tinnion / *Preece*	Bent/Agostino Watson/Gouck
27	Welch / *Marriott*	Carey / *Brace*	Edwards / *Hardy*	Barnard / *Phillips^*	Paterson / *Jones B*	Kuhl / *McGregor*	Maskell* / *Skimer*	Hewlett / *Russell^*	Nugent / *Connolly*	Owers / *Watkin*	Tinnion / *Hughes*	Agostino Owen/Morris
28	Welch / *Andrews*	Carey^ / *Oldbury^*	Barnard / *Beardsmore*	McLeary / *Morris*	Bryant / *Casper*	Kuhl / *Bailey*	Bent* / *Holland*	Hewlett / *Mean^*	Seal / *Jones*	Agostino / *Robinson*	Tinnion / *Brisett*	Plummer/Hansen Victory/Santos/'R'son
29	Welch / *Edwards*	Carey / *Seabury*	Barnard / *Boden*	Barnard / *Taylor*	Bryant / *Whiston*	Kuhl / *Scott*	Bent / *Dempsey*	Hewlett / *Stevens*	Seal / *Anthrobus*	Agostino / *Walton*	Tinnion / *Berkley**	Woods
30	Welch / *Dearden*	Carey / *Harvey*	Barnard / *Anderson*	Barnard / *Hutchings*	Bryant / *Bates*	Kuhl / *McGhee*	Bent* / *Canham**	Hewlett / *Smith*	Seal / *Forster*	Agostino / *Bent^*	Tinnion / *Taylor*	Martin/Omigie
31	Welch / *Sheffield*	Carey* / *Bastham*	Barnard / *Clark*	McLeary / *Sedgemore*	Bryant / *Foran*	Kuhl / *Heald*	Bent* / *Martindale*	Hewlett* / *Ebdon*	Seal / *Farrell*	Agostino" / *Charlery*	Tinnion / *Carter*	Owers Plum'r/Owers/Nugent
32	Welch / *Ward*	Carey* / *Liburd*	Barnard / *Brightwell*	McLeary / *Mohan*	Bryant / *Kernaghan*	Kuhl / *Mitchell*	Hewlett / *Wright*	Owers / *Duxbury*	Seal / *Showler**	Agostino / *Stallard**	Tinnion / *Murray^*	Bent/Nugent O'royll/Jewell/Shutt
33	Welch / *Rust*	Owers / *Myall*	Barnard / *Chapman*	McLeary / *Parris*	Bryant / *Johnson*	Kuhl / *McCarthy*	Bent / *Mundee^*	Hewlett / *Byrne^*	Seal^ / *Minton*	Agostino / *Storer*	Tinnion / *McDonald*	Nugent McDougald/Fox
34	Welch / *Freestone*	Owers / *Clode*	Barnard / *Cook*	McLeary / *Molby*	Bryant / *Edwards**	Kuhl / *Ampadu^*	Bent* / *Hodge"*	Hewlett / *Chapple*	Seal^ / *Torpey*	Agostino / *Comforth*	Tinnion / *Penney*	Nugent Walker/Coates/Th'mas

Match reports

24 CREWE — This hugely entertaining encounter is settled entirely against the run of play by Nugent, who buries a superb left-foot shot in the corner of Mark Gayle's net. City's win is entirely down to their resilience as skilful Crewe dominated the play with their measured passing football

25 BRISTOL ROV — Fiasco at the Gate with many thousands, including season ticket holders, locked out. Despite the mayhem, three gates trampled down and fans standing in the aisles, the kick-off is only delayed 15 mins. Peter Beadle's tap-in and superb angled-drive secures a deserved win for Rovers.

26 BLACKPOOL — Jordan was unrepentant after his on-pitch protest to the referee following Nugent's 20th-minute sending off for supposedly elbowing Phil Brown in the face. City are often exposed by Mark Bonner, and his cross to Tony Ellis sees the striker up-ended by McLeary for Pool's pen.

27 WREXHAM — In sub-zero temperatures at the Racecourse Ground, Paterson is a rock at the heart of City's defence as they weather Wrexham's early storm. After the break City have the best of things, but Owers fires wide from the edge of the box and Agostino screws a twelve-yard effort wide.

28 BOURNEMOUTH — With rival boardroom factions battling for control and City losing £9K per week, at least the thrilling action in this match brings back the smiles. Sandwiched between Seal's stunning volley and Agostino's shot into an open net, Tinnion's head is the unlikely source of City's second.

29 SHREWSBURY — After passing a fitness test on his injured leg an hour before the kick-off, Bent is City's star as he sends in a stream of crosses. Agostino gets on the end of a deep centre to head City in front, before finding it necessary to use his head again to put away a high spinning ball.

30 BRENTFORD — Champagne football from City, but failure to kill off the opposition makes the bubbles go flat. Despite 17 goal attempts City have to be content with Agostino equalising David McGhee's headed opener by side-footing in a rebound, and Barnard curling a 20-yard free-kick into the net.

31 PETERBOROUGH — The errors that made the first half of the season so disappointing return to haunt City as they gift the Posh all three points. Bent and Seal both miss good chances, before Bryant dithers on the ball to allow Ken Charlery to nip in and fire an angled shot into the far corner of the net.

32 BRADFORD C — Kuhl's powerful header in finishing off Barnard's cross settles this fiercely-contested encounter. A cruel result for Bradford, who were on top throughout most of the match and deservedly levelled Seal's hard-driven opener, when Tommy Wright's lob found the back of the net.

33 BRIGHTON — Kuhl misses out on a hat-trick, but he isn't displeased as previous visits to the Goldstone had brought the misery of red cards. His hooked shot from the edge of the box puts City in front, then he is perfectly placed to drill home a loose ball to make sure of victory.

34 SWANSEA — Jan Molby, Swansea's player-boss, bestrides this game with a performance that exudes authority, poise and elegance. After Shaun Chapple's stunning 25-yard opener, Molby doubles the Swans' advantage with a free-kick that smashes into the back of the net before Welch can move.

No	H/A	Date	Club	Att	Pos	Pts	HT	Res	FT	Lge Pos
35	H	9/3	BURNLEY	6,612	15	44	0-0	L	0-1	11
36	A	16/3	BRISTOL ROV	8,622	7	47	2-1	W	4-2	11
37	A	19/3	STOCKPORT	3,713	8	48	0-0	D	0-0	11
38	H	23/3	WREXHAM	6,141	9	51	1-0	W	3-1	11
39	H	30/3	SWINDON	11,370	2	52	0-0	D	0-0	12
40	A	2/4	HULL	2,641	24	55	0-0	W	3-2	11
41	A	6/4	WALSALL	4,142	13	55	1-2	L	1-2	12
42	A	8/4	YORK	7,512	19	56	0-0	D	1-1	12
43	A	13/4	CHESTERFIELD	4,619	6	57	1-0	W	1-0	11
44	H	20/4	OXFORD	7,674	3	57	0-2	L	0-2	13
45	H	27/4	ROTHERHAM	6,101	15	60	1-1	W	4-3	13
46	A	4/5	CARLISLE	5,925	20	60	1-2	L	1-2	13

Home Average 7,017 — Away 4,908

---

35. BURNLEY (H) 9/3 — L 0-1
City: Welch, Owers, Barnard, McLeary, Bryant, Kuhl, Hewlett, Bent*, Seal, Agostino*, Tinnion — subs Nugent/Fowler
Burnley: Beresford, Parkinson, Vinnicombe, Harrison*, Winstanley, Thompson, Weller, Joyce, Smith', Nogan, Eyres — subs Hoyland/Robinson
Scorers: Nogan 83
Ref: S Bennett
City waste their chances, Seal rattling a post, and then having his 74th-minute spot-kick saved, but Agostino's failure from two yards is by far the worst. He wants the ground to open up as he misses the ball completely with his attempt at an extravagant back-heel just after the interval.

36. BRISTOL ROV (A) 16/3 — W 4-2
City: Welch, Owers, Barnard, McLeary, Bryant, Kuhl, Hewlett, Bent*, Nugent, Agostino*, Tinnion — subs Fowler/Seal
Bristol Rov: Collett, Gurney, Morgan, Browning, Clark, Tillson, Miller, Sterling, Stewart, Channing*, Beadle — sub French
Scorers: Nugent 9, Hewlett 45, Agostino 60, [Seal 85]; Gurney 29, Clarke 86
Ref: J Rushton
In one of the most entertaining of derbies, City's textbook away performance brings their first League win at Twerton. Hewlett's right-foot shot is deflected past the helpless Andy Collett to change the course of the game, but the pick of the goals is Agostino's stylish header.

37. STOCKPORT (A) 19/3 — D 0-0
City: Welch, Edwards, Barnard, McLeary, Bryant, Kuhl, Hewlett, Bent*, Nugent, Agostino, Tinnion — sub Fowler
Stockport: Connolly, Todd, Marsden, Flynn, Durkan, Bound, Ware, Mutch, Armstrong, Jeffers
Ref: J Kirkby
At Edgeley Park, City dent Stockport's play-off ambitions with a gutsy display. After Barnard brings a super save out of Neil Edwards, City have lady luck on their side when the lively Alun Armstrong crashes Stockport's best chance against a post a few minutes before half-time.

38. WREXHAM (H) 23/3 — W 3-1
City: Welch, Owers, Barnard, McLeary*, Bryant, Kuhl, Hewlett, Bent*, Nugent, Agostino*, Tinnion — subs Fowler/Seal/Carey
Wrexham: Marriott, McGregor, Hardy*, Phillips*, Humes!, Jones B, Russell, Chalk, Connolly, Jones L, Ward — subs Watkin/Hunter
Scorers: Nugent 18, 84, Tinnion 62; Connolly 66
Ref: G Barber
With the new board installed, Nugent slips in City's opener after Karl Connolly had been denied by a goal-line clearance nine minutes earlier. Following Connolly's diving header, Nugent's angled shot ties up the points, just prior to Tony Humes' dismissal for his second booking.

39. SWINDON (H) 30/3 — D 0-0
City: Welch, Talia, Barnard, McLeary, Bryant, Kuhl, Hewlett, Bent*, Nugent, Agostino*, Tinnion — sub Seal
Swindon: Culverhouse, Bodin, Leitch, Allen, Taylor, Robinson, O'Sullivan, Thorne, Allison, Harlock
Ref: I Hemley
City's professional performance that thwarts Swindon suggests that they now have what it takes to be a Second Division force next season. It's all City for the final 20 mins and it takes Paul Bodin's clearance to prevent Seal's lob finding the back of the net shortly before the call of time.

40. HULL (A) 2/4 — W 3-2
City: Welch, Carroll, Barnard, McLeary, Bryant, Kuhl, Fowler, Fowler*, Nugent, Agostino*, Tinnion — sub Seal
Hull: Humphries!, Graham, Wilkinson, Allison, Quigley, Peacock, Wharton*, Mann, Williams, Gordon/Lawford
Scorers: Hewlett 56, Agostino 67, Seal 81; Gordon 72, Mann 82
Ref: R Poulain
A deserved victory as Seal replaces his compatriot Agostino to lob in City's third goal 13 minutes later. Agostino powers in City's second, after setting up Hewlett to shoot in the opener, but substitute Gavin Gordon tucks away his first senior goal to bring Hull back into the game.

41. WALSALL (A) 6/4 — L 1-2
City: Welch, Walker, Carey, McLeary, Bryant, Kuhl, Hewlett, Fowler*, Nugent, Seal*, Tinnion — subs Bent/Agostino
Walsall: Ntamark*, Daniel, Viveash, Evans, Mountfield, Keister, Bradley, Lightbourne!, Wilson, Houghton, Marsh
Scorers: Seal 33; Nugent 2 (og), Bradley 90
Ref: A Leake
Nugent's despair as the ball cannons off him into City's net is matched by Tinnion 20 mins later when his spot-kick crashes against the legs of the diving James Walker. Kyle Lightbourne receives his marching orders for time wasting, shortly after Bradley heads in the Saddlers' winner.

42. YORK (A) 8/4 — D 1-1
City: Welch, Kiely, Barnard, McLeary, Bryant*, Kuhl, Hewlett, Bent*, Seal*, Agostino, Tinnion — subs Pat'son/Plum'r/B'clay
York: McMillan, Atkinson, Pepper, Sharples, Barras, Jordan, Murty*, Naylor, Bull — subs Stephenson*/Bushell/Peverall
Scorers: Kuhl 56p; Bull 90
Ref: M Fletcher
Kuhl ends City's penalty jinx as, at their fourth attempt this season, he buries their first successful kick. He celebrates with a marathon run of delight, but York snatch a point at the death. City's defence dithers and Gary Bull swivels to crash the ball into the roof of the net.

43. CHESTERFIELD (A) 13/4 — W 1-0
City: Welch, Beasley, Barnard, McLeary, Bryant, Kuhl, Hewlett, Fowler*, Nugent, Agostino*, Tinnion — subs Bent/Seal
Chesterfield: Hewitt, Dyche, Curtis, Williams, Law, Hazel, McDougald, Lormor, Holland, Jules
Scorers: Owers 19; McDougald 60
Ref: D Orr
Impressive in the first half when Owers finishes off an interchange of passes with Nugent to hammer an angled shot into the bottom corner of the net, City are shaken by Chesterfield's resurgence after the break. Kuhl twice kicks off the line before Junior McDougald shoots past Welch.

44. OXFORD (H) 20/4 — L 0-2
City: Welch, Whitehead, Barnard, McLeary, Bryant, Kuhl, Hewlett, Bent, Nugent, Agostino*, Tinnion — subs Plummer/Barclay
Oxford: Robinson, Ford M, Smith, Elliott, Gilchrist, Rush, Gray, Moody, Beauchamp, Massey
Scorers: Rush 56, Moody 73
Ref: P Rejer
Dennis Smith's Oxford notch up their fourth-successive League win over City. McLeary's error in losing possession turns the game as David Rush pounces to slide in a low-angled shot. Then Paul Moody makes sure of the points with a left-foot volley from Joey Beauchamp's cross.

45. ROTHERHAM (H) 27/4 — W 4-3
City: Welch, Clarke, Barnard, Paterson, Bryant*, Kuhl, Hewlett, Bent, Partridge, Agostino, Tinnion — sub Fowler*
Rotherham: Smith, Hurst, McGlashan, Breckin, Moore, Jemson, Bowyer, Hayward, Goater, Roscoe* — sub Barry
Scorers: Partridge 15, Agostino 47, 49, Kuhl 79; Jemson 14, Berry 68, McGlashan 88
Ref: M Pierce
A thrilling home finale in which Agostino takes the eye with his two goals in City's narrow, but deserved win. He holds off three challengers before slipping in a left-foot shot past Matt Clarke, then follows this with a 25-yard drive which squeezes into the bottom corner of the net.

46. CARLISLE (A) 4/5 — L 1-2
City: Welch, Carey*, Barnard, Paterson, McLeary, Kuhl, Owers, Hewlett, Nugent, Agostino, Tinnion* — subs Partridge/Edwards
Carlisle: Caig, Edmondson, Robinson, Delap, Bennett, Thomas, Hayward, Currie!, Reeves, Conway, Thorpe — sub McAlindon
Scorers: Robinson 22 (og); Conway 10, Hayward 28p
Ref: S Mathieson
Caught ball-watching as Paul Conway volleys in from six yards, City equalise when Jamie Robinson deflects Paul Agostino's low cross into the net. McLeary's felling of Rod Thomas in the area proves conclusive as City, apart from Owers firing against the crossbar, offer little else.

ENDSLEIGH DIVISION 2 (CUP-TIES)   Manager: Joe Jordan   SEASON 1995-96

Coca-Cola Cup

		F-A	H-T	Scorers, Times, and Referees	1	2	3	4	5	6	7	8	9	10	11	subs used
1:1 A COLCHESTER 15/8	L	1-2	1-2	Seal 2 / Adcock 15, Kinsella 16 / Ref: P Taylor / 2,831	Welch	Hansen	Munro*	Dryden	McLeary	Kuhl	Barber	Bent	Agostino	Seal	Partridge^	Shail/Fowler
					Emberson	*Locke*	*Betts*	*McCarthy*	*Caesar*	*Cawley*	*Kinsella*	*English*	*Whitton*	*Adcock*	*Cheetham*	

Ever the fall guys, City are Colchester's first victims in the League Cup for twelve years. After Seal's half-volley opener after just 132 secs, Tony Adcock's 20-yard strike, and Munro's deflection of Mark Kinsella's shot leaves City the need to redeem themselves in the second leg.

		F-A	H-T	Scorers, Times, and Referees	1	2	3	4	5	6	7	8	9	10	11	subs used
1:2 H COLCHESTER 22/8	W	2-1 aet	1-0	Seal 28, 81 / Cheetham 61 / Ref: G Barber / (City won on penalties 5-3) / 3,468	Welch	Hansen^	Shail	McLeary	Dryden	Kuhl	Bent	Fowler	Seal	Agostino"	Barber*	Plum'r/Bryant/P'tridge
					Emberson	*Locke*	*Betts*	*McCarthy*	*Caesar*	*Cawley*	*Kinsella*	*English*	*Whitton*	*Adcock**	*Cheetham^*	*Fry/Reinelt*

A standing ovation for gallant Colchester as they succumb in the penalty shoot-out. Despite a history in such deciders that didn't offer any hope, Kuhl, Dryden, Bent, Bryant and Seal give City a full house, whilst full-back Simon Betts blasts Colchester's third against the crossbar.

		F-A	H-T	Scorers, Times, and Referees	1	2	3	4	5	6	7	8	9	10	11	subs used
2:1 H NEWCASTLE 19/9	L	0-5	0-3	[Gillespie 46, Lee 85] Peacock 8, Sellars 22, Ferdinand 31, / Ref: K Burge / 22, 15,952 P:1	Kite	Hansen	Edwards	Dryden	Bryant	Kuhl	Bent	Plummer*	Seal	Agostino	Munro	Hewlett
					*Hislop**	*Barton^*	*Elliott*	*Fox*	*Peacock*	*Howey*	*Lee*	*Gillespie"*	*Ferdinand*	*Ginola*	*Sellars*	*Srnicek/Hottig/W'son*

After Darren Peacock heads in the Magpies' opener from Scott Sellars' corner, magnificent Newcastle hardly need to break sweat in this easy win. So outclassed are City that even the referee shows compassion as he allows Kite to escape with a booking after handling outside the box.

		F-A	H-T	Scorers, Times, and Referees	1	2	3	4	5	6	7	8	9	10	11	subs used
2:2 A NEWCASTLE 4/10	L	1-3	1-0	Agostino 14 / Barton 48, Albert 55, Ferdinand 65 / Ref: J Kirkby / (City lost 1-8 on aggregate) / 22, 36,357 P:1	Kite	Hansen	Edwards	Dryden	Bryant	Paterson	Owers	Kuhl	Bent	Seal*	Agostino"	Partridge/Plummer
					Hislop	*Hottiger*	*Albert*	*Clark*	*Peacock*	*Watson*	*Barton*	*Brayson^*	*Ferdinand*	*Gillespie*	*Sellars**	*Holland/Crawford*

City rediscover their pride and passion to deservedly lead at the break, courtesy of Agostino's header from Bent's cross. After the interval Newcastle take control and Warren Barton's half-volley – together with headers from Philippe Albert and Les Ferdinand, clinch their success.

FA Cup

		F-A	H-T	Scorers, Times, and Referees	1	2	3	4	5	6	7	8	9	10	11	subs used
1 A BOURNEMOUTH 11/11	D	0-0	0-0	Ref: G Barber / 19, 5,304 11	Welch	Paterson	Edwards	Dryden	Shail	Kuhl	Bent*	Owers	Nugent	Barnard	Carey	Partridge
					Moss	*Young*	*Beardsmore*	*Morris*	*Murray*	*Pennock*	*Holland*	*Bailey**	*Jones*	*Fletcher*	*Brissett*	*Robinson*

The last time Welch left a football field he was flat on his back on a stretcher – this time it should have been shoulder high. In a traditional early-round tie with more puff than poise, Welch's save from Steve Jones' 80th-minute volley to keep City in the Cup was on another plane.

		F-A	H-T	Scorers, Times, and Referees	1	2	3	4	5	6	7	8	9	10	11	subs used
1R H BOURNEMOUTH 21/11	L	0-1	0-1	Robinson 5 / Ref: G Barber / 20, 5,069 10	Welch	Carey	Edwards	Bryant	Shail	Kuhl	Bent	Owers*	Nugent	Barnard	Carey	Tinnion
					Moss	*Young*	*Beardsmore*	*Morris*	*Murray*	*Pennock*	*Bailey*	*Robinson*	*Jones*	*Fletcher*	*Brissett**	*Mean*

A cruel defeat for City who dominate this thrilling replay with 30 goal attempts (eleven on target). Poor finishing, outstanding saves, and sheer bad luck thwart City's attempts to redress Steve Robinson's header as Bournemouth equal a club record of seven successive clean sheets.

League Table

Pos	Team	P	Home W	D	L	F	A	Away W	D	L	F	A	Pts
1	Swindon	46	12	10	1	37	16	13	7	3	34	18	92
2	Oxford	46	17	4	2	52	14	7	7	9	24	25	83
3	Blackpool	46	14	5	4	41	20	9	8	6	26	20	82
4	Notts Co	46	14	6	3	42	21	7	9	7	21	18	78
5	Crewe	46	13	3	7	40	24	9	4	10	37	36	73
6	Bradford C *	46	15	4	4	41	25	7	3	13	30	44	73
7	Chesterfield	46	14	6	3	39	21	6	6	11	17	30	72
8	Wrexham	46	12	6	5	51	27	6	10	7	25	28	70
9	Stockport	46	8	9	6	30	20	11	4	8	31	27	70
10	Bristol Rov	46	12	4	7	29	28	8	6	9	28	32	70
11	Walsall	46	12	7	4	38	20	5	5	11	22	25	69
12	Wycombe	46	9	8	6	36	26	6	7	10	27	33	60
13	BRISTOL CITY	46	10	6	7	28	22	5	9	9	27	38	60
14	Bournemouth	46	12	5	6	33	25	4	5	14	18	45	58
15	Brentford	46	12	6	5	24	15	3	7	13	19	34	58
16	Rotherham	46	11	7	5	31	20	3	7	13	23	42	56
17	Burnley	46	9	8	6	35	28	5	5	13	21	40	55
18	Shrewsbury	46	9	8	6	32	29	6	6	11	26	41	53
19	Peterborough	46	9	6	8	40	27	4	7	12	19	39	52
20	York	46	8	6	9	28	29	5	7	11	30	44	52
21	Carlisle	46	11	6	6	35	20	1	7	15	22	52	49
22	Swansea	46	8	8	7	27	29	3	6	14	16	50	47
23	Brighton	46	6	7	10	25	31	3	3	16	21	38	40
24	Hull	46	4	8	11	26	37	1	8	14	10	41	31
		1104	259	153	140	840	574	140	153	259	574	840	1503

* promoted
after play-offs

Appearances and Goals

Player	Lge	Sub	LC	Sub	FAC	Sub	Goals Lge	LC	FAC	Tot
Agostino, Paul	29	11	4				10	1		11
Armstrong, Gordon	6									
Baird, Ian	1									
Barber, Phil	3		2							
Barnard, Darren	33	1			2		4			4
Barclay, Dominic		2								
Bent, Junior	33	7	4		2		2			2
Bryant, Matt	31	1	2	1	2					
Carey, Louis	23	1			2					
Dryden, Richard	17	1	4		1		1			1
Dykstra, Sieb	8									
Edwards, Rob	18	1	2		2					
Fowler, Jason	6	4		1						
Hansen, Vergard	7	1	4							
Hewlett, Matt	27	1			1		2			2
Kite, Phil	3		2							
Kuhl, Martin	46		4		2		6			6
McLeary, Alan	30	1	2	2						
Maskell, Craig	5						1			1
Munro Stuart	3	2								
Nugent, Kevin	29	5	2		2		8			8
Owers, Gary	34	3	1		2		2			2
Partridge, Scott	3	6	1	2		1	1			1
Paterson, Scott	16	2	1		1		1			1
Plummer, Dwayne	1	10				2				
Seal, David	19	11	4		1		10		3	13
Shail, Mark	9	3	1	1	1	2				
Starbuck, Phil	5									
Tinnion, Brian	28	3					1			1
Welch, Keith	35		2		2		3			3
(own-goals)							3			3
30 players used	508	75	44	8	22	2	55		4	59

Odds & ends

Double wins: (2) Hull, Rotherham.
Double losses: (2) Walsall, Oxford.

Won from behind: (3) Chesterfield (h), Rotherham (a), Rotherham (h).
Lost from in front: (2) Shrewsbury (a), Crewe (a).

High spots: Beating Hull 4-0 at Ashton Gate on 14 October.
Beating Bristol Rov 4-2 at Twerton Park on 16 March.
Winning the penalty shoot-out to beat Colchester in the League Cup.
A brilliant FA Cup replay against Bournemouth at Ashton Gate even though City lose 0-1.

Low spots: A humiliating 1-4 defeat at Gay Meadow on 29 August.
Cancellation of this season's Gloucestershire Cup.

Player of the year: Martin Kuhl.
Ever-presents: (1) Martin Kuhl.
Hat-tricks: (0).
Leading scorer: David Seal (13).

NATIONWIDE LEAGUE DIVISION 2

Manager: Jordan ⇒ John Ward   SEASON 1996-97

Column key: No | | | Att | Pos | Pt | F-A | H-T | Scorers, Times, and Referees | 1 | 2 | 3 | 4 | 5 | 6 | 7 | 8 | 9 | 10 | 11 | subs used

---

1 — A GILLINGHAM — 17/8 | Att 7,212 | Pt 0 | L 2-3 | H-T 0-1
Scorers: Fortune-West 13, Harris 81, Piper 90. Ref: A Butler

1	2	3	4	5	6	7	8	9	10	11	subs used
Naylor	Owers	Barnard	McLeary	Edwards	Kuhl	Bent*	Hewlett	Nugent*	Goater	Tinnion	Agostino/Partridge
Stannard	*Humphrey*	*Ford*	*Hessenthaler*	*Harris*	*Bryant*	*Chapman^*	*Ratcliffe*	*Fortune-West*	*Butler^*	*Onuora^*	*Puttnam/Bailey/Piper*

Sub Lenny Piper breaks City hearts in the second minute of injury-time when he blasts in the Gills' winner from Denis Bailey's cross. A cruel blow for City whose superiority after the break was confirmed by Goater's low, hard shot past Jim Stannard, and Bent's close-range prod.

---

2 — H BLACKPOOL — 24/8 | Att 9,417 | Pt 0 | L 0-1 | H-T 0-1
Scorers: Ellis 21. Ref: D Orr

1	2	3	4	5	6	7	8	9	10	11	subs used
Welch	Owers	Barnard	Cundy	Shail	Kuhl	Bent*	Hewlett*	Agostino^	Goater*	Tinnion	Carey/Partridge/Nugent
Banks	*Bryan*	*Barlow*	*Butler*	*Linighan I*	*Brabin*	*Bonner*	*Mellon I*	*Quinn^*	*Ellis^*	*Philpott^*	*Dixon/Thorpe/Preece*

With second bookable offences depriving Blackpool of the services of Dave Linighan just after half-time and Micky Mellon seven minutes before the end, it is a mystery how City lost. Despite 17 efforts on goal and a corner count of 13, City cannot level Tony Ellis' low drive.

---

3 — H LUTON — 27/8 | Att 7,028 | Pos 15 | Pt 3 | W 5-0 | H-T 2-0
Scorers: Goodridge 11, 51, Nugent 41, Goater 46, [Cundy 63]. Ref: S Bennett

1	2	3	4	5	6	7	8	9	10	11	subs used
Welch	Owers	Barnard	Cundy	Shail	Kuhl	Goodridge*	Carey	Nugent	Goater*	Tinnion	Seal/Partridge
Feuer	*James*	*Thomas*	*Waddock*	*Davis*	*Patterson*	*Showler**	*Hughes*	*Oldfield^*	*Grant^*	*Thorpe I*	*Alexander/Fotiadis/Guentchev*

A five-star debut for Greg Goodridge, who has Luton in constant disarray with his speed down the flanks, and accurate crossing, as well as twice getting on the scoresheet. His left-footed rocket shot from the edge of the box is followed by a right-footed effort from fully 15 yards.

---

4 — A BURY — 31/8 | Att 4,160 | Pos 18 | Pt 3 | L 0-4 | H-T 0-1
Scorers: Johnson 35, Carter 48, Jackson 50, [Johnrose 87]. Ref: K Lynch

1	2	3	4	5	6	7	8	9	10	11	subs used
Welch	Owers	Barnard	Cundy	Shail	Kuhl	Goodridge*	Carey	Nugent	Goater	Tinnion	Agostino
Kiely	*West*	*Reid*	*Daws*	*Butler*	*Jackson*	*Hughes*	*Johnson*	*Matthews**	*Johnrose*	*Carter*	*Rigby^/Stant*

After this humiliating defeat a City fan contacted the radio phone-in to complain that he was unable to get out of the ground 30 minutes before time. He had to stay and suffer with the rest as Lennie Johnrose ties up Bury's easy success by heading in Michael Jackson's knock-back.

---

5 — H PRESTON — 7/9 | Att 8,016 | Pos 12 | Pt 6 | W 2-1 | H-T 1-0
Scorers: Nugent 17, 79; Kilbane 46. Ref: K Leach

1	2	3	4	5	6	7	8	9	10	11	subs used
Naylor	Owers	Barnard	Cundy	Edwards	Kuhl	Goodridge*	Carey	Nugent	Agostino^	Tinnion	Seal/Hewlett
Mimms	*Kay*	*Barrick*	*McDonald^*	*Wilcox**	*Moyes*	*Davey*	*Astcroft*	*Saville*	*Wilkinson*	*Kilbane^*	*Kidd/Bryson/Atkinson*

City are the only team in it during the first half, but ride their luck later. Kevin Kilbane's 20-yard drive in off a post brings Preston level, but Nugent kills them off. He adds to his opening close-range shot with another easy effort after Bobby Mimms had clawed out Seal's effort.

---

6 — A SHREWSBURY — 10/9 | Att 2,502 | Pos 16 | Pt 6 | L 0-1 | H-T 0-0
Scorers: Stevens 76. Ref: P Taylor

1	2	3	4	5	6	7	8	9	10	11	subs used
Naylor	Owers	Edwards*	Cundy	Taylor	Kuhl	Barnard	Carey	Nugent*	Goater	Tinnion	Goodridge/Agostino
Gall	*Seabury*	*Nielsen*	*Spink*	*Taylor L**	*Taylor M*	*Scott*	*Stevens*	*Anthrobus*	*Evans*	*Berkley*	*Rowbotham*

Is he kidding or not? After another miserable away performance, Shrewsbury boss Fred Davies voices his opinion that City could prove to be the team to catch this season! Punchless City are punished for their profligacy by Ian Stevens who scores with a fierce shot from twelve yards.

---

7 — A ROTHERHAM — 14/9 | Att 2,546 | Pos 15 | Pt 7 | D 2-2 | H-T 0-0
Scorers: Owers 65, 80; Berry 48, Richardson 56p. Ref: D Laws

1	2	3	4	5	6	7	8	9	10	11	subs used
Naylor	Owers	Barnard	Cundy	Taylor	Hewlett	Goodridge	Carey	Nugent	Goater	Tinnion	Agostino
Cherry	*Smith*	*Hurst*	*Garner*	*Richardson*	*Breckin*	*Berry**	*Bowyer*	*Monington*	*Hayward*	*Wilson*	*Roscoe/McGlashan*

With chairman Davidson voicing his concern over City's performances, things looked black for Jordan when Neil Richardson's penalty, after Naylor brings down Mark Monington, puts Rotherham two up. Owers saves the day with a magnificent 25-yarder, followed by an easy header.

---

8 — H WALSALL — 21/9 | Att 7,412 | Pos 13 | Pt 10 | W 4-1 | H-T 2-1
Scorers: Goater 30, 44, Hewlett 73, Goodridge 90; Lightbourne 16. Ref: R Harris

1	2	3	4	5	6	7	8	9	10	11	subs used
Naylor	Owers	Barnard	Edwards	Taylor	Hewlett	Goodridge	Carey*	Agostino^	Goater	Tinnion	Kuhl/Nugent
Walker	*Ntamark*	*Viveash*	*Watson*	*Marsh*	*Richardson*	*Blake*	*Bradley*	*Wilson*	*Lightbourne*	*Butler*	*Butler*

'That's for you' Goater tells under-pressure Jordan after leading the goal charge to bury woeful Walsall. After Kyle Lightbourne shoots in with a first-time shot from an Owers cross, and then puts City ahead with an angled drive.

---

9 — A BURNLEY — 28/9 | Att 9,587 | Pos 10 | Pt 13 | W 3-2 | H-T 1-1
Scorers: Goater 12, 62, Taylor 79; Gleghorn 44, Weller 55. Ref: M Bailey

1	2	3	4	5	6	7	8	9	10	11	subs used
Naylor	Owers	Barnard	Edwards	Taylor	Hewlett	Goodridge^	Carey	Agostino^	Goater	Tinnion	Kuhl/Nugent
Beresford	*Parkinson**	*Vinnicombe*	*Watson*	*Winstanley*	*Hoyland*	*Weller*	*Smith*	*Nogan*	*Barnes*	*Gleghorn*	*Cooke*

A thrill a minute game in which Burnley miss their chances – Weller incredibly hitting the bar from just two yards, and Paul Smith having a goal disallowed. Goater is City's goalscoring hero, an angled drive in off the far post, and a crisp header into the top corner of Burnley's net.

---

10 — H BRENTFORD — 1/10 | Att 9,520 | Pos 10 | Pt 13 | L 1-2 | H-T 1-1
Scorers: Goodridge 38; Asaba 12, Edwards 72 (og). Ref: A Wiley

1	2	3	4	5	6	7	8	9	10	11	subs used
Naylor	Owers	Barnard	Edwards	Taylor	Hewlett	Goodridge	Carey	Agostino^	Goater	Tinnion	Kuhl/Nugent
Dearden	*Hurdle*	*Anderson*	*Ashby*	*McGhee*	*Hutchings*	*Asaba^*	*Smith*	*Forster*	*Abrahams^*	*Taylor*	*Harvey/Bent*

Edwards not only blatantly chops down the rampaging Nick Forster as he surges goalwards, but then succeeds in slicing the same player's header from the resultant free-kick into his own net.

---

11 — A CHESTERFIELD — 5/10 | Att 4,438 | Pos 13 | Pt 14 | D 1-1 | H-T 0-1
Scorers: Owers 90; Lormor 21. Ref: E Wolstenholme

1	2	3	4	5	6	7	8	9	10	11	subs used
Naylor	Owers	Barnard	Edwards	Taylor	Hewlett	Kuhl*	Carey	Agostino^	Goater	Tinnion	Goodridge/Nugent
Leaning	*Hewitt*	*Rogers*	*Curtis*	*Law*	*Dyche*	*Beaumont*	*Gaughan^*	*Howard^*	*Lormor*	*Jules*	*Perkins/Holland*

Furious Chesterfield players protest that Owers had re-enacted Maradona's hand of God con trick when notching City's injury-time lifesaver. Owers insists it was his head, whilst Nugent claims the goal for himself as he says his header was over the line before Owers followed up.

Match 12 — YORK (H) 11/10 — 2–0 (Pos 9, W, 20, 17) Att 9,308

Naylor · Owers · Barnard · Edwards · Taylor · Hewlett · Goodridge˘ · Carey* · Nugent · Goater · Tinnion !
Clarke · McMillan · Atkinson · Pepper · Tutill! · Barras · Murty · Randall˘ · Tolson · Bull · Stephenson · Bushell/Pouton · Kuhl/Agostino*

Nugent 3, Goodridge 47
Ref: B Knight

After Goodridge crosses for Nugent to touch home from close range in City's first attack, the chances go begging until City's winger runs 60 yards before shooting past Tim Clarke. Sending offs for Tinnion (retaliation) on 53 mins and Steve Tutill (second booking) during injury-time.

Match 13 — WYCOMBE (H) 15/10 — 3–0 (Pos 8, W, 22, 20) Att 7,325

Naylor · Owers · Barnard · Edwards · Taylor · Hewlett · Goodridge · Carey · Agostino · Goater · Tinnion
Parkin ! · Cousins · Bell · McCarthy · Patterson · Carroll · Brown · Farrell˜ · Williams ˜ · McGavin · De Souza/Crossley

Agostino 18, Barnard 59, Tinnion 75
Ref: D Pugh

After Agostino's opening header, City cruise to victory over a poor Wycombe side handicapped by Brian Parkin's 72nd-minute sending off for handling the ball outside the area – Tinnion punishing Parkin's aberration by sending the resultant free-kick past stand-in keeper Stan Brown.

Match 14 — PLYMOUTH (A) 19/10 — 0–0 (Pos 9, D, 21, 21) Att 9,645

Naylor · Owers · Barnard · Edwards · Taylor · Hewlett* · Goodridge* · Carey · Agostino · Goater* · Tinnion
Grobbelaar · Billy · Williams · Mauge · Heathcote · James · Simpson · Corazzin · Evans · Barlow · Illman · Kuhl/McLeary/Seal*

Ref: P Richards

A third-successive clean sheet for City after this uninspiring West Country clash. Bruce Grobbelaar supplies the entertainment in the Argyle goal, catching balls behind his back and sometimes controlling the ball on his chest. Goater comes closest for City with a diving header.

Match 15 — NOTTS CO (H) 26/10 — 4–0 (Pos 9, W, 22, 24) Att 9,540

Naylor · Owers · Barnard · Edwards · Taylor · Hewlett" · Goodridge · Carey · Agostino" · Goater* · Tinnion
Ward · Wilder · Baraclough · Derry · Murphy · Hogg · Gallagher · Hunt · Battersby˜ · Jones · Kuhl · Nugent/Seal/Plummer · Agana

Goater 7, 23, 45, Agostino 17
Ref: A Bates

In contrast to Goodridge's extravagant somersaults in goal celebration, Goater comes up with a less athletic compromise of taking a camera and snapping his team-mates. After registering with two headers, Goater claims his hat-trick with a firm drive into the back of County's net.

Match 16 — BOURNEMOUTH (A) 29/10 — 2–0 (Pos 5, W, 21, 27) Att 4,197

Naylor · Owers · Barnard · Edwards · Taylor · Kuhl* · Goodridge · Carey · Agostino˘ · Goater · Brennan^
Marshall · Young · Beardsmore · Coll˜ · Cox · Bailey · Robinson · Holland · Fletcher · Watson˘ · Dean · McLeary/Partridge/Seal · Brissett/Omoyimmi

Barnard 79p, Agostino 82
Ref: M Pierce

Kuhl keeps his own record intact as City's unbeaten run stretches to six games, and five successive clean sheets. He has never missed from the spot in professional soccer and it as City's penalty, after Goater was fouled by Owen Coll, which finally breaks Bournemouth's resistance.

Match 17 — STOCKPORT (A) 2/11 — 1–1 (Pos 7, D, 10, 28) Att 6,654

Naylor · Owers · Barnard · Edwards · Taylor · Blackmore · Goodridge · Carey · Agostino · Goater* · Brennan^
Jones · Connelly · Todd · Bennett · Flynn · Dinning · Durkan˘ · Marsden · Angell · Cavaco˘ · Jeffers · Seal/Partridge · Mutch/Searle

Blackmore 43 · Bennett 83
Ref: T Jones

Clayton Blackmore (on loan from Middlesbrough) is City's goal hero, though he admits that Agostino's cross goes in off his shoulder. Defending stoutly after the break, City are caught out as Tom Bennett taps in an easy chance to maintain Stockport's run of late goals.

Match 18 — MILLWALL (H) 9/11 — 1–1 (Pos 9, D, 1, 29) Att 12,517

Naylor · Owers · Barnard · Edwards · Taylor* · Blackmore · Goodridge˘ · Carey · Agostino · Goater" · Tinnion
Carter · Newman · Harle · Savage · Witter · Fitzgerald · Bowry · Neill · Crawford · Dair · Hartley · Paterson/Partridge/Seal · Lavin*

Barnard 82 · Crawford 77
Ref: S Baines

Barnard produces a contender for goal of the season with his floated 20-yard free-kick that earns City a point from this gripping tussle with the leaders. With 14 shots overall compared to Millwall's nine, City possibly deserved more than to equalise Steve Crawford's driven-in opener.

Match 19 — PETERBOROUGH (H) 23/11 — 2–0 (Pos 8, W, 21, 32) Att 12,312

Naylor · Owers · Barnard · Edwards · Taylor · Kuhl* · Blackmore · Carey · Agostino* · Goater · Tinnion
Sheffield · Boothroyd · Clark · Edson · Heald · Bodley · O'Connor · Payne · Carruthers · Charlery · Houghton˜ · Goodridge/Nugent · Willis/Rowe*

Goater 35, Goodridge 87
Ref: T Lunt

City play well below their best, but eventually win through with a display of persistence and hard work. Goater holds off two defenders as he races through the middle to send the ball over the advancing keeper, then Blackmore sets up Goodridge to clinically fire in an angled shot.

Match 20 — NOTTS CO (A) 30/11 — 0–2 (Pos 11, L, 22, 32) Att 4,693

Naylor · Owers · Barnard · Edwards* · Paterson · Kuhl · Blackmore · Carey · Agostino" · Goater" · Shaill/Hewlett/Seal
Ward · Wilder · Baraclough · Hogg · Strudder · Derry · Kennedy · Robinson · Arkins · Jones · Finnan · Agana*

Arkins 65, Robinson 75
Ref: M Fletcher

Despite County's lowly position, City rarely look like extending their unbeaten run to ten games. Unlucky perhaps when Vince Arkins' close-range shot is adjudged to have crossed the line, City are exposed when Phil Robinson bursts through their defence to round Naylor and tap in.

Match 21 — WATFORD (H) 3/12 — 1–1 (Pos 11, D, 8, 33) Att 9,097

Naylor · Owers · Barnard · Blackmore · Paterson · Hewlett · Goodridge* · Carey · Agostino* · Nugent · Tinnion
Miller · Gibbs · Robinson · Palmer · Millen · Page · Bazeley · Slater˜ · Noel-Williams · Pennice · Mooney · Seal · White/Andrews

Barnard 71p · Noel-Williams 56
Ref: G Cain

For all City's crisp, sharp and speedy football, they have to be satisfied with a draw gained by Barnard's penalty, after Gary Penrice brings down Hewlett. A poor reward for their attacking display which produces 22 shots (twelve on target) compared to Watford's ten (three).

Match 22 — BRISTOL ROV (H) 15/12 — 1–1 (Pos 10, D, 13, 34) Att 18,642

Naylor · Owers · Barnard · Edwards ! · Taylor · Hewlett · Blackmore* · Carey · Agostino" · Goater · Tinnion
Collett · Pritchard · Martin · Browning · Clark" · Tillson · Holloway · Hayfield^ · Harris · Lockwood · Beadle · Carey/Goater · Archer/Cureton/Skinner*

Agostino 16 · Beadle 90
Ref: D Orr

Violence mars this game on Sky TV as some so-called fans are unable to take victory being snatched from ten-man City's grasp by Peter Beadle's tap-in. City should have had the game well won by then, but squander their chances to add to Agostino's brilliant right-footed strike.

Match 23 — WREXHAM (A) 21/12 — 1–2 (Pos 11, L, 5, 34) Att 4,618

Naylor · Owers · Barnard · Paterson · Taylor · Hewlett · Goodridge* · Carey* · Agostino · Nugent" · Tinnion
Marriott · McGregor · Hardy · Hughes · Humes · Jones B · Chalk · Owen˘ · Watkin · Morris · Ward · Bent/Goater · Russell

Hewlett 79 · Watkin 15p, Hughes 68
Ref: G Laws

A frustrating afternoon for City as controversial decisions prove costly. Hewlett is twice hard done by, as the referee awards a penalty after he wins the ball cleanly in a tackle on Bryan Hughes, then in the last seconds his point saver is disallowed for a supposed handball offence.

NATIONWIDE LEAGUE DIVISION 2

Manager: Jordan ⇨ John Ward   SEASON 1996-97

No	Date				Att	Pos	Pt	F-A	H-T	Scorers, Times, and Referees	1	2	3	4	5	6	7	8	9	10	11	subs used
24	26/12	H	SHREWSBURY	9,803	9	37	3-2	1-2	Agostino 18, Barnard 57p, Owers 87 / Stevens 32, Nielsen 45 / Ref: R Styles	Naylor	Owers	Barnard	Edwards*	Taylor	Hewlett	Goodridge*	Carey	Agostino	Goater*	Tinnion	Bent/Kuhl/Nugent
										Edwards	*Seabury*	*Nielsen*	*Spink*	*Taylor*	*Whiston*	*Brown*	*Stevens*	*Anthrobus*	*Evans*	*Dempsey*	

City rediscover their goal touch, but poor defending keeps the game on a knife-edge right until the end. It takes a fortunate penalty to get City level after Shrewsbury recover from Agostino's headed opener, then Owers clinches the points with a six-yard shot into the top corner.

No	Date				Att	Pos	Pt	F-A	H-T	Scorers, Times, and Referees	1	2	3	4	5	6	7	8	9	10	11	subs used
25	28/12	A	PRESTON	10,905	16	40	2-0	1-0	Agostino 17, Goater 66 / Ref: T Heilbron	Naylor	Owers	Barnard	Kuhl	Taylor	Hewlett	Bent*	Carey	Agostino	Goater*	Tinnion	Nugent
										Mimms	*Gage**	*Barrick**	*Davey*	*Kidd*	*Gregan*	*Ashcroft*	*McDonald*	*Reeves*	*Bennett*	*Kilbane*	*Squires/Rankine*

Pace, aggression, invention, allied to superb organisation and steely determination, prove too much for North End. Shots from Agostino and Goater earn City only their fourth win in 31 visits to Deepdale, despite Preston moving up a gear after the break when they forced 13 corners.

No	Date				Att	Pos	Pt	F-A	H-T	Scorers, Times, and Referees	1	2	3	4	5	6	7	8	9	10	11	subs used
26	11/1	H	BURNLEY	10,013	8	43	2-1	1-1	Bent 19, Goater 68 / Smith 36 / Ref: M Halsey	Naylor !	Owers	Barnard	Kuhl	Taylor	Hewlett	Bent	Carey	Agostino	Goater*	Tinnion	Paterson
										Russell	*Parkinson^*	*Vinnicombe*	*Harrison*	*Swan*	*Brass*	*Little**	*Smith*	*Cooke*	*Barnes*	*Gleghorn*	*Nogan/Weller*

Despite being nonplussed when Paul Smith throws himself at the ball and sends it into the net with a quick flip of his ankle, City recover to take the points. Tinnion is not unduly troubled in goal following Naylor's 77th-minute sending off for bringing down Kurt Nogan outside the box.

No	Date				Att	Pos	Pt	F-A	H-T	Scorers, Times, and Referees	1	2	3	4	5	6	7	8	9	10	11	subs used
27	18/1	A	BRENTFORD	7,606	1	44	0-0	0-0	Ref: S Bennett	Naylor	Owers	Barnard	Allen	Taylor	Hewlett	Bent	Carey*	Agostino	Goater*	Tinnion	Paterson/Nugent
										Dearden	*Hurdle*	*Anderson*	*Ashby*	*Bates*	*McGhee*	*Asaba*	*Smith*	*Forster*	*Statham*	*Taylor*	

Paul Allen, signed from Swindon until the end of the season, inspires City to a point in this titanic struggle. The ref Steve Bennett has touchline words with boss Jordan who struggles to contain his fury when City are denied a clear penalty after Bent is dragged down by Ijah Anderson.

No	Date				Att	Pos	Pt	F-A	H-T	Scorers, Times, and Referees	1	2	3	4	5	6	7	8	9	10	11	subs used
28	25/1	H	BOURNEMOUTH	10,434	15	44	0-1	0-1	Cox 42 / Ref: A Leake	Naylor	Owers	Barnard	Paterson	Taylor	Hewlett	Bent*	Allen	Agostino	Nugent*	Tinnion	Seal/Goodridge
										Glass	*Young*	*Vincent*	*Beardsmore*	*Cox*	*Bailey*	*Holland*	*Robinson**	*Rawlinson*	*Fletcher*	*Brisett*	*Town*

Shades of City's match at Newport 15 years ago, but this time it is Bournemouth who are possibly playing their last game as the receivers ponder a £4.5 million debt. Ian Cox nips in at the near post to steer in Mark Rawlinson's free-kick to give the South Coast club a deserved win.

No	Date				Att	Pos	Pt	F-A	H-T	Scorers, Times, and Referees	1	2	3	4	5	6	7	8	9	10	11	subs used
29	1/2	A	MILLWALL	9,158	9	47	2-0	1-0	Goater 15p, 64 / Ref: D Pugh	Naylor	Owers	Barnard	Paterson	Taylor	Hewlett	Bent	Allen	Agostino	Goater	Tinnion	Kuhl
										Carter	*Newman**	*Rogan*	*Savage**	*Witter*	*Stevens**	*Neill*	*Bowry*	*Crawford*	*Dair*	*Dolby*	*Harle/Hartley/Sadler*

Goater returns to City's frontline wearing a brace to hold his teeth together, a five-stitch repair inside his mouth and swelling on one side of his face. By the end he had another whack on the other side to even things up and two goals, his penalty being followed by a great 15-yard header.

No	Date				Att	Pos	Pt	F-A	H-T	Scorers, Times, and Referees	1	2	3	4	5	6	7	8	9	10	11	subs used
30	7/2	H	STOCKPORT	13,186	8	48	1-1	0-1	Goater 46 / Armstrong 26 / Ref: A Butler	Naylor	Owers	Barnard	Edwards	Taylor	Hewlett	Bent	Allen*	Agostino	Goater	Tinnion	Kuhl
										Jones	*Connelly*	*Todd*	*Bennett*	*Flynn*	*Gannon*	*Durkan**	*Dinning*	*Angell*	*Armstrong*	*Cavaco*	*Nash*

Stockport show all the qualities that have taken them into the semi-finals of the League Cup and on the fringe of the promotion zone. Alan Armstrong drills the ball into the net to give the Hatters the lead, after Sean Connelly's shot was deflected off the referee straight into his path.

No	Date				Att	Pos	Pt	F-A	H-T	Scorers, Times, and Referees	1	2	3	4	5	6	7	8	9	10	11	subs used
31	15/2	A	PETERBOROUGH	4,221	21	48	1-3	0-1	Barnard 83p / Willis 15, 86, Otto 90 / Ref: C Finch	Naylor	Owers	Barnard	Edwards	Taylor	Hewlett	Bent	Allen*	Agostino*	Goater*	Carey*	Nugent/Goodridge
										Griemink	*Boothroyd*	*Clark*	*Edwards*	*Heald*	*Ramage*	*Donowa*	*Payne*	*Willis*	*Charlery*	*Otto*	

Fortunate to get back on terms with Barnard's pen, after Andy Edwards was adjudged to have held down Nugent, City succumb to late goals. Roger Willis exploits poor defending to head in from a flag kick, then Ricky Otto breaks clear and fires a breathtaking shot into the far corner.

No	Date				Att	Pos	Pt	F-A	H-T	Scorers, Times, and Referees	1	2	3	4	5	6	7	8	9	10	11	subs used
32	22/2	H	CREWE	11,306	5	51	3-0	0-0	Goater 59, Agostino 86, Westw'd 89 (og) / Ref: P Taylor	Naylor	Owers	Barnard	Carey	Taylor	Hewlett	Bent*	Allen	Agostino	Goater*	Tinnion	Agostino/Goodridge
										Kearton	*Lightfoot*	*Unsworth*	*Westwood*	*Macauley*	*Whalley*	*Garvey*	*Savage*	*Tierney*	*Murphy*	*Barr*	

Declining the chance to play for Bermuda in the Caribbean tournament, Goater sets City off on the winning trial with a first-time shot from the edge of the box. Agostino then gets in on the act by firing in the second, before unleashing the shot which Ashley Westwood deflects in.

No	Date				Att	Pos	Pt	F-A	H-T	Scorers, Times, and Referees	1	2	3	4	5	6	7	8	9	10	11	subs used
33	1/3	A	WATFORD	8,539	6	51	0-3	0-2	Phillips 10, 25, 78 / Ref: G Frankland	Naylor	Owers	Barnard	Carey	Taylor	Hewlett	Bent	Allen	Agostino	Goater	Tinnion*	Goodridge Noel-Williams
										Miller	*Gibbs*	*Robinson*	*Easton*	*Millen*	*Page*	*Bazeley*	*Scott**	*Phillips*	*Johnson*	*Penrice*	

Pint-sized striker Kevin Phillips' hat-trick, all shot in from close range, rips a giant hole in City's promotion bid. Lacklustre City are hurt by sloppy defending and the skilful play of Darren Bazeley on the right flank. City fail to muster a single shot on target during the second half.

No	Date				Att	Pos	Pt	F-A	H-T	Scorers, Times, and Referees	1	2	3	4	5	6	7	8	9	10	11	subs used
34	4/3	A	WALSALL	4,322	6	51	0-2	0-1	Lightbourne 35, 76 / Ref: B Coddington	Naylor	Owers	Barnard	Carey	Taylor	Edwards	Bent	Allen*	Agostino	Goater*	Tinnion	Kuhl/Nugent
										Walker	*Ntamark*	*Evans*	*Viveash*	*Marsh*	*Mountfield*	*Thomas*	*Keister*	*Lightbourne*	*Watson**	*Hodge*	*Ricketts*

With Walsall desperately hanging onto Kyle Lightbourne's hat-trick, all shot in from acute-angle opener, Goater shoots wide with only the keeper to beat. Unfortunately Lightbourne makes his chances count and his powerful header finishes off John Hodge's cross to ensure Walsall's success.

No		Date	Opponent	Att				Res	FT	HT	Scorers / Opp scorers / Ref
35	A	16/3	BRISTOL ROV	8,078	9	20	54	W	2-1	1-0	Agostino 30, Goater 72 / Alsop 80 / Ref: C Wilkes
36	H	18/3	ROTHERHAM	10,646	9	23	54	L	0-2	0-0	Garner 68, Jean 72 / Ref: A Wiley
37	A	22/3	BLACKPOOL	4,518	10	12	54	L	0-1	0-0	Preece 53 / Ref: D Laws
38	A	25/3	CREWE	3,687	9	6	57	W	2-1	1-0	Bent 36, Goater 73 / Westwood 46 / Ref: P Reger
39	H	29/3	GILLINGHAM	11,276	9	13	57	L	0-1	0-0	Onuora 74p / Ref: A Bates
40	A	1/4	LUTON	7,550	9	3	58	D	2-2	2-1	Goater 3, Agostino 40 / Davis 45, Thorpe 73 / Ref: G Singh
41	H	5/4	BURY	10,274	8	1	61	W	1-0	0-0	Barnard 66 / Ref: M Fletcher
42	H	15/4	WREXHAM	9,817	7	10	64	W	2-1	1-0	Barnard 30p, Goater 88 / Morris 71 / Ref: S Baines
43	A	19/4	YORK	3,344	6	20	67	W	3-0	1-0	Goater 5, 53, Nugent 47 / Ref: A Leake
44	H	26/4	PLYMOUTH	15,368	6	18	70	W	3-1	1-1	Barnard 35, 61p, Nugent 75 / Williams 17 / Ref: J Kirkby
45	H	30/4	CHESTERFIELD	16,195	5	12	73	W	2-0	2-0	Goater 7, Barnard 38p / Ref: E Lomas
46	A	3/5	WYCOMBE	7,240	5	18	73	L	0-2	0-2	Carroll 25, McGavin 45 / Ref: G Cain

Average: Home 10,802 / Away 6,062

35. BRISTOL ROV
City lineup: Naylor, Owers, Edwards*, Barnard, Taylor, Hewlett, Bent, Carey, Agostino, Goater, Brennan, Paterson/Nugent
Opponents: Collett, Pritchard, Skinner*, Power*, White, Tillson, Holloway, Miller*, Cureton, Martin, Beadle, Bennett/Alsop/Hayfield
City lay on the transportation for the limited number of their supporters with tickets for the first League derby at the Memorial Ground. They see a deserved win for their favourites as Goater's angled shot puts City in control, following Naylor's save of Peter Beadle's 40th-minute pen.

36. ROTHERHAM
City lineup: Naylor, Owers, Paterson, Barnard, Taylor*, Hewlett*, Bent, Carey, Agostino, Goater, Brennan*, Kuhl/Goodridge/Nugent
Opponents: Pilkington, Breckin, Dillon, Bain, Bowman, Roscoe, Berry*, Garner, Hayward, McKenzie, McDougald, Jean
It looks black for boss Jordan, as chairman Davidson condemns City's performance as appalling. Against the side with the worst away record, Naylor prevents an even heavier defeat, but he can do nothing about Darren Garner's 25-yard drive that crashes in off the underside of the bar.

37. BLACKPOOL
City lineup: Naylor, Owers, Edwards, Barnard, Kuhl!, Hewlett*, Bent, Carey, Agostino*, Goater, Brennan, Allen/Nugent
Opponents: Banks, Bryan, Butler, Barlow, Linighan, Clarkson, Bonner, Mellon, Quinn !, Ellis*, Preece, Bradshaw
Prior to Kuhl's injury-time dismissal following his second booking, City fail to make their numerical superiority count, after Jimmy Quinn's 61st-min sending off for elbowing. Naylor saves Quinn's 20th-min pen before a teasing cross allows Andy Preece to toe-poke in the only goal.

38. CREWE
City lineup: Naylor, Owers, Paterson, Barnard, Kuhl, Hewlett*, Bent, Carey, Agostino*, Goater*, Allen*, Goater
Opponents: Kearton, Smith S, Westwood, Unsworth, Lightfoot, Charnock*, Savage, Garvey, Anthrobus, Murphy, Tierney*, Little/Rivers
Following Jordan's Monday-night sacking, temporary boss Gerry Sweeney plots this win that rekindles City's promotion hopes. Upset by his omission from the starting line-up, Goater comes off the bench to score the winning goal by finishing off Barnard's cross with a firm header.

39. GILLINGHAM
City lineup: Welch, Owers, Edwards, Barnard, Paterson, Hewlett, Bent, Carey, Goater*, Nugent, Allen*, Agostino/Hewlett
Opponents: Stannard, Galloway, Pennock, Butters, Green, Bryant, Hessenthaler, Ratcliffe, Onuora*, Akinbiyi*, Chapman, Bailey/Butler
New boss John Ward gets off to a disappointing start, as resilient Gillingham take the points at Ashton Gate. Paterson's tug on Iffy Onuora inside the area, enables the No 9 to put away the decisive penalty, as City lack the invention to break down opponents with five at the back.

40. LUTON
City lineup: Welch, Owers, Paterson, Barnard, Shail, Hewlett*, Carey, Goater*, Agostino*, Allen*, Bent/Nugent
Opponents: Feuer, McGowan*, Thomas, Waddock, Davis, Johnson, Alexander, Hughes, Oldfield*, Thorpe, Guentchev*, Marshall/McLaren/Grant
Despite John Ward giving City the lead from his penalty rebound, and Agostino tapping in Allen's cross to double the advantage, it takes a battling rearguard action to secure a point. Headers by Steve Davis and Tony Thorpe set up a rousing finale with City hanging on for their lives.

41. BURY
City lineup: Welch, Owers, Paterson, Barnard, Shail, Edwards, Hewlett*, Carey, Goater*, Agostino, Allen*, Nugent/Brennan
Opponents: Kiely, West*, Armstrong* Daws, Lucketti, Woodward, Butler, Randall, Johnson, Johnrose, Jepson, Scott/Carter
Barnard (he of the red boots) keeps a play-off place in sight as he registers with one of City's two shots on target. His left-foot shot into the top corner of Dean Kiely's net from 15 yards, ends Bury's five-match winning run, during which time they hadn't conceded a single goal.

42. WREXHAM
City lineup: Welch, Owers, Shail, Barnard, Paterson, Hewlett*, Carey, Goater, Agostino*, Allen*, Plummer/Bent/Seal
Opponents: Marriott, McGregor, Jones P*, Phillips, Ridler, Jones B, Russell, Connolly, Skinner, Brammer, Cross/Morris
City all but end Wrexham's play-off ambitions with this nail-biting win achieved by Goater's looped header into the far corner. City escaped to victory that didn't look likely for much of the second half, when Steve Morris headed the visitors deservedly level from Karl Connolly's cross.

43. YORK
City lineup: Welch, Owers, Paterson, Barnard, Shail, Edwards, Hewlett*, Carey, Nugent*, Goater*, Bent/Seal
Opponents: Warrington, McMillan, Bushell, Atkinson, Sharples, Barras, Stephenson, Tinkler, Tolson, Bull, Gilbert*, Greening
Sporting an all-white kit, City outclass York to move up into a play-off position. After Goater gives City an early lead with a near-post header from Barnard's centre, it takes the save of the game by Welch in the 43rd min to keep out Neil Tolson's dipping shot from the edge of the box.

44. PLYMOUTH
City lineup: Welch, Owers, Paterson, Barnard, Shail, Edwards, Hewlett*, Carey, Nugent*, Goater*, Tinnion/Agostino
Opponents: Dungey, Billy, Williams, Saunders*, Heathcote, Perkins*, Rowbotham, Logan, Littlejohn*, Collins, Mauge, Illman/Clayton/Curran
Plymouth threaten to tear City apart after Paul Williams shoots in off the underside of the bar from four yards, but Barnard's cross ends up in the net for a fortunate equaliser. Barnard puts his spot-kick to the keeper's left as the picture in programme shows his Wrexham pen went right.

45. CHESTERFIELD
City lineup: Welch, Owers, Shail, Barnard, Paterson, Hewlett*, Carey, Nugent*, Goater*, Kuhl, Tinnion/Agostino
Opponents: Leaning, Perkins, Jules, Curtis, Williams, Dyche, Beaumont*, Davies, Morris, Ebdon, Howard, Rogers/Lormor
The fans celebrate as though promotion was already achieved as City clinch a play-off place. Their classy first-half display is rewarded by Goater blasting home from six yards, and Barnard sending Andy Leaning the wrong way from the spot after Sean Dyche's handball offence.

46. WYCOMBE
City lineup: Welch, Owers, Shail, Barnard, Paterson, Tinnion, Carey, Nugent, Goater*, Kuhl*, Agostino/Goodridge
Opponents: Parkin, Cousins !, Bell, Kavanagh, McCarthy, Forsyth, Scott*, Stallard, McGavin*, Brown, Read/Evans/Simpson
With boss Ward winning the Manager of the Month, this flop is disappointing and also worrying with the play-offs on the horizon. Two almost identical long-range efforts had the game well won for Wycombe, when Jason Cousins is sent off for his second booking in the 67th minute.

NATIONWIDE DIVISION 2 (CUP-TIES) Manager: Jordan ⇨ John Ward SEASON 1996-97

Coca-Cola Cup

				F-A	H-T	Scorers, Times, and Referees
1:1	A	TORQUAY	20/8 2,824	D 3-3	0-1	Goater 52, Agostino 69, Partridge 83 / Baker 43p, 46, 56 / Ref: M Fletcher

1	2	3	4	5	6	7	8	9	10	11	subs used
Naylor	Owers	Barnard	McLeary	Edwards	Kuhl	Bent*	Hewlett	Nugent*	Goater	Tinnion	Agostino/Partridge
Newland	*Mitchell*	*Barrow*	*McCall'*	*Gittens*	*Watson*	*Oatway*	*Nelson*	*Baker*	*Jack'*	*Hancox*	*Adcock/Hawthorne*

A typical poacher's goal for Partridge after Jon Gittens loses control in the box, saves City's blushes. Naylor's challenge on Garry Nelson starts the hectic goal action as the resultant pen is the prelude to Paul Baker's powerful header, before Goater fires in City's reply from close range.

				F-A	H-T	
1:2	H	TORQUAY	3/9 4,513 3:5	W 1-0	0-0	Barnard 69 / Ref: G Singh (City won 4-3 on aggregate)

1	2	3	4	5	6	7	8	9	10	11	subs used
Naylor	Owers	Barnard	Edwards	McCall	Kuhl*	Paterson	Carey	Nugent*	Goater*	Tinnion	Agostino/Hewlett
Newland	*Winter*	*Barrow'*	*McCall*	*Gittens*	*Watson*	*Oatway*	*Baker*	*Mitchell**	*Jack*	*Hancox*	*Hathaway/Nelson*

City take a firm grip of the game and rarely look like loosing against poor Torquay. Barnard's right-footed effort that curls into the opposite corner of the net from the edge of the box decides the issue, but later Agostino is unlucky with a stunning header that crashes against the bar.

				F-A	H-T	
2:1	H	BOLTON	18/9 6,351 1:1	D 0-0	0-0	Ref: G Pooley

1	2	3	4	5	6	7	8	9	10	11	subs used
Naylor	Owers	Barnard	McLeary	Edwards	Hewlett	Goodridge	Carey*	Agostino	Goater*	Tinnion	Kuhl/Nugent
Branagan	*McAnespie*	*Phillips*	*Frandsen*	*Taggart*	*Fairclough*	*Johansen*	*Lee**	*Blake*	*McGinlay*	*Thompson*	*Todd*

City's hard-working display leaves all to play for in the second leg. With both sides content to shoot from long range, chances are few and far between, though at the death John McGinlay should perhaps have done better than shave a post with his volley from McAnespie's centre.

				F-A	H-T	
2:2	A	BOLTON	24/9 6,367 1:1 aet	L 1-3	0-0	Owers 57 / McGinlay 47, Blake 92, Thompson 107 / Ref: R Pearson (City lost 1-3 on aggregate)

1	2	3	4	5	6	7	8	9	10	11	subs used
Naylor	Owers	Barnard	Bergsson	McLeary	Hewlett	Goodridge	Carey	Agostino*	Goater*	Tinnion*	Seal/Nugent/Kuhl
Branagan	*Phillips*	*Frandsen*	*Taggart*	*Fairclough*	*Johansen'*	*Lee**	*Blake*	*McGinlay*	*Thompson*		*Sellars/Taylor/Todd*

Heartbreak at Burden Park as Nathan Blake's prod-in and Alan Thompson's breakaway in extra-time dump City out of the League Cup. Both sides had their chances to win in normal time, which ended all square, with Owers side-footed curler countering John McGinley's 15-yard shot.

FA Cup

				F-A	H-T	
1	A	SWANSEA	16/11 5,629 3:20	D 1-1	1-0	Kuhl 45 / Torpey 71 / Ref: A Wiley

1	2	3	4	5	6	7	8	9	10	11	subs used
Naylor	Owers	Barnard	Edwards	Taylor	Kuhl	Goodridge	Carey	Agostino	Goater	Tinnion	Hewlett/Nugent
Freestone	*Brown'*	*Clode*	*Moreira*	*Edwards*	*Jones*	*Jenkins*	*Penney*	*Torpey*	*Ampadu !*	*Coates'*	*Thomas*

A thrilling end-to-end cup-tie sees City ahead at the break thanks to Kuhl's perfectly stroked 25-yard shot into the left corner of the net, secs after Naylor had pushed a close-range shot onto the bar. Torpey earns Swansea a deserved replay with a diving header to Mark Clode's cross.

				F-A	H-T	
1R	H	SWANSEA	26/11 8,017 3:14	W 1-0	1-0	Agostino 1 / Ref: A Wiley

1	2	3	4	5	6	7	8	9	10	11	subs used
Naylor	Owers	Barnard	Edwards	Taylor*	Kuhl	Goodridge	Carey	Agostino	Goater*	Tinnion	Hewlett/Nugent
Freestone	*O'Leary*	*Clode**	*Moreira*	*Edwards*	*Jones*	*Heggs*	*Penney*	*Torpey*	*Ampadu*	*Coates*	*Thomas*

Agostino strikes for City after just 17 seconds when pouncing on a loose ball 25 yards out and lifting a composed shot over Roger Freestone. Despite all the possession no further goals ensue, Goodridge ending a strong run in the second half by disappointingly shooting wide.

				F-A	H-T	
2	H	ST ALBANS CITY	7/12 7,136 11:17	W 9-2	5-0	Goodridge 13, Agostino 22, 41, 48, 77, Clark 54, Daly 67 / Kuhl 25, Hewlett 42, 56, Nugent 81 / Ref: G Barber

1	2	3	4	5	6	7	8	9	10	11	subs used
Naylor	Howells	Barnard	Kuhl*	Paterson	Hewlett	Goodridge	Carey	Nugent	Goater*	Tinnion	Doherty
Howell'	*Mudd*	*Polston*	*Coleman'*	*Daly*	*Bashir*	*Evans*	*Cobb*	*Howell'*	*Haworth'*	*Clark*	*Blackman/Risley/Martin*

Goals galore at Ashton Gate with eleven in a match equalling that for the 1st round game against Chichester City on Guy Fawkes' day in 1960. This time, though, City allow the opposition to notch two, with Steve Clark and Jon Daly heading in at the Covered End for spirited St Albans.

				F-A	H-T	
3	A	CHESTERFIELD	14/1 5,193 7	L 0-2	0-0	Howard 69, 88 / Ref: E Wolstenholme

1	2	3	4	5	6	7	8	9	10	11	subs used
Naylor	Owers	Barnard!	Kuhl*	Paterson	Hewlett	Bent*	Carey	Agostino*	Goater*	Tinnion	Edwards/Nugent/Goodridge
Mercer	*Hewitt*	*Jules*	*Curtis*	*Williams*	*Dyche*	*Davies*	*Holland*	*Lornor*	*Howard*	*Morris*	

Naylor is City's hero following Barnard's 18th-min sending off for hauling down Billy Mercer, Naylor saves all that Chesterfield can offer, until Jon Howard stoops to head in a left-wing centre.

Play-offs

				F-A	H-T	
SF 1	H	BRENTFORD	11/5 15,581	L 1-2	1-2	Owers 28 / Smith 14, Taylor 30 / Ref: U Rennie

1	2	3	4	5	6	7	8	9	10	11	subs used
Welch	Owers	Barnard	Shail	Paterson	Edwards	Hewlett*	Allen	Nugent*	Goater	Kuhl*	Tinnion/Agostino/Carey
Dearden	*Hurdle*	*Anderson*	*Statham*	*Bates*	*McGhee*	*Asaba*	*Smith*	*Bent*	*Hutchings*	*Taylor*	

At a wet Ashton Gate, it's like turning the clock back twenty years or more as the admirable referee Uriah Rennie allows a real old-fashioned blood and thunder contest. Rob Taylor's nod of the head gives Brentford a deserved win after Owers had glanced in Bristol City's equaliser.

				F-A	H-T	
SF 2	A	BRENTFORD	14/5 9,496	L 1-2	0-0	Barnard 49 / Taylor 67, Bent 78 / Ref: J Kirkby (City lost 2-4 on aggregate)

1	2	3	4	5	6	7	8	9	10	11	subs used
Welch	Owers	Barnard	Shail*	Hutchings	Edwards	Hewlett	Allen	Nugent	Goater	Tinnion*	Carey"/Goodridge/Bent
Dearden	*Hurdle*	*Anderson*	*Hutchings*	*Bates*	*McGhee*	*Dennis**	*Smith*	*Bent*	*Statham*	*Taylor*	*Canham*

City spurn their chances at Griffin Park as they threaten to turn the tables. On top throughout the first half, they are rewarded shortly after the break. Barnard's 15-yard cross-shot finds the net, but Goater misses opportunities and Rob Taylor's curler punishes City for their wastefulness.

#	Team	P	Home					Away					Pts
			W	D	L	F	A	W	D	L	F	A	
1	Bury	46	18	5	0	39	7	6	7	10	23	31	84
2	Stockport	46	15	5	3	31	14	8	8	7	28	27	82
3	Luton	46	13	7	3	38	14	8	8	7	33	31	78
4	Brentford	46	8	11	4	26	22	12	3	8	30	21	74
5	BRISTOL CITY	46	14	4	5	43	18	7	6	10	26	33	73
6	Crewe *	46	15	4	4	38	15	7	3	13	18	32	73
7	Blackpool	46	13	7	3	41	21	5	8	10	19	26	69
8	Wrexham	46	11	9	3	37	28	6	9	8	17	22	69
9	Burnley	46	14	3	6	48	27	5	8	10	23	28	68
10	Chesterfield	46	10	9	4	25	18	8	5	10	17	21	68
11	Gillingham	46	13	3	7	37	25	6	7	10	23	34	67
12	Walsall	46	12	8	3	35	21	7	2	14	19	32	67
13	Watford	46	10	8	5	24	14	6	11	6	21	24	67
14	Millwall	46	12	4	7	27	22	4	9	10	23	33	61
15	Preston	46	14	5	4	33	19	4	2	17	16	36	61
16	Bournemouth	46	8	9	6	24	20	7	6	10	25	25	60
17	Bristol Rov	46	13	4	6	34	22	2	2	14	13	28	56
18	Wycombe	46	13	4	6	31	14	2	6	15	20	42	55
19	Plymouth	46	7	11	5	19	18	5	7	11	28	40	54
20	York	46	8	6	9	27	31	5	7	11	20	37	52
21	Peterborough	46	7	7	9	38	34	4	7	12	17	39	47
22	Shrewsbury	46	8	6	9	27	32	3	7	13	22	42	46
23	Rotherham	46	4	7	12	17	29	3	7	13	22	41	35
24	Notts Co	46	4	9	10	20	25	3	5	15	13	34	35
		1104	264	155	133	759	510	133	155	264	510	759	1501

* promoted
after play-offs

Appearances / Goals

Player	Appearances						Goals			
	Lge	Sub	LC	Sub	FAC	Sub	Lge	LC	FAC	Tot
Agostino, Paul	34	10	2	2	4		9	1	5	15
Allen, Paul	13	1								
Barnard, Darren	44		4		4		11		1	12
Bent, Junior	17	5	1		1		3			3
Blackmore, Clayton	5						1			1
Brennan, Jim	7	1								
Carey, Louis	40	2	3		4					
Cundy, Jason	6		2				1			1
Doherty, Tommy						1				
Edwards, Rob	31		4		2	1				
Goater, Shaun	39	3	4		3		23		1	24
Goodridge, Greg	19	9	3		3	1	6	1		7
Hewlett, Matt	33	3	3	1	2	1	2	2		4
Kuhl, Martin	22	9	2		4	1	1			1
McLeary, Alan	1	2			3					
Naylor, Stuart	35		4		4					
Nugent, Kevin	19	17	2	2	1		6		1	7
Owers, Gary	46		4		4		4	1		5
Partridge, Scott		6				1			1	1
Paterson, Scott	15	4	1		1					
Plummer, Dwayne		2								
Seal, David		12		1						
Shail, Mark	10	1								
Taylor, Shaun	29				3		1			1
Tinnion, Brian	30	2	4		4		1			1
Welch, Keith	11									
(own-goals)										1
26 players used	506	89	44	9	44	6	69	5	10	84

Odds & ends

Double wins: (4) Preston, Burnley, York, Crewe.

Double losses: (2) Gillingham, Blackpool.

Won from behind: (4) Walsall (h), Burnley (a), Shrewsbury (h), Plymouth (h).

Lost from in front: (0).

High spots: Greg Goodridge's brilliant display on his debut v Luton (h).
Winning 3-2 at Turf Moor on 28 September.
Beating Bristol Rovers 2-1 on our first visit to the Memorial Ground.
Hammering 9 goals against St Albans in the FA Cup.
Shaun Goater's 81st-minute goal against Bristol Rov at Ashton Gate on 6 August to bring City their 54th win in the Gloucestershire Cup Final.
Winning the Herefordshire Cup by beating Hereford 3-2 on 31 July.

Low spots: Losing at Wycombe on 3 May.
Losing in the semi-finals of the promotion play-offs 2-4 on aggregate against Brentford.
Succumbing 0-2 at Chesterfield in the FA Cup.

Player of the year: Shaun Taylor.

Ever-presents: (1) Gary Owers.

Hat-tricks: (2) Shaun Goater (1), Paul Agostino (1).

Leading scorer: Shaun Goater (24).

Manager: John Ward

No	Date	Att	Pos	Pt	F-A	H-T	Scorers, Times, and Referees	1	2	3	4	5	6	7	8	9	10	11	subs used
1	A GRIMSBY 9/8	6,479		D 1	1-1	1-0	Torpey 27 / Widdrington 74; Ref: G Frankland	Welch	Carey	Bell	Paterson	Taylor	Edwards	Hewlett	Owers	Goater	Torpey*	Tinnion	Cramb*/Barclay
	Grimsby							Davison	McDermott	Gallimore*	Handyside	Lever	Widdrington	Donovan	Black*	Livingstone	Nogan	Groves	Jobling/Woods
2	H BLACKPOOL 16/8	9,043		W 4	2-0	0-0	Cramb 48, Goater 87; Ref: G Singh	Welch	Locke	Bell	Paterson	Taylor	Edwards	Hewlett	Owers	Goater	Cramb*	Tinnion*	Bent/Tisdale
	Blackpool							Banks	Bryan*	Bradshaw	Butler	Lydiate	Brabin	Bonner	Clarkson	Malkin	Philpott	Preece	Linighan
3	A NORTHAMPTON 23/8	6,217	14	L 4	1-2	1-2	Cramb 4 / Seal 23, Gayle 44; Ref: P Taylor	Welch	Carey	Bell	Paterson*	Taylor	Edwards	Hewlett*	Owers	Goater	Cramb*	Tinnion	Torpey/Tisdale/Bent
	Northampton							Woodman	Clarkson	Frain	Sampson	Warburton	Brightwell	Parrish	Conway*	Seal*	Gayle	Hunter	Peel/Heggs
4	H WIGAN 30/8	9,255	15	W 7	3-0	3-0	Goater 26, 37, 39p; Ref: M Pierce	Welch	Carey	Bell	Paterson	Taylor	Edwards*	Hewlett	Owers	Goater*	Cramb	Tinnion*	Langan/Tisdale/Barclay
	Wigan							Carroll	Green	Johnson	Greenall	McGibbon	Martinez	Lee	Jones*	O'Connell*	Kilford	Lowe*	Saville/Sharp/Warne
5	H FULHAM 2/9	10,293	9	L 7	0-2	0-1	/ Newhouse 14, Carpenter 79; Ref: R Harris	Welch		Bell	Paterson*	Taylor	Edwards	Hewlett*	Owers	Goater	Cramb	Tinnion*	Barclay/Locke
	Fulham							Walton	Lawrence	Herrera	Cullip	Smith	Blake	Newhouse*	Hayward	Moody*	Morgan	Cockerill*	Carpenter/Scott/Brooker
6	A WREXHAM 13/9	3,181	16	L 7	1-2	0-1	Goater 68 / Spink 13, Watkin 59; Ref: A Bates	Welch	Tisdale	Bell	Paterson	Taylor	Edwards*	Hewlett*	Owers	Goater*	Cramb	Tinnion	Carey/Torpey/Goodridge
	Wrexham							Marriott	McGregor	Hardy	Phillips	Humes*	Carey	Skinner	Owen	Connelly	Spink*	Brammer	Jones/Watkin
7	H BOURNEMOUTH 20/9	8,330	7	D 8	1-1	1-0	Goater 26 / Robinson 83; Ref: M Fletcher	Welch	Carey	Bell	Tisdale	Taylor	Edwards	Hewlett*	Owers	Goater	Torpey	Tinnion	Barclay/Doherty
	Bournemouth							Glass	Young	Vincent	Howe	Cox	Bailey	Beardsmore	Robinson	O'Neill*	Fletcher	Tomlinson*	Brissett/Rawlinson
8	H LUTON 27/9	8,509	23	W 11	3-0	3-0	Bell 5p, Torpey 27, 30 / Ref: E Lomas	Welch	Locke	Bell	Dyche	Taylor	Edwards	Goodridge*	Owers	Goater	Cramb*	Tinnion	Barclay/Doherty
	Luton							Davis K	Evers	Small	White	Harvey	McLaren	Waddock*	Davies	George*	Thorpe	Oldfield	Spring/Kean
9	A GILLINGHAM 4/10	6,201	7	L 11	0-2	0-2	/ Akinbiyi 6, 44; Ref: A D'Urso	Welch	Locke	Bell	Dyche	Taylor	Edwards	Goodridge	Owers	Torpey	Doherty*	Tinnion	Goater
	Gillingham							Moss	Green	Butters	Smith	Ashby	Bryant*	Hessenthaler	Ratcliffe	Butler*	Akinbiyi*	Corbett*	Gall'way/Fort*/West/Onuora
10	A SOUTHEND 11/10	3,218	21	W 14	2-0	1-0	Barnard 34, Hails 56 (og) / Ref: D Orr	Welch	Barnard	Bell	Dyche	Taylor	Shail	Doherty*	Owers	Torpey	Cramb*	Tinnion	Goater/Plummer
	Southend							Royce	Hails*	Jones	Marsh*	Lewis	Perkins	Allen	Byrne*	Rammell	Dublin	Clarke	Gridelet/Coulbault/Thomson
11	H YORK 17/10	9,568	8	W 17	2-1	0-1	Cramb 68, Torpey 81 / Rowe 37; Ref: M Halsey	Welch	Locke	Bell	Dyche	Taylor	Shail*	Doherty*	Owers	Torpey	Cramb	Tinnion	Goodridge/Edwards
	York							Samways	McMillan	Hall	Bushell	Reed	Barras	Murty	Tinkler	Tolson	Rowe	Stephenson	

Match notes

1. Torpey's crisp shot on the turn gets the promotion favourites off to a good start, before a clash of heads brings about the early departure of City's £400,000 signing. Town deservedly equalise when Tommy Widdrington slides the ball in after Welch parries Paul Groves' effort.

2. City's 5-3-2 formation is a major talking point amongst the fans, but few complaints in this game as Locke and Bell convincingly go forward. Cramb's firm header from Tinnion's centre gives City the lead, before Goater's poor penalty is pushed round the post by Steve Banks.

3. John Ward drops a howler in giving permission for on-loan David Seal to turn out for the Cobblers in this game. After Cramb hooks in from Bell's cross to put City ahead, Seal lobs in Town's leveller, and then rubs further salt in the wound with his pass for John Gayle's winner.

4. Goater, with his fastest hat-trick, and Bell impress as City dominate the first half. Goater heads in from Carey's cross to open his account, and then runs onto Cramb's through-ball, before completing his fifth hat-trick, when he shoots in from the spot after Owers is up-ended.

5. Out-of-sorts City are taken to task after a minute's silence in memory of Princess Diana and the Fulham Chairman's son Dodi Fayed. Shortly after Moody hits the bar, Newhouse heads in, whilst Carpenter is on hand to make the game safe when Welch is unable to hold Moody's drive.

6. Another flop as Wrexham lead with an opportunist strike by Dean Spink. Welch has to be at his best to keep City in the game, but he cannot prevent Steve Watkin registering with a diving header. Goater gives City hope, but despite a hectic finale the equaliser doesn't come.

7. Boss John Ward is stunned by the jeering reaction of the City fans when Steve Robinson converts Jason Brissett's pass to snatch a point for the Cherries. The critics complain that Ward's system of play is too negative as City are unable to build on Goater's early side-foot strike.

8. Goodridge's return brings back the smiles, though Ward still retains a 5-3-2 formation. The woodwork denies both Taylor and Edwards as well as twice thwarting Goodridge, but Bell's spot-kick, after Cramb is bundled over, and Torpey's header and shot bring a convincing success.

9. Welch saves City from a heavy defeat as they are well beaten by Ade Akinbiyi's close-range shot and his well-taken effort on the turn. City, for whom Goodridge fires against a post, again incur the jeers of their fans on the final whistle after being out-battled by robust opponents.

10. With Doherty controlling the midfield, City notch up their first away win of the campaign. After Barnard (£150,000 ex Wycombe) strikes with a brilliant 25-yard free-kick to quell United's bright start, Julian Hails ties up the points for City by slotting Locke's cross past his own keeper.

11. The boo-boys make themselves heard at half-time with City fortunate to be only losing to Rowe's shot, as shortly afterwards Bushell wastes a great chance. Cramb seizes on Reed's attempted back-header to slot in the equaliser and Torpey heads in the winner as City switch to 4-4-2.

12 | H | 21/10 | PRESTON — 9,039 | 6 | W | 11 | 20 | 2-1 | 0-0
Bell 64p, Goodridge 89 / Dyche 68 (og) / Ref: R Styles

Welch	Locke	Dyche	Taylor	Edwards	Goodridge	Doherty	Torpey	Cramb	Tinnion
Moilanen	*Parkinson* *Kidd*	*Murdock*	*Moyes*	*Appleton*	*Cartwright* *Ashcroft*		*Reeves*	*Rankine*	*Barrick*

Goodridge puts Kidd off balance with his trademark step-over before cutting inside to unleash an unstoppable shot into the top of the net and deprive Preston of a deserved point. Dyche diverts the ball into his own net to make up for City's lucky penalty for an unseen handball offence.

---

13 | A | 25/10 | WALSALL — 4,618 | 7 | D | 19 | 21 | 0-0 | 0-0
Ref: C Foy

Welch	Locke	Dyche	Taylor	Edwards	Goodridge*	Doherty	Torpey	Cramb*	Tinnion
Walker	*Marsh* *Evans*	*Viveash*	*Mountfield* *Peron*	*Platt**	*Skinner*	*Keates* *Watson*	*Hodge*	*Goater/Hewlett*	*Ricketts*

City should have won this game after controlling most of the play. Walsall's best effort comes from City's Doherty, whose header from a John Hodge cross has Welch flying to tip the ball onto the crossbar. Taylor comes closest to ending the deadlock with two powerful headers.

---

14 | A | 29/10 | MILLWALL — 7,026 | 3 | W | 5 | 24 | 2-0 | 1-0
Torpey 9, Locke 54 / Ref: F Stretton

Welch	Locke	Dyche	Taylor	Edwards	Hewlett	Doherty	Torpey	Cramb	Tinnion
Spink	*Brown* *Newman*	*Bowry*	*Law* *McLeary*	*Black*	*Shaw*	*Wilkinson* *Grant**	*Allen**	*Savage/Hockton*	

Locke produces a stirring performance at the New Den. Not only does his cross lay on a simple header for the opening goal, but he grabs the other himself with a volley from Tinnion's centre. Hewlett's return to City's side is marred by his missing an open net with an early header.

---

15 | H | 1/11 | OLDHAM — 10,221 | 2 | W | 8 | 27 | 1-0 | 0-0
Bell 61p / Ref: D Crick

Welch	Locke	Dyche	Taylor	Edwards	Hewlett	Carey	Torpey	Cramb	Tinnion*
Pollitt	*Redmond* *Serrant*	*Graham* *Hodgson*	*McNiven**	*Rush**	*Duxbury*	*McCarthy** *Rickers*	*Reid*	*Ritchie/Wright/Hughes*	

City benefit from a moment of madness by defender Doug Hodgson after withstanding Oldham's aerial bombardment. With no real danger he palms away Tinnion's corner to concede a penalty. Bell sends Mike Pollitt the wrong way to add to Ward's Manager of the Month award.

---

16 | A | 4/11 | BRISTOL ROV — 7,552 | 2 | W | 12 | 30 | 2-1 | 1-0
Goater 27, 49 / Tillson 85 / Ref: M Bailey

Welch	Brennan	Dyche	Taylor	Edwards	Hewlett	Carey	Torpey	Goater*	Tinnion
Collett	*Pritchard* *Lockwood*	*Penrice* *Gayle**	*Tillson*	*Holloway*	*French**	*Beadle* *Cureton*	*Hayles*	*White/Alsop*	

City could hardly ever win at Twerton, but are developing a liking for the Memorial ground with a third success in as many visits. Goater collects Locke's long ball down the right to shoot in the opener, and his angled drive doubles the advantage before Tilson fires in for Rovers.

---

17 | A | 8/11 | BRENTFORD — 6,162 | 2 | W | 24 | 33 | 4-1 | 2-0
Torpey 31, Goater 32, 67, Doherty 77 / Reina 84 / Ref: P Danson

Welch	Dearden	Dyche	Taylor	Edwards*	Hewlett	Carey	Torpey	Goater	Tinnion
	Hurdle *Anderson*	*Hutchings* *Bates*	*Oatway*	*McGhee*	*Cockerill**	*Bent* *Reina*	*Taylor*	*Denys*	

City spoil the first match for new Brentford boss Mickey Adams. A creative midfield and strong defending against long-ball tactics bring City success. After Doherty shoots in his first half rebounds off the keeper, poor marking allows Ricky Reina to head home for the Bees.

---

18 | H | 18/11 | PLYMOUTH — 10,867 | 2 | W | 17 | 36 | 2-1 | 2-0
Bell 33, 34 / Corazzin 83 / Ref: A Wiley

Welch	Locke	Dyche	Taylor	Edwards*	Hewlett	Doherty	Torpey	Goater	Tinnion*
Sheffield	*Logan* *Williams*	*Mauge* *Wotton**	*Barlow*	*Jean**	*Littlejohn*	*Corazzin* *Billy*	*Brennan/Langan*	*Saunders/Wilson*	

City's one-touch passing style rips Argyle apart in the first half. Goater has an early effort ruled out for offside, while Torpey hits the post and Taylor's header is cleared off the line. Carlo Corazzin shoots in for Plymouth after Bell has secured City's points with two brilliant free-kicks.

---

19 | H | 22/11 | WYCOMBE — 11,129 | 2 | W | 16 | 39 | 3-1 | 1-0
Hewlett 38, 59, Torpey 67 / Scott 82p / Ref: K Lynch

Welch	Locke*	Dyche	Taylor	Edwards	Hewlett	Carey	Torpey	Goater*	Tinnion*
Taylor	*Cousins* *Beeton*	*Ryan* *Mohan*	*Comforth**	*Kavanagh* *Scott*	*Read**	*McGavin* *Brown*		*McCarthy/Harkin*	

Hewlett replies to his critics by netting a glorious shot from just outside the box, and then notches his second when cutting in from the right to stroke the ball past the diving Martin Taylor. Brennan's handball gives the visitors their late penalty, after Torpey's header has City cruising.

---

20 | A | 29/11 | CARLISLE — 5,044 | 2 | W | 24 | 42 | 3-0 | 1-0
Goater 19, 53, Goodridge 59 / Ref: M Pike

Welch	Locke	Goodridge*	Taylor	Edwards	Hewlett	Doherty*	Goater	Cramb	Tinnion*
Caig	*Barr* *Boertien*	*Hoyland* *Prokas*	*Pounewat'y* *Harrison**	*Anthony*	*Stevens*	*Dobie* *Wright*		*Brennan/Edwards/Barclay* *McAllindon*	

Goodridge rifles in the rebound as Caig's brilliant save denies Goater a hat-trick. Off-form City have Goater to thank for their eighth win in a row. From point-blank range he fires in Anthony's miscued clearance to add to his precision shot opener which had left the keeper helpless.

---

21 | H | 2/12 | BURNLEY — 11,136 | 2 | W | 22 | 45 | 3-1 | 0-1
Goodridge 48, 83, Bell 71p / Barnes 29 / Ref: A Bates

Welch	Locke	Goodridge*	Taylor	Edwards	Hewlett	Doherty	Goater	Cramb*	Tinnion*
Beresford	*Brass* *Vinnicombe**	*Harrison* *Blatherwick* *Moore*	*Waddle**	*Ford*	*Howey*	*Barnes* *Weller*	*Brennan*	*Matthew/Cooke*	*Barclay*

Burnley surprise City early on and deserve the half-time advantage gained by a Paul Barnes' thunderous half volley. Goodridge puts on a dazzling display to turn the tide, firing in two rockets to beat Marlon Beresford, who needlessly brings down Cramb to concede Bell's penalty.

---

22 | A | 13/12 | WATFORD — 16,072 | 2 | D | 1 | 46 | 1-1 | 0-0
Goater 54 / Noel-Williams 84 / Ref: B Knight

Welch	Locke	Goodridge	Taylor	Edwards	Hewlett	Carey	Goater	Cramb*	Tinnion
Chamberlain *Gibbs*	*Kennedy* *Page*	*Millen*	*Palmer*	*Mooney* *Hyde*	*Lee*	*Johnson* *Rosenthal**	*Noel-Williams*	*Dyche*	

Noel-Williams' shot takes a deflection to wrong-foot Welch and end City's bid to better their 1905-06 side, who share the League record of 14 successive wins. City take the lead when Doherty's long ball finds Cramb, whose flick on allows Goater to burst clear and shoot into the net.

---

23 | H | 20/12 | CHESTERFIELD — 11,792 | 2 | W | 8 | 49 | 1-0 | 1-0
Bell 13p / Ref: A D'Urso

Welch	Locke	Bell	Goodridge*	Taylor	Carey	Hewlett	Goater	Cramb*	Tinnion
Mercer	*Hewitt* *Jules**	*Beaumont* *Williams*	*Brackin*	*Wilkinson**	*Holland*	*Reeves* *Ebdon*	*Perkins*	*Murray/Paterson* *Curtis/Willis*	

City are lucky when Chesterfield hit the bar, but they dominate the first half after Bell's clinical penalty punishes Mark Williams for tugging at Goater's shirt. The Spireites take control after the break, but despite all their possession they rarely look capable of forcing an equaliser.

NATIONWIDE LEAGUE DIVISION 2 — Manager: John Ward — SEASON 1997-98

No	Date		Scorers, Times, and Referees	Att	Pos	Res	Pt	F-A	H-T	1	2	3	4	5	6	7	8	9	10	11	subs used
24	26/12	H MILLWALL	Cramb 10, Edwards 17, Tinnion 59, Veart 53 [Taylor 68] — Ref: R Harris	16,128	2 (6)	W	52	4-1	2-0	Welch / Spink	Locke / Brown	Bell / Law	Goodridge* / Bowry	Taylor / Fitzgerald	Carey / Savage	Edwards / Newman	Doherty / Neil^	Goater* / Shaw	Cramb / Grant	Tinnion / Veart	Murray/Torpey / Sturges
25	28/12	A FULHAM	Moody 50 — Ref: J Robinson	13,275	2 (6)	L	52	0-1	0-0	Welch / Taylor	Locke* / Lawrence	Bell / Herrera*	Goodridge / Trollope	Taylor / Coleman	Carey / Neilson	Edwards / Smith^	Doherty* / Bracewell	Goater / Moody	Cramb / Peschisolido Hayward	Tinnion /	Murray/Torpey / Cullip/Carpenter
26	10/1	H GRIMSBY	Cramb 1, 39, Taylor 5, Goater 47, Groves 82 — Ref: E Wolstenholme	12,567	1 (6)	W	55	4-1	3-0	Welch / Davison	Locke* / McDermott Gallimore	Bell / Rodger*	Goodridge / Lever	Taylor / Jobling	Carey /	Edwards / Donovan	Doherty^ / Black	Goater* / Livingstone Clare^	Cramb / Groves	Tinnion /	Murray/Hewlett/Torpey / Burnett/Woods
27	17/1	A WIGAN	Doherty 3, Tinnion 23, Goater 71 — Ref: D Laws	5,078	1 (16)	W	58	3-0	2-0	Welch / Butler	Locke / Bradshaw^ Morgan	Bell /	Goodridge* / Greenall	Taylor / McGibbon^ Martinez	Carey /	Edwards / Lee	Doherty / Rogers	Goater /	Cramb^ / Fitzhenry*	Tinnion / Lowe	Hewlett/Torpey / Smeets/Sharp/Warne
28	24/1	H NORTHAMPTON	Ref: D Hine	14,753	2 (5)	D	59	0-0	0-0	Welch / Woodman	Murray / Hill	Bell / Frain	Goodridge / Sampson	Taylor / Warburton	Carey / Brightwell	Hewlett / Hunt	Doherty / Dozzell	Goater* / Freestone^	Cramb* / Gayle	Tinnion / Hunter	Torpey / Gibb
29	31/1	H WREXHAM	Goater 5, Roberts 48 — Ref: P Danson	11,741	2 (13)	D	60	1-1	1-0	Welch / Marriott	Murray / McGregor Hardy	Bell / Phillips	Goodridge* / Ridler	Taylor /	Carey / Carey	Edwards / Spink	Doherty^ / Owen	Goater / Connelly^	Cramb^ / Roberts	Tinnion / Brammer	Hewlett/Torpey / Skinner
30	3/2	A BLACKPOOL	Hewlett 66, 77, Preece 54, Bent 88 — Ref: G Frankland	3,724	2 (14)	D	61	2-2	0-0	Welch / Banks	Murray / Bryan	Bell / Hills	Goodridge / Butler	Taylor / Strong	Carey / Linighan	Edwards / Bonner	Hewlett / Clarkson	Goater / Malin*	Cramb* / Bent	Tinnion / Preece	Torpey / Philpott
31	7/2	A BOURNEMOUTH	Fletcher 41 — Ref: P Rejer	6,673	2 (8)	L	61	0-1	0-1	Welch / Glass	Murray / Young Vincent	Bell / Rolling	Goodridge* / Cox	Taylor /	Carey / Bailey	Edwards / O'Neill	Hewlett / Robinson	Goater / Warren	Torpey* / Fletcher^ S	Tinnion / Brissett*	Locke / Barclay/Teather
32	14/2	H GILLINGHAM	Corbett 48, Southall 71 — Ref: A Hall	11,781	2 (9)	L	61	0-2	0-0	Welch / Stannard	Locke^ / Corbett	Bell / Pennock	Goodridge* / Smith	Taylor / Ashby	Owers / Butters	Edwards / Hessenthaler	Hewlett / Southall	Goater / Butler^	Johansen* / Akinbiyi	Tinnion / Galloway^	Torpey/Murray / Bryant^/Ratcliffe/Onuora, Teather
33	21/2	A LUTON	Ref: K Leach	6,978	2 (21)	D	62	0-0	0-0	Welch / Davis K	Locke / Patterson Thomas	Bell / Thomas	Goodridge* / Evers^	Taylor / Davis S	Carey / White	Edwards / Allen C^	Hewlett / McLaren	Goater / Oldfield	Johansen* / Gray	Tinnion / Alexander	Murray/Cramb / Fotiadis/Marshall
34	24/2	A YORK	Bell 65p — Ref: B Coddington	3,770	2 (13)	W	65	1-0	0-0	Welch / Samways	Locke / McMillan Murty	Bell / Bushell	Murray /	Taylor / Jones	Carey / Barras	Edwards / Pouton	Hewlett* / Tinkler	Goater* / Bull*	Torpey / Rowe	Tinnion / Stephenson	Owers/Cramb / Greening

Match reports

24 — A large crowd, not deterred by the mid-day kick-off, are thrilled as Cramb finishes off Bell's near-post cross and Edwards heads in Goodridge's long throw. Tinnion's strike from a 30-yard free-kick, and Taylor's header ensure a sparkling City win after Carl Veart shoots in for the Lions.

25 — City's 15-game unbeaten League run comes to an end as money-bags Fulham complete the double. City go down fighting, but do not produce much in the way of flowing football. Goater thumps a shot against the bar shortly before Paul Moody's glancing header settles the contest.

26 — Cramb's first-time shot from Goodridge's cross goes in after just 17 seconds as City get off to a good start to end Grimsby's 13-match unbeaten run. Taylor's bullet header and shots by Cramb and Goater overwhelm the Mariners, before Groves heads in a late response.

27 — Another excellent display by City after pint-sized Doherty heads in from a corner, and Tinnion strokes the ball past Lee Butler, following an exchange of passes with Cramb. After the break, Welch is forced to make three excellent saves, before Goater shoots in from twelve yards.

28 — The scantily-clad England Monarch cheerleaders provide the only entertainment at Ashton Gate as City's new goal-celebration music doesn't get an airing. John Gayle hits the crossbar for the Cobblers, but generally City miss the chances – Hewlett failing from less than a yard.

29 — Wrexham's refreshing display of attacking football gains them a deserved point. Goater's chip over Andy Marriott gets City off to a great start, but after Cramb has a shot cleared off the line play becomes more even. Neil Roberts capitalises on a rare Carey error to slot in the equaliser.

30 — Junior Bent, renowned for his inability to put the ball in the net whilst at Ashton Gate, breaks City's hearts with a lob that finds the back of the net. A topsy-turvy encounter sees Hewlett's header and shot give City a rather fortunate lead, after Andy Preece had fired Blackpool in front.

31 — City lose at Dean Court for the third time this season, but whilst they were unfortunate before, this time they get what they deserve. City fail to force Jimmy Glass to make a single testing save as they lose to Steve Fletcher's angled drive after Taylor blocks Christer Warren's shot.

32 — After a bright start, City are made to pay for their missed chances, when Iffy Onuora carves his way through to lay on Jim Corbett's opener. Taylor's passing error seals City's fate as the live-wire Onuora capitalises again. This time, against opponents with the Second Division's worst home record, they are constantly thwarted by Kelvin Davis as Luton make light of the gap between the teams to play a full part in a close encounter.

33 — City remain the division's top scorers despite the recent goals scarcity. (continued in match report)

34 — City keep up their good record at Bootham Crescent to end a spell of six games without a win. They are fortunate when Gary Bull heads over shortly before Bell cracks his spot-kick past Mark Samways, who is lucky to escape with a yellow card after bringing down Murray in the box.

Bristol City 1997–98 — Match-by-Match Record (Matches 35–46)

No.	Venue / Date	Opponent	Att.	A	Pos	Res	Pts	FT	HT	Scorers / Ref
35	H 28/2	SOUTHEND	12,049	2	23	W	68	1-0	1-0	Cramb 44 — Ref: R Styles
36	H 3/3	BRENTFORD	10,398	2	22	D	69	2-2	0-1	Torpey 54, Cockerill 61 (og); *Bryan 44, Rapley 79* — Ref: J Brandwood
37	H 14/3	BRISTOL ROV	17,086	1	8	W	72	2-0	1-0	Bell 35p, Goater 59 — Ref: E Lomas
38	A 21/3	PLYMOUTH	7,622	2	19	L	72	0-2	0-0	*Saunders 50, Conlon 77* — Ref: M Fletcher
39	A 28/3	WYCOMBE	6,326	2	16	W	75	2-1	1-0	Cramb 41, 84; *Harkin 57* — Ref: R Furnandiz
40	A 31/3	OLDHAM	4,543	1	14	W	78	2-1	0-1	Goodridge 52, Roberts 53; *Rush 23* — Ref: D Pugh
41	H 4/4	CARLISLE	12,578	1	23	W	81	1-0	0-0	Goodridge 53 — Ref: M Pierce
42	A 11/4	BURNLEY	10,820	1	22	L	81	0-1	0-1	*Payton 7p* — Ref: A Butler
43	H 13/4	WATFORD	19,141	1	2	D	82	1-1	0-0	Edwards 68; *Lee 64* — Ref: A Wiley
44	A 18/4	CHESTERFIELD	5,085	1	9	L	82	0-1	0-1	*Williams 43* — Ref: R Pearson
45	H 25/4	WALSALL	15,059	1	19	W	85	2-1	1-1	Owers 3, Tinnion 80; *Tholot 23* — Ref: S Mathieson
46	A 2/5	PRESTON	12,067	2	15	L	85	1-2	1-2	McCarthy 9; *Ashcroft 5, Eyres 10* — Ref: C Foy

Away 6,858 · Home 11,846 · Average 11,846

Line-ups, substitutes & match notes

35 — H SOUTHEND (W 1-0)
City: Welch, Locke, Bell, Murray, Taylor, Carey, Edwards, Doherty*, Torpey*, Cramb*, Tinnion*
Southend: Royce, Dublin, Hails, Gridelet, Jobson, Coleman, Maher, Jones!, Rammell, Aldridge*, Clarke; subs Owers/Johansen, Thomson/Stimson
"Already-booked Nathan Jones earns himself a red card for his dying swan act in attempting to win a pen when challenged by Murray. Despite a one-man advantage for two thirds of this game, City can only manage a solitary goal, when Cramb's header leaves Simon Royce motionless."

36 — H BRENTFORD (D 2-2)
City: Welch, Locke, Bell, Murray, Taylor, Carey, Edwards, Doherty, Torpey, Cramb*, Tinnion
Brentford: Dearden, Hutchings, Watson, Cullip, Cockerill*, Hogg, Oatway*, McGhee, Bryan*, Aspinall, Taylor; subs Thompson/Rapley/Canham
"Goater wastes the chance of a 3-1 lead, as he fails to appreciate that receiving the ball from a Brentford defender negates Cramb's offside position. Carl Hutchings' long throw twelve minutes later allows Kevin Rapley to net with an overhead kick to deprive City of two points."

37 — H BRISTOL ROV (W 2-0)
City: Welch, Locke, Bell, Murray, Taylor, Carey, Edwards, Hewlett, Torpey*, Goater, Tinnion
Bristol Rov: Collett, Pritchard, Power*, Penrice, Foster, Tillson, Holloway, Ramasut, Beadle, Cureton, Low*; subs Bennett/Hayfield
"An appalling first half is redeemed in the eyes of City fans as Goater wins a lucky penalty, when Dave Pritchard is judged to have nudged him in the back. Murray ties up the points when, after chasing a lost cause, he centres for Goater to shoot in his unlikely centre at the near post."

38 — A PLYMOUTH (L 0-2)
City: Welch, Locke, Bell, Murray, Taylor, Carey, Edwards*, Hewlett, Goater, Cramb, Tinnion
Plymouth: Sheffield, Williams*, Saunders, Heathcote, Wotton, Barlow, Starbuck, Conlon, Corazzin*, Billy; subs Rowbotham/Phillips, Doherty/Barclay
"Home Park has become a bogey ground again after City's sequence of success at this venue in the 1960s. Out-of-sorts City never look like turning the clock back, and they are outplayed as shots by Mark Saunders and Barry Conlon consign them to their eighth League defeat."

39 — A WYCOMBE (W 2-1)
City: Welch, Locke, Bell, Goodridge*, Taylor, Carey, Edwards, Hewlett*, McCarthy, Cramb*, Tinnion
Wycombe: Taylor, Kavanagh, Beeton, Ryan, Comforth, Mohan, Carroll*, Scott, McGavin*, Brown; subs Harkin/Reed
"A spirited performance at Adams Park after the shock sale of Goater. City's first-half display is their sharpest for weeks, as Cramb and loan signing McCarthy link up effectively. Cramb fires in a great 25-yard goal and then poaches City's winner by heading in Tinnion's cross."

40 — A OLDHAM (W 2-1)
City: Welch, Locke, Bell, Goodridge, Taylor, Carey, Owers, Hewlett, Roberts*, Cramb*, Tinnion
Oldham: Kelly, McNiven*, Holt, Garnett, Boxall, Rickers, Rush*, Duxbury, Hodgson!, Littlejohn*; subs Allott/Tipton/Redmond, Reid
"In front of the Sky TV cameras, City recover from Matthew Rush's superb strike to win in some style, before Doug Hodgson is sent off for kicking at Doherty. After Hewlett's shot is blocked, then Roberts shoots home the winner with some style, before Doug Hodgson is sent off for kicking at Doherty."

41 — H CARLISLE (W 1-0)
City: Welch, Locke, Bell, Goodridge, Taylor, Carey, Owers, Hewlett*, McCarthy*, Cramb*, Tinnion
Carlisle: Caig, Liburd*, Prokas, Thorpe, Varty, Foster, Anthony, Pounewat'y, Stevens, Wright; subs Roberts/Doherty, Smart, Couzens
"An inspired performance by Tony Caig in the swirling wind and torrential rain, but his one error allows City to extend their top of the table advantage to four points as Watford lose 2-3 at Wigan. He allows Goodridge's dipping shot from the edge of the box to slither under his body."

42 — A BURNLEY (L 0-1)
City: Welch, Locke, Bell, Goodridge, Taylor, Carey, Owers, Hewlett*, McCarthy*, Cramb, Tinnion
Burnley: Woods, Weller, Winstanley, Harrison, Moore, Little*, Waddle*, Mullin, Cooke, Payton*; subs Vinnicombe/Hoyland/Brass, Matthew, Doherty/Murray
"With promotion assured by Grimsby's failure to win yesterday, City are unable to capitalise against a committed Burnley side. Carey brings down Glen Little to concede the match-winning penalty, but Locke is unlucky when his great cross-shot in the final minutes is disallowed."

43 — H WATFORD (D 1-1)
City: Welch, Locke, Bell, Goodridge*, Taylor*, Carey, Owers, Doherty*, McCarthy, Cramb, Tinnion
Watford: Chamberlain, Kennedy, Page, Millen, Mooney, Hyde, Lee, Palmer, Hazan*; subs Edwards/Hewlett/Murray, Noel-Williams
"On a pitch bearing evidence of the recent American Football game, City are unable to make home advantage tell against their championship rivals. Jason Lee taps in after Welch is unable to hold Peter Kennedy's drive, but Edwards fires home from close range to salvage a point."

44 — A CHESTERFIELD (L 0-1)
City: Welch*, Locke, Bell, Goodridge, Edwards, Carey, Owers, Doherty*, McCarthy, Cramb, Tinnion
Chesterfield: Mercer, Perkins, Curtis, Williams, Carr*, Willis, Howard, Reeves, Wilkinson*, Beaumont; subs Paterson/Murray, Breckin/Lomas
"With Taylor out of action, City run into more trouble at Saltergate, as Welch is forced off early on with a groin injury. Tinnion gives an accomplished, but unorthodox, display between the sticks as City dominate territorially, and is only beaten when Mark Williams volleys in."

45 — H WALSALL (W 2-1)
City: Naylor, Locke, Bell, Goodridge, Paterson, Carey, Owers, Doherty, McCarthy, Cramb, Tinnion
Walsall: Walker, Evans, Viveash, Roper, Thomas*, Ricketts, Keister, Tholot, Porter, Hodge; subs Murray/Hewlett, Platt
"A great start as Owers heads in, but Locke is forced to clear off the line before Didlier Tholot outstrips the City defence to notch a fine leveller. Goodridge then has to follow Locke's example to keep Walsall at bay, but after the break Tinnion's free-kick brings City a hard-earned win."

46 — A PRESTON (L 1-2)
City: Naylor, Locke, Bell, Goodridge, Edwards, Carey, Owers, Doherty, McCarthy*, Cramb*, Tinnion
Preston: Moilanen, Parkinson, Barrick, Vieash, Jackson, Gregan, McKenna, Rankine, Davey, Macken; subs Murray/Hewlett, Ashcroft, Eyres
"With the fate of the championship in their own hands, City lack a cutting edge at Deepdale and lose out as Watford win at Fulham. After Lee Ashcroft's brilliant volley for North End, McCarthy levels by shooting into an open net, but David Eyres is at the far post to end City's hopes."

NATIONWIDE DIVISION 2 (CUP-TIES)   Manager: John Ward   SEASON 1997-98

Coca-Cola Cup

		F-A	H-T	Scorers, Times, and Referees	1	2	3	4	5	6	7	8	9	10	11	subs used
1:1 H BRISTOL ROV 12/8	9,341	D 0-0	0-0	Ref: G Cain	Welch	Locke	Bell	Paterson	Taylor	Edwards	Hewlett*	Owers	Goater	Cramb*	Tinnion	Tisdale/Bent
					Collett	*Perry*	*Foster*	*Beadle**	*Gayle*	*Tillson*	*Holloway*	*Penrice*	*Alsop*	*Cureton*	*Hayles*	*Bennett*

City's early superiority is matched by the Rovers after the break, as they fight out an even contest. Mickey Bell is the star performer, but City's midfield still lacks creativity. Bent's perfect cross sets up City's best chance near the end, but Goater heads tamely straight at Andy Collett.

		F-A	H-T	Scorers, Times, and Referees	1	2	3	4	5	6	7	8	9	10	11	subs used
1:2 A BRISTOL ROV 26/8	5,872	W 2-1 aet	0-0	Taylor 59, Bent 117 / *Alsop 48* / Ref: P Rejer (City won 2-1 on aggregate)	Welch	Locke	Bell	Paterson^	Taylor	Edwards	Hewlett	Owers	Goater	Cramb*	Tinnion	Bent/Carey
					Collett	*Perry*	*Pritchard*	*Bennett*	*Gayle*	*Tillson*	*Holloway*	*Penrice*	*Alsop**	*Cureton^*	*Hayles*	*Beadle/Lockwood*

Outplayed in the first half, City recover to put on one of their best derby displays, after Julian Alsop sends the ball looping into their net. After Taylor's emphatic header takes the tie into extra-time, substitute Bent latches onto a return pass from Owers to burst clear and settle the issue.

		F-A	H-T	Scorers, Times, and Referees	1	2	3	4	5	6	7	8	9	10	11	subs used
2:1 A LEEDS 17/9	8,806	L 1-3	0-1	Wetherall 19, Hasselb'k 69p, Ribeiro 90 / *Martyn 90p* / Ref: G Poll	Welch	Carey	Bell	Paterson	Taylor	Tisdale	Hewlett	Owers	Goater*	Torpey	Tinnion	Goodridge
					Martyn	*Halle*	*Robertson*	*Kelly*	*Radebe*	*Wetherall*	*Hopkin*	*Wallace*	*Hasselbaink**	*Kewell*	*Molenaar*	*Ribeiro*

After Goater pounces on David Wetherall's woeful back header to slide the ball under former Bristol Rovers keeper Nigel Martyn, a super 30-yard shot by Bruno Ribeiro ends City's hopes. Wetherall is fully involved, as he heads the opener and is fouled by Paterson for the penalty.

		F-A	H-T	Scorers, Times, and Referees	1	2	3	4	5	6	7	8	9	10	11	subs used
2:2 H LEEDS 30/9	10,857	W 2-1	1-1	Goodridge 41, Taylor 61 / *Hasselbaink 8* / Ref: N Barry (City lost 3-4 on aggregate)	Welch	Locke	Bell	Dyche	Taylor	Edwards	Goodridge	Owers	Torpey	Doherty*	Tinnion	Barclay
					Martyn	*Molenaar**	*Robertson*	*Kelly*	*Radebe*	*Wetherall*	*Hopkin*	*Wallace*	*Hasselbaink^*	*Haaland^*	*Bowyer*	*Halle/Lilley*

Taylor towers above a mêlée of players to plant a bullet header past Nigel Martyn, to give City hope of overturning Leeds' first-leg advantage. Jimmy Hasselbaink shoots past Welch to get United off to a great start, but his 30th-minute sending off for flooring Tinnion aids City's cause.

FA Cup

		F-A	H-T	Scorers, Times, and Referees	1	2	3	4	5	6	7	8	9	10	11	subs used
1 H MILLWALL 15/11	8,413	W 2-1	1-0	Taylor 24 / Ref: M Fletcher	Welch	Locke	Bell	Goodridge*	Taylor	Carey	Hewlett	Doherty	Torpey	Goater	Tinnion	Langan
					Spink	*Brown*	*Sturgess"*	*Bowry*	*Law*	*McLeary*	*Newman*	*Savage*	*Wilkinson*	*Allen^*	*Doyle**	*Grant/Hockton/Bircham*

City dominate the first half, but are called upon to give a resilient performance after the break, when Millwall make a determined effort to save the game. Goodridge gives a brilliant display of his dribbling skills, but the tie is won by Taylor's unstoppable header from Tinnion's corner.

		F-A	H-T	Scorers, Times, and Referees	1	2	3	4	5	6	7	8	9	10	11	subs used
2 A BOURNEMOUTH 7/12	5,687	L 1-3	0-1	Cramb 83 / *Carey 14 (og), O'Neill 80, Fletcher 90* / Ref: M Halsey	Welch	Locke	Bell	Goodridge	Taylor	Carey	Edwards	Tisdale^	Goater	Cramb	Brennan*	Tinnion/Barclay
					Glass	*Young*	*Vincent*	*Howe*	*Cox*	*Bailey*	*Beardsmore**	*Robinson*	*Warren*	*Fletcher*	*O'Neill*	*Rawlinson*

In front of the Sky TV cameras City dominate this thrilling cup-tie at Dean Court, but the plucky Cherries give them a lesson in finishing. Jimmy Glass keeps City at bay with a great display between the sticks, and it isn't until near the end that Cramb's diving header beats him.

Final League Table

		P	W	D	L	F	A	W	D	L	F	A	Pts
					Home					Away			
1	Watford	46	13	7	3	36	22	11	9	3	31	19	88
2	**BRISTOL CITY**	46	16	5	2	41	17	9	5	9	28	22	85
3	Grimsby *	46	11	7	5	30	14	7	11	5	25	23	72
4	Northampton	46	14	5	4	33	17	5	9	9	19	20	71
5	Bristol Rov	46	13	2	8	43	33	7	8	8	27	31	70
6	Fulham	46	12	7	4	31	14	7	6	10	29	29	70
7	Wrexham	46	10	10	3	31	23	8	6	9	24	28	70
8	Gillingham	46	13	7	3	30	18	6	6	11	22	29	70
9	Bournemouth	46	11	8	4	28	15	6	7	10	29	37	66
10	Chesterfield	46	13	7	3	31	19	4	7	12	15	25	65
11	Wigan	46	12	5	6	41	31	4	9	10	23	35	62
12	Blackpool	46	13	6	4	35	24	4	5	14	24	43	62
13	Oldham	46	13	7	3	43	23	3	6	14	19	31	61
14	Wycombe	46	10	10	3	32	20	4	8	11	19	33	60
15	Preston	46	10	6	7	29	26	5	8	10	27	30	59
16	York	46	9	7	7	26	21	6	7	10	26	37	59
17	Luton	46	7	7	9	35	38	8	5	10	25	26	57
18	Millwall	46	7	8	8	23	23	7	5	11	20	31	55
19	Walsall	46	10	8	5	26	16	3	7	13	17	36	54
20	Burnley	46	10	9	4	34	23	3	4	16	21	42	52
21	Brentford	46	9	7	7	33	29	3	7	13	17	42	50
22	Plymouth	46	10	5	8	36	30	2	8	13	19	40	49
23	Carlisle	46	8	5	10	27	28	3	6	14	30	45	44
24	Southend	46	8	7	8	29	30	3	3	17	18	49	43
		1104	262	162	128	783	554	128	162	262	554	783	1494

* promoted after play-offs

Odds & ends

Double wins: (7) Wigan, Southend, York, Millwall, Oldham, Bristol Rov, Wycombe.

Double losses: (2) Fulham, Gillingham.

Won from behind: (3) York (h), Burnley (h), Oldham (a).

Lost from in front: (1) Northampton (a).

High spots: Eight consecutive League victories. Brilliant home win over Grimsby. Colin Cramb's two goals at Wycombe. Recovering from half-time deficit to beat Oldham at Boundary Park. Doing the double over Bristol Rovers. Celebrations following the Walsall game at Ashton Gate.

Low spots: The loss of Taylor and Welch through injury and the transfer of Shaun Goater during the promotion run-in. Losing at Northampton, despite taking an early lead. Twice succumbing to Fulham. Poor display at Preston that lost the Championship. Inability to beat Bournemouth in four attempts (League, FA Cup and Autowindscreens Shield). The disgraceful decision by both Bristol City and Bristol Rovers not to contest what would have been the 100th Gloucestershire Senior Cup Final.

Player of the year: Shaun Taylor.

Ever-presents: (0).

Hat-tricks: Shaun Goater (1).

Leading scorer: Shaun Goater (18).

Appearances and Goals

Player	Lge	Sub	LC	Sub	FAC	Sub	Lge	LC	FAC	Tot
Barclay, Dominic										
Bell, Mickey	44		4		2		10			10
Bent, Junior		8		2						
Brennan, Jim	4	2		1						
Carey, Louis	37	1	1		1				1	1
Cramb, Colin	34	6	2		1		9	1		10
Doherty, Tom	22	8	1	1	1		2			2
Dyche, Sean	10	1	1		1					
Edwards, Rob	34	3	3		1		2			2
Goater, Shaun	28		5		3		17	1		18
Goodridge, Greg	28	3	3	1	1	1	6	1		7
Hewlett, Matt	27	7	3		3		4			4
Johansen, Stig	2	1								
Langan, Kevin		3				1				
Locke, Adam	35	2	2		2		1			1
McCarthy, Shaun	7						1			1
Murray, Scott	10	13					1			1
Naylor, Stuart	2		2							
Owers, Gary	20	2	4		1		1			1
Paterson, Scott	7	3	3		1					
Plummer, Dwayne	1	1								
Roberts, Jason		2								
Shail, Mark	2									
Taylor, Shaun	43		4		2		2	2	1	5
Tinnion, Brian	44		4		1	1	3			3
Tisdale, Paul	2	3	1	1	1					
Torpey, Steve	19	10	2	2	1		8			8
Welch, Keith	44		4		2					
(own-goals)							2			2
28 players used	506	86	44	6	22	3	69	5	2	76

Results

No	Date	Opponent	Att	Pos	Result	Pt	F-A	H-T	Scorers, Times, and Referees
1	H 8/8	OXFORD	13,729		D	1	2-2	2-1	Andersen 26, 44 / Murphy 18, Windass 48 — Ref: R Furnandiz
2	A 15/8	QP RANGERS	13,337		D	2	1-1	1-0	Hewlett 28 / Ready 90 — Ref: A Wiley
3	H 22/8	WATFORD (3)	13,063	17	L	2	1-4	0-1	Andersen 59 / Johnson 8, 61, Yates 58, Hazan 79 — Ref: B Knight
4	A 29/8	TRANMERE (22)	5,960	16	D	3	1-1	1-1	Akinbiyi 32 / Parkinson 7 — Ref: W Burns
5	H 31/8	HUDDERSFIELD (9)	11,801	19	L	3	1-2	1-0	Goodridge 12 / Horne 48, Stewart 52 — Ref: A Butler
6	A 5/9	SWINDON (18)	8,537	21	L	3	2-3	0-3	Akinbiyi 65, Bell 79p / Walters 2p, Ndah 5, Onuora 9 — Ref: P Rejer
7	A 8/9	SUNDERLAND (2)	32,745	20	D	4	1-1	0-1	Andersen 88 / Phillips 13 — Ref: D Pugh
8	H 13/9	WEST BROM (6)	13,761	22	L	4	1-3	0-2	Watts 69 / Hughes 11, 33, Quinn 52 — Ref: S Baines
9	A 19/9	IPSWICH (10)	13,657	23	L	4	1-3	0-2	Akinbiyi 88 / Johnson 13, 90, Scowcroft 33 — Ref: P Danson
10	H 26/9	CREWE (20)	9,810	22	W	7	5-2	3-0	Doherty 13, Goodridge 29, Murray 37, [Akin' 78, Hut' 89] / Anthrobus 72, 85 — Ref: R Styles
11	H 29/9	BARNSLEY (14)	12,005	22	D	8	1-1	0-0	Sheridan 74 / Bell 69 — Ref: A Leake

Line-ups (City top row, opponents in italic) and match notes

1 — OXFORD (H) 8/8

1	2	3	4	5	6	7	8	9	10	11	subs used
Welch	Locke	Bell	Hewlett	Watts	Dyche*	Goodridge"	Hutchings	Akinbiyi	Anders'n S*	Tinnion	Carey/Thorpe/Doherty
Whitehead	*Robinson*	*Marsh*	*Gray*	*Davis**	*Gilchrist*	*Banger"*	*Windass*	*Thomson"*	*Murphy*	*Beauchamp*	*Powell/Weatherstone/Smith*

City's attack looks proficient enough, but against more skilful opponents their defence gives cause for concern as Murphy is unmarked when he turns in Banger's cross. In the wilting heat Hewlett and Hutchings strike the woodwork either side of Andersen's tapped-in early equaliser.

2 — QP RANGERS (A) 15/8

1	2	3	4	5	6	7	8	9	10	11	subs used
Welch	Locke	Bell	Hewlett	Watts	Dyche*	Goodridge	Hutchings	Akinbiyi	Andersen S*	Tinnion	Thorpe/Dyche
Harper	*Heinola*	*Baraclough*	*Yates**	*Ready*	*Maddix*	*Murray*	*Peacock*	*Sheron*	*Gallen"*	*Scully*	*Slade/Rowland*

Despite Akinbiyi being given offside when he puts the ball in the net, City look set for their first win of the season by virtue of Hewlett's strike when he is played in by Andersen. Unfortunately, the defence falters in final seconds as the unmarked Karl Ready fires into the bottom corner.

3 — WATFORD (H) 22/8

1	2	3	4	5	6	7	8	9	10	11	subs used
Welch	Locke	Bell	Hewlett*	Watts*	Carey	Goodridge	Hutchings	Akinbiyi	Andersen S	Tinnion	Thorpe/Dyche
Chamberlain	*Kennedy*	*Bazeley*	*Palmer*	*Millen**	*Yates*	*Smart"*	*Hyde*	*Ngonge"*	*Johnson*	*Robinson*	*Hazan/Noel-Williams/Daley*

Watford demonstrate the art of finishing as they expose City's poor defending. Shortly after Andersen's powerful shot hauls City back into the game, Richard Johnson adds to his 30-yard opener with another screamer, but this time from only 25 yards. City are well beaten by the end.

4 — TRANMERE (A) 29/8

1	2	3	4	5	6	7	8	9	10	11	subs used
Welch	Locke	Bell	Hewlett	Watts	Carey	Edwards R	Hutchings	Akinbiyi	Andersen S*	Tinnion	Goodridge
Coyne	*Morgan"*	*Thompson*	*Allen*	*Hill*	*Irons*	*Morrissey"*	*O'Brien*	*Jones G*	*Parkinson*	*Jones L"*	*Koumas/Mellon/Russell*

In a contest that fades badly after an action-packed opening, Akinbiyi shows just why City paid a record £1.2 million for him. After Andy Parkinson drives in from John Morrissey's corner, Akinbiyi finishes off Tinnion's inviting free-kick with an unstoppable headed equaliser.

5 — HUDDERSFIELD (H) 31/8

1	2	3	4	5	6	7	8	9	10	11	subs used
Welch	Locke	Bell	Hewlett	Watts	Carey	Goodridge	Edwards R*	Akinbiyi	Andersen S*	Tinnion	Thorpe/Doherty
Vaesen	*Jenkins*	*Edwards*	*Johnson*	*Morrison*	*Collins*	*Browning"*	*Horne*	*Stewart*	*Allison*	*Thornley*	*Richardson*

Marcus Stewart nips in between Bell and Welch to fire home Town's winner as City pay yet again for their defensive shortcomings. Goodridge fires in from 15 yards for the opener, but City's failure to close down opponents allows Barry Horne to net with a screamer just after the break.

6 — SWINDON (A) 5/9

1	2	3	4	5	6	7	8	9	10	11	subs used
Welch	Bell	Edwards	Doherty	Watts	Dyche	Murray	Edwards R*	Akinbiyi	Thorpe*	Tinnion	Hewlett/Cramb
Talia	*Kerslake*	*Hall*	*Leitch"*	*Reeves*	*Borrows**	*Walters*	*Noah*	*Onuora*	*Bullock*	*Gooden*	*Davis !/Hulbert !*

City are lifted by their magnificent fans and nearly complete a stirring comeback. Shortly after Sol Davis is sent off for bringing down Murray to concede City's penalty, Akinbiyi almost breaks the bar with a close-range shot. Hulbert walks at the death for his second bookable offence.

7 — SUNDERLAND (A) 8/9

1	2	3	4	5	6	7	8	9	10	11	subs used
Welch	Locke	Bell	Doherty	Watts*	Dyche	Murray	Hewlett	Akinbiyi	Carey	Tinnion"	Andersen S/Goodridge
Sorensen	*Williams*	*Gray M*	*Ball*	*Melville*	*Butler"*	*Summerbee*	*Mullin*	*Dichio*	*Phillips*	*Johnson*	

A fortuitous point at the Stadium of Light, thanks to Andersen's magnificent shot on the turn. Welch, who saves a 24th-minute penalty from Kevin Phillips, is in great form between the sticks. In front of the Sky TV audience he saves City's over-run side from complete humiliation.

8 — WEST BROM (H) 13/9

1	2	3	4	5	6	7	8	9	10	11	subs used
Welch	Locke	Bell	Doherty	Carey	Dyche	Murray"	Hewlett"	Akinbiyi	Andersen S	Tinnion"	Goodridge/Watts/Cramb
Miller	*McDermott*	*Van Blerk*	*Flynn*	*Raven*	*Carbon*	*Quinn*	*De Frietas"*	*Hughes"*	*Kilbane*	*Sneekes*	*Bortolazzi/Mardon*

A 22-hour postponement of this game, due to yesterday's return of The Matthew to home waters, fails to save City from a rout. Watts heads in to give City hope after being caught square time and time again by the pace of Albion's strikers following Lee Hughes' tapped-in opener.

9 — IPSWICH (A) 19/9

1	2	3	4	5	6	7	8	9	10	11	subs used
Welch	Locke	Bell	Zwijnenb'rg	Watts	Carey	Brennan"	Hutchings"	Akinbiyi	Andersen S	Tinnion	Edwards R/Cramb/Murray
Wright	*Stockwell*	*Taricco*	*Clapham*	*Thetis"*	*Tanner*	*Dyer*	*Holland*	*Johnson*	*Scowcroft*	*Petta**	*Sonner/Holster*

Welch saves City from an even heavier defeat as they run out of ideas. Starting with a 5-3-2 formation, they progress through a conventional 4-4-2 to finish in 4-3-3 mode, but all to no avail. David Johnson lobs Welch in injury-time to extinguish hopes raised by Akinbiyi's header.

10 — CREWE (H) 26/9

1	2	3	4	5	6	7	8	9	10	11	subs used
Welch	Murray	Bell	Doherty	Watts	Carey	Goodridge	Edwards R*	Akinbiyi	Cramb*	Tinnion	Andersen S/Hutchings
Kearton	*Bignot*	*Smith S*	*Unsworth*	*Walton*	*Charnock**	*Wright*	*Johnson**	*Jack*	*Anthrobus*	*Rivers*	*Little/Lunt*

The message on Akinbiyi's and Goodridge's tee-shirts demonstrate City's great team spirit as they romp to their first League win of the season. The goal highlights are a spectacular volley from the edge of the box by Steve Anthrobus for his first, and Goodridge's thunderous 25-yarder.

11 — BARNSLEY (H) 29/9

1	2	3	4	5	6	7	8	9	10	11	subs used
Welch	Murray	Bell	Doherty	Watts	Carey	Goodridge*	Hutchings	Akinbiyi	Cramb"	Tinnion	Zwijnenberg/Andersen S
Leese	*Eaden*	*De Zeeuw*	*Richardson**	*Morgan*	*Appleby"*	*Hendrie*	*McClare*	*Ward*	*Bullock M*	*Barnard*	*Sheridan/Liddell/Fjortoft*

Bell's unstoppable free-kick from just outside the box gives City a surprise lead against a Barnsley side who control the play for long periods. Darren Sheridan brings Barnsley a deserved equaliser with a left-foot volley bent beyond Welch's dive into the top corner from fully 25 yards.

12 — A 3/10 BURY — 4,794 — 19 W — 12 11 — 1-0 (0-0)

Bell 67p

Ref: A Wiley

Welch	Murray	Bell	Doherty	Watts	Carey	Goodridge*	Hutchings	Akinbiyi	Cramb	Tinnion
Kiely	Woodward	Barrick	Daws	Lucketti	Redmond	Swailes C*	Matthews^	Billy	Patterson	Preece

Edwards R

Baldry^/Avdiu/Jemson

City's leaky defence somehow survives a battering at Gigg Lane, and it takes a conga on the terraces by their travelling fans to inspire some attacking ideas. Akinbiyi is brought down outside the area, but the referee's award of a penalty condemns Bury to their first home defeat.

13 — H 10/10 PORTSMOUTH — 13,056 — 18 D — 15 12 — 2-2 (1-1)

Murray 11, Andersen 85
Igoe 18, Claridge 70

Ref: A D'Urso

Welch	Murray	Bell	Doherty	Watts	Carey	Goodridge	Hutchings	Akinbiyi	Cramb*	Tinnion
Flahavan	Thogersen	Simpson F	Hillier	Whitbread	Awford	Perrett	Peron	Aloisi*	Claridge	Igoe

Andersen S/Edwards R

Durnin

Andersen rescues a point from this noon encounter against a skilful Pompey side prompted by the inspirational Sammy Igoe. He shoots past the advancing keeper to equalise Steve Claridge's header, after Murray's thunderous opener had been countered by Igoe's rounding of Welch.

14 — A 17/10 PORT VALE — 6,691 — 20 L — 15 12 — 2-3 (0-1)

Murray 55, Akinbiyi 59
Beesley 1, Ainsworth 47, 86

Ref: K Leach

Welch	Murray	Bell	Doherty	Watts	Carey	Goodridge*	Edwards R	Akinbiyi	Cramb	Tinnion
Musselwhite	Carragher	Tankard	Bogie	Barnett	Beesley	Ainsworth	Barker	Beadle	Foyle*	McGlinchey

Hutchings/Cramb

Snijders

City's spirited fight-back is of no avail as Tinnion's hapless defensive header sets up the Vale winner, with Ainsworth weaving past three men before firing in. After conceding the day's earliest goal, and another straight after the break, Murray's wickedly-deflected shot sparks City.

15 — A 20/10 GRIMSBY — 5,082 — 22 L — 5 12 — 1-2 (1-0)

Andersen 33
Groves 50, 60p

Ref: C Foy

Welch	Murray	Bell	Docherty*	Watts	Carey	Goodridge*	Edwards R	Akinbiyi	Andersen S	Tinnion
Davison	McDermott	Gallimore	Smith R	Lever	Widdrington	Donovan*	Smith D*	Nogan	Black	Groves

Thorpe/Hutchings

Lester/Livingstone

City's defence is all of a dither as their old inability to deal with corners allows Paul Groves to net with a stooping header, and then Kevin Donovan wins a penalty without falling down. Andersen punishes the Mariners' lax defending as he is free in the box to head in City's opener.

16 — H 23/10 BOLTON — 12,026 — 18 W — 7 15 — 2-1 (2-1)

Akinbiyi 28, Bell 45p
Gunnlaugsson 5

Ref: M Halsey

Welch	Murray*	Bell	Hutchings	Watts	Carey	Goodridge	Edwards R	Akinbiyi*	Andersen S*	Tinnion
Branagan	Cox	Whitlow	Jensen	Todd	Fish	Johansen	Frandsen^	Blake	Gardner*	Gunn'gsson

Thorpe/Zwijnenberg

Holdsworth/Taylor

Rip-roaring tussle in front of the Sky cameras after a 30-second silence for war victims. City refuse to be dismayed following Bolton's brilliant early strike. After Akinbiyi's poorly-hit shot finds the net with the aid of a deflection, Andersen is flattened for City's match-winning penalty.

17 — A 31/10 BRADFORD C — 14,468 — 21 L — 8 15 — 0-5 (0-2)

[Beagrie 58, Blake 90]
Mills 8, Carey 15 (og), Rankin 51,

Ref: A Bates

Welch	Walsh	Bell	Jacobs	Watts	Carey	Goodridge	Edwards R	Akinbiyi	Andersen S	Tinnion
Todd	Moore	Dreyer	Rankin	Blake	Mills*	Whalley	Beagrie^			

Shail

Lawrence/Watson/O'Brien

A cruel introduction to English football for new boss Benny Lennartsson as City are ripped to shreds at Valley Parade. In contrast to last week's heroics, a gutless performance as defensive frailties resurface. Mills starts the rot by firing in after receiving Moore's 50-yard pass.

18 — H 7/11 WOLVES — 15,432 — 21 L — 8 15 — 1-6 (1-2)

[Robinson 80] Hutchings 12
Whittingham 19, Connolly 21, 57, 67, 77,

Ref: P Taylor

Welch	Murray*	Bell*	Hutchings	Watts	Carey	Goodridge*	Thorpe*	Akinbiyi	Andersen S*	Tinnion
Stowell	Muscat*	Naylor	Emblen	Sedgley	Corica	Fernando*	Connolly^			

Cramb/Hill/Torpey

Robinson/Ferguson/Jones

Wolves inflict on an inept and passionless City side their worst home League loss for almost 50 years. Connolly thrives on the amount of space behind Bell to notch a deserved hat-trick. The sponsors show a fine appreciation of irony in their choice of Tinnion as City Man of the Match.

19 — A 14/11 CRYS PALACE — 17,821 — 23 L — 11 15 — 1-2 (1-2)

Andersen 35
Bradbury 5, Jansen 88

Ref: R Furnandiz

Welch	Murray*	Bell*	Hutchings	Watts	Carey	Goodridge	Edwards R	Akinbiyi*	Andersen S*	Tinnion
Digby	Austin*	Jihal	Petric	Burton	Foster	Lombardo	Rizzo^	Bradbury*	Jansen	Mullins

Tuttle/Curcic/Morrison

City battle back well after conceding an early goal. Carey's failure to cut out a through-ball allows Bradbury to curl in a shot past Welch, but Andersen levels with a delightful chip. Unfortunately, straight after Akinbiyi hits the post Jansen finds himself free to head powerfully home.

20 — H 21/11 STOCKPORT — 11,032 — 23 D — 17 16 — 1-1 (1-0)

Thorpe 43
Angell 53

Ref: P Rejer

Welch	Murray	Bell*	Hutchings	Watts	Carey	Goodridge	Thorpe*	Akinbiyi	Andersen S*	Tinnion
Nash	Connelly	Woodthorpe Cook*	Flynn	McIntosh	Gannon*	Angell^	Matthews^			

Cooper/Wilbraham/Dinning

Goodridge/Tinnion
Branch

Akinbiyi's failure to score, perhaps put off by the innovation of a yellow ball, when clean through on a through-ball, costs City the points in a game where all the good football is played by Stockport. For the second successive home match Bell fails to make a worthwhile tackle.

21 — A 28/11 BIRMINGHAM — 17,577 — 23 L — 4 16 — 2-4 (2-3)

Thorpe 4, Andersen 45
Johnson M 5, Ndlovu 14, Forster 42, 72

Ref: B Coddington

Welch	Murray	Bell*	Hutchings	Watts	Carey	Goodridge*	Edwards R*	Akinbiyi	Andersen S*	Tinnion
Poole	Rowett	Charlton*	Purse	Grainger	Johnson M	McCarthy	Holland	Forster^	Robinson	Ndlovu

Goodridge/Tinnion

Hughes/Johnson A

For once it is City who take an early lead as Thorpe's half-volley finds the net, but straight away Michael Johnson's header loses them the advantage. Nicky Forster punishes dominant City for spurning many chances after the break by heading in following Akinbiyi's bad miss.

22 — H 5/12 SHEFFIELD UTD — 11,134 — 23 W — 9 19 — 2-0 (1-0)

Bell 33p, Akinbiyi 65

Ref: A Hall

Phillips	Brennan	Bell	Hutchings	Watts	Carey	Goodridge	Edwards R*	Akinbiyi	Andersen S*	Tinnion
Tracey	O'Connor	Quinn	Henry	Derry	Sandford	Ford	Hamilton	Marcelo	Devlin*	Woodhouse

Murray/Doherty

Twiss

United, weakened by the loss of eight regulars, have Henry sent off in the 85th minute for his blatant late challenge on Phillips. The crowd are mystified by City's penalty award as Hamilton is adjudged to have pulled Thorpe's shirt. Akinbiyi cracks the points with a powerful header.

23 — H 12/12 CRYS PALACE — 13,014 — 23 D — 14 20 — 1-1 (1-1)

Akinbiyi 25
Bell 23 (og)

Ref: E Wolstenholme

Phillips	Murray	Bell	Hutchings	Watts	Carey	Edwards R	Thorpe	Akinbiyi*	Andersen S	Tinnion
Miller	Amsalem	Crowe	Petric*	Burton	Foster	Rodger	Mullins	Svensson^	Jansen	Tuttle

Goodridge/Doherty

Bradbury/Thomson
Brown

A case of two points lost against a Crystal Palace team who run out of steam after the half-time break. Bell supplies the cross for Akinbiyi's headed equaliser within a couple of minutes of conceding an own-goal in his attempts to clear Craig Foster's toe-poke over the diving Phillips.

NATIONWIDE LEAGUE DIVISION 1

Manager: Ward ⇨ Benny Lennartsson   SEASON 1998-99

No	H/A	Opponent	Date	Att	Pos	OppPos	Res	Pt	F-A	H-T	Scorers, Times, and Referees	1	2	3	4	5	6	7	8	9	10	11	subs used
24	A	NORWICH	19/12	17,022	23	5	L	20	1-2	1-2	Akinbiyi 20 / Roberts 18, 36 / Ref: J Brandwood	Phillips / Watt	Brennan / Kenton	Bell / Mackay	Hutchings / Grant	Shail / Wilson	Carey / Jackson	Edwards R* / Adams*	Thorpe / Eadie	Akinbiyi / Roberts	Murray / Russell*	Goodridge / Llewellyn	Andersen S/Torpey, Sutch/Marshall
25	A	WATFORD	26/12	15,081	23	3	L	20	0-1	0-0	Smart 57 / Ref: R Styles	Phillips / Chamberlain	Brennan / Bazeley	Bell / Kennedy	Hutchings* / Page	Shail / Palmer	Edwards C / Iroha	Murray* / Smart	Tistimet'u / Hyde	Akinbiyi / Ni'i Williams	Torpey / Johnson	Andersen S / Gudmundss'n	Thorpe/Doherty/Goodridge
26	H	SWINDON	28/12	16,257	23	15	W	23	3-1	1-0	Torpey 8, 51, Akinbiyi 75 / Ndah 46 / Ref: M Pierce	Phillips / Talia	Brennan* / Robinson*	Bell / Hall	Doherty / Hulbert	Shail / Taylor	Edwards C / Ndah	Murray / Walters	Tistimetanu / Hay^	Akinbiyi / Onuora^	Torpey / Bullock	Andersen S / Davis	Hutchings, Watson/Cowe/Reeves
27	A	OXFORD	9/1	9,434	23	21	D	24	0-0	0-0	Ref: A Leake	Phillips / Gerrard	Brennan / Robinson	Bell / Powell	Murray / Warren	Shail / Watson	Edwards C / Gilchrist	Hewlett* / Remy	Tistimetanu / Murphy	Akinbiyi / Banger	Torpey / Windass	Andersen S / Beauchamp	Locke
28	H	TRANMERE	16/1	13,217	21	16	D	25	1-1	1-1	Locke 25 / Mahon 8 / Ref: M Warren/S Castle	Phillips / Coyne	Brennan / Allen	Bell / Thompson^ / McGreal	Locke* / Challinor	Shail / —	Carey / Irons	Murray / Mahon	Tistimetanu / O'Brien^	Akinbiyi / Parkinson*	Torpey / Hill	Andersen S* / Taylor	Tinnion/Hutchings, Jones L/Jones G
29	A	HUDDERSFIELD	30/1	14,034	22	10	D	26	2-2	1-1	Akinbiyi 16, Locke 62 / Phillips 3, Johnson 60 / Ref: G Frankland	Phillips / Vaesen	Brennan / Jenkins	Bell / Edwards	Locke / Johnson^	Shail / Collins^	Carey / Gray^	Edwards R / Beech	Tistimetanu* / Phillips	Akinbiyi / Stewart	Torpey / Allison	Tinnion / Thornley	Murray/Andersen S, Hessey/Beresford
30	H	QP RANGERS	5/2	13,841	22	17	D	27	0-0	0-0	Ref: J Kirkby	Phillips / Miklosko	Brennan / Heinola*	Bell / Baraclough^	Locke / Morrow	Shail / Ready	Carey / Maddix	Murray* / Plummer	Tistimetanu / Peacock	Akinbiyi / Dowie	Torpey / Gallen	Tinnion / Kiwomya	Goodridge, Murray/Scully
31	H	SUNDERLAND	13/2	15,736	23	1	L	27	0-1	0-0	Phillips 89p / Ref: K Styles	Phillips / Sorensen	Brennan / Makin	Bell* / Gray M	Locke / Ball	Shail / Melville	Carey / Butler	Murray / Summerbee	Tistimetanu / Clark	Edwards R* / Quinn*	Torpey* / Johnston	Tinnion / Phillips	Sebok/Andersen S, Dichio
32	A	WEST BROM	20/2	16,343	23	9	D	28	2-2	0-1	Akinbiyi 60, 85 / Hughes 32, 90 / Ref: P Walton	Phillips / Whitehead	Brennan / Holmes	Bell* / Van Blerk	Locke / Bortolazzi^	Shail* / Murphy	Carey / Raven	Brown / Quinn	Tistimetanu* / Sneekes	Akinbiyi / De Freitas*	Torpey / Hughes	Tinnion / Kilbane	Sebok/Andersen S, Flynn/Angel
33	H	IPSWICH	27/2	14,065	23	3	L	28	0-1	0-0	Naylor 56 / Ref: B Knight	Phillips / Wright	Brennan / Wilnis*	Bell* / Thetis	Sebok / Clapham	Shail / Mowbray	Carey / Venus	Brown / Dyer	Edwards R* / Holland	Akinbiyi / Naylor	Torpey / Harewood^	Andersen S* / Magilton	Hill, Stockwell/Petta
34	H	BURY	9/3	11,606	23	22	D	29	1-1	0-1	Andersen 80 / D'Jaffo 17 / Ref: A D'Urso	Phillips / Kiely	Brennan / West	Langan^ / Serrant	Locke / Daws	Shail* / Lucketti	Carey / Redmond	Brown* / Swailes C	Edwards R / Hall	Akinbiyi / D'Jaffo*	Torpey / Billy	Doherty / Littlejohn^	Andersen S/Murray/Hill, Jamson/Preece

Match reports

24 — Norwich: Akinbiyi is the early hero when latching onto Edwards' through-pass to slide the ball under Michael Watt, but turns villain at the death. He misses two relatively simple chances to equalise, after Iwan Roberts deflects in Matt Jackson's goalward header, to add to his headed opener.

25 — Watford: City have the better of the early play as Ben Iroha almost heads Bell's centre into his own net. Hutchings has his header cleared off the line, and Andersen's 25-yard drive hits the bar. Watford resort to time-wasting tactics at the end as they hang on to Allan Smart's 15-yard winner.

26 — Swindon: Torpey is City's hero with a bizarre opening goal as his swinging left foot connects 30 yards out to send the ball looping over the advancing Frank Talia to bounce high into the net. George Ndah expertly beats Phillips, but Torpey's header and Akinbiyi's drive tie up City's win.

27 — Oxford: City show few attacking ideas as they end a poor away run. Phillips is in top form to deny Oxford, making a point-blank stop as early as the second minute, while Bell and Murray both effect clearances off the goal-line. Paul Gerrard's finger-tip save denies Torpey a headed goal.

28 — Tranmere: Challinor's missile-like throws cause City problems, but Locke equalises Mahon's early shot, by driving in a loose ball. Steve Castle (a 48th-minute replacement for the injured Mark Warren) harshly sends off Andy Thompson for his second bookable offence near the call of time.

29 — Huddersfield: The strength, courage and determination of Akinbiyi allows City to recover from the early shock of David Phillips' breathtaking 30-yard strike. He powerfully heads an equaliser, and then, shortly after Grant Johnson had fired Town back in front, flicks on a cross for Locke to stab in.

30 — QP Rangers: Creativity is at a minimum as these struggling sides fail to serve up a Friday night treat for the live Sky TV audience. City have the best of the chances, Brennan's 20-yarder skimming the bar in the 62nd minute, but the killer touch is lacking as the fear of defeat dominates the action.

31 — Sunderland: The dark blue of Sunderland's shirts forces the officials to turn out in green shirts, whilst the keepers perform in yellow jerseys. City are denied a deserved share of the spoils as Kevin Phillips on his namesake Kevin gifts Sunderland their match-winning penalty.

32 — West Brom: In the seventh minute of injury-time, City's sloppy defending allows Lee Hughes to shoot in the Baggies' equaliser. Torpey hits the woodwork before Hughes heads Albion's opener, but Akinbiyi makes amends for early misses by firing in, either side of Brown being denied by a post.

33 — Ipswich: City's poor finishing, allied to the excellent form of keeper Richard Wright, allows Ipswich to keep their 19th clean sheet of the campaign with this smash and grab win. After Akinbiyi puts his header wide from just six yards, Richard Naylor has time and space to shoot in Dyer's pass.

34 — Bury: A lacklustre display by shapeless City in this aerial encounter. Laurent D'Jaffo's seventh-minute strike is ruled out for handball, but no escape for City shortly after, when his low swerving drive gives Bury a deserved lead. Substitute Andersen rescues a point with his six-yard header.

35 — A 13/3 WOLVES 25,237 — L 0-3 (23, 6, 29)

Scorers: Flo 14, 84, Sebok 53 (og). Ref: D Crick

Phillips	Brennan	Murray	Sebok	Locke*	Carey	Andersen S	Edwards R	Torpey	Tinnion^	Doherty/Heaney
Stowell	Atkins	Gilkes	Richards	Sedgley	Curle	Simpson^	Emblem*	Flo	Keane	Osborn^

Robinson/Corica/Connolly

City's improved display is thwarted by Phillips as he misses his kick in attempting to deal with Sebok's simple back-pass. A long crossfield ball allows Haavard Flo to slide home Wolves' opener, and he adds his second with a clinical volley for a somewhat flattering victory margin.

36 — H 20/3 BRADFORD C 10,870 — L 2-3 (24, 3, 29)

Scorers: Akinbiyi 51, Andersen 81; Mills 30, Jacobs 40, Whalley 83. Ref: W Jordan

Phillips	Brennan	Sebok	Doherty	Locke*	Carey	Heaney^	Edwards R*	Akinbiyi	Torpey	Tinnion^
Walsh	Todd	Jacobs	McCall	Moore	Dreyer	Lawrence	Windass*	Mills	Whalley	Beagrie

Locke/Murray · Rankin

City's early ineptitude brings down the fans wrath on Benny Lennartsson, but a second-half recovery almost saves the game. Unfortunately, after superb headed goals from Akinbiyi and Andersen, the defence dithers and allows Gareth Whalley the time to drill in Bradford's winner.

37 — A 23/3 BARNSLEY 14,741 — L 0-2 (24, 15, 29)

Scorers: Dyer 32, Hignett 89. Ref: G Laws

Andersen B	Brennan	Murray	Shail	Locke	Carey	Heaney^	Brown^	Akinbiyi	Andersen	Tinnion
Bullock T	Eaden	De Zeeuw	Richardson	Moses	Appleby	Van der L*^	Hignett	Sheron	Dyer^	Jones

Goodridge/Hewlett · Blackmore/Hristov

With both sides seeking their first League win in three months, it is City who find themselves in their all-familiar role as the fall guys. After Bruce Dyer shoots in Barnsley's opener, Craig Hignett kills off City by steering the ball in from Mike Sheron's cross to round off a fine move.

38 — H 3/4 PORT VALE 11,039 — W 2-0 (24, 22, 32)

Scorers: Akinbiyi 31, Howells 36. Ref: S Bennett

Andersen B	Brennan	Sebok	Taylor	Locke	Carey	Howells*	Brown	Akinbiyi	Torpey	Tinnion
Musselwhite	Aspin	Tankard	Brammer	Butler^	Awford	Talbot	Bent	Foyle	Widdrington^	Smith/Lee/Beesley

Goodridge

Shaun Taylor's return inspires City to their first win of the year, but Vale are far from being outplayed. Brennan has to clear off the line, while both Stewart Taylor and Alan Lee are denied by the woodwork. Akinbiyi's header and a brilliant half-volley by Howells clinch the spoils.

39 — A 5/4 PORTSMOUTH 13,026 — W 1-0 (24, 18, 35)

Scorers: Locke 87. Ref: F Stretton

Andersen B	Brennan	Sebok	Taylor	Locke	Carey	Howells	Brown	Akinbiyi	Torpey*	Tinnion
Knight	Robinson	Simpson	McLoughlin	Whitbread	Awford	Nightingale^	Peron	Viachos	Claridge^	Igoe

Andersen S · Durnin/Phillips

City fans are in dreamland as Locke clinches victory at Fratton Park, when he is unmarked at the far post to head in Tinnion's corner. City ride their luck in injury-time as Matthew Robinson's header hits the bar, but straight away Akinbiyi races clear at the other end and only to shoot wide.

40 — H 10/4 GRIMSBY 11,616 — W 4-1 (23, 13, 38)

Scorers: Torpey 21, Akinbiyi 43, 62, Tinnion 55; Ashcroft 13. Ref: S Mathieson

Andersen B	Brennan	Sebok	Taylor^	Locke	Carey	Howells*	Black	Akinbiyi	Torpey^	Tinnion
Love	McDermott*	Gallimore	Livingstone	Lever	Burnett^	Caldicott	Ashcroft	Claridge^	Lester^	Groves

Goodridge/Andersen S/Shail · Butterfield/Nogan/Clare

Refusing to be put out of their stride by Lee Ashcroft's stunning 25-yard strike, City hit back as Torpey shoots in at the near post. Grimsby have no answer to City's onslaught as a header and a shot by Akinbiyi, as well as Tinnion's great strike, raise hopes of escape from relegation.

41 — A 13/4 BOLTON 14,459 — L 0-1 (23, 5, 38)

Scorers: Gudjohnsen 7. Ref: A Hall

Andersen B	Brennan	Sebok	Taylor	Locke	Carey	Howells	Brown^	Akinbiyi*	Torpey	Tinnion
Banks	Cox	Phillips	Frandsen	Todd	Fish	Johnansen	Jensen	Gudjohnsen	Taylor	Gardner

Andersen S/Goodridge

At the Reebok Stadium City are caught cold early on as Eidur Gudjohnsen blasts home from close in. Bolton are rampant in the first half, but after the break City make a more even game of it against opponents with only one win in ten games. Locke nets on 51 minutes, but is offside.

42 — A 17/4 STOCKPORT 7,602 — D 2-2 (23, 14, 39)

Scorers: Brennan 58, Tinnion 77; Ellis 56, 69. Ref: B Coddington

Andersen B	Brennan	Sebok	Taylor	Locke	Carey	Howells	Brown*	Andersen S^	Torpey	Tinnion
Nash	Gannon	Dinning	Smith	Flynn	McIntosh	Cooper	Matthews*	Angell	Ellis	Woodthorpe/Moore

Goodridge/Cramb

Brennan's shot into the far corner and Tinnion's scorching drive enable City to retain an unbeaten record at Edgeley Park that goes back 86 years. Torpey performs wonders to divert Mike Flynn's header for a corner midway through the first half as County threaten to tear City apart.

43 — H 24/4 BIRMINGHAM 15,845 — L 1-2 (24, 4, 39)

Scorers: Akinbiyi 46; Grainger 48p, Ndlovu 70. Ref: M Dean

Andersen B	Brennan	Sebok	Taylor	Locke	Carey	Howells	Brown^	Akinbiyi	Torpey^	Doherty*
Poole	Rowett	Grainger	Hyde	Holdsworth	Johnson	Bass	Robinson*	Bradbury^	Hughes	Ndlovu

Goodridge/Cramb/Shail · McCarthy/Furlong

The referee reaches the height of notoriety, giving a pen as Ndlovu is challenged outside the box, after previously disallowing Akinbiyi's 26th-min tap-in and Lee Bradbury's 41st-min header, as well as ignoring Jonathan Bass's handball. Howells' weak back-pass gives away the points.

44 — A 27/4 CREWE 5,579 — L 0-1 (24, 19, 39)

Scorers: Johnson 23. Ref: C Foy

Andersen B	Brennan	Shail	Taylor	Locke	Carey	Howells^	Brown*	Akinbiyi	Torpey	Tinnion
Kearton	Wright D	Smith S	Macauley	Walton	Charnock	Wright J	Johnson	Jack*	Murphy	Rivers

Doherty/Edwards R/Cramb · Street

City control most of this game against fellow strugglers, but their inability to get behind Crewe's rearguard all but makes relegation a certainty. Lennartsson bemoans the loss of Brennan and Sebok on international duty as Rodney Jack's cross sets up Seth Johnson to ram the ball home.

45 — A 1/5 SHEFFIELD UTD 17,316 — L 1-3 (24, 8, 39)

Scorers: Akinbiyi 61; Marcelo 44, Morris 55, 64. Ref: D Pugh

Andersen B	Brennan	Shail^	Taylor*	Locke	Carey	Howells^	Brown	Akinbiyi	Torpey	Tinnion
Kelly	Derry	Kozluk	Dellas	Sandford*	Tebily	Donis	Hunt^	Marcelo^	Devlin	Morris

Goodridge/Doherty/Cramb · Jacobsen/Quinn/Katchouro

At the last chance saloon Marcelo shoots the Blades ahead as five defenders back off, while City's only reply to two strikes by Morris is Akinbiyi's header. After Doherty's 88th-min sending off for handling Tebily's goal-bound shot, Morris has his penalty saved by Bo Andersen.

46 — H 9/5 NORWICH 10,856 — W 1-0 (24, 9, 42)

Scorers: Pinamonte 40. Ref: M Halsay

Anderson B	Brennan	Sebok	Doherty	Jordan	Carey	Goodridge*	Brown	Akinbiyi	Torpey	Pinamonte
Marshall A	Kenton	Fugelstad	Marshall L	Jackson	Mackay	Arselin^	Bellamy	Roberts	Devlin	Mulryne

Bell* · Andersen S/Meechan · Llewellyn · Carey

A typical end-of-season non-event enlivened by City's amazing fans who form congas in the stands. Reserve top scorer Lorenzo Pinamonte shows a true striker's instincts, sticking out a foot to divert Akinbiyi's header into the net for a close-range debut goal on his 21st birthday.

Home 12,818 · Away 13,502 · Average 13,502

NATIONWIDE DIVISION 1 (CUP-TIES)　Manager: Ward ⇨ Benny Lennartsson　SEASON 1998-99

Worthington Cup

		F-A	H-T	Scorers, Times, and Referees	1	2	3	4	5	6	7	8	9	10	11	subs used
1:1 H SHREWSBURY	W	4-0	3-0	Hutchings 13, Akinbiyi 14, 54.	Welch	Locke	Bell	Hewlett	Watts˘	Carey	Goodridge"	Hutchings	Akinbiyi	Andersen S*	Tinnion	Thorpe/Dyche/Murray
3,585				Ref: P Taylor	*Edwards* [Andersen 21]	*Seabury*	*Hanmer*	*Jobling*	*Wilding*	*Gayle*	*Craven*	*Kerrigan˘*	*Steele**	*Evans*	*Preece**	*Jagielka/White/Williams*

City put on a classy show on a night where nearly everything goes right. Hutchings opens the scoring with a perfectly-timed run and jump to meet Tinnion's free-kick and angle a header into the bottom corner, and then supplies the pass for Akinbiyi to fire in from the edge of the area.

		F-A	H-T	Scorers, Times, and Referees	1	2	3	4	5	6	7	8	9	10	11	subs used
1:2 A SHREWSBURY	L	3-4	2-2	Thorpe 4, Akinbiyi 30, 54, Hewlett 88.	Welch	Locke	Brennan	Hewlett	Dyche	Carey !	Murray*	Doherty	Akinbiyi"	Thorpe^	Tinnion	Watts/Edwards R/Cramb
1,011				Evans 39p, 43, 47p, Jobling 69. Ref: M Dean	*Edwards*	*Seabury*	*Hanmer*	*Herbert*	*Wilding*	*Gayle*	*Craven*	*Jagielka*	*White*	*Evans*	*Jobling*	
				(City won 7-4 on aggregate)												

After Thorpe's tap-in and Akinbiyi's conversion of Murray's low centre for a 6-0 aggregate lead, City lose their way. Handball by Akinbiyi and Dyche concede pens, whilst Paul Evans nets in Beckham-like style after the sending off of Carey for his professional foul on Jagielka.

		F-A	H-T	Scorers, Times, and Referees	1	2	3	4	5	6	7	8	9	10	11	subs used
2:1 H CREWE 22	D	1-1	1-1	Akinbiyi 15.	Welch	Locke	Bell	Hutchings	Watts	Carey*	Goodridge^	Brennan	Akinbiyi	Andersen S	Tinnion	Edwards R/Murray
3,082 18				Rivers 21. Ref: M Fletcher	*Kearton*	*Bignot**	*Smith S*	*Wicks*	*Charnock"*	*Unsworth*	*Rivers*	*Street*	*Little"*	*Wright J*	*Smith P*	*Wright D/Foster/Lunt*

A bore for the fans as boss Ward makes no apology for sacrificing entertainment to halt City's poor run. Akinbiyi has the easiest of tap-ins to put the Robins ahead, but poor defending allows Mark Rivers to collect Colin Little's through-pass and lift the ball over the stranded Welch.

		F-A	H-T	Scorers, Times, and Referees	1	2	3	4	5	6	7	8	9	10	11	subs used
2:2 A CREWE 23	L	0-2	0-0	Rivers 62, 64.	Welch	Murray	Bell	Doherty*	Zwijnenberg	Watts	Goodridge	Edwards R	Akinbiyi	Cramb^	Tinnion	Hutchings/Andersen S
3,089 11				Ref: R Pearson	*Kearton*	*Bignot*	*Smith S*	*Unsworth*	*Walton*	*Charnock*	*Wright J*	*Johnson*	*Little^*	*Anthrobus*	*Rivers*	*Street*
				(City lost 1-3 on aggregate)												

In a tight first half City, looking solid at the back, have the better chances, but after the interval Mark Rivers, who switches flanks to escape Murray, turns the game. Watts is deceived by his shot on the turn and a few minutes later he taps the ball over the goal-line after Welch saves.

FA Cup

		F-A	H-T	Scorers, Times, and Referees	1	2	3	4	5	6	7	8	9	10	11	subs used
3 H EVERTON 23	L	0-2	0-0	Bakayoko 86, 88.	Phillips	Locke*	Bell	Murray	Shail	Carey	Hewlett*	Tistimetanu	Akinbiyi	Torpey	Andersen S	Goodridge/Hutchings
19,608 P:14				Ref: J Winter	*Myhre*	*Dunne*	*Ball*	*Bilic*	*Watson*	*Unsworth*	*Cadamarei"*	*Barmby**	*Bakayoko*	*Dacourt**	*Hutchison*	*Grant/Oster/Branch*

Hewlett hits the post as City dominate this game in front of the Match of the Day cameras, but Everton snatch a late win, much as they did four years previously. Unlucky when ref fails to consult linesman flagging for a penalty, City's hearts are broken by Ibrahim Bakayoko's free-kick.

League Table

		P	Home					Away					Pts
			W	D	L	F	A	W	D	L	F	A	
1	Sunderland	46	19	3	1	50	20	12	9	2	41	18	105
2	Bradford City	46	15	4	4	48	20	11	5	7	34	27	87
3	Ipswich	46	16	1	6	37	15	10	7	6	32	17	86
4	Birmingham	46	12	7	4	32	15	11	5	7	34	22	81
5	Watford *	46	12	7	4	30	19	9	7	7	35	37	77
6	Bolton	46	13	6	4	44	25	7	10	6	34	34	76
7	Wolves	46	11	10	2	37	19	8	6	9	27	24	73
8	Sheffield Utd	46	12	6	5	42	29	6	7	10	29	37	67
9	Norwich	46	7	12	4	34	28	8	5	10	28	33	62
10	Huddersfield	46	11	6	6	38	23	4	10	9	24	48	61
11	Grimsby	46	11	6	6	25	18	5	7	11	15	34	61
12	West Brom	46	12	4	7	43	33	4	7	12	26	43	59
13	Barnsley	46	7	9	7	35	30	7	8	8	24	26	59
14	Crys Palace	46	11	10	2	43	26	3	6	14	15	45	58
15	Tranmere	46	7	9	7	37	30	5	11	7	26	31	56
16	Stockport	46	7	9	7	24	21	5	8	10	25	39	53
17	Swindon	46	7	8	8	40	44	6	3	14	19	37	50
18	Crewe	46	8	6	9	27	35	4	6	13	27	43	48
19	Portsmouth	46	10	5	8	34	26	3	3	17	23	47	47
20	QP Rangers	46	9	7	7	34	22	3	4	16	18	39	47
21	Port Vale	46	10	3	10	22	28	3	5	15	23	47	47
22	Bury	46	9	7	7	24	27	3	4	16	11	33	47
23	Oxford	46	7	8	8	31	30	3	6	14	17	41	44
24	BRISTOL CITY	46	7	8	8	35	36	2	7	14	22	44	42
		1104	250	163	139	846	609	139	163	250	609	846	1493

* promoted after play-offs

Appearances / Goals

	Appearances						Goals			
	Lge	Sub	LC	Sub	FAC	Sub	Lge	LC	FAC	Tot
Akinbiyi, Ade	44		4			1	19	4		23
Andersen, Bo	10									
Andersen, Soren	26	13	2	1	1		10	1		11
Bell, Mickey	33		3		1		5			5
Brennan, Jim	29		2				1			1
Brown, Aaron	14				1					
Carey, Louis	40	1	3		1					
Cramb, Colin	4	9	1	1	1		1			1
Doherty, Tom	15	8	2		1		1			1
Dyche, Sean	4	2	1		1					
Edwards, Christian	3									
Edwards, Rob	19	4	1	2						
Goodridge, Greg	15	15	3			1	2			2
Heaney, Neil	2	1								
Hewlett, Matt	8	2	2		1		1		1	2
Hill, Matt	8	3								
Howells, David	8						1			1
Hutchings, Carl	16	5	2	1	1	1	2	1		3
Jordan, Andrew	1									
Langan, Kevin	1									
Locke, Adam	26	2	3		1		3			3
Meechan, Alex		1								
Murray, Scott	27	5	2	2	1		3			3
Phillips, Steve	15		2	1	1					
Pinamonte, Lorenzo	1									
Sebok, Vilmos	10	2								
Shail, Mark	21	3			1					
Taylor, Shaun	8									
Thorpe, Tony	9	7	1	1	1		2	1		3
Tinnion, Brian	32	3	4				2			2
Tistimetanu, Ivan	8					1				
Torpey, Steve	19	2	2	1	1		3			3
Watts, Julian	16	1	3	1			1			1
Welch, Keith	21		4							
Zwijnenberg, Clem'		2	1							
35 players used	**506**	**91**	**44**	**10**	**11**	**2**	**57**	**8**		**65**

Odds & ends

Double wins: (0).

Double loses: (5) Watford, Ipswich, Bradford City, Wolves, Birmingham.

Won from behind: (2) Bolton (h), Grimsby (h).

Lost from in front: (5) Huddersfield (h), Grimsby (a), Wolves (h). Birmingham (a), Birmingham (h).

High spots: Keith Welch's brilliant goalkeeping display and Soren Anderson's great strike at Sunderland.

Beating Bolton 2-1 at Ashton Gate.

Adam Locke's late winner at Portsmouth.

Ade Akinbiyi's enthusiastic play.

The tremendous support given by City fans in a difficult season.

The half-time punch-up between the mascots (Wolfie, Cat and the sponsors' three little pigs) at the Wolves game on 7 November.

Low spots: Being savaged by the Wolves at Ashton Gate.

Dispirited performance in 0-5 defeat at Bradford City.

Inability to get behind Crewe's defence at Gresty Road.

The departure of John Ward.

The failure of Benny Lennartsson to improve results or produce a side playing other than route-one football.

Player of the Year: Ade Akinbiyi.

Ever-presents: (0).

Hat-tricks: (0).

Leading scorer: Ade Akinbiyi (23).

NATIONWIDE LEAGUE DIVISION 2   Manager: Tony Pulis   SEASON 1999-2000

Results

No	Date	H/A	Opponent	Scorers, Times, and Referees	F-A	H-T	Result	Att	Pos	Pt
1	7/8	A	READING	Brebner 15, Crawford 85, Tinnion 78. Ref: G Cain	1-2	0-1		13,348	–	0
2	14/8	H	BOURNEMOUTH	Akinbiyi 24, 44, Brennan 47, O'Neill 77. Ref: S Mathieson	3-1	2-0	W	11,315	–	3
3	21/8	A	WIGAN	Thorpe 72p, Barlow 8, Haworth 90. Ref: B Burns	1-2	0-1	L	7,103	14 (2)	3
4	28/8	H	BURY	Taylor 90, Littlejohn 67. Ref: A Butler	1-1	0-0	D	9,537	15 (13)	4
5	4/9	H	BLACKPOOL	Bell 48, Thorpe 70, 79, Hutchings 83, [Brenn'n 89], Ormerod 15, Murphy 85. Ref: W Jordan	5-2	0-1	W	8,439	12 (20)	7
6	11/9	H	MILLWALL	Ref: A Bates	0-0	0-0	D	9,893	14 (22)	8
7	18/9	A	SCUNTHORPE	Jones 79, Taylor 84, Guinan 56. Ref: P Rejer	2-1	0-0	W	4,542	11 (20)	11
8	25/9	H	BURNLEY	Ref: M Jones	0-0	0-0	D	11,510	13 (2)	12
9	2/10	A	OXFORD	Ref: P Richards	0-3	0-2	L	6,638	14 (15)	12
10	9/10	A	PRESTON	Mathie 37. Ref: J Kirby	0-1	0-1	L	10,042	15 (7)	12
11	17/10	H	BRISTOL ROV	Ref: T Heilbron	0-0	0-0	D	16,011	15 (1)	13

Line-ups (Bristol City players / *opponents*)

No	1	2	3	4	5	6	7	8	9	10	11	subs used
1	Phillips / *Howie*	Lavin! / *Gurney*	Brennan / *Gray*	Mortimer / *Caskey*	Taylor / *Hunter*	Carey / *Polston*	Goodridge* / *McLaren*	Hutchings" / *Brebner*	Akinbiyi" / *Scott"*	Brown" / *Williams*	Tinnion / *Hodges**	Murray/Shail/Pinamonte / *McIntyre/Crawford*
2	Phillips / *Ovendale*	Carey / *Young*	Brennan / *Warren*	Sebok / *Cox*	Taylor / *Howe*	Mortimer / *Mean**	Goodridge / *Hayter"*	Hutchings / *Rawlinson**	Akinbiyi / *Fletcher*	Torpey* / *Stein*	Tinnion / *Jorgensen*	Pinamonte/Murray / *Hughes/Huck/O'Neill*
3	Phillips / *Carroll*	Carey / *Green*	Brennan / *Bowen*	Sebok / *Kilford**	Taylor / *McGibbon*	Murray / *Balmer*	Goodridge / *O'Neil**	Hutchings / *Sheridan*	Akinbiyi / *Haworth*	Torpey* / *Liddell*	Tinnion / *Barlow*	Thorpe / *Porter, Lee*
4	Phillips / *Kenny*	Brennan / *Billy*	Bell / *Williams*	Sebok / *Collins*	Taylor / *Swailes C*	Murray* / *Daws*	Goodridge / *Richardson**	Hutchings* / *Reid*	Thorpe* / *Littlejohn*	Torpey / *Lawson*	Tinnion / *James*	Doherty/Meechan/Pinamonte / *Bulloch*
5	Phillips / *Caig*	Lavin / *Bryan*	Bell* / *Hills*	Mortimer" / *Clarkson*	Taylor / *Carlisle*	Carey / *Hughes**	Goodridge / *Bent"*	Hutchings / *Cousins*	Thorpe / *Murphy*	Torpey* / *Ormerod*	Tinnion / *Forsyth*	Pinamonte/Brennan/Murray / *Robinson I/Nowland*
6	Phillips / *Warner*	Lavin* / *Neill*	Brennan / *Stuart*	Mortimer / *Cahill*	Taylor / *Fitzgerald*	Carey* / *Nethercott*	Goodridge / *Reid**	Murray / *Bircham*	Thorpe* / *Sadler*	Torpey / *Moody**	Tinnion / *Gilkes"*	Sebok/Bell/Jones / *Livermore/Harris/Ryan*
7	Phillips / *Evans*	Brennan / *Harsley*	Lavin / *Hope*	Sebok / *Wilcox*	Taylor / *Dawson*	Mortimer! / *Hodges**	Goodridge! / *Guinan*	Sparrow / *Stanton*	Thorpe* / *Calvo-G'cia*	Torpey* / *Ipoua*	Tinnion / *Gayle*	Bell/Thorpe
8	Phillips / *Crichton*	Brennan / *Davis*	Lavin / *West*	Sebok / *Armstrong*	Taylor / *Thomas*	Mortimer / *Cook**	Goodridge / *Little**	Holland* / *Mellon*	Thorpe / *Branch**	Pinamonte* / *Payton*	Tinnion / *Smith*	Hutchings/Thorpe / *Mullin/Johnrose/Jepson*
9	Phillips / *Lundin*	Lavin* / *Folland*	Brennan / *Powell*	Sebok / *Robinson*	Taylor / *Watson*	Hutchings* / *Murphy*	Goodridge* / *Lambert**	Jones / *Lilley*	Thorpe* / *Anthrobus*	Bell* / *Fear*	Bell / *Beauchamp*	Tistimetanu/Torpey/Murray / *Cook/Abbey*
10	Phillips / *Moilanen*	Lavin / *Alexander*	Bell / *Edwards*	Carey* / *Jackson*	Taylor / *Kidd*	Hutchings* / *Rankine*	Goodridge* / *Cartwright*	Jones / *Gregan*	Jones / *Mathie**	Pinamonte / *Macken*	Tinnion / *McKenna**	Murray/Sebok/Meechan / *Eyres/Nogan*
11	Phillips / *Taylor*	Lavin / *Pethick*	Brennan / *Challis*	Carey* / *Thomson*	Taylor / *Tillson*	Mortimer / *Foster*	Goodridge* / *Hillier*	Hutchings / *Mauge*	Jones / *Cureton**	Thorpe* / *Roberts*	Tinnion / *Pritchard**	Brown M/Murray/Sebok / *Bryant/Ellington/Leoni*

Match reports

1. READING (A) — 7/8: For both Davidson and Pulis it proves to be a case of engaging the tongue before the brain. They are forced to backtrack from their immediate post-match comments that Lavin would not play for the club again after his 28th-minute dismissal for kicking the ball into the home crowd.

2. BOURNEMOUTH (H) — 14/8: After missing early chances, Akinbiyi fires in Tinnion's cross for the opener, before Mortimer's 40-yard pass sets him free to coolly slide in his second. Brennan's angled drive just after the break allows City to turn on the style, but John O'Neill runs through for the visitors' consolation.

3. WIGAN (A) — 21/8: At Wigan's new home, the magnificent JJB Stadium, City should have been two up before Stuart Barlow struck with a curled shot. Thorpe levels from the spot after being felled by Roy Carroll, but in injury-time Simon Haworth drills in a rebound off the bar from Barlow's drive.

4. BURY (H) — 28/8: Despite Taylor's late headed leveller for his 50th League goal, both sides squander further chances during minutes of injury-time. A poor game, in which the ball is often in the air, looked as though it was settled when the lively Adrian Littlejohn brushed past Brennan and shot in.

5. BLACKPOOL (H) — 4/9: The 48th-minute dismissal of Phil Robinson for hauling back Thorpe and Bell's registering from the resulting free-kick changes the course of this game. Brennan adds to his goal for Canada in midweek by netting a real screamer from a narrow angle after his dash down the left flank.

6. MILLWALL (H) — 11/9: Head injuries to Carey and Lavin in separate incidents early in the second half help to produce 13 minutes of injury-time in this exciting game. Millwall keeper Tony Warner turns in a Kevin Keelan type performance to deny City who make 19 goal attempts and twice hit the woodwork.

7. SCUNTHORPE (A) — 18/9: Perhaps Glanfield Park is more to City's liking than the Old Show Ground. Despite Mortimer's 44th-minute red card for a high kick, City notch up their first-ever away win over Scunthorpe. Jones' angled shot and Taylor's header tie up the points after Steve Guinan blasted Iron in front.

8. BURNLEY (H) — 25/9: A dire travesty of a match, the only entertainment being a display by the youngsters of King Edmund Gymnastic Club at half-time. Apart from a Taylor header that rebounds off the base of the post, the keepers are rarely troubled, though Paul Crichton does well to save from Goodridge.

9. OXFORD (A) — 2/10: City are made to pay for squandering a hatful of chances as they commit suicide at the back. How they miss the departed Welch's assurance on the ball as Phillips is dispossessed in his attempt to dribble round Derek Lilley, who squares the ball for Joey Beauchamp to tap in the opener.

10. PRESTON (A) — 9/10: City's failure to score for the fourth successive game rekindles fears of another relegation fight. Despite City's hard work, the inability of their front players to hold the ball up makes it easy for Preston, who should have registered more than Alex Mathie's shot on the turn from the left.

11. BRISTOL ROV (H) — 17/10: A much smaller crowd than expected see City dominate this Sky TV game without being able to end their goal drought. Too much air-ball in the first half when Jones heads against the bar, and then after the interval Goodridge's header suffers the same fate as City turn on the style.

#		Opponent	Date	Att.	Pos			Res	FT	HT	Scorers	Ref
12	H	COLCHESTER	19/10	7,777	15	23	14	D	1-1	1-0	Tinnion 34 / Duguid 58	Ref: M Warren
13	A	BURNLEY	23/10	10,175	16	5	14	L	0-2	0-1	Cook 6, Cooke 61	Ref: K Leach
14	A	GILLINGHAM	2/11	6,892	17	8	15	L	0-3	0-0	Taylor 60, 63, 89	Ref: G Laws
15	H	CAMBRIDGE	6/11	8,646	17	22	15	D	1-1	1-1	Jones 35 / Butler 2	Ref: T Parkes
16	A	STOKE	14/11	10,775	17	7	16	D	1-1	0-0	Tinnion 85 / Mohan 65	Ref: R Beeby
17	H	OLDHAM	23/11	8,214	19	15	17	D	1-1	1-0	Beadle 39 / Allott 84	Ref: G Barber
18	A	NOTTS CO	27/11	5,374	19	6	18	D	4-4	1-2	Bell 20, 76, Tistimetanu 60, Beadle 64 / Hollt 30 (og), St'll'd 31, Dy'r 72, Wr'r'n 87	Ref: P Walton
19	H	READING	4/12	8,936	14	21	21	W	3-1	1-0	Torpey 45, Taylor 50, Beadle 76 / Caskey 56	Ref: P Dowd
20	A	CHESTERFIELD	7/12	2,254	14	24	24	W	2-0	1-0	Galloway 45 (og), Tistimetanu 61	Ref: E Wolstenholme
21	H	WYCOMBE	17/12	8,195	13	12	25	D	0-0	0-0		Ref: A Wiley
22	A	BRENTFORD	26/12	6,942	14	9	25	L	1-2	0-0	Beadle 90 / Owusa 46, Rowlands 50	Ref: S Bennett
23	H	LUTON	28/12	11,832	14	12	26	D	0-0	0-0		Ref: M Ryan

12 — COLCHESTER
Line-up: Phillips, Lavin, Brennan, Sebok", Taylor, Mortimer, Goodridge*, Hutchings, Jones, Beadle", Tinnion. Subs: Thorpe/Murray/Brown M, McGavin/Moralee.
Opposition: Brown, Farley, Keith, Greene, Skelton*, Arnott*, Wilkins, Gregory, Duguid, Dazzell, Lua Lua.
Tinnion ends City's 490-minute barren spell by driving in a simple chance at the Wedlock Stand end after David Greene got in a tangle. Karl Duguid steers in a well-earned leveller for enterprising Colchester as City's truly appalling performance brought them the jeers they deserved.

13 — BURNLEY
Line-up: Phillips, Lavin, Brennan, Sebok", Taylor, Mortimer, Murray, Hutchings, Jones*, Beadle", Tinnion. Subs: Branch/Mellon/Jepson, Goodridge/Thorpe/Torpey.
Opposition: Crichton, West, Smith, Davis, Thomas, Cook", Little, Mullin", Cooke*, Payton, Johnrose.
City more than match high-riding Burnley, except in the art of goalscoring. After Paul Cook's 30-yard opener, both Mortimer and Jones miss easy chances before Beadle (£200k ex Notts) heads against the post just prior to the interval. Andy Cooke's curler ties up the Clarets' victory.

14 — GILLINGHAM
Line-up: Mercer, Lavin, Bartram... , Hutchings, Taylor, Mortimer, Murray, Holland, Jones, Meechan*, Tinnion. Subs: Taylor/Hodge/Lewis, Thorpe.
Opposition: Bartram, Southall, Edge, Pennock, Ashby, Butters, Saunders", Hessenthaler, Omoyimni*, Thomson", Smith.
Pulis' return to his old club ends in disappointment after City dominate the first half. Robert Taylor comes off the bench to destroy City after the break. New keeper Mercer, a £275,000 signing from Chesterfield, has no chance as Taylor notches his hat-trick with three fine shots.

15 — CAMBRIDGE
Line-up: Mercer, Lavin*, Bell, Hutchings, Taylor, Mortimer, Holland, Jones, Beadle, Tinnion". Subs: Goodridge"/Meechan/Burns, Taylor.
Opposition: Marshall, Ashbee, Wilson, McNeil, Joseph, Mustoe, MacKenzie, Wanless, Benjamin*, Butler, Kyd.
Against the run of play Jones levels Martin Butler's spectacular 20-yard opener, with a first-time shot from eight yards. Unlucky with Jones' header cleared off the line and a Mortimer shot kept out by a post, City fully deserve the boos at the finish for what in truth was a dire display.

16 — STOKE
Line-up: Mercer, Murray*, Bell, Hutchings, Taylor, Holland, Tistimetanu", Jones, Beadle, Mortimer*. Subs: Jacobson/Robinson/Oldfield, Goodridge.
Opposition: Ward, Short*, Clarke, Mohan, Dryden, Kavanaugh, Keen", O'Connor, Lightbourne, Thorne, Bullock*.
Stoke boss Gary Megson, in his last game following an Icelandic take-over, is cheered by Nicky Mohan's bullet header that gives his side the lead. City save a point with Tinnion's superb 35-yard lob, but they should have won as Goodridge puts a last minute point-blank header wide.

17 — OLDHAM
Line-up: Mercer, Murray, Bell, Millen, Taylor, Holland, Tistimetanu", Jones", Beadle, Mortimer*. Subs: Lavin/Torpey/Goodridge, Tipton/Walsh.
Opposition: Kelly, Rickers, Holt, McNiven, Garnett, Hotte, Duxbury, Whitehall*, Allott, Sheridan, Innes".
City are booed off after being outplayed by the Latics, but it should have been a different story after Beadle bundled in his first goal for the club. Oldham, unbeaten away since losing to the Rovers in September, fully deserved to extend their own, courtesy of Mark Allott's towering header.

18 — NOTTS CO
Line-up: Mercer, Lavin*, Bell, Millen, Taylor, Holland, Tistimetanu, Jones*, Beadle, Tinnion. Subs: Torpey/Murray.
Opposition: Ward, Holmes*, Pearce, Warren, Fenton", Redmile, Hughes, Allsopp, Owers, Ramage, Stallard/Dyer/Tierney.
City's early dominance is sabotaged by the 27th-minute introduction of substitute Mark Stallard, but after the half-time interval they regain control. Bell's 25-yard screamer should have been a worthy winner, but they fail to close down Mark Warren, who fires in a 30-yard leveller.

19 — READING
Line-up: Mercer, Bell, Millen, Taylor, Tistimetanu", Goodridge", Beadle", Torpey, Holland, Tinnion. Subs: Holland/Murray/Hutchings, Mortimer*.
Opposition: Howie, Gurney, Primus, Polston, Caskey, Grant", McIntyre, Williams, Bernal, Evers*, Smith/Lisbie.
Moments after Taylor gets away with his handball to keep out Jimmy McIntyre's shot, Torpey's 18-yarder sets City up for their first League win in twelve attempts. Darren Caskey's free-kick has City rocking until Beadle races through. Mercer saves Caskey's last-minute penalty.

20 — CHESTERFIELD
Line-up: Mercer, Bell, Millen, Taylor, Tistimetanu", Goodridge*, Beadle, Torpey, Holland, Tinnion. Subs: Holland/James.
Opposition: Gayle, Williams D, Williams R, Pearce*, Payne, Blatherwick, Galloway", Howard, Reeves, D'Auria, Beaumont, Hewitt/Breckin.
Moldovan international Tistimetanu's 25-yard wonder volley lights up a dismal game. City have the better first half, but are fortunate to take the lead when Mick Galloway deflects Lavin's cross into his own net. The post aids City on 72 minutes by keeping out Jon Howard's header.

21 — WYCOMBE
Line-up: Mercer, Lavin, Taylor, Hutchings*, Taylor, Millen, Black*, Beadle, Holland, Tinnion. Subs: Holland/James.
Opposition: Taylor, Lawrence, Ablett, Simpson, Cousins, Bates, Carroll", Baird!, Devine*, Ryan, Brown, Bulman/Senda.
Hutchings, on 31 minutes and loan-signing Black (Arsenal) early in the second half are both denied by a post in an absorbing contest in which the visitors are always a threat. Baird is sent off on 72 minutes after a tangle with man-of-the-match Black brought forth a second yellow card.

22 — BRENTFORD
Line-up: Mercer, Lavin, Bell, Hutchings, Taylor*, Millen, Black, Holland, Beadle, Tistimetanu". Subs: Goodridge/Torpey/Mortimer, Agyemang/Charles.
Opposition: Woodman, Quinn, Ingimarsson, Mahon, Marshall, Clement, Evans, Theobald, Partridge", Rowlands, Owusa".
At Griffin Park keeper Mercer is the fall guy in a slapstick comedy of errors as woeful City lose their seven-match unbeaten League run. He spills a long shot into the path of Lloyd Owusa, and shortly after is beaten by Martin Rowlands' great angled drive from the edge of the area.

23 — LUTON
Line-up: Mercer, Lavin*, Bell, Millen, Taylor, Mortimer, Black, Hutchings", Beadle, Torpey". Subs: Goodridge"/Tinnion/Thorpe, Fotiadis.
Opposition: Abbey, Taylor, Boyce, Johnson, Watts, Docherty, Spring, Gray, White, Douglas*, Locke.
Pulis hardly encourages the fans to return with his post-match comment that his side are playing good football. Most fans would disagree after witnessing yet another poor game. Luton have their chances, though City are unlucky with Beadle's first-half effort which cannons off the bar.

(Up to 31 December 1999)

NATIONWIDE DIVISION 2 (CUP-TIES) Manager: Tony Pulis SEASON 1999-2000

Worthington Cup

					F-A	H-T	Scorers, Times, and Referees

1:1 A CAMBRIDGE 10/8   2,813   D   2-2   0-0
Hutchings 51, Mortimer 90
Butler 50, 86
Ref: P Taylor

1	2	3	4	5	6	7	8	9	10	11	subs used
Phillips	Carey	Brennan	Sebok	Taylor	Mortimer	Murray^	Hutchings^	Akinbiyi	Torpey*	Tinnion	Torpey/Doherty/Goodridge
Van Heusden Chenery	*Van Heusden Chenery*	*Wilson*	*Duncan*	*Eustace*	*Russell*	*Mustoe^*	*Ashbee*	*Benjamin*	*Butler*	*Kyd**	*Taylor/Graham*

Mortimer's late header leaves all to play for in the 2nd leg, but in truth City squandered numerous chances. In the first half Murray hits a post and Martin Butler is unfortunate with his shot that hits the crossbar, but makes amends by bundling in the opener and heading the U's in front.

1:2 H CAMBRIDGE 24/8   5,352 17   W   2-1   2-0
Torpey 18, Thorpe 36
Ref: C Wilkes
(City won 4-3 on aggregate)

1	2	3	4	5	6	7	8	9	10	11	subs used
Phillips	Carey	Brennan	Sebok	Taylor	Murray	Goodridge	Hutchings	Thorpe	Torpey*	Tinnion	Pinamonte
Van Huesden Chenery	*Van Huesden Chenery*	*Wilson*	*Eustace*	*Duncan*	*Ashbee*	*Wanless^*	*Mustoe**	*Benjamin*	*Benjamin*	*Kyd**	*Taylor/Youngs/Cassidy*

With Akinbiyi away on international duty, Thorpe has the chance to show his pace. Only the goalkeeping of Arjan Van Huesden, fortunate when an early shot cannons off his crossbar, thwarts City, but he can do nothing when Torpey and Thorpe are presented with easy tap-ins.

2:1 A NOTT'M FOREST 15/9   5,015 1:9   L   1-2   1-1
Jordan 13
Harewood 12, Rogers 56
Ref: M Messias

1	2	3	4	5	6	7	8	9	10	11	subs used
Phillips	Sebok	Brennan	Jordan	Taylor	Mortimer^	Murray	Meechan*	Jones	Tinnion	Bell	Brown-M/ Brown A
*Crossley**	*Louis-Jean*	*Chettle*	*Scimeca^*	*Hjelde*	*Burns*	*Petrachi**	*Freedman^*	*Harewood*	*Quashie*	*Rogers*	*Allou/Bonalair/Merino*

Marvin Brown's 73rd-minute sub appearance makes him City's youngest-ever player at 16 years, 71 days. Forest's poor finishing keeps City in with a chance after sharp-eyed officials ruled Jordan's header over the line just after Marlon Harewood's low driven opener from 15 yards.

2:2 H NOTT'M FOREST 22/9   8,259 1:11   D   0-0   0-0
Ref: P Durkin
(City lost 1-2 on aggregate)

1	2	3	4	5	6	7	8	9	10	11	subs used
Phillips	Lavin	Brennan	Sebok	Taylor	Mortimer	Goodridge*	Murray*	Jones	Pinamonte^	Tinnion	Brown A/Thorpe/Torpey
*Crossley**	*Louis-Jean*	*Doig*	*Bonalair*	*Hjelde*	*Pratton*	*Allou^*	*Freedman*	*Harewood*	*Quashie*	*Rogers*	*Beasant/Gray*

Despite Forest's superior skill City with 14 shots on goal (five on target), have the chances to win this exciting game. Dave Beasant took over between the sticks for Forest when Mark Crossley lands awkwardly after tipping over Goodridge's teasing 35-yard dipper in the 16th minute.

FA Cup

1 H MANSFIELD 30/10   5,411 3:18   W   3-2   1-1
Tinnion 44, 50, Murray 65
Lormor 10p, Blake 89
Ref: R Oliver

1	2	3	4	5	6	7	8	9	10	11	subs used
Phillips	Lavin	Bell	Hutchings	Taylor !	Mortimer*	Murray	Beadle*	Jones*	Holland	Tinnion	Meechan/Goodridge/Tistimetanu
Bowling	*Hassell**	*Porter*	*Richardson*	*Linighan*	*Clarke*	*Williams^*	*Disby^*	*Lormor*	*Blake*	*Roscoe*	*Asher/Boulding/Bacon*

One short and trailing to Lormor's penalty following Taylor's dismissal for keeping the ball out with his hand, Meechan's 25th-minute entry as sub for the injured Jones transforms home fortunes. Tinnion's rarely used right foot fires in the equaliser, then his left-foot chip puts City ahead.

2 A BOURNEMOUTH 20/11   5,223 13   W   2-0   1-0
Murray 22, 53
Ref: W Jordan

1	2	3	4	5	6	7	8	9	10	11	subs used
Mercer	Murray	Bell	Millen	Taylor	Holland	Tistimetanu*	Beadle	Jones	Mortimer	Tinnion	Hutchings
Ovendale	*Young*	*Warren**	*Broadhurst*	*Cox*	*Day*	*Jorgensen*	*Robinson*	*Stein*	*Fletcher S*	*Fletcher C !*	*Watson*

Third time lucky for Bristol City, as they avenge recent FA Cup defeats by the Cherries. Carl Fletcher is dismissed on 72 minutes for his second bookable offence, but by then Murray's brilliant cross-shots from the left had clinched victory, his second a great 16-yarder into the top corner.

3 A SHEFFIELD WED 11/12   11,644 P:20   L   0-1   0-1
Booth 25
Ref: M Reed

1	2	3	4	5	6	7	8	9	10	11	subs used
Mercer	Lavin^	Bell	Millen	Taylor	Hutchings	Tistimetanu^	Beadle	Torpey	Holland	Tinnion	Murray/Jones
Smicek	*Nolan*	*Atherton*	*Thome*	*Walker*	*Hinchcliffe**	*Alexandersson*	*De Bilde*	*Booth*	*Jonk^*	*Sonner*	*McKeever/Sibon/Quinn!*

Against opponents lacking in confidence, City's failure to get behind Wednesday's defence often proves costly as they succumb to Andy Booth's first-half header. The Owls' 88th-minute sub Alan Quinn is red carded almost immediately when he clatters into Taylor with a raised arm.